West's Law School Advisory Board

ENVIRONMENTAL LAW IN CONTEXT

CASES AND MATERIALS

Third Edition

■ ■ ■

By

Robin Kundis Craig

University of Utah S.J. Quinney College of Law

AMERICAN CASEBOOK SERIES®

WEST®

A Thomson Reuters business

Mat #41046231

610 Opperman Drive
St. Paul, MN 55123
1–800–313–9378

Printed in the United States of America

ISBN: 978–0–314–26607–1

For Mom,
who first taught me the basics of writing
and who encouraged me to get into teaching, with love.

PREFACE TO THE THIRD EDITION

The Third Edition of *Environmental Law in Context* continues to keep students up-to-date on developments in federal environmental law. It reflects most of the major developments in federal environmental law over the last four years, including:

- A reorganized introduction to environmental justice in the RCRA materials for Chapter 1 that emphasizes the EPA's new environmental justice programs.
- A significant reorganization of the CERCLA section of Chapter 1, to include the three newest Supreme Court decisions and to more clearly present the issues in choosing between Section 107 cost recovery actions and Section 113 contribution actions, including the roles of joint and several liability and equitable apportionment in each.
- In Chapter 2, the Supreme Court's recent decision in *Monsanto* regarding NEPA remedies, plus updates on the various NEPA cases and the CEQ's categorical exclusions guidance.
- In Chapter 3, updates regarding the Northern spotted owl's recovery plan and implementation of protections for the delta smelt, plus a new case and more recent case that better presents the issues involved in designating ESA critical habitat.
- Comprehensive updates in Chapter 4 discussing the EPA's increasing use of its Clean Air Act authority to address greenhouse gas emissions from both mobile and stationary sources, plus a summary of the merits in *American Electric Power Co. v. Connecticut.* Revisions to Chapter 4 also include a new chart detailing the revised NAAQS and updated figures throughout.
- In Chapter 5, two new Supreme Court cases discussing Clean Water Act permitting—*Entergy Corp.*, which discusses the Act's intake water requirements; and the Coeur Alaska gold mine case, which explores the differences between the Section 402 and Section 404 permitting programs. The revisions also update the EPA's continuing efforts to regulate CAFOs.
- Finally, in Chapter 6, the Supreme Court's standing decision in *Summers v. Earth Island Institute* standing decision and a discussion of the Court's (brief) discussion of state standing in *AEP v. Connecticut.*

ROBIN KUNDIS CRAIG
Professor of Law
University of Utah
College of Law

Acknowledgments

The students in several years' worth of Environmental Law classes at the Western New England College School of Law, the Indiana University School of Law, Indianapolis, and the Florida State University College of Law, have given me feedback on progressive drafts of this casebook and new cases for inclusion in the Second Edition, and I am grateful for their indulgence and their honesty regarding what worked (and what didn't) for them. I have no doubt that future classes will similarly refine the approach of, and materials included within, this textbook, and I thank those future students in advance.

I would like to thank Professors Daniel Cole and Andrew Klein at the Indiana University School of Law for their extensive and critical reviews of, in Professor Cole's case, the Introduction and Chapter 4, and, in Professor Klein's case, Chapter 1. I nevertheless retain full responsibility for all errors made.

From the First Edition, I would like to thank my fast-working team of proofreaders, all students at the Indiana University School of Law: Amanda Bailor; Joseph Buitron; Lindsay Carlberg; Bre Conway; Lauren Dougherty; Margaret Esler; Teresa Finn; Daniel Gibson; Josh Harrison; William Hogg; Andrea Impicciche; Trina Kissel; Marcus Knotts; Andrew Kossack; Sarah Lashua; Julia Maness; Jennifer McCoy; Matt McQuillan; Dana Rifai; Quincy Sauer; Gina Sciortino; Stephanie Thielen; Brandon Tomey; Eva Wailes; and Emily Yates.

For the Second Edition, I would like to thank my Research Assistants, Morgan Bourdat and Sarah Naf, for their tireless work in helping me to update this textbook. Both are Class of 2008 graduates of the Florida State University College of Law.

For the Third Edition, I gratefully acknowledge the assistance of Lori Beail–Farkas and my fall 2011 Environmental Law class at the Florida State University College of Law.

Summary of Contents

TABLE OF CONTENTS

TABLE OF CASES

The principal cases are in bold type. Cases cited or discussed in the text are in roman type. References are to pages. Cases cited in principal cases and within other quoted materials are not included.

ENVIRONMENTAL LAW IN CONTEXT

CASES AND MATERIALS

Third Edition

INTRODUCTION: STUDYING ENVIRONMENTAL LAW IN CONTEXT

■ ■ ■

I. WHAT *IS* THE ENVIRONMENT, AND WHAT MOTIVATED PEOPLE TO PROTECT IT?

—What makes it so hard to organize the environment sensibly is that everything we touch is hooked up to everything else.

Isaac Asimov, ISAAC ASIMOV'S BOOK OF SCIENCE AND NATURE QUOTATIONS (1998)

At its most basic, environmental law is law related to "the environment." Arguably, "the environment" is everything—the planet Earth and all of its processes, attributes, species, and ecosystems, plus: (1) the sun, which supplies much of the energy upon which life on earth depends; (2) the moon, which drives the ocean tides; (3) comets and meteors, which sprinkle the Earth with rare elements and occasionally have even greater effects, like causing the mass extinctions of the dinosaurs; and (4) all of the other astronomical bodies that exert gravitational influences on the Earth.

From a physical-ecological perspective, that definition of "the environment" may be appropriate and useful. However, from an environmental law perspective, it is almost certainly too broad. Environmental law, like every other kind of law, regulates *human* behavior. Science fiction movies notwithstanding, many astronomical and geological processes are simply beyond the scope of meaningful human influence, at least at the moment.

As a result, "the environment," at least for purposes of an environmental law course, tends to refer to the biological, chemical, and physical processes that occur on or near the surface of the Earth or in its atmosphere. Water, land, air, species, ecosystems, minerals, and other natural resources are the primary subjects of environmental law.

What about humans? Are human beings part of "the environment"? You might be tempted to say "no"—humans are the technological creatures who have separated themselves from "the environment." However, any such claim would ignore the fact that human prosperity ultimately depends on the environment—the quality of water, the quality of air, and the continuing availability of natural resources and the services that ecosystems provide.

Indeed, it was humans' increasing awareness in the 1960s and 1970s of their connections to the environment that helped to inspire federal environmental law. The Environmental Protection Agency (EPA) has outlined some of the significant events that helped to inspire the enactment of environmental law in the United States as follows:

MAJOR EVENTS BEFORE EARTH DAY THAT RAISED ENVIRONMENTAL CONSCIOUSNESS

1962
Rachel Carson's book, *Silent Spring*, alerts the general public to the hidden dangers associated with pesticide use. *Silent Spring* becomes a cornerstone of the environmental movement, highlighting the causal relationship between human action and adverse changes to human health and the environment.

1968
Apollo 8 transmits the first images of the Earth as a luminous blue sphere in the otherwise dark void of outer space. The images of our planet from the Apollo moon missions give rise to feelings that our Earth's environment is something fragile and precious that must be protected -- providing inspiration to a nascent environmental movement.

Earth as seen by the Apollo astronauts

1969
An explosion on an oil platform six miles off the coast of Santa Barbara, California, spills 200,000 gallons of crude oil -- creating an 800 mile oil slick that mars 35 miles of the California coast. Incoming tides wash the corpses of dead seals and dolphins on shore; nearly 3,700 birds are estimated to have died.

In Cleveland, Ohio, the Cuyahoga River catches fire and burns due to chemical contamination. This event galvanizes growing public concerns about the threats of unregulated toxic chemical use and disposal.

1970
The National Environmental Policy Act of 1969 (NEPA) is signed into law by President Richard Nixon on January 1, 1970. Heralded as the *Magna Carta* of the country's environmental movement, NEPA established a framework for the Federal government to assess the environmental effects of its major decisions.

Membership in the Sierra Club grows from 15,000 in 1960 to 113,000 in 1970 -- an increase of more than 700 percent. The National Audubon Society also sees its membership grow significantly during the decade -- from 32,000 in 1960 to 148,000 in 1970.

U.S. ENVIRONMENTAL PROTECTION AGENCY, SUPERFUND: 20 YEARS OF PROTECTING HUMAN HEALTH AND THE ENVIRONMENT 1–1 (Dec. 11, 2000), *available at* http://www.epa.gov/superfund/20years/index.htm (last updated September 19, 2007).

Beyond the particular historical circumstances that led to federal environmental regulation in the United States, however, are more general issues regarding why the environment should be protected. When people ask why governments should regulate humans' use of the environment, they are usually asking one of two questions. First, they might be asking whether the government needs to regulate humans' use of the environment in order to protect *humans*. In other words, is there some evidence that unchecked human use is damaging the environment in ways that impact human lives to an unacceptable degree? Regulation of air and water resources came about largely as a result of perceived harms to humans from non-regulation—"killer fogs" from air pollution, contaminated drinking water supplies, rivers so polluted that they caught on fire. This first question reflects the ***anthropocentric*** (i.e., human-centered) view of environmental regulation—the view that all environmental regulation is ultimately about human beings and human values.

Second, when people ask why the government should regulate humans' use of the environment, they might be asking whether the government needs to regulate human use of the environment to protect *the environment itself*. This second question arguably reflects a broader view of the world—a ***biocentric*** (life-centered), ***ecocentric*** (ecosystem-centered), or even ***geocentric*** (Earth-centered) view that sees value in protecting the environment for itself. These views help to explain statutes that protect imperiled species, such as the federal Endangered Species Act and Marine Mammal Protection Act.

Nevertheless, the anthropocentric and ecocentric views of the environment form more of a continuum than opposing choices. Some environmental problems, like smog or disease-infected water, have direct and obvious consequences for human beings. However, humans, as members of particular ecosystems, also suffer less directly and/or less obviously from more general ecosystem degradation, as the discipline of ***ecological economics*** has attempted to demonstrate through the concept of ***ecosystem services***. Moreover, as a practical matter, it is humans who enact environmental laws, and they are much more likely to do so if they perceive some benefit to themselves—especially given that much environmental regulation imposes restrictions on human activity.

II. WHY SHOULD THE *FEDERAL* GOVERNMENT PROTECT THE ENVIRONMENT?

The focus of this book is *federal* environmental law, raising the issues of why the federal government became involved in environmental regulation and whether regulation at the federal level is appropriate. As you will learn in later chapters, environmental regulation began with the states.

Indeed, the earliest federal environmental statutes were largely vehicles for encouraging states to address certain fundamental environmental problems. Unfortunately, states generally greeted such statutes unenthusiastically, and little progress was made.

There are at least two reasons why states were reluctant to regulate environmental pollution independently. First, environmental regulation is expensive for states to implement. States have to create, staff, and fund environmental agencies, hire enforcement personnel, and pay for enforcement proceedings. Second, environmental compliance is often (or often perceived to be) expensive and burdensome for the regulated entities, such as industry. As a result, without some guarantee that *all* states had to enact similar environmental requirements, some states feared that job- and income-providing companies would simply relocate to states that did not impose requirements on them to protect the environment. The states' resulting refusal to enact "excessive" environmental requirements is sometimes referred to as the ***race to the bottom***.

In addition, environmental degradation is, legitimately, a *national* problem involving *national* public welfare. Rivers flow downstream, often through several states. For example, pollution problems in the Gulf of Mexico originate in part from water pollution in Illinois, Indiana, and Wisconsin. Air currents carry air pollution with the prevailing winds. For example, eastern states suffer from acid rain and smog caused by air pollution generated in the Midwest. Toxins seep through soil into groundwater, forming toxic plumes that can flow for miles underground. Species and ecosystems cross state borders.

In a sense, therefore, the entire United States is one big commons, shared by all the people who live here. In 1968, Garrett Hardin published his theory of ***the tragedy of the commons***, postulating that unregulated and unchecked use of a common environment almost inevitably leads to environmental degradation. His argument was that, in the absence of regulation or other controlling mechanisms, each individual will seek to maximize his or her own gain from the commons, adding cows to common grazing pasture, for example, or seeking to catch as many fish as possible from common lakes or the ocean. However, if all users of the commons behave the same way—and it is in their self-interest to do so—eventually the users will overwhelm the system and destroy the commons. Garrett Hardin, *The Tragedy of the Commons*, 168 SCIENCE 1243 (1968). Overexploitation of public lands for grazing and the collapse of fisheries all over the world testify to the viability of Hardin's theory.

In modern economic parlance, use of the commons creates ***externalities*** or ***external costs*** for which the rancher or fisher does not have to pay. Environmental law can force people who use the commons to ***internalize*** the value of the commons by requiring users to pay for permits and/or to pay to minimize the harm to the environment. Alternatively, environmental law and regulation can control access to the commons, limiting use to ***sustainable*** levels.

III. SOURCES OF FEDERAL ENVIRONMENTAL LAW: A FEW INTRODUCTORY PRACTICALITIES

A. FEDERAL STATUTES

1. The United States Code (U.S.C.)

The focus of this textbook is federal environmental law. Federal environmental law begins with federal environmental ***statutes***—the Clean Air Act, the Clean Water Act, the Resource Conservation and Recovery Act, and so on. Once legislation becomes federal law, it is codified into the ***United States Code*** **(U.S.C.)**. (NOTE: The *official* version of federal statutes is found in the United States Code, which the federal government publishes. However, unofficial versions of the federal statutes, such as West's United States Code Annotated (U.S.C.A.), can be more helpful to researchers because they contain notes on how courts have interpreted the statutes.) The United States Code is divided into ***titles*** and ***sections***. Titles are major divisions in the United States Code and represent general subject matter distinctions. For example, general statutes governing administrative agencies are found in Title 5, while provisions governing federal courts are found in Title 28. Most federal environmental and natural resources statutes are found in Title 7 (agriculture), Title 16 (conservation), Title 33 (water-related legislation), Title 42 (public health and welfare), and Title 43 (public lands).

Each title has many kinds of subdivisions, but the ones you will use most frequently are statutory ***sections***. Each section number refers to a particular set of legal provisions. Sections are often subdivided into subsections, which can contain sub-subsections, and so on. Ordinarily, the numbering hierarchy for a particular federal statutory section is as follows:

§ XXXX: Title of Statutory Section

- (a) Subsection
  - (1) Sub-subsection
    - (A) sub-sub-subsection
      - (i) sub-sub-sub-subsection
      - (ii) sub-sub-sub-subsection
    - (B)sub-sub-subsection
  - (2) Sub-subsection
- (b) Subsection
- . . . and so on.

If you know a federal statutory provision's title and section numbers (and subsection numbers, if you need to be more specific), you can identify it for anyone else: XX U.S.C. § YYYY. For example, the Endangered Species Act's provision for listing new endangered species is found at 16 U.S.C. § 1533, while the Clean Water Act's major prohibition on discharges is found at 33 U.S.C. § 1311(a).

Environmental law practitioners, however, also use another set of numbers to refer to specific statutory provisions: the ***public law numbers***. After Congress enacts a federal statute, that statute first appears as a public law. Each piece of legislation has its own public law number, and the provisions of that statute each have a public law section number. These public law section numbers usually have no correlation to the United States Code section numbers that will eventually be assigned to each statutory provision.

As a result, to practice environmental law (and, more immediately, to be able to read environmental law cases), you will have to be able to cross-correlate the public law section references and the United States Code section references. In the examples above, the Endangered Species Act's listing provision is also § 4 of the Endangered Species Act, while the Clean Water Act's major prohibition is found in § 301(a) of the Clean Water Act. Fortunately, at the very end of every United States Code statutory section is a reference to the public law section number. This textbook will give you both references, in the following format: ESA § 4, 16 U.S.C. § 1533.

2. Studying Statutory Law: The Basics

There are four aspects of any federal environmental law (indeed, any statute) that you should learn as quickly as possible. These four aspects allow you to outline the scope and applicability of that statute. The four "must know" aspects of any statute are:

A. The Statutory "Trigger": To what factual and/or legal circumstances does the statute apply? What event must occur, or what condition must exist, before that statute's requirements govern a particular situation?

B. The Basic Definitions: Most statutes have a definition section that defines many of the statute's key terms; if not, courts have usually filled in the gaps. These definitions are usually most important in refining the statutory trigger. For example, it's all well and good to know that the federal Resource Conservation and Recovery Act (RCRA) applies to "solid waste," but you still won't get very far until you know that Congress defined "solid waste" to be "discarded materials" and to include semisolids, liquids, and contained gases.

C. Major Exemptions and Exceptions: Once you've figured out when a statute applies, you then need to know whether there are any statutory exemptions, exclusions, or exceptions—situations that might appear to fit within the statute's scope but that Congress, for whatever reason (and there are many), has chosen to explicitly remove from the statute's scope.

D. Major Requirements/Prohibitions/Liabilities: If the statute is triggered, what happens next? Is some activity forbidden? Must the regulated entity get a permit? Must the regulating agency follow certain procedures? What happens if the statute is violated?

Of course, other provisions of the statute are also important, such as the details regarding what compliance requires. However, you will most quickly understand a new statutory regime if you learn when the statute applies, when it doesn't apply, and the basic requirements it imposes.

B. FEDERAL REGULATIONS

Federal environmental law-making does not end at the statutory level. Almost every federal environmental statute assigns to some federal agency—the EPA, the U.S. Fish & Wildlife Service, the Department of the Interior, the U.S. Army Corps of Engineers, *etc.*—the power and duty to implement the statute. Such powers and duties usually fall into three categories: (1) ***rulemaking***, which is the process of promulgating administrative regulations that can then have the force of law; (2) ***investigation and recordkeeping***, the processes through which a federal agency oversees the persons and industries regulated under the statute; and (3) ***enforcement***, which can include the power to ***adjudicate*** violations of the law within the agency, the power to impose ***administrative penalties*** on violators, and the power to refer cases to the ***Department of Justice*** for civil or criminal prosecution in court.

The most general level of federal agency lawmaking occurs through rulemaking. In order for agency rules to have the force of law, they must meet several requirements. First, for the agency's lawmaking to be constitutional, Congress must ***delegate*** rulemaking authority to the agency through a statute and give the agency some sort of standard to use in exercising its authority—the so-called ***intelligible principle test***. This ***nondelegation doctrine*** recognizes that the U.S. Constitution gives federal lawmaking power exclusively to Congress; the intelligible principle test ensures that Congress maintains some control over its delegations of lawmaking authority to administrative agencies.

Second, federal agency rules are legally binding on regulated entities only if the agency follows the correct procedures in promulgating those rules. While a particular environmental statute may specify what procedures the agency has to follow, most federal agency rulemaking follows the "informal" rulemaking procedures in the federal ***Administrative Procedure Act* (APA)**, 5 U.S.C. §§ 551–559, 701–706. The APA delineates a three-step process for informal rulemaking, also known as ***notice-and-comment rulemaking***: (1) notice of the proposed rule published in the Federal Register; (2) an opportunity for interested persons to comment on the proposed rule to the agency, either through written (or, increasingly, electronic) comments (most commonly) or through public hearings or both; and (3) publication of the final rule and an explanation of the final rule in the Federal Register at least 30 days before the rule goes into effect. 5 U.S.C. § 553.

The ***Federal Register*** is thus an important source of environmental law. The federal government publishes the Federal Register daily, and each daily issue contains all of the federal agency notices for that day. Because the Federal Register is organized on the basis of date of notice, searching the paper version of the Federal Register is extraordinarily laborious. Fortunately, the Federal Register is now available in a far more searchable format on-line and through electronic legal search services such as Westlaw.

Once a year, all of the currently legally effective federal regulations are organized by subject matter and agency and published in the ***Code of Federal Regulations*** **(C.F.R.)**. The Code of Federal Regulations is many volumes long—indeed, it rivals the United States Code in length. All of the regulations that a given agency promulgates in a given area of law are collected and organized into the same volume. For example, most of the EPA's environmental regulations are collected in volume 40 of the Code of Federal Regulations. In addition, each individual regulation receives a specific section number. For example, the regulations implementing the National Environmental Policy Act (NEPA) are found in Title 40 of the Code of Federal Regulations, Parts 1500 to 1508. If you then wanted to find the regulatory definition of "major Federal actions requiring the preparation of environmental impact statements," you would look at 40 C.F.R. § 1502.3.

If the federal agency does not follow the required procedural steps for rulemaking, the resulting agency pronouncements are not legally binding on the regulated entities. Nevertheless, the resulting documents—generally referred to as ***policy statements*** and ***guidance documents***—are still important for the implementation of the statute, because they warn regulated entities of how the agency plans to interpret and apply the law.

C. FEDERAL COURT DECISIONS

Despite the number of statutory provisions and agency regulations, some environmental issues remain unresolved until litigation. As a result, ***federal courts*** also help to fashion federal environmental law by interpreting statutes and regulations and clarifying how those statutes apply to specific factual situations. In addition, the federal courts ensure that environmental statutes and federal agencies comply with the U.S. Constitution and that federal agencies follow the procedures that Congress has dictated that they must follow in promulgating rules, conducting investigations, holding administrative hearings (adjudications), issuing permits, and imposing administrative sanctions and penalties.

Another important aspect of federal environmental litigation is the ***citizen suit***. Almost all federal environmental statutes include provisions that allow individual citizens to bring civil lawsuits against persons who violate those statutes or against the federal agencies that are supposed to implement the environmental statute, or both. In addition, the federal APA contains judicial review provisions that allow citizens to sue federal agencies if the citizens are "adversely affected or aggrieved" by a federal agency's actions, including rulemaking and enforcement actions. As a result, private citizens and interest groups can directly influence the interpretation and application of federal environmental law.

TO RECAP: Federal environmental law consists of the ***federal statutory provisions*** designated through ***United States Code*** (U.S.C.) or ***public law*** sections; ***federal administrative regulations***, announced and explained in the ***Federal Register*** and then codified into sections in the ***Code of Federal Regulations*** (C.F.R.); administrative ***policy statements*** and ***guidance documents***; and decisions of the ***federal courts***.

IV. THE OTHER INFLUENCES ON FEDERAL ENVIRONMENTAL LAW

Even though federal environmental law derives most directly from statutes, it does not exist in isolation from other kinds of law, from science and technological developments, from economic and social considerations, or from politics. You will most fully appreciate the depth and challenges of practicing environmental law if you study it with an awareness of how these other influences affect environmental regulation.

A. COMMON LAW

While much federal environmental law is statutory law, common law, especially torts, remains relevant for several reasons. First, many of the statutory principles that Congress enacted derive directly from legal principles found in common law, such as public and private nuisance. In addition, environmental liability often reflects common-law distinctions between civil and criminal liability and, in the civil context, between strict liability, negligence, and intentional conduct.

Second, when Congress leaves a gap in an environmental statute, courts will often look to the common law to supply the relevant requirements or standards. For example, in the Comprehensive Environmental Response, Compensation, and Liability Act (CERCLA), Congress specified neither the causation standard required to prove that a person contributed to a hazardous substance clean-up problem, nor the liability standard when more than one person contributes to releases of hazardous substances on the same property. Courts have turned to common-law torts principles to establish these standards.

Third, however, Congress also often enacts statutes to *change* the common law. For example, one of the reasons that Congress enacted CERCLA and the Resource Conservation and Recovery Act (RCRA) was that common-law nuisance was proving to be an inadequate vehicle for preventing hazardous waste contamination, as Chapter 1 will discuss.

B. ADMINISTRATIVE LAW

As was discussed in Part III, federal administrative agencies like the EPA implement most federal environmental statutes. The law governing actions of administrative agencies and courts' review of those agency actions is collectively referred to as ***administrative law***. Administrative law includes a number of constitutional and procedural requirements that define the proper roles for and limitations upon administrative agencies.

Regarding constitutional law, for example, the U.S. Constitution does not explicitly address administrative agencies. Federal agencies like the EPA are generally considered to be part of the Executive Branch because they execute—administer and enforce—the law. However, as Part III discussed, administrative agencies also often write law, in the form of administrative regulations, and they often adjudicate individual cases. Thus, administrative agencies blend legislative and judicial elements with executive elements. One part of administrative law, therefore, consists of the constitutional interpretations that allow federal agencies to exist without violating the Constitution's principle of separation of powers.

On the procedural side, administrative law governs the procedures that agencies must use in carrying out their various functions. For federal administrative agencies, the default set of procedural requirements are found in the federal ***Administrative Procedure Act* (APA)**. However, Congress remains free to subject agencies to more particular procedural requirements in specific statutes, and Congress has exercised that option in several environmental statutes, such as the Endangered Species Act and the Clean Air Act.

Figure I-1: Influences on Environmental Law

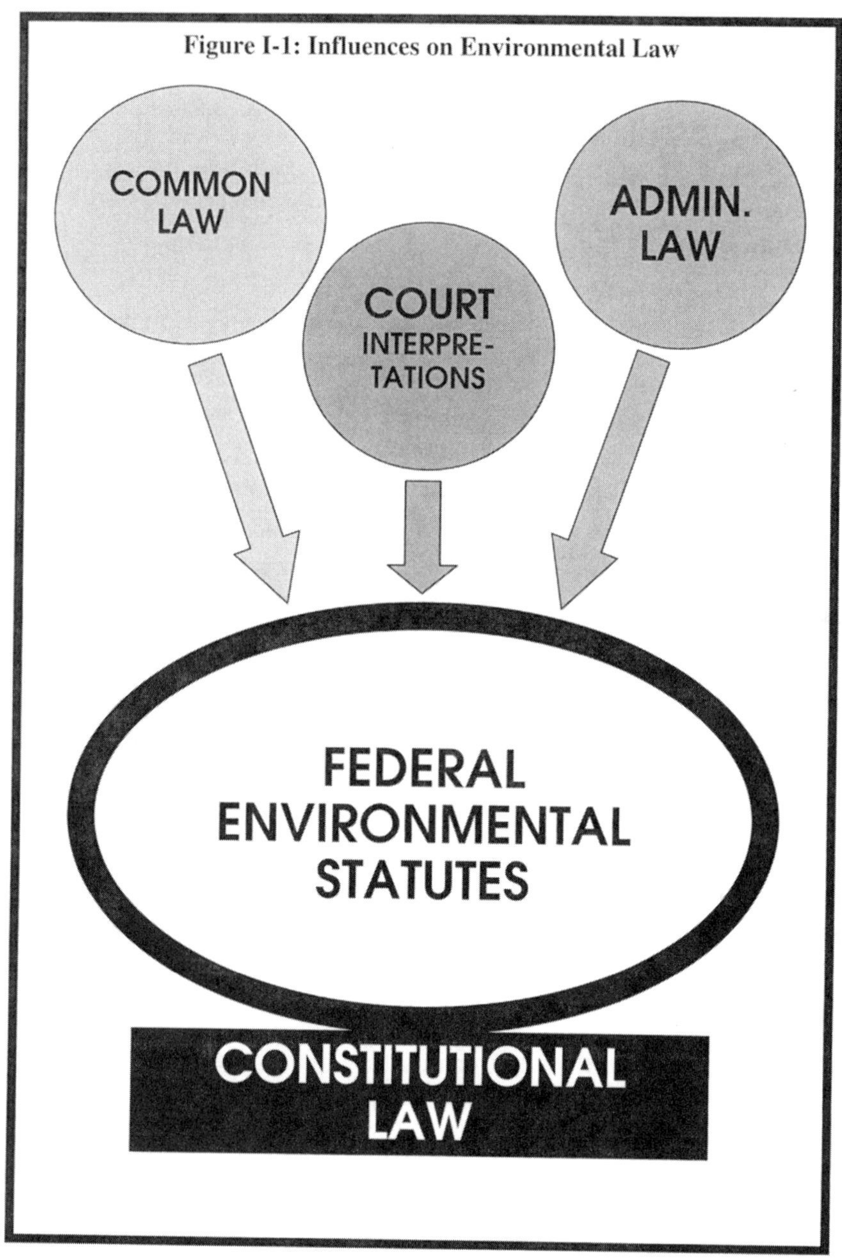

Administrative law is thus highly relevant to the actual implementation of federal environmental law. It governs the procedures that agencies must follow when writing environmental regulations, the procedures and standards that they must use when taking enforcement actions against people who violate environmental requirements, and the standards that federal courts must use when evaluating the agencies' actions. It is no exaggeration to view federal environmental law as applied administrative law.

C. CONSTITUTIONAL LAW

No federal statute, including federal environmental statutes, can violate the U.S. Constitution, either on its face or as applied to particular factual situations. Constitutional law has become an increasingly important component of environmental law. In particular, four constitutional provisions have repeatedly generated challenges regarding the scope of federal environmental law.

First, the ***Commerce Clause*** gives Congress the power to enact federal statutes that regulate interstate commerce. Congress enacted almost all of the federal environmental statutes pursuant to its Commerce Clause powers. In the 1960s and 1970s, when Congress enacted most of the environmental statutes, this reliance was not a problem, because the Supreme Court had not invalidated a federal statute on Commerce Clause grounds in decades. However, in 1995, the Supreme Court decided *United States v. Lopez*, 514 U.S. 549 (1995), invalidating the Gun–Free School Zones Act of 1990 on the grounds that Congress had exceeded its Commerce Clause authority. In reaching its decision, the *Lopez* Court held that the Commerce Clause authorizes Congress to regulate "three broad categories of activity":

> First, Congress may regulate the use of the channels of interstate commerce. Second, Congress is empowered to regulate and protect the instrumentalities of interstate commerce, or persons or things in interstate commerce, even though the threat may come only from intrastate activities. Finally, Congress' commerce authority includes the power to regulate those activities having a substantial relation to interstate commerce, *i.e.*, those activities that substantially affect interstate commerce.

Id. at 558–59 (citations omitted). The *Lopez* decision has exposed federal environmental statutes to numerous Commerce Clause challenges.

Second, most federal environmental statutes encourage states to participate in environmental regulation, an arrangement known as ***cooperative federalism***. Under the ***Tenth Amendment***, however, the federal government cannot *force* states to participate. As a result, many environmental statutes contain provisions that encourage states to adopt certain standards but provide that the federal government will regulate if the states do not.

Third, the U.S. Supreme Court's recent interpretations of the ***Eleventh Amendment*** have made it increasingly difficult for federal courts to entertain suits by members of the public against states that have, at the state level, violated federal environmental laws. Eleventh Amendment jurisprudence is thus most relevant to environmental ***citizen suits***, which is where this textbook will explore that constitutional provision further.

Finally, various versions of the constitutional ***separation of powers doctrine*** influence federal environmental law. Most prominently, this concept was a key component of the U.S. Supreme Court's ***standing*** jurisprudence, which limits the federal courts' ability to entertain environmental citizen suits. In addition, defendants in citizen suits have argued that the whole concept of a citizen suit violates the separation of powers doctrine because citizen suits interfere with the Executive's power to execute the law.

D. INTERNATIONAL LAW AND POLICY

Just as the United States is, in some senses, a single commons, the entire world can also be considered a commons. As the international ramifications of pollution become more obvious, and as international trade and environmental issues become increasingly intertwined, and as it becomes increasingly obvious that countries' actions can have environmental effects in other parts of the world, international law and policy have become increasingly important to the United States' environmental law.

International considerations can take several forms. First, United States agencies and companies may act in ways that can affect other countries' natural resources and environments, raising issues of whether U.S. domestic environmental laws, such as the National Environmental Policy Act (NEPA), apply to that overseas conduct. Second, many federal environmental statutes contain specific provisions to address international environmental problems, such as transboundary pollution. For example, section 115 of the Clean Air Act, 42 U.S.C. § 7415, specifically addresses international air pollution. As Chapter 4 will cover in more detail, Canada has used this provision to challenge the United States' control of its ozone pollution. Finally, and perhaps most importantly, federal environmental laws can implement international treaties related to the environment. Treaties are agreements among various nations to implement certain policies in pursuit of shared goals. In the environmental context, these goals might include preservation of endangered species and biodiversity, reduction of oil spills at sea, or combating global warming by reducing carbon dioxide emissions, among others. Once a nation has ratified a treaty, it usually must then implement that treaty through domestic legislation. As Chapter 3 will explore in more detail, for example, the federal Endangered Species Act implements for the United States the international Convention on International Trade in Endangered Species of Fauna and Flora (CITES).

E. STATUTORY INTERPRETATION

Federal environmental law comes from statutes, and federal courts have developed a collection of informal judicial "rules" to interpret such statutes. As usually stated, the overall goal of statutory interpretation is to ***effectuate congressional intent***. Because Congress has the constitutional authority to write federal law, federal courts should not depart from the legal requirements that Congress intended to apply.

As a general rule, the best evidence of what Congress intended is the language of the statute itself. Thus, one principle of statutory interpretation is the ***plain meaning rule***: courts will first examine the language of the statute itself and, if the meaning is plain and unambiguous, apply that meaning. An important tool for determining a statute's plain meaning is the statute's ***definition section***. As noted in Part III, most federal environmental statutes have at least one section in which Congress defined key statutory terms. These definitions can be some of the best indications of what Congress intended, because they often include not only a definition but also examples and exclusions. When the statute fails to define a key word or phrase, however, the Supreme Court has been relying on ***dictionaries*** to supply the "ordinary meaning" of words.

Another set of tools for discerning the statute's "plain meaning" are the ***canons of statutory construction***. Most canons are common-sense guidelines for what language probably means under certain circumstances. One canon, for instance, dictates that words are given their ordinary meaning unless Congress clearly indicates otherwise. Thus, in *Nix v. Hedden*, 149 U.S. 304 (1893), the U.S. Supreme Court decided that a tomato was a "vegetable," not a "fruit," for purposes of the Tariff Act of 1883 (and hence subject to duties), because even though tomatoes technically are fruits, most people ordinarily consider them to be vegetables. Other canons of statutory construction include: *noscitur a sociis* ("a thing shall be known by its associates"), which dictates that a word takes meaning from the words with which it is grouped; *expresio unius est exclusion alterius* ("the expression of one thing suggests the exclusion of all others"), which indicates that if Congress explicitly mentioned one thing, it meant to exclude everything else; *the rule of the last antecedent*, which dictates that a modifier refers back only to the last word it could describe or modify, unless the statute's punctuation dictates otherwise; and *the and/or rule*, which indicates that, generally, Congress uses "and" to indicate that *all* items in a series are included or required, while it uses "or" to indicate that items in a series are alternatives or separate considerations.

Despite statutory definition sections, dictionaries, and canons, statutory language often remains ambiguous, particularly with respect to how a statutory requirement should apply to an unusual or unanticipated situation. As one recent example, it took a U.S. Supreme Court decision to resolve the issue of whether the greenhouse gases that contribute to climate change are "pollutants" for purposes of the Clean Air Act. If the language of the statute does not adequately reveal Congress's intent, courts have several other tools of statutory construction to work with. First, courts will consider any ***agency interpretations*** from the implementing agency. The U.S. Supreme Court has developed a series of rules and guidelines to govern how federal courts should deal with federal agency interpretations of the statutes they implement. In general, however, the agency's interpretation is entitled to respect, and federal courts will usually defer to the agency's interpretation if it is reasonable. Second, as has already been discussed with reference to the common law, one such tool is legal ***borrowing***—if a statutory concept or principle is closely related to a concept or principle from the common law or from a related statute, a court may "borrow" the interpretations from common law or the related statute and import them into the statute that it is analyzing.

A third tool to resolve ambiguous language is the statute's ***legislative history***—the history of Congress's dealing with the legislation that can sometimes give insights into what Congress intended the legislation to do. As you know, the two branches of Congress—the House of Representatives and the Senate—are responsible for enacting all federal statutes. Federal statutes begin as bills introduced into each house. As bills wend their way through various committees for approval, congresspersons write reports explaining what the bill is and what the bill does. In addition, Representatives and Senators often debate various provisions of the bills when they come up for discussion before the full body. Sometimes the Senate and House versions of a particular piece of legislation are identical or nearly so, but more often they differ in some significant way. As a result, the proposed legislation often goes to a joint conference committee, which irons out the differences, writes a joint committee report, and sends the joint bill to each house for a vote. If both the House and the Senate pass the legislation, it goes to the President. If the President signs the legislation, it becomes federal law. Occasionally the President will issue an explanation of why he is signing the legislation. Committee reports, congressional debates, and presidential commentaries are three forms of legislative history. As you will see in the cases, courts consider committee reports, and especially the joint committee reports, to be the most persuasive form of legislative history. However, the current Supreme Court is split regarding whether courts should examine legislative history at all. Justice Scalia, in particular, dislikes legislative history and only rarely considers it.

F. ENVIRONMENTAL JUSTICE

"Environmental justice" is the term used to refer to the civil rights aspects of environmental law. Richard O. Brooks, for example, has defined "environmental justice" broadly to include "the proper distribution of environmental amenities, the fair correction and retribution of environmental abuses, the fair restoration of nature, and the environmentally fair exchange of resources." Richard O. Brooks, *A New Agenda for Modern Environmental Law* 6 J. ENVTL. L. & LITIG. 1, 26 (1991). More commonly, however, "environmental justice" refers to "the demands of poor and minority communities for equitable environmental enforcement and facility siting * * *." KENNETH A. MANASTER, ENVIRONMENTAL PROTECTION AND JUSTICE 21 n.1 (2d ed. 2000). Such demands arose because poor and minority communities perceived discrimination in the ways that the EPA and other federal agencies implemented the various environmental laws. For example:

> In a comprehensive survey of every U.S. environmental lawsuit concluded in the past seven years, the NLJ [National Law Journal] found penalties against pollution law violators in minority areas are lower than those imposed for violations in largely white areas. In an analysis of every residential toxic waste site in the 12–year-old Superfund program, the NLJ also discovered the government takes longer to address hazards in minority communities, and it accepts solutions less stringent than those recommended by the scientific community.
>
> This racial imbalance, the investigation found, often occurs whether the community is wealthy or poor.
>
> The following are key National Law Journal findings, gathered over an eight-month period, and based on a computer-assisted analysis of the census data, the civil court case docket of the Environmental Protection Agency, and the agency's own record of performance at 1,177 Superfund toxic waste sites:
>
> - Penalties under hazardous waste laws at sites having the greatest white population were about 500 percent higher than penalties at sites with the greatest minority population. Hazardous waste, meanwhile, is the type of pollution experts say is most concentrated in minority communities.
> - For all the federal laws aimed at protecting citizens from air, water and waste pollution, penalties in white communities were 46 percent higher than in minority communities.
> - Under the giant Superfund clean-up program, abandoned hazardous waste sites in minority areas take 20 percent longer to be placed on the national priority action list than those in white areas.
> - In more than half of the 10 autonomous regions that administer EPA programs around the country, action on cleanup at Superfund sites begins from 12 percent to 42 percent later at minority sites than at white sites.
> - At the minority sites, the EPA chooses "containment," the capping or walling off of a hazardous dump site, 7 percent more frequently than the cleanup method preferred under the law, permanent "treatment," to eliminate the waste or rid it of its toxins. At white sites, the EPA orders treatment 22 percent more often than containment.

Marianne Lavelle *et al.*, *Unequal Protection: The Racial Divide in Environmental Law*, NATIONAL L.J. (Sept. 21, 1992), at S2.

The National Law Journal's study, and other studies like it, did not go unchallenged. *See, e.g.*, Mary Bryant, *Unequal Justice? Lies, Damn Lies, and Statistics Revisited*, ABA SECTION OF NATURAL RESOURCES, ENERGY, AND ENVIRONMENTAL LAW NEWS (Sept./Oct. 1993), at 3. Nevertheless, they did inspire official recognition that environmental law is not necessarily even-handed in its regulation and that certain communities may already be disadvantaged by a history of decisions that effectively concentrated hazardous waste treatment facilities and certain kinds of industrial facilities within those communities. In response, the EPA established an Office of Environmental Equity. More comprehensively, in 1994, President Bill Clinton issued Executive Order No. 12898, 59 Fed. Reg. 7629 (Feb. 11, 1994). This order, entitled "Federal Actions to Address Environmental Justice in Minority Populations and Low Income Populations," requires all federal agencies, including the EPA and other environmental agencies, to study and assess the effects of their actions on minority, Native American, and low-income communities.

In recognition of the 20th anniversary of this Executive Order, the EPA is pursuing "Plan EJ 2014." The goals of this plan are: (1) "Protect health in communities overburdened by pollution"; (2) "Empower communities to take action to improve their health and environment"; and (3) "Establish partnerships with local, state, tribal, and federal organizations to achieve healthy and sustainable communities." EPA, *Environmental Justice: Plan EJ 2014*, http://www.epa.gov/environmentaljustice/plan-ej/index.html. The plan includes development of legal tools to effectuate environmental justice.

Because environmental justice issues arose most dramatically in the context of hazardous waste, this textbook will first address such issues in depth in Chapter 1.

G. THE ECONOMICS OF ENVIRONMENTAL REGULATION AND COST-BENEFIT ANALYSES

Environmental law tends to be restrictive law, particularly as it applies to individuals: environmental statutes usually prevent people from doing things with, in, and to the environment or require that people conduct their activities more carefully than had previously been allowed. Such restrictions come with associated ***costs***—the costs of not being able to acquire resources on demand, the costs of having to install pollution control equipment, the costs of having to engage in monitoring and reporting results to the government, the costs of having to go through permitting processes, and so forth. In enacting environmental legislation and rules, regulators assess the benefits from protecting the environment against the costs (financial, political, and otherwise) of increased regulation. As a result, legislators and the people that elect them generally regulate environmental issues only after the harms become fairly obvious, after the scientific proof is fairly certain, and after the ***benefits*** of such legislation are fairly clear.

As a practical matter, some kind of cost-benefit analysis, explicit or implicit, rigorous or "gut-level," occurred among congresspersons before they enacted every federal environmental statute. However, the term "***cost-benefit analysis***" usually refers to the more formal and detailed analyses that agencies perform before implementing particular environmental provisions or programs. At the federal level, every President since Ronald Reagan has ordered federal agencies like the EPA to perform cost-benefit analyses for every major regulation they write. Most recently, President Obama affirmed the role of cost-benefit analysis in federal regulation. Improving Regulation and Regulatory Review, Exec. Order No. 13,563, 76 Fed. Reg. 3821 (Jan. 18, 2011).

Cost-benefit analysis is an inherently rational approach to regulation: Why bother to regulate if the benefits of the regulation will not outweigh the costs? In the environmental context, however, cost-benefit analysis can rarely be precise. How much is a tree worth left in the forest, as compared to a tree cut down and turned into lumber? The latter calculation is fairly easy, but the former is extremely difficult, because usually no ***markets*** exist to set ***prices*** for intact ecosystems and the services that they provide. As a result, historically, analysts (including regulators) often valued extractive uses of the environment more highly than intact ecosystems.

Value is an inherently ***anthropocentric*** (human-centered) issue: the environment is valuable because and to the extent that it is important to humans. Nevertheless, there are many kinds of value that humans can assign to the environment. Most obviously, the environment has ***use value***. For example, the environment supplies ***goods*** that people use and sell in various markets, such as trees for firewood and lumber, minerals for industry and construction, fish for food, water for drinking and irrigation, and so on. Use values can be further subdivided into ***direct use values*** and ***indirect use values***. Direct uses of the environment, especially environmental goods, generally have the advantage of being easy to value in terms of dollars because they are sold on the open market. The values of goods are direct use values. Indirect use values, in turn, reflect the value of environmental processes that support direct uses, such as the plankton that feed the fish that fishermen catch. Another type of use value is the value of the environment for hiking, camping, boating, birdwatching, photography, and other forms of ***recreation***. The values of these uses are not quite as easy to ***monetize***—translate into dollar values—as those for goods, but approximations are still relatively easy to generate through entrance and lodging fees, travel expenses, and equipment costs.

While use values provide a good starting point for valuing the environment, relying exclusively on use values would reduce the value of the environment to the sum of its parts. Most people acknowledge that intact ecosystems are often worth more than just the goods they produce, and one way of assessing these other benefits is through ***non-use values***. Non-use values include such things as the ***spiritual*** and ***aesthetic*** value of the environment. The most controversial non-use value is the ***existence value*** of the environment—the value a person attaches to just knowing that humpback whales, or Yellowstone Park, or the Great Barrier Reef, or old-growth forests, exist somewhere in the world, regardless of whether the person actually plans to visit or use these facets of the environment. While existence value is undoubtedly real—indeed, it helps explain the wide appeal of "Save the Whales" and "Save the Tigers" and "Save the Coral Reefs" campaigns—it is notoriously difficult to measure. One method of attempting to assess the existence value of the environment, for example, is the ***"willingness-to-pay" survey***, where researchers actually poll people regarding how much those people would be willing to pay to ensure a particular environmental benefit or to avoid a particular environmental harm.

Recently, certain schools of economics have suggested another means of valuing the intact environment. They measure environmental value not just in terms of goods and direct uses but also in terms of ***ecosystem services***. Ecosystem services are the services that intact ecosystems provide and that humans depend upon. For example, intact wetlands and clean soils are very good at filtering water. In the mid–1990s, New York City chose to restore and manage the Catskills Mountains watershed, which supplies the city's drinking water, rather than build a new drinking water treatment plant. The reason was easy: it was cheaper for the city to restore the environment, which could then filter the city's drinking water naturally, than it would have been for the city to build a new treatment plant.

New York City's drinking water provides an easy example of how ecosystem services can be valued in dollar amounts, because the city knew both the cost of the ***technological replacement*** for the treatment system and the ***restoration costs***. Other means of calculating the value of ecosystem services are possible. In a controversial 1997 study, for example, a group of ecological economists estimated that the total value of the world's ecosystem services was about $33 trillion (the median value)—far more than the combined gross domestic products of all of the nations on Earth. *See* Robert Constanza *et al.*, *The Value of the World's Ecosystem Services and Natural Capital*, 387 NATURE 253 (1997). While that figure is disputable on several grounds (although, notably, the authors purposefully chose *conservative* estimates throughout their calculations), it at least serves the authors' basic purpose of emphasizing, in dollar figures, that intact, functional ecosystems are quite valuable—more valuable *in toto* than the goods that humans can extract from them.

In addition, many of the benefits derived from environmental protection relate to the preservation and improvement of human health, but calculating the dollar value of these benefits is not necessarily any easier than calculating the dollar value of environmental harm. How much is a life worth? How about a life with some debilitating disease, as compared to a healthy life? How do we value a decreased risk of cancer?

Despite these monetization difficulties, however, environmental cost-benefit analyses are commonplace. The EPA, for example, analyzed the costs and benefits of 20 years of regulation under the Clean Air Act, from 1970 to 1990. As shown in Figure I–2, it easily charted the costs of compliance with the Clean Air Act and the amount of pollutants eliminated. Benefits, however, were more difficult to calculate, because they consisted mainly of improvements in health as a result of the reductions in air pollutants. The EPA began by identifying health consequences avoided in the 20 years of Clean Air Act regulation, as shown in Figure I–3. However, the EPA also admitted that certain benefits could not be ***monetized***. These non-monetized benefits are presented in Figure I–4. Nevertheless, the EPA could assign dollar values to certain health benefits, as shown in Figure I–5.

Figure I-2: Direct Costs of Compliance with the Clean Air Act

EPA graph.

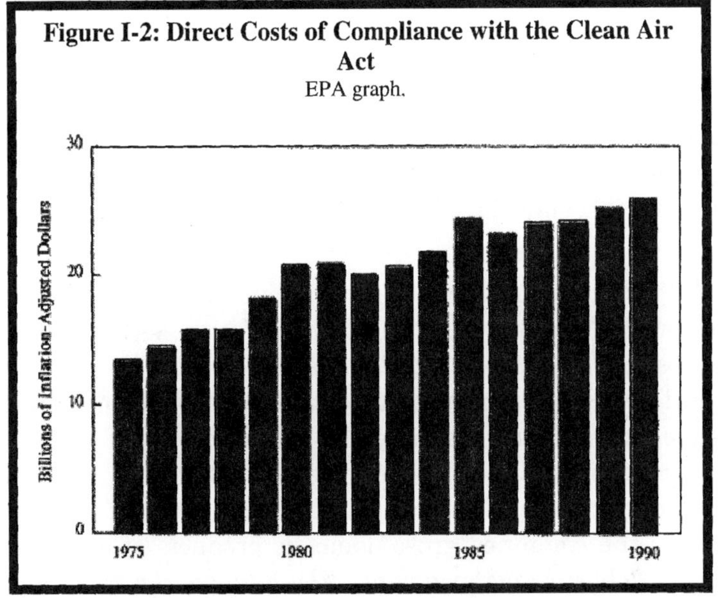

Using these figures, the EPA calculated that the total benefits of the Clean Air Act were worth somewhere between $5.6 and $49.4 trillion, with a central estimate of $22.2 trillion, while the costs of compliance amounted to only $0.5 trillion. In other words, regulation under the Clean Air Act clearly produced a net benefit for the country. Summarized from U.S. E.P.A., *Executive Summary*, FINAL REPORT TO CONGRESS ON BENEFITS AND COSTS OF THE CLEAN AIR ACT (EPA 410–R–97–002) (Oct. 1997), *available at* http://www.epa.gov/oar/sect812/812exec2.pdf.

In 2003, the federal Office of Management and Budget (OMB) performed cost-benefit analyses of major federal environmental regulations and determined that, for both the single year 2001–2002 and the ten-year period from 1992–2002, benefits of environmental regulation far outweighed the costs. For example, estimates of benefits from EPA's major rules from October 1, 2001, to September 30, 2002, ranged from $1.25 to $4.8 billion, whereas those same rules imposed costs of only $192 million. OFFICE OF INFORMATION AND REGULATORY AFFAIRS, OFFICE OF MANAGEMENT AND BUDGET, INFORMING REGULATORY DECISIONS: 2003 REPORT TO CONGRESS ON THE COSTS AND BENEFITS OF FEDERAL REGULATIONS AND UNFUNDED MANDATES ON STATE, LOCAL, AND TRIBAL ENTITIES 6 (2003). Over the ten-year period from October 1, 1992, to September 30, 2002, major EPA rules imposed estimated costs of about $23.4 to $26.6 billion while producing estimated benefits of $120.8 to $193.2 billion. *Id.* at 7. This report thus suggested, like the Clean Air Act study, that environmental regulation is a net benefit for the United States.

The OMB's latest cost-benefit report on federal regulations appeared in June 2011. OMB, 2011 REPORT TO CONGRESS ON THE BENEFITS AND COSTS OF FEDERAL REGULATIONS AND UNFUNDED MANDATES ON STATE, LOCAL, AND TRIBAL ENTITIES (June 2011). Notably, for all federal regulations from October 1, 2000, to September 30, 2010, "the air pollution rules from the Environmental Protection Agency (EPA) produced 62 to 84 percent of the benefits and 46 to 53 percent of the costs." *Id.* at 3. In total, 32 major EPA rules during this period imposed $23.3 to $28.5 billion in costs (in 2001 dollars) to achieve $81.8 to $550.7 billion in benefits, *id.* at 13 table 1-1, again suggesting that environmental regulation provides a net benefit to the United States. Among EPA programs, moreover, air regulations produced the greatest ratio of benefits to costs, followed by water regulations. *Id.* at 15 table 1-2.

Figure I-3: Health Consequences Avoided Through Clean Air Act Regulation
EPA chart.

Endpoint	Pollutant(s)	Affected Population	Annual Effects Avoided[a] (thousands)			Unit
			5th %ile	Mean	95th %ile	
Premature Mortality	PM[a]	30 and over	112	184	257	cases
Premature Mortality	Lead	all	7	22	54	cases
Chronic Bronchitis	PM	all	498	674	886	cases
Lost IQ Points	Lead	children	7,440	10,400	13,000	points
IQ less than 70	Lead	children	31	45	60	cases
Hypertension	Lead	men 20-74	9,740	12,600	15,600	cases
Coronary Heart Disease	Lead	40-74	0	22	64	cases
Atherothrombotic brain infarction	Lead	40-74	0	4	15	cases
Initial cerebrovascular accident	Lead	40-74	0	6	19	cases
Hospital Admissions						
All Respiratory	PM & Ozone	all	75	89	103	cases
Chronic Obstructive Pulmonary Disease & Pneumonia	PM & Ozone	over 65	52	62	72	cases
Ischemic Heart Disease	PM	over 65	7	19	31	cases
Congestive Heart Failure	PM & CO	65 and over	28	39	50	cases
Other Respiratory-Related Ailments						
Shortness of breath, days	PM	children	14,800	68,000	133,000	days
Acute Bronchitis	PM	children	0	8,700	21,600	cases
Upper & Lower Respiratory Symptoms	PM	children	5,400	9,500	13,400	cases
Any of 19 Acute Symptoms	PM & Ozone	18-65	15,400	130,000	244,000	cases
Asthma Attacks	PM & Ozone	asthmatics	170	850	1,520	cases
Increase in Respiratory Illness	NO2	all	4,840	9,800	14,000	cases
Any Symptom	SO2	asthmatics	26	264	706	cases
Restricted Activity and Work Loss Days						
Minor Restricted Activity Days	PM & Ozone	18-65	107,000	125,000	143,000	days
Work Loss Days	PM	18-65	19,400	22,600	25,600	days

[a] The following additional human welfare effects were quantified directly in economic terms: household soiling damage, visibility impairment, decreased worker productivity, and agricultural yield changes.

[a] The 5th and 95th percentile outcomes represent the lower and upper bounds, respectively, of the 90 percent credible interval for each effect as estimated by uncertainty modeling. The mean is the arithmetic average of all estimates derived by the uncertainty modeling. See Chapter 7 and Appendix I for details.

[a] In this analysis, PM is used as a proxy pollutant for all non-Lead (Pb) criteria pollutants which may contribute to premature mortality. See Chapter 5 and Appendix D for additional discussion.

Figure I-4: Nonmonetized Effects of Air Pollution

EPA chart.

Pollutant	Nonmonetized Adverse Effects
Particulate Matter	Large Changes in Pulmonary Function Other Chronic Respiratory Diseases Inflammation of the Lung Chronic Asthma and Bronchitis
Ozone	Changes in Pulmonary Function Increased Airway Responsiveness to Stimuli Centroacinar Fibrosis Inflammation of the Lung Immunological Changes Chronic Respiratory Diseases Extrapulmonary Effects (i.e., other organ systems) Forest and other Ecological Effects Materials Damage
Carbon Monoxide	Decreased Time to Onset of Angina Behavioral Effects Other Cardiovascular Effects Developmental Effects
Sulfur Dioxide	Respiratory Symptoms in Non-Asthmatics Hospital Admissions Agricultural Effects Materials Damage Ecological Effects
Nitrogen Oxides	Increased Airway Responsiveness to Stimuli Decreased Pulmonary Function Inflammation of the Lung Immunological Changes Eye Irritation Materials Damage Eutrophication (e.g., Chesapeake Bay) Acid Deposition
Lead	Cardiovascular Diseases Reproductive Effects in Women Other Neurobehavioral, Physiological Effects in Children Developmental Effects from Maternal Exposure, inc IQ Loss [/1] Ecological Effects
Air Toxics	All Human Health Effects Ecological Effects

[/1] IQ loss from direct, as opposed to maternal, exposure is quantified and monetized. See Tables ES-1 And ES-3.

Figure I-5: Monetized Benefits from Clean Air Act Regulation

EPA chart.

Endpoint	Pollutant	Valuation (mean est.)	
Mortality	PM & Lead	$4,800,000	per case /1
Chronic Bronchitis	PM	$260,000	per case
IQ Changes			
Lost IQ Points	Lead	$3,000	per IQ point
IQ less than 70	Lead	$42,000	per case
Hypertension	Lead	$680	per case
Strokes /2	Lead	$200,000 $150,000	per case-males[3] per case-females[3]
Coronary Heart Disease	Lead	$52,000	per case
Hospital Admissions			
Ischemic Heart Disease	PM	$10,300	per case
Congestive Heart Failure	PM	$8,300	per case
COPD	PM & Ozone	$8,100	per case
Pneumonia	PM & Ozone	$7,900	per case
All Respiratory	PM & Ozone	$6,100	per case
Respiratory Illness and Symptoms			
Acute Bronchitis	PM	$45	per case
Acute Asthma	PM & Ozone	$32	per case
Acute Respiratory Symptoms	PM, Ozone, NO_2, SO_2	$18	per case
Upper Respiratory Symptoms	PM	$19	per case
Lower Respiratory Symptoms	PM	$12	per case
Shortness of Breath	PM	$5.30	per day
Work Loss Days	PM	$83	per day
Mild Restricted Activity Days	PM & Ozone	$38	per day
Welfare Benefits			
Visibility	DeciView	$14	per unit change in DeciView
Household Soiling	PM	$2.50	per household per PM-10 change
Decreased Worker Productivity	Ozone	$1	/4
Agriculture (Net Surplus)	Ozone	Change in Economic Surplus	

/1 Alternative results, based on assigning a value of $293,000 for each life-year lost are presented on pg. ES-9.

/2 Strokes are comprised of atherothrombotic brain infarctions and cerebrovascular accidents; both are estimated to have the same monetary value.

/3 The different valuations for stroke cases reflect differences in lost earnings between males and females. See Appendix G for a more complete discussion of valuing reductions in strokes.

/4 Decreased productivity valued as change in daily wages: $1 per worker per 10% decrease in ozone.

H. RISK ASSESSMENT

Legislatures tend to regulate more quickly (and more stringently) when environmental problems pose direct and serious risks to human health and welfare. As noted, Congress first enacted most of the federal environmental statutes in the 1960s and 1970s. At that point, certain environmental harms—and their potential effect on humans—had become obvious. Many rivers throughout the country were so polluted that they could and did catch fire. Heavy industry in increasingly concentrated cities pumped millions of tons of air pollutants into the atmosphere every year, creating haze, smog, and "killer fogs." In contrast, Congress has not regulated as quickly or effectively environmental problems that remained difficult to discern or adequately prove, such as climate change, ozone holes, and loss of ocean biodiversity.

Congress's responses to obvious problems reflect one form of risk assessment, a "calculation" that these problems were "bad enough" to require regulation. More scientifically, ***risk assessment*** is the process of calculating the risk that an individual will experience some sort of harm based on a population's exposure to the cause of that harm. A few environmental statutes, notably the Clean Air Act and statutes involving toxic pollutants, explicitly adopt a ***health-based, risk assessment approach*** to regulation and require federal agencies to set regulatory standards to protect human health, regardless of the cost. Most statutes, however, combine risk assessment and cost-benefit analyses. One component of such analyses will be the seriousness of the risks involved, as outlined in Figure I–6.

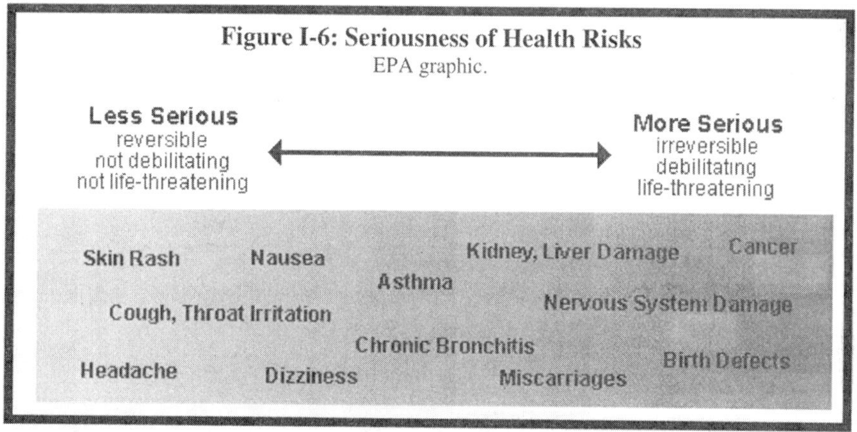

Figure I-6: Seriousness of Health Risks
EPA graphic.

Another component of risk-based regulation will be the level of risk reduction required. It is rarely realistically or economically possible to eliminate all risk from a given type of activity without simply prohibiting the activity—and such prohibitions come with their own costs. How much risk is allowed to remain is often a combination of several factors, including public perception of the risk and the resulting politics, technological capacity to reduce the risk, the importance and utility of the activity, *etc.* However, a common thread running through both Congress's statutes and the EPA's regulations is that, in general, the risk of cancer or acute toxic poisoning should be reduced to one chance in a million. Think about that baseline as you look at Figure I–7.

Figure I-7: Risks of Common Events
EPA graphic.

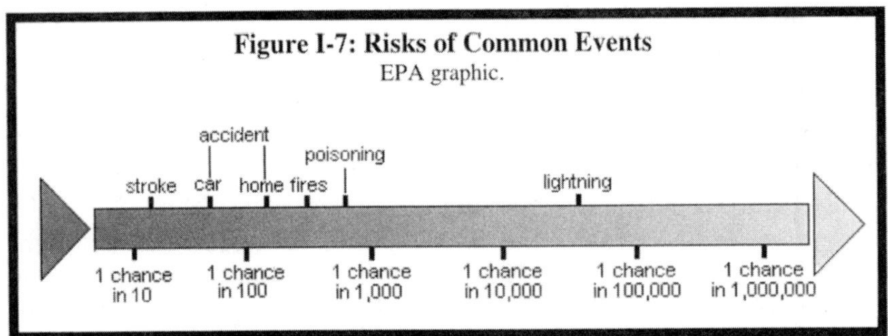

A risk of one chance in a million is more generally denoted as 1 X 10^{-6} . The EPA has explained this notation as follows:

> Risk analysts describe risks numerically in scientific notation, for example 1 x 10^{-5}, which means that there is one chance in 100,000 of an event occurring. It is important to note that these risk statistics are population averages, while risk analysts usually estimate risk to the maximum exposed individual. * * *

U.S. EPA, *Air Pollution and Health Risk*, EPA 450/3–90–022 (March 1991), *available at* http://www.epa.gov/ttn/atw/3_90_022.html (last updated June 6, 2007).

The process of identifying and quantifying risks is known as ***risk assessment***. Figure I–8 shows the four-step risk assessment process that the EPA follows. At the ***hazard identification*** step, the EPA identifies which pollutants may be of concern and what problems they might cause, especially to human health. As noted, toxics and carcinogens (cancer-causing pollutants) tend to be of the most concern. The evidence that the EPA uses to identify the hazard can itself be a point of contention. Human studies are the most convincing in demonstrating that a pollutant poses a health hazard to humans, but such studies are rare. As a result, the EPA often has to rely on animal studies, creating potential uncertainties regarding how well animal responses correlate to human responses. (Of course, if the EPA is worried about hazards to fish and wildlife, such animal studies may become more convincing.)

At the ***exposure assessment*** step, the EPA estimates both how much of a pollutant people (or fish and wildlife) are exposed to and how many people (or animals) are exposed. Monitoring and computer modeling often supply this information.

Figure I-8: The Risk Assessment Process
EPA graphic.

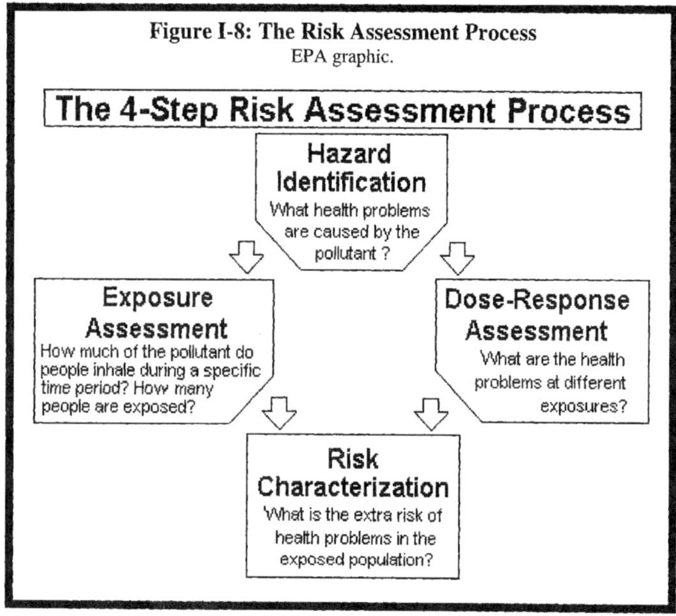

The ***dose-response relationship*** describes the effects from exposure to a given amount of a pollutant over a given period of time. Various relationships are possible. For example, a ***linear*** dose-response relationship exists if the negative effects of a pollutant get steadily worse with a more concentrated and/or longer exposure. Often more problematic for regulators are ***non-linear*** dose-response relationships, where small amounts of pollutant exposure cause no apparent problems until a threshold exposure is reached, at which point the negative effects are dramatic and, in the worst cases, irreversible. As in hazard identification, the EPA uses human and animal studies to establish dose-response relationships.

These preliminary analyses allow the EPA to characterize the risk. A ***risk characterization*** presents a standardized, and hence comparable, measurement of the risk added as a result of exposure to a pollutant. The EPA might characterize the risk to an individual or to a population. One common risk characterization, for example, is the ***maximum individual lifetime cancer risk***, which the EPA calculates by multiplying the maximum estimated lifetime exposure to a carcinogen by the dose-response relationship. At the population level, in turn, the EPA might be interested in the ***distribution of individual risks***, an analysis that recognizes that not all exposed individuals will be exposed at the maximum exposure. Figure I–9 gives an example of a risk distribution graphic. However, because of information limitations and the use of assumptions in modeling and data extraction, risk characterizations inevitably include a certain amount of ***uncertainty***. This uncertainty often leaves the EPA's final regulations open to legal attack, especially if the regulated community concludes that the EPA is being too over-protective.

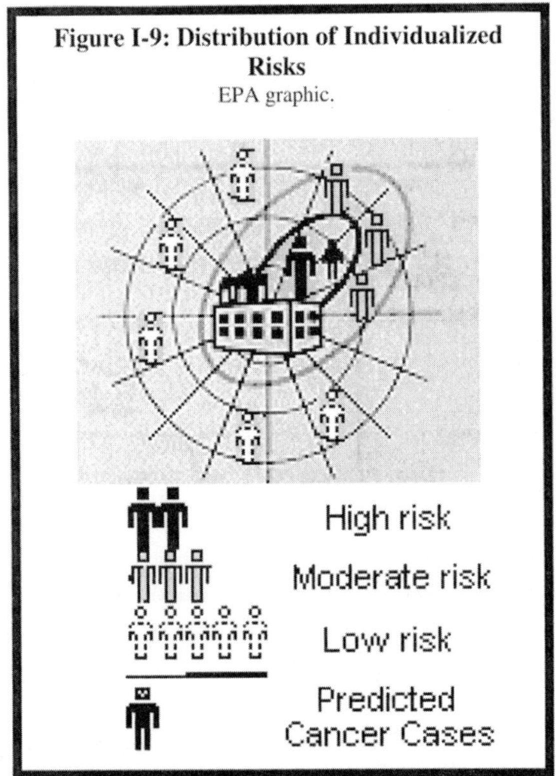

Figure I-9: Distribution of Individualized Risks
EPA graphic.

On the subject of overprotection, Thomas McGarity has noted that "[i]n the Benzene Case (*Industrial Union Department, AFL-CIO v. American Petroleum Institute*, 448 U.S. 607 (1980)), the U.S. Supreme Court suggested that a one-in-one-billion chance of developing cancer was not a significant risk, but that a one-in-one-thousand chance of dying was. *Id.* at 655. However, the court did not consider exposure rates when talking about risk." Thomas O. McGarity, *The Story of the Benzene Case, in* RICHARD J. LAZARUS & OLIVER A. HOUCK, EDS., ENVIRONMENTAL LAW STORIES 141, 164 (Foundation Press 2005). Professor McGarity credits the Benzene Case with making quantitative risk assessment a routine part of environmental law. *Id.* at 165–69.

I. SCIENTIFIC AND TECHNOLOGICAL DEVELOPMENTS

Accurate risk assessment and cost-benefit analyses depend on accurate science. Without adequate studies of whether and how various activities cause various environmental effects, or whether and how various environmental conditions contribute to human health or ecosystem problems, Congress and the environmental agencies are unlikely to be able to create rational or adequate environmental statutes and regulations. As a result, environmental law has tended to evolve as scientific information becomes more detailed and more accurate.

In addition, various environmental statutes impose science-related requirements on the implementing agencies. For example, the EPA sets the national standards for air quality to protect human health, and the Clean Air Act requires it to rely on science in assessing what standards are required. Similarly, the Secretaries of the Interior and Commerce, acting through the U.S. Fish & Wildlife Service and the National Marine Fisheries Service (now NOAA Fisheries), respectively, list species for protection under the Endangered Species Act on the basis of the best scientific evidence available.

Most recently, Congress imposed generally scientific requirements on agency decisionmaking through the ***Data Quality Act***, also known as the Information Quality Act, 44 U.S.C. § 3516, Historical and Statutory Notes (as added by Pub. L. No.106–554, § 1(a)(3) (Title V, § 515), 114 Stat. 2763, 2763A–153 (Dec. 21, 2000)). This statute required the Director of the federal Office of Management and Budget (OMB) to issue guidelines "that provide policy and procedural guidance to Federal agencies for ensuring and maximizing the quality, objectivity, utility and integrity of information (including statistical information) disseminated by Federal agencies * * *." *Id.* The OMB issued its final guidelines in January 2002. Guidelines for Ensuring and Maximizing the Quality, Objectivity, Utility, and Integrity of Information Disseminated by Federal Agencies, 67 Fed. Reg. 369 (Jan. 3, 2002). In addition to requiring that agencies substantiate the substantive quality of their scientific information, the OMB guidelines also require federal agencies to allow affected persons and entities to "seek and obtain, where appropriate, correction of information disseminated by the agency that does not comply with the OMB or agency guidelines." *Id.* As a result, the OMB guidelines effectively allow any affected person to challenge the scientific and technical information that any federal agency—including the environmental agencies—uses in implementing its statutory duties. Nevertheless, litigation decisions involving the Act have been limited—fewer than 30 from federal courts as of June 2011.

Technology also plays an important role in environmental regulation. Most pollution controls, for example, are technological—"scrubbers" that can remove air pollutants from industrial emissions, filters that can remove pollutants from liquid effluent before it enters a waterway, treatment processes that can detoxify waste, catalytic converters that can reduce pollution emissions from automobiles and other vehicles. Many of the pollution-control requirements that you will encounter in the federal environmental statutes are ***technology-based***: the EPA sets pollution control requirements on the basis of some technological standard, such as the ***Maximum Achievable Control Technology*** **(MACT)** or the ***Best Available Technology*** **(BAT)** or ***Reasonably Available Control Technology*** **(RACT)**.

As these labels suggest, technology-based pollution control requirements can vary considerably in how well they reduce pollution—and in how expensive the pollution control equipment is. As you will see, Congress tends to require the most stringent technology-based pollution controls from ***new polluters*** in areas known to have pollution problems and for control of ***toxic pollutants***. On occasion, however, Congress also engages in ***technology-forcing regulation***, setting environmental requirements at levels that force the regulated parties and industries to develop new technologies that will allow them to meet those requirements.

V. THE COMPLEXITIES OF THE ENVIRONMENT: CLIMATE CHANGE AND OTHER CHALLENGES FOR REGULATORS

As the quotation that opened this chapter acknowledged, everything in the "environment" is connected to everything else. However, as you proceed through this casebook, you'll notice that federal environmental and natural resources statutes rarely actively acknowledge those connections. Instead, Congress tends to organize environmental and natural resources statutes around a particular medium or resource (land, species, air, water).

Since the 1960s and 1970s, however, it has become increasingly clear that this segmented approach to regulation can accomplish only so much. Multi-media, multi-jurisdiction problems strain the limits of the existing statutes. For example, atmospheric deposition of pollutants such as mercury and nutrients is a major water quality problem. Because the sources discharge their pollutants into the air, they would seem to fall within the jurisdiction of the Clean Air Act. However, as you'll find, the Clean Air Act is structured to achieve National Ambient *Air* Quality Standards—not water quality standards. As a result, these air emissions, when they fall into water, can cause violations of the Clean Water Act, but the sources aren't directly regulated under the Clean Water Act.

The largest *uber*-problem currently challenging federal environmental law is global climate change, and this casebook will from time to time show you how climate change considerations challenge traditional applications of the federal environmental statutes. As you probably know, the scientific community is in general consensus that human emissions of carbon dioxide (CO_2) and other greenhouse gases are altering the planet's climate. As a regulatory matter, one immediate problem is that the whole world is contributing to the problem, raising issues of whether the EPA's regulation of greenhouse gases under the United States' Clean Air Act is even allowed, as you'll read in Chapter 4's excerpt from *Massachusetts v. EPA*. However, climate change is also altering how federal agencies analyze the environmental effects of their actions, both under the National Environmental Policy Act (NEPA, Chapter 2) and the Endangered Species Act (Chapter 3). Finally, because climate change creates widespread risks that affect everyone all at once, it creates procedural challenges for citizens trying to sue to correct the problem, as this casebook explores in Chapter 6.

The larger point, however, is that you should constantly be looking for the ways in which Congress and the federal agencies have responded to newly recognized and newly emerging environmental problems. Sometimes, as in the Clean Air Act, Congress has repeatedly amended the statute to address previously unrecognized air pollution problems, such as nonattainment and acid rain. Other times, the EPA and the courts have adopted expansive interpretations of the most relevant statute in order to address the problem—or have *refused* such interpretations, leaving the recognized problem outside of the scope of federal regulation. See if you can identify certain common characteristics among these reactions—keeping in mind, of course, that the politics surrounding environmental and natural resources law and policy have also changed several times over the last 40 years.

CHAPTER 1

ENVIRONMENTAL LAW AND THE COMMON LAW: HAZARDOUS WASTE, RCRA, AND CERCLA

■ ■ ■

I. COMMON LAW ENVIRONMENTAL ACTIONS AND WASTE DISPOSAL

A. COMMON LAW ENVIRONMENTAL ACTIONS

Before Congress wrote any federal environmental statutes, individuals directly harmed by pollution or other environmental damage could try to bring a lawsuit under any of several common-law tort theories, many of which you may have already studied in your Torts and Property courses. These theories include ***strict liability***, ***negligence***, ***trespass***, and ***nuisance***.

Strict liability often arises when a defendant engages in inherently dangerous activities or abnormally dangerous conduct. Many inherently dangerous activities have environmental consequences. For example, in one of the first applications of strict liability in England, in *Rylands v. Fletcher*, the court found a defendant liable for damages when large quantities of water the defendant was storing on his land flooded the neighboring plaintiff's land. More recently, some courts have held defendants strictly liable for problems arising from the defendant's storage or transportation of hazardous waste, while other courts have refused to impose strict liability on defendants who store gasoline. Thus, what activities are considered "abnormally" dangerous can vary from region to region.

Unlike strict liability, ***negligence*** is a fault-based approach to liability. Before a defendant is liable in negligence, the defendant's conduct must have violated some duty or standard of care, generally set as the care a reasonable person would use. The defendant's unreasonable conduct must also be the factual and legal (proximate) cause of the plaintiff's harm. In the environmental context, negligence is the foundation of most ***toxic torts.***

Trespass is a tort cause of action arising from the defendant's ***physical invasion*** of the plaintiff's real property. Environmental trespass occurs only if the defendant does something physical to plaintiff's land—noise pollution is generally insufficient, but air pollution that settles on the plaintiff's land, or water pollution that contaminates plaintiff's water or land, can satisfy the elements of trespass.

The most important common-law precursor to the environmental statutes is ***nuisance***. A nuisance is classically defined as an unreasonable interference with the plaintiff's use and enjoyment of plaintiff's real property, and hence nuisance can encompass more kinds of environmental harms, such as noise, than trespass.

Two kinds of nuisance exist: ***public nuisance*** and ***private nuisance***. Public nuisance is an unreasonable interference with rights held by the public in general. Usually, state or local governments bring public nuisance actions against the defendant on behalf of the general public. Private individuals also can bring public nuisance actions, but—in the majority of states—only if the plaintiff's injury differs in *kind* from the injury that the general public suffered. Private nuisance, in contrast, is an unreasonable interference with the rights of a plaintiff who has a possessory interest in the land affected. Either the landowner or the tenant can sue to abate a private nuisance.

Classically, the remedy for a proven nuisance was an injunction that ended the nuisance. More recently, successful nuisance plaintiffs can receive damages, as well.

B. NUISANCE AND WASTE DISPOSAL

Many environmental nuisance cases arise in the context of ***waste disposal***—someone suffers an unreasonable interference with his or her use of property because someone else is trying to get rid of noxious by-products or other waste. Centuries ago in England, the courts recognized that noxious waste disposal could constitute a public nuisance. For example, in *The Prior of Southwark's Case*, Y.B. Trin., 13 Hen. 7, f. 26, pl. 4 (1498), at least one English judge determined that the plaintiff, the Prior of Southwark, had stated a claim when the defendant's lime pit, used for curing calf skins and sheep skins, polluted a stream that the Prior's tenants used "to dye their clothes, to water their beasts, to bake and to brew, and for other easements." *Id., as translated in* CECIL HERBERT STUART FIFOOT, HISTORY AND SOURCES OF THE COMMON LAW: TORT AND CONTRACT (London: Stevens & Sons Limited, 1949).

In the United States, before Congress enacted the federal environmental statutes, nuisance continued to be the most important of the common-law controls on waste disposal in the United States. However, in light of the problems that improper waste disposal can cause, many state and local governments began to enact statutes and ordinances specifying that certain kinds of waste disposal constituted *nuisance per se* and requiring government review and/or permitting before certain kinds of disposal activities could occur. These statutes acknowledged that, as a basis for comprehensive environmental regulation, nuisance has several distinct shortcomings. Consider those shortcomings—and the advantages of hazardous waste statutes—in the following case.

OREGON DEPARTMENT OF ENVIRONMENTAL QUALITY v. CHEMICAL WASTE STORAGE AND DISPOSITION, INC.

528 P.2d 1076 (Or. App. 1974).

LANGTRY, JUDGE.

Acting by and through the Department of Environmental Quality (DEQ), the State of Oregon initiated this injunctive proceeding seeking to compel compliance by defendant corporation with the provisions of the Environmentally Hazardous Wastes Statutes (ORS 459.410 through 459.690), and to have the "disposal site" owned by the defendant declared a public nuisance. * * *

* * * Evidence, elicited at the hearing below, shows that in 1969 defendant purchased approximately 6,000 acres of the Alkali Lake bed located in southeastern Oregon after its president completed some three years of study concerning a "safe" disposition of pesticide wastes. Preliminary research had indicated that these waste materials could be successfully biodegraded into the soil, and that the most preferable site for such an operation would be one situated in a remote area where the soil was alkaline and where spillage would not contaminate a watershed. Having acquired the Alkali property which met essentially all of these requirements, Chemical Waste began early in 1969—pursuant to a contract with Rhodia, Inc., of Portland—to transport residue materials to that tract. These materials were contained in 55-gallon steel drums which were themselves stored within a ten-acre plot of the Alkali property.

* * * In 1971 the legislature passed and the Governor signed Oregon Laws 1971, ch. 699 (ORS 459.410 through 459.690) creating the Department of Environmental Quality which was to assume jurisdiction over the control of "environmentally hazardous wastes," the proposed definition of which encompassed those materials present at Alkali Lake. After considering the impact of this new law, the directors of Chemical Waste decided that its anticipated operations were no longer feasible and determined that the biodegrading of the materials acquired pursuant to its contract with Rhodia would have to be completed before the terms of that law became applicable. Steps were then taken to that end, including the fencing of a 400-acre area to be used for the biodegrading and the installation of vats, mixing machinery and electricity.

Although the specific terms of the Act indicated that any preexisting disposal site could be maintained without a license from the DEQ until 60 days after rules and regulations governing the form and contents of license applications were adopted, Chemical Waste was notified by the DEQ in December of 1971—some three months before any such regulations were, in fact, formulated—that no additional waste materials could be brought onto the Alkali site and that further disposal of materials already present was prohibited. As a result of this action, defendant terminated its operations, paid all creditors, and transferred the assets of the corporation—with the exception of the ten acres upon which the barrels containing the waste materials were stored—to the stockholders in exchange for their stock. At the time this suit was initiated by the state, therefore, Chemical Waste was a corporate "shell," with the ten-acre parcel constituting its sole asset.

* * * We are directed by ORS 19.125(3) to try "anew upon the record" this suit and to make our own independent study of the record and to arrive at our own conclusions. Consideration of the evidence disclosed by this record as well as issues involved leads us to the conclusions that (1) contrary to the finding of the lower court the storage of the waste materials on the defendant's Alkali Lake property does not constitute a public nuisance, and (2) because those waste materials fall within the statutory definition of "environmentally hazardous" materials (ORS 459.410(6)), the defendant is currently operating a "disposal site," the maintenance of which is subjected to statutory provisions with which both the defendant and the state must comply.

"The term 'nuisance' is incapable of an exact and exhaustive definition which will fit all cases, because the controlling facts are seldom alike, and because of the wide range of subject matter embraced under the term. There is no exact rule or formula by which the existence of a nuisance may be determined, but each case must stand on its own facts and special circumstances." 58 AM. JUR. 2D 553–54, Nuisances § 1. Acknowledging their essentially amorphous character, the Supreme Court of Oregon has declined to "define" the elements of either private—affecting an individual or limited number of individuals—or public—those prejudicial to the health, comfort or safety of citizens at large—nuisances. [T]he court found this analysis to be persuasive:

> "The law of nuisance affords no rigid rule to be applied in all instances. It is elastic. It undertakes to require only that which is fair and reasonable under all the circumstances. . . ." [*E. St. Johns Shingle Co. et al. v. Portland*, 195 Or. 505, 522, 246 P.2d 554, 561 (1952),] quoting *Stevens v. Rockport Granite Co.*, 216 Mass. 486, 488, 104 N.E. 371 (1914).

and quoted with approval from *Schott v. Appleton Brewery Co.*, 205 S.W.2d 917, 920 (Mo. App. 1947):

> ". . . What is a reasonable use and whether a particular use is a nuisance . . . depends upon the facts of each particular case, such as

location, character of the neighborhood, nature of the use, extent and frequency of the injury, the effect upon the enjoyment of life, health, and property, and the like. The use of property in one locality and under some circumstances may be lawful and reasonable, which under other circumstances would be unlawful, unreasonable, and a nuisance. 39 AM. JUR. pp. 298, 299, § 16...." 195 Or. at 520, 246 P.2d at 560–61.

[Moreover, in 1960, the Oregon Supreme Court] held:

"... Each case then must be decided on its own peculiar facts, balancing the interests before the court.

"...

"... The flexibility of nuisance law enables the trial judge to take into consideration ... all relevant factors which will assist him in balancing the interests of the parties before the court in light of relevant public interest." [*Atkinson et al. v. Bernard Inc.*, 223 Or. 624, 631, 633, 355 P.2d 229, 232, 233 (1960).]

Here, the "nuisance" complained of conceivably falls into only that category of nuisance defined * * * as " ... [c]ases involving harm to human comfort, safety or health by reason of the maintenance by a defendant upon his land of noxious or dangerous instrumentalities...." Although the court below gave no indication of the grounds upon which its conclusion that "(t)he condition existing at the site does constitute a nuisance ..." was based, it is evident that the decision was necessarily founded on the determination that the site is harmful to "human comfort, safety, or health."

While, as we note below, defendant has been "operating" the site in violation of the Environmentally Hazardous Wastes Statutes from the time they became effective in early 1972, that continuing violation does not require a finding that the site constitutes a public nuisance. We find nothing in ORS 459.410 through 459.690 declaring such a site to be a nuisance *per se*. These statutes do direct tight control of the operation or maintenance of such sites and provide sanctions to be imposed where compliance is lacking; they do not, however, serve to make that a nuisance which is not so in fact.

The cases from which we have quoted lead to the conclusion that the peculiar locations and surroundings involved in the cases are of great significance and may in many cases be determinative of whether any nuisances exist. * * * It is undisputed that the ten-acre storage site involved here is located amidst the high desert of eastern Oregon, some three miles from the nearest "residence or farm or anything," and some two to three miles from the nearest public road.

The state alleges, however, that in spite of the site's remote location it should be condemned as a nuisance to the public on the ground that there are presently dangers of harm which may result from (1) human or animal contact with the waste materials, (2) contamination of water in the Alkali

Lake Basin, and (3) an interference with the public comfort caused by odors emitting from the site.

In light of the fact that the entire ten-acre site is surrounded by a trench and enclosed by a woven-wire, "stock-tight" fence topped with three lines of barbed wire, kept locked at all times, the first, and probably the second, of the "dangers" alluded to by the state do not appear to be substantial. With reference to the second, much testimony was introduced below relative to the effect of heavy rainfall upon the disposal site where many of the steel drums have deteriorated to the point of being less than water tight. The point of that testimony appears to have been to suggest that such rainfall might produce a "run-off" capable of contaminating water sources in the area. Apart from the facts that the possibility of a rainfall substantial enough to cause such a run-off is extremely remote, that the ten acres is surrounded by a trench and that the wastes in the drums are about 90 percent solid, the evidence also indicates that the site is located within the "sump" of a 30–by–35 mile sink into which all surface drainage moves and that the only potable water to be found in the entire basin—99 percent of which is owned by the former stockholders of Chemical Waste—is located on private property and enclosed by a fence with locked gates designed to deter public use.

Although the record includes some reference to public complaints concerning the presence of a "phenolic" odor characteristic of the materials stored on defendant's land, additional testimony revealed that there was no evidence that the "source" of the offensive odors had ever been traced to the site and may well have been due to the fact that roadside weeds and "many hundreds of acres of sagebrush ..." unassociated with defendant's property had been sprayed with 2,4–D which produces an identical distinct odor. Testimony did, in fact, indicate that the odors associated with the storage site extended for a distance of no greater than one-fourth mile. In light of the fact that the nearest public road or habitation is some three miles from the storage location, this evidence tends to minimize the possibility that the site presently causes any public discomfort.

Taken as a whole this record does not indicate that defendant's storage site constitutes a nuisance at this time.

The record does indicate, however, that the defendant is presently "operating" a disposal site without the license required by the legislature. Because the defendant is apparently unwilling and unable to meet conditions which are a prerequisite to obtaining such a license (specifically those included in ORS 459.530(3), and 459.590(1) and (2)(f)), it is evident that any application submitted would be inadequate and thus refused.

ORS 459.520(2) provides:

> "If the license is refused, the licensee must cease operations within a time set by the commission that allows reasonable opportunity for the licensee to take such steps for the security or disposition of stored material as the commission deems necessary. The commission shall

> not direct removal of stored material unless an alternate site has been designated as suitable for disposal of it."

The Environmental Quality Commission may, therefore, proceed to communicate to the defendant those "steps" it deems necessary "for the security or disposition" of the pesticide wastes now stored on the Alkali Lake property. These "steps" may, dependent on prevailing circumstances, include the removal of those materials if an alternate site is designated as suitable for the storage or disposition of the materials in accordance with the Environmental Hazardous Wastes Statutes (ORS 459.410 through 459.690).

If Chemical Waste fails to comply with any order issued by the Commission—not an unlikely possibility in light of defendant's current financial status—an equitable proceeding may then be initiated pursuant to ORS 459.690 at which the respective obligations and responsibilities of the parties will be judicially determined. * * *

NOTES

1. **The Public Nuisance Claim.** Did Chemical Waste's property constitute a public nuisance? Why or why not? Note that, as a government body, Oregon did not have to show any special injury in order to bring its public nuisance action. Did that fact help its case? Why or why not?

2. **Common Law Burdens of Proof.** Where does the common law put the burden of proof? What is the practical effect of that burden of proof allocation? Is there a more effective way to ensure that pollution of the environment does not occur?

3. **The Statutory Claim.** Why did Oregon win this case? What was the relationship between public nuisance and the Oregon statutes? What advantages did the statutes give the State of Oregon over common-law public nuisance in regulating waste disposal?

4. **The Limitations of Nuisance: An Environmental Nuisance Problem.** Professor Daniel H. Cole created the following hypothetical to illustrate the limitations of nuisance in addressing environmental pollution. What problems would arise in a public or private nuisance claim on behalf of one of the gardeners in this hypothetical?

> Consider a stylized case involving the hypothetical air pollutant, pollutox. Pollutox is a by-product of many industrial activities and internal combustion engines. It is a pervasive pollutant known to harm human health and the environment. Virtually every medium-sized city in the country of Freeland has several sources of pollutox emissions. Plants that emit pollutox, in order to be good neighbors, build tall smokestacks to place their pollutox emissions high into the prevailing winds, which carry them away from the source. This avoids creating local air pollution problems. The winds carry the pollutox emissions hundreds of miles away. It is very difficult (and, therefore, expensive) to determine where the pollutox emissions from any given source ultimately fall from the sky. But where and when they do, they cause health and environmental

problems. Automobiles are another major source of pollutox emissions. Every single car emits a very small amount of pollutox—too little by itself to cause any significant harm. But tens of thousands of cars within a thirty-mile or so radius can cumulatively produce enough pollutox to create a local public health threat.

One day, several residents of Urbania, a large city in the State of Caladonia in the country of Freeland, were working in their gardens, when they began to suffer acute respiratory problems and were hospitalized—some for a few hours, others for several days. The doctors determined the cause of their respiratory problems was pollutox inhalation.

DANIEL H. COLE, POLLUTION AND PROPERTY 101 (Cambridge University Press 2002).

* * *

II. THE FEDERAL RESOURCE CONSERVATION AND RECOVERY ACT (RCRA)

A. TRIGGERING RCRA: THE DEFINITION OF "SOLID WASTE"

By way of background, Thomas Merrill has noted that "in the early 1980s, . . . the municipal garbage disposal industry began to undergo a major transformation. The driving force behind this transformation was a shift in public attitudes about wastes buried in the ground." Thomas W. Merrill, *The Story of* SWANCC*: Federalism and the Politics of Locally Unwanted Land Uses, in* RICHARD J. LAZARUS & OLIVER A. HOUCK, ENVIRONMENTAL LAW STORIES 283, 284 (2005). This shift in attitude regarding land disposal of waste is also evident in RCRA.

Congress originally enacted the ***Solid Waste Disposal Act*** **(SWDA)**, 42 U.S.C. §§ 6901–6992k, in 1976, but it was the 1980 amendments to this statute in the ***Resource Conservation and Recovery Act*** **(RCRA)** that gave the statute its more common name. In the SWDA and RCRA, Congress sought to address the problem of solid and hazardous waste. Specifically, Congress found that "although land is too valuable a national resource to be needlessly polluted by discarded materials, most solid waste is disposed of on land in open dumps and sanitary landfills" and that "disposal of solid waste and hazardous waste in or on the land without careful planning and management can present a danger to human health and the environment * * *." RCRA § 1002(b)(1), (2), 42 U.S.C. § 6901(b)(1), (2).

RCRA applies to "solid waste," which the statute defines as:

> any garbage, refuse, sludge from a waste treatment plant, water supply treatment plant, or air pollution control facility and other discarded material, including solid, liquid, semisolid, or contained gaseous material resulting from industrial, commercial, mining, and agricultural operations, and from community activities, but does not

> include solid or dissolved material in domestic sewage, or solid or dissolved materials in irrigation return flows or industrial sources which are point sources subject to permits under section 1342 of Title 33 [the Clean Water Act], or source, special nuclear, or byproduct material as defined by the Atomic Energy Act of 1954, as amended * * *.

RCRA § 1004(27), 42 U.S.C. § 6903(27). Several aspects of this definition are noteworthy. First, "solid waste" does not have to be solid—liquids, semisolids, and even some gaseous materials qualify. Second, "solid waste" *does* have to be waste—that is, ***discarded material***. Finally, Congress expressly exempted from RCRA wastes that certain other statutes, notably the Clean Water Act, already regulated.

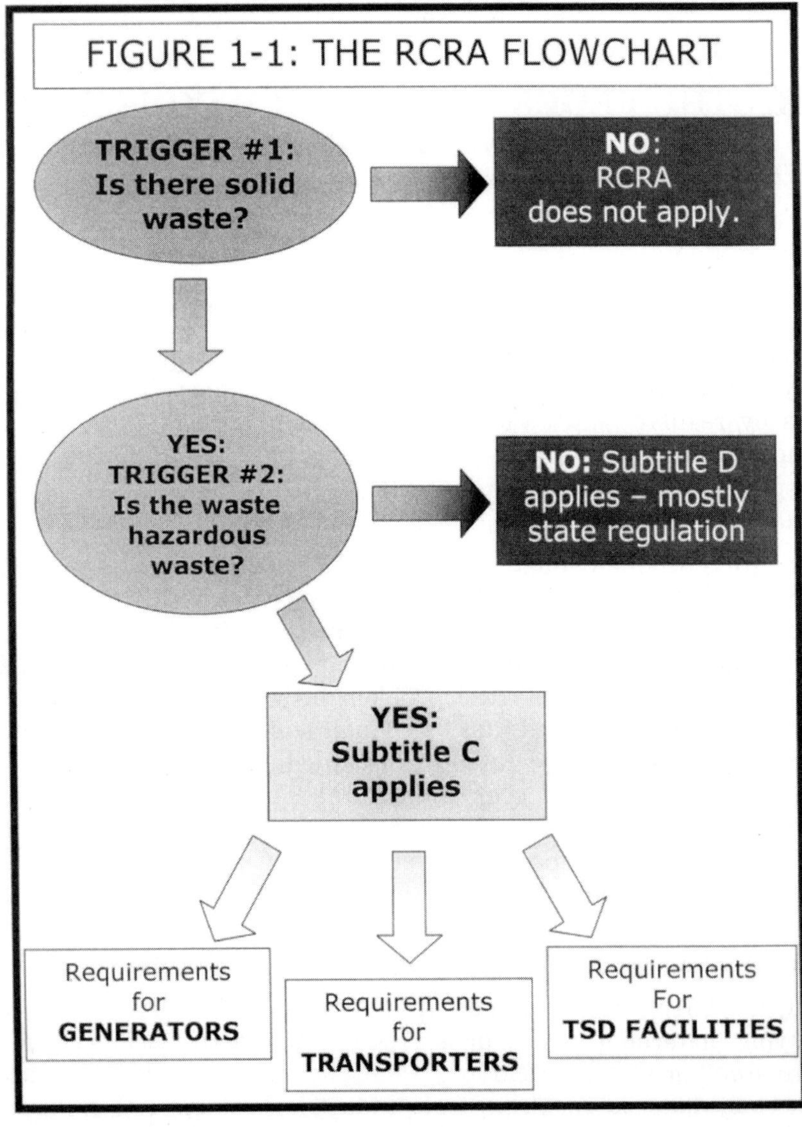
FIGURE 1-1: THE RCRA FLOWCHART
TRIGGER #1: Is there solid waste?
NO: RCRA does not apply.
YES: TRIGGER #2: Is the waste hazardous waste?
NO: Subtitle D applies – mostly state regulation
YES: Subtitle C applies
Requirements for GENERATORS
Requirements for TRANSPORTERS
Requirements For TSD FACILITIES

The EPA has further defined "solid waste" in its RCRA regulations. As is generally the case for RCRA, the regulatory definitions are far more complex than the statutory definitions. However, the EPA, like Congress, has emphasized that "solid waste" is "discarded material." Specifically:

(1) A solid waste is any discarded material that is not excluded by § 261.4(a) or that is not excluded by variance granted under §§ 260.30 and 260.31.

(2) A discarded material is any material which is:

(i) Abandoned * * *; or

(ii) Recycled * * *; or

(iii) Considered inherently waste-like * * *; or

(iv) A military munition identified as a solid waste in 40 C.F.R. § 266.202.

40 C.F.R. § 261.2(a).

1. When Is Material "Discarded"?

While RCRA's definition of "solid waste" is broad, it does raise the issue of timing: *when* do materials that humans put in contact with the environment qualify as "discarded"—that is, as "solid wastes" subject to regulation under RCRA? The EPA regulation above offers four options: materials are "discarded" when they are "abandoned," "recycled," "considered inherently waste-like," or military munitions identified as solid wastes by regulation. The EPA further defines two of these categories, "considered inherently waste-like" and military munitions, through long, very specific regulatory provisions in, respectively, 40 C.F.R. § 261.2(d) and 40 C.F.R. § 266.202, the EPA's ***Military Munitions Rule***. "Abandoned" and "recycled" materials, however, have been subject to more general discussions.

Abandonment is a very old concept in law, which you may have explored in your Property course. At common law, abandonment of property requires: (1) an intent to abandon; and (2) overt acts that constitute abandonment. Under the EPA's regulatory definition of "solid waste," materials are considered "discarded materials"—and therefore "solid wastes" subject to RCRA—if "they are abandoned by being:"

(1) Disposed of; or

(2) Burned or incinerated; or

(3) Accumulated, stored, or treated (but not recycled) before or in lieu of being abandoned by being disposed of, burned, or incinerated.

40 C.F.R. § 261.2(b). Burning and incineration are clear enough. However, to say that material is "discarded" because it is "abandoned" because it is "disposed of" or accumulated to be disposed of seems rather circular. As a result, cases like the following have further elucidated this prong of the "solid waste" definition.

NO SPRAY COALITION, INC. v. CITY OF NEW YORK

252 F.3d 148 (2d Cir. 2001).

PER CURIAM:

In an effort to control West Nile Virus—a fatal, mosquito-borne disease—the City of New York last summer undertook an insecticide spraying program, and may renew that program in the summer of 2001. Plaintiffs appeal an order of the United States District Court for the Southern District of New York (Martin, J.), denying, *inter alia*, a preliminary injunction against the renewed spraying and dismissing their claim under the citizen suit provision of the Resource Conservation Recovery Act ("RCRA"), 42 U.S.C. §§ 6972(a)(1)(A) and (B). * * *

I.

The RCRA provides for an injunction where:

> the past or present handling, storage, treatment, transportation, or *disposal* of *any solid* or hazardous *waste* [] may present an *imminent and substantial endangerment* to health or the environment....

Id. § 6972(a) (emphasis added). The term "solid waste"

> means any garbage, refuse, sludge, from a waste treatment plant, water supply treatment plant, or air pollution control facility and *other discarded material*....

Id. § 6903(27) (emphasis added).

Plaintiffs claim, in essence, that (i) the spraying of the pesticides constitutes the "disposal" of a "solid waste" in a manner that renders it "discarded material" causing "imminent and substantial endangerment" to people, and (ii) the spraying into the air of densely populated areas is in violation of the label instructions and this improper use constitutes disposal of a hazardous solid waste without a permit, in violation of 42 U.S.C. § 6925(a).

II.

* * * The district court did not abuse its discretion in denying injunctive relief. Plaintiffs argue that "[o]nce pesticides are sprayed onto or into the air, land, and waters of New York City, they become discarded solid wastes within the meaning of RCRA § 1004(27)." But we have indicated that material is not discarded until after it has served its intended purpose. *Cf. Connecticut Coastal Fishermen's Assoc. v. Remington Arms Co.*, 989 F.2d 1305, 1316 (2d Cir. 1993). We therefore agree with the district court that the pesticides are not being "discarded" when sprayed into the air with the design of effecting their intended purpose: reaching and killing mosquitoes and their larvae. * * *

Notes

1. **The Definition of "Disposed Of."** When is a substance "disposed of" for purposes of triggering RCRA, according to the Second Circuit? Why didn't the sprayed pesticides qualify as "discarded materials"?

2. **RCRA Abandonment and Common Law Abandonment:** How did the Second Circuit's view of "discarded materials" comport with the common-law concept of abandonment? Does this gloss on "discarded material" make sense? Why or why not?

3. **Pesticide Spraying as a Nuisance.** Consider this case as a nuisance case. Could the plaintiffs have won on a public nuisance theory? Why or why not? Could the plaintiffs have won on a private nuisance theory? Why or why not?

4. **Environmental Law and Federal Court Procedures**. In this case, the plaintiffs were requesting a preliminary injunction. In a part of the case not reproduced above, the Second Circuit enumerated the standard elements for a preliminary injunction—irreparable harm and likelihood of success on the merits—but also noted that federal courts will apply that standard differently when government action is involved. *No Spray Coalition*, 252 F.3d at 150. The government action was the state spraying program to eliminate disease-carrying mosquitoes, and the Second Circuit required that "when the injunction sought 'will alter rather than maintain the status quo,' the movant must show 'clear' or 'substantial' likelihood of success." *Id.* (quoting *Rodriguez v. DeBuono*, 175 F.3d 227, 233 (2d Cir. 1999)).

In contrast, in other types of litigation, federal courts will "relax" the preliminary injunction standard in favor of protecting the environment, particularly when it is the government that requests the injunction and particularly when the environmental harm would be irreparable if it occurs. For example, federal judges in the Pacific Northwest states (Oregon, Washington, and Idaho) usually grant preliminary injunctions in litigation regarding the legality of logging, reasoning that if the logging turns out to be illegal, the court will be unable to restore the forest, whereas if the logging is legal, the trees will still be there at the end of the litigation. *See, e.g.*, *Idaho Sporting Congress, Inc. v. Alexander*, 222 F.3d 562, 565 (9th Cir. 2000) (noting that irreparable harm and probability of success on the merits exist on a sliding scale, so that a strong showing of one can reduce the showing necessary for the other). Nevertheless, when the U.S. Supreme Court addressed the issue of a preliminary injunction in a lawsuit involving the National Environmental Policy Act (NEPA, addressed in Chapter 2) in 2008, it emphasized that "[a] preliminary injunction is an extraordinary remedy never awarded as of right." *Winter v. Natural Resources Defense Council, Inc.*, 555 U.S. 7, 24 (2008).

5. **Environmental Citizen Suits**. *No Spray Coalition* is this textbook's first example of an environmental ***citizen suit***. Almost all of the federal environmental statutes include provisions that allow individual members of the public to file suit against persons who violate that statute, or against federal agencies for failure to carry out mandatory statutory duties. This textbook will explore citizen suits in greater detail in Chapter 6.

6. **The Timing of Disposal.** In *Connecticut Coastal Fishermen's Association v. Remington Arms Co.*, 989 F.2d 1305 (2d Cir. 1993), cited in *No Spray Coalition*, the Second Circuit had addressed a similar issue to the one in *No Spray Coalition* but reached the opposite conclusion. The case involved a skeet and trap shooting club that had been operating on Long Island Sound since 1945. As club members pursued their shooting activities, clay targets and lead shot fell into the Sound, accumulating there for over 55 years. Plaintiffs, in another citizen suit, argued that the club owners had violated both RCRA and the federal Clean Water Act because they had disposed of the targets and shot without proper permits. The Second Circuit agreed that the citizens had a claim under RCRA that the club "has created an 'imminent and substantial endangerment' to human health and the environment under § 6972(a)(1)(B)." *Id.* at 1316. Relying heavily on the EPA's amicus brief, the Second Circuit concluded that "the EPA states that the materials are discarded because they have been 'left to accumulate long after they have served their intended purpose.' Without deciding how long materials must accumulate before they become discarded—that is, when the shot is fired or at some later time—we agree that the lead shot and clay targets in Long Island Sound have accumulated long enough to be considered solid waste." *Id.* How can you explain the differences in outcome between *No Spray Coalition* and *Connecticut Coastal Fishermen's Association*?

* * *

WATER KEEPER ALLIANCE v. UNITED STATES DEPARTMENT OF DEFENSE

152 F. Supp. 2d 163 (D. Puerto Rico 2001).

LAFFITTE, CHIEF JUDGE.

This lawsuit presents claims under the Resource Conservation and Recovery Act ("RCRA") [in connection with the Department of Defense's target practice on Vieques Island, near Puerto Rico. The target practice not only destroyed large portions of the island but also resulted in accumulated ordnance.] * * * For reasons that follow, the Court hereby grants Defendants' Motion to Dismiss.

DISCUSSION

* * * 1. RCRA Claims

The parties agree that RCRA allows any person to file suit "against any person, including the United States . . . , who has contributed or who is contributing to the past or present handling, storage, treatment, transportation, or *disposal of any solid or hazardous waste* which may present an imminent and substantial endangerment to health or the environment." 42 U.S.C. § 6972(a)(1)(B) (emphasis added). The parties further agree that for Plaintiffs to succeed on their RCRA claims, they must demonstrate that Defendants are disposing of, or have disposed of, solid waste in Vieques.

a. Fired Ordnance as "Solid Waste" Under RCRA

Plaintiffs argue that as soon as ordnance is fired and makes contact with the land in the Live Impact Area ("LIA"), it becomes solid waste, and the Defendants have disposed of it. Both "solid waste" and "disposal" are statutorily-defined terms. Solid waste is

> any garbage, refuse, sludge from a waste treatment plant, water supply treatment plant, or air pollution control facility and other *discarded* material, including solid, liquid, semisolid, or contained gaseous material resulting from industrial, commercial, mining, and agricultural operations, and from community activities.

Figure 1-2: Vieques Island
EPA map.

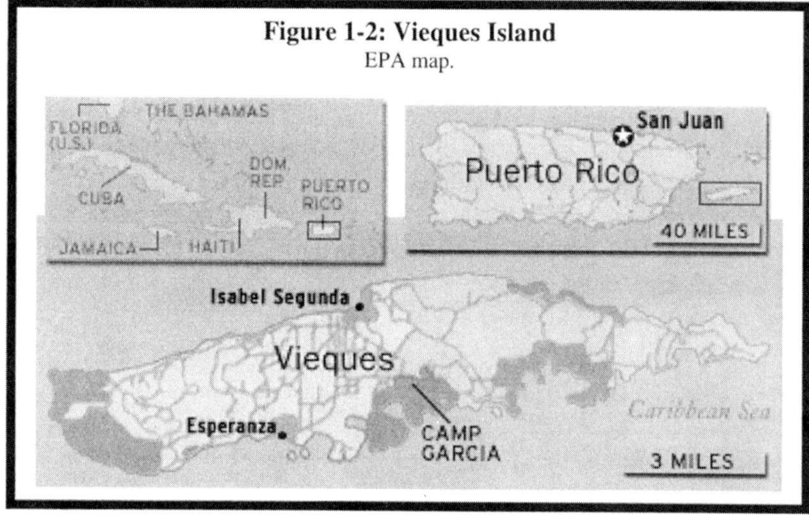

42 U.S.C. § 6903(27) (emphasis added). Disposal is

> the discharge, deposit, injection, dumping, spilling, leaking, or placing of any solid waste ... into or on any land or water so that such solid waste ... or any constituent thereof may enter the environment or be emitted into the air or discharged into any waters, including ground waters.

42 U.S.C. § 6903(3).

Defendants argue that disposal requires placing onto land of solid waste and that solid waste must be "discarded material" under the statute. Plaintiffs do not dispute this position. Thus, the parties' disagreement can be distilled to the following: whether as soon as ordnance is fired and makes contact with the land it is "discarded material." If it is not discarded material, it is not solid waste, and Plaintiffs can not bring suit on the basis of the firing of ordnance in the LIA under RCRA's citizen suit provision.

Defendants contend that ordnance is not discarded material as soon as it is fired onto the LIA. The essence of Defendants' argument is that the firing of munitions and their subsequent contact with the LIA are precisely the intended use of the munitions. In other words,

> [t]he very purpose of the ordnance in the training exercises at issue is to be fired from a plane or ship and to hit the ground, either to explode or to raise dust, depending on whether it is live or inert, so that the observers can evaluate the accuracy of the pilot or gunner.

Thus, Defendants are not discarding ordnance when they fire it at the LIA.

In support of this asseveration, Defendants cite *Connecticut Coastal Fishermen's Ass'n v. Remington Arms Co.,* 989 F.2d 1305 (2nd Cir. 1993), for the proposition that ordnance does not become discarded material until some time after it has served its intended purpose. Plaintiffs agree with Defendants that the Second Circuit's decision was based in large part on the Environmental Protection Agency's ("EPA") *amicus curiae* argument that munitions "eventually" become discarded material by being "left to accumulate long after they have served their intended purpose." Plaintiffs point out, however, that "[s]ince it was uncontroverted that the fired ordnance would remain on the ground without immediate remediation the Court stated that it need not decide whether the ordnance was discarded as soon as the shot was fired, or at some other point."

Plaintiffs argue that this means that ordnance becomes discarded material as soon as it is fired. The Second Circuit's decision in *Connecticut Coastal Fishermen's Ass'n,* however, points to precisely the opposite conclusion. The court stated,

> [w]ithout deciding how long materials must accumulate before they become discarded—that is, when the shot is fired or at some later time—we agree that the lead shot and clay targets in Long Island Sound have accumulated long enough to be considered solid waste.

Connecticut Coastal Fishermen's Ass'n, 989 F.2d at 1316. Thus, the court's language strongly suggests that munitions must "accumulate" for an unspecified amount of time before they can be considered discarded material and thus solid waste.

* * * Finally, Defendants cite *No Spray Coalition v. City of New York,* 2000 WL 1401458 (S.D.N.Y. 2000), in support of their position that munitions do not become discarded material upon being fired. * * * In their opposition, Plaintiffs make no attempt to distinguish the facts in *No Spray Coalition* from the facts in the instant case. The Southern District's analysis persuasively supports the notion that neither insecticide nor munitions become discarded at the time of their release; rather, they can not be considered discarded until some time after they have served their intended purpose.

Undaunted, Plaintiffs present an alternative argument in support of their contention that ordnance becomes discarded material immediately upon being discharged. They assert that even if ordnance does not become discarded material until after it has served its intended purpose, the ordnance being used in the LIA is not serving its intended purpose. Thus, the argument goes, the ordnance is discarded material as soon as it is fired.

Defendants assert that the intended use of their munitions "is to be fired from a plane or ship and to hit the ground, either to explode or to raise dust, depending on whether [they are] live or inert, so that the observers can evaluate the accuracy of the pilot or gunner." Plaintiffs counter that because inert bombs sometimes "skip" off of the range and into the water, Defendants' munitions are not being used for their intended purpose.

Simply because some ordnance fails to fulfill its purpose of landing on the LIA and raising a dust cloud can not, as Plaintiffs would have it, mean that the ordnance is discarded material immediately upon being fired. Regardless of whether the ordnance performs as the gunner or bomber wishes, it is most certainly being used for its intended purpose and is thus not discarded material under RCRA. To hold otherwise would torture the meaning of the term discarded material.

Further, if Plaintiffs' contention were taken to its logical conclusion, every piece of ordnance that did not land precisely where it was intended would be considered discarded material immediately upon being fired. Further, a court faced with the facts in *Connecticut Coastal Fishermen's Ass'n,* in which shotguns were used to shoot lead pellets at clay targets, would have to differentiate between the lead pellets that actually hit the targets and those that did not in determining which lead pellets were discarded material under RCRA. A court dealing with the spraying of insecticides, as in *No Spray Coalition,* would have to determine which airborne droplets of insecticide actually made contact with and killed mosquitos and which did not. Taken further, the court would have to determine whether the mosquitos killed were actually carriers of the West Nile Virus, in determining whether the droplets were being used for their intended purpose. This extreme result can not have been within Congress' contemplation in drafting RCRA.

Thus, RCRA does not support Plaintiffs' contention that munitions become discarded material immediately upon being fired. Not being discarded material, these munitions can not be considered solid waste. Accordingly, the Court hereby dismisses Plaintiffs' claim that Defendants' firing of ordnance onto the LIA constitutes "*disposal of any solid or hazardous waste* which may present an imminent and substantial endangerment to health or the environment." 42 U.S.C. § 6972(a)(1)(B) (emphasis added). * * *

NOTES

1. **Finding Legal Authority.** Puerto Rico is in the First Circuit, not the Second. Nevertheless, the U.S. District Court of Puerto Rico analyzed the ordnance issue using *Connecticut Coastal Fishermen's Association* and *No*

Spray Coalition. Why, do you suppose? How did the district court apply those cases? In particular, how did *Connecticut Coastal Fisherman's Association*—which found that the clay targets and lead shot *were* "solid wastes" under RCRA—support the Department of Defense's argument that its ordnance was *not* "solid waste"?

2. **Timing of RCRA "Solid Waste."** Do you agree with the district court that the ordnance was not "solid waste"? Why or why not? Given the district court's reasoning, will the ordnance *ever* become solid waste? If so, when?

3. **Environmental Law and the Military.** The Department of Defense and the various branches of the armed services have a long history of resisting the application of environmental law to their activities—despite the fact that many of the most contaminated sites in the United States are military bases. In the wake of the September 11, 2001, terrorist attacks, the military sought—and, in the National Defense Authorization Act for Fiscal Year 2004, partially received—statutory waivers from federal environmental statutes, particularly the Endangered Species Act and the Marine Mammal Protection Act. Pub. L. No. 108–136, §§ 318, 319, 117 Stat. 1392, 1433–35 (Nov. 24, 2003). The Department of Defense also sought exemptions from RCRA and CERCLA for munitions left on active "operational ranges" (which presumably would eliminate cases like this one), but Congress has yet to agree—although it has asked for studies regarding the effects of RCRA and CERCLA on military readiness. *Id.* § 320, 117 Stat. 1435–37. More commonly, however, Congress has required the military to comply with CERCLA with respect to specific military bases.

The U.S. Supreme Court has also acknowledged that the military is "special" when it comes to environmental law. Most recently, in *Winter v. Natural Resources Defense Council*, 555 U.S. 7 (2008), the Court reversed the lower courts' granting of preliminary injunctions against the U.S. Navy's use of mid-frequency active sonar (MFAS), which is believed by many to harm marine mammals such as dolphins and whales. The Navy uses MFAS as an improved means of finding submarines, but the Natural Resources Defense Council (NRDC) and other environmental groups challenged the Navy's MFAS training exercises as violating several environmental statutes. The Supreme Court emphasized, first, that plaintiffs seeking an injunction must show that irreparable harm is *likely* if the injunction does not issue. *Id.* at 22. More importantly, it determined that, even if the plaintiffs had shown irreparable harm, the benefits of the Navy's training exercises outweighed the harms to the environment:

> [The national security interests at stake] must be weighed against the possible harm to the ecological, scientific, and recreational interests that are legitimately before this Court. Plaintiffs have submitted declarations asserting that they take whale watching trips, observe marine mammals underwater, conduct scientific research on marine mammals, and photograph these animals in their natural habitats. Plaintiffs contend that the Navy's use of MFA sonar will injure marine mammals or alter their behavioral patterns, impairing plaintiffs' ability to study and observe the animals.

> While we do not question the seriousness of these interests, we conclude that the balance of equities and consideration of the overall public interest in this case tip strongly in favor of the Navy. For the plaintiffs, the most serious possible injury would be harm to an unknown number of the marine mammals that they study and observe. In contrast, forcing the Navy to deploy an inadequately trained antisubmarine force jeopardizes the safety of the fleet. Active sonar is the only reliable technology for detecting and tracking enemy diesel-electric submarines, and the President—the Commander in Chief—has determined that training with active sonar is "essential to national security."
>
> The public interest in conducting training exercises with active sonar under realistic conditions plainly outweighs the interests advanced by the plaintiffs. Of course, military interests do not always trump other considerations, and we have not held that they do. In this case, however, the proper determination of where the public interest lies does not strike us as a close question.

Id. at 25–26.

4. **Statutory Interpretation and Policy Considerations.** What concerns influence the Puerto Rico District Court's view of "solid waste" in this case? What difficulties does it seek to avoid? Do these policy considerations make sense?

* * *

CORDIANO v. METACON GUN CLUB, INC.

575 F.3d 199 (2d Cir. 2009).

DEBRA ANN LIVINGSTON, CIRCUIT JUDGE:

* * * Plaintiffs–Appellants are Simsbury–Avon Preservation Society, LLC, a group of homeowners who live near Defendants–Appellees' shooting range, and Gregory Silpe, a member thereof (collectively referred to as "SAPS"). Defendants–Appellees Metacon Gun Club, Inc., and its members and guests (collectively referred to as "Metacon") operate a shooting range that, according to SAPS, engages in the discharge and accumulation of lead munitions on Metacon's site in violation of the RCRA * * *.

I. The Metacon Site

Metacon has operated a private outdoor shooting range at its present location on 106 Nod Road in Simsbury, Connecticut since the mid–1960s. Metacon's range is located on 137 acres of woods, meadows, wetlands and mountainside, and is situated on a flood plain of the Farmington River Valley. The site is bounded to the north by the Connecticut State Police pistol and rifle ranges, to the west by Nod Road and the Farmington River, to the south by a residence and a golf course, and to the east by a cliff that runs along the entire eastern property boundary.

* * * Metacon has a 100–yard shooting range at the back of which stands an engineered earthen berm for bullet containment. * * *

II. Evidence of Lead Contamination at Metacon

SAPS provided evidence of lead accumulation on Metacon's site based on a SAPS member's non-specific observation of a "tremendous amount of spent ammunition on the ground," and Metacon's admission in a related state lawsuit that "[t]housands of pounds of lead are deposited at the Site[.]" Meanwhile, Metacon provided evidence that, for at least the last ten years, it has conducted "regular clean-ups," where members rake the range to collect materials such as spent casings and munitions.

Several rounds of expert testing have been performed on Metacon's site. In November 2003, the State of Connecticut Department of Environmental Protection ("CTDEP") indicated that groundwater and surface water samples from the Metacon site exceeded Connecticut's Remediation Standard Regulation ("RSR") protection criterion for lead in groundwater and surface water. However, given time constraints on the testing and the fact that standard sampling protocol was not followed, CTDEP indicated that the result could be "skewed[,] . . . potentially resulting in higher concentrations of metals parameters." As a result, CTDEP requested that Metacon retain a consultant to resample the monitoring wells and surface water east of the berm using an appropriate sampling methodology, and report back to the Department.

Metacon hired Leggette, Brashears & Graham, Inc. ("LBG"), which provides professional groundwater and environmental engineering services, to conduct the requested testing. In an April 2004 report, LBG found that "the ground water beneath the shooting range has not been impacted by lead from the shooting range," and that, with respect to wetland surface water, "the dissolved lead findings demonstrate that lead is not leaching out of the soil or surface water to contaminate the surface water." In sum, the sampling "demonstrated that the shoo[t]ing activities at the Metacon property [have] not resulted in lead contamination of the ground water or surface water at the Metacon site." Based on this report, the CTDEP concluded that "[a]ll the results indicate[] that lead was not detected or was present at concentrations in groundwater and surface water below action levels."

SAPS disputed these findings with a May 2005 report produced by its own expert, Advanced Environmental Interface, Inc. ("AEI"). Unlike the LBG study, which tested only groundwater and wetland surface water samples, AEI tested soil samples and wetland sediment samples, as well as wetland surface water samples from the range and area surrounding the berm. With respect to soil samples, all samples collected from the backstop berm area, and all but one sample collected from locations between the firing line and berm, contained total lead concentrations that exceeded the CTDEP Direct Exposure Criterion ("DEC") for residential sites, with several samples exceeding the CTDEP Significant Environmental Hazard ("SEH") notification threshold. Some of these samples were subject to a leaching procedure, with results indicating that "the lead is leachable and may over time pose a threat to ground water quality." With respect to wetland sediment samples, the total lead concentration for all samples exceeded the CTDEP DEC for residential sites. As to the wetland surface water samples, the report found different results in filtered and unfiltered samples. As to the unfiltered samples, the total lead concentrations exceeded the CTDEP chronic aquatic life criterion, with some samples exceeding the acute aquatic life criterion. However, the dissolved lead in the filtered samples was non-detect, meaning that the total lead concentrations in the unfiltered samples were likely "the result of either turbidity caused by suspended lead-bearing particles or colloidal matter." The AEI report does not specifically explain the relevance of the distinction between the results from the filtered and unfiltered wetland surface water samples.

The AEI report states that "[s]pent ammunition from typical firing range activities has contaminated various environmental media on the Metacon Gun Club site." Although the report notes that "firing-range-related contaminants on the site ... represent[ ] a potential exposure risk to both humans and wildlife," it concludes that "[a] risk assessment utilizing the data obtained during this investigation would be necessary to evaluate the degree of risk to humans and wildlife."

It is undisputed that Metacon does not have a hazardous waste disposal permit under the RCRA, 42 U.S.C. § 6925 * * *.

* * *DISCUSSION

* * *II. RCRA

A. Statutory Background

RCRA is a "comprehensive environmental statute that governs the treatment, storage, and disposal of solid and hazardous waste." *Meghrig v. KFC W., Inc.*, 516 U.S. 479, 483 (1996). "RCRA's primary purpose ... is to reduce the generation of hazardous waste and to ensure the proper treatment, storage, and disposal of that waste which is nonetheless generated, 'so as to minimize the present and future threat to human health and the environment.' "*Id.* (quoting 42 U.S.C. § 6902(b)). The statute contains a citizen suit provision, 42 U.S.C. § 6972, "which permits private citizens to enforce its provisions in some circumstances." *Id.* at 484.

* * * RCRA defines solid waste as "any garbage ... and other *discarded material* ... resulting from industrial, commercial, mining, and agricultural operations, and from community activities." 42 U.S.C. § 6903(27) (emphasis added). In order for waste to be classified as hazardous under RCRA, "it must first qualify as a solid waste" pursuant to the statute. *Conn. Coastal Fishermen's Ass'n v. Remington Arms Co.*, 989 F.2d 1305, 1313 (2d Cir. 1993); *see also* 42 U.S.C. § 6903(5) ("The term 'hazardous waste' means a solid waste [that also has additional characteristics.]"). * * *

* * * The definition of solid waste in the RCRA regulations governing permitting violations and other related matters "is narrower than its statutory counterpart." * * *

B. The Permitting Claim

SAPS claims that Metacon is operating a hazardous waste disposal facility without a permit in violation of 42 U.S.C. § 6925(a). Hazardous waste within the meaning of 42 U.S.C. § 6925(a) must meet the narrower regulatory definition of solid waste. Thus, to prevail, SAPS must allege and prove that the lead deposited on the Metacon site is a "discarded material," 42 U.S.C. § 6903(27), which 40 C.F.R. § 261.2(a)(2)(i)(A) defines in relevant part as any material which is "abandoned" by being "[d]isposed of" or by being "[a]ccumulated, stored, or treated (but not recycled) before or in lieu of being abandoned by being disposed of." 40 C.F.R. § 261.2(b). SAPS argues that the maintenance of a shooting range where lead shot accumulates involves "discarded material" within the meaning of the RCRA permitting regulations.

The district court dismissed this claim pursuant to Fed. R. Civ. P. 12(b)(6). The court noted that the EPA took the position in *amicus* briefs * * * that the ordinary use of lead shot on a shooting range does not fall within the regulatory definition of solid waste because "[s]pent rounds of ammunition and target fragments are not ... 'discarded material' within the meaning of the regulation, because they have not been 'abandoned,' ... [but] come to rest on land ... as a result of their proper and expected use." The court observed further that the EPA's guidance manual, Best Management Practices for Lead at Outdoor Shooting Ranges, published in 2001, states that "[l]ead shot is not considered a hazardous waste subject to RCRA at the time it is discharged from a firearm because it is used for its intended purpose. As such, shooting lead shot (or bullets) is not regulated *nor is a RCRA permit required* to operate a shooting range." *Id.* (quoting EPA Doc. No. EPA–902–B–01–001). The court concluded that the EPA's interpretation of its regulations was reasonable and entitled to deference. *Id.* at *6.

In response to a request from this Court, the United States has submitted an *amicus* brief addressing whether lead shot discharged at a shooting range falls within the regulatory definition of solid waste set forth in 40 C.F.R. § 261.2. The United States maintains that the "EPA ... has consistently taken the position that the discharge of lead shot as part of the normal use of that product (i.e., being fired from a gun at a firing range) does not render the materials 'discarded' within the meaning of the RCRA subtitle C permitting regulations under 42 U.S.C. § 6925(a)," and further that the "EPA has repeatedly stated that its regulatory jurisdiction under RCRA does not apply to products that are applied to the land in the ordinary manner of use, because such products are being used, not 'abandoned.' "

We conclude that this interpretation of 40 C.F.R. § 261.2 by the EPA is entitled to deference. The regulation is ambiguous as to whether lead shot discharged into a shooting range's berm, or the range itself, constitutes "discarded material." A person shooting a gun into a berm clearly knows that his spent ammunition will remain there unless removed. But has he therefore discarded it? Or has he instead merely used the ammunition in its intended manner, with the result that it is left on the land? The text of 40 C.F.R. § 261.2 provides no definitive answer.

In such circumstances we will generally defer to an agency's interpretation of its own regulations, including one presented in an *amicus* brief, so long as the interpretation is not plainly erroneous or inconsistent with law.

Here, the agency reasonably determined that lead shot put to its ordinary, intended use, i.e., discharged at a shooting range, is neither "material which is . . . abandoned by being . . . [d]isposed of," nor "[a]ccumulated . . . before or in lieu of being abandoned by being disposed of." 40 C.F.R. § 261.2(a)(2)(i), (b). The EPA's distinction between "abandonment" of lead shot, which falls within the regulatory definition of solid waste, and the normal, intended use of lead shot at a shooting range, which does not, is consistent with related RCRA regulations. For example, 40 C.F.R. § 261.2(c)(ii) provides that certain "commercial chemical products . . . are not solid wastes if they are applied to the land and that is their ordinary manner of use." Similarly, "[a] military munition is not a solid waste when . . . [u]sed for its intended purpose," while an "unused military munition is a solid waste when . . . [t]he munition is abandoned by being disposed of." 40 C.F.R. § 266.202(a), (b) * * * . More generally, the EPA's position that materials put to their ordinary, intended use are not "abandoned" under the regulatory definition of solid waste, and hence are not subject to the permitting requirements of 42 U.S.C. § 6925(a), is consistent with the RCRA. As this Court has recognized, the words of the statute "contemplate that the EPA would refine and narrow the definition of solid waste," *Conn. Coastal,* 989 F.2d at 1315, for the purpose of the more stringent regulatory treatment afforded to hazardous wastes in Subchapter III, where the permitting provisions are located. The EPA's interpretation of its regulations—excluding from the more stringent permitting requirements of § 6925(a) those materials deposited on the land as part of their intended use—does just that.

We also note the consistency of the EPA's interpretation of 40 C.F.R. § 261.2 over time. The EPA took the position that lead munitions discharged at a shooting range do not fall within the regulatory definition of solid waste in an *amicus* brief to this Court in *Connecticut Coastal,* 989 F.2d at 1315, decided in 1993, and again in an *amicus* brief to a district court in *Long Island Soundkeeper Fund, Inc.,* 1996 WL 131863 at *8–9, decided in 1996. Furthermore, in the "Best Management Practices" manual the EPA makes clear that while spent lead shot left in the environment "is subject to the broader definition of solid waste" employed elsewhere in the RCRA, "[l]ead shot is not considered a hazardous waste subject to RCRA at the time it is discharged from a firearm . . . nor is a RCRA permit required to operate a shooting range."

* * ***IV. Conclusion**

For the above reasons, the judgment of the district court in favor of Metacon is AFFIRMED.

NOTES

1. **Regulations versus Statutes.** Notice that the U.S. Court of Appeals for the Second Circuit in this case focuses on the *regulatory* definition of "solid waste" rather than the *statutory* definition. Why, do you suppose? What is the overall effect of the regulations, according to the court? Is that effect consistent with Congress's purposes in enacting RCRA? Why or why not?

2. **The Role of the EPA and Deference.** The EPA gets a considerable amount of deference in the Second Circuit's decision. As you may have learned in Administrative Law, federal agencies are entitled to a considerable amount of deference, generally termed *Chevron* deference, when they interpret the statutes they administer through regulations. Federal agencies get even *more* deference when they interpret their own regulations, a deference standard generally known as *Auer* deference. Which kind of deference was in play in *Metacon Gun Club*? Do you agree with the EPA's view of firing ranges and RCRA? Why or why not?

3. **Battles of Experts in Environmental Litigation.** Notice that both sides presented competing reports regarding the effects of lead contamination on the property. There are three important points to make here. First, the existence of demonstrated environmental harm is rarely required to establish basic liability under the federal pollution control statutes. Thus, if the lead shot had qualified as "solid waste" and "hazardous waste," Metacon would have been strictly liable for disposing of hazardous waste without a permit, *regardless* of the effects on the environment. Why would Congress have changed the burden of proof from nuisance law in this way?

Second, even though environmental harm may not be relevant to basic regulatory liability, it *is* often relevant to the level of liability that a defendant faces—for example, civil versus criminal—and to the magnitude of the penalty that the defendant may have to pay and/or cleanup effort that the defendant will have to undertake. Thus, when environmental harm exists, it is still very relevant to the overall scope of environmental enforcement efforts.

Third, environmental harm often needs to be proved through experts. As a result, all of the issues associated with expert testimony that you may have learned about in Evidence can be relevant to an environmental case, especially if causation is at issue.

* * *

2. Recycling and RCRA

Like products that are still serving their useful life after being released into the environment, industrial ***recycling*** can raise many issues regarding the existence of "solid waste" and hence the applicability of RCRA. The issue of recycling is one of the most complex regarding RCRA solid wastes. To get some sense of this complexity, consider the EPA's regulatory treatment of recycled materials. While the EPA generally considers recycled materials to be discarded, 40 C.F.R. § 261.2(a), its regulation explains "recycling" as follows:

(c) Materials are solid wastes if they are recycled—or accumulated, stored, or treated before recycling—as specified in paragraphs (c)(1) through (c)(4) of this section.

(1) Used in a manner constituting disposal.

(i) Materials noted with a " * " in Column 1 of Table I are solid wastes when they are:

(A) Applied to or placed on the land in a manner that constitutes disposal; or

(B) Used to produce products that are applied to or placed on the land or are otherwise contained in products that are applied to or placed on the land (in which cases the product itself remains a solid waste).

(ii) However, commercial chemical products listed in § 261.33 are not solid wastes if they are applied to the land and that is their ordinary manner of use.

(2) Burning for energy recovery.

(i) Materials noted with a " * " in column 2 of Table 1 are solid wastes when they are:

(A) Burned to recover energy;

(B) Used to produce a fuel or are otherwise contained in fuels (in which cases the fuel itself remains a solid waste).

(ii) However, commercial chemical products listed in § 261.33 are not solid wastes if they are themselves fuels.

(3) Reclaimed. Materials noted with a " * " in column 3 of Table 1 are solid wastes when reclaimed * * *. Materials noted with a "—" in column 3 of Table 1 are not solid wastes when reclaimed.

(4) Accumulated speculatively. Materials noted with a " * " in column 4 of Table 1 are solid wastes when accumulated speculatively.

Table 1

	Use constituting disposal (§ 261.2(c)(1))	Energy recovery/fuel (§ 261.2(c)(2))	Reclamation (§ 261.2(c)(3)) (except as provided in 261.4(a)(17) for mineral processing secondary materials)	Speculative accumulation (§ 261.2(c)(4))
	1	2	3	4
Spent Materials	*	*	*	*
Sludges (listed in 40 CFR Part 261.31 or 261.32	*	*	*	*

	1	2	3	4
Sludges exhibiting a characteristic of hazardous waste	*	*	—	*
By-products (listed in 40 CFR 261.31 or 261.32)	*	*	*	*
By-products exhibiting a characteristic of hazardous waste	*	*	—	*
Commercial chemical products listed in 40 CFR 261.33	*	*	—	—
Scrap metal other than excluded scrap metal (see 261.1(c)(9))	*	*	*	*

40 C.F.R. § 261.2(c).

The federal courts have also wrestled with the difficult issue of recycled materials and the applicability of RCRA. As was emphasized in the previous two cases, in order to qualify as RCRA "solid waste," material must be "discarded." Do spent materials and by-products destined for recycling qualify as "discarded" materials? Does it matter whether they are reused in-house or sold to another business? Does it matter whether they are reused immediately or stored for several months? The D.C. Circuit has addressed these issues in a series of RCRA cases.

AMERICAN MINING CONGRESS v. UNITED STATES ENVIRONMENTAL PROTECTION AGENCY

824 F.2d 1177 (D.C. Cir. 1987).

STARR, CIRCUIT JUDGE:

These consolidated cases arise out of EPA's regulation of hazardous wastes under the Resource Conservation and Recovery Act of 1976 ("RCRA"), as amended, 42 U.S.C. §§ 6901–6933 (1982 & Supp. III 1985). Petitioners, trade associations representing mining and oil refining interests, challenge regulations promulgated by EPA that amend the definition of "solid waste" to establish and define the agency's authority to regulate secondary materials reused within an industry's ongoing production process. In plain English, petitioners maintain that EPA has exceeded its regulatory authority in seeking to bring materials that are not discarded or otherwise disposed of within the compass of "waste."

I

RCRA is a comprehensive environmental statute under which EPA is granted authority to regulate solid and hazardous wastes. * * *

Congress' "overriding concern" in enacting RCRA was to establish the framework for a national system to insure the safe management of hazardous waste. In passing RCRA, Congress expressed concern over the "rising tide" in scrap, discarded, and waste materials. 42 U.S.C. § 6901 (a)(2). As the statute itself puts it, Congress was concerned with the need "to reduce the amount of waste and unsalvageable materials and to provide for proper and economical solid waste disposal practices." *Id.* § 6901(a)(4). Congress thus crafted RCRA "to promote the protection of health and the environment and to conserve valuable material and energy resources." *Id.* § 6902.

RCRA includes two major parts: one deals with non-hazardous solid waste management and the other with hazardous waste management. Under the latter, EPA is directed to promulgate regulations establishing a comprehensive management system. *Id.* § 6921. EPA's authority, however, extends only to the regulation of "hazardous waste." Because "hazardous waste" is defined as a subset of "solid waste," *id.* § 6903(5), the scope of EPA's jurisdiction is limited to those materials that constitute "solid waste." That pivotal term is defined by RCRA as

> any garbage, refuse, sludge from a waste treatment plant, water supply treatment plant, or air pollution control facility *and other discarded material,* including solid, liquid, semisolid or contained gaseous material, resulting from industrial, commercial, mining, and agricultural operations, and from community activities....

42 U.S.C. § 6903(27) (emphasis added). As will become evident, this case turns on the meaning of the phrase, "and other discarded material," contained in the statute's definitional provisions.

EPA's interpretation of "solid waste" has evolved over time. * * * [In its 1983 proposed rules, one thing] seemed clear: EPA was drawing a line between discarding and ultimate recycling, on the one hand, and a continuous or ongoing manufacturing process with on-site "recycling," on the other. If the activity fell within the latter category, then the materials were not deemed to be "discarded."

After receiving extensive comments, EPA issued its final rule on January 4, 1985. 50 Fed. Reg. 614 (1985). Under the final rule, materials are considered "solid waste" if they are abandoned by being disposed of, burned, or incinerated; or stored, treated, or accumulated before or in lieu of those activities. In addition, certain recycling activities fall within EPA's definition. EPA determines whether a material is a RCRA solid waste when it is recycled by examining both the material or substance itself and the recycling activity involved. The final rule identifies five categories of "secondary materials" (spent materials, sludges, by-products, commercial chemical products, and scrap metal). These "secondary materials" constitute "solid waste" when they are disposed of; burned for energy recovery or used to produce a fuel; reclaimed; or accumulated speculatively. *Id.* at 618–19, 664. Under the final rule, if a material constitutes "solid waste," it is subject to RCRA regulation *unless* it is directly reused as an ingredient or as an effective substitute for a commercial product, or is returned as a raw material substitute to its original manufacturing process. *Id.* In the jargon of the trade, the latter category is known as the "closed-loop" exception. In either case, the material must not first be "reclaimed" (processed to recover a usable product or regenerated). *Id.* EPA exempts these activities "because they are like ordinary usage of commercial products." *Id.* at 619.

II

Petitioners, American Mining Congress ("AMC") and American Petroleum Institute ("API"), challenge the scope of EPA's final rule. Relying upon the statutory definition of "solid waste," petitioners contend that EPA's authority under RCRA is limited to controlling materials that are *discarded* or *intended for discard.* They argue that EPA's reuse and recycle rules, as applied to in-process secondary materials, regulate materials that have not been discarded, and therefore exceed EPA's jurisdiction.

To understand petitioners' claims, a passing familiarity with the nature of their industrial processes is required.

Petroleum. Petroleum refineries vary greatly both in respect of their products and their processes. Most of their products, however, are complex mixtures of hydrocarbons produced through a number of interdependent and sometimes repetitious processing steps. In general, the refining process starts by "distilling" crude oil into various hydrocarbon streams or "fractions." The "fractions" are then subjected to a number of processing steps. Various hydrocarbon materials derived from virtually all stages of processing are combined or blended in order to produce products such as gasoline, fuel oil, and lubricating oils. Any hydrocarbons that are not usable in a particular form or state are returned to an appropriate stage in the refining process so they can eventually be used. Likewise, the hydrocarbons and materials which escape from a refinery's production vessels are gathered and, by a complex retrieval system, returned to appropriate parts of the refining process. Under EPA's final rule, this reuse and recycling of materials is subject to regulation under RCRA.

Mining. In the mining industry, primary metals production involves the extraction of fractions of a percent of a metal from a complex mineralogical matrix (*i.e.*, the natural material in which minerals are embedded). Extractive metallurgy proceeds incrementally. Rome was not built in a day, and all metal cannot be extracted in one fell swoop. In consequence, materials are reprocessed in order to remove as much of the pure metal as possible from the natural ore. Under EPA's final rule, this reprocessed ore and the metal derived from it constitute "solid waste." What is more, valuable metal-bearing and mineral-bearing dusts are often released in processing a particular metal. The mining facility typically recaptures, recycles, and reuses these dusts, frequently in production processes different from the one from which the dusts were originally emitted. The challenged regulations encompass this reprocessing, to the mining industry's dismay.

Against this factual backdrop, we now examine the legal issues presented by petitioners' challenge.

III

We observe at the outset of our inquiry that EPA's interpretation of the scope of its authority under RCRA has been unclear and unsteady. * * * We emphasize, therefore, that we are confronted with neither a consistent nor a longstanding agency interpretation. Under settled doctrine, "[a]n agency interpretation of a relevant provision which conflicts with the agency's earlier interpretation is 'entitled to considerably less deference' than a consistently held agency view."

A

* * * As we are confronted in this case with a "pure" question of statutory construction, we remain mindful of the fact that "[t]he judiciary is the final authority on issues of statutory construction.... If a court, employing traditional tools of statutory construction, ascertains that Congress had an intention on the precise question at issue, that intention is the law and must be given effect."

B

Guided by these principles, we turn to the statutory provision at issue here. Congress, it will be recalled, granted EPA power to regulate "solid waste." Congress specifically defined "solid waste" as "discarded material." EPA then defined "discarded material" to include materials destined for reuse in an industry's *ongoing* production processes. The challenge to EPA's jurisdictional reach is founded, again, on the proposition that in-process secondary materials are outside the bounds of EPA's lawful authority. Nothing has been *discarded,* the argument goes, and thus RCRA jurisdiction remains untriggered.

1

The first step in statutory interpretation is, of course, an analysis of the language itself. * * * In pursuit of Congress' intent, we "start with the assumption that the legislative purpose is expressed by the ordinary meaning of the words used." These sound principles governing the reading of statutes seem especially forceful in the context of the present case. Here, Congress defined "solid waste" as "discarded material." The ordinary, plain-English meaning of the word "discarded" is "disposed of," "thrown away" or "abandoned." Encompassing materials retained for immediate reuse within the scope of "discarded material" strains, to say the least, the everyday usage of that term.

* * * [However], a complete analysis of the statutory term "discarded" calls for more than resort to the ordinary, everyday meaning of the specific language at hand. For, "the sense in which [a term] is used in a

statute must be determined by reference to the purpose of the particular legislation." The statutory provision cannot properly be torn from the law of which it is a part; context and structure are, as in examining any legal instrument, of substantial import in the interpretive exercise.

As we previously recounted, the broad objectives of RCRA are "to promote the protection of health and the environment and to conserve valuable material and energy resources...." 42 U.S.C. § 6902. But that goal is of majestic breadth, and it is difficult * * * to pour meaning into a highly specific term by resort to grand purposes. Somewhat more specifically, we have seen that RCRA was enacted in response to Congressional findings that the "rising tide of scrap, discarded, and waste materials" generated by consumers and increased industrial production had presented heavily populated urban communities with "serious financial, management, intergovernmental, and technical problems in the disposal of solid wastes." *Id.* § 6901(a). In light of this problem, Congress determined that "[f]ederal action through financial and technical assistance and leadership in the development, demonstration, and application of new and improved methods and processes to reduce the amount of waste and unsalvageable materials and to provide for proper and economical solid waste disposal practices" was necessary. *Id.* Also animating Congress were its findings that "disposal of solid and hazardous waste" without careful planning and management presents a danger to human health and the environment; that methods to "separate usable materials from solid waste" should be employed; and that usable energy can be produced from solid waste. *Id.* § 6901(b), (c), (d).

The question we face, then, is whether, in light of the National Legislature's expressly stated objectives and the underlying problems that motivated it to enact RCRA in the first instance, Congress was using the term "discarded" in its ordinary sense—"disposed of" or "abandoned"—or whether Congress was using it in a much more open-ended way, so as to encompass materials no longer useful in their original capacity though destined for immediate reuse in another phase of the industry's ongoing production process.

For the following reasons, we believe the former to be the case. RCRA was enacted, as the Congressional objectives and findings make clear, in an effort to help States deal with the ever-increasing problem of solid waste *disposal* by encouraging the search for and use of alternatives to existing methods of disposal (including recycling) and protecting health and the environment by regulating hazardous wastes. To fulfill these purposes, it seems clear that EPA need not regulate "spent" materials that are recycled and reused in an *ongoing* manufacturing or industrial process. These materials have not yet become part of the waste disposal problem; rather, *they are destined for beneficial reuse or recycling in a continuous process by the generating industry itself.*

* * * EPA's regulation of in-process materials * * * seems to us an effort to get at the same evil (albeit, very broadly defined) that Congress

had identified by extending the agency's regulatory compass, rather than * * * an attempt to reach activities that if left unregulated would sabotage the agency's regulatory mission. We are thus not presented with a situation in which Congress likely intended that the pivotal jurisdictional term be read in its broadest sense, detached from everyday parlance; instead, we have a situation in which Congress, perhaps through the process of legislative compromise which courts must be loathe to tear asunder, employed a term with a widely accepted meaning to define the materials that EPA could regulate under RCRA. And it was that term which the Congress of the United States passed and the President ultimately signed into law.

2

Our task in analyzing the statute also requires us to determine whether other provisions of RCRA shed light on the breadth with which Congress intended to define "discarded." * * *

* * * 3

* * * [The definition of "solid waste"], we believe, indicates clear Congressional intent to limit EPA's authority. First, the definition of "solid waste" is situated in a section containing thirty-nine separate, defined terms. This is definitional specificity of the first order. The very care evidenced by Congress in defining RCRA's scope certainly suggests that Congress was concerned about delineating and thus cabining EPA's jurisdictional reach.

Second, the statutory definition of "solid waste" is quite specific. Although Congress well knows how to use broad terms and broad definitions, * * * the definition here is carefully crafted with specificity. It contains three specific terms and then sets forth the broader term, "other discarded material." That definitional structure brings to mind a long-standing canon of statutory construction, *ejusdem generis*. Under that familiar canon, where general words follow the enumeration of particular classes of things, the general words are most naturally construed as applying only to things of the same general class as those enumerated. * * * Here, the three particular classes—garbage, refuse, and sludge from a waste treatment plant, water supply treatment plant, or air pollution control facility—contain materials that clearly fit within the ordinary, everyday sense of "discarded." It is most sensible to conclude that Congress, in adding the concluding phrase "other discarded material," meant to grant EPA authority over similar types of waste, but not to open up the federal regulatory reach of an entirely new category of materials, *i.e.*, materials neither disposed of nor abandoned, but passing in a continuous stream or flow from one production process to another.

In sum, our analysis of the statute reveals clear Congressional intent to extend EPA's authority only to materials that are truly discarded, disposed of, thrown away, or abandoned. EPA nevertheless submits that the legislative history evinces a contrary intent. * * * Although we find

RCRA's statutory language unambiguous, and can discern no exceptional circumstances warranting resort to its legislative history, we will nonetheless in an abundance of caution afford EPA the benefit of consideration of those secondary materials.

4

EPA points first to damage incidents cited by Congress in 1976 as justification for establishing a hazardous waste management system. *See* H.R. REP. No. 1491, 94th Cong., 2d Sess. at 18, 22 (1976). Neither of the incidents noted by EPA, however, involved commercial, in-process reuse or recycling activities. Instead, both incidents provide clear examples of waste *disposal,* which, of course, indisputably falls within EPA's jurisdiction conferred by RCRA.

EPA next asserts that the "most significant" aspect of the 1976 legislative history is the sense that Congress enacted broad grants of regulatory authority in order to " 'eliminate[] the last remaining loophole in environmental law.' " EPA, however, neglects to favor us with the entire sentence, and thereby misses the thrust of this passage. In pertinent part, the Report states as follows: "[The Committee] believes that the approach taken by this legislation eliminates the last remaining loophole in environmental law, that of *unregulated land disposal of discarded materials and hazardous wastes.*" *Id.* (emphasis added).

* * * Thus, * * * EPA is unable to point to any portion of the legislative history which supports its expansive and counterintuitive interpretation of the pivotal term, "discarded."

To the contrary, a fair reading of the legislative history reveals intimations of an intent to regulate under RCRA only materials that have truly been discarded. Not only is the language of the legislative history fully consistent with the use of "discarded" in the sense of "disposed of," but it strains the language to read it otherwise. Most significantly, in discussing its choice of the words "discarded materials" to define "solid waste," the House Committee stated:

> Not only solid wastes, but also liquid and contained gaseous wastes, semi-solid wastes and sludges are the subjects of this legislation. Waste itself is a misleading word in the context of the committee's activity. *Much industrial and agricultural waste is reclaimed or put to new use and is therefore not a part of the discarded materials disposal problem the committee addresses.*

H.R. REP. No. 1491, 94th Cong., 2d Sess. at 2, U.S. Code Cong. & Admin. News 1976, p. 6240 (emphasis added). The Committee then went on to explain that "the term discarded materials is used to identify collectively those substances often referred to as industrial, municipal or post-consumer waste; *refuse, trash, garbage, and sludge.*" *Id.* (emphasis added). Later in the Report, the Committee stated: "The overwhelming concern of the Committee, however, is the effect on the population and environment of the *disposal* of discarded hazardous wastes.... Unless neutralized or otherwise properly managed in their *disposal,* hazardous wastes present a clear danger. . . . " *Id.* at 3, U.S. Code Cong. & Admin. News 1976, p. 6241 (emphasis added). Throughout the Report, the Committee refers time and again to the problem motivating the enactment of RCRA as the *disposal* of waste.

In the Senate, a brief discussion took place as to the scope of the definition of "solid waste." In response to Senator Domenici's expression of concern that RCRA be aimed only at "the *disposal* of municipal and industrial wastes and not at the regulation of mining," Senator Randolph, the chairman of the Committee, unequivocally stated: "The bill definitely is directed at the *disposal* of municipal and industrial wastes." 122 Cong. Rec. 21,424 (1976) (emphasis added). To the extent this colloquy has probative value, it cuts squarely against expansive agency notions of the breadth of its jurisdictional reach.

After all is said and done, we are satisfied that the legislative history, rather than evincing Congress' intent to define "discarded" to include in-process secondary materials employed in an ongoing manufacturing process, confirms that the term was employed by the Article I branch in its ordinary, everyday sense.

IV

We are constrained to conclude that, in light of the language and structure of RCRA, the problems animating Congress to enact it, and the relevant portions of the legislative history, Congress clearly and unambiguously expressed its intent that "solid waste" (and therefore EPA's regulatory authority) be limited to materials that are "discarded" by virtue of being disposed of, abandoned, or thrown away. While we do not lightly overturn an agency's reading of its own statute, we are persuaded that by regulating in-process secondary materials, EPA has acted in contravention of Congress' intent. * * *

Notes

1. **Types of Recycling.** What kind of recycling was at issue in this case? Was this a relatively easy recycling case as a result? Why or why not? Are other types of recycled materials still subject to RCRA? Why or why not?

2. **Statutory Interpretation and "Solid Waste."** The D.C. Circuit engaged in a lengthy process of statutory interpretation in this case, the first such extended analysis presented in this textbook. Where did the D.C. Circuit begin its process of interpreting "solid waste"? Upon what definitions of "solid waste" and "discarded material" did it rely? How did the *context* of the term "solid waste" relate to its meaning, according to the D.C. Circuit? How did that context influence the D.C. Circuit's specific interpretation of "solid waste"? How did the structure of RCRA help the D.C. Circuit to determine the scope of "solid waste"? What did that structure indicate about the scope of the EPA's authority? What is the role of RCRA's purposes and objectives in statutory interpretation, according to the D.C. Circuit? What did those pur-

poses and objectives indicate about the definition and scope of "solid waste"? How did the D.C. Circuit treat RCRA's legislative history? Why did the EPA want to examine the legislative history? Did the legislative history suggest a different interpretation than the statute itself? Why or why not? What canon of statutory construction did the D.C. Circuit rely on? What does this canon mean? How did the D.C. Circuit apply it to help construe the term "solid waste"?

3. ***American Mining Congress*, Part II:** In 1990, the D.C. Circuit decided *American Mining Congress v. U.S. Environmental Protection Agency*, 907 F.2d 1179 (D.C. Cir. 1990) (*AMC II*), in which the industry petitioners challenged the EPA's classification of six kinds of mining wastes, including wastewater sludges, as hazardous wastes subject to RCRA. According to AMC, under *AMC I* "sludges from wastewater that are stored in surface impoundments and that *may* at some time in the future be reclaimed are not 'discarded.' " *Id.* at 1186. The D.C. Circuit, however, disagreed:

> Petitioners read *AMC* too broadly. *AMC*'s holding concerned only materials that are "destined for *immediate reuse* in another phase of the industry's ongoing production process," and that "have not yet become part of the waste disposal problem[.]" Nothing in *AMC* prevents the agency from treating as "discarded" the wastes at issue in this case, which are managed in land disposal units that *are* part of wastewater treatment systems, which *have* therefore become "part of the waste disposal problem," and which are *not* part of ongoing industrial processes.

Id. Are *AMC I* and *AMC II* reconcilable? Why or why not? How does *AMC II* refine the recycling problem for RCRA "solid wastes"?

4. **Speculatively Accumulated Materials.** As the *AMC II* case suggests, used or byproduct materials (***secondary materials***) that a company accumulates because there is a *possibility* that the company will reuse those materials in the future are still considered "discarded materials" for RCRA purposes. *See* 40 C.F.R. § 261.2(c)(4). The closed-loop recycling exemption generally applies *only* if the company *immediately* reuses the materials in an on-going manufacturing process. More specifically, the EPA will consider used materials to be speculatively accumulated, and hence subject to RCRA regulation, if: (1) there is no viable market for those materials; or (2) the regulated entity has not used 75% of the accumulated materials within a calendar year. OFFICE OF SOLID WASTE, U.S. E.P.A., RCRA ORIENTATION MANUAL III–7 (March 2006), *available at* http://www.epa.gov/epaoswer/general/orientat/.

5. **Sham Recycling.** Because RCRA's regulatory requirements can be burdensome and expensive, especially for hazardous wastes, potentially regulated entities might seek to "hide" their discarded secondary materials by injecting them back, uselessly, into ongoing manufacturing processes. The EPA considers such tactics ***sham recycling***, and it will continue to regard any of the discarded materials involved as RCRA "solid wastes." In determining whether claimed recycling is legitimate recycling or sham recycling, the EPA considers a number of factors, "includ[ing] whether the secondary material is effective for the claimed use, if secondary material is used in excess of the amount necessary, and whether or not the facility has maintained records of the recycling transactions." OFFICE OF SOLID WASTE, U.S.

E.P.A., RCRA ORIENTATION MANUAL III–9 (March 2006), *available at* http://www.epa.gov/epaoswer/general/orientat/.

6. **Stored Materials and Eventual Reuse.** A decade after *AMC II*, the D.C. Circuit held that stored materials destined for eventual reuse are not RCRA "solid wastes" because those materials have not yet been "discarded." *Association of Battery Recyclers, Inc. v. U.S. E.P.A.*, 208 F.3d 1047, 1050–54 (D.C. Cir. 2000). How can you distinguish the *Battery Recyclers* decision from the D.C. Circuit's decision in *AMC II*, given the D.C. Circuit's view of recycling in *AMC I*?

7. **Recycling and the Timing of RCRA "Solid Wastes."** In determining whether reused materials can be RCRA "solid wastes," the D.C. Circuit tends to emphasize, as it did in *AMC II*, whether the reused materials have "become part of the waste disposal problem." The D.C. Circuit has thus articulated a more refined answer to the problem addressed by the Second Circuit in *No Spray Coalition* and by the Puerto Rico District Court in *Water Keeper Alliance*: when, exactly, do materials that can potentially come in contact with the environment qualify as "discarded" materials subject to regulation under RCRA?

In the recycling context, other timing decisions are possible. Consider the following facts: In steel production, crushed limestone (calcium carbonate) is added to the molten steel while it is in the furnace to remove impurities. In performing this function, the limestone produces a "slag," which floats to the surface and is removed. Steel companies then "cure" the slag over several months and sell it as road building and construction material. Is this reused "slag" a "solid waste" for purposes of RCRA? Why or why not? *See Owen Electrical Steel Company of South Carolina, Inc. v. Browner*, 37 F.3d 146 (4th Cir. 1994).

8. **Wastewaters and RCRA Recycling.** In 2000, the D.C. Circuit again considered the issue of recycling in the context of wastewater treatment. In *American Petroleum Institute v. United States Environmental Protection Agency*, 216 F.3d 50 (D.C. Cir. 2000), the issues were whether oil-bearing wastewaters and petrochemical recovered oil could qualify as RCRA "solid wastes." With respect to oil bearing wastewaters, the issue was *when* those wastewaters became "solid waste"—before or after petroleum refiners treated the wastewaters to remove excess oil. The EPA argued that the petroleum refiners engaged in such treatment primarily to comply with the federal Clean Water Act and hence that the wastewaters were RCRA "solid wastes" as soon as that treatment began. The refiners, in contrast, argued that they removed the oil from the wastewaters primarily to recover the valuable oil (up to 1000 barrels per day) and that they would have engaged in such recovery regardless of the Clean Water Act, so that the wastewaters did not become RCRA "solid wastes" until after this treatment. According to the D.C. Circuit:

> It may be permissible for EPA to determine that the predominant purpose of primary treatment is discard. Legal abandonment of property is premised on determining the intent to abandon, which requires an inquiry into facts and circumstances. Where an industrial by-product may be characterized as discarded or "in process" material, EPA's choice of characterization is entitled to deference. However, the record must reflect

> that EPA engaged in reasoned decisionmaking to decide which characterization is appropriate. The record in this case is deficient in that regard. EPA has noted two purposes of primary treatment and concludes, "[c]learly, wastewater treatment is the main purpose." As English teachers have long taught, a conclusion is not "clear" or "obvious" merely because one says so.

Id. at 57. The court remanded the question to the EPA for further evaluation. *Id.*

Does *American Petroleum Institute* change the legal analysis for distinguishing legitimate recycling and discarded materials? In particular, does the case create a "primary purpose" test, or add an intent element to the evaluation of "solid waste"? Or, as was suggested in connection with *No Spray Coalition*, has that element been there all along? What is the relationship of intent to recycling?

9. **New "Solid Waste" Regulations.** In October 2008, the EPA finalized new "solid waste" regulations to try to better address the RCRA recycling issue. Revisions to the Definition of Solid Waste, 73 Fed. Reg. 64,668 (Oct. 30, 2008). These regulations left the sham recycling and speculative accumulation limitations in place. However, the regulations also created certain exclusions from RCRA, including an exclusion for hazardous materials legitimately reclaimed under the control of the generator and another for hazardous materials transferred to someone else for the purpose of legitimate reclamation. *Id.* at 64,669–70. In addition, the regulations created a process whereby a person who thought he or she should be excluded from RCRA regulation could ask the EPA for a "non-waste" determination. *Id.* at 64,670.

In July 2011, the EPA proposed revisions to the 2008 "solid waste" regulations. Definition of Solid Waste, 76 Fed. Reg. 44,094 (July 22, 2011). These proposed regulations would revise some of the exclusions created in 2008 to better protection human health and the environment. For example, the proposed regulations would eliminate the exclusion for hazardous materials transferred to someone else for reclamation and replace it with an alternative Subtitle C regulation for hazardous recyclable materials, because the EPA has become convinced that only limited categories of such transfers do not involving discarding. *Id.* at 44,096. Under the alternative regulation, "the hazardous recyclable materials must be managed according to the current RCRA Subtitle C requirements, including manifesting and hazardous waste permits for storage, except that generators may accumulate hazardous recyclable materials for up to a year without a RCRA permit if the generator makes advance arrangements for legitimate reclamation and documents those arrangements in a reclamation plan." *Id.* For reclamation by the generator, the EPA is proposing more limited revisions but strengthening the legitimacy criteria to ensure that the recycling/reclamation is legitimate. *Id.*

The EPA is also tightening up its RCRA regulation of secondary materials used as fuels. In June 2010, for example, the EPA withdrew a 2008 regulation that exempted "Emission Comparable Fuels" (ECF) from RCRA regulation. In essence, under the 2008 rule, hazardous secondary materials that produced essentially the same emissions as fuel oil when burned were deemed not discarded and hence not solid waste for RCRA purposes. By June 2010, however, the EPA had reconsidered the potential harmful effects of that exclusion and concluded:

> The fundamental premise of the ECF rule is that ECF is no more hazardous than burning fuel oil, because combustion of this material will have comparable emissions. However, to ensure that the material does not pose greater risks, EPA felt compelled to promulgate a very detailed set of conditions—the equivalent of a detailed regulatory scheme—for both the storage and combustion of ECF. As discussed in the proposed rule, * * * the existing subtitle C permitting process provides for the necessary review on the operation of the combustion units and the storage units to assure that the appropriate storage and combustion conditions are met.

Withdrawal of the Emission–Comparable Fuel Exclusion Under RCRA, 75 Fed. Reg. 33,712, 33,713 (June 15, 2010).

More generally, in March 2011, the EPA promulgated final regulations that defined when non-hazardous secondary materials used as fuels or ingredients in combustion units qualify as "solid waste." Identification of Non–Hazardous Secondary Materials That Are Solid Waste, 76 Fed. Reg. 15,456 (March 21, 2011). This rule identifies six categories of secondary materials—"any material that is not the primary product of a manufacturing or commercial process," *id.* at 15,458—that are *not* "solid waste" when legitimately used as fuels or ingredients in a combustion unit. The six categories are: (1) secondary materials that remain within the control of the generator and are used as fuel; (2) scrap tires that are managed by established tire collection programs and used as fuel; (3) resinated wood used as fuel; (4) secondary materials that are used as ingredients (as in *AMC I*); (5) discarded secondary materials that have undergone processing to produce fuel or ingredient products; and (6) secondary materials that are used as fuels and for which a non-waste determination has been granted. *Id.* at 15,459. The "legitimacy" of the use is judged through application of the EPA's legitimacy criteria. According to the EPA:

> To meet the *fuel* legitimacy criteria, the non-hazardous secondary material must be managed as a valuable commodity, have a meaningful heating value and be used as a fuel in a combustion unit that recovers energy, and contain contaminants at levels comparable to or lower than those in traditional fuels which the combustion unit is designed to burn.

Id. at 15,460 (emphasis added). Similarly:

> To meet the ingredient legitimacy criteria, the non-hazardous secondary material must be managed as a valuable commodity, provide a useful contribution to the production or manufacturing process, be used to produce a valuable product or intermediate, and must result in products that contain contaminants at levels that are comparable to or lower than those found in traditional products that are manufactured without the non-hazardous secondary material.

Id. Finally, like the 2008 regulations governing reclamation, the 2011 fuel regulations include a procedure whereby generators and handlers can petition the EPA for a "non-waste determination." *Id.* at 15,538–40.

What do these recent regulations suggest about the trend in the EPA's thinking about reuse and recycling under RCRA? Are they consistent with *AMC I*? Why or why not? What are the potential advantages and disadvantages for both the EPA and the regulated entities of the petition processes for non-waste declarations?

B. REGULATION OF NON–HAZARDOUS SOLID WASTES: RCRA SUBTITLE D

1. Basic Requirements and Liabilities

RCRA divides its regulation of solid wastes between two subtitles. ***Subtitle D*** governs non-hazardous solid waste, while ***Subtitle C*** governs hazardous waste. Although primarily concerned with hazardous waste, Congress included Subtitle D in RCRA in recognition of the growing non-hazardous waste disposal problem. Much of this waste is ***municipal solid waste***—that is, waste collected and disposed of by local governments. In 2000, the United States generated 232 tons of municipal solid waste, 15% of which was disposed of through combustion and 30% of which was disposed of through recycling. OFFICE OF SOLID WASTE, U.S. E.P.A., RCRA ORIENTATION MANUAL II–4, fig. II–3 (March 2006), *available at* http://www.epa.gov/epaoswer/general/orientat/. The remaining municipal solid waste—55% of the total generated—was disposed of on land, generally in ***landfills***. *Id.*

Compared to Subtitle C, Subtitle D's regulation of non-hazardous solid waste is not very onerous. States received the primary authority under RCRA to regulate non-hazardous solid waste. Under RCRA § 4003, states were expected to enact ***state solid waste management plans***. 42 U.S.C. § 6943. In order to receive federal approval, these state plans had to meet six statutory requirements. Most importantly, states had to forbid new open dumps within their borders and provide for the closing or upgrading of all existing open dumps. RCRA § 4003(a)(2), (3), 42 U.S.C. § 6943(a)(2), (3). As part of these controls, states were expected to implement permit programs for ***solid waste management facilities*** to control their intake of hazardous waste. RCRA § 4005(c)(1), 42 U.S.C. § 6945(c)(1). In addition, new disposal could only occur at ***sanitary landfills***. RCRA § 4004(b), 42 U.S.C. § 6944(b).

Congress also imposed new requirements for sanitary landfills. All new, replacement, and expanded landfills had to be built with at least two liners and leachate collection systems and had to provide for groundwater monitoring. RCRA § 3004(*o*), 42 U.S.C. § 6924(*o*). These requirements reflect Congress's recognition that one of the biggest problems from open dumps and nonsanitary landfills is contamination of groundwater.

Figure 1-3: Cross Section of a Sanitary Landfill
EPA graphic.

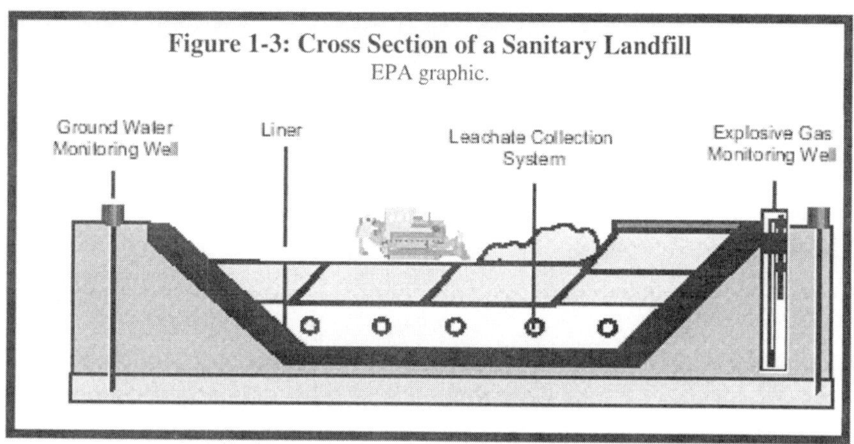

As a general principle of constitutional federalism, the federal government cannot force states to regulate in any particular way. Therefore, to induce states to enact solid waste management plans, Congress provided ***federal financial assistance*** to states that submitted qualifying plans on time. RCRA § 4007(b), 42 U.S.C. § 6947(b). Congress also provided special assistance to rural communities. RCRA § 4009, 42 U.S.C. § 6949.

Just because waste is "non-hazardous" solid waste, however, does not mean that no environmental issues can arise regarding its disposal. In recognition of this fact, Congress included the Subtitle D requirements within the scope of RCRA's ***citizen suit provision***, which states that:

> [A]ny person may commence a civil action on his own behalf—
>
> (1) (A) against any person (including (a) the United States, and (b) any other governmental instrumentality or agency, to the extent permitted by the eleventh amendment to the Constitution) who is alleged to be in violation of any permit, standard, regulation, condition, requirement, prohibition, or order which has become effective pursuant to this chapter, or
>
> (B) against any person, including the United States and any other governmental instrumentality or agency, to the extent permitted by the eleventh amendment to the Constitution, and including any past or present generator, past or present transporter, or past or present owner or operator of a treatment, storage, or disposal facility, *who has contributed or who is contributing to the past or present handling, storage, treatment, transportation, or disposal of any solid* or hazardous *waste which may present an imminent and substantial endangerment to health or the environment*; or
>
> (2) against the Administrator [of the EPA] where there is alleged a failure of the Administrator to perform any act or duty under this chapter which is not discretionary with the Administrator.

42 U.S.C. § 6972(a) (emphasis added). The plaintiffs in the following case brought their nonhazardous solid waste RCRA citizen suit pursuant to section (1)(B).

COX v. CITY OF DALLAS, TEXAS

256 F.3d 281 (5th Cir. 2001).

KING, CHIEF JUDGE:

* * * This case involves two consolidated citizen suits brought pursuant to the Resource Conservation and Recovery Act ("RCRA"), 42 U.S.C. § 6901 *et seq.*, concerning two open garbage dumps in Dallas, Texas—an 85–acre lot located at 523 Deepwood Street (the "Deepwood dump") and an adjacent 40–acre lot (the "South Loop 12 dump").

Zoned for residential use, the Deepwood and South Loop 12 dumps have been used for sand and gravel mining and illegal dumping for over twenty-five years. Substantial deposits of uncovered solid waste, including household waste, tires, demolition debris, insulation, asphalt shingles, abandoned automobiles, jugs and bottles labeled "sulfuric acid" and "nitric acid," 55–gallon drums, and syringes, are on the properties.[1] The dumps adjoin residential neighborhoods and a tributary to the Trinity River and are partially in the flood plain of the Trinity River. Neither dump has been upgraded or closed according to sanitary landfill criteria. *See* 42 U.S.C. § 6944(a). Residents adjacent to the dumps report the appearance of snakes and rats in their backyards since the beginning of the illegal dumping, and the dumps are easily accessible to children in the neighborhood. Since at least 1976, the State of Texas and the City of Dallas, Texas (the "City") have been aware of open dumping on both sites.

A. *History of the Deepwood Dump*

In August 1976, officials from the Texas Natural Resource Conservation Commission (the "TNRCC") and the City's sanitation department visited the Deepwood dump and prepared a report that called for continuing surveillance of the site. In 1983, the City conducted soil and water tests at the Deepwood dump in response to complaints from nearby residents that illegal dumping was taking place. The City's report and test results, which made clear that the Deepwood dump was being used for the disposal of solid waste, were sent to the State for analysis.

1. "Solid waste" includes "any garbage, refuse, sludge ... and other discarded material." 42 U.S.C. § 6903(27). From the RCRA's inception, Congress made clear that it intended the term "solid waste" to be viewed with a wide lens * * *.

Figure 1-4: An Open Dump
EPA photo.

In 1987, the City filed suit in state court against the owners of the Deepwood dump for dumping solid waste without a state permit and joined the TNRCC as a necessary party. In December 1989, the state court entered a final judgment, requiring the Deepwood dump owners to submit and implement a plan for closure of the site. An April 1991 inspection revealed that the Deepwood dump had not been cleaned up or closed, and the City filed a contempt motion. This motion was not heard by the state court, and no further action was taken by the State or the City to enforce the judgment.

During this time, the City contracted with Billy Nabors and Dallas Demolition Excavating Co. ("Dallas Demolition") to conduct demolitions of City property. These City contractors disposed of their debris at the Deepwood dump. The City's contracts with Dallas Demolition did not specify that waste materials generated by City activities must be properly disposed of in a legal landfill. The City was aware that Dallas Demolition dumped at the Deepwood dump. However, even after the City's attorneys had learned of Dallas Demolition's illegal acts, the City continued to use Dallas Demolition.

Also, the City designed and implemented a plan to reclaim the area from the flood plain by depositing fill material in the low spots. The plan's objective was to collect more tax revenue from the area by eventually rezoning it for industrial purposes. In 1982, Terry Van Sickle began operating the Deepwood dump with land use and fill permits issued by the City. Van Sickle overtly stated his intention to dump solid waste at the Deepwood dump when he submitted his application to the City: "Fill old pits with solid waste 'means all putrescible and non-putrescible discarded materials or unwanted rock, dirt, metal, sand gravel wood etc. [*sic*].' " The City subsequently issued a certificate-of-occupancy permit based on this application. While this certificate stated that the use was to be for the "mining of sand and gravel," it did not specifically restrict the types of fill material. Furthermore, the City's Public Works Department later granted Van Sickle "[p]ermission to fill the mined areas." This grant also did not restrict the types of fill material, although Van Sickle had made his intentions clear regarding the solid waste fill he wished to employ in the dump. In its own documents, the City admits that "control at the site[s] has been loose and in a few cases improper material has been used for fill ... [and] some approved flood plain areas have had large amounts of decomposable material placed in them."

At a Board of Adjustment hearing, the City considered the impact of operations at the Deepwood dump on the community. Although residents adjacent to the dump provided information about the illegal dumping and the hazards at the dump and requested that the Board put an end to the use of the dump, the Board did not act to terminate the dumping. * * * Until the district court's injunction, the City had never revoked the certificate-of-occupancy permit for the Deepwood site.

Herman Nethery, the current owner of the Deepwood dump, operated an illegal open dump at the Deepwood site from 1994 through 1997. The State inspected the Deepwood dump several times from 1995 to 1997 and discovered massive illegal dumping, including asbestos, benzene, and medical waste. The State also noted in its own reports that there was an imminent threat of the discharge of municipal solid waste into Elam Creek, a tributary of the Trinity River, because of the concentrated dumping. In addition, the State observed that shingles and construction and demolition debris at the dump may cause contamination of surface and ground water through the leaching of contaminates from the debris by rainwater. For several months during 1988 and during 1997, the Deepwood dump caught fire and burned, and a significant fire hazard still exists at the site.

Despite this history, in August 1994, the City granted Nethery a permit allowing mining use of the Deepwood dump. The City failed to follow its own procedures of issuing permits: no inspection was conducted prior to the issuance of the permit, and no test zone was established around the areas where illegal solid waste had been deposited.

In 1995, the City filed suit against Nethery in state court alleging violations of the Texas Solid Waste Disposal Act (the "TSWDA"), and the State intervened. The state court entered judgment against Nethery for $15,000,000. The judgment does not require that any of the imposed civil penalties be used for cleaning up the dump. In addition to the state civil actions, the State criminally prosecuted Nethery and Herman Lee Gibbons, an operator at the Deepwood dump. Both were convicted of violating

Texas organized crime laws relating to the financing of the illegal dump, and both were incarcerated in Texas on those charges.

The City informed the State and the United States Environmental Protection Agency ("EPA") that the Deepwood dump poses long-term fire and health hazards for the neighborhood and requested funds to remediate the dump. The State and the EPA refused to provide funds to clean up the dump.

B. History of the South Loop 12 Dump

In 1964, the City entered into an agreement to use the South Loop 12 site as a sanitary landfill. In 1972, the then-owner of the site excluded the City from dumping because the City had not complied with the conditions in the agreement (*i.e.*, to cover the refuse that it had dumped with at least eighteen inches of compact soil). In addition, the City never canceled this agreement. In 1989, the City and the State sued the owners of the South Loop 12 dump in state court for violating the TSWDA. The state court entered an Agreed Final Judgment in 1990, ordering the owners to clean up the dump. An April 1991 inspection found that no corrective action had been taken, but the City and State did nothing to gain compliance with the 1990 judgment. As was the case with the Deepwood dump, there currently exists a substantial danger of fires from the solid waste present on the site, and the dump is also easily accessible to children. The South Loop 12 site remains an open dump, and the State has not cleaned, and does not intend to clean up, the site.

C. Procedural History of Current Litigation

In February 1997, Plaintiffs, homeowners in residential areas adjoining these dumps, brought a citizens suit in federal court against the owners of the Deepwood dump[] and the City for injunctive relief under the RCRA, 42 U.S.C. § 6972(a)(1). This suit was consolidated with Plaintiffs' July 1998 citizens suit against the City * * * regarding the South Loop 12 dump. Plaintiffs alleged, *inter alia,* that the City violated 42 U.S.C. § 6972(a)(1)(B) by "contributing to" illegal open dumping at both sites * * *.

* * * The Final Judgment, entered on August 27, 1999, granted Plaintiffs injunctive relief against the City on both dumps, finding that the City had "contributed to" illegal open dumping * * *. The district court's injunction required the City, *inter alia,* to (1) erect a fence around both sites, (2) monitor the sites for methane gas and fire hazards, (3) prevent future open dumping, (4) remove all solid waste from the sites without harming adjoining properties, and (5) restore the sites to non-hazardous conditions.

* * * III. THE CITY'S APPEAL

In the district court, Plaintiffs asserted the following four claims against the City: (1) "contributing to" liability under 42 U.S.C. § 6972(a)(1)(B) at the Deepwood dump, (2) "contributing to" liability under § 6972(a)(1)(B) at the South Loop 12 dump, (3) liability under § 6945(a) at the Deepwood dump, and (4) liability under § 6945(a) at the South Loop 12 dump. The district court found the City liable under § 6972(a)(1)(B) for both the Deepwood and South Loop 12 dumps, but found that Plaintiffs had not met their burden as to their § 6945(a) claims. Plaintiffs are not appealing the district court's decision on the § 6945(a) claims, but the City is appealing the liability findings under § 6972(a)(1)(B).

In order to supply a better understanding of the RCRA, we provide at the outset a brief description of nuisance at common law. We then lay out the statutory framework of "contributing to" liability under § 6972(a)(1)(B). Finally, we assess whether the district court's ruling that the City fell within the statutory reach of § 6972(a)(1)(B) was in error.

A. *Nuisance at Common Law*

Nuisance principles form the core doctrinal foundation for modern environmental statutes, including the RCRA. The nuisance action originated in the twelfth century. *See* RESTATEMENT (SECOND) OF TORTS § 821D cmt. a (1979). Courts first recognized "private" nuisances, *see id.*, and by the sixteenth century, began to recognize "public" nuisances, *id.* § 821C cmt. a. "A private nuisance is a nontrespassory invasion of another's interest in the private use and enjoyment of land." *Id.* § 821D. A public nuisance, on the other hand, involves an unreasonable interference with a right common to the general public. *See id.* § 821B. In determining whether conduct amounts to a public nuisance, courts consider, *inter alia,* whether the conduct involves a significant interference with public health, safety, peace, comfort, or convenience. *See id.* Private and public nuisances are not set apart in rigid, mutually exclusive categories. On the contrary, "[w]hen the nuisance, in addition to interfering with the public right, also interferes with the use and enjoyment of the plaintiff's land, it is a private nuisance as well as a public one." *Id.* § 821C cmt. e.

These interests (*i.e.*, in a public right and in the use and enjoyment of one's land) "may be invaded by any one of the types of conduct that serve in general as bases for all tort liability." RESTATEMENT (SECOND) OF TORTS § 822 cmt. a. The Restatement explains that one is subject to liability for a private nuisance (1) if one's conduct is the legal cause of an invasion of another's interest and (2) if the invasion is either (a) "intentional and unreasonable" or (b) "unintentional and otherwise actionable under the rules controlling liability for negligent or reckless conduct, or for abnormally dangerous conditions or activities." *Id.* § 822. The rules of strict liability, *i.e.*, liability imposed without regard to the defendant's negligence or intent to harm, are frequently applied to abnormally dangerous activities, *see* RESTATEMENT (SECOND) OF TORTS § 519 (1977), although they are imposed in other nuisance situations as well.

The private nuisance liability framework of Restatement § 822 is also generally applicable in public nuisance situations. *See* RESTATEMENT (SEC-

OND) OF TORTS § 822 cmt. a. However, public nuisance law tends to impose liability more often on the basis of strict liability.

Two basic remedies are available in nuisance actions—damages and injunctions. *See* Restatement (Second) of Torts § 821B cmt. i; *id.* § 821C * * *; *id.* § 821F * * *; *id.* § 822 cmt. d * * *.

The theory of nuisance lends itself naturally to combating the harms created by environmental problems. One commentator succinctly described environmental jurisprudence, stating: "The deepest doctrinal roots of modern environmental law are found in principles of nuisance.... Nuisance actions have involved pollution of all physical media—air, water, land—by a wide variety of means.... Nuisance actions have challenged virtually every major industrial and municipal activity which is today the subject of comprehensive environmental regulation.... Nuisance theory and case law is the common law backbone of modern environmental and energy law." WILLIAM H. RODGERS, JR., HANDBOOK ON ENVIRONMENTAL LAW § 2.1, at 100 (1977).

Specifically, as regards the RCRA, Congress indicated that the statute embodied common law concepts of nuisance.

* * * *B. Section 6972(a)(1)(B)*

Section 6972(a)(1)(B) of the RCRA provides in relevant part:

> [A]ny person may commence a civil action on his own behalf—against any person, including the United States and any other governmental instrumentality or agency, to the extent permitted by the eleventh amendment to the Constitution, and including any past or present generator, past or present transporter, or past or present owner or operator of a treatment, storage, or disposal facility, *who has contributed or who is contributing to* the past or present handling, storage, treatment, transportation, or disposal of any solid or hazardous waste which may present an imminent and substantial endangerment to health or the environment.

42 U.S.C. § 6972(a)(1)(B) (emphasis added).

Parsing the language of § 6972(a)(1)(B), we find it contains essentially three elements. To prevail on a "contributing to" claim, a plaintiff is required under § 6972(a)(1)(B) to demonstrate: (1) that the defendant is a person, including, but not limited to, one who was or is a generator or transporter of solid or hazardous waste or one who was or is an owner or operator of a solid or hazardous waste treatment, storage, or disposal facility; (2) that the defendant has contributed to or is contributing to the handling, storage, treatment, transportation, or disposal of solid or hazardous waste; and (3) that the solid or hazardous waste may present an imminent and substantial endangerment to health or the environment.

We turn now to the district court's finding that the City falls within the statutory reach of § 6972(a)(1)(B) for both the Deepwood and South Loop 12 dumps.

1. Any Person

First, the RCRA states that "any person" may be held liable, "including" past or present generators, transporters, owners, or operators. *See* 42 U.S.C. § 6972(a)(1)(B).

[I]t is undisputed that the City has been and is a generator of solid waste. Municipal activities, such as basic office operations in city buildings, demolition, and construction, generate waste. * * * Specifically, on this record, the City generated solid waste through its demolition activities.

2. Has Contributed to or Is Contributing to

Second, the district court did not err as a matter of law in interpreting the "contributing to" prong of § 6972(a)(1)(B). In addition, its finding that the City satisfied the requirements of the provision was not clear error. In so concluding, we first lay out the basic framework that will guide our analysis and then examine the evidence relating to each dump.

a. Construction of the Term "Contribute"

The RCRA does not define the term "contribute" or any variation thereof. "This silence compels us to 'start with the assumption that the legislative purpose is expressed by the ordinary meaning of the words used.' "

Webster's Dictionary defines "contribute" as to "have a share in any act or effect." WEBSTER'S THIRD NEW INTERNATIONAL DICTIONARY 496 (unabridged) (1963); *see also* OXFORD ENGLISH DICTIONARY 849 (2d ed. 1989) ("to have a part or share in producing [an effect]"); THE AMERICAN HERITAGE DICTIONARY OF THE ENGLISH LANGUAGE 410 (3d ed. 1992) ("to help bring about a result").

Our sister circuits have drawn upon the plain meaning of the word "contribute" and on the legislative history as well to interpret the "contributing to" phrase under the analogous § 6973 provision. The Court of Appeals for the Fourth Circuit aptly summarized congressional intent regarding interpretations of phrases such as "contributing to":

> [Congress has mandated] that the former common law of nuisance, as applied to situations in which a risk of harm from solid or hazardous wastes exists, shall include new terms and concepts which shall be developed in a liberal, not a restrictive, manner. This ensures that problems that Congress could not have anticipated when passing the [RCRA] will be dealt with in a way minimizing the risk of harm to the environment and the public.

[*United States v.*] *Waste Indus.*, 734 F.2d [159,] 167 [(4th Cir. 1984)] (citations omitted). Therefore, we follow our sister circuits' lead and interpret "contribute" to mean "have a part or share in producing an effect."

b. The Required Level of Fault

As to the fault standard under which such "contributions" are held actionable, we note that the one circuit that has addressed this specific issue has held that the RCRA imposes strict liability, *i.e.*, liability imposed without regard to the defendant's negligence or intent to harm. Some other courts have also come to the same conclusion.

We have no reason to consider here whether strict liability may be a basis for liability under the RCRA. The district court did not hold the City strictly liable for the waste that it generated and that was deposited in the Deepwood and South Loop 12 dumps. In the case of the South Loop 12 dump, the City did not dispute that it used the site as a municipal dump. In the case of the Deepwood dump, the district court found, and we agree, that there is a compelling case on the record that the City's actions were negligent, *i.e.*, that the City failed to exercise due care in selecting or instructing the entity actually conducting the disposal of the City's waste.

c. The Evidence Regarding the Deepwood and South Loop 12 Dumps

We now examine the evidence regarding each dump and conclude that the district court did not commit clear error in finding that the evidence established § 6972(a)(1)(B) "contributing to" liability for the City.

i. Deepwood Dump

The RCRA creates, at the very least, a duty on the part of generators not to dispose of their waste in such a manner that it may present an imminent and substantial endangerment to health or the environment. Negligent oversight of disposal is actionable under the RCRA. As described *supra* in Part I.A, the City contracted with Billy Nabors and Dallas Demolition to conduct demolitions of City property. These City contractors dumped loads of debris at the Deepwood dump. The City's contracts with Dallas Demolition did not specify that waste materials generated by the City's activities must be properly disposed of in a legal landfill. The City was aware that Dallas Demolition engaged in illegal dumping and operated its own unauthorized waste site. Furthermore, the City's attorneys were informed that Dallas Demolition dumped at the Deepwood dump. However, even *after* the City's attorneys had learned that Dallas Demolition had been dumping illegally in Dallas, the City continued to work with Dallas Demolition. The district court did not clearly err in finding that this "lax oversight" of its contractors and their disposal of City waste is evidence of the City's "contributing to" liability.

The City argues that there is no evidence in the record that the City's waste actually went into the Deepwood dump. The City asserts, instead, that the contracts simply demonstrate that it could have used Billy Nabors or Dallas Demolition to haul trash, but that there is no evidence that it actually did do so (and, even if it did utilize these haulers, that the City's particular waste was taken to the Deepwood dump). We find little merit in this argument.

First, the district court reasonably inferred that the City's waste went into the Deepwood dump, and on this record, this inference is not clear error. The City Council allocated funds for the demolition actions, and the City Council, subsequent to a bidding process, awarded specific contracts to Dallas Demolition and Billy Nabors, even after City attorneys knew that they were dumping illegally at the Deepwood dump. Given that the City specifically hired these contractors to perform certain jobs, a logical conclusion is that the City used them for those jobs. A mere assertion from the City that the jobs might not have been performed is insufficient to alter this conclusion.

The City's actions therefore snugly fit the "failed to exercise due care in selecting or instructing the entity actually conducting the disposal" statement from S. REP. NO. 96–172, at 5 (1979), *reprinted in* 1980 U.S.C.C.A.N. 5019, 5023. This situation also closely parallels an example considered in a 1979 House Committee Report and a 1979 Senate Report, *i.e.*, that a generator of solid waste is subject to liability even when someone else conducted the disposal at the generator's request. *See* S. REP. NO. 96–172, at 5 (1979), *reprinted in* 1980 U.S.C.C.A.N. 5019, 5023; H.R. COMM. PRINT NO. 96–IFC 31, at 31 (1979).

Therefore, the district court did not err in assessing § 6972(a)(1)(B) liability against the City based on the City's negligent actions regarding the disposal of its waste.

ii. South Loop 12 Dump

The City does not dispute that it used the South Loop 12 site as a municipal landfill from 1964 until at least 1972. An owner of South Loop 12 fenced the site and hired a guard to stop the City from dumping because the City would not properly cover the refuse it had dumped there. The City's primary argument is that because its use ended in 1972 and because the RCRA was not enacted until 1976, it cannot be held liable under § 6972(a)(1)(B). We do not agree.

Section 6972(a)(1)(B) is clear that it applies to *both* past and present acts, as the adjectives "past and present" are specifically included. We have also previously confirmed that "[w]e understand [the] language [of § 6972(a)(1)(B)] to provide a claim for injunctive relief based on either *past or present* conduct."

"In short, the disposal of wastes [as wholly past acts] can constitute a continuing violation as long as no proper disposal procedures are put into effect or as long as the waste has not been cleaned up and the environmental effects remain remediable." The continued presence of this municipal waste in the South Loop 12 dump (so long as it presents an imminent and substantial endangerment to health or the environment, *see infra* Part III.B.3), is actionable under § 6972(a)(1)(B).

3. *Imminent and Substantial Endangerment to Health or Environment*

Lastly, the district court did not err in concluding that an imminent and substantial endangerment to health or the environment existed at both dumps. At the outset, we note that the operative word in § 6972(a)(1)(B) is "may." Thus, Plaintiffs must demonstrate that the waste "may present" such a danger.

The Supreme Court has also pointed out that the phrase "may present" communicates another idea: It "quite clearly excludes waste that no longer presents" the harm contemplated by § 6972(a)(1)(B). "[T]his language 'implies that there must be a threat which is present *now,* although the impact of the threat may not be felt until later.' " As such, "under an imminent hazard citizen suit, the endangerment must be ongoing, but the conduct that created the endangerment need not be."

Because the RCRA does not define "imminent," the Supreme Court, as is its customary practice, ... looked to the plain meaning of the term: "An endangerment can only be 'imminent' if it 'threaten[s] to occur immediately.' " The legislative history supports interpreting "imminent" in accordance with this plain meaning. * * * And finally, an endangerment is "substantial" if it is "serious."

With this framework in place, we now examine the evidence regarding the imminent and substantial endangerment to health and the environment at each dump.

a. Deepwood Dump

The district court did not clearly err in concluding that the Deepwood dump "may present an imminent and substantial endangerment to health or the environment." The evidence includes the following: The Deepwood dump is adjacent to residences and is partially in the flood plain of the Trinity River; the dump is easily accessible to children; the Deepwood dump twice caught fire and burned, with the resulting fumes polluting the neighborhood air; a significant fire hazard continues to exist at the dump; the State's reports reveal that there is an imminent threat of the discharge of municipal solid waste into Elam Creek, a tributary of the Trinity River, because of the massive illegal dumping; the State itself has noted that waste at the Deepwood dump may cause contamination of surface water and ground water through the leaching of contaminates from the debris by rainwater; asbestos, benzo(a)athracene, and benzene (in excess of state limits) have been detected at the Deepwood dump; and the City itself has long maintained that the Deepwood dump poses a hazard to the public health.

b. South Loop 12 Dump

On appeal, the City argues that the material it dumped at the South Loop 12 dump presents no danger to health or the environment; yet, the City points to nothing in the record to support this assertion. The district court concluded that Plaintiffs have adequately demonstrated that the City's contributions played a role in the creation of the dangers at the

South Loop 12 dump, and, as will be explained below, the record well supports this conclusion.

The district court did not clearly err in finding that the South Loop 12 dump satisfies the endangerment standard of § 6972(a)(1)(B). First, as the district court noted, the City itself had previously admitted that the South Loop 12 dump was a "hazard to the public health in its present condition." Furthermore, the City's state court judgment against the owners stated that the judgment was "necessary for the maintenance of the public health and environment."

In addition, the State's documents themselves describe the very danger of old landfills, like the South Loop 12 dump, that were established before any of the proper closure requirements were in place: As the old waste decomposes, the cover soil can settle, ground and surface water can become contaminated with leachate, and dangerous gases can form and migrate underground. This meets the "may present an imminent and substantial endangerment" standard. Moreover, as the City failed to adhere even to the less stringent requirements in effect during the time it was dumping at the South Loop 12 dump, the dangers described in the State's plan are even more likely to materialize.

Therefore, the district court's finding that the City was liable under § 6972(a)(1)(B) for the Deepwood and South Loop 12 dumps was not clearly erroneous. * * *

NOTES

1. **RCRA "Contributing to" Liability.** What are the statutory elements of RCRA "contributing to" liability? How did the Fifth Circuit define each element? Why did the Fifth Circuit affirm the district court in finding that the City of Dallas was liable for the Deepwood Dump? Why did the Fifth Circuit affirm the district court in finding that the City of Dallas was liable for the South Loop 12 dump? What, according to the City, was the weakest element of its "contributing to" liability for each dump?

2. **Nuisance Law and RCRA.** Why did the Fifth Circuit review nuisance law as an aid to assessing the City's RCRA liability? What evidence did it have that Congress intended nuisance to be relevant in interpreting and applying RCRA's provisions? Did the Deepwood and South Loop 12 dumps qualify as nuisances under common law? Why or why not? According to the Fifth Circuit, is RCRA liability broader than common law nuisance liability or narrower than common law nuisance liability? In other words, is it easier or harder to make out a RCRA "contributing to" claim, compared to common law nuisance?

3. **RCRA and the Standard of Fault.** Note that the Fifth Circuit avoided the issue of whether RCRA imposes a strict liability or a negligence standard, asserting instead that even if negligence is required, the City of Dallas was in fact negligent. The majority of federal courts that have addressed this issue have concluded that RCRA imposes a ***strict liability*** standard for civil violations of the Act. (Criminal violations, of course, require

a higher threshold of liability.) *United States v. Northeastern Pharmaceutical & Chemical Co.*, 810 F.2d 726, 740 (8th Cir. 1986), *cert. denied* 484 U.S. 848 (1987) (holding that RCRA cleanup liability under RCRA § 7003(a), 42 U.S.C. § 6973(a), is strict); *United States v. Domestic Industries, Inc.*, 32 F. Supp. 2d 855, 866–67 (E.D. Va. 1999) (holding that RCRA's used oil provisions impose strict liability); *United States v. Valentine*, 885 F.Supp. 1506, 1511 (D. Wyo. 1995) (holding that RCRA cleanup liability under RCRA § 7003(a), 42 U.S.C. § 6973(a), is strict); *Western Greenhouses v. United States*, 878 F.Supp. 917, 930 (N.D. Tex. 1995) (holding that both RCRA and CERCLA are strict liability statutes); *Zands v. Nelson*, 797 F.Supp. 805, 809 (S.D. Cal. 1992) ("Individuals are liable under RCRA without regard to fault or negligence."); *United States v. Allegan Metal Finishing Co.*, 696 F.Supp. 275, 287 (W.D. Mich. 1988) (holding that "civil violations of RCRA provisions are properly characterized as strict liability offenses"); *United States v. Bliss*, 667 F.Supp. 1298, 1313 (E.D. Mo. 1987) ("Section 7003(a) of RCRA imposes liability without fault or negligence"); *United States v. Ottati & Goss, Inc.*, 630 F.Supp. 1361, 1400–01 (D.N.H. 1985) (holding that RCRA cleanup liability under RCRA § 7003(a), 42 U.S.C. § 6973(a), is strict); *United States v. Liviola*, 605 F.Supp. 96, 100 (D. Ohio 1985) (holding that civil penalties under RCRA are strict liability offenses); *United States v. Hardage*, 18 E.R.C. 1685, 1686 (W.D. Okla. 1982) (holding that RCRA cleanup liability under RCRA § 7003(a), 42 U.S.C. § 6973(a), is strict). Why would the federal courts so interpret RCRA? How does a strict liability standard promote Congress's intent and purposes in enacting RCRA?

4. **Plaintiffs' Section 6945(a) Claims.** As the Fifth Circuit mentioned at the beginning of *Cox*, the plaintiffs in this case also brought claims against the City that alleged that it had violated section 6945(a) of RCRA. Section 6945 is the section of Subtitle D that governs the upgrading of open dumps. Subsection (a) provides that, after the EPA establishes criteria for preventing open dumping, "any solid waste management practice or disposal of solid waste or hazardous waste which constitutes the open dumping of solid waste or hazardous waste is prohibited * * *. The prohibition contained in the preceding sentence shall be enforceable under section 6972 of this title against persons engaged in the act of open dumping." 42 U.S.C. § 6945(a). Thus, section 6945 explicitly makes the open dumping prohibitions enforceable through RCRA citizen suits. Why do you suppose that plaintiffs' section 6945 claims failed in this case?

5. **Refining "Contributing To" Liability.** In order for a RCRA defendant to be liable pursuant to RCRA's "contributing to" provisions, that defendant must "ha[ve] contributed to or [be] contributing to the past or present handling, storage, treatment, transportation, or disposal of any solid or hazardous waste.... " 42 U.S.C. § 6972(a)(1)(B). How direct and active must the defendant's contribution be? Suppose, for example, that the defendant manufactures a machine that other people use in their businesses. In the process of using the machine, solid and hazardous wastes are inevitably created. Should the machine manufacturer be liable for "contributing to" liability under RCRA? Why or why not? *See Hinds Investments, L.P. v. Angioli*, 654 F.3d 846, 850–51 (9th Cir. 2011) (answering "no" and requiring active control of in the production and handling of wastes for RCRA liability).

Is this an example of notions of proximate cause slipping back into RCRA's liability scheme?

6. **RCRA Subtitle D, Landfills, and Climate Change.** Notice that, as part of Subtitle D's requirements, sanitary landfills have to monitor for methane emissions. Methane is a potent greenhouse gas, more than 20 times more effective at trapping heat in the atmosphere than carbon dioxide (CO_2). Landfills are thus potentially relevant to climate change.

In April 2009, in response to the Supreme Court's decision in *Massachusetts v. EPA* (see Chapter 4), the EPA proposed a regulation that would impose mandatory reporting of greenhouse gas emissions. Mandatory Reporting of Greenhouse Gases, 74 Fed. Reg. 16,448 (April 10, 2009). The rule was finalized in October 2009. Mandatory Reporting of Greenhouse Gases, 74 Fed. Reg. 56,260 (Oct. 30, 2009). Under the original rule, municipal solid waste landfills had to report their methane emissions if those emissions exceeded 25,000 metric tons of carbon dioxide equivalents per year. *Id.* at 56,267. The EPA later established industrial solid waste landfills as a separate category of sources subject to mandatory greenhouse gas reporting and established separate reporting requirements for them. 75 Fed. Reg. 39,736, 39,746–50 (July 10, 2010). In August 2011, however, the EPA proposed substantial revisions to the reporting rules, including for landfills. 76 Fed. Reg. 47,392, 47,403–04 (Aug. 4, 2011).

7. **The Rest of the Story.** Thomas W. Merrill has discussed the effects of environmental concerns on the handling of municipal household wastes.

> The garbage industry in 1980 was highly decentralized, characterized by large numbers [of] public and private entities operating large numbers of dumps under regulatory standards that were uneven at best. In the next two decades, the industry was transformed into one dominated by a handful of corporate waste disposal firms operating out of a much smaller number of tightly-regulated mega-sites. Accompanying the consolidation in the industry was a shift in the location of sites. Virtually all new disposal sites today are located in rural areas outside the path of urban development. Perhaps the biggest adjustment associated with the change in the solid waste industry has been coming to terms with the higher costs of transporting garbage to these areas for burial.

Thomas W. Merrill, *The Story of* SWANCC*: Federalism and the Politics of Locally Unwanted Land Uses, in* RICHARD J. LAZARUS & OLIVER A. HOUCK, ENVIRONMENTAL LAW STORIES 283, 284 (Foundation Press 2005).

* * *

2. Constitutional Limitations on States' Handling of Solid Waste

In a series of decisions spanning almost 20 years, the U.S. Supreme Court has repeatedly emphasized that waste disposal is a commercial or economic activity and thus that, under the "dormant" or "negative" Commerce Clause, state and local governments cannot discriminate against out-of-state waste in their waste disposal plans. *See, e.g.*, *C & A Carbone, Inc. v. Town of Clarkstown, N.Y.*, 511 U.S. 383 (1994) (holding that a town ordinance that required handling of solid waste at the town's transfer station violated the dormant Commerce Clause); *Oregon Waste Systems, Inc. v. Department of Environmental Quality of Oregon*, 511 U.S. 93 (1994) (holding that Oregon violated the dormant Commerce Clause by imposing a $2.50 per ton surcharge on in-state disposal of waste generated out of the state); *Fort Gratiot Sanitary Landfill, Inc. v. Michigan Department of Natural Resources*, 504 U.S. 353 (1992) (holding that a Michigan statute that prohibited private landfill operators from accepting solid waste that originated outside of the county in which the landfill was located violated the dormant Commerce Clause); *Chemical Waste Management, Inc. v. Hunt*, 504 U.S. 334 (1992) (finding that an Alabama statute that imposed an additional fee on all hazardous wastes generated outside Alabama discriminated against interstate commerce in violation of the Constitution); *City of Philadelphia v. New Jersey*, 437 U.S. 617 (1978) (holding that a New Jersey statute that prohibited importation of most solid and liquid waste that originated or was collected outside of the state violated the dormant Commerce Clause). *But see Minnesota v. Clover Leaf Creamery Co.*, 449 U.S. 456 (1981) (upholding a Minnesota statute that banned the retail sale of milk in plastic, nonreturnable, nonrefillable containers). In the context of RCRA Subtitle D, what practical difficulties might these constitutional decisions cause states?

In April 2007, the U.S. Supreme Court revisited the issue of solid waste management and flow control statutes in the following case. As you read this decision, consider what this decision might mean for state and local government authority to manage solid waste.

UNITED HAULERS ASSOCIATION, INC. v. ONEIDA-HERKIMER SOLID WASTE MANAGEMENT AUTHORITY

550 U.S. 330, (2007).

CHIEF JUSTICE ROBERTS delivered the opinion of the Court, except as to Part II–D.

"Flow control" ordinances require trash haulers to deliver solid waste to a particular waste processing facility. In *C & A Carbone, Inc. v. Clarkstown,* 511 U.S. 383 (1994), this Court struck down under the Commerce Clause a flow control ordinance that forced haulers to deliver waste to a particular *private* processing facility. In this case, we face flow control ordinances quite similar to the one invalidated in *Carbone*. The only salient difference is that the laws at issue here require haulers to bring waste to facilities owned and operated by a state-created public benefit corporation. We find this difference constitutionally significant. Disposing of trash has been a traditional government activity for years, and laws that favor the government in such areas—but treat every private business, whether in-state or out-of-state, exactly the same—do not discriminate against interstate commerce for purposes of the Commerce Clause. Applying the Commerce Clause test reserved for regulations that do not discriminate against interstate commerce, we uphold these ordinances because any incidental burden they may have on interstate commerce does not outweigh the benefits they confer on the citizens of Oneida and Herkimer Counties.

I

Located in central New York, Oneida and Herkimer Counties span over 2,600 square miles and are home to about 306,000 residents. Traditionally, each city, town, or village within the Counties has been responsible for disposing of its own waste. Many had relied on local landfills, some in a more environmentally responsible fashion than others.

By the 1980's, the Counties confronted what they could credibly call a solid waste " 'crisis.' " Many local landfills were operating without permits and in violation of state regulations. Sixteen were ordered to close and remediate the surrounding environment, costing the public tens of millions of dollars. These environmental problems culminated in a federal clean-up action against a landfill in Oneida County; the defendants in that case named over 600 local businesses and several municipalities and school districts as third-party defendants.

The "crisis" extended beyond health and safety concerns. The Counties had an uneasy relationship with local waste management companies, enduring price fixing, pervasive overcharging, and the influence of organized crime. Dramatic price hikes were not uncommon: In 1986, for example, a county contractor doubled its waste disposal rate on six weeks' notice.

Responding to these problems, the Counties requested and New York's Legislature and Governor created the Oneida–Herkimer Solid Waste Management Authority (Authority), a public benefit corporation. The Authority is empowered to collect, process, and dispose of solid waste generated in the Counties. To further the Authority's governmental and public purposes, the Counties may impose "appropriate and reasonable limitations on competition" by, for instance, adopting "local laws requiring that all solid waste ... be delivered to a specified solid waste management-resource recovery facility." § 2049–tt(3).

In 1989, the Authority and the Counties entered into a Solid Waste Management Agreement, under which the Authority agreed to manage all solid waste within the Counties. Private haulers would remain free to pick up citizens' trash from the curb, but the Authority would take over the job of processing the trash, sorting it, and sending it off for disposal. To fulfill its part of the bargain, the Authority agreed to purchase and develop facilities for the processing and disposal of solid waste and recyclables generated in the Counties.

The Authority collected "tipping fees" to cover its operating and maintenance costs for these facilities.[2] The tipping fees significantly

2. Tipping fees are disposal charges levied against collectors who drop off waste at a processing facility. They are called "tipping" fees because garbage trucks literally tip their back

exceeded those charged for waste removal on the open market, but they allowed the Authority to do more than the average private waste disposer. In addition to landfill transportation and solid waste disposal, the fees enabled the Authority to provide recycling of 33 kinds of materials, as well as composting, household hazardous waste disposal, and a number of other services. If the Authority's operating costs and debt service were not recouped through tipping fees and other charges, the agreement provided that the Counties would make up the difference.

As described, the agreement had a flaw: Citizens might opt to have their waste hauled to facilities with lower tipping fees. To avoid being stuck with the bill for facilities that citizens voted for but then chose not to use, the Counties enacted "flow control" ordinances requiring that all solid waste generated within the Counties be delivered to the Authority's processing sites. Private haulers must obtain a permit from the Authority to collect waste in the Counties. Penalties for noncompliance with the ordinances include permit revocation, fines, and imprisonment.

Petitioners are United Haulers Association, Inc., a trade association made up of solid waste management companies, and six haulers that operated in Oneida and Herkimer Counties when this action was filed. In 1995, they sued the Counties and the Authority under * * * 42 U.S.C. § 1983, alleging that the flow control laws violate the Commerce Clause by discriminating against interstate commerce. They submitted evidence that without the flow control laws and the associated $86–per-ton tipping fees, they could dispose of solid waste at out-of-state facilities for between $37 and $55 per ton, including transportation.

The District Court read our decision in *Carbone,* 511 U.S. 383, as categorically rejecting nearly all flow control laws. The court ruled in the haulers' favor, enjoining enforcement of the Counties' laws. The Second Circuit reversed, reasoning that *Carbone* and our other dormant Commerce Clause precedents allow for a distinction between laws that benefit public as opposed to private facilities. * * * The court remanded to let the District Court decide whether the Counties' ordinances nevertheless placed an incidental burden on interstate commerce, and if so, whether the ordinances' benefits outweighed that burden.

On remand and after protracted discovery, a Magistrate Judge and the District Court found that the haulers did not show that the ordinances imposed *any* cognizable burden on interstate commerce. The Second Circuit affirmed, assuming that the laws exacted some toll on interstate commerce, but finding any possible burden "modest" compared to the "clear and substantial" benefits of the ordinances. Because the Sixth Circuit had recently issued a conflicting decision holding that a flow control ordinance favoring a public entity *does* facially discriminate against interstate commerce, we granted certiorari.

---

end to dump out the carried waste. As of 1995, haulers in the Counties had to pay tipping fees of at least $86 per ton, a price that ballooned to as much as $172 per ton if a particular load contained more than 25% recyclables.

II

A

The Commerce Clause provides that "Congress shall have Power . . . [t]o regulate Commerce with foreign Nations, and among the several States." U.S. CONST., Art. I, § 8, cl. 3. Although the Constitution does not in terms limit the power of States to regulate commerce, we have long interpreted the Commerce Clause as an implicit restraint on state authority, even in the absence of a conflicting federal statute.

To determine whether a law violates this so-called "dormant" aspect of the Commerce Clause, we first ask whether it discriminates on its face against interstate commerce. In this context, " 'discrimination' simply means differential treatment of in-state and out-of-state economic interests that benefits the former and burdens the latter." *Oregon Waste Systems, Inc. v. Department of Environmental Quality of Ore.,* 511 U.S. 93, 99 (1994); *New Energy Co. of Ind. v. Limbach,* 486 U.S. 269, 273 (1988). Discriminatory laws motivated by "simple economic protectionism" are subject to a "virtually *per se* rule of invalidity," *Philadelphia v. New Jersey,* 437 U.S. 617, 624 (1978), which can only be overcome by a showing that the State has no other means to advance a legitimate local purpose, *Maine v. Taylor,* 477 U.S. 131, 138 (1986).

B

Following the lead of the Sixth Circuit in *Daviess County,* the haulers argue vigorously that the Counties' ordinances discriminate against interstate commerce under *Carbone.* In *Carbone,* the town of Clarkstown, New York, hired a private contractor to build a waste transfer station. According to the terms of the deal, the contractor would operate the facility for five years, charging an above-market tipping fee of $81 per ton; after five years, the town would buy the facility for one dollar. The town guaranteed that the facility would receive a certain volume of trash per year. To make good on its promise, Clarkstown passed a flow control ordinance requiring that all nonhazardous solid waste within the town be deposited at the transfer facility.

This Court struck down the ordinance, holding that it discriminated against interstate commerce by "hoard[ing] solid waste, and the demand to get rid of it, for the benefit of the preferred processing facility." The dissent pointed out that all of this Court's local processing cases involved laws that discriminated in favor of *private* entities, not public ones. According to the dissent, Clarkstown's ostensibly private transfer station was "essentially a municipal facility," and this distinction should have saved Clarkstown's ordinance because favoring local government is by its nature different from favoring a particular private company. The majority did not comment on the dissent's public-private distinction.

The parties in this case draw opposite inferences from the majority's silence. The haulers say it proves that the majority agreed with the dissent's characterization of the facility, but thought there was no difference under the dormant Commerce Clause between laws favoring private entities and those favoring public ones. The Counties disagree, arguing that the majority studiously avoided the issue because the facility in *Carbone* was private, and therefore the question whether *public* facilities may be favored was not properly before the Court.

We believe the latter interpretation of *Carbone* is correct. As the Second Circuit explained, "in *Carbone* the Justices were divided over the *fact of whether* the favored facility was public or private, rather than on the import of that distinction." The *Carbone* dissent offered a number of reasons why public entities should be treated differently from private ones under the dormant Commerce Clause. It is hard to suppose that the *Carbone* majority definitively rejected these arguments without explaining why.

* * * C

The flow control ordinances in this case benefit a clearly public facility, while treating all private companies exactly the same. Because the question is now squarely presented on the facts of the case before us, we decide that such flow control ordinances do not discriminate against interstate commerce for purposes of the dormant Commerce Clause.

Compelling reasons justify treating these laws differently from laws favoring particular private businesses over their competitors. * * * States and municipalities are not private businesses—far from it. Unlike private enterprise, government is vested with the responsibility of protecting the health, safety, and welfare of its citizens. These important responsibilities set state and local government apart from a typical private business.

Given these differences, it does not make sense to regard laws favoring local government and laws favoring private industry with equal skepticism. As our local processing cases demonstrate, when a law favors in-state business over out-of-state competition, rigorous scrutiny is appropriate because the law is often the product of "simple economic protectionism." Laws favoring local government, by contrast, may be directed toward any number of legitimate goals unrelated to protectionism. Here the flow control ordinances enable the Counties to pursue particular policies with respect to the handling and treatment of waste generated in the Counties, while allocating the costs of those policies on citizens and businesses according to the volume of waste they generate.

The contrary approach of treating public and private entities the same under the dormant Commerce Clause would lead to unprecedented and unbounded interference by the courts with state and local government. The dormant Commerce Clause is not a roving license for federal courts to decide what activities are appropriate for state and local government to undertake, and what activities must be the province of private market competition. * * * It is not the office of the Commerce Clause to control the decision of the voters on whether government or the private sector should provide waste management services. * * *

We should be particularly hesitant to interfere with the Counties' efforts under the guise of the Commerce Clause because "[w]aste disposal is both typically and traditionally a local government function." 261 F.3d, at 264 (case below) (Calabresi, J., concurring) * * *. Congress itself has recognized local government's vital role in waste management, making clear that "collection and disposal of solid wastes should continue to be primarily the function of State, regional, and local agencies." Resource Conservation and Recovery Act of 1976, 90 Stat. 2797, 42 U.S.C. § 6901(a)(4). The policy of the State of New York favors "displac[ing] competition with regulation or monopoly control" in this area. N.Y. PUB. AUTH. LAW ANN. § 2049–tt(3). We may or may not agree with that approach, but nothing in the Commerce Clause vests the responsibility for that policy judgment with the Federal Judiciary.

Finally, it bears mentioning that the most palpable harm imposed by the ordinances—more expensive trash removal—is likely to fall upon the very people who voted for the laws. Our dormant Commerce Clause cases often find discrimination when a State shifts the costs of regulation to other States, because when "the burden of state regulation falls on interests outside the state, it is unlikely to be alleviated by the operation of those political restraints normally exerted when interests within the state are affected." *Southern Pacific Co. v. Arizona ex rel. Sullivan,* 325 U.S. 761, 767–768, n. 2 (1945). Here, the citizens and businesses of the Counties bear the costs of the ordinances. There is no reason to step in and hand local businesses a victory they could not obtain through the political process.

We hold that the Counties' flow control ordinances, which treat in-state private business interests exactly the same as out-of-state ones, do not "discriminate against interstate commerce" for purposes of the dormant Commerce Clause.

D

The Counties' flow control ordinances are properly analyzed under the test set forth in *Pike v. Bruce Church, Inc.,* 397 U.S. 137, 142 (1970), which is reserved for laws "directed to legitimate local concerns, with effects upon interstate commerce that are only incidental." *Philadelphia v. New Jersey,* 437 U.S., at 624. Under the *Pike* test, we will uphold a nondiscriminatory statute like this one "unless the burden imposed on [interstate] commerce is clearly excessive in relation to the putative local benefits." 397 U.S., at 142.

After years of discovery, both the Magistrate Judge and the District Court could not detect *any* disparate impact on out-of-state as opposed to in-state businesses. * * * We find it unnecessary to decide whether the ordinances impose any incidental burden on interstate commerce because any arguable burden does not exceed the public benefits of the ordinances.

The ordinances give the Counties a convenient and effective way to finance their integrated package of waste-disposal services. * * *

At the same time, the ordinances are more than financing tools. They increase recycling in at least two ways, conferring significant health and environmental benefits upon the citizens of the Counties. First, they create enhanced incentives for recycling and proper disposal of other kinds of waste. Solid waste disposal is expensive in Oneida–Herkimer, but the Counties accept recyclables and many forms of hazardous waste for free, effectively encouraging their citizens to sort their own trash. Second, by requiring all waste to be deposited at Authority facilities, the Counties have markedly increased their ability to enforce recycling laws. If the haulers could take waste to any disposal site, achieving an equal level of enforcement would be much more costly, if not impossible. For these reasons, any arguable burden the ordinances impose on interstate commerce does not exceed their public benefits.

* * *

The Counties' ordinances are exercises of the police power in an effort to address waste disposal, a typical and traditional concern of local government. The haulers nevertheless ask us to hold that laws favoring public entities while treating all private businesses the same are subject to an almost *per se* rule of invalidity, because of asserted discrimination. In the alternative, they maintain that the Counties' laws cannot survive the more permissive *Pike* test, because of asserted burdens on commerce. There is a common thread to these arguments: They are invitations to rigorously scrutinize economic legislation passed under the auspices of the police power. There was a time when this Court presumed to make such binding judgments for society, under the guise of interpreting the Due Process Clause. See *Lochner v. New York,* 198 U.S. 45 (1905). We should not seek to reclaim that ground for judicial supremacy under the banner of the dormant Commerce Clause.

The judgments of the United States Court of Appeals for the Second Circuit are affirmed.

It is so ordered.

JUSTICE SCALIA, concurring in part.

I join Part I and Parts II–A through II–C of the Court's opinion. I write separately to reaffirm my view that "the so-called 'negative' Commerce Clause is an unjustified judicial invention, not to be expanded beyond its existing domain." *General Motors Corp. v. Tracy,* 519 U.S. 278, 312 (1997) (SCALIA, J., concurring). * * *

JUSTICE ALITO, with whom JUSTICE STEVENS and JUSTICE KENNEDY join, dissenting.

In *C & A Carbone, Inc. v. Clarkstown,* 511 U.S. 383 (1994), we held that "a so-called flow control ordinance, which require[d] all solid waste to be processed at a designated transfer station before leaving the municipality," discriminated against interstate commerce and was invalid under the Commerce Clause because it "depriv[ed] competitors, including out-of-state firms, of access to a local market." *Id.,* at 386. Because the provisions challenged in this case are essentially identical to the ordinance invalidated in *Carbone,* I respectfully dissent. * * *

NOTES

1. **Federalism and the Dormant Commerce Clause.** The constitutional and regulatory relationship between the states and the federal government in the United States is referred to as ***federalism***. The Commerce Clause of the U.S. Constitution, in both its positive and its dormant forms, is one of the constitutional provisions that helps to define this complex relationship. How does the U.S. Supreme Court address federalism issues in *United Haulers*? Why does it focus on issues of local government function?

2. **RCRA and the Dormant Commerce Clause.** How was RCRA relevant to the Supreme Court's decision? Does this decision further the goals and purposes of Subtitle D? Why or why not?

3. **The Supreme Court, Waste Handling, and the Commerce Clause.** States' and local governments' handling of solid and hazardous waste has generated a surprising number of dormant Commerce Clause decisions from the Supreme Court, and over several decades. Besides *Carbone* and *United Haulers*, these decisions include: *City of Philadelphia v. New Jersey*, 437 U.S. 617 (1978) (invalidating a New Jersey statute that prohibited the importation of out-of-state waste); *Chemical Waste Management v. Hunt*, 504 U.S. 334 (1992) (invalidating Alabama's imposition of an additional disposal fee on hazardous waste generated outside the state but disposed of within Alabama); *Fort Gratiot Sanitary Landfill, Inc. v. Michigan Department of Natural Resources*, 504 U.S. 353 (1992) (invalidating the provisions of Michigan's Solid Waste Management Act that restricted landfill's ability to accept out-of-state waste); and *Oregon Waste Systems, Inc. v. Oregon Department of Environmental Quality*, 511 U.S. 93 (1994) (invalidating Oregon's increased per-ton surcharge on waste generated in other states). Notice that, until *United Haulers*, state attempts to control importation of out-of-state waste universally failed. Nevertheless, states kept trying to impose such controls despite very clear decisions from the Supreme Court that any such discrimination against out-of-state waste was likely to be unconstitutional.

What does this continual struggle between states and the Supreme Court suggest about the realities—financial and otherwise—of waste management and the burdens that out-of-state waste can impose on in-state landfills and other facilities? As a policy matter, should solid and hazardous waste be treated as articles of commerce, the same as wine or widgets or any other product? Why or why not?

* * *

C. RCRA'S REGULATION OF HAZARDOUS SOLID WASTES: SUBTITLE C

1. What Is a "Hazardous Waste"?

RCRA's most stringent regulatory provisions apply to ***hazardous wastes***. RCRA hazardous wastes are a ***subset*** of RCRA solid wastes. In other words, in order to qualify as a "hazardous waste," materials must first qualify as "solid wastes," as shown in Figure 1–5.

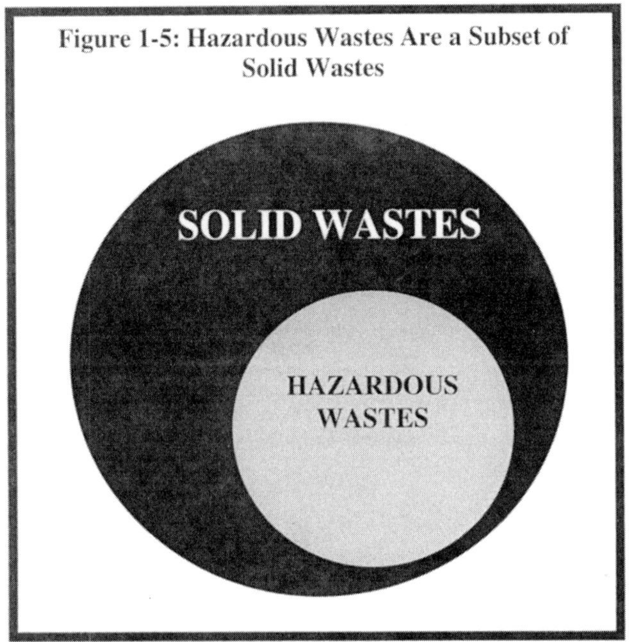

Like "solid waste," "hazardous waste" is defined by the statute itself. A "hazardous waste" is "a solid waste, or combination of solid wastes, which because of its quantity, concentration, or physical, chemical, or infectious characteristics may—"

(A) cause, or significantly contribute to an increase in mortality or an increase in serious irreversible, or incapacitating reversible, illness; or

(B) pose a substantial present or potential hazard to human health or the environment when improperly treated, stored, transported, or disposed of, or otherwise managed.

RCRA § 1004(5), 42 U.S.C. § 6903(5).

Figure 1-6: The World of RCRA Hazardous Wastes

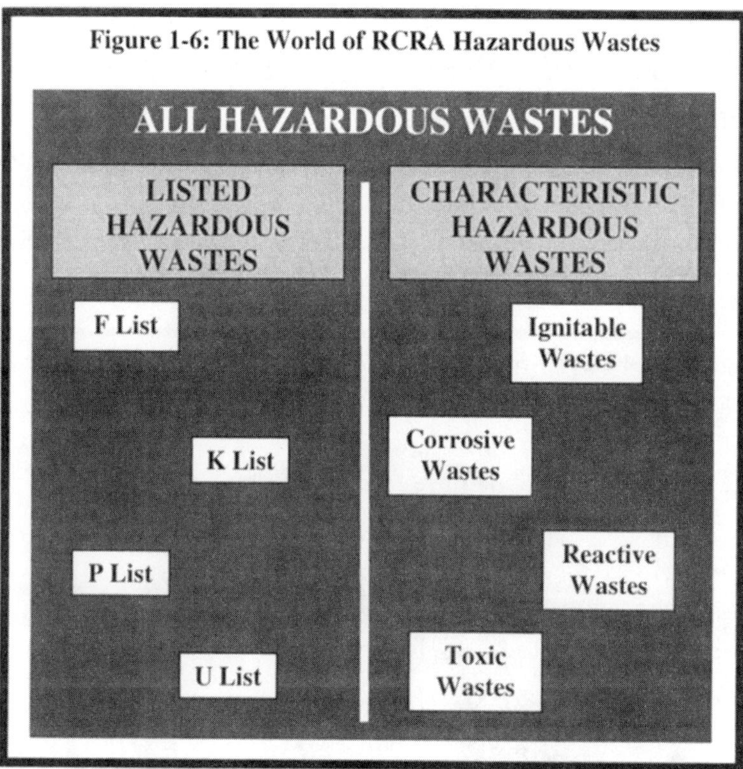

The EPA had the responsibility to "develop and promulgate criteria for identifying the characteristics of hazardous waste, and for listing hazardous waste" and to actually list hazardous wastes subject to RCRA's subtitle C requirements, "taking into account toxicity, persistence, and degradability in nature, potential for accumulation in tissue, and other related factors such as flammability, corrosiveness, and other hazardous characteristics." RCRA § 3001(a), (b)(1), 42 U.S.C. § 6921(a), (b)(1). In addition, State Governors can petition the EPA to add particular materials to the hazardous waste lists. RCRA § 3001(c), 42 U.S.C. § 6921(c).

As a result of the EPA's rulemaking, there are two basic ways that a solid waste qualifies as a hazardous waste: (1) the solid waste may be a ***characteristic hazardous waste*** because it exhibits one of four regulatory characteristics; or (2) the solid waste may be a ***listed hazardous waste*** because the EPA specifically listed that waste as hazardous in the EPA's regulations. 40 C.F.R. § 261.3(a). A solid waste qualifies as a ***characteristic hazardous waste*** if it exhibits any one of four regulatory characteristics: ***ignitability***; ***corrosivity***; ***reactivity***; or ***toxicity***, as illustrated in Figure 1–6.

The EPA's regulations classify a solid waste as an ***ignitable hazardous waste*** if: (1) the waste is a liquid with a flash point of less than 140°F; (2) the waste is a non-liquid that can catch fire at normal temperatures and pressures; (3) the waste is an ignitable condensed gas; *or* (4) the waste is an oxidizer. 40 C.F.R. § 261.21(a). Ignitable hazardous wastes are identified as **D001** hazardous wastes. *Id.* § 261.21(b).

Under the EPA's regulations, a solid waste is a ***corrosive hazardous waste*** **(D002)** if: (1) it has a pH of less than or equal to 2 or greater than or equal to 12.5 (*i.e.*, it is either a strong acid or a strong base); or (2) it corrodes steel at rate faster than 6.35 millimeters per year at 130°F. 40 C.F.R. § 261.22.

Reactive hazardous wastes **(D003)** are solid wastes that are "normally unstable" and that "undergo[] violent change" or "react[] violently with water," that generate toxic gases when mixed with water, or that can detonate or explode. 40 C.F.R. § 261.23.

Finally, solid wastes qualify as characteristic ***toxic hazardous wastes*** **(D004 to D043)** through ***Toxicity Characteristic Leachate Procedure*** **(TCLP)**. 40 C.F.R. § 261.24. Under this procedure, water is run through the waste to generate a ***leachate***, which is then tested for 39 chemicals. The waste is considered a characteristic hazardous waste if its leachate contains any of the chemicals listed in Figure 1–7 in concentrations equal to or greater than the thresholds indicated.

The EPA has designated ***listed hazardous wastes*** in three regulations and four lists. The ***F list*** designates general hazardous wastes that can derive from a variety of sources, like F001, spent halogenated solvents. 40 C.F.R. § 261.31. The ***K list,*** in contrast, specifies hazardous wastes that derive from very specific sources. 40 C.F.R. § 261.32. K175, for example, identifies "wastewater treatment sludges from the production of vinyl chloride monomer using mercuric chloride catalyst in an acetylene-based process." *Id.* ***P list*** and ***U list*** hazardous wastes designate discarded commercial chemical products, such as arsenic oxide (P012), barium cyanide (P013), calcium chromate (U032), or vinyl chloride (U043). 40 C.F.R. § 261.33.

Characteristic and listed hazardous wastes differ in how long they are potentially subject to regulation under RCRA Subtitle C. In general, characteristic hazardous wastes, especially ignitable, corrosive, and reactive wastes, are subject to RCRA Subtitle C only so long as they exhibit the characteristic(s) that made them hazardous. For example, concentrated hydrochloric acid and concentrated sodium hydroxide both qualify as corrosive hazardous wastes. Thus, if you have a gallon of discarded concentrated hydrochloric acid and a gallon of discarded concentrated sodium hydroxide, stored separately, you have two gallons of hazardous waste. If you mix them together (carefully!), you'll end up with two gallons of salt water—and no RCRA hazardous wastes.

Figure 1-7: Toxicity Characteristic Constituents and Regulatory Levels, in Milligrams per Liter (mg/l)

EPA chart.

Waste Code	Contaminants	Concentration
D004	Arsenic	5.0
D005	Barium	100.0
D018	Benzene	0.5
D006	Cadmium	1.0
D019	Carbon tetrachloride	0.5
D020	Chlordane	0.03
D021	Chlorobenzene	100.0
D022	Chloroform	6.0
D007	Chromium	5.0
D023	o-Cresol*	200.0
D024	m-Cresol*	200.0
D025	p-Cresol*	200.0
D026	Total Cresols*	200.0
D016	2,4-D	10.0
D027	1,4-Dichlorobenzene	7.5
D028	1,2-Dichloroethane	0.5
D029	1,1-Dichloroethylene	0.7
D030	2,4-Dinitrotoluene	0.13
D012	Endrin	0.02
D031	Heptachlor (and its epoxide)	0.008
D032	Hexachlorobenzene	0.13
D033	Hexachlorobutadiene	0.5
D034	Hexachloroethane	3.0
D008	Lead	5.0
D013	Lindane	0.4
D009	Mercury	0.2
D014	Methoxychlor	10.0
D035	Methyl ethyl ketone	200.0
D036	Nitrobenzene	2.0
D037	Pentachlorophenol	100.0
D038	Pyridine	5.0
D010	Selenium	1.0
D011	Silver	5.0
D039	Tetrachloroethylene	0.7
D015	Toxaphene	0.5
D040	Trichloroethylene	0.5
D041	2,4,5-Trichlorophenol	400.0
D042	2,4,6-Trichlorophenol	2.0
D017	2,4,5-TP (Silvex)	1.0
D043	Vinyl chloride	0.2

In contrast, listed hazardous wastes tend to remain hazardous wastes forever because of two special EPA rules. Under the EPA's ***mixture rule***, when listed hazardous waste is mixed with other materials, even non-hazardous materials, the entire resulting mixture is a listed hazardous waste. 40 C.F.R. § 261.3(a)(2)(iv), (b)(2). Moreover, under the ***derived from rule***, any material derived from a listed hazardous waste is also a listed hazardous waste. 40 C.F.R. § 261.3(c)(2)(i). Thus, once a facility generates listed hazardous waste, it is unlikely that the facility will be able to change the classification of that material. The EPA *has* created a ***treatment exemption*** for listed hazardous wastes that it listed because those wastes are ignitable, reactive, or corrosive (***ICR wastes***). 40 C.F.R. § 261.3(g)(1), (2). However, that exemption has limited application because the EPA listed most listed hazardous wastes on the basis of their *toxicity*.

2. RCRA's Cradle-to-Grave Regulation of Hazardous Wastes

In Subtitle C, Congress aimed to address the country's hazardous waste problem through a ***cradle-to-grave*** regulatory and tracking program. As a result, as Figure 1–8 illustrates, Subtitle C regulates hazardous waste ***generators***, hazardous waste ***transporters***, and hazardous waste ***treatment, storage, and disposal* (TSD) *facilities***.

Figure 1-8: RCRA's Cradle-to-Grave Regulation of Hazardous Waste
EPA graphic.

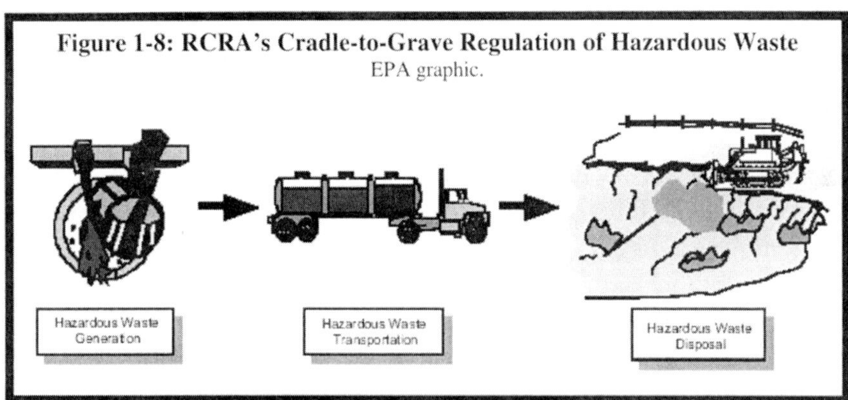

Hazardous waste ***generation*** is "the act or process of producing hazardous waste." RCRA § 1004(6), 42 U.S.C. § 6903(6). RCRA requires the EPA to regulate hazardous waste generators "to protect human health and the environment." RCRA § 3002(a), 42 U.S.C. § 6922(a). Specifically, hazardous waste generators must:

- keep records that accurately identify the hazardous wastes generated;
- properly label containers of hazardous waste for transportation, storage, treatment, or disposal;
- use appropriate containers to store the hazardous waste;
- furnish information about the hazardous waste's chemical composition;
- begin the manifest system to track the hazardous waste from generation through transport to a TSD facility; and
- file reports with the EPA.

Id.

The EPA also regulates hazardous waste ***transporters*** "to protect human health and the environment." RCRA § 3003(a), 42 U.S.C. § 6923(a). The Act does not define "transport" or "transporter," but nevertheless transporters must:

- keep records about the hazardous waste they transport, including the source and point of delivery;
- refuse to transport improperly labeled hazardous waste;
- continue the manifest system started by the generators; and
- transport hazardous waste only to a permitted TSD facility designated on the manifest.

Id.

Subtitle C's most onerous requirements apply to ***treatment, storage, and disposal* (TSD) *facilities***. Hazardous waste ***treatment*** is:

> any method, technique, or process, including neutralization, designed to change the physical, chemical, or biological character or composition of any hazardous waste so as to neutralize such waste or so as to render such waste nonhazardous, safer for transport, amenable for recovery, amenable for storage, or reduced in volume.

RCRA § 1004(34), 42 U.S.C. § 6903(34). "***Storage***," in turn, is "the containment of hazardous waste, either on a temporary basis or for a period of years, in such a manner as not to constitute disposal of such hazardous waste." RCRA § 1004(33), 42 U.S.C. § 6903(33). Finally, "***disposal***" is:

> the discharge, deposit, injection, dumping, spilling, leaking, or placing or any solid waste or hazardous waste into or on any land or water so that such solid waste or hazardous waste or any constituent thereof may enter the environment or be emitted into the air or discharged into any waters, including ground waters.

RCRA § 1004(3), 42 U.S.C. § 6924(3). Any facility that treats, stores, or disposes of hazardous waste is subject to RCRA Subtitle C's provisions for TSD facilities. TSD facilities must:

- maintain records of all hazardous wastes that they treat, store, and/or dispose of, including the manner in which those wastes were treated, stored, or disposed of;
- comply with reporting, monitoring, and inspection requirements;
- complete the manifest started by the generator;
- treat, store, and/or dispose of hazardous waste in accordance with EPA's regulations;
- comply with EPA's requirements regarding the location, design, and construction of the facility;
- generate contingency plans in case of emergencies;
- comply with financial responsibility requirements; and

- get a RCRA permit.

RCRA § 3004(a), 42 U.S.C. § 6924(a). In addition, TSD facilities become liable for ***corrective actions***—that is, for cleanups at the TSD facility and beyond the TSD facility if hazardous wastes escape from the TSD facility. RCRA § 3004(v), 42 U.S.C. § 6924(v).

3. Avoiding TSD Status

Given the numerous and expensive requirements imposed on TSD facilities, facilities that handle solid waste often strive to avoid TSD facility status. There are a number of arguments that facilities can make. First, a facility can argue that it does not handle "solid waste." As we have already seen, if material is not "solid waste," it cannot be "hazardous waste." Second, a facility can argue that it handles only "solid waste," not "hazardous waste." If so, Subtitle C does not apply to the facility.

Even facilities handling "hazardous waste," however, have several arguments for avoiding TSD status. For example, under the EPA's regulations implementing RCRA, generators can store hazardous waste for up to 90 days without becoming TSD facilities, so long as they follow the EPA's storage and labeling requirements. 40 C.F.R. § 262.34(a). Another way for facilities to avoid TSD status is the statutory ***household waste exclusion.*** The Supreme Court addressed the scope of that exclusion, found in RCRA § 3001(i), 42 U.S.C. § 6921(i), in the following case.

CITY OF CHICAGO v. ENVIRONMENTAL DEFENSE FUND

511 U.S. 328 (1994).

JUSTICE SCALIA delivered the opinion of the Court.

We are called upon to decide whether, pursuant to § 3001(i) of the Solid Waste Disposal Act (Resource Conservation and Recovery Act of 1976 (RCRA)), the ash generated by a resource recovery facility's incineration of municipal solid waste is exempt from regulation as a hazardous waste under Subtitle C of RCRA.

I

Since 1971, petitioner city of Chicago has owned and operated a municipal incinerator, the Northwest Waste-to-Energy Facility, that burns solid waste and recovers energy, leaving a residue of municipal waste combustion (MWC) ash. The facility burns approximately 350,000 tons of solid waste each year and produces energy that is both used within the facility and sold to other entities. The city has disposed of the combustion residue—110,000 to 140,000 tons of MWC ash per year—at landfills that are not licensed to accept hazardous wastes.

Figure 1-9: A Municipal Waste Incinerator
EPA photo.

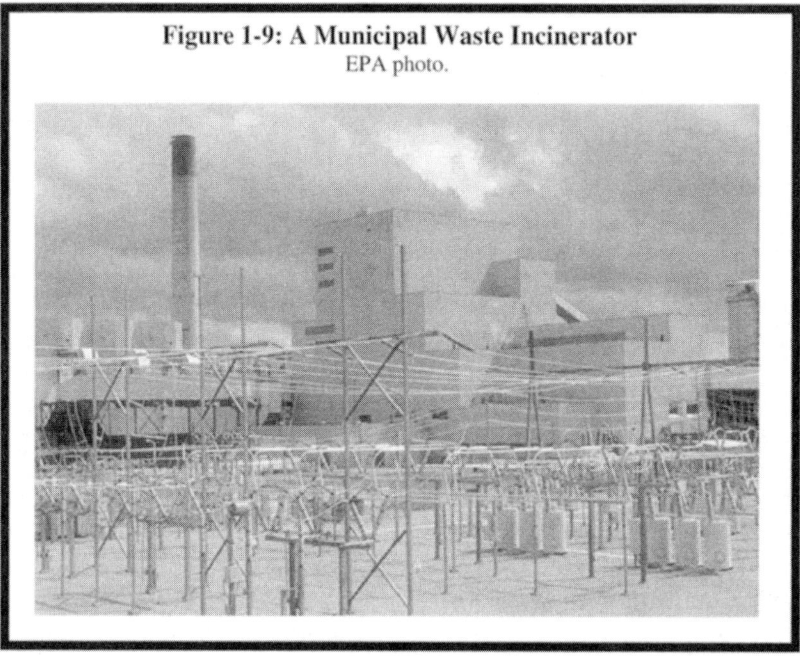

In 1988, respondent Environmental Defense Fund (EDF) filed a complaint against the petitioners, city of Chicago and its mayor, under the citizen suit provisions of RCRA, 42 U.S.C. § 6972, alleging that they were violating provisions of RCRA and of implementing regulations issued by the Environmental Protection Agency (EPA). Respondent alleged that the MWC ash generated by the facility was toxic enough to qualify as a "hazardous waste" under EPA's regulations, 40 CFR pt. 261 (1993). It was uncontested that, with respect to the ash, petitioners had not adhered to any of the requirements of Subtitle C, the portion of RCRA addressing hazardous wastes. Petitioners contended that RCRA § 3001(i), 42 U.S.C. § 6921(i), excluded the MWC ash from those requirements. The District Court agreed with that contention and subsequently granted petitioners' motion for summary judgment.

The Court of Appeals reversed, concluding that the "ash generated from the incinerators of municipal resource recovery facilities is subject to regulation as a hazardous waste under Subtitle C of RCRA." * * *

* * * II

RCRA is a comprehensive environmental statute that empowers EPA to regulate hazardous wastes from cradle to grave, in accordance with the rigorous safeguards and waste management procedures of Subtitle C, 42 U.S.C. §§ 6921–6934. (Nonhazardous wastes are regulated much more loosely under Subtitle D, 42 U.S.C. §§ 6941–6949.) Under the relevant provisions of Subtitle C, EPA has promulgated standards governing hazardous waste generators and transporters, see 42 U.S.C. §§ 6922 and

6923, and owners and operators of hazardous waste treatment, storage, and disposal facilities (TSDF's), *see* § 6924. Pursuant to § 6922, EPA has directed hazardous waste generators to comply with handling, recordkeeping, storage, and monitoring requirements, see 40 CFR pt. 262 (1993). TSDF's, however, are subject to much more stringent regulation than either generators or transporters, including a 4–to–5 year permitting process, *see* 42 U.S.C. § 6925, 40 CFR pt. 270 (1993), burdensome financial assurance requirements, stringent design and location standards, and, perhaps most onerous of all, responsibility to take corrective action for releases of hazardous substances and to ensure safe closure of each facility, *see* 42 U.S.C. § 6924; 40 CFR pt. 264 (1993). "[The] corrective action requirement is one of the major reasons that generators and transporters work diligently to manage their wastes so as to avoid the need to obtain interim status or a TSD permit." 3 ENVIRONMENTAL LAW PRACTICE GUIDE § 29.06[3][d] (M. Gerrard ed. 1993) (hereinafter PRACTICE GUIDE).

RCRA does not identify which wastes are hazardous and therefore subject to Subtitle C regulation; it leaves that designation to EPA. 42 U.S.C. § 6921(a). When EPA's hazardous waste designations for solid wastes appeared in 1980, *see* 45 Fed. Reg. 33084, they contained certain exceptions from normal coverage, including an exclusion for "household waste," defined as "any waste material ... derived from households (including single and multiple residences, hotels and motels)," *id.* at 33120, *codified as amended at* 40 CFR § 261.4(b)(1) (1993). Although most household waste is harmless, a small portion—such as cleaning fluids and batteries—would have qualified as hazardous waste. The regulation declared, however, that "[h]ousehold waste, including household waste that has been collected, transported, stored, treated, disposed, recovered (*e.g.*, refuse-derived fuel) or reused" is not hazardous waste. *Ibid.* Moreover, the preamble to the 1980 regulations stated that "residues remaining after treatment (*e.g.*, incineration, thermal treatment) [of household waste] are not subject to regulation as a hazardous waste." 45 Fed. Reg. 33099. By reason of these provisions, an incinerator that burned only household waste would not be considered a Subtitle C TSDF, since it processed only nonhazardous (*i.e.*, household) waste, and it would not be considered a Subtitle C generator of hazardous waste and would be free to dispose of its ash in a Subtitle D landfill.

The 1980 regulations thus provided what is known as a "waste stream" exemption for household waste, *ibid.*, *i.e.*, an exemption covering that category of waste from generation through treatment to final disposal of residues. The regulation did not, however, exempt MWC ash from Subtitle C coverage if the incinerator that produced the ash burned anything *in addition to* household waste, such as what petitioners' facility burns: nonhazardous industrial waste. Thus, a facility like petitioners' would qualify as a Subtitle C hazardous waste generator if the MWC ash it produced was sufficiently toxic, *see* 40 CFR §§ 261.3, 261.24 (1993)—though it would still not qualify as a Subtitle C TSDF, since all the waste it took in would be characterized as nonhazardous. (An ash can be hazardous, even though the product from which it is generated is not, because in the new medium the contaminants are more concentrated and more readily leachable, *see* 40 CFR §§ 261.3, 261.24, and pt. 261, App. II (1993).)

Four years after these regulations were issued, Congress enacted the Hazardous and Solid Waste Amendments of 1984, which added to RCRA the "Clarification of Household Waste Exclusion" as § 3001(i), § 223, 98 Stat. 3252. The essence of our task in this case is to determine whether, under that provision, the MWC ash generated by petitioners' facility—a facility that would have been considered a Subtitle C generator under the 1980 regulations—is subject to regulation as hazardous waste under Subtitle C. We conclude that it is.

Section 3001(i), 42 U.S.C. § 6921(i), entitled "Clarification of household waste exclusion," provides:

> "A resource recovery facility recovering energy from the mass burning of municipal solid waste shall not be deemed to be treating, storing, disposing of, or otherwise managing hazardous wastes for the purposes of regulation under this subchapter, if—
>
> "(1) such facility—
>
> "(A) receives and burns only—
>
> "(i) household waste (from single and multiple dwellings, hotels, motels, and other residential sources), and
>
> "(ii) solid waste from commercial or industrial sources that does not contain hazardous waste identified or listed under this section, and
>
> "(B) does not accept hazardous wastes identified or listed under this section, and
>
> "(2) the owner or operator of such facility has established contractual requirements or other appropriate notification or inspection procedures to assure that hazardous wastes are not received at or burned in such facility."

The plain meaning of this language is that so long as a facility recovers energy by incineration of the appropriate wastes, *it* (the *facility*) is not subject to Subtitle C regulation as a facility that treats, stores, disposes of, or manages hazardous waste. The provision quite clearly does *not* contain any exclusion for the *ash itself*. Indeed, the waste the facility produces (as opposed to that which it receives) is not even mentioned. There is thus no express support for petitioners' claim of a waste-stream exemption.

Petitioners contend, however, that the practical effect of the statutory language is to exempt the ash by virtue of exempting the facility. If, they argue, the facility is not deemed to be treating, storing, or disposing of hazardous waste, then the ash that it treats, stores, or disposes of must itself be considered nonhazardous. There are several problems with this argument. First, as we have explained, the only exemption provided by the terms of the statute is for the *facility*. It is the facility, *not the ash,* that "shall not be deemed" to be subject to regulation under Subtitle C. *Unlike* the preamble to the 1980 regulations, which had been in existence for four years by the time § 3001(i) was enacted, § 3001(i) does not explicitly exempt MWC ash generated by a resource recovery facility from regulation as a hazardous waste. In light of that difference, and given the statute's express declaration of national policy that "[w]aste that is ... generated should be treated, stored, or disposed of so as to minimize the present and future threat to human health and the environment," 42 U.S.C. § 6902(b), we cannot interpret the statute to permit MWC ash sufficiently toxic to qualify as hazardous to be disposed of in ordinary landfills.

Moreover, as the Court of Appeals observed, the statutory language does not even exempt the *facility* in its capacity as a *generator* of hazardous waste. RCRA defines "generation" as "the act or process of producing hazardous waste." 42 U.S.C. § 6903(6). There can be no question that the creation of ash by incinerating municipal waste constitutes "generation" of hazardous waste (assuming, of course, that the ash qualifies as hazardous under 42 U.S.C. § 6921 and its implementing regulations, 40 CFR pt. 261 (1993)). Yet although § 3001(i) states that the exempted facility "shall not be deemed to be treating, storing, disposing of, or otherwise managing hazardous wastes," it significantly omits from the catalog the word "*generating.*" Petitioners say that because the activities listed as exempt encompass the full scope of the facility's operation, the failure to mention the activity of generating is insignificant. But the statute itself refutes this. Each of the three specific terms used in § 3001(i)—"treating," "storing," and "disposing of"—is separately defined by RCRA, and none covers the production of hazardous waste. The fourth and less specific term ("otherwise managing") is also defined, to mean "collection, source separation, storage, transportation, processing, treatment, recovery, and disposal," 42 U.S.C. § 6903(7)—just about every hazardous waste-related activity *except* generation. We think it follows from the carefully constructed text of § 3001(i) that while a resource recovery facility's management activities are excluded from Subtitle C regulation, its generation of toxic ash is not.

Petitioners appeal to the legislative history of § 3001(i), which includes, in the Senate Committee Report, the statement that "[a]ll waste management activities of such a facility, including the *generation,* transportation, treatment, storage and disposal of waste shall be covered by the exclusion." S. REP. NO. 98–284, p. 61 (1983) (emphasis added). But it is the statute, and not the Committee Report, which is the authoritative expression of the law, and the statute prominently *omits* reference to generation. * * * Petitioners point out that the activity by which they "treat" municipal waste is the very same activity by which they "generate" MWC ash, to wit, incineration. But there is nothing extraordinary about an activity's being exempt for some purposes and nonexempt for others. The incineration here is exempt from TSDF regulation, but subject to regulation as hazardous waste generation. (As we have noted, the latter is much less onerous.)

Our interpretation is confirmed by comparing § 3001(i) with another statutory exemption in RCRA. In the Superfund Amendments and Reauthorization Act of 1986, Congress amended 42 U.S.C. § 6921 to provide that an "owner and operator of equipment used to recover methane from a landfill shall not be deemed to be managing, generating, transporting, treating, storing, or disposing of hazardous or liquid wastes within the meaning of" Subtitle C. This provision, in contrast to § 3001(i), provides a complete exemption by including the term "generating" in its list of covered activities. * * * We agree with respondents that this provision "shows that Congress knew how to draft a waste stream exemption in RCRA when it wanted to."

Petitioners contend that our interpretation of § 3001(i) turns the provision into an "empty gesture," since even under the pre-existing regime an incinerator burning household waste and nonhazardous industrial waste was exempt from the Subtitle C TSDF provisions. If § 3001(i) did not extend the waste-stream exemption to the product of such a combined household/nonhazardous-industrial treatment facility, petitioners argue, it did nothing at all. But it is not nothing to codify a household waste exemption that had previously been subject to agency revision; nor is it nothing (though petitioners may value it as less than nothing) to *restrict* the exemption that the agency previously provided—which is what the provision here achieved, by withholding all waste-stream exemption for waste processed by resource recovery facilities, even for the waste stream passing through an exclusively household waste facility.

We also do not agree with petitioners' contention that our construction renders § 3001(i) ineffective for its intended purpose of promoting household/nonhazardous-industrial resource recovery facilities, see 42 U.S.C. §§ 6902(a)(1), (10), (11), by subjecting them "to the potentially enormous expense of managing ash residue as a hazardous waste." It is simply not true that a facility which is (as our interpretation says these facilities are) a hazardous waste "generator" is also deemed to be "managing" hazardous waste under RCRA. Section 3001(i) clearly exempts these facilities from Subtitle C TSDF regulations, thus enabling them to avoid the "full brunt of EPA's enforcement efforts under RCRA." PRACTICE GUIDE § 29.05[1].

* * * RCRA's twin goals of encouraging resource recovery and protecting against contamination sometimes conflict. It is not unusual for legislation to contain diverse purposes that must be reconciled, and the most reliable guide for that task is the enacted text. * * * Section 3001(i) simply cannot be read to contain the cost-saving waste-stream exemption petitioners seek. * * *

JUSTICE STEVENS, with whom JUSTICE O'CONNOR joins, dissenting.

The statutory provision in question is a 1984 amendment entitled "Clarification of Household Waste Exclusion." To understand that clarification, we must first examine the "waste exclusion" that the amendment clarified and, more particularly, the ambiguity that needed clarification. * * *

I

When Congress enacted the Resource Conservation and Recovery Act of 1976 (RCRA), it delegated to the Environmental Protection Agency (EPA) vast regulatory authority over the mountains of garbage that our society generates. The statute directed the EPA to classify waste as hazardous or nonhazardous and to establish regulatory controls over the disposition of the two categories of waste pursuant to Subtitles C and D of RCRA. 42 U.S.C. § 6921(a). To that end, the EPA in 1980 promulgated detailed regulations establishing a federal hazardous waste management system pursuant to Subtitle C.

Generally, though not always, the EPA regulations assume that waste is properly characterized as hazardous or nonhazardous when it first becomes waste. Based on that characterization, the waste is regulated under either Subtitle C or D. * * *

Section 261.4(b)(1) of the EPA's 1980 regulations first established the household waste exclusion. *See* 45 Fed. Reg. 33120 (1980). The relevant text of that regulation simply provided that solid wastes derived from households (including single and multiple residences, hotels, and motels) were "not hazardous wastes." The regulation itself said nothing about the status of the residue that remains after the incineration of such household waste. An accompanying comment, however, unambiguously explained that "residues remaining after treatment (*e.g.*, incineration, thermal treatment) are not subject to regulation as hazardous waste." *Id.*, at 33099. Thus, the administrative history of the 1980 regulation, rather than its text, revealed why a municipal incinerator burning household waste was not treated as a generator of hazardous waste.

The EPA's explanatory comment contained an important warning: If household waste was "mixed with other hazardous wastes," the entire mixture would be deemed hazardous. Yet neither the comment nor the regulation itself identified the consequences of mixing household waste with other wastes that are entirely *nonhazardous*. * * * The EPA's failure to comment expressly on the significance of adding 100 percent nonhazardous commercial or industrial waste nevertheless warranted further clarification.

Congress enacted that clarification in 1984. Elaborating upon the EPA's warning in 1980, the text of the 1984 amendment—§ 3001(i) of RCRA, 42 U.S.C. § 6921(i)—made clear that a facility treating a mixture of household waste and "solid waste from commercial or industrial sources that does not contain hazardous waste," § 6921(i)(1)(A)(ii), shall not be deemed to be treating hazardous waste. In other words, the addition of *non*hazardous waste derived from other sources does not extinguish the household waste exclusion.

The parallel between the 1980 regulation and the 1984 statutory amendment is striking. * * * Moreover, the title's description of the amendment as a "clarification" identifies an intent to codify its counterpart in the 1980 regulation.

The Report of the Senate Committee that recommended the enactment of § 3001(i) demonstrates that the sponsors of the legislation understood it to have the same meaning as the 1980 EPA regulation that it "clarified." * * * The Report explains that resource recovery facilities frequently take in household wastes that are mixed with other nonhazardous waste streams from a variety of commercial and industrial sources, and emphasizes the importance of encouraging commercially viable resource recovery facilities. To that end, "[n]ew section [3001(i)] clarifies the original intent to include within the household waste exclusion activities of a resource recovery facility which recovers energy from the mass burning of household waste and non-hazardous waste from other sources." The Report further explains:

> "All waste management activities of such a facility, including the generation, transportation, treatment, storage and disposal of waste shall be covered by the exclusion, if the limitations in paragraphs (1) and (2) of [the amendment] are met. * * *." *Ibid.*

These comments referred to the Senate bill that became law after a majority of the Senate followed the Committee's recommendation "that the bill (as amended) do pass." *Id.*, at 1. Given this commentary, it is quite unrealistic to assume that the omission of the word "generating" from the particularized description of management activities in the statute was intended to render the statutory description any less inclusive than either the 1980 regulation or the Committee Report. It is even more unrealistic to assume that legislators voting on the 1984 amendment would have detected any difference between the statutory text and the Committee's summary just because the term "generating" does not appear in the 1984 amendment. A common-sense reading of the statutory text in the light of the Committee Report and against the background of the 1980 regulation reveals an obvious purpose to *preserve,* not to change, the existing rule.

* * * II

* * * The majority's decision today may represent sound policy. Requiring cities to spend the necessary funds to dispose of their incinerator residues in accordance with the strict requirements of Subtitle C will provide additional protections to the environment. It is also true, however, that the conservation of scarce landfill space and the encouragement of the recovery of energy and valuable materials in municipal wastes were major concerns motivating RCRA's enactment. Whether those purposes will be disserved by regulating municipal incinerators under Subtitle C and, if so, whether environmental benefits may nevertheless justify the

costs of such additional regulation are questions of policy that we are not competent to resolve. Those questions are precisely the kind that Congress has directed the EPA to answer. The EPA's position, first adopted unambiguously in 1980 and still maintained today, was and remains a correct and permissible interpretation of the EPA's broad congressional mandate.

Accordingly, I respectfully dissent.

NOTES

1. **Competing Interpretations and the Role of Regulatory and Legislative History.** What was the import of Congress's clarification of the household waste exclusion, according to the majority? What tools of statutory construction did the majority use to arrive at its conclusion? Why did Justices Stevens and O'Connor dissent? What tools did they rely on to reach a different interpretation of § 3001(i) than the majority? In particular, what role did the regulatory and statutory history of the household waste exclusion play in their analysis?

2. **RCRA Exclusions and Environmental Policy.** What policy considerations are at odds in this case? Why did the majority and dissent reconcile those policies differently?

3. **Congress's Response.** Congress amended RCRA § 3001 in 1996, about two years after the Supreme Court decided this case. Pub. L. No. 104–119, § 4, 110 Stat. 833 (March 26, 1996) (amending 42 U.S.C. § 6921). However, Congress left section 3001(i), the provision at issue in this case, unchanged. Does that mean that the majority in the *City of Chicago* case was correct in its interpretation, and that Justices Stevens and O'Connor were wrong?

4. **Conditionally Exempt Small Generators.** As *City of Chicago* indicates, there are advantages to being just a RCRA generator instead of a RCRA TSD facility. Under the EPA's regulations, moreover, generators of small quantities of hazardous wastes—no more than 100 kilograms per month—can be exempted from many of the requirements for hazardous waste generators. 40 C.F.R. § 261.5(a). Is this exemption likely to help municipal incinerators like the one that the City of Chicago operates? Why or why not?

5. **A TSD Problem.** Plaintiff purchased an industrial facility from Defendant. Before the sale, the Defendant installed a new natural gas heating systems, but it also left the old heating system in place. The old heating system was insulated with asbestos-containing material, and asbestos is a hazardous waste under RCRA. Plaintiff sued Defendant, alleging that Defendant has violated RCRA by disposing of hazardous wastes without a TSD facility permit. How should the court rule, and why? *See Sycamore Industrial Park Associates v. Ericsson, Inc.*, 546 F.3d 847, 853–54 (7th Cir. 2008).

6. **TSD Exclusions, Climate Change and RCRA: A Hazardous Waste Exclusion for Carbon Storage and Sequestration?** In August 2011, the EPA proposed a regulation that would conditionally exempt carbon sequestration and storage from RCRA hazardous waste regulation. Hazardous

Waste Management System: Identification and Listing of Hazardous Waste: Carbon Dioxide (CO_2) Streams in Geologic Sequestration Activities, 76 Fed. Reg. 48,073 (Aug. 8, 2011). Carbon sequestration and storage is a technological means of reducing greenhouse gas emissions, especially carbon dioxide emissions, by capturing greenhouse gases during industrial processes and then sequestering them underground. The technique remains unproven at large scale but is nevertheless touted by many as one way of mitigating climate change.

RCRA issues arise because carbon sequestration and storage is a form of waste disposal, and RCRA applies to contained gaseous materials, as the statutory definition of "solid waste" makes clear. The EPA's regulation would conditionally exempt carbon sequestration and storage from RCRA. As the EPA itself explained in the Federal Register notice proposing the new rule:

> The Environmental Protection Agency (EPA or the Agency) is proposing to revise the regulations for hazardous waste management under the Resource Conservation and Recovery Act (RCRA) to conditionally exclude carbon dioxide (CO_2) streams that are hazardous from the definition of hazardous waste, provided these hazardous CO_2 streams are captured from emission sources, are injected into Class VI Underground Injection Control (UIC) wells for purposes of geologic sequestration (GS), and meet certain other conditions. EPA is taking this action because the Agency believes that the management of these CO_2 streams under the proposed conditions does not present a substantial risk to human health or the environment, and therefore additional regulation pursuant to RCRA's hazardous waste regulations is unnecessary. EPA expects that this amendment will substantially reduce the uncertainty associated with identifying these CO_2 streams under RCRA subtitle C, and will also facilitate the deployment of GS by providing additional regulatory certainty.

76 Fed. Reg. at 48,074.

Should federal agencies use exemptions from RCRA (and other environmental law statutes) to promote certain kinds of responses to climate change? Why or why not? What if experience with carbon sequestration and storage proves that the technique poses significant risks to human health and the environment, such as carbon dioxide escaping and suffocating large areas?

* * *

4. Permitting RCRA TSD Facilities: The Permit Process

The EPA has flow-charted the RCRA TSD facility permitting process, as shown in Figure 1–10.

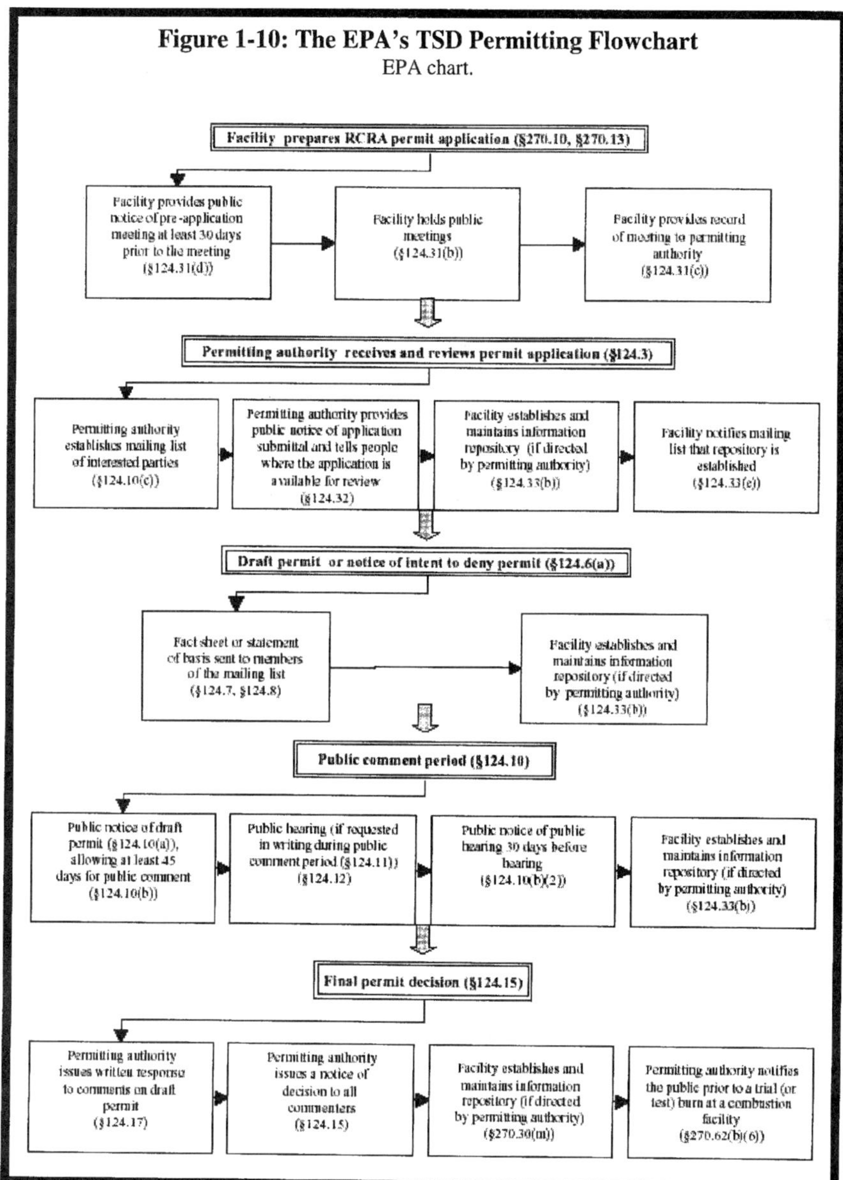

Figure 1-10: The EPA's TSD Permitting Flowchart
EPA chart.

5. Permitting RCRA TSD Facilities: Facility Siting, Risk Assessment, and Environmental Justice

As was noted in the Introduction to this textbook, risk assessment is an important component of environmental law and policy. Because, by definition, a RCRA TSD facility handles hazardous wastes, its location and treatment, storage, and disposal processes could affect the health and safety of the people and businesses, as well as the property values, within its vicinity. For these and other reasons, community groups often oppose TSD facilities' decisions to locate within their communities, viewing the hazardous waste TSD facilities as ***NIMBYs*** (from Not In My Back Yard) or ***LULUs*** (Locally Undesirable Land Uses).

One aspect of siting TSD facilities, related to both risk assessment and civil rights, is review of the effects that a TSD facility might have on minority and/or low-income communities in the vicinity. The ethical principle that governments and industry should avoid overburdening these communities with dangerous and/or undesirable facilities and should actively correct such discrimination from the past is known as ***environmental justice***. According to the EPA:

> Environmental Justice is the fair treatment and meaningful involvement of all people regardless of race, color, national origin, or income with respect to the development, implementation, and enforcement of environmental laws, regulations, and policies. **Fair treatment** means that no group of people, including a racial, ethnic, or a socioeconomic group, should bear a disproportionate share of the negative environmental consequences resulting from industrial, municipal, and commercial operations or the execution of federal, state, local, and tribal programs and policies. **Meaningful involvement** means that: (1) potentially affected community residents have an appropriate opportunity to participate in decisions about a proposed activity that will affect their environment and/or health; (2) the public's contribution can influence the regulatory agency's decision; (3) the concerns of all participants involved will be considered in the decision making process; and (4) the decision makers seek out and facilitate the involvement of those potentially affected.
>
> In sum, environmental justice is the goal to be achieved for all communities and persons across this Nation. Environmental justice is achieved when everyone, regardless of race, culture, or income, enjoys the same degree of protection from environmental and health hazards and equal access to the decision-making process to have a healthy environment in which to live, learn, and work.

EPA, *Environmental Justice Home Page*, http://www.epa.gov/compliance/environmentaljustice/index.html. As this statement suggests, giving effect to environmental justice principles often depends on opportunities for public participation, and thus the public participation aspects of RCRA permitting—and other environmental permitting—can be critical in meeting environmental justice goals.

President Bill Clinton sought to promote environmental justice in federal agency decision making. He issued the following Executive Order to further environmental justice.

EXECUTIVE ORDER 12898 FEDERAL ACTIONS TO ADDRESS ENVIRONMENTAL JUSTICE IN MINORITY POPULATIONS AND LOW-INCOME POPULATIONS

59 Fed. Reg. 7629 (Feb. 11, 1994).

By the authority vested in me as President by the Constitution and the laws of the United States of America, it is hereby ordered as follows:

Section 1–1. Implementation.

1–101. Agency Responsibilities. To the greatest extent practicable and permitted by law, and consistent with the principles set forth in the report on the National Performance Review, each Federal agency shall make achieving environmental justice part of its mission by identifying and addressing, as appropriate, disproportionately high and adverse human health or environmental effects of its programs, policies, and activities on minority populations and low-income populations in the United States and its territories and possessions, the District of Columbia, the Commonwealth of Puerto Rico, and the Commonwealth of the Mariana Islands.

* * * 1–103. Development of Agency Strategies.

(a) Except as provided in section 6–605 of this order, each Federal agency shall develop an agency-wide environmental justice strategy * * * that identifies and addresses disproportionately high and adverse human health or environmental effects of its programs, policies, and activities on minority populations and low-income populations. The environmental justice strategy shall list programs, policies, planning and public participation processes, enforcement, and/or rulemakings related to human health or the environment that should be revised to, at a minimum: (1) promote enforcement of all health and environmental statutes in areas with minority populations and low-income populations; (2) ensure greater public participation; (3) improve research and data collection relating to the health of and environment of minority populations and low-income populations; and (4) identify differential patterns of consumption of natural resources among minority populations and low-income populations. In addition, the environmental justice strategy shall include, where appropriate, a timetable for undertaking identified revisions and consideration of economic and social implications of the revisions.

* * * Sec. 2–2. Federal Agency Responsibilities for Federal Programs. Each Federal agency shall conduct its programs, policies, and activities that substantially affect human health or the environment, in a manner that ensures that such programs, policies, and activities do not have the effect of excluding persons (including populations) from participation in, denying persons (including populations) the benefits of, or subjecting

persons (including populations) to discrimination under, such programs, policies, and activities, because of their race, color, or national origin.

* * * Sec. 5–5. Public Participation and Access to Information.

(a) The public may submit recommendations to Federal agencies relating to the incorporation of environmental justice principles into Federal agency programs or policies. Each Federal agency shall convey such recommendations to the Working Group.

(b) Each Federal agency may, whenever practicable and appropriate, translate crucial public documents, notices, and hearings relating to human health or the environment for limited English speaking populations.

(c) Each Federal agency shall work to ensure that public documents, notices, and hearings relating to human health or the environment are concise, understandable, and readily accessible to the public.

(d) The Working Group shall hold public meetings, as appropriate, for the purpose of fact-finding, receiving public comments, and conducting inquiries concerning environmental justice. The Working Group shall prepare for public review a summary of the comments and recommendations discussed at the public meetings.

Sec. 6–6. General Provisions.

6–601. Responsibility for Agency Implementation. The head of each Federal agency shall be responsible for ensuring compliance with this order. Each Federal agency shall conduct internal reviews and take such other steps as may be necessary to monitor compliance with this order.

* * * 6–604. Scope. For purposes of this order, Federal agency means any agency on the Working Group, and such other agencies as may be designated by the President, that conducts any Federal program or activity that substantially affects human health or the environment. Independent agencies are requested to comply with the provisions of this order.

6–605. Petitions for Exemptions. The head of a Federal agency may petition the President for an exemption from the requirements of this order on the grounds that all or some of the petitioning agency's programs or activities should not be subject to the requirements of this order.

6–606. Native American Programs. Each Federal agency responsibility set forth under this order shall apply equally to Native American programs. In addition, the Department of the Interior, in coordination with the Working Group, and, after consultation with tribal leaders, shall coordinate steps to be taken pursuant to this order that address Federally-recognized Indian Tribes.

6–607. Costs. Unless otherwise provided by law, Federal agencies shall assume the financial costs of complying with this order.

6–608. General. Federal agencies shall implement this order consistent with, and to the extent permitted by, existing law.

6–609. Judicial Review. This order is intended only to improve the internal management of the executive branch and is not intended to, nor does it create any right, benefit, or trust responsibility, substantive or procedural, enforceable at law or equity by a party against the United States, its agencies, its officers, or any person. This order shall not be construed to create any right to judicial review involving the compliance or noncompliance of the United States, its agencies, its officers, or any other person with this order.

WILLIAM CLINTON
THE WHITE HOUSE,
February 11, 1994.

NOTES

1. **What Is An Executive Order?** Executive orders are some of the most interesting creations of the federal government, because they have no official status. At their most basic, executive orders are directions from the President to an agency or agencies within the Executive Branch of the federal government. However, because the U.S. Constitution vests law-making power in Congress, executive orders cannot violate existing statutes—as most executive orders make clear.

2. **Applicability of Executive Order No. 12898.** To which agencies does Executive Order No. 12898 apply? What does it require them to do? How does this executive order promote the principles of environmental justice?

* * *

Enforcing environmental justice is a different matter. Read § 6–609 of the Executive Order carefully. If a federal agency decides not to comply with Executive Order No. 12898, does an affected community have any recourse in the courts? Consider the recent opinion of the U.S. Court of Appeals for the Fifth Circuit in a challenge to the Housing Authority of New Orleans (HANO) and the U.S. Department of Housing and Urban Development (HUD) regarding environmental justice challenges to the way housing revitalization was handled in New Orleans after Hurricane Katrina. According to the Fifth Circuit:

> Executive Order 12898 instructs agencies to consider the environmental justice impacts of their actions. Exec. Order No. 12898, 59 *Fed. Reg.* 7629 § 6–609 (1994). The Order does not, however, create a private right of action. Thus, we review the agency's consideration of environmental justice issues under the APA's deferential "arbitrary and capricious" standard. *See, e.g., Communities Against Runway Expansion, Inc. (CARE) v. F.A.A.*, 355 F.3d 678, 688 (D.C. Cir. 2004). Leaving aside legalisms, we see in this record no administrative insensitivity to racial or economic inequality. Instead, we see a project that HUD perceived reasonably as a community effort, endorsed initially by some who now

oppose it, to renovate a deteriorating public housing project for the ultimate and enduring benefit of the community.

> HUD's environmental justice study, completed in September 2002, looked at the area in which the project is being built and determined that those who return to live in the "new" St. Thomas will benefit from safer, more sanitary living conditions and an improved economic environment. It considers the problems of displacement, including the fact that residents still living in the project would be eligible for relocation under the Uniform Relocation Act. Furthermore, HUD's study reflected that St. Thomas residents had numerous complaints about the housing project and were at risk from pest infestations, asbestos, drug paraphernalia, lead exposure, and raw sewage. It notes, based on the comments received from then-residents, that many had complaints about the St. Thomas development and while some would stay there if conditions and amenities were improved, others would prefer to become home owners outside of the project. Over 200 lawsuits had been filed over lead exposure in the housing units, and that 99% of residents belonged to a minority group.
>
> The record also indicates that HUD received and responded to comments made at a public meeting by Mr. Brod Bagert, whose master's thesis had been highly critical of the HOPE IV program, and of the broader "market revitalization" approach to improving urban areas. His comments and his study use the St. Thomas project as an example to attack that particular theory of urban planning. HUD responded to Mr. Bagert's comments, indicating that while it understood the basis of his criticism of the HOPE IV approach to urban revitalization, the HOPE IV approach is clearly supported by Congressional mandate.
>
> Plaintiffs offer Mr. Bagert's comments, and evidence of problems with residential relocations under the Uniform Relocation Act, for the proposition that HUD's evaluation of the project's impacts is entirely contradicted by the evidence. The record in front of us is hardly so clear cut, and certainly reveals that HUD gave attention to the issues plaintiffs raise, for all they disagree with the conclusions. Beyond their allegations and Mr. Bagert's comments, which HUD clearly took under consideration, plaintiffs offer no evidence suggesting that the environmental justice study was arbitrary or capricious in its choice of methodology. We cannot, therefore, say that they have met their burden of showing that HUD's consideration of environmental justice concerns was arbitrary and capricious.

Colliseum Square Association, Inc. v. Jackson, 465 F.3d 215, 232–33 (5th Cir. 2006). Thus, while the Fifth Circuit allowed judicial review of environmental justice complaints through the federal Administrative Procedure Act (APA), it was—as is typical under the APA—highly deferential to the agency's analysis and decision.

It is worth noting, too, that environmental justice concerns can play a role at the state level, as well. Thus, for example, the U.S. District Court for the Northern District of Georgia upheld a county's denial of a landfill operator's application for expansion against a due process challenge in part because environmental justice concerns—in conjunction with concerns about groundwater contamination and increased odors—legitimated the rationality of the county's decision. *BFI Waste System of North America v. Dekalb County, Georgia*, 303 F. Supp. 2d 1335, 1351–52 (N.D. Ga. 2004).

The most viable arena for pressing environmental justice concerns based on the Executive Order, however, is during the various levels of permitting processes that various federal agencies—including the EPA—follow, including during administrative review of permitting decisions. This includes RCRA TSD permitting and appeals within the EPA to the Environmental Appeals Board. *See In re Ash Grove Cement Company*, 7 Envtl. Appeals Decisions (E.A.D.) 387 (EPA Envtl. Appeals Bd. Nov. 14, 1997), 1997 WL 732000. In general, under RCRA, EPA TSD permitting starts in the appropriate EPA regional offices. People dissatisfied with the region's permitting decision can appeal to the EPA's Environmental Appeals Board. After completing the agency's internal appeals process, RCRA dictates that parties must appeal decisions regarding RCRA TSD facility permits to "the Circuit Court of Appeals of the United States for the Federal judicial district in which such person resides or transacts business * * *." 42 U.S.C. § 6976(b). Moreover, parties must appeal within 90 days of the EPA's final decision on the permit, *id.*, which comes only *after* the parties have exhausted (by use or lapse of time) the EPA's own internal review procedures. Thus, RCRA TSD permitting provides contestants with several forums for raising environmental justice issues.

In addition, the EPA has recently revitalized its environmental justice program, with an emphasis on renewed attention to environmental justice in environmental permitting. *See generally* EPA, *Environmental Justice*, http://www.epa.gov/environmentaljustice/ (as updated Nov. 8, 2011). In honor of the 20th Anniversary of Executive Order No. 12898, the EPA has released *Plan EJ 2014*. EPA, *Environmental Justice: Plan EJ 2014*, http://www.epa.gov/environmentaljustice/plan-ej/index.html (as updated Nov. 2, 2011). The Plan emphasizes five cross-agency areas where the EPA plans to expand its consideration and incorporation of environmental justice issues:

(1) Incorporating Environmental Justice into Rulemaking.

(2) Considering Environmental Justice in Permitting.

(3) Advancing Environmental Justice through Compliance and Enforcement.

(4) Supporting Community–Based Action Programs.

(5) Fostering Administration–Wide Action on Environmental Justice.

Id. At the end of the plan, in 2014, EPA will assess its progress in meeting environmental justice goals and come up with next steps.

With respect to the goal of considering environmental justice in permitting, the EPA is pursuing three strategies. First, it wants to develop tools that will allow overburdened communities to participate more fully and effectively in EPA permitting processes. Second, it wants to develop tools that will allow permitting authorities to more effectively address environmental justice issues during the permitting process. Finally, it plans to implement these tools in its own permitting processes and to encourage other authorities—like state, local, and tribal permitting authorities—to do the same. *Id.*

How might TSD facility permitting under RCRA raise environmental justice issues? Consider first issues that might arise given where a particular TSD facility is sited. Should poor and minority communities have to put up with more than their "fair share" of facilities and industries generating and handling hazardous materials? Next consider the fact that many TSD facilities treat and dispose of hazardous waste by burning it. What environmental justice issues could such treatment raise? Finally, consider that hazardous waste often needs to be transported to TSD facilities. What hazards could such transportation raise for the surrounding communities?

6. The RCRA Hazardous Waste "Land Ban"

Another issue for TSD facilities, particularly those facilities that *dispose* of hazardous wastes, is the RCRA ***land ban***. Congress enacted the so-called "land ban"—severe restrictions on disposal of hazardous wastes into landfills—in the 1984 amendments to RCRA. Under these amendments, "after November 8, 1984 * * * the land disposal of the hazardous wastes referred to in paragraph (2) is prohibited unless the Administrator determines the prohibition on one or more methods of land disposal of such waste is not required in order to protect human health and the environment for as long as the waste remains hazardous * * *." RCRA § 3004(d)(2), 42 U.S.C. § 6924(d)(1). Hazardous wastes subject to the land ban include:

(A) Liquid hazardous wastes * * * containing free cyanides at concentrations greater than or equal to 1,000 mg/l.

(B) Liquid hazardous wastes [containing high concentrations of arsenic, cadmium, chromium, lead, mercury, nickel, selenium, thallium, or their compounds].

(C) Liquid hazardous wastes having a pH less than or equal to two (2.0).

(D) Liquid hazardous wastes containing polychlorinated biphenyls at concentrations greater than or equal to 50 ppm.

(E) Hazardous wastes containing halogenated organic compounds in total concentration greater than or equal to 1,000 mg/kg.

RCRA § 3004(d)(2), 42 U.S.C. § 6924(d)(2).

In addition, Congress required the EPA to enact regulations regarding land disposal of all of the listed hazardous wastes by May 8, 1990. RCRA § 3004(g)(5), (6)(C), 42 U.S.C. § 6924(g)(5), (6)(C). The EPA was to work in thirds, with the first one-third of the regulations to be promulgated by August 8, 1988, the second third by June 8, 1989, and the "third third" by May 8, 1990. *Id.* § 3004(g)(6)(A)-(C), 42 U.S.C. § 6924(g)(6)(A)-(C). The last third consisted mostly of the characteristic hazardous wastes. Congress also stated that if the EPA failed to meet the final deadline, "such hazardous waste shall be prohibited from land disposal." *Id.* § 3004(g)(6)(C), 42 U.S.C. § 6924(g)(6)(C). This last provision is known as the land ban ***"hammer provision,"*** which Congress used to induce the EPA to promulgate the regulations on time.

Under the standards of the 1984 amendments to RCRA, in order to allow disposal of hazardous wastes on land, the EPA had to ensure that the waste would be treat to minimize the short-term and long-term threats to human health and the environment posed by toxic and hazardous constituents. RCRA § 3004(m), 42 U.S.C. § 6924(m). Alternatively, land disposal of hazardous wastes would be allowed if the EPA could find that no migration of hazardous constituents from the facility will occur after disposal. *Id.* § 3004(g)(5), 42 U.S.C. § 6924(g)(5). More specifically, under the 1984 Amendments, the EPA's final regulations had to

> prohibit[] one or more methods of land disposal of the hazardous wastes listed on such schedule except for methods of land disposal which the Administrator determines will be protective of human health and the environment for as long as the waste remains hazardous * * *. For the purposes of this paragraph, a method of land disposal may not be determined to be protective of human health and the environment (except with respect to a hazardous waste which has complied with the pretreatment regulations promulgated under subsection (m) of this section) unless, upon application by an interested person, it has been demonstrated to the Administrator, to a reasonable degree of certainty, that there will be no migration of hazardous constituents from the disposal unit or injection zone for as long as the wastes remain hazardous.

RCRA § 3004(g)(5), 42 U.S.C. § 6924(g)(5).

The EPA finished the land disposal regulations on time, *see* 55 Fed. Reg. 22,520–720 (1990) (promulgating the "third-third" rules), although not without controversy. In particular, the EPA imposed treatment standards on some characteristic hazardous wastes that required treatment to below the level that would have made the waste hazardous in the first place. Nevertheless, the D.C. Circuit upheld these requirements in *Chemical Waste Management, Inc. v. United States Environmental Protection Agency*, 976 F.2d 2 (D.C. Cir. 1992), reasoning that in adding Sections 3004(g)(5) and 3004(m), Congress gave the EPA this additional authority in the 1984 amendments.

7. Enforcement of Subtitle C

RCRA expressly gives the EPA authority to take enforcement actions against people who violate Subtitle C's requirements for hazardous waste. RCRA §§ 3008, 7003, 42 U.S.C. §§ 6928, 6973. Civilly,

> whenever on the basis of any information the Administrator determines that any person has violated or is in violation of any requirement of this subchapter, the Administrator may issue an order assessing a civil penalty for any past or current violation, requiring compliance immediately or within a specified time period, or both, or the Administrator may commence a civil action in the United States district court in the district in which the violation occurred for appropriate relief, including a temporary or permanent injunction.

RCRA § 3008(a)(1), 42 U.S.C. § 6928(a)(1).

According to RCRA itself, civil penalties can be up to $25,000 per day of violation. *Id.* § 3008(c), 42 U.S.C. § 6928(c). However, in 1996, in the Debt Collection Improvement Act of 1996, 28 U.S.C. § 2461, Congress allowed the EPA to increase RCRA civil penalties by up to 10 percent. The EPA exercised this authority in May 1997, so that the maximum civil penalties under RCRA (and most other pollution control statutes) increased to $27,500. For more information, see the EPA's June 2003 RCRA Civil Penalty Policy, *available at* http://www.nmenv.state.nm.us/HWB/Guidance_docs/EPA_RCRA_Civil_Penalty_Policy_2003.pdf. Moreover, the EPA has continued to increase civil penalty maximums to account for inflation. Through January 12, 2009, maximum penalties for most statutes were increased to $32,500. After January 12, 2009, those maximum penalties increased to $37,500. EPA, *Civil Monetary Penalty Inflation Adjustment Rule*, 74 Fed. Reg. 626, 626–27 (Jan. 7, 2009).

In addition, the EPA can seek injunctions:

> upon receipt of evidence that the past or present handling, storage, treatment, transportation or disposal of any solid waste or hazardous waste may present an imminent and substantial endangerment to health or the environment, the Administrator may bring suit on behalf of the United States in the appropriate district court against any person (including any past or present generator, past or present transporter, or past or present owner or operator of a treatment, storage, or disposal facility) who has contributed or who is contributing to such handling, storage, treatment, transportation or disposal to restrain such person from such handling, storage, treatment, transportation, or disposal, to order such person to take such other action as may be necessary, or both.

RCRA § 7003(a), 42 U.S.C. § 6973(a). Persons who violate the Administrator's orders are subject to fines of up to $5000 per day. *Id.* § 7003(b), 42 U.S.C. § 6973(b). As was discussed above, civil liability under RCRA is ***strict liability***.

RCRA also subjects violators to criminal liability for several kinds of ***"knowing"*** violations of its provisions, such as when a person "knowingly transports or causes to be transported any hazardous waste * * * to a facility that does not have a permit," "knowingly treats, stores, or disposes of any hazardous waste" without a RCRA permit or in knowing violation of a permit, or knowingly transports hazardous wastes without a manifest. RCRA § 3008(d)(1), (2), (5), 42 U.S.C. § 6928(d)(1), (2), (5). In addition, section 3008 recognizes the crime of ***"knowing endangerment,"*** creating criminal liability for "[a]ny person who knowingly transports, treats, stores, disposes of, or exports any hazardous waste * * * who knows at the time that he thereby places another person in imminent danger of death or serious bodily injury * * *." *Id.* § 3008(e), 42 U.S.C. § 6928(e). According to section 3008, "[a] person's state of mind is knowing with respect to—"

(A) his conduct, if he is aware of the nature of his conduct;

(B) an existing circumstance, if he is aware or believes that the circumstance exists; or

(C) a result of his conduct, if he is aware or believes that his conduct is substantially certain to cause danger or death or serious bodily injury.

RCRA § 3008(f)(1), 42 U.S.C. § 6928(f)(1).

The following is an example of a criminal prosecution for violations of RCRA Subtitle C.

UNITED STATES v. HANSEN

262 F.3d 1217 (11th Cir. 2001).

PER CURIAM:

Alfred R. Taylor, Christian A. Hansen, and Randall W. Hansen appeal their convictions for conspiracy to commit environmental crimes, violating the Clean Water Act, violating the Resource Conservation and Recovery Act, and violating the Comprehensive Environmental Response, Compensation, and Liability Act. On appeal, they each assert several alleged trial and sentencing errors. Finding no merit to their claims, we AFFIRM.

I. BACKGROUND

Christian Hansen ("Hansen") founded the Hanlin Group ("Hanlin") in 1972, and served as its President, Chief Executive Officer, and Chairman of the Board until early April 1993. Hanlin operated an industrial plant in Brunswick, Georgia, as LCP Chemicals–Georgia ("LCP"), and Hansen served as the plant manager for approximately two months in 1993. Randall Hansen ("Randall"), Hansen's son, was hired as an executive vice president in 1992. He became Chief Executive Officer in April 1993 and served in that capacity until November 1993. Alfred Taylor ("Taylor") began working for LCP in 1979, and became the Brunswick operations manager in 1991. He served as plant manager from February until July 1993. * * *

Hanlin purchased the Brunswick plant in 1979. The plant, which is on a site adjacent to tidal marshes and Purvis Creek, operated continuously year-round, manufacturing caustic soda, hydrogen gas, hydrochloric acid, and chlor-alkali bleach. About 150 people worked at the plant in two "cell buildings" or "cellrooms." Each cellroom was about the size of a football field and contained fifty mercury "cells," the units used to produce the bleach, soda, gas, and acid ultimately sold by LCP. "The production process generated hazardous wastes, including elemental mercury, mercury-contaminated sludge (or 'muds'), wastewater, chlorine contaminated wastewater, and extremely caustic wastes with high pH values." The wastes were subject to various environmental regulations, including wastewater limitations on pH, mercury, and chlorine set forth in LCP's National Pollutant Discharge Elimination System ("NPDES") [under the Clean Water Act], and to regulations of the Resource Conservation and Recovery Act ("RCRA"), 42 U.S.C. § 6928(d)(2).

Figure 1-11: LCP Chemicals Plant in Brunswick, Georgia
National Oceanic & Atmospheric Administration photo.

* * * The plant was authorized to store wastewater which was awaiting treatment in the wastewater treatment plant on the floor of the cellrooms. The cellrooms were constructed of concrete, with a downward slope which diverted the wastewaters to a sump and then to the wastewater treatment holding tanks. If the cellroom became incapable of holding the wastewater, it leaked out onto the ground and accumulated in a lake. LCP also used "Bunker C" oil tanks for additional wastewater storage. Due to accidental spills, bleach sometimes accumulated on the Cellroom 1 floor. During the early 1990s, the maintenance at the plant began deteriorating. Replacement parts were not made available, and wastewater began accumulating around the plant.

The operations were subject to Occupational Safety and Health Administration ("OSHA") regulations for the protection and safety of the employees. The workers exposed to mercury vapors in the mercury cell process were provided with liquids to drink in order to stay hydrated and deplete the mercury, and their exposure was periodically monitored through an extensive mercury urinalysis procedure. Employees who showed exposure to excess mercury were not allowed to return to work until they were seen by a medical physician, and were then relocated to other plant locations away from the mercury cells.

In August 1992, OSHA inspected the plant "due to an employee complaint about safety hazards associated with water on cell room floors." OSHA found this to be a "willful violation and demanded that no employees be allowed to work in contact with the water while the equipment was energized," and "forced" LCP "to erect a boardwalk system above the water level around all the equipment until the water c[ould] be eliminated permanently." LCP added wooden elevated walkways in the cellrooms to prevent the workers from having contact with the water on the floor and to reduce the workers' risk of electrical shock or chemical burns. The chemicals used in LCP's operations were very alkaline and caustic and could irritate and burn skin. To minimize the workers' risk of skin irritations and burns, LCP held routine safety meetings, encouraged and received safety inspections, and provided the employees with training, protective equipment to preclude skin contact, and first aid stations and showers to relieve inadvertent contact. All employees, including those assigned to the cellrooms, were authorized to work elsewhere in the plant if they were concerned about their safety.

* * * In July and August 1993, Hansen directed the plant employees to begin pumping the wastes into the large "bunker" tanks that had once been used to store oil although he knew that the wastewater mixed with oil could not be run through the wastewater treatment system. The plant environmental/safety manager reported the use of the tanks to Randall in July. After the EPD moved to revoke the plant's [Clean Water Act NPDES] permit, Hansen advised the employees to "increase the flow on the wastewater treatment system to a level that was to keep the water from running out the [cellroom] door" and into the lake. During their respective terms as plant manager, Hansen and Taylor were advised of and observed "water[] flow[ing] out the back door of the cellroom" as a result of a break in the cellroom berms, and "overflow[ing] on the ground." The employees complained to Hansen, Taylor, and Randall about "the water condition, the deterioration of the plant with the pipes, the leaks, and the safety equipment," and, despite assurances that conditions would improve "[a]s soon as [the plant] g[o]t some money," the plant did not get "any money" and conditions did not change.

* * * During this same period of time, Allied Signal and HoltraChem indicated interest as buyers, and a financial agreement was worked out in which Allied Signal would provide needed money, personnel, and raw materials or maintenance parts for the plant, including an extra wastewater treatment facility. With the influx of Allied Signal's resources, conditions at the plant improved. The purchase agreement eventually fell through and shortly thereafter the facility closed. * * *

The Georgia EPD turned the closed plant over to the U.S. Environmental Protection Agency (EPA) for cleanup and EPA estimated that the cleanup will cost more than $50 million. * * *

The government indicted Christian Hansen, Randall Hansen, Douglas Brent Hansen, and Alfred R. Taylor for conspiracy to commit environmental crimes at the site between 1 July 1985, and 1 February 1994, 18 U.S.C. § 371, (Count 1), and various substantive crimes. The charges included: violating the Clean Water Act ("CWA"), 33 U.S.C. § 1319(c)(2)(A) and 18 U.S.C. § 2, by exceeding the NPDES permit between June 1993 and January 1994 (Counts 2–21); violating the Resource Conservation and Recovery Act ("RCRA"), 42 U.S.C. §§ 6928(d)(2)(A) and (e), and 18 U.S.C. § 2, by storing wastewater on the cellroom floor and permitting some to escape into the environment between 29 May 1993 and 1 February 1994 (Counts 22–32), storing wastewater in the Bunker "C" tanks between 23 July 1993 and 1 February 1994 (Count 33), and knowingly endangering employees by exposing them to impermissibly stored wastes and wastewaters between 29 May 1993 and 1 February 1994 (Count 34); violating the Comprehensive Environmental Response, Compensation, and Liability Act ("CERCLA"), 42 U.S.C. § 9603(b)(3), by failing to notify the U.S. government of unpermitted releases of chlorine or wastewater into the environment between 21 July and 23 October 1993 (Counts 35–41); and violating the Endangered Species Act, 16 U.S.C. § 1538(a)(1)(B), 1538(g), and 1540(b)(1), by taking an endangered species, a Wood Stork, as a result of discharging mercury into the marsh, Purvis Creek, and the Turtle River (Count 42). * * * At the conclusion of the defendants' case, the district judge granted their motion for acquittal as to Count 42 but denied the motion as to all other charges. Hansen was convicted of all counts, Randall was convicted of all charged counts, and Taylor was convicted of Counts 1–3, 10–11, 22–26, 29–32, 34–35, and 38–41. * * *

II. DISCUSSION

* * * B. *Insufficiency of the Evidence*

* * * 2. Hazardous substances or materials

Taylor and Hansen argue that the government failed to prove that the untreated wastewater contained enough mercury and caustic to meet the environmental laws' definition of hazardous substances or materials, or that the untreated wastewater was improperly stored.

a. *Hazardous substances as defined*

OSHA chemist Clinton Leroy Merrell testified that samples which were submitted from LCP on 9 September 1992 tested as containing 8 to 30 parts per million of mercury, and six to ten-percent caustic, with a pH of 14. Former LCP plant manager Hugh Leroy Croom testified that, in January 1993, the untreated wastewater may have had "a high pH, and ... some mercury," but would not have contained mercury sludge. He said that the pH could be high enough to be a danger "at times" but that it did not stay high and varied according to the spills. However, he testified that muds containing mercury and caustic were washed onto the cellroom floors every three or four days when the treatment system's filters were back washed. When asked whether the wastewater on the cellroom floors would be considered a hazardous waste, Croom responded "[m]ost of the time, probably it was."

Dr. Teitelbaum testified that a fall and submersion into caustic soda with a pH of 14 would cause a third-degree burn over the entire body with a likelihood of death. LCP former employee Duane Carver testified that, some time between 1987 and 1993, he stepped into the cellroom sump hole and went in up to his waist. He knew that the pH was "pretty high" because he quickly felt it. He showered and was able to get most of it off so that he "didn't get burned all the way" and did not seek medical attention. * * *

The Waste Water Treatment Operators Logs for the periods of the indictment showed that the wastewater often contained more than 200 parts per billion of mercury. Former LCP employee Dunn testified that Taylor directed the employees to "put a sign up" labeling the wastewater in the rail cars as "[h]azardous waste materials." Taylor testified that the pH of the plant's wastewater was normally between seven and ten, and in concentration of eight to ten percent.

A "hazardous waste" is defined as

> a solid waste, or combination of solid wastes, which because of its quantity, concentration, or physical, chemical, or infectious characteristics may—
>
> (A) cause, or significantly contribute to an increase in mortality or an increase in serious irreversible, or incapacitating reversible, illness; or
>
> (B) pose a substantial present or potential hazard to human health or the environment when improperly treated, stored, transported, or disposed of, or otherwise managed.

42 U.S.C. § 6903(5). Hazardous wastes are categorized as either "listed" hazardous substances or "characteristic" hazardous substances. 40 C.F.R. § 261.3(a). * * * Wastewater containing mercury is classified as a characteristic hazardous substance when the water contains 200 parts per billion or more of mercury. *Id.* at § 261.24(a), Table. "Wastewater treatment sludge from the mercury cell process in chlorine production" is listed as hazardous waste K106. *Id.* at § 261.32. Wastewater containing caustic is classified as a characteristic hazardous substance when the water "has a pH less than or equal to 2 or greater than or equal to 12.5." *Id.* at § 261.22(a)(1). Once solid wastes are mixed with sludge or caustic, they are defined as hazardous. *Id.* at § 261.3(a)(2)(iv).

Where there is no sampling of the actual wastes, the government may prove the hazardous nature of the material by inventories, hazardous waste logs, internal memoranda, and trial testimony. The government is not required to prove that material is hazardous by EPA testing. We find that the testimony of the former LCP employees and the wastewater logs were sufficient for the jury to find that the untreated wastewater contained enough mercury and caustic to meet the environmental laws' definition of hazardous substances or materials.

b. Storage of hazardous materials.

Taylor and Hansen maintain that the accumulation of wastewater on the cellroom floors did not violate federal law because the wastewaters were not stored there for the statutory requisite of 90 days. * * *

Hazardous waste generators are permitted to "accumulate hazardous waste on-site for 90 days or less without a permit" if "the waste is placed" in tanks visibly marked with "[t]he date upon which each period of accumulation begins" and clearly labeled as "Hazardous Waste." 40 C.F.R. § 262.34(a)(1)(ii), (2), and (3). A "tank" is "a stationary device, designed to contain an accumulation of hazardous waste which is constructed primarily of non-earthen materials ... which provide structural support." 40 C.F.R. § 260.10.

There was no evidence that suggested that the cellrooms, in which earthen berms were constructed to contain the wastewater, were marked with the date of accumulation or labeled as containing hazardous wastes and thus qualified as "tanks." The testimony and logs indicate that the wastewater, which may have abated in cellroom one during various periods of time, remained in cellroom two and was present for more than 90 days. Therefore, the evidence was sufficient for the jury to find that the wastewater was improperly stored.

3. Knowing Endangerment Under RCRA

Hansen, Randall, and Taylor argue that the evidence was insufficient to convict them for knowing endangerment. They acknowledge that the government may have shown that they "could have been aware" of the inherent dangers of working in a chlor-alkali plant, but argue that it failed to show that they knew and had an actual belief that the conduct which allegedly violated the environmental laws was substantially certain to cause death or serious bodily injury to others. * * *

For a conviction of knowing endangerment under the RCRA, the government must prove that the defendants knowingly caused the illegal treatment, storage, or disposal of hazardous wastes while knowing that such conduct placed others in imminent danger of death or serious injury. 42 U.S.C. § 6928(e). A defendant acts "knowingly" "if he is aware or believes that his conduct is substantially certain to cause danger of death or serious bodily injury." *Id.* at 6928(f)(1)(C). The defendant must have possessed "actual awareness or actual belief." *Id.* at 6928(f)(2)(A). Circumstantial evidence, "including evidence that the defendant took affirmative steps to shield himself from relevant information," may be used to prove the defendant's awareness or belief. *Id.* The knowing endangerment statute was drafted to "assure to the extent possible that persons are not prosecuted or convicted unjustly for making difficult business judgments where such judgments are made without the necessary scienter" "however dire may be the danger in fact created." S. REP. 96–172, at 37–38 (1979), *reprinted in* 1980 U.S.C.C.A.N. 5019, 5036–38. The penalties imposed by the knowing endangerment section were "designed for the occasional case where the defendant's knowing conduct shows that his respect for human life is utterly lacking and it is merely fortuitous that his conduct may not have caused a disaster." *Id.* at 38, 1980 U.S.C.C.A.N. at 5038. We have held that "[t]he government need only prove that a defendant had knowledge of the general hazardous character of the chemical" and knew "that the chemicals have the potential to be harmful to others or to the environment." "[W]hile knowledge of prior illegal activity is not conclusive as to whether a defendant possessed the requisite knowledge of later illegal activity, it most certainly provides circumstantial evidence of the defendant's later knowledge from which the jury may draw the necessary inference."

The statute defines "serious bodily injury" as "(A) bodily injury which involves a substantial risk of death; (B) unconsciousness; (C) extreme physical pain; (D) protracted and obvious disfigurement; or (E) protracted loss or impairment of the function of a bodily member, organ, or mental faculty." 42 U.S.C. § 6928(f)(6). A condition which may cause one of the statutorily defined conditions is sufficient to show "serious bodily injury."

a. The Evidence of Endangerment

Former LCP employees testified that they suffered serious skin and respiratory conditions from the wastewater on the cellroom floors. A November 1992 memorandum from Taylor to Randall showed Taylor's concern for needed repairs "to avert severe safety and environmental problems." The urinalysis testing on employees showed "an increase" in the number with mercury levels which exceeded the 150 action level from 1986 to 1993. Taylor admitted that most of the employees in the cellroom were removed to other plant locations "before any medical condition occurred" but said that he did not see any "reason to draw any correlation between" the rise in the number of employees exposed to excess mercury and the dumping of hazardous wastes and mercury.

Expert testimony and reports linked exposure to mercury and caustic to a variety of serious health problems. The National Institute for Occupational Safety and Health (NIOSH) report on sodium hydroxide caustic indicated that local contact with caustic could result in "extensive damage to tissues, with resultant blindness, cutaneous burns, and perforations of the alimentary tract," with potential for development of "squamous cell carcinomas." The NIOSH report on inorganic mercury warned of the effects of mercury and mercury vapors to the central nervous system. Dr. Teitelbaum testified that exposure to caustic could cause burns ranging from first-to third-degree and could be lethal, and that exposure to mercury could cause mild tremors, personality changes, some detectable neurological abnormalities, changes in kidney function to severe kidney damage with potential death, and immune system problems. Dr. Teitelbaum opined that the employees were "in danger of death or serious bodily injury." The evidence was sufficient for the jury to find that the defendants placed others in danger of death or serious bodily injury.

b. The Evidence of Mens Rea

The evidence showed that Hansen, Randall, and Taylor knew that the conditions of the plant were dangerous and that the conditions posed a serious danger to the employees. LCP former employee Wilbur Duane Outhwaite testified that he voiced his opposition to the use of the Bunker "C" storage with Hansen, and that Hansen responded that it was "his decision to make, and he decided to use them." LCP acting plant manager Hugh Croom discussed his concerns regarding the dangerous conditions in the cellroom and the danger to the employees with Randall. Croom and LCP former employee Outhwaite testified that Randall received daily reports from the plant managers concerning plant operations and "safety problems." Randall was aware of the water on the cellroom floor and "wouldn't say that [he] wasn't unaware of the hazard," but thought that the walkway was "an acceptable resolution" to "eliminating the hazard to the employees while we worked to dry the cellroom floor." He conceded that he was aware that the company was cited for willful violation of OSHA safety regulations as a result of water on cellroom floors. Jesse Jones, a former LCP employee and a union representative, met with Randall to discuss the employees' safety issues, and Randall promised the needed repairs. He said that he discussed the safety concerns, specifically "the water condition, the deterioration of the plant with the pipes, the leaks, and the safety equipment[]" with Hansen and Taylor. Between 3 August 1993, and 4 February 1994, Randall was sent 22 reports listing 110 different violations of the NPDES standards. As LCP's environmental manager, Brent Hanson regularly advised Randall of the plant's environmental problems "[w]henever he was interested in things" and by monthly reports.

As early as 1988, NIOSH informed Taylor that the plant employees had "extremely high" levels of mercury in their bodies which created "an unacceptably high potential for health effects," and that the mercury-contaminated wastes should be kept in vapor-proof containers. Despite this, the employees' exposure to high levels of mercury continued. In 1992, Taylor addressed his concerns about "severe safety" problems in a memorandum to Randall. Taylor was aware that, during the spring of 1993, 23 cellroom employees were removed from their duty in the cellrooms due to their high levels of mercury and that the mercury level in the workplace increased. Taylor was aware of and concerned by the mercury-contaminated waste which was stored in drums in the cellrooms' basement and which was emitting elevated levels of mercury fumes. He admitted that the mercury-contaminated mud on the cellroom floors posed a health risk and needed to be monitored. He testified that, on occasion, he would get into the water wearing protective equipment to make repairs and improvements to the pumps, and admitted that, if the wastewater got onto bare skin and was caustic, "you would start to feel a little burning or a little heat sensation" but that it could be neutralized by washing with the safety solution. He said that such burns were "not unusual" in a caustic soda manufacturing plant through employee carelessness and equipment failures.

c. Consent to the Risks

The RCRA knowing endangerment provision can be affirmatively defended if "the conduct charged was consented to by the person endangered and that the danger and conduct charged were reasonably foreseeable hazards of—(A) an occupation, a business, or a profession." 42 U.S.C. § 6928(f)(3). The evidence showed that the plant's environmental violations seriously endangered the employees and were not typical to chlor-alkali plants. * * * LCP environmental manager Brent Hanson noted that, although covering mercury with water to limit mercury vapors was an accepted practice within the chlor-alkali industry, it was usually practiced "in a little more confined manner" than the condition of the cellrooms, it was not an industry practice to allow such quantities of mercury to accumulate on the cellroom floors, and he knew of no other chlor-alkali plants that permitted such a condition to exist. Dr. Teitelbaum testified that, although he did not think that "you can get a zero risk" in a chlor-alkali plant, he thought "you can make chlor-alkali plants safe so that workers under everyday conditions are extremely unlikely to be hurt."

The employees also did not freely consent to conditions at the plant. They complained to management, including Hansen, Randall, and Taylor, about the dangerous working conditions, and refused to work in the cellrooms. Union representative and former plant employee Jesse Jones testified that LCP suspended nine employees who refused to "go underneath the cellroom to repair the pump" because of the wastewater on the cellroom floor. Jones said that he discussed his concerns about the working conditions with Hansen, Randall, and Taylor. Former employee Larry Barwick said that he complained "to whoever would listen," including the LCP management, about the fumes[3] and visible mercury in the cell buildings. He refused to go into the cellrooms, and was once sent home for the day based on his refusal. The evidence, therefore, was sufficient to show that the defendants knew that the plant's violations of the CWA and RCRA violations were inevitable, that the plant was incapable of complying with environmental standards, and that the employees were endangered while working within this environment without consenting to the risk. * * *

NOTES

1. **Statutory Interactions.** This case provides a good example of how one basic environmental problem—an inability to properly treat wastewater—can violate several federal environmental (and other) statutes. LCP Chemi-

3. Barwick said that:

[T]he fumes from the acid burners were coming down and you couldn't breathe without wearing a respirator.

It would burn your skin. It would take the hair off of your arms. It would get in your eyes, under your goggles. And everything—it had caustic. It had bleach. It had acid fumes.... After probably the last year or year and a half, that was probably a regular everyday thing almost, that you would get gas somewhere in [the cell building].

cals–Georgia's wastewater problems led not only to its RCRA liability, but also to liability under the Comprehensive Environmental Response, Compensation, and Liability Act (CERCLA), the Clean Water Act, and the Endangered Species Act. In addition, LCP was subject to the federal Occupational Safety and Health Act (OSH Act), administered by the Occupational Safety and Health Administration (OSHA). The OSH Act is not an environmental statute, *per se*; instead, its purpose is to keep workers safe on the job. Why was the OSH Act nevertheless relevant to the defendants' RCRA liability?

2. **Triggering RCRA.** Looking back at the definition of "solid waste," why did the mercury and caustic qualify as "solid wastes" for purposes of RCRA?

3. **Triggering Subtitle C: Mercury.** Mercury is a toxic heavy metal that causes brain damage. For RCRA purposes, is mercury a listed hazardous waste or a characteristic hazardous waste? What is the regulatory standard? For purposes of this case, was the mercury a listed or a characteristic hazardous waste? What evidence in this case demonstrated the presence of mercury at concentrations that made it hazardous?

4. **Triggering Subtitle C: Caustic.** "Caustic" is another name for strongly basic materials—materials with a pH above 7. (On the 14–point pH scale, 7 is neutral, like distilled water. Materials with a pH below 7 are acids; the strongest acids have pH values of 1 or 2.) Is caustic a listed hazardous waste or a characteristic hazardous waste? What is the regulatory standard? What evidence in this case demonstrated that the defendants' wastewater met that standard?

5. **TSD Facility Status.** Why did LCP Chemicals–Georgia, the facility at issue in this case, qualify as a TSD facility? What exception did the defendants try to use? Why didn't that tactic work?

6. **Knowing Endangerment.** What are the elements of knowing endangerment, according to the Eleventh Circuit? Why was the evidence sufficient to prove each of those elements beyond a reasonable doubt? Do you agree with the jury in this case that the defendants knowingly endangered their employees? Why or why not?

7. **RCRA and the Common–Law Defense of Consent.** As you may remember from Torts, consent can be a valid common-law defense to a tort action. For example, boxers who agree to participate in a boxing match cannot later sue their opponents for battery based on the punches thrown in the match, at least so long as the punches were the kind a boxer would normally anticipate. Employees can also consent to hazardous employment conditions. Why did the consent defense, which Congress expressly incorporated into RCRA, not work in this case?

8. **Sentencing for Environmental Crimes.** Nearly all of the federal environmental statutes create criminal liability for certain kinds of environmental violations, and nearly all of those criminal provisions specify the penalties for conviction. For example, RCRA specifies that a person convicted of knowing endangerment will "be subject to a fine of not more than $250,000 or imprisonment for not more than fifteen years, or both," while "[a] defendant that is an organization shall * * * be subject to a fine of not more

than $1,000,000." RCRA § 3008(e), 42 U.S.C. § 6928(e). Nevertheless, once the ***Federal Sentencing Guidelines*** took effect, they superseded these statute-specific penalties, and convicted environmental criminals were subject to the standard federal sentencing matrix. However, in January 2005, the Supreme Court decided that mandatory Federal Sentencing Guidelines violate criminal defendants' Sixth Amendment right to a jury trial, and thus it made the Guidelines advisory only. *United States v. Booker*, 543 U.S. 220 (2005). In accordance with the Supreme Court's view of the Sentencing Guidelines as advisory, some federal Courts of Appeal have continued to consider the Guidelines when sentencing and fining defendants criminally convicted of violating the federal environmental statutes. *See, e.g.*, *United States v. Mancuso*, 2011 WL 2580228 (2d Cir. 2011); *United States v. Rushing*, 239 Fed. Appx. 322, 323 (9th Cir. 2007); *United States v. Kinard*, 472 F.3d 1294, 1296–97 (11th Cir. 2006); *United States v. Hillyer*, 457 F.3d 347, 352–53 (4th Cir. 2006). Notably, the Guidelines allow for a sentencing enhancement for any defendant found to be discharging or mishandling hazardous substances in violation of RCRA, CERCLA, or the Clean Water Act. *United States v. Kinard*, 472 F.3d at 1296. Nevertheless, other courts have concluded that the Sentencing Guidelines no longer apply in environmental law. *See United States v. Southern Union Co.*, 630 F.3d 17, 39 (1st Cir. 2010) (holding that the statute, not the Sentencing Guidelines, controls the amount of fine imposed on a corporation pursuant to RCRA).

* * *

III. THE COMPREHENSIVE ENVIRONMENTAL RESPONSE, COMPENSATION, AND LIABILITY ACT (CERCLA)

A. TRIGGERING CERCLA LIABILITY

Congress designed RCRA to prevent hazardous wastes from escaping into the environment by regulating such wastes from their generation to their disposal. However, RCRA took effect in 1976, and hazardous wastes had already escaped into the environment at many sites throughout the country. The problems with these pre-RCRA sites became very clear to Congress and the public in the 1978 Love Canal problem:

> At Love Canal, over 21,000 tons of chemical wastes were deposited in a landfill. The landfill closed in 1952, and was then covered over the next year. Over time, a community grew around the abandoned landfill. Under the old scenario of "out of sight-out of mind," that should have been the end of the story.
>
> However, more than two decades later, increasing numbers of Love Canal residents began complaining of health problems, including chronic headaches, respiratory discomforts, and skin ailments. Residents also noticed high incidents of cancer and deafness. The State of New York investigated and found high levels of chemical contaminants in the soil and air—with a high incidence of birth defects and

miscarriages in the immediate area around the Love Canal landfill. President Jimmy Carter declared a State of Emergency in 1978, and Federal funds were used to permanently relocate 239 families in the first two rows of houses that encircled the landfill area.

But the tragedy did not end. A New York State investigation found "extensive migration of potentially toxic materials outside the immediate canal area." In 1979, 300 additional families in a 10–block area around the site were relocated because of health problems from chemical exposures. In 1980, EPA announced the results of blood tests that showed chromosome damage in Love Canal residents. Residents were told that this could mean an increased risk of cancer, reproductive problems, and genetic damage. Later that year, President Carter issued a second State of Emergency—providing funding for the permanent relocation of all 900 residents of the Love Canal area.

U.S. E.P.A., SUPERFUND: 20 YEARS OF PROTECTING HUMAN HEALTH AND THE ENVIRONMENT 1–4 (Dec. 11, 2000), *available at* http://www.epa.gov/superfund/20years/index.htm.

To deal with problems like Love Canal, in 1980, Congress enacted the ***Comprehensive Environmental Response, Compensation, and Liability Act of 1980* (CERCLA)**, 42 U.S.C. §§ 9601–9675. Together, RCRA and CERCLA comprehensively deal with hazardous waste problems. CERCLA is triggered whenever there is a ***release of a hazardous substance from a facility***. The statute defines "***release***" broadly to be:

> any spilling, leaking, pumping, pouring, emitting, emptying, discharging, injecting, escaping, leaching, dumping, or disposing into the environment (including the abandonment or discarding of barrels, containers, and other closed receptacles containing any hazardous substance or pollutant or contaminants) * * *.

CERCLA § 101(22), 42 U.S.C. § 9601(22). However, the definition of "release" also explicitly excludes releases that are regulated under other environmental statutes—workplace releases covered by the Occupational Safety and Health Act (OSH Act); engine emissions from cars, trucks, airplanes, and pipeline pumping station engines, which are regulated through a variety of federal statutes, especially the Clean Air Act; releases of nuclear and radioactive materials covered by the Atomic Energy Act of 1954's financial protection requirements; and the normal application of fertilizer. *Id.* In addition, people cannot be liable *under CERCLA* for releases of pesticides regulated by the Federal Insecticide, Fungicide, and Rodenticide Act (FIFRA), 7 U.S.C. §§ 136 *et seq.*, or for releases of materials already permitted under other federal statutes. CERCLA § 107(i), (j), 42 U.S.C. § 9607(i), (j).

CERCLA defines "***hazardous substance***" largely through reference to other federal statutes. CERCLA § 101(14), 42 U.S.C. § 9601(14). Thus, hazardous substances include:

- oil and associated pollutants regulated under the Clean Water Act;
- hazardous wastes regulated under RCRA;
- toxic pollutants regulated under the Clean Water Act;
- hazardous air pollutants regulated under the Clean Air Act; and
- imminently hazardous chemicals regulated under the Toxic Substances Control Act (TSCA).

Id. In addition, the EPA can designate other substances as "hazardous substances" under CERCLA itself. *Id.* There are two major statutory exceptions to this list, however. "Hazardous substance" does not include: (1) "petroleum, including crude oil or any fraction thereof which is not otherwise specifically listed or designated as a hazardous substance"; or (2) "natural gas, natural gas liquids, liquified natural gas, or synthetic gas usable for fuel (or mixtures of natural gas and such synthetic gas)." *Id.*

FIGURE 1-12: A FLOW CHART OF CERCLA

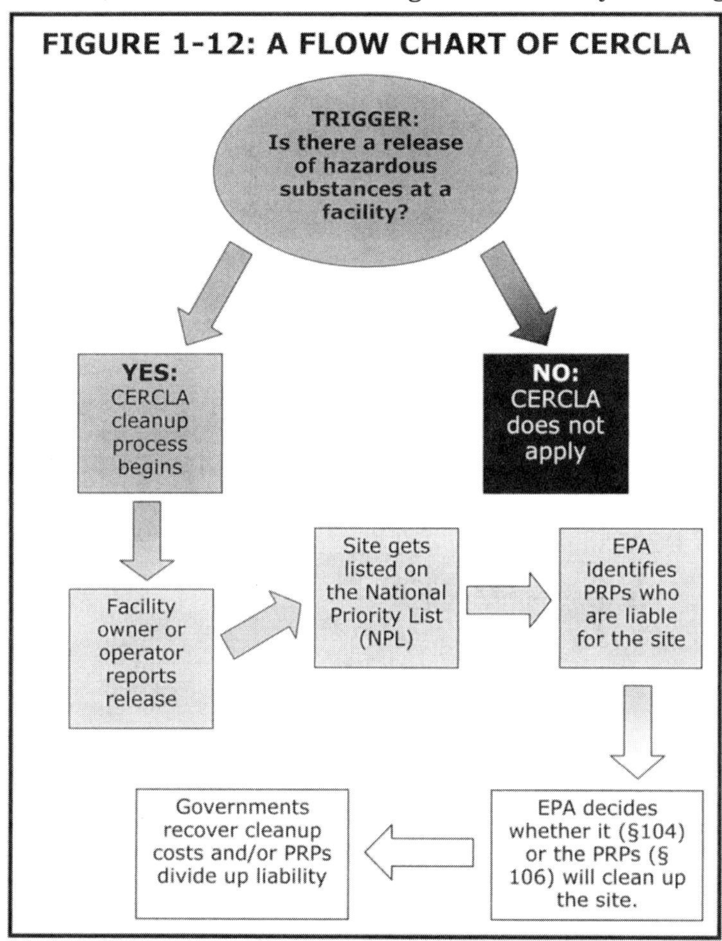

Finally, a "***facility***" is:

(A) any building, structure, installation, equipment, pipe or pipeline (including any pipe into a sewer or publicly owned treatment works), well, pit, pond, lagoon, impoundment, ditch, landfill, storage container, motor vehicle, rolling stock, or aircraft, or (B) any site or area where a hazardous substance has been deposited, stored, disposed of, or placed, or otherwise come to be located; but does not include any consumer product in consumer use or any vessel.

CERCLA § 101(9), 42 U.S.C. § 9601(9).

As many courts have noted, CERCLA is a ***remedial statute***, designed to correct an existing and recognized problem. As a result, courts interpret the statute broadly. The breadth of CERCLA begins with its trigger. As the following case demonstrates, the government need not show very much—nowhere near the traditional requirements of tort law, including nuisance—to make an entity a ***potentially responsible party* (PRP)** for the cleanup.

UNITED STATES v. ALCAN ALUMINUM CORP.

964 F.2d 252 (3rd Cir. 1992).

GREENBERG, CIRCUIT JUDGE.

This matter is before the court on appeal by Alcan Aluminum Corporation ("Alcan") from a summary judgment entered in favor of the United States (the "Government") for response costs incurred by the Government in cleaning the Susquehanna River.

* * * On November 24, 1989, the Government filed a complaint in the United States District Court for the Middle District of Pennsylvania under section 107(a) of the Comprehensive Environmental Response, Compensation and Liability Act, 42 U.S.C. § 9607(a) ("CERCLA") against 20 defendants, including Alcan, for the recovery of clean-up costs it incurred in response to a release of hazardous substances into the Susquehanna River. On October 11, 1990, the Government moved for summary judgment against Alcan, the only non-settling defendant, and on November 13, 1990, Alcan cross-moved for summary judgment.

* * * [O]n May 8, 1991, the court entered judgment against Alcan in the amount of $473,790.18, which was the difference between the full response costs the Government had incurred in cleaning the Susquehanna River and the amount the Government had recovered from the settling defendants.

* * * I. FACTS AND PROCEDURAL HISTORY

Virtually all of the facts in this case to the extent developed at this point are undisputed. The Butler Tunnel Site (the "Site") is listed on the National Priorities List established by the Environmental Protection Agency ("EPA") under section 105 of CERCLA, 42 U.S.C. § 9605. The Site includes a network of approximately five square miles of deep underground mines and related tunnels, caverns, pools and waterways bordering the east bank of the Susquehanna River in Pittston, Pennsylvania. The mine workings at the Site are drained by the Butler Tunnel (the "Tunnel"), a 7500 foot tunnel which feeds directly into the Susquehanna River.

The mines are accessible from the surface by numerous air shafts or boreholes. One borehole (the "Borehole") is located on the premises of Hi–Way Auto Service, an automobile fuel and repair station situated above the Tunnel. The Borehole leads directly into the mine workings at the Site.

In the late 1970's, the owner of Hi–Way Auto Service permitted various liquid waste transport companies, including those owned and controlled by Russell Mahler (the "Mahler Companies"), to deposit oily liquid wastes containing hazardous substances into the Borehole. The Mahler Companies collected the liquid wastes from numerous industrial facilities located in the northeastern United States and, in total, disposed of approximately 2,000,000 gallons of oily wastes containing hazardous substances through the Borehole. Apparently, it was contemplated that the waste would remain at the Site indefinitely.

Alcan is an Ohio corporation which manufactures aluminum sheet and plate products in Oswego, New York. From 1965 through at least 1989, Alcan's manufacturing process involved the hot-rolling of aluminum ingots. To keep the rolls cool and lubricated during the hot-rolling process, Alcan circulated an emulsion through the rolls, consisting of 95% deionized water and 5% mineral oil. At the end of the hot-rolling process, Alcan removed the used emulsion and replaced it with unused emulsion.

During the rolling process, fragments of the aluminum ingots, which also contained copper, chromium, cadmium, lead and zinc, hazardous substances under CERCLA, broke off into the emulsion. In an effort to remove those fragments, Alcan then filtered the used emulsion prior to disposing of it, but the filtering process was imperfect and hence some fragments remained. According to Alcan, however, the level of these compounds in the post-filtered, used emulsion was "far below the EP toxic or TCLP toxic levels and, indeed, orders of magnitude below ambient or naturally occurring background levels. Moreover, the trace quantities of metal compounds in the emulsion [were] immobile...." * * *

From mid–1978 to late 1979, Alcan contracted with the Mahler Companies to dispose of at least 2,300,950 gallons of used emulsion from its Oswego, New York, facility. During that period, the Mahler Companies disposed of approximately 32,500–37,500 gallons (or five 6500–7500 gallon loads) of Alcan's liquid waste through the Borehole into the Site.

In September 1985, approximately 100,000 gallons of water contaminated with hazardous substances were released from the Site into the Susquehanna River. It appears that this discharge was composed of the wastes deposited into the Borehole in the late 1970's. Between September 28, 1985, and January 7, 1987, EPA incurred significant response costs due to the release and the threatened release of hazardous substances from the Site. According to the Government, EPA's response actions included "containing an oily material on the river through the use of absorbent booms; immediately removing and disposing of 161,000 pounds (over 80 tons) of oil and chemical-soaked debris and soil, monitoring, sampling and analysis of air and water, and conducting hydrogeologic studies."

* * * In November 1989, the Government filed a complaint against 20 defendants, including Alcan, for the recovery of costs incurred as a result of the release of hazardous wastes from the Site into the Susquehanna River. In response, 17 of the 20 defendants executed a consent decree, reimbursing the Government for certain removal costs, and the district court entered that decree on January 17, 1990. On June 8, 1990, two of the three remaining defendants entered into a second consent decree with the Government, which the district court approved on July 25, 1990.

The Government then moved for summary judgment against Alcan, the only non-settling defendant, to collect the balance of its response costs. Alcan cross-moved for summary judgment, arguing that its emulsion did not constitute a "hazardous substance" as defined by CERCLA due to its below-ambient levels of copper, cadmium, chromium, lead and zinc, and further contending that its emulsion could not have caused the release or any response costs incurred by the Government.

On January 9, 1991, the district court * * * held that Alcan was jointly and severally liable for the removal costs because Alcan's waste contained identifiable levels of hazardous substances and was present at the Site from which there was a release. * * *

* * * II. DISCUSSION

A. CERCLA Framework

In response to widespread concern over the improper disposal of hazardous wastes, Congress enacted CERCLA, a complex piece of legislation designed to force polluters to pay for costs associated with remedying their pollution. As numerous courts have observed, CERCLA is a remedial statute which should be construed liberally to effectuate its goals.

CERCLA, as amended by the Superfund Amendments and Reauthorization Act of 1986, grants broad authority to the executive branch of the federal government to provide for the clean-up of hazardous substance sites. Specifically, section 104 authorizes the President to respond to a release or substantial threat of a release of hazardous substances into the environment by: (1) removing or arranging for the removal of hazardous substances; (2) providing for remedial action relating to such hazardous substances; and (3) taking any other response measure consistent with the National Contingency Plan that the President deems necessary to protect the public health or welfare or the environment. 42 U.S.C. § 9604(a). The President has delegated most of his authority under CERCLA to EPA.

CERCLA's bite lies in its requirement that responsible parties pay for actions undertaken pursuant to section 104. Under section 107, CERCLA liability is imposed where the plaintiff establishes the following four elements:

(1) the defendant falls within one of the four categories of "responsible parties";

(2) the hazardous substances are disposed at a "facility";

(3) there is a "release" or threatened release of hazardous substances from the facility into the environment;

(4) the release causes the incurrence of "response costs".

42 U.S.C. § 9607.

Reimbursement for response costs can be obtained in a variety of ways. For example, the Government can clean the sites itself using monies in the Hazardous Substance Response Trust Fund established by section 221 of CERCLA, 42 U.S.C. § 9631 and now the Hazardous Substance Superfund or "Superfund" (*see* 26 U.S.C. § 9507); EPA can then seek reimbursement from responsible parties, as it has done in this case. In addition, section 106(a) permits EPA to request the Attorney General to "secure such relief as may be necessary to abate such danger or threat" by filing a civil action in federal district court. That section also permits EPA to issue administrative orders "as may be necessary to protect public health and welfare and the environment."

Finally, and of great significance in this case, CERCLA imposes strict liability on responsible parties. 42 U.S.C. § 9601(32).

B. CERCLA Contains No Quantitative Requirement in its Definition of "Hazardous Substance"

Alcan argues that it should not be held liable for response costs incurred by the Government in cleaning the Susquehanna River because the level of hazardous substances in its emulsion was below that which naturally occurs and thus could not have contributed to the environmental injury. * * *

The Government responds that under a plain reading of the statute, there is no quantitative requirement in the definition of "hazardous substance." Therefore, the Government asserts that Alcan's argument that substances containing below-ambient levels of hazardous substances are not really "hazardous" is properly directed at Congress, not the judiciary. * * *

* * * *1. Plain Meaning*

Section 9601(14) sets forth CERCLA's definition of "hazardous substance" as:

> 'hazardous substance' means (A) any substance designated pursuant to section 1321(b)(2)(A) of Title 33, (B) any element, compound, mixture, solution, or substance designated pursuant to section 9602 of

this title, (C) any hazardous waste having the characteristics identified under or listed pursuant to section 3001 of the Solid Waste Disposal Act [42 U.S.C.A. § 6921] (but not including any waste the regulation of which under the Solid Waste Disposal Act [42 U.S.C.A. § 6901 et seq.] has been suspended by Act of Congress), (D) any toxic pollutant listed under section 1317(a) of Title 33, (E) any hazardous air pollutant listed under section 112 of the Clean Air Act [42 U.S.C.A. § 7412], and (F) any imminently hazardous chemical substance or mixture with respect to which the Administrator has taken action pursuant to section 2606 of Title 15. The term does not include petroleum, including crude oil or any fraction thereof which is not otherwise specifically listed or designated as a hazardous substance under subparagraphs (A) through (F) of this paragraph....

Hence, the statute does not, on its face, impose any quantitative requirement or concentration level on the definition of "hazardous substances." Rather, the substance under consideration must simply fall within one of the designated categories.

2. Legislative History

Since the statute is plain on its face, we need not resort to legislative history to uncover its meaning. In any event, the legislative history is barren of any remarks directly revealing Congress' intent vis-á-vis a threshold requirement on the definition of hazardous substances. Significantly, however, the available legislative history of CERCLA *does* indicate that Congress created the statute to force all polluters to pay for their pollution. It is difficult to imagine that Congress intended to impose a quantitative requirement on the definition of hazardous substances and thereby permit a polluter to add to the total pollution but avoid liability because the amount of its own pollution was minimal.

3. Jurisprudence

In addition, courts that have addressed this issue have almost uniformly held that CERCLA liability does not depend on the existence of a threshold quantity of a hazardous substance.

4. Congressional Matter

It may be that Congress did not intend such an all-encompassing definition of "hazardous substances," but this argument is best directed at Congress itself. If Congress had intended to impose a threshold requirement, it could easily have so indicated. We should not rewrite the statute simply because the definition of one of its terms is broad in scope.

C. The District Court's Definition of "Hazardous Substance" is not Inconsistent With EPA Regulations and Policy

* * * In Alcan's view, the district court's construction of the statute is at odds with environmental policy because it imposes liability on generators of allegedly "hazardous" substances although the substances

pose no real threat to the environment. Alcan's argument, though superficially appealing, is flawed. First, as noted above, the Government responds to "releases" that threaten environmental safety. Thus, it is the *release alone* that must justify the response costs, not the particular waste generated by one given defendant. Here, there is no question but that a release occurred. Second, the fact that a single generator's waste would not in itself justify a response is irrelevant in the multi-generator context, as this would permit a generator to escape liability where the amount of harm it engendered to the environment was minimal, though it was significant when added to other generators' waste. Accordingly, we find that the district court's construction of the statute furthers important environmental goals.

D. Causation

Alcan maintains that, if we decline to construe the determination of "hazardous substance" to encompass a concentration threshold, we must at least require the Government to prove that *Alcan's emulsion* caused or contributed to the release or the Government's incurrence of response costs. The Government contends * * * that the statute imposes no such causation requirement, but rather requires that the plaintiff in a CERCLA proceeding establish that the *release* or *threatened release* caused the incurrence of response costs; it underscores the difficulty CERCLA plaintiffs would face in the multi-generator context if required to trace the cause of the response costs to each responsible party.

1. Plain Meaning

The plain meaning of the statute supports the Government's position. As noted above, section 107 imposes liability upon a generator of hazardous substances who contracts with another party to dispose of the hazardous substances at a facility "from which there is a *release, or threatened release which causes the incurrence of response costs.*" 42 U.S.C. § 9607 (emphasis supplied). The statute does not, on its face, require the plaintiff to prove that the generator's *hazardous substances* themselves caused the release or caused the incurrence of response costs; rather, it requires the plaintiff to prove that the *release or threatened release* caused the incurrence of response costs, and that the defendant is a generator of hazardous substances at the facility.

2. Legislative History

The legislative history also supports the Government's position that CERCLA does not require the plaintiff to establish a specific causal relationship between a generator's waste and the release or the plaintiff's incurrence of response costs. It appears that the early House of Representatives' version of CERCLA imposed liability upon those persons who "caused or contributed to the release or threatened release." H.R. 7020, 96th Cong., 2d Sess. § 3071(a)(D), 126 Cong. Rec. 26,779. However, the version ultimately passed by Congress deleted the causation requirement and instead imposed liability upon a *class* of responsible persons without regard to whether the person specifically caused or contributed to the release and the resultant response costs. *See* 126 Cong. Rec. 31,981–82. Moreover, Congress added three limited defenses to liability based on causation which are contained in 42 U.S.C. § 9607(b): acts of God, acts of war, and acts or omissions of a contractually unrelated third party when the defendant exercised due care and took appropriate responses. Imputing a specific causation requirement would render these defenses superfluous.

* * * *3. Jurisprudence*

Further, virtually every court that has considered this question has held that a CERCLA plaintiff need not establish a direct causal connection between the defendant's hazardous substances and the release or the plaintiff's incurrence of response costs. * * *

* * * Decisions rejecting a causation requirement between the defendant's waste and the release or the incurrence of response costs are well-reasoned, consistent with the plain language of the statute and consistent with the legislative history of CERCLA. Accordingly, we reject Alcan's argument that the Government must prove that Alcan's emulsion deposited in the Borehole caused the release or caused the Government to incur response costs. Rather, the Government must simply prove that the defendant's hazardous substances were deposited at the site from which there was a release and that the *release* caused the incurrence of response costs.

E. Petroleum Exclusion

Alcan further argues that its emulsion constitutes "petroleum" within the meaning of 42 U.S.C. § 9601 and is thus excluded from CERCLA liability. Section 9601(14) provides: "[t]he term [hazardous substance] does not include *petroleum, including crude oil or any fraction thereof which is not otherwise specifically listed or designated as a hazardous substance under subparagraphs (A) through (F) of this paragraph*...." (emphasis supplied). According to Alcan, EPA has interpreted the petroleum exclusion to extend to "used oil" containing concentrations of hazardous substances at levels equal to or less than that found in virgin oil. Alcan contends that its emulsion is "used oil" with concentration levels of cadmium, chromium, copper, lead and zinc that are lower than the levels of these compounds in virgin oil and therefore falls within the petroleum exclusion. Although this argument has superficial appeal, it cannot withstand close scrutiny.

First, and most importantly, EPA has distinguished between oil that naturally contains low levels of hazardous substances and oil to which hazardous substances have been added through use. Although EPA has extended the petroleum exclusion to the former category of oily substances, it has specifically declined to extend such protection to the latter category. * * * Moreover, EPA's interpretation of the petroleum exclusion comports with the relevant legislative history which indicates that the exclusion was intended for oil spills, not for releases of oil which has become infused with hazardous substances through use. *See* S. REP. NO. 848, 96th Cong., 2d Sess. 30–31 (1987).

Alcan has admitted that the hot-rolling process adds hazardous substances to the emulsion. Thus, it has effectively conceded that its emulsion does not fall within the scope of the petroleum exclusion as construed by EPA.

[As a result, the Third Circuit deemed that Alcan Aluminum was responsible for the costs of cleanup.]

NOTES

1. **Triggering CERCLA.** What was the *release* in this CERCLA case? What was the *facility*? What were the *hazardous substances*? Which of these elements was Alcan Aluminum contesting with respect to its wastes?

2. **The Elements of a CERCLA Case.** What are the elements of a CERCLA case against a PRP, according to the Third Circuit? What *doesn't* the government have to prove? How does the CERCLA standard of proof compare to the standard of proof in a typical tort case? Why would Congress make such a change to common-law tort principles?

3. **Fault in a CERCLA Case.** Notice that the Third Circuit characterized CERCLA as a strict liability statute. As with RCRA, imposition of strict liability is a nearly universal federal court interpretation of CERCLA. Does CERCLA strict liability reflect an *adoption* by Congress of common law tort principles or a *rejection* of them? Why?

4. **CERCLA and Causation.** As we will see in the second half of this case, discussed in section III.E: Reducing Individual PRP Liability, CERCLA liability is not *entirely* free from causation issues.

5. **The Petroleum Exclusion**. Congress excluded releases of petroleum from CERCLA because other statutes—in 1980, Clean Water Act § 311, 33 U.S.C. § 1321; now, the Oil Pollution Act of 1990, 33 U.S.C. §§ 2701–2753—existed to regulate the clean up of and liability for oil spills. Nevertheless, the petroleum exclusion in CERCLA's definition of "hazardous substances" has been one of the most litigated provisions of CERCLA because it represents a potential defense to CERCLA liability. According to the Third Circuit and the EPA, when does a hazardous substance qualify for the petroleum exclusion? Are *all* petroleum products excluded? Why or why not?

6. **The Rest of the Story**. The Butler Mine Tunnel site was added to CERCLA's National Priorities List for cleanup on July 22, 1987, after a damaging flushout of oil from the tunnel in 1985. At the time that the site was proposed for listing, the EPA described conditions there as follows:

> The Butler Mine Tunnel in Pittston, Luzerne County, Pennsylvania, was originally constructed about 50 years ago as a collection and discharge point for mine drainage from an estimated 5–square-mile area of under-

> ground coal mines. In addition, hazardous materials were disposed in the tunnel, which discharges directly to the Susquehanna River.
>
> On July 30, 1979, an oily discharge coming from the tunnel created an oil slick from bank to bank on the Susquehanna River. EPA tracked the contaminants from this initial discharge 60 miles downstream to a municipal water intake that is the sole source of drinking water for approximately 11,700 residents of Danville, Pennsylvania. The primary source of the contaminants entering the river was traced, via State enforcement actions, to the illegal dumping of hazardous chemicals into a 4–inch borehole 3.5 miles inland from the river. The borehole discharges into the labyrinth of underground mines which the tunnel drains. The State identified as responsible parties the owner of the Hi–Way Auto Service Station where the borehole was located, the president of the waste transporting company, and the dispatcher of the company. All three received jail sentences.
>
> In 1979, EPA emergency personnel responded to the Butler discharge under the Clean Water Act. Booms were installed to collect the oily substances on the surface. They continued to operate until December 5, 1980, collecting 160,000 gallons of oil, which contained approximately 13,000 pounds of dichlorobenzene. After the booms were removed, an automated detection system was installed. The cost of the emergency action was $2.2 million. The State operated the system until 1984, during which time there was no evidence of any discharge from the tunnel.
>
> On October 23, 1981, EPA announced the Interim Priorities List (IPL), which included the Butler Mine Tunnel. The IPL was a preliminary list developed prior to formal proposal of the first NPL. In February 1982, the State indicated that no further response actions were warranted based on monitoring of existing conditions. On December 30, 1982, the first NPL was proposed. Butler Mine Tunnel was not included because EPA had determined that all appropriate Fund-financed cleanup had been completed. Therefore, the Butler Mine Tunnel satisfied one of the criteria for deleting a site from the NPL.
>
> In September 1985, approximately 100,000 gallons of waste oil containing 1 to 3 percent of bis(2–ethylhexyl)phthalate were released at the Butler Mine Tunnel following heavy rains associated with Hurricane Gloria. Once again EPA responded, this time using CERCLA emergency funds. EPA installed booms, is disposing of the collected waste and contaminated soil, and is reinstalling the automatic detection system.

EPA, *National Priorities List (NPL): NPL Site Narrative for Butler Mine Tunnel*, http://www.epa.gov/superfund/sites/npl/nar1414.htm (as updated Aug. 9, 2011). Nevertheless, the CERCLA cleanup process for the Butler Mine Tunnel site is nearly complete. EPA Region 3 has summarized cleanup progress at the site as follows:

> In 1985, approximately 100,000 gallons of waste oil were discharged from the Butler Mine Tunnel, following the heavy rains associated with Hurricane Gloria. EPA once again responded by installing booms on the river and collecting the contaminated oil. The existing monitoring boreholes were sampled, and contaminated vegetation was removed.

> In 1987, the potentially responsible parties (PRPs), under EPA oversight, began an investigation to determine the extent of the contamination and to identify the alternative technologies available for cleanup. The investigation is complete and the Record of Decision was issued in 1996.
>
> A Consent Decree was negotiated with the potentially responsible parties (PRPs) who agreed to implement the clean up remedy identified in the Record of Decision. The PRPs completed the remedial design for cleanup in December 2003.
>
> The remedial action at the site (including construction of anchors and purchasing response materials) was completed in September 2005. During the spring 2007, the PRPs performed a training exercise in the Susquehanna River, to test the elements of the flushout-response system, including mobilization of equipment, and boom deployment. Future activities at the Site will include on-river training exercises, tunnel monitoring, and flushout-response system deployments for actual or potential flush outs.

EPA Region 3, *Mid-Atlantic Superfund: Butler Mine Tunnel*, http://www.epa.gov/reg3hwmd/npl/PAD980508451.htm (as updated June 16, 2011). Many of the documents associated with the site, including the Preliminary Public Health Assessment, are available from EPA Region 3 at http://www.epa.gov/reg3hwmd/super/sites/PAD980508451/index.htm.

* * *

B. PRPS AND CERCLA LIABILITY

1. Reportable Quantities and the Duty of Notification

CERCLA required that within 180 days of its effective date (that is, by June 1981), all facilities storing hazardous substances notify the EPA of their existence, on penalty of $10,000 for failure to report, unless the facility was already operating pursuant to a RCRA permit or was storing and applying pesticides in compliance with the Federal Insecticide, Fungicide, and Rodenticide Act (FIFRA). CERCLA § 103(c), (e), 42 U.S.C. § 9603(c), (e). The EPA could then subject such facilities to recordkeeping and reporting requirements. CERCLA § 103(d), 42 U.S.C. § 9603(d).

At the same time, the EPA was busy promulgating regulations regarding the ***reportable quantity*** of hazardous substances. CERCLA § 102(a), 42 U.S.C. § 9602(a). The reportable quantity is the minimum amount of a given hazardous substance that must be released before CERCLA's requirements apply. Before the EPA's designations of reportable quantities took effect, Congress set statutory default reportable quantities of either one pound or the reportable quantity established under the Clean Water Act's hazardous substance provisions, 33 U.S.C. § 1321(b). CERCLA § 102(b), 42 U.S.C. § 9602(b).

CERCLA liability begins when a facility or vessel releases a hazardous substance in a reportable quantity. The person in charge of the facility or vessel must immediately give notice of the release to the ***National Response Center***, which then notifies all appropriate government agencies, including the Governor of the affected state. CERCLA § 103(a), 42 U.S.C. § 9603(a). Failure to notify is punishable through fines or imprisonment. *Id.* § 103(b), 42 U.S.C. § 9603(b).

After notification of a release, the EPA has two choices. First, under ***section 104***, the EPA itself can respond to the release. 42 U.S.C. § 9604(a). The EPA's response must be consistent with the ***National Contingency Plan* (NCP)**, which "establish[es] procedures and standards for responding to releases of hazardous substances, pollutants, and contaminants * * *." CERCLA § 105(a), 42 U.S.C. § 9605(a). Alternatively, under ***section 106***, the EPA can order the responsible persons to undertake the clean-up in an ***abatement action***. *Id.* § 106(a), 42 U.S.C. § 9606(a).

Either way, responses to the release are either ***removal actions*** or ***remedial actions***. Removal actions are immediate actions taken "to prevent, minimize, or mitigate damage to the public health or welfare or to the environment, which may otherwise result from the release or threat of release," such as measures to restrict access or contain large spills. CERCLA § 101(23), 42 U.S.C. § 9601(23). Remedial actions, in turn, are the actions taken to effect a permanent solution to the release—*i.e.*, the cleanup. CERCLA § 101(24), 42 U.S.C. § 9601(24).

2. Overview of PRPs

The heart of most CERCLA litigation—and most CERCLA controversies—is the Act's liability provision. Section 107 establishes four categories of ***potential responsible parties* (PRPs)**:

(1) the owner or operator of a vessel or a facility,

(2) any person who at the time of disposal of any hazardous substance owned or operated any facility at which such hazardous substances were disposed of,

(3) any person who by contract, agreement, or otherwise arranged for disposal or treatment, or arranged with a transporter for transport for disposal or treatment, of hazardous substances owned or possessed by such person, by any other party or entity, at a facility or incineration vessel owned or operated by another party or entity and containing such hazardous substances, and

(4) any person who accepts or accepted any hazardous substances for transport to disposal or treatment facilities, incineration vessels or sites selected by such person, from which there is a release, or a threatened release which causes the incurrence of response costs, of a hazardous substance * * *.

CERCLA § 107(a), 42 U.S.C. § 9607(a). Moreover, section 107 creates only three general defenses to CERCLA liability:

(1) an act of God;

(2) an act of war; or

(3) an act or omission of a third party other than an employee or agent of the defendant, or than one whose act or omission occurs in connection with a contractual relationship, existing directly or indirectly, with the defendant (except where the sole contractual relationship arises from a published tariff and acceptance for carriage by a common carrier by rail) if the defendant establishes by a preponderance of the evidence that (a) he exercised due care with respect to the hazardous substance concerned, taking into consideration the characteristics of such hazardous substance, in light of all relevant facts and circumstances, and (b) he took precautions against foreseeable acts or omissions of any such third party and the consequences that could foreseeably result from such acts or omissions * * *.

CERCLA § 107(b), 42 U.S.C. § 9607(b).

3. Current Owner or Operator Liability

Under section 107(a), the *current* owner or operator of the site is liable for any release of hazardous substances on the premises, regardless of the time the release occurred or the current owner or operator's fault in causing the release. CERCLA § 107(a)(1), 42 U.S.C. § 9607(a)(1). CERCLA's definitions of "***owner***" and "***operator***" are not very helpful—the owner is the person who owns a facility or vessel, while the operator is the person who operates the facility or vessel. CERCLA § 101(20)(A), 42 U.S.C. § 9601(20)(A). Nevertheless, owners and operators are generally fairly easy to identify.

Certain kinds of property relationships, however, can create ambiguities regarding CERCLA owners and operators. For example, state and local governments can acquire contaminated properties involuntarily, through operation of law, such as through abandonment or tax delinquency. Are they then CERCLA owners, subject to CERCLA liability? Similarly, banks often take mortgages on properties as security for loans, never intending to own or operate the property in the usual sense, even though the bank may acquire a deed to the property as part of the mortgage process. Is the bank then an owner or operator of the property? What happens if the bank has to foreclose in order to protect its interests?

In 1996, Congress amended CERCLA's definition of "owner or operator" to deal with many of these problems. For governments, "[t]he term 'owner or operator' does not include a unit of State or local government which acquired ownership or control involuntarily through bankruptcy, tax delinquency, abandonment, or other circumstances in which the government involuntarily acquires title by virtue of its function as sovereign." CERCLA § 101(20)(D), 42 U.S.C. § 9601(20)(D). Instead, in such cases, "any person who owned, operated, or otherwise controlled activities at such facility immediately 'beforehand' is deemed the owner or operator." CERCLA § 101(20)(A), 42 U.S.C. § 9601(20)(A). However, this exclusion does *not* apply if the state or local government caused or contributed to the release or threatened release of hazardous substances, in which case the government is liable like any other PRP. CERCLA § 101(20)(D), 42 U.S.C. § 9601(20)(D).

As for banks and other creditors, "owner or operator" "does not include a person who, without participating in the management of a vessel or facility, holds indicia of ownership primarily to protect his security interest in the vessel or facility." CERCLA § 101(20)(A), (E)(i), 42 U.S.C. § 9601(20)(A), (E)(i). The definition of "owner or operator" contains an extended definition of "participation in management," which essentially imposes an ***actual participation***—as opposed to ***capacity to control***—test on the security holder's activities. CERCLA § 101(20)(F), 42 U.S.C. § 9601(20)(F). Congress specified the test in order to resolve a split among the federal Courts of Appeal that had confronted this issue. Moreover, the person holding the security interest can foreclose on the property without becoming an owner or operator for CERCLA liability purposes, so long as "the person seeks to sell, re-lease (in the case of a lease finance transaction), or otherwise divest the person of the vessel or facility at the earliest practicable, commercially reasonable time, on commercially reasonable terms, taking into account market conditions and legal and regulatory requirements." CERCLA § 101(20)(E)(ii), 42 U.S.C. § 9601(20)(E)(ii).

One problem that CERCLA does not directly address is the potential ambiguity regarding "owners" and "operators" among parent and subsidiary corporations. The Supreme Court confronted this issue in the following case.

UNITED STATES v. BESTFOODS

524 U.S. 51 (1998).

JUSTICE SOUTER delivered the opinion of the Court.

The United States brought this action for the costs of cleaning up industrial waste generated by a chemical plant. The issue before us, under the Comprehensive Environmental Response, Compensation, and Liability Act of 1980 (CERCLA) is whether a parent corporation that actively participated in, and exercised control over, the operations of a subsidiary may, without more, be held liable as an operator of a polluting facility owned or operated by the subsidiary. We answer no, unless the corporate veil may be pierced. But a corporate parent that actively participated in, and exercised control over, the operations of the facility itself may be held directly liable in its own right as an operator of the facility.

I

In 1980, CERCLA was enacted in response to the serious environmental and health risks posed by industrial pollution. * * * The term "person" is defined in CERCLA to include corporations and other business organizations, *see* 42 U.S.C. § 9601(21), and the term "facility" enjoys a broad and detailed definition as well, *see* § 9601(9). The phrase "owner or operator" is defined only by tautology, however, as "any person owning or operating" a facility, § 9601(20)(A)(ii), and it is this bit of circularity that prompts our review.

II

In 1957, Ott Chemical Co. (Ott I) began manufacturing chemicals at a plant near Muskegon, Michigan, and its intentional and unintentional dumping of hazardous substances significantly polluted the soil and ground water at the site. In 1965, respondent CPC International Inc. incorporated a wholly owned subsidiary to buy Ott I's assets in exchange for CPC stock. The new company, also dubbed Ott Chemical Co. (Ott II), continued chemical manufacturing at the site, and continued to pollute its surroundings. CPC kept the managers of Ott I, including its founder, president, and principal shareholder, Arnold Ott, on board as officers of Ott II. Arnold Ott and several other Ott II officers and directors were also given positions at CPC, and they performed duties for both corporations.

In 1972, CPC sold Ott II to Story Chemical Company, which operated the Muskegon plant until its bankruptcy in 1977. Shortly thereafter, when respondent Michigan Department of Natural Resources (MDNR) examined the site for environmental damage, it found the land littered with thousands of leaking and even exploding drums of waste, and the soil and water saturated with noxious chemicals. MDNR sought a buyer for the property who would be willing to contribute toward its cleanup, and after extensive negotiations, respondent Aerojet–General Corp. arranged for transfer of the site from the Story bankruptcy trustee in 1977. Aerojet created a wholly owned California subsidiary, Cordova Chemical Company (Cordova/California), to purchase the property, and Cordova/California in turn created a wholly owned Michigan subsidiary, Cordova Chemical Company of Michigan (Cordova/Michigan), which manufactured chemicals at the site until 1986.

By 1981, the federal Environmental Protection Agency had undertaken to see the site cleaned up, and its long-term remedial plan called for expenditures well into the tens of millions of dollars. To recover some of that money, the United States filed this action under § 107 in 1989, naming five defendants as responsible parties: CPC, Aerojet, Cordova/California, Cordova/Michigan, and Arnold Ott. (By that time, Ott I and Ott II were defunct.) * * * Because the parties stipulated that the Muskegon plant was a "facility" within the meaning of 42 U.S.C. § 9601(9), that hazardous substances had been released at the facility, and that the United States had incurred reimbursable response costs to clean up the site, the trial focused on the issues of whether CPC and Aerojet, as the parent corporations of Ott II and the Cordova companies, had "owned or operated" the facility within the meaning of § 107(a)(2).

The District Court said that operator liability may attach to a parent corporation both directly, when the parent itself operates the facility, and indirectly, when the corporate veil can be pierced under state law. * * *

* * * [A] divided panel of the Court of Appeals for the Sixth Circuit reversed in part * * *. [In a divided *en banc* decision, the Sixth Circuit held that:]

> "[W]here a parent corporation is sought to be held liable as an operator pursuant to 42 U.S.C. § 9607(a)(2) based upon the extent of its control of its subsidiary which owns the facility, the parent will be liable only when the requirements necessary to pierce the corporate veil [under state law] are met. In other words, . . . whether the parent will be liable as an operator depends upon whether the degree to which it controls its subsidiary and the extent and manner of its involvement with the facility, amount to the abuse of the corporate form that will warrant piercing the corporate veil and disregarding the separate corporate entities of the parent and subsidiary."

[*United States v. Cordova/Michigan*, 113 F.3d 572, 580 (6th Cir. 1997).]

Applying Michigan veil-piercing law, the Court of Appeals decided that neither CPC nor Aerojet was liable for controlling the actions of its subsidiaries, since the parent and subsidiary corporations maintained separate personalities and the parents did not utilize the subsidiary corporate form to perpetrate fraud or subvert justice.

We granted certiorari to resolve a conflict among the Circuits over the extent to which parent corporations may be held liable under CERCLA for operating facilities ostensibly under the control of their subsidiaries. We now vacate and remand.

III

It is a general principle of corporate law deeply "ingrained in our economic and legal systems" that a parent corporation (so-called because of control through ownership of another corporation's stock) is not liable for the acts of its subsidiaries. * * * Although this respect for corporate distinctions when the subsidiary is a polluter has been severely criticized in the literature, nothing in CERCLA purports to reject this bedrock principle, and against this venerable common-law backdrop, the congressional silence is audible. The Government has indeed made no claim that a corporate parent is liable as an owner or an operator under § 107 simply because its subsidiary is subject to liability for owning or operating a polluting facility.

But there is an equally fundamental principle of corporate law, applicable to the parent-subsidiary relationship as well as generally, that the corporate veil may be pierced and the shareholder held liable for the corporation's conduct when, *inter alia,* the corporate form would otherwise be misused to accomplish certain wrongful purposes, most notably fraud, on the shareholder's behalf. Nothing in CERCLA purports to rewrite this well-settled rule, either. * * * The Court of Appeals was accordingly correct in holding that when (but only when) the corporate veil may be pierced, may a parent corporation be charged with derivative CERCLA liability for its subsidiary's actions.

IV

A

If the Act rested liability entirely on ownership of a polluting facility, this opinion might end here; but CERCLA liability may turn on operation as well as ownership, and nothing in the statute's terms bars a parent corporation from direct liability for its own actions in operating a facility owned by its subsidiary. * * * CERCLA's "operator" provision is concerned primarily with direct liability for one's own actions. It is this direct liability that is properly seen as being at issue here.

Under the plain language of the statute, any person who operates a polluting facility is directly liable for the costs of cleaning up the pollution. See 42 U.S.C. § 9607(a)(2). This is so regardless of whether that person is the facility's owner, the owner's parent corporation or business partner, or even a saboteur who sneaks into the facility at night to discharge its poisons out of malice. If any such act of operating a corporate subsidiary's facility is done on behalf of a parent corporation, the existence of the parent-subsidiary relationship under state corporate law is simply irrelevant to the issue of direct liability.

This much is easy to say: the difficulty comes in defining actions sufficient to constitute direct parental "operation." Here of course we may again rue the uselessness of CERCLA's definition of a facility's "operator" as "any person ... operating" the facility, 42 U.S.C. § 9601(20)(A)(ii), which leaves us to do the best we can to give the term its "ordinary or natural meaning." In a mechanical sense, to "operate" ordinarily means "[t]o control the functioning of; run: *operate a sewing machine.*" AMERICAN HERITAGE DICTIONARY 1268 (3d ed. 1992); *see also* WEBSTER'S NEW INTERNATIONAL DICTIONARY 1707 (2d ed. 1958) ("to work; as, to *operate* a machine"). And in the organizational sense more obviously intended by CERCLA, the word ordinarily means "[t]o conduct the affairs of; manage: *operate a business.*" AMERICAN HERITAGE DICTIONARY, *supra,* at 1268; *see also* WEBSTER'S NEW INTERNATIONAL DICTIONARY, *supra,* at 1707 ("to manage"). So, under CERCLA, an operator is simply someone who directs the workings of, manages, or conducts the affairs of a facility. To sharpen the definition for purposes of CERCLA's concern with environmental contamination, an operator must manage, direct, or conduct operations specifically related to pollution, that is, operations having to do with the leakage or disposal of hazardous waste, or decisions about compliance with environmental regulations.

B

With this understanding, we are satisfied that the Court of Appeals correctly rejected the District Court's analysis of direct liability. But we also think that the appeals court erred in limiting direct liability under the statute to a parent's sole or joint venture operation, so as to eliminate any possible finding that CPC is liable as an operator on the facts of this case.

1

By emphasizing that "CPC is directly liable under section 107(a)(2) as an operator because CPC actively participated in and exerted significant control over Ott II's business and decision-making," the District Court applied the "actual control" test of whether the parent "actually operated the business of its subsidiary," as several Circuits have employed it.

The well-taken objection to the actual control test, however, is its fusion of direct and indirect liability; the test is administered by asking a question about the relationship between the two corporations (an issue going to indirect liability) instead of a question about the parent's interaction with the subsidiary's facility (the source of any direct liability). If, however, direct liability for the parent's operation of the facility is to be kept distinct from derivative liability for the subsidiary's own operation, the focus of the enquiry must necessarily be different under the two tests. "The question is not whether the parent operates the subsidiary, but rather whether it operates the facility, and that operation is evidenced by participation in the activities of the facility, not the subsidiary. Control of the subsidiary, if extensive enough, gives rise to indirect liability under piercing doctrine, not direct liability under the statutory language." The District Court was therefore mistaken to rest its analysis on CPC's relationship with Ott II, premising liability on little more than "CPC's 100–percent ownership of Ott II" and "CPC's active participation in, and at times majority control over, Ott II's board of directors." The analysis should instead have rested on the relationship between CPC and the Muskegon facility itself. * * *

NOTES

1. **The Rest of the Story.** According to EPA Region 5:

> The Ott/Story/Cordova site located in Muskegon, Dalton Township, Muskegon County, Michigan, is a former organic chemical production facility that operated under at least three owners from 1957 until 1985 and used as many as five unlined seepage lagoons to dispose of industrial wastewaters and production vessel residues. These practices resulted in contamination of groundwater, soils, and nearby Little Bear Creek and its unnamed tributary. Approximately 10,000 drums of waste material, some of which contained phosgene gas, were also stockpiled onsite. The former production area is approximately 20 acres in size, surrounded by wooded undeveloped land and a semirural residential area with approximately 300 to 500 residents in a one-mile radius of the site.

EPA Region 5, *Region 5 Superfund (SF): Ott/Story/Cordova Chemical Co.*, http://www.epa.gov/R5Super/npl/michigan/MID060174240.htm (as updated Nov. 10, 2011). According to Region 5's updates in November 2011, cleanup at this site is expected to last at least until 2030, and the State of Michigan will bear most of the expense:

> A partial removal was conducted between 1977 and 1979 by the State of Michigan and former site owner Cordova Chemical Co. By that time a

> contaminant plume, containing at least 40 organic chemicals, migrated approximately one mile to the southeast, contaminating the Creek and several private wells. Residents received bottled water until the 1982 installation of a municipal water system by potentially responsible parties in settlement of a citizens' suit. The United States Environmental Protection Agency (U.S. EPA) completed a Remedial Investigation/Feasibility Study and signed a Record of Decision (ROD) on September 29, 1989, for groundwater containment by at least five extraction wells. A second ROD signed on September 29, 1990, requires aquifer restoration by using additional extraction wells and treatment by a Groundwater Treatment Facility (GWTF). On September 27, 1993, U.S. EPA signed a third ROD, selecting Low Temperature Thermal Desorption as the remedy for approximately 10,000 cubic yards of soil and sediment. A ROD Amendment for Creek monitoring and excavation and offsite disposal of approximately 4,000 cubic yards of that soil was signed on February 26, 1998. The soil cleanup was completed under the authority of the State of Michigan. Except for the soil remedy, all cleanup activity has been done under federal and state cost share agreements. The GWTF design was completed on September 29, 1992, which started treating contaminated groundwater on February 24, 1996, and has removed approximately 9800 pounds of contaminants from approximately 4,570,000,000 gallons of groundwater; system operational and functional status was achieved on September 14, 2000. The Long–Term Response Action (LTRA) and Operation & Maintenance (O & M), started on that date, should be completed by September 30, 2030, and also estimates approximately 31,000 pounds of contaminant, removed from approximately 14,500,000,000 gallons of water treated. The soil RA (Operable Unit #3) under the authority of the State of Michigan was completed on March 21, 2002. The State of Michigan should assume 100 percent of the remedy that has been constructed and operating by Spring 2011. Confirmatory sampling was started in 2009 to certify the remedy's effectiveness, to support transfer of the project, and to address remaining outstanding remedy issues.

Id. The 1993 Record of Decision for this site is available at http://www.epa.gov/superfund/sites/rods/fulltext/r0593243.pdf.

After the Supreme Court's decision, in 2000, the U.S. District Court for the Western District of Michigan approved a consent decree negotiated among the United States, the State of Michigan, Aerojet, Cordova Chemical Company, and Cordova Chemical Company of Michigan. *United States v. Cordova Chemical Co. of Michigan*, 2000 WL 1238926 (W.D. Mich. Aug. 24, 2000). Under this consent decree, Aerojet was credited with having spent $2.6 million to remediate contaminated soil at the site, but the decree required it to pay an addition $5.5 million. This represents about 8 percent of the EPA's projected total cleanup costs of $100 million. Nevertheless, the Michigan Court of Appeals had previously held that the State of Michigan would be obligated under its contracts to protect Aeroject from these costs.

In November 2001, the Western District of Michigan found that CPC could not be held liable as an operator of the facility or as a result of corporate successor liability. *See generally Bestfoods v. Aerojet–General Corp.*, 173 F.

Supp. 2d 729 (W.D. Mich. 2001). It applied Michigan's corporations law in reaching these conclusions (see Note 6).

2. **Federal Statutes and State Corporation Law.** What is the relationship between CERCLA and state corporations law, according to the Supreme Court? What does Congress have to do in a federal statute in order to displace state common law?

3. **Parent Corporations as Owners of Subsidiaries' CERCLA Facilities.** When is a parent corporation liable as an *owner* for its subsidiary's releases of hazardous substances, according to the U.S. Supreme Court? How is this liability referred to in corporations law? What is the test for holding a parent corporation liable as an owner for a facility that its subsidiary owns and operates?

4. **Parent Corporations as Operators of Subsidiaries' CERCLA Facilities.** When is a parent corporation liable as an *operator* for releases of hazardous substances at a facility that the subsidiary owns, according to the U.S. Supreme Court? *What* must the parent corporation be operating?

5. **Defining "Operate" for CERCLA.** How did the Supreme Court define "operate"? What tools of statutory interpretation does it use?

6. **The Corporate Form and Piercing the Corporate Veil.** ***Corporations*** are the subject of special law courses in Business Associations or Corporations. In general, however, people form corporations to protect the individual owners—stockholders—from personal liability for the corporation's debts and other kinds of liabilities. In general, as the Supreme Court indicates, CERCLA respects the corporate form, and the EPA will not pursue individual stockholders or the Board of Directors for a corporation's violation of CERCLA. However, if owners misuse the corporate form, such as to accomplish a fraud, state corporations law allows ***piercing of the corporate veil*** so that individual owners or stockholders can be held liable. In the case of parent and subsidiary corporations, piercing the veil of the subsidiary corporation allows the parent corporation to be held liable, as the owner of the subsidiary corporation, for the subsidiary's misdeeds.

As noted, the law governing the formation of corporations and corporate veil piercing is *state* law. One question left after the *Bestfoods* case is whether corporate veil piercing for CERCLA purposes should be judged on a national standard, or whether the applicable state standard should be used. Why might the choice matter? For a recent, thorough review of this issue that nevertheless failed to choose between state and national law, *see New York v. National Service Industries, Inc.*, 460 F.3d 201, 206–09 (2d Cir. 2006).

7. **Owner and Operator Exemptions: Brownfields and Bona Fide Prospective Purchasers.** In 2002, Congress enacted the Small Business Liability Relief and Brownfields Revitalization Act ("the Brownfields Act"), Pub. L. No. 107–118, 115 Stat. 2356 (Jan. 11, 2002), which amended CERCLA § 107(a)(1) owner or operator liability to encourage people to purchase lightly contaminated commercial properties, known as ***brownfields***, and to redevelop them for commercial use. A "***brownfield***," under these amendments, is "real property, the expansion, redevelopment, or reuse of which may be complicated by the presence or potential presence of a hazardous substance,

pollutant, or contaminant." CERCLA § 101(39)(A), 42 U.S.C. § 9601(39)(A). Congress sought to encourage purchases and redevelopments of brownfields by exempting ***bona fide prospective purchasers*** from normal CERCLA "owner or operator" liability. Thus, section 107 now specifies that "[n]otwithstanding subsection (a)(1) of this section, a bona fide prospective purchaser whose potential liability for a release or threatened release is based solely on the purchaser's being considered to be an owner or operator of the facility shall not be liable as long as the bona fide prospective purchaser does not impede the performance of a response action or natural resource restoration." CERCLA § 107(r)(1), 42 U.S.C. § 9607(r)(1). To qualify as a ***bona fide prospective purchaser***, the buyer must establish eight conditions by a preponderance of the evidence, including the facts that "[a]ll disposal of hazardous substances at the facility occurred before the person acquired the facility," "[t]he person made all appropriate inquiries into the previous ownership and uses of the facility," "[t]he person exercises appropriate care with respect to the hazardous substances found at the facility," and the person cooperates with all cleanup actions. CERCLA § 101(40), 42 U.S.C. § 9601(40). In addition, if the United States does not recover all of its response costs from cleaning up the brownfield property, it can put a lien on the property up to the amount of those unrecovered response costs, to the extent that the cleanup increased the value of the former brownfields property. CERCLA § 107(r)(2)–(4), 42 U.S.C. § 9607(r)(2)-(4).

The EPA issued proposed regulations regarding the requirements for "all appropriate inquiry" in August 2004. EPA, Standards and Practices for All Appropriate Inquiry, 69 Fed. Reg. 52,543 (Aug. 26, 2004). Final regulations appeared on November 1, 2005, and took effect on November 1, 2006. EPA, Standards and Practices for All Appropriate Inquiries, 70 Fed. Reg. 66,070 (Nov. 1, 2005).

* * *

4. The Liability of Past Owners and Operators

In addition to designating current owners and operators as PRPs, CERCLA also establishes that "any person who at the time of disposal of any hazardous substance owned or operated any facility at which such hazardous substances were disposed of" is also a PRP. CERCLA § 107(a)(2), 42 U.S.C. § 9607(a)(2). Thus, past owners and operators are liable if they owned or operated the facility at the time when a release occurred. CERCLA's imposition of liability on past owners and operators raises two main issues: (1) the issue of ***retroactive application*** of the statute—that is, the later imposition of liability for conduct that was perfectly legal at the time it occurred; and (2) what it means for an past owner to have been the owner "at the time of disposal."

a. CERCLA's Retroactive Liability

As the Supreme Court has repeatedly declared, in light of due process requirements, there is a presumption against the retroactive application of new statutes. Congress can overcome this presumption, however, if it clearly intends to have the statute apply retroactively. Because CERCLA imposes liability on past owners and operators, federal courts have usually determined that CERCLA applies retroactively. Nevertheless, retroactive application of the Act remains controversial, as the following case demonstrates.

ALLIEDSIGNAL, INC. v. AMCAST INTERNATIONAL CORP.

177 F. Supp. 2d 713 (S.D. Ohio 2001).

RICE, CHIEF JUDGE.

For a number of years, the Plaintiff disposed of waste from a coal tar products plant it operated in an abandoned sand and gravel pit in Ironton, Ohio, known as the Goldcamp Disposal Area ("GDA"). The Defendant, which operated a foundry in Ironton, also dumped wastes into the GDA. After the United States Environmental Protection Agency ("EPA") placed the GDA on the National Priorities List ("NPL"), Plaintiff entered into two agreements with the EPA, under which it agreed to investigate the environmental hazards at the GDA and to clean up that facility. Through December 31, 1994, the Plaintiff had incurred response costs in excess of $12,000,000 to comply with those agreements, and it is estimated that the total cost will be $30,000,000. The Plaintiff brought this action, seeking to recover a portion of the more than $12,000,000 that it had expended through 1994, under §§ 107(a) and 113(f) of the Comprehensive Environmental Response, Compensation and Liability Act of 1980 ("CERCLA"), 42 U.S.C. §§ 9607(a) and 9613(f). In addition, the Plaintiff seeks a declaratory judgment that the Defendant is liable for costs it has incurred since 1994 and that it will incur in the future, as well as prejudgment interest. The Defendant has asserted a counterclaim against the Plaintiff, seeking contribution from the latter, pursuant to § 113(f) of CERCLA. * * *

II. OPINION

In its Complaint, the Plaintiff sets forth a claims under §§ 107(a) and 113(f) of CERCLA, 42 U.S.C. §§ 9607(a) and 9613(f), requesting that the Court order the Defendant to pay for a portion of the expenses it (Plaintiff) had incurred through December 31, 1994. In addition, the Plaintiff requests that the Court enter a Declaratory Judgment, requiring the Defendant to pay a portion of the costs it (Plaintiff) has incurred since the end of 1994 and will incur in the future, and, finally, that the Court award it prejudgment interest. As a protective measure, the Defendant has asserted a counterclaim against the Plaintiff, seeking contribution. To resolve the Plaintiff's claims and Defendant's counterclaim, the Court must address the following categories of issues, to wit: 1) may CERCLA be applied retroactively and is that statute constitutional; 2) is the Plaintiff's claim one for contribution, under § 113(f), or is it entitled to maintain a cost recovery action under § 107(a); 3) is the Defendant liable under CERCLA; 4) for what portion of the expenses Plaintiff had incurred through the trial of this litigation is the Defendant liable; and 5) is the Plaintiff entitled to the requested declaratory relief and/or prejudgment interest? The Court will address those issues in the above order.

A. Retroactive Application and Constitutionality of CERCLA

On September 30, 1996, this Court entered an Order, in which it invited the parties to submit memoranda addressing *United States v. Olin,* 927 F. Supp. 1502 (S.D. Ala. 1996), *reversed,* 107 F.3d 1506 (11th Cir. 1997), in which the District Court had concluded that CERCLA could not be applied retroactively to activity which occurred before its effective date, December 11, 1980, and that Congress had exceeded the authority granted to it by the Commerce Clause, Article I, § 8, Clause 3, of the United States Constitution, when it enacted CERCLA. The parties have submitted their memoranda. * * * Since a conclusion either that CERCLA cannot be applied retroactively or that Congress exceeded the authority granted to it by the Commerce Clause when it enacted that statute would prevent the Court from holding the Defendant liable under that statute, the Court will resolve the two issues addressed in *Olin,* before turning to the merits of the Plaintiff's claim under Cercla. * * *

* * * *1. Retroactivity*

In *Olin,* the District Court noted that all federal courts which had considered the question had concluded that CERCLA could be applied retroactively. Nevertheless, the *Olin* court did not consider those decisions to be persuasive, because those decisions predated *Landgraf v. USI Film Products,* 511 U.S. 244 (1994), which, according to the *Olin* court, "demolishe[d] the interpretive premises on which prior cases had concluded that CERCLA is retroactive." In *Landgraf,* the Supreme Court concluded that the Civil Rights Act of 1991 could not be applied retroactively (*i.e.*, to conduct occurring before its effective date) and set forth the analytical framework which must be followed to determine whether a statute may be applied retroactively:

> When a case implicates a federal statute enacted after the events in suit, the court's first task is to determine whether Congress has expressly prescribed the statute's proper reach. If Congress has done so, of course, there is no need to resort to judicial default rules. When, however, the statute contains no such express command, the court must determine whether the new statute would have retroactive effect, *i.e.*, whether it would impair rights a party possessed when he acted, increase a party's liability for past conduct, or impose new duties with respect to transactions already completed. If the statute would operate retroactively, our traditional presumption teaches that it does not govern absent clear congressional intent favoring such a result.

511 U.S. at 280. When it enacted CERCLA, Congress did not expressly indicate that said statute was to be applied retroactively or that it was not to be so applied. Section 302(a) of CERCLA provides that "[u]nless

otherwise provided, all provisions of this Act shall be effective on the date of the enactment of this Act." 94 Stat. 2767, 2808. In *Landgraf,* the Supreme Court concluded that a provision of the Civil Rights Act of 1991, which contained similar language, did not constitute such an express statement. *Id.* at 257–65. To impose CERCLA liability upon the Defendant in this case would be to give "retroactive effect" to that statute. The GDA was closed in 1977; however, CERCLA did not become effective until December 11, 1980. In other words, the Plaintiff is seeking to impose liability upon the Defendant for conduct which did not violate CERCLA when the latter engaged in it, since that statute was not in effect when the Defendant so acted. *Landgraf,* 511 U.S. at 269–70 (noting that a statute applies retroactively when it "attaches new legal consequences to events completed before its enactment"). Consequently, the Court must apply the presumption against retroactive application "absent clear congressional intent favoring such result." For reasons which follow, the Court concludes that both the text of CERCLA and its legislative history furnish such intent.

The first indication that Congress intended that CERCLA would be applied retroactively is the preamble to that statute, which provides that it is an act "[t]o provide for liability, compensation, cleanup and emergency responses for hazardous substances released into the environment and the cleanup of inactive hazardous waste disposal sites." 94 Stat. 2767. It is not possible "[t]o provide for liability ... for ... the cleanup of inactive hazardous waste disposal sites" without applying Cercla retroactively. A "cleanup" necessarily contemplates action on a site to remediate a condition already in existence. Therefore, if this Court did not so apply that statute, it would be required to deny one of the Congressionally declared purposes of that enactment. The text of CERCLA also lends support to the conclusion that it is to be applied retroactively. For instance, § 107(a) of CERCLA, 42 U.S.C. § 9607(a), imposes liability upon responsible parties for three types of costs, to wit: removal and remedial actions, other necessary response costs and damages to natural resources. However, in § 107(f) of that statute, Congress expressly prohibited the imposition of liability for damages to natural resources "where such damages and the release of a hazardous substance from which such damages resulted have occurred wholly before the enactment of this Act." 94 Stat. 2767, 2783. If Congress had not intended that liability for the remaining costs, *i.e.*, removal and remedial actions and for other response costs, to be imposed for conduct occurring before the effective date of CERCLA, it would have not been necessary to create an exemption for liability for damage to natural resources based upon conduct occurring before that date. Several other courts have relied upon the negative implication of the exemption contained in § 107(f) in order to conclude that Congress clearly intended that CERCLA would be applied retroactively. In addition, § 107(a), which is the provision of CERCLA under which liability is imposed upon responsible parties, is phrased in the past tense. *See* 42 U.S.C. § 9607(a)(2) (imposing liability upon any person "who at the time of disposal of any hazardous substance owned or operated any facility into which hazardous substances were disposed of"); *id.* at § 9607(a)(3) (imposing liability upon any person who "arranged" for the transportation or disposal of any hazardous substances); *id.* at § 9607(a)(4) (imposing liability upon person who accepts or "accepted" hazardous waste for disposal). After *Landgraf,* other courts have found that the use of the past tense in this key provision of CERCLA demonstrates clear Congressional intent that such statute is to be applied retroactively. Additionally, the Eleventh Circuit, when it reversed the District Court's decision in *Olin,* noted that § 103(c) of CERCLA, 42 U.S.C. § 9603(c), required any person, who owned or operated a facility at the time when hazardous substances had been disposed of, to notify the EPA within 180 days of the effective date of CERCLA. The Eleventh Circuit concluded that § 103(c) addressed conduct that had occurred before the enactment of that statute and that, therefore, Congress had intended that statute to be applied retroactively.

In addition to the text of CERCLA, its legislative history is indicative of clear Congressional intent that the statute should be applied retroactively. CERCLA was enacted to fill a gap left by the Resource Conservation and Recovery Act of 1976 ("RCRA"), 42 U.S.C. § 6901 *et seq.,* a statute, the purpose of which is to prevent future harm, rather than to remediate that which has occurred in the past. H. REP. 96–106, Part I, at 17, *reprinted in,* 1980 U.S.C.C.A.N. 6119, 6120. Rather than focusing on the future, CERCLA looks to the past. That statute addresses what the House Report called the "tragic consequences" of the "inactive hazardous waste site problem." *Id.* To address that problem, CERCLA directs the Administrator of the EPA to take emergency actions with respect to such sites and creates a federal, strict liability cause of action "to enable the Administrator to pursue rapid recovery of costs incurred for the costs of such actions undertaken by him from the persons liable therefor and to induce such persons voluntarily to pursue appropriate environmental response actions with respect to inactive hazardous waste sites." *Id.* It is simply not possible to fulfill the second purpose identified by the House Report (*i.e.,* allowing the government to recover the costs it has incurred to remediate inactive hazardous waste sites from the persons responsible), unless CERCLA is applied retroactively (*i.e.,* to conduct which occurred before its effective date). In short, use of the term "inactive hazardous waste sites" presupposes a site which at a prior point in time, *i.e.,* prior to the enactment of the legislation, was active by being utilized for disposal.

In sum, this Court agrees with the overwhelming majority of federal courts, including the Eleventh Circuit in *Olin,* which have concluded, both before and after *Landgraf,* that Congress clearly intended that CERCLA be applied so as to impose liability for conduct which occurred before December 11, 1980, the effective date of that statute. Accordingly, the Court holds that the Defendant can be liable herein, despite the fact that its actions, upon which liability would be predicated, occurred before CERCLA was enacted.

2. Constitutionality of CERCLA

The District Court in *Olin,* relying upon *United States v. Lopez,* 514 U.S. 549 (1995), also concluded that CERCLA violates the Commerce Clause, Article I, § 8, Clause 3, of the United States Constitution. In *Lopez,* the Supreme Court concluded that, by enacting the Gun–Free School Zones Act of 1990, 18 U.S.C. § 922(q)(1)(A), Congress had exceeded the authority bestowed upon it by the Commerce Clause. The *Lopez* Court summarized the Supreme Court's Commerce Clause jurisprudence by restating the "three broad categories of activity that Congress may regulate under its commerce power:"

> First, Congress may regulate the use of the channels of interstate commerce.... Second, Congress is empowered to regulate and protect the instrumentalities of interstate commerce, or persons or things in interstate commerce, even though the threat may come only from intrastate activities.... Finally, Congress' commerce authority includes the power to regulate those activities having a substantial relation to interstate commerce, ... *i.e.*, those activities that substantially affect interstate commerce.

Id. at 558–59 (citations omitted). * * *

Herein, the Court need not consider whether CERCLA regulates the channels of interstate commerce, the instrumentalities of interstate commerce, or persons or things in interstate commerce. Rather, for reasons which follow, the Court concludes that CERCLA regulates activities that substantially affect interstate commerce. Before engaging in this analysis, the Court believes that it is appropriate to set forth certain principles which inform that analytical framework. In the context of a challenge to a statute on the basis that, by enacting it, Congress exceeded the powers granted to it by the Commerce Clause, the Supreme Court has said that "[i]t is established beyond peradventure that legislative Acts adjusting the burdens and benefits of economic life come to [a court] with a presumption of constitutionality...." In addition, the issue to resolve is whether Congress had a rational basis for believing that the activity regulated by CERCLA substantially affects interstate commerce. Lastly, in the wake of *Lopez,* the Sixth Circuit has sounded the cautionary note that "the history of Commerce Clause jurisprudence 'still counsels great restraint.' "

In *Olin,* the District Court concluded that the activity regulated by CERCLA did not substantially affect interstate commerce, because that statute did not regulate economic activity. Rather, since the case before it was a proposed consent decree which would have provided for the remediation of a closed landfill, that court concluded that CERCLA related strictly to real estate, the regulation of which was traditionally left to the states. Like every court which has subsequently considered the question, this Court disagrees with the analysis employed and the conclusion reached by the District Court in *Olin.* The fact that environmental legislation enacted by Congress impacts upon the use of land does not mean that said statute violates the Commerce Clause. * * * Accordingly, the Court turns to the question of whether the disposal of hazardous substances affects interstate commerce.

An important purpose of CERCLA is to protect groundwater from contamination caused by inactive, hazardous waste sites. 42 U.S.C. § 9618 (high priority shall be given to cleaning up hazardous waste sites from which the release of hazardous substances has contaminated or threatens to contaminate groundwater). *See also* H. REP. 96–1016, Part I, at 18, *reprinted in*, 1980 U.S.C.C.A.N. 6119, 6122 (noting the harm that inactive landfills have caused to groundwater, rendering local water supplies unusable). The Supreme Court has recognized that groundwater is an article of interstate commerce. Certainly, Congress could have rationally believed that the number of inactive waste sites, leaking hazardous substances into the groundwater, would affect the quality of a product that moved in interstate commerce. In addition, the Eleventh Circuit concluded that CERCLA regulates activity that substantially affects interstate commerce, since the growth of the chemical industry, coupled with the concomitant increased disposal of the waste that it generated, had caused significant harm to a number of interstate industries, such as agriculture and fishing.

Based upon the foregoing, the Court concludes that Congress did not exceed its power under the Commerce Clause when it enacted CERCLA.

[The liability aspect of this case will be examined in part III.E.]

NOTES

1. **The *Landgraf* Test for Retroactivity.** What test has the U.S. Supreme Court established to determine whether federal statutes may be applied retroactively?

2. **CERCLA's Retroactivity.** Why did the district court in *Olin* decide that CERCLA failed the *Landgraf* test? Why did the Southern District of Ohio disagree?

The Southern District of Ohio is in the decided majority of courts, both pre-and post-*Landgraf*, that have determined that CERCLA liability for response costs (cleanup costs) applies retroactively. *See United States v. Olin Corp.*, 107 F.3d 1506, 1511–15 (11th Cir. 1997); *Virginia Properties, Inc. v. Home Insurance Co.*, 74 F.3d 1131, 1132 (11th Cir. 1996); *Velsicol Chemical Corp. v. Enenco, Inc.*, 9 F.3d 524, 528–30 (6th Cir. 1993); *United States v. Monsanto*, 858 F.2d 160, 174 (4th Cir. 1988); *United States v. Northeastern Pharmaceutical & Chemical Co.*, 810 F.2d 726, 732–34 (8th Cir. 1986); *Combined Properties/Greenbriar Ltd. Partnership v. Morrow*, 58 F. Supp. 2d 675, 676–77 (E.D. Va. 1999); *In re Tutu Wells Contamination Litigation*, 994 F.Supp. 638, 660–61 (D.V.I. 1998); *Raytheon Co. v. McGraw–Edison Co.*, 979 F.Supp. 858, 863–64 (E.D. Wis. 1997); *Continental Title Co. v. Peoples Gas Light & Coke Co.*, 959 F.Supp. 893, 893–901 (N.D. Ill. 1997); *The Ninth Avenue Remedial Group v. Fiberbond Corp.*, 946 F.Supp. 651, 651–64 (N.D. Ind. 1996); *Nova Chems., Inc. v. GAF Corp.*, 945 F.Supp. 1098, 1100–05 (E.D. Tenn. 1996); *Gould Inc. v. A & M Battery & Tire Service*, 933 F.Supp. 431,

438 (M.D. Pa. 1996); *Matter of Reading Co.*, 900 F.Supp. 738, 742 (E.D. Pa. 1995); *New York v. SCA Services, Inc.*, 785 F.Supp. 1154, 1157 (S.D.N.Y. 1992); *United States v. Sharon Steel Corp.*, 681 F.Supp. 1492, 1495–96 (D. Utah 1987).

3. **CERCLA Retroactivity and Natural Resources Damages.** As the Southern District of Ohio noted, CERCLA's natural resource damages provision states that there "shall be no recovery [of natural resource damages] where such damages and the release of a hazardous substance from which such damages resulted have occurred wholly before December 11, 1980" (CERCLA's effective date). CERCLA § 107(f)(1), 42 U.S.C. § 9607(f)(1). Given the *Landgraf* analysis and the discussion above, is PRP liability for natural resource damages also retroactive? Why or why not? *See United States v. Olin Corp.*, 107 F.3d 1506, 1513 (11th Cir. 1997); *Artesian Water Co. v. Government of New Castle County*, 851 F.2d 643, 650 (3rd Cir. 1988); *Montana v. Atlantic Richfield Co.*, 266 F. Supp. 2d 1238, 1242, 1244 (D. Mont. 2003); *Continental Title Co. v. Peoples Gas Light & Coke Co.*, 959 F.Supp. 893, 895–96 (N.D. Ill. 1997); *The Ninth Ave. Remedial Group v. Fiberbond Corp.*, 946 F.Supp. 651, 659 (N.D. Ind. 1996); *Nova Chemicals, Inc. v. GAF Corp.*, 945 F.Supp. 1098, 1101 (E.D. Tenn. 1996); *Nevada Dep't of Transportation v. United States*, 925 F.Supp. 691, 694–95 (D. Nev. 1996); *Idaho v. Bunker Hill Co.*, 635 F.Supp. 665, 674 (D. Idaho 1986).

4. **CERCLA's Commerce Clause Constitutionality.** Why did the Southern District of Ohio determine that CERCLA was within Congress's Commerce Clause authority? What analysis did it use?

5. **Other Possible Constitutional Issues.** As noted, retroactive application of statutes inherently raises due process concerns. In addition, in *Eastern Enterprises v. Apfel*, 524 U.S. 498 (1998), four Justices of the Supreme Court concluded that the retroactive provisions of the Coal Industry Retiree Health Benefit Act of 1992 violated the Takings Clause of the Fifth Amendment. Nevertheless, federal courts addressing these two constitutional issues—due process and takings—in the context of CERCLA have nearly unanimously upheld CERCLA as constitutional. *See, e.g.*, *Franklin County Convention Facilities Authority v. American Premier Underwriters, Inc.*, 240 F.3d 534, 552–53 (6th Cir. 2001); *United States v. Dico*, 266 F.3d 864, 880 (8th Cir. 2001); *United States v. Manzo*, 182 F. Supp. 2d 385, 407–08 (D.N.J. 2000); *United States v. Alcan Aluminum Corp.*, 49 F. Supp. 2d 96, 99–101 (N.D.N.Y. 1999); *United States v. Vertac Chemical Corp.*, 33 F. Supp. 2d 769, 784–85 (E.D. Ark. 1998); *United States v. Rohm & Haas Co.*, 939 F.Supp. 1142, 1152 (D.N.J. 1996); *American Color & Chemical Corp. v. Tenneco Polymers, Inc.*, 918 F.Supp. 945, 960 (D.S.C. 1995); *United States v. Shell Oil Co.*, 841 F.Supp. 962, 974 (C.D. Cal. 1993), *aff'd* 281 F.3d 812 (9th Cir. 2002), *opinion superseded on other grounds*, 294 F.3d 1045 (9th Cir. 2002); *United States v. Iron Mountain Mines, Inc.*, 812 F.Supp. 1528, 1544–45 (E.D. Cal. 1992); *United States v. Kramer*, 757 F.Supp. 397, 429–31 (D.N.J. 1991); *Kelley v. Thomas Solvent Co.*, 714 F.Supp. 1439, 1443–45 (W.D. Mich. 1989); *United States v. Hooker Chemicals & Plastics Corp.*, 680 F.Supp. 546, 556–57 (W.D.N.Y. 1988); *United States v. Dickerson*, 640 F.Supp. 448, 451 (D. Md. 1986); *United States v. Ottati & Goss, Inc.*, 630 F.Supp. 1361, 1397–99

(D.N.H. 1985); *United States v. Conservation Chemical Co.*, 619 F.Supp. 162, 218–22 (D. Mo. 1985); *United States v. Shell Oil Co.*, 605 F.Supp. 1064, 1069–73 (D. Colo. 1985); *United States v. South Carolina Recycling & Disposal, Inc.*, 653 F.Supp. 984, 997–98 (D.S.C. 1984); *State ex rel. Brown v. Georgeoff*, 562 F.Supp. 1300, 1306–12 (D. Ohio 1983).

6. **The Rest of the Story.** The Goldcamp Disposal Area at issue in the main case was part of a larger and more complex CERCLA site. As EPA Region 5 has explained:

> The 95–acre Allied Chemical and Ironton Coke site lies on the banks of the Ohio River near the point where the Ohio, Kentucky and West Virginia borders converge. The facility produced a number of products during its 83–year history including crude tar, coke, light oil, ammonia, creosote, pitch and naphthalene. The result of operations and waste disposal practices was extensive contamination of soil and ground water, sediment (mud) in nearby Ice Creek and Ohio River. The site was placed on EPA's National Priorities List in 1983.
>
> The site actually is made up of three distinct cleanup areas, referred to as operable units. They are the former tar plant, a former disposal area for tar plant waste and foundry sand called the Goldcamp Disposal Area, and the former coke plant and waste lagoons. *With the exception of ground water monitoring and routine maintenance, the Goldcamp Disposal Area, former coke plant and waste lagoons have been cleaned up.* A portion of the land formerly occupied by the coke plant has been redeveloped into a maintenance facility for Ohio Department of Transportation.

EPA Region 5, *Region 5 Cleanup Sites: Background*, http://www.epa.gov/region5/cleanup/alliedchemical/background.htm (as updated Aug. 3, 2011) (emphasis added).

The last area requiring cleanup is the site of the former tar plant, which ceased operations in 2000. In August 2003, the EPA and Honeywell International (the owner of the property) signed an Administrative Order on Consent requiring Honeywell to complete a site investigation. The EPA issued its final cleanup decision in August 2007, *see* http://www.epa.gov/region5/cleanup/alliedchemical/pdfs/rod200709.pdf, and the cleanup plan will address contamination of the soils, sediment, and air. A list of contaminants of concern for the site is available at http://cfpub.epa.gov/supercpad/SiteProfiles/index.cfm?fuseaction=second.contams&id=0504336.

Pursuant to a settlement announced on March 31, 2010, Honeywell International is responsible for the cleanup of the tar plant site, a settlement worth about $10 million, according to the U.S. Department of Justice. Through settlements with Honeywell and other parties, the United States secured over $75 million total in cleanup work at the three cleanup areas. The Department of Justice's press release regarding the settlement is available at http://www.justice.gov/opa/pr/2010/March/10–enrd–351.html.

* * *

b. *Ownership or Operation "at the Time of Disposal"*

CARSON HARBOR VILLAGE, LTD. v. UNOCAL CORPORATION

270 F.3d 863 (9th Cir. 2001) (*en banc*).

MCKEOWN, CIRCUIT JUDGE:

This appeal stems from the environmental cleanup of a contaminated wetlands site used originally for petroleum production and later as a mobile home park. The current property owner, Carson Harbor Village, Ltd. ("Carson Harbor"), brought suit principally under the Comprehensive Environmental Response, Compensation, and Liability Act ("CERCLA"), 42 U.S.C. § 9601 *et seq.,* for reimbursement of costs associated with the cleanup. We are called upon to determine whether, as a matter of law, * * * certain of the defendants are "potentially responsible parties" ("PRPs") under CERCLA § 107(a), 42 U.S.C. § 9607(a).

* * * Parsing the meaning of the term "disposal" in § 9607(a)(2) lies at the heart of ["whether defendants Carson Harbor Village Mobile Home Park, Richard G. Braley, and Walker Smith, Jr. (the 'Partnership Defendants') are PRPs; if not, summary judgment was ... appropriate."] We conclude that the migration of contaminants on the property does not fall within the statutory definition of "disposal." Thus, in the CERCLA claim, we affirm the district court's grant of summary judgment for the Partnership Defendants.

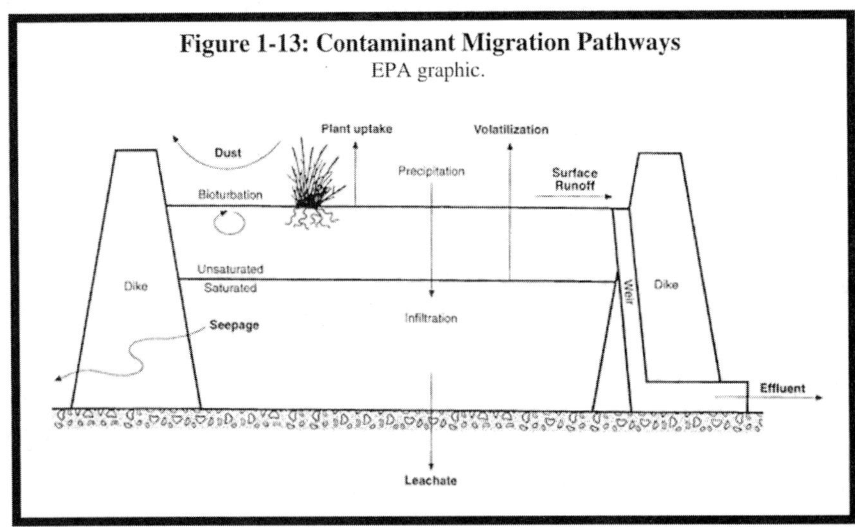

Figure 1-13: Contaminant Migration Pathways
EPA graphic.

* * * BACKGROUND

Carson Harbor owns and operates a mobile home park on seventy acres in the City of Carson, California. From 1977 until 1983, prior to Carson Harbor's ownership, defendant Carson Harbor Village Mobile Home Park, a general partnership controlled by defendants Braley and

Smith (the "Partnership Defendants"), owned the property. They, like Carson Harbor, operated a mobile home park on the property. Beginning over thirty years earlier, however, from 1945 until 1983, Unocal Corporation held a leasehold interest in the property and used it for petroleum production, operating a number of oil wells, pipelines, above-ground storage tanks, and production facilities.

* * * While attempting to refinance the property in 1993, Carson Harbor discovered hazardous substances on the site. The prospective lender commissioned an environmental assessment, which revealed tar-like and slag materials in the wetlands area of the property. Subsequent investigation revealed that the materials were a waste or by-product of petroleum production and that they had been on the property for several decades prior to its development as a mobile home park.

* * * As required by law, Carson Harbor's environmental consultants reported their findings to the appropriate agencies. * * *

The tar-like and slag materials were removed from the property in 1995. Over the course of five days, 1,042 tons of material were removed. * * *

In 1997, Carson Harbor brought suit against the Partnership Defendants, the Government Defendants, and Unocal seeking relief under * * * CERCLA * * *. Carson Harbor sought to recover the costs of its cleanup (which totaled approximately $285,000) as well as damages arising from its inability to refinance the property. According to Carson Harbor, Unocal is responsible for dumping the tar-like and slag materials on the property; the Partnership Defendants are liable as past owners of the property; and the Government Defendants and Caltrans are liable for lead on the property that resulted from lead-contaminated storm water runoff, which may have contributed either to the lead found in the tar-like and slag materials or the elevated lead levels outside those materials.

The parties * * * cross-moved for summary judgment * * *. [W]ith respect to the Partnership Defendants, the district court held that they were not PRPs within the meaning of 42 U.S.C. § 9607(a)(2) because "disposal warranting CERCLA liability requires a showing that hazardous substances were affirmatively introduced into the environment." *Id.* at 1195. * * *

* * * Carson Harbor appealed the district court's rulings on the CERCLA claim * * *. Following the issuance of a panel opinion, we agreed to hear this case *en banc*.

DISCUSSION

We review de novo the district court's grant of summary judgment. Similarly, "[t]he district court's interpretation of a statute is a question of law which we review *de novo*."

I. CERCLA OVERVIEW

CERCLA "generally imposes strict liability on owners and operators of facilities at which hazardous substances were disposed." To achieve that end, CERCLA "authorizes private parties to institute civil actions to recover the costs involved in the cleanup of hazardous wastes from those responsible for their creation."

To prevail in a private cost recovery action, a plaintiff must establish that (1) the site on which the hazardous substances are contained is a "facility" under CERCLA's definition of that term, Section 101(9), 42 U.S.C. § 9601(9); (2) a "release" or "threatened release" of any "hazardous substance" from the facility has occurred, 42 U.S.C. § 9607(a)(4); (3) such "release" or "threatened release" has caused the plaintiff to incur response costs that were "necessary" and "consistent with the national contingency plan," 42 U.S.C. §§ 9607(a)(4) and (a)(4)(B); and (4) the defendant is within one of four classes of persons subject to the liability provisions of Section 107(a).

The * * * fourth of these elements [is] at issue here.

With respect to th[at] fourth element, 42 U.S.C. § 9607(a) sets out the "four classes of persons subject to the liability provisions." *Id.* Those persons are "potentially responsible parties" or "PRPs." We must decide in this case whether the Partnership Defendants fit within the second PRP category; namely, whether they owned the contaminated property "at the time of disposal of any hazardous substance." 42 U.S.C. § 9607(a)(2).

* * * III. THE CONTAMINANT MIGRATION AT ISSUE HERE IS NOT A DISPOSAL UNDER CERCLA

* * * To determine whether the Partnership Defendants are PRPs, we must decide whether there was a "disposal" during their ownership of the property. This inquiry rests on our interpretation of the statutory definition of "disposal." Based upon the plain meaning of the statute, we conclude that there was no disposal during the Partnership Defendants' ownership. Therefore, they are not PRPs, and they are not subject to liability. Accordingly, the district court did not err in granting summary judgment in their favor on the CERCLA issue.

A. *PRPs, The Meaning of "Disposal," and Circuit Court Interpretations*

Section 9607(a), which sets out the four PRP categories, provides:

(1) the owner and operator of a vessel or a facility,

(2) any person who *at the time of disposal* of any hazardous substance owned or operated any facility at which such hazardous substances were disposed of,

(3) any person who by contract, agreement, or otherwise arranged for disposal or treatment, or arranged with a transporter for transport for disposal or treatment, of hazardous substances owned or

possessed by such person, by any other party or entity, at any facility or incineration vessel owned or operated by another party or entity and containing such hazardous substances, and

(4) any person who accepts or accepted any hazardous substances for transport to disposal or treatment facilities, incineration vessels or sites selected by such person, from which there is a release, or a threatened release which causes the incurrence of response costs, of a hazardous substance, shall be liable. . . .

42 U.S.C. § 9607(a) (emphasis added). Carson Harbor argues that the Partnership Defendants fit within the second PRP category as owners of the property "at the time of disposal" under § 9607(a)(2).

CERCLA defines "disposal" for purposes of § 9607(a) with reference to the definition of "disposal" in RCRA, *see* 42 U.S.C. § 9601(29), which in turn defines "disposal" as follows:

> The term "disposal" means the *discharge, deposit, injection, dumping, spilling, leaking, or placing* of any solid waste or hazardous waste into or on any land or water so that such solid waste or hazardous waste or any constituent thereof may enter the environment or be emitted into the air or discharged into any waters, including ground waters.

42 U.S.C. § 6903(3) (emphasis added). Under this definition, for the Partnership Defendants to be PRPs, there must have been a "discharge, deposit, injection, dumping, spilling, leaking, or placing" of contaminants on the property during their ownership. *Id.*

Although we have previously concluded that RCRA's definition of "disposal" is "clear," whether the definition includes passive soil migration is an issue of first impression in this circuit. Other circuit courts have taken a variety of approaches. * * *

The first circuit court to face the question was the Fourth Circuit in *Nurad*[*, Inc. v. William E. Hooper & Sons Co.*, 966 F.2d 837 (4th Cir. 1992)]. There, the court addressed whether leaking from underground storage tanks is a "disposal." 966 F.2d at 844–46. The current owner brought suit against two prior owners for reimbursement costs under CERCLA, claiming that the past owners were PRPs under § 9607(a)(2). *Id.* at 840. The court rejected the "active-only" approach. * * * The Fourth Circuit concluded "that § 9607(a)(2) imposes liability not only for active involvement in the 'dumping' or 'placing' of hazardous waste at the facility, but for ownership of the facility at a time that hazardous waste was 'spilling' or 'leaking.' " *Id.* at 846; *accord Crofton Ventures Ltd. P'ship v. G & H P'ship*, 258 F.3d 292, 300 (4th Cir. 2001) (holding that, "[g]iven the breadth of the statutory definition of 'disposal,' the district court must be able to conclude that the buried drums did not leak" when the defendants owned or operated the facility "to make a finding that [they] were not liable under § 9607(a)(2)").

Four years later, in [*United States v.*] *CDMG Realty,* [96 F.3d 706 (3rd Cir. 1996),] the Third Circuit addressed whether the spread of contamination within a landfill is a "disposal." 96 F.3d at 710. There, as in *Nurad,* the current owner of contaminated property sought contribution from the prior owner, asserting that the prior owner was a PRP under § 9607(a)(2). *Id.* The Third Circuit held, based on the plain meaning of the words used to define "disposal" and the structure and purposes of CERCLA, *see id.* at 714–18, that "the passive migration of contamination dumped in the land prior to [the past owner's] ownership does not constitute disposal," *id.* at 711. The court specifically declined, however, "to reach the question whether the movement of contaminants unaided by human conduct can ever constitute 'disposal,' " *id.,* concluding that "[w]hile 'leaking' and 'spilling' may not require affirmative human conduct, neither word denotes the gradual spreading of contamination alleged here." *Id.* at 714.

The next year, the Second Circuit, in *ABB Industrial Systems,* [*Inc. v. Prime Tech., Inc.,* 120 F.3d 351 (2d Cir. 1997),] similarly addressed whether a current owner could recover cleanup costs under § 9607(a)(2) from several companies that had previously controlled the property. 120 F.3d at 353. As in *CDMG Realty,* the Second Circuit addressed whether there was a "disposal" where hazardous chemicals "continued to gradually spread underground" while the defendants controlled the property. *Id.* at 357. The Second Circuit, relying on the Third Circuit's analysis of CERCLA's language, structure, and purposes in *CDMG Realty,* affirmed the district court's grant of summary judgment to the defendants, holding "that prior owners and operators of a site are not liable under CERCLA for mere passive migration." *Id.* at 359. The Second Circuit, however, "express[ed] no opinion" on whether "prior owners are liable if they acquired a site with leaking barrels [and] the prior owner's actions are purely passive." *Id.* at 358 n. 3.

In [*United States v.*] *150 Acres of Land,* [204 F.3d 698 (6th Cir. 2000),] the Sixth Circuit interpreted "disposal" for purposes of the "innocent landowner" defense. 204 F.3d at 704–05. In that context, the Sixth Circuit explicitly required active conduct for a "disposal." *See id.* at 706. The court concluded that the current owners, whose status as PRPs arises under § 9607(a)(1), acquired the property after the "disposal" under § 9601(35), because there is no "disposal" "[i]n the absence of any evidence that there was human activity involved in whatever movement of hazardous substances occurred on the property since [the current owners] have owned it." *Id.; see also Bob's Beverage, Inc. v. Acme, Inc.,* 264 F.3d 692, 697–98 (6th Cir. 2001).

In sum, although all of the cases reference the active/passive distinction in some manner, there is no clear dichotomy among the cases that have interpreted "disposal." Rather, the cases fall in a continuum, with the Sixth Circuit taking an "active-only" approach in *150 Acres of Land;* the Third Circuit, in *CDMG Realty,* and the Second Circuit, in *ABB Industrial Systems,* addressing only the spread of contamination (and leaving open whether migration must always be "active" to be a "disposal"); and, finally, the Fourth Circuit in *Nurad,* concluding that "disposal" includes passive migration, at least in the context of leaking underground storage tanks.

We have not addressed whether "disposal" in § 9607(a) includes the passive movement of contamination. We have held, however, that the movement of contamination that *does* result from human conduct is a "disposal." *See Kaiser Aluminum & Chem. Corp.,* 976 F.2d at 1342 (holding that "disposal" under § 9607(a)(2) includes a party's movement and spreading of contaminated soil to uncontaminated portions of property and that "Congress did not limit ['disposal'] to the initial introduction of hazardous material onto property"). In another context, we have held that "disposal" refers "only to an affirmative act of discarding a substance as waste, and not to the productive use of the substance." *3550 Stevens Creek Assocs.,* 915 F.2d at 1362 (concluding that there was no "disposal" of asbestos in a building when it was installed for use as insulation and fire retardant). We have also held that the definition of "disposal" is the same under § 9607(a)(2) and § 9607(a)(3).

B. Statutory Construction

When interpreting a statute, "[o]ur task is to construe what Congress has enacted." *Duncan v. Walker,* 533 U.S. 167 (2001). "[W]e look first to the plain language of the statute, construing the provisions of the entire law, including its object and policy, to ascertain the intent of Congress." *Northwest Forest Res. Council v. Glickman,* 82 F.3d 825, 830 (9th Cir. 1996) (internal quotation marks and citation omitted). We will resort to legislative history, even where the plain language is unambiguous, "where the legislative history clearly indicates that Congress meant something other than what it said." *Perlman v. Catapult Entm't, Inc. (In re Catapult Entm't, Inc.),* 165 F.3d 747, 753 (9th Cir. 1999). The plain meaning of the terms used to define "disposal" compels the conclusion that there was no "disposal" during the Partnership Defendants' ownership, because the movement of the contamination, even if it occurred during their ownership, cannot be characterized as a "discharge, deposit, injection, dumping, spilling, leaking, or placing." 42 U.S.C. § 6903(3). This approach is consistent with CERCLA's purposes, minimizes internal inconsistency in the statute, and presents no conflict with CERCLA's legislative history.

1. Plain Meaning

"We begin, as always, with the language of the statute." *Duncan,* 121 S.Ct. at 2124; *accord Perlman,* 165 F.3d at 750. In examining the statutory language, we follow the Supreme Court's instruction and adhere to the "Plain Meaning Rule":

> It is elementary that the meaning of a statute must, in the first instance, be sought in the language in which the act is framed, and if that is plain, ... the sole function of the courts is to enforce it according to its terms.

> Where the language is plain and admits of no more than one meaning the duty of interpretation does not arise, and the rules which are to aid doubtful meanings need no discussion.

Caminetti v. United States, 242 U.S. 470, 485 (1917) (citations omitted); *accord Negonsott v. Samuels,* 507 U.S. 99, 104–05 (1993).

"When a statute includes an explicit definition, [however,] we must follow that definition, even if it varies from that term's ordinary meaning." *Stenberg v. Carhart,* 530 U.S. 914, 942 (2000). Therefore, we return to the definition of "disposal." Under § 6903(3), there is a "disposal" when there has been a

- discharge,
- deposit,
- injection,
- dumping,
- spilling,
- leaking, or
- placing

of solid or hazardous wastes on the property. 42 U.S.C. § 6903(3). CERCLA does not define these terms, but we gain some insight into their statutory meaning by examining CERCLA's definition of "release," which includes some of the words used to define "disposal," as well as the word "disposing":

> The term "release" means any *spilling, leaking, pumping, pouring, emitting, emptying, discharging, injecting, escaping, leaching, dumping, or disposing* into the environment (including the abandonment or discarding of barrels, containers, and other closed receptacles containing any hazardous substance or pollutant or contaminant)....

42 U.S.C. § 9601(22) (emphasis added).

"We must presume that words used more than once in the same statute have the same meaning." *Boise Cascade Corp. v. United States Envtl. Prot. Agency,* 942 F.2d 1427, 1432 (9th Cir. 1991). Therefore, from these definitions, we can conclude that "release" is broader than "disposal," because the definition of "release" includes "disposing" (also, it includes "passive" terms such as "leaching" and "escaping," which are not included in the definition of "disposal"). But, at the same time, the definitions of "disposal" and "release" have several words in common: "discharge"/"discharging"; "injection"/"injecting"; "dumping"; "spilling"; and "leaking."

We thus focus on the plain meanings of the terms used to define "disposal." We first note that one can find both "active" *and* "passive" definitions for nearly all of these terms in any standard dictionary. We therefore reject the absolute binary "active/passive" distinction used by some courts. * * *

Instead of focusing solely on whether the terms are "active" or "passive," we must examine each of the terms in relation to the facts of the case and determine whether the movement of contaminants is, under the plain meaning of the terms, a "disposal." Put otherwise, do any of the terms fit the hazardous substance contamination at issue?

Examining the facts of this case, we hold that the gradual passive migration of contamination through the soil that allegedly took place during the Partnership Defendants' ownership was not a "discharge, deposit, injection, dumping, spilling, leaking, or placing" and, therefore, was not a "disposal" within the meaning of § 9607(a)(2). The contamination on the property included tar-like and slag materials. The tar-like material was highly viscous and uniform, without any breaks or stratification. The slag material had a vesicular structure and was more porous and rigid than the tar-like material. There was some evidence that the tar-like material moved through the soil and that lead and/or TPH may have moved from that material into the soil. If we try to characterize this passive soil migration in plain English, a number of words come to mind, including gradual "spreading," "migration," "seeping," "oozing," and possibly "leaching." But certainly none of those words fits within the plain and common meaning of "discharge, ... injection, dumping, ... or placing." 42 U.S.C. § 6903(3). Although these words generally connote active conduct, even if we were to infuse passive meanings, these words simply do not describe the passive migration that occurred here. Nor can the gradual spread here be characterized as a "deposit," because there was neither a deposit by someone, nor does the term deposit encompass the gradual spread of contaminants. The term "spilling" is likewise inapposite. Nothing spilled out of or over anything. Unlike the spilling of a barrel or the spilling over of a holding pond, movement of the tar-like and slag materials was not a spill.

Of the terms defining "disposal," the only one that might remotely describe the passive soil migration here is "leaking." But under the plain and common meaning of the word, we conclude that there was no "leaking." The circumstances here are not like that of the leaking barrel or underground storage tank envisioned by Congress, * * * or a vessel or some other container that would connote "leaking." Therefore, there was no "disposal," and the Partnership Defendants are not PRPs. On this basis, we affirm the district court's grant of summary judgment to the Partnership Defendants on the CERCLA claim.

* * * 2. *Reading the Statute as a Whole*

No statutory provision is written in a vacuum. Complex regulatory statutes, in particular, often create a web—or, in the case of CERCLA, perhaps a maze—of sections, subsections, definitions, exceptions, defenses, and administrative provisions. Thus, we examine the statute as a whole, including its purpose and various provisions.

* * * A. *Statutory Purpose*

"CERCLA was enacted to protect and preserve public health and the environment by facilitating the expeditious and efficient cleanup of hazardous waste sites." But CERCLA also has a secondary purpose-assuring that "responsible" persons pay for the cleanup * * *. "We construe CERCLA liberally to achieve these goals." At the same time, we have cautioned that "we must reject a construction that the statute on its face does not permit, and the legislative history does not support."

Our conclusion that "disposal" does not include passive soil migration but that it may include other passive migration that fits within the plain meaning of the terms used to define "disposal" is consistent with CERCLA's dual purposes. Holding passive owners responsible for migration of contaminants that results from their conduct *and* for passive migration ensures the prompt and effective cleanup of abandoned storage tanks, which * * * is one of the problems Congress sought to address when enacting CERCLA. Indeed, if "disposal" is interpreted to exclude all passive migration, there would be little incentive for a landowner to examine his property for decaying disposal tanks, prevent them from spilling or leaking, or to clean up contamination once it was found.

B. Internal Consistency and Avoiding Illogical Results

Our plain-language interpretation of "disposal" also makes sense within the liability provisions of CERCLA—the sections identifying the parties that are "potentially responsible." As explained in section III.A, CERCLA creates four categories of PRPs: current owners or operators, owners or operators at the time of a disposal, arrangers, and transporters. *See* 42 U.S.C. § 9607(a). This categorization makes the best sense only under a plain-meaning interpretation of "disposal;" the extreme positions on either side render the structure awkward. For example, had Congress intended *all* passive migration to constitute a "disposal," then disposal is nearly always a perpetual process. Hence, every landowner after the first disposal would be liable, and there would be no reason to divide owners and operators into categories of former and current. On the other extreme, had Congress intended "disposal" to include only releases directly caused by affirmative human conduct, then it would make no sense to establish a strict liability scheme assigning responsibility to "any person who at the time of disposal . . . owned or operated any facility." 42 U.S.C. § 9607(a)(2). Rather, the statute would have a straightforward causation requirement.

* * * CERCLA next allows certain PRPs to avoid liability by asserting various defenses. Most relevant here is the so-called "innocent owner" defense, which absolves from liability landowners who can show that "the real property on which the facility concerned is located was acquired by the defendant after the disposal or placement of the hazardous substance on, in, or at the facility" and that "[a]t the time the defendant acquired the facility the defendant did not know and had no reason to know that any hazardous substance which is the subject of the release or threatened release was disposed of on, in, or at the facility." 42 U.S.C. § 9601(35)(A).

Our interpretation of "disposal" preserves the purpose and role of this defense within the statutory structure. The alternatives, on the other hand, would render the defense either impossible to present or entirely superfluous.

Were we to adopt an interpretation of "disposal" that encompassed all subsoil passive migration, the innocent landowner defense would be essentially eliminated. As discussed above, in all but a tiny fraction of cases, such an interpretation would lead to the conclusion that disposal is a never-ending process, rendering liable every landowner after the initial disposal. For those subsequent landowners, the innocent landowner defense would be available only if one could show that the land was purchased after the hazardous substances were "placed" there. Thus, the defense would only be available to a small portion of the landowners who have no actual culpability in the disposal of the hazardous substances.

* * * The opposite extreme is no better fit. Were we to interpret "disposal" to include only actions caused by affirmative human conduct, we would eliminate the need for an innocent landowner defense altogether. Such an interpretation of "disposal" would exclude from liability even a landowner whose facilities "spill" or "leak" without affirmative human conduct—that is, anything short of an intentional dump during an owner's tenure. Under this interpretation, there would exist no landowner capable of presenting an innocent landowner defense who would not already be excluded from liability in the first place. We doubt, even in the uncertain world of CERCLA, that Congress went to the trouble of amending the statute to create a defense that no one would need.

* * * Based on this analysis, we conclude that the plain meaning interpretation of "disposal" is consistent with the statute both in its constituent parts and as a whole.

3. Legislative History

Because the conclusion we reach is compelled by the plain meaning of the statute's text, our inquiry into legislative history is strictly limited. * * * [T]he available materials demonstrate that the public, the EPA, and drafters of the legislation used and understood the words "discharge, deposit, injection, dumping, spilling, leaking, or placing" in their ordinary, plain-meaning sense, encompassing events both caused by affirmative human conduct and, particularly in the case of "spill" and "leak," occurring solely in a passive context as well. Because we find no indication that Congress intended anything other than what it said, we present here only a few brief examples.

A. CERCLA

Any inquiry into CERCLA's legislative history is somewhat of a snark hunt. Like other courts that have examined the legislative history, we have found few truly relevant documents. This is not surprising, given the circumstances surrounding the bill's passage.[4] One searches in vain for committee reports or floor statements explaining the purpose of subtle or even dramatic changes from early versions of the bill to final passage. Nevertheless, those materials that do exist confirm the plain-meaning interpretation of "disposal."

As an initial matter, it is evident that CERCLA's primary targets included spills and leaks from abandoned sites—sites at which there was no longer any affirmative human activity. The two incidents of hazardous substance contamination that most prominently prompted congressional action—Love Canal and the Valley of the Drums—were both abandoned hazardous waste sites that were described as spilling or leaking with no affirmative human conduct.

Hearing testimony further confirmed that both the EPA and the legislators understood that hazardous substances legislation would deal with a wide range of disposal events, not predicated on an "active/passive" dichotomy. * * *

In addition, the primary legislative sponsors and relevant committees regularly used the words "spill" or "leak" to describe passive events at abandoned sites. * * *

B. SARA

In 1986 Congress enacted the Superfund Amendments and Reauthorization Act ("SARA"), aimed at speeding cleanup and forcing quicker action by the EPA. Most significantly for our purposes, Congress created the innocent landowner defense that we have already discussed. *See* 42 U.S.C. § 9601(35)(A). It did not do so, however, by creating a straightforward exception to CERCLA liability. In a single stroke, SARA first clarified that one who purchases land from a polluting owner or operator cannot present a third-party defense, then set conditions under which this limit would not apply—that is, if the property were purchased after disposal or placement, and the purchaser did not know and had no reason to know that hazardous substances were disposed of there. The plain-meaning interpretation of "disposal" we adopt leaves in place the narrow applicability of the defense. * * * Accordingly, the legislative history of the innocent owner defense does not contradict the plain meaning interpretation of "disposal," but rather is consistent with this formulation.

4. By November 1980, Congress had considered emergency response and hazardous substance cleanup proposals for at least three years. The bill that ultimately became law was an eleventh-hour compromise hastily assembled by a bipartisan leadership group of senators; it was introduced and passed by the Senate with only days remaining in a lame-duck session, and went to the house for an up-or-down vote. Statements in both houses reflected members' belief that the bill was flawed, but was the best that might pass given the circumstances; the pressure on both houses to pass something was compounded by the impending party switch in the Senate and the presidency. *See* letter from Senators Robert T. Stafford and Jennings Randolph to Representative James J. Florio (December 2, 1980), *reprinted at* 1 SENATE COMMITTEE ON ENVIRONMENT AND PUBLIC WORKS, 97TH CONG., A LEGISLATIVE HISTORY OF THE COMPREHENSIVE ENVIRONMENTAL RESPONSE, COMPENSATION, AND LIABILITY ACT OF 1980 (SUPERFUND) 774–75 (Committee Print 1983) (hereinafter "Committee Print").

C. Conclusion

In sum, we hold that, in light of the plain meaning of the terms used to define "disposal" in § 6903(3), the alleged passive migration of contaminants through soil during the Partnership Defendants' ownership was not a "disposal" under § 9607(a)(2). This plain-meaning approach is consistent with the statute as a whole and its legislative history. The Partnership Defendants are thus entitled to summary judgment on the CERCLA claim. * * *

NOTES

1. **Defining "Disposal."** Why did the Ninth Circuit have to define "disposal" in order to determine whether the past owner and operator defendants are liable for contribution under CERCLA? How did the Ninth Circuit define "disposal"? What tools of statutory construction did it use?

2. **CERCLA Cross–Referencing.** Where does CERCLA's definition of "disposal" come from? Does that cross-referencing make sense? Why or why not?

3. **Overlapping Terms.** As the Ninth Circuit indicated, a CERCLA case requires that there be a "release" of hazardous substances at the facility, but a "disposal" is only relevant if the plaintiff tries to establish that the defendants are PRPs under section 107(a)(2) (past owners and operators) or section 107(a)(3) (arrangers). What is the relationship between "release" and "disposal," according to the Ninth Circuit? Does the distinction between the two terms make sense in light of CERCLA's larger goals and purposes?

4. **CERCLA's Purposes and the Definition of "Disposal."** The principal case was an *en banc* decision of the Ninth Circuit, decided when the Ninth Circuit agreed to rehear the case after a normal three-judge appellate panel had already issued a decision. In that three-judge opinion, *Carson Harbor Village, Ltd. v. Unocal Corp.*, 227 F.3d 1196 (9th Cir. 2000), *withdrawn and superseded on rehearing en banc*, the court found that the passive migration in this case *did* constitute "disposal" under CERCLA, emphasizing the remedial purposes of CERCLA and the fact that its terms should be construed liberally to effectuate the Act's purposes. *Id.* at 1206–10. On rehearing, how did the *en banc* panel define CERCLA's purposes? How did those purposes inform its interpretation of "disposal"? Which view of CERCLA's purposes, and which interpretation of "disposal," seems most likely to prompt cleanup of contaminated sites? Why?

5. **The Rest of the Story.** On remand from the Ninth Circuit, the Central District of California decided that the Ninth Circuit's conclusion that the Partnership Defendants were not PRPs under CERCLA was the law of the case, and it refused to disturb that finding. *Carson Harbor Village v. Unocal Corp.*, 287 F. Supp. 2d. 1118, 1131 n. 40 (C.D. Cal. 2003). Moreover, in an extensive and detailed analysis, the district court also concluded that Carson Harbor's remediation work did not comply with the National Contingency Plan. *Id.* at 1153–77. As a result, Carson Harbor could not recover from *any* PRPs pursuant to CERCLA. The Ninth Circuit affirmed. *Carson Harbor Village v. County of Los Angeles Corp.*, 433 F.3d 1260 (9th Cir. 2006).

However, the district court did leave open the possibility that Carson Harbor may recover under state law through indemnification contracts.

6. **Is There A Circuit Split Regarding Passive Migration? A CERCLA Passive Migration Problem.** The Supreme Court denied *certiorari* in this case, *Carson Harbor Village, Ltd. v. Braley*, 535 U.S. 971 (2002), leaving the differences among the federal circuits unresolved. According to the Ninth Circuit, the federal Courts of Appeals are less split in their views of "disposal" than spread over a continuum. Where on this continuum did the Ninth Circuit place itself? Can the current decisions be reconciled?

Consider this CERCLA problem: In 1940, Landowner C owns Parcel 1 and knows that previous owners Landowner A and Landowner B buried drums of hazardous substances on the property (which was perfectly legal at the time). However, Landowner C herself handles no hazardous waste during her ownership and does nothing to disturb the drums. Nevertheless, the drums were cheaply made and in 1960 the drums, which had been corroding through natural processes, begin to leak hazardous wastes into the soil. Unaware of the problem, Landowner C sells Parcel 1 to Landowner D in 1965. During Landowner D's ownership, hazardous wastes continue to flow out of the drums into the soil, draining the drums, so that by the time Landowner D sells Parcel 1 to Landowner E (who knows nothing about the problem) in 1972, the drums themselves are completely empty. Nevertheless, during Landowner E's ownership, the hazardous wastes continue to migrate through the soil to groundwater, which they reach in 1978. Landowner E sells Parcel 1 to Landowner F in 1979, and the groundwater and soil contamination are finally discovered in 1985, after CERCLA has taken effect. Which past owners are liable under CERCLA section 107(a)(2) in the Second and Third Circuits? In the Fourth? In the Sixth? In the Ninth?

7. **CERCLA Defenses: The Innocent Purchaser Defense.** As was discussed above, there are only three defenses that PRPs can assert to CERCLA liability: act of God, act of war, and the innocent landowner defense. The last of these is the most complex and requires the PRP to show that "the release or threat of release of hazardous substances and the damages resulting therefrom":

- were caused *solely*
- by an act or omission of a third party
- who is someone *other than an employee or agent of the PRP*
- and someone *other than someone in a contractual relationship with the PRP*
- if the PRP establishes by a preponderance of the evidence
- that the PRP exercised "due care" with respect to the hazardous substances involved
- and that the PRP "took precautions against foreseeable acts or omissions of any such third party and the consequences that could foreseeably result from such acts or omissions * * *."

CERCLA § 107(b)(3), 42 U.S.C. § 9607(b)(3). Moreover, courts construe the defense narrowly to effectuate CERCLA's purposes. What is the relationship between the innocent landowner defense and past "disposal" of hazardous substances, according to the Ninth Circuit? How did this defense affect the court's interpretation of "disposal"?

Consider again the CERCLA problem in Note 6. Assuming that Landowners D through F knew nothing about the hazardous substances or the problems with the corroding drums when they purchased Parcel 1, can any of them use the innocent purchaser defense? Why or why not?

8. **The Non-Appealing Defendant, UNOCAL:** Why did UNOCAL not appeal its CERCLA liability in the principal case? Was it a different kind of past owner or operator than the other defendants? Why or why not?

9. **CERCLA's Drafting and Legislative History and Statutory Interpretation.** As the Ninth Circuit explained in footnote 13, Congress drafted and passed CERCLA extremely quickly in 1980 in order to enact the statute before the Reagan Administration replaced the Carter Administration in January 1981. As might be expected, the resulting statute is not as clear as it could have been, and CERCLA's legislative history is particularly unilluminating among federal environmental statutes. However, as the Ninth Circuit also indicates, the federal courts are well aware of these circumstances and, as a result, are more likely to "adjust" CERCLA's plain meaning than they are for most other statutes. Do the circumstances of CERCLA's drafting and enactment make a difference to the Ninth Circuit's interpretation of "disposal"?

* * *

5. Arranger Liability

The third category of CERCLA PRPs includes "any person who by contract, agreement, or otherwise arranged for disposal or treatment, or arranged with a transporter for transport for disposal or treatment, of hazardous substances owned or possessed by such person, by any other party or entity, at a facility or incineration vessel owner or operated by another party or entity and containing such hazardous substances * * *." CERCLA § 107(a)(3), 42 U.S.C. § 9607(a)(3). This so-called "arranger" liability is the most complex of the PRP provisions, and the Supreme Court addressed it in 2009.

BURLINGTON NORTHERN AND SANTA FE RAILWAY COMPANY v. UNITED STATES

556 U.S. 599 (2009).

STEVENS, J., delivered the opinion of the Court, in which ROBERTS, C.J., and SCALIA, KENNEDY, SOUTER, THOMAS, BREYER, and ALITO, JJ., joined. GINSBURG, J., filed a dissenting opinion.

In 1980, Congress enacted the Comprehensive Environmental Response, Compensation, and Liability Act (CERCLA), 94 Stat. 2767, as amended, 42 U.S.C. §§ 9601–9675, in response to the serious environmental and health risks posed by industrial pollution. The Act was designed to promote the " 'timely cleanup of hazardous waste sites' " and to ensure that the costs of such cleanup efforts were borne by those responsible for the contamination. These cases raise the questions whether and to what extent a party associated with a contaminated site may be held responsible for the full costs of remediation.

I

In 1960, Brown & Bryant, Inc. (B & B), began operating an agricultural chemical distribution business, purchasing pesticides and other chemical products from suppliers such as Shell Oil Company (Shell). Using its own equipment, B & B applied its products to customers' farms. B & B opened its business on a 3.8 acre parcel of former farmland in Arvin, California, and in 1975, expanded operations onto an adjacent .9 acre parcel of land owned jointly by the Atchison, Topeka & Santa Fe Railway Company, and the Southern Pacific Transportation Company (now known respectively as the Burlington Northern and Santa Fe Railway Company and Union Pacific Railroad Company) (Railroads). Both parcels of the Arvin facility were graded toward a sump and drainage pond located on the southeast corner of the primary parcel. Neither the sump nor the drainage pond was lined until 1979, allowing waste water and chemical runoff from the facility to seep into the ground water below.

During its years of operation, B & B stored and distributed various hazardous chemicals on its property. Among these were the herbicide dinoseb, sold by Dow Chemicals, and the pesticides D–D and Nemagon, both sold by Shell. Dinoseb was stored in 55–gallon drums and 5–gallon containers on a concrete slab outside B & B's warehouse. Nemagon was stored in 30–gallon drums and 5–gallon containers inside the warehouse. Originally, B & B purchased D–D in 55–gallon drums; beginning in the mid–1960's, however, Shell began requiring its distributors to maintain bulk storage facilities for D–D. From that time onward, B & B purchased D–D in bulk.

When B & B purchased D–D, Shell would arrange for delivery by common carrier, f.o.b. destination.[2] When the product arrived, it was transferred from tanker trucks to a bulk storage tank located on B & B's primary parcel. From there, the chemical was transferred to bobtail trucks, nurse tanks, and pull rigs. During each of these transfers leaks and spills could—and often did—occur. Although the common carrier and B & B used buckets to catch spills from hoses and gaskets connecting the tanker trucks to its bulk storage tank, the buckets sometimes overflowed or were knocked over, causing D–D to spill onto the ground during the transfer process.

Aware that spills of D–D were commonplace among its distributors, in the late 1970's Shell took several steps to encourage the safe handling of

2. F.o.b. destination means "the seller must at his own expense and risk transport the goods to [the destination] and there tender delivery of them.... " U.C.C. § 2–319(1)(b) (2001). The District Court found that B & B assumed "stewardship" over the D–D as soon as the common carrier entered the Arvin facility.

its products. Shell provided distributors with detailed safety manuals and instituted a voluntary discount program for distributors that made improvements in their bulk handling and safety facilities. Later, Shell revised its program to require distributors to obtain an inspection by a qualified engineer and provide self-certification of compliance with applicable laws and regulations. B & B's Arvin facility was inspected twice, and in 1981, B & B certified to Shell that it had made a number of recommended improvements to its facilities.

Despite these improvements, B & B remained a " '[s]loppy' [o]perator." Over the course of B & B's 28 years of operation, delivery spills, equipment failures, and the rinsing of tanks and trucks allowed Nemagon, D–D and dinoseb to seep into the soil and upper levels of ground water of the Arvin facility. In 1983, the California Department of Toxic Substances Control (DTSC) began investigating B & B's violation of hazardous waste laws, and the United States Environmental Protection Agency (EPA) soon followed suit, discovering significant contamination of soil and ground water. Of particular concern was a plume of contaminated ground water located under the facility that threatened to leach into an adjacent supply of potential drinking water.

Although B & B undertook some efforts at remediation, by 1989 it had become insolvent and ceased all operations. That same year, the Arvin facility was added to the National Priority List, see 54 Fed. Reg. 41027, and subsequently, DTSC and EPA (Governments) exercised their authority under 42 U.S.C. § 9604 to undertake cleanup efforts at the site. By 1998, the Governments had spent more than $8 million responding to the site contamination; their costs have continued to accrue.

In 1991, EPA issued an administrative order to the Railroads directing them, as owners of a portion of the property on which the Arvin facility was located, to perform certain remedial tasks in connection with the site. The Railroads did so, incurring expenses of more than $3 million in the process. Seeking to recover at least a portion of their response costs, in 1992 the Railroads brought suit against B & B in the United States District Court for the Eastern District of California. In 1996, that lawsuit was consolidated with two recovery actions brought by DTSC and EPA against Shell and the Railroads.

The District Court conducted a 6–week bench trial in 1999 and four years later entered a judgment in favor of the Governments. In a lengthy order supported by 507 separate findings of fact and conclusions of law, the court held that both the Railroads and Shell were potentially responsible parties (PRPs) under CERCLA—the Railroads because they were owners of a portion of the facility, see 42 U.S.C. §§ 9607(a)(1)-(2), and Shell because it had "arranged for" the disposal of hazardous substances through its sale and delivery of D–D, see § 9607(a)(3).

* * * The Governments appealed the District Court's apportionment, and Shell cross-appealed the court's finding of liability. The Court of Appeals acknowledged that Shell did not qualify as a "traditional" arran-

ger under § 9607(a)(3), insofar as it had not contracted with B & B to directly dispose of a hazardous waste product. Nevertheless, the court stated that Shell could still be held liable under a " 'broader' category of arranger liability" if the "disposal of hazardous wastes [wa]s a foreseeable byproduct of, but not the purpose of, the transaction giving rise to" arranger liability. Relying on CERCLA's definition of "disposal," which covers acts such as "leaking" and "spilling," 42 U.S.C. § 6903(3), the Ninth Circuit concluded that an entity could arrange for "disposal" "even if it did not intend to dispose" of a hazardous substance. 520 F.3d, at 949.

Applying that theory of arranger liability to the District Court's findings of fact, the Ninth Circuit held that Shell arranged for the disposal of a hazardous substance through its sale and delivery of D–D * * * . Under such circumstances, the court concluded, arranger liability was not precluded by the fact that the purpose of Shell's action had been to transport a useful and previously unused product to B & B for sale.

The Railroads and Shell moved for rehearing *en banc*, which the Court of Appeals denied over the dissent of eight judges. We granted certiorari to determine whether Shell was properly held liable as an entity that had "arranged for disposal" of hazardous substances within the meaning of § 9607(a)(3) * * * . [W]e now reverse.

II

CERCLA imposes strict liability for environmental contamination upon four broad classes of PRPs:

"(1) the owner and operator of a vessel or a facility,

"(2) any person who at the time of disposal of any hazardous substance owned or operated any facility at which such hazardous substances were disposed of,

"(3) any person who by contract, agreement, or otherwise arranged for disposal or treatment, or arranged with a transporter for transport for disposal or treatment, of hazardous substances owned or possessed by such person, by any other party or entity, at any facility or incineration vessel owned or operated by another party or entity and containing such hazardous substances, and

"(4) any person who accepts or accepted any hazardous substances for transport to disposal or treatment facilities, incineration vessels or sites selected by such person, from which there is a release, or a threatened release which causes the incurrence of response costs, of a hazardous substance.... " 42 U.S.C. § 9607(a).

Once an entity is identified as a PRP, it may be compelled to clean up a contaminated area or reimburse the Government for its past and future response costs.

In these cases, it is undisputed that the Railroads qualify as PRPs under both §§ 9607(a)(1) and 9607(a)(2) because they owned the land leased by B & B at the time of the contamination and continue to own it now. The more difficult question is whether Shell also qualifies as a PRP under § 9607(a)(3) by virtue of the circumstances surrounding its sales to B & B.

To determine whether Shell may be held liable as an arranger, we begin with the language of the statute. As relevant here, § 9607(a)(3) applies to an entity that "arrange[s] for disposal ... of hazardous substances." It is plain from the language of the statute that CERCLA liability would attach under § 9607(a)(3) if an entity were to enter into a transaction for the sole purpose of discarding a used and no longer useful hazardous substance. It is similarly clear that an entity could not be held liable as an arranger merely for selling a new and useful product if the purchaser of that product later, and unbeknownst to the seller, disposed of the product in a way that led to contamination. Less clear is the liability attaching to the many permutations of "arrangements" that fall between these two extremes—cases in which the seller has some knowledge of the buyers' planned disposal or whose motives for the "sale" of a hazardous substance are less than clear. In such cases, courts have concluded that the determination whether an entity is an arranger requires a fact-intensive inquiry that looks beyond the parties' characterization of the transaction as a "disposal" or a "sale" and seeks to discern whether the arrangement was one Congress intended to fall within the scope of CERCLA's strict-liability provisions.

Although we agree that the question whether § 9607(a)(3) liability attaches is fact intensive and case specific, such liability may not extend beyond the limits of the statute itself. Because CERCLA does not specifically define what it means to "arrang[e] for" disposal of a hazardous substance, we give the phrase its ordinary meaning. In common parlance, the word "arrange" implies action directed to a specific purpose. Consequently, under the plain language of the statute, an entity may qualify as an arranger under § 9607(a)(3) when it takes intentional steps to dispose of a hazardous substance.

The Governments do not deny that the statute requires an entity to "arrang[e] for" disposal; however, they interpret that phrase by reference to the statutory term "disposal," which the Act broadly defines as "the discharge, deposit, injection, dumping, spilling, leaking, or placing of any solid waste or hazardous waste into or on any land or water." 42 U.S.C. § 6903(3); see also § 9601(29) (adopting the definition of "disposal" contained in the Solid Waste Disposal Act). The Governments assert that by including unintentional acts such as "spilling" and "leaking" in the definition of disposal, Congress intended to impose liability on entities not only when they directly dispose of waste products but also when they engage in legitimate sales of hazardous substances knowing that some disposal may occur as a collateral consequence of the sale itself. Applying that reading of the statute, the Governments contend that Shell arranged for the disposal of D–D within the meaning of § 9607(a)(3) by shipping D–D to B & B under conditions it knew would result in the spilling of a portion of the hazardous substance by the purchaser or common carrier.

Because these spills resulted in wasted D–D, a result Shell anticipated, the Governments insist that Shell was properly found to have arranged for the disposal of D–D.

While it is true that in some instances an entity's knowledge that its product will be leaked, spilled, dumped, or otherwise discarded may provide evidence of the entity's intent to dispose of its hazardous wastes, knowledge alone is insufficient to prove that an entity "planned for" the disposal, particularly when the disposal occurs as a peripheral result of the legitimate sale of an unused, useful product. In order to qualify as an arranger, Shell must have entered into the sale of D–D with the intention that at least a portion of the product be disposed of during the transfer process by one or more of the methods described in § 6903(3). Here, the facts found by the District Court do not support such a conclusion.

Although the evidence adduced at trial showed that Shell was aware that minor, accidental spills occurred during the transfer of D–D from the common carrier to B & B's bulk storage tanks after the product had arrived at the Arvin facility and had come under B & B's stewardship, the evidence does not support an inference that Shell intended such spills to occur. To the contrary, the evidence revealed that Shell took numerous steps to encourage its distributors to *reduce* the likelihood of such spills, providing them with detailed safety manuals, requiring them to maintain adequate storage facilities, and providing discounts for those that took safety precautions. Although Shell's efforts were less than wholly successful, given these facts, Shell's mere knowledge that spills and leaks continued to occur is insufficient grounds for concluding that Shell "arranged for" the disposal of D–D within the meaning of § 9607(a)(3). Accordingly, we conclude that Shell was not liable as an arranger for the contamination that occurred at B & B's Arvin facility.

* * * IV

For the foregoing reasons, we conclude that the Court of Appeals erred by holding Shell liable as an arranger under CERCLA for the costs of remediating environmental contamination at the Arvin, California facility. * * * The judgment is reversed, and the cases are remanded for further proceedings consistent with this opinion.

It is so ordered.

Justice GINSBURG, dissenting.

Although the question is close, I would uphold the determinations of the courts below that Shell qualifies as an arranger within the compass of the Comprehensive Environmental Response, Compensation and Liability Act (CERCLA). See 42 U.S.C. § 9607(a)(3). As the facts found by the District Court bear out, Shell "arranged for disposal . . . of hazardous substances" owned by Shell when the arrangements were made.

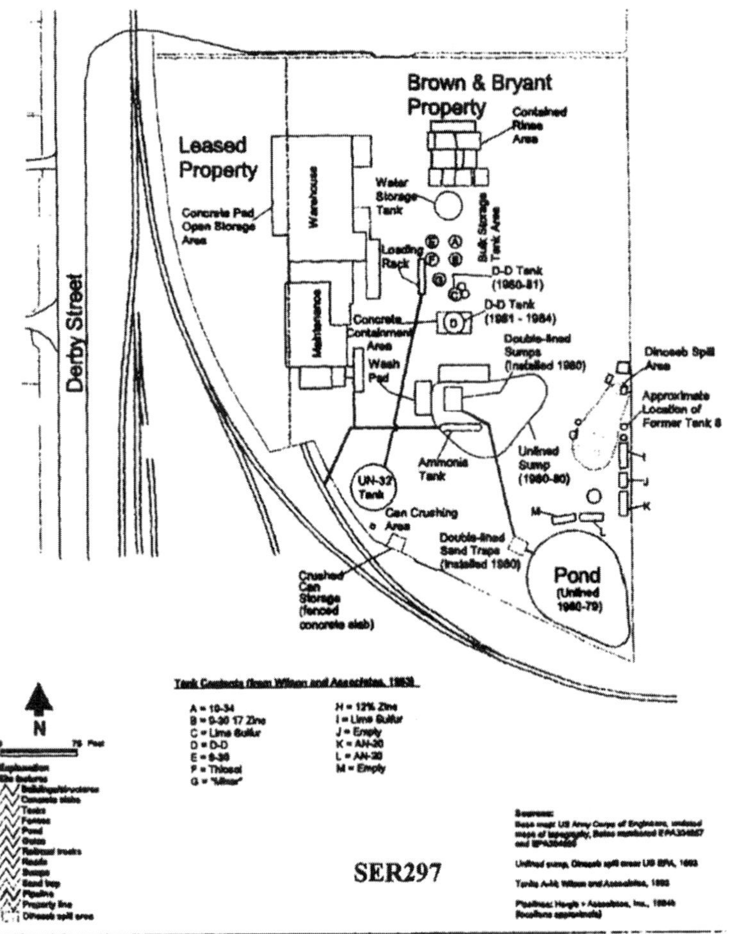

In the 1950's and early 1960's, Shell shipped most of its products to Brown and Bryant (B & B) in 55–gallon drums, thereby ensuring against spillage or leakage during delivery and transfer. Later, Shell found it economically advantageous, in lieu of shipping in drums, to require B & B to maintain bulk storage facilities for receipt of the chemicals B & B purchased from Shell. By the mid–1960's, Shell was delivering its chemical to B & B in bulk tank truckloads. As the Court recognizes, "bulk storage of the chemical led to numerous tank failures and spills as the chemical rusted tanks and eroded valves."

Shell furthermore specified the equipment to be used in transferring the chemicals from the delivery truck to B & B's storage tanks. In the process, spills and leaks were inevitable, indeed spills occurred every time deliveries were made.

That Shell sold B & B useful products, the Ninth Circuit observed, did not exonerate Shell from CERCLA liability, for the sales "necessarily and immediately result[ed] in the leakage of hazardous substances." The deliveries, Shell was well aware, directly and routinely resulted in disposals of hazardous substances (through spills and leaks) for more than 20 years. "[M]ere knowledge" may not be enough, but Shell did not simply know of the spills and leaks without contributing to them. Given the control rein held by Shell over the mode of delivery and transfer, the lower courts held and I agree, Shell was properly ranked an arranger. Relieving Shell of any obligation to pay for the cleanup undertaken by the United States and California is hardly commanded by CERCLA's text, and is surely at odds with CERCLA's objective—to place the cost of remediation on persons whose activities contributed to the contamination rather than on the taxpaying public.

* * *

NOTES

1. **Defining "Arranger" Liability.** How does the majority define arranger liability in *Burlington Northern*? Why does Shell *not* qualify as a PRP under that definition? Who *would* qualify, according to the Court? How does the dissent's view of arranger liability differ from the majority's? Why *would* Shell be an arranger under that definition?

2. **Resolving a Jumbled Litigation History for Arranger Liability?** The differences between the majority's view and the dissenter's view of arranger liability reflects in part a long-term split in the federal Courts of Appeals regarding how broadly CERCLA's arranger liability should be. All courts—including the Supreme Court in *Burlington Northern*—agree that people who explicitly and consciously arrange for the disposal of hazardous substances qualify as arrangers under this provision of CERCLA. Thus, for example, persons who ship RCRA hazardous wastes to a TSD facility that later experiences a release of hazardous substances would clearly be PRPs. However, courts have also applied arranger liability in other contexts, such as when a party ships raw materials to another party for processing, and the processor's site becomes contaminated. *United States v. Aceto Agricultural Chemicals Corp.*, 872 F.2d 1373 (8th Cir. 1989). However, the Ninth Circuit concluded that the United States could *not* be held liable as an arranger in connection with sites contaminated through the production of military aviation fuel ("avgas") during World War II, despite the fact that the United States government was the main consumer of such fuel and fuel production was decidedly influenced by government wartime policies. *United States v. Shell Oil Co.*, 294 F.3d 1045 (9th Cir. 2002).

Does the *Burlington Northern* decision resolve the ambiguities that prior case law had created regarding the scope of arranger liability? Why or why not?

3. **The Other PRPs in *Burlington Northern*.** Be sure to note that the *Burlington Northern* decision involved other PRPs besides Shell. Why were the statuses of these other PRPs not nearly as problematic as Shell's? Did those other PRPs have any apparent defenses to CERCLA liability?

* * *

6. Transporter Liability

CERCLA's fourth category of PRPs creates liability for "any person who accepts or accepted any hazardous substances for transport to disposal or treatment facilities, incineration vessels or sites selected by such person, from which there is a release, or a threatened release * * *." CERCLA § 107(a)(4), 42 U.S.C. § 9607(a)(4). Is the transporter still liable if the transporter did *not* select the disposal or treatment facility to which he or she transported the hazardous substances? Consider the following case.

TIPPINS INCORPORATED v. USX CORPORATION

37 F.3d 87 (3rd Cir. 1994).

BECKER, CIRCUIT JUDGE.

These appeals from two orders of the district court in a contribution action involving the allocation of response costs under the Comprehensive Environmental Response, Compensation, and Liability Act ("CERCLA"), 42 U.S.C.A. §§ 9601–75 (1983 & Supp. 1994), present an interesting question of first impression in the courts of appeals concerning transporter liability under CERCLA § 107(a)(4), 42 U.S.C.A. § 9607(a)(4). * * * The court found USX liable as an arranger and Petroclean liable as a transporter. * * *

Appellants raise a number of issues. We write solely on Tippins' argument that a transporter is liable even if it does not select the facility at which the waste was disposed, and on Petroclean's argument that it cannot be held liable as a transporter unless the court finds that it made the ultimate decision to select Four County as the disposal facility. * * *

We reject Tippins' argument that under § 107(a)(4) a transporter is liable as a responsible party even if it does not "select" the disposal "facility" (in contrast to a "site"). We also reject Petroclean's assertion that it cannot be liable unless the court finds that it made the ultimate selection of the facility as the disposal location regardless of whether it contributed to the selection of the facility ultimately utilized. We basically agree with Tippins that § 107(a)(4) applies if the transporter's advice was a substantial contributing factor in the decision to dispose of the hazardous waste at a particular facility. As we interpret that section, a transporter selects the disposal facility when it actively and substantially participates in the decision-making process which ultimately identifies a facility for disposal. Since there is no dispute that Petroclean did so—Petroclean had considerable input into the selection process and, importantly, Tippins relied upon Petroclean's expertise in hazardous waste management when making its disposal decision—Petroclean is liable as a transporter. Accordingly, we will also affirm the grant of summary judgment against Petroclean on transporter liability.

I. FACTS AND PROCEDURAL HISTORY

In September 1987, Tippins signed an agreement with Sydney Steel Corporation of Nova Scotia to provide equipment for electric arc furnace ("EAF") steelmaking. Included in this agreement was a provision that required Tippins to furnish and install an EAF baghouse.[5] * * *

As a result of USX's manufacturing and processing of steel at the Duquesne Works, EAF dust was present in and around the baghouse. To effect cleanup of the EAF dust, Tippins solicited bids from contractors to pick up and transport the dust for disposal. Tippins eventually contracted with Petroclean, which is licensed to haul hazardous waste and specializes in the transport and disposal of hazardous substances, to transport the dust for disposal. The transportation agreement provided that Petroclean would supply the labor, equipment, and material for removal and transport of the EAF dust as well as obtain a provisional EPA identification number for the generation of the hazardous waste.

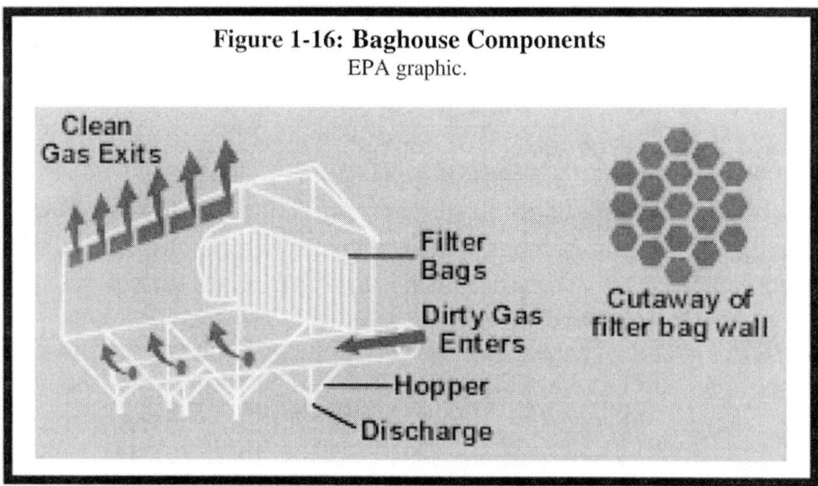

Figure 1-16: Baghouse Components
EPA graphic.

The CECOS International facility in Williamsburg, Ohio was chosen after Petroclean gathered information on the site and submitted a proposal to Tippins based on certain cost parameters. * * * The parties subsequently learned that the CECOS site would accept EAF dust only if

5. EAF dust is a byproduct of the manufacture of steel using electric furnaces. A baghouse, a large, fabricated structure, vacuums contaminated air inside to filter out the EAF dust. The dust is collected inside a hopper or dumpster, and clean air is exhausted from the structure. The EPA listed EAF dust as a hazardous substance in 1980, designating it as K061. *See* 40 C.F.R. § 261.32.

packaged in its own containers. Since those containers were "prohibitively" expensive, Tippins and Petroclean agreed to transport the dust to another disposal site. Petroclean, having surveyed substitute disposal sites, identified two landfills that would accept the dust, the Four County Landfill in Rochester, Indiana and Wayne Disposal, Inc. in Detroit, Michigan. Petroclean contacted each site, gathered financial information as to disposal costs, and offered Tippins both sites as possible disposal locations from which Tippins could choose. Tippins subsequently picked Four County, where Petroclean disposed of the EAF dust.

Later, both the EPA and the Indiana Department of Environmental Management requested the owner of Four County to participate in a program to monitor and close the landfill. The EPA thereafter notified Tippins that it was a potentially responsible party for environmental contamination at Four County. Tippins then made written demands upon Petroclean and USX, advising them of their potential liability under CERCLA for remedial investigation and response costs incurred by Tippins arising from the monitoring and closing of the landfill. Petroclean and USX denied CERCLA liability.

In August 1992, Tippins filed an action in the District Court for the Western District of Pennsylvania against Petroclean and USX pursuant to CERCLA §§ 107(a) and 113(f), 42 U.S.C.A. §§ 9607(a), 9613(f), and the Declaratory Judgment Act, 28 U.S.C.A. § 2201 (1994), seeking indemnity and contribution for past response costs and a declaratory judgment apportioning future response costs arising from the remedial action at Four County. Tippins * * * alleged that Petroclean was liable as a transporter under § 107(a)(4).

* * * II. DISCUSSION

Congress enacted CERCLA to facilitate the cleanup of potentially dangerous hazardous waste sites, with a view to the preservation of the environment and human health. CERCLA, a strict liability statute, has its "bite" in holding responsible parties financially accountable for the costs associated with a remedial or removal action at hazardous waste facilities. Section 107(a)(4)(B) provides that a responsible party, as defined in subsections 107(a)(1)-(4), shall be liable for "any other necessary costs of response incurred by any other person consistent with the national contingency plan." Section 113(f)(1), as amended by the Superfund Amendments and Reauthorization Act of 1986 ("SARA"), Pub. L. No. 99–499, 100 Stat. 1613 (Oct. 17, 1986), provides for an express right of contribution "from any other person who is liable or potentially liable" under § 107(a). To succeed under either section, a plaintiff must establish that the defendant is a responsible party. One basis for establishing a party's responsibility is transporter liability.

Petroclean contends that the district court erred when it concluded that Petroclean was liable as a transporter under § 107(a)(4), which provides that

> any person who accepts or accepted any hazardous substances for transport to disposal or treatment facilities, incineration vessels or sites selected by such person, from which there is a release, or a threatened release which causes the incurrence of response costs, of a hazardous substance, shall be liable....

Specifically, Petroclean asserts that it cannot be liable unless the court finds that Petroclean made the ultimate selection of Four County as the disposal location. Petroclean further submits that the record is "vague at best" regarding its role in site selection and, thus, that a genuine issue of material fact exists as to this issue.

In response, Tippins argues that § 107(a)(4) does not mandate that a transporter make the ultimate decision to select the disposal facility. Tippins claims that the phrase "selected by such person" found in § 107(a)(4) only modifies the term "sites," but not "facilities." Since Four County is a "facility," under Tippins' construction, Petroclean need not have participated in the selection of Four County as the disposal location at all for CERCLA liability to attach; its act of transportation would, standing alone, suffice. Tippins alternatively contends that, even if liability attaches only to transporters who "select" a facility, the record demonstrates that, as a matter of fact, Petroclean did select the Four County facility.

A. *Application of the Phrase "Selected by Such Person"*

It is axiomatic that the starting point for interpreting a statute is the language of the statute itself. Thus, to determine whether the phrase "selected by such person" just modifies "sites," or also applies to "facilities," we turn to the language of § 107(a)(4), *quoted supra*. Under any parsing of the statute, a person who transports a hazardous substance to a "site" is liable under § 107(a)(4) only if it selected that disposal location. But there abides within an ambiguity as to whether selection is a necessary prerequisite to transporter liability where the hazardous waste is deposited at a "facility." Namely, in view of the absence of a comma after "sites," the phrase "selected by such person" can be interpreted to modify only "sites," as opposed to also modifying "facilities" and "incineration vessels." The fact that two divergent interpretations of § 107(a)(4) are plausible underscores the oft repeated notion that "CERCLA is not a paradigm of clarity or precision," *Artesian Water Co. v. Government of New Castle County,* 851 F.2d 643, 648 (3d Cir. 1988), but "is riddled with inconsistencies and redundancies," *Alcan Aluminum,* 964 F.2d at 258 n. 5 (citation omitted).

A general canon of statutory construction holds that, absent a clear intention to the contrary, a modifier's reference is to the closest noun. *See* NORMAN J. SINGER, SUTHERLAND STATUTORY CONSTRUCTION § 47.33 (4th ed. 1985) (stating that "referential and qualifying words and phrases, where no contrary intention appears, refer solely to the last antecedent"). Because of the inartful crafting of CERCLA in general, however, reliance solely upon general canons of statutory construction must be more tempered than usual; such canons are more appropriately applied to divine intent from statutes carefully worded and assiduously compiled than from the imprecise statutory language such as that found in § 107(a)(4). We believe that, notwithstanding the canon, the phrase "selected by such person" can, as the statute is grammatically constructed, also be construed to refer to "facilities" and "incineration vessels." A number of district courts have adopted such a construction, along with several commentators.

The distinction Tippins advances would be illusory at best and nonsensical at worst, as CERCLA broadly defines "facility" to include any "site" containing a hazardous substance. *See* 42 U.S.C.A. § 9601(9). Thus, Tippins' reading would lead to a curious result. On the one hand, a transporter would be liable if it transported the waste to a virgin site (one containing no hazardous substances) only if it selected that site. On the other hand, a transporter would be liable if it transported the waste to a site containing hazardous substances (thereby a "facility") whether or not it selected that location. The oddness of this result is aggravated by the fact that the very first shipment to a virgin site would deflower it, and the transporter would be liable for any subsequent shipments even if it had not selected that site. * * *

We conclude then that a transporter must select the disposal facility to be held liable under § 107(a)(4). This conclusion is based on our finding that the subordinate clause "selected by such person" modifies the referents "facilities" and "incineration vessels" along with the referent "sites." We must now consider what acts by a transporter constitute selection of the disposal facility.

B. The Meaning of "Selection"

Since a transporter must select the disposal location to be liable under § 107(a)(4), we must determine whether Petroclean selected Four County as the disposal facility. Tippins argues that Petroclean selected the site because it was actively involved in the selection process. Not surprisingly, Petroclean counters this contention and would construe § 107(a)(4) narrowly to hold a transporter liable only when it made the final decision to select the disposal facility. CERCLA does not unequivocally resolve the question of what particular acts by a transporter constitute selection, as it does not define the term "select." Nor did the drafters of CERCLA or SARA provide any explanation for the site selection language.

* * * Construing the term "selected" to encompass those persons whose participation in the selection process is as described takes no liberties with the statute. * * * In a case such as this, where the statute does not define the term at issue and the legislative history is unavailing, we must define the term "selected" in light of its ordinary use and the overall policies and objectives of CERCLA.

First, we note that our construction of "selected" is within the term's ordinary meaning. To "select" is "to choose from a number or group usu[ally] by fitness, excellence, or other distinguishing feature." WEBSTER'S THIRD NEW INTERNATIONAL DICTIONARY 2058 (Philip B. Gove ed. 1966). When a transporter with a knowledge and understanding of the industry superior to its customer's investigates a number of potential disposal sites and suggests several to the customer from which it may pick, and the customer relies upon the transporter's knowledge and experience by choosing one of the winnowed sites, the transporter has performed a selection. Although the transporter has not made the ultimate decision, it has made the penultimate one; for all intents and purposes, the transporter has selected the facility by presenting it as one of a few disposal alternatives. In such cases of cooperation, the customer and transporter have jointly selected an appropriate disposal facility.

The "active participation" standard advances the objectives of CERCLA by recognizing the reality that transporters often play an influential role in the decision to dispose waste at a given facility. Generators undoubtedly regularly rely upon a transporter's expertise in hazardous waste management when considering disposal alternatives. A sophisticated transporter specializing in the transportation of hazardous material is accordingly frequently in the best position to ensure safe and proper disposal of the waste. There is no sound reason for such parties to escape CERCLA liability while the generators, owners, and operators are held liable, when they essentially determined the disposal location subjected to the remedial actions and incurring the response costs. This approach also comports with the need to interpret a remedial statute such as CERCLA liberally.

We emphasize that for liability to attach, a transporter must be so involved in the selection process that it has substantial input into the disposal decision. A transporter clearly does not select the disposal site merely by following the directions of the party with which it contracts. * * * To be held liable under § 107(a)(4), the transporter must be so engaged in the selection process that holding it liable furthers one of CERCLA's central objectives: to hold all persons actively involved in the storage or disposal of hazardous waste financially accountable for the cost of remedying resulting harm to the human health or environment.

C. Petroclean's Putative Selection of the Four County Landfill

Applying this standard to the instant case, we conclude that the district court appropriately granted summary judgment against Petroclean since there is no genuine issue of material fact as to Petroclean's active participation in the decision to dispose of the EAF dust at Four County. Petroclean admits that it did more than merely pick up the dust and transport it to the landfill. As a company specializing in site remediation and hazardous waste and transportation services, Petroclean had substantial input into the selection process, and Tippins clearly relied on its special expertise in ultimately choosing Four County.

Petroclean first identified the CECOS facility as the disposal site for the EAF dust and subsequently contracted with Tippins to dispose of the waste there. Later, after discussions with CECOS about disposal costs, Petroclean learned that CECOS accepted waste only if packaged in special disposal bags which Petroclean considered "prohibitively" expensive. Petroclean thereafter surveyed alternative landfills and completed applications for two possible disposal locations, Wayne Disposal and Four County. After receiving estimated disposal costs for the EAF dust from those sites, Petroclean forwarded the financial information to Tippins, which relied upon it to make its final selection of Four County as the disposal facility.

Although Petroclean did not make the *final* decision to dispose of the dust at Four County, it substantially contributed to and shared in that decision by locating and submitting a limited number of potential disposal sites from which Tippins could select. Moreover, it is evident from the record that Tippins at all times relied upon Petroclean's expertise in the field of hazardous waste management when deciding the appropriate means and location to dispose of the EAF dust. On these facts, Petroclean was far more than a mere conduit of the hazardous waste; rather, it actively participated in the site selection decision, such that Petroclean and Tippins, working together, selected Four County as the disposal site. Consequently, Petroclean is liable under CERCLA § 107(a)(4) as a transporter which selected the disposal facility.

NOTES

1. **Section 107(a)(4)'s Ambiguities.** What are the two ambiguities in section 107(a)(4), according to Tippins and Petroclean?

2. **CERCLA and the Use of Canons of Statutory Construction.** What canon of statutory construction did Tippins rely on in its argument that Petroclean is liable under CERCLA as a transporter? Why did that canon help Tippins' argument? How did the Third Circuit treat canons of statutory construction in the context of CERCLA? Did its view of CERCLA comport with any other case that you have read? Did the Third Circuit in fact apply the canon at issue here? Why or why not?

3. **Interpreting "Select."** What two possible definitions of "select" were offered in this case? Why did the Third Circuit's choice of definition matter to the outcome? Which definition did the Third Circuit choose? Why?

4. **The "De Micromis" Exemption for Arrangers and Transporters.** As part of the 2002 Brownfields Act, Pub. L. No 107–118, 115 Stat. 2356 (Jan. 11, 2002), Congress amended section 107 of CERCLA to add a "de micromis" exemption from liability for persons who would otherwise qualify as ***arrangers or transporters*** under section 107(a). Under this new provision, "a person shall not be liable, with respect to response costs at a facility on the National Priorities List, under this chapter if liability is based solely on paragraph (3) or (4) of subsection (a), and the person * * * can demonstrate that—"

(A) the total amount of material containing hazardous substances that the person arranged for disposal or treatment of, arranged with a transporter for transport for disposal or treatment of, or accepted for transport for disposal or treatment, at the facility was less than 110 gallons of liquid materials or less than 200 pounds of solid materials (or such greater or lesser amounts as the Administrator [of the EPA] may determine by regulation); and

(B) all or part of the disposal, treatment, or transport concerned occurred before April 1, 2001.

CERCLA § 107(*o*)(1), 42 U.S.C. § 9607(*o*)(1). The exemption does not apply if the arranger or transporter has already been criminally convicted for the activities in question, or if the President determines that the hazardous substances involved "have contributed significantly or could contribute significantly, either individually or in the aggregate, to the cost of response action or natural resource restoration with respect to the facility" or that the person has impeded the cleanup process. CERCLA § 107(*o*)(2), 42 U.S.C. § 9607(*o*)(2).

Why would Congress add this exemption to CERCLA? Why would Congress limit it to activities that occurred before April 1, 2001? What effect do you think that this exemption will have on PRP litigation?

* * *

C. THE CERCLA CLEANUP PROCESS

Cleaning up a site contaminated with hazardous substances is a long, multi-step process. The EPA has summarized those steps as follows.

SITE DISCOVERY

General description:
Process begins when a hazardous substance release (*e.g.*, spill, abandoned site) is identified and reported to EPA.

CERCLIS

General description:
Site is listed in the Comprehensive Environmental Response Compensation and Liability Information System (CERCLIS), which inventories and tracks releases providing comprehensive information to response agencies.

PRELIMINARY ASSESSMENT (PA)

General description:
This is the first stage of a site assessment. Preliminary Assessments are conducted to determine if an Emergency Removal Action is necessary, and to establish Site Inspection priorities.

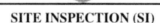

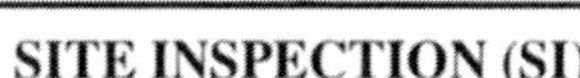

General description:
The second stage of a site assessment involves on-site investigations to ascertain the extent of a release or potential for release. The Site Inspection usually involves sample collection and may also include the installation of ground water monitoring wells.

REMOVAL ACTION*

General description:
A short-term, fast-track Federal response to prevent, minimize, or mitigate damage at sites where hazardous materials have been released or pose a threat of release. Removal Actions may occur at any step of the response process.

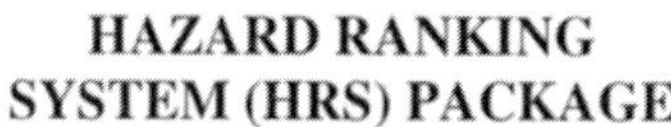

General description:
Site assessment information is then used in the Hazard Ranking System (HRS). HRS is a screening system to evaluate environmental hazards of a site.

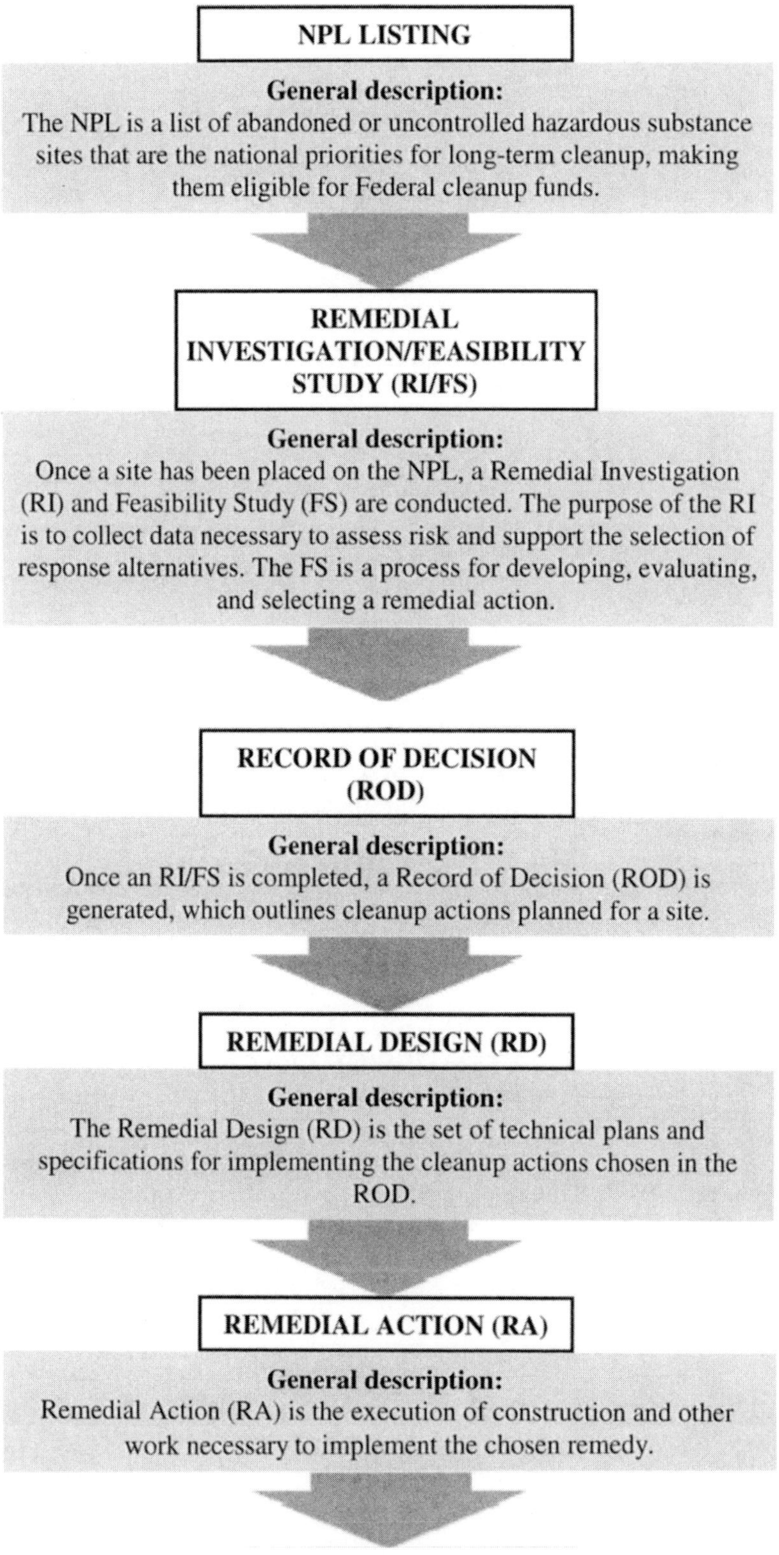

NPL LISTING

General description:
The NPL is a list of abandoned or uncontrolled hazardous substance sites that are the national priorities for long-term cleanup, making them eligible for Federal cleanup funds.

↓

REMEDIAL INVESTIGATION/FEASIBILITY STUDY (RI/FS)

General description:
Once a site has been placed on the NPL, a Remedial Investigation (RI) and Feasibility Study (FS) are conducted. The purpose of the RI is to collect data necessary to assess risk and support the selection of response alternatives. The FS is a process for developing, evaluating, and selecting a remedial action.

↓

RECORD OF DECISION (ROD)

General description:
Once an RI/FS is completed, a Record of Decision (ROD) is generated, which outlines cleanup actions planned for a site.

↓

REMEDIAL DESIGN (RD)

General description:
The Remedial Design (RD) is the set of technical plans and specifications for implementing the cleanup actions chosen in the ROD.

↓

REMEDIAL ACTION (RA)

General description:
Remedial Action (RA) is the execution of construction and other work necessary to implement the chosen remedy.

↓

CONSTRUCTION COMPLETION

General description:
Construction completion is where physical construction of all cleanup remedies is complete, all immediate threats have been addressed, and all long-term threats are under control.

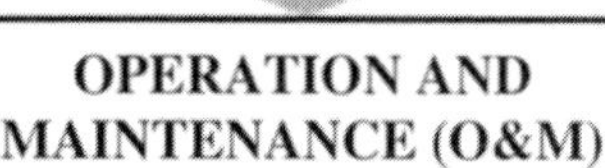

General description:
Operation and Maintenance are activities conducted at a site after remedial construction activities have been completed to ensure the cleanup methods are working properly.

DELETION FROM NPL

General description:
When EPA, in conjunction with the State, has determined that all appropriate response actions have been implemented and no further remedial measures are necessary, a Notice of Final Action to Delete is published in the Federal Register. If EPA receives no significant adverse or critical comments from the public within the 30-day comment period, the site is deleted from the NPL.

*[R]emovals can occur whenever they are determined to be necessary, and not during a specific stage in the cleanup process.

Adapted from U.S. E.P.A., SUPERFUND: 20 YEARS OF PROTECTING HUMAN HEALTH AND THE ENVIRONMENT 4–2 to 4–3 (Dec. 11, 2000), *available at* http://www.epa.gov/superfund/20years/index.htm (last updated Oct. 21, 2003).

In addition to listing the site on the NPL and devising a site-specific remedial action plan, the EPA also searches for PRPs to participate in cleanup and/or to help pay for that cleanup. *Id.* at 4–5 to 4–6.

How clean is clean enough? The EPA sets the clean-up standards for the remedial action on the basis of ***applicable or relevant and appropriate requirements*** **(ARARs)**. CERCLA § 121(d)(2)(A), 42 U.S.C. § 9621(d)(2)(A)(ii). ARARs can come from other federal environmental statutes such as the Clean Water Act, the Safe Drinking Water Act, or the Toxic Substances Control Act, or from state environmental law requirements. *Id.* For example, when PRPs had contaminated groundwater under the Rose Site in Michigan with polychlorinated biphenyls (PCBs), lead, arsenic, and other toxic materials, the Sixth Circuit upheld the imposition of the State of Michigan's water-quality related antidegradation laws as ARARs for the site. *United States v. Akzo Coatings of America, Inc.*, 949 F.2d 1409, 1421 n.9, 1442–48 (6th Cir. 1991).

D. THE FOUR CATEGORIES OF CERCLA DAMAGES

Pursuant to section 107(a), CERCLA PRPs are liable for four kinds of damages:

(A) all costs of removal or remedial action incurred by the United States Government or a State or Indian Tribe not inconsistent with the national contingency plan;

(B) any other necessary costs or response incurred by any other person consistent with the national contingency plan;

(C) damages for injury to, destruction of, or loss of natural resources, including the reasonable costs of assessing such injury, destruction, or loss resulting from such release; and

(D) the costs of any health assessment or health effects study carried out under section 9604(i) of this title.

CERCLA § 107(a)(1), 42 U.S.C. § 9607(a)(1). We will explore these categories in turn.

1. Response Costs

a. Consistency With the NCP

In order for response costs to be recoverable, they must be consistent with the ***national contingency plan*** **(NCP)**. However, as quoted above, CERCLA distinguishes between costs recoverable by governments—the United States, States, and Tribes—and costs recoverable by private PRPs. Governments can recover remedial and removal costs that are "not inconsistent" with the NCP, while private PRPs can only recover necessary and response costs that are "consistent" with the NCP. How do those differences affect the following two cases?

CALIFORNIA v. NEVILLE CHEMICAL COMPANY

358 F.3d 661 (9th Cir. 2004).

BERZON, CIRCUIT JUDGE:

* * * FACTUAL BACKGROUND

For 35 years, Neville Chemical Company (Neville) manufactured at its industrial facility in Santa Fe Springs, California, various chemical compounds for use in insecticides, solvents, metal working lubricants, and flame retardants. These activities contaminated the groundwater and soil at the facility. In 1986, the California Department of Toxic Substances Control (the Department) issued a Remedial Action Order, directing Neville to (1) begin the process of cleaning the site; (2) conduct a remedial investigation and feasibility study; (3) submit a draft remedial action plan (RAP); and, once the draft RAP was finalized, (4) implement the plan.

The Department sent Neville a letter on September 29, 1989, informing Neville of its obligation to pay an "activity fee" to the Department. The letter explained that the activity fee—$46,636.38—was "to partially cover the Department's cost of overseeing [Neville's] actions to characterize and satisfactorily remediate this site." At that time, the Department had a formal policy of "only collect[ing] direct program expenditures (generally laboratory or contract expenditures) beyond activity fees in cases where the responsible parties are being cooperative." In 1992, the Department rescinded this policy in favor of pursuing the full cost recovery of overseeing a clean-up, regardless of whether the responsible party was recalcitrant or cooperative.

In August 1991, Neville presented the Department with preliminary findings from the Remedial Investigation. In October 1991, the Department directed Neville to prepare a Groundwater Removal Action Proposal (the Proposal), in which Neville was to propose an expedited response to the contamination. The Department stated that the Proposal "should be consistent with a final cleanup strategy for groundwater as it may ultimately become the final remedy presented in the Remedial Action Plan." Neville submitted its Proposal on September 1, 1992. It included "three major components: an extraction system, a temporary on-site treatment system, and an effluent disposal system."

The Department reviewed the Proposal and, in January 1993, directed Neville to implement the extraction and treatment system. * * *

Neville submitted a Feasibility Study Technical Memorandum in August 1993, listing alternative possible remedies. * * *

Neville began to excavate three extraction wells at the site in April 1994. A month later, Neville submitted a Draft Feasibility Study, again proposing several alternative remedies. The Department responded with comments to this draft in June of 1994 * * *. In October of the same year, the Department sent Neville a letter expressing concern because Neville had not started construction of the Groundwater Removal System. * * *

Neville submitted a final Feasibility Study, discussing seven alternative groundwater remedial options, in December of 1994. Later that month the Department approved it.

Neville then submitted a draft remedial action plan. On May 8, 1995, after having circulated the draft for public review and comment and holding a public meeting to discuss the plan, the Department approved the final remedial action plan. The groundwater containment and treatment system originally designed as an interim removal action remained part of the final RAP.

ANALYSIS

* * * II. NEVILLE'S DEFENSES ON THE MERITS

Neville raised an affirmative defense—waiver and estoppel—in the district court. The argument was that Neville cannot be liable under CERCLA for the costs of overseeing the clean-up incurred by the Department because the Department had promised that it would not sue Neville for full recovery costs if Neville conducted the research, planning, and clean-up of the site. [The Department asserted that Neville owed $760,000 for the cleanup, plus attorneys' fees and costs. Neville argued that he owed only the original $46,636.38.] * *

CERCLA section 107(a) and (b), 42 U.S.C. § 9607(a) and (b), allow for only three defenses to CERCLA liability. A covered person is liable under the statute "subject only to the defenses set forth in subsection (b) of this section." 42 U.S.C. § 9607(a). Subsection (b) lists three defenses "(1) an act of God; (2) an act of war; [and] (3) an act or omission of a third party...." 42 U.S.C. § 9607(b)(1)-(3). * * *

Every court of appeals that has considered the precise question whether § 9607 permits equitable defenses has concluded that it does not, as the statutory defenses are exclusive. * * * [W]e conclude that the three statutory defenses are the only ones available, and that traditional equitable defenses are not. The district court was correct, therefore, in holding that Neville could not raise equitable defenses to liability under CERCLA.

* * * Neville makes one last defensive argument: The Department may not sue for its recovery costs, Neville contends, because those costs were not consistent with the national contingency plan. Whether a party can recover certain costs under § 9607 depends on whether or not those costs were incurred consistently with the "national contingency plan." 42 U.S.C. § 9607(a)(4)(A) (providing that a covered person who violates CERCLA "shall be liable for ... all costs of removal or remedial action incurred by the ... State ... *not inconsistent with the national contingency plan*") (emphasis added). The national contingency plan is promulgated by the EPA and "provide[s] the organizational structure and procedures for preparing and responding to ... releases of hazardous substances." 40 C.F.R. § 300.1. * * * To show that the Department's actions were inconsistent with the national contingency plan, the burden is on Neville to show that the Department acted in an arbitrary and capricious manner in choosing a particular response action. * * * When a state is seeking recovery of response costs, consistency with the national contingency plan is presumed. * * *

Neville has provided no evidence that the Department acted "arbitrarily and capriciously *in choosing a particular response action* to respond to a hazardous waste site." * * * In fact, Neville does not challenge any response action taken by the Department. Neville challenges instead the

Department's attempt to recover the full oversight costs after suggesting that, should Neville cooperate and conduct the clean-up itself, the Department would only require Neville to pay an "activity fee." This change in policy and pursuit of the full costs of oversight cannot be "inconsistent with" the national contingency plan, as the national contingency plan does not direct the state to limit its recovery of response costs in any way. *See* 40 C.F.R. §§ 300.1 *et seq.* The district court, therefore, did not err by finding that Neville was responsible for all the Department's response costs. * * *

NOTES

1. **CERCLA and Common–Law Defenses.** What is the relationship between CERCLA and common-law defenses to liability, according to the Ninth Circuit? Did that decision make sense? Why might Congress have wanted to eliminate PRPs' common law defenses to CERCLA liability? Do you think that the language of section 107(a) and (b) is sufficient to eliminate these defenses, given what you've learned about how courts treat the relationship between statutes and the common law? Why or why not?

2. **Government Recovery and Consistency.** What test did the Ninth Circuit use to evaluate whether California's response costs were "consistent" enough with the NCP to warrant California being able to recover them from Neville? Why did Neville fail this test?

3. **CERCLA's Statute of Limitations for Section 107 Response Costs.** CERCLA specifies a statute of limitations for actions under section 107 to recover response costs. Actions to recover removal costs "must be commenced * * * within 3 years after the completion of the removal action," unless there is a waiver or unless "the remedial action is initiated within 3 years after the completion of the removal action * * *." CERCLA § 113(g)(2), 42 U.S.C. § 9613(g)(2). In turn, an action for remedial costs "must be commenced * * * within 6 years after initiation of physical on-site construction of the remedial action * * *." CERCLA § 113(g)(2)(B), 42 U.S.C. § 9613(g)(2)(B). In a part of *California v. Neville Chemical Co.* not reproduced above, the Ninth Circuit determined that this six-year statute of limitations does not start to run until the relevant government agency (the EPA or the state) has approved the remedial action plan. *Id.* Why did this decision make sense, especially remembering that it was California seeking to recover response costs from Neville?

* * *

b. Using Section 107 for Cost Recovery

CERCLA includes provisions both for cost recovery in Section 107 and for contribution in Section 113. In two recent cases, the U.S. Supreme Court has sharply distinguished these provisions in terms of their use for cost recovery. As you read these cases, see if you can categorize the types of plaintiffs who can use each provision to recover their response costs.

COOPER INDUSTRIES, INC. v. AVIALL SERVICES, INC.

543 U.S. 157 (2004).

THOMAS, J., delivered the opinion of the Court, in which REHNQUIST, C.J., and O'CONNOR, SCALIA, KENNEDY, SOUTER, and BREYER, JJ., joined. GINSBURG, J., filed a dissenting opinion, in which STEVENS, J., joined.

Section 113(f)(1) of the Comprehensive Environmental Response, Compensation, and Liability Act of 1980 (CERCLA) allows persons who have undertaken efforts to clean up properties contaminated by hazardous substances to seek contribution from other parties liable under CERCLA. Section 113(f)(1) specifies that a party may obtain contribution "during or following any civil action" under CERCLA § 106 or § 107(a). The issue we must decide is whether a private party who has not been sued under § 106 or § 107(a) may nevertheless obtain contribution under § 113(f)(1) from other liable parties. We hold that it may not.

I

Under CERCLA, 94 Stat. 2767, the Federal Government may clean up a contaminated area itself, see § 104, or it may compel responsible parties to perform the cleanup, see § 106(a). In either case, the Government may recover its response costs under § 107, 42 U.S.C. § 9607 (2000 ed. and Supp. I), the "cost recovery" section of CERCLA. Section 107(a) lists four classes of potentially responsible persons (PRPs) and provides that they "shall be liable" for, among other things, "all costs of removal or remedial action incurred by the United States Government ... not inconsistent with the national contingency plan." § 107(a)(4)(A). Section 107(a) further provides that PRPs shall be liable for "any other necessary costs of response incurred by any other person consistent with the national contingency plan." § 107(a)(4)(B).

After CERCLA's enactment in 1980, litigation arose over whether § 107, in addition to allowing the Government and certain private parties to recover costs from PRPs, also allowed a PRP that had incurred response costs to recover costs from other PRPs. More specifically, the question was whether a private party that had incurred response costs, but that had done so voluntarily and was not itself subject to suit, had a cause of action for cost recovery against other PRPs. Various courts held that § 107(a)(4)(B) and its predecessors authorized such a cause of action.

After CERCLA's passage, litigation also ensued over the separate question whether a private entity that had been sued in a cost recovery action (by the Government or by another PRP) could obtain contribution from other PRPs. As originally enacted in 1980, CERCLA contained no provision expressly providing for a right of action for contribution. A number of District Courts nonetheless held that, although CERCLA did not mention the word "contribution," such a right arose either impliedly from provisions of the statute, or as a matter of federal common law. That conclusion was debatable in light of two decisions of this Court that refused to recognize implied or common-law rights to contribution in other federal statutes.

Congress subsequently amended CERCLA in the Superfund Amendments and Reauthorization Act of 1986 (SARA), 100 Stat. 1613, to provide an express cause of action for contribution, codified as CERCLA § 113(f)(1):

> "Any person may seek contribution from any other person who is liable or potentially liable under section 9607(a) of this title, during or following any civil action under section 9606 of this title or under section 9607(a) of this title. Such claims shall be brought in accordance with this section and the Federal Rules of Civil Procedure, and shall be governed by Federal law. In resolving contribution claims, the court may allocate response costs among liable parties using such equitable factors as the court determines are appropriate. Nothing in this subsection shall diminish the right of any person to bring an action for contribution in the absence of a civil action under section 9606 of this title or section 9607 of this title." *Id.,* at 1647, as codified in 42 U.S.C. § 9613(f)(1).

SARA also created a separate express right of contribution, § 113(f)(3)(B), for "[a] person who has resolved its liability to the United States or a State for some or all of a response action or for some or all of the costs of such action in an administrative or judicially approved settlement." In short, after SARA, CERCLA provided for a right to cost recovery in certain circumstances, § 107(a), and separate rights to contribution in other circumstances, §§ 113(f)(1), 113(f)(3)(B).

II

This case concerns four contaminated aircraft engine maintenance sites in Texas. Cooper Industries, Inc., owned and operated those sites until 1981, when it sold them to Aviall Services, Inc. Aviall operated the four sites for a number of years. Ultimately, Aviall discovered that both it and Cooper had contaminated the facilities when petroleum and other hazardous substances leaked into the ground and ground water through underground storage tanks and spills.

Aviall notified the Texas Natural Resource Conservation Commission (Commission) of the contamination. The Commission informed Aviall that it was violating state environmental laws, directed Aviall to clean up the site, and threatened to pursue an enforcement action if Aviall failed to undertake remediation. Neither the Commission nor the EPA, however, took judicial or administrative measures to compel cleanup.

Aviall cleaned up the properties under the State's supervision, beginning in 1984. Aviall sold the properties to a third party in 1995 and 1996, but remains contractually responsible for the cleanup. Aviall has incurred approximately $5 million in cleanup costs; the total costs may be even greater. In August 1997, Aviall filed this action against Cooper in the United States District Court for the Northern District of Texas, seeking to recover cleanup costs. The original complaint asserted a claim for cost recovery under CERCLA § 107(a), a separate claim for contribution under CERCLA § 113(f)(1), and state-law claims. Aviall later amended the complaint, combining its two CERCLA claims into a single, joint CERCLA claim. That claim alleged that, pursuant to § 113(f)(1), Aviall was entitled to seek contribution from Cooper, as a PRP under § 107(a), for response costs and other liability Aviall incurred in connection with the Texas facilities. Aviall continued to assert state-law claims as well.

Both parties moved for summary judgment, and the District Court granted Cooper's motion. The court held that Aviall, having abandoned its § 107 claim, sought contribution only under § 113(f)(1). The court held that § 113(f)(1) relief was unavailable to Aviall because it had not been sued under CERCLA § 106 or § 107. Having dismissed Aviall's federal claim, the court declined to exercise jurisdiction over the state-law claims.

A divided panel of the Court of Appeals for the Fifth Circuit affirmed. The majority, relying principally on the "during or following" language in the first sentence of § 113(f)(1), held that "a PRP seeking contribution from other PRPs under § 113(f)(1) must have a pending or adjudged § 106 administrative order or § 107(a) cost recovery action against it." The dissent reasoned that the final sentence of § 113(f)(1), the saving clause, clarified that the federal common-law right to contribution survived the enactment of § 113(f)(1), even absent a § 106 or § 107(a) civil action.

On rehearing en banc, the Fifth Circuit reversed by a divided vote, holding that § 113(f)(1) allows a PRP to obtain contribution from other PRPs regardless of whether the PRP has been sued under § 106 or § 107. The court held that "[s]ection 113(f)(1) authorizes suits against PRPs in both its first and last sentence[,] which states without qualification that 'nothing' in the section shall 'diminish' any person's right to bring a contribution action in the absence of a section 106 or section 107(a) action." The court reasoned in part that "may" in § 113(f)(1) did not mean "may only." Three members of the en banc court dissented for essentially the reasons given by the panel majority. We granted certiorari, and now reverse.

III

A

Section 113(f)(1) does not authorize Aviall's suit. The first sentence, the enabling clause that establishes the right of contribution, provides: "Any person *may* seek contribution ... *during or following* any civil action under section 9606 of this title or under section 9607(a) of this title," 42 U.S.C. § 9613(f)(1) (emphasis added). The natural meaning of this sentence is that contribution may only be sought subject to the specified conditions, namely, "during or following" a specified civil action.

Aviall answers that "may" should be read permissively, such that "during or following" a civil action is one, but not the exclusive, instance in which a person may seek contribution. We disagree. First, as just noted, the natural meaning of "may" in the context of the enabling clause is that it authorizes certain contribution actions—ones that satisfy the subsequent specified condition—and no others.

Second, and relatedly, if § 113(f)(1) were read to authorize contribution actions at any time, regardless of the existence of a § 106 or § 107(a) civil action, then Congress need not have included the explicit "during or following" condition. In other words, Aviall's reading would render part of the statute entirely superfluous, something we are loath to do. Likewise, if § 113(f)(1) authorizes contribution actions at any time, § 113(f)(3)(B), which permits contribution actions after settlement, is equally superfluous. There is no reason why Congress would bother to specify conditions under which a person may bring a contribution claim, and at the same time allow contribution actions absent those conditions.

The last sentence of § 113(f)(1), the saving clause, does not change our conclusion. That sentence provides: "Nothing in this subsection shall diminish the right of any person to bring an action for contribution in the absence of a civil action under section 9606 of this title or section 9607 of this title." 42 U.S.C. § 9613(f)(1). The sole function of the sentence is to clarify that § 113(f)(1) does nothing to "diminish" any cause(s) of action for contribution that may exist independently of § 113(f)(1). In other words, the sentence rebuts any presumption that the express right of contribution provided by the enabling clause is the exclusive cause of action for contribution available to a PRP. The sentence, however, does not itself establish a cause of action; nor does it expand § 113(f)(1) to authorize contribution actions not brought "during or following" a § 106 or § 107(a) civil action; nor does it specify what causes of action for contribution, if any, exist outside § 113(f)(1). Reading the saving clause to authorize § 113(f)(1) contribution actions not just "during or following" a civil action, but also before such an action, would again violate the settled rule that we must, if possible, construe a statute to give every word some operative effect.

Our conclusion follows not simply from § 113(f)(1) itself, but also from the whole of § 113. As noted above, § 113 provides two express avenues for contribution: § 113(f)(1) ("during or following" specified civil actions) and § 113(f)(3)(B) (after an administrative or judicially approved settlement that resolves liability to the United States or a State). Section 113(g)(3) then provides two corresponding 3–year limitations periods for contribution actions, one beginning at the date of judgment, § 113(g)(3)(A), and one beginning at the date of settlement, § 113(g)(3)(B). Notably absent from § 113(g)(3) is any provision for starting the limitations period if a judgment or settlement never occurs, as is the case with a purely voluntary cleanup. The lack of such a provision supports the conclusion that, to assert a contribution claim under § 113(f), a party must satisfy the conditions of either § 113(f)(1) or § 113(f)(3)(B).

Each side insists that the purpose of CERCLA bolsters its reading of § 113(f)(1). Given the clear meaning of the text, there is no need to resolve this dispute or to consult the purpose of CERCLA at all. * * * Section 113(f)(1), 100 Stat. 1647, authorizes contribution claims only "during or following" a civil action under § 106 or § 107(a), and it is undisputed that Aviall has never been subject to such an action. Aviall therefore has no § 113(f)(1) claim.

B

Aviall and *amicus* Lockheed Martin contend that, in the alternative to an action for contribution under § 113(f)(1), Aviall may recover costs under § 107(a)(4)(B) even though it is a PRP. The dissent would have us so hold. We decline to address the issue. Neither the District Court, nor the Fifth Circuit panel, nor the Fifth Circuit sitting en banc considered Aviall's § 107 claim. * * *

C

In addition to leaving open whether Aviall may seek cost recovery under § 107, we decline to decide whether Aviall has an implied right to contribution under § 107. * * *

* * *

We hold only that § 113(f)(1) does not support Aviall's suit. We therefore reverse the judgment of the Fifth Circuit and remand the case for further proceedings consistent with this opinion.

It is so ordered.

JUSTICE GINSBURG, with whom JUSTICE STEVENS joins, dissenting.

Aviall Services, Inc., purchased from Cooper Industries, Inc., property that was contaminated with hazardous substances. Shortly after the purchase, the Texas Natural Resource Conservation Commission notified Aviall that it would institute enforcement action if Aviall failed to remediate the property. Aviall promptly cleaned up the site and now seeks reimbursement from Cooper. In my view, the Court unnecessarily defers decision on Aviall's entitlement to recover cleanup costs from Cooper.

* * * In its original complaint, Aviall identified § 107 as the federal-law basis for an independent cost-recovery claim against Cooper, and § 113 as the basis for a contribution claim. In amended pleadings, Aviall alleged both §§ 107 and 113 as the federal underpinning for its contribution claim. Aviall's use of §§ 113 and 107 in tandem to assert a contribution claim conformed its pleading to then-governing Fifth Circuit precedent, which held that a CERCLA contribution action arises through the joint operation of §§ 107(a) and 113(f)(1). A party obliged by circuit precedent to plead in a certain way can hardly be deemed to have waived a plea the party could have maintained had the law of the circuit permitted him to do so.

* * * I see no cause for protracting this litigation by requiring the Fifth Circuit to revisit a determination it has essentially made already: Federal courts, prior to the enactment of § 113(f)(1), had correctly held that PRPs could "recover [under § 107] a proportionate share of their costs in actions for contribution against other PRPs," 312 F.3d, at 687; nothing in § 113 retracts that right. Accordingly, I would not defer a definitive ruling by this Court on the question whether Aviall may pursue a § 107 claim for relief against Cooper.

* * *

UNITED STATES v. ATLANTIC RESEARCH CORPORATION

551 U.S. 128 (2007).

THOMAS, J., delivered the opinion for a unanimous Court.

Two provisions of the Comprehensive Environmental Response, Compensation, and Liability Act of 1980 (CERCLA)—§§ 107(a) and 113(f)—allow private parties to recover expenses associated with cleaning up contaminated sites. 42 U.S.C. §§ 9607(a), 9613(f). In this case, we must decide a question left open in *Cooper Industries, Inc. v. Aviall Services, Inc.,* 543 U.S. 157, 161 (2004): whether § 107(a) provides so-called potentially responsible parties (PRPs), 42 U.S.C. §§ 9607(a)(1)-(4), with a cause of action to recover costs from other PRPs. We hold that it does.

I

A

Courts have frequently grappled with whether and how PRPs may recoup CERCLA-related costs from other PRPs. The questions lie at the intersection of two statutory provisions—CERCLA §§ 107(a) and 113(f). Section 107(a) defines four categories of PRPs, 42 U.S.C. §§ 9607(a)(1)-(4), and makes them liable for, among other things:

> "(A) all costs of removal or remedial action incurred by the United States Government or a State or an Indian tribe not inconsistent with the national contingency plan; [and]
>
> "(B) any other necessary costs of response incurred by any other person consistent with the national contingency plan." §§ 9607(a)(4)(A)-(B).

Enacted as part of the Superfund Amendments and Reauthorization Act of 1986 (SARA), 100 Stat. 1613, § 113(f) authorizes one PRP to sue another for contribution in certain circumstances. 42 U.S.C. § 9613(f).

Prior to the advent of § 113(f)'s express contribution right, some courts held that § 107(a)(4)(B) provided a cause of action for a private party to recover voluntarily incurred response costs and to seek contribution after having been sued. After SARA's enactment, however, some Courts of Appeals believed it necessary to "direc[t] traffic between"

§ 107(a) and § 113(f). As a result, many Courts of Appeals held that § 113(f) was the exclusive remedy for PRPs. But as courts prevented PRPs from suing under § 107(a), they expanded § 113(f) to allow PRPs to seek "contribution" even in the absence of a suit under § 106 or § 107(a).

In *Cooper Industries,* we held that a private party could seek contribution from other liable parties only after having been sued under § 106 or § 107(a). This narrower interpretation of § 113(f) caused several Courts of Appeals to reconsider whether PRPs have rights under § 107(a)(4)(B), an issue we declined to address in *Cooper Industries*. After revisiting the issue, some courts have permitted § 107(a) actions by PRPs. However, at least one court continues to hold that § 113(f) provides the exclusive cause of action available to PRPs. Today, we resolve this issue.

B

In this case, respondent Atlantic Research leased property at the Shumaker Naval Ammunition Depot, a facility operated by the Department of Defense. At the site, Atlantic Research retrofitted rocket motors for petitioner United States. Using a high-pressure water spray, Atlantic Research removed pieces of propellant from the motors. It then burned the propellant pieces. Some of the resultant wastewater and burned fuel contaminated soil and ground water at the site.

Atlantic Research cleaned the site at its own expense and then sought to recover some of its costs by suing the United States under both §§ 107(a) and 113(f). After our decision in *Cooper Industries* foreclosed relief under § 113(f), Atlantic Research amended its complaint to seek relief under § 107(a) and federal common law. The United States moved to dismiss, arguing that § 107(a) does not allow PRPs (such as Atlantic Research) to recover costs. The District Court granted the motion to dismiss, relying on a case decided prior to our decision * * *.

The Court of Appeals for the Eighth Circuit reversed. Recognizing that *Cooper Industries* undermined the reasoning of its prior precedent, the Court of Appeals joined the Second and Seventh Circuits in holding that § 113(f) does not provide "the exclusive route by which [PRPs] may recover cleanup costs." The court reasoned that § 107(a)(4)(B) authorized suit by any person other than the persons permitted to sue under § 107(a)(4)(A). Accordingly, it held that § 107(a)(4)(B) provides a cause of action to Atlantic Research. To prevent perceived conflict between §§ 107(a)(4)(B) and 113(f)(1), the Court of Appeals reasoned that PRPs that "have been subject to §§ 106 or 107 enforcement actions are still required to use § 113, thereby ensuring its continued vitality." We granted certiorari, and now affirm.

II

A

The parties' dispute centers on what "other person[s]" may sue under § 107(a)(4)(B). The Government argues that "any other person" refers to any person not identified as a PRP in §§ 107(a)(1)-(4). In other words, subparagraph (B) permits suit only by non-PRPs and thus bars Atlantic Research's claim. Atlantic Research counters that subparagraph (B) takes its cue from subparagraph (A), not the earlier paragraphs (1)-(4). In accord with the Court of Appeals, Atlantic Research believes that subparagraph (B) provides a cause of action to anyone except the United States, a State, or an Indian tribe—the persons listed in subparagraph (A). We agree with Atlantic Research.

Statutes must "be read as a whole." Applying that maxim, the language of subparagraph (B) can be understood only with reference to subparagraph (A). The provisions are adjacent and have remarkably similar structures. Each concerns certain costs that have been incurred by certain entities and that bear a specified relationship to the national contingency plan. Bolstering the structural link, the text also denotes a relationship between the two provisions. By using the phrase "other necessary costs," subparagraph (B) refers to and differentiates the relevant costs from those listed in subparagraph (A).

In light of the relationship between the subparagraphs, it is natural to read the phrase "any other person" by referring to the immediately preceding subparagraph (A), which permits suit only by the United States, a State, or an Indian tribe. The phrase "any other person" therefore means any person other than those three. See 42 U.S.C. § 9601(21) (defining "person" to include the United States and the various States). Consequently, the plain language of subparagraph (B) authorizes cost-recovery actions by any private party, including PRPs.

The Government's interpretation makes little textual sense. In subparagraph (B), the phrase "any other necessary costs" and the phrase "any other person" both refer to antecedents—"costs" and "person[s]"—located in some previous statutory provision. Although "any other necessary costs" clearly references the costs in subparagraph (A), the Government would inexplicably interpret "any other person" to refer not to the persons listed in subparagraph (A) but to the persons listed as PRPs in paragraphs (1)-(4). Nothing in the text of § 107(a)(4)(B) suggests an intent to refer to antecedents located in two different statutory provisions. Reading the statute in the manner suggested by the Government would destroy the symmetry of §§ 107(a)(4)(A) and (B) and render subparagraph (B) internally confusing.

Moreover, the statute defines PRPs so broadly as to sweep in virtually all persons likely to incur cleanup costs. Hence, if PRPs do not qualify as "any other person" for purposes of § 107(a)(4)(B), it is unclear what private party would. The Government posits that § 107(a)(4)(B) authorizes relief for "innocent" private parties—for instance, a landowner whose land has been contaminated by another. But even parties not responsible for contamination may fall within the broad definitions of PRPs in §§ 107(a)(1)-(4). See 42 U.S.C. § 9607(a)(1) (listing "the owner and operator of a . . . facility" as a PRP); see also *United States v. Alcan Aluminum*

Corp., 315 F.3d 179, 184 (C.A.2 2003) ("CERCLA § 9607 is a strict liability statute"). The Government's reading of the text logically precludes all PRPs, innocent or not, from recovering cleanup costs. Accordingly, accepting the Government's interpretation would reduce the number of potential plaintiffs to almost zero, rendering § 107(a)(4)(B) a dead letter.

According to the Government, our interpretation suffers from the same infirmity because it causes the phrase "any other person" to duplicate work done by other text. In the Government's view, the phrase "any other necessary costs" "already precludes governmental entities from recovering under" § 107(a)(4)(B). Even assuming the Government is correct, it does not alter our conclusion. The phrase "any other person" performs a significant function simply by clarifying that subparagraph (B) excludes the persons enumerated in subparagraph (A). In any event, our hesitancy to construe statutes to render language superfluous does not require us to avoid surplusage at all costs. It is appropriate to tolerate a degree of surplusage rather than adopt a textually dubious construction that threatens to render the entire provision a nullity.

B

The Government also argues that our interpretation will create friction between §§ 107(a) and 113(f), the very harm courts of appeals have previously tried to avoid. In particular, the Government maintains that our interpretation, by offering PRPs a choice between §§ 107(a) and 113(f), effectively allows PRPs to circumvent § 113(f)'s shorter statute of limitations. See 42 U.S.C. §§ 9613(g)(2)–(3). Furthermore, the Government argues, PRPs will eschew equitable apportionment under § 113(f) in favor of joint and several liability under § 107(a). Finally, the Government contends that our interpretation eviscerates the settlement bar set forth in § 113(f)(2).

We have previously recognized that §§ 107(a) and 113(f) provide two "clearly distinct" remedies. "CERCLA provide[s] for a *right to cost recovery* in certain circumstances, § 107(a), and *separate rights to contribution* in other circumstances, §§ 113(f)(1), 113(f)(3)(B)." The Government, however, uses the word "contribution" as if it were synonymous with any apportionment of expenses among PRPs. This imprecise usage confuses the complementary yet distinct nature of the rights established in §§ 107(a) and 113(f).

Section 113(f) explicitly grants PRPs a right to contribution. Contribution is defined as the "tortfeasor's right to collect from others responsible for the same tort after the tortfeasor has paid more than his or her proportionate share, the shares being determined as a percentage of fault." BLACK'S LAW DICTIONARY 353 (8th ed. 2004). Nothing in § 113(f) suggests that Congress used the term "contribution" in anything other than this traditional sense. The statute authorizes a PRP to seek contribution "during or following" a suit under § 106 or § 107(a). 42 U.S.C. § 9613(f)(1). Thus, § 113(f)(1) permits suit before or after the establishment of common liability. In either case, a PRP's right to contribution under § 113(f)(1) is contingent upon an inequitable distribution of common liability among liable parties.

By contrast, § 107(a) permits recovery of cleanup costs but does not create a right to contribution. A private party may recover under § 107(a) without any establishment of liability to a third party. Moreover, § 107(a) permits a PRP to recover only the costs it has "incurred" in cleaning up a site. 42 U.S.C. § 9607(a)(4)(B). When a party pays to satisfy a settlement agreement or a court judgment, it does not incur its own costs of response. Rather, it reimburses other parties for costs that those parties incurred.

Accordingly, the remedies available in §§ 107(a) and 113(f) complement each other by providing causes of action "to persons in different procedural circumstances." Section 113(f)(1) authorizes a contribution action to PRPs with common liability stemming from an action instituted under § 106 or § 107(a). And § 107(a) permits cost recovery (as distinct from contribution) by a private party that has itself incurred cleanup costs. Hence, a PRP that pays money to satisfy a settlement agreement or a court judgment may pursue § 113(f) contribution. But by reimbursing response costs paid by other parties, the PRP has not incurred its own costs of response and therefore cannot recover under § 107(a). As a result, though eligible to seek contribution under § 113(f)(1), the PRP cannot simultaneously seek to recover the same expenses under § 107(a). Thus, at least in the case of reimbursement, the PRP cannot choose the 6–year statute of limitations for cost-recovery actions over the shorter limitations period for § 113(f) contribution claims.

For similar reasons, a PRP could not avoid § 113(f)'s equitable distribution of reimbursement costs among PRPs by instead choosing to impose joint and several liability on another PRP in an action under § 107(a). The choice of remedies simply does not exist. In any event, a defendant PRP in such a § 107(a) suit could blunt any inequitable distribution of costs by filing a § 113(f) counterclaim. Resolution of a § 113(f) counterclaim would necessitate the equitable apportionment of costs among the liable parties, including the PRP that filed the § 107(a) action. 42 U.S.C. § 9613(f)(1) ("In resolving contribution claims, the court may allocate response costs among liable parties using such equitable factors as the court determines are appropriate").

Finally, permitting PRPs to seek recovery under § 107(a) will not eviscerate the settlement bar set forth in § 113(f)(2). That provision prohibits § 113(f) contribution claims against "[a] person who has resolved its liability to the United States or a State in an administrative or judicially approved settlement.... " 42 U.S.C. § 9613(f)(2). The settlement bar does not by its terms protect against cost-recovery liability under § 107(a). For several reasons, we doubt this supposed loophole would discourage settlement. First, as stated above, a defendant PRP may trigger equitable apportionment by filing a § 113(f) counterclaim. A district court applying traditional rules of equity would undoubtedly consider any prior settlement as part of the liability calculus. Second, the settlement bar continues to provide significant protection from contribution suits by PRPs that have inequitably reimbursed the costs incurred by another party. Third, settlement carries the inherent benefit of finally resolving liability as to the United States or a State.

III

Because the plain terms of § 107(a)(4)(B) allow a PRP to recover costs from other PRPs, the statute provides Atlantic Research with a cause of action. We therefore affirm the judgment of the Court of Appeals.

It is so ordered.

NOTES

1. **The Meaning of It All.** So, who can bring a Section 107 cost recovery action, and when? Why would PRP plaintiffs prefer a cost recovery action? Who can bring a Section 113(f) contribution action, and when? What are the differences in remedy between the two sections? What are the two different statutes of limitation? Which provision will governments almost always use? Why are governments different from PRPs, most of the time, in pursuing costs under CERCLA?

2. **Incentives Under CERCLA.** As has been true throughout this chapter, Congress has used federal statutes to change the incentives created under the common law pertaining to waste disposal problems, especially nuisance. An argument can be made that the Supreme Court in *Cooper Industries v. Aviall Services* did not adequately consider the disincentives it was (at least potentially) creating. Specifically, there was a real possibility after *Cooper Industries* that PRPs (such as the current owner) who voluntarily cleaned up a contaminated property would have *no* statutory basis for seeking any part of the cleanup costs from other PRPs. Does *Atlantic Research* adequately "fix" that potential disincentive to voluntary cleanups? Why or why not?

3. **Interpreting Section 113(f).** How did the majority in *Cooper Industries* interpret Section 113(f)? What was the key wording of this provision, according to the majority? Why is the history of that contribution provision relevant, according to the majority? Do you agree with this interpretation? Is it significant that the dissenters do not really disagree with the majority's interpretation of Section 113(f)?

4. **Interpreting Section 107.** How did the unanimous Supreme Court interpret Section 107 in *Atlantic Research*? What phrase was the key phrase in Section 107, according to the Court? What interpretation did the government try to offer? Why was that interpretation problematic, according to the Court?

5. **Cost Recovery, Joint and Several Liability, Contribution, and Equitable Apportionment.** In *Atlantic Research*, the government argues that one of the key differences between Section 107 and Section 113 is that Section 107 operates under principles of joint and several liability, while

Section 113 operates under principles of equitable apportionment. One of the more confusing aspects of CERCLA is the multiple manners in which CERCLA liability is finally distributed among the PRPs, because CERCLA simultaneously incorporates tort conceptions of joint and several liability, divisibility of harm, and equitable apportionment. We will discuss the interplay of those concepts in Part E.

* * *

2. Natural Resources Damages

a. *Statutory Provisions*

Besides response costs, CERCLA PRPs are liable for "damages for injury to, destruction of, or loss of natural resources, including the reasonable costs of assessing such injury, destruction, or loss resulting from such a release * * *." CERCLA § 107(a)(C), 42 U.S.C. § 9607(a)(C). "Natural resources" are "land, fish, wildlife, biota, air, water, ground water, drinking water supplies, and other such resources belonging to, managed by, held in trust by, appertaining to, or otherwise controlled by the United States * * *, any State or local government, any foreign government, any Indian tribe, or, if such resources are subject to a trust restriction on alienation, any member of an Indian tribe." CERCLA § 101(16), 42 U.S.C. § 9601(16). Thus, CERCLA requires PRPs to pay for injury to *public* natural resources, but not for injury to private property and private natural resources. As a result, only government or tribal trustees can sue to recover ***natural resources damages*** **(NRDs)**. CERCLA § 107(f)(1), (2), 42 U.S.C. § 9607(f)(1), (2). Moreover, as was discussed in connection with past owner and operator liability, PRP liability for CERCLA NRDs is not retroactive. Instead, PRPs are liable only for NRDs that occurred after December 11, 1980, CERCLA's effective date. CERCLA § 107(f)(1), 42 U.S.C. § 9607(f)(1).

Public trustees must sue for NRDs within three years of "[t]he date of the discovery of the loss and its connection to the release in question" or the date on which the EPA promulgates NRD regulations, whichever is *later*. CERCLA § 113(g)(1), 42 U.S.C. § 9613(g)(1). Congress structured the NRD statute of limitations this way because the EPA took a very long time to promulgate the CERCLA NRD regulations, not issuing the first set until 1986, and Congress did not want PRPs to escape liability for NRDs that they caused between 1980 and the time the regulations were promulgated.

b. *The NRD Regulations*

The CERCLA NRD regulations are a good example not only of agency delay in promulgating environmental regulations (remember the land ban "hammer" provisions under RCRA?), but also the multiple rounds of litigation to which most complex and/or expense-incurring regulations are subject. Shortly after the EPA promulgated the 1986 NRD regulations, they were challenged in the District of Columbia Court of Appeals (D.C.

Circuit). Addressing 11 substantive issues, the D.C. Circuit invalidated key portions of the 1986 regulations. *Ohio v. United States Department of the Interior*, 880 F.2d 432 (D.C. Cir. 1989). Most importantly, the D.C. Circuit invalidated the EPA's use of the "lesser of" rule. The EPA's regulations required that NRDs be measured by the *lesser of* the costs of restoring the natural resources or the resources' use value. The D.C. Circuit stressed that, as a practical matter, the "lesser of" rule meant that public trustees would rarely recover the full costs of restoring the environment:

> [W]e initially stress the enormous practical significance of the "lesser of" rule. A hypothetical example will illustrate the point: imagine a hazardous substance spill that kills a rookery of fur seals and destroys a habitat for seabirds at a sealife reserve. The lost use value of the seals and seabird habitat would be measured by the market value of the fur seals' pelts (which would be approximately $15 each) plus the selling price per acre of land comparable in value to that on which the spoiled bird habitat was located. Even if, as likely, that use value turns out to be far less than the cost of restoring the rookery and seabird habitat, it would nonetheless be the only measure of damages eligible for the presumption of recoverability under the Interior rule.

Id. at 442. Determining that in the CERCLA NRD provisions Congress had expressed a distinct preference for restoration, the D.C. Circuit invalidated the "lesser of" rule and remanded the NRD regulations to the EPA for amendment to emphasize that the basic measure of NRDs should be the costs of restoration. *Id.* at 459.

The EPA amended its NRD regulations in March 1994. The new regulations, like the 1986 regulations, were subject to immediate court challenge by both industry representatives and by states, and the D.C. Circuit eventually resolved their challenges in *Kennecott Utah Copper Corp. v. U.S. Department of the Interior*, 88 F.3d 1191 (D.C. Cir. 1996). Some of the more important decisions in that case were as follows:

- Under the 1986 Regulations, trustees had to choose the most cost-effective restoration option as the measure of damages. 43 C.F.R. § 11.82(f)(1) (1986); 51 Fed. Reg. at 27,749. The 1994 Regulations eliminated this provision. Instead, the 1994 regulations instruct natural resources trustees to evaluate each option on the basis of its cost-effectiveness, but also to consider nine other listed factors and "all relevant considerations." The D.C. Circuit upheld this change on the ground that nothing in CERCLA requires the most cost-effective restoration option.
- The D.C. Circuit rejected the Industry Petitioners' argument that the EPA had to adopt a "gross disproportionality" standard in order to avoid restoration solutions that cost far more than the value of the restored resources.
- The D.C. Circuit allowed natural resources damages to be measured in terms of the loss of ecosystem services, but it remanded the regulations to the EPA so that the EPA could make clear that

natural resources trustees were not allowed to recover *both* the costs of restoring the ecosystem services *and* the costs of restoring the resources themselves.

- Against Montana's argument that there should be a preference for restoring and rehabilitating the damaged resources over acquisition of replacement resources, the D.C. Circuit instead concluded that Congress had not clearly expressed such a preference.

Notice that the D.C. Circuit resolved both sets of challenges to the natural resources damages regulations. Parties to environmental lawsuits may occasionally choose to litigate in the D.C. Circuit for strategic reasons, because the D.C. Circuit is often perceived to be more "neutral" (and certainly less liberal) than other federal circuits. With respect to CERCLA regulations, however, challengers have no choice regarding their forum. Section 113 specifies:

> Review of any regulation promulgated under this chapter may be had upon application by any interested person only in the Circuit Court of Appeals of the United States for the District of Columbia. Any such application shall be made within ninety days from the date of promulgation of such regulations. Any matter with respect to which review could have been obtained under this subsection shall not be subject to judicial review in any civil or criminal proceeding for enforcement or to obtain damages of recovery of response costs.

CERCLA § 113(a), 42 U.S.C. § 9613(a). Forum designation provisions appear in several federal environmental statutes, including the Clean Air Act, CAA § 307(b), 42 U.S.C. § 7607(b), and the Clean Water Act, CWA § 509(b)(1), 33 U.S.C. § 1369(b)(1). To the extent that such provisions can be generalized, they usually require that petitions to review specific administrative actions by the implementing agency be filed in particular Courts of Appeal—often, as with CERCLA, the D.C. Circuit—rather than in the federal district courts. However, such provisions can be highly specific and can become a trap for the unwary lawyer who files a lawsuit in the wrong court, because, as with the CERCLA provision above, the forum designation provisions can require filing of lawsuits within relative short periods of time—only 90 days for CERCLA regulations.

c. *Assessing NRDs in the Real World: The* Exxon Valdez *Oil Spill*

Responsible parties are liable for NRDs not only under CERCLA but also under the companion oil spill provisions in the Clean Water Act, CWA § 311, 33 U.S.C. § 1321, and the Oil Pollution Act of 1990, 33 U.S.C. §§ 2701–2720, 2731–2738, 2751–2752. The most extensive efforts in assessing NRDs have come in connection with the 1989 *Exxon Valdez* oil spill in Alaska, in which the *Exxon Valdez* oil tanker released approximately 11 million gallons of crude oil (enough to fill 125 Olympic-sized pools) into Prince William Sound, affecting 1300 miles of Alaska's shoreline. Exxon claims to have spent $2.1 billion to clean up the spill; it was also assessed $150 million in criminal fines ($125 million of which the court forgave in light of Exxon's cleanup efforts) and $100 million in criminal restitution.

Figure 1-14: A Protective Boom Around a Salmon Hatchery After the *Exxon Valdez* Oil Spill
National Oceanic & Atmospheric Administration photo.

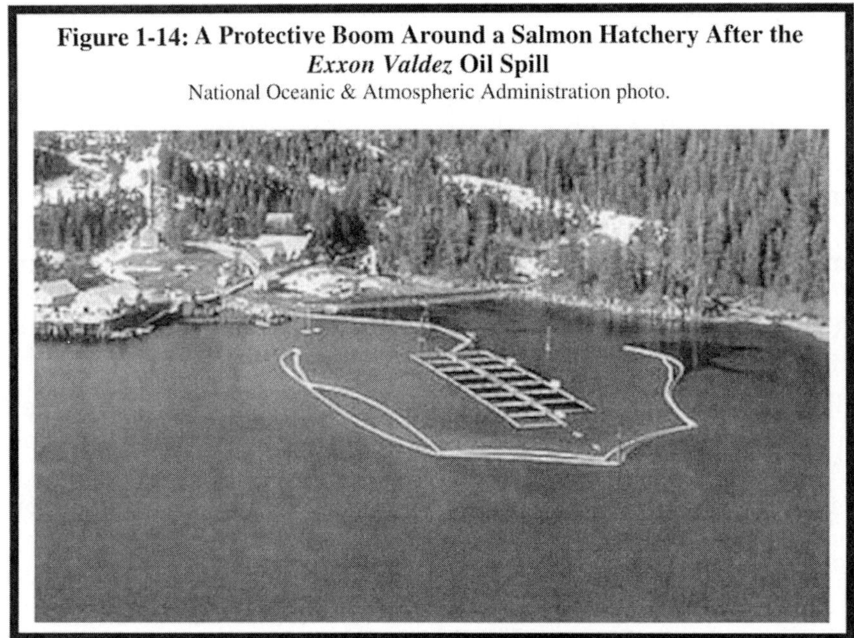

Exxon settled the NRDs with the government trustees, agreeing to pay at least $900 million over 10 years to restore the damaged natural resources, and including an additional $100 million "reopener" if the original payments weren't enough. Exxon's last regularly scheduled NRD payment was in 2001, although cleanup and restoration efforts continue. See the Exxon Valdez Oil Spill Trustee Council web site, http://www.evostc.state.ak.us, for more information on the trustees' efforts to assess and value the damages from the oil spill, including efforts to assign a value to marine creatures ranging from sea gulls to sea otters to orcas and humpback whales.

* * *

3. Health Assessments and Health Effects Studies

The fourth, rather limited category of CERCLA liability states that PRPs are liable for "the costs of any health assessment or health effects study carried out under section 9604(i) of this title." CERCLA § 107(a)(D), 42 U.S.C. § 9607(a)(D). The referenced section created the ***Agency for Toxic Substances and Disease Registry*** **(ATSDR)** within the U.S. Public Health Service. CERCLA § 104(i)(1), 42 U.S.C. § 9604(i)(1). The Administrator of the ATSDR must complete a ***health assessment*** for every site on the National Priority List (NPL) within a year of the site being listed. *Id.* § 104(i)(6)(A), 42 U.S.C. § 9604(i)(6)(A). This health assessment

> shall include preliminary assessments of the potential risk to human health posed by individual sites and facilities, based on such factors as the nature and extent of contamination, the existence of potential pathways of human exposure (including ground or surface water contamination, air emissions, and food chain contamination), the size and potential susceptibility of the community within the likely pathways of exposure, the comparison of expected human exposure levels to the short-term and long-term health effects associated with identified hazardous substances and any available recommended exposure or tolerance limits for such hazardous substances, and the comparison of existing morbidity and mortality data on diseases that may be associated with the observed levels of exposure.

Id. § 104(i)(6)(F), 42 U.S.C. § 9604(i)(6)(F). The Administrator of the ATSDR is also supposed to finish the assessment "promptly, and, to the maximum extent practicable, before the completion of the remedial investigation and feasibility study at the facility concerned." *Id.* § 104(i)(6)(D), 42 U.S.C. § 9604(i)(6)(D). In other words, the health assessment is supposed to inform the EPA's decision regarding the remedial action taken at the site.

The Administrator of the ATSDR can also, "on the basis of the results of a health assessment, * * * conduct a pilot ***study of health effects*** for selected groups of exposed individuals in order to determine the desirability of conducting full scale epidemiological or other health studies of the entire exposed population." CERCLA § 104(i)(7)(A), 42 U.S.C. § 9604(i)(7)(A). If the pilot studies indicate that full-scale studies are warranted, "the Administrator shall conduct such full scale epidemiological or other health studies as may be necessary to determine the health effects on the population exposed to hazardous substances from a release or threatened release." *Id.* § 104(i)(7)(B), 42 U.S.C. § 9604(i)(7)(B). If these studies reveal "a significant increased risk of adverse health effects in humans from exposure to hazardous substances," the ATSDR must initiate a ***health surveillance program*** for the exposed population, including periodic medical testing and a referral system for treatment. *Id.* § 104(i)(9), 42 U.S.C. § 9604(i)(9).

4. Non–CERCLA Damages: Private Damages

Notice that, although PRPs are liable for the costs of public NRDs, health assessments. and health effects studies, they are *not* liable under CERCLA for any private damages, such as damage to private property or the actual costs of medical treatment. Does that mean that PRPs are off the hook for these damages—*i.e.*, that CERCLA eliminated state-law tort liability? No.

Because federal environmental statutes generally do not redress every kind of harm that can arise from a violator's unlawful conduct, most such statutes contain general ***savings provisions*** that preserve private litigants' state statutory and common-law causes of action. The Clean Water Act, for example, provides explicitly in its citizen suit provision that "[n]othing in this section shall restrict any right which any person (or class of persons) may have under any statute or common law to seek enforcement of any effluent standard or limitation or to seek other relief * * *." CWA § 505(e), 33 U.S.C. § 1365(e). RCRA contains an almost identical provision. RCRA § 7002(f), 42 U.S.C. § 6972(f).

CERCLA's citizen suit provision also contains a savings clause, which provides that "[t]his chapter does not affect or otherwise impair the rights of any person under Federal, State, or common law, *except with respect to the timing of review as provided in section [113(h),] 9613(h) of this title or as otherwise provided in section [309,] 9658 of this title*." CERCLA § 310(h), 42 U.S.C. § 9659(h) (emphasis added). Section 113(h) limits the availability of judicial review until after the site is cleaned up, stating that "[n]o Federal court shall have jurisdiction under Federal law * * * to review any challenges to removal or remedial action selected under section 9604 of this title, or to review any order issued under section 9606(a) of this title * * *." CERCLA § 113(h), 42 U.S.C. § 9613(h).

Section 309, in turn, changes the commencement date for any state statute of limitations for "any action brought under State law for personal injury, or property damages, which are caused or contributed to by exposure to any hazardous substance" to the federal discovery rule. CERCLA § 309(a)(1), (b)(4), 42 U.S.C.§ 9658(a)(1), (b)(4). Specifically, "if the applicable limitations period for such action [under state law] * * * provides a commencement date which is earlier than the federally required commencement date, such period shall commence at the federally required commencement date in lieu of the date specified in such State statute." *Id.* § 309(a)(1), 42 U.S.C. § 9658(a)(1). In other words, Congress ***preempted*** the commencement rules in state statutes of limitation for state-law causes of action brought in connection with CERCLA releases of hazardous substances. The "federally required commencement date" is "the date the plaintiff knew (or reasonably should have known) that the personal injury or property damages * * * were caused or contributed to by the hazardous substance or pollutant or contaminant concerned." *Id.* § 309(b)(4), 42 U.S.C. § 9658(b)(4).

CERCLA thus complicates the "saving" of state-law causes of action. However, once the "federally required commencement date" is established, state law still dictates both the length of the limitations period and the causes of action that may be available to the plaintiff. *See, e.g.*, *Freier v. Westinghouse Electric Corp.*, 303 F.3d 176 (2d Cir. 2002) (discussing the availability of wrongful death, survival, and loss of consortium claims under New York law in connection with exposure to hazardous substances deposited in a landfill).

In addition, adjudication of CERCLA liability can often help plaintiffs bringing pendant state-law causes of action, especially if those state-law actions are also strict liability offenses. For example, in *Scribner v. Summers*, 84 F.3d 554 (2d Cir. 1996), the defendant's previously-determined liability under CERCLA for releases of barium chloride supported the plaintiff's claims for property damages based on trespass and private nuisance.

E. DIVIDING CERCLA LIABILITY: JOINT AND SEVERAL LIABILITY, CONTRIBUTION, EQUITABLE APPORTIONMENT, AND SETTLEMENT

As many of the prior cases demonstrate, CERCLA PRPs often try to find ways to reduce their liability. One way that an established PRP can reduce its CERCLA liability is to share that liability with other PRPs. Given the multiple categories of PRPs in Section 107(a) and CERCLA's retroactive application, almost all major CERCLA sites have more than one PRP.

However, context matters. As the Supreme Court noted in *Atlantic Research*, Section 107 cost recovery actions traditionally differ from Section 113(f) contribution actions in how willing courts are to apportion liability among PRPs. In particular, when a *government* brings a cost recovery action under Section 107, courts usually turn to tort principles of joint and several liability to ensure that the government can recover all of its response costs.

In 2009, the U.S. Supreme Court discussed the use of joint and several liability in CERCLA cost recovery actions.

BURLINGTON NORTHERN AND SANTA FE RAILWAY COMPANY v. UNITED STATES

556 U.S. 599 (2009).

STEVENS, J., delivered the opinion of the Court, in which ROBERTS, C.J., and SCALIA, KENNEDY, SOUTER, THOMAS, BREYER, and ALITO, JJ., joined. GINSBURG, J., filed a dissenting opinion.

[NOTE: The facts of this case were presented in Part B.5, discussing arranger liability. The Supreme Court also addressed joint and several liability under CERCLA and the availability of equitable apportionment, presented here.]

I

The District Court conducted a 6–week bench trial in 1999 and four years later entered a judgment in favor of the Governments. In a lengthy order supported by 507 separate findings of fact and conclusions of law, the court held that both the Railroads and Shell were potentially responsible parties (PRPs) under CERCLA—the Railroads because they were owners of a portion of the facility, see 42 U.S.C. §§ 9607(a)(1)-(2), and Shell because it had "arranged for" the disposal of hazardous substances through its sale and delivery of D–D, see § 9607(a)(3).

Although the court found the parties liable, it did not impose joint and several liability on Shell and the Railroads for the entire response cost incurred by the Governments. The court found that the site contamination created a single harm but concluded that the harm was divisible and therefore capable of apportionment. Based on three figures—the percentage of the total area of the facility that was owned by the Railroads, the duration of B & B's business divided by the term of the Railroads' lease, and the Court's determination that only two of three polluting chemicals spilled on the leased parcel required remediation and that those two chemicals were responsible for roughly two-thirds of the overall site contamination requiring remediation—the court apportioned the Railroads' liability as 9% of the Governments' total response cost. Based on estimations of chemicals spills of Shell products, the court held Shell liable for 6% of the total site response cost.

The Governments appealed the District Court's apportionment, and Shell cross-appealed the court's finding of liability. * * * On the subject of apportionment, the Court of Appeals found "no dispute" on the question whether the harm caused by Shell and the Railroads was capable of apportionment. The court observed that a portion of the site contamination occurred before the Railroad parcel became part of the facility, only some of the hazardous substances were stored on the Railroad parcel, and "only some of the water on the facility washed over the Railroads' site." With respect to Shell, the court noted that not all of the hazardous substances spilled on the facility had been sold by Shell. Given those facts, the court readily concluded that "the contamination traceable to the Railroads and Shell, with adequate information, would be allocable, as would be the cost of cleaning up that contamination." Nevertheless, the Court of Appeals held that the District Court erred in finding that the record established a reasonable basis for apportionment. Because the burden of proof on the question of apportionment rested with Shell and the Railroads, the Court of Appeals reversed the District Court's apportionment of liability and held Shell and the Railroads jointly and severally liable for the Governments' cost of responding to the contamination of the Arvin facility.

The Railroads and Shell moved for rehearing *en banc*, which the Court of Appeals denied over the dissent of eight judges. We granted certiorari to determine * * * whether Shell and the Railroads were properly held liable for all response costs incurred by EPA and the State of California. [W]e now reverse.

* * * III

Having concluded that Shell is not liable as an arranger, we need not decide whether the Court of Appeals erred in reversing the District Court's apportionment of Shell's liability for the cost of remediation. We must, however, determine whether the Railroads were properly held jointly and severally liable for the full cost of the Governments' response efforts.

The seminal opinion on the subject of apportionment in CERCLA actions was written in 1983 by Chief Judge Carl Rubin of the United States District Court for the Southern District of Ohio. *United States v. Chem–Dyne Corp.,* 572 F. Supp. 802. After reviewing CERCLA's history, Chief Judge Rubin concluded that although the Act imposed a "strict liability standard," it did not mandate "joint and several" liability in every case. Rather, Congress intended the scope of liability to "be determined from traditional and evolving principles of common law[.]" The *Chem-Dyne* approach has been fully embraced by the Courts of Appeals.

Following *Chem-Dyne,* the courts of appeals have acknowledged that "[t]he universal starting point for divisibility of harm analyses in CERCLA cases" is § 433A of the RESTATEMENT (SECOND) OF TORTS. Under the RESTATEMENT,

> "when two or more persons acting independently caus[e] a distinct or single harm for which there is a reasonable basis for division according to the contribution of each, each is subject to liability only for the portion of the total harm that he has himself caused. RESTATEMENT (SECOND) OF TORTS, §§ 433A, 881 (1976); Prosser, LAW OF TORTS, pp. 313–314 (4th ed.1971).... But where two or more persons cause a single and indivisible harm, each is subject to liability for the entire harm. RESTATEMENT (SECOND) OF TORTS, § 875; Prosser, at 315–316."

In other words, apportionment is proper when "there is a reasonable basis for determining the contribution of each cause to a single harm." RESTATEMENT (SECOND) OF TORTS § 433A(1)(b), p. 434 (1963–1964).

Not all harms are capable of apportionment, however, and CERCLA defendants seeking to avoid joint and several liability bear the burden of proving that a reasonable basis for apportionment exists. When two or more causes produce a single, indivisible harm, "courts have refused to make an arbitrary apportionment for its own sake, and each of the causes is charged with responsibility for the entire harm." RESTATEMENT (SECOND) OF TORTS § 433A, Comment *i,* p. 440 (1963–1964).

Neither the parties nor the lower courts dispute the principles that govern apportionment in CERCLA cases, and both the District Court and Court of Appeals agreed that the harm created by the contamination of the Arvin site, although singular, was theoretically capable of apportionment. The question then is whether the record provided a reasonable basis for the District Court's conclusion that the Railroads were liable for only 9% of the harm caused by contamination at the Arvin facility.

The District Court criticized the Railroads for taking a " 'scorched earth,' all-or-nothing approach to liability," failing to acknowledge any responsibility for the release of hazardous substances that occurred on their parcel throughout the 13–year period of B & B's lease. According to the District Court, the Railroads' position on liability, combined with the Governments' refusal to acknowledge the potential divisibility of the harm, complicated the apportioning of liability. Yet despite the parties' failure to assist the court in linking the evidence supporting apportionment to the proper allocation of liability, the District Court ultimately concluded that this was "a classic 'divisible in terms of degree' case, both as to the time period in which defendants' conduct occurred, and ownership existed, and as to the estimated maximum contribution of each party's activities that released hazardous substances that caused Site contamination." Consequently, the District Court apportioned liability, assigning the Railroads 9% of the total remediation costs.

The District Court calculated the Railroads' liability based on three figures. First, the court noted that the Railroad parcel constituted only 19% of the surface area of the Arvin site. Second, the court observed that the Railroads had leased their parcel to B & B for 13 years, which was only 45% of the time B & B operated the Arvin facility. Finally, the court found that the volume of hazardous-substance-releasing activities on the B & B property was at least 10 times greater than the releases that occurred on the Railroad parcel, and it concluded that only spills of two chemicals, Nemagon and dinoseb (not D–D), substantially contributed to the contamination that had originated on the Railroad parcel and that those two chemicals had contributed to two-thirds of the overall site contamination requiring remediation. The court then multiplied .19 by .45 by .66 (two-thirds) and rounded up to determine that the Railroads were responsible for approximately 6% of the remediation costs. "Allowing for calculation errors up to 50%," the court concluded that the Railroads could be held responsible for 9% of the total CERCLA response cost for the Arvin site.

The Court of Appeals criticized the evidence on which the District Court's conclusions rested, finding a lack of sufficient data to establish the precise proportion of contamination that occurred on the relative portions of the Arvin facility and the rate of contamination in the years prior to B & B's addition of the Railroad parcel. The court noted that neither the duration of the lease nor the size of the leased area alone was a reliable measure of the harm caused by activities on the property owned by the Railroads, and—as the court's upward adjustment confirmed—the court had relied on estimates rather than specific and detailed records as a basis for its conclusions.

Despite these criticisms, we conclude that the facts contained in the record reasonably supported the apportionment of liability. The District Court's detailed findings make it abundantly clear that the primary pollution at the Arvin facility was contained in an unlined sump and an unlined pond in the southeastern portion of the facility most distant from the Railroads' parcel and that the spills of hazardous chemicals that occurred on the Railroad parcel contributed to no more than 10% of the total site contamination, some of which did not require remediation. With those background facts in mind, we are persuaded that it was reasonable for the court to use the size of the leased parcel and the duration of the lease as the starting point for its analysis. Although the Court of Appeals faulted the District Court for relying on the "simplest of considerations: percentages of land area, time of ownership, and types of hazardous products," these were the same factors the court had earlier acknowledged were *relevant* to the apportionment analysis.

The Court of Appeals also criticized the District Court's assumption that spills of Nemagon and dinoseb were responsible for only two-thirds of the chemical spills requiring remediation, observing that each PRP's share of the total harm was not necessarily equal to the quantity of pollutants that were deposited on its portion of the total facility. Although the evidence adduced by the parties did not allow the court to calculate precisely the amount of hazardous chemicals contributed by the Railroad parcel to the total site contamination or the exact percentage of harm caused by each chemical, the evidence did show that fewer spills occurred on the Railroad parcel and that of those spills that occurred, not all were carried across the Railroad parcel to the B & B sump and pond from which most of the contamination originated. The fact that no D–D spills on the Railroad parcel required remediation lends strength to the District Court's conclusion that the Railroad parcel contributed only Nemagon and dinoseb in quantities requiring remediation.

The District Court's conclusion that those two chemicals accounted for only two-thirds of the contamination requiring remediation finds less support in the record; however, any miscalculation on that point is harmless in light of the District Court's ultimate allocation of liability, which included a 50% margin of error equal to the 3% reduction in liability the District Court provided based on its assessment of the effect of the Nemagon and dinoseb spills. Had the District Court limited its apportionment calculations to the amount of time the Railroad parcel was in use and the percentage of the facility located on that parcel, it would have assigned the Railroads 9% of the response cost. By including a two-thirds reduction in liability for the Nemagon and dinoseb with a 50% "margin of error," the District Court reached the same result. Because the District Court's ultimate allocation of liability is supported by the evidence and comports with the apportionment principles outlined above, we reverse the Court of Appeals' conclusion that the Railroads are subject to joint and several liability for all response costs arising out of the contamination of the Arvin facility.

IV

For the foregoing reasons, we conclude * * * that the District Court reasonably apportioned the Railroads' share of the site remediation costs at 9%. The judgment is reversed, and the cases are remanded for further proceedings consistent with this opinion.

It is so ordered.

Justice GINSBURG, dissenting.

* * * As to apportioning costs, the District Court undertook an heroic labor. The Railroads and Shell, the court noted, had pursued a " 'scorched earth,' all-or-nothing approach to liability. Neither acknowledged an iota of responsibility.... Neither party offered helpful arguments to apportion

liability." Consequently, the court strived "independently [to] perform [an] equitable apportionment analysis." Given the party presentation principle basic to our procedural system, it is questionable whether the court should have pursued the matter *sua sponte*.

The trial court's mode of procedure, the United States urged before this Court, "deprived the government of a fair opportunity to respond to the court's theories of apportionment and to rebut their factual underpinnings—an opportunity the governmen[t] would have had if those theories had been advanced by petitioners themselves." I would return these cases to the District Court to give all parties a fair opportunity to address that court's endeavor to allocate costs. Because the Court's disposition precludes that opportunity, I dissent from the Court's judgment.

NOTES

1. **Joint and Several Liability under CERCLA.** When is joint and several liability appropriate under CERCLA, according to the Supreme Court? Why does it borrow from the RESTATEMENT OF TORTS? How is CERCLA liability similar to tort liability? Does it matter that the original sponsors of CERCLA in the House and Senate consciously deleted language from the act that would have specified joint and several liability?

2. **Apportionment in *Burlington Northern*.** Note that, despite acknowledging that the use of joint and several liability can be appropriate in CERCLA cases and that the PRPs have the burden of proving divisible harm, the Supreme Court upholds the district court's apportionment of liability in *Burlington Northern*. Why? Note also that the district court apportioned the liability even though the PRPs refused to cooperate in its efforts *and* there was groundwater contamination at the site, which would seem to be the quintessential indivisible harm. What factors did the district court use as its basis for apportionment?

Under § 433A of the RESTATEMENT, damages for harm can be apportioned where "there are distinct harms" *or* where "there is a reasonable basis for determining the contribution of each cause to a single harm." RESTATEMENT (SECOND) OF TORTS, § 433A. Does this detail help to explain the district court's and Supreme Court's decision? Why or why not?

3. **The Refusal to Remand.** Why did Justice Ginsburg dissent from the majority's conclusion on divisibility in *Burlington Northern*? Given that the burden of proof was on the PRPs, isn't she right that a remand would have been more appropriate, especially considering the differences of opinion between the district court and the court of appeals regarding the legal availability of apportionment?

* * *

Unlike Section 107, Section 113 explicitly allows for equitable apportionment among PRPs in contribution actions. Section 113(f)(1), 42 U.S.C. § 9613(f)(1). CERCLA's contribution provisions encourage sharing of liability by providing that "[a]ny person may seek contribution from any other person who is liable or potentially liable under section 9607(a) of this title, during or following any civil action under section 9606 of this title or under section 9607(a) of this title. * * * In resolving contribution claims, the court may allocate response costs among liable parties using equitable factors as the court determines are appropriate." CERCLA § 113(f)(1), 42 U.S.C. § 9613(f)(1). However, "[a] person who has resolved its liability to the United States or a State in an administrative or judicially approved settlement shall not be liable for claims of contribution for matters addressed in the settlement." *Id.* § 1013(f)(2), 42 U.S.C. § 9613(f)(2).

One thing that PRPs *cannot* do, however, is prospectively contract away their CERCLA liability—at least so far as EPA and state enforcement are concerned. The Act expressly provides that "no indemnification, hold harmless, or similar agreement or conveyance shall be effective to transfer from the owner or operator of any vessel or facility or from any person who may be liable for a release or threat of release under this section, to any other person the liability imposed under this section." CERCLA § 107(e)(1), 42 U.S.C. § 9607(e)(1). The indemnification agreement remains valid, however, as between the two contracting parties. *Id.*

Contribution actions among multiple PRPs raise a number of issues that CERCLA does not resolve: How is the federal court to apportion liability fairly among the PRPs? What if a particular PRP contributed hazardous substances to the site that did not contribute to the actual release? How is such causation (or lack of causation) to be factored into the PRP's status as a PRP?

ALLIEDSIGNAL, INC. v. AMCAST INTERNATIONAL CORP.

177 F. Supp. 2d 713 (S.D. Ohio 2001).

RICE, CHIEF JUDGE.

* * * I. FINDINGS OF FACT

A. The Parties, their Operations and the GDA

1. Plaintiff AlliedSignal, Inc. ("Plaintiff" or "Allied"), is a Delaware corporation, whose principal place of business is located within the state of New Jersey. Plaintiff is the successor corporation to Allied Chemical Corporation.

2. Defendant Amcast Corporation ("Defendant" or "Amcast") is an Ohio corporation, whose principal place of business is located within this state. * * *

3. At all relevant times, Plaintiff operated two, related industrial facilities in Ironton, to wit: a coke plant and a coal tar plant. At the latter facility, Plaintiff processed coal tar, a by-product of its coking operations. This litigation arises out of the Plaintiff's activities at its coal tar plant, and the disposal of the wastes generated at that facility. Plaintiff produced coal tar pitch, creosote oils, phthalic anhydride, anthracene and naphthal-

ene at the coal tar plant. Those processes generated high levels of hazardous waste, including polycyclic aromatic hydrocarbons ("PAHs"), some of which were carcinogenic. The PAHs generated at Allied's coal tar plant included benzo(a)pyrene, benzo(b)fluoranthene, benzo(k)fluoranthene, dibenzo(ah)anthracene, chrysene, acenaphthlene, anthracene, fluorene, fluoranthene, naphthalene, phenanthrene, pyrene and 2 methylnapthalene. Of those PAHs, benzo(a)pyrene, benzo(b)fluoranthene, benzo(k)fluoranthene, dibenzo(ah)anthracene and chrysene were carcinogenic. In addition, the Plaintiff's processes generated ammonia and chlorides.

4. Beginning in 1916, and continuing through December, 1983, Defendant operated a malleable iron foundry in Ironton. At that facility, the Defendant manufactured products by pouring molten metal into sand molds. The sand molds were prepared by mixing together sand, water, bentonite clay, seacoal and either cereal (such as flour) or sawdust. Defendant's facility, like other foundries, recycled the sand that it used in the molds, so that the sand would be repeatedly used. After a point, however, all sand used by the Defendant was discarded and replaced by new sand.

5. During the Defendant's manufacturing process, molten metal would be poured into a sand mold, which contained a small amount of seacoal. When the molten metal came into contact with the seacoal, much of that material was completely burned. A second portion did not ignite at all. A third portion of the seacoal was partially burned and, thus, was transformed into PAHs, through a process called pyrolysis. The PAHs generated through that process are the same as those which were generated through the Plaintiff's industrial processes. Thus, the Defendant generated the following carcinogenic PAHs, to wit: benzo(a)pyrene, benzo(b)fluoranthene, benzo(k)fluoranthene, dibenzo(ah)anthracene and chrysene. However, the quantity of those chemicals formed by the Defendant's processes was much smaller than that which resulted from the Plaintiff's operations.

6. Beginning in 1945 and continuing until 1977, Plaintiff disposed of all of the industrial wastes which were generated at its coal tar plant in the Goldcamp Disposal Area ("GDA"), an abandoned sand and gravel pit. * * * Beginning in approximately 1950 and continuing through 1977, Defendant disposed some of its foundry wastes in the GDA. In 1955, Plaintiff purchased the GDA from its former owners, Henry and Margaret Goldcamp, after which Plaintiff exercised control over the waste disposed of at that site. Over the years, other entities also disposed of very small quantities of waste at the GDA.

7. In 1977, all waste disposal at the GDA ceased. In 1979, the Plaintiff, under the supervision of the Ohio Environmental Protection Agency ("OEPA"), closed the GDA and covered it with a semi-permeable cap.

B. Waste Disposed of at the GDA

8. Between 1945 and 1977, the Plaintiff disposed of all the waste it generated from its coal tar plant into the GDA. The Plaintiff's waste was largely organic. A substantial portion of that waste was in a semisolid or liquid state. The Plaintiff disposed of 29,759 tons of anthracene residue, which had a 65% PAH content. In addition, the Plaintiff disposed of 9,000 tons of anthracene salts, which consisted of 100% PAHs. Plaintiff also disposed of 2,000 tons of creosote spillage, 1,592 tons of coal tar residues and 32,005 tons of coal tar pitch, all of which had a 10% PAH content.

9. Between 1950 and 1977, the Defendant dumped a significant amount of waste into the GDA. The Defendant's waste was largely inorganic, comprised primarily of sand. The Defendant delivered that waste to the GDA in dump trucks, which its employees unloaded. That waste included spent foundry sand, broken cores which Defendant had used in its casting process, waste from the foundry's cupolas and other miscellaneous waste generated at that facility. Included with the spent foundry sand were small quantities of the following carcinogenic PAHs, to wit: benzo(a)pyrene, benzo(b)fluoranthene, benzo(k)fluoranthene, dibenzo(ah)anthracene and chrysene. When the Defendant dumped its spent foundry sand into the GDA, the carcinogenic PAHs were bonded to the individual grains of sand. The Defendant's waste also included phenolics.

10. The wastes of both parties were deposited into the GDA, side by side. In other words, Plaintiff's waste was not placed in one area of the facility, with Defendant disposing of its waste in another. Frequently, the waste of the two parties was mixed together by a bulldozer operated by employees of the Plaintiff.

11. PAHs are not normally soluble. As a result, the PAHs that were bonded to the spent foundry sand that the Defendant had deposited into the GDA were not likely to leach, i.e., to migrate from that sand to the groundwater which lay below that waste site, through the normal action of rainwater. However, the Plaintiff deposited anthracene waste into the GDA, in liquid form and at a high temperature. When that hot, liquid anthracene waste mixed with the spent foundry sand deposited by the Defendant, it had the effect of scrubbing off the PAHs bonded to that sand. The PAHs contained in the Defendant's waste stream then became mixed with and indistinguishable from those compounds which the Plaintiff had deposited into the GDA, producing "mixed PAHs."

12. Some of the mixed PAHs, which had been contributed to the GDA by both the Plaintiff and the Defendant, then migrated through the soil and were able to reach the groundwater in the aquifer which lay below the GDA. Being insoluble, those compounds did not mix with the water; rather, they sank until they reached the bedrock at the bottom of the aquifer, since the molecular weight of the PAHs was greater than that of the water in the aquifer. Those PAHs, referred to as nonaqueous phase liquids, remain at the bottom of the aquifer and constitute the NAPS layer.

13. By volume, Plaintiff contributed 72% of the waste to the GDA, while Defendant deposited 28% of that waste. In addition to depositing a greater quantity of waste into the GDA, the hazardous component of Plaintiff's waste was much greater. Although the waste streams generated by the Plaintiff and the Defendant both contained PAHs, the Plaintiff deposited 97% to 98% of the total amount of those compounds that went into the GDA, while Defendant was responsible for the remaining 2% to 3%. In addition, Plaintiff's practice of depositing hot, liquid anthracene waste allowed the PAHs, which had been formed during the Defendant's industrial processes, to be released from the spent foundry sand and ultimately to reach the groundwater in the aquifer.

14. The parties have stipulated that the carcinogenic PAHs, deposited into the GDA and released into the groundwater from it, are hazardous substances under CERCLA.

C. The Cleanup of the GDA

15. In 1982, the OEPA had demanded that Allied and Amcast jointly pay $35 million to clean up the GDA. Subsequently, the OEPA withdrew its demand that Defendant fund the cleanup. In 1983, the EPA placed the Allied Chemical/Ironton Coke facility on the NPL. The EPA divided that hazardous waste site into two operable units, to wit: the GDA and the coke plant/lagoons area. This litigation involves only the GDA.

16. On April 11, 1984, Plaintiff entered into an Administrative Consent Order with the EPA and the OEPA, under which it agreed to perform and to fund a Remedial Investigation/Feasibility Study ("RI/FS") at the GDA. Defendant is not a party to that Order. Plaintiff expended approximately $1,162,000 to complete the RI/FS. Defendant has not paid any portion of the funds so paid. The Plaintiff performed the RI/FS under the close direction and supervision of the EPA and the OEPA.

17. During the RI/FS, Plaintiff did not characterize the waste that parties other than itself and Defendant had deposited at the GDA. In addition, Plaintiff did not document any analytical testing of either its wastes or those of Defendant that had been so deposited.

18. On September 29, 1988, the EPA issued a Record of Decision ("ROD") for the GDA. That document adopted a remedy that is composed of three major components. *First,* the ROD requires that a cap, which complies with the Resource Conservation and Recovery Act, be placed over the surface of that facility. *Second,* the ROD requires that a low permeability slurry wall be constructed to surround the GDA. That slurry wall must extend from the surface to the bedrock below the GDA, in order to prevent hazardous substances released from that facility from migrating further into the environment. *Third,* the groundwater, both inside and outside the slurry wall containment system, must be extracted and treated, until stipulated cleanup standards are achieved.

19. In addition, the ROD required that a study be conducted of the NAPS layer. The Plaintiff conducted that study between November, 1990,

and February, 1993, at a cost of $800,000, a sum to which the Defendant contributed nothing. As a result of that study, the EPA has not altered the selected remedy for the GDA hazardous waste site.

20. The primary concern at the GDA hazardous waste site is the groundwater. The ROD established cleanup standards for seven chemicals, to wit: ammonia, which must be reduced to 0.5 parts per million; chloride, which must be reduced to 250 parts per million; total cyanide, which must be reduced to 0.2 parts per million; phenolics, which must be reduced to between 0.3 and 3.5 parts per million; benzene, which must be reduced to 0.005 parts per million; naphthalene, which must be reduced to 0.69 parts per million; and benzo(a)pyrene, a carcinogenic PAH, which must be reduced to 0.005 parts per *billion*. Given that the cleanup standard for benzo(a)pyrene, a carcinogenic PAH, is so much more stringent than that for any other substance, that carcinogenic PAH is driving the cleanup of the groundwater that lies below that hazardous waste site. In other words, when the benzo(a)pyrene has been sufficiently removed from the groundwater, the remedy at that facility will have been completed. Except for benzo(a)pyrene, Defendant's waste either did not contain the chemicals for which cleanup standards were established in the ROD, or the concentrations of those chemicals which were contained therein were below those standards.

21. On March 9, 1989, the EPA issued an Administrative Order, directing both the Plaintiff and the Defendant to implement the remedy selected by the EPA and set forth in the ROD. In particular, the Plaintiff and the Defendant were ordered to submit, within 60 days of the entry of the order, a plan for the remedial design/remedial action ("RD/RA") phase of the cleanup. Plaintiff has complied with that order, while the Defendant has declined to participate. On a number of occasions, Plaintiff has asked the EPA to take action against the Defendant for its refusal to participate the RD/RA phase of the cleanup. The EPA has not taken any such action against the Defendant.

22. Through December 31, 1994, the Plaintiff had expended the sum of $12,423,137, in connection with the cleanup of the GDA. That sum is composed of $1,162,000, to conduct the RI/FS; $800,000, to study the NAPS layer; and $10,461,137, to implement the ROD by conducting the RD/RA. It is expected that the total cost of cleaning up the GDA will be $30,000,000. The Defendant has not contributed any money to the cleanup process.

D. Defendant's Liability under CERCLA

23. Defendant arranged for the disposal of hazardous substances, including the carcinogenic PAH, benzo(a)pyrene, at the GDA.

24. The GDA is a site where hazardous substances, including the carcinogenic PAH, benzo(a)pyrene, have been deposited.

25. The hazardous substances deposited into the GDA, including those contributed by the Defendant, have migrated from the GDA to the groundwater which lies below that facility.

26. As a result of the release of hazardous substances from the GDA, the Plaintiff, through December 31, 1994, had incurred necessary response costs in the sum of $12,423,137, has continued to incur those costs after that date and will continue to incur such costs in the future.

27. The Plaintiff has incurred its response costs in compliance with the two orders issued by the EPA, pursuant to § 106 of CERCLA, 42 U.S.C. § 9606. Indeed, the EPA and the OEPA have closely directed and supervised the activities of the Plaintiff with regard to the RI/FS, the study of the NAPS layer and the implementation of the ROD.

28. The Plaintiff has incurred those costs in substantial compliance with the National Contingency Plan ("NCP").

29. Defendant is liable for 2% of the response costs incurred by the Plaintiff, through December 31, 1994, for all tasks except the cap for the GDA. Defendant is liable for 28% of the cost of the cap.

II. OPINION

In its Complaint, the Plaintiff sets forth a claims under §§ 107(a) and 113(f) of CERCLA, 42 U.S.C. §§ 9607(a) and 9613(f), requesting that the Court order the Defendant to pay for a portion of the expenses it (Plaintiff) had incurred through December 31, 1994. In addition, the Plaintiff requests that the Court enter a Declaratory Judgment, requiring the Defendant to pay a portion of the costs it (Plaintiff) has incurred since the end of 1994 and will incur in the future, and, finally, that the Court award it prejudgment interest. As a protective measure, the Defendant has asserted a counterclaim against the Plaintiff, seeking contribution. To resolve the Plaintiff's claims and Defendant's counterclaim, the Court must address the following categories of issues, to wit: 1) may CERCLA be applied retroactively and is that statute constitutional; 2) is the Plaintiff's claim one for contribution, under § 113(f), or is it entitled to maintain a cost recovery action under § 107(a); 3) is the Defendant liable under CERCLA; 4) for what portion of the expenses Plaintiff had incurred through the trial of this litigation is the Defendant liable; and 5) is the Plaintiff entitled to the requested declaratory relief and/or prejudgment interest? The Court will address those issues in the above order.

A. *Retroactive Application and Constitutionality of CERCLA*

[The court's opinion on these issues is presented in section III.B.2: Liability of Past Owners and Operators.]

* * * D. *Equitable Allocation*

Having concluded that the Defendant is liable under CERCLA, the Court now turns to the issue of equitable allocation, pursuant to § 113(f)(1), of the response costs that the Plaintiff has incurred. The

Plaintiff argues that the Court should allocate a "substantial" share of the response costs to the Defendant, while the latter asserts that it should be held liable for no more than 1% of those costs. The Court begins that analysis by examining the factors that courts have considered, when making such an allocation.

Section 113(f)(1) provides that, in resolving contribution claims, "the court may allocate response costs among liable parties using such equitable factors as the court determines appropriate." 42 U.S.C. § 9613(f)(1). * * * Of course, that discretion is not without limit, since a District Court may not require any party to contribute more than its equitable share of the entire cleanup costs. Courts have frequently noted that some or all of the so-called "Gore factors" may be employed when exercising the broad discretion with which they are invested to make an equitable apportionment under § 113(f)(1). The Gore factors are:

1. the ability of the parties to demonstrate that their contribution to a discharge, release, or disposal of a hazardous waste can be distinguished;
2. the amount of hazardous waste involved;
3. the degree of toxicity of the hazardous waste;
4. the degree of involvement by the parties in the generation, transportation, treatment, storage, or disposal of the hazardous waste;
5. the degree of care exercised by the parties with respect to the hazardous waste concerned, taking into account the characteristics of such hazardous waste; and
6. the degree of cooperation by the parties with Federal, State, or local officials to prevent any harm to the public health or the environment.

For reasons that follow, this Court finds that, applying its broad discretion to the totality of the circumstances giving rise to the need to remediate the GDA, the Defendant should be required to pay for 2% of the response costs incurred by the Plaintiff, with the exception of those costs associated with the cap for that facility. With respect to the cap, the Court finds that the Defendant is responsible for 28% of the costs incurred by the Plaintiff. As a means of analysis, the Court will initially set forth its reasons for finding that the Defendant is liable for 2% of the Plaintiff's response costs for all items with the exception of the cap, following which it will set forth its reasoning relating to the cap.

1. Plaintiff's Response Costs for Items Other Than the Cap

Excluding the cap, the Plaintiff has incurred response costs to conduct the RI/FS, to study the NAPS layer and to execute the remedy selected by the EPA in the ROD, by engaging in the RD/RA. The environmental risk posed by the GDA is one to the groundwater in the aquifer below it. Some of the carcinogenic PAHs disposed of in the GDA, typified by benzo(a)pyrene, have migrated to and contaminated the groundwater. Indeed, the NAPS layer is composed of PAHs, including the carcinogenic variety. The remedy selected by the EPA included the construction of the slurry wall and the pumping and treating of the contaminated groundwater, both within and outside the slurry wall. The slurry wall will prevent the further spread of carcinogenic PAHs, while the "pump and treat" component of the remedy will, over time, remove those hazardous substances from the groundwater. Thus, the evidence presented at trial points to the inescapable conclusion that the remedy at the GDA is being driven by the presence of carcinogenic PAHs, typified by benzo(a)pyrene, in the groundwater below that hazardous waste site. * * *

* * * Since the cleanup of the GDA is being driven by the presence of carcinogenic PAHs at the GDA, a logical basis for equitably and fairly allocating the response costs that the Plaintiff has and will incur is to require each party to bear the portion of the total costs which equal the percentage of the carcinogenic PAHs that came from the waste each deposited in the GDA. The difficulty with that approach is that the Court is not able to conclude, based upon the evidence presented at trial, what percentage of those hazardous substances is attributable to each of the parties. * * *

An alternative to allocating response costs on the basis of the percentage of carcinogenic PAHs in the groundwater below the GDA attributable to each party is to focus upon the percentage of PAHs, whether carcinogenic or otherwise, which each of the parties contributed to the GDA. While this method does not tie allocation of response costs to the precise hazardous substances driving the cleanup of the GDA (i.e., carcinogenic PAHs), there was no reliable evidence introduced at trial that the PAHs contributed by one party had a higher concentration of such carcinogenic compounds than those originating with the other. Moreover, it should be noted that the PAHs contributed by the parties originated from similar processes. The Plaintiff created PAHs through its coking operations, during which coal was burned in an oxygen deficient environment. Coal tar, which was the waste product of the coking operations and which was processed at the coal tar plant, has a high PAH content. The PAHs which the Defendant disposed of at the GDA were created by the process known as pyrolysis, when seacoal in the molding sand partially burned in an atmosphere from which the oxygen had been removed. There was no evidence that either party's processes would have caused a greater concentration of carcinogenic PAHs to be created (when compared to the non-carcinogenic variety of those compounds). Therefore, the Court concludes that the total percentage of PAHs disposed of by each party (whether carcinogenic or not), which each of the parties contributed to the GDA, is an equitable and fair manner of allocating the Plaintiff's response costs. Based upon the testimony of Bern, the Court finds that the Defendant disposed of between 2% and 3% of the PAHs at the GDA, while the Plaintiff was responsible for the remainder. * * * Accordingly, the Court finds that the Defendant is liable for between 2% and 3% of the Plaintiff's response costs.

Having concluded that the percentage of PAHs that each party contributed to the GDA is the equitable and fair factor to employ to allocate the response costs for the RI/FS, the study of the NAPS layer and the implementation of the remedy selected by the EPA in the ROD, the Court must now determine what that percentage is. Is it 2%, 3% or some figure between those two? The Court finds that 2% is the equitable and fair amount of response costs to allocate to the Defendant. Two factors cause this Court to select the 2% figure. *First,* for more than 20 years, the Plaintiff exercised control over the activities of the GDA, as the owner and operator of that facility. The fourth Gore factor provides that courts should consider, *inter alia,* the degree of control that the parties have exercised over the hazardous waste facility. Moreover, courts have recognized that ownership and control of a hazardous waste site is an appropriate factor to consider when equitably allocating response costs. As the owner and operator of the GDA, the Plaintiff had the ability to prevent the disposal of waste at that site, in the manner in which it was done, a manner which permitted hazardous chemicals to be released to the environment. The Plaintiff's failure to do so supports limiting Defendant's liability for response costs to 2%. *Second,* the Plaintiff facilitated the release of the PAHs contained in the waste disposed of by the Defendant, by mixing hot, liquid wastes originating from the operations of the coal tar plant with the foundry wastes disposed of by the Defendant. The PAHs that the Defendant contributed to the GDA were created by the process known as pyrolysis, when some of the seacoal, contained in the mixture of sand and other material of which the molds were composed, heated in an oxygen deficient environment. The PAHs in Defendant's foundry waste were bound to the sand. Since PAHs are insoluble, it is unlikely that a significant portion of those substances bound to the sand in Defendant's waste would have migrated to the groundwater if the Plaintiff had not mixed its hot, liquid waste with the foundry sand which the Defendant had disposed of in the GDA. Therefore, the actions of the Plaintiff are partially responsible for the Defendant's contribution of PAHs to the groundwater below that site. This fact further buttresses the Court's conclusion that the Defendant should be liable for only 2% of the response costs, rather than for 3% or for some amount between 2% and 3%.

* * * An analysis of the "Gore factors" supports the Court's conclusion that the Defendant is liable for 2% of the response costs that the Plaintiff has incurred (other than costs associated with the cap). The first factor, the ability of the parties to demonstrate that their contributions to the release of hazardous substances can be distinguished, does not alter that conclusion. Simply stated, there is no way to distinguish the molecules of carcinogenic PAHs that came from the Plaintiff's waste, from those that originated with the Defendant. The second through fourth factors require the Court to consider the amount of hazardous waste deposited by each of the parties; the degree of toxicity of their waste; and

the degree of their involvement in the generation, transportation, treatment, storage, or disposal of that waste. Above, the Court has discussed how those considerations influence its conclusion that the Defendant is liable for 2% of the response costs for all aspects of the cleanup of the GDA other than the cap. The Court will not repeat that discussion. The parties did not present any evidence on the fifth Gore factor, the degree of care exercised by the parties with respect to the hazardous substances. Therefore, that factor does not cause the Court to alter its conclusion regarding the level of the Defendant's responsibility.

The Plaintiff argues that the sixth Gore factor, the degree of cooperation by the parties with federal, state and local officials to prevent harm to the public health and the environment, serves as the basis for the Court to allocate a greater portion of the response costs to the Defendant. In particular, the Plaintiff argues that the Defendant not only failed to cooperate with the EPA and the OEPA, by ignoring the unilateral order to implement the ROD, but also misled those agencies, by mischaracterizing the content of the waste that it had disposed of in the GDA. The Plaintiff also notes that it has complied with the orders of the EPA to conduct the RI/FS and to implement the ROD, and, thus, that it has borne the entire cost of remediation to date, while the Defendant has contributed nothing. Given the facts of this case, the Court cannot agree with the Plaintiff that the sixth Gore factor is the basis for allocating an increased share of liability to the Defendant.

With respect to Defendant's alleged mischaracterization of the content of its waste, the Plaintiff relies upon a number of letters that Defendant sent to the OEPA during the 1980's, in which it indicated that its foundry waste did not include hazardous substances. The Plaintiff points out that the statements contained in those letters were false, since it is uncontroverted that the Defendant's foundry waste contained carcinogenic PAHs. The Court does not agree. The statements in those letters were based on an analysis of its foundry sand that the Defendant had conducted. In addition, the Plaintiff's argument ignores the fact that the Defendant did not know that its waste contained carcinogenic PAHs, when, in the 1980's, it sent letters to that regulatory agency, indicating that its waste did not include such hazardous substances. Indeed, in the Remedial Investigation, the Plaintiff itself did not indicate that the Defendant's waste contained that type of substances. Moreover, Robert Ford, who had been involved in the RI/FS as Plaintiff's director of site remediation, testified that he was surprised that the EPA had ordered the Defendant to implement the ROD. Therefore, this Court cannot find that the Defendant knowingly misled any regulatory agency concerning the content of the waste it had disposed of at the GDA. Moreover, the Plaintiff did not present any evidence that the Defendant's failure to inform the EPA and the OEPA that its waste contained small quantities of carcinogenic PAHs affected, in any manner, the remedy selected for the GDA or caused the RI/FS to be more difficult or expensive. The remedy for the GDA is being driven by the presence carcinogenic PAHs in the groundwater below that hazardous waste site. The regulatory agencies were fully aware that the Plaintiff's waste contained significant quantities of those substances.

With respect to the Defendant's failure to comply with the order of the EPA to implement the ROD and to contribute to the costs of the remediation of the GDA, the Court likewise cannot conclude that this is the basis for allocating a greater share of responsibility to the Defendant. This is not a case where the cleanup has been performed by one of two parties that share relatively equal responsibility for the conditions at a hazardous waste site. On the contrary, the Plaintiff was the owner and operator of the GDA. It deposited the overwhelming majority of hazardous substances into that facility. Its waste was largely organic, with a high content of PAHs, while the Defendant's waste was composed overwhelmingly of inorganic sand which posed no risk to the environment. Defendant's waste had a small PAH content. The fact that the Defendant, whose responsibility for the conditions at the GDA pales in comparison to that of Plaintiff, chose not to comply with an order from the EPA does not cause this Court to allocate a greater share of responsibility to that non-complying party. * * *

Thus, while the Court is in complete agreement with the Plaintiff that, in the appropriate case, a party's failure to cooperate with the cleanup of a hazardous waste site could serve as the basis for equitably allocating a greater share of the response costs, for reasons discussed above, the Court does not find this to be such an appropriate case.

In sum, all tasks associated with the cleanup of the GDA, except for the cap, is being driven by the presence of carcinogenic PAHs in that facility and in the groundwater below it. Although there was no reliable evidence from which the Court could find the percentage of those substances which were deposited by each of the parties, there was reliable evidence as to the percentage of PAHs (whether carcinogenic or otherwise) for which each is responsible. Accordingly, based upon foregoing, the Court finds that the Defendant is liable for 2% of the Plaintiff's response costs, except for the costs associated with the cap.

2. Plaintiff's Response Costs for the Cap

Unlike the other tasks performed by the Plaintiff, for which it has incurred response costs, the cap is not remedy driven. Rather, the Court finds that construction of the cap on the GDA would have been required, even if carcinogenic PAHs had not migrated to the groundwater. In other words, the need to place a cap on the GDA is driven by the fact that waste has been disposed of in that facility. * * * Since the need for a cap on the GDA is not being driven by the contents contained therein, it is neither equitable nor fair to allocate response costs for that aspect of the remedy selected by the EPA on the basis of the percentage of PAHs contributed by each of the parties. Rather, the most equitable manner is to allocate responsibility for the cost of the cap on the basis of the percentage of their total contribution of waste to the GDA. Since the Defendant disposed of

28% of the waste in that facility, the Court finds that it is liable for 28% of the cost of the cap. * * *

NOTES

1. **The Gore Factors.** What are the Gore factors? How did they apply in this case?

2. **Divisibility of the Harm.** Why was the harm in this case indivisible?

3. **Equitable Apportionment.** Why did the district court distinguish the contribution assessment for the cap from the contribution assessment for all other aspects of the cleanup? On which Gore factors did it heavily rely? Did its assessment seem fair and justified to you? this case? Why?

* * *

F. ORPHAN SITES AND SUPERFUND

Because CERCLA's liability is retroactive, contaminated sites exist for which no PRPs remain, or remain able to pay. To cover such situations, Congress created the ***Superfund***. CERCLA § 111, 42 U.S.C. § 9611. Superfund, a trust fund, was funded through taxes on petroleum and certain chemicals. Congress originally assigned $8.5 billion for cleanups between October 17, 1986, and October 1, 1991, and $5.1 billion for cleanups between October 1, 1991, and September 30, 1994. CERCLA § 111(a), 42 U.S.C. § 9611(a).

According to CERCLA, "[n]o claim may be asserted against the Fund * * * unless such claim is presented in the first instance to the owner, operator, or guarantor of the vessel or facility from which a hazardous substance has been released, if known to the claimant, and to any other person known to the claimant who may be liable under section 9607 of this title." CERCLA § 112(a), 42 U.S.C. § 9612(a). If the claim is not satisfied by these PRPs within 60 days, the claimant may proceed with its claim against the fund. *Id.* However, "[n]o claim may be presented under this section for the recovery of the *costs* referred to in section 9607(a) of this title after the date 6 years after the date of completion of all response action." CERCLA § 112(d)(1), 42 U.S.C. § 9612(d)(1) (emphasis added). Moreover:

> No claim may be present under this section for recovery of the *damages* referred to in section 9607(a) of this title unless the claim is presented within 3 years after the later of the following:
>
> (A) The date of the discovery of the loss and its connection with the release in question.
>
> (B) The date on which final regulations are promulgated under section 9651(c) of this title [which empowers the EPA to promulgate regulations respecting the assessment of NRDs].

CERCLA § 112(d)(2), 42 U.S.C. § 9612(d)(2). Finally, Congress imposed additional restrictions on the use of Superfund to cover NRDs, such as the requirement that "[n]o money in the Fund may be used * * * where the injury, destruction, or loss of natural resources and the release of hazardous substances from which such damages resulted have occurred wholly before December 11, 1980," CERCLA § 111(d)(1), 42 U.S.C. § 9611(d)(1)—one reason that the Montana District Court determined that CERCLA's NRD cost recovery provisions are not retroactive.

The tax that funds Superfund expired in 1995, and, by spring 2003, the funds remaining had dropped to $400 million. Despite recurring attempts in Congress to reinstate the tax, as of November 2011, the tax had not been reinstated—although Democratic presidential hopeful Hillary Clinton announced in October 2007 that she would seek re-enactment of the tax. In the interim, Congress has been funding the Superfund through appropriations.

G. PROGRESS IN CERCLA CLEANUPS UNDER SUPERFUND

CERCLA has now been in effect for over 20 years. Over 1500 sites have been listed on the NPL, many of which remain on the NPL. The EPA has charted its yearly progress through early 2012 as follows:

Number of National Priorities List (NPL) Site Actions and Milestones by Fiscal Year

Action	2003	2004	2005	2006	2007	2008	2009	2010	2011	2012
Sites Proposed to the NPL	14	26	12	10	17	17	23	8	35	0
Sites Finalized on the NPL	20	11	18	11	12	18	20	20	25	0
Sites Deleted from the NPL	9	16	18	7	7	9	8	7	7	2
Milestone	**2003**	**2004**	**2005**	**2006**	**2007**	**2008**	**2009**	**2010**	**2011**	**2012**
Partial Deletions*	7	7	5	3	3	3	3	5	3	0
Construction Completions	40	40	40	40	24	30	20	18	22	1

A fiscal year is October 1 through September 30. Fiscal year 2012 includes actions and milestones achieved from October 1, 2011 to the present. Partial deletion totals are not applicable until fiscal year 1996, when the policy was first implemented.

* These totals represent the total number of partial deletions by fiscal year and may include multiple partial deletions at a site. Currently, there are 71 partial deletions at 57 sites.

Notice that more sites are being added to the NPL than are being removed from it. What does that fact suggest about land contamination in the United States—or about the difficulty of restoring land and groundwater once contamination has occurred?

CHAPTER 2

ENVIRONMENTAL PROCEDURES AND JUDICIAL REVIEW: NEPA AND THE APA

■ ■ ■

I. NEPA AND THE APA: BASIC REQUIREMENTS AND JUDICIAL REVIEW

A. INTRODUCTION TO THE FEDERAL ADMINISTRATIVE PROCEDURE ACT (APA)

As was noted in the Introduction to this textbook, federal agencies such as the EPA implement most federal environmental statutes through rulemaking and enforcement. If the relevant environmental statute provides the agency with rulemaking and/or enforcement procedures to follow, the agency will follow those specific statutory procedures. For example, the Clean Air Act provides specific procedures for the EPA to follow for many types of rulemaking under that statute. CAA § 307(d), 42 U.S.C. § 7607(d).

However, if the environmental statute does *not* supply procedures, then the agency will use the default procedures in the federal ***Administrative Procedure Act*** **(APA)**, 5 U.S.C. §§ 551–559, 701–706. The APA defines "agency" broadly to include "each authority of the Government of the United States, whether or not it is within or subject to review by another agency * * *." APA §§ 2(1), 10(b)(1), 5 U.S.C. §§ 551(1), 701(b)(1). However, the definition of "agency" then exempts several federal authorities from the APA's provisions, including Congress, the federal courts (including courts martial), and military authority exercised in time of war. *Id.* Oddly, the APA does not explicitly exempt the President of the United States, but the Supreme Court has determined that the President is in fact exempt. *Franklin v. Massachusetts*, 505 U.S. 788, 800–01 (1992).

The APA then provides the public with several provisions for acquiring information about and from the federal government. These include the Freedom of Information Act, APA § 3, 5 U.S.C. § 552, which allows any person to obtain agency records from any federal agency for any purpose; the Privacy Act, 5 U.S.C. § 552a, which provides protections to individuals regarding the federal government's records about them; and the Government in Sunshine Act, 5 U.S.C. § 552b, which opens many meetings of federal agencies to public participation.

The rest of the APA divides into three categories: rulemaking procedures; adjudication procedures; and judicial review procedures. ***Rulemaking*** is the process whereby agencies write regulations of general applicability and future effect—that is, rules to guide a large number of regulated entities in shaping their future behavior to comply with a federal statute. Agency ***rules*** can take several forms and include: ***procedural rules*** that the agency writes to govern its own internal procedures; ***interpretive rules*** that suggest how the agency plans to interpret ambiguous provisions in the statute or its other regulations; and ***policy statements*** and ***guidance documents***, which inform the general public of how the agency intends to apply the statute or its regulations to various kinds of behavior or activities. However, if the agency intends a rule to be immediately enforceable against the regulated public, the agency must follow at least the ***informal rulemaking procedures*** outlined in APA § 4, 5 U.S.C. § 553. These procedures require the agency to: (1) give ***notice*** of the proposed rule in the Federal Register; (2) provide an opportunity to the interested public to submit ***comments*** on the rule (although not necessarily in person—most comments are submitted by mail or e-mail or through the internet); and (3) publish the final rule, together with "a concise general statement of [its] basis and purpose," in the Federal Register at least 30 days before the rule takes effect. APA § 4, 5 U.S.C. § 553. Occasionally, agencies must follow the more time-consuming and expensive ***formal rulemaking*** procedures in the APA, which require that the agency write the regulations and take comments in a trial-like proceeding. APA §§ 4(c), 7, 8, 5 U.S.C. §§ 553(c), 556, 557.

In an agency ***adjudication***, the federal agency determines how the statute involved applies to individual persons or businesses based on particular facts—should this person get a permit? If so, what should the permit say? Did this business violate the statute or the regulations? If so, how? Adjudications end with the agency issuing an administrative ***order*** of some kind. Because individual rights are often at stake in adjudications, Congress usually prefers for adjudications to be fairly formal procedurally, a preference Congress signals in the relevant statute by requiring the agency's decision "to be determined on the record after opportunity for an agency hearing * * *." APA § 5(a), 5 U.S.C. § 554(a). ***Formal adjudications*** are very similar to trials—the parties can be represented by attorneys, the decisionmaker cannot be the investigator, *ex parte* contacts are strictly forbidden, the parties present arguments orally before the decisionmaker as well as submit briefs making their arguments, the parties may subpoena and call witnesses, and the parties may submit reliable evidence. APA §§ 6(b), 7, 8, 5 U.S.C. §§ 555(b), 556, 557. In APA formal adjudications, "the proponent of a rule or order has the burden of proof." APA § 7(d), 5 U.S.C. § 556(d). As a result, the agency usually has the burden of proof.

Figure 2-1: Applying the Federal APA

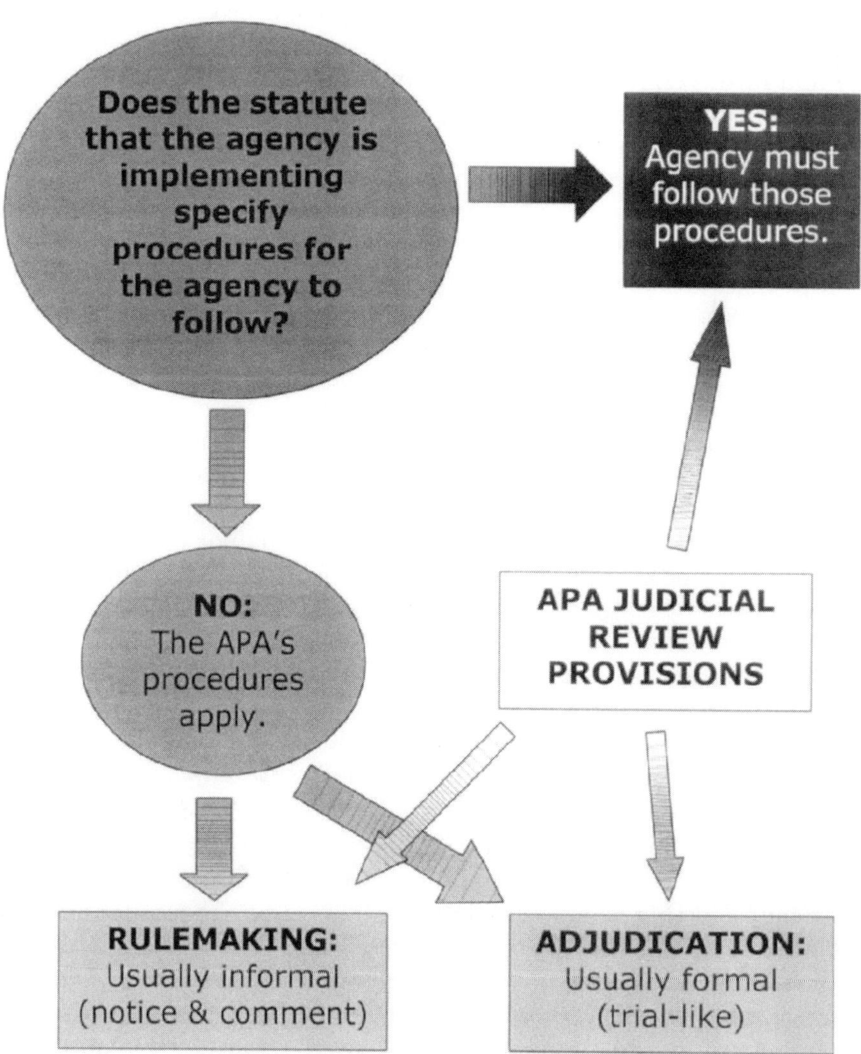

Finally, through its ***judicial review*** provisions, the APA gives the public access to federal courts to challenge agency actions. The plaintiff must be "suffering legal wrong because of an agency action, or [be] adversely affected or aggrieved by agency action within the meaning of the relevant statute" and must seek "relief other than money damages"—*i.e.*, a declaratory judgment and/or an injunction. APA § 10a, 5 U.S.C. § 702. Moreover, the plaintiff can sue only if the relevant statute does not preclude judicial review and only if the agency's action is not committed to its absolute discretion, APA § 10(a), 5 U.S.C. § 701(a), but federal courts interpret these exemptions narrowly and presume that judicial review is available. Judicial review is available only for "[a]gency action made reviewable by statute and final agency action for which there is no other adequate remedy in court * * *." APA § 10c, 5 U.S.C. § 704. An agency action is final if the agency is at the end of its decisionmaking process, but the APA's "no other adequate remedy" requirement means that APA lawsuits are a default remedy—if the plaintiff has another cause of action against the agency, he or she must use it.

The APA also provides the federal courts with ***standards of review*** for evaluating federal agency actions. APA § 10e, 5 U.S.C. § 706, states:

> **Scope of Review**. To the extent necessary to make a decision and when presented, the reviewing court shall decide all relevant questions of law, interpret constitutional and statutory provisions, and determine the meaning and applicability of the terms of an agency action. The reviewing court shall—
>
> (1) compel agency action unlawfully withheld or unreasonably delayed; and
>
> (2) hold unlawful and set aside agency action, findings, and conclusions found to be—
>
> (A) arbitrary, capricious, an abuse of discretion, or otherwise not in accordance with law;
>
> (B) contrary to constitutional right, power, privilege, or immunity;
>
> (C) in excess of statutory jurisdiction, authority, or limitations, or short of statutory right;
>
> (D) without observance of procedure required by law; [or]
>
> (E) unsupported by substantial evidence in a case subject to sections 556 and 557 of this title or otherwise reviewed on the record of an agency hearing provided by statute * * *.

Id. Section 706 thus introduces the concept of ***deference*** to certain kinds of federal agency determination. Under section 706, the reviewing federal court has complete authority—a ***de novo*** standard of review that gives *no* deference to the agency—to determine the ***legal*** issues of whether the agency followed the correct procedures, acted within its statutory authority, and complied with the U.S. Constitution. In contrast, the reviewing court evaluates the federal agency's determination of ***facts*** according to one of two highly deferential standards of review. If the agency made factual determinations through *informal procedures*, such as informal rulemaking, then its decisions are subject to the ***arbitrary and capri-***

cious standard of review. If the agency made factual determinations through *formal procedures*, such a formal adjudication, then its decisions are subject to the ***substantial evidence*** standard of review.

B. INTRODUCTION TO THE NATIONAL ENVIRONMENTAL POLICY ACT (NEPA)

On January 1, 1970, Congress enacted the National Environmental Policy Act of 1969 (NEPA), 42 U.S.C. §§ 4321–4370e, in order "[t]o declare a national policy which will encourage productive and enjoyable harmony between man and his environment; to promote efforts which will prevent or eliminate damage to the environment and biosphere and stimulate the health and welfare of man; to enrich the understanding of the ecological systems and natural resources important to the Nation; and to establish a Council on Environmental Quality." NEPA § 2, 42 U.S.C. § 4321. While it is the ***Council on Environmental Quality*** **(CEQ)** that writes the NEPA regulations, NEPA § 204, 42 U.S.C. § 4344, every federal agency is responsible for complying with NEPA's environmental review requirements.

The most important of these requirements is buried in NEPA § 102(2)(C), 42 U.S.C. § 4332(2)(C). This statutory provision requires that "all agencies of the Federal Government shall * * * include in every recommendation or report on proposals for legislation and other major Federal actions significantly affecting the quality of the human environment, a detailed statement by the responsible official on * * * the environmental impact of the proposed action * * *." *Id.* This statement has become known as the ***environmental impact statement*** **(EIS)**.

Unlike many environmental statutes, NEPA does not have a citizen suit provision. Thus, interested citizens *must* use the APA to challenge a federal agency's compliance with NEPA.

Under CEQ's regulations, a federal agency's NEPA analysis proceeds in several stages. A federal agency undertaking an action that may qualify as "a major Federal action significantly affecting the quality of the human environment" determines first whether that action is the type that normally requires an EIS, normally does not require an EIS, or is too distinctive to tell. 40 C.F.R. § 1501.4(a). If the action is of the type that normally requires an EIS, the CEQ's regulations directs the federal agency to go ahead and prepare the EIS. *Id.* § 1501.4(b).

If the action does not normally require an EIS but has not been categorically excluded from the NEPA process, or if the action is too distinctive for the agency to know whether an EIS is required, the agency will prepare an ***environmental assessment*** **(EA).** *Id.* §§ 1501.4(c), 1501.3. An EA is a "concise public document" that "[b]riefly provide[s] sufficient evidence and analysis for determining whether to prepare an environmental impact statement or a finding of no significant impact" and briefly discusses "the need for the proposal, [] alternatives * * *, [and] the environmental impacts of the proposed action and alternatives * * *." 40 C.F.R. § 1508.9. In short, the EA is a mini-EIS.

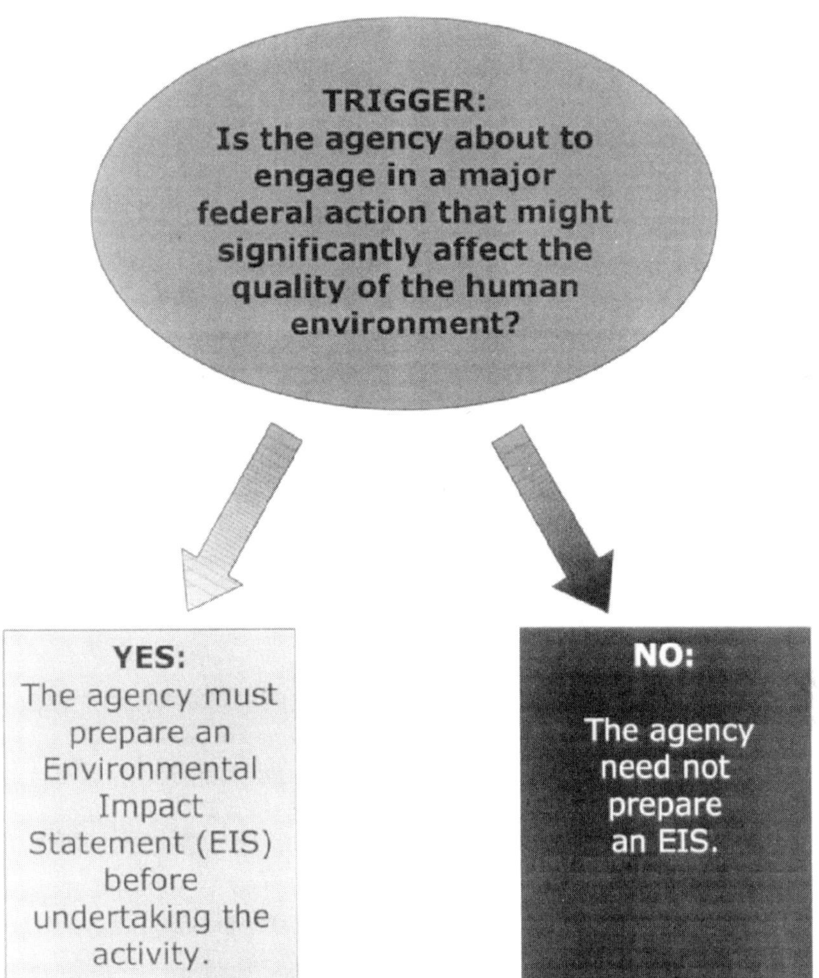

Figure 2-2: Triggering NEPA
TRIGGER:
Is the agency about to engage in a major federal action that might significantly affect the quality of the human environment?
YES:
The agency must prepare an Environmental Impact Statement (EIS) before undertaking the activity.
NO:
The agency need not prepare an EIS.

If, at the end of the EA, the agency concludes that its action is "a major Federal action significantly affecting the quality of the human environment," it will then extend its EA analysis into an EIS. 40 C.F.R. § 1501.4(c). If, on the other hand, the agency concludes that its action is *not* "a major Federal action significantly affecting the quality of the human environment," it prepares ***a finding of no significant impact*** **(FONSI)**. *Id.* § 1501.4(e).

Both an EIS and a FONSI, as final agency actions, are subject to judicial review pursuant to the APA. In addition, the federal agency is supposed to allow public comment and review during the entire NEPA process. 40 C.F.R. Part 1503.

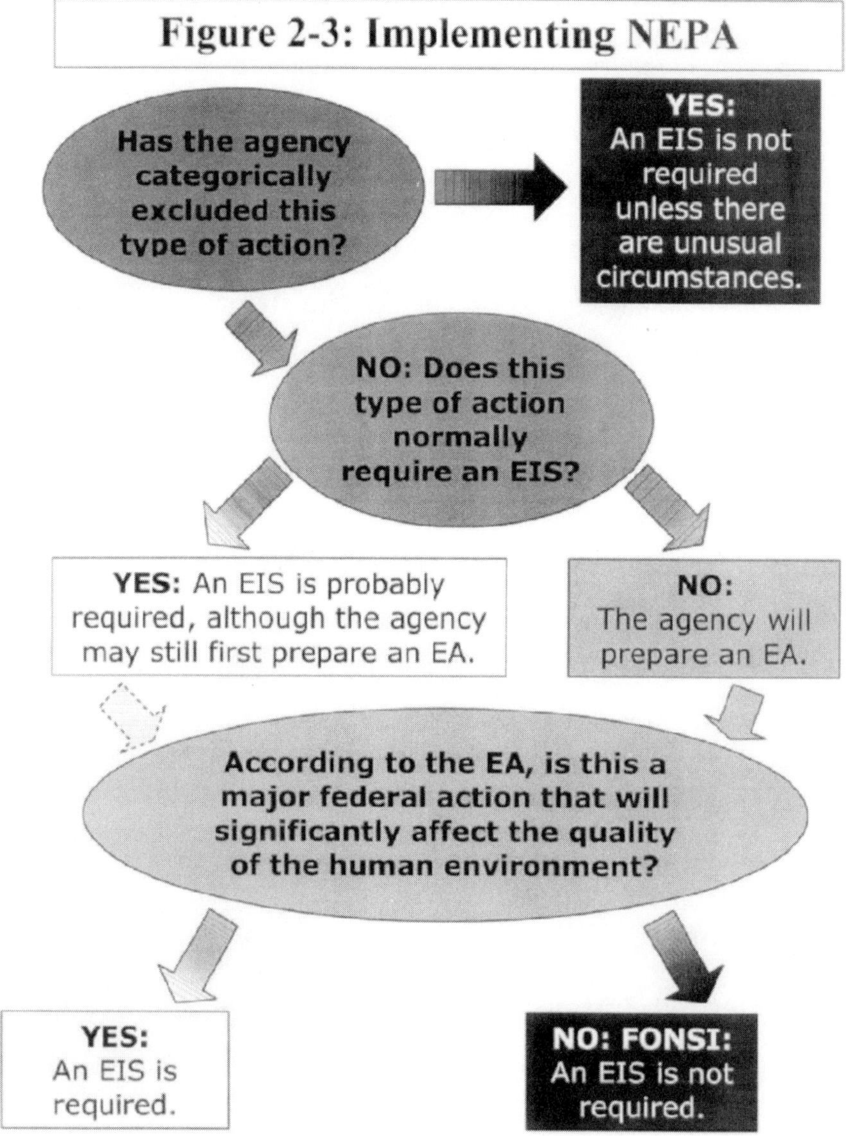
Figure 2-3: Implementing NEPA
Has the agency categorically excluded this type of action?
YES: An EIS is not required unless there are unusual circumstances.
NO: Does this type of action normally require an EIS?
YES: An EIS is probably required, although the agency may still first prepare an EA.
NO: The agency will prepare an EA.
According to the EA, is this a major federal action that will significantly affect the quality of the human environment?
YES: An EIS is required.
NO: FONSI: An EIS is not required.

II. IMPLEMENTING NEPA

A. THE TIMING OF THE NEPA EVALUATION

The CEQ's regulations provide that "[a]gencies shall integrate the NEPA process with other planning at the earliest possible time to insure that planning and decisions reflect environmental values, to avoid delays later in the process, and to head off potential conflicts." 40 C.F.R. § 1501.2. They emphasize, moreover, that

> An agency shall commence preparation of an environmental impact statement as close as possible to the time the agency is developing or is presented with a proposal * * * so that preparation can be completed in time for the final statement to be included in any recommendation or report on the proposal. The statement shall be prepared early enough so that it can serve practically as an important contribution to the decisionmaking process and will not be used to rationalize or justify decisions already made * * *.

40 C.F.R. § 1502.5. Moreover, while the agency is working on its NEPA assessments, it cannot take any actions respecting the proposed action that would "[h]ave an adverse environmental impact" or "[l]imit the choice of reasonable alternatives." 40 C.F.R. § 1506.1.

Thus, an agency must determine whether its proposed action is a major federal action that significantly affects the quality of the human environment—and hence is an action that will require an EIS—very early in the action planning process. The goal, as the CEQ's regulations indicate, is to ensure that federal agencies consider environmental values while those agencies are still free to change their minds about proposed actions. This goal of influencing federal agency decision making is also one reason that NEPA requires federal agencies to consider alternative actions and methods in the EIS. What happens if an agency engages in the NEPA evaluation process *after* it has already decided what it wants to do?

METCALF v. DALEY

214 F.3d 1135 (9th Cir. 2000).

TROTT, CIRCUIT JUDGE:

Appellants Jack Metcalf *et al.* appeal the district court's grant of summary judgment in favor of appellees William Daley, Secretary of Commerce; James Baker, Administrator of National Oceanic and Atmospheric Administration; Rolland A. Schmitten, Director of National Marine Fisheries Service (collectively "Federal Defendants"); and the Makah Indian Tribe ("Makah" or "Tribe"). Appellants argue that in granting the Makah authorization to resume whaling, the Federal Defendants violated the National Environmental Policy Act ("NEPA") by (1) preparing an Environmental Assessment ("EA") that was both untimely and inadequate, and (2) declining to prepare an Environmental Impact Statement ("EIS"). * * * We have jurisdiction pursuant to 28 U.S.C. § 1291, and we REVERSE and REMAND to the district court.

I. FACTUAL BACKGROUND

The Makah, who reside in Washington state on the northwestern Olympic Peninsula, have a 1500 year tradition of hunting whales. In particular, the Makah target the California gray whale ("gray whale"), which annually migrates between the North Pacific and the coast of Mexico. During their yearly journey, the migratory gray whale population travels through the Olympic Coast National Marine Sanctuary ("Sanctuary"), which Congress established in 1993 in order to protect the marine environment in a pristine ocean and coastal area. A small sub-population of gray whales, commonly referred to as "summer residents," live in the Sanctuary throughout the entire year.

In 1855, the United States and the Makah entered into the Treaty of Neah Bay, whereby the Makah ceded most of their land on the Olympic Peninsula to the United States in exchange for "[t]he right of taking fish and of whaling or sealing at usual and accustomed grounds and stations...." Treaty of Neah Bay, 12 Stat. 939, 940 (1855). Despite their long history of whaling and the Treaty of Neah Bay, however, the Makah ceased whaling in the 1920s because widespread commercial whaling had devastated the population of gray whales almost to extinction. Thus, the Tribe suspended whale hunting for seventy years, notwithstanding the important cultural role this practice played in their community.

Figure 2-4: Calfornia Gray Whale
NOAA photo.

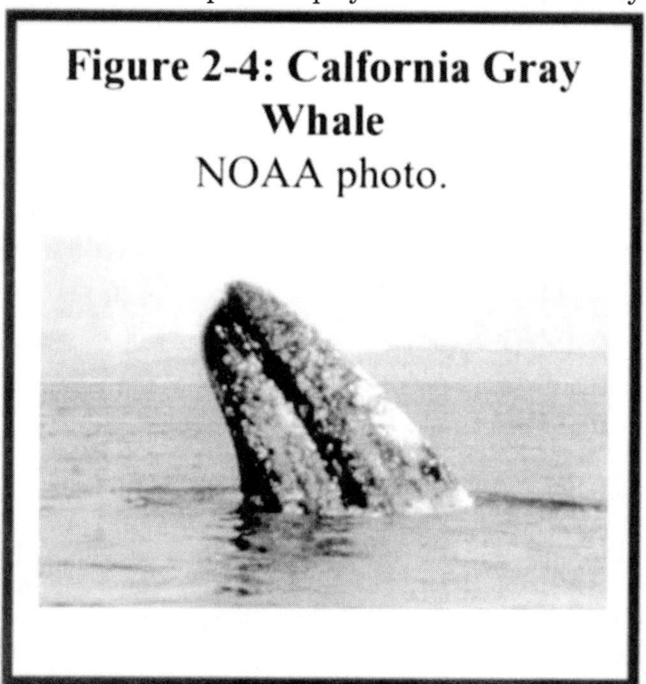

Because the gray whale had become virtually extinct, the United States signed in 1946 the International Convention for the Regulation of Whaling in order "to provide for the proper conservation of whale stocks and thus make possible the orderly development of the whaling industry...." International Convention for the Regulation of Whaling, 62 Stat. 1716, 1717 (1946). The International Convention for the Regulation of

Whaling enacted a schedule of whaling regulations ("Schedule") and established the International Whaling Commission ("IWC"), which was to be composed of one member from each signatory nation. * * *

Subsequently, in 1949, Congress passed the Whaling Convention Act to implement domestically the International Convention for the Regulation of Whaling. *See* 16 U.S.C.A. § 916 *et seq*. (1985). The Whaling Convention Act prohibits whaling in violation of the International Convention for the Regulation of Whaling, the Schedule, or any whaling regulation adopted by the Secretary of Commerce. *See id.* § 916c. In addition, the National Oceanic and Atmospheric Administration ("NOAA") and the National Marine Fisheries Service ("NMFS"), branches of the Department of Commerce, have been tasked with promulgating regulations to implement the provisions of the Whaling Convention Act. *See id.* § 916 *et seq*.; 50 C.F.R. § 230.1 (1998).

When the IWC was established on December 2, 1946, it took immediate action to protect the beleaguered mammal. Specifically, the IWC amended the Schedule to impose a complete ban on the taking or killing of gray whales. 62 Stat. at 1723. However, the IWC included an exception to the ban "when the meat and products of such whales are to be used exclusively for local consumption by the aborigines." *Id.* This qualification is referred to as the "aboriginal subsistence exception."

In addition to being shielded from commercial whaling under international law, the gray whale received increased protection in 1970 when the United States designated the species as endangered under the Endangered Species Conservation Act of 1969, the predecessor to the Endangered Species Act of 1973 ("ESA"). In 1993, however, NMFS determined that the eastern North Pacific stock of gray whales had recovered to near its estimated original population size and was no longer in danger of extinction. As such, this stock of gray whales was removed from the endangered species list in 1994. * * *

After these gray whales were removed from the endangered species list, the Makah decided to resume the hunting of whales that migrated through the Sanctuary. * * * The Tribe asked representatives from the Department of Commerce to represent it in seeking approval from the IWC for an annual quota of up to five gray whales.

As evidenced in an internal e-mail message written by an NMFS representative, the United States agreed in 1995 to "work with" the Makah in obtaining an aboriginal subsistence quota from the IWC. It was too late, however, to present the Makah's request formally at the IWC annual meeting scheduled to take place in May 1995. Nevertheless, the

Figure 2-5: Historic Native American Marine Mammal Hunting
NOAA image.

United States took the opportunity at the annual meeting to inform the Commission that: (1) the Makah had expressed an interest in harvesting up to five gray whales for ceremonial and subsistence purposes; and (2) the United States intended to submit in the future a formal proposal requesting such a quota.

After the 1995 annual meeting, NOAA prepared an internal report evaluating the merits of the Tribe's proposal in order to determine whether the United States should support its request for a gray whale quota. * * *

In January 1996, Will Martin, an NOAA representative, sent an e-mail message to his colleagues informing them that "we now have interagency agreement to support the Makah's application in IWC for a whaling quota of 5 grey whales." Shortly thereafter, on March 22, 1996, NOAA entered into a formal written Agreement with the Tribe, which provided that "[a]fter an adequate statement of need is prepared [by the Makah], NOAA, through the U.S. Commissioner to the IWC, will make a formal proposal to the IWC for a quota of gray whales for subsistence and ceremonial use by the Makah Tribe." * * * [T]he Agreement provided that within thirty days of IWC approval of a quota, "NOAA will revise its regulations to address subsistence whaling by the Makah Tribe, and the Council will adopt a management plan and regulations to govern the harvest * * *." The Agreement was signed by the Chairman of the Makah Tribal Council, Hubert Markishtum, and the Under Secretary for Oceans and Atmosphere, D. James Baker.

Pursuant to the Agreement, the Makah prepared an adequate statement of need, and the United States presented a formal proposal to the IWC for a quota of gray whales for the Tribe at the IWC annual meeting in June 1996. * * * Ultimately, the United States realized that it did not have the three-quarters majority required to approve it. Thus, after consulting with the Makah, the United States withdrew the proposal in order to give the Tribe an opportunity to address the delegates' concerns.

In June 1997, an attorney representing the organizations Australians for Animals and BEACH Marine Protection wrote a letter to NOAA and NMFS alleging that the United States Government had violated NEPA by authorizing and promoting the Makah whaling proposal without preparing an EA or an EIS. In response, the Administrator for NOAA wrote to Australians for Animals and BEACH Marine Protection on July 25, 1997, informing them that an EA would be prepared. Twenty-eight days later, on August 22, 1997, a draft EA was distributed for public comment.

On October 13, 1997, NOAA and the Makah entered into a new written Agreement, which, in most respects, was identical to the Agreement signed in 1996. * * * Four days later, and after the signing of this new Agreement, NOAA/NMFS issued, on October 17, 1997, a final EA and a Finding of No Significant Impact ("FONSI").

The 1997 IWC annual meeting was held on October 18, 1997, one day after the final EA had been issued. * * * After conferring, the United States and the Russian Federation decided to submit a joint proposal for a five-year block quota of 620 whales. The total quota of 620 assumed an average annual harvest of 120 whales by the Chukotka and an average annual harvest of four whales by the Makah. We note in passing that because "not every gray whale struck will be landed," the EA eventually concluded that the cumulative impact of the removal of injured gray whales by the Makah would total not just twenty whales over a five-year period, but forty-one. The EA makes no explicit mention of the decision to submit this joint proposal to the IWC, which would include a block quota of 620 whales for the Chukotka.

* * * [T]he quota was approved by consensus with no objections.

On April 6, 1998, NOAA issued a Federal Register Notice setting the domestic subsistence whaling quotas for 1998. *See* Notice of Aboriginal Subsistence Whaling Quotas, 63 Fed. Reg. 16, 701 (1998). The Notice stated that the Makah's subsistence and cultural needs had been recognized by both the United States and the IWC. *Id.* at 16,704. Accordingly, the Notice allowed the Makah to engage in whaling pursuant to the IWC-approved quota and Whaling Convention Act regulations. *Id.*

II. Procedural Background

On October 17, 1997, the same day as the release of the FONSI, appellants, including, *inter alia*, Congressman Metcalf, Australians for Animals, and BEACH Marine Protection, filed a complaint against the Federal Defendants in the United States District Court for the District of Columbia. Appellants alleged that the Federal Defendants had violated NEPA, the Whaling Convention Act, and the Administrative Procedures [*sic*] Act in connection with their support of the Makah whaling proposal. * * *

* * * Ultimately, the parties filed cross-motions for summary judgment on the merits, which were briefed and argued during the spring and summer of 1998. On September 21, 1998, the district court denied appellants' motion for summary judgment and granted the Federal Defendants' and the Makah's motions for summary judgment. Appellants now appeal.

III. Standard of Review

We review the district court's decision to grant or deny a motion for summary judgment de novo. However, we review substantive agency decisions concerning NEPA under the "arbitrary and capricious" standard, meaning we must determine whether the decision by NOAA/NMFS was "based on a consideration of the relevant factors," or whether their actions were "arbitrary, capricious, an abuse of discretion, or otherwise not in accordance with law." *Blue Mountains Biodiversity Project v. Blackwood*, 161 F.3d 1208, 1211 (9th Cir. 1998) (quoting the Administrative Procedures [*sic*] Act, 5 U.S.C. § 706(2)(A)). "NEPA does not mandate particular results, but simply provides the necessary process to ensure that federal agencies take a hard look at the environmental consequences of their actions." *Muckleshoot Indian Tribe v. United States Forest Serv.*, 177 F.3d 800, 814 (9th Cir. 1999). Under this deferential standard, we must defer to an agency's decision that is "fully informed and well-considered," *Save the Yaak Comm. v. Block*, 840 F.2d 714, 717 (9th Cir. 1988), but we need not forgive a "clear error of judgment." *Marsh v. Oregon Natural Resources Council*, 490 U.S. 360, 378, 385 (1989).

IV. NEPA Claim

A.

NEPA sets forth a "national policy which will encourage productive and enjoyable harmony between man and his environment ... [and]

promote efforts which will prevent or eliminate damage to the environment and biosphere and stimulate the health and welfare of man." 42 U.S.C.A. § 4321 (1994). NEPA does not set out substantive environmental standards, but instead establishes "action-forcing" procedures that require agencies to take a "hard look" at environmental consequences. *Robertson v. Methow Valley Citizens Council*, 490 U.S. 332, 348 (1989). We have characterized the statute as "primarily procedural," and held that "agency action taken without observance of the procedure required by law will be set aside." *Save the Yaak*, 840 F.2d at 717. In this respect, we have observed in connection with the preparation of an EA that "[p]roper timing is one of NEPA's central themes. An assessment must be 'prepared early enough so that it can serve practically as an important contribution to the decisionmaking process and will not be used to rationalize or justify decisions already made.' " *Id.* at 718 (quoting 40 C.F.R. § 1502.5 (1987)).

The phrase "early enough" means "at the earliest possible time to insure that planning and decisions reflect environmental values." *Andrus v. Sierra Club*, 442 U.S. 347, 351 (1979). *See also* 40 C.F.R. § 1501.2 (1999). The Supreme Court in referring to NEPA's requirements as "action forcing," *Andrus*, 442 U.S. at 350, has embraced the rule that for projects directly undertaken by Federal agencies, environmental impact statements "shall be prepared at the feasibility analysis (go-no go) stage and may be supplemented at a later stage if necessary." *Id.* at 351 n.3; *see also* 40 C.F.R. § 1502.5(a) (1999).

All of these rules notwithstanding, NEPA does not require that agency officials be "subjectively impartial." The statute does require, however, that projects be objectively evaluated. * * * In summary, the comprehensive "hard look" mandated by Congress and required by the statute must be timely, and it must be taken objectively and in good faith, not as an exercise in form over substance, and not as a subterfuge designed to rationalize a decision already made. * * *

NEPA requires that an EIS be prepared for all "major Federal actions significantly affecting the quality of the human environment." 42 U.S.C.A. § 4332(2)(C) (1994). However, if, as here, an agency's regulations do not categorically require the preparation of an EIS, then the agency must first prepare an EA to determine whether the action will have a significant effect on the environment. *See* 40 C.F.R. § 1501.4 (1991); *Salmon River Concerned Citizens v. Robertson*, 32 F.3d 1346, 1356 (9th Cir. 1994). If, in light of the EA, the agency determines that its action will significantly affect the environment, then an EIS must be prepared; if not, then the agency issues a FONSI. *See* 40 C.F.R. §§ 1501.4, 1508.9 (1999); *Salmon River*, 32 F.3d at 1356. "If an agency decides not to prepare an EIS, it must supply a 'convincing statement of reasons' to explain why a project's impacts are insignificant." *Blue Mountain*, 161 F.3d at 1211 (quoting *Save the Yaak*, 840 F.2d at 717).

In this case, the Federal Defendants did (1) prepare an EA, (2) decide that the Makah whaling proposal would not significantly affect the environment, and (3) issue a FONSI, but they did so after already having signed two agreements binding them to support the Tribe's proposal. Appellants assert that, in so doing, the Federal Defendants violated NEPA in several ways. Appellants argue that, although NOAA/NMFS ultimately prepared an EA, they violated NEPA because they prepared the EA too late in the process. * * * Additionally, appellants contend that the Federal Defendants violated NEPA by preparing an inadequate EA, and by issuing a FONSI instead of preparing an EIS.

B.

We begin by considering appellants' argument that the Federal Defendants failed timely and in the proper sequence to comply with NEPA. As provided in the regulations promulgated to implement NEPA, "[a]gencies shall integrate the NEPA process with other planning *at the earliest possible time* to insure that planning and decisions reflect environmental values, to avoid delays later in the process, and to head off potential conflicts." 40 C.F.R. § 1501.2 (emphasis added); *see also id.* § 1502.5 ("An agency shall commence preparation of an [EIS] as close as possible to the time the agency is developing or is presented with a proposal...."). Furthermore, this court has interpreted these regulations as requiring agencies to prepare NEPA documents, such as an EA or an EIS, "before any irreversible and irretrievable commitment of resources." *Conner v. Burford*, 848 F.2d 1441, 1446 (9th Cir. 1988); *see also EDF v. Andrus*, 596 F.2d 848, 852 (9th Cir. 1979). Thus, the issue we must decide here is whether the Federal Defendants prepared the EA too late in the decision-making process, *i.e.*, after making an irreversible and irretrievable commitment of resources. We conclude that they did.

The purpose of an EA is to provide the agency with sufficient evidence and analysis for determining whether to prepare an EIS or to issue a FONSI. 40 C.F.R. § 1508.9. Because the very important decision whether to prepare an EIS is based solely on the EA, the EA is fundamental to the decision-making process. In terms of timing and importance to the goals of NEPA, we see no difference between an EA and an EIS in connection with when an EA must be integrated into the calculus. In the case at bar, the Makah first asked the Federal Defendants to help them secure IWC approval for a gray whale quota in 1995; however, NOAA/NMFS did not prepare an EA until 1997. During these two years, the United States and the Makah worked together toward obtaining a gray whale quota from the IWC. In January 1996, an NOAA representative informed his colleagues that "we now have interagency agreement to support the Makah's application in IWC for a whaling quota of 5 grey whales." More importantly, in March 1996, more than a year before the EA was prepared, NOAA entered into a contract with the Makah pursuant to which it committed to (1) making a formal proposal to the IWC for a quota of gray whales for subsistence and ceremonial use by the Makah and (2) participating in the management of the harvest. To demonstrate the firmness of this commitment, we need only to look at the EA, which says, "In early 1996, [NOAA and the Makah Tribal Council] signed an agreement in which the United States committed to make a formal request to the IWC...."

The Federal Defendants did not engage the NEPA process "at the earliest possible time." Instead, the record makes clear that the Federal Defendants did not even consider the potential environmental effects of the proposed action until long after they had already committed in writing to support the Makah whaling proposal. The "point of commitment" in this case came when NOAA signed the contract with the Makah in March 1996 and then worked to effectuate the agreement. It was at this juncture that it made an "irreversible and irretrievable commitment of resources." * * * Although it could have, NOAA did not make its promise to seek a quota from the IWC and to participate in the harvest conditional upon a NEPA determination that the Makah whaling proposal would not significantly affect the environment.

Had NOAA/NMFS found after signing the Agreement that allowing the Makah to resume whaling would have a significant effect on the environment, the Federal Defendants would have been required to prepare an EIS, and they may not have been able to fulfill their written commitment to the Tribe. As such, NOAA would have been in breach of contract. * * *

It is highly likely that because of the Federal Defendants' prior written commitment to the Makah and concrete efforts on their behalf, the EA was slanted in favor of finding that the Makah whaling proposal would not significantly affect the environment. * * * The EA itself somewhat disingenuously claims in 1997 that the "decision to be made" is "whether to support the Makah Tribe in its effort to continue its whaling tradition," when in point of fact that decision had already been made in contract form. To quote the 1996 Agreement, "after an adequate statement of need is prepared, NOAA ... will make a formal proposal to the IWC for a quota of gray whales...." The Makah satisfied its part of the bargain in 1996, binding the Federal Defendants to deliver on theirs, as they did at the IWC meeting in June 1996. Also, NOAA/NMFS's statement in the EA that "[a]ny perception that the U.S. Government is trying to withdraw its support for Makah whaling would likely plunge the Tribe into a difficult controversy with the United States" strongly suggests that the Federal Defendants were predisposed to issue a FONSI.

NEPA's effectiveness depends entirely on involving environmental considerations in the initial decisionmaking process. *See* 40 C.F.R. §§ 1501.2, 1502.5; *see also Methow Valley*, 490 U.S. at 349 (explaining that NEPA "ensures that the agency, in reaching its decision, will have available, and will carefully consider, detailed information concerning significant environmental impacts"). Moreover, the Supreme Court has clearly held that treaty rights such as those at stake in this case "may be regulated ... in the interest of conservation ..., provided the regulation ... does not discriminate against the Indians." *Puyallup Tribe v. Department of Game of Wash.*, 391 U.S. 392, 398 (1968). Here, before preparing an EA, the Federal Defendants signed a contract which obligated them both to make a proposal to the IWC for a gray whale quota and to participate in the harvest of those whales. We hold that by making such a firm commitment before preparing an EA, the Federal Defendants failed to take a "hard look" at the environmental consequences of their actions and, therefore, violated NEPA.

* * * V. REMEDY

Appellees argue that, even if the Federal Defendants did violate NEPA by preparing the EA after deciding to support Makah whaling, the issue is moot because the only relief that the court could order is the preparation of an adequate EA, which, appellees contend, already has been done. * * *

* * * [A]ppellants here do not concede that the EA that ultimately was prepared is adequate. To the contrary, appellants contend that the EA is demonstrably suspect because the process under which the EA was prepared was fatally defective—*i.e.*, the Federal Defendants were predisposed to finding that the Makah whaling proposal would not significantly affect the environment. We agree. Moreover, appellants vigorously maintain that the EA is deficient with respect to its content and conclusions.

Our conclusions about the EA in this case raise an obvious question: Having already committed in writing to support the Makah's whaling proposal, can the Federal Defendants now be trusted to take the clear-eyed hard look at the whaling proposal's consequences required by the law, or will a new EA be a classic Wonderland case of first-the-verdict, then-the-trial? In order to avoid this problem and to ensure that the law is respected, must we—and can we—set aside the FONSI and require the Federal Defendants to proceed directly to the preparation of an Environmental Impact Statement? On reflection, and in consideration of our limited role in this process, we have decided that it is appropriate only to require a new EA, but to require that it be done under circumstances that ensure an objective evaluation free of the previous taint. Unlike many of the disputes we are called on to resolve, time here is not of the essence. Although the doctrine of laches cannot defeat Indian rights recognized in a treaty, the Makah's seventy year hiatus in connection with whale hunting suggests that a modest delay occasioned by the need to respect NEPA's commands will cause no harm.

The manner of ensuring that the process for which we remand this case is accomplished objectively and in good faith shall be left to the relevant agencies. Should a new EA come back to the courts for additional scrutiny, however, the burden shall be on the Federal Defendants to demonstrate to the district court that they have complied with this requirement. * * *

NOTES

1. **The Rest of the Story.** After the district court in this case granted summary judgment in favor of the Makah, but before the Ninth Circuit issued

the opinion presented here, the Makah Tribe hunted and killed one gray whale on May 17, 1999, to much outcry and protest. Pictures of that hunt, and the Makahs' justifications for it, are available through the Makah Indian Nation's home page, http://www.makah.com.

After the Ninth Circuit issued the decision presented here, NOAA and NMFS withdrew their agreement with the Makah regarding whaling. However, in January 2001—mere months after the Ninth Circuit's decision—these agencies issued a new draft EA. On July 12, 2001, NOAA and NMFS issued their final EA, concluding that whaling according to the Makahs' management plan would have no significant impact on the quality of the human environment. The agencies issued another FONSI. These Environmental Assessments (EAs) are available through NOAA's web site at http://www.nmfs.noaa.gov/prot_res/PR2/Conservation_and_Recovery_Program/makah_EA.html. The Makahs' management plan, on which the new EA was based, required the hunters to strike no more than 33 gray whales between 1998 and 2002 and to strike no more than 14 whales in 2001 and 2002. In addition, during 2001 and 2002, the Makah would strike no more than five whales during the whales' migration or in the Strait of Juan de Fuca, off Washington State.

In December 2001, NOAA and NMFS announced that the Makah Tribe could land five gray whales in 2001 and 2002. 66 Fed. Reg. 64,378 (Dec. 13, 2001). In January 2002, environmental groups and animals' rights organizations filed a lawsuit challenging that decision, and a few months later the district court again granted summary judgment in favor of the Makah. The challengers appealed, and in December 2002 the Ninth Circuit determined that the second FONSI was also arbitrary and capricious, although not for reasons of timing. *Anderson v. Evans*, 314 F.3d 1006, 1017–23 (9th Cir. 2002), *amended by* 350 F.3d 815, 831–37 (9th Cir. 2003). In December 2003, the Ninth Circuit denied the Tribe's petition for an *en banc* review but nevertheless ruled that the Tribe could file another such petition. As of May 2004, the Makah Tribe had filed its second petition for *en banc* review and was awaiting the Ninth Circuit's decision.

The federal government's decision to allow the Makah to whale also caused problems for the Tribe under the federal Marine Mammal Protection Act (MMPA), 16 U.S.C. §§ 1361–1432h. This Act prohibits the "take" of marine mammals, MMPA § 102(a), 16 U.S.C. § 1372(a), a prohibition that extends to both killing and harassing whales. However, the Act allows for permitted exceptions to the "take" prohibition. MMPA § 104, 16 U.S.C. § 1374.

In 2002, the Ninth Circuit concluded that the federal government's decision to allow the Makah to hunt whales violated both NEPA and the MMPA. The decision violated NEPA because NOAA had failed to adequately address the effects of hunting on the *local* population of gray whales. *Anderson v. Evans*, 314 F.3d 1006, 1018–19 (9th Cir. 2002). Moreover, the Makah qualified for no exemption from the MMPA's "take" prohibition, and the Ninth Circuit concluded that the MMPA should apply to the Tribe, even though it was enacted after the Treaty of Neah Bay, because of a "conservation necessity." *Id.* At 1023–29 (see Note 10). Although the Ninth Circuit took the unusual step of amending its opinion twice over the next two years—*Anderson v. Evans*, 350 F.3d 815 (9th Cir. 2003); *Anderson v. Evans*, 371 F.3d 475 (9th Cir. 2004)—it did not change its final conclusions.

As a result of these decisions, the Makah applied for a waiver from the MMPA's "take" prohibition, including the necessary permits and NOAA regulations, on February 14, 2005. The waiver application itself triggered the need for another EIS under NEPA. Public comment on the proposed EIS closed on March 29, 2006. On May 9, 2008, NOAA released its Draft EIS. Comments on the Draft EIS were due by August 15, 2008. As of late November 2011, NOAA had not released the Final EIS.

In the meantime, on September 8, 2007, several tribal members shot and killed a gray whale without NOAA's permission and apparently without tribal authorization. Federal prosecutors indicted five tribal members who engaged in the hunt on October 4, 2007 for misdemeanor counts. The leader served five months in prison.

The IWC has estimated, given the continuing recovery of the gray whale species, that 407–670 individual whales could be taken sustainably each year, without harm to the species. The gray whale's status—and aboriginal hunting quotas—were issues at the IWC's July 2011 meeting.

2. **Identifying the Procedures Used.** What NEPA procedures did the National Oceanic and Atmospheric Administration (NOAA) and the National Marine Fisheries Service (NMFS; now known as NOAA Fisheries) follow?

3. **The Ninth Circuit's Standard of Review.** What APA standard did the Ninth Circuit use to review NOAA's and NMFS's compliance with NEPA? Why would it use that standard? How did the Ninth Circuit describe this standard of judicial review?

4. **NEPA as a Procedural Statute.** According to the Ninth Circuit, does NEPA impose any *substantive* requirements on federal agencies? For instance, does a federal agency have to choose the alternative with the least environmental impact? Why or why not? *See Strycker's Bay Neighborhood Council, Inc. v. Karlen*, 444 U.S. 223, 227–28 (1980); *Vermont Yankee Nuclear Power Corp. v. NRDC*, 435 U.S. 519, 558 (1978); *Kleppe v. Sierra Club,* 427 U.S. 390, 410 n.21 (1976).

5. **Timing of NEPA Evaluations.** How has case law elaborated upon the CEQ's timing requirement? When *exactly* must federal agencies engage in the NEPA process? What kinds of events indicate that the analysis comes too late?

6. **The Federal Defendants' NEPA Violation.** Why, given the standard of review that the Ninth Circuit used, did that court invalidate the FONSI? How had NOAA and NMFS violated the NEPA timing requirements in this case?

7. **The Remedy for NEPA Violations.** What remedy did the Ninth Circuit give to the plaintiffs? Does this remedy seem very satisfactory? Why or why not?

8. **International Legal Protections for Whales.** As this case made clear, the Makahs' attempts to hunt whales had international law ramifica-

tions for the United States. How are whales protected under international law? How has the United States implemented those international protections? How could NOAA and NMFS champion the Makah Tribe's whaling proposal without putting the United States in violation of international law?

9. **Other Domestic Legal Protections for Gray Whales.** As the Ninth Circuit mentioned, gray whales were at one time protected not only under international law but also under the United States' Endangered Species Act (ESA), 16 U.S.C. §§ 1531–1544, which you will study more thoroughly in Chapter 3. NMFS determined that gray whales were nearing extinction as a result of extensive hunting and listed the species as an endangered species under the ESA. However, the eastern North Pacific (California) gray whale population is one of the ESA's great success stories. With hunting eliminated, this population's numbers began to increase, and in 1984 NMFS upgraded its status from endangered to threatened. 49 Fed. Reg. 44,774 (Nov. 9, 1984). By the early 1990s, this population of gray whales had recovered to near its original numbers, and NMFS removed it from the endangered species list entirely in 1994. 59 Fed. Reg. 31,094 (June 16, 1994). NOAA estimated in 2002 that there are 17,000 to 26,000 whales in the eastern North Pacific gray whale stock and that the stock is near its full carrying capacity.

Nevertheless, as discussed in Note 1, gray whales remain subject to the federal Marine Mammal Protection Act (MMPA), 16 U.S.C. §§ 1361–1423h, which prohibits the "taking" of marine mammals. 16 U.S.C. § 1371(a). However, the MMPA also declares that its prohibitions are subject to existing international treaty rights. 16 U.S.C. § 1372(a)(2). In its 2002 decision regarding the Makahs' whaling, the Ninth Circuit held that the Makah could not make use of this provision, because the 1997 IWC schedules that allowed the Makah to hunt gray whales were not "existing" international treaty rights as of 1972, when Congress enacted the MMPA. *See Anderson v. Evans*, 314 F.3d 1006, 1023–26 (9th Cir. 2002), *amended by* 350 F.3d 815, 837–41 (9th Cir. 2003).

10. **Indian Treaty Rights and Environmental Law.** As the Ninth Circuit pointed out in *Metcalf v. Daley*, the Makah Tribe has a right, pursuant to its treaty with the United States, to engage in whaling at its accustomed grounds. As one federal judge has observed, "[e]very statute and treaty designed to protect animals or birds has a specific exemption for Native Alaskans who hunt the species for subsistence purposes. These statutes have been construed as specifically imposing on the Federal government a trust responsibility to protect the Alaskan Natives' rights of subsistence hunting." *North Slope Borough v. Andrus*, 486 F. Supp. 332, 344 (D.D.C. 1980); *see also* MMPA, 16 U.S.C. § 1371(b); ESA, 16 U.S.C. § 1539(e). However, these exemptions generally do not help non-Alaskan Tribes like the Makah.

Courts rely on various doctrines to apply federal environmental statutes to non-Alaskan Tribes. The Ninth Circuit prefers the "conservation necessity" doctrine, which it has twice applied to the Makah Tribe. The most controversial part of the Ninth Circuit's 2002 decision regarding Makah gray whale hunting, for instance, was its decision that the MMPA applies to the Makah Tribe, regardless of the Tribe's treaty rights, as a conservation necessity. According to the Ninth Circuit, "the MMPA may regulate any pre-existing Makah Tribe whaling rights under treaty if (1) the United States has jurisdiction where the whaling occurs; (2) the MMPA applies in a non-discriminatory manner to treaty and non-treaty persons alike; and (3) the application of the statute is necessary to achieve its conservation purposes." *Anderson v. Evans*, 314 F.3d 1006, 1026 (9th Cir. 2002). The court concluded that all three elements were met and thus "that the issuance by NOAA of a gray whale quota to the Tribe, absent compliance with the MMPA, violates federal law." *Id.* at 1028. *See also Midwater Trawlers Co-operative v. Department of Commerce*, 282 F.3d 710, 716–20 (9th Cir. 2002) (holding that the Magnuson–Stevens Fisheries Conservation and Management Act, 16 U.S.C. §§ 1801–1883, applies to the Makah Tribe's treaty fishing, despite the Treaty of Neah Bay, under the conservation necessity doctrine).

More strictly, however, abrogation of tribal treaty rights should be an issue of congressional intent. Under the U.S. Supreme Court's jurisprudence, Congress can abrogate tribal treaty rights through legislation. *Santa Clara Pueblo v. Martinez*, 436 U.S. 49, 56–57 (1978); *Federal Power Comm'n v. Tuscarora Indian Nation*, 362 U.S. 99, 116 (1960); *United States v. Kagama*, 118 U.S. 375, 379–81, 383–84 (1886). Deciding whether Congress has actually done so, however, can result in complex analyses of congressional intent. The issue of whether Congress has intentionally abrogated the Makah Tribe's treaty right to whale, either through implementation of the International Whaling Convention or through the MMPA, remains an undecided issue as of early 2008.

* * *

B. DEFINING NEPA'S TRIGGER: "MAJOR FEDERAL ACTIONS"

Once the agency properly begins the NEPA evaluation process, it must determine whether it must prepare an EIS for the action it is considering. As has been noted, a federal agency triggers NEPA's EIS requirement if the agency proposes "a major Federal action significantly affecting the quality of the human environment." NEPA § 102(C), 42 U.S.C. § 4332(C). The CEQ has defined almost every word in this phrase in its regulations.

According to the CEQ, a federal action is ***"major"*** if it *might* be major. 40 C.F.R. § 1508.18. In other words, uncertainty about the action's effects cuts *in favor* of the EIS. Otherwise, "[m]ajor reinforces but does not have a meaning independent of significantly * * *." *Id.* Thus, a federal action is "major" if it significantly affects the quality of the human environment. ***"Significantly,"*** in turn, refers to both the context and the intensity of the agency action—that is, to the type of environment actually affected and to the severity of that impact. 40 C.F.R. § 1508.27.

"Actions" "include new and continuing activities * * *; new or revised agency rules, regulations, plans, policies, or procedures; and legislative proposals * * *." 40 C.F.R. § 1508.18(a). However, "[a]ctions do not include bringing judicial or administrative civil or criminal enforcement actions." *Id.* Thus, environmental enforcement actions do not trigger the NEPA EIS requirement.

An action is ***"federal"*** if it is "entirely or partly financed, assisted, conducted, regulated, or approved by federal agencies," but federal funding qualifies an action as "federal" only if the federal agency retains control over those funds. *Id.* According to the CEQ, "Federal actions tend to fall within one of [four] categories": adoption of official policy and regulations; adoption of formal plans; adoption of programs; and approval of specific projects. 40 C.F.R. § 1508.18(b).

Some actions are clearly "federal" actions for NEPA purposes, such as when the EPA writes regulations or the U.S. Forest Service adopts plans for a national forests. However, NEPA potentially applies to actions with a far less direct federal connection, such as when federal agencies fund or permit projects carried out by non-federal actors. As a result, litigants often argue that NEPA applies to actions undertaken by non-federal entities, as in the following case.

MAYAGUEZANOS POR LA SALUD Y EL AMBIENTE v. UNITED STATES

198 F.3d 297 (1st Cir. 1999).

LYNCH, CIRCUIT JUDGE.

On February 3, 1998, the *Pacific Swan*, a British-flag freighter carrying a cargo of vitrified high-level nuclear waste, passed through the Mona Passage, a stretch of seas between the islands of Puerto Rico and Hispaniola. It was bound for Japan, by way of the Panama Canal, from France. A day earlier, a group of fishermen and environmental organizations from western Puerto Rico, fearing an accident or maritime disaster, brought this action for an injunction to stop the shipment until the United States filed an Environmental Impact Statement (EIS) in accordance with the National Environmental Policy Act (NEPA), 42 U.S.C. § 4321 *et seq.* After the parties filed cross-motions for summary judgment, the district court denied the claim for injunctive relief and dismissed the action. We affirm on different reasoning.

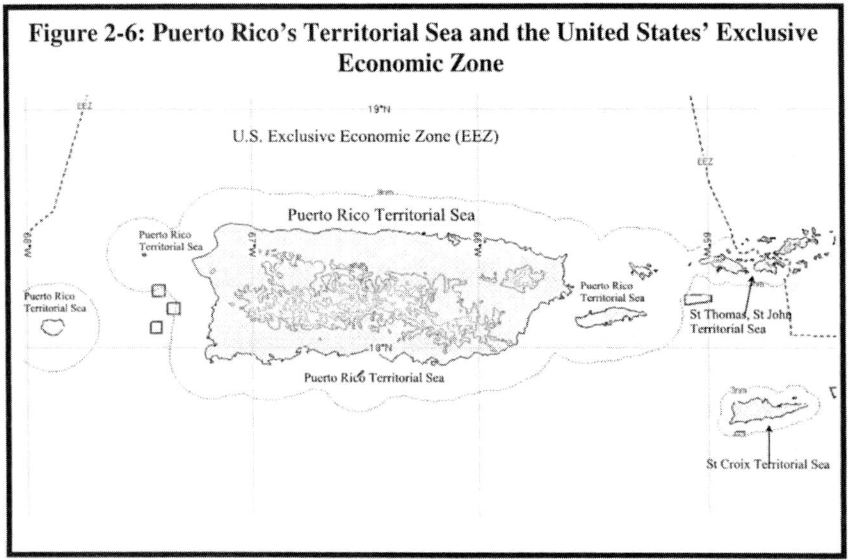

Figure 2-6: Puerto Rico's Territorial Sea and the United States' Exclusive Economic Zone

I

The voyage of the *Pacific Swan* is part of a modern circumferential trade. Uranium from the United States is sent to Japan to fuel nuclear energy reactors. Japan ships the reactors' spent fuel to COGEMA, a French nuclear power company, for recycling at its La Hague plant. This process recovers a substantial portion of reusable fissionable material, which is turned into nuclear fuel (either RepU fuel, comprising uranium, or MOX fuel, comprising plutonium and uranium). It also generates high-level nuclear waste, which includes trace amounts of uranium and plutonium. The waste is vitrified according to specifications that have been approved by French and Japanese governments and placed in casks that meet criteria set forth by the International Atomic Energy Agency in its Regulations for the Safe Transport of Radioactive Material.[1] Both the waste and the fuel are returned to Japan on board specially designed ships that meet the standards of the International Maritime Organization's Code for the Safe Carriage of Irradiated Nuclear Fuel, Plutonium and High–Level Radioactive Wastes in Flasks on Board Ships. The private shippers choose the return route to Japan from three options: the Cape of Good Hope, Cape Horn, or the Panama Canal.

The U.S. connection to this trade occurs in two ways. First, the United States supplies the uranium to Japan under a 1988 agreement between the two countries. Second, the transport of the nuclear waste shipments through the Mona Passage means that the ship traverses

1. The vitrification process turns the waste into a solid glass form, thereby "immobilizing" it. According to Frederick F. McGoldrick, the State Department's Principal Deputy Director of Nuclear Energy Affairs, the vitrified waste is "very insoluble in water, resistant to heat, and extremely stable."

waters in which the United States has some interest, even if they are not territorial waters.

II

Because these waste-laden voyages through the Mona Passage continue, the case is not moot, which the United States appropriately concedes. Review of entry of summary judgment is de novo; further, the issues presented are ones of law and our review is plenary.

On appeal, Mayaguezanos has refined its argument to a single attack: the federal courts have jurisdiction to consider this action under NEPA and the United States's failure to regulate the passage of such nuclear waste through its Exclusive Economic Zone (EEZ) waters is a "major federal action" within the meaning of NEPA. Mayaguezanos argues that there is a major federal action because the United States is required to play some role in the transport of this waste under various international agreements and customary international law. This complex of interests and responsibilities, they contend, suffices to establish "major federal action" under NEPA. The United States rejoins that the shipment of waste is the "action," it is not being carried out by a federal agency but by private parties, and the facts do not meet the tests to determine if there is federal action where the primary action is carried out by private players.

Under NEPA, all U.S. agencies are required to "include in every recommendation or report on proposals for legislation and other major Federal actions significantly affecting the quality of the human environment" a "detailed statement." 42 U.S.C. § 4332(2). This detailed statement, known as an EIS, must address the environmental impact of proposed actions and alternatives. * * * NEPA's aims are two-fold: to "place[] upon an agency the obligation to consider every significant aspect of the environmental impact of a proposed action" and to "ensure[] that the agency will inform the public that it has indeed considered environmental concerns in its decisionmaking process." *Baltimore Gas & Elec. Co. v. Natural Resources Defense Council, Inc.*, 462 U.S. 87, 97 (1983) (internal quotation marks and citations omitted); *see also Robertson v. Methow Valley Citizens Council*, 490 U.S. 332, 349 (1989).

Mayaguezanos has described the significance of a maritime accident or incident involving this waste and the government has responded that all safety precautions have been taken.[7] Arguments about the safety of

7. Mayaguezanos asserts that "[t]he serial transportation of [this waste] through the Mona Passage is likely to cause loss of marine habitat, degradation of water quality, and irreparable damages to the ecosystem of the West Coast of Puerto Rico, as well as to threaten rare plant and animal species in Mona Island and to impair long-term scientific research projects in the area." The United States says that it is "keenly interested in ensuring that the transportation of [vitrified high-level nuclear waste] be carried out safely in accordance with applicable international standards . . . , particularly when the transportation route approaches United States territory," and that it has "every reason to believe that this and future shipments will be completed in a safe and secure manner, and that the shipments do not pose any significant risk to 'health, safety, or the environment.' " It points to the conclusion of Charles D. Massey of Sandia National Laboratories that "the risk that there would be any significant environmental impact from marine transport of vitrified high level waste is less than one chance in a billion."

such shipments may be made to a variety of bodies, both in the United States and internationally. Before, however, U.S. courts may speak to the safety matter, they must first decide whether they have any authority to address such issues, a question that turns on whether NEPA applies at all.

The arguments seem to contain two implicit assumptions: that NEPA applies to actions outside territorial U.S. lands and waters and that NEPA's "major federal action" requirement would work in the same fashion in the domestic and the international contexts. We are skeptical. These are difficult problems, but because Mayaguezanos's claims fail even under the "major federal action" tests used in domestic cases, we need not inquire into the validity of these assumptions. Consequently, we turn to the domestic case law.

This circuit has not recently addressed the criteria to be used in domestic cases to determine when private activities may be deemed to be major federal actions under NEPA. In *Citizens for Responsible Area Growth v. Adams,* 680 F.2d 835 (1st Cir. 1982), this court held that construction of an airport hangar by private parties with private monies was not federal action for NEPA purposes and that the mere appearance of the proposed construction on a federally approved Airport Layout Plan did not create sufficient federal involvement to require an EIS. *See id.* at 839–40. The court acknowledged that the need for a federal license or approval could sometimes trigger NEPA, but not where the approval did not involve close scrutiny of the action or anything more than notice for safety purposes. *See id.* at 840.

Additional guidance comes from the definition articulated by the Council on Environmental Quality (CEQ). The regulations of the CEQ suggest that actions by non-federal actors "with effects that may be major and which are potentially subject to Federal control and responsibility" can be major federal actions. 40 C.F.R. § 1508.18. Under CEQ regulations, "actions" include "projects and programs entirely or partly financed, assisted, conducted, regulated, or approved by federal agencies." 40 C.F.R. § 1508.18(a). The "CEQ's interpretation of NEPA is entitled to substantial deference." *Andrus v. Sierra Club*, 442 U.S. 347, 358 (1979).

There are two situations that generally will not constitute major federal actions under NEPA. The first situation is governmental inaction, where that failure to act is not otherwise subject to review by the courts or administrative agencies under the Administrative Procedure Act or other laws. *See* 40 C.F.R. § 1508.18. The second situation is mere approval by the federal government of action by a private party where that approval is not required for the private party to go forward. This latter category encompasses, and disposes of, the portion of Mayaguezanos's argument that is based on the shippers having voluntarily notified the Coast Guard of the *Pacific Swan*'s transit through the Mona Passage.

There are various situations that may constitute major federal action under NEPA. In cases, such as this one, where there is no claim that the non-federal project is being federally funded, the circuits have articulated different formulations of "major federal action," but the focus has been on the indicia of control over the private actors by the federal agency. For example, this circuit found "major federal action" where a federal agency approved the release of funds from a trust held by the agency that were necessary for a project to go forward. The effect of this action was explicitly to permit the private actor to decommission a nuclear facility.

The Fourth Circuit has held that "a non-federal project is considered a 'federal action' if it cannot begin or continue without prior approval by a federal agency and the agency possesses authority to exercise discretion over the outcome." *Sugarloaf Citizens Ass'n v. Federal Energy Regulatory Comm'n*, 959 F.2d 508, 513–14 (4th Cir. 1992). The Tenth Circuit found that there is a major federal action when "the federal government has actual power to control the project." *Ross v. Federal Highway Admin.*, 162 F.3d 1046, 1051 (10th Cir. 1998) (internal quotation marks and citation omitted). The Eighth Circuit held in *Ringsred v. City of Duluth*, 828 F.2d 1305, 1308 (8th Cir. 1987), that "federal action [must be] a legal condition precedent to the [private event]." The Third Circuit has said that the federal agency's action must be a legal pre-condition that authorizes the other party to proceed with action. *See NAACP v. Medical Ctr., Inc.*, 584 F.2d 619, 628 n.15 (3d Cir. 1978).

Like the Fourth Circuit, we look to whether federal approval is the prerequisite to the action taken by the private actors and whether the federal agency possesses some form of authority over the outcome. Mayaguezanos makes two arguments that the United States has effectively authorized the shipments. First, the United States has implicitly consented to such shipments, they say, under the U.S.–EURATOM Agreement and generally has acted under the Atomic Energy Act and the Nuclear Non–Proliferation Act. Secondly, they contend that the United States has the power to stop such shipments through its EEZ waters, has chosen not to do so, and so has implicitly authorized the shipments. We evaluate each argument in turn.

III

The Treaties

Mayaguezanos's core argument is that the United States granted or was required to grant specific authorization for the shipments of this nuclear waste from France to Japan under the provisions of the U.S.–EURATOM Agreement.

Under § 123 of the Atomic Energy Act of 1954 (AEA), 42 U.S.C. § 2153, certain foreign commerce in nuclear materials must be governed by "agreement[s] for cooperation" that contain particular safeguards. *See id.* § 2153(a)(1). This framework was enhanced with the 1978 enactment of the Nuclear Non–Proliferation Act (NNPA), 22 U.S.C. § 3201 *et seq.*, which intended to ensure "effective controls by the United States over its exports of nuclear materials and equipment and of nuclear technology." 22 U.S.C. § 3202(d). Acting under this authority, the United States in

1988 entered the U.S.–Japan Agreement. Pursuant to this agreement, the United States has sold uranium to Japan; the nuclear waste at issue in this case derived from one of these sales.

Once the irradiated material leaves Japan for reprocessing it is governed by another § 123 agreement, commonly called the U.S.–EURATOM Agreement. The EURATOM signatories are fifteen European countries, including France and the United Kingdom. That agreement includes certain "safeguards," a term of art for systems to verify that the nuclear material will not be diverted to weaponry or illicit uses.

Article 5.2 of the U.S.–EURATOM Agreement provides that certain nuclear materials may be removed from the governance of the Agreement through procedures set out in an Administrative Arrangement. Once the material in question has been determined, under agreed-upon procedures, to be "no longer usable for any nuclear activity relevant from the point of view of international safeguards or [has] become practically irrecoverable," then the material is no longer governed by the Agreement.

Here, the appropriate authority, which was not the United States, made the determination that the waste at issue was "practically irrecoverable," and, as a result, no longer governed by the Agreement. In addition, the International Atomic Energy Agency terminated its safeguards because the reprocessed waste was "practically irrecoverable." As such, the Agreement does not cover such waste materials and so there is no U.S. federal action involved.

* * * *The Waters*

Mayaguezanos maintains as well that the *Pacific Swan*'s passage through U.S. EEZ waters in the Mona Passage activates NEPA's major federal action requirement. The boundaries of the United States extend, by a 1989 Presidential Proclamation, to twelve nautical miles offshore, an area called the territorial sea. Since the distance between Mona Island and the island of Puerto Rico is about thirty-nine miles, there are at least fifteen miles of international waters and twenty-four miles of territorial sea in that part of the Mona Passage that runs between the two islands. Under customary international law, the United States has sovereignty and jurisdiction over its territorial seas, subject to the right of innocent passage.

In addition to the territorial seas, the United States has an interest in the two-hundred-mile EEZ. This case concerns the EEZ, as it is undisputed that the *Pacific Swan* did not enter U.S. territorial waters. The interests of a coastal state in its EEZ largely have to do with development of natural resources and the availability of scientific research. A coastal state has limited powers in the EEZ under customary international law. * * * Foreign ships do not require the permission of the United States to pass through its EEZ.

Whatever the scope of the United States's potential powers, either multilaterally or unilaterally, over the EEZ, it is clear that the United

States has not exercised any such powers with respect to the transport of nuclear waste. Simply stated, the United States has chosen not to regulate shipments of nuclear waste through its EEZ—there is no requirement that it do so, nor is it immediately evident that it would have that authority if it so chose. Under these circumstances, there is no major federal action.

IV

Where this country's multilateral relationships are involved there is a particularly heavy burden on Mayaguezanos to demonstrate a "major federal action" for NEPA purposes, and thus to involve the courts. It has not come close. That is not to say that Mayaguezanos's concerns about the safety of the shipments are frivolous, a matter that we do not judge, only that such concerns should be presented elsewhere. * * *

NOTES

1. **Lack of Major Federal Action.** Why did the activities involved in this case not constitute major federal action for purposes of NEPA? What two arguments did the citizens' group make?

2. **Standard of Review.** Did the First Circuit use an APA standard of review in this case? If so, what was it? If not, why not?

3. **Extraterritorial Application of NEPA**. The usual presumption is that the United States' domestic laws do not apply in foreign countries. *Sale v. Haitian Centers Council, Inc.*, 509 U.S. 155, 173–74 (1993); *Lujan v. Defenders of Wildlife*, 504 U.S. 555, 585–89 & n.4 (1992); *EEOC v. Arabian American Oil Co.*, 499 U.S. 244, 248 (1991); *Foley Bros., Inc. v. Filardo*, 336 U.S. 281, 285 (1949). However, because NEPA affects federal agency *decision-making*, environmental groups have argued that NEPA should always apply to the decisions of United States agencies, regardless of where the proposed actions will finally occur. Following this logic, the D.C. Circuit in 1993 held that NEPA applied to the National Science Foundation's incineration of food wastes in Antarctica because the presumption against extraterritoriality "does not apply where the conduct regulated by the statute occurs primarily, if not exclusively, in the United States, and the alleged extraterritorial effect of the statute will be felt in Antarctica—a continent without a sovereign, and an area over which the United States has a great measure of legislative control." *Environmental Defense Fund, Inc. v. Massey*, 986 F.2d 528, 529, 532 (D.C. Cir. 1993); *but see NEPA Coalition of Japan v. Aspin*, 837 F.Supp. 466, 467 (D.D.C. 1993) (holding that NEPA did not apply to U.S. military installations in Japan because Department of Defense (DOD) "operations in Japan are governed by complex and long-standing treaty arrangements" and the court would risk intruding on this treaty relationship "[b]y requiring DOD to prepare EISs * * *.").

The State Department has similarly concluded that NEPA should apply to the decisions of United States agencies to take action outside of the United States in areas, such as Antarctica, where other nations' sovereignty would not be offended, because:

> application of [NEPA] to actions occurring outside the jurisdiction of any State, including the United States, would not conflict with the primary purpose underlying this venerable rule of interpretation—to avoid ill-will and conflict between nations arising out of one nation's encroachments upon another's sovereignty * * *. There are at least three general areas: The high seas, outer space, and Antarctica.

Memorandum of C. Herter, Special Assistant to the Secretary of State for Environmental Affairs, *reprinted in Administration of the National Environmental Policy Act: Hearing Before the Subcommittee on Fisheries and Wildlife Conservation of the House Committee on Merchant Marine and Fisheries,* 91st Cong., 2d Sess. 551 (1970). In addition, the President and the courts have agreed that if an extraterritorial action is a major federal action "and there is a risk of significant environmental damage *in the United States*," NEPA applies. *Hirt v. Richardson*, 127 F. Supp. 2d 833, 844–45 (W.D. Mich. 1999) (emphasis added); *see also* Executive Order No. 1211–4, §§ 3–5 (Jan. 4, 1979).

Under these guidelines, was the National Aeronautics and Space Administration (NASA) required to comply with NEPA before it sent the "Opportunity" and "Spirit" rovers to the planet Mars? Why or why not? As you may recall, both rovers successfully landed on Mars and explored the Martian surface at NASA's direction. *See* 67 Fed. Reg. 75,863 (Dec. 10, 2002); 67 Fed. Reg. 48,490 (July 24, 2002); 66 Fed. Reg. 11,184 (Feb. 22, 2001).

4. **Extraterritorial Activities and Environmental Justice.** Consider the environmental justice ramifications of the principal case: Three highly developed nations—Great Britain, France, and Japan—are engaging in activities (or, in the case of Great Britain, have flagships engaged in activities) that the residents of Puerto Rico—a mostly minority territory of the United States—believe may harm them environmentally. Should environmental justice concerns be a part of international treaties? Consider the fact that, in the pursuit of environmental justice, the EPA is currently engaged in projects to address pesticide regulatory problems in Central America, to develop (in concert with the United Nations Environmental Programme (UNEP)) a Chemical Information Exchange Network to provide Africa and Central America more information about chemical pollutants, and to address cross-border pollution and development issues with Mexico. OFFICE OF ENVIRONMENTAL JUSTICE, U.S. E.P.A., ENVIRONMENTAL JUSTICE BIENNIAL REPORT 2002, at 36–39 (2002), *available at* http://www.epa.gov/Compliance/resources/publications/ej/annual-project-reports/ej-biennial-report–2002.pdf.

5. **NEPA's Application in the Exclusive Economic Zone (EEZ).** As this case discussed, the United States asserts federal authority over the first 200 nautical miles of ocean waters. The first 12 nautical miles from shore are the United States' *territorial sea*—waters where the United States is sovereign. The next 188 nautical miles are known as the exclusive economic zone (EEZ), where the United States can regulate to manage the environmental resources resources found there but over which the United States does not exercise complete sovereignty. In 2002, the United States District Court for the Central District of California decided that NEPA applies to major federal actions that occur in the EEZ, even if those activities occur outside of the United States' territorial sea. *Natural Resources Defense Council, Inc. v. U.S.*

Department of the Navy, 2:01–CV–07781, Slip op. at 16 (C.D. Cal. Sept. 17, 2002). Did the Central District of California create a conflict with the First Circuit's decision in *Mayaguezanos*? Why or why not?

6. **Environmental Impact Assessments Internationally.** The idea of an environmental impact assessment (EIA) is one of the most important environmental law concepts that the United States has exported to the world. NEPA "was the first EIA statute enacted in the world." William L. Andreen, "Comparative Environmental Impact Assessment," *presented at* Association of American Law Schools, *Environmental Law in a Global Context*, Portland, Oregon (June 16, 2004). According to Professor Andreen:

> NEPA has likely been the most successful US legal export in history. It has served as a model for over 100 countries, dozens of political subdivisions (states and provinces), and a number of multilateral organizations, all of which have adopted some form of EIA, whether by legislation, regulation, or informal policy guidance.
>
> Most of the early development took place in a number of developed countries such as Australia and Canada, although it was also adopted in Colombia in 1974 and in the Philippines in 1978.
>
> Most adoptions of EIA processes took place after the mid–1980s. Almost all developed countries now have EIA procedures, as do a great many developing and transitional countries. During the 1990s, nearly half of the 48 countries in Sub–Saharan Africa adopted legislation on EIA.

Id. What does this proliferation of EIA procedures suggest about the need for a United States NEPA analysis for the shipment of nuclear waste at issue in *Mayaguezanos*? Why would Puerto Rican citizens nevertheless fight for a NEPA EIS? Might environmental justice problems nevertheless remain?

Puerto Rico, by the way, also has its own territorial "mini-NEPA" requirement, as do 19 states within the United States and the District of Columbia. Andreen, *supra*; *see also* 12 L.P.R.A. § 1124(c)(1) (Puerto Rico's EIS requirement); 12 L.P.R.A. § 241e (specifically requiring an EIS for projects that might negatively impact coral reefs); 12 L.P.R.A. § 1143h (specifically requiring an EIS for any project that affects caves, caverns, or sinkholes). Why wasn't Puerto Rico's own legislation sufficient to address the citizens' concerns in *Mayaguezanos*?

7. **Federal Involvement in State Highway Projects and a Test for "Federal" Actions.** Highway projects, which are often jointly funded by federal and state governments, often raise NEPA issues regarding whether a "major federal action" is involved. As the CEQ's regulations indicate, the federal funding may be insufficient, in and of itself, to create major *federal* action if no federal agency, like the Federal Highway Administration, exercises continuing control over the project. Even so, state highway projects may still require several different kinds of federal permits from different federal agencies—permits from the Army Corps of Engineers under the Clean Water Act to dredge and fill wetlands and waterways, permits from the National Park Service to cross a national park, and so on. Courts have wrestled in such situations to determine how much federal involvement is enough to trigger

NEPA. After reviewing case law from the Fourth and D.C. Circuits, the Sixth Circuit concluded

> that there are two alternative bases for finding that a non-federal project constitutes a "major Federal action" such that NEPA requirements apply: (1) when the non-federal project restricts or limits the statutorily prescribed federal decision-makers' choice of reasonable alternatives; or (2) when the federal decision-makers have authority to exercise sufficient control or responsibility over the non-federal project so as to influence the outcome of the project. If either test is satisfied, the non-federal project must be considered a major federal action. Both tests require a situation-specific and fact-intensive analysis.

Southwest Williamson County Community Ass'n, Inc. v. Slater, 243 F.3d 270, 281 (6th Cir. 2001). How does the Sixth Circuit's approach compare with the First Circuit's in *Mayaguezanos*?

8. **Federal Agency Activities That Are Not NEPA "Actions."** It is important to remember that "action" is also a defined term for purposes of NEPA and that not every federal agency activity qualifies. In 1979, for example, the Supreme Court decided that an agency's requests for appropriations from Congress are not "federal actions" for purposes of NEPA because they are neither proposals for legislation nor proposals for agency actions. *Andrus v. Sierra Club*, 442 U.S. 347, 355–57 (1979).

9. **NEPA's Reach and the Bush Administration**. The CEQ is housed within the White House. *See* CEQ home page, http://www.whitehouse.gov/ceq. After taking office in 2001, President George W. Bush quietly tried to limit NEPA's scope, opposing in court its "extension" to the EEZ and lobbying Congress for amendments that would exempt ocean activities (such as offshore oil drilling) from the NEPA process. Congress, however, has been reluctant to grant such exemptions and limitations.

* * *

C. DEFINING NEPA'S TRIGGER: "SIGNIFICANTLY AFFECTING THE QUALITY OF THE HUMAN ENVIRONMENT"

1. Introduction: The CEQ's Regulations

In addition to being a "major federal action," a proposed action must significantly affect the quality of the human environment before it is subject to NEPA's EIS requirement. According to the CEQ's regulations, ***"significantly"*** "requires considerations of both context and intensity." 40 C.F.R. § 1508.27. ***Context*** considerations require

> that the significance of an action be analyzed in several contexts such as society as a whole (human, national), the affected region, the affected interests, and the locality. Significance varies with the setting of the proposed action. For instance, in the case of a site-specific action, significance would usually depend upon the effects in the

> locale rather than in the world as a whole. Both short- and long-term effects are relevant.

Id. § 1508.27(a). ***Intensity***, in turn, "refers to the severity of impact." *Id.* § 1508.27(b). The CEQ lists several factors that agencies should consider in evaluating intensity, including the fact that impacts can be either beneficial or adverse; public health or safety effects; "unique characteristics of the geographic area"; controversy over the effects on the quality of the human environment; uncertainty or unique or unknown risks; the status of the action as precedent for future actions; cumulative impacts with other projects; effects on historically, scientifically, or culturally important resources; effects on endangered or threatened species or critical habitat; and the project's compliance with federal, state, and local environmental laws. *Id.*

"***Affecting*** means will or *may* have an effect on." 40 C.F.R. § 1508.3 (emphasis added). As a result, actions that *may* significantly affect the quality of the human environment are still subject to NEPA. The CEQ more expansively defines ***"effects"***:

> *Effects* include:
>
> (a) Direct effects, which are caused by the action and occur at the same time and place.
>
> (b) Indirect effects, which are caused by the action and are later in time or farther removed in distance, but are still reasonably foreseeable. Indirect effects may include growth inducing effects and other effects related to induced changes in the pattern of land use, population density or growth rate, and related effects on air and water and other natural systems, including ecosystems.
>
> Effects and impacts as used in these regulations are synonymous. Effects includes ecological (such as the effects on natural resources and on the components, structures, and functioning of affected ecosystems), aesthetic, historic, cultural, economic, social, or health, whether direct, indirect, or cumulative. Effects may also include those resulting from actions which may have both beneficial and detrimental effects, even if on balance the agency believes that the effect will be beneficial.

40 C.F.R. § 1508.8.

The CEQ defines ***"human environment"*** broadly. The term "shall be interpreted comprehensively to include the natural and physical environment and the relationship of people with that environment." 40 C.F.R. § 1508.14.

2. Non-Environmental Impacts

Overall, the regulations discussed above suggest that NEPA requires agencies to look broadly in determining whether a proposed action might significantly affect the quality of the human environment. The agency must take into account positive as well as negative effects and take into account cultural, social, and historical effects as well as ecological effects. Nevertheless, many federal actions that are "significant," in the ordinary sense of that word, do not necessarily qualify as actions that "significantly affect the quality of the human environment" for purposes of NEPA, as the following Supreme Court decision makes clear.

METROPOLITAN EDISON COMPANY v. PEOPLE AGAINST NUCLEAR ENERGY

460 U.S. 766 (1983).

JUSTICE REHNQUIST delivered the opinion of the Court.

The issue in these cases is whether petitioner Nuclear Regulatory Commission (NRC) complied with the National Environmental Policy Act, 42 U.S.C. § 4321 *et seq.* (NEPA), when it considered whether to permit petitioner Metropolitan Edison Co. to resume operation of the Three Mile Island Unit 1 nuclear power plant (TMI–1). The Court of Appeals for the District of Columbia Circuit held that the NRC improperly failed to consider whether the risk of an accident at TMI–1 might cause harm to the psychological health and community well-being of residents of the surrounding area. We reverse.

Metropolitan owns two nuclear power plants at Three Mile Island near Harrisburg, Pennsylvania. Both of these plants were licensed by the NRC after extensive proceedings, which included preparation of Environmental Impact Statements (EIS). On March 28, 1979, TMI–1 was not operating; it had been shut down for refueling. TMI–2 was operating, and it suffered a serious accident that damaged the reactor. Although, as it turned out, no dangerous radiation was released, the accident caused widespread concern. The Governor of Pennsylvania recommended an evacuation of all pregnant women and small children, and many area residents did leave their homes for several days.

After the accident, the NRC ordered Metropolitan to keep TMI–1 shut down until it had an opportunity to determine whether the plant could be operated safely. 44 Fed. Reg. 40461 (1979). The NRC then published a notice of hearing specifying several safety related issues for consideration. 10 N.R.C. 141 (1979). The notice stated that the Commission had not determined whether to consider psychological harm or other indirect effects of the accident or of renewed operation of TMI–1. It invited

Figure 2-7: Three Mile Island Nuclear Power Plant
Centers for Disease Control photo.

interested parties to submit briefs on this issue. *Id.,* at 148. Petitioner People Against Nuclear Energy (PANE), intervened and responded to this invitation. PANE is an association of residents of the Harrisburg area who are opposed to further operation of either TMI reactor. PANE contended that restarting TMI–1 would cause both severe psychological health damage to persons living in the vicinity, and serious damage to the stability, cohesiveness, and well-being of the neighboring communities.

The NRC decided not to take evidence concerning PANE's contentions. PANE filed a petition for review in the Court of Appeals, contending that * * * NEPA * * * require[s] the NRC to address its contentions. Metropolitan intervened on the side of the NRC.

The Court of Appeals [found] that NEPA requires the NRC to evaluate "the potential psychological health effects of operating" TMI–1 which have arisen since the original EIS was prepared. It also held that, if the NRC finds that significant new circumstances or information exist on this subject, it shall prepare a "supplemental [EIS] which considers not only the effects on psychological health but also effects on the well being of the communities surrounding Three Mile Island." We granted certiorari.

All the parties agree that effects on human health can be cognizable under NEPA, and that human health may include psychological health. * * * PANE * * * contends that because the psychological health damage to its members would be caused by a change in the environment (renewed operation of TMI–1), NEPA requires the NRC to consider that damage. Although these arguments are appealing at first glance, we believe they skip over an essential step in the analysis. They do not consider the closeness of the relationship between the change in the environment and the "effect" at issue.

Section 102(C) of NEPA, 42 U.S.C. 4332(C), directs all federal agencies to

> "include in every recommendation or report on proposals for legislation and other major Federal actions significantly affecting the quality of the human environment, a detailed statement by the responsible official on—
>
> (i) the environmental impact of the proposed action, [and]
>
> (ii) any adverse environmental effects which cannot be avoided should the proposal be implemented. . . ."

To paraphrase the statutory language in light of the facts of this case, where an agency action significantly affects the quality of the human environment, the agency must evaluate the "environmental impact" and any unavoidable adverse environmental effects of its proposal. The theme of § 102 is sounded by the adjective "environmental": NEPA does not require the agency to assess *every* impact or effect of its proposed action, but only the impact or effect on the environment. If we were to seize the word "environmental" out of its context and give it the broadest possible definition, the words "adverse environmental effects" might embrace virtually any consequence of a governmental action that some one thought "adverse." But we think the context of the statute shows that Congress was talking about the physical environment—the world around us, so to speak. NEPA was designed to promote human welfare by alerting governmental actors to the effect of their proposed actions on the physical environment.

* * * To determine whether § 102 requires consideration of a particular effect, we must look at the relationship between that effect and the change in the physical environment caused by the major federal action at issue. For example, if the Department of Health and Human Services were to implement extremely stringent requirements for hospitals and nursing homes receiving federal funds, many perfectly adequate hospitals and homes might be forced out of existence. The remaining facilities might be so limited or so expensive that many ill people would be unable to afford medical care and would suffer severe health damage. Nonetheless, NEPA would not require the Department to prepare an EIS evaluating that health damage because it would not be proximately related to a change in the physical environment.

Some effects that are "caused by" a change in the physical environment in the sense of "but for" causation, will nonetheless not fall within

§ 102 because the causal chain is too attenuated. For example, residents of the Harrisburg area have relatives in other parts of the country. Renewed operation of TMI–1 may well cause psychological health problems for these people. They may suffer "anxiety, tension and fear, a sense of helplessness," and accompanying physical disorders because of the risk that their relatives may be harmed in a nuclear accident. However, this harm is simply too remote from the physical environment to justify requiring the NRC to evaluate the psychological health damage to these people that may be caused by renewed operation of TMI–1.

Our understanding of the congressional concerns that led to the enactment of NEPA suggests that the terms "environmental effect" and "environmental impact" in § 102 be read to include a requirement of a reasonably close causal relationship between a change in the physical environment and the effect at issue. This requirement is like the familiar doctrine of proximate cause from tort law. *See generally* W. PROSSER, LAW OF TORTS ch. 7 (4th ed. 1971). The issue before us, then, is how to give content to this requirement. This is a question of first impression in this Court.

The federal action that affects the environment in this case is permitting renewed operation of TMI–1. The direct effects on the environment of this action include release of low-level radiation, increased fog in the Harrisburg area (caused by operation of the plant's cooling towers), and the release of warm water into the Susquehanna River. The NRC has considered each of these effects in its EIS, and again in the EIA. Another effect of renewed operation is a risk of a nuclear accident. The NRC has also considered this effect.

We emphasize that in this case we are considering effects caused by the risk of an accident. The situation where an agency is asked to consider effects that will occur if a risk is realized, for example, if an accident occurs at TMI–1, is an entirely different case. The NRC considered, in the original EIS and in the most recent EIA for TMI–1, the possible effects of a number of accidents that might occur at TMI–1.

PANE argues that the psychological health damage it alleges "will flow directly from the risk of [a nuclear] accident." But a *risk* of an accident is not an effect on the physical environment. A risk is, by definition, unrealized in the physical world. In a causal chain from renewed operation of TMI–1 to psychological health damage, the element of risk and its perception by PANE's members are necessary middle links. We believe that the element of risk lengthens the causal chain beyond the reach of NEPA.

Risk is a pervasive element of modern life; to say more would belabor the obvious. Many of the risks we face are generated by modern technology, which brings both the possibility of major accidents and opportunities for tremendous achievements. Medical experts apparently agree that risk can generate stress in human beings, which in turn may rise to the level of serious health damage. For this reason among many others, the question whether the gains from any technological advance are worth its attendant risks may be an important public policy issue. Nonetheless, it is quite different from the question whether the same gains are worth a given level of alteration of our physical environment or depletion of our natural resources. The latter question rather than the former is the central concern of NEPA.

Time and resources are simply too limited for us to believe that Congress intended to extend NEPA as far as the Court of Appeals has taken it. The scope of the agency's inquiries must remain manageable if NEPA's goal of "ensur[ing] a fully informed and well considered decision" is to be accomplished.

* * * Anyone who fears or dislikes a project may find himself suffering from "anxiety, tension, fear, [and] a sense of helplessness." Neither the language nor the history of NEPA suggest that it was intended to give citizens a general opportunity to air their policy objections to proposed federal actions. The political process, and not NEPA, provides the appropriate forum in which to air policy disagreements.

We do not mean to denigrate the fears of PANE's members, or to suggest that the psychological health damage they fear could not, in fact, occur. Nonetheless, it is difficult for us to see the differences between someone who dislikes a government decision so much that he suffers anxiety and stress, someone who fears the effects of that decision so much that he suffers similar anxiety and stress, and someone who suffers anxiety and stress that "flow directly," from the risks associated with the same decision. It would be extraordinarily difficult for agencies to differentiate between "genuine" claims of psychological health damage and claims that are grounded solely in disagreement with a democratically adopted policy. Until Congress provides a more explicit statutory instruction than NEPA now contains, we do not think agencies are obliged to undertake the inquiry.

* * * For these reasons, we hold that the NRC need not consider PANE's contentions. NEPA does not require agencies to evaluate the effects of risk, *qua* risk. The judgment of the Court of Appeals is reversed, and the case is remanded with instructions to dismiss the petition for review.

NOTES

1. **Standard of Review.** What standard did the Supreme Court use to review the Nuclear Regulatory Commission's (NRC's) decision that it did not have to take evidence of psychological effects? Was it using an arbitrary and capricious standard? Why or why not?

2. **NEPA and the Common Law.** What common law concept did the Supreme Court import into NEPA in this case? What statutory terms was it interpreting? Why is that common-law concept necessary, according to the Court, in order to effectuate congressional intent? Do you agree?

3. **NEPA and Psychological Effects.** According to the Court, are psychological effects irrelevant to an agency's NEPA analysis? Why or why not? How does an agency determine whether psychological effects are relevant in determining whether its action will "significantly affect the quality of the human environment"? If you were an agency official or a lower court, would you feel comfortable in applying this case to future decisions? Why or why not?

Consider the following facts: After completing an EIS, the U.S. Forest Service Forest Supervisor declines to lease certain lands within the Lewis & Clark National Forest for oil and gas development, citing in part that National Forest's "value of place" to the people who use it. The Independent Petroleum Association of America challenges that decision in court, alleging that the Forest Supervisor had improperly considered the psychological effects of the oil and gas leasing, violating NEPA. Given the Supreme Court's decision in *Metropolitan Edison*, should the federal court rule that the Forest Supervisor was arbitrary and capricious in applying NEPA? Why or why not? *See Rocky Mountain Oil & Gas Ass'n v. U.S. Forest Service*, 12 Fed. Appx. 498, 500 (9th Cir. 2001).

4. **NEPA and Socioeconomic Effects.** Can socioeconomic impacts from a proposed federal agency action be sufficiently significant, alone, to warrant an EIS? The CEQ's definition of "effects" suggests that they might be, because that definition specifically lists "cultural, economic, [and] social" effects as being included within NEPA's scope. However, the CEQ's definition of "human environment" indicates otherwise: "economic or social effects are not intended by themselves to require preparation of an environmental impact statement." 40 C.F.R. § 1508.14. Nevertheless, "[w]hen an environmental impact statement is prepared and economic or social and natural or physical environmental effects are interrelated, then the environmental impact statement will discuss all of these effects on the human environment." *Id.*

When the proposed action clearly affects the physical environment in some way, agencies routinely discuss the socioeconomic impacts, direct or indirect, of the proposed action as well as the physical and ecological impacts. Changes of use in urban areas, however, can raise issues of whether the action's significance is environment-based or purely socioeconomic. For example, suppose the federal Bureau of Prisons wants to convert a former state mental hospital into a federal prison hospital, a change of use that will require only insignificant changes to the building and its grounds. Citizens in the surrounding community, however, complain that the change will result in the "introduction of weapons and drugs into the area, an increase in crime, and a decrease or halt in neighborhood development." Are these effects sufficient to trigger NEPA's EIS requirement? See *Olmsted Citizens for a Better Community v. United States*, 793 F.2d 201, 205–06 (8th Cir. 1986). Consider this statement by the U.S. District Court for the District of New Jersey: "The case law is clear that an EIS is not required unless the primary impact of the project is on the natural environment. Once this threshold requirement is met, secondary socio-economic effects should be considered. However, socio-economic effects alone are insufficient to trigger the requirement of an EIS." *Azzolina v. U.S. Postal Service*, 602 F.Supp. 859, 862 (D.N.J. 1985) (citing *Goodman Group, Inc. v. Dishroom*, 679 F.2d 182 (9th Cir. 1982); *Image of Greater San Antonio, Texas v. Brown*, 570 F.2d 517 (5th Cir. 1978); *Breckinridge v. Rumsfeld*, 537 F.2d 864 (6th Cir. 1976), *cert. denied*, 429 U.S. 1061 (1977); *Township of Dover v. U.S. Postal Service*, 429 F.Supp. 295 (D.N.J. 1977)).

5. **NEPA and Environmental Justice Effects.** Given Executive Order No. 12898, discussed in Chapter 1 in connection with RCRA permitting, must federal agencies consider the environmental justice effects of their actions in connection with NEPA? *See Morongo Band of Mission Indians v. FAA*, 161 F.3d 569, 575–76 (9th Cir. 1998); *One Thousand Friends of Iowa v. Mineta*, 250 F. Supp. 2d 1075, 1084 (S.D. Iowa 2002); *Citizens Concerned About Jet Noise, Inc. v. Dalton*, 48 F. Supp. 2d 582, 604 (E.D. Va. 1999).

* * *

3. Uncertainty, Controversy, Intensity, Cumulative Impacts, Alternatives, and Agency Discretion

Under the CEQ's regulations, as part of the intensity element of whether a proposed action will "significantly" affect the quality of the human environment, the federal agency must consider

> [w]hether the action is related to other actions with individually insignificant but cumulatively significant impacts. Significance exists if it is reasonable to anticipate a cumulatively significant impact on the environment. Significance cannot be avoided by terming an action temporary or by breaking it down into small component parts.

40 C.F.R. § 1508.27(b)(7). The resulting "cumulative impacts analysis" can thus reveal that an agency action will "significantly affect the quality of the human environment" when viewed in a broader context than just the proposed action itself.

Global climate change is becoming an interesting and important testing ground for the concepts of agency responsibility, cumulative impacts, and controversy and uncertainty regarding both the environmental and regulatory effects of agency actions. We will see these themes again in the sections of Chapter 4 (Clean Air Act) and Chapter 6 (citizen suits) that present the U.S. Supreme Court's April 2007 decision in *Massachusetts v. EPA*. However, climate change discussions are also becoming important aspects of the implementation of other statutes, such as the Endangered Species Act (Chapter 3) and NEPA.

As you read the following case, pay particular attention to the reasons *why* the Ninth Circuit concludes that the National Highway Traffic Safety Administration (NHTSA) must produce a full Environmental Impact Statement (EIS) in connection with its new fuel economy standards for light trucks and SUVs. Does the Ninth Circuit believe that more stringent standards will reverse global climate change? If not, what is the value of a full NEPA analysis? What are the "significant effects" of the new fuel economy standards?

CENTER FOR BIOLOGICAL DIVERSITY v. NATIONAL HIGHWAY TRAFFIC SAFETY ADMINISTRATION

508 F.3d 508 (9th Cir. 2007).

B. FLETCHER, CIRCUIT JUDGE:

Eleven states, the District of Columbia, the City of New York, and four public interest organizations petition for review of a rule issued by the National Highway Traffic Safety Administration (NHTSA) entitled "Average Fuel Economy Standards for Light Trucks, Model Years 2008–2011," 71 Fed. Reg. 17,566 (Apr. 6, 2006) ("Final Rule") (codified at 49 C.F.R. pt. 533). Pursuant to the Energy Policy and Conservation Act of 1975 (EPCA), 49 U.S.C. §§ 32901–32919 (2007), the Final Rule sets corporate average fuel economy (CAFE) standards for light trucks, defined by NHTSA to include many Sport Utility Vehicles (SUVs), minivans, and pickup trucks, for Model Years (MYs) 2008–2011. For MYs 2008–2010, the Final Rule sets new CAFE standards using its traditional method, fleet-wide average (Unreformed CAFE). For MY 2011 and beyond, the Final Rule creates a new CAFE structure that sets varying fuel economy targets depending on vehicle size and requires manufacturers to meet different fuel economy levels depending on their vehicle fleet mix (Reformed CAFE).

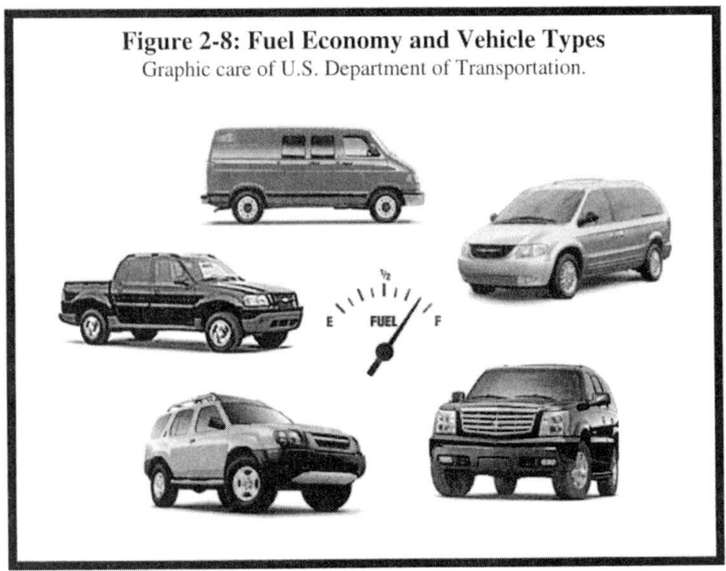

Figure 2-8: Fuel Economy and Vehicle Types
Graphic care of U.S. Department of Transportation.

* * * Petitioners argue that NHTSA's Environmental Assessment is inadequate under NEPA because it fails to take a "hard look" at the

greenhouse gas implications of its rulemaking and fails to analyze a reasonable range of alternatives or examine the rule's cumulative impact. Petitioners also argue that NEPA requires NHTSA to prepare an Environmental Impact Statement. * * *

I. FACTUAL AND PROCEDURAL BACKGROUND

A. CAFE Regulation Under the Energy Policy and Conservation Act

In the aftermath of the energy crisis created by the 1973 Mideast oil embargo, Congress enacted the Energy Policy and Conservation Act of 1975, Pub. L. No. 94–163, 89 Stat. 871, 901–16. Congress observed that "[t]he fundamental reality is that this nation has entered a new era in which energy resources previously abundant, will remain in short supply, retarding our economic growth and necessitating an alteration in our life's habits and expectations." *Id.* at 1763. The goals of the EPCA are to "decrease dependence on foreign imports, enhance national security, achieve the efficient utilization of scarce resources, and guarantee the availability of domestic energy supplies at prices consumers can afford." S. REP. NO. 94–516 (1975) (Conf. Rep.), *as reprinted in* 1975 U.S.C.C.A.N. 1956, 1957. These goals are more pressing today than they were thirty years ago: since 1975, American consumption of oil has risen from 16.3 million barrels per day to over 20 million barrels per day, and the percentage of U.S. oil that is imported has risen from 35.8 to 56 percent.

In furtherance of the goal of energy conservation, Title V of the EPCA establishes automobile fuel economy standards. An "average fuel economy standard" (often referred to as a CAFE standard) is "a performance standard specifying a minimum level of average fuel economy applicable to a manufacturer in a model year." 49 U.S.C. § 32901(a)(6) (2007). Only "automobiles" are subject to fuel economy regulation, and passenger automobiles must meet a statutory standard of 27.5 mpg, 49 U.S.C. § 32902(b), whereas non-passenger automobiles must meet standards set by the Secretary of Transportation, *id.* § 32902(a). Congress directs the Secretary to set fuel economy standards at "the maximum feasible average fuel economy level that the Secretary decides the manufacturers can achieve in that model year." *Id.* § 32902(a). Under this subsection, the Secretary is authorized to "prescribe separate standards for different classes of automobiles." *Id.* Congress also provides that "[w]hen deciding maximum feasible average fuel economy under this section, the Secretary of Transportation shall consider technological feasibility, economic practicability, the effect of other motor vehicle standards of the Government on fuel economy, and the need of the United States to conserve energy." *Id.* § 32902(f).

* * * For MYs [Model Years] 1996 to 2004, Congress froze the light truck CAFE standard at 20.7 mpg. After the legislative restrictions were lifted, NHTSA set new light truck CAFE standards in April 2003: 21.0 mpg for MY 2005, 21.6 mpg for MY 2006, and 22.2 mpg for MY 2007.

In response to a request from Congress, the National Academy of Sciences (NAS) published in 2002 a report entitled "Effectiveness and Impact of Corporate Average Fuel Economy (CAFE) Standards." The NAS committee made several findings and recommendations. It found that from 1970 to 1982, CAFE standards helped contribute to a 50 percent increase in fuel economy for new light trucks. In the subsequent decades, however, light trucks became more popular since domestic manufacturers faced less competition in the light truck category and could generate greater profits. * * * As the market share of light trucks has increased, the overall average fuel economy of the new light duty vehicle fleet (light trucks and passenger automobiles) has declined "from a peak of 25.9 MPG in 1987 to 24.0 MPG in 2000." Vehicle miles traveled (VMT) by light trucks has also been growing more rapidly than passenger automobile travel.

* * * Significantly, the committee found that of the many reasons for improving fuel economy, "[t]he most important ... is concern about the accumulation in the atmosphere of so-called greenhouse gases, principally carbon dioxide. Continued increases in carbon dioxide emissions are likely to further global warming." In addition, the committee found "externalities of about $0.30/gal of gasoline associated with the combined impacts of fuel consumption on greenhouse gas emissions and on world oil market conditions" that "are not necessarily taken into account when consumers purchase new vehicles."

B. National Environmental Policy Act

NEPA requires a federal agency "to the fullest extent possible," to prepare "a detailed statement on ... the environmental impact" of "major Federal actions significantly affecting the quality of the human environment." 42 U.S.C. § 4332(2)(C)(i) (2007); *see also* 40 C.F.R. § 1500.2 (2007). The purpose of NEPA is twofold: " 'ensure[] that the agency ... will have available, and will carefully consider, detailed information concerning significant environmental impacts[, and] guarantee[] that the relevant information will be made available to the larger [public] audience.' " *Idaho Sporting Cong. v. Thomas,* 137 F.3d 1146, 1149 (9th Cir. 1998) (quoting *Robertson v. Methow Valley Citizens Council,* 490 U.S. 332, 349 (1989)); *see also* 40 C.F.R. § 1500.1(b) (stating that environmental information must be provided "before decisions are made and before actions are taken."). * * *

If there is a substantial question whether an action "may have a significant effect" on the environment, then the agency must prepare an Environmental Impact Statement (EIS). *See, e.g., Blue Mountains Biodiversity Project v. Blackwood,* 161 F.3d 1208, 1212 (9th Cir. 1998) (internal quotation marks omitted). An EIS should contain a discussion of significant environmental impacts and alternatives to the proposed action. *See* 40 C.F.R. §§ 1502.1, 1502.14, 1508.7. As a preliminary step, an agency may prepare an Environmental Assessment (EA) in order to determine whether a proposed action may "significantly affect[]" the environment and thereby trigger the requirement to prepare an EIS. *See* 40 C.F.R. § 1508.9(a)(1) (2007). An EA is "a concise public document" that "[b]riefly provide[s] sufficient evidence and analysis for determining whether to prepare an environmental impact statement or a finding of no significant impact." *Id.* An EA "[s]hall include brief discussions of the need for the proposal, of alternatives as required by sec. 102(2)(E), of the environmental impacts of the proposed action and alternatives, and a listing of agencies and persons consulted." *Id.* § 1508.9(b).

Whether an action may "significantly affect" the environment requires consideration of "context" and "intensity." *Id.* § 1508.27; *see also Nat'l Parks & Conservation Ass'n v. Babbitt,* 241 F.3d 722, 731 (9th Cir. 2001). "Context ... delimits the scope of the agency's action, including the interests affected." *Nat'l. Parks & Conservation Ass'n,* 241 F.3d at 731. Intensity refers to the "severity of impact," which includes both beneficial and adverse impacts, "[t]he degree to which the proposed action affects public health or safety," "[t]he degree to which the effects on the quality of the human environment are likely to be highly controversial," "[t]he degree to which the possible effects on the human environment are highly uncertain or involve unique or unknown risks," and "[w]hether the action is related to other actions with individually insignificant but cumulatively significant impacts." 40 C.F.R. § 1508.27(b)(2), (4), (5), (7).

C. NHTSA's Proposed Rulemaking and Draft Environmental Assessment

On December 29, 2003, NHTSA published an advance notice of proposed rulemaking (ANPRM) that solicited comments on several proposed regulatory changes intended to increase fuel economy, including a proposal to modernize the light truck/car distinction and a proposal to increase the GVWR limit on vehicles subject to CAFE standards. 68 Fed. Reg. 74,908 (Dec. 29, 2003). * * * The Draft EA [that accompanied this rulemaking] noted that "CO2 ... has started to be viewed as an issue of concern for its global climate change potential." With regard to biological resources, the Draft EA stated, "emissions of criteria pollutants and greenhouse gases could result in ozone layer depletion and promote climate change that could affect species and ecosystems." The projected lifetime fuel savings for MY 2008–2011 light trucks under Alternatives B and C would "rang[e] from 1.3% to 1.7% of their fuel compared to the baseline, corresponding to 4.7–6.0 billion gallons." The estimated lifetime emissions of CO2 ranged from 1,341.4 million metric tons (mmt) under baseline to 1,306.4 and 1,304.0 mmt under Alternatives B and C, respectively. The Draft EA concluded that the proposed standards would "result in reduced emissions of CO2, the predominant greenhouse gas emitted by motor vehicles," "reductions in contamination of water resources," and "minor reductions in impacts to biological resources." In addition, "the cumulative effects estimated to result from both the 2005–2007 and 2008–2011 light truck rulemakings over the lifetimes of the vehicles they would affect are projected to be very small."

NHTSA received over 45,000 comments on the NPRM and Draft EA from states, consumer and environmental organizations, automobile manufacturers and associations, members of Congress, and private individuals. *See* 71 Fed. Reg. at 17,577. * * * The states and environmental and consumer organizations generally argued that * * * NHTSA's draft EA is inadequate and fails to consider the proposed rule's impact on climate change.

Commenters also submitted to NHTSA numerous scientific reports and studies regarding the relationship between climate change and greenhouse gas emissions and the expected impacts on the environment. Emissions from light trucks make up about eight percent of annual U.S. greenhouse gas emissions. [According to the NAS, t]he transportation sectors account for about 31 percent of human-generated CO2 emissions in the U.S. economy. "Overall, U.S. light-duty vehicles [passenger cars and light trucks] produce about 5 percent of the entire world's greenhouse gases." The NAS committee concluded, "Since the United States produces about 25 percent of the world's greenhouse gases, fuel economy improvements could have a significant impact on the rate of CO2 accumulation in the atmosphere."

The Intergovernmental Panel on Climate Change (IPCC)'s "Third Assessment Report," published in 2001, presented the consensus view of hundreds of scientists on key issues relating to climate change. The IPCC concluded that "CO2 concentrations increasing over [the] 21st century [are] virtually certain to be mainly due to fossil-fuel emissions," and that "[s]tabilization of atmospheric CO2 concentrations at 450, 650, or 1,000 ppm would require global anthropogenic CO2 emissions to drop below year 1990 levels, within a few decades, about a century, or about 2 centuries, respectively, and continue to decrease steadily thereafter to a small fraction of current emissions." The average earth surface temperature has increased by about 0.6 degree Celsius since the late 19th century; snow and ice cover have decreased about 10 percent since the late 1960s; and global average sea level has risen between 10 to 20 cm during the 20th century. The IPCC also developed a range of emissions scenarios as its basis for predicting the environmental effect of increased emissions.

More recent evidence shows that there have already been severe impacts in the Arctic due to warming, including sea ice decline. Global warming has already affected plants, animals, and ecosystems around the world. Some scientists predict that "on the basis of mid-range climate-warming scenarios for 2050, that 15–37% of species in our sample of regions and taxa will be 'committed to extinction.' " In addition, there will be serious consequences for human health, including the spread of infectious and respiratory diseases, if worldwide emissions continue on current trajectories. Sea level rise and increased ocean temperatures are also associated with increasing weather variability and heightened intensity of storms such as hurricanes. Past projections have underestimated sea level rise. Several studies also show that climate change may be non-linear, meaning that there are positive feedback mechanisms that may push global warming past a dangerous threshold (the "tipping point").

D. The Final Rule: CAFE Standards for Light Trucks MYs 2008–2011

NHTSA issued the Final Rule on April 6, 2006. 71 Fed. Reg. at 17,566. NHTSA set the CAFE standards for MY 2008–2010 (Unreformed CAFE) at the same levels as proposed in the NPRM. * * * NHTSA monetized some externalities such as emission of criteria pollutants during gasoline refining and distribution and crash and noise costs associated with driving. However, NHTSA did not monetize the benefit of reducing carbon dioxide emissions, which it recognized was the "the main greenhouse gas emitted as a result of refining, distribution, and use of transportation fuels." NHTSA acknowledged the estimates suggested in the scientific literature, *see* 71 Fed. Reg. at 17,638, but concluded:

> [T]he value of reducing emissions of CO2 and other greenhouse gases [is] too uncertain to support their explicit valuation and inclusion among the savings in environmental externalities from reducing gasoline production and use. There is extremely wide variation in published estimates of damage costs from greenhouse gas emissions, costs for controlling or avoiding their emissions, and costs of sequestering emissions that do occur, the three major sources for developing estimates of economic benefits from reducing emissions of greenhouse gases.

71 Fed. Reg. at 17,638.

* * * II. STANDARD OF REVIEW

The Administrative Procedure Act (APA), 5 U.S.C. §§ 701–706 (2007), provides that agency action must be set aside by the reviewing court if it is " 'arbitrary, capricious, an abuse of discretion, or otherwise not in accordance with law.' " *Competitive Enter. Inst. v. NHTSA* (*CEI III*), 45 F.3d 481, 484 (D.C. Cir. 1995) (quoting 5 U.S.C. § 706(2)(A)) (applying the APA to review a rulemaking under the EPCA). The scope of review is narrow, but "the agency must examine the relevant data and articulate a satisfactory explanation for its action including a 'rational connection between the facts found and the choice made.' " *Motor Vehicle Mfrs. Ass'n v. State Farm Mut. Auto. Ins. Co.,* 463 U.S. 29, 43 (1983) (citation omitted). An agency rule would normally be arbitrary and capricious if:

> the agency has relied on factors which Congress has not intended it to consider, entirely failed to consider an important aspect of the problem, offered an explanation for its decision that runs counter to the evidence before the agency, or is so implausible that it could not be ascribed to a difference in view or the product of agency expertise.

Id. The reviewing court " 'may not supply a reasoned basis for the agency's action that the agency itself has not given.' " *Id.* (quoting *SEC v. Chenery Corp.,* 332 U.S. 194, 196 (1947)). * * *

III. DISCUSSION

* * * *B. National Environmental Policy Act*

1. The EPCA does not limit NHTSA's NEPA obligations

NHTSA argues both that it has broad discretion to balance the factors of 49 U.S.C. § 32902(f) in setting fuel economy standards and that the EPCA constrains it from considering more stringent alternatives in the EA. NHTSA can't have it both ways. Its hands are not tied, as demonstrated by its discretionary, substantive decisions to, among other things, value the benefit of carbon emissions reduction at zero, peg its Unreformed CAFE standard to the least capable manufacturer with a substantial share of the market, apply technologies only until marginal cost equals marginal benefit, reject weight reduction as a cost-effective technology for vehicles between 4,000 and 5,000 lbs. curb weight, not adopt a backstop.

* * * NHTSA clearly has statutory authority to impose or enforce fuel economy standards, 49 U.S.C. § 32902(a), (c), and it could have, in exercising its discretion, set higher standards if an EIS contained evidence that so warranted. Although NEPA does not demand substantive environmental outcomes, NHTSA possesses the power to act on whatever information might be contained in an EIS. * * *

Moreover, the CAFE standard will affect the level of the nation's greenhouse gas emissions and impact global warming. NHTSA does not dispute that light trucks account for a significant percentage of the U.S. transportation sector, that the U.S. transportation sector accounts for about six percent of the world's greenhouse gases, and that "fuel economy improvements could have a significant impact on the rate of CO2 accumulation in the atmosphere," which would affect climate change.

In sum, the EPCA does not limit NHTSA's duty under NEPA to assess the environmental impacts, including the impact on climate change, of its rule. * * *

2. Sufficiency of the Environmental Assessment

We examine the EA with two purposes in mind: to determine whether it has adequately considered and elaborated the possible consequences of the proposed agency action when concluding that it will have no significant impact on the environment, and whether its determination that no EIS is required is a reasonable conclusion.

Even though an EA need not "conform to all the requirements of an EIS," it must be "sufficient to establish the reasonableness of th[e] decision" not to prepare an EIS. *Found. for N. Am. Wild Sheep,* 681 F.2d at 1178 n. 29 (1982); *see also* 40 C.F.R. § 1508.9(a)(1). An EA "[s]hall include brief discussions of the need for the proposal ... [and] the environmental impacts of the proposed action and alternatives." 40 C.F.R. § 1508.9(b). An EA "must in some circumstances include an analysis of the cumulative impacts of a project.... An EA may be deficient if it fails to include a cumulative impact analysis...." *Native Ecosystems Council v. Dombeck,* 304 F.3d 886, 895 (9th Cir. 2002); *see also Klamath–Siskiyou*

Wildlands Ctr. v. Bureau of Land Mgmt., 387 F.3d 989, 993–94 (9th Cir. 2004); *Kern v. U.S. Bureau of Land Mgmt.*, 284 F.3d 1062, 1076–78 (9th Cir. 2002).

a. Cumulative impacts of greenhouse gas emissions on climate change and the environment

A cumulative impact is defined as "the impact on the environment which results from the incremental impact of the action when added to other past, present, and reasonably foreseeable future actions regardless of what agency . . . or person undertakes such other actions. Cumulative impacts can result from individually minor but collectively significant actions taking place over a period of time." 40 C.F.R. § 1508.7. In *Klamath–Siskiyou Wildlands Center*, this court held that:

> Cumulative impacts of multiple projects can be significant in different ways. The most obvious way is that the greater total magnitude of the environmental effects . . . may demonstrate by itself that the environmental impact will be significant. Sometimes the total impact from a set of actions may be greater than the sum of the parts.

387 F.3d at 994.

The EA catalogues the total tonnage of CO2 emissions for light trucks for MYs 2005–2011. Table 4–5 of the Final EA lists the amount of fuel consumption and emissions of criteria pollutants and CO2 emissions. For example, it shows that under Unreformed CAFE, the lifetime CO2 emissions for light trucks MY 2005–2011 would be 4,979 million metric tons (mmt). Under Reformed CAFE, including MDPVs in MY 2011, CO2 emissions would be 4,966 million metric tons. NHTSA estimated that:

> together with the previous action raising MY 2005–07 light truck CAFE standards, the various alternatives for the current action will reduce lifetime carbon dioxide (CO2) emissions from MY 2005–11 light trucks by 122 to 196 million metric tons, or by 2.4 to 3.8 percent *from their level if neither action had been taken.* . . . MY 2008–11 light truck CAFE standards are projected to result in cumulative reductions from the previous and current actions ranging from 0.2 to 0.3 percent of U.S. greenhouse gas emissions over the lifetimes of MY 2005–11 light trucks.

Id. at 36–37 (emphasis added).

We conclude that the EA's cumulative impacts analysis is inadequate. While the EA quantifies the expected amount of CO2 emitted from light trucks MYs 2005–2011, it does not evaluate the "incremental impact" that these emissions will have on climate change or on the environment more generally in light of other past, present, and reasonably foreseeable actions such as other light truck and passenger automobile CAFE standards. The EA does not discuss the *actual* environmental effects resulting from those emissions or place those emissions in context of other CAFE rulemakings. * * *

NHTSA does not dispute that the CAFE standard will have an effect on global warming due to an increase in greenhouse gas emissions. The new rule will not actually result in a decrease in carbon emissions, but potentially only a decrease in the rate of growth of carbon emissions. NHTSA concedes that "the new CAFE standards will not entirely offset the projected effect of increases in the number of light trucks." * * *

* * * We agree with Petitioners that "[b]y allowing particular fuel economy levels, which NHTSA argues translate directly into particular tailpipe emissions, NHTSA's regulations are the proximate cause of those emissions just as EPA Clean Air Act rules permitting particular smokestack emissions are the proximate cause of those air pollutants and are unquestionably subject to NEPA's cumulative impacts requirements." Thus, the fact that "climate change is largely a global phenomenon that includes actions that are outside of [the agency's] control ... does not release the agency from the duty of assessing the effects of *its* actions on global warming within the context of other actions that also affect global warming." The cumulative impacts regulation specifically provides that the agency must assess the "impact of the action when added to other past, present, and reasonably foreseeable future actions *regardless of what agency (Federal or non-Federal) or person undertakes such other actions.*" 40 C.F.R. § 1508.7.

The impact of greenhouse gas emissions on climate change is precisely the kind of cumulative impacts analysis that NEPA requires agencies to conduct. Any given rule setting a CAFE standard might have an "individually minor" effect on the environment, but these rules are "collectively significant actions taking place over a period of time." 40 C.F.R. § 1508.7. Thus, NHTSA must provide the necessary contextual information about the cumulative and incremental environmental impacts of the Final Rule in light of other CAFE rulemakings and other past, present, and reasonably foreseeable future actions, regardless of what agency or person undertakes such other actions.

b. Reasonable alternatives

NHTSA must "[r]igorously explore and objectively evaluate all reasonable alternatives." 40 C.F.R. § 1502.14(a). The alternatives section is the "heart" of an EIS. *Id.* § 1502.14. Although "an agency's obligation to consider alternatives under an EA is a lesser one than under an EIS," *Native Ecosystems Council v. U.S. Forest Serv.*, 428 F.3d 1233, 1246, 1245 (9th Cir. 2005), "NEPA requires that alternatives ... be given full and meaningful consideration," whether the agency prepares an EA or an EIS, *id.* at 1245 (alteration in original; internal quotation marks omitted). The agency must "provide sufficient evidence and analysis for determining whether to prepare an environmental impact statement or a finding of no significant impact." 40 C.F.R. § 1508.9.

In the EA, NHTSA considered a very narrow range of alternatives. All the alternatives evaluated were derived from NHTSA's cost-benefit analysis. The alternatives presented in the EA are as follows:

- *Alternative A* ("Baseline"): MY 2007 standard of 22.2 mpg for MYs 2008–2011.
- *Alternative B:* Unreformed CAFE for MYs 2008–2010 and Reformed CAFE for MY 2011 with fuel economy targets set using continuous function. MDPVs [Medium Duty Passenger Vehicle] included in MY 2011 only.
- *Alternative C:* Reformed CAFE for MYs 2008–2011 with fuel economy targets set using continuous function. Impacts are shown including MDPVs for MY 2011 only and excluding MDPVs altogether.
- *Alternative D:* Reformed CAFE as described in NPRM, with fuel economy targets set using step function (six footprint categories). Entirely excludes MDPVs.
- *Alternative E:* Reformed CAFE described in NPRM, with revised fuel economy targets for each of its six footprint categories. Impacts are shown including MDPVs for MY 2011 only and excluding MDPVs altogether.

The alternative NHTSA ultimately chose is a mix between Alternatives B and C: NHTSA adopted Reformed CAFE beginning in MY 2011 and Unreformed CAFE for MYs 2008–2010, but it allowed a transition period to Reformed CAFE in MY 2011, so manufacturers may choose to continue to follow Unreformed CAFE in MYs 2008–2010. The adopted alternative includes MDPVs for MY 2011 only.

These alternatives are hardly different from the option that NHTSA ultimately adopted. * * * NHTSA acknowledged that "the range of impacts from the considered alternatives is very narrow and minimal." However, the agency justified its choice of range and refusal to consider other alternatives on the ground that "standards more stringent than those represented by the alternatives would not satisfy the statutory requirement to establish standards ... that are both technologically feasible and economically practicable.... NEPA's requirements must be applied in light of the constraints placed on the agency by EPCA." Once again, NHTSA falls back on its contention that it had no discretion to consider setting higher CAFE standards. As before, we conclude that this argument is flawed.

NHTSA also erroneously contends that Petitioners have not identified any specific alternative the agency should have considered. To the contrary, Environmental Defense submitted a detailed appendix to its comment titled, "Revised Benefit–Cost Analysis for Calculating Optimal CAFE Targets." In this document, Environmental Defense performed a marginal cost-benefit analysis, using a variety of different assumptions and inputs. Table A–1 set forth 28 different possible CAFE standards for MY 2011 (including NHTSA's figure). On the basis of its calculations, it recommended a final rule that would increase CAFE standards at a rate of 4% per year and achieve a standard of 26 mpg by MY 2011.

We also disagree with NHTSA that Petitioners' suggested alternatives would not be reasonably related to the project's purpose. The purpose of the Final Rule is to set CAFE standards for light trucks for MYs 2008–2011. 71 Fed. Reg. at 17,566. NHTSA itself describes the scope of the EA as "analyz[ing] the environmental impacts associated with various alternatives to the existing CAFE program." Final EA at 4. Since EPCA's overarching goal is energy conservation, consideration of more stringent fuel economy standards that would *conserve more energy* is clearly reasonably related to the purpose of the CAFE standards. Energy conservation and environmental protection are not coextensive, but they often overlap. The Supreme Court has recently recognized as much.

3. NHTSA must prepare an Environmental Impact Statement

An agency must prepare an EIS "if 'substantial questions are raised as to whether a project ... *may* cause significant degradation of some human environmental factor.'" *Idaho Sporting Cong. v. Thomas,* 137 F.3d 1146, 1149 (9th Cir. 1998). Petitioners "need not show that significant effects *will in fact occur,*" but only that there are "substantial questions whether a project may have a significant effect." *Id.* at 1150 (internal quotation marks omitted). "If an agency decides not to prepare an EIS, it must supply a 'convincing statement of reasons' to explain why a project's impacts are insignificant. 'The statement of reasons is crucial to determining whether the agency took a 'hard look' at the potential environmental impact of a project.'" *Blue Mountains Biodiversity Project,* 161 F.3d at 1212 (quoting *Save the Yaak Comm. v. Block,* 840 F.2d 714, 717 (9th Cir. 1988)).

"Whether there may be a significant effect on the environment requires consideration of two broad factors: 'context and intensity.'" *Nat'l Parks & Conservation Ass'n,* 241 F.3d at 731 (quoting 40 C.F.R. § 1508.27). A number of factors should be considered in evaluating intensity, including, "[t]he degree to which the proposed action affects public health or safety," "[t]he degree to which the effects on the quality of the human environment are likely to be highly controversial," "[t]he degree to which the possible effects on the human environment are highly uncertain or involve unique or unknown risks," "[t]he degree to which the action may establish a pre for future actions with significant effects or represents a decision in principle about a future consideration," "[w]hether the action is related to other actions with individually insignificant but cumulatively significant impacts," and "[t]he degree to which the action may adversely affect an endangered or threatened species or its habitat." 40 C.F.R. § 1508.27(b)(2), (4), (5), (6), (7), (9). An action may be "significant" if one of these factors is met.

* * * We conclude that NHTSA's FONSI is arbitrary and capricious and the agency must prepare an EIS because the evidence raises a substantial question as to whether the Final Rule may have a significant impact on the environment. Moreover, NHTSA has failed to provide a convincing statement of reasons for its finding of insignificance.

Petitioners have raised a "substantial question" as to whether the CAFE standards for light trucks MYs 2008–2011 "*may* cause significant degradation of some human environmental factor," particularly in light of the compelling scientific evidence concerning "positive feedback mechanisms" in the atmosphere. Among the evidence Petitioners presented to the agency was the following:

- The IPCC Third Assessment Report, which discusses the history of anthropogenic interference with the climate system, the projected increase in climate variability and extreme weather events, and the projected effects on various ecological systems. * * *
- The IPCC Working Group I Technical Summary provided: "The possibility for rapid and irreversible changes in the climate system exists, but there is a large degree of uncertainty about the mechanisms involved and hence also about the likelihood or time-scales of such transitions. The climate system involves many processes and feedbacks that interact in complex non-linear ways. *This interaction can give rise to thresholds in the climate system that can be crossed if the system is perturbed sufficiently.*"
- "The American Meteorological Society, the American Geophysical Union, and the American Association for Advancement of Science, among many, many other scientific organizations have all concluded that the evidence of human induced warming is compelling.... In an April 2004 article, leading NASA and Department of Energy scientists stated that emissions of carbon dioxide and other heat-trapping gases have warmed the oceans and led to an energy imbalance that is causing and will continue to cause, significant warming, increasing the urgency of reducing CO2 emissions."
- The Climate Change Futures Report published by the Center for Health and the Global Environment at Harvard Medical School, which analyzed in detail climate change scenarios that "will affect the health of humans as well as the ecosystems and species on which we depend."

Finally, Petitioners have satisfied several of the "intensity" factors listed in 40 C.F.R. § 1508.27(b) for determining "significant effect." For example, the Final Rule clearly may have an "individually insignificant but cumulatively significant" impact with respect to global warming. Evidence that Petitioners submitted in the record also shows that global warming will have an effect on public health and safety. Petitioners do not claim (nor do they have to show) that NHTSA's Final Rule would be the *sole* cause of global warming, and that is NHTSA's only response on this point.

Petitioners have also satisfied the "controversy" factor. *See* 40 C.F.R. § 1508.27(b)(4). NHTSA received over 45,000 individual submissions on its proposal. We reject NHTSA's argument that "petitioners' controversy does not concern the 'size, nature, or effect' of the new CAFE standards, but rather the desire of some commenters for different regulations that they have not described in any detail." The entire dispute between Petitioners and NHTSA centers on the *stringency* of the MY 2008–2011 light truck CAFE standards—their "size" or "effect."

In light of the evidence in the record, it is hardly "self-evident" that a 0.2 percent decrease in carbon emissions (as opposed to a greater decrease) is not significant. NHTSA's conclusion that a small reduction (0.2% compared to baseline) in the growth of carbon emissions would not have a significant impact on the environment was unaccompanied by any analysis or supporting data, either in the Final Rule or the EA.

Nowhere does the EA provide a "statement of reasons" for a finding of no significant impact, much less a "convincing statement of reasons." For example, the EA discusses the amount of CO2 emissions expected from the Rule, but does not discuss the potential impact of such emissions on climate change. In the "Affected Environment" section of the EA, NHTSA states that "[i]ncreasing concentrations of greenhouse gases are likely to accelerate the rate of climate change." The agency notes that "[t]he transportation sector is a significant source of greenhouse gas (GHG) emissions, accounting for approximately 28 percent of all greenhouse gas emissions in the United States." From this, NHTSA jumps to the conclusion that "[c]oupled with the effects resulting from the 2003 light truck rule, the effects resulting from the agency's current action are expected to lessen the GHG impacts discussed above."

Table 3–2 of the EA, which shows the potential health effects of criteria air pollutants, is similarly devoid of meaningful analysis or a statement of reasons why the effects would be insignificant. * * *

Nor is there any analysis or statement of reasons in the section of the EA that discusses environmental impacts. The EA states that reduction in fuel production and consumption would reduce "contamination of water resources," acid rain, risk of oil spills and contamination, and "lead to minor reductions in impacts to biological resources ... includ[ing] habitat encroachment and destruction, air and water pollution, greenhouse gases, and oil contamination from petroleum refining and distribution."

NHTSA's EA "shunted aside [significant questions] with merely conclusory statements," failed to "directly address[]" "substantial questions," and most importantly, "provide[d] no foundation" for the important inference NHTSA draws between a decrease in the rate of carbon emissions growth and its finding of no significant impact. *Found. for N. Am. Wild Sheep,* 681 F.2d at 1179. NHTSA makes "vague and conclusory statements" unaccompanied by "supporting data," and the EA "do[es] not constitute a 'hard look' at the environmental consequences of the action as required by NEPA." *Great Basin Mine Watch v. Hankins,* 456 F.3d 955, 973 (9th Cir. 2006). Thus, the FONSI is arbitrary and capricious.

* * * Petitioners have raised a substantial question of whether the Final Rule *may* significantly affect the environment. NHTSA acknowledges that carbon emissions contribute to global warming, and it does not dispute the scientific evidence that Petitioners presented concerning the

significant effect of incremental increases in greenhouses gases. NHTSA has not provided a "statement of reasons *why* potential effects are insignificant," much less a "convincing statement of reasons." *See Blue Mountains Biodiversity Project,* 161 F.3d at 1211 (emphasis added) (internal quotation marks omitted). It asserts simply that the insignificance of the effects is "self-evident[]." In order that the public and the agency be fully advised, we remand and order the agency to prepare a full EIS. * * *

NOTES

1. **Federal Action.** What was the action that triggered NEPA review in this case? Was there any argument that this action was not federal? Why or why not?

2. **NEPA and Climate Change.** Why is climate change relevant in general to NEPA analyses? Why in particular was climate change relevant to the NHTSA's NEPA evaluation of the new CAFE standards for SUVs and light trucks? Do you agree with the Ninth Circuit that climate change effects should be part of the NEPA analysis? Why or why not? How did the NHTSA try to argue that climate change effects should not be part of its required analysis?

NOTE: On February 28, 2008, the International Center for Technology Assessment, the Natural Resources Defense Council, and the Sierra Club filed a formal petition for rulemaking with the CEQ, requesting that climate change analyses be made a formal requirement for all NEPA analyses. The petition is available at http://www.icta.org/doc/CEQ_Petition_Final_Version_2-28-08.pdf.

3. **Evaluating "Significant" Effect.** Which of the CEQ's factors for determining "significance" were relevant in this case? What was the context of the NHTSA's rulemaking? Did that context matter to the Ninth Circuit's decision? How? Which of the CEQ's intensity factors were relevant to the Ninth Circuit's decision? Did the Ninth Circuit discuss all of these factors? Why did the NHTSA nevertheless issue a FONSI?

4. **Controversy.** Under the CEQ's regulations, federal agencies must prepare an EIS whenever a federal action is "controversial." According to case law, a federal action is controversial when "substantial questions are raised as to whether a project ... may cause significant degradation of some human environmental factor," *Northwest Environmental Defense Center v. Bonneville Power Administration*, 117 F.3d 1520, 1539 (9th Cir. 1997), or "a substantial dispute [about] the nature, size, or effect of the major Federal action" exists. *Blue Mountains Biodiversity Project v. Blackwood*, 161 F.3d 1208, 1212 (9th Cir. 1998), *cert. denied*, 527 U.S. 1003 (1999) (citations omitted). What was controversial about the NHTSA's new CAFE standard regulations, for NEPA purposes? What was the evidence of that controversy?

5. **What Does an Environmental Assessment Look Like?** The Department of Transportation's (DOT's) 2002 Draft Environmental Assessment for the then-current CAFE standards can be viewed at http://www.nhtsa.dot.gov/cars/rules/rulings/CAFE/EnvAssess-d/Index.html. As the CEQ intended, this is a fairly short document. It considers only two alternatives—

no action and the proposed CAFE standards—but already contains a fairly extensive (at least in comparison to other analyses) discussion of climate change and carbon dioxide. Would this draft EA have survived the Ninth's Circuit's analysis? Why or why not?

6. **FONSI Standard of Review.** What standard did the Ninth Circuit use to review the NHTSA's decision not to prepare an EIS? Why? How did the Ninth Circuit describe that standard?

7. **Makah Whaling, Revisited.** As was noted in connection with *Metcalf v. Daley*, in 2002 the Ninth Circuit invalidated NOAA/NMFS's second FONSI regarding the Makah Tribe's whaling. The Ninth Circuit determined, on uncertainty and controversy grounds, that NMFS and NOAA had to prepare an EIS:

> There is no disagreement in this case concerning the EA's conclusion that the impact of the Makah Tribe's hunt on the overall California gray whale population will not be significant. What is in hot dispute is the possible impact on the whale population in the local area where the Tribe wants to hunt. In our view, the answer to this question * * * is sufficiently uncertain and controversial to require the full EIS protocol.
>
> Our reasoning in this regard is as follows: The government agrees that a relatively small group of whales comes into the area of the Tribe's hunt each summer, and that about sixty percent of them are returning whales (although, again, not necessarily whales returning annually). Even if the eastern Pacific gray whales overall or the smaller PCFA group of whales are not significantly impacted by the Makah Tribe's whaling, the summer whale population in the *local* Washington area may be significantly affected. Such local effects are a basis for a finding that there will be a significant impact from the Tribe's hunts. *See* 40 C.F.R. § 1508.27(a). Thus, if there are substantial questions about the impact on the number of whales who frequent the Strait of Juan de Fuca and the northern Washington Coast, an EIS must be prepared.
>
> The crucial question, therefore, is whether the hunting, striking, and taking of whales from this smaller group could significantly affect the environment in the local area. The answer to this question is, we are convinced, both uncertain and controversial within the meaning of NEPA. No one, including the government's retained scientists, has a firm idea what will happen to the local whale population if the Tribe is allowed to hunt and kill whales pursuant to the approved quota and Makah Management Plan. There is at least a substantial question whether killing five whales from this group either annually or every two years, which the quota would allow, could have a significant impact on the environment.
>
> * * * In short, the record establishes that there are "substantial questions" as to the significance of the effect on the *local* area. Despite the commendable care with which the EA addresses other questions, the EA simply does not adequately address the highly uncertain impact of the Tribe's whaling on the *local* whale population and the local ecosystem. This major analytical lapse is, we conclude, a sufficient basis for holding that the agencies' finding of no significant impact cannot survive the level

> of scrutiny applicable in this case. And because the EA simply does not adequately address the local impact of the Tribe's hunt, an EIS is required.

Anderson v. Evans, 350 F.3d 815, 832–35 (9th Cir. 2003). How did the CEQ's context and intensity factors play out in this decision? Specifically, how did the Ninth Circuit's focus on *context* affect its analysis of the uncertainty and controversy involved in the Makahs' whaling?

8. **NEPA "Significant Effects" and Mitigation Measures.** The CEQ's regulations define "mitigation" to include:

> (a) Avoiding the impact altogether by not taking a certain action or parts of an action.
>
> (b) Minimizing impacts by limiting the degree or magnitude of the action and its implementation.
>
> (c) Rectifying the impact by repairing, rehabilitating, or restoring the affected environment.
>
> (d) Reducing or eliminating the impact over time by preservation and maintenance operations during the life of the action.
>
> (e) Compensating for the impact by replacing or providing substitute resources or environments.

40 C.F.R. § 1508.20.

The CEQ's regulations make it clear that an agency must discuss mitigation measures if it prepares an EIS. 40 C.F.R. §§ 1502.14(f), 1502.16(h). Less clear from the regulations, however, is whether an agency can use mitigation measures to avoid an EIS altogether—*i.e.*, at the EA stage, can an agency include as part of its proposed action measures that would mitigate the effects of a project that would otherwise clearly "significantly affect the quality of the human environment" and issue a FONSI as a result? The federal Courts of Appeals are in substantial agreement that it can. *Spiller v. White*, 352 F.3d 235, 241 (5th Cir. 2003); *Wetlands Action Network v. U.S. Army Corps of Engineers*, 222 F.3d 1105, 1121 (9th Cir. 2000); *Audubon Soc'y of Cent. Arkansas v. Dailey*, 977 F.2d 428, 435–36 (8th Cir. 1992); *Roanoke River Basin Ass'n v. Hudson*, 940 F.2d 58, 62 (4th Cir. 1991); *C.A.R.E. Now, Inc. v. FAA*, 844 F.2d 1569, 1575 (11th Cir. 1988); *Cabinet Mountains Wilderness v. Peterson*, 685 F.2d 678, 682–83 (D.C. Cir. 1982). Does this rule effectuate NEPA's purposes? Why or why not? How might controversy and uncertainty affect an agency's ability to rely on such mitigation measures to avoid preparing an EIS?

9. **Segmentation and Cumulative Impacts.** Federal agencies will occasionally try to avoid a finding of significant impact by ***segmenting*** their projects into smaller projects that do not, individually, significantly affect the quality of the human environment. How does the cumulative impacts analysis attempt to avoid that result?

Agency segmentation of federal projects forces courts to identify projects that really are separate and hence can be analyzed independently from those that are truly linked and must be analyzed together. The federal Courts of Appeals have approached this issue in a variety of ways. For example, according to the Fifth Circuit, in the context of federal highway projects, "Segmentation analysis functions to weed out projects which are pretextually segmented, and for which that is no independent reason to exist. When the segmentation project has no independent jurisdiction, no life of its own, or is simply illogical when viewed in isolation, the segmentation will be held invalid." *Save Barton Creek Association v. Federal Highway Administration*, 950 F.2d 1129, 1139 (5th Cir. 1992). "Segmentation becomes suspect, however, only after an evaluation of such factors as whether the proposed segment (1) has logical termini; (2) has substantial independent utility; (3) does not foreclose the opportunity to consider alternatives' and (4) does not irretrievably commit federal funds for closely related projects." *Id.* at 1140. The Fourth Circuit has adopted a substantial similar analysis for highway projects. *Wilds v. South Carolina Department of Transportation*, 9 Fed. Appx. 114 (4th Cir. 2001). In contrast, in the context of salvage logging sales, the Ninth Circuit has said that future sales in the same forest must be included in the cumulative impacts analysis if those future sales are reasonably foreseeable. *Blue Mountains Biodiversity Project v. Blackwood*, 161 F.3d 1208 (9th Cir. 1998).

10. **Cumulative Impacts and NEPA Scoping.** Besides significance, cumulative impacts are also relevant to the NEPA scoping process. "Scope" refers to "the range of actions, alternatives, and impacts to be considered in an environmental impact statement. * * * To determine the scope of environmental impact statements, agencies shall consider 3 types of actions, 3 types of alternatives, and 3 types of impacts." 40 C.F.R. § 1508.25. Cumulative impacts are one of the three types of impacts that the CEQ lists. *Id.* § 1508.25(c)(3).

11. **NEPA Tiering.** Agencies also occasionally try to avoid preparing an EIS through *tiering*—in general, by relying on more general programmatic EISs that the agency has already prepared at an earlier planning stage. Under the CEQ's regulations, tiering allows federal agencies to prepare successive EISs with progressively more specificity. *See* 40 C.F.R. § 1508.28. Indeed, "[a]gencies are encouraged to tier their environmental impact statements to eliminate repetitive discussions of the same issues and to focus on the actual issues ripe for decision at each level of environmental review * * *." 40 C.F.R. § 1502.20.

Tiering is particularly useful when a federal agency addresses resource use at a variety of levels. For example, the Forest Service must issue management plans—and accompanying EISs—for entire National Forests. These plans describe overall goals for and general uses allowed within particular National Forests, which can occupy large tracts of land. Areas within a National Forest may be subject to more specific planning—and hence a more specific EIS. Finally, individual projects may occur within a particular National Forest, such as fire recovery actions. Through tiering, the more specific EAs and EISs can rely on the more general analyses already conducted in the EISs for the more general plans and programs. "Whenever a broad environmental impact statement has been prepared (such as a program or policy statement) and a subsequent statement or environmental assessment is then prepared on an action included within the entire program or policy (such as a site-specific action) the subsequent statement or environmental assessment need only summarize the issues discussed in the broader statement * * *." 40 C.F.R. § 1502.20.

12. **Exhaustion of Administrative Remedies.** Because NEPA contains no citizen suit provision and challengers seek review of an agency's NEPA decisions through the federal APA, NEPA review is subject to the APA's limitations. In general, courts require litigants to exhaust their administrative remedies before bringing their claims to federal court. *Darby v. Cisneros*, 509 U.S. 137, 153–54 (1993). However, "the exhaustion doctrine [applies] as a matter of judicial discretion," and Congress can eliminate it by statute. *Id.* In 1993, the U.S. Supreme Court determined that Congress had eliminated the exhaustion requirement for APA lawsuits and that, in such suits, "an appeal to 'superior agency authority' is a prerequisite to judicial review *only* when expressly required by statute or when an agency rule requires appeal before review and the administrative action is made inoperative pending that review." *Id.*

Thus, the exhaustion requirement will vary from agency to agency. For example, with respect to APA lawsuits against the Forest Service, the federal courts are in wide agreement that both the U.S. Department of Agriculture Reorganization Act of 1994, 7 U.S.C. § 6912(e), and the Department of Agriculture's regulations, 36 C.F.R. § 215.20, require litigants to exhaust their administrative remedies before suing the Forest Service in federal court for NEPA violations. (The Forest Service is housed within the Department of Agriculture.) *Idaho Sporting Congress v. Rittenhouse*, 305 F.3d 957, 965–66 (9th Cir. 2002); *Kleissler v. U.S. Forest Service*, 183 F.3d 196, 200–02 (3rd Cir. 1999); *Sharps v. U.S. Forest Service*, 28 F.3d 851, 853–55 (8th Cir. 1994); *Biodiversity Assocs. v. U.S. Forest Service*, 226 F. Supp. 2d 1270, 1313–14 (D. Wyo. 2002); *Utah Environmental Congress v. Zieroth*, 190 F. Supp. 2d 1265, 1272 (D. Utah 2002); *Gregson v. U.S. Forestry Service*, 19 F. Supp. 2d 925, 929 (E.D. Ark. 1998).

13. **Emergencies and NEPA Review.** The CEQ's regulations provide that "[w]here emergency circumstances make it necessary to take an action with significant environmental impact without observing the provisions of these regulations, the Federal agency taking the action should consult with the Council about alternative arrangements. Agencies and the Council will limit such arrangements to actions necessary to control the immediate impacts of the emergency. Other actions remain subject to NEPA review." 40 C.F.R. § 1506.11.

* * *

D. CATEGORICAL EXCLUSIONS

If an agency repeatedly undertakes similar actions that do not significantly affect the quality of the human environment, it may seek to ***categorically exclude*** that kind of action from the NEPA review process. A ***categorical exclusion*** is "a category of actions which do not individually or cumulatively have a significant effect on the human environment and which have been found to have no such effect in procedures adopted by a Federal agency in implementation of these regulations * * * and for which, therefore, neither an environmental assessment nor an environmental impact statement is required." 40 C.F.R. § 1508.4. However, in setting up a categorical exclusion, the agency must "provide for extraordinary circumstances in which a normally excluded action may have a significant environmental effect." *Id.* Moreover, the agency remains free to prepare an EA for any particular excluded action if the agency so desires. *Id.*

It should be remembered, however, that the agency's issuance of criteria for categorical exclusions, the categorical exclusions themselves, and the procedures for identifying categorical exclusions (see 40 C.F.R. § 1507.3) are themselves generally major federal actions subject to NEPA review. Moreover, challengers remain free to argue that "extraordinary circumstances" exist that require any activity that otherwise fits a categorical exclusion to undergo NEPA review, or that the proposed action did not fit the claimed exclusion.

UTAH ENVIRONMENTAL CONGRESS v. BOSWORTH

443 F.3d 732 (10th Cir. 2006).

TYMKOVICH, CIRCUIT JUDGE.

In 2004, the United States Forest Service approved a 123–acre timber-thinning project to treat beetle-infested trees in Utah's Fishlake National Forest. Its approval was made pursuant to a categorical exclusion, a streamlined process allowing minor projects to be quickly implemented so long as they have no significant effect on the environment. As a result of this decision, Utah Environmental Congress ("UEC") appealed to the district court arguing that the project violated a number of environmental and regulatory provisions. We agree with the district court that the Forest Service properly implemented this project under a categorical exclusion.

Exercising jurisdiction pursuant to 28 U.S.C. § 1291, we AFFIRM.

Figure 2-9: Fishlake National Forest
U.S. Forest Service photo.

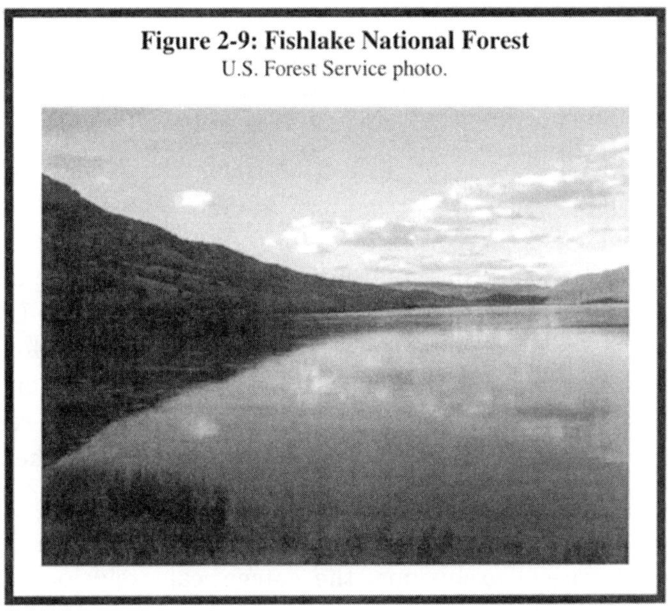

I. BACKGROUND

A. *Statutory and Regulatory Framework*

1. National Environmental Policy Act

The National Environmental Policy Act ("NEPA") requires federal agencies such as the Forest Service to analyze environmental consequences before initiating actions that potentially affect the environment. In conducting this analysis, the Forest Service must prepare one of the following: (1) an environmental impact statement, (2) an environmental assessment, or (3) a categorical exclusion. An environmental impact statement involves the most rigorous analysis, and is required if a proposed action will "significantly affect[] the quality of the human environment." 42 U.S.C. § 4332(2)(C); 40 C.F.R. § 1502.4.

If an agency is uncertain whether the proposed action will significantly affect the environment, it may prepare a considerably less detailed environmental assessment. 40 C.F.R. § 1508.9. An environmental assessment provides "sufficient evidence and analysis" to determine whether a proposed project will create a significant effect on the environment. *Id.* If so, the agency must then develop an environmental impact statement; if not, the environmental assessment results in a "Finding of No Significant Impact," and no further agency action is required. *Id.*

In certain narrow instances, however, an agency is not required to prepare either an environmental assessment or an environmental impact statement. This occurs when the proposed action falls within a categorical exclusion, *i.e.*, those actions predetermined not to "individually or cumulatively have a significant effect on the human environment." *Id.* § 1508.4. The Forest Service has created a list of 24 such categories. Examples include small acreage timber-thinning and harvesting, as well as the construction of trails, utility lines, and meteorological sampling sites.

Federal law limits categorical exclusions in one critical respect: a proposed action is precluded from categorical exclusion if "extraordinary circumstances" exist such that "a normally excluded action may have a significant environmental effect." 40 C.F.R. § 1508.4. Extraordinary circumstances may exist, for example, where a proposed action—albeit small in scope—significantly affects inventoried roadless areas, archaeological sites, flood plains, or federally listed threatened or endangered species habitat.

** * * B. The Seven Mile Project*

The Seven Mile Spruce Beetle Management Project ("Seven Mile Project" or "Project") sitting within the 1,424,479 acres of the Fishlake National Forest in south-central Utah, is located approximately 22 miles east of Richfield, Utah. * * * The Project involves a selective harvest of beetle-infested mature, dead, diseased, or dying Englemann spruce timber stands covering approximately 123 acres. By implementing the Project, the Forest Service plans to prevent an epidemic infestation of spruce beetle from spreading into adjacent stands and killing the spruce. In so doing, the Forest Service hopes to protect mature stands, preserve wildlife habitat, and reduce the risk of wildfire.

The Forest Service ultimately approved the Seven Mile Project under categorical exclusion 14 ("Category 14") in 2004. * * * Category 14 applies to small acreage timber-thinning projects. Specifically, it excludes from NEPA review "commercial and noncommercial sanitation harvest of trees to control insects or disease not to exceed 250 acres, requiring no more than 1/2 mile of temporary road construction, including removal of infested/infected trees and adjacent live uninfested/uninfected trees as determined necessary to control the spread of insects or disease."

Finding Category 14 would apply to the Seven Mile Project, the Fishlake National Forest district ranger issued a Decision Memorandum in May 2004. He concluded that "[Category 14] is appropriate in this situation because there are no extraordinary circumstances related to the proposed action." The district ranger replaced the original Decision Memorandum in October 2004 with a new Memorandum, but left the project largely unmodified.

Figure 2-10: The Spruce Beetle
U.S. Department of Agriculture photo.

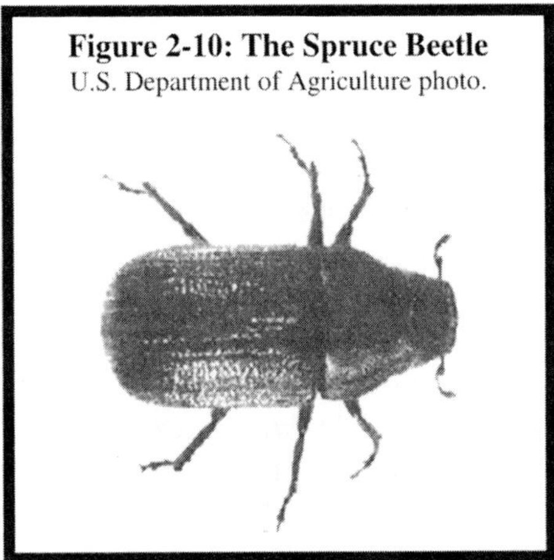

In sum, the local forest officials found "that the spruce beetle infestation in the Seven Mile Project area has escalated substantially during the past 8 years ... [and] at least 80 percent mortality will occur in non-infested spruce in the absence of thinning." *Id.* at 551. The district manager assured that (1) "three snags per acre will be retained ... [as well as] snags containing nest cavities or offering potential nesting opportunities ... to provide for [foraging and nesting] for three-toed woodpeckers;" (2) although "no sensitive species are known to occur in the project area, and suitable habitat has not been found," local forest rangers "will continue to survey the project area for all sensitive species during pre- and post-treatment activities;" and (3) if any goshawk are discovered during the "ongoing surveys [] being conducted for the northern goshawk," the Forest Service will act appropriately "to conserve this species."

* * * II. STANDARD OF REVIEW

Because neither NEPA nor NFMA provide a private right of action, this court reviews the Forest Service's approval of the Seven Mile Project as a final agency action under the APA. We consider the district court's decision de novo. However, we will not overturn the agency's decision unless it is "arbitrary, capricious, an abuse of discretion, or otherwise not in accordance with law." 5 U.S.C. § 706(2)(A).

While administrative agencies generally are afforded a presumption of regularity, an agency's decision will nonetheless be arbitrary and capricious "if the agency ... entirely failed to consider an important aspect of the problem, offered an explanation for its decision that runs counter to the evidence before the agency, or is so implausible that it could not be ascribed to a difference in view or the product of agency expertise." *Motor Vehicle Mfrs. Ass'n v. State Farm Mut. Auto. Ins. Co.*, 463 U.S. 29, 43 (1983). Furthermore, we must determine whether the disputed decision was based on consideration of the relevant factors and whether there has been a clear error of judgment. *Id.* Deference to the agency is especially strong where the challenged decisions involve technical or scientific matters within the agency's area of expertise. *Marsh v. Or. Natural Res. Council*, 490 U.S. 360, 378 (1989).

* * * III. ANALYSIS

UEC [argues that] the Forest Service acted arbitrarily and capriciously by failing to consider the cumulative impact of the Seven Mile Project on fish and wildlife * * *.

A. Categorical Exclusion of the Seven Mile Project

We first address UEC's argument that the Forest Service acted arbitrarily and capriciously by authorizing the Seven Mile Project pursuant to Category 14's exclusion. UEC raises two separate claims: (1) the Seven Mile Project should not have been categorically excluded because use of an exclusion is appropriate only when the Forest Service first conducts a preliminary analysis determining that the proposed project will have no significant or cumulative effects on the environment, and (2) the existence of extraordinary circumstances here precludes categorical exclusion of the Seven Mile Project.

1. Cumulative Impact

UEC's first claim is that "in order for an agency to determine whether a project may be categorically excluded, the agency must [definitively] determine, based on cumulative effects, whether categorical exclusion is appropriate." Specifically, UEC asserts the Seven Mile Project should not have been categorically excluded because the Forest Service conducted an inadequate analysis of the Project's cumulative effects on the forest. UEC points to three specific omissions by the Forest Service, which it contends, demonstrate the failure to conduct an adequate cumulative impact analysis. The Forest Service failed to (1) analyze the Project's effect on management indicator species; (2) create an appropriate cumulative effects boundary encompassing the entire Project area and areas adjacent to the Project where the Project's effects could be perceived; and (3) analyze the Project's effect on sensitive species located outside the Project area but nonetheless still within the cumulative effects boundary as well as analyze the impact of other projects occurring within the cumulative effects boundary. In addressing this argument, the Forest Service counters that UEC's argument would effectively render useless the purpose of categorical exclusions generally. We agree.

Federal regulations define the term "categorical exclusion" as:

> [A] category of actions which do not individually or cumulatively have a significant effect on the human environment and which have been found to have no such effect in procedures adopted by a Federal agency in implementation of these regulations.... Any procedures under this section shall provide for extraordinary circumstances in

which a normally excluded action may have a significant environmental effect.

40 C.F.R. § 1508.4 (2003) (emphasis added). By definition, then, a categorical exclusion does not create a significant environmental effect; consequently, the cumulative effects analysis required by an environmental assessment need not be performed. That assessment has already been conducted as a part of the creation of the exclusion, which UEC does not challenge in this action.

Because the Seven Mile Project fell within the general confines of Category 14, a point that UEC also does not dispute, the Project was predetermined to have no significant effect. Under the regulation, only if extraordinary circumstances were present would the Forest Service need to perform further analysis in the form of an environmental assessment.

We agree that it may be conceptually possible for a large number of small projects to collectively create conditions that could significantly effect the environment. But the regulation itself contains a provision to address that concern, namely the extraordinary circumstances exception. And the extraordinary circumstances safety-valve is more than capable of addressing specific harms allegedly created by specific projects, which we turn to next.

Accordingly, the Forest Service did not act arbitrarily in failing to conduct any cumulative effects analysis unrelated to the existence of extraordinary circumstances.

2. Extraordinary Circumstances

UEC next claims that even if the Forest Service was not required to do a preliminary cumulative effects analysis, the Forest Service nonetheless exhibited a clear error in judgment in failing to find extraordinary circumstances. To determine whether extraordinary circumstances exist, the Forest Service must consider if the proposed action may have a potentially significant impact on certain "resource conditions." The resource conditions are defined in the Forest Service Handbook as follows:

(a) Federally listed threatened or endangered species or designated critical habitat, species proposed for federal listing or proposed critical habitat, or proposed critical habitat, or Forest Service sensitive species.

(b) Floodplains, wetlands, or municipal watersheds.

(c) Congressionally designated areas such as wilderness, wilderness study areas, or national recreation areas.

(d) Inventoried roadless areas.

(e) Research natural areas.

(f) American Indians' and Alaska Natives' religious or cultural sites.

(g) Archaeological sites, or historic properties or areas.

Here, UEC claims subpart (a) is triggered because the Seven Mile Project will have "guaranteed effects" on the three-toed woodpecker and the northern goshawk. Therefore, UEC argues, the Forest Service was required to perform an environmental assessment. In particular, UEC claims the Forest Service, while finding "no impact" on the northern goshawk, conceded in its Decision Memorandum that the Project "may affect" the three-toed woodpecker. In light of the Forest Service's uncertainty, UEC argues, it should invoke the extraordinary circumstances exception. The Forest Service, on the other hand, interprets the applicable regulations to require a significant environmental effect, not just any effect as asserted by UEC.

The regulatory language guides our analysis. In general, environmental regulations do not place a heavy burden on federal agencies to detail actions which will have only insignificant effects on the health of the environment. For example, "a detailed statement by the responsible official on the environmental impact of [a] proposed action" is required only for "Federal actions significantly affecting the quality of the human environment. . . ." 42 U.S.C. § 4332(C) (emphasis added); see 68 Fed. Reg. 44,598, 44,600 (July 29, 2003) (noting that the Forest Service's "scarce resources" should be concentrated on "major Federal actions and not expend[ed] ... analyzing agency actions where experience has demonstrated the insignificance of effects") (emphasis added).

The analysis is no different with regard to the Forest Service's use of categorical exclusions. As we already discussed, the presence of an extraordinary circumstance precludes the application of a categorical exclusion. And such a circumstance exists only where a proposed action "may have a significant environmental effect." 40 C.F.R. § 1508.4 (emphasis added).

This language plainly requires that an action first may produce a significant effect before a federal agency engage in further analysis. This is only logical given the substantial analytical and evidentiary burdens triggered when a project is ineligible for categorical exclusion. By relying on categorical exclusions, the Forest Service promotes efficiency in its NEPA review process while avoiding unnecessary analysis.

UEC contends that despite this provision, an effect need not be significant, but merely predicted by the Forest Service, to trigger extraordinary circumstances. Thus, even a *de minimis* effect on a threatened species would bar application of the exclusion. In support of this proposition, it cites two statements from the Forest Service Handbook. First, the Handbook notes that "[t]he mere presence of one or more [] resource conditions does not preclude use of a categorical exclusion; instead, [i]t is the degree of the potential effect of a proposed action on these resource conditions that determines whether extraordinary circumstances exist." Second, the Handbook requires the Forest Service to prepare an environmental assessment if, based on its evaluation, "it is uncertain whether the proposed action may have a significant effect on the environment."

While it is true that the Handbook refers to the "degree of the potential effect of a proposed action on a resource condition," the regulation itself requires the potential for a "significant environmental effect." We must interpret the language found in the Handbook in light of the entire regulation and its accompanying policy. We must also be careful not to disrupt the plain language of the regulation itself. Considering the purpose of categorical exclusions in light of these factors and affording the agency's interpretation substantial deference, we conclude that an extraordinary circumstance is found only when there exists a potential for a significant effect on a resource condition.

In this light, we review UEC's contention that the Forest Service erred in evaluating whether the Seven Mile Project would significantly affect the three-toed woodpecker and the northern goshawk. The Forest Service found that although the Seven Mile Project will have "no impact" on the northern goshawk, it "may affect, but is not likely to result in a trend toward federal listing or loss of viability for the three-toed woodpecker."

Although UEC argues the Forest Service expressed "uncertainty" with regard to the two species, the Forest Service decision can hardly be construed to express such doubt. In evaluating the Seven Mile Project's effect on the northern goshawk, the Forest Service relied on helicopter and ground surveys documenting and confirming the lack of goshawk habitat in the proposed area. Explaining the lack of effect on the three-toed woodpecker, the Forest Service stated that while "it may impact individuals, individual territories, and cause displacement within the project area," the Project "would not contribute to a trend towards federal listing or a loss of population viability," since adequate woodpecker habitat would be preserved throughout the forest, and the Project would provide some long-term habitat improvements where intermediate harvesting or under-burning occurred.

These conclusions were based on a review of the species and habitat conducted as a part of the analysis leading to the agency's Decision Memorandum, including a biological evaluation of both species. Additionally, the species monitoring performed by the Forest Service, although not consistently conducted on an annual basis, was more than ample to determine whether extraordinary circumstances existed.

Accordingly, the Forest Service did not violate the APA when it categorically excluded the Seven Mile Project. * * *

NOTES

1. **Identifying the Categorical Exclusion.** What general categorical exclusion(s) had the U.S. Forest Service established? What action did the Forest Service conclude was categorically excluded? Why?

2. **Standard of Review.** What standard of review did the Tenth Circuit use to review the Forest Service's decision that an action fits within a categorical exclusion? Why?

3. **Cumulative Impacts and Categorical Exclusions.** Why did the Utah Environmental Congress argue that the NEPA cumulative impacts analysis was relevant to the Forest Service's ability to use a categorical exclusion? What is the relationship between the cumulative impacts analysis and categorical exclusions, according to the Tenth Circuit? Do you agree?

4. **Categorical Exclusions and Extraordinary Circumstances.** How has the Forest Service defined "extraordinary circumstances" for purposes of Categorical Exclusion 14? How did the Utah Environmental Congress try to argue that extraordinary circumstances existed with respect to the project at issue? How did the Tenth Circuit approach its evaluation of whether extraordinary circumstances existed?

5. **New CEQ Guidance on Categorical Exclusions.** On September 14, 2006, the CEQ issued its proposed new *Guidance on Categorical Exclusions*, which is available at http://ceq.eh.doe.gov/ntf/Proposed_CE_guidance_91406.pdf. The finalized Guidance appeared on November 23, 2010, and is available at http://ceq.hss.doc.gov/ceq_regulations/NEPA_CE_Guidance_Nov232010.pdf. According to the CEQ, "Categorical exclusions are not exemptions or waivers of NEPA review; they are simply one type of NEPA review." CEQ, *Establishing, Applying, and Revising Categorical Exclusions Under the National Environmental Policy Act* 2 (2010).

6. **Other Exceptions to NEPA's Procedures:** A few other exceptions to NEPA's procedures exist. For example, the CEQ by regulation has provided for an emergency circumstances exception. Specifically, "[w]here emergency circumstances make it necessary to take an action with significant environmental impact without observing" normal NEPA procedures, "the Federal agency taking the action should consult with the Council about alternative arrangements." 40 C.F.R. § 1506.11. Application of this exception was set to be tested in *Winter v. NRDC*, 555 U.S. 7 (2008), when the CEQ granted the U.S. Navy permission to use alternative procedures to comply with NEPA in connection with the Navy's training exercises off the coast of southern California involving active sonar, which allegedly can harm marine mammals and other marine species. The basis of the "emergency circumstances" was the district court's injunction restricting how the Navy trained with its sonar. However, the U.S. Supreme Court did not reach the issue of whether the Navy's use of the "emergency circumstances" exception was proper.

* * *

III. THE EIS PROCESS AND THE ADEQUACY OF THE EIS

A. OVERVIEW

Once an agency determines that its proposed project is a major federal action that may significantly affect the quality of the human environment, it must prepare an EIS. To prepare the EIS, the agency must first define the ***scope*** of the EIS. Procedurally, an agency will ordinarily publish a notice of its intent to prepare an EIS in the Federal Register, soliciting comments regarding the scope of that EIS. Substantively, "*[s]cope* consists of the range of actions, alternatives, and impacts to be considered in an environmental impact statement." 40 C.F.R. § 1508.25. The CEQ's regulation further specifies that:

> To determine the scope of environmental impact statements, agencies shall consider 3 types of actions, 3 types of alternatives, and 3 types of impacts. They include:
>
> (a) Actions (other than unconnected single actions) which may be:
>
> (1) Connected actions, which means that they are closely related and therefore should be discussed in the same impact statement. Actions are connected if they:
>
> (i) Automatically trigger other actions which may require environmental impact statements.
>
> (ii) Cannot or will not proceed unless other actions are taken previously or simultaneously.
>
> (iii) Are interdependent parts of a larger action and depend on the larger action for their justification.
>
> (2) Cumulative actions, which when viewed with other proposed actions have cumulatively significant impacts and should therefore be discussed in the same impact statement.
>
> (3) Similar actions, which when viewed with other reasonably foreseeable or proposed agency actions, have similarities that provide a basis for evaluating their environmental consequences together, such as common timing or geography. * * *
>
> (b) Alternatives, which include:
>
> (1) No action alternative.
>
> (2) Other reasonable courses of action.
>
> (3) Mitigation measures (not in the proposed action).
>
> (c) Impacts, which may be:
>
> (1) Direct;
>
> (2) Indirect;
>
> (3) Cumulative.

Id.

Once scoping is complete, the agency prepares a ***draft EIS*** **(DEIS)**. The agency will usually notify the public of the DEIS by publishing a notice of its availability in the Federal Register. Agencies are also increasingly making NEPA documents available through their web sites. The agency must ***circulate*** the DEIS to: "[a]ny Federal agency which has jurisdiction by law or special expertise with respect to any environmental impact involved"; all appropriate Federal, State, and local agencies that can develop environmental standards; "[t]he applicant, if any; [and] [a]ny person, organization, or agency requesting the EIS * * *." 40 C.F.R. § 1502.19. It also must actively invite ***comments*** on the DEIS from all of these groups, from the general public, and from Indian tribes if the proposed action could affect a Tribal reservation. 40 C.F.R. § 1503.1. In general, the agency must allow at least 45 days for comments. 40 C.F.R. § 1506.10(c).

The ***final EIS*** **(FEIS)** often looks very much like the DEIS, except that the agency must respond to the comments it receives on the DEIS as it prepares the FEIS. 40 C.F.R. § 1503.4. When the agency has completed the FEIS, it must circulate it to the same entities to which it sent the DEIS, plus send it to "any person, organization, or agency that commented on the draft EIS." 40 C.F.R. § 1502.19. In addition, the agency will again publish a notice of the FEIS's availability in the Federal Register.

The final step in the EIS process is the ***record of decision*** **(ROD)**. The record of decision is a public document that the agency issues in connection with the decision-making process that: (1) states what the agency's decision is; (2) identifies all of the alternatives that the agency considered, including identifying which were most environmentally preferable; and (3) states "whether all practicable means to avoid or minimize environmental harm from the alternative selected have been adopted, and if not, why they were not." 40 C.F.R. § 1505.2. However, the agency cannot make a final decision on the proposed action until: (1) 90 days after it publishes notice of the DEIS; and (2) 30 days after it publishes notice of the FEIS. 40 C.F.R. § 1506.10(b).

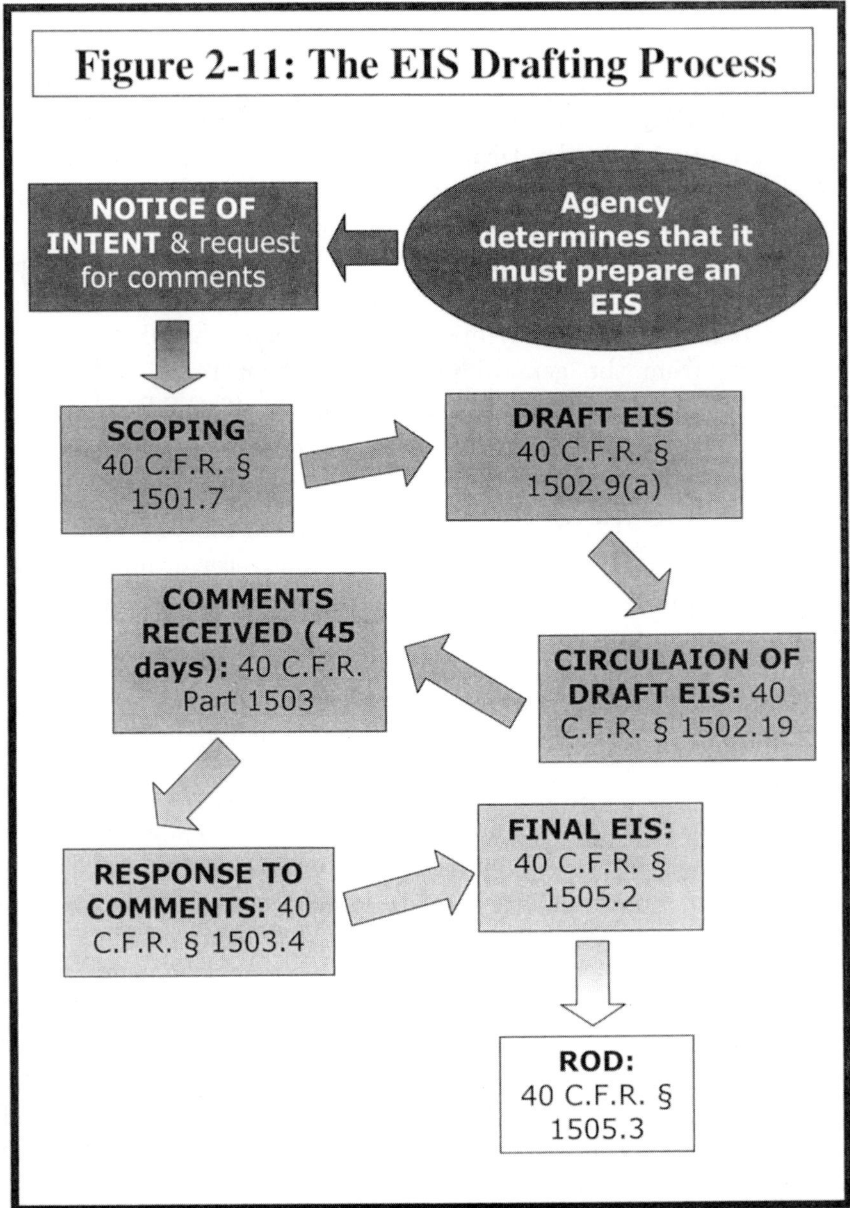

B. CONTENTS OF THE EIS

NEPA itself specifies five elements that any EIS must discuss:

(i) the environmental impact of the proposed action,

(ii) any adverse environmental effects which cannot be avoided should the proposal be implemented,

(iii) alternatives to the proposed action,

(iv) the relationship between local short-term uses of man's environment and the maintenance and enhancement of long-term productivity, and

(v) any irreversible and irretrievable commitments of resources which would be involved in the proposed action should it be implemented.

NEPA § 102(2)(C), 42 U.S.C. § 4332(2)(C).

Under the CEQ's recommended ***format***, the draft and final EISs consist of a cover sheet, a summary, a table of contents, a description of the purpose of and need for the action, an analysis of alternatives, a description of the affected environment, an analysis of the environmental consequences of the proposed action and each of the alternatives, a list of preparers, a list of agencies to whom the EIS is sent, an index, and appendices. 40 C.F.R. § 1502.10. The CEQ's regulations suggest that EISs should normally be less than 150 pages long. 40 C.F.R. § 1502.7. However, EISs for controversial or complex actions rarely meet this suggested length limit.

The "heart of the environmental impact statement" is its ***analysis of alternatives***. 40 C.F.R. § 1502.14. According to the CEQ's regulations, this section "should present the environmental impacts of the proposal and the alternatives in comparative form, thus sharply defining the issues and providing a clear basis for choice among options by the decision-maker and the public." *Id.* Agencies are supposed to "[r]igorously explore and objectively evaluate all reasonable alternatives" and explain why certain alternatives have been eliminated as options. *Id.* § 1502.14(a). One of the alternatives must be the "no action" alternative, *id.* § 1502.14(d), which ensures that the agency at least compares the environmental effects of doing nothing to the environmental effects of its proposed action. In addition, the agency is supposed to identify its preferred alternative in both the draft and final versions of the EIS, *id.* § 1502.14(e), and to "[i]nclude appropriate mitigation measures not already included in the proposed action or alternatives." *Id.* § 1502.14(f).

Two other important elements of the EIS include the ***description of the affected environment*** and the ***description of environmental consequences***. The CEQ's regulations emphasize that the description of the affected environment need not be elaborate. Instead, the EIS "shall succinctly describe the environment of the area(s) to be affected or created by the alternatives under consideration. The descriptions shall be no longer than is necessary to understand the effects of the alternatives." 40 C.F.R. § 1502.15. Thus, the alternatives selected will determine the adequacy of the description of the affected environment. However, the CEQ regulation stresses that "[v]erbose descriptions of the affected environment are themselves no measure of the adequacy of an environmental impact statement." *Id.*

The description of environmental consequences, in turn, "forms the scientific and analytic basis for the comparisons" of the alternatives. 40 C.F.R. § 1502.16. This section of the EIS is supposed to address the issues outlined in subsections (i), (ii), (iv), and (v) of NEPA § 102(2)(C), quoted above. *Id*. More specifically, this section is supposed to discuss:

(a) Direct effects and their significance (§ 1508.8).

(b) Indirect effects and their significance (§ 1508.8).

(c) Possible conflicts between the proposed action and the objectives of Federal, regional, State, and local (and in the case of a reservation, Indian tribe) land use plans, policies and controls for the area concerned (*See* § 1506.2(d)).

(d) The environmental effects of alternatives including the proposed action. * * *

(e) Energy requirements and conservation potential of various alternatives and mitigation measures.

(f) Natural or depletable resource requirements and conservation potential of various alternatives and mitigation measures.

(g) Urban quality, historic and cultural resources, and the design of the built environment, including the reuse and conservation potential of various alternatives and mitigation measures.

(h) Means to mitigate adverse environmental impacts (if not fully covered under § 1502.14(f)).

40 C.F.R. § 1502.16.

Must an EIS include anything beyond these statutory and regulatory requirements? In the following case, the Supreme Court addressed arguments for two such additional requirements—the "worst case" analysis requirement and the mitigation plan requirement.

ROBERTSON v. METHOW VALLEY CITIZENS COUNCIL

490 U.S. 332 (1989).

JUSTICE STEVENS delivered the opinion of the Court.

We granted certiorari to decide two questions of law. As framed by petitioners, they are:

> "1. Whether the National Environmental Policy Act requires federal agencies to include in each environmental impact statement: (a) a fully developed plan to mitigate environmental harm; and (b) a 'worst case' analysis of potential environmental harm if relevant information concerning significant environmental effects is unavailable or too costly to obtain.
>
> "2. Whether the Forest Service may issue a special use permit for recreational use of national forest land in the absence of a fully developed plan to mitigate environmental harm."

Pet. for Cert. i.

Concluding that the Court of Appeals for the Ninth Circuit misapplied the National Environmental Policy Act of 1969 (NEPA), 83 Stat. 852, 42 U.S.C. § 4321 *et seq.*, and gave inadequate deference to the Forest Service's interpretation of its own regulations, we reverse and remand for further proceedings.

I

The Forest Service is authorized by statute to manage the national forests for "outdoor recreation, range, timber, watershed, and wildlife and fish purposes." 74 Stat. 215, 16 U.S.C. § 528. *See also* 90 Stat. 2949, 16 U.S.C. § 1600 *et seq*. Pursuant to that authorization, the Forest Service has issued "special use" permits for the operation of approximately 170 Alpine and Nordic ski areas on federal lands.

* * * Sandy Butte is a 6,000–foot mountain located in the Okanogan National Forest in Okanogan County, Washington. At present Sandy Butte, like the Methow Valley it overlooks, is an unspoiled, sparsely populated area that the District Court characterized as "pristine." In 1968, Congress established the North Cascades National Park and directed the Secretaries of the Interior and Agriculture to agree on the designation of areas within, and adjacent to, the park for public uses, including ski areas. A 1970 study conducted by the Forest Service pursuant to this congressional directive identified Sandy Butte as having the highest potential of any site in the State of Washington for development as a major downhill ski resort.

Figure 2-12: Okanogan National Forest
U.S. Forest Service map.

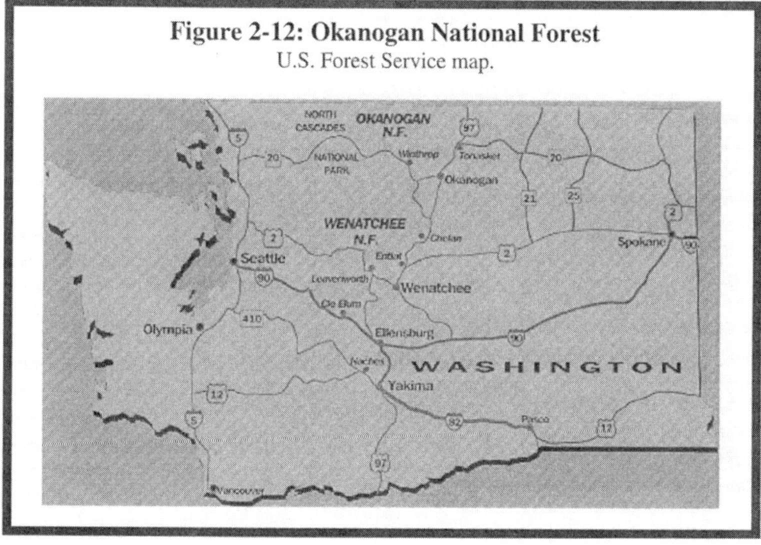

In 1978, Methow Recreation, Inc. (MRI), applied for a special use permit to develop and operate its proposed "Early Winters Ski Resort" on Sandy Butte and an 1,165–acre parcel of land it had acquired adjacent to the National Forest. The proposed development would make use of approximately 3,900 acres of Sandy Butte; would entice visitors to travel long distances to stay at the resort for several days at a time; and would stimulate extensive commercial and residential growth in the vicinity to accommodate both vacationers and staff.

In response to MRI's application, the Forest Service, in cooperation with state and county officials, prepared an EIS known as the Early Winters Alpine Winter Sports Study (Early Winters Study or Study). The stated purpose of the EIS was "to provide the information required to evaluate the potential for skiing at Early Winters" and "to assist in making a decision whether to issue a Special Use Permit for downhill skiing on all or a portion of approximately 3900 acres of National Forest System land." A draft of the Study was completed and circulated in 1982, but release of the final EIS was delayed as Congress considered including Sandy Butte in a proposed wilderness area. When the Washington State Wilderness Act of 1984 was passed, however, Sandy Butte was excluded from the wilderness designation, and the EIS was released.

The Early Winters Study is a printed document containing almost 150 pages of text and 12 appendices. It evaluated five alternative levels of development of Sandy Butte that might be authorized, the lowest being a "no action" alternative and the highest being development of a 16–lift ski area able to accommodate 10,500 skiers at one time. The Study considered the effect of each level of development on water resources, soil, wildlife, air quality, vegetation, and visual quality, as well as land use and transportation in the Methow Valley, probable demographic shifts, the economic market for skiing and other summer and winter recreational activities in the Valley, and the energy requirements for the ski area and related developments. The Study's discussion of possible impacts was not limited to on-site effects, but also, as required by Council on Environmental Quality (CEQ) regulations, *see* 40 CFR § 1502.16(b) (1987), addressed "off-site impacts that each alternative might have on community facilities, socio-economic and other environmental conditions in the Upper Methow Valley." As to off-site effects, the Study explained that "due to the uncertainty of where other public and private lands may become developed," it is difficult to evaluate off-site impacts, and thus the document's analysis is necessarily "not site-specific[]." Finally, the Study outlined certain steps that might be taken to mitigate adverse effects, both on Sandy Butte and in the neighboring Methow Valley, but indicated that these proposed steps are merely conceptual and "will be made more specific as part of the design and implementation stages of the planning process."

The effects of the proposed development on air quality and wildlife received particular attention in the Study. In the chapter on "Environmental Consequences," the first subject discussed is air quality. As is true of other subjects, the discussion included an analysis of cumulative impacts over several years resulting from actions on other lands as well as from the development of Sandy Butte itself. The Study concluded that although the construction, maintenance, and operation of the proposed ski area "will not have a measurable effect on existing or future air quality," the off-site development of private land under all five alternatives—including the "no action" alternative—"will have a significant effect on air quality during severe meteorological inversion periods." The burning of wood for space heat, the Study explained, would constitute the primary cause of diminished air quality, and the damage would increase incrementally with each of the successive levels of proposed development. * * * The Study cautioned that without efforts to mitigate these effects, even under the "no action" alternative, the increase in automobile, fireplace, and wood stove use would reduce air quality below state standards, but added that "[t]he numerous mitigation measures discussed" in the Study "will greatly reduce the impacts presented by the model."

In its discussion of air-quality mitigation measures, the EIS identified actions that could be taken by the county government to mitigate the adverse effects of development, as well as those that the Forest Service itself could implement at the construction stage of the project. The Study suggested that Okanogan County develop an air quality management plan, requiring weatherization of new buildings, limiting the number of wood stoves and fireplaces, and adopting monitoring and enforcement measures. In addition, the Study suggested that the Forest Service require that the master plan include procedures to control dust and to comply with smoke management practices.

In its discussion of adverse effects on area wildlife, the EIS concluded that no endangered or threatened species would be affected by the proposed development and that the only impact on sensitive species was the probable loss of a pair of spotted owls and their progeny. With regard to other wildlife, the Study considered the impact on 75 different indigenous species and predicted that within a decade after development vegetational change and increased human activity would lead to a decrease in population for 31 species, while causing an increase in population for another 24 species on Sandy Butte. Two species, the pine marten and nesting goshawk, would be eliminated altogether from the area of development.

In a comment in response to the draft EIS, the Washington Department of Game voiced a special concern about potential losses to the State's largest migratory deer herd, which uses the Methow Valley as a critical winter range and as its migration route. The state agency estimated that the total population of mule deer in the area most likely to be affected was "better than 30,000 animals" and that "the ultimate impact on the Methow deer herd could exceed a 50 percent reduction in numbers." * * * Because the deer harvest is apparently proportional to the size of the herd, the state agency predicted that "Washington business can expect to lose over $3 million annually from reduced recreational opportunity." The Forest Service's own analysis of the impact on the deer herd was more modest. It first concluded that the actual operation of the ski hill would have only a "minor" direct impact on the herd, but then recognized that the off-site effect of the development "would noticeably reduce numbers of deer in the Methow [Valley] with any alternative." Although its estimate indicated a possible 15 percent decrease in the size of the herd, it summarized the State's contrary view in the text of the EIS, and stressed that off-site effects are difficult to estimate due to uncertainty concerning private development.

As was true of its discussion of air quality, the EIS also described both on-site and off-site mitigation measures. Among possible on-site mitigation possibilities, the Study recommended locating runs, ski lifts, and roads so as to minimize interference with wildlife, restricting access to selected roads during fawning season, and further examination of the effect of the development on mule deer migration routes. Off-site options discussed in the Study included the use of zoning and tax incentives to limit development on deer winter range and migration routes, encouragement of conservation easements, and acquisition and management by local government of critical tracts of land. As with the measures suggested for mitigating the off-site effects on air quality, the proposed options were primarily directed to steps that might be taken by state and local government.

Ultimately, the Early Winters Study recommended the issuance of a permit for development at the second highest level considered—a 16–lift ski area able to accommodate 8,200 skiers at one time. On July 5, 1984, the Regional Forester decided to issue a special use permit as recommended by the Study. In his decision, the Regional Forester found that no major adverse effects would result directly from the federal action, but that secondary effects could include a degradation of existing air quality and a reduction of mule deer winter range. He therefore directed the supervisor of the Okanogan National Forest, both independently and in cooperation with local officials, to identify and implement certain mitigating measures.

Four organizations (respondents) opposing the decision to issue a permit appealed the Regional Forester's decision to the Chief of the Forest Service. After a hearing, he affirmed the Regional Forester's decision. * * *

Thereafter, respondents brought this action under the Administrative Procedure Act, 5 U.S.C. §§ 701–706, to obtain judicial review of the Forest Service's decision. Their principal claim was that the Early Winters Study did not satisfy the requirements of NEPA, 42 U.S.C. § 4332. With the consent of the parties, the case was assigned to a United States Magistrate. After a trial, the Magistrate filed a comprehensive written opinion and concluded that the EIS was adequate. * * *

Concluding that the Early Winters Study was inadequate as a matter of law, the Court of Appeals reversed. The court held that the Forest Service could not rely on " 'the implementation of mitigation measures' " to support its conclusion that the impact on the mule deer would be minor, "since not only has the effectiveness of these mitigation measures not yet been assessed, but the mitigation measures themselves have yet to be developed." It then added that if the agency had difficulty obtaining adequate information to make a reasoned assessment of the environmental impact on the herd, it had a duty to make a so-called "worst case analysis." Such an analysis is " 'formulated on the basis of available information, using reasonable projections of the worst possible consequences of a proposed action.' "

The court found a similar defect in the EIS's treatment of air quality. * * *

* * * II

Section 101 of NEPA declares a broad national commitment to protecting and promoting environmental quality. 83 Stat. 852, 42 U.S.C. § 4331. To ensure that this commitment is "infused into the ongoing programs and actions of the Federal Government, the act also establishes some important 'action-forcing' procedures." 115 Cong. Rec. 40416 (remarks of Sen. Jackson). *See also* S. REP. NO. 91–296, p. 19 (1969) U.S. Code Cong. & Admin. News 1969 p. 2751; *Andrus v. Sierra Club*, 442 U.S. 347, 350 (1979); *Kleppe v. Sierra Club*, 427 U.S. 390, 409 and n.18 (1976). Section 102 thus, among other measures

> "directs that, to the fullest extent possible ... all agencies of the Federal Government shall—
>
> ...
>
> "(C) include in every recommendation or report on proposals for legislation and other major Federal actions significantly affecting the quality of the human environment, a detailed statement by the responsible official on—
>
> "(i) the environmental impact of the proposed action,
>
> "(ii) any adverse environmental effects which cannot be avoided should the proposal be implemented,
>
> "(iii) alternatives to the proposed action,
>
> "(iv) the relationship between local short-term uses of man's environment and the maintenance and enhancement of long-term productivity, and
>
> "(v) any irreversible and irretrievable commitments of resources which would be involved in the proposed action should it be implemented." 83 Stat. 853, 42 U.S.C. § 4332.

The statutory requirement that a federal agency contemplating a major action prepare such an environmental impact statement serves NEPA's "action-forcing" purpose in two important respects. It ensures that the agency, in reaching its decision, will have available, and will carefully consider, detailed information concerning significant environmental impacts; it also guarantees that the relevant information will be made available to the larger audience that may also play a role in both the decisionmaking process and the implementation of that decision.

Simply by focusing the agency's attention on the environmental consequences of a proposed project, NEPA ensures that important effects will not be overlooked or underestimated only to be discovered after resources have been committed or the die otherwise cast. Moreover, the strong precatory language of § 101 of the Act and the requirement that agencies prepare detailed impact statements inevitably bring pressure to bear on agencies "to respond to the needs of environmental quality." 115 Cong. Rec. 40425 (1969) (remarks of Sen. Muskie).

Publication of an EIS, both in draft and final form, also serves a larger informational role. It gives the public the assurance that the agency "has indeed considered environmental concerns in its decisionmaking process," *Baltimore Gas & Electric Co.* [*v. Natural Resources Defense Council*], 462 U.S. [87,] 97 [(1983)], and, perhaps more significantly, provides a springboard for public comment, *see* L. CALDWELL, SCIENCE AND THE NATIONAL ENVIRONMENTAL POLICY ACT 72 (1982). * * *

The sweeping policy goals announced in § 101 of NEPA are thus realized through a set of "action-forcing" procedures that require that agencies take a " 'hard look' at environmental consequences," *Kleppe*, 427 U.S. at 410, n.21 (citation omitted), and that provide for broad dissemination of relevant environmental information. Although these procedures are almost certain to affect the agency's substantive decision, it is now well settled that NEPA itself does not mandate particular results, but simply prescribes the necessary process. * * *

To be sure, one important ingredient of an EIS is the discussion of steps that can be taken to mitigate adverse environmental consequences. The requirement that an EIS contain a detailed discussion of possible mitigation measures flows both from the language of the Act and, more expressly, from CEQ's implementing regulations. Implicit in NEPA's demand that an agency prepare a detailed statement on "any adverse environmental effects which cannot be avoided should the proposal be implemented," 42 U.S.C. § 4332(C)(ii), is an understanding that the EIS will discuss the extent to which adverse effects can be avoided. * * *

There is a fundamental distinction, however, between a requirement that mitigation be discussed in sufficient detail to ensure that environmental consequences have been fairly evaluated, on the one hand, and a substantive requirement that a complete mitigation plan be actually formulated and adopted, on the other. In this case, the off-site effects on air quality and on the mule deer herd cannot be mitigated unless nonfederal government agencies take appropriate action. Since it is those state and local governmental bodies that have jurisdiction over the area in which the adverse effects need be addressed and since they have the authority to mitigate them, it would be incongruous to conclude that the Forest Service has no power to act until the local agencies have reached a final conclusion on what mitigating measures they consider necessary. Even more significantly, it would be inconsistent with NEPA's reliance on procedural mechanisms—as opposed to substantive, result-based standards—to demand the presence of a fully developed plan that will mitigate environmental harm before an agency can act.

We thus conclude that the Court of Appeals erred, first, in assuming that "NEPA requires that 'action be taken to mitigate the adverse effects of major federal actions,'" and, second, in finding that this substantive requirement entails the further duty to include in every EIS "a detailed explanation of specific measures which *will* be employed to mitigate the adverse impacts of a proposed action[]."

III

The Court of Appeals also concluded that the Forest Service had an obligation to make a "worst case analysis" if it could not make a reasoned assessment of the impact of the Early Winters project on the mule deer herd. Such a "worst case analysis" was required at one time by CEQ regulations, but those regulations have since been amended. Moreover, although the prior regulations may well have expressed a permissible application of NEPA, the Act itself does not mandate that uncertainty in predicting environmental harms be addressed exclusively in this manner. Accordingly, we conclude that the Court of Appeals also erred in requiring the "worst case" study.

* * * IV

The Court of Appeals also held that the Forest Service's failure to develop a complete mitigation plan violated the agency's own regulations. Those regulations require that an application for a special use permit include "measures and plans for the protection and rehabilitation of the environment during construction, operation, maintenance, and termination of the project," 36 CFR § 251.54(e)(4) (1988), and that "[e]ach special use authorization ... contain ... [t]erms and conditions which will ... minimize damage to scenic and esthetic values and fish and wildlife habitat and otherwise protect the environment," § 251.56(a)(1)(ii). Applying those regulations, the Court of Appeals concluded that "[s]ince the mitigation 'plan' here at issue is so vague and undeveloped as to be wholly inadequate, ... the Regional Forester's decision to grant the special use permit could be none other than arbitrary, capricious and an abuse of discretion." We disagree.

The Early Winters Study made clear that on-site effects of the development will be minimal and will be easily mitigated. * * * Given the limited on-site effects of the proposed development, the recommended ameliorative steps—which, for example, called for "prompt revegetation of all disturbed areas," and suggested locating "new service roads away from water resources and fawning cover,"—cannot be deemed overly vague or underdeveloped.

The Court of Appeals' conclusion that the Early Winters Study's treatment of possible mitigation measures is inadequate apparently turns on the court's review of the proposed off-site measures. Although NEPA and CEQ regulations require detailed analysis of both on-site and off-site mitigation measures, *see, e.g.*, 40 CFR § 1502.16(b) (1987), there is no basis for concluding that the Forest Service's own regulations must also be read in all cases to condition issuance of a special use permit on consideration (and implementation) of off-site mitigation measures. The Forest Service regulations were promulgated pursuant to a broad grant of authority "to permit the use and occupancy of suitable areas of land within the national forests ... for the purpose of constructing or maintaining hotels, resorts, and any other structures or facilities necessary or desirable for recreation, public convenience, or safety," 16 U.S.C. § 497, and were not based on the more direct congressional concern for environmental quality embodied in NEPA. *See* H.R. REP. NO. 99–709, pt. 1, p. 2 (1986). As is clear from the text of the permit issued to MRI, the Forest Service has decided to implement its mitigation regulations by imposing appropriate controls over MRI's actual development and operation during the term of the permit. It was surely not unreasonable for the Forest Service in this case to have construed those regulations as not extending to actions that might be taken by Okanogan County or the State of Washington to ameliorate the off-site effects of the Early Winters project on air quality and the mule deer herd. This interpretation of the agency's own regulation is not "plainly erroneous or inconsistent with the regulation," and is thus controlling. *Bowles v. Seminole Rock & Sand Co.*, 325 U.S. 410, 414 (1945). *See also Lyng v. Payne*, 476 U.S. 926, 939 (1986); *Udall v. Tallman*, 380 U.S. 1, 16–17 (1965).

V

In sum, we conclude that NEPA does not require a fully developed plan detailing what steps *will* be taken to mitigate adverse environmental impacts and does not require a "worst case analysis." In addition, we hold that the Forest Service has adopted a permissible interpretation of its own regulations. The judgment of the Court of Appeals is accordingly reversed, and the case is remanded for further proceedings consistent with this opinion.

NOTES

1. **The EIS Standard of Review.** What standard of review did the Supreme Court use to assess the adequacy of the Forest Service's EIS in this case? Why?

2. **The Length of An EIS.** Notice the length of the Early Winters Study challenged in this case. An EIS can be a very lengthy document, despite the CEQ's admonitions that it should be short and concise. Why would agencies write such lengthy documents when the regulations do not require—indeed, actively discourage—them?

3. **Discussion of Mitigation in the EIS.** Do NEPA and the CEQ's regulations impose *any* mitigation-related duties on the agency? If so, why did the plaintiffs' mitigation challenge not succeed in this case? How did the Supreme Court's decision on mitigation relate to its view of NEPA as imposing primarily procedural requirements?

4. **The Forest Service's Own Regulations and Mitigation.** In addition to complying with federal statutes that apply to their actions, federal agencies must comply with their own regulations. How did the plaintiffs try to challenge the Forest Service's mitigation plan based on the Forest Service's own regulations? Why did that challenge not succeed? How much deference did the Supreme Court give to the Forest Service's interpretation of its own regulations?

5. **NEPA and the Worst Case.** As the Supreme Court recounted, the CEQ at one point required agencies to engage in a "worst case" analysis. Why would the CEQ impose such a requirement? How does such a requirement further NEPA's purposes?

6. **Changes in Agency Regulations.** Notice that the CEQ had changed its regulations regarding the "worst case" analysis. Just as Congress can amend and change federal statutes, agencies can amend and change their regulations. Occasionally, however, federal courts will accord less deference to an agency when that agency "changes its mind," particularly if the agency appears to be inconsistent in its reasoning. What level of deference did the Supreme Court give to the CEQ's new regulation in this case? Why?

7. **The Adequacy of the EIS: Choice of Alternatives.** An EIS is inadequate and the agency's decision is thus subject to reversal under the APA if the EIS does not contain a required analysis—hence the plaintiffs' arguments in *Methow Valley* that the EIS had to contain a worst case analysis and a full mitigation plan.

Agencies rarely completely omit a required element from an EIS. Nevertheless, even if an agency technically includes all of the required elements in its EIS, challengers can still assert that the agency's execution of those elements is inadequate—*i.e.*, arbitrary and capricious. Much NEPA litigation of this type has been devoted to the agency's choice of alternatives to analyze, especially when the agency appears to have ignored a possible alternative. The one required alternative, as discussed above, is the "no action" alternative. 40 C.F.R. § 1502.14(d). Notice that in *Methow Valley* the EIS at issue did include this alternative.

Otherwise, the federal courts are in general agreement that 40 C.F.R. § 1502.14 (discussed at length at the beginning of this section) "recognizes that a detailed statement of alternatives cannot as a practical matter 'include every alternative device and thought conceivable by the mind of man.' " *City of Bridgeton v. FAA*, 212 F.3d 448, 455 (8th Cir. 2000) (quoting *Vermont Yankee Nuclear Power Corp. v. Natural Resources Defense Council, Inc.*, 435 U.S. 519, 551 (1978)). As such, "[a]n agency * * * is 'entitled to identify *some* parameters and criteria—related to Plan standards—for generating alternatives to which it would devote serious consideration. Without such criteria, an agency could generate countless alternatives.' " *Morongo Band of Mission Indians v. F.A.A.*, 161 F.3d 569, 575 (9th Cir. 1998) (quoting *Resources Ltd. v.*

Robertson, 35 F.3d 1300, 1307 (9th Cir. 1993)). According to the Ninth Circuit, "[t]he 'touchstone for our inquiry is whether an EIS's selection and discussion of alternatives fosters informed decision-making and informed public participation.' " *Id.* (quoting *City of Angoon v. Hodel*, 803 F.2d 1016, 1020 (9th Cir. 1986)). Nevertheless, the "existence of a viable but unexamined alternative renders an environmental impact statement inadequate." *Idaho Conservation League v. Mumma*, 956 F.2d 1508, 1519 (9th Cir. 1992); *see also Dubois v. U.S. Department of Agriculture*, 102 F.3d 1273, 1287 (1st Cir. 1996) (citing the Ninth Circuit for the same proposition).

Given these legal parameters, consider the following facts: The Loon Mountain Recreation Corp. (LMRC) operates a ski resort in the White Mountain National Forest in New Hampshire pursuant to a permit from the U.S. Forest Service. As part of that permit, LMRC can use water from Loon Pond, a pristine mountain lake classified as an "outstanding resource water," for snowmaking. However, under its original permit, LMRC could only "draw down" Loon Pond a total of 18 inches. Skiing at the Loon Mountain facility was booming, and LMRC sought to expand its operations, which required another permit from the Forest Service. In its permit application, LMRC sought to increase its use of Loon Pond for snowmaking; specifically, it sought to be able to draw down the pond a total of 20 feet. The Forest Service prepared a draft EIS that discussed five alternatives, all of which located the expanded ski facilities at the Loon Mountain site and all of which allowed LMRC to increase its draw down of Loon Pond. Commenters expressed consistent concern about the increased use of Loon Pond, for water quality and ecological reasons, and suggested that LMRC should be required to build artificial water storage ponds to supply its snowmaking machines from captured rainfall and snowmelt. Forest Service scientists also expressed concern about increased draw down of Loon Pond. When the Forest Service issued its final EIS, it discussed six alternatives, but all six still located the expanded ski facilities on Loon Mountain and still allowed LMRC to take more water from Loon Pond. In its Record of Decision, the Forest Service decided to implement Alternative #6, which allowed LMRC to draw down Loon Pond a total of 15 feet but mitigated the direct water quality effects on the pond by requiring LMRC to take its water from the more polluted East Branch. Neither the final EIS nor the ROD addressed the storage pond comments, but both the draft and final EISs declared in a single sentence that building an entirely new ski resort somewhere else in the White Mountains National Forest would be prohibitively expensive and have greater adverse environmental impacts on the National Forest as a whole than simply expanding the existing facilities.

If you wanted to challenge the Forest Service's decision on the basis that it had inadequately discussed alternatives in its EIS, what would you argue? Do you think that the court would find the Forest Service's decision to be arbitrary and capricious? *See Dubois v. U.S. Department of Agriculture*, 102 F.3d 1273, 1288 (1st Cir. 1996).

8. **Adequacy of the EIS: Other Arbitrary and Capricious Arguments.** Opponents to proposed federal agency actions have challenged the adequacy of EISs on a variety of grounds. How could you argue that the EIS

was inadequate, and the resulting agency decision arbitrary and capricious, when:

- The U.S. Coast Guard, the U.S. Army Corps of Engineers, the Federal Highway Administration, and the Maine Department of Transportation prepared an EIS for a new port facility on Sears Island, Maine, that limited its secondary impacts analysis to the four light industries that a target market report identified as the most likely tenants of the resulting industrial park, despite designation of the park as being for heavy industry? *See Sierra Club v. Marsh*, 976 F.2d 763, 775–76 (1st Cir. 1992).
- In its ROD, the General Services Administration chose its original location for a federal building project even though the EIS for that project recognized that the selected site was located in a community that was 80% minority and recognized that the building could have impacts on minority-owned businesses?
- In implementing the Truckee Carson Pyramid Lake Water Rights Settlement Act's requirement that the Department of the Interior acquire sufficient water and water rights to sustain 25,000 acres of wetlands in Lahontan Valley, the Department of the Interior prepared an EIS that recognized that agriculture would bear the brunt of the Department's acquisition of water rights but did not estimate the total reduction in agricultural acreage? *See Churchill County v. Norton*, 276 F.3d 1060, 1079–80 (9th Cir. 2001).
- In a Forest Service timber sale, the Forest Service's own scientists concluded that the cumulative impacts of this and other timber sales on lynx, wolverines, fishers, boreal owls, goshawks, flammulated owls, and white-headed woodpeckers had to be assessed with respect to those species' large "landscape scale" range, but the resulting EIS assessed such cumulative impacts instead based on the species' smaller "home scale" range? *See Idaho Sporting Congress, Inc. v. Rittenhouse*, 305 F.3d 957, 973–74 (9th Cir. 2002).

* * *

C. SUPPLEMENTAL ENVIRONMENTAL IMPACT STATEMENTS (SEISS)

Federal agency actions can take a long time to implement and can evolve over time. As a result, a federal agency will sometimes prepare a ***supplemental EIS* (SEIS)** to address evolving environmental issues or new information regarding the environmental impacts of its project.

Is a SEIS ever *required*? According to the CEQ's regulations, agencies:

(1) Shall prepare supplements to either draft or final environmental impact statements if:

(i) The agency makes substantial changes in the proposed action that are relevant to environmental concerns; or

(ii) There are significant new circumstances or information relevant to environmental concerns and bearing on the proposed action or its impacts.

(2) May also prepare supplements when the agency determines that the purposes of the Act will be furthered by doing so.

(3) Shall adopt procedures for introducing a supplement into its formal administrative record, if such a record exists.

(4) Shall prepare, circulate, and file a supplement to a statement in the same fashion (exclusive of scoping) as a draft and final statement unless alternative procedures are approved by the Council.

40 C.F.R. § 1502.9(c).

When is new information sufficient to require a new EIS? The Supreme Court addressed that question in the following case.

MARSH v. OREGON NATURAL RESOURCES COUNCIL

490 U.S. 360 (1989).

JUSTICE STEVENS delivered the opinion of the Court.

This case is a companion to *Robertson v. Methow Valley Citizens Council,* 490 U.S. 332 * * *. It arises out of a controversial decision to construct a dam at Elk Creek in the Rogue River Basin in southwest Oregon. In addition to the question whether an Environmental Impact Statement (EIS) prepared pursuant to the National Environmental Policy Act of 1969 (NEPA), 83 Stat. 852, 42 U.S.C. § 4321 *et seq.,* must contain a complete mitigation plan and a "worst case analysis," which we answered in *Robertson,* it presents the question whether information developed after the completion of the EIS requires that a supplemental EIS be prepared before construction of the dam may continue.

I

In the 1930's in response to recurring floods in the Rogue River Basin, federal and state agencies began planning a major project to control the water supply in the Basin. In 1961 a multiagency study recommended the construction of three large dams: the Lost Creek Dam on the Rogue River, the Applegate Dam on the Applegate River, and the Elk Creek Dam on the Elk Creek near its confluence with the Rogue River. The following year, Congress authorized the Army Corps of Engineers (Corps) to construct the project in accordance with the recommendations of the 1961 study. The Lost Creek Dam was completed in 1977, and the Applegate Dam was completed in 1981.

Plans for the Elk Creek Dam describe a 238–foot-high concrete structure that will control the run-off from 132 square miles of the 135–square-mile Elk Creek watershed. When full, the artificial lake behind the dam will cover 1,290 acres of land, will have an 18–mile shoreline, and will hold 101,000 acre-feet of water. The dam will cost approximately $100 million to construct and will produce annual benefits of almost $5 million. It will be operated in coordination with the nearby Lost Creek Dam, where the control center for both dams will be located. Its "multiport" structure, which will permit discharge of water from any of five levels, makes it possible to regulate, within limits, the temperature, turbidity, and volume of the downstream flow. Although primarily designed to control flooding along the Rogue River, additional project goals include enhanced fishing, irrigation, and recreation.

In 1971, the Corps completed its EIS for the Elk Creek portion of the three-dam project and began development by acquiring 26,000 acres of land and relocating residents, a county road, and utilities. Acknowledging incomplete information, the EIS recommended that further studies concerning the project's likely effect on turbidity be developed. The results of these studies were discussed in a draft supplemental EIS completed in 1975. However, at the request of the Governor of Oregon, further work on the project was suspended, and the supplemental EIS was not filed to make it possible to analyze the actual consequences of the construction of the Lost Creek Dam, which was nearing completion, before continuing with the Elk Creek project. Following that analysis and the receipt of a statement from the Governor that he was "extremely interested in pursuing construction of the Elk Creek Dam," the Corps completed and released its final Environmental Impact Statement, Supplement No. 1 (FEISS), in December 1980.

Because the Rogue River is one of the Nation's premier fishing grounds, the FEISS paid special heed to the effects the dam might have on water quality, fish production, and angling. In its chapter on the environmental effects of the proposed project, the FEISS explained that water quality studies were prepared in 1974 and in 1979 and that "[w]ater temperature and turbidity have received the most attention." Using computer simulation models, the 1974 study predicted that the Elk Creek Dam might, at times, increase the temperature of the Rogue River by one to two degrees Fahrenheit and its turbidity by one to three JTU's [Jackson Turbidity Units, a measure of the suspended matter in water]. The 1979 study took a second look at the potential effect of the Elk Creek Dam on turbidity and, by comparing the 1974 study's predictions concerning the effects of the Lost Creek Dam with actual measurements taken after that dam became operational, it "increased technical confidence in the mathematical model predictions ... and reinforced the conclusions of the 1974 [study]." Based on these studies, the FEISS predicted that changes in the "turbidity regime" would not have any major effect on fish production, but that the combined effect of the Lost Creek and Elk Creek Dams on the turbidity of the Rogue River might, on occasion, impair fishing.

Figure 2-13: The Elk Creek Dam
U.S. Army Corps of Engineers drawing.

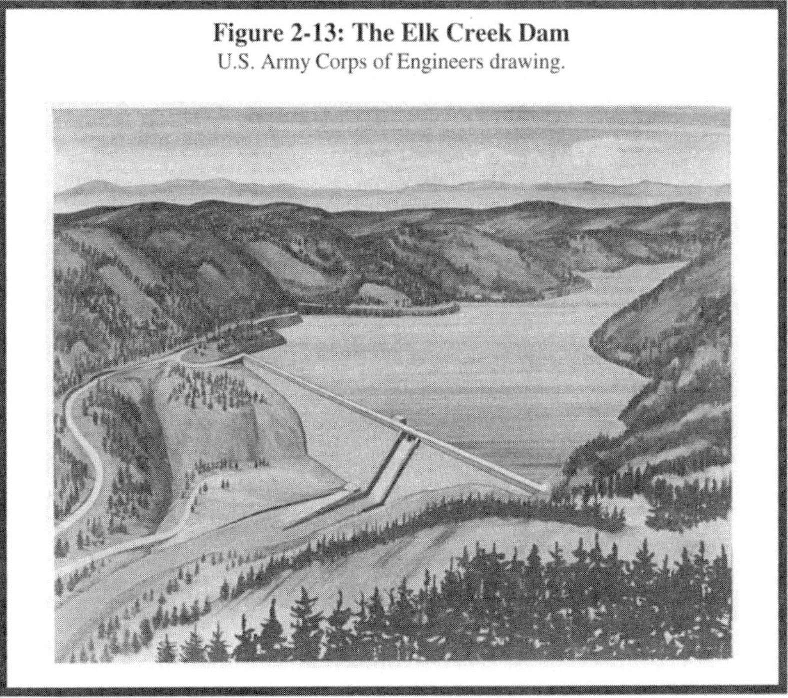

Other adverse effects described by the FEISS include the displacement of wildlife population—including 100 black-tailed deer and 17 elk—and the loss of forest land and vegetation resulting from the inundation of 1,290 acres of land with the creation of the artificial lake. Most significantly, it is perfectly clear that the dam itself would interfere with the migration and spawning of a large number of anadromous fish, but this effect has been mitigated by the construction of a new hatchery. Finally, the FEISS found that no endangered or threatened species would be affected by the project.

On February 19, 1982, after reviewing the FEISS, the Corps' Division Engineer made a formal decision to proceed with construction of the Elk Creek Dam, "subject to the approval of funds by the United States Congress." In his decision, he identified the mitigation measures that had already been taken with respect to the loss of anadromous fish spawning habitat, as well as those that would "most likely" be taken to compensate for the loss of other wildlife habitat. He concluded that the benefits that would be realized from the project "outweigh the economic and environmental costs" and that completion would serve "the overall public interest." In August 1985, Congress appropriated the necessary funds. The dam is now about one-third completed and the creek has been rechanneled through the dam.

II

In October 1985, four Oregon nonprofit corporations filed this action in the United States District Court for the District of Oregon seeking to enjoin construction of the Elk Creek Dam. Their principal claims were that the Corps violated NEPA by failing (1) to consider the cumulative effects of the three dams on the Rogue River Basin in a single EIS; (2) adequately to describe the environmental consequences of the project; (3) to include a "worst case analysis" of uncertain effects; and (4) to prepare a second supplemental EIS to review information developed after 1980.

* * * The new information relied upon by respondents is found in two documents. The first, an internal memorandum prepared by two Oregon Department of Fish and Wildlife (ODFW) biologists based upon a draft ODFW study, suggested that the dam will adversely affect downstream fishing, and the second, a soil survey prepared by the United States Soil Conservation Service (SCS), contained information that might be taken to indicate greater downstream turbidity than did the FEISS. As to both documents, the District Judge concluded that the Corps acted reasonably in relying on the opinions of independent and Corps experts discounting the significance of the new information. * * *

The Court of Appeals reversed. * * * With regard to the failure to prepare a second supplemental EIS, the Court of Appeals concluded that the ODFW and SCS documents brought to light "significant new information" concerning turbidity, water temperature, and epizootic fish disease; that this information, although "not conclusive," is "probably accurate;" and that the Corps' experts failed to evaluate the new information with sufficient care. The court thus concluded that a second supplemental EIS should have been prepared. * * *

III

The subject of postdecision supplemental environmental impact statements is not expressly addressed in NEPA. Preparation of such statements, however, is at times necessary to satisfy the Act's "action-forcing" purpose. NEPA does not work by mandating that agencies achieve particular substantive environmental results. Rather, NEPA promotes its sweeping commitment to "prevent or eliminate damage to the environment and biosphere" by focusing Government and public attention on the environmental effects of proposed agency action. 42 U.S.C. § 4321. By so focusing agency attention, NEPA ensures that the agency will not act on incomplete information, only to regret its decision after it is too late to correct. *See Robertson*, 490 U.S. at 349. Similarly, the broad dissemination of information mandated by NEPA permits the public and other government agencies to react to the effects of a proposed action at a meaningful time. 490 U.S. at 349–350. It would be incongruous with this approach to environmental protection, and with the Act's manifest concern with preventing uninformed action, for the blinders to adverse environmental effects, once unequivocally removed, to be restored prior to the completion of agency action simply because the relevant proposal has received initial approval. As we explained in *TVA v. Hill*, 437 U.S. 153, 188, n.34 (1978), although "it would make sense to hold NEPA inapplicable at some point in the life of a project, because the agency would no longer have a meaningful opportunity to *weigh* the benefits of the project versus the detrimental effects on the environment," up to that point, "NEPA cases have generally required agencies to file environmental impact statements when the remaining governmental action would be environmentally 'significant.' "

This reading of the statute is supported by Council on Environmental Quality (CEQ) and Corps regulations, both of which make plain that at times supplementation is required. The CEQ regulations, which we have held are entitled to substantial deference, *see Robertson*, 490 U.S. at 355–356; *Andrus v. Sierra Club*, 442 U.S. 347, 358 (1979), impose a duty on all federal agencies to prepare supplements to either draft or final EIS's if there "are significant new circumstances or information relevant to environmental concerns and bearing on the proposed action or its impacts." Similarly, the Corps' own NEPA implementing regulations require the preparation of a supplemental EIS if "new significant impact information, criteria or circumstances relevant to environmental considerations impact on the recommended plan or proposed action."[17]

The parties are in essential agreement concerning the standard that governs an agency's decision whether to prepare a supplemental EIS. They agree that an agency should apply a "rule of reason," and the cases they cite in support of this standard explicate this rule in the same basic terms. These cases make clear that an agency need not supplement an EIS every time new information comes to light after the EIS is finalized. To require otherwise would render agency decisionmaking intractable, always awaiting updated information only to find the new information outdated by the time a decision is made. On the other hand, and as the petitioners concede, NEPA does require that agencies take a "hard look" at the environmental effects of their planned action, even after a proposal has received initial approval. Application of the "rule of reason" thus turns on the value of the new information to the still pending decisionmaking process. In this respect the decision whether to prepare a supplemental EIS is similar to the decision whether to prepare an EIS in the first instance: If there remains "major Federal actio[n]" to occur, and if the new information is sufficient to show that the remaining action will "affec[t] the quality of the human environment" in a significant manner

---

17. The Corps regulations provide in relevant part:

"*Supplements.* A Supplement to the draft or final EIS on file will be prepared whenever significant impacts resulting from changes in the proposed plan or new significant impact information, criteria or circumstances relevant to environmental considerations impact on the recommended plan or proposed action as discussed in 40 CFR 1502.9(c). A supplement to a draft EIS will be prepared, filed and circulated in the same manner as a draft EIS. * * * A supplement to a final EIS will be prepared and filed first as a *draft* supplement and then as a *final* supplement. * * * "

33 CFR § 230.11(b) (1987).

or to a significant extent not already considered, a supplemental EIS must be prepared. *Cf.* 42 U.S.C. § 4332(2)(C).

The parties disagree, however, on the standard that should be applied by a court that is asked to review the agency's decision. Petitioners argue that the reviewing court need only decide whether the agency decision was "arbitrary and capricious," whereas respondents argue that the reviewing court must make its own determination of reasonableness to ascertain whether the agency action complied with the law. In determining the proper standard of review, we look to § 10(e) of the Administrative Procedure Act (APA), 5 U.S.C. § 706, which empowers federal courts to "hold unlawful and set aside agency action, findings, and conclusions" if they fail to conform with any of six specified standards. We conclude that review of the narrow question before us whether the Corps' determination that the FEISS need not be supplemented should be set aside is controlled by the "arbitrary and capricious" standard of § 706(2)(A).

* * * The question presented for review in this case is a classic example of a factual dispute the resolution of which implicates substantial agency expertise. Respondents' claim that the Corps' decision not to file a second supplemental EIS should be set aside primarily rests on the contentions that the new information undermines conclusions contained in the FEISS, that the conclusions contained in the ODFW memorandum and the SCS survey are accurate, and that the Corps' expert review of the new information was incomplete, inconclusive, or inaccurate. The dispute thus does not turn on the meaning of the term "significant" or on an application of this legal standard to settled facts. Rather, resolution of this dispute involves primarily issues of fact. Because analysis of the relevant documents "requires a high level of technical expertise," we must defer to "the informed discretion of the responsible federal agencies." *Kleppe v. Sierra Club*. 427 U.S. 390, 412 (1976). Under these circumstances, we cannot accept respondents' supposition that review is of a legal question and that the Corps' decision "deserves no deference." Accordingly, as long as the Corps' decision not to supplement the FEISS was not "arbitrary or capricious," it should not be set aside.

* * * IV

Respondents' argument that significant new information required the preparation of a second supplemental EIS rests on two written documents. The first of the documents is the so-called "Cramer Memorandum," an intraoffice memorandum prepared on February 21, 1985, by two scientists employed by ODFW. The Cramer Memorandum, in turn, relied on a draft ODFW study describing the effects of the Lost Creek Dam on fish production. The second document is actually a series of maps prepared in 1982 by SCS to illustrate the composition of soil near the Elk Creek shoreline. The information was provided to the Corps for use in managing the project. Although respondents contend that the maps contained data relevant to a prediction of the dam's impact on downstream turbidity, the maps do not purport to shed any light on that subject. Nor do they purport to discuss any conditions that had changed since the FEISS was completed in 1980. The Corps responded to the claim that these documents demonstrate the need for supplementation of the FEISS by preparing a formal Supplemental Information Report, dated January 10, 1986 * * * (hereinafter SIR). The SIR explained: "While it is clear based upon our review that this information does not require additional NEPA documentation, Corps regulations provide that a Supplemental Information Report can be used to disseminate information on points of concern regarding environmental impacts set forth in the EIS."

The significance of the Cramer Memorandum and the SCS survey is subject to some doubt. Before respondents commenced this litigation in October 1985, no one had suggested that either document constituted the kind of new information that made it necessary or appropriate to supplement the FEISS. Indeed, the record indicates that the Corps was not provided with a copy of the Cramer Memorandum until after the lawsuit was filed. Since the probative value of that document depends largely on the expert qualification of its authors, the fact that they did not see fit to promptly apprise the Corps of their concern—or to persuade ODFW to do so—tends to discount the significance of those concerns. Similarly, the absence of any pretrial expression of concern about the soil characteristics described in the 1982 SCS survey is consistent with the view that it shed little, if any, new light on the turbidity potential of the dam. Yet, even if both documents had given rise to prompt expressions of concern, there are good reasons for concluding that they did not convey significant new information requiring supplementation of the FEISS.

The Court of Appeals attached special significance to two concerns discussed in the Cramer Memorandum: the danger that an increase in water temperature downstream during fall and early winter will cause an early emergence and thus reduce survival of spring chinook fry and the danger that the dam will cause high fish mortality from an epizootic disease. Both concerns were based partly on fact and partly on speculation.

With respect to the first, the Cramer Memorandum reported that the authors of the draft ODFW study had found that warming of the Rogue River caused by the Lost Creek Dam had reduced the survival of spring chinook fry; however, the extent of that reduction was not stated, nor did the memorandum estimate the extent of warming to be expected due to closure of the Elk Creek Dam. Instead, the memorandum estimated that an increase of only one degree centigrade in river temperature in January would decrease survival of spring chinook "from 60–80%." The authors of the memorandum concluded that because the Elk Creek Dam is likely to increase the temperature of the Rogue River, further evaluation of this effect should be completed "before ODFW sets its final position on this project."

The Corps' response to this concern in its SIR acknowledged that the "biological reasoning is sound and has been recognized for some time," but then explained why the concern was exaggerated. The SIR stressed that because the model employed by ODFW had not been validated, its predictive capability was uncertain. Indeed, ODFW scientists subsequently recalculated the likely effect of a one-degree centigrade increase in temperature, adjusting its estimate of a 60–to–80 percent loss downward to between 30 and 40 percent. Moreover, the SIR supplied a variable missing in the Cramer Memorandum, suggesting that the Elk Creek Dam would, in most cases, either reduce or leave unchanged the temperature of the Rogue River. Discernible increases were only found in July, August, and December of the study year, and even during those months the maximum temperature increase was only 0.6 degrees centigrade. Finally, the SIR observed that the Cramer Memorandum failed to take into account the dam's beneficial effects, including its ability to reduce peak downstream flow during periods of egg incubation and fry rearing and its ability to reduce outflow temperature through use of the multiport structure. Given these positive factors, the Corps concluded that any adverse effects of the 0.6–degree temperature increase can be offset.

With respect to the second concern emphasized by the Court of Appeals, the Cramer Memorandum reported the fact that "an unprecedented 76% of the fall chinook in 1979 and 32% in 1980 were estimated to have died before spawning" and then speculated that the Lost Creek Dam, which had been completed in 1977, was a contributing cause of this unusual mortality. The Corps responded to this by pointing out that the absence of similar epizootics after the closure of the Applegate Dam and the evidence of prespawning mortality in the Rogue River prior to the closing of the Lost Creek Dam were inconsistent with the hypothesis suggested in the Cramer Memorandum. In addition, the Corps noted that certain diseased organisms thought to have been the cause of the unusually high mortality rates were not found in the outflow from the Lost Creek Dam.

In thus concluding that the Cramer Memorandum did not present significant new information requiring supplementation of the FEISS, the Corps carefully scrutinized the proffered information. Moreover, in disputing the accuracy and significance of this information, the Corps did not simply rely on its own experts. Rather, two independent experts hired by the Corps to evaluate the ODFW study on which the Cramer Memorandum was premised found significant fault in the methodology and conclusions of the study. We also think it relevant that the Cramer Memorandum did not express the official position of ODFW. In preparing the memorandum, the authors noted that the agency had "adopted a neutral stand on Elk Creek Dam" and argued that new information raised the question whether "our agency should continue to remain neutral." The concerns disclosed in the memorandum apparently were not sufficiently serious to persuade ODFW to abandon its neutral position.

The Court of Appeals also expressed concern that the SCS survey, by demonstrating that the soil content in the Elk Creek watershed is different than assumed in the FEISS, suggested a greater turbidity potential than indicated in the FEISS. In addition, the court observed that ODFW scientists believe that logging and road building in the Elk Creek watershed has caused increased soil disturbance resulting in higher turbidity than forecast by the FEISS. As to this latter point, the SIR simply concluded that although turbidity may have increased in the early 1980's due to logging, "watershed recovery appears to have occurred to reduce the turbidity levels back to those of the 1970's." The implications of the SCS soil survey are of even less concern. As discussed in the FEISS, water quality studies were conducted in 1974 and 1979 using computer simulation models. The 1974 study indicated that turbidity in the Rogue River would increase by no more than one to three JTU's as a result of the Elk Creek Dam, and the 1979 study verified this result. These studies used water samples taken from Elk Creek near the proposed dam site and from near the Lost Creek Dam, and thus did not simply rely on soil composition maps in drawing their conclusions. Although the SIR did not expressly comment on the SCS survey, in light of the in-depth 1974 and 1979 studies, its conclusion that "the turbidity effects are not expected to differ from those described in the 1980 EISS" surely provided a legitimate reason for not preparing a supplemental FEISS to discuss the subject of turbidity.

There is little doubt that if all of the information contained in the Cramer Memorandum and SCS survey was both new and accurate, the Corps would have been required to prepare a second supplemental EIS. It is also clear that, regardless of its eventual assessment of the significance of this information, the Corps had a duty to take a hard look at the proffered evidence. However, having done so and having determined based on careful scientific analysis that the new information was of exaggerated importance, the Corps acted within the dictates of NEPA in concluding that supplementation was unnecessary. Even if another decisionmaker might have reached a contrary result, it was surely not "a clear error of judgment" for the Corps to have found that the new and accurate information contained in the documents was not significant and that the significant information was not new and accurate. As the SIR demonstrates, the Corps conducted a reasoned evaluation of the relevant information and reached a decision that, although perhaps disputable, was not "arbitrary or capricious." * * *

NOTES

1. **The Rest of the Story.** Given the Supreme Court's decision in this case, one would expect that the Army Corps finished the Elk Creek dam. Instead, growing concern about the salmon runs in Elk Creek—Oregon's governor, the Oregon Department of Fish and Wildlife, and the U.S. Fish & Wildlife Service (USFWS) were all calling for the dam's removal to protect the salmon and steelhead runs—led the Army Corps to prepare a second SEIS in 1991. The Oregon Natural Resources Council (ONRC) challenged this SEIS in the federal courts, arguing that it violated NEPA. Although the Oregon

District Court upheld the SEIS, the Ninth Circuit reversed in April 1995, deciding that the SEIS was too limited in the scope of its cumulative impacts analysis. The Ninth Circuit also awarded attorney fees to ONRC. *See generally Oregon Natural Resources Council v. Marsh*, 52 F.3d 1485 (9th Cir. 1995). According to the Army Corps, "Due to the cost and time required to respond to the Ninth Circuit court opinion without any certainty of success, and the current restrictive federal budgeting climate, the Corps decided not to perform the NEPA studies necessary to remove the [Ninth Circuit's 1995] injunction against completion of the project." Operations Division, Portland District, U.S. Army Corps of Engineers, *Rogue River Basin Projects*, https://www.nwp.usace.army.mil/op/r/home.asp (last updated April 27, 2006). The Army Corps proposed instead to provide for fish passage through the unfinished dam by cutting a 150–foot-wide notch through it, and when Congress passed the Energy and Water Development Appropriations Act for fiscal year 1997, it provided the Army Corps with funds to complete the project. Fish passage became a priority in June 1977, when the USFWS and National Marine Fisheries Service (NMFS) listed the coho salmon as a threatened species under the Endangered Species Act.

However, nothing is ever easy when it comes to breaching a dam, even a partially completed one. Despite ONRC's March 2000 lawsuit alleging that the dam was violating the Endangered Species Act and NMFS's January 2001 Biological Opinion concluding that anything other than notching the dam risked jeopardizing the continued existence of the Elk Creek coho salmon, Representative Greg Walden (R–OR) actively opposed notching the dam for fish passage, and Jackson County, Oregon, wanted to preserve the option of completing the dam so that the county could use the resulting reservoir for water storage. In early March 2003, President George W. Bush signed a law that prohibited the Army Corps from notching the dam. Instead, the Army Corps had to catch adult salmon and steelhead at the dam's base and truck them upstream to their spawning grounds. At the time, the Army Corps expected to finish more permanent facilities for catching and transporting salmon and steelhead by fall 2006, at an estimated cost of $8 million to build the facilities and $150,000 per year to operate them.

By late 2007, $100 million had been spent on the Elk Creek Dam, which would require an additional $70 million to complete. Notching the dam, in contrast, would cost $7 million, and the Army Corps had expressed a strong preference that the dam be removed. Nevertheless, in December 2007 the Jackson County Board of Commissioners and Shady Grove City Council resisted, arguing that no flood control studies had been done since before the building of the dams. These two local governments even tried to persuade the Federal Emergency Management Agency (FEMA) to become involved in the debate.

However, the Elk Creek Dam debate is finally over. On January 24, 2008, the federal government announced that it would notch the Elk Creek Dam to improve fish passage. The blast to notch the dam occurred on July 15, 2008, opening Elk Creek to both fish and recreational boaters. WaterWatch of Oregon provides both a video of the blast and photos of the re-opened river. *Notching the Elk Creek Dam*, http://waterwatch.org/programs/freeing-the-rogue-river/notching-the-elk-creek-dam.

2. **The CEQ Standard for Preparing a Supplemental EIS.** When, in general, is a SEIS required, according to the Supreme Court? How does this standard, which purports to interpret the CEQ's regulation, actually compare to the CEQ's regulations?

3. **The Army Corps' Standard for Preparing a Supplemental EIS.** When must the Army Corps prepare a SEIS, according to its own regulations? How does this standard compare to the standard in the CEQ's regulations? How does it compare to the Supreme Court's standard?

4. **The Standard of Review.** According to the Supreme Court, what standard of review should federal courts use to review an agency's decision not to prepare a SEIS? Why? How did conflicting expert opinions affect its application of this standard?

5. **The Army Corps' Decision Not to Prepare a SEIS.** This is a good case for seeing the practical effects of the APA standard of review. The Supreme Court did *not* decide whether the Army Corps of Engineers was "correct" in any absolute sense, or even whether the Army Corps made the "best" decision, given the facts. It merely determined whether the Army Corps' assessment of the facts in deciding whether or not to prepare the SEIS was "arbitrary and capricious." As the Supreme Court noted, however, the Army Corps did have a duty to take a "hard look" at the new evidence and to explain its decision not to prepare a SEIS on the basis of that evidence. Why did the Supreme Court uphold the Army Corps' decision not to prepare a SEIS? Could the Army Corps have legitimately reached the opposite conclusion?

6. **Supplemental EAs.** Might an agency have to supplement an EA/FONSI in light of new information? Although the CEQ's regulations do not directly address this issue, the federal Courts of Appeals are in wide agreement that significant new information can require re-evaluation of an EA and FONSI. *Highway J Citizens Group v. Mineta*, 349 F.3d 938, 959–60 (7th Cir. 2003); *Southern Utah Wilderness Alliance v. Norton*, 301 F.3d 1217, 1238 (10th Cir. 2002); *Price Road Neighborhood Ass'n, Inc. v. U.S. Department of Transportation*, 113 F.3d 1505, 1509–10 (9th Cir. 1997); *Town of Orangetown v. Ruckelshaus*, 740 F.2d 185, 189–90 (2d Cir. 1984). *But see Newton County Wildlife Ass'n v. Rogers*, 141 F.3d 803, 808 (8th Cir. 1998) (holding that plaintiffs could not use post-sale evidence to challenge Forest Service timber sales under NEPA). There is also significant agreement that "[t]he standard for preparing a supplemental EA is the same as for preparing an SEIS." *Southern Utah Wilderness Alliance v. Norton*, 301 F.3d 1217, 1238 n.19 (10th Cir. 2002); *see also Idaho Sporting Congress v. Thomas*, 137 F.3d 1146, 1152 (9th Cir. 1998) (setting the same standard). Why would the federal courts be so willing to require such re-evaluation? How does this rule serve the purposes of NEPA?

* * *

IV. REMEDIES FOR NEPA VIOLATIONS

As the Makah whaling case made clear, crafting adequate remedies for violations of NEPA's procedural requirements can be difficult. As a general matter, courts will generally declare a federal agency's decision made in violation of NEPA invalid and send the agency back to comply with NEPA. However, what happens if regulated entities are already acting in reliance on that prior decision? How far can a court act to un-do the agency decision that violated NEPA?

The U.S. Supreme Court recently addressed these issues in the following case. As you read the Court's decision, try to determine what remedy the district court *could* have issued instead.

MONSANTO CO. v. GEERTSON SEED FARMS

___ U.S. ___, 130 S.Ct. 2743 (2010).

ALITO, J., delivered the opinion of the Court, in which ROBERTS, C.J., and SCALIA, KENNEDY, THOMAS, GINSBURG, and SOTOMAYOR, JJ., joined. STEVENS, J., filed a dissenting opinion. BREYER, J., took no part in the consideration or decision of the case.

This case arises out of a decision by the Animal and Plant Health Inspection Service (APHIS) to deregulate a variety of genetically engineered alfalfa. The District Court held that APHIS violated the National Environmental Policy Act of 1969 (NEPA), 42 U.S.C. § 4321 *et seq.*, by issuing its deregulation decision without first completing a detailed assessment of the environmental consequences of its proposed course of action. To remedy that violation, the District Court vacated the agency's decision completely deregulating the alfalfa variety in question; ordered APHIS not to act on the deregulation petition in whole or in part until it had completed a detailed environmental review; and enjoined almost all future planting of the genetically engineered alfalfa pending the completion of that review. The Court of Appeals affirmed the District Court's entry of permanent injunctive relief. The main issue now in dispute concerns the breadth of that relief. For the reasons set forth below, we reverse and remand for further proceedings.

I

A

The Plant Protection Act (PPA), 7 U.S.C. § 7701 *et seq.*, provides that the Secretary of the Department of Agriculture (USDA) may issue regulations "to prevent the introduction of plant pests into the United States or the dissemination of plant pests within the United States." § 7711(a). The Secretary has delegated that authority to APHIS, a division of the USDA. 7 CFR §§ 2.22(a), 2.80(a)(36) (2010). Acting pursuant to that delegation, APHIS has promulgated regulations governing "the introduction of organisms and products altered or produced through genetic engineering that are plant pests or are believed to be plant pests." See § 340.0(a)(2) and n. 1. Under those regulations, certain genetically engineered plants are presumed to be "plant pests"—and thus "regulated articles" under the PPA—until APHIS determines otherwise. However, any person may petition APHIS for a determination that a regulated article does not present a plant pest risk and therefore should not be subject to the applicable regulations. 7 U.S.C. § 7711(c)(2); 7 CFR § 340.6. APHIS may grant such a petition in whole or in part. § 340.6(d)(3).

In deciding whether to grant nonregulated status to a genetically engineered plant variety, APHIS must comply with NEPA, which requires federal agencies "to the fullest extent possible" to prepare an environmental impact statement (EIS) for "every recommendation or report on proposals for legislation and other major Federal actio[n] significantly affecting the quality of the human environment." 42 U.S.C. § 4332(2)(C). * * *

B

This case involves Roundup Ready Alfalfa (RRA), a kind of alfalfa crop that has been genetically engineered to be tolerant of glyphosate, the active ingredient of the herbicide Roundup. Petitioner Monsanto Company (Monsanto) owns the intellectual property rights to RRA. Monsanto licenses those rights to co-petitioner Forage Genetics International (FGI), which is the exclusive developer of RRA seed.

APHIS initially classified RRA as a regulated article, but in 2004 petitioners sought nonregulated status for two strains of RRA. In response, APHIS prepared a draft EA assessing the likely environmental impact of the requested deregulation. It then published a notice in the Federal Register advising the public of the deregulation petition and soliciting public comments on its draft EA. After considering the hundreds of public comments that it received, APHIS issued a Finding of No Significant Impact and decided to deregulate RRA unconditionally and without preparing an EIS. Prior to this decision, APHIS had authorized almost 300 field trials of RRA conducted over a period of eight years.

Approximately eight months after APHIS granted RRA nonregulated status, respondents (two conventional alfalfa seed farms and environmental groups concerned with food safety) filed this action against the Secretary of Agriculture and certain other officials in Federal District Court, challenging APHIS's decision to completely deregulate RRA. Their complaint alleged violations of NEPA, the Endangered Species Act of 1973 (ESA), 16 U.S.C. § 1531 *et seq.*, and the PPA. Respondents did not seek preliminary injunctive relief pending resolution of those claims. Hence, RRA enjoyed nonregulated status for approximately two years. During that period, more than 3,000 farmers in 48 States planted an estimated 220,000 acres of RRA.

In resolving respondents' NEPA claim, the District Court accepted APHIS's determination that RRA does not have any harmful health effects on humans or livestock. Nevertheless, the District Court held that APHIS violated NEPA by deregulating RRA without first preparing an EIS. * * * In light of its determination that the deregulation decision ran afoul of NEPA, the District Court dismissed without prejudice respondents' claims under the ESA and PPA.

* * * III

A

The District Court sought to remedy APHIS's NEPA violation in three ways: First, it vacated the agency's decision completely deregulating RRA; second, it enjoined APHIS from deregulating RRA, in whole or in part, pending completion of the mandated EIS; and third, it entered a nationwide injunction prohibiting almost all future planting of RRA. Because petitioners and the Government do not argue otherwise, we assume without deciding that the District Court acted lawfully in vacating the deregulation decision. We therefore address only the latter two aspects of the District Court's judgment. Before doing so, however, we provide a brief overview of the standard governing the entry of injunctive relief.

B

"[A] plaintiff seeking a permanent injunction must satisfy a four-factor test before a court may grant such relief. A plaintiff must demonstrate: (1) that it has suffered an irreparable injury; (2) that remedies available at law, such as monetary damages, are inadequate to compensate for that injury; (3) that, considering the balance of hardships between the plaintiff and defendant, a remedy in equity is warranted; and (4) that the public interest would not be disserved by a permanent injunction." The traditional four-factor test applies when a plaintiff seeks a permanent injunction to remedy a NEPA violation.

* * * An injunction should issue only if the traditional four-factor test is satisfied. In contrast, the [petitioners] appear to presume that an injunction is the proper remedy for a NEPA violation except in unusual circumstances. No such thumb on the scales is warranted. * * *

* * * [T]he injunctive relief granted here cannot stand.

C

We first consider whether the District Court erred in enjoining APHIS from partially deregulating RRA during the pendency of the EIS process.

The relevant part of the District Court's judgment states that, "[b]efore granting Monsanto's deregulation petition, *even in part,* the federal defendants shall prepare an environmental impact statement." The plain text of the order prohibits *any* partial deregulation, not just the particular partial deregulation embodied in APHIS's proposed judgment. We think it is quite clear that the District Court meant just what it said. * * *

In our view, none of the traditional four factors governing the entry of permanent injunctive relief supports the District Court's injunction prohibiting partial deregulation. To see why that is so, it is helpful to understand how the injunction prohibiting a partial deregulation fits into the broader dispute between the parties.

Respondents in this case brought suit under the APA to challenge a particular agency order: APHIS's decision to *completely* deregulate RRA. The District Court held that the order in question was procedurally defective, and APHIS decided not to appeal that determination. At that point, it was for the agency to decide whether and to what extent it would pursue a *partial* deregulation. If the agency found, on the basis of a new EA, that a limited and temporary deregulation satisfied applicable statutory and regulatory requirements, it could proceed with such a deregulation even if it had not yet finished the onerous EIS required for complete deregulation. If and when the agency were to issue a partial deregulation order, any party aggrieved by that order could bring a separate suit under the Administrative Procedure Act to challenge the particular deregulation attempted. See 5 U.S.C. § 702.

* * * The District Court may well have acted within its discretion in refusing to craft a judicial remedy that would have *authorized* the continued planting and harvesting of RRA while the EIS is being prepared. It does not follow, however, that the District Court was within its rights in *enjoining* APHIS from allowing such planting and harvesting pursuant to the authority vested in the agency by law. When the District Court entered its permanent injunction, APHIS had not yet exercised its authority to partially deregulate RRA. Until APHIS actually seeks to effect a partial deregulation, any judicial review of such a decision is premature.

* * * Based on the analysis set forth above, it is clear that the order enjoining any deregulation whatsoever does not satisfy the traditional four-factor test for granting permanent injunctive relief. Most importantly, respondents cannot show that they will suffer irreparable injury if APHIS is allowed to proceed with any partial deregulation, for at least two independent reasons.

First, if and when APHIS pursues a partial deregulation that arguably runs afoul of NEPA, respondents may file a new suit challenging such action and seeking appropriate preliminary relief. See 5 U.S.C. §§ 702, 705. Accordingly, a permanent injunction is not now needed to guard against any present or imminent risk of likely irreparable harm.

Second, a partial deregulation need not cause respondents any injury at all, much less irreparable injury; if the scope of the partial deregulation is sufficiently limited, the risk of gene flow to their crops could be virtually nonexistent. * * * In any case, the District Court's order prohibiting *any* partial deregulation improperly relieves respondents of their burden to make the requisite evidentiary showing.

* * * In sum, we do not know whether and to what extent APHIS would seek to effect a limited deregulation during the pendency of the EIS process if it were free to do so; we do know that the vacatur of APHIS's deregulation decision means that virtually no RRA can be grown or sold until such time as a new deregulation decision is in place, and we also know that any party aggrieved by a hypothetical future deregulation decision will have ample opportunity to challenge it, and to seek appropri-

ate preliminary relief, if and when such a decision is made. In light of these particular circumstances, we hold that the District Court did not properly exercise its discretion in enjoining a partial deregulation of any kind pending APHIS's preparation of an EIS. It follows that the Court of Appeals erred in affirming that aspect of the District Court's judgment.

D

We now turn to petitioners' claim that the District Court erred in entering a nationwide injunction against planting RRA. * * *

First, the impropriety of the District Court's broad injunction against planting flows from the impropriety of its injunction against partial deregulation. If APHIS may partially deregulate RRA before preparing a full-blown EIS—a question that we need not and do not decide here—farmers should be able to grow and sell RRA in accordance with that agency determination. Because it was inappropriate for the District Court to foreclose even the possibility of a partial and temporary deregulation, it necessarily follows that it was likewise inappropriate to enjoin any and all parties from acting in accordance with the terms of such a deregulation decision.

Second, respondents have represented to this Court that the District Court's injunction against planting does not have any meaningful practical effect independent of its vacatur. An injunction is a drastic and extraordinary remedy, which should not be granted as a matter of course. If a less drastic remedy (such as partial or complete vacatur of APHIS's deregulation decision) was sufficient to redress respondents' injury, no recourse to the additional and extraordinary relief of an injunction was warranted.

E

In sum, the District Court abused its discretion in enjoining APHIS from effecting a partial deregulation and in prohibiting the possibility of planting in accordance with the terms of such a deregulation. Given those errors, this Court need not express any view on whether injunctive relief of some kind was available to respondents on the record before us. Nor does the Court address the question whether the District Court was required to conduct an evidentiary hearing before entering the relief at issue here. The judgment of the Ninth Circuit is reversed, and the case is remanded for further proceedings consistent with this opinion.

It is so ordered.

JUSTICE STEVENS, dissenting.

The Court does not dispute the District Court's critical findings of fact: First, Roundup Ready Alfalfa (RRA) can contaminate other plants. Second, even planting in a controlled setting had led to contamination in some instances. Third, the Animal and Plant Health Inspection Service (APHIS) has limited ability to monitor or enforce limitations on planting. And fourth, genetic contamination from RRA could decimate farmers' livelihoods and the American alfalfa market for years to come. Instead, the majority faults the District Court for "enjoining APHIS from partially deregulating RRA."

In my view, the District Court may not have actually ordered such relief, and we should not so readily assume that it did. Regardless, the District Court did not abuse its discretion when, after considering the voluminous record and making the aforementioned findings, it issued the order now before us. * * *

* * * [T]he District Court's judgment can be understood as a reasonable response to the nature of the risks posed by RRA. Separate and apart from NEPA's requirement of an EIS, these risks were sufficiently serious, in my view, that the court's injunction was a permissible exercise of its equitable authority.

The District Court found that gene transfer can and does occur, and that if it were to spread through open land the environmental and economic consequences would be devastating. Although "a mere possibility of a future nuisance will not support an injunction," courts have never required proof "that the nuisance *will* occur"; rather, "it is sufficient ... that the *risk* of its happening is greater than a reasonable man would incur." Once gene transfer occurred in American fields, it "would be difficult—if not impossible—to reverse the harm."

Additional considerations support the District Court's judgment. It was clear to the court that APHIS had only limited capacity to monitor planted RRA, and some RRA had already been planted. The marginal threat posed by additional planting was therefore significant. * * * Under these circumstances, it was not unreasonable for the court to conclude that the most equitable solution was to allocate the limited amount of potentially safe RRA to the farmers who had already planted that crop.

The Court suggests that the injunction was nonetheless too sweeping because "a partial deregulation need not cause respondents any injury at all ... if the scope of the partial deregulation is sufficiently limited, the risk of gene flow to their crops could be virtually nonexistent." The Court appears to reach this conclusion by citing one particular study (in a voluminous record), rather than any findings of fact. Even assuming that this study is correct, the Court ignores the District Court's findings that gene flow is likely and that APHIS has little ability to monitor any conditions imposed on a partial deregulation. Limits on planting or harvesting may operate fine in a laboratory setting, but the District Court concluded that many limits will not be followed and cannot be enforced in the real world.

Against that background, it was perfectly reasonable to wait for an EIS. * * * It was reasonable for the court to conclude that planting could not go forward until more complete study, presented in an EIS, showed that the known problem of gene flow could, in reality, be prevented.

NOTES

1. **Remedying NEPA Violations: The Vacatur.** Notice that none of the parties challenge, nor does the Supreme Court upset, the district court's decision to vacate APHIS's decision to completely de-regulate Roundup Ready Alfala (RRA). Why not, do you suppose? Is this the basic minimum of NEPA remedies? Why or why not? Or, to think of the question another way, if the courts do not do at least this much, would NEPA have any real meaning at all?

2. **Remedying the NEPA Violations: The Injunctions.** Where did the district court go wrong in issuing its injunctions, according to the Supreme Court majority? What do the plaintiffs have to show, and the district court find, in order for an injunction to issue? Why did Justice Stevens disagree with the majority's assessment?

The district court did issue rather broad and nationwide injunctions in this case. Could the district court have fashioned more narrowly tailored injunctions that would have satisfied the Supreme Court majority? If so, how? If not, why not? Does *Geertson Seed Farms* preclude the use of injunctions as NEPA remedies? Why or why not?

3. **Balancing the Harms and Disservice to the Public.** Of what relevance is it to this case that farmers had already bought RRA seeds and were planting RRA crops? Notice that this case, like many cases involving environmental regulation, presents more than two (plaintiff and defendant) sets of interests. Here there are at least four: (1) the interests of the public, represented by APHIS; (2) the interests of Monsanto and FGI, the parties with property rights in RRA; (3) the interests of commercial alfalfa growers who grow (or want to grow) RRA crops; and (4) the interests of the organic alfalfa growers and environmental groups, who want to stop the spread of the modified genes in RRA. How should a court evaluate the appropriateness of an injunction in the face of these divergent interests, all of whom will be or could be directly impacted (and usually financially) by the outcome of the case and most of whom are basically "innocent bystanders" to APHIS's decision?

4. **Timing and NEPA Injunctions.** Notice that the majority classifies the district court's remedy as a "permanent" injunction, while Justice Stevens characterizes it more as an injunction until APHIS properly complies with NEPA. Does the duration of the injunction matter in *Geertson Seed Farms*? Why or why not? Could it matter in a different NEPA case? Why or why not?

* * *

Chapter 3

Protecting Endangered and Threatened Species in the United States and Globally

■ ■ ■

I. THE DUAL FOCUS OF THE FEDERAL ENDANGERED SPECIES ACT

A. THE INTERACTION OF INTERNATIONAL AND DOMESTIC LAW IN GENERAL

As you may recall from the Makah whaling case (*Metcalf v. Daley*) in Chapter 2, actions within the United States that affect the environment can implicate international law as well as the United States' domestic laws. In that case, the Makah Tribe wanted to resume subsistence hunting of gray whales pursuant to their tribal treaty rights with the United States. However, in 1946, the United States had signed the International Convention for the Regulation of Whaling, Dec. 2, 1946, 161 U.N.T.S. 72, 62 Stat. 1716 (Nov. 10, 1948), and in 1949 Congress passed the Whaling Convention Act, 16 U.S.C. §§ 916 *et seq.*, which prohibits whaling in violation of the Convention or the Convention's Schedule of whaling regulations. The International Whaling Commission amended the Schedule to prohibit all taking and killing of gray whales. As a result, the United States faced a potential conflict between its treaty trust responsibility to the Makah and its international obligations. Resolution of that conflict required the United States to seek an subsistence hunting exemption for the Makah from the International Whaling Commission. However, the Makahs' attempts to whale also implicated the United States' National Environmental Policy Act (NEPA) and the Marine Mammal Protection Act (MMPA), resulting in domestic law litigation.

The International Convention for the Regulation of Whaling provides a fairly typical example of how domestic and international environmental law intersect in the United States. International law exists through the ***consent*** of participating countries. Each country in the world is an independent nation, entitled to full sovereignty over its territory free from interference from other countries. To create an international regulatory regime, each country must agree to give up some of its inherent sovereignty and to be bound by common rules.

There are many sources of international law. One such source is ***customary international law***, which consists of the rules that almost all nations follow as a matter of custom and informal understandings, despite a lack of treaties or other agreements. A nation's consent to follow these rules can be inferred from that nation's past behavior and the universality of the rules.

Far more important for environmental issues, however, are ***international conventions, treaties, and agreements***. According to the Vienna Convention on the Law of Treaties, May 23, 1969, 1155 U.N.T.S. 331—itself a treaty that has become so widely accepted that its principles are generally deemed to be customary law even for non-parties—a "treaty" is "an international agreement concluded between States in written form and governed by international law, whether embodied in a single instrument or in two or more related instruments and whatever its particular designation." *Id.* art 2.1(a). In essence, a treaty functions as a formal contract between two or more nations. To be governed by the Vienna Convention, treaties must be in writing, but, like the Vienna Convention itself, they do not have to be explicitly labelled "treaties," and hence treaties are often referred to as "conventions" or "agreements." Treaties can be ***bilateral*** (involving only two countries), ***trilateral*** (involving three countries), or ***multilateral*** (involving multiple countries). For example, the International Convention for the Regulation of Whaling is a multilateral treaty, but the United States has also entered a number of bilaterial and trilateral treaties, such as the 1909 Boundary Waters Treaty between the United States and Canada, which governs the Great Lakes, or the 1988 United States–Japan Agreement regarding uranium and nuclear waste.

A number of treaties now govern a variety of international environmental issues. Treaties related to air pollution, for example, include: (1) the Convention on Long–Range Transboundary Air Pollution, Nov. 13, 1979, T.I.A.S. No. 10,541, 34 U.S.T. 3043, 18 I.L.M. 1442 (1979), which entered into force on March 16, 1983; (2) the Vienna Convention for the Protection of the Ozone Layer, March 2, 1985, 26 I.L.M. 1529 (1987), which entered into force Sept. 22, 1988, together with the Montreal Protocol on Substances that Deplete the Ozone Layer, Sept.16, 1987, 26 I.L.M. 1550 (1987), and the London Adjustments and Amendments to the Montreal Protocol on Substances that Deplete the Ozone Layer, 30 I.L.M. 537 (1990); (3) the Canada–United States Agreement on Air Quality, March 13, 1991, 30 I.L.M. 676 (1991), which entered into force March 13, 1991; and (4) the United Nations Framework Convention on Climate Change, May 9, 1992, 31 I.L.M. 848 (1992), which entered into force June 4, 1992, and its Kyoto Protocol, Dec. 10, 1997, 1997 WL 1048455, which entered into force on February 16, 2005.

More relevant to this chapter, a number of international treaties govern issues related to biodiversity and species protection. In addition to the International Whaling Convention, these treaties include:

- The Antarctic Treaty, Dec. 1, 1959, T.I.A.S. No. 4780, 12 U.S.T. 794, 402 U.N.T.S. 71, 19 I.L.M. 860 (1959), which entered into force June 23, 1961, and its Protocol on Environmental Protection, Oct. 4, 1991, 30 I.L.M. 1461, which entered into force Jan. 14, 1998.
- The Convention on Wetlands of International Importance Especially as Waterfowl Habitat (the "Ramsar Convention"), Feb. 2, 1971, T.I.A.S. No. 11084, 996 U.N.T.S. 245, which entered into force Dec. 21, 1975.
- The Convention for the Protection of the World Cultural and Natural Heritage (the "World Heritage Convention"), Nov. 16, 1972, T.I.A.S. No. 8226, 27 U.S.T. 37, 1037 U.N.T.S. 151, which entered into force Dec. 17, 1975.
- The Convention on International Trade in Endangered Species of Wild Fauna and Flora (CITES), March 3, 1973, T.I.A.S. No. 8249, 27 U.S.T. 1087, which entered into force July 1, 1975.
- The United Nations Convention on the Law of the Sea (UNCLOS III), Dec. 10, 1982, 21 I.L.M. 1261, which entered into force Nov. 16, 1994, although the United States is not a party, and the Agreement for Implementation of the Provisions of the United Nations Convention on the Law of the Sea of December 10, 1982 Relating to the Conservation and Management of Straddling Fish Stocks and Highly Migratory Migratory Fish Stocks (Dec. 4, 1995), 34 I.L.M. 1542 (1995).
- The United Nations Convention of Biological Diversity (the "Biodiversity Convention"), June 2, 1992, 31 I.L.M. 818 (1992), and the Cartagena Protocol on Biosafety to the Convention on Biological Diversity, Jan. 29, 2000, 39 I.L.M. 1027 (2000).

As this list suggests, the international community has agreed to protect biodiversity and threatened species in a number of ways: by prohibiting hunting and killing of species of concern; by establishing clear regulatory authority over particular species and/or geographic areas; by protecting important habitat; and by regulating potentially damaging trade and products.

As a general rule, treaties govern the relations among nations instead of regulating individual private parties. To make treaty provisions applicable to individuals, ratifying nations generally must enact ***implementing***

domestic legislation. In international law terms, therefore, most treaties are *not* ***self-executing***. This non-self-executing quality of most treaties explains why, after becoming a party to the International Convention for the Regulation of Whaling, the United States had to enact the Whaling Convention Act. Moreover, private parties within the United States who whale in violation of the Convention are liable for violating the *Act*, not the Convention itself.

The International Whaling Convention and the Whaling Convention Act are also examples of how, in the United States, Congress and the President interact both to make the United States a party to a treaty and to implement treaties domestically. Under the U.S. Constitution, the President has the "Power, by and with the Advice and Consent of the Senate, to make Treaties, provided two-thirds of the Senators present concur." U.S. CONST., art. II, § 2, cl.2. Congress, in turn, has the powers "[t]o define and punish * * * Offenses against the Law of Nations" and "[t]o make all Laws which shall be necessary and proper for carrying into Execution the foregoing Powers, and all other Powers vested by this Constitution in the Government of the United States, or in any Department of Officer thereof." *Id.* art I, § 8, cls. 10, 18. However, the President must sign any legislation that Congress passes, unless two-thirds of the House agrees to override a presidential veto. *Id.* art I, § 7, cl. 2.

In addition, the U.S. Constitution specifies that it, "and the Laws of the United States which shall be made in Pursuance thereof; *and all Treaties made*, or which shall be made, under the Authority of the United States, shall be the supreme Law of the Land; and the Judges in every State shall be bound thereby, any Thing in the Constitution or Laws of any State to the Contrary notwithstanding." U.S. CONST., art VI, c. 2 (emphasis added). This provision, known as the ***Supremacy Clause***, requires the federal Constitution, federal laws, and treaties to trump—***preempt***—state constitutions and statutes. Within the three kinds of federal law, however, the U.S. Constitution is superior to both federal statutes and international treaties; indeed, federal courts generally treat treaties like federal statutes. *American Insurance Ass'n v. Garamendi*, 539 U.S. 396, 123 S. Ct. 2374, 2387–88 (2003); *DeCanas v. Bica*, 424 U.S. 351, 354 n.5 (1976).

B. THE ENDANGERED SPECIES ACT'S DUAL FOCUS

When Congress enacted the Endangered Species Act of 1973 (ESA), 16 U.S.C. §§ 1531–1544, it did so to effectuate both domestic and international goals for conserving endangered and threatened species. For the United States, Congress found that "various species of fish, wildlife, and plants in the United States have been rendered extinct as a consequence of economic growth and development untempered by adequate concern and conservation;" that "other species of fish, wildlife, and plants have been so depleted in numbers that they are in danger of or threatened with extinctions;" and that "these species of fish, wildlife, and plants are of esthetic, ecological, educational, historical, recreational, and scientific value to the Nation and its people." ESA § 2(a)(1)–(3), 16 U.S.C. § 1531(a)(1)–(3). At the same time, Congress recognized that "the United States has pledged itself as a sovereign state in the international community to conserve to the extent practicable the various species of fish or wildlife or plants facing extinction * * *." *Id.* § 2(a)(4), 16 U.S.C. § 1531(a)(4).

The ESA's dual national and international focus is also evident in Congress's statement of the statute's purposes, which are "to provide a means whereby the ecosystems upon which endangered species and threatened species depend may be conserved, to provide a program for the conservation of such endangered species and threatened species, and to take steps as may be appropriate to achieve the purposes of [certain] treaties and conventions * * *." ESA § 2(b), 16 U.S.C. § 1531(b). Specifically, Congress listed six treaties, conventions, and groups of treaties and conventions that it intended the ESA to implement or help to implement:

(A) migratory bird treaties with Canada and Mexico;

(B) the Migratory and Endangered Bird Treaty with Japan;

(C) the Convention on Nature Protection and Wildlife Preservation in the Western Hemisphere;

(D) the International Convention for the Northwest Atlantic Fisheries;

(E) the International Convention for the High Seas Fisheries of the North Pacific Ocean; [and]

(F) the Convention on International Trade in Endangered Species of Wild Fauna and Flora[.]

ESA § 2(a)(4), 16 U.S.C. § 1531(a)(4).

This chapter will begin by examining how the ESA protects endangered and threatened species domestically. It will then examine the ESA's role in implementing international protections for endangered and threatened species and finish by examining other issues that have arisen regarding international trade and endangered species.

II. THE ENDANGERED SPECIES ACT AND THE UNITED STATES'S DOMESTIC REGULATION OF ENDANGERED AND THREATENED SPECIES

A. AN OVERVIEW OF THE ENDANGERED SPECIES ACT (ESA)

The ESA divides domestic regulatory responsibility over endangered and threatened species between the Secretaries of the Interior, of Commerce, and of Agriculture. ESA § 3(15), 16 U.S.C. § 1532(15). The Secretary of Agriculture's sole responsibilities relate to the importation and exportation of plants. *Id.* The Secretary of the Interior is responsible for implementing the ESA with respect to ***terrestrial species*** and has delegated its responsibilities to the ***United States Fish and Wildlife Serves* (USFWS or FWS)**. The Secretary of Commerce is responsible for implementing the ESA with respect to ***marine species*** and has delegated its authority to the ***National Marine Fisheries Service* (NMFS)**, now known as ***NOAA Fisheries***.

The ESA protects endangered and threatened species both from federal agency actions that could further harm such species, ESA § 7, 16 U.S.C. § 1536, and from certain private actions. ESA § 9, 16 U.S.C. § 1538. However, none of the ESA's protections apply to a species until the USFWS has ***listed*** that species pursuant to section 4. ESA § 4, 16 U.S.C. § 1533; *see also* Figure 3–1. At the time of listing, the appropriate agency also determines whether a species is an ***endangered species*** or ***threatened species***. An "endangered species" is a "species which is in danger of extinction throughout all or a significant portion of its range" but cannot include insects determined to be pests. ESA § 3(6), 16 U.S.C. § 1532(6). A "threatened species" is a "species which is likely to become an endangered species within the foreseeable future throughout all or a significant portion of its range." ESA § 3(20), 16 U.S.C. § 1532(20). In addition, the listing agency is also supposed to determine the species' ***critical habitat***—that is, habitat both inside and outside the species' range at the time of listing that is essential to the conservation of the species. *See* ESA § 3(5), 16 U.S.C. § 1532(5).

The USFWS keeps track of all the species listed for protection, and the complete list is available through the agency's web site at http://endangered.fws.gov/wildlife.html#Species.

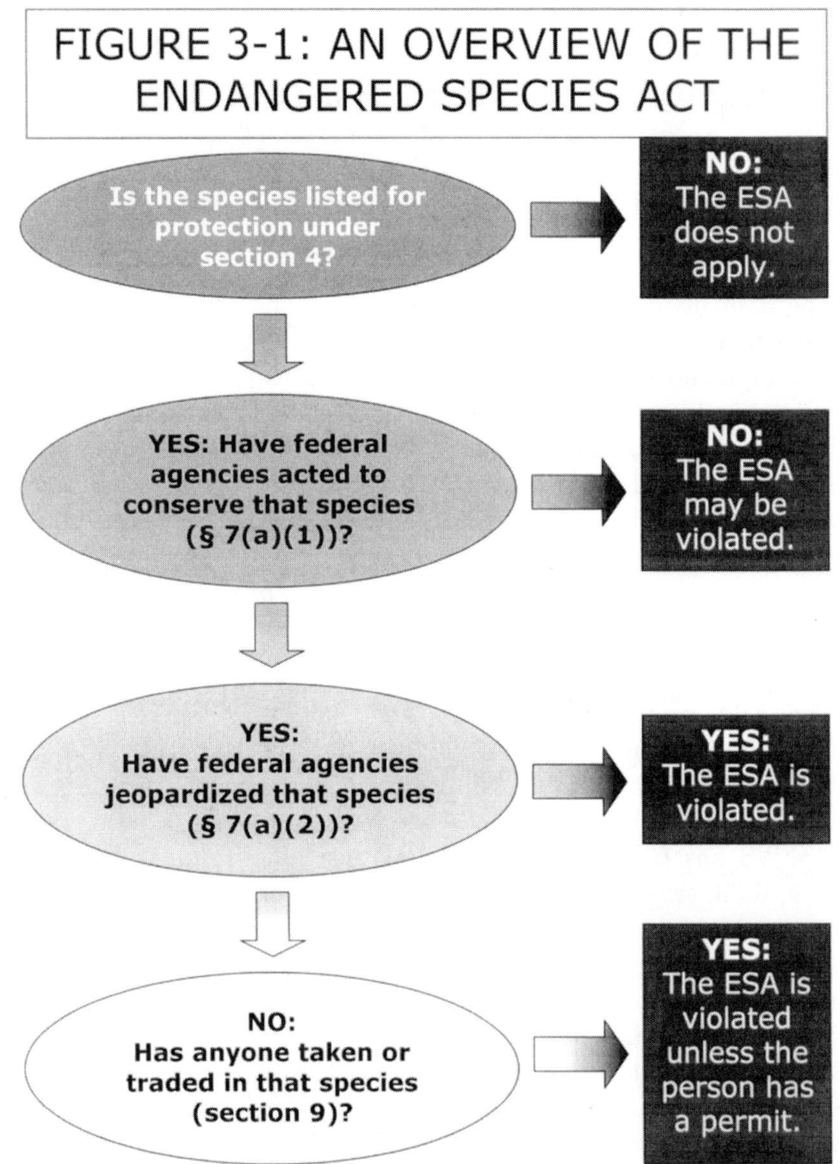
FIGURE 3-1: AN OVERVIEW OF THE ENDANGERED SPECIES ACT
Is the species listed for protection under section 4?
NO: The ESA does not apply.
YES: Have federal agencies acted to conserve that species (§ 7(a)(1))?
NO: The ESA may be violated.
YES: Have federal agencies jeopardized that species (§ 7(a)(2))?
YES: The ESA is violated.
NO: Has anyone taken or traded in that species (section 9)?
YES: The ESA is violated unless the person has a permit.

B. THE DOMESTIC PURPOSES OF THE ENDANGERED SPECIES ACT

Statutory interpretation is important for all federal environmental statutes, but interpretive issues have been particularly determinative for the Endangered Species Act. The following case is the U.S. Supreme Court's first interpretation of the ESA, which emphasized Congress's broad conservation purposes in enacting the ESA. *TVA v. Hill* remains good law. Moreover, it is the case with which all federal courts must continue to wrestle as they interpret the ESA.

TENNESSEE VALLEY AUTHORITY v. HILL

437 U.S. 153 (1978).

Mr. CHIEF JUSTICE BURGER delivered the opinion of the Court.

The questions presented in this case are (a) whether the Endangered Species Act of 1973 requires a court to enjoin the operation of a virtually completed federal dam—which had been authorized prior to 1973—when, pursuant to authority vested in him by Congress, the Secretary of the Interior has determined that operation of the dam would eradicate an endangered species; and (b) whether continued congressional appropriations for the dam after 1973 constituted an implied repeal of the Endangered Species Act, at least as to the particular dam.

I

The Little Tennessee River originates in the mountains of northern Georgia and flows through the national forest lands of North Carolina into Tennessee, where it converges with the Big Tennessee River near Knoxville. The lower 33 miles of the Little Tennessee takes the river's clear, free-flowing waters through an area of great natural beauty. Among other environmental amenities, this stretch of river is said to contain abundant trout. Considerable historical importance attaches to the areas immediately adjacent to this portion of the Little Tennessee's banks. To the south of the river's edge lies Fort Loudon, established in 1756 as England's southwestern outpost in the French and Indian War. Nearby are also the ancient sites of several native American villages, the archeological stores of which are to a large extent unexplored. These include the Cherokee towns of Echota and Tennase, the former being the sacred capital of the Cherokee Nation as early as the 16th century and the latter providing the linguistic basis from which the State of Tennessee derives its name.

In this area of the Little Tennessee River the Tennessee Valley Authority, a wholly owned public corporation of the United States, began constructing the Tellico Dam and Reservoir Project in 1967, shortly after Congress appropriated initial funds for its development. Tellico is a multipurpose regional development project designed principally to stimulate shoreline development, generate sufficient electric current to heat 20,000 homes, and provide flatwater recreation and flood control, as well as improve economic conditions in "an area characterized by underutilization of human resources and outmigration of young people." Hearings on Public Works for Power and Energy Research Appropriation Bill, 1977, before a Subcommittee on the House Committee on Appropriations, 94th Cong., 2d Sess., pt. 5, p. 261 (1976). Of particular relevance to this case is one aspect of the project, a dam which TVA determined to place on the Little Tennessee, a short distance from where the river's waters meet with the Big Tennessee. When fully operational, the dam would impound water covering some 16,500 acres—much of which represents valuable and productive farmland—thereby converting the river's shallow, fast-flowing waters into a deep reservoir over 30 miles in length.

The Tellico Dam has never opened, however, despite the fact that construction has been virtually completed and the dam is essentially ready for operation. Although Congress has appropriated monies for Tellico every year since 1967, progress was delayed, and ultimately stopped, by a tangle of lawsuits and administrative proceedings. After unsuccessfully urging TVA to consider alternatives to damming the Little Tennessee, local citizens and national conservation groups brought suit in the District Court, claiming that the project did not conform to the requirements of the National Environmental Policy Act of 1969 (NEPA), 83 Stat. 852, 42 U.S.C. § 4321 *et seq*. After finding TVA to be in violation of NEPA, the District Court enjoined the dam's completion pending the filing of an appropriate environmental impact statement. The injunction remained in effect until late 1973, when the District Court concluded that TVA's final environmental impact statement for Tellico was in compliance with the law.

A few months prior to the District Court's decision dissolving the NEPA injunction, a discovery was made in the waters of the Little Tennessee which would profoundly affect the Tellico Project. Exploring the area around Coytee Springs, which is about seven miles from the mouth of the river, a University of Tennessee ichthyologist, Dr. David A. Etnier, found a previously unknown species of perch, the snail darter, or *Percina (Imostoma) tanasi*. This three-inch, tannish-colored fish, whose numbers are estimated to be in the range of 10,000 to 15,000, would soon engage the attention of environmentalists, the TVA, the Department of the Interior, the Congress of the United States, and ultimately the federal courts, as a new and additional basis to halt construction of the dam.

Until recently the finding of a new species of animal life would hardly generate a cause celebre. This is particularly so in the case of darters, of which there are approximately 130 known species, 8 to 10 of these having been identified only in the last five years. The moving force behind the snail darter's sudden fame came some four months after its discovery, when the Congress passed the Endangered Species Act of 1973 (Act), 87 Stat. 884, 16 U.S.C. § 1531 *et seq*. (1976 ed.). This legislation, among other things, authorizes the Secretary of the Interior to declare species of animal life "endangered" and to identify the "critical habitat" of these creatures. When a species or its habitat is so listed, the following portion of the Act—relevant here—becomes effective:

> "The Secretary [of the Interior] shall review other programs administered by him and utilize such programs in furtherance of the purposes of this chapter. All other Federal departments and agencies shall, in consultation with and with the assistance of the Secretary, utilize their authorities in furtherance of the purposes of this chapter by carrying out programs for the conservation of endangered species and

threatened species listed pursuant to section 1533 of this title and *by taking such action necessary to insure that actions authorized, funded, or carried out by them do not jeopardize the continued existence of such endangered species and threatened species or result in the destruction or modification of habitat of such species* which is determined by the Secretary, after consultation as appropriate with the affected States, to be critical." 16 U.S.C. § 1536 (1976 ed.) (emphasis added).

In January 1975, the respondents in this case and others petitioned the Secretary of the Interior to list the snail darter as an endangered species. After receiving comments form various interested parties, including TVA and the State of Tennessee, the Secretary formally listed the snail darter as an endangered species on October 8, 1975. 40 Fed. Reg. 47505–47506; see 50 C.F.R. § 17.11(i) (1976). In so acting, it was noted that "the snail darter is a living entity which is genetically distinct and reproductively isolated from other fishes." 40 Fed. Reg. 47505. More important for the purposes of this case, the Secretary determined that the snail darter apparently lives only in that portion of the Little Tennessee River which would be completely inundated by the reservoir created as a consequence of the Tellico Dam's completion. *Id.* at 47506. The Secretary went on to explain the significance of the dam to the habitat of the snail darter:

"[T]he snail darter occurs only in the swifter portions of shoals over clean gravel substrate in cool, low-turbidity water. Food of the snail darter is almost exclusively snails which require a clean gravel substrate for their survival. *The proposed impoundment of water behind the proposed Tellico Dam would result in total destruction of the snail darter's habitat.*" *Ibid.* (emphasis added).

Subsequent to this determination, the Secretary declared the area of the Little Tennessee which would be affected by the Tellico Dam to be the "critical habitat" of the snail darter. 41 Fed. Reg. 13926–13928 (1976) (to be certified as 50 CFR § 17.81). Using these determinations as a predicate, and notwithstanding the near completion of the dam, the Secretary declared that pursuant to § 7 of the Act, "all Federal agencies must take such action as is necessary to insure that actions authorized, funded, or carried out by them do not result in the destruction or modification of this critical habitat area." 41 Fed. Reg. 13928 (1976) (to be codified as 50 CFR § 17.81(b)). This notice, of course, was pointedly directed at TVA and clearly aimed at halting completion or operation of the dam.

* * * Meanwhile, Congress had also become involved in the fate of the snail darter. Appearing before a Subcommittee of the House Committee on Appropriations in April 1975—some seven months before the snail darter was listed as endangered—TVA representatives described the discovery of the fish and the relevance of the Endangered Species Act to the Tellico Project. At that time TVA presented a position which it would advance in successive forums thereafter, namely, that the Act did not prohibit the completion of a project authorized, funded, and substantially

constructed before the Act was passed. TVA also described its efforts to transplant the snail darter, but contended that the dam should be finished regardless of the experiment's success. Thereafter, the House Committee on Appropriations, in its June 20, 1975, Report, stated the following in the course of recommending that an additional $29 million be appropriated for Tellico:

> "The *Committee* directs that the project, for which an environmental impact statement has been completed and provided the Committee, should be completed as promptly as possible . . . ." H.R. REP. NO. 94–319, p. 76 (1975). (Emphasis added).

Congress then approved the TVA general budget, which contained funds for continued construction of the Tellico Project. In December 1975, one month after the snail darter was declared an endangered species, the President signed the bill into law.

In February 1976, pursuant to § 11(g) of the Endangered Species Act, 87 Stat. 900, 16 U.S.C. § 1540(g) (1976 ed.), respondents filed the case now under review, seeking to enjoin completion of the dam and impoundment of the reservoir on the ground that those actions would violate the Act by directly causing the extinction of the species *Percina (Imostoma) tanasi*. The District Court denied respondents' request for a preliminary injunction and set the matter for trial. Shortly thereafter the House and Senate held appropriations hearings which would include discussions of the Tellico budget.

* * * The District Court found that closure of the dam and the consequent impoundment of the reservoir would "result in the adverse modification, if not complete destruction, of the snail darter's critical habitat," making it "highly probable" that "the continued existence of the snail darter" would be "jeopardize[d]." Despite these findings, the District Court declined to embrace the plaintiffs' position on the merits: that once a federal project was shown to jeopardize an endangered species, a court of equity is compelled to issue an injunction restraining violation of the Endangered Species Act.

* * * Less than a month after the District Court decision, the Senate and House Appropriations Committees recommended the full budget request of $9 million for continued work on Tellico. * * * On June 29, 1976, both Houses of Congress passed TVA's general budget, which included funds for Tellico; the President signed the bill on July 12, 1976.

Thereafter, in the Court of Appeals, respondents argued that the District Court had abused its discretion by not issuing an injunction in the face of "a blatant statutory violation." *Hill v. TVA*, 549 F.2d 1064, 1069 (CA6 1977). The Court of Appeals agreed, and on January 31, 1977, it reversed, remanding "with instructions that a permanent injunction issue halting all activities incident to the Tellico Project which may destroy or modify the critical habitat of the snail darter." *Id.*, at 1075. * * *

* * * Following the issuance of the permanent injunction, members of TVA's Board of Directors appeared before Subcommittees of the House and Senate Appropriations Committees to testify in support of continued appropriations for Tellico. * * * Both Appropriations Committees subsequently recommended the full amount requested for completion of the Tellico Project. In its June 2, 1977, Report, the House Appropriations Committee stated:

> "It is *the Committee's view* that the Endangered Species Act was not intended to halt projects such as these in their advanced stage of completion, and [the Committee] strongly recommends that these projects not be stopped because of misuse of the Act." H.R. REP. NO. 95–379, p. 104. (Emphasis added).

[Moreover, r]eporting to the Senate on these measures, the Appropriations Committee took a particularly strong stand on the snail darter issue:

> "This *committee has not viewed* the Endangered Species Act as preventing the completion and use of these projects which were well under way at the time the affected species were listed as endangered. If the act has such an effect which is contrary to *the Committee's understanding* of the intent of Congress in enacting the Endangered Species Act, funds should be appropriated to allow these projects to be completed and their benefits realized in the public interest, the Endangered Species Act notwithstanding." S. REP. NO. 95–301, p. 99 (1977). (Emphasis added).

TVA's budget, including funds for completion of Tellico and relocation of the snail darter, passed both Houses of Congress and was signed into law on August 7, 1977.

We granted certiorari to review the judgment of the Court of Appeals.

II

We begin with the premise that operation of the Tellico Dam will either eradicate the known population of snail darters or destroy their critical habitat. Petitioner does not now seriously dispute this fact. * * *

Starting from [this] premise, two questions are presented: (a) Would TVA be in violation of the Act if it completed and operated the Tellico Dam as planned? (b) If TVA's actions would offend the Act, is an injunction the appropriate remedy for the violation? For the reasons stated hereinafter, we hold that both questions must be answered in the affirmative.

(A)

It may seem curious to some that the survival of a relatively small number of three-inch fish among all the countless millions of species extant would require the permanent halting of a virtually completed dam for which Congress has expended more than $100 million. The paradox is not minimized by the fact that Congress continued to appropriate large sums of public money for the project, even after congressional Appropriations Committees were apprised of its apparent impact upon the survival of the snail darter. We conclude, however, that the explicit provisions of the Endangered Species Act require precisely that result.

One would be hard pressed to find a statutory provision whose terms were any plainer than those in § 7 of the Endangered Species Act. Its very words affirmatively command all federal agencies "to *insure* that actions *authorized, funded,* or *carried out* by them do not *jeopardize* the continued existence" of an endangered species or "*result* in the destruction or modification of habitat of such species . . . ." 16 U.S.C. § 1536 (1976 ed.). (Emphasis added.) This language admits of no exception. Nonetheless, petitioner urges, as do the dissenters, that the Act cannot reasonably be interpreted as applying to a federal project which was well under way when Congress passed the Endangered Species Act of 1973. To sustain that position, however, we would be forced to ignore the ordinary meaning of plain language. It has not been shown, for example, how TVA can close the gates of the Tellico Dam without "carrying out" an action that has been "authorized" and "funded" by a federal agency. Nor can we understand how such action will "*insure*" that the snail darter's habitat is not disrupted. Accepting the Secretary's determinations, as we must, it is clear that TVA's proposed operation of the dam will have precisely the opposite effect, namely the *eradication* of an endangered species.

Concededly, this view of the Act will produce results requiring the sacrifice of the anticipated benefits of the project and of many millions of dollars in public funds. But examination of the language, history, and structure of the legislation under review here indicates beyond doubt that Congress intended endangered species to be afforded the highest of priorities.

When Congress passed the Act in 1973, it was not legislating on a clean slate. The first major congressional concern for the preservation of the endangered species had come with passage of the Endangered Species Act of 1966, 80 Stat. 926, repealed, 87 Stat. 903. * * * Declaring the preservation of endangered species a national policy, the 1966 Act directed all federal agencies both to protect these species and "*insofar as is practicable and consistent with the[ir] primary purposes,*" § (b), 80 Stat. 926, "preserve the habitats of such threatened species on lands under their jurisdiction." *Ibid.* (Emphasis added.) * * *

In 1969 Congress enacted the Endangered Species Conservation Act, 83 Stat. 275, repealed, 87 Stat. 903, which continued the provisions of the 1966 Act while at the same time broadening federal involvement in the preservation of endangered species. Under the 1969 legislation, the Secretary was empowered to list species "threatened with worldwide extinction," § 3(a), 83 Stat. 275; in addition, the importation of any species so recognized into the United States was prohibited. § 2, 83 Stat. 275. An indirect approach to the taking of endangered species was also adopted in the Conservation Act by way of a ban on the transportation and sale of wildlife taken in violation of any federal, state, or foreign law. §§ 7(a)-(b), 83 Stat. 279.

Despite the fact that the 1966 and 1969 legislation represented "the most comprehensive of its type to be enacted by any nation" up to that time, Congress was soon persuaded that a more expansive approach was needed if the newly declared national policy of preserving endangered species was to be realized. By 1973, when Congress held hearings on what would later become the Endangered Species Act of 1973, it was informed that species were still being lost at the rate of about one per year, and "the pace of disappearance of species" appeared to be "accelerating." H.R. REP. NO. 93–412, p. 4 (1973). Moreover, Congress was also told that the primary cause of this trend was something other than the normal process of natural selection[.]

* * * The legislative proceedings in 1973 are, in fact, replete with expressions of concern over the risk that might lie in the loss of *any* endangered species. Typifying these sentiments is the Report of the House Committee on Merchant Marine and Fisheries on H.R. 37, a bill which contained the essential features of the subsequently enacted Act of 1973; in explaining the need for the legislation, the Report stated:

> "As we homogenize the habitats in which these plants and animals evolved, and as we increase the pressure for products that they are in a position to supply (usually unwillingly) we threaten their—and our own—genetic heritage.
>
> "*The value of this genetic heritage is, quite literally, incalculable.*
>
> * * * "From the most narrow possible point of view, *it is in the best interests of mankind to minimize the losses of genetic variations.* The reason is simple: they are potential resources. They are keys to puzzles which we cannot solve, and may provide answers to questions which we have not yet learned to ask.
>
> "To take a homely, but apt, example: one of the critical chemicals in the regulation of ovulations in humans was found in a common plant. Once discovered, and analyzed, humans could duplicate it synthetically, but had it never existed—or had it been driven out of existence before we knew its potentialities—we would never have tried to synthesize it in the first place.
>
> "Who knows, or can say, what potential cures for cancer or other scourges, present or future, may lie locked up in the structures of plants which may yet be undiscovered, much less analyzed? * * * Sheer self-interest impels us to be cautious.
>
> "*The institutionalization of that caution* lies at the heart of H.R. 37 ...." H.R. REP. NO. 93–412, pp. 4–5 (1973). (Emphasis added.)

As the examples cited here demonstrate, Congress was concerned about the *unknown* uses that endangered species might have and about the *unforeseeable* place such creatures may have in the chain of life on this planet.

In shaping legislation to deal with the problem thus presented, Congress started from the finding that "[t]he two major causes of extinction are hunting and destruction of natural habitat." S. REP. NO. 93–307, p. 2 (1973) U.S. Code Cong. & Admin. News 1973, pp. 2989, 2990. Of these twin threats, Congress was informed that the greatest was destruction of natural habitats. Virtually every bill introduced in Congress during the 1973 session responded to this concern by incorporating language similar, if not identical, to that found in the present § 7 of the Act. * * *

As it was finally passed, the Endangered Species Act of 1973 represented the most comprehensive legislation for the preservation of endangered species ever enacted by any nation. Its stated purposes were "to provide a means whereby the ecosystems upon which endangered species and threatened species depend may be conserved," and "to provide a program for the conservation of such ... species ...." 16 U.S.C. § 1531(b) (1976 ed.). In furtherance of these goals, Congress expressly stated in § 2(c) that "all Federal departments and agencies *shall* seek *to conserve endangered species* and threatened species ...." 16 U.S.C. § 1531(c) (1976 ed.). (Emphasis added.) Lest there be any ambiguity as to the meaning of this statutory directive, the Act specifically defined "conserve" as meaning "to use and the use of *all methods and procedures which are necessary* to bring *any endangered species or threatened species* to the point at which the measures provided pursuant to this chapter are no longer necessary." § 1532(2). (Emphasis added.) Aside from § 7, other provisions indicated the seriousness with which Congress viewed this issue: Virtually all dealings with endangered species, including taking, possession, transportation, and sale, were prohibited, 16 U.S.C. § 1538 (1976 ed.), except in extremely narrow circumstances see § 1539(b). The Secretary was also given extensive power to develop regulations and programs for the preservation of endangered and threatened species, § 1533(d). Citizen involvement was encouraged by the Act, with provisions allowing interested persons to petition the Secretary to list a species as endangered or threatened, § 1533(c)(2), and bring civil suits in United States district courts to force compliance with any provision of the Act, §§ 1540(c) and (g).

Section 7 of the Act, which of course is relied upon by respondents in this case, provides a particularly good gauge of congressional intent. As we have seen, this provision had its genesis in the Endangered Species Act of 1966, but that legislation qualified the obligation of federal agencies by stating that they should seek to preserve endangered species only "*insofar as is practicable and consistent with the[ir] primary purposes* ...." Likewise, every bill introduced in 1973 contained a qualification similar to that found in the earlier statutes. * * * This type of language did not go unnoticed by those advocating strong endangered species legislation. A representative of the Sierra Club, for example, attacked the use of the phrase "consistent with the primary purpose" in proposed H.R. 4758, cautioning that the qualification "could be construed to be a declaration of congressional policy that other agency purposes are necessarily more important than protection of endangered species and would always prevail if conflict were to occur." 1973 House Hearings 335 (statement of the Chairman of the Sierra Club's National Wildlife Committee); see *id.*, at 251 (statement for the National Audubon Society).

What is very significant in this sequence is that the final version of the 1973 Act carefully omitted all of the reservations described above. * * * In explaining the expected impact of this provision * * * on federal agencies, the House Committee's Report states:

> "This subsection *requires* the Secretary and the heads of all other Federal departments and agencies to use their authorities in order to carry out programs for the protection of endangered species, and it further *requires* that those agencies take *the necessary action* that will *not jeopardize* the continuing existence of endangered species or result in the destruction of critical habitat of those species." H.R. REP. NO. 93–412, p. 14 (1973). (Emphasis added.)

While the Conference Report made no specific reference to this choice of provisions, the House manager of the bill, Representative Dingell, provided an interpretation of what the Conference bill would require, making it clear that the mandatory provisions of § 7 were not casually or inadvertently included:

> "[Section 7] substantially amplifie[s] the obligation of [federal agencies] to take steps within their power to carry out the purposes of this act. A recent article ... illustrates the problem which might occur absent this new language in the bill. It appears that the whooping cranes of this country, perhaps the best known of our endangered species, are being threatened by Air Force bombing activities along the gulf coast of Texas. Under existing law, the Secretary of Defense has some discretion as to whether or not he will take the necessary action to see that this threat disappears .... [O]nce the bill is enacted, [the Secretary of Defense] *would be required to take the proper steps* ....
>
> "Another example ... [has] to do with the continental population of grizzly bears which may or may not be endangered, but which is surely threatened .... Once this bill is enacted, the appropriate Secretary, whether of Interior, Agriculture or whatever, *will have to take action* to see that this situation is not permitted to worsen, and that these bears are not driven to extinction. The purposes of the bill included the conservation of the species and of the ecosystems upon which they depend, and *every agency of government is committed* to see that those purposes are carried out. ... [T]he agencies of Government can no longer plead that they can do nothing about it. *They can, and they must. The law is clear.*" 119 Cong. Rec. 42913 (1973). (Emphasis added.)

It is against this legislative background that we must measure TVA's claim that the Act was not intended to stop operation of a project which, like Tellico Dam, was near completion when an endangered species was discovered in its path. While there is no discussion in the legislative history of precisely this problem, the totality of congressional action makes it abundantly clear that the result we reach today is wholly in accord with both the words of the statute and the intent of Congress. The plain intent of Congress in enacting this statute was to halt and reverse the trend toward species extinction, whatever the cost. This is reflected not only in the stated policies of the Act, but in literally every section of the statute. All persons, including federal agencies, are specifically instructed not to "take" endangered species, meaning that no one is "to harass, harm, pursue, hunt, shoot, wound, kill, trap, capture, or collect" such life forms. 16 U.S.C. § 1532(14), 1538(a)(1)(B) (1976 ed.). Agencies in particular are directed by §§ 2(c) and 3(2) of the Act to "use . . . *all methods* and procedures which are necessary" to preserve endangered species. 16 U.S.C. §§ 1531(c), 1532(2) (emphasis added) (1976 ed.). In addition, the legislative history undergirding § 7 reveals an explicit congressional decision to require agencies to afford first priority to the declared national policy of saving endangered species. The pointed omission of the type of qualifying language previously included in endangered species legislation reveals a conscious decision by Congress to give endangered species priority over the "primary missions" of federal agencies.

* * * Furthermore, it is clear Congress foresaw that § 7 would, on occasion, require agencies to alter ongoing projects in order to fulfill the goals of the Act. Congressman Dingell's discussion of Air Force practice bombing, for instance, obviously pinpoints a particular activity—intimately related to the national defense—which a major federal department would be obliged to alter in deference to the strictures of § 7. * * *

One might dispute the applicability of these examples to the Tellico Dam by saying that in this case the burden on the public through the loss of millions of unrecoverable dollars would greatly outweigh the loss of the snail darter. But neither the Endangered Species Act nor Art. III of the Constitution provides federal courts with authority to make such fine utilitarian calculations. On the contrary, the plain language of the Act, buttressed by its legislative history, shows clearly that Congress viewed the value of endangered species as "incalculable." Quite obviously, it would be difficult for a court to balance the loss of a sum certain—even $100 million—against a congressionally declared "incalculable" value, even assuming we had the power to engage in such a weighing process, which we emphatically do not.

In passing the Endangered Species Act of 1973, Congress was also aware of certain instances in which exceptions to the statute's broad sweep would be necessary. Thus, § 10, 16 U.S.C. § 1539 (1976 ed.), creates a number of limited "hardship exemptions," none of which would even remotely apply to the Tellico Project. In fact, there are no exemptions in the Endangered Species Act for federal agencies, meaning that under the maxim *expressio unius est exclusio alterius*, we must presume that these were the only "hardship cases" Congress intended to exempt.

Notwithstanding Congress' expression of intent in 1973, we are urged to find that the continuing appropriations for Tellico Dam constitute an implied repeal of the 1973 Act, at least insofar as it applies to the Tellico Project. * * * [T]hose Reports generally reflected the attitude of the *Committees* either that the Act did not apply to Tellico or that the dam should be completed regardless of the provisions of the Act. Since we are unwilling to assume that these latter Committee statements constituted advice to ignore the provisions of a duly enacted law, we assume that these Committees believed that the Act simply was not applicable in this situation. But even under this interpretation of the Committees' actions, we are unable to conclude that the Act has been in any respect amended or repealed.

* * * It is true that the *Committees* repeated their earlier expressed "view" that the Act did not prevent completion of the Tellico Project. Considering these statements in context, however, it is evident that they " 'represent only the personal views of these legislators,' " and "however explicit, [they] cannot serve to change the legislative intent of Congress expressed before the Act's passage." *Regional Rail Reorganization Act Cases*, 419 U.S. 102, 132 (1974).

(B)

Having determined that there is an irreconcilable conflict between operation of the Tellico Dam and the explicit provisions of § 7 of the Endangered Species Act, we must now consider what remedy, if any, is appropriate. It is correct, of course, that a federal judge sitting as a chancellor is not mechanically obligated to grant an injunction for every violation of law. As a general matter it may be said that "[s]ince all or almost all equitable remedies are discretionary, the balancing of equities and hardships is appropriate in almost any case as a guide to the chancellor's discretion." D. DOBBS, REMEDIES 52 (1973).

But these principles take a court only so far. Our system of government is, after all, a tripartite one, with each branch having certain defined functions delegated to it by the Constitution. While "[i]t is emphatically the province and duty of the judicial department to say what the law is," *Marbury v. Madison*, 1 Cranch. 137, 177 (1803), it is equally—and emphatically—the exclusive province of the Congress not only to formulate legislative policies and mandate programs and projects, but also to establish their relative priority for the Nation. Once Congress, exercising its delegated powers, has decided the order of priorities in a given area, it is for the Executive to administer the laws and for the courts to enforce them when enforcement is sought.

Here we are urged to view the Endangered Species Act "reasonably," and hence shape a remedy "that accords with some modicum of common sense and the public weal." But is that our function? We have no expert knowledge on the subject of endangered species, much less do we have a mandate from the people to strike a balance of equities on the side of the Tellico Dam. Congress has spoken in the plainest of words, making it abundantly clear that the balance has been struck in favor of affording endangered species the highest of priorities, thereby adopting a policy which it described as "institutionalized caution."

Our individual appraisal of the wisdom or unwisdom of a particular course consciously selected by the Congress is to be put aside in the process of interpreting a statute. Once the meaning of an enactment is discerned and its constitutionality determined, the judicial process comes to an end. We do not sit as a committee of review, nor are we vested with the power of veto. * * *

We agree with the Court of Appeals that in our constitutional system the commitment to the separation of powers is too fundamental for us to pre-empt congressional action by judicially decreeing what accords with "common sense and the public weal." Our Constitution vests such responsibilities in the political branches. * * *

NOTES

1. **Interactions Between NEPA and the ESA.** How did NEPA and the ESA interact to help the plaintiffs' attempt to halt construction of the Tellico Dam? Why would the plaintiffs have relied on NEPA first?

2. **The Rest of the Story**. Professor Zygmunt J.B. Plater, who was the petitioner and lead counsel in the Tellico Dam litigation, has recounted the history of *TVA v. Hill* and outlined the environmental litigation issues that it revealed in his article, *Law and the Fourth Estate: Endangered Nature, the Press, and the Dicey Game of Democratic Governance*, 32 ENVIRONMENTAL LAW 1–36 (Winter 2002). According to Professor Plater:

> At the heart of TVA's project justifications for Tellico was a decision to acquire large areas of land that would never be flooded by the long, winding, shallow lake [that the dam would create]—more than twice as much private land was to be condemned than was needed for the reservoir, 340 family farms—and the theory was that this land would be re-sold and redeveloped as a model industrial city to be called "Timberlake New Town." At a cost of $850 million, including at least $145 million in additional "infrastructure grant" subsidies that Congress would be asked to provide at some later date, TVA and its partner, the Boeing Corporation, said the hypothetical city would bring 50,000 people and 26,000 new jobs to the area. The "shoreland development" benefits of this plan, along with even greater hypothesized recreational benefits, allowed TVA to claim a 1.70/1.00 benefit-cost ratio (later modified downward). * * * Despite the inevitable image of the controversy, the Tellico Project was fundamentally not a hydroelectric dam project. The dam was just the dubious central feature of a federal recreational and land-development project.

Id. at 6–7. In contrast, citizens in the area—"a motley little coalition of farmers, fishermen, Native Americans, historians, archaeologists, and others," *id.* at 7—emphasized the loss of "more than 300 family farms on some of the richest agricultural soils in the world," of the "best big river trout fishing resource east of the Mississippi,'' of an archaeological site that had been inhabited for over 10,000 years and that had been the heart of the Cherokee civilization, and of the potential tourism and cultural values of the area. *Id.* at 7–8.

According to Professor Plater, ''[i]n retrospect, the dam was quite certainly a mistake.'' *Id.* at 8. In 1979, the newly created Endangered Species Committee (see Note 3) agreed, refusing to grant an exemption for the Tellico Dam. Jared des Rosiers, Note, *The Exemption Process Under the Endangered Species Act: How the ''God Squad'' Works and Why*, 66 NOTRE DAME L. REV. 825, 843–48 (1991). Nevertheless, Congress passed an appropriations rider to allow the Tellico Dam to be completed. Energy and Water Development Appropriations Act of 1980, Pub. L. No. 96–367, 94 Stat. 1331 (1980). Marc Reisner has reported on the passage of this legislation:

> June 18, 1979 was a dull day on the floor of the House, even duller than most. Little was going on, so hardly anyone was there. Bob Edgar was one of the many who were absent, and he still hates himself for it. He was one of the few Congressmen who might have been suspicious enough to stop what was about to take place. ''[Congressman James] Duncan walked in waving a piece of paper,'' Edgar recalls. ''He said, 'Mr. Speaker! Mr. Speaker! I have an amendment to offer to the public-works appropriations bill.' [Congressmen] Tom Bevill and John Myers of the Appropriations Committee both happened to be there. I wonder why. Bevill says, 'I've seen the amendment. It's good.' Myers says, 'I've seen the amendment. It's a good one.' And that was that. It was approved by voice vote! No one even knew what they were voting for! *They were voting to exempt Tellico Dam from all laws.* All laws! They punched a loophole big enough to shove a $100 million dam through it, and then they scattered threats all through Congress so we couldn't muster votes to shove it back out. I tried—lots of people tried—but we couldn't get the rider out of the bill. The speeches I heard on the floor were the angriest I've heard in elective office. Senator [Howard] Baker and Representative Duncan couldn't have cared less. They got their dam.''
>
> A few days later, the House passed the appropriations bill with the Tellico rider still in it. The Senate followed suit, 48–44, despite two earlier votes against the dam. ''That,'' said Edgar with sardonic disgust, ''is the democratic process at work.''

MARC REISNER, CADILLAC DESERT: THE AMERICAN WEST AND ITS DISAPPEARING WATER 328 (New York, NY: Penguin Books 1993).

TVA completed the dam. However, the asserted benefits never materialized. ''The Timberlake model city was never feasible, and Boeing pulled out in 1976, scuttling that part of the project.'' Plater, *supra*, at 8. The snail darter, however, has survived. Indeed, ''[t]hrough massive transplantation and discovery of several small relict populations, the darter's ultimate survival seems assured, and it has been downgraded to 'threatened' status.'' *Id.* at 8 n.22. However, ''its prime natural habitat and the function the darter served in that habitat as a legal bellwether for rational decisionmaking have been wastefully lost.'' *Id.* at 8.

Figure 3-2: The Completed Tellico Dam & Reservoir
TVA photo.

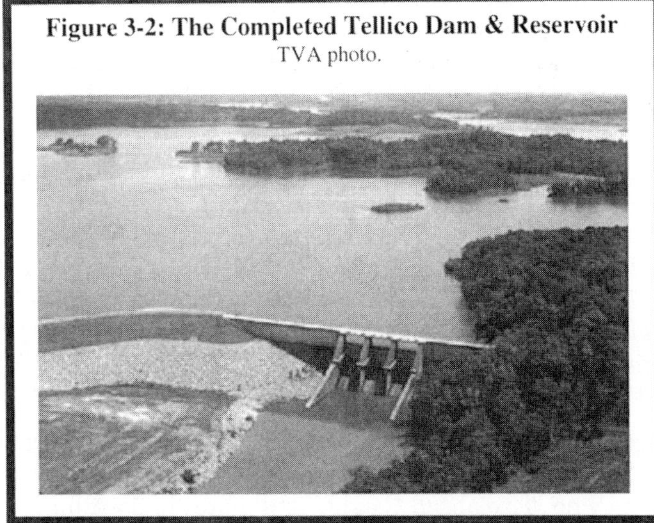

3. **Post *TVA v. Hill* Amendments to the ESA: The God Squad.** In the wake of *TVA v. Hill*, Congress amended section 7 to add an exemption procedure whereby federal agencies could seek permission from the seven-member Endangered Species Committee to go ahead with actions that would jeopardize the continued existence of species. Endangered Species Act Amendments of 1978, Pub. L. No, 95–632, 92 Stat. 3751 (Nov. 10, 1978). The Committee consists of the Secretary of Agriculture, the Secretary of the Army, the Chairman of the Council of Economic Advisors, the Administrator of the EPA, the Secretary of the Interior, the Administrator of the NOAA, and one individual from the affected state, who is appointed by the President. *Id.* § 7(e)(3), 16 U.S.C. § 1536(e)(3). Because of its power over the fate of species, this Committee has become known as the "God Squad."

The section 7 exemption procedure is long and complex, *see id.* § 7(g), (h), (i), (*l*), 16 U.S.C. § 1536(g),, (h), (i), (*l*), and the Endangered Species Committee's final decision is rendered through a formal APA adjudication process. *Id.* § 7(g)(4), 16 U.S.C. § 1536(g)(4). The God Squad can grant an exemption from section 7 only if it determines on the administrative record that:

> (i) there are no reasonable and prudent alternatives to the agency action;
>
> (ii) the benefits of such action clearly outweigh the benefits of alternative courses of action consistent with conserving the species or its critical habitat, and such action is in the public interest;
>
> (iii) the action is of regional or national significance; and
>
> (iv) neither the Federal agency concerned nor the exemption applicant made any irreversible or irretrievable commitments of resources * * *.

ESA § 7(h)(2)(A), 16 U.S.C. § 1536(h)(2)(A). In addition, the Committee must "establish such reasonable mitigation and enhancement measures * * * as are necessary and appropriate to minimize the adverse effects of the agency action upon the endangered species, threatened species, or critical habitat concerned." *Id.* § 7(h)(2)(B), 16 U.S.C. § 1536(h)(2)(B). However, "[n]otwithstanding any other provision of this chapter, the Committee *shall* grant an exemption for any agency action if the Secretary of Defense finds that such exemption is necessary for reasons of national security." *Id.* § 7(j), 16 U.S.C. § 1536(j) (emphasis added).

Finally, decisions to grant an exemption require a supermajority vote within the God Squad of at least five to two. ESA § 7(h)(1), 16 U.S.C. § 1536(h)(1). However, given the extensive review by the Committee of the environmental effects of any such exemption, Congress determined that "[a]n exemption decision by the Committee * * * shall not be a major Federal action for purposes of the National Environmental Policy Act of 1969: *Provided*, That an environmental impact statement which discusses the impacts upon endangered species or threatened species or their critical habitats shall have been previously prepared with respect to any agency action exempted by such order." *Id.* § 7(k), 16 U.S.C. § 1536(k).

The Tellico Dam was one of two projects congressionally mandated to proceed through Endangered Species Committee review; the other was the Grayrocks Dam project on the Laramie River in Wyoming, which was jeopardizing the listed whooping crane. *See* 16 U.S.C. § 1539(i)(1) (Supp. III 1979). By unanimous vote, the Endangered Species Committee *granted* the exemption for the Grayrocks Dam, allowing its completion. In contrast, also by unanimous vote, the Committee *denied* an exemption for the Tellico Dam, largely on cost-benefit grounds. As Professor Plater recounts, the Endangered Species Committee "concluded unanimously, in the words of Charles Schultze of the Council of Economic Advisors, that '[t]he interesting phenomenon is that here is a project that is *95% complete*, and if one takes *just the cost of finishing it* against the [*total*] benefits, and does it properly, *it doesn't pay*.' " Plater, *supra* Note 1, at 9 (quoting Charles Schultze, Chairman of the Council on Economic Advisors, Endangered Species Committee, *Tellico Dam and Reservoir Project* 25–26 (Jan. 13, 1979)); *see also* REISNER, *supra* Note 1, at 327. Reisner also notes that "Cecil Andrus added, 'Frankly, I hate to see the snail darter get the credit for delaying a project that was so ill-conceived and uneconomic in the first place.' * * * Tellico was a loser—it didn't deserve to be finished." REISNER, *supra* Note 1, at 327–28.

Since the Grayrocks Dam and Tellico Dam projects, federal agencies have rarely invoked the Endangered Species Committee, and the "God Squad" has never granted an exemption that would allow the complete eradication of a species. In 1991, for example, the Bureau of Land Management (BLM) applied for a section 7 exemption for 44 timber sales in Oregon for FY1991, which otherwise would have jeopardized the threatened Northern Spotted Owl. The Endangered Species Committee, by a 5–2 vote, granted an exemption—but only for 13 of the proposed sales. 57 Fed. Reg. 23405 (June 3, 1992). Moreover, even that limited exemption was lost when the Ninth Circuit overturned the Committee's decision, determining that it had violated the

APA's prohibition on *ex parte* contacts during formal adjudications. *Portland Audubon Society v. Endangered Species Committee*, 984 F.2d 1534, 1543–51 (9th Cir. 1993). In the interim, President William J. Clinton replaced President George H.W. Bush, and the Clinton Administration's BLM withdrew its request for exemptions.

Most recently, in July 2001, the Department of the Interior refused the Pacific Legal Foundation's application to the Endangered Species Committee, on behalf of the Klamath and Tulelake Irrigation Districts, for a section 7 exemption for the Klamath River irrigation project in northern California and southern Oregon. *See* U.S. Dept. of the Interior, *Department of the Interior Issues Endangered Species Committee Decision* (press release) (July 13, 2001), *available at* http://www.doi.gov/news/010713g.html. Release of water from this project to ranchers and farmers in the area had been found to jeopardize two listed species of suckers (fish) in the river system. However, according to the Department, the Pacific Legal Foundation was not a proper party to seek Committee review because it was neither the federal agency involved nor a permittee. Conflicts over Klamath River water continue, however, and it is likely that another application for Endangered Species Committee review—from more appropriate parties—will occur.

4. **The Supreme Court's Construction of the ESA.** As was discussed in the Introduction to this textbook, statutory interpretation is the process through which courts decide the meaning of a particular statute. Statutory interpretation issues usually arise when the court, or the implementing agency in an enforcement action, or a citizen in a citizen suit, attempts to apply the statute to a particular set of facts that create an unusual or borderline regulatory situation.

You have already seen many of the federal courts' ***tools of statutory construction*** in practice. Federal courts start with the presumption that the actual words Congress chose to use in the statute are the best indication of congressional intent. If Congress did not further define these words in the statute, then, under the ***plain meaning rule***, courts will assume that Congress intended the everyday, ordinary meaning of the words—increasingly often as defined by ***dictionaries***—to apply. ***Canons of statutory construction*** also help courts to discern the "plain meaning" of a statutory provision. Of course, if Congress did define particular words to give them particular meanings for the statute at issue, the courts will give effect to those congressional definitions. Often, however, the statutory definitions just move the interpretive issue to another level. For example, in Chapter 1 we saw that Congress defined "solid waste" in RCRA to mean "discarded material." Nevertheless, courts still had to determine what qualified as "discarded material" in a variety of factual contexts.

Courts will also look at the ***context*** of the statutory provision at issue in order to help discern its meaning. Context can include not only the immediately surrounding words and provisions but also the more general ***purposes*** and ***structure*** of the statute. The ***statutory history***—the history of amendments and other revisions to the statute—can also shed light on congressional intent.

Finally, most federal courts will still at least consider a federal statute's ***legislative history*** in interpreting that statute, particularly if Congress and its relevant committees thoroughly considered and explained their reasoning behind the statutory provision at issue. As was noted in the Introduction, however, certain Justices on the U.S. Supreme Court do not favor the use of legislative history, and hence lower courts are increasingly unlikely to rest an interpretive decision entirely on this tool.

TVA v. Hill is the most important federal case to construe the ESA. What was the precise issue of statutory interpretation that confronted the Supreme Court in that case? What was the Court's view of the *plain meaning* of section 7? How do the proponents of the dam argue that section 7 should not apply to the dam? What word becomes the focus of the Court's exercise in statutory interpretation? How does the Court's emphasis on the *purposes* of the ESA inform its interpretation of section 7 of the statute?

The *TVA v. Hill* Court relied on a variety of statutory interpretation tools besides the plain meaning of section 7 and the ESA's general purposes. What were these other tools, and how did the Court blend them into a single interpretation? How did these tools reinforce the Court's view of section 7's plain meaning and Congress's purposes?

5. **Valuing Endangered Species.** One of the most often quoted sentences from *TVA v. Hill* is that "[t]he plain intent of Congress in enacting this statute was to halt and reverse the trend toward species extinction, whatever the cost." Why did Congress value endangered species, according to the Supreme Court? What kind of a cost-benefit balance did it strike in the ESA? Why? Do the post-*TVA v. Hill* amendments discussed in Note 3 represent a different cost-benefit balancing by Congress? Why or why not? How does the Supreme Court's perception of Congress's cost-benefit balancing ultimately affect the federal courts' abilities to fashion equitable remedies in section 7 cases? Why does the Supreme Court reach that conclusion regarding ESA remedies? How does its perception of Congress's cost-benefit balancing relate to constitutional separation of powers principles?

6. **Statutory Interpretation and Congressional Appropriations.** Why didn't the repeated funding of the Tellico Dam project indicate a congressional intent not to apply section 7 to the Tellico Dam? Were such appropriations "legislative history," as that term is used in statutory interpretation? Why or why not? Did the appropriations legislation partially repeal the ESA with respect to the Tellico Dam? Why or why not?

* * *

C. SECTION 4 OF THE ENDANGERED SPECIES ACT: THE LISTING DECISION

1. Scientific Basis of the Listing Decision

As noted above, the ESA's protections do not apply to a species until the USFWS lists that species for protection (with NMFS's/NOAA Fisheries' recommendation if the species is a marine species). Thus, unlike many environmental statutes, the ESA's trigger is not an event that occurs in the regulated community but rather a purposeful decision on the part of the federal agencies that implement the Act. As a result, listing determinations can be critical to the preservation of species.

The USFWS lists species through the ***informal rulemaking*** procedures of the federal ***Administrative Procedures Act*** **(APA)**; the ESA specifies that, with certain exceptions for emergencies, "the provisions of section 553 of Title 5 (relating to rulemaking procedures), shall apply to any regulations promulgated to carry out the purposes of this chapter." ESA § 4(b)(4), 16 U.S.C. § 1533(b)(4). As you may recall from Chapter 2, the APA's informal rulemaking procedures require the USFWS to publish ***notice*** of its listing decisions in the Federal Register, to allow the general public to ***comment*** on its proposed decisions, and then to publish its final determinations, with explanations, in the Federal Register. *See* 5 U.S.C. § 553.

However, section 4 also imposes particular requirements on the listing process that affect how the USFWS conducts its notice-and-comment rulemaking for listings. For example, section 4 imposes scientific requirements on the agencies' listing decisions. Under section 4, the USFWS can list a species on the basis of any of five factors:

(A) the present or threatened destruction, modification, or curtailment of its habitat or range;

(B) overutilization for commercial, recreational, scientific, or educational purposes;

(C) disease or predation;

(D) the inadequacy of existing regulatory mechanisms; or

(E) other natural or manmade factors affecting its continued existence.

ESA § 4(a)(1), 16 U.S.C. § 1533(a)(1). However, listing decisions must be made "solely on the basis of the best scientific and commercial data available * * * after conducting a review of the status of the species and after taking into account those effort, if any, being made by any State of foreign nation, or any political subdivision of a State or foreign nation, to protect such species * * *." ESA § 4(b)(1)(A), 16 U.S.C. § 1533(b)(1)(A). Economic considerations and cost-benefit analyses are not supposed to play any role in the listing process.

The following case addresses the scientific requirements for listing endangered and threatened species.

NORTHERN SPOTTED OWL (*STRIX OCCIDENTALIS CAURINA*) v. HODEL

716 F.Supp. 479 (W.D. Wash. 1988).

ZILLY, DISTRICT JUDGE.

A number of environmental organizations bring this action against the United States Fish & Wildlife Service ("Service") and others, alleging that the Service's decision not to list the northern spotted owl as endangered or threatened under the Endangered Species Act of 1973, as amended, 16 U.S.C. § 1531 *et seq.* ("ESA" or "the Act"), was arbitrary and capricious or contrary to law.

Figure 3-3: Northern Spotted Owl
USFWS photo.

Since the 1970s the northern spotted owl has received much scientific attention, beginning with comprehensive studies of its natural history by Dr. Eric Forsman, whose most significant discovery was the close association between spotted owls and old-growth forests. This discovery raised concerns because the majority of remaining old-growth owl habitat is on public land available for harvest.

In January 1987, plaintiff Greenworld, pursuant to Sec. 4(b)(3) of the ESA, 16 U.S.C. § 1533(b)(3), petitioned the Service to list the northern spotted owl as endangered. In August 1987, 29 conservation organizations filed a second petition to list the owl as endangered both in the Olympic Peninsula in Washington and in the Oregon Coast Range, and as threatened throughout the rest of its range.

The ESA directs the Secretary of the Interior to determine whether any species have become endangered or threatened due to habitat destruction, overutilization, disease or predation, or other natural or manmade factors. 16 U.S.C. § 1533(a)(1). The Act was amended in 1982 to ensure that the decision whether to list a species as endangered or threatened was based solely on an evaluation of the biological risks faced by the species, to the exclusion of all other factors. *See* Conf. Report 97–835, 97th

Cong, 2d Sess. (Sept. 17, 1982) at 19, *reprinted in* 1982 U.S. Code Cong. & Admin. News 2807, 2860.[3]

The Service's role in deciding whether to list the northern spotted owl as endangered or threatened is to assess the technical and scientific data in the administrative record against the relevant listing criteria in section 4(a)(1) and then to exercise its own expert discretion in reaching its decision.

In July 1987, the Service announced that it would initiate a status review of the spotted owl and requested public comment. 52 Fed. Reg. 34396 (Sept. 11, 1987). The Service assembled a group of Service biologists, including Dr. Mark Shaffer, its staff expert on population viability, to conduct the review. The Service charged Dr. Shaffer with analyzing current scientific information on the owl. Dr. Shaffer concluded that:

> the most reasonable interpretation of current data and knowledge indicate continued old growth harvesting is likely to lead to the extinction of the subspecies in the foreseeable future which argues strongly for listing the subspecies as threatened or endangered at this time.

M. Shaffer, letter of November 11, 1987, to Jay Gore, U.S. Fish and Wildlife Service, Region 1, Endangered Species, attached to *Final Assessment of Population Viability Projects for the Northern Spotted Owl* [Administrative Record at III.A.1].

The Service invited a peer review of Dr. Shaffer's analysis by a number of U.S. experts on population viability, all of whom agreed with Dr. Shaffer's prognosis for the owl, although each had some criticisms of his work.

The Service's decision is contained in its 1987 Status Review of the owl ("Status Review") [Administrative Record at II.C] and summarized in its Finding on Greenworld's petition ("Finding") [Administrative Record at I.D.1]. The Status Review was completed on December 14, 1987, and on December 17 the Service announced that listing the owl as endangered under the Act was not warranted at that time. 52 Fed. Reg. 48552, 48554 (Dec. 23, 1987). This suit followed. Both sides now move for summary judgment on the administrative record before the Court.

* * * This Court reviews the Service's action under the "arbitrary and capricious" standard of the Administrative Procedure Act ("APA"), 5 U.S.C. § 706(2)(A). This standard is narrow and presumes the agency action is valid, but it does not shield agency action from a "thorough, probing, in-depth review," *Citizens to Preserve Overton Park v. Volpe*, 401 U.S. 402, 415 (1971). Courts must not "rubber-stamp the agency decision

---

3. In its only opinion construing the Act the Supreme Court declared that "[t]he plain intent of Congress in enacting [the ESA] was to halt and reverse the trend toward species extinction, whatever the cost." *Tennessee Valley Authority v. Hill*, 437 U.S. 153, 184 (1978) (further construction of nearly completed dam was permanently enjoined after discovery that the completed dam would eliminate the remaining habitat of an endangered species, the snail darter).

as correct." *Ethyl Corp. v. EPA*, [541 F.2d 1,] 34 [(D.C. Cir.), *cert. denied*, 426 U.S. 941 (1976)].

> Rather, the reviewing court must assure itself that the agency decision was "based on a consideration of the relevant factors ...." Moreover, it must engage in a "substantial inquiry" into the facts, one that is "searching and careful." This is particularly true in highly technical cases ....

Id. at 35–35 (citations and footnotes omitted). Agency action is arbitrary and capricious where the agency has failed to "articulate a satisfactory explanation for its action including a 'rational connection between the facts found and the choice made.' " *Motor Vehicles Mfns. Ass'n v. State Farm Mut. Auto Ins.*, 463 U.S. 29, 43 (1983) (citations omitted).

The Status Review and the Finding to the listing petition offer little insight into how the Service found that the owl currently has a viable population. Although the Status Review cites extensive empirical data and lists various conclusions, it fails to provide any analysis. The Service asserts that it is entitled to make its own decision, yet it provides no explanation for its findings. An agency must set forth clearly the grounds on which it acted. Judicial deference to agency expertise is proper, but the Court will not do so blindly. The Court finds that the Service has not set forth the grounds for its decision against listing the owl.

The Service's documents also lack any expert analysis supporting its conclusion. Rather, the expert opinion is entirely to the contrary. The only reference in the Status Review to an actual opinion that the owl does not face a significant likelihood of extinction is a mischaracterization of a conclusion of Dr. Mark Boyce:

> Boyce (1987) in his analysis of the draft preferred alternative concluded that there is a low probability that the spotted owls will go extinct. He does point out that population fragmentation appears to impose the greatest risks to extinction.

Status Review at 24. * * * Dr. Boyce responded to the Service:

> I did not conclude that the Spotted Owl enjoys a low probability of extinction, and I would be very disappointed if efforts to preserve the Spotted Owl were in any way thwarted by a misinterpretation of something I wrote.

M. Boyce, letter of February 18, 1988, to Rolf Wallenstrom, U.S. Fish and Wildlife Service, Region 1, exhibit 7 to Complaint.

Numerous other experts on population viability contributed to or reviewed drafts of the Status Review, or otherwise assessed spotted owl viability. Some were employed by the Service; others were independent. None concluded that the northern spotted owl is not at risk of extinction. * * *

The Service invited a peer review of Dr. Shaffer's analysis. Drs. Michael Soule, Bruce Wilcox, and Daniel Goodman, three leading U.S.

experts on population viability, reviewed and agreed completely with Dr. Shaffer's prognosis for the owl.

* * * The Court will reject conclusory assertions of agency "expertise" where the agency spurns unrebutted expert opinions without itself offering a credible alternative explanation. Here, the Service disregarded all the expert opinion on population viability, including that of its own expert, that the owl is facing extinction, and instead merely asserted its expertise in support of its conclusions.

The Service has failed to provide its own or other expert analysis supporting its conclusions. Such analysis is necessary to establish a rational connection between the evidence presented and the Service's decision. Accordingly, the United States Fish and Wildlife Service's decision not to list at this time the northern spotted owl as endangered or threatened under the Endangered Species Act was arbitrary and capricious and contrary to law.

The Court further finds that it is not possible from the record to determine that the Service considered the related issue of whether the northern spotted owl is a threatened species. This failure of the Service to review and make an express finding on the issue of threatened status is also arbitrary and capricious and contrary to law.

In deference to the Service's expertise and its role under the Endangered Species Act, the Court remands this matter to the Service, which has 90 days from the date of this order to provide an analysis for its decision that listing the northern spotted owl as threatened or endangered is not currently warranted. Further, the Service is ordered to supplement its Status Review and petition Finding consistent with this Court's ruling.

NOTES

1. **The Politics and Economics of the Northern Spotted Owl Listing**. The Northern Spotted Owl listing was one of the most controversial ESA listing decisions ever made, because the owl occupies old-growth forests in the Pacific Northwest (northern California, Oregon, and Washington)—forests that are particularly valuable for timber harvesting. Because these forests are largely under the control of the United States Forest Service and Bureau of Land Management, who are subject to the restrictions in section 7 of the ESA discussed in *TVA v. Hill*, listing of the Northern Spotted Owl had the potential to halt much of the timber harvesting on federal land within the owl's range. People aligned with timber interests made their opposition to the spotted owl listing known in a variety of ways, including through bumper stickers that stated: "I like the spotted owl—FRIED."

In June 1990, the USFWS finally listed the Northern Spotted Owl as a threatened species. It used 80 Federal Register pages to justify its decision. 55 Fed. Reg. 26114–26194 (June 26, 1990). More than a year and a half later, the USFWS established critical habitat for the Northern Spotted Owl. 57 Fed. Reg. 1796–1838 (January 15, 1992).

The Northern Spotted Owl listing remains one of the most controversial ESA listings. The owl's critical habitat ranges from northern California to the State of Washington and encompasses many private lands. Citizens continue to petition the USFWS to de-list the species, *see, e.g.*, 65 Fed. Reg. 5298 (Feb. 3, 2000), and litigation regarding the ESA's protections for the owl continues more than 15 years after its listing. *See, e.g.*, *Oregon Natural Resources Council v. Allen*, 476 F.3d 1031, 1037–41 (9th Cir. 2007) (declaring invalid an incidental take statement issued pursuant to Section 7 of the ESA that would allow take of the Northern spotted owl in connection with a timber sale and harvest on federal land).

The USFWS began its five-year review of the owl's status in April 2003. 68 Fed. Reg. 19569 (April 21, 2003). It wasn't until 2007, however, that the USFWS issued a Draft Recovery Plan for the Northern Spotted Owl, 72 Fed. Reg. 20,865 (April 26, 2007). See Note 6 for the results of that process.

Do you think that the economics and politics of a decision to list the spotted owl affect the USFWS's decision not to list the species, in spite of the ESA's commandment that the agency rely only on the best scientific data? Is there anything in the way that the USFWS handled the listing decision that suggests such an influence?

The Northwest spotted owl also became embroiled in the allegations that former Deputy Assistant Secretary of the Interior Julie MacDonald interfered with the scientific and agency evaluations of species in 13 Endangered Species Act cases. Specifically, a lawsuit in the U.S. District Court for the District of Columbia, *Carpenters Industrial Council v. Salazar*, alleged that Ms. MacDonald improperly interfered with the revisions of the spotted owl's recovery plan and critical habitat designation. On March 31, 2009, the U.S. Departments of Justice and the Interior asked for both to be remanded to the USFWS.

2. **The Federal Court's Standard of Review.** What standard does the Western District of Washington use to review the USFWS's decision to *not* list the Northern Spotted Owl? Why? In what two ways did the USFWS fail to meet that standard? Why?

3. **The ESA's Scientific Standard.** According to the Ninth Circuit, what standard does the ESA actually impose on the USFWS in listing species? Does the USFWS have to follow the scientific consensus? Why or why not? Is such an interpretation consistent with *TVA v. Hill*? Why or why not?

4. **The Administrative Record.** Notice the references to the administrative record throughout the *Northern Spotted Owl* case. As part of any informal rulemaking, but particularly in listing decisions pursuant to the ESA, a federal agency will compile the information generated as part of the rulemaking procedure into an ***administrative record*** of its decision. This record includes the proposed rule, the comments received during the comment period, internal agency documents that the agency relied on, the final rule, and the agency's explanation of the final rule. In the case of ESA listing decisions, this record includes the scientific data compiled by the agency regarding the species at issue. As the Western District of Washington notes, moreover, the the record that the agency relied on must support the agency's explanation of why it promulgated the rule it did. Why, based on the northern

spotted owl administrative record, did the Western District of Washington reverse the USFWS's decision here? Would it have made a difference to the outcome of this case if one scientist had submitted an opinion that the owl was not endangered? Five scientists? Most of the scientists on record? What else might a federal court look at when assessing the reasonableness of the agency's explanation of scientific issues?

5. **Species as Plaintiffs.** Notice the official plaintiff in this case. ESA cases are some of the few cases where species appear to sue in their own names. Does that mean that species have standing to bring federal lawsuits? *See The Cetacean Community v. Bush*, 386 F.3d 1169, 1174–76 (9th Cir. 2004) (upholding the U.S. District Court for the District of Hawai'i in finding that animals do not have standing to sue in federal court).

6. **Recovery for the Northern Spotted Owl?** In June 2011, the Fish & Wildlife Service issued its Revised Recovery Plan for the Northern Spotted Owl. U.S. FISH & WILDLIFE SERVICE, REVISED RECOVERY PLAN FOR THE NORTHERN SPOTTED OWL (*STRIX OCCIDENTALIS CAURINA*) (June 28, 2011), *available at* http://www.fws.gov/arcata/es/birds/NSO/documents/USFWS2011RevisedRecoveryPlanNorthernSpottedOwl.pdf. This Plan indicates that populations of the owl are still declining and that habitat loss remains an important impediment to the owl's recovery. However, the Northern spotted owl now faces a new threat, as well: competition from the barred owl. As a result, the recovery plan emphasizes not just "[h]abitat conservation and active forest restoration" but also "[b]arred owl management." *Id.* at vii. More specifically:

> The second step in this recovery strategy is to move forward with a scientific evaluation of potential management options to reduce the impact of barred owls on spotted owls. Barred owls pose perhaps the most significant short-term threat to spotted owl recovery. This threat is better understood now than when the spotted owl was listed. Barred owls have reduced spotted owl site occupancy, reproduction, and survival. Because the abundance of barred owls continues to increase, effectively addressing this threat depends on initiating action as soon as possible. The recovery actions address research involving the competition between spotted and barred owls, experimental control of barred owls and, if recommended by research, management of barred owls.

Id. at II–4. The Service is also cognizant of climate change in implementing the owl's recovery plan:

> There is significant overlap between many of the spotted owl recovery goals described in this Revised Recovery Plan and opportunities to mitigate impacts due to climate change. The Service is applying Secretarial Order No. 3289: *Addressing the Impacts of Climate Change on America's Water, Land, and Other Natural and Cultural Resources* into our forest management activities. This Secretarial Order directs DOI agencies to analyze potential climate change impacts when undertaking long-range

> planning exercises, developing multi-year management plans, and making major decisions regarding potential use of resources under the Service's purview. This direction applies to this Revised Recovery Plan, which includes a detailed treatment of climate change and its potential impact on spotted owl recovery.

Id. at II–5 to II–6. The Service estimates that it will take at least 30 years and $127.1 million to bring the Northern spotted owl back to the point where it can be delisted from the Endangered Species Act. *Id.* at viii.

* * *

2. Timing of Agency Listing Decisions

The second way in which Congress altered the APA informal rulemaking process for ESA listing decisions was by specifying the timing of ESA listing procedures. First, the USFWS must publish the proposed listing at least 90 days before it takes effect. ESA § 4(b)(5)(A), 16 U.S.C. § 1533(b)(5)(A). Interested persons have 45 days from the date of publication to request a public hearing on the listing decision. ESA § 4(b)(5)(E), 16 U.S.C. § 1533(b)(5)(E). Within a year of publishing the proposed listing, the agency must publish either a final regulation to implement its proposed determination; a final regulation implementing a revision; notice that the one-year period is being extended; or notice that the proposed regulation is being withdrawn, with an explanation of why it is being withdrawn. ESA § 4(b)(6)(A), 16 U.S.C. § 1533(b)(6)(A). Extensions of the one-year period are limited to six months, and the USFWS can extend the listing period only if "there is substantial disagreement regarding the sufficiency or accuracy of the available data" relevant to the listing. ESA § 4(b)(6)(B)(i), 16 U.S.C. § 1533(b)(6)(B)(i). At the end of the six-month extension, the agency must publish either a final rule listing the species or a withdrawal of the proposed listing. ESA § 4(b)(6)(B)(iii), 16 U.S.C. § 1533(b)(6)(B)(iii). To withdraw a proposed listing at either time, the USFWS must conclude that "there is not sufficient evidence to justify the action proposed * * *." ESA § 4(b)(6)(B)(ii), 16 U.S.C. § 1533(b)(6)(B)(ii).

The ESA also contains an exception to its timing requirements. Neither the APA's informal rulemaking procedures nor the ESA's timing requirements "apply to any regulation issued by the [agency] in regard to any emergency posing a significant risk to the well-being of any species of fish or wildlife or plants * * *." ESA § 4(b)(7), 16 U.S.C. § 1533(b)(7). However, such emergency rules are only valid if the USFWS publishes detailed reasons why the emergency rule is necessary and it gives actual notice of the rule to the relevant state agencies. *Id.* In addition, the regulation takes effect immediately upon publication but remains effective for only 240 days, unless the USFWS complies with the normal listing procedures in the interim. *Id.*

3. Timing of Citizen Petitions to List Species

Timing requirements become even more complex if a member of the public petitions the USFWS to list (or de-list) a species or to change its categorization as endangered or threatened. First, within 90 days of receiving the petition, the agency is supposed to "make a finding as to whether the petition presents substantial scientific or commercial information indicating that the petitioned action may be warranted." ESA § 4(b)(3)(A), 16 U.S.C. § 1533(b)(3)(A). If the petition contains such information, the agency begins a status review. If it does not contain sufficient information, the agency can deny the petition. Either way, the agency must publish its 90—day findings in the Federal Register.

Second, if the petition contains sufficient information to prompt a status review, then within 12 months of receiving the petition, the agency must make one of three findings:

> (i) The petitioned action is not warranted, in which case the [agency] shall promptly publish such finding in the Federal Register.
>
> (ii) The petitioned action is warranted, in which case the [agency] shall promptly publish in the Federal Register a general notice and the complete text of a proposed regulation to implement such action [and starting the beginning of the rulemaking process described above].
>
> (iii) The petitioned action is warranted, but that—
>
> (I) the immediate proposal and timely promulgation of a final regulation implementing the petitioned action * * * is precluded by pending proposals to determine whether any species is an endangered species or a threatened species, and
>
> (II) expeditious progress is being made to add qualified species to either of the lists * * * and to remove from such lists species for which the protections of this chapter are no longer necessary,
>
> in which case the [agency] shall promptly publish such finding in the Federal Register together with a description and evaluation of the reasons and data on which the finding is based.

ESA § 4(b)(3)(B), 16 U.S.C. § 1533(b)(3)(B).

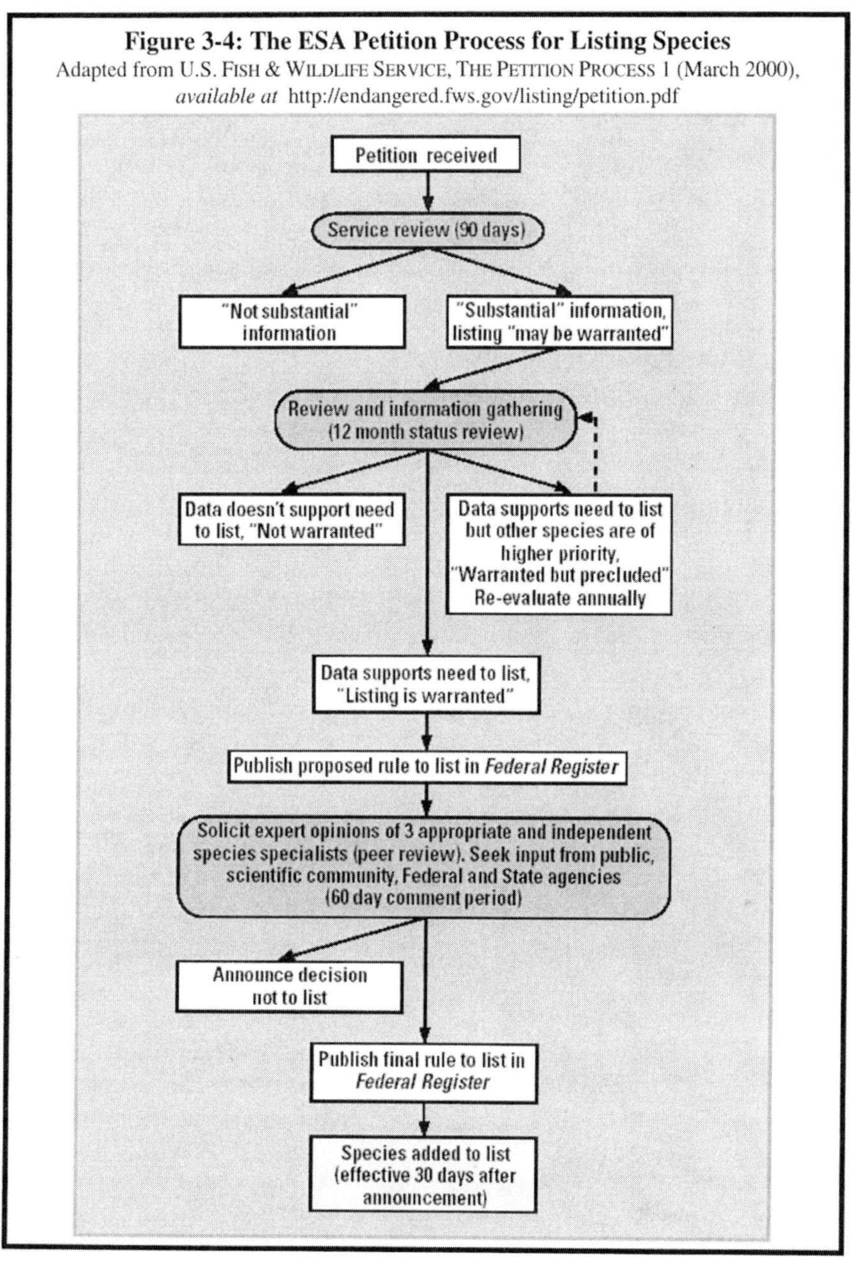

Figure 3-4: The ESA Petition Process for Listing Species
Adapted from U.S. FISH & WILDLIFE SERVICE, THE PETITION PROCESS 1 (March 2000), *available at* http://endangered.fws.gov/listing/petition.pdf

Third, if the USFWS determines that the petitioned action is "***warranted but precluded***," the ESA treats the petition as though it were resubmitted to the agency, and the USFWS must make new findings on the petition every year until it determines that the listing is warranted or not warranted. *See* ESA § 4(b)(3)(C)(i), 16 U.S.C. § 1533(b)(3)(C)(i). Moreover, all agency determinations on the petition, except the determination that listing is warranted, are subject to judicial review under the APA. ESA § 4(b)(3)(C)(ii), 16 U.S.C. § 1533(b)(3)(C)(ii).

The USFWS's flow chart of the petition process appears in Figure 3–4.

4. Litigating Timing

The USFWS often fails to meet the timing requirements for listing species. The following case discusses the legal effect of such failures.

IDAHO FARM BUREAU FEDERATION v. BABBITT

58 F.3d 1392 (9th Cir. 1995).

TANG, SENIOR CIRCUIT JUDGE:

Idaho Conservation League and Committee for Idaho's High Desert ("ICL/CIHD"), intervenors in the district court proceedings, appeal from a district court judgment setting aside the final rule listing the Bruneau Hot Springs Snail as an endangered species. The judgment was entered after a hearing on cross-motions for summary judgment. The district court determined that the listing rule was arbitrary and capricious because the United States Fish and Wildlife Service ("FWS") committed several procedural errors during the period between the initial proposal and the final listing.

* * * On the merits this appeal raises [a] major issue[:] does the Endangered Species Act ("ESA"), 16 U.S.C. § 1533(b)(6), proscribe listing a species as endangered once the statutory twelve or eighteen month time limits have passed? We conclude that it does not. Legislative history indicates that Congress established time limits to speed up the listing process so that more species would be listed. The time limits were designed as an impetus to act rather than as a bar on subsequent action. * * *

* * * The Bruneau Hot Springs Snail is a species of very small snails first identified in the early 1950's. Thus far, the species has been found only in a narrow band of thermal springs and seeps along a 5.28 mile stretch of the Bruneau River and a tributary, Hot Creek, in Owyhee County in southwest Idaho. Government agencies and other researchers have been unsuccessful in their attempts to locate other Springs Snail habitat. On August 21, 1985, FWS published a proposal to list the snail as an endangered species. 50 Fed. Reg. 33,803 (1983). The proposal was made under the Endangered Species Act ("ESA"), 16 U.S.C. § 1533. At that time, the Springs Snail was known to exist only in two springs in the Bruneau River area. According to FWS, a declining water table, resulting from ground water pumping, had reduced the springs' flow to less than ten percent of the 1954 flow. Reduced habitat due to the lower spring flow posed the primary threat to the Springs Snail. *Id.* at 33,803–05.

Initially, FWS provided a sixty-day comment period, from August 21 to October 21, 1985. FWS also published notice of the proposal in the *Idaho Statesman,* a newspaper serving southwest Idaho. Responding to a request for a public hearing, FWS set an additional comment period, from

October 31 to December 31, 1985. 50 Fed. Reg. 45,443 (1985). FWS held one public hearing in Boise on December 10, 1985, and a second public hearing on January 15, 1986, near Bruneau. FWS also extended the comment period through February 1, 1986. 50 Fed. Reg. 51,894 (1985).

In December of 1986, over sixteen months after the initial notice, FWS announced that there was substantial disagreement in the data regarding the status of the Springs Snail and extended the period of consideration for six months. 51 Fed. Reg. 47,033 (1986). FWS set another period of public comment from December 30, 1986, to February 6, 1987.

One year later, by letter dated February 23, 1988, the United States Senators for Idaho, James McClure and Steve Symms, wrote the FWS director and asked that he not proceed with listing the Springs Snail. The Senators expressed concern that the listing could have "devastating effects" on the local agricultural community and added that "listing would be meaningless to protection of the snail's natural habitat if the hydrologic cause of the habitat's decline is not fully understood." They urged FWS to determine the connection between pumping of the aquifer and decreasing water levels in the Indian Bathtub spring, and to determine whether Springs Snails existed in other springs. The Senators added that they would assist in securing the funding necessary to conduct further studies. The FWS director agreed to delay listing the Springs Snail pending funding of conservation activities that might eliminate the need for an ESA listing.

Thereafter Congress provided FWS with $400,000 in funding for two additional studies. One study conducted by Idaho State University (ISU) and completed in May, 1992, found 126 previously unknown colonies of Springs Snails in spring and seep sites along a 5.28 mile section of the Bruneau River. The study stated that because information provided by the United States Geological Survey indicated that all springs in the area arise from a common aquifer, the threat to the species posed by depletion of the aquifer was not reduced by finding additional snail colonies in those springs.

A second study, conducted by the United States Geological Survey ("USGS"), analyzed the hydrology of the geothermal system in the Bruneau River valley to determine the cause of declining spring flows. A provisional draft was completed in 1992. USGS gave FWS the draft but did not release the report to the public. The provisional draft is contained in the administrative record. Nonetheless, the record indicates the public did not have access to the report. * * *

* * * By 1992, FWS still had not made a final decision on the proposed listing. In July, 1992, Idaho Conservation League and Committee for Idaho's High Desert ("ICL/CIHD") (intervenors-appellants in the present action), filed suit to compel a final ruling on the proposed listing. On November 24, 1992, the district court approved a settlement in that action. In the settlement, FWS committed to rendering a final decision on

the Springs Snail listing proposal by January 15, 1993 and publishing the decision by February 1, 1993.

* * * FWS issued its final rule listing the Springs Snail as an endangered species on January 25, 1993, seven and one-half years after FWS first proposed the listing on August 21, 1985. 58 Fed. Reg. 5938 (1993). FWS concluded that the Springs Snail risks extinction because agricultural ground water withdrawal has depleted the geothermal aquifer in the Bruneau area, thereby reducing or eliminating the springs constituting Springs Snail habitat.

Idaho Farm Bureau Federation ("IFB") filed a complaint for declaratory and injunctive relief against the Secretary of the Interior and the FWS national director, regional director and Boise field supervisor. On cross-motions for summary judgment, the district court set aside the FWS final rule listing the Springs Snail as an endangered species. The court found the listing to be arbitrary and capricious because FWS had committed a number of procedural violations in the course of listing the Springs Snail. ICL/CIHD appeal the district court judgment.

* * * III. DOES THE ENDANGERED SPECIES ACT PROHIBIT THE SECRETARY FROM LISTING ANY SPECIES AS ENDANGERED MORE THAN EIGHTEEN MONTHS AFTER THE LISTING IS FIRST PROPOSED?

FWS listed the Springs Snail as an endangered species well past the eighteen month time requirement set forth in the ESA. We must determine whether the ESA, 16 U.S.C. § 1533(b)(6), proscribes listing a species as endangered once the statutory time limits have passed. We interpret the statutory provisions of the ESA *de novo*.

The ESA imposes specific deadlines on the Secretary for acting on a proposal to list a species. Within one year of publishing a proposed listing rule, the Secretary "shall" publish either a final listing rule, notice that the proposed rule is being withdrawn on grounds of insufficient evidence, or notice that the one-year period is being extended by six months to gather additional data because there is substantial disagreement regarding the existing data relevant to the listing determination. 16 U.S.C. § 1533(b)(6)(A)(i)(I)–(IV), (b)(6)(B)(i)–(ii). If the Secretary extends the decision by six months, he "shall" publish at the end of the six months either the rule or a notice withdrawing the rule, together with the finding on which withdrawal is based. 16 U.S.C. § 1533(b)(6)(B)(iii).

Although the statutory term "shall" suggests that the limits are mandatory, failure of an agency to act within a statutory time frame does not bar subsequent agency action absent a specific indication that Congress intended the time frame to serve as a bar. * * *

Legislative history accompanying the 1982 amendments to the ESA indicates that Congress passed the amendments due to concern about the low number of additions to the list of endangered species. "The Endangered Species Act was enacted in 1973 as a response to mounting concern over the extinction of fish, wildlife, and plants in the United States." H.R.

REP. No. 567, 97th Congress, 2d Sess., *reprinted in* 1982 U.S.C.C.A.N. 2807, 2809. In evaluating the ESA, "[o]ne of the principal problems noted was the decline in the pace of listing species which has occurred in recent years. Since 1981, only two species have passed through the entire proposal and listing processes." *Id.* at 2811.

In response, Congress attempted to find ways to expedite listing endangered species. "These amendments are intended to expedite the decisionmaking process and to ensure prompt action in determining the status of the many species which may require the protections of the Act." H.R. CONF. REP. No. 385, 97th Congress, 2d Sess., *reprinted in* U.S.C.C.A.N. 2807, 2809. As one means of expediting the listing process, Congress shortened the time frames for action. "To ensure that proposals ... are acted upon quickly, the Committee adopted a provision, new section 4(b)(6)(A), to shorten the allowable time for final action on section 4 proposals to list or delist a species from 2 years to one year from date of proposal." *Id.* at 2864. "Unless explicitly qualified, the time periods set forth in section 4, as amended, must be strictly adhered to by the Secretary." *Id.*

The legislative history's emphasis on the importance of the time limitations must be interpreted in light of the purpose of the amendments—to facilitate addition of endangered species to the endangered species list. A conclusion that the Secretary is prohibited from acting after passage of the prescribed time requirements would be inconsistent with this purpose. [T]he time requirements are designed to be an impetus to act rather than a prohibition on action taken after the time expires. Therefore, the Secretary can still list a species after expiration of the eighteen month statutory time requirement.

Our conclusion is bolstered by the fact that * * * the ESA does not provide any consequences for failure to act within the prescribed time. Further, the ESA provides a less drastic remedy—IFB could have filed a citizen suit to compel a decision. The availability of citizen suits makes it even less likely that Congress intended to create the more drastic remedy of revoking agency listing authority after passage of time requirements. Considering these factors together, the ESA did not preclude the FWS from listing the Springs Snail as an endangered species even after the eighteen month time requirement had passed.

We are well aware that the period between the initial proposed listing and the final listing, seven years, is exceptionally long. Such passage of time is a disservice to potentially endangered species and to the public. However, we also recognize that FWS faced a situation not anticipated in the standard listing process established in the ESA. Idaho's senators asked FWS to delay the listing, at least until FWS determined the cause of decline in Springs Snail habitat. The Senators agreed to help obtain the funding necessary to conduct additional studies. Congress thereafter provided funding for two separate studies. As long as FWS followed the mandated procedures after obtaining the studies, the passage of time does not render FWS's conduct arbitrary and capricious. * * *

NOTES

1. **The Rest of the Story.** Despite its decision on timing, the Ninth Circuit reversed the snail's listing on the grounds that the USFWS had not made the USGS study available during the public comment period. On September 12, 1995, the USFWS published a notice in the Federal Register announcing that the USGS Report and other scientific data and studies were available for public comment for 60 days. 60 Fed. Reg. 47,339. The USFWS then extended the comment period until December 15, 1995. 60 Fed. Reg. 56,976 (Nov. 13, 1995). The snail's listing then became subjected to the 1995 listing moratorium (see Note 7), delaying the USFWS in addressing the snail again until 1997. *See* 63 Fed. Reg. 32,981, 32,985 (June 17, 1998). By then, over a year had passed since the public comment period has closed, so the USFWS opened a second public comment period in January 1997 that eventually ended on June 9, 1997. 62 Fed. Reg. 3493 (Jan. 23, 1997); 62 Fed. Reg. 14,101 (March 25, 1997). In mid-June 1998, almost 13 years after the USFWS originally proposed listing the snail, the USFWS issued a notice in the Federal Register that it would retain the Bruneau Hot Springs Snail's "endangered" status. 63 Fed. Reg. 32,981, 32,981 (June 17, 1998).

2. **The Impetus for the Listing Decision and the Required Procedures.** How was the ESA listing in this case initiated? What procedures was the USFWS required to follow as a result? Did it follow all of those procedures? How did the USFWS violate the ESA's timing requirements in its listing decision? *Why* did it violate those requirements?

3. **The Consequences of Timing Violations.** Does violation of the timing requirements prevent the USFWS from listing the proposed species, according to the Ninth Circuit? Why or why not? Is this decision in accord with *TVA v. Hill*? Why or why not? What tools of statutory interpretation did the Ninth Circuit rely upon to reach its decision?

4. **The Economics and Politics of Listing Decisions, Revisited.** As noted, economic concerns are not, as a *legal* matter, supposed to influence the USFWS's ESA listing decisions. What does the involvement of Idaho's Senators in this listing decision suggest about the role of economics and politics as a *practical* matter? Why did the Senators become involved? What were their concerns? What effect did their involvement have on the listing process? Did the Idaho Senators act improperly? Why or why not? Did they ask the USFWS to act improperly? *Did* the USFWS act improperly? Why or why not?

5. **ESA Listing Decisions and Environmental Justice.** Think again about the Idaho Senators' concerns about the listing of the Bruneau Hot Springs Snail under the ESA, and about the controversy surrounding the listing of the Northern Spotted Owl. Do agency decisions to list species under the ESA affect all Americans equally? Why or why not? Who stood to be hurt by each of those listing decisions? Why? Under Executive Order No. 12898, on Environmental Justice, discussed in Chapter 1, *should* the USFWS consider environmental justice issues when making ESA listing decisions? Why or why

not? Legally, *can* it consider environmental justice issues when making ESA listing decisions? Why or why not?

6. **Other Procedures: NEPA and Endangered Species Act Listing Decisions.** As was examined in Chapter 2, the National Environmental Policy Act (NEPA) imposes procedural requirements on any major federal action that could substantially affect the quality of the human environment. 42 U.S.C. § 4332(2)(C). ESA listing decisions—like most environmental rulemakings—would normally qualify as "major federal actions substantially affecting the quality of the human environment" and thus trigger NEPA, requiring the USFWS to assess the environmental impacts of its listing decisions, at least through an ***Environmental Assessment*** **(EA)** and perhaps more extensively through an ***Environmental Impact Statement*** **(EIS)**.

However, because section 4 of the ESA also imposes extensive procedural and evaluative requirements on the USFWS, it has consistently argued that NEPA does not apply to its decisions to list endangered or threatened species or to designate critical habitat. The two leading federal Courts of Appeals decisions on this issue reached opposite conclusions. The Ninth Circuit, in *Douglas County v. Babbitt*, 48 F.3d 1495 (9th Cir. 1995), concluded that the ESA's procedures displaced NEPA's procedures, so that only the ESA analysis was required in listing decisions. A year later, the Tenth Circuit explicitly disagreed with the Ninth Circuit in *Catron County Board of Commissioners, New Mexico v. U.S Fish & Wildlife Service*, 75 F.3d 1429 (10th Cir. 1996), requiring both NEPA and ESA section 4 analyses in listing and critical habitat decisions. This circuit split remains unresolved.

The only time that Congress explicitly addressed the applicability of NEPA to ESA decisions was in the context of the Endangered Species Committee's section 7 exemption decisions. ESA § 7(k), 16 U.S.C. § 1536(k). What does the existence of this provision suggest for section 4, as a matter of statutory interpretation?

7. **The 1995 Listing Moratorium.** The effects of certain ESA listing decisions, like the Northern Spotted Owl decision, have made the ESA a highly controversial statute. In 1994, after the Republican party won a majority of seats in both houses of Congress, Congress attempted to institute a number of "reforms" in federal law, the so-called Contract with (or Contract on, depending on your politics) America. One result of this Republican activism was Public Law No. 104–06, 109 Stat. 73, 86 (April 10, 1995). While Public Law 104–06 did not repeal the ESA, it did eliminate the funding available to the USFWS to list species for protection under the ESA, creating in a backlog of petitions to list and proposed listings from which that agency is only now beginning to recover.

In *Environmental Defense Center v. Babbitt*, 73 F.3d 867 (9th Cir. 1995), the Ninth Circuit had to decide how the moratorium affected the USFWS's legal duties to list endangered species in the context of citizen petitions to list the California red-legged frog as an endangered species. As the Ninth Circuit noted, "[t]he Secretary admits that he failed to make a final determination on the red-legged frog by the statutory deadline. He contends, however, that he currently is unable to do so because Public Law 104–06 rescinds funding for the making of a final determination that a species is endangered." *Id.* at 870. Relying on the moratorium's origin in an appropriations rider, the Ninth Circuit determined that the moratorium did not affect the USFWS's legal duties under the ESA. *Id.* at 871. However, the Ninth Circuit also determined that no remedy for the delay in listing the frog was then available, given the moratorium. *Id.* at 871–72.

As a result of continuing congressional resolutions, the spending moratoria eventually lasted 13 months, from April 1995 through April 1996. However, when Congress again enacted a listing moratorium in the Omnibus Consolidated Rescissions and Appropriations Act of 1996, Pub. L. No. 104–134, 110 Stat. 1321 (April 26, 1996), it allowed the President to waive that moratorium. "President Clinton waived the moratorium the day he signed the bill into law," providing the USFWS with approximately $4 million for its listing and critical habitat designations for the rest of FY 1996. *Forest Guardians v. Babbitt*, 174 F.3d 1178, 1183 (10th Cir. 1999).

The moratoria's effects were felt long after 1996. "Because of the moratoria, between October 1995 and April 1996, the Service expended only $233,000 on the entire nationwide listing program—a modest sum compared to the nearly $4 million it received for the first six months of FY 1995." *Id.* As late as 1999, the USFWS still referred to the spending moratoria when arguing that it was "impossible" for it to fulfill its ESA listing responsibilities. *Id.* Moreover, because ESA citizen suits continued throughout the moratoria, resulting in judgments such as the one the Ninth Circuit issued in *Environmental Defense Center v. Babbitt*, the USFWS emerged from the moratoria with a long list of court judgments to satisfy. As a result, ESA listings since 1995 have been driven almost entirely by litigation, not by sound scientific priorities.

8. **Reaction to the Listing Moratoria: The PMG Policy.** As part of its own responsibilities for protecting species, the USFWS identifies ***candidate species*** for listing. "Candidate species are plants and animals for which the Fish and Wildlife Service * * * has sufficient information on their biological status and threats to propose them as endangered or threatened under the Endangered Species Act, but for which development of a proposed listing regulation is precluded by higher priority listing activities. The National Marine Fisheries Service (NMFS), which has jurisdiction over most marine species, defines candidate species more broadly to include species whose status is of concern but more information is needed before they can be proposed for listing." U.S. FISH & WILDLIFE SERVICE, THE ENDANGERED SPECIES ACT AND CANDIDATE SPECIES 1 (Sept. 2001), *available at* http://training.fws.gov/library/Pubs9/esa_cand01.pdf. For the USFWS, therefore, candidate species are the agency-generated equivalent of the "warranted but precluded" species generated pursuant to the petition process. Like warranted-but-precluded species, moreover, candidate species receive none of the ESA's protections because they have not been officially listed pursuant to section 4.

After the congressional spending moratoria expired, one of the ways that the USFWS attempted to deal with the backlog of petitions to list species was through its 1996 ***Petition Management Guidance*** **(PMG policy).** The PMG policy attempted to merge the USFWS's own candidate identification program with the petition process. Specifically, as described by the Ninth Circuit,

> [t]he policy provides that '[a] petition for an action on a species or critical habitat "identical" or "equivalent" to a petition *still pending (or active)* requires only a prompt (i.e., within 30 days) response informing the submitter of the prior petition and its status; Federal Register publication of this response is not required.' * * * The PMG policy equates species identified as candidates for listing with those designated 'warranted but precluded' under 16 U.S.C. § 1533(b)(3)(B)(iii). Candidate species are thus 'consider[ed] * * * as under petition,' and a petition to list a candidate species is deemed 'redundant.' Consequently, the Secretary now treats petitions to list species already identified as candidates for protection as second petitions and does not—ever—fulfill the statutory obligations described above that ordinarily attach to initial petitions.

Center for Biological Diversity v. Norton, 254 F.3d 833, 836 (9th Cir. 2001).

In *Center for Biological Diversity*, decided in the context of petitions to list the Chiricahua leopard frog and the Gila chub, the Ninth Circuit invalidated the PMG policy on grounds that it conflicted with congressional intent. In response to these petitions, the USFWS, citing to its PMG policy, responded merely that the two species were already candidate species for protection. It did not make the 90–day findings or issue the 12–month determinations for either species, characterizing the 90–day findings in particular as "superfluous." Under *de novo* review, the Ninth Circuit concluded that the ESA's timing requirements for petitions are clear and impose unmistakable requirements ("shall") on the USFWS. Candidate status did not satisfy these requirements:

> A "warranted but precluded" finding has two components. First, it is an admission by the Secretary that a species qualifies for protection—and that protection is "warranted"—under the ESA, an admission which, as noted, might be met by a candidate designation under the PMG policy's revised definition of candidate species. Second, the finding also states that a final rule cannot be issued right away, for administrative reasons, thereby temporarily excusing the Secretary from issuing a final rule. The circumstances under which the Secretary may invoke that excuse, however, are narrowly defined * * *. Specifically, the Secretary must show that she is "actively working on other listings and delistings and must determine and publish a finding that such other work has resulted in pending proposals which *actually* preclude[d] [her] proposing the petitioned action at that time." * * *
>
> When the Secretary, acting on her own initiative, designates a species for candidate status, she need not—and does not—explain why more immediate action is not appropriate. To the extent the PMG policy allows the Secretary to avoid this explanation in response to a citizen-sponsored petition, it is inconsistent with the express requirements of the ESA.

Id. at 838–39. As a result, candidate status also did not provide federal courts with an adequate basis for judicial review, like the 90–day findings and 12–month determinations do. *Id.* Finally, candidate status did not fulfill the ESA's mandatory deadlines. *Id. See also American Lands Alliance v. Norton*,

242 F. Supp. 2d 1, 13–18 (D.D.C. 2003) (following the Ninth Circuit's decision).

* * *

D. SECTION 4 OF THE ENDANGERED SPECIES ACT: ESTABLISHING CRITICAL HABITAT

The USFWS is supposed to designate ***critical habitat*** for each species that it lists at the same time of the listing, "to the maximum extent prudent and determinable * * *." ESA § 4(a)(3), 16 U.S.C. § 1533(a)(3); *see also* ESA § 4(b)(6)(C), 16 U.S.C. § 1533(b)(6)(C). A species' "critical habitat" is:

> (i) the specific area within the geographical area occupied by the species, at the time it is listed in accordance with the provisions of section 1533 of this title, on which are found those physical or biological features (I) essential to the conservation of the species and (II) which may require special management considerations or protection; and
>
> (ii) specific areas outside the geographical area occupied by the species at the time it is listed in accordance with the provisions of section 1533 of this title, upon a determination by the Secretary that such areas are essential for the conservation of the species.

ESA § 3(5)(A), 16 U.S.C. § 1532(5)(A). However, "[e]xcept in circumstances determined by the Secretary, critical habitat shall not include the entire geographical area which can be occupied by the threatened or endangered species." *Id.* § 3(5)(C), 16 U.S.C. § 1532(5)(C).

Critical habitat designation is thus tied to the overall goal of conserving the listed species, and the ESA defines "conservation" to mean "to use and the use of all methods and procedures which are necessary to bring any endangered species or threatened species to the point at which the measures provided pursuant to this chapter are no longer necessary." ESA § 3(3), 16 U.S.C. § 15342(3). The USFWS designates critical habitat "on the basis of the best scientific data available and after taking into consideration the economic impact, and any other relevant impact, of specifying any particular area as critical habitat." ESA § 4(b)(2), 16 U.S.C. § 1533(b)(2).

Thus, while the agency makes listing decisions purely on the basis of the scientifically-determined status of the species, critical habitat designations can consider the economic costs involved. Moreover, the USFWS

> may exclude any area from critical habitat if [it] determines that the benefits of such exclusion outweigh the benefits of specifying such area as part of the critical habitat, unless [it] determines, on the basis of the best scientific and commercial data available, that the failure to

designate such area as critical habitat will result in the extinction of the species concerned.

Id. Finally, the USFWS need not publish the critical habitat designation concurrently with the listing if:

> (i) it is essential to the conservation of such species that the regulation implementing [the listing] determination be promptly published; or
>
> (ii) critical habitat of such species is not then determinable, in which case the [agency], with respect to the proposed regulation to designate such habitat, may extend the one-year period * * * by not more than one additional year, but not later than the close of such additional year the [agency] must publish a final regulation, based on such data as may be available at that time, designating, to the maximum extent prudent, such habitat.

Id.

Members of the public can petition the USFWS to add or remove areas as critical habitat, using the same process as petitions to add or remove species from the list. ESA § 4(b)(3)(D), 16 U.S.C. § 1533(b)(3)(D). As with petitions to list or de-list species, the USFWS has 90 days to determine "whether the petition presents substantial scientific information indicating that the revision may be warranted." ESA § 4(b)(3)(D)(i), 16 U.S.C. § 1533(b)(3)(D)(i). That finding must be published in the Federal Register. Moreover, if the agency finds that the petition contained sufficient information, it must make and publish a proposed decision on the critical habitat petition within 12 months of receiving the petition. ESA § 4(b)(3)(D)(ii), 16 U.S.C. § 1533(b)(3)(D)(ii).

Because the ESA allows the USFWS to consider economic costs and other factors, and because the critical habitat designation provisions include qualifiers like "prudent," the USFWS has more discretion in making its critical habitat designations than it does in its listing decisions. The next case explores the limits of that discretion.

OTAY MESA PROPERTY, L.P. v. UNITED STATES DEPARTMENT OF THE INTERIOR

646 F.3d 914 (D.C. Cir. 2011).

KAVANAUGH, CIRCUIT JUDGE:

This case concerns the San Diego fairy shrimp, an aquatic animal found in southern California. The San Diego fairy shrimp is the size of an ant and has a life span of about 30 days. In 1997, the Fish and Wildlife Service listed the San Diego fairy shrimp as an endangered species under the Endangered Species Act. That Act authorizes the Fish and Wildlife Service to designate property as "critical habitat" for the endangered species if the property was "occupied" by the species when the species was listed as endangered (and if certain other requirements are met).

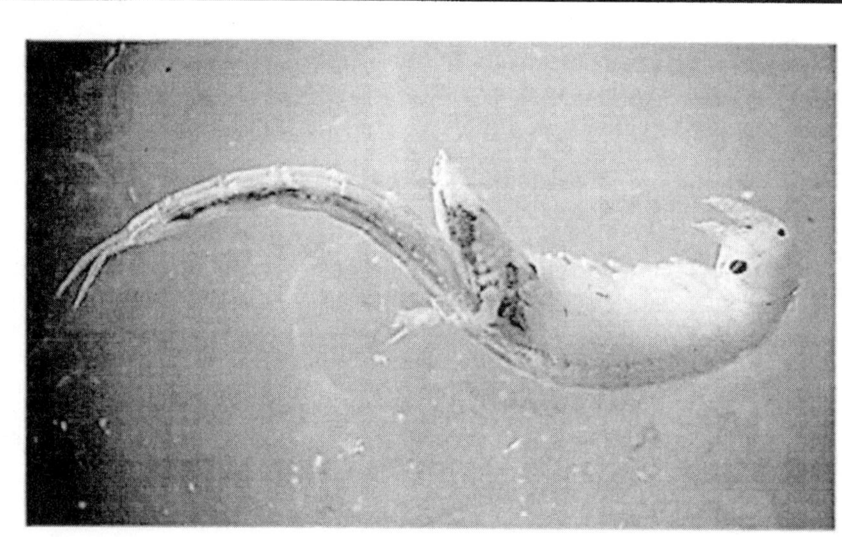

Figure 3-5: San Diego Fairy Shrimp
Photo care of U.S. Fish & Wildlife Service (Dwight Harvey)

Plaintiffs are companies that own land along the California–Mexico border. In 2007, acting pursuant to the Endangered Species Act, the Fish and Wildlife Service designated 143 acres of plaintiffs' property as critical habitat for the San Diego fairy shrimp. The Fish and Wildlife Service based that critical habitat designation on a single 2001 sighting of four ant-sized San Diego fairy shrimp on the 143 acres of plaintiffs' property. The four San Diego fairy shrimp were observed in a tire rut on a dirt road on plaintiffs' property. Because the Fish and Wildlife Service has not reasonably explained how that one, isolated observation demonstrates that plaintiffs' property was "occupied" by the San Diego fairy shrimp in 1997 (the relevant statutory date), we reverse the judgment of the District Court and remand. On remand, the District Court should vacate the designation of plaintiffs' property as critical habitat for the San Diego fairy shrimp and remand the matter to the agency.

I

The landmark Endangered Species Act of 1973 authorizes the Department of the Interior to take measures to protect species at risk of extinction. The Fish and Wildlife Service, an agency within the Department, implements this important Act, as do other agencies. The Fish and Wildlife Service may list species at risk of extinction as "threatened" or "endangered." 16 U.S.C. § 1533. Once a species is so designated, it may be unlawful for anyone to "take" (i.e., kill) members of that species. *Id.* § 1538(a)(1)(B).

In addition, the Fish and Wildlife Service may designate land, including private property, as "critical habitat" for a threatened or endangered species. The Act states:

The term "critical habitat" for a threatened or endangered species means—

(i) the specific areas within the geographical area *occupied by* the species, *at the time it is listed* [as a threatened or endangered species], on which are found those physical or biological features (I) essential to the conservation of the species and (II) which may require special management considerations or protection; and

(ii) specific areas outside the geographical area occupied by the species at the time it is listed [as a threatened or endangered species], upon a determination by the Secretary that such areas are essential for the conservation of the species.

16 U.S.C. § 1532(5)(A) (emphases added).

Designation of private property as critical habitat can impose significant costs on landowners because federal agencies may not authorize, fund, or carry out actions that are likely to "result in the destruction or adverse modification" of critical habitat. *Id.* § 1536(a)(2).

Plaintiffs Otay Mesa Property, L.P., Rancho Vista Del Mar, and Otay International, LLC, own property along the California–Mexico border. In 2007, the Fish and Wildlife Service designated 143 acres of plaintiffs' property as critical habitat for the San Diego fairy shrimp.

San Diego fairy shrimp are tiny aquatic animals—about the size of ants. They live in "vernal pools" in southern California and northwestern Mexico. Those pools are typically large puddles or small seasonal ponds that form during the winter and then dry out as summer approaches. The life span of San Diego fairy shrimp is only about 30 days. If the shrimp lay eggs, those eggs can lie dormant in the bottom of a dry pool for months or years. When the pool re-fills again, the eggs can hatch.

In 1997, the Fish and Wildlife Service listed San Diego fairy shrimp as an endangered species. 62 Fed. Reg. 4925 (Feb. 3, 1997). But the Service did not designate plaintiffs' property as critical habitat at that time. In 2001, an environmental consulting company surveyed a 3300–acre area along the California–Mexico border, searching for fairy shrimp. The surveyed area included plaintiffs' property. The company conducted eight surveys between January and May 2001, when vernal pools are normally full and San Diego fairy shrimp can be found. Those eight surveys produced one confirmed observation of San Diego fairy shrimp on plaintiffs' property: On February 7, 2001, surveyors observed four adult San Diego fairy shrimp in a tire rut on a dirt road.

The Fish and Wildlife Service became aware of this report and, in 2003, included plaintiffs' property in its proposed critical habitat designation for San Diego fairy shrimp. During the ensuing notice and comment period, plaintiffs submitted letters objecting to the designation of their property. The Fish and Wildlife Service rejected those comments and in 2007 published a final rule designating as critical habitat 391 acres of southeast Otay Mesa, including plaintiffs' property, on the justification that the area was "occupied by the [San Diego fairy shrimp] at the time of listing [as an endangered species in 1997]," and that "the species continues to occur" in the designated area. 72 Fed. Reg. 70,648, 70,674 (Dec. 12, 2007).

In 2008, plaintiffs sued to challenge the designation of their property as critical habitat. The District Court granted summary judgment to the Fish and Wildlife Service, although the court described the Fish and Wildlife Service's support for its conclusion as "distinctly thin." We review the District Court's decision de novo. We review the Fish and Wildlife Service's underlying decision pursuant to the standards set forth in the Administrative Procedure Act. *See* 5 U.S.C. § 706. The question here is whether substantial evidence supports the Fish and Wildlife Service's determination that plaintiffs' land was occupied by the San Diego fairy shrimp at the time of listing in 1997. Substantial evidence is a deferential standard. But deference is not abdication. This case illustrates the significance of that distinction.

II

According to the Fish and Wildlife Service, plaintiffs' property meets the statutory definition of critical habitat because the property was "occupied" by the San Diego fairy shrimp in 1997—the year the San Diego fairy shrimp was listed as an endangered species. 16 U.S.C. § 1532(5)(A)(i).

Several factors taken together point to a lack of substantial evidence for the Fish and Wildlife Service's determination that plaintiffs' property was "occupied" by the San Diego fairy shrimp in 1997.

First, surveyors identified San Diego fairy shrimp on plaintiffs' property only in one location. On February 7, 2001, surveyors found four San Diego fairy shrimp in a tire rut on a dirt road on plaintiffs' land. That is the sole confirmed observation of San Diego fairy shrimp on plaintiffs' property.

Second, after the one survey that found San Diego fairy shrimp on plaintiffs' property, surveyors searched plaintiffs' property six more times in 2001 for San Diego fairy shrimp. Having once found San Diego fairy shrimp, it might have been thought that surveyors would again find San Diego fairy shrimp on plaintiffs' property. That did not happen. The failure to observe *any* San Diego fairy shrimp in later surveys of plaintiffs' property is in tension with the suggestion that the property was occupied by the San Diego fairy shrimp in 2001. It is likewise in tension with the agency's conclusion that the property was occupied in 1997 and the "species continue[d] to occur" in 2007.

On appeal to this Court, the Fish and Wildlife Service explains that San Diego fairy shrimp may live for only 30 days, but they can leave behind buried eggs that do not hatch for months or even years. It appears that the Service might believe (i) that wherever adult San Diego fairy shrimp are observed, one can assume that the shrimp have left behind eggs and (ii) that a property with dormant, buried eggs is by definition "occupied" by the San Diego fairy shrimp. But if that's the theory behind the Fish and Wildlife Service's determination that plaintiffs' property is occupied by San Diego fairy shrimp, the theory cannot be found in the final rule. This Court of course "may not supply a reasoned basis for the agency's action that the agency itself has not given."

Third, the lone sighting in this case was in 2001, but the relevant date for purposes of the designation is 1997. Critical habitat includes "specific areas within the geographical area occupied by the species, *at the time it is listed.*" 16 U.S.C. § 1532(5)(A) (emphasis added). The San Diego fairy shrimp was listed as an endangered species in 1997. But the Service has provided no evidence of sightings on plaintiffs' land in 1997. Although the Service has tried to explain why a single sighting in 2001 means that the San Diego fairy shrimp occupied plaintiffs' property as of 1997, that reasoning is at best strained. *See* 72 Fed. Reg. at 70,666. For their part, plaintiffs believe that the San Diego fairy shrimp may have been brought onto plaintiffs' property after 1997 by a truck tire.

Separately, the Fish and Wildlife Service suggests that plaintiffs' property is part of a "vernal pool complex" that supports the San Diego fairy shrimp population in the general area. At oral argument, counsel for the Fish and Wildlife Service stated that maps in the record show a stream running from plaintiffs' property to a pool not on plaintiffs' land where San Diego fairy shrimp have been observed (albeit, again, only one time).

But the potential existence of San Diego fairy shrimp *outside* plaintiffs' property does not itself show that San Diego fairy shrimp occupy plaintiffs' property, and occupation of plaintiffs' property was the rationale supplied in the agency's final rule. To be sure, the Endangered Species Act allows designation of critical habitat both for land occupied by the species in question and for "specific areas outside the geographical area occupied by the species ... upon a determination by the Secretary that such areas are essential for the conservation of the species." 16 U.S.C. § 1532(5)(A)(ii). But the Fish and Wildlife Service here designated plaintiffs' land as critical habitat on the basis that it was *occupied,* not on the basis that it was a "specific area[] outside the geographical area occupied by the species ... essential for the conservation of the species." *See, e.g.,* 72 Fed. Reg. at 70,664 ("All areas designated as critical habitat for San Diego fairy shrimp are occupied.... "). If the Fish and Wildlife Service believes that plaintiffs' land is critical habitat not because it is occupied, but rather because it is "essential for the conservation of the species," then it must say so in its agency decision and justify that determination.

The Fish and Wildlife Service also contends that the evidence here suffices because the Endangered Species Act requires the Fish and Wildlife Service to make critical habitat designations "on the basis of the best scientific data available." 16 U.S.C. § 1533(b)(2). The Fish and Wildlife Service argues, correctly, that it has no affirmative obligation to conduct its own research to supplement existing data. But the absence of a requirement for the Service to collect more data on its own is not the same as an authorization to act without data to support its conclusions, even acknowledging the deference due to agency expertise.

Here, the Fish and Wildlife Service relies on eight surveys of plaintiffs' property. Seven of those surveys found no confirmed San Diego fairy shrimp on the property. One survey in 2001 resulted in identification of the species' presence in one location. The "best scientific data available" fails to demonstrate, without further explanation, that plaintiffs' property was "occupied" by San Diego fairy shrimp in 1997.

We emphasize that it is the combination of all the above factors that leads us to vacate the Fish and Wildlife Service's designation of plaintiffs' property. We rely on no single factor alone. On remand, moreover, the Fish and Wildlife Service may be able to justify a re-designation. Our conclusion in this case is thus quite narrow: The current record is simply too thin to justify the action the Service took.

NOTES

1. **Delays in Critical Habitat Listing.** Notice the delay in this case between the FWS's listing of the San Diego fairy shrimp under the ESA and the actual designation of critical habitat—about a decade. FWS has long considered critical habitat designations to be of limited value in protecting species. Why would that be, do you suppose? Consider this question again as you study the protections provided in Section 7 and Section 9, and remember the role of critical habitat in *TVA v. Hill*. If critical habitat designations were as toothless as the FWS believed, would property owners like the ones in this case fight so hard to have their properties un-designated?

2. **Standard of Review.** Which APA standard of review does the U.S. Court of Appeals use to review the FWS's decision regarding critical habitat in this case? How does that standard different from "arbitrary and capricious" review? Did the D.C. Circuit use the correct standard, based on what you know of administrative law? Why or why not?

3. **Habitat Currently Occupied vs. Future Habitat.** As the D.C. Circuit acknowledges, FWS can designate unoccupied habitat as critical habitat under the ESA. Why then did the D.C. Circuit vacate FWS's inclusion of the plaintiffs' property as critical habitat for the San Diego fairy shrimp? On remand, could FWS again decide to designate this property as critical habitat? If so, on what basis?

4. **The Economics of Critical Habitat Designations.** The ESA requires the USFWS to analyze the economic effects of a critical habitat

designation. ESA § 4(b)(2), 16 U.S.C. § 1533(b)(2). The USFWS has a Division of Economics, which conducts these analyses.

As noted, however, the USFWS is *not* supposed to consider economics when deciding whether to *list* a species. To reconcile these two commands, the USFWS for many years used an ***incremental baseline approach*** to determine the economic effects of critical habitat designations. Under this approach, the USFWS considered only those economic effects caused by the critical habitat designation itself—*not* any of the effects caused by the listing—in its economic analyses of the critical habitat designation. Because the ESA's protections are tied mainly to the fact of listing, the USFWS's baseline approach meant that few critical habitat designations incurred costs that outweighed their benefits.

In 2001, the Tenth Circuit invalidated the incremental baseline approach. *New Mexico Cattle Growers Ass'n v. U.S. Fish & Wildlife Service*, 248 F.3d 1277, 1283–85 (10th Cir. 2001). Addressing the issue of "whether the FWS must analyze all of the economic impacts of the critical habitat designation (regardless of whether the impacts are co-extensive with other causes), or only those impacts that are a 'but for' result" of the designation, *id.* at 1284, the Tenth Circuit emphasized that "[t]he root of the problem lies in the FWS's long held policy position that [critical habitat designations] are unhelpful, duplicative, and unnecessary." *Id.* at 1283. According to the Tenth Circuit, "The statutory language is plain in requiring some kind of consideration of economic impact in the [critical habitat designation] phase." *Id.* at 1285. Moreover, "[b]ecause economic analysis done using the FWS's baseline model is rendered essentially without meaning * * *, we conclude Congress intended that the FWS conduct a full analysis of all economic impacts of a critical habitat designation, regardless of whether those impacts are attributable co-extensively to other causes." *Id.*

Several federal district courts have adopted the Tenth Circuit's decision, often in response to the USFWS's request for a voluntary remand of its critical habitat designations in the face of industry challenges to such designations. *See, e.g.*, *Home Builders Ass'n of Northern California v. U.S. Fish & Wildlife Service*, 268 F. Supp. 2d 1197, 1225–30 (E.D. Cal. 2003) (Alameda whipsnake); *Natural Resources Defense Council, Inc. v. U.S. Dep't of the Interior*, 275 F. Supp. 2d 1136, 1140–45 (C.D. Cal. 2002) (California gnatcatcher and San Diego fairy shrimp); *Home Builders Ass'ns of Northern California v. Norton*, 293 F. Supp. 2d 1, 3–4 (D.D.C. 2002) (California red-legged frog); *Building Industry Legal Defense Foundation v. Norton*, 231 F. Supp. 2d 100, 102–07 (D.D.C. 2002) (Riverside fairy shrimp and arroyo southwestern toad). What kinds of parties does the Tenth Circuit's decision favor? Would it tend to be better for species or for developers? Why?

* * *

E. SECTION 7 OF THE ENDANGERED SPECIES ACT

1. Introduction and Overview

Once the USFWS lists a species under section 4 of the ESA, that species receives the Act's protections. The most significant of these protections are found in section 7, 16 U.S.C. § 1536, and section 9, 16 U.S.C. § 1538.

Section 7 applies only to federal agencies and imposes two requirements on them. First, all "Federal agencies shall, in consultation with and with the assistance of [the USFWS and NMFS/NOAA Fisheries], utilize their authorities in furtherance of the purposes of this chapter by carrying out programs for the conservation of endangered species and threatened species listed pursuant to section 1533 of this title." ESA § 7(a)(1), 16 U.S.C. § 1536(a)(1). "Conservation," in turn, is "the use of all methods and procedures which are necessary to bring any endangered species or threatened species to the point at which the measures provided pursuant to this chapter are no longer necessary." ESA § 3(3), 16 U.S.C. § 1532(3).

Second, "[e]ach Federal agency shall, in consultation with and with the assistance of [USFWS or NMFS], insure that any action authorized, funded, or carried out by such agency * * * is not likely to jeopardize the continued existence of any endangered species or threatened species or result in the destruction or adverse modification of [critical] habitat, * * * unless such agency has been granted an exemption for such action by the [Endangered Species] Committee pursuant to subsection (h) of this section." ESA § 7(a)(2), 16 U.S.C. § 1536(a)(2).

Let's examine each of these provisions in turn.

2. Section 7(a)(1) and Conservation of Listed Species

Section 7(a)(1) was the later of section 7's two requirements to achieve practical significance. The following case is the first appellate level case recognizing the independent legal force of section 7(a)(1).

CARSON-TRUCKEE WATER CONSERVANCY DISTRICT v. CLARK

741 F.2d 257 (9th Cir. 1984).

PREGERSON, CIRCUIT JUDGE:

[SUMMARY OF FACTS: "The Little Truckee River flows into the Truckee River, which then flows from California into Nevada and into Pyramid Lake." Pyramid Lake is home to two species of fish, the cui-ui fish and the Lahontan cutthroat trout, that were listed for protection under the Endangered Species Act (ESA). However, water flowing through the Truckee River system to Pyramid Lake is controlled by Stampede Dam, "located on the Little Truckee in California." Congress authorized the building of the dam as a source of water supply. Although Congress intended the water stored behind the dam to be used primarily for agricultural irrigation, in fact the only real use for the water by the 1980s was municipal and industrial (M & I) use. The Washoe Project Act, 43 U.S.C. §§ 614–614d, governs the Secretary of the Interior's sales of water from the dam project, but, unlike many reclamation acts (so named because water supplies allowed settlers to reclaim dry lands from being desert), the Washoe Act did not absolutely require the Secretary to sell all of the project's water. As a result, pursuant to ESA § 7(a)(1), the Secretary of the Interior had been refusing to sell water from the project to the the Carson–Truckee Water Conservancy District and Sierra Pacific Power Company in order to conserve the two listed species of fish in Pyramid Lake. Specifically, by not selling the water, the Secretary guaranteed a greater supply of water to those fish.]

Carson–Truckee Water Conservancy District and Sierra Pacific Power Company (appellants) sought a declaratory judgment that the Secretary of the Interior (Secretary) violated the Washoe Project Act, 43 U.S.C.A. §§ 614–614d (West 1964), and related reclamation laws in refusing to sell water from the Stampede Dam and Reservoir on the Little Truckee River for municipal and industrial (M & I) use in Reno and Sparks.

* * * Appellants concede that the Secretary's obligations under ESA supersede his obligations under the Washoe Project Act and related federal reclamation laws. Appellants, however, challenge the extent of the Secretary's obligations under ESA.

* * * II. ANALYSIS

We affirm and adopt all but one of the district court's holdings for the reasons ably stated by Judge Solomon in his two learned opinions. * * *

* * * We feel constrained to elaborate our reasons for rejecting appellants' arguments against two of the district court's holdings. Those holdings are that (1) ESA requires the Secretary to give priority to the conservation of threatened and endangered species, and (2) the Secretary did not abuse his discretion both in determining that there was no excess water to sell for M & I purposes after his obligations under ESA were fulfilled, and in rejecting appellants' alternate plan for operating Stampede Dam. * * *

(1) ESA's requirements.

Appellants urge a reading of ESA that would lead to a result at odds with the statute's clearly stated objectives. Appellants contend that the Secretary's authority is defined solely by ESA § 7(a)(2), 16 U.S.C. § 1536(a)(2). Thus, they argue that the Secretary is authorized only to take actions that avoid "jeopardizing" the continued existence of a species. Appellants contend that the Secretary may not do more than that.

In addition to its § 7(a)(2) "jeopardy" provision, however, ESA also directs the Secretary to conserve threatened and endangered species to the extent that they are no longer threatened or endangered. Appellants, relying *solely* on § 7(a)(2), would have us ignore the other sections of ESA directly applicable here and relied on by the district court. ESA § 2(b), (c), & § 3(3), 16 U.S.C. § 1531(b), (c), & § 1532(3). ESA § 7(a)(1), moreover, specifically directs that the Secretary "shall" use programs administered by him to further the conservation purposes of ESA. 16 U.S.C. § 1536(a)(1). Those sections, as the district court found, direct that the

Secretary actively pursue a species conservation policy. *See also Tennessee Valley Authority v. Hill,* 437 U.S. 153, 184 (1978) (ESA requires the Secretary to give highest priority to the preservation of endangered species; Congress intended to "halt *and reverse* the trend toward species extinction, whatever the cost." (emphasis added)).

The purpose of ESA § 7(a)(2) is to ensure that the federal government does not undertake actions, such as building a dam or highway, that incidentally jeopardize the existence of endangered or threatened species. See *TVA v. Hill*, 437 U.S. 153, for an example of § 7(a)(2)'s application. Contrary to appellants' contention, ESA § 7(a)(2) is inapplicable here because the Secretary has not undertaken a project that threatens an endangered species. Instead, following the mandate of ESA § 7(a)(1), § 2(b), (c), & § 3(3), 16 U.S.C. § 1536(a)(1), § 1531(c), (b), & § 1532(3), the Secretary actively seeks to conserve endangered species. Thus, the district court properly applied ESA § 2(b), (c), & § 3(3) rather than ESA § 7(a)(2) to this case.

Applying the proper code sections to this case, the Secretary's decision is well-justified. The Washoe Project Act anticipates but does not require the Secretary to sell water to recover project construction costs. ESA, on the other hand, directs the Secretary to use programs under his control for conservation purposes where threatened or endangered species are involved. Following this directive, the Secretary here decided to conserve the fish and not to sell the project's water. Given these circumstances, the ESA supports the Secretary's decision to give priority to the fish until such time as they no longer need ESA's protection.[5]

NOTES

1. **Identifying the Proper Subsection of Section 7.** Why was this a section 7(a)(1) case and not a section 7(a)(2) jeopardy case? Could the Secretary of the Interior's decisions to sell or not sell water from the Washoe Project ever raise section 7(a)(2) issues? How?

2. ***TVA v. Hill* as Precedent.** How does the Ninth Circuit use *TVA v. Hill* in this decision? Were the Secretary of the Interior's actions consistent with *TVA v. Hill*, according to the Ninth Circuit? Why or why not? Is the Ninth Circuit's decision in this case consistent with *TVA v. Hill*? Why or why not?

3. **Competing Obligations and Conflicts Among Statutes.** Why was there no conflict between the Washoe Project Act and the ESA in this case? What would the courts have done if the Washoe Project Act required the Secretary to sell "as much water as possible" from the Stampede Dam

5. Because we hold that the Washoe Project Act does not require the Secretary to sell water for M & I use, we need not reach the question whether, given competing mandatory statutory directives, the Secretary would be required to use the project's water entirely for conservation purposes under ESA § 2(b), (c), § 3(3), & § 7(a)(1). Similarly, because the Secretary actively seeks to use the project for conservation purposes, we need not consider the extent of his affirmative obligations under ESA § 2(b), (c), § 3(3), & § 7(a)(1) had he decided neither to sell the water nor to protect the fish.

reservoir? What would the courts have done if the Washoe Project Act required the Secretary to sell a certain amount of acre-feet (the unit for measuring large quantities of water, which is the amount of water that will cover one acre of ground to one foot in depth of water) from the project every year? Does it matter that Congress enacted the Washoe Project Act in 1956 and the ESA in 1973?

4. **The Endangered Species Act and Water: A Thought Problem on Policy Balancing.** *Carson-Truckee Water Conservancy District* was not only the first case to test section 7(a)(1), it was also a harbinger of an increasingly important source of conflict with the ESA: water use. In the eastern half of the United States, year-round rainfall and groundwater are likely to be sufficient to sustain humans, farms, industry, *and* species listed for protection under the ESA—although conflicts are beginning to arise even there. In the arid West, in contrast, cities, industry, and agriculture flourish only because of the many federally financed reclamation projects that exist there. These projects generally constructed dams, creating reservoirs that could store the winter and spring rains for use during the summer and early fall, when little to no rain falls, and during drought years. Occasionally, however, such projects transported water from one part of the country to another. Marc Reisner has expertly told the tale of water development in the American West in his book CADILLAC DESERT: THE AMERICAN WEST AND ITS DISAPPEARING WATER (original: New York, NY: Viking Penguin 1986; revised edition: New York, NY: Penguin Books 1993).

Recall that *TVA v. Hill* also involved a water project and dam. However, the problem in that case was loss of the snail darter's habitat—not loss of water *per se*. Increasingly, species protected under the ESA are competing with humans for the *water itself*. Would the Supreme Court have reached the same conclusion in *TVA v. Hill*, do you think, if enjoining the dam would have deprived city dwellers of drinking water and farmers of irrigation water? How could the Court have interpreted section 7 differently than it did? More broadly, how should courts and Congress balance humans' and imperiled species' needs for water?

Consider the following facts: Since 1909, the Bureau of Reclamation has operated the Klamath Irrigation Project, one of the oldest federal reclamation schemes, in northern California and southern Oregon. The Secretary of the Interior undertook this project pursuant to the Reclamation Act of 1902, 43 U.S.C. § 371 *et seq*., and the Act of February 9, 1905, 33 Stat. 714. This project uses the Upper Klamath Lake for its primary water storage. Water then flows through the Klamath River past a series of dams, the last of which is the Iron Gate Dam. Storage in Upper Klamath Lake is limited, hampering the project's ability to supply sufficient water to meet all needs in drought years. Nevertheless, the project irrigates 200,000 acres of land, and the irrigators all have repayment contracts with the Bureau of Reclamation. These contracts, under the Reclamation Act, are supposed to insure that the water users eventually repay the cost of the Klamath Irrigation Project. 43 U.S.C. §§ 412, 462, 501.

The Klamath Irrigation Project operated largely without conflict until 1988, when the USFWS listed the Lost River Sucker (*Deltistes luxatus*) and the Shortnose Sucker (*Chasmistes brevirostri*) as endangered species under the federal ESA. These two fish live only in the Upper Klamath Lake and nearby project waters. 53 Fed. Reg. 27,130, 27131–32 (July 18, 1988). In 1992, the Bureau of Reclamation notified the USFWS that operation of the project might affect these two fish.

In addition, in 1997, the USFWS and NMFS listed the coho salmon as a threatened species under the ESA. The coho lives in the Klamath River, and it warranted protection under the ESA in part because the Klamath Irrigation Project had degraded the coho's habitat by diverting water away from the river. 62 Fed. Reg. 24,588, 24,592 (May 6, 1997). In 1999, the two agencies determined that the Klamath River below the Iron Gate Dam was critical habitat for the coho. 64 Fed. Reg. 24,049, 24,049 (May 5, 1999).

While the Bureau of Reclamation generally can balance the water needs of the fish and the farmers, despite the Upper Klamath Lake's limited storage, 2001 was a "critically dry" year for the Klamath River area, and the USFWS and NMFS determined that normal delivery of irrigation water to farmers by the Bureau would jeopardize the continued existence of all three species of fish. As a result, when the Bureau of Reclamation wrote the Klamath Reclamation Project 2001 Operations Plan, it provided that water elevations in the Upper Klamath Lake and water flows below the Iron Gate Dam would be maintained to support the endangered suckers and threatened coho salmon. No irrigation water would be delivered to the majority of land served by the reclamation project, even though it was estimated that the resulting agricultural losses would run to the millions of dollars.

When farmers sued the Bureau, demanding release of the water, what should the federal district judge have done? Does it matter to your answer that the listed fish are of profound cultural significance to various Tribes in the region and provide subsistence food to their members? Why or why not? Does it matter to your answer that commercial fishermen in California and Oregon make their livings off the Klamath River coho runs? Why or why not? Does it matter to your answer that dams and irrigation projects have endangered almost all species of salmon in California, Oregon, and Washington, not just the coho? Why or why not? Does it matter to your answer that the Bureau of Reclamation still has not sought an exemption for its operation of the Klamath Irrigation Project from the Endangered Species Committee? Why or why not? *See Kandra v. United States*, 145 F. Supp. 2d 1192 (D. Or. 2001); *see also Pacific Coast Federation of Fishermen's Ass'ns v. U.S. Bureau of Reclamation*, 138 F. Supp. 2d 1228 (N.D. Cal. 2001).

5. Section 7(a)(1) as a Sword. In *Carson-Truckee Water Conservancy District*, the Department of the Interior used section 7(a)(1) as a ***shield***—that is, as a defense to liability for not selling more water pursuant to the Washoe Project Act. More recently, environmental challengers have begun to use section 7(a)(1) as a ***sword***—that is, as a means of forcing federal agencies to more actively conserve species listed for protection under the ESA. For example, in *Sierra Club v. Glickman*, 156 F.3d 606 (5th Cir. 1998), the Sierra Club claimed that the Department of Agriculture had violated section 7(a)(1) with respect to five listed species—the fountain darter, the San Marcos gambusia, the San Marcos salamander, the Texas blind salamander, and Texas wild rice—that inhabit the San Marcos Springs and the Comal Springs in central Texas. These springs are fed by the Edwards Aquifer, an underground source of water, and the Sierra Club sought to force the Department of Agriculture to use its authority under various federal statutes to encourage or require farmers to reduce the amount of water that the farmers pumped out of the Edwards Aquifer, delivering more water to the ESA-protected species.

The Fifth Circuit upheld the district court in concluding that section 7(a)(1) imposes affirmative obligations on federal agencies "to carry out programs for the conservation" of listed species and to consult with the USFWS regarding such programs. *Id.* at 618. Moreover, the court considered insufficient the USDA's "argument that it has complied with the requirements of § 7(a)(1) because the Edwards-dependent species have experienced incidental benefits from national USDA programs designed and carried out for other purposes." *Id.* As a result, because "there is no real dispute that the USDA has never fulfilled its obligations under § 7(a)(1) with respect to the Edwards-dependent species," the Sierra Club prevailed, requiring the USDA to develop, in consultation with the USFWS, an organized program for conserving those species. *Id.*

Given this decision, does section 7(a)(1) created purely procedural requirements for federal agencies, or does it include substantive requirements as well?

* * *

3. Section 7(a)(2) and the Jeopardy Determinations

a. The Section 7 Consultation Process

The "jeopardy" or critical habitat destruction determination process is a complex one. First, when an ***action agency*** is considering whether to authorize, fund, or carry out a new action, it begins an ***informal consultation process*** with the USFWS and NMFS/NOAA Fisheries—the ***expert agencies***—to determine whether any species listed for protection under the ESA are present in the action area. ESA § 7(a)(3), 16 U.S.C. § 1536(a)(3). If such species are present, then the *action agency* prepares a ***Biological Assessment* (BA)**, ESA § 7(c), 16 U.S.C. § 1536(c), to determine whether its action is likely to *adversely affect* any listed species or critical habitat. The relevant *expert agency* then reviews the BA. If the action agency concludes in its BA that its action will not adversely affect any species or critical habitat, and the relevant expert agency concurs, then the action agency's consultation duties under section 7 are complete.

In their *Endangered Species Consultation Handbook*, the USFWS and NMFS/NOAA Fisheries flowchart the informal consultation process as shown in Figure 3–6. As that flowchart indicates, if during informal consultation the action agency concludes in its BA that its proposed action will adversely affect a listed species and/or critical habitat, the action agency and the expert agencies must proceed through the ***formal consultation process***. ESA § 7(b), 16 U.S.C. § 1536(b).

The USFWS and NMFS/NOAA Fisheries flowchart the formal consultation process as shown in Figure 3–7. As this flowchart indicates, in formal consultation, after all information is assembled, the ***expert agency*** has 90 days in which to formulate its ***Biological Opinion*** **(BO or BiOp)**. The BO is the expert agency's advice to the action agency regarding whether the expert agency's proposed action will jeopardize the continued existence of a listed species or destroy or adversely modify critical habitat. In addition, if the expert agency concludes that the proposed action will not jeopardize the species but will result in ***incidental take*** of the species, the BO can include an ***incidental take statement*** that relieves the action agency of liability under section 9. To be effective, the incidental take statement must be a written statement that:

> (i) specifies the impact of such incidental taking on the species,
>
> (ii) specifies those reasonable and prudent measures that the [expert agency] considers necessary or appropriate to minimize such impact,

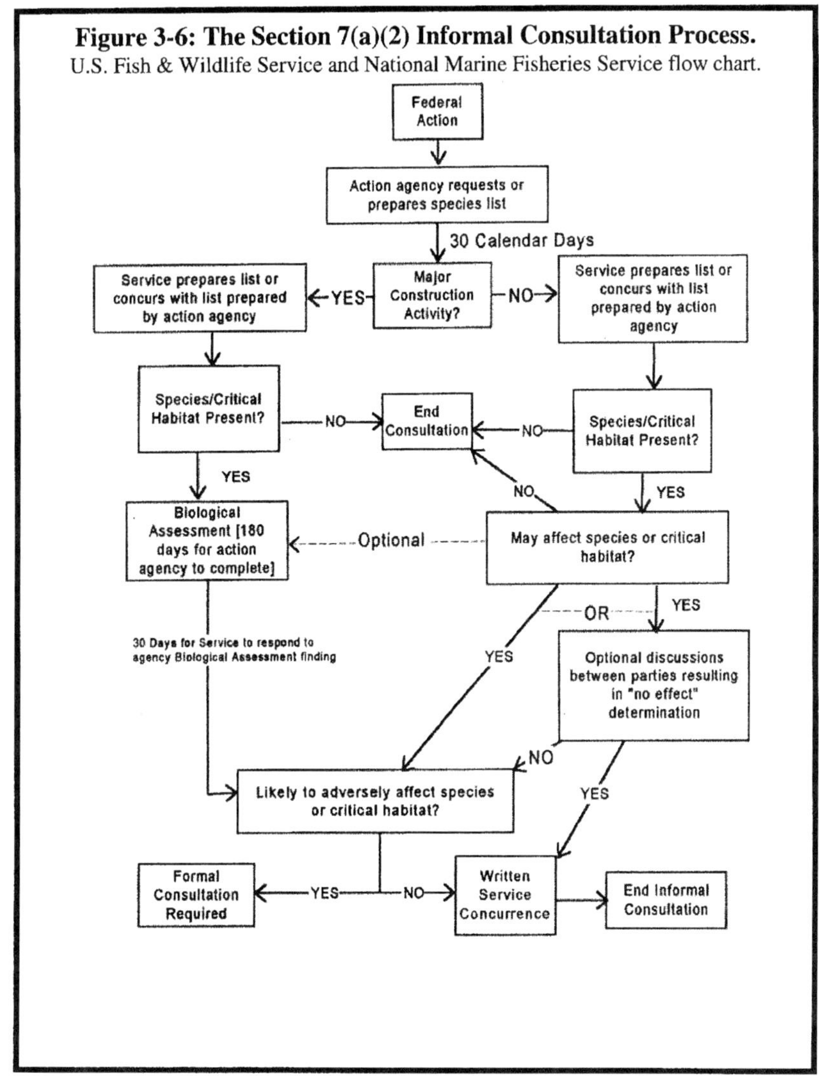

Figure 3-6: The Section 7(a)(2) Informal Consultation Process.
U.S. Fish & Wildlife Service and National Marine Fisheries Service flow chart.

Figure 3-7: The Section 7(a)(2) Formal Consultation Process
U.S. Fish & Wildlife Service and National Marine Fisheries Service flow chart.

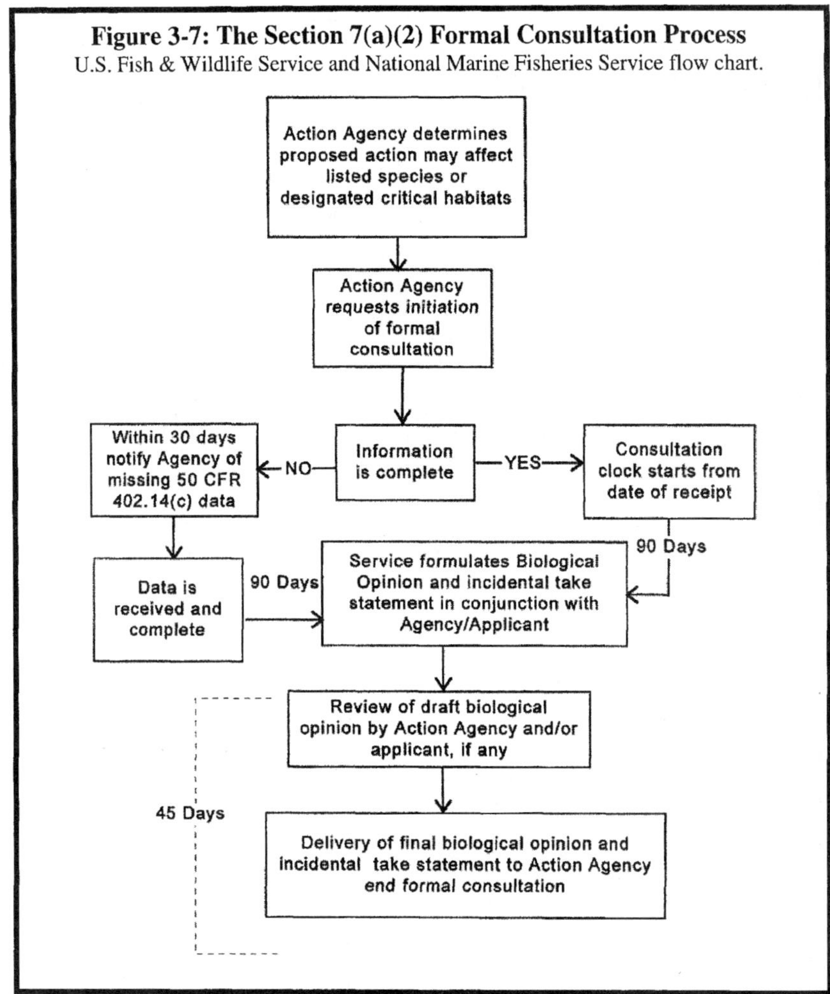

(iii) in the case of marine mammals, specifies those measures that are necessary to comply with [the Marine Mammal Protection Act] with regard to such taking, and

(iv) sets forth the conditions (including, but not limited to, reporting requirements) that must be complied with by the Federal agency or applicant (if any), or both, to implement the measures specified under clauses (ii) and (iii).

ESA § 7(b)(4), 16 U.S.C. § 1536(b)(4).

Regardless of what the expert agency's BO concludes, the decision whether to proceed with the proposed action always remains with the ***action agency***. However, if the USFWS or NMFS/NOAA Fisheries concludes that the action agency's action will violate section 7, the action agency will almost certainly be reversed in court if it chooses to go ahead with its proposed action as proposed.

As was discussed in detail in the notes after *TVA v. Hill*, in 1978 Congress amended section 7 so that if the expert agency concludes that jeopardy will occur, the action agency or any permit applicant can apply to the Endangered Species Committee ("God Squad") for an exemption from section 7(a)(2). ESA § 7(e)–(h), 16 U.S.C. § 1536(e)–(h).

The U.S. Fish & Wildlife Service and NMFS established most of the Section 7 consultation process through regulations. *See* 51 Fed. Reg. 19,926 (June 3, 1986). As a result, the details of the consultation process can be altered by these agencies. A political battle ensued in 2008 when the agencies, in the last days of the Bush Administration, proposed new consultation regulations to take effect January 15, 2009—*i.e.*, right before President Obama took office. On May 4, 2009, the Obama Administration withdrew the new consultation regulations and reinstated, with some minor amendments, the 1986 regulations. *See* 74 Fed. Reg. 20,421 (May 4, 2009).

b. Applying Section 7(a)(2): Agency Discretion

In footnote 5 of the *Carson–Truckee Water Conservancy District* decision, the Ninth Circuit emphasized that Secretary of the Interior was not obligated to sell the project's water for municipal and industrial use. As a result, the Secretary had ***discretion*** to act in favor of the listed species pursuant to Section 7(a)(1).

Despite the mandatory language of Section 7(a)(2)'s "no jeopardy" requirement, agency discretion may be important here, as well. In 2007, the U.S. Supreme Court took up this issue when it decided how the EPA's obligations under the Endangered Species Act should be interpreted in light of its obligations under the Clean Water Act.

NATIONAL ASSOCIATION OF HOME BUILDERS v. DEFENDERS OF WILDLIFE

551 U.S. 644 (2007).

JUSTICE ALITO delivered the opinion of the Court.

These cases concern the interplay between two federal environmental statutes. Section 402(b) of the Clean Water Act requires that the Environmental Protection Agency transfer certain permitting powers to state authorities upon an application and a showing that nine specified criteria have been met. Section 7(a)(2) of the Endangered Species Act of 1973 provides that a federal agency must consult with agencies designated by the Secretaries of Commerce and the Interior in order to "insure that any action authorized, funded, or carried out by such agency . . . is not likely to jeopardize the continued existence of any endangered species or threatened species." The question presented is whether § 7(a)(2) effectively operates as a tenth criterion on which the transfer of permitting power under the first statute must be conditioned. We conclude that it does not. The transfer of permitting authority to state authorities—who will exercise that authority under continuing federal oversight to ensure compliance with relevant mandates of the Endangered Species Act and other federal environmental protection statutes—was proper. We therefore reverse the judgment of the United States Court of Appeals for the Ninth Circuit.

I

A

1

The Clean Water Act of 1972 (CWA), 33 U.S.C. § 1251 *et seq.*, established a National Pollution Discharge Elimination System (NPDES) that is designed to prevent harmful discharges into the Nation's waters. The Environmental Protection Agency (EPA) initially administers the NPDES permitting system for each State, but a State may apply for a transfer of permitting authority to state officials. If authority is transferred, then state officials—not the federal EPA—have the primary responsibility for reviewing and approving NPDES discharge permits, albeit with continuing EPA oversight.

Under § 402(b) of the CWA, * * * the EPA "shall approve each submitted program" for transfer of permitting authority to a State "unless [it] determines that adequate authority does not exist" to ensure that nine specified criteria are satisfied. These criteria all relate to whether the state agency that will be responsible for permitting has the requisite authority under state law to administer the NPDES program.[2] If the criteria are met, the transfer must be approved.

2

The Endangered Species Act of 1973 (ESA), 16 U.S.C. § 1531 et seq., is intended to protect and conserve endangered and threatened species and their habitats. Section 4 of the ESA directs the Secretaries of Commerce and the Interior to list threatened and endangered species and to designate their critical habitats. § 1533. The Fish and Wildlife Service (FWS) administers the ESA with respect to species under the jurisdiction of the Secretary of the Interior, while the National Marine Fisheries Service (NMFS) administers the ESA with respect to species under the

2. The State must demonstrate that it has the ability: (1) to issue fixed-term permits that apply and ensure compliance with the CWA's substantive requirements and which are revocable for cause; (2) to inspect, monitor, and enter facilities and to require reports to the extent required by the CWA; (3) to provide for public notice and public hearings; (4) to ensure that the EPA receives notice of each permit application; (5) to ensure that any other State whose waters may be affected by the issuance of a permit may submit written recommendations and that written reasons be provided if such recommendations are not accepted; (6) to ensure that no permit is issued if the Army Corps of Engineers concludes that it would substantially impair the anchoring and navigation of navigable waters; (7) to abate violations of permits or the permit program, including through civil and criminal penalties; (8) to ensure that any permit for a discharge from a publicly owned treatment works includes conditions requiring the identification of the type and volume of certain pollutants; and (9) to ensure that any industrial user of any publicly owned treatment works will comply with certain of the CWA's substantive provisions. §§ 1342(b)(1)–(9).

jurisdiction of the Secretary of Commerce. See 50 CFR §§ 17.11, 222.101(a), 223.102, 402.01(b) (2006).

Section 7 of the ESA prescribes the steps that federal agencies must take to ensure that their actions do not jeopardize endangered wildlife and flora. Section 7(a)(2) provides that "[e]ach Federal agency shall, in consultation with and with the assistance of the Secretary [of Commerce or the Interior], insure that any action authorized, funded, or carried out by such agency (hereinafter in this section referred to as an 'agency action') is not likely to jeopardize the continued existence of any endangered species or threatened species." 16 U.S.C. § 1536(a)(2).

Once the consultation process contemplated by § 7(a)(2) has been completed, the Secretary is required to give the agency a written biological opinion "setting forth the Secretary's opinion, and a summary of the information on which the opinion is based, detailing how the agency action affects the species or its critical habitat." § 1536(b)(3)(A); see also 50 CFR § 402.14(h). If the Secretary concludes that the agency action would place the listed species in jeopardy or adversely modify its critical habitat, "the Secretary shall suggest those reasonable and prudent alternatives which he believes would not violate [§ 7(a)(2)] and can be taken by the Federal agency ... in implementing the agency action." 16 U.S.C. § 1536(b)(3)(A); see also 50 CFR § 402.14(h)(3). Regulations promulgated jointly by the Secretaries of Commerce and the Interior provide that, in order to qualify as a "reasonable and prudent alternative," an alternative course of action must be able to be implemented in a way "consistent with the scope of the Federal agency's legal authority and jurisdiction." § 402.02. * * * The regulations also provide that "Section 7 and the requirements of this part apply to all actions in which there is discretionary Federal involvement or control." 50 CFR § 402.03.

B

1

In February 2002, Arizona officials applied for EPA authorization to administer that State's NPDES program. The EPA initiated consultation with the FWS to determine whether the transfer of permitting authority would adversely affect any listed species.

The FWS regional office concluded that the transfer of authority would not cause any direct impact on water quality that would adversely affect listed species. However, the FWS office was concerned that the transfer could result in the issuance of more discharge permits, which would lead to more development, which in turn could have an indirect adverse effect on the habitat of certain upland species, such as the cactus ferruginous pygmy-owl and the Pima pineapple cactus. Specifically, the FWS feared that, because § 7(a)(2)'s consultation requirement does not apply to permitting decisions by state authorities, the transfer of authority would empower Arizona officials to issue individual permits without considering and mitigating their indirect impact on these upland species.

The FWS regional office therefore urged that, in considering the proposed transfer of permitting authority, those involved in the consultation process should take these potential indirect impacts into account.

The EPA disagreed, maintaining that "its approval action, which is an administrative transfer of authority, [would not be] the cause of future non-discharge-related impacts on endangered species from projects requiring State NPDES permits." As a factual matter, the EPA believed that the link between the transfer of permitting authority and the potential harm that could result from increased development was too attenuated. And as a legal matter, the EPA concluded that the mandatory nature of CWA § 402(b)—which directs that the EPA "shall approve" a transfer request if that section's nine statutory criteria are met—stripped it of authority to disapprove a transfer based on any other considerations.

Pursuant to procedures set forth in a memorandum of understanding between the agencies, the dispute was referred to the agencies' national offices for resolution. In December 2002, the FWS issued its biological opinion, which concluded that the requested transfer would not cause jeopardy to listed species. * * *

The EPA concluded that Arizona had met each of the nine statutory criteria listed in § 402(b) and approved the transfer of permitting authority. In the notice announcing the approval of the transfer, the EPA noted that the issuance of the FWS's biological opinion had "conclude[d] the consultation process required by ESA section 7(a)(2) and reflects the [FWS'] agreement with EPA that the approval of the State program meets the substantive requirements of the ESA."

2

On April 2, 2003, respondents filed a petition in the United States Court of Appeals for the Ninth Circuit seeking review of the transfer * * *. * * *

A divided panel of the Ninth Circuit held that the EPA's approval of the transfer was arbitrary and capricious because the EPA "relied during the administrative proceedings on legally contradictory positions regarding its section 7 obligations." * * * The panel did not dispute that Arizona had met the nine criteria set forth in § 402(b) of the CWA, but the panel nevertheless concluded that § 7(a)(2) of the ESA provided an "affirmative grant of authority to attend to [the] protection of listed species," in effect adding a tenth criterion to those specified in § 402(b). The panel dismissed the argument that the EPA's approval of the transfer application was not subject to § 7(a)(2) because it was not a "discretionary action" within the meaning of 50 CFR § 402.03 (interpreting § 7(a)(2) to apply only to agency actions "in which there is discretionary Federal involvement and control"). * * * On these grounds, the court granted the petition and vacated the EPA's transfer decision.

* * * The Ninth Circuit denied rehearing and rehearing *en banc*. * * *

The Ninth Circuit's construction of § 7(a)(2) is at odds with that of other Courts of Appeals. Compare 420 F.3d 946 (case below), with *Platte River Whooping Crane Critical Habitat Maintenance Trust v. FERC*, 962 F.2d 27, 33–34 (C.A.D.C. 1992), and *American Forest & Paper Association v. EPA*, 137 F.3d 291, 298–299 (C.A.5 1998). We granted certiorari to resolve this conflict, and we now reverse.

* * * III

A

* * * Section 402(b) of the CWA provides, without qualification, that the EPA "shall approve" a transfer application unless it determines that the State lacks adequate authority to perform the nine functions specified in the section. 33 U.S.C. § 1342(b). By its terms, the statutory language is mandatory and the list exclusive; if the nine specified criteria are satisfied, the EPA does not have the discretion to deny a transfer application. Neither respondents nor the Ninth Circuit has ever disputed that Arizona satisfied each of these nine criteria.

The language of § 7(a)(2) of the ESA is similarly imperative: it provides that "[e]ach Federal agency shall, in consultation with and with the assistance of the Secretary, insure that any action authorized, funded, or carried out by such agency ... is not likely to jeopardize" endangered or threatened species or their habitats. 16 U.S.C. § 1536(a)(2). This mandate is to be carried out through consultation and may require the agency to adopt an alternative course of action. As the author of the panel opinion below recognized, applying this language literally would "ad[d] one [additional] requirement to the list of considerations under the Clean Water Act permitting transfer provision." 450 F.3d, at 404, n. 2 (Berzon, J., concurring in denial of rehearing *en banc*) (emphasis in original). That is, it would effectively repeal the mandatory and exclusive list of criteria set forth in § 402(b), and replace it with a new, expanded list that includes § 7(a)(2)'s no-jeopardy requirement.

B

While a later enacted statute (such as the ESA) can sometimes operate to amend or even repeal an earlier statutory provision (such as the CWA), "repeals by implication are not favored" and will not be presumed unless the "intention of the legislature to repeal [is] clear and manifest." *Watt v. Alaska*, 451 U.S. 259, 267 (1981) (internal quotation marks omitted). We will not infer a statutory repeal "unless the later statute 'expressly contradict[s] the original act' " or unless such a construction "is absolutely necessary ... in order that [the] words [of the later statute] shall have any meaning at all." *Traynor v. Turnage*, 485 U.S. 535, 548 (1988) (quoting *Radzanower v. Touche Ross & Co.*, 426 U.S. 148, 153 (1976), in turn quoting T. SEDGWICK, THE INTERPRETATION AND CONSTRUCTION OF STATUTORY AND CONSTITUTIONAL LAW 98 (2d ed. 1874)). Outside these limited circumstances, "a statute dealing with a narrow, precise, and specific subject is not submerged by a later enacted statute covering a more generalized spectrum." *Radzanower, supra*, at 153.

Here, reading § 7(a)(2) as the Court of Appeals did would effectively repeal § 402(b)'s statutory mandate by engrafting a tenth criterion onto the CWA. Section 402(b) of the CWA commands that the EPA "shall" issue a permit whenever all nine exclusive statutory prerequisites are met. Thus, § 402(b) does not just set forth minimum requirements for the transfer of permitting authority; it affirmatively mandates that the transfer "shall" be approved if the specified criteria are met. The provision operates as a ceiling as well as a floor. By adding an additional criterion, the Ninth Circuit's construction of § 7(a)(2) raises that floor and alters § 402(b)'s statutory command.

The Ninth Circuit's reading of § 7(a)(2) would not only abrogate § 402(b)'s statutory mandate, but also result in the implicit repeal of many additional otherwise categorical statutory commands. Section 7(a)(2) by its terms applies to "any action authorized, funded, or carried out by" a federal agency—covering, in effect, almost anything that an agency might do. Reading the provision broadly would thus partially override every federal statute mandating agency action by subjecting such action to the further condition that it pose no jeopardy to endangered species. While the language of § 7(a)(2) does not explicitly repeal any provision of the CWA (or any other statute), reading it for all that it might be worth runs foursquare into our presumption against implied repeals.

C

1

The agencies charged with implementing the ESA have attempted to resolve this tension through regulations implementing § 7(a)(2). The NMFS and FWS, acting jointly on behalf of the Secretaries of Commerce and the Interior and following notice-and-comment rulemaking procedures, have promulgated a regulation stating that "Section 7 and the requirements of this part apply to all actions in which there is discretionary Federal involvement or control." 50 CFR § 402.03 (emphasis added). Pursuant to this regulation, § 7(a)(2) would not be read as impliedly repealing nondiscretionary statutory mandates, even when they might result in some agency action. Rather, the ESA's requirements would come into play only when an action results from the exercise of agency discretion. This interpretation harmonizes the statutes by giving effect to the ESA's no-jeopardy mandate whenever an agency has discretion to do so, but not when the agency is forbidden from considering such extrastatutory factors.

* * * In this situation, it is appropriate to look to the implementing agency's expert interpretation, which cabins § 7(a)(2)'s application to "actions in which there is discretionary Federal involvement or control." 50 CFR § 402.03. This reading harmonizes the statutes by applying

§ 7(a)(2) to guide agencies' existing discretionary authority, but not reading it to override express statutory mandates.

* * * 3

* * * In short, we read § 402.03 to mean what it says: that § 7(a)(2)'s no-jeopardy duty covers only discretionary agency actions and does not attach to actions (like the NPDES permitting transfer authorization) that an agency is required by statute to undertake once certain specified triggering events have occurred. This reading not only is reasonable, inasmuch as it gives effect to the ESA's provision, but also comports with the canon against implied repeals because it stays § 7(a)(2)'s mandate where it would effectively override otherwise mandatory statutory duties.

D

Respondents argue that our opinion in *TVA v. Hill*, 437 U.S. 153 (1978), supports their contrary position. * * * *TVA v. Hill*, however, had no occasion to answer the question presented in these cases. That case was decided almost a decade before the adoption in 1986 of the regulations contained in 50 CFR § 402.03. And in any event, the construction project at issue in *TVA v. Hill*, while expensive, was also discretionary. The TVA argued that by continuing to make lump-sum appropriations to the TVA, some of which were informally earmarked for the Tellico Dam project, Congress had implicitly repealed § 7's no-jeopardy requirement as it applied to that project. *See* 437 U.S., at 189–193. The Court rejected this argument, concluding that "[t]he Appropriations Acts did not themselves identify the projects for which the sums had been appropriated" and that reports by congressional committees allegedly directing the TVA to complete the project lacked the force of law. *Id.*, at 189, n. 35. Central to the Court's decision was the conclusion that Congress did not mandate that the TVA put the dam into operation; there was no statutory command to that effect; and there was therefore no basis for contending that applying the ESA's no-jeopardy requirement would implicitly repeal another affirmative congressional directive.

TVA v. Hill thus supports the position, expressed in § 402.03, that the ESA's no-jeopardy mandate applies to every discretionary agency action—regardless of the expense or burden its application might impose. But that case did not speak to the question whether § 7(a)(2) applies to non-discretionary actions, like the one at issue here. The regulation set forth in 50 CFR § 402.03 addressed that question, and we defer to its reasonable interpretation.

IV

Finally, respondents and their amici argue that, even if § 7(a)(2) is read to apply only to "discretionary" agency actions, the decision to transfer NPDES permitting authority to Arizona represented such an exercise of discretion. They contend that the EPA's decision to authorize a transfer is not entirely mechanical; that it involves some exercise of judgment as to whether a State has met the criteria set forth in § 402(b); and that these criteria incorporate references to wildlife conservation that bring consideration of § 7(a)(2)'s no-jeopardy mandate properly within the agency's discretion.

The argument is unavailing. While the EPA may exercise some judgment in determining whether a State has demonstrated that it has the authority to carry out § 402(b)'s enumerated statutory criteria, the statute clearly does not grant it the discretion to add another entirely separate prerequisite to that list. * * *

* * *

[W]e defer to the agency's reasonable interpretation of ESA § 7(a)(2) as applying only to "actions in which there is discretionary Federal involvement or control." 50 CFR § 402.03. Since the transfer of NPDES permitting authority is not discretionary, but rather is mandated once a State has met the criteria set forth in § 402(b) of the CWA, it follows that a transfer of NPDES permitting authority does not trigger § 7(a)(2)'s consultation and no-jeopardy requirements. Accordingly, the judgment of the Court of Appeals for the Ninth Circuit is reversed, and these cases are remanded for further proceedings consistent with this opinion.

JUSTICE STEVENS, with whom JUSTICE SOUTER, JUSTICE GINSBURG, and JUSTICE BREYER join, dissenting.

These cases present a problem of conflicting "shalls." On the one hand, § 402(b) of the Clean Water Act (CWA) provides that the Environmental Protection Agency (EPA) "shall" approve a State's application to administer a National Pollution Discharge Elimination System (NPDES) permitting program unless it determines that nine criteria are not satisfied. 33 U.S.C. § 1342(b). On the other hand, shortly after the passage of the CWA, Congress enacted § 7(a)(2) of the Endangered Species Act of 1973 (ESA), which commands that federal agencies "shall" insure that their actions do not jeopardize endangered species. 16 U.S.C. § 1536(a)(2).

When faced with competing statutory mandates, it is our duty to give full effect to both if at all possible. The Court fails at this task. * * *

In the celebrated "snail darter" case, *TVA v. Hill*, 437 U.S. 153 (1978), we held that the ESA "reveals a conscious decision by Congress to give endangered species priority over the 'primary missions' of federal agencies," *id.*, at 185. Consistent with that intent, Chief Justice Burger's exceptionally thorough and admirable opinion explained that § 7 "admits of no exception." *Id.*, at 173. Creating precisely such an exception by exempting nondiscretionary federal actions from the ESA's coverage, the Court whittles away at Congress' comprehensive effort to protect endangered species from the risk of extinction and fails to give the Act its intended effect. * * *

I

* * * Our opinion in *Hill* explained at length why § 7 imposed obligations on "all federal agencies" to ensure that "actions authorized, funded, or carried out by them do not jeopardize the continued existence of endangered species." 437 U.S., at 173 (emphasis deleted; internal quotation marks omitted). Not a word in the opinion stated or suggested that § 7 obligations are inapplicable to mandatory agency actions that would threaten the eradication of an endangered species. Nor did the opinion describe the Tennessee Valley Authority's (TVA) attempted completion of the Tellico Dam as a discretionary act. * * * Moreover, after observing that the ESA creates only a limited number of "hardship exemptions," see 16 U.S.C. § 1539—none of which would apply to federal agencies—we applied the maxim *expressio unius est expression alterius* to conclude that "there are no exemptions in the Endangered Species Act for federal agencies," 437 U.S., at 188.

Today, however, the Court countenances such an exemption. It erroneously concludes that the ESA contains an unmentioned exception for nondiscretionary agency action and that the statute's command to enjoin the completion of the Tellico Dam depended on the unmentioned fact that the TVA was attempting to perform a discretionary act. But both the text of the ESA and our opinion in *Hill* compel the contrary determination that Congress intended the ESA to apply to "all federal agencies" and to all "actions authorized, funded, or carried out by them." *Id.*, at 173 (emphasis deleted).

A transfer of NPDES permitting authority under § 402(b) of the CWA is undoubtedly one of those "actions" that is "authorized" or "carried out" by a federal agency. * * * It follows from *Hill* that § 7(a)(2) applies to such NPDES transfers—whether they are mandatory or discretionary.

* * * III

There are at least two ways in which the CWA and the ESA can be given full effect without privileging one statute over the other.

A

The text of § 7(a)(2) itself provides the first possible way of reconciling that provision with § 402(b) of the CWA. * * * If the biological opinion concludes that the agency action would put a listed species in jeopardy, * * * the ESA contains a process for resolving the competing demands of agency action and species protection. The ESA provides that "the Secretary shall suggest those reasonable and prudent alternatives which he believes would not violate subsection (a)(2) and can be taken by the Federal agency or applicant in implementing the agency action." 16 U.S.C. § 1536(b)(3)(A); *see also* 50 CFR § 402.14(h)(3). * * * Thus, in the face of any conflict between the ESA and another federal statute, the ESA and its implementing regulations encourage federal agencies to work out a reasonable alternative that would let the proposed action move forward "consistent with [its] intended purpose" and the agency's "legal authority," while also avoiding any violation of § 7(a)(2).

* * * [F]or the rare case in which no "reasonable and prudent alternative" can be found, Congress has provided yet another mechanism for resolving any conflicts between the ESA and a proposed agency action. In 1978, shortly after our decision in *Hill*, Congress amended the ESA to create the "Endangered Species Committee," which it authorized to grant exemptions from § 7(a)(2). 16 U.S.C. § 1536(e). Because it has the authority to approve the extinction of an endangered species, the Endangered Species Committee is colloquially described as the "God Squad" or "God Committee." In light of this weighty responsibility, Congress carefully laid out requirements for the God Committee's membership, procedures, and the factors it must consider in deciding whether to grant an exemption. * * *

B

EPA's regulations offer a second way to harmonize the CWA with the ESA. After EPA has transferred NPDES permitting authority to a State, the agency continues to oversee the State's permitting program. If a state permit is "outside the guidelines and the requirements" of the CWA, EPA may object to it and block its issuance. *See* 33 U.S.C. § 1342(d)(2); 66 Fed. Reg. 11206 (2001). Given these ongoing responsibilities, EPA has enacted a regulation that requires a State to enter into a Memorandum of Agreement (MOA) that sets forth the particulars of the agency's oversight duties. *See* 40 CFR § 123.24(a) (2006).

* * * Like the § 7(a)(2) consultation process described above, MOAs provide a potential mechanism for giving effect to § 7 of the ESA while also allowing the transfer of permitting authority to a State. * * * EPA might negotiate a provision in the MOA that would require a State to abide by the ESA requirements when issuing pollution permits. Alternatively, "EPA could require the state to provide copies of draft permits for discharges in particularly sensitive habitats such as those of ESA-listed species or for discharges that contain a pollutant that threatens ESA-listed wildlife." Or the MOA might be drafted in a way that would allow the agency to object to state permits that would jeopardize any and all endangered species. These are just three of many possibilities. I need not identify other ways EPA could use the MOA process to comply with the ESA; it is enough to observe that MOAs provide a straightforward way to give the ESA its full effect without restricting § 7(a)(2) in the way the Court does. * * *

NOTES

1. **What is the Supreme Court Deciding?** How does the majority frame the main issue to be decided in this case? How does the dissent describe the Court's task? Are these differences significant to the outcome of the case? In particular, how do the majority and the dissent differ in their approach to addressing the relationship of apparently conflicting statutes?

2. **Limitations on Section 7 Consultations.** How does the majority limit the reach of Section 7(a)(2)? Is this limitation consistent with the language of Section 7(a)(2)? Why or why not? Is this limitation consistent with *TVA v. Hill*? Why or why not? What does it mean for an agency action to be "mandatory" or "discretionary" after this decision? Are you sure?

3. **Reconciling Statutes.** Justice Stevens emphasizes in his dissent that, faced with apparently conflicting statutes, the duty of the federal courts is to first try to reconcile the statutes. What is the apparent conflict between the Endangered Species Act and the Clean Water Act? Is that conflict real or merely apparent? Are there ways to reconcile the two statutes? What do you think of the majority's resolution? What do you think of Justice Stevens' suggested means of reconciling the statutes?

4. **The Stakes of the Litigation.** By the time the U.S. Supreme Court decided this case in 2007, the EPA had already delegated NPDES permitting authority to 45 of the 50 states, with varying attention to the Endangered Species Act. If a majority of Justices had agreed with Defenders of Wildlife that the Endangered Species Act's consultation requirement applied to the EPA's delegations of permitting authority to states, would that decision have rendered the 45 prior delegations at least potentially invalid? Why or why not?

Or is this case "really" about the Clean Water Act at all? Is the *National Association of Home Builders* decision limited to Clean Water Act permit delegations? Why or why not? HINT: What were the other, conflicting, cases that the majority mentions at the beginning of the case about?

5. ***TVA v. Hill* as Precedent.** How do the majority and the dissent treat *TVA v. Hill* as precedent for this decision? Which treatment do you find more convincing? Why?

6. **States and Section 7.** The USFWS was concerned about the delegation of NPDES permitting authority to Arizona because states, unlike federal agencies, are not subject to Section 7. However, states *are* subject to Section 9, discussed *infra*.

7. **The Discretionary Action Regulation.** The ESA regulations currently state: "Section 7 and the requirements of this part apply to all actions in which there is discretionary Federal involvement or control." 50 C.F.R. § 402.03. Does this regulation clearly rule out the applicability of Section 7 to *other* Federal actions? Why or why not? How will/should the courts treat the agencies' view of this regulation?

* * *

c. *Applying Section 7(a)(2): Science, Climate Change, and Biological Opinions*

NATURAL RESOURCES DEFENSE COUNCIL v. KEMPTHORNE

506 F. Supp. 2d 322 (E.D. Cal. 2007).

OLIVER W. WANGER, DISTRICT JUDGE.

I. INTRODUCTION

This case concerns the effect on a threatened species of fish, the Delta smelt (*Hypomesus transpacificus*), of the coordinated operation of the federally-managed Central Valley Project ("CVP") and the State of California's State Water Project ("SWP"), among the world's largest water diversion projects. Both projects divert large volumes of water from the California Bay (Sacramento–San Joaquin) Delta ("Delta") and use the Delta to store water.

For over thirty years, the projects have been operated pursuant to a series of cooperation agreements. In addition, the projects are subject to ever-evolving statutory, regulatory, contractual, and judicially-imposed requirements. The Long–Term Central Valley Project and State Water Project Operations Criteria and Plan ("2004 OCAP" or "OCAP") surveys how the projects are currently managed in light of these evolving circumstances. At issue in this case is a 2005 biological opinion ("BiOp"), issued by the United States Fish and Wildlife Service ("FWS" or "Service") pursuant to the Endangered Species Act ("ESA"), which concludes that current project operations described in the OCAP and certain planned future actions will not jeopardize the continued existence of the Delta smelt or adversely modify its critical habitat.

The Delta smelt is a small, slender-bodied fish endemic to the Delta. Historically, Delta smelt could be found throughout the Delta. Although abundance data on the smelt indicates that the population has fluctuated wildly in the past, it is undisputed that, overall, the population has declined significantly in recent years, to its lowest reported volume in fall 2004.

Figure 3-8: Central Valley Project
Map care of Congressional Budget Office

In this case, Plaintiffs, a coalition of environmental and sportfishing organizations, challenge the 2005 BiOp's no jeopardy and no adverse modification findings as arbitrary, capricious, and contrary to law under the Administrative Procedure Act, 5 U.S.C. §§ 702 et seq. Before the court for decision is Plaintiffs' motion for summary judgment. * * *

II. THE ENDANGERED SPECIES ACT

A recent Ninth Circuit opinion in *National Wildlife Federation v. National Marine Fisheries Service,* 481 F.3d 1224 (9th Cir. 2007) [hereinafter "*NWF v. NMFS*"], succinctly summarizes the relevant provisions of the ESA:

> The ESA requires federal agencies to "insure that any action authorized, funded, or carried out by such agency ... is not likely to

Figure 3-9: Delta smelt
U.S. Fish & Wildlife Service photo.

jeopardize the continued existence of any endangered species or threatened species or result in the destruction or adverse modification of [designated critical] habitat. . . ." 15 U.S.C. § 1536(a)(2). The ESA imposes a procedural consultation duty whenever a federal action may affect an ESA-listed species. *Thomas v. Peterson,* 753 F.2d 754, 763 (9th Cir. 1985). To that end, the agency planning the action, usually known as the "action agency," must consult with the consulting agency. This process is known as a "Section 7" consultation. The process is usually initiated by a formal written request by the action agency to the consulting agency. After consultation, investigation, and analysis, the consulting agency then prepares a biological opinion. *See generally Ariz. Cattle Growers' Ass'n v. U.S. Fish & Wildlife,* 273 F.3d 1229, 1239 (9th Cir. 2001). * * *

The consulting agency evaluates the effects of the proposed action on the survival of species and any potential destruction or adverse modification of critical habitat in a biological opinion, 16 U.S.C. § 1536(b), based on "the best scientific and commercial data available," *id.* § 1536(a)(2). The biological opinion includes a summary of the information upon which the opinion is based, a discussion of the effects of the action on listed species or critical habitat, and the consulting agency's opinion on "whether the action is likely to jeopardize the continued existence of a listed species or result in the destruction or adverse modification of critical habitat...." 50 C.F.R. § 402.14(h)(3). In making its jeopardy determination, the consulting agency evaluates "the current status of the listed species or critical habitat," the "effects of the action," and "cumulative effects." *Id.* § 402.14(g)(2)-(3). * * * If the biological opinion concludes that jeopardy is not likely and that there will not be adverse modification of critical habitat, or that there is a "reasonable and prudent alternative[]" to the agency action that avoids jeopardy and adverse modification and that the incidental taking of endangered or threatened species will not violate section 7(a)(2), the consulting agency can issue an "Incidental Take Statement" which, if followed, exempts the action agency from the prohibition on takings found in Section 9 of the ESA. 16 U.S.C. § 1536(b)(4); *ALCOA v. BPA,* 175 F.3d 1156, 1159 (9th Cir. 1999).

* * * *Id.* at 1230.

III. FACTUAL BACKGROUND

For over thirty years the state and federal agencies charged with management of the CVP and SWP have operated the projects in an increasingly coordinated manner pursuant to a Coordinated Operating Agreement ("COA"). The COA, which dates to 1986, has evolved over time to reflect, among other things, changing facilities, delivery requirements, and regulatory restrictions. The most recent document surveying how the COA is implemented in light of these evolving circumstances is the 2004 Operating Criteria and Plan ("2004 OCAP" or "OCAP") issued June 30, 2004.

A. Overview of the 2004 OCAP.

The OCAP begins with a "Purpose of Document" section * * *. * * * As the OCAP's "Purpose of Document" section explains, the immediate objective of the OCAP is to lay out all such regulatory and other operational information so that ESA Section 7 consultation can proceed to evaluate how project operations will affect the Delta smelt under various projected future conditions.

B. Applying the ESA to Project Operations.

Because endangered and/or threatened species, including the Delta smelt, reside in the area affected by the CVP and SWP, the 2004 OCAP, administered on behalf of the federal government by the Bureau of Reclamation ("Bureau"), must comply with various provisions of the ESA. Specifically, prior to authorizing, funding, or carrying out any action, the acting federal agency (in this case, the Bureau) must first consult with FWS and/or NMFS to "insure that [the] action ... is not likely to jeopardize the continued existence of any endangered species or threatened species or result in the destruction or adverse modification of habitat of such species which is determined ... to be critical...." 16 U.S.C. § 1536(a)(2) [ESA § 7(a)(2)]. This form of consultation is called "formal consultation," and concludes with the issuance of a biological opinion. 50 C.F.R. § 402.02.

* * * In this case, the 2004 OCAP BiOp contemplates increases in water diversions and the construction of new facilities in the Delta. * * * Water transfers resulting in an annual 200,000 to 600,000 acre-feet increase in Delta exports will result.

The Bureau submitted some of these operational changes for formal consultation with FWS concerning their impact on the Delta smelt, while other changes were subject only to early consultation * * *.

C. *History of This Lawsuit.*

On July 30, 2004, FWS issued a Biological Opinion (the "2004 OCAP BiOp"), addressing both formal and early consultation for the above-described OCAP actions.

* * * Plaintiffs in this case, a coalition of non-profit conservation organizations, filed suit on February 15, 2005, alleging that the 2004 OCAP BiOp was legally inadequate * * * and should be invalidated. Plaintiffs named as defendants the Department of the Interior and the FWS.

On February 16, 2005, FWS issued an amended BiOp (the "2005 OCAP BiOp," "OCAP BiOp," or "BiOp"), which superseded the 2004 OCAP BiOp. The 2005 OCAP BiOp concludes that the coordinated operation of the SWP and CVP, including the proposed future actions, will not jeopardize the Delta smelt's continued existence. Although the BiOp recognizes that *existing* protective measures may be inadequate, the FWS concluded that certain *proposed* protective measures, including the EWA and a proposed "adaptive management" protocol would provide adequate protection.

Since the filing of this complaint, Federal Defendants have reinitiated § 7 consultation * * *.

Plaintiffs filed a supplemental complaint on May 20, 2005, challenging the amended BiOp on various grounds.

D. *Delta Smelt Abundance.*

Smelt once were one of the most common pelagic fish in the Delta, having previously occupied the waters from "Suisun Bay and Montezuma Slough, upstream to at least Verona on the Sacramento River, and Mossdale on the San Joaquin River." Smelt abundance has "declined irregularly" for at least the past 20 years. FWS relies primarily upon two indices to monitor Delta smelt abundance, calculated from the Summer Tow Net Survey ("TNS") and the Fall Midwater Trawl ("FMWT"). * * * Since 1983, except for three years (1986, 1993, and 1994), the TNS has remained consistently lower than ever previously recorded. * * *

E. Relationship Between Abundance and Project Operations.

The BiOp cites several reasons for the smelt's decline. First, since the mid 1800s, mining, agricultural use, and levee construction caused the loss of a large portion of smelt habitat. Second, recreational boating in the Delta has resulted in the presence and propagation of "predatory non-native fish" and an increase in the rate of smelt erosion resulting from boat wakes. Third, reduced water quality "from agricultural runoff, effluent discharge and boat effluent has the potential to harm the pelagic larvae and reduce the availability of the planctonic food source." Finally, the BiOp acknowledges that "delta smelt have been increasingly subject to entrainment, upstream or reverse flows of waters in the Delta and San Joaquin River, and constriction of low salinity habitat to deep-water river channels of the interior Delta." The BiOp acknowledges that these final adverse effects are *"primarily a result of the steadily increasing proportion of river flow being diverted from the Delta by the Projects, and occasional droughts."* The BiOp in no way quantifies the contribution of each of these factors to the smelt's decline. The parties dispute the extent to which project operations jeopardize the smelt.

F. Relationship Between Smelt and "X2."

Smelt are euryhaline (tolerant of a wide range of salinities), but generally occur in water with less than 10–12 parts per thousand (ppt) salinity. For a large part of its life span, Delta smelt are thought to be associated with the "freshwater edge of the mixing zone," where the salinity is approximately 2 parts per thousand (often referred to as "X2"). The summer TNS index increases dramatically whenever X2 is located between Chipps and Roe islands. Whenever the location of X2 shifts upstream of the confluence of the Sacramento and San Joaquin, either as a result of water diversions or natural conditions, smelt abundance decreases.

G. The Concept of "Salvage."

The BiOp's "no jeopardy" conclusion relies on the concept of "salvage," which refers generally to the process of using mechanical devices to screen fish that would otherwise be entrained in project facilities (e.g., pumps) into holding tanks for transport to other parts of the Delta. Unlike many other fish species in the Delta, Delta smelt do not survive the salvage process, "either due to stress and injury from handling, trucking and release, or from predation in or near the salvage facilities, the release sites, or in Clifton Court Forebay." As a result, for Delta smelt, FWS uses the terms salvage and entrainment essentially interchangeably.

More recently, project managers, fisheries officials, and other experts came to the consensus that the salvage approach was insufficient on its own. * * *

* * * *H. "Conservation Measures."*

The "conservation measures" contemplated are listed in the Summary of Effects section of the BiOp and include: (1) the Environmental

Water Account ("EWA"); (2) Central Valley Project Improvement Act (b)(2) water; (3) State Water Resource Control Board's Water Rights Decision 1641; (4) the Vernalis Adaptive Management Plan ("VAMP"); and (5) the DSRAM adaptive management plan.

1. CVPIA (b)(2) Water.

According to the 1992 Central Valley Project Improvement Act, the CVP must "dedicate and manage annually 800,000 acre-feet of Central Valley Project yield for the primary purpose of implementing the fish, wildlife, and habitat restoration purposes and measures authorized by this title; to assist the State of California in its efforts to protect the waters of the San Francisco Bay/Sacramento–San Joaquin Delta Estuary; and to help to meet such obligations as may be legally imposed upon the Central Valley Project under State or Federal law following the date of enactment of this title, including but not limited to additional obligations under the Federal Endangered Species Act." Title XXXXIV of the Reclamation Projects Authorization and Adjustment Act of 1992, Pub. L. 102–575, 106 Stat. 4600, 4706 (1992).

FWS, in consultation with the Bureau and other agencies, may use this "(b)(2) water" to meet Water Quality Control Plan (WQCP) obligations and any other requirements imposed by law after 1992. * * *

The base CVP yield committed to fish restoration is fixed by statute and is mandatory. This fixed supply is subject to reduction up to 25% in critically dry years under CVPIA § 3406(b)(2)(C).

2. Environmental Water Account.

The Environmental Water Account ("EWA") is "an adaptive management tool that aims to protect both fish and water users as it modifies water project operations in the Bay–Delta."

The EWA provides water for the protection and recovery of fish beyond that which would be available through the existing baseline of regulatory protection related to project operations. The EWA buys water from willing sellers or diverts surplus water when safe for fish, then banks, stores, transfers and releases it as needed to protect fish and compensate water users for deferred diversions.

The EWA has been used to benefit smelt by allowing for the curtailment of project export pumping during critical time periods. The EWA could also be used to increase in-stream flows or increase outflows in the Delta, both of which would benefit the smelt. The EWA is not fixed by statute nor is annual funding assured, and the water supply it provides, though reasonably anticipated, is not immutable.

3. Water Rights Decision 1641.

State Water Resource Control Board Decision 1641 (D–1641) imposes certain minimum flow and water quality objectives upon the projects[.] * * * The D–1641 requirements are mandatory under the projects' operating permits. The water to satisfy D–1641 comes from 3406(b)(2) yield and supplemental sources the Bureau utilizes.

4. Vernalis Adaptive Management Plan (VAMP).

The Vernalis Adaptive Management Plan (VAMP) is an experimental program that had its origin in D–1641. It provides for flows on the lower San Joaquin River and export curtailments at the projects. VAMP's purpose is to "provide pulse flows on the San Joaquin River and improve habitat conditions in the Delta by reducing exports at the CVP and SWP" over a 31 day period in April and May for the benefit of Chinook salmon and Delta smelt. * * * VAMP flows "allow larval and juvenile smelt to avoid becoming entrained at the export facilities and to move downstream to Suisun Bay."

The VAMP water supply is not irrevocably fixed or assured.

I. Delta Smelt Risk Assessment Matrix (DSRAM).

The BiOp's other, primary protection for the smelt is the implementation of a new adaptive management protocol, known as the Delta Smelt Risk Assessment Matrix ("DSRAM"). The DSRAM utilizes a list of trigger criteria to precipitate responses. The criteria are:

(1) the previous year's FMWT index;

(2) the risk of smelt entrainment based upon the location of X2;

(3) the estimated duration of the smelt spawning period, based on water temperature;

(4) the presence of spawning female smelt;

(5) the proximity of the smelt to project pumping facilities; and

(6) a salvage trigger for adult and juvenile smelt.

1. The DSRAM Process.

If any trigger criteria is met or exceeded, a Delta Smelt Working Group ("DSWG") is convened. The DSWG consists of representatives from FWS, the California Department of Fish and Game, DWR, the United States Environmental Protection Agency, the Bureau, and the California Bay–Delta Authority. The DSWG then recommends corrective actions to a Water Operations Management Team ("WOMT"). The OCAP BiOp identifies four specific actions that the DSWG and WOMT must consider taking if one or more trigger criteria occur: (1) export reductions at one or both of the projects; (2) changes in the south Delta barrier operations; (3) changes in San Joaquin River flows; and (4) changes in the operation of the Delta cross channel. The DSRAM does not contain defined action criteria, but instead leaves any response wholly to the discretion of the two groups who administer the DSRAM (DSWG and WOMT).

2. *DSRAM Implementation.*

The BiOp acknowledges although FWS is "confident that use of the DSRAM will reduce the frequency with which actual salvage exceeds the median predicted salvage, the exceedence frequency could be as high as 50%." There is no analysis of the duration or consequences from such exceedence. The DSRAM provides no operating criteria or action schedule, specifying when mitigation actions must be taken. It is not possible to predict what, how and when DSRAM measures will be implemented.

* * * *K. Recent Procedural History.*

The Federal Defendants acknowledge that "[s]hortly before the 2005 OCAP BiOP was completed, a fall midwater trawl survey of delta smelt revealed a substantial decline in the population index for the species" to the lowest ever. The Federal Defendants do not concede that the existence of this data renders the BiOp arbitrary and capricious, because "limited analysis of this data existed, and the Service relied on the raw data, and its own professional judgments as the best available scientific and commercial data available." Nevertheless, "the CALFED agencies have continued to assemble and analyze new data and information." * * *

On July 6, 2006, the Bureau requested that the FWS re-initiate consultation concerning the impact of the OCAP on the Delta smelt. In a July 6, 2006 letter to the FWS, the Bureau acknowledged that "emerging data indicates an apparent substantial decline in the Delta smelt population index." * * *

* * * VI. SUMMARY OF PLAINTIFFS' MOTION

Plaintiffs move for summary judgment on the following grounds:

* * * [T]he BiOp did not utilize the Best Available Science by * * * failing to consider the possible effects that climate change might have on the smelt's habitat. * * *

* * * VII. DISCUSSION

* * * *C. Best Available Science.*

The § 7 formal consultation process is designed to "insure" that any agency action "is not likely to jeopardize the continued existence of any endangered species or threatened species or result in the destruction or adverse modification of habitat of such species which is determined ... to be critical...." 16 U.S.C. § 1536(a)(2). "In fulfilling the requirements of this paragraph each agency shall use the best scientific and commercial data available." *Id.*

An agency has wide discretion to determine what is "the best scientific and commercial data available." *San Luis v. Badgley,* 136 F. Supp. 2d 1136, 1151 (E.D. Cal. 2000). Yet, an agency must make its decision about jeopardy based on the best science available at the time of the decision, and may not defer that jeopardy analysis by promising future studies to assess whether jeopardy is occurring. While uncertainty is not necessarily fatal to an agency decision, an agency may not entirely fail to develop appropriate projections where data "was available but [was] simply not analyzed," *Greenpeace v. NMFS,* 80 F. Supp. 2d 1137, 1149–50 (W.D. Wash. 2000). Here, EWS maintains the necessary data cannot be obtained.

1. Does a "Benefit of the Doubt to the Species" Presumption Apply?

The parties debate at length whether the best available scientific information principle includes a requirement that the agency "give the benefit of the doubt to the species." This language has its origins in the legislative history of the ESA, H.R. CONF. REP. NO. 96–697, 96th Cong., 1st Sess. 12, *reprinted in* 1979 U.S.C.C.A.N. 2572, 2576:

> Section 7(b) of the act requires the fish and wildlife service and the national marine fisheries service to render biological opinions which advise whether or not proposed agency actions would violate section 7(a)(2). Courts have given substantial weight to these biological opinions as evidence of an agency's compliance with section 7(a). The amendment would not alter this state of the law or lessen in any way an agency's obligation under section 7(a)(2).
>
> * * * *This language continues to give the benefit of the doubt to the species,* and it would continue to place the burden on the action agency to demonstrate to the consulting agency that its action will not violate section 7(a)(2). Furthermore, the language will not absolve federal agencies from the responsibility of cooperating with the wildlife agencies in developing adequate information upon which to base a biological opinion. If a federal agency proceeds with the action in the face of inadequate knowledge or information, the agency does so with the risk that it has not satisfied the standard of section 7(a)(2) and that new information might reveal that the agency has not satisfied the standard of section 7(a)(2).

(emphasis added).

In *Conner v. Burford,* 848 F.2d 1441, 1454 (9th Cir. 1988), the Ninth Circuit applied this "benefit of the doubt" language to hold that FWS violated the ESA by "failing to use the best information available to prepare comprehensive biological opinions considering all stages of the agency action...." At dispute in *Conner* was a biological opinion reviewing the proposed sale of oil and gas leases on National Forest land. * * *

> In light of the ESA requirement that the agencies use the best scientific and commercial data available to insure that protected species are not jeopardized, 16 U.S.C. § 1536(a)(2), the FWS cannot ignore available biological information or fail to develop projections of oil and gas activities which may indicate potential conflicts between development and the preservation of protected species. We hold that the FWS violated the ESA by failing to use the best information available to prepare comprehensive biological opinions considering all stages of the agency action, and thus failing to adequately assess whether the agency action was likely to jeopardize the continued

> existence of any threatened or endangered species, as required by section 7(a)(2). *To hold otherwise would eviscerate Congress' intent to "give the benefit of the doubt to the species."*

Id. (emphasis added). *Conner* does not directly support the broader interpretation urged by Plaintiffs, that the agency should err on the side of the species when evaluating uncertain evidence. *Conner* stands for the proposition that an agency cannot abdicate its responsibility to evaluate the impacts of an action on a species by labeling available information "uncertain," because doing so violates Congress' intent that the agencies "give the benefit of the doubt to the species."

Center for Biological Diversity v. Lohn, 296 F. Supp. 2d 1223, 1239 (W.D. Wash. 2003) (*rev'd on other grounds*, 483 F.3d 984 (9th Cir. 2007)), applied the *Conner* holding in conformity with Plaintiffs' interpretation. * * *

Another case Plaintiffs cite, *Rock Creek Alliance v. U.S. Fish & Wildlife Service,* 390 F. Supp. 2d 993, 1003 (D. Mont. 2005), does not support imposing a "benefit of the doubt" presumption to uncertain scientific evidence:

> Though the agency has discretion to make decisions based in its expertise, the ESA expresses a legislative mandate "to require agencies to afford first priority to the declared national policy of saving endangered species.... Congress has spoken in the plainest of words, making it abundantly clear that the balance has been struck in favor of affording endangered species the highest of priorities, thereby adopting a policy which it described as 'institutionalized caution.'"

Id. (quoting *Tennessee Valley Authority v. Hill,* 437 U.S. 153, 185 (1978)). However, as in *Center for Biological Diversity,* this language was part of a general discussion of the legal framework; the *Rock Creek* court never applied a benefit of the doubt presumption in the manner Plaintiffs suggest it should be applied here.

In response, Defendant Intervenors cite *Oceana, Inc. v. Evans,* 384 F. Supp. 2d 203 (D.D.C. 2005), a challenge to NMFS's choice between two estimates of how much take a particular type of fishing gear would cause. The agency chose the lower estimate, reasoning that it was the "best estimate possible." The plaintiff argued that this estimate failed to give the "benefit of the doubt" to the species. *Id.* at 228. Although the lower estimate was uncertain, the district court reasoned that "the ESA does not require the agency to reject the 'best estimate possible' in favor of a more 'conservative' estimate that, according to the scientists, would be lacking in support." *Id.*

Lohn and *Oceana* appear irreconcilable, but, they can be harmonized. *Lohn* rejected an agency's decision to follow the taxonomy in the face of significant and compelling scientific evidence favoring a different conclusion. To side with the agency under such circumstances would "not give the benefit of the doubt to the species...." *Id.* at 1239. In contrast,

Oceana, concerned an agency's choice of the "best estimate possible" over a more "conservative" estimate that lacked scientific support. The *Oceana* court refused to ignore the general rule that an agency must choose the best available science, simply because the ESA commands that the agency give the "benefit of the doubt" to the species. *Both* cases stand for the proposition that the agency must carefully examine the available scientific data and models and rationally choose the most reliable.

* * * *3. Global Climate Change Evidence.*

Plaintiffs next argue that the BiOp ignored data about Global Climate Change that will adversely affect the Delta smelt and its habitat. This is potentially significant because the BiOp's conclusions are based in part on the assumption that the hydrology of the water bodies affected by the OCAP will follow historical patterns for the next 20 years.

In a July 28, 2004 comment letter, Plaintiff NRDC directed FWS's attention to several studies on the potential effects of climate change on water supply reliability, urging that the issue be considered in the BiOp. The comment letter stated:

> The best scientific data available today establishes that global climate change is occurring and will affect western hydrology. At least half a dozen models predict warming in the western United States of several degrees Celsius over the next 100 years (Redmond, 2003). Such sophisticated regional climate models must be considered as part of the FWS' consideration of the best available scientific data.
>
> Unfortunately, the Biological Assessment provided by the Bureau to FWS entirely ignores global climate change and existing climate change models. Instead, the BA projects future project impacts in explicit reliance on seventy-two years of historical records. In effect, the Biological Assessment assumes that neither climate nor hydrology will change. This assumption is not supportable.
>
> In California, a significant percentage of annual precipitation falls as snow in the high Sierra Nevada mountains. Snowpack acts as a form of water storage by melting to release water later in the spring and early summer months (Minton, 2001). The effects of global climate change are expected to have a profound effect on this dynamic. *Among other things, more precipitation will occur as rain rather than snow, less water will be released slowly from snowpack "storage" during spring and summer months, and flooding is expected to increase* (Wilkinson, 2002; Dettinger, 2003). *These developments will make it more difficult to fill the large reservoirs in most years, reducing reservoir yields and will magnify the effect of CVP operations on downstream fishes* (Roos, 2001). These developments will also dramatically increase the cost of surface storage relative to other water supply options, such as conservation.
>
> While the precise magnitude of these changes remains uncertain, judgments about the likely range of impacts can and have been made.

> *See e.g.*, U.S. Global Climate Action Report–2002; Third National Communication of the United States Under the United Nations Framework Convention on Climate Change at 82, 101 (2002). The Service can and must evaluate how that range of likely impacts would affect CVP operations and impacts, including the Bureau's ability to provide water to contractors while complying with environmental standards. We therefore request that the Service review and consider the work cited above, as well as the background and Dettinger presentation at a recent climate change conference held in Sacramento, June 9–11, 2004 [citation omitted] and climate change reports [citation omitted].

(emphasis added).

A second presentation by Michael Dettinger at a December 8–9, 2004 CALFED meeting, attended by FWS staff, concluded that "warming is already underway . . ."; that this would result in earlier flows, more floods, and drier summers; and that "California water supplies/ecosystems are likely to experience [] changes earliest and most intensely." Following Dettinger's presentation, members of CALFED noted "the need to reevaluate water storage policies and ERP [Ecosystem Recovery Program] recovery strategies, all of which would be affected by projected climate changes." The record reflects that extreme water temperatures can have dramatic impacts upon smelt abundance.

In addition to the specific studies and data cited by NRDC, FWS scientists recognized the issue of climate change warranted further consideration. At a June 2003 symposium entitled "Framing the issues for Environmental and Ecological Effects of Proposed Changes in Water Operations: Science Symposium on the State of Knowledge," a number of questions regarding climate change were raised, including: "How does the proposed operations plan account for the potential effects of climate change (e.g., El Nino or La Nina, long term changes in precipitation and runoff patters, or increases in water temperature)?"

Plaintiffs argue that, despite this evidence that climate change could seriously impact the smelt by changing Delta hydrology and temperature, the BiOp "did not so much as mention the probable effects of climate change on the delta smelt, its habitat, or the magnitude of impacts that could be expected from the 2004 OCAP operations, much less analyze those effects." Defendants and Defendant–Intervenors respond by arguing (1) that the evidence before FWS at the time the BiOp was issued was inconclusive about the impacts of climate change; and (2) that, far from ignoring climate change, the issue is built into the BiOp's analysis through the use of X2 as a proxy for the location and distribution of Delta smelt.

a. *Inconclusive Nature of Available Information Regarding the Impacts of Global Climate Change on Precipitation.*

Federal Defendants and the State Water Contractors characterize Mr. Dettinger's presentation, as reflecting "a great deal of uncertainty that climate change will impact future precipitation." The presentation is entitled "Climate Change Uncertainties and CALFED Planning." Dettinger acknowledges that, although current climate models "yield consistent warming scenarios for California", there is no similar consensus regarding the impact of warming on future precipitation. Federal Defendants suggest that FWS "responsibly refused to engage in sheer guesswork, and properly declined to speculate as to how global warming might affect delta smelt." But, the NRDC letter cited a number of studies in addition to Mr. Dettinger's presentations, all of which predict that anticipated climate change will adversely impact future water availability in the Western United States.

At the very least, these studies suggest that climate change will be an "important aspect of the problem" meriting analysis in the BiOp. *Pacific Coast Fed'n,* 265 F.3d at 1034. However, as with the 2004 FMWT data, the climate change issue was not meaningfully discussed in the biological opinion, making it impossible to determine whether the information was rationally discounted because of its inconclusive nature, or arbitrarily ignored.

b. *X2 as a Proxy for Climate Change.*

The State Water Contractors argue that the approaches taken in the DSRAM are "more than adequate to deal with the projected impacts of climate change—assuming they occur." For example, Plaintiffs' suggestion that climate change will produce earlier flows, more floods, and drier summers is addressed by the DSRAM's X2 trigger. Flow level changes will be reflected in the position of X2. If climate change alters water temperatures, DSRAM also includes a temperature trigger, that monitors the temperature range within which successful Delta smelt spawning occurs.

The DSRAM offers no assurance that any mitigating fish protection actions will be implemented if the X2 criteria is triggered. That X2 indirectly monitors climate change does not assuage Plaintiffs' concerns that the BiOp has not adequately analyzed the potential impact of climate change on the smelt.

The BiOp does not gauge the potential effect of various climate change scenarios on Delta hydrology. Assuming, *arguendo,* a lawful adaptive management approach, there is no discussion when and how climate change impacts will be addressed, whether existing take limits will remain, and the probable impacts on CVP–SWP operations.

FWS acted arbitrarily and capriciously by failing to address the issue of climate change in the BiOp. This absence of *any* discussion in the BiOp of how to deal with any climate change is a failure to analyze a potentially "important aspect of the problem."

Plaintiffs' motion for summary adjudication is **GRANTED** as to this claim. * * *

NOTES

1. **The Rest of the Story.** "[T]he Delta is a maze of channels and levess that drains most of the central valley watersheds into the Pacific Ocean." Tom Chandler, "The California Water Wars: Pumping the Delta Smelt Into Oblivion," *The Trout Underground*, http://troutunderground.com/2007/07/08/the-california-water-wars-pumping-the-delta-smelt-into-oblivion/ (July 8, 2007). Withdrawals of water from the Bay Delta provide drinking water to about 25 million Californians and irrigation water for about 750,000 acres of crops. At full capacity, the pumping of water from the Delta is so intensive that it can reverse the flow of water into the Delta.

Survey trawls conducted in Spring 2007, immediately before this decision, found only 25 juvenile Delta smelt in the system, down from 326 smelt in 2006. Moreover, in late May 2007, as Judge Wanger was issuing this decision, juvenile smelt were found entrained (caught and damaged) in pumping facilities for California's State Water Project (SWP). As a result, on May 31, 2007, the California Department of Water Resources announced that it would stop pumping at SWP facilities in order to provide the maximum benefit to the Delta smelt. In addition, pumping in the CVP was reduced to 100 cubic feet per second in June 2007, about 90 percent less than normal. Nevertheless, an additional 609 Delta smelt were killed in CVP pumps in July 2007, well after Judge Wanger's decision.

Judge Wanger issued his initial remedy decision for this case on August 31, 2007, after a seven-day evidentiary hearing held August 21–24 and August 29–31. The judge finalized his decision on December 14, 2007, and the final order is available at http://www.earthjustice.org/library/legal_docs/delta-smelt-final-remedy-order.pdf. His decision: (1) remands the 2005 OCAP BiOp to the U.S. Fish & Wildlife Service, with instructions to produce a new BiOp in conformance with the opinion by September 15, 2008; (2) declines vacatur, "[t]o avoid the potentially draconian consequences of operating the CVP and SWP without incidental take authority"; (3) issues a preliminary injunction requiring the federal agencies' compliance with "interim remedial measures to prevent the extinction of the Delta smelt"; (4) prohibits the Bureau of Reclamation from entering into any new water contracts to provide water from the CVP; (5) prohibits the Bureau from undertaking any new construction projects; (6) prohibits the Bureau from increasing the amount of water exported from the Delta; and (7) requires a status report by April 30, 2008. The required interim remedial measures include: (1) increased Delta smelt surveys; (2) increased sampling for Delta smelt entrained at the Jones Pumping Plant, including monitoring for larval and juvenile Delta smelt; (3) flow restrictions to protect spawning Delta smelt and larval and juvenile Delta smelt; (4) continued implementation of the Vernalis Adaptive Management Plan; and (5) restrictions on the installation of barriers within the water system.

The flow restrictions in Judge Wanger's decision could have reduced the amount of water withdrawn from the Delta by up to 35 percent. In combination with the significant droughts that were occurring in the West from about 2000 until about 2010, Judge Wanger's decision, and other measures to protect the Delta smelt, forced some water rationing in some of central California.

People affected by this rationing brought their own challenge to the use of the Endangered Species Act to protect the Delta smelt, arguing that these federally induced measures violated the Commerce Clause of the U.S. Constitution because the Delta smelt is a wholly intrastate species not traded in commerce. In March 2011, the Ninth Circuit denied the constitutional challenge, concluding that actions taken to prevent the "take" of Delta smelt did not violate the Commerce Clause. *San Luis & Delta–Mendota Water Authority v. Salazar*, 638 F.3d 1163, 1175–77 (9th Cir. 2011). The Supreme Court denied *certiorari* on Halloween. *Stewart & Jasper Orchards v. Salazar*, ___ U.S. ___, 132 S.Ct. 498 (2011).

While this challenge was wending its way through the federal courts, California experienced its wettest winter (2010–2011) in a decade. The September 2011 counts of Delta smelt were the highest they had been since 2001—although still very low by historical standards. That same month, shortly before retiring from the bench, Judge Wanger both allowed the Delta pumps to run at 80 percent capacity and criticized the Fish & Wildlife Services' scientists, calling them "zealots" who were not acting in good faith.

2. **Science and Biological Opinions.** What does ESA § 7(a)(2) require with respect to the expert agencies' use of science in Biological Opinions? How have Congress, the Ninth Circuit, and various federal district courts interpreted this requirement? Is this view of science in Biological Opinions consistent with the U.S. Supreme Court's decision in *TVA v. Hill*? Why or why not? How are expert agencies supposed to deal with scientific uncertainty in their Biological Opinions?

3. **Climate Change and the Delta Smelt.** Why is climate change potentially relevant to the Delta smelt's survival? Why didn't the U.S. Fish & Wildlife Service discuss climate change in its Biological Opinion? Why was the Eastern District of California's view of science and Section 7(a)(2) relevant to the U.S. Fish & Wildlife Service's treatment of climate change in its Biological Opinion?

4. **Formal Consultation, Biological Opinions, and Incidental Take Statements.** In a portion of the opinion not reproduced above, Judge Wanger noted that the Biological Opinions at issue allowed the CVP/SWP system to "incidentally take" delta smelt. This incidental take could be significant—over 45,000 delta smelt in June, for example, if water flows are normal, but still over 30,000 fish if flows are below normal. When may expert agencies like the U.S. Fish & Wildlife Service include an incidental take statement with their Biological Opinions? What does an incidental take statement do for the action agency? Does an incidental take statement seem appropriate in the case of the Delta smelt? Why or why not?

Note that in the remedy phase of this litigation, *supra* note 1, Judge Wanger refused to vacate the 2005 Biological Opinion because vacatur would eliminate the incidental take statement, a result that the judge viewed as "draconian." Why would the judge take this approach to an invalid Biological Opinion? Why would elimination of the incidental take statement result in potentially "draconian" consequences for the Bureau of Reclamation?

5. **Water Law, Federal Water Projects, and the ESA.** Regulation of withdrawals of water, the subject of a course in Water Law, is generally the province of the states. However, in much of the West (and to a lesser extent in some places in the East), Congress authorized many massive federal ***reclamation, water storage, and flood control projects***, generally consisting of the building of dams and the creation of large reservoirs, such as Hoover Dam and Lake Mead on the Colorado River. The federal agencies involved—often the U.S. Bureau of Reclamation and the U.S. Army Corps of Engineers—receive the original water rights for the projects from the relevant state. Congress then often authorizes the relevant federal agency to sell water made available from the project. For example, in *Natural Resources Defense Council v. Kempthorne*, the Bureau of Reclamation was authorized to enter into water contracts for water made available from the Central Valley Project (CVP), which includes 20 dams and reservoirs such as Shasta Dam and Trinity Dam.

Such federal involvement, however, also subjects these water projects to Section 7 of the ESA, and conflicts between the ESA and federal water projects are becoming increasingly common throughout the United States. Some examples include litigation to protect coho salmon, shortnose suckerfish, and Lost River suckerfish from federally authorized water withdrawals in the Klamath River, along the border of California and Oregon; litigation to protect pallid sturgeon from federal projects along the Missouri River; and litigation to protect Gulf sturgeon and listed mussel species from the federal water projects in the Apalachicola–Chattahoochee–Flint River basin in Alabama, Florida, and Georgia.

6. **Climate Change and Other Aspects of the Endangered Species Act:** Climate change impacts now routinely influence the ESA listing process, as well. In the first six months of 2009, for example, climate change played a role—sometimes significant—in the agencies' determinations that: (1) the black abalone should be listed as an endangered species, 74 Fed. Reg. 1937, 1939, 1941 (Jan. 14, 2009); (2) a petition to list the Wyoming pocket gopher was warranted, 74 Fed. Reg. 6558, 6562–63 (Feb. 10, 2009); (3) the Pacific eulachon should be proposed as a threatened species, 74 Fed. Reg. 10,857, 10,869, 10,870–74 (March 13, 2009); (4) a petition to list the Tehachapi slender salamander was warranted, 74 Fed. Reg. 18,336, 18,340–41 (April 22, 2009); and (5) a petition to list the American pika was warranted, 74 Fed. Reg. 21,301, 21,304–09 (May 7, 2009). Climate change impacts have also been argued less successfully in several other listing processes. *See* 74 Fed. Reg. 27,226, 27,270 (June 9, 2009) (Narrowleaf evening primrose); 74 Fed. Reg. 23,376, 23,381–84 (May 19, 2009) (Coaster brook trout); 74 Fed. Reg. 12,932, 12,939, 12,944–47, 12,960–62 (March 25, 2009) (Yellow-billed loon); 73 Fed. Reg. 79,822, 79,824–27 (Dec. 30, 2008) (Ribbon seal).

Climate change is also playing a role in critical habitat decisions. It has been relevant, for example, for the Frosted Flatwoods and Reticulated Flatwoods salamanders, 74 Fed. Reg. 6700, 6716 (Feb. 10, 2009); the Canada lynx, 74 Fed. Reg. 8616, 8617, 8621 (Feb. 25, 2009); the Louisiana black bear, 74 Fed. Reg. 10,350, 10,356 (March 10, 2009); the Desert Bighorn sheep, 74 Fed. Reg. 17,288, 17,297, 17,303–05, 17,309 (April 14, 2009); and the Piping plover in Texas, 74 Fed. Reg. 23,476, 23,480–81, 23,488 (May 19, 2009).

* * *

F. THE SECTION 9 "TAKE" PROHIBITION

1. Overview of Section 9

Section 9 of the ESA, 16 U.S.C. § 1538, establishes prohibitions that apply to "any person." A "person," for purposes of the ESA, is "an individual, corporation, partnership, trust, association, or any other private entity; or any officer, employee, agency, department, or instrumentality of the Federal Government, of any State, municipality, or political subdivision of a State, or of any foreign government; any State, municipality, or political subdivision of a State; or any other entity subject to the jurisdiction of the United States." ESA § 3(13), 16 U.S.C. § 1532(13). Thus, federal agencies are subject to section 9 as well as section 7, but section 9 is far broader than section 7 in its applicability.

With regard to endangered species of fish and wildlife, section 9 makes it unlawful for any person to:

(A) import any such species into, or export any such species from the United States;

(B) take any such species within the United States or the territorial sea of the United States;

(C) take any such species upon the high seas;

(D) possess, sell, deliver, carry, transport, or ship, by any means whatsoever, any such species taken in violation of subparagraphs (B) and (C);

(E) deliver, receive, carry, transport, or ship in interstate or foreign commerce, by any means whatsoever and in the course of commercial activity, any such species;

(F) sell or offer for sale in interstate or foreign commerce any such species; or

(G) violate any regulation pertaining to such species or to any threatened species of fish or wildlife listed pursuant to section 1533 of this title and promulgated by [USFWS or NMFS/NOAA Fisheries] pursuant to authority provided by this chapter.

ESA § 9(a)(1), 16 U.S.C. § 1538(a)(1). The prohibitions for endangered *plants* are slightly different. For them, the ESA makes it unlawful for any person to:

(A) import any such species into, or export any such species from, the United States;

(B) remove and reduce to possession any such species from areas under Federal jurisdiction; maliciously damage or destroy any such species on any such area; or remove, cut, dig up, or damage or destroy any such species on any other area in knowing violation of any law or regulation of any State or in the course of any violation of a State criminal trespass law;

(C) deliver, receive, carry, transport, or ship in interstate or foreign commerce, by any means whatsoever and in the course of a commercial activity, any such species;

(D) sell or offer for sale in interstate or foreign commerce any such species; or

(E) violate any regulation pertaining to such species or to any threatened species of plants listed pursuant to section 1533 of this title and promulgated by [USFWS or NMFS/NOAA Fisheries] pursuant to authority provided by this chapter.

ESA § 9(a)(2), 16 U.S.C. § 1538(a)(2).

Notice that section 9's prohibitions apply most directly to *endangered* species; the only prohibition for threatened species is to not violate the agencies' regulations. Under section 4(d), when a species is listed as "threatened" rather than endangered, the USFWS or NMFS/NOAA Fisheries "shall issue such regulations as [it] deems necessary or advisable to provide for the conservation of such species." 16 U.S.C. § 1533(d). The agencies have promulgated § 4(d) regulations for some threatened species. For example, in June 2004, the USFWS proposed to exempt international, foreign, and interstate commerce in beluga sturgeon products (*i.e.*, caviar) from the ESA section 9 prohibitions. 69 Fed. Reg. 38,863, 38,863 (June 29, 2004). NOAA promulgated a section 4(d) rule for threatened species of salmon to accommodate tribal treaty rights to fish for these listed species. 65 Fed. Reg. 42,481, 42,481 (July 10, 2000), *codified at* 50 C.F.R. § 223.209. The USFWS's section 4(d) rules are codified at 50 C.F.R. §§ 17.40 to 17.48.

Most threatened species, however, receive all of the statutory section 9 protections through an USFWS rule that confers all of the protections in section 9 on all threatened species, unless special section 4(d) rules apply to that species. 50 C.F.R. § 17.31(a), (c). In general, therefore, threatened species receive exactly the same protections that endangered species do.

2. The "Take" Prohibition

a. Habitat Modification as "Harm"

Of section 9's prohibitions, the most controversial is the "take" prohibition. The ESA defines "take" to mean "to harass, harm, pursue, hunt, shoot, wound, kill, capture, or collect, or to attempt to engage in any such conduct." ESA § 3(19), 16 U.S.C. § 1538(19). The USFWS has further elaborated on the definition of "harm" in its regulations, which became the subject of the following U.S. Supreme Court decision.

BABBITT v. SWEET HOME CHAPTER OF COMMUNITIES FOR A GREAT OREGON

515 U.S. 687 (1995).

JUSTICE STEVENS delivered the opinion of the Court.

The Endangered Species Act of 1973 (ESA or Act), 87 Stat. 884, 16 U.S.C. § 1531 (1988 ed. and Supp. V), contains a variety of protections designed to save from extinction species that the Secretary of the Interior designates as endangered or threatened. Section 9 of the Act makes it unlawful for any person to "take" any endangered or threatened species. The Secretary has promulgated a regulation that defines the statute's prohibition on takings to include "significant habitat modification or degradation where it actually kills or injures wildlife." This case presents the question whether the Secretary exceeded his authority under the Act by promulgating that regulation.

I

Section 9(a)(1) of the Act provides the following protection for endangered species:

> "Except as provided in sections 1535(g)(2) and 1539 of this title, with respect to any endangered species of fish or wildlife listed pursuant to section 1533 of this title it is unlawful for any person subject to the jurisdiction of the United States to—
>
> . . .
>
> "(B) take any such species within the United States or the territorial sea of the United States." 16 U.S.C. § 1538(a)(1).

Section 3(19) of the Act defines the statutory term "take":

> "The term 'take' means to harass, harm, pursue, hunt, shoot, wound, kill, trap, capture, or collect, or to attempt to engage in any such conduct." 16 U.S.C. § 1532(19).

The Act does not further define the terms it uses to define "take." The Interior Department regulations that implement the statute, however, define the statutory term "harm":

> "*Harm* in the definition of 'take' in the Act means an act which actually kills or injures wildlife. Such act may include significant habitat modification or degradation where it actually kills or injures wildlife by significantly impairing essential behavioral patterns, including breeding, feeding, or sheltering." 50 CFR § 17.3 (1994).

This regulation has been in place since 1975.

A limitation on the § 9 "take" prohibition appears in § 10(a)(1)(B) of the Act, which Congress added by amendment in 1982. That section authorizes the Secretary to grant a permit for any taking otherwise prohibited by § 9(a)(1)(B) "if such taking is incidental to, and not the purpose of, the carrying out of an otherwise lawful activity." 16 U.S.C. § 1539(a)(1)(B).

In addition to the prohibition on takings, the Act provides several other protections for endangered species. Section 4, 16 U.S.C. § 1533, commands the Secretary to identify species of fish or wildlife that are in danger of extinction and to publish from time to time lists of all species he determines to be endangered or threatened. Section 5, 16 U.S.C. § 1534, authorizes the Secretary, in cooperation with the States, to acquire land to aid in preserving such species. Section 7 requires federal agencies to ensure that none of their activities, including the granting of licenses and permits, will jeopardize the continued existence of endangered species "or result in the destruction or adverse modification of habitat of such species which is determined by the Secretary ... to be critical." 16 U.S.C. § 1536(a)(2).

Respondents in this action are small landowners, logging companies, and families dependent on the forest products industries in the Pacific Northwest and in the Southeast, and organizations that represent their interests. They brought this declaratory judgment action against petitioners, the Secretary of the Interior and the Director of the Fish and Wildlife Service, in the United States District Court for the District of Columbia to challenge the statutory validity of the Secretary's regulation defining "harm," particularly the inclusion of habitat modification and degradation in the definition. Respondents challenged the regulation on its face. Their complaint alleged that application of the "harm" regulation to the red-cockaded woodpecker, an endangered species, and the northern spotted owl, a threatened species, had injured them economically.

Respondents advanced three arguments to support their submission that Congress did not intend the word "take" in § 9 to include habitat modification, as the Secretary's "harm" regulation provides. First, they correctly noted that language in the Senate's original version of the ESA would have defined "take" to include "destruction, modification, or curtailment of [the] habitat or range" of fish or wildlife, but the Senate deleted that language from the bill before enacting it. Second, respondents argued that Congress intended the Act's express authorization for the Federal Government to buy private land in order to prevent habitat degradation in § 5 to be the exclusive check against habitat modification on private property. Third, because the Senate added the term "harm" to the definition of "take" in a floor amendment without debate, respondents argued that the court should not interpret the term so expansively as to include habitat modification.

The District Court considered and rejected each of respondents' arguments, finding "that Congress intended an expansive interpretation of the word 'take,' an interpretation that encompasses habitat modification." * * * The District Court therefore entered summary judgment for petitioners and dismissed respondents' complaint.

A divided panel of the Court of Appeals initially affirmed the judgment of the District Court. After granting a petition for rehearing, however, the panel reversed. After acknowledging that "[t]he potential breadth of the word 'harm' is indisputable," the majority concluded that the immediate statutory context in which "harm" appeared counseled against a broad reading; like the other words in the definition of "take," the word "harm" should be read as applying only to "the perpetrator's direct application of force against the animal taken . . . The forbidden acts fit, in ordinary language, the basic model 'A hit B.' " The majority based its reasoning on a canon of statutory construction called *noscitur a sociis,* which holds that a word is known by the company it keeps.

* * * The Court of Appeals' decision created a square conflict with a 1988 decision of the Ninth Circuit that had upheld the Secretary's definition of "harm." See *Palila v. Hawaii Dept. of Land and Natural Resources,* 852 F.2d 1106 (1988) (*Palila II*). The Court of Appeals neither cited nor distinguished *Palila II,* despite the stark contrast between the Ninth Circuit's holding and its own. We granted certiorari to resolve the conflict. Our consideration of the text and structure of the Act, its legislative history, and the significance of the 1982 amendment persuades us that the Court of Appeals' judgment should be reversed.

II

* * * The text of the Act provides three reasons for concluding that the Secretary's interpretation is reasonable. First, an ordinary understanding of the word "harm" supports it. The dictionary definition of the verb form of "harm" is "to cause hurt or damage to: injure." WEBSTER'S THIRD NEW INTERNATIONAL DICTIONARY 1034 (1966). In the context of the ESA, that definition naturally encompasses habitat modification that results in actual injury or death to members of an endangered or threatened species.

Respondents argue that the Secretary should have limited the purview of "harm" to direct applications of force against protected species, but the dictionary definition does not include the word "directly" or suggest in any way that only direct or willful action that leads to injury constitutes "harm." Moreover, unless the statutory term "harm" encompasses indirect as well as direct injuries, the word has no meaning that does not duplicate the meaning of other words that § 3 uses to define "take." A reluctance to treat statutory terms as surplusage supports the reasonableness of the Secretary's interpretation.

Second, the broad purpose of the ESA supports the Secretary's decision to extend protection against activities that cause the precise harms Congress enacted the statute to avoid. In *TVA v. Hill,* 437 U.S. 153 (1978), we described the Act as "the most comprehensive legislation for the preservation of endangered species ever enacted by any nation." *Id.*, at 180. Whereas predecessor statutes enacted in 1966 and 1969 had not contained any sweeping prohibition against the taking of endangered species except on federal lands, *id.*, at 175, the 1973 Act applied to all land in the United States and to the Nation's territorial seas. As stated in § 2 of the Act, among its central purposes is "to provide a means whereby the ecosystems upon which endangered species and threatened species depend may be conserved ...." 16 U.S.C. § 1531(b).

In *Hill,* we construed § 7 as precluding the completion of the Tellico Dam because of its predicted impact on the survival of the snail darter. *See* 437 U.S., at 193. Both our holding and the language in our opinion stressed the importance of the statutory policy. "The plain intent of Congress in enacting this statute," we recognized, "was to halt and reverse the trend toward species extinction, whatever the cost. This is reflected not only in the stated policies of the Act, but in literally every section of the statute." *Id.*, at 184. Although the § 9 "take" prohibition was not at issue in *Hill,* we took note of that prohibition, placing particular emphasis on the Secretary's inclusion of habitat modification in his definition of "harm." In light of that provision for habitat protection, we could "not understand how TVA intends to operate Tellico Dam without 'harming' the snail darter." *Id.*, at 184 n.30. Congress' intent to provide comprehensive protection for endangered and threatened species supports the permissibility of the Secretary's "harm" regulation.

Respondents advance strong arguments that activities that cause minimal or unforeseeable harm will not violate the Act as construed in the "harm" regulation. Respondents, however, present a facial challenge to the regulation. Thus, they ask us to invalidate the Secretary's understanding of "harm" in every circumstance, even when an actor knows that an activity, such as draining a pond, would actually result in the extinction of a listed species by destroying its habitat. Given Congress' clear expression of the ESA's broad purpose to protect endangered and threatened wildlife, the Secretary's definition of "harm" is reasonable.[13]

Third, the fact that Congress in 1982 authorized the Secretary to issue permits for takings that § 9(a)(1)(B) would otherwise prohibit, "if such taking is incidental to, and not the purpose of, the carrying out of an otherwise lawful activity," 16 U.S.C. § 1539(a)(1)(B), strongly suggests that Congress understood § 9(a)(1)(B) to prohibit indirect as well as deliberate takings. * * * No one could seriously request an "incidental" take permit to avert § 9 liability for direct, deliberate action against a member of an endangered or threatened species, but respondents would read "harm" so narrowly that the permit procedure would have little more than that absurd purpose. "When Congress acts to amend a statute,

13. The dissent incorrectly asserts that the Secretary's regulation (1) "dispenses with the foreseeability of harm" and (2) "fail[s] to require injury to particular animals[.]" As to the first assertion, the regulation merely implements the statute, and it is therefore subject to the statute's "knowingly violates" language, see 16 U.S.C. §§ 1540(a)(1), (b)(1), and ordinary requirements of proximate causation and foreseeability. Nothing in the regulation purports to weaken those requirements. To the contrary, the word "actually" in the regulation should be construed to limit the liability about which the dissent appears most concerned, liability under the statute's "otherwise violates" provision. The Secretary did not need to include "actually" to connote "but for" causation, which the other words in the definition obviously require. As to the dissent's second assertion, every term in the regulation's definition of "harm" is subservient to the phrase "an act which actually kills or injures wildlife."

we presume it intends its amendment to have real and substantial effect." *Stone v. INS*, 514 U.S. 386, 397 (1995). Congress' addition of the § 10 permit provision supports the Secretary's conclusion that activities not intended to harm an endangered species, such as habitat modification, may constitute unlawful takings under the ESA unless the Secretary permits them.

The Court of Appeals made three errors in asserting that "harm" must refer to a direct application of force because the words around it do. First, the court's premise was flawed. Several of the words that accompany "harm" in the § 3 definition of "take," especially "harass," "pursue," "wound," and "kill," refer to actions or effects that do not require direct applications of force. Second, to the extent the court read a requirement of intent or purpose into the words used to define "take," it ignored § 11's express provision that a "knowin[g]" action is enough to violate the Act. Third, the court employed *noscitur a sociis* to give "harm" essentially the same function as other words in the definition, thereby denying it independent meaning. The canon, to the contrary, counsels that a word "gathers meaning from the words around it." *Jarecki v. G.D. Searle & Co.*, 367 U.S. 303, 307 (1961). The statutory context of "harm" suggests that Congress meant that term to serve a particular function in the ESA, consistent with, but distinct from, the functions of the other verbs used to define "take." The Secretary's interpretation of "harm" to include indirectly injuring endangered animals through habitat modification permissibly interprets "harm" to have "a character of its own not to be submerged by its association." *Russell Motor Car Co. v. United States*, 261 U.S. 514, 519 (1923).

* * * We need not decide whether the statutory definition of "take" compels the Secretary's interpretation of "harm," because our conclusions that Congress did not unambiguously manifest its intent to adopt respondents' view and that the Secretary's interpretation is reasonable suffice to decide this case. The latitude the ESA gives the Secretary in enforcing the statute, together with the degree of regulatory expertise necessary to its enforcement, establishes that we owe some degree of deference to the Secretary's reasonable interpretation.

III

Our conclusion that the Secretary's definition of "harm" rests on a permissible construction of the ESA gains further support from the legislative history of the statute. The Committee Reports accompanying the bills that became the ESA do not specifically discuss the meaning of "harm," but they make clear that Congress intended "take" to apply broadly to cover indirect as well as purposeful actions. The Senate Report stressed that " '[t]ake' is defined . . . in the broadest possible manner to include every conceivable way in which a person can 'take' or attempt to 'take' any fish or wildlife." S. REP. NO. 93–307, p. 7 (1973). U.S. Code Cong. & Admin. News 1973, pp. 2989, 2995. The House Report stated that "the broadest possible terms" were used to define restrictions on takings.

H.R. REP. NO. 93–412, p.15 (1973). The House Report underscored the breadth of the "take" definition by noting that it included "harassment, *whether intentional or not.*" *Id.*, at 11 (emphasis added). The Report explained that the definition "would allow, for example, the Secretary to regulate or prohibit the activities of birdwatchers where the effect of those activities might disturb the birds and make it difficult for them to hatch or raise their young." *Ibid.* These comments, ignored in the dissent's welcome but selective foray into legislative history, support the Secretary's interpretation that the term "take" in § 9 reached far more than the deliberate actions of hunters and trappers.

Two endangered species bills, S. 1592 and S. 1983, were introduced in the Senate and referred to the Commerce Committee. Neither bill included the word "harm" in its definition of "take," although the definitions otherwise closely resembled the one that appeared in the bill as ultimately enacted. Senator Tunney, the floor manager of the bill in the Senate, subsequently introduced a floor amendment that added "harm" to the definition, noting that this and accompanying amendments would "help to achieve the purposes of the bill." 119 Cong. Rec. 25683 (1973). Respondents argue that the lack of debate about the amendment that added "harm" counsels in favor of a narrow interpretation. We disagree. An obviously broad word that the Senate went out of its way to add to an important statutory definition is precisely the sort of provision that deserves a respectful reading.

The definition of "take" that originally appeared in S. 1983 differed from the definition as ultimately enacted in one other significant respect: It included "the destruction, modification, or curtailment of [the] habitat or range" of fish and wildlife. Respondents make much of the fact that the Commerce Committee removed this phrase from the "take" definition before S. 1983 went to the floor. *See* 119 Cong. Rec. 25663 (1973). We do not find that fact especially significant. The legislative materials contain no indication why the habitat protection provision was deleted. That provision differed greatly from the regulation at issue today. Most notably, the habitat protection provision in S. 1983 would have applied far more broadly than the regulation does because it made adverse habitat modification a categorical violation of the "take" prohibition, unbounded by the regulation's limitation to habitat modifications that actually kill or injure wildlife. The S. 1983 language also failed to qualify "modification" with the regulation's limiting adjective "significant." We do not believe the Senate's unelaborated disavowal of the provision in S. 1983 undermines the reasonableness of the more moderate habitat protection in the Secretary's "harm" regulation.

The history of the 1982 amendment that gave the Secretary authority to grant permits for "incidental" takings provides further support for his reading of the Act. The House Report expressly states that "[b]y use of the word 'incidental' the Committee intends to cover situations in which it is known that a taking will occur if the other activity is engaged in but such taking is incidental to, and not the purpose of, the activity." H.R.

REP. NO. 97–567, p. 31 (1982). U.S. Code Cong. & Admin. News 1982, pp. 2807, 2831. This reference to the foreseeability of incidental takings undermines respondents' argument that the 1982 amendment covered only accidental killings of endangered and threatened animals that might occur in the course of hunting or trapping other animals. Indeed, Congress had habitat modification directly in mind: Both the Senate Report and the House Conference Report identified as the model for the permit process a cooperative state-federal response to a case in California where a development project threatened incidental harm to a species of endangered butterfly by modification of its habitat. *See* S. REP. NO. 97–418, p. 10 (1982); H.R. CONF. REP. NO. 97–835, pp. 30–32 (1982). Thus, Congress in 1982 focused squarely on the aspect of the "harm" regulation at issue in this litigation. Congress' implementation of a permit program is consistent with the Secretary's interpretation of the term "harm."

IV

When it enacted the ESA, Congress delegated broad administrative and interpretive power to the Secretary. See 16 U.S.C. §§ 1533, 1540(f). The task of defining and listing endangered and threatened species requires an expertise and attention to detail that exceeds the normal province of Congress. Fashioning appropriate standards for issuing permits under § 10 for takings that would otherwise violate § 9 necessarily requires the exercise of broad discretion. The proper interpretation of a term such as "harm" involves a complex policy choice. When Congress has entrusted the Secretary with broad discretion, we are especially reluctant to substitute our views of wise policy for his. In this case, that reluctance accords with our conclusion, based on the text, structure, and legislative history of the ESA, that the Secretary reasonably construed the intent of Congress when he defined "harm" to include "significant habitat modification or degradation that actually kills or injures wildlife."

In the elaboration and enforcement of the ESA, the Secretary and all persons who must comply with the law will confront difficult questions of proximity and degree; for, as all recognize, the Act encompasses a vast range of economic and social enterprises and endeavors. These questions must be addressed in the usual course of the law, through case-by-case resolution and adjudication.

The judgment of the Court of Appeals is reversed.

It is so ordered.

JUSTICE O'CONNOR, concurring.

My agreement with the Court is founded on two understandings. First, the challenged regulation is limited to significant habitat modification that causes actual, as opposed to hypothetical or speculative, death or injury to identifiable protected animals. Second, even setting aside difficult questions of scienter, the regulation's application is limited by ordinary principles of proximate causation, which introduce notions of foreseeability. These limitations, in my view, call into question *Palila v. Hawaii Dept.*

of Land and Natural Resources, 852 F.2d 1106 (CA9 1988) (*Palila II*), and with it, many of the applications derided by the dissent. Because there is no need to strike a regulation on a facial challenge out of concern that it is susceptible of erroneous application, however, and because there are many habitat-related circumstances in which the regulation might validly apply, I join the opinion of the Court.

* * * In my view, * * * the "harm" regulation applies where significant habitat modification, by impairing essential behaviors, proximately (foreseeably) causes actual death or injury to identifiable animals that are protected under the Endangered Species Act. Pursuant to my interpretation, *Palila II*—under which the Court of Appeals held that a state agency committed a "taking" by permitting mouflon sheep to eat mamane-naio seedlings that, when full grown, might have fed and sheltered endangered palila—was wrongly decided according to the regulation's own terms. Destruction of the seedlings did not proximately cause actual death or injury to identifiable birds; it merely prevented the regeneration of forest land not currently sustaining actual birds.

This case, of course, comes to us as a facial challenge. We are charged with deciding whether the regulation on its face exceeds the agency's statutory mandate. I have identified at least one application of the regulation (*Palila II*) that is, in my view, inconsistent with the regulation's *own* limitations. That misapplication does not, however, call into question the validity of the regulation itself. One can doubtless imagine questionable applications of the regulation that test the limits of the agency's authority. However, it seems to me clear that the regulation does not on its terms exceed the agency's mandate, and that the regulation has innumerable valid habitat-related applications. Congress may, of course, see fit to revisit this issue. And nothing the Court says today prevents the agency itself from narrowing the scope of its regulation at a later date.

With this understanding, I join the Court's opinion.

Justice SCALIA, with whom THE CHIEF JUSTICE and JUSTICE THOMAS join, dissenting.

I think it unmistakably clear that the legislation at issue here (1) forbade the hunting and killing of endangered animals, and (2) provided federal lands and federal funds *for the acquisition of private lands,* to preserve the habitat of endangered animals. The Court's holding that the hunting and killing prohibition incidentally preserves habitat on private lands imposes unfairness to the point of financial ruin—not just upon the rich, but upon the simplest farmer who finds his land conscripted to national zoological use. I respectfully dissent.

I

The Endangered Species Act of 1973 (Act), 16 U.S.C. § 1531 *et seq.* (1988 ed. and Supp. V), provides that "it is unlawful for any person subject to the jurisdiction of the United States to take—. . . any [protected] species within the United States." § 1538(a)(1)(B). The term "take" is defined as "to harass, *harm,* pursue, hunt, shoot, wound, kill, trap, capture, or collect, or to attempt to engage in any such conduct." § 1532(19) (emphasis added). The challenged regulation defines "harm" thus:

> "*Harm* in the definition of 'take' in the Act means an act which actually kills or injures wildlife. Such act may include significant habitat modification or degradation where it actually kills or injures wildlife by significantly impairing essential behavioral patterns, including breeding, feeding or sheltering." 50 CFR § 17.3 (1994).

* * * The regulation has three features which, for reasons I shall discuss at length below, do not comport with the statute. First, it interprets the statute to prohibit habitat modification that is no more than the cause-in-fact of death or injury to wildlife. *Any* "significant habitat modification" that in fact produces that result by "impairing essential behavioral patterns" is made unlawful, regardless of whether that result is intended or even foreseeable, and no matter how long the chain of causality between modification and injury.

Second, the regulation does not require an "act": The Secretary's officially stated position is that an *omission* will do. The previous version of the regulation made this explicit. When the regulation was modified in 1981 the phrase "or omission" was taken out, but only because (as the final publication of the rule advised) "the [Fish and Wildlife] Service feels that 'act' is inclusive of either commissions or omissions which would be prohibited by section [1538(a)(1)(B)]." 46 Fed. Reg. 54748, 54750 (1981). In their brief here petitioners agree that the regulation covers omissions.

The third and most important unlawful feature of the regulation is that it encompasses injury inflicted, not only upon individual animals, but upon populations of the protected species. "Injury" in the regulation includes "significantly impairing essential behavioral patterns, including *breeding,*" 50 CFR § 17.3 (1994) (emphasis added). Impairment of breeding does not "injure" living creatures; it prevents them from propagating, thus "injuring" *a population* of animals which would otherwise have maintained or increased its numbers. * * *

None of these three features of the regulation can be found in the statutory provisions supposed to authorize it. The term "harm" in § 1532(19) has no legal force of its own. An indictment or civil complaint that charged the defendant with "harming" an animal protected under the Act would be dismissed as defective, for the only *operative* term in the statute is to "take." If "take" were not elsewhere defined in the Act, none could dispute what it means, for the term is as old as the law itself. To "take," when applied to wild animals, means to reduce those animals, by killing or capturing, to human control. This is just the sense in which "take" is used elsewhere in federal legislation and treaty. And that meaning fits neatly with the rest of § 1538(a)(1), which makes it unlawful not only to take protected species, but also to import or export them, § 1538(a)(1)(A); to possess, sell, deliver, carry, transport, or ship any taken species, § 1538(a)(1)(D); and to transport, sell, or offer to sell them in interstate or foreign commerce, §§ 1538(a)(1)(E), (F). The taking prohibition, in other words, is only part of the regulatory plan of § 1538(a)(1), which covers all the stages of the process by which protected wildlife is reduced to man's dominion and made the object of profit. It is obvious that "take" in this sense—a term of art deeply embedded in the statutory and common law concerning wildlife—describes a class of acts (not omissions) done directly and intentionally (not indirectly and by accident) to particular animals (not populations of animals).

The Act's definition of "take" does expand the word slightly (and not unusually), so as to make clear that it includes not just a completed taking, but the process of taking, and all of the acts that are customarily identified with or accompany that process ("to harass, harm, pursue, hunt, shoot, wound, kill, trap, capture, or collect"); and so as to include attempts. § 1532(19). The tempting fallacy—which the Court commits with abandon—is to assume that *once defined,* "take" loses any significance, and it is only the definition that matters. The Court treats the statute as though Congress had directly enacted the § 1532(19) definition as a self-executing prohibition, and had not enacted § 1538(a)(1)(B) at all. But § 1538(a)(1)(B) *is* there, and if the terms contained in the definitional section are susceptible of two readings, one of which comports with the standard meaning of "take" as used in application to wildlife, and one of which does not, an agency regulation that adopts the latter reading is necessarily unreasonable, for it reads the defined term "take"—the only operative term—out of the statute altogether.

* * * "Harm" is merely one of 10 prohibitory words in § 1532(19), and the other 9 fit the ordinary meaning of "take" perfectly. To "harass, pursue, hunt, shoot, wound, kill, trap, capture, or collect" are all affirmative acts (the provision itself describes them as "conduct," see § 1532(19)) which are directed immediately and intentionally against a particular animal—not acts or omissions that indirectly and accidentally cause injury to a population of animals. The Court points out that several of the words ("harass," "pursue," "wound," and "kill") "refer to actions or effects that do not require direct *applications of force.*" That is true enough, but force is not the point. Even "taking" activities in the narrowest sense, activities traditionally engaged in by hunters and trappers, do not all consist of direct applications of force; pursuit and harassment are part of the business of "taking" the prey even before it has been touched. What the nine other words in § 1532(19) have in common—and share with the narrower meaning of "harm" described above, but not with the Secretary's ruthless dilation of the word—is the sense of affirmative conduct intentionally directed against a particular animal or animals.

* * * I would call it *noscitur a sociis,* but the principle is much the same: The fact that "several items in a list share an attribute counsels in favor of interpreting the other items as possessing that attribute as well," *Beecham v. United States*, 511 U.S. 368, 371 (1994). In any event, the Court's contention that "harm" in the narrow sense adds nothing to the

other words underestimates the ingenuity of our own species in a way that Congress did not. To feed an animal poison, to spray it with mace, to chop down the very tree in which it is nesting, or even to destroy its entire habitat in order to take it (as by draining a pond to get at a turtle), might neither wound nor kill, but would directly and intentionally harm. * * *

NOTES

1. **Tracking Section 9's Operative Language and Regulatory Interpretations.** What does ESA § 9 actually prohibit? How does the Secretary of the Interior define "harm" for purposes of the "take" prohibition? What part of this definition is controversial? Why?

2. **As-Applied v. Facial Challenges to Regulations.** What kind of challenge do the plaintiffs bring again the Secretary of the Interior's regulatory definition of harm—an "as applied" challenge or a "facial" challenge? What is the difference between these two kinds of challenges? Does the type of challenge make a difference to the outcome of the case? Why or why not?

3. ***TVA v. Hill* as Precedent.** How does the majority use *TVA v. Hill* in making its decision? Is its decision consistent with *TVA v. Hill*, in your opinion? Why or why not?

4. **Interpreting "Take."** What tools of statutory contraction does the majority rely upon in upholding the Secretary's definition of "harm"? How does the majority view the word "take," especially in contrast to Justice Scalia's view of the word "take" in dissent? Is Justice Scalia trying to limit "take" to its historical meaning? Why or why not? Is the majority's decision consistent with the historical meaning of "take"? Why or why not? What canon of statutory construction do the majority and Justice Scalia discuss? How does each opinion view and apply that canon?

5. **Justice O'Connor v. Justice Scalia Regarding the ESA and Private Property.** Both Justice O'Connor, in her concurring opinion, and Justice Scalia, in his dissenting opinion, are concerned about limiting the scope of the Secretary of the Interior's harm regulation. Why would both Justices be concerned about habitat modification constituting a "take" of endangered and threatened species? Most explicitly, who is Justice Scalia trying to protect? Which policies and values are implicitly at odds in *both* of these Justices' opinions? How does Justice O'Connor resolve that tension? Upon what common-law principle does she rely? How would Justice Scalia resolve that tension? Why? Which is the better approach, in your opinion?

6. **Private Property and the ESA's Perverse Incentives.** According to Professor Daniel H. Cole, "[i]n the United States, nearly 90 percent of endangered species have some or all of their critical habitat on private lands; more than half have at least 81 percent of their critical habitat on non-federal land; and between one-third and one-half are found *exclusively* on private property." DANIEL H. COLE, POLLUTION AND PROPERTY 150 (Cambridge University Press 2002) (citing U.S. GOVERNMENT ACCOUNTING OFFICE, ENDANGERED SPECIES ACT: INFORMATION ON SPECIES PROTECTION ON NONFEDERAL LANDS, GAO/RCED–95–16 (1993)); Daniel S. Wilkove, et al., *Rebuilding the Ark: Toward a More Effective Endangered Species Act for Private Land* (Environmental Defense

Fund 1996), *available at* http://www.environmentaldefense.org/documents/483_Rebuilding_the_Ark.htm. Moreover, an Environmental Defense Fund study indicates that endangered species recover less well when their habitat is privately owned than when their habitat is publicly owned. *Id.*

What are the implications of the Secretary of the Interior's regulatory definition of "harm" and the U.S. Supreme Court's *Sweet Home* decision for private landowners whose property may be habitat for endangered and threatened species? Recall the USFWS's concern in critical habitat designations that species listings and critical habitat designations under the ESA can provoke deliberate vandalism. Does the habitat modification rule create any similar perverse incentives that might actually interfere with the ESA's goals of species recovery? If so, does the creation of those perverse incentives mean that the regulation actually undermines the ESA's purposes?

7. **Harm to Listed Species, Breeding, and *Palila*.** As the majority notes in its opinion, the D.C. Circuit's decision in *Sweet Home*, overturning the Secretary of the Interior's "harm" regulation, created a circuit split with the Ninth Circuit, which had upheld that regulation in *Palila v. Hawaii Department of Land & Natural Resources*, 852 F.2d 1106 (9th Cir. 1988). The Palila is "a six-inch long finch-billed bird * * * found only on the slopes of Mauna Kea on the island of Hawaii." *Id.* at 1107. The USFWS listed the bird as an endangered species. "The Palila is totally dependent on the mamane-naio woodlands. Its preferred food is the pods of the mamane tree, but the bird will also eat mamane flowers, buds, and leaves, and the berries of the naio tree. The Palila also relies on the mamane for shelter and nesting sites." *Id.* at 1107 n.2.

Figure 3-10: The Palila
U.S. Geologial Survey photo.

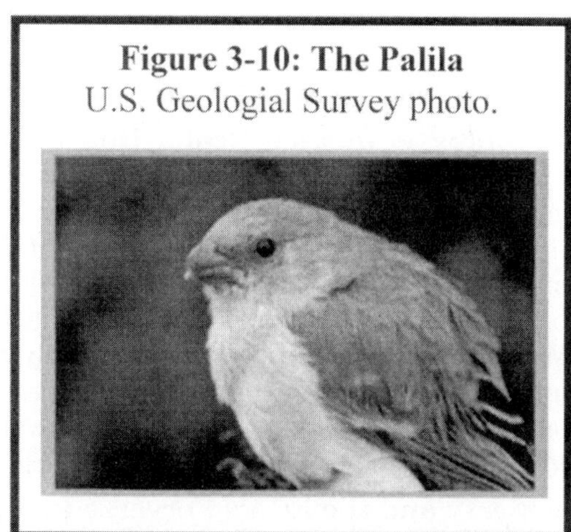

The Palila was the subject of a long series of ESA litigation battles against the Hawaii Department of Land and Natural Resources (DLNR). Because the DLNR is a *state* agency, section 7 was not available to the plaintiffs, so they relied on section 9 of the ESA. Originally, in 1978, the Sierra Club and others sued the DLNR "claiming that the Department's practice of maintaining feral goats and sheep (animals that originally were domesticated but were allowed to run wild) in the Palila's critical habitat constituted an unlawful 'taking' under the Act." *Id.* at 1107. In 1984, the Sierra Club amended its complaint to add claims that the DLNR had effected a "taking" of the Palila as a result of the mouflon sheep that it had introduced in 1962 and 1966 as game for sport hunters, because the mouflon sheep fed on the mamane trees in the Palila's critical habitat.

The Ninth Circuit in 1988 upheld the district court in holding "that habitat destruction that could drive the Palila to extinction constitutes 'harm.'" *Id.* at 1108. This interpretation "serves the overall purpose of the Act, which is 'to provide a means whereby the ecosystems upon which endangered species and threatened species depend may be conserved,'" because "it conserves the Palila's threatened ecosystem (the mamane-naio woodland)." *Id.* (quoting 16 U.S.C. § 1531(b)). Because evidence showed that the Palila's population had remained static over the long term despite the DLNR's many efforts to recover it, and because it takes 25 years before mamane trees grow to the point of providing food and shelter for the Palila but mouflon sheep can eat the trees to death for the first 10–15 years they grow, the Ninth Circuit determined that a taking had occurred. *Id.* at 1109.

If the Ninth Circuit were deciding the *Palila* case *after* the Supreme Court's decision in *Sweet Home*, could it have still found that a taking of the Palila had occurred in violation of section 9? Why or why not? What does Justice O'Connor indicate about the status of the *Palila* decision in her opinion? What specific issues does *Palila* raise that trouble her? Would the other five members of the majority agree? Why or why not?

* * *

b. Causation and Section 9

One of the issues that Justice O'Connor and Justice Scalia debate in *Sweet Home* is the issue of ***causation*** in ESA taking liability. The Justices debated this issue in the context of habitat modification and destruction, arguing about when habitat destruction was a sufficiently direct cause of harm to a species to incur ESA liability. As was true for CERCLA, moreover, the Justices in *Sweet Home*—especially Justice O'Connor—borrowed common-law conceptions of causation, notably foreseeability and proximate cause, to inform their interpretation of the ESA.

Nevertheless, the section 9 "take" prohibition does not specify the causation standard to be applied, and the *Sweet Home* Court did not decide the causation issue. Section 9 does specify that "[i]t is unlawful for any person subject to the jurisdiction of the United States to attempt to commit, solicit another to commit, or cause to be committed, any offense defined in this section." ESA § 9(g), 16 U.S.C. § 1538(g). Does this provision shed any light on ESA causation? Why or why not?

Consider that question as you read the next case, where, shortly after the *Sweet Home* decision, the First Circuit squarely faced the issue of causation in ESA takings.

STRAHAN v. COXE

127 F.3d 155 (1st Cir. 1997).

TORRUELLA, CHIEF JUDGE.

In April 1995, Richard Strahan ("Strahan") filed suit against Trudy Coxe, Secretary of the Massachusetts Executive Office of Environmental Affairs, John Phillips, Commissioner of the Massachusetts Department of Fisheries, Wildlife, and Environmental Law Enforcement, and Philip Coates, Director of the Massachusetts Division of Marine Fisheries (together "defendants"), claiming that these Massachusetts state officers were violating the federal Endangered Species Act ("ESA"), 16 U.S.C. § 1531 *et seq.* * * *. Strahan sought a preliminary injunction ordering the Commonwealth to revoke licenses and permits it had issued authorizing gillnet and lobster pot fishing and barring the Commonwealth from issuing such licenses and permits in the future unless it received "incidental take" * * * permits from the National Marine Fisheries Service ("NMFS") under the ESA * * *. Defendants moved to dismiss Strahan's complaint and, in the alternative, for summary judgment.

On September 24, 1996, the district court: (1) denied defendants' motion for summary judgment on Strahan's ESA claims; * * * and (3) granted summary judgment on Strahan's ESA claims in Count IV of Strahan's amended complaint. * * *

BACKGROUND

I. *Status of the Northern Right whale*

Strahan is an officer of GreenWorld, Inc., an organization dedicated to the preservation and recovery of endangered species. Strahan brought suit on behalf of the Northern Right whale, listed as an endangered species by the federal government. *See* 50 C.F.R. § 222.23(a). Northern Right whales are the most endangered of the large whales, presently numbering around 300, 62 Fed. Reg. 39157, 39158 (1997). Entanglement with commercial fishing gear has been recognized as a major source of human-caused injury or death to the Northern Right whale. Collision with ships is also a significant cause of Northern Right whale death.

The majority of Northern Right whales are present in Massachusetts waters only during spring feeding. The district court found, based on statements made by defendants as well as on affidavits from three scientists, that Northern Right whales have been entangled in fixed fishing gear in Massachusetts coastal waters at least nine times. Moreover, a Northern Right whale mortality was reported off Cape Cod, Massachusetts in May 1996. 61 Fed. Reg. 41116, 41117 (Aug. 7, 1996).

The NMFS issued a final interim rule proposing to close off entirely the critical habitat of the Northern Right whale and to modify fishing practices to enhance the viability of the Northern Right whale. The report accompanying the proposed rule recognized that entanglement with fishing gear is one of the leading causes of the depletion of the Northern Right whale population and indicated that more than half of the Northern Right whale population bear scars indicating unobserved and unrecorded earlier entanglement. The report calls for a ban on gillnet fishing and lobster pot fishing, the two manners of fishing at issue in this case, during the Northern Right whales' high season in the Cape Cod Bay Critical Habitat from January 1 to May 15 of each year, and in the Great South Channel from April 1 to June 30, until modified fishing equipment is developed that will diminish the risk of injury and death to the Northern Right whale.

Figure 3-11: Right Whale Entangled in Fishing Gear
NOAA photo.

II. Massachusetts' regulatory authority scheme

The Massachusetts Division of Marine Fisheries ("DMF") is vested with broad authority to regulate fishing in Massachusetts's coastal waters, Mass. Gen. L. c. 130, which extend three nautical miles from the shoreline. Nearly all commercial fishing vessels must receive a permit from DMF in order to take fish, including shellfish, from Massachusetts coastal waters. DMF is a division of the Department of Fisheries, Wildlife and Environmental Law Enforcement, which is part of the Executive Office of Environmental Affairs. The Division of Fisheries and Wildlife, a subcomponent of the Department of Fisheries, Wildlife and Environmental Law Enforcement, "has authority over all endangered species of Massachusetts including marine mammals."

The DMF has limited the use of gillnets and lobster pot fishing gear in certain areas. * * * In addition, the DMF has established a 500-yard "buffer zone" around Northern Right whales in Massachusetts coastal waters. 322 C.M.R. § 12.00–12.05 (1993). Defendant Coates admitted that he had "issued a limited number of scientific research permits to some whale watch vessels exempting them from the 500 yard buffer zone surrounding right whales for scientific research purposes upon application."

STANDARD OF REVIEW

In ruling on a motion for preliminary injunction, a district court is charged with considering:

> (1) the likelihood of success on the merits; (2) the potential for irreparable harm if the injunction is denied; (3) the balance of relevant impositions, *i.e.*, the hardship to the nonmovant if enjoined as contrasted with the hardship to the movant if no injunction issues; and (4) the effect (if any) of the court's ruling on the public interest.

Ross-Simons of Warwick, Inc. v. Baccarat, Inc., 102 F.3d 12, 15 (1st Cir. 1996). Under the ESA, however, the balancing and public interest prongs have been answered by Congress' determination that the "balance of hardships and the public interest tips heavily in favor of protected species." *National Wildlife Fed'n v. Burlington Northern R.R.*, 23 F.3d 1508, 1510 (9th Cir. 1994). Our review of the district court's ruling on a motion for preliminary injunction is deferential and, "unless the appellant can show that the lower court misapprehended the law or committed a palpable abuse of discretion, the court of appeals will not intervene." *Ross-Simons of Warwick, Inc.*, 102 F.3d at 16.

DISCUSSION

* * * *II. Endangered Species Act*

A. Statutory and regulatory background

The Endangered Species Act was enacted with the purpose of conserving endangered and threatened species and the ecosystems on which they depend. *See* 16 U.S.C. § 1531. The ESA is "the most comprehensive legislation for the preservation of endangered species ever enacted by any nation." *TVA v. Hill,* 437 U.S. 153, 180 (1978). The Act empowers the Secretary of Commerce to recommend to the Secretary of the Interior that a species be listed as endangered or threatened and that the species' habitat be listed as a critical habitat. *See* § 1533(a)(2)(A). The Secretary of the Interior, if he concurs, shall implement the designation. *See* § 1533(a)(3)(A). The Act further requires the Secretary to develop and implement plans for the conservation and survival of an endangered or threatened species. *See* § 1533(f). The Northern Right whale has been listed as endangered pursuant to the ESA. *See* 50 C.F.R. § 222.23(a).

As it relates to this litigation, the ESA prohibits any person from "tak[ing] any [endangered] species within the United States or the territorial sea of the United States." § 1538(a)(1)(B). In addition, the ESA makes it unlawful for any person "to attempt to commit, solicit another to commit, or cause to be committed, any offense defined" in the ESA. *See* § 1538(g). The term " 'take' means to harass, harm, pursue, hunt, shoot, wound, kill, trap, capture, or collect, or to attempt to engage in any such conduct." § 1532(19). " 'Take' is defined ... in the broadest possible manner to include every conceivable way in which a person can 'take' or attempt to 'take' any fish or wildlife." S. REP. NO. 93–307, at 7 (1973); *see also Babbitt v. Sweet Home Chapter of Communities for a Great Oregon,*

515 U.S. 687, 703–04 (1995) (citing Senate and House Reports indicating that "take" is to be defined broadly). The Secretary of the Interior has defined "harm" as "an act which actually kills or injures wildlife. Such act may include significant habitat modification or degradation where it actually kills or injures wildlife by significantly impairing essential behavioral patterns, including breeding, feeding, or sheltering." *See* 50 C.F.R. § 17.3 (1994); *Sweet Home*, at 695–701 (upholding the regulation as a reasonable interpretation of the statutory language). The term "person" includes "any officer, employee, agent, department, or instrumentality ... of any State, municipality, or political subdivision of a State ... [or] any State, municipality, or political subdivision of a State...." 16 U.S.C. § 1532(13).

Under the ESA regulatory scheme, the National Marine Fisheries Service ("NMFS"), part of the National Oceanic and Atmospheric Administration ("NOAA") within the Department of Commerce, is responsible for species of the order *Cetacea* (whales and dolphins) under the ESA * * * * * *

On August 31, 1995, the NMFS implemented a prohibition on any taking of a Northern Right whale incidental to commercial fishing operations. In addition, the NMFS recently implemented a ban on approaches within 500 yards of a Northern Right whale. This restriction brings the federal approach distance in line with the Massachusetts 500 yard approach prohibition. *See* 322 Code. Mass. Reg. § 12.05.

* * * *B. Legal challenges*

The district court's reasoning, in finding that Massachusetts' commercial fishing regulatory scheme likely exacted a taking in violation of the ESA, was founded on two provisions of the ESA read in conjunction. The first relates to the definition of the prohibited activity of a "taking," *see* § 1538(a)(1)(B), and the second relates to the solicitation or causation by a third party of a prohibited activity, such as a taking, *see* § 1538(g). The district court viewed these provisions, when read together, to apply to acts by third parties that allow or authorize acts that exact a taking and that, but for the permitting process, could not take place. Indeed, the district court cited several opinions that have also so held. The statute not only prohibits the acts of those parties that directly exact the taking, but also bans those acts of a third party that bring about the acts exacting a taking. We believe that, contrary to the defendants' argument on appeal, the district court properly found that a governmental third party pursuant to whose authority an actor directly exacts a taking of an endangered species may be deemed to have violated the provisions of the ESA.

The defendants argue that the statute was not intended to prohibit state licensure activity because such activity cannot be a "proximate cause" of the taking. The defendants direct our attention to long-standing principles of common law tort in arguing that the district court improperly found that its regulatory scheme "indirectly causes" these takings. Specifically, the defendants contend that to construe the proper meaning of "cause" under the ESA, this court should look to common law principles of causation and further contend that proximate cause is lacking here. The defendants are correct that when interpreting a term in a statute which is, like "cause" here, well-known to the common law, the court is to presume that Congress intended the meaning to be interpreted as in the common law. We do not believe, however, that an interpretation of "cause" that includes the "indirect causation" of a taking by the Commonwealth through its licensing scheme falls without the normal boundaries.

The defendants protest this interpretation. Their first argument is that the Commonwealth's licensure of a generally permitted activity does not cause the taking any more than its licensure of automobiles and drivers solicits or causes federal crimes, even though automobiles it licenses are surely used to violate federal drug laws, rob federally insured banks, or cross state lines for the purpose of violating state and federal laws. The answer to this argument is that, whereas it is possible for a person licensed by Massachusetts to use a car in a manner that does not risk the violations of federal law suggested by the defendants, it is not possible for a licensed commercial fishing operation to use its gillnets or lobster pots in the manner permitted by the Commonwealth without risk of violating the ESA by exacting a taking. Thus, the state's licensure of gillnet and lobster pot fishing does not involve the intervening independent actor that is a necessary component of the other licensure schemes which it argues are comparable. Where the state has licensed an automobile driver to use that automobile and her license in a manner consistent with both state and federal law, the violation of federal law is caused only by the actor's conscious and independent decision to disregard or go beyond the licensed purposes of her automobile use and instead to violate federal, and possibly state, law. The situation is simply not the same here. In this instance, the state has licensed commercial fishing operations to use gillnets and lobster pots in specifically the manner that is likely to result in a violation of federal law. The causation here, while indirect, is not so removed that it extends outside the realm of causation as it is understood in the common law.

* * * C. *Factual challenges*

We review the district court's findings of fact for clear error. The district court found that entanglement with fishing gear in Massachusetts waters caused injury or death to Northern Right whales. Indeed, the district court cited several of the Commonwealth's documents in support of this finding, including its statement that " '[f]ive right whales have been found entangled in fixed fishing gear in Massachusetts waters; three in gillnets and two in lobster lines.' " The court further cited to affidavits of three scientists that suggested that entanglement of Northern Right whales had harmed, injured, or killed those whales. The court cited eleven occasions on which Northern Right whales had been found entangled in fishing gear in Massachusetts waters between 1978 and 1995. The court also indicated that at least fifty-seven percent of all Northern right whales have scars indicating prior entanglement with fishing gear and noted that, even where the whale survives, the entanglement still wounds the whale. Although these findings indicate only that entanglements have occurred in Massachusetts waters, the district court determined that three whales had been found entangled in gear deployed in Massachusetts waters.

The defendants contend that the factual evidence before the district court did not support a finding that the Commonwealth has perpetrated a taking. The defendants' main contention is that the "District Court made its 'taking' determination ... based on speculation that Northern Right whales have become entangled in fishing gear: (1) deployed in Massachusetts coastal waters; and (2) licensed by the Commonwealth." The defendants first state that they submitted affidavit evidence indicating that no deaths of Northern Right whales had occurred in Massachusetts coastal waters. While this may be true, it answers only half the taking question, which bars not only killings of, but also injuries to, Northern Right whales. Because the district court need not have made a determination as to whale deaths in determining whether the Commonwealth exacted a taking, we find no error.

The defendants acknowledge that the district court relied on a scientist's affidavit that was supplied by amicus curiae Conservation Law Foundation. The defendants do not challenge the factual statements asserted in the affidavit, including the one relied upon by the district court that "[t]hree of the entanglements of endangered whales ... clearly involved fishing gear that was deployed in Massachusetts waters." Despite the defendants' protests that the district court was engaging in speculation when it found that whales have become entangled in fishing gear deployed in Commonwealth's waters, in fact the district court relied on the unchallenged factual assertion in the scientific affidavit. Thus, the defendants' first challenge to the district court's fact-finding speculation is not valid.

With respect to the district court's determination that these entanglements involved gear licensed by the Commonwealth, the district court relied on the affidavit regarding the three entanglements that occurred in Massachusetts waters. The affidavit explained that the whales were found entangled in gear "fixed" in Massachusetts waters such that the whale could not escape because it could not break free of the gear. The district court's inference that gear fixed in Massachusetts waters was licensed by the Commonwealth, and was not set illegally or brought into Massachusetts waters from another area by the whale, was reasonable and we find no clear error in that inference.

The defendants next contend that the district court ignored evidence of the significant efforts made by the Commonwealth to "minimize Northern Right Whale entanglements in fishing gear," and evidence of other causes of takings of Northern Right whales. With respect to the determination of whether a taking has occurred, the district court quite rightly disregarded such evidence. Given that there was evidence that any entanglement with fishing gear injures a Northern Right whale and given that a single injury to one whale is a taking under the ESA, efforts to minimize such entanglements are irrelevant. For the same reasons, the existence of other means by which takings of Northern Right whales occur is irrelevant to the determination of whether the Commonwealth has engaged in a taking.

Finding neither any error of law nor any clear error with respect to the factual findings, we believe that the district court properly applied the ESA to the facts presented and was correct in enjoining the Commonwealth so as to prevent the taking of Northern Right whales in violation of the ESA. * * *

NOTES

1. **Tracking This Case Through Section 9.** What is the species at issue in this case? Has it been listed for protection under the ESA? How do you know? Who does Strahan argue has violated the Section 9 "take" prohibition? What did that entity do? Why is causation at issue in this case? Do other defendants exist that could be liable for the Section 9 "takings" alleged in this case? If so, who are they?

2. **The First Circuit's Use of Supreme Court Precedent.** How does the First Circuit use *TVA v. Hill* to support its decision in this case? Is its decision consistent with *TVA v. Hill*'s view of the ESA? Why or why not?

How does the First Circuit use the *Sweet Home* decision? Does the use of fishing gear qualify as "habitat modification" under the Secretary of the Interior's harm regulation? Does it have to, for the First Circuit to decide this case? Is the First Circuit's decision in *Strahan* consistent with the majority's opinion in *Sweet Home*? Why or why not? Is the First Circuit's decision consistent with Justice O'Connor's concurring opinion? Why or why not? How would Justice Scalia have viewed this decision? Was the harm that occurred here consistent with his view of "take" in *Sweet Home*?

3. **Legal Causation in *Strahan v. Coxe*.** What legal standard of causation does the First Circuit adopt for ESA taking causation? Why? Why is that legal standard met in this case? How does Massachusetts' licensing of fishing gear differ from its licensing of automobiles regarding legal causation, according to the First Circuit? Do you agree?

4. **Factual Causation in *Strahan v. Coxe*.** What factual challenges does the defendant raise regarding the causation issue? How does the First Circuit decide those issues? Why? What evidence showed factual causation of ESA "takings" in this case?

5. **Implications of Third–Party Section 9 Liability.** Think back to *National Association of Home Builders v. Defenders of Wildlife*, presented *supra* in connection with the discussion of Section 7(a)(2). What are the implications of *Strahan v. Coxe* for Arizona's assumption of the Clean Water Act permitting program? Will Arizona have to worry about ESA-listed species when it issues NPDES permits? Why or why not?

* * *

G. SECTION 10 EXEMPTIONS FROM THE SECTION 9 "TAKE" PROHIBITION

As was discussed in connection with section 7, the USFWS and NMFS/NOAA Fisheries can relieve *federal agencies* from the "take" prohibition through a section 7 "incidental take statement." Private parties, in contrast, can apply for any one of a number of "take" permits under section 10, 16 U.S.C. § 1539. The USFWS and NMFS/NOAA Fisheries can issue permits to allow a person to "take" an endangered or threatened species: (1) "for scientific purposes or to enhance the propagation or survival of the affected species," ESA § 10(a)(1)(A), 16 U.S.C. § 1539(a)(1)(A); (2) for hardships arising from contract obligations entered before a relevant species was listed, ESA § 10(b), 16 U.S.C. § 1539(b); (3) for subsistence takings of certain species by Alaska natives, ESA § 10(e), 16 U.S.C. § 1539(e); (4) for trade in sperm whale oil and scrimshaw products created before the ESA took effect, ESA § 10(f), 16 U.S.C. § 1539(f); (5) for trade in antique objects at least 100 years old, ESA § 10(h), 16 U.S.C. § 1539(h); and (6) for experimental populations released outside the current range of the species in order to conserve the species. ESA § 10(j), 16 U.S.C. § 1539(j).

However, the most common—and the most procedurally complex—section 10 permits are permits for the incidental taking of endangered or threatened species, discussed in both *Sweet Home* and *Strahan v. Coxe*. 16 U.S.C. § 1539(a)(1)(B). In order to receive a section 10 ***incidental take permit*** **(ITP)**, the applicant must submit a ***habitat conservation plan*** **(HCP)** to the USFWS or NMFS/NOAA Fisheries "that specifies—"

> (i) the impact which will likely result from the taking;
>
> (ii) what steps the applicant will take to minimize and mitigate such impacts, and the funding that will be available to implement such steps;
>
> (iii) what alternative actions to such taking the applicant considered and the reasons why such alternatives are not being utilized; and
>
> (iv) such other measures that [the USFWS or NMFS/NOAA Fisheries] may require as being necessary or appropriate for purposes of the plan.

ESA § 10(a)(2)(A), 16 U.S.C. § 1539(a)(2)(A). The HCP is then subject to public comment, and the USFWS or NMFS/NOAA Fisheries can issue the incidental take permit only if it finds that:

(i) the taking will be incidental;

(ii) the applicant will, to the maximum extent practicable, minimize and mitigate the impacts of such taking;

(iii) the applicant will ensure that adequate funding for the plan will be provided;

(iv) the taking will not appreciably reduce the likelihood of the survival and recovery of the species in the wild; and

(v) the measures, if any, required under subparagraph (A)(iv) will be met * * *.

ESA § 10(a)(2)(B), 16 U.S.C. § 1539(a)(2)(B). Moreover, the agencies retain the authority to revoke the permit if the permittee is not complying with its terms and conditions. ESA § 10(a)(2)(C), 16 U.S.C. § 1539(a)(2)(C).

1. Issuing the ITP

SIERRA CLUB v. BABBITT

15 F. Supp. 2d 1274 (S.D. Ala. 1998).

BUTLER, CHIEF JUDGE.

This action commenced in April of 1997 in the United States District Court of the District of Columbia when the original plaintiff's [*sic*] filed this action seeking declaratory injunctive relief regarding two incidental take permits ("ITP's") issued by the Fish & Wildlife Service ("FWS") for the construction of two separate high density housing complexes in habitat of the endangered Alabama Beach Mouse ("ABM"), alleging that the FWS violated numerous provisions of the Endangered Species Act ("ESA") * * *. The case was transferred to this Court on June 26th, 1997 pursuant to 28 U.S.C. § 1404(a), and on August 6th of 1997, the parties stipulated that the plaintiff's motion for preliminary injunction would be treated as a motion for summary judgment and that the defendants would file their opposition thereto and cross motion for summary judgment. They have done this, and the Court heard oral argument on these motions on May 21, 1998, and the case is now ripe for ruling.

* * * Because this case involves a challenge to the final administrative action of the FWS in issuing the two ITPs in question, the appropriate standard of review is whether actions of the FWS were "arbitrary, capricious, an abuse of discretion, or otherwise not in accordance with the law," as set forth in 5 U.S.C. § 706(2)(A). Thus, this Court's review is limited to the two voluminous sets of Administrative Records. In reviewing the agency's action, the Court considers whether the agency acted within the scope of its legal authority, whether it has explained its decision, whether the facts on which it purports to rely have some basis in the record, and whether the agency considered the relevant factors.

* * * "It is rudimentary administrative law that discretion as to the substance of the ultimate decision does not confer discretion to ignore the required procedures of decision making." *Bennett,* 520 U.S. 154; *see SEC v. Chenery Corp.,* 318 U.S. 80, 94–95 (1943). When an administrative agency fails to provide an adequate basis in the Administrative Record for its action, such action is arbitrary and capricious. * * *

This Court has spent a considerable amount of time carefully reviewing the Administrative Record in order to ascertain whether the agency supplied a sufficient basis for the Court to determine whether the ICPs and HCPs "minimize and mitigate" the projects' harm to the ABM "to the maximum extent practicable" as required by ESA § 10(a)(2)(B)(ii). In making this determination the Court must first look to the substantive law (ESA § 10(a)(2)(B)(ii)) to ascertain what is required of the agency, and then to the Administrative Record to determine whether the agency has complied with the law.

Against the ESA statutory framework and the FWS's regulations regarding Endangered Wildlife (50 C.F.R., § 17.21, et. seq.) it is unlawful to "take" an endangered species without first obtaining, from the FWS, an ITP pursuant to ESA § 10(a)(1)(B). The ITP must include, among other things, "a conservation plan", and the steps the applicant will take to minimize and mitigate the impact to the species or its habitat. (50 C.F.R. § 17.22(b)(1)). The director of the FWS considers certain criteria and "shall issue" the permit if he finds that: "(i) the taking will be incidental; (ii) the applicant will, to the maximum extent practicable, minimize and mitigate the impact of such taking; (iii) the applicant will insure that adequate funding for the conservation plan . . . will be provided; (iv) the taking will not appreciably reduce the likelihood of the survival . . . of the species. . . ." (50 C.F.R. 17.22(b)(2)). It is criteria (ii) around which this dispute largely focuses: whether "to the maximum extent practicable" the developers' HCPs adequately minimize and mitigate the impacts likely to result from the proposed takings. Once an application for an ITP is submitted, the FWS must conduct a biological assessment (BA) in accordance with ESA § 7(b)(3)(4) (50 C.F.R. 402.14(h)-(i)) which must include a discussion of the effects of the action on the ABM and the FWS's opinion of whether the action is likely to jeopardize the continued existence of the ABM or result in the destruction or adverse modification of critical habitat. FWS has developed a handbook which guides them through the statutory and regulatory maze involved in the permit process and requires early coordination between the regional office and the applicable field office.

Figure 3-12: Alabama Beach Mouse
U.S. Fish & Wildlife Service photo.

The ABM was listed as endangered in 1985, and at that time the FWS concluded that the species' habitat was being drastically destroyed "by residential and commercial development, recreational activity, and tropical storms". 50 Fed. Reg. 23872 (June 6, 1985). The FWS determined that on the portion of the Alabama coast known as the Fort Morgan Peninsula, there was in 1985 a total baseline habitat of approximately 671 acres of which approximately 402 are known as fore dunes, 269 scrub dunes. Between 1985, when the ABM was listed, and January 1996, when the FWS issued an ITP for construction of the first of the two developments at issue in this case—the 52 acre Aronov project—another 8.5% of dwindling ABM habitat was lost due to additional commercial development and damage from Hurricane Opal. Indeed, during that time, the FWS issued four other ITPs allowing further habitat loss in the area * * *. According to the FWS, the four ITPs issued prior to Aronov resulted in the destruction of a total of 41.3 acres of ABM habitat. The remaining ABM habitat has also been reduced by a series of hurricanes, and in January 1996 the FWS concluded that the "designated critical habitat may be an inadequate area for ABM recovery and delisting". In the final biological opinion, the FWS noted that the net direct effect of the Fort Morgan project will be the permanent destruction of 37 acres of currently occupied ABM habitat, of which 25 are scrub dunes habitat and an undetermined number of ABM will be incidentally taken during destruction. The FWS also determined that as to the Aronov Project the net direct effect will be the permanent destruction of 7.5 acres currently occupied by ABM, 6.5 of which is scrub dune habitat, and an undetermined number of ABM incidentally taken during construction. * * *

The primary bone of contention in this lawsuit evolves around the proposals in the HCPs incorporated into the Aronov Realty Management,

Inc. ITP at paragraph H(5) that there be $60,000 collected from the developer for offsite, mitigation "to acquire property of quantity and quality sufficient to compensate for and minimize unavoidable impacts of the project area", and incorporated in the Fort Morgan ITP at paragraph G(5) that there be $150,000 collected from the developer for offsite mitigation. The plaintiffs first contend that the level of off site mitigation funding is inadequate, and cannot be supported by any rational basis in the Administrative Record. In addition, the plaintiffs challenge the inconsistent application of the FWS's off site mitigation policies. Finally, the Plaintiffs contend that the FWS's reliance on speculative unnamed sources to contribute additional funds in order to make up for the inadequacy of the amounts of off site mitigation funding the FWS required the developers to pay is arbitrary and capricious, and otherwise not in accordance with the law.

First, the plaintiffs maintain that the level of mitigation funding for both projects is inadequate, and that the agency's determination of these amounts is arbitrary and capricious. The lack of any analysis in the Administrative Record concerning whether the amount or level of offsite mitigation funding is to the maximum extent practicable supports the plaintiff's contention. Moreover, the Jackson field office supervisor voiced much concern over the inadequacy of the level of funding for offsite mitigation required by the HCP for the Fort Morgan project: "Overall, our primary concern is the amount or level of mitigation provided". The field office based these concerns on consideration of the biological effects of the project and a comparison of such effects to the level of mitigation provided by other ITPs with high density real estate development. Based on these considerations the field office stated that, "we believe the amount of mitigation provided is low". Moreover, the field office noted that, "the biological effects of the Joint Venture project are the single most largest (sic) of any ABM HCP to date", and "the project provides the least mitigation for the effects of high density development of any previous ABM HCP or ITP". Furthermore, although the field office failed to voice similar concerns over the Aronov project's HCP and ITP, the record nevertheless shows that the FWS failed to support the level or amount of offsite mitigation funding with a clearly articulated analysis demonstrating whether the amount or level of funding is rationally based on the relevant facts. * * * Remarkably, the FWS simply ignored the clearly expressed concerns of the experts Congress intended the agency to rely upon in making such discretionary decisions. This is further illustrated by the complete lack of subsequent consideration or explanation of the amount of mitigation funding in the final BO, HCP, and ITP. As the Court finds that there is no sufficient basis in the Administrative Record to support the amount of offsite mitigation funding, the issuance of the ITPs was arbitrary and capricious.

In addition, the plaintiffs contend that the inconsistency in the amounts of offsite mitigation funding that the FWS has required for various high density developments on the Alabama coast[5] indicates that the FWS has failed to develop an appropriate standard for determining what levels of mitigation will mitigate the effects of these two projects to the maximum extent practicable. The FWS's Habitat Conservation Planning Handbook is intended to guide the agency through complex determinations such as the establishment of mitigation measures for HCP. The Handbook states that "[m]itigation measures required by individual FWS or NMFS offices should be as consistent as possible for the same species", and that consistency is "essential". The Handbook goes on further and states that consistency is to be accomplished by (1) establishing good communication between offices, and (2) establishing "specific standards". Moreover, "*[t]he Service should not apply inconsistent mitigation policies for the same species, unless differences are based on biological or other good reasons and are clearly explained*" (emphasis original). The Court can find no evidence that the FWS paid any attention to its own guidelines. * * * Although neither Congress nor the FWS Handbook requires the FWS to develop one specific formula for determining the level of mitigation required for all projects, the Administrative Record must contain some analysis of why the level or amount selected is appropriate for the particular project at issue, and the FWS should not apply inconsistent mitigation policies for the same species in the same geographic area, unless differences are based on biological or other good reasons and are clearly explained. The Court finds on the basis of the record for these two projects that the agency's inconsistent application of offsite mitigation measures for the same species in the same geographic area is arbitrary and capricious, as the record is devoid of any "biological or other good reasons to justify such findings".

Finally, the FWS's speculative reliance on other unnamed sources to contribute funds to make up for the inadequacy of the amounts of offsite mitigation funding required is simply contrary to the law and unsupported by any factually reliable basis in the Administrative Record. In the Biological Opinions the FWS states that the Applicant's offsite mitigation funding would have to be combined with additional funds from a non-profit organization in order to purchase a large tract or several tracts for mitigation purposes. The BO does not establish how much those funds would be, who they would come from, or whether it is likely they could be acquired. Nevertheless, the FWS issued the two ITPs at issue by relying on funding from an unknown source for an unknown amount, and accepts that this will "minimize and mitigate" the effects of the projects to the maximum extent practicable. Because the Administrative Record does not establish what level of funding has been offered by "other sources", the FWS cannot demonstrate any basis in the Administrative Record upon which the level or amount of offsite mitigation measures are "to the maximum extent practicable". Moreover, the law establishes that the FWS

5. The following identifies the projects since 1985 on the Alabama Coast for which an ITP was issued, the number of acres of ABM the project destroyed, and the amount of off site mitigation funding the FWS required: (Laguna Key/19/None), (Kiva Dunes/14 /None), (Phoenix/1.4 /$80 K), (Sage/7/$50 K), (Aronov/7.5/$60 K), (Fort Morgan/37/$150 K).

cannot comply with the strict ESA mandate that the HCP "minimize and mitigate" the effects of the projects to the "maximum extent practicable" simply by relying on speculative future actions by others.

Based upon all of the above considerations, the Court finds that the Administrative Record is devoid of any rational basis upon which the FWS could have reasonably relied in deciding to issue the ITPs for these two projects. Therefore, because the Court finds that the permits at issue fall short of both the ESA and APA standards, they must be remanded to the agency for review and re-issuance. * * *

NOTES

1. **Standard of Review for the USFWS's ITP Decisions.** What standard does the Southern District of Alabama use to review the USFWS's decision to issue the ITPs? Why is that standard appropriate? How does the district court define that standard of review? Where does it focus its attention in determining whether the USFWS's decision met that standard?

2. **The Intersection of Section 10 and Section 7.** Why does the USFWS have to comply with section 7 as well as section 10 in issuing an ITP? What section 7 procedures did the USFWS follow in this case? What did it conclude about its own potential liability under section 7? How does the section 7 standard for the USFWS relate to the section 10 requirements for an ITP? Why did the USFWS issue *both* the Biological Assessment (BA) and the Biological Opinion (BO)? How do these documents affect the court's review of the USFWS's decision on the ITPs?

3. **The Mitigation Issue.** Why, legally, did the USFWS have to ensure that the developers adequately mitigated their housing complexes' effects on the Alabama Beach Mouse? Where does the mitigation issue arise in the ITP process? What is the role of the USFWS's Handbook? What kind of agency document is the Handbook? How does it affect the court's review?

4. **The Sierra Club's Arguments.** What three arguments did the Sierra Club make about the ITPs that the USFWS issued in this case? How does the Southern District of Alabama resolve each of the issues that the Sierra Club raises? Why does the Sierra Club win its lawsuit?

5. **Multiplying ITPs.** Consider the number of ITPs that the USFWS had issued for this area of Alabama Beach Mouse habitat and the effect that those ITPs were having on the mouse's critical habitat. What criticism could be made of the ITP program? How did the ITPs issued in Alabama arguably interfere with the Alabama Beach Mouse's ability to cope with natural disasters?

6. **ESA Takings and Fifth Amendment Takings.** The facts of this case suggest that the USFWS will eventually have to stop issuing ITPs for this area of Alabama coast if the USFWS is going to fulfill its own section 7 responsibilities to ensure that the mouse's continued existence is not jeopardized. What will it mean for private landowners who want to develop their properties if ITPs are no longer available?

The Fifth Amendment to the U.S. Constitution provides that the federal government shall not take "private property * * * for public use, without just compensation." U.S. CONST., amend. V. Historically, such Fifth Amendment takings of private property involved the federal government's *physical* takeover and occupation of private property for public purposes—for example, to build a Post Office or other federal building. In such cases, the United States government almost always proceeds through formal ***condemnation proceedings***, which include an award of appropriate compensation to the private landowner.

However, in 1922 the U.S. Supreme Court recognized that *government regulation* could also effect a taking of private property in violation of the Fifth Amendment, for federal regulations, or the Fourteenth Amendment, for state regulations. *Pennsylvania Coal Co. v. Mahon*, 260 U.S. 393, 415 (1922); *see also Penn Central Transportation Co. v. New York City*, 438 U.S. 104, 124–37 (1978). However, no ***regulatory taking*** will occur unless the government regulation deprives the landowner of "*all* economically viable use" of that private property, *Lucas v. South Carolina Coastal Council*, 505 U.S. 1003, 1019 (1992), or unless a complex balancing of factors indicates that the government has intruded "too far" upon private rights. *Tahoe-Sierra Preservation Council, Inc. v. Tahoe Regional Planning Agency*, 535 U.S. 302, 321, 325 n.19 (2002).

Would the USFWS's inability to issue ITPs for development of the Alabama Beach Mouse's habitat constitute a "taking" of private property in violation of the Fifth Amendment? Why or why not? Should the landowner have to apply for an ITP before being able to bring a Fifth Amendment claim against the United States? Why or why not? *See generally Morris v. United States*, 58 Fed. Cl. 95 (2003); *Seiber v. United States*, 53 Fed. Cl. 570 (2002).

* * *

2. The Scope of an ITP

LOGGERHEAD TURTLE v. COUNTY COUNCIL OF VOLUSIA COUNTY, FLORIDA

148 F.3d 1231 (11th Cir. 1998).

HATCHETT, CHIEF JUDGE:

The loggerhead sea turtle (*Caretta caretta*) and green sea turtle (*Chelonia mydas*) with appellants Shirley Reynolds and Rita Alexander (collectively the Turtles) challenge the district court's dismissal of their case brought pursuant to the Endangered Species Act (ESA), 16 U.S.C. §§ 1531–1544 (1994). They present [] an issue of first impression, whether the incidental take permit exception to the ESA's "take" prohibition applies to an activity performed as a purely mitigatory measure upon which the issuing agency conditions the permit[.] * * *

I. BACKGROUND

In 1978, the United States Fish and Wildlife Service (Service) listed the loggerhead sea turtle as a threatened species and the green sea turtle as an endangered species. *See* 50 C.F.R. § 17.11(h) (1997). Adjoining the Atlantic Ocean for nearly forty miles in northeast Florida, Volusia County's beaches play host to both humans and sea turtles. * * * Female adult sea turtles come ashore in the spring, deposit eggs in the sand and return to the ocean. Months later, when sea turtle hatchlings break out of their shells at night, they instinctively crawl toward the brightest light on the horizon. On an undeveloped beach, the brightest light is the moon's reflection off the surf. On a developed beach, the brightest light can be an inland artificial source.

Figure 3-13: Green Sea Turtle
NOAA photo.

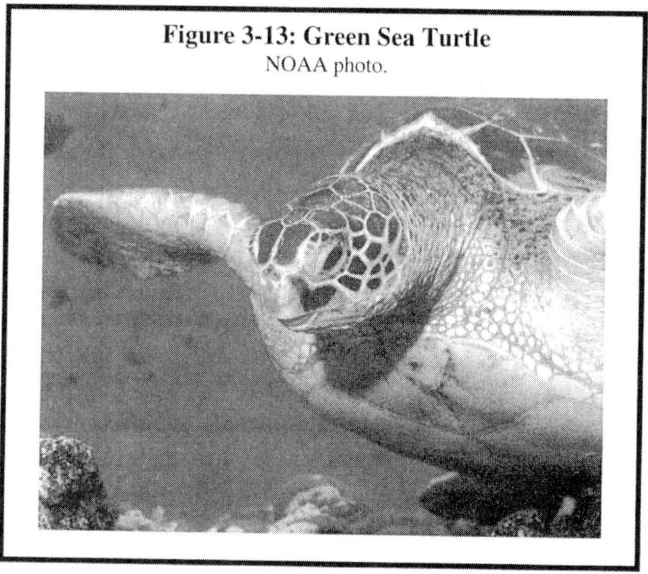

* * * On June 8, 1995, the Turtles instituted this lawsuit in the United States District Court for the Middle District of Florida under the citizen-suit provision of the ESA, 16 U.S.C. § 1540(g)(1)(A). Seeking declaratory, permanent injunctive and—in a separate, contemporaneously-filed motion—preliminary injunctive relief, the Turtles alleged that appellee County Council of Volusia County, Florida's (Volusia County) "refusal to ban beach driving during sea turtle nesting season and ban beachfront artificial light sources that adversely impact sea turtles" violates the ESA's "take" prohibition, 16 U.S.C. § 1538(a)(1)(B). The Turtles quoted excerpts from their federally-issued recovery plans that "[a]rtificial beachfront lighting from buildings, streetlights, dune crossovers, vehicles and other types of beachfront lighting have been documented in the disorientation (loss of bearings) and misorientation (incorrect orientation) of hatchling turtles" and that "nesting females avoided areas where beachfront lights were the most intense" or "abort[] nesting attempts at a greater frequency in lighted areas." (Quoting United States Fish & Wildlife Serv., Dep't of the Interior; Nat'l Marine Fisheries Serv., Dep't of Commerce, *Recovery Plan for U.S. Population of Loggerhead Turtle* (*Caretta caretta*) (1991), at 6–7; United States Fish & Wildlife Serv., Dep't of the Interior;

Nat'l Marine Fisheries Serv., Dep't of Commerce, *Recovery Plan for U.S. Population of Atlantic Green Turtle* (*Chelonia mydas*) (1991), at 4–5.) As exhibits, the Turtles advanced reports of fatal "disorientations" and "misorientations," as well as "false crawls" (aborted nesting attempts) that volunteer "Turtle Patrol" members had witnessed throughout Volusia County.

* * * [T]he Service issued the county an incidental take permit on November 21, 1996. The next day, Volusia County moved the district court to dissolve the preliminary injunction and dismiss the Turtles' case, contending that the permit mooted further proceedings. Although conceding that the permit authorized incidental takes through beach driving, the Turtles contended that it did not authorize incidental takes through artificial beachfront lighting. The district court agreed with Volusia County and closed the case. This appeal follows.

II. ISSUES

We address * * * whether the district court erred in concluding that Volusia County's incidental take permit excepted it from liability for taking protected sea turtles through artificial beachfront lighting * * *. Our standard of review for th[is] issue[] is *de novo*.

III. CONTENTIONS

[T]he Turtles contend that Volusia County's incidental take permit authorizes only incidental takes of sea turtles from beach driving, not from artificial beachfront lighting. The Turtles argue that to fall within the incidental take permit exception to the "take" prohibition, the Service's permission must be express and activity-specific. The Turtles also assert that the district court could not infer such permission from the Service's conditioning the permit on lighting-related mitigatory measures.

Volusia County responds that under the permit, it must survey every light source, study their impacts and implement methods to correct light sources that misorient sea turtles. Volusia County argues that given those extensive mitigatory requirements, the Service clearly contemplated that it be excepted from liability for any incidental takes that artificial beachfront lighting causes during the life of the permit.

* * * IV. DISCUSSION

Under the ESA, it is unlawful to "take" endangered or threatened wildlife unless a statutory exception applies. 16 U.S.C. § 1538(a)(1)(B) (1994) (the "take" prohibition); *see* 50 C.F.R. § 17.31(a) (1997) (the "take" prohibition applies to threatened as well as endangered wildlife). Defined broadly, "take" means "to harass, harm, pursue, hunt, shoot, wound, kill, trap, capture, or collect[.]" 16 U.S.C. § 1532(19); *see Babbitt v. Sweet Home Chapter of Communities for a Great Or.,* 515 U.S. 687 (1995) ("Congress intended 'take' to apply broadly to cover indirect as well as purposeful actions."). It is equally unlawful "to attempt to commit, solicit another to commit, or cause to be committed" a "take." 16 U.S.C. § 1538(g).

"Harass" and "harm," within the meaning of "take," are defined through regulation. The Secretary of the Interior, through the Service, has construed "harass" as "an intentional or negligent act or omission which creates the likelihood of injury to wildlife by annoying it to such an extent as to significantly disrupt normal behavioral patterns which include, but are not limited to, breeding, feeding or sheltering." 50 C.F.R. § 17.3; *see* 16 U.S.C. § 1533(d) (delegating regulatory authority to the "Secretary"); *Sweet Home*, 515 U.S. 687, 115 S.Ct. at 2410 & n. 2 (noting that the Secretary of the Interior, through the Director of the Service, promulgated 50 C.F.R. § 17.3).

The crux of the Turtles' artificial beachfront lighting allegations centered on "harm," "an act which actually kills or injures wildlife" that may include "significant habitat modification or degradation where it actually kills or injures wildlife by significantly impairing essential behavioral patterns, including breeding, feeding or sheltering." 50 C.F.R. § 17.3 (the "harm" regulation). At the preliminary injunction stage, the district court found "overwhelming[]" evidence that artificial beachfront lighting "harms" sea turtles on Volusia County's beaches. Similarly, at the summary judgment stage, the district court found a genuine factual dispute "as to whether the artificial beachfront lighting controlled by Volusia County is responsible for 'taking' sea turtles."

A.

The incidental take permit exception to the "take" prohibition and its regulatory constructions, including the "harm" regulation, can be found in 16 U.S.C. § 1539(a). As relevant to this case, the Service "may permit, under such terms and conditions as [it] shall prescribe ... any taking otherwise prohibited by section 1538(a)(1)(B) of [the ESA] if such taking is incidental to, and not the purpose of, the carrying out of an otherwise lawful activity." 16 U.S.C. § 1539(a)(1)(B). As a prerequisite to receiving an incidental take permit, the applicant must submit a habitat conservation plan that specifies: "(i) the impact which will likely result from such taking; (ii) what steps the applicant will take to minimize and mitigate such impacts, and the funding that will be available to implement such steps; (iii) what alternative actions to such taking the applicant considered and the reasons why such alternatives are not being utilized; and (iv) such other measures that the [issuing agency] may require as being necessary or appropriate for purposes of the plan." 16 U.S.C. § 1539(a)(2)(A). Service regulations further instruct the applicant to include a "complete description of the activity sought to be authorized" and "[t]he common and scientific names of the species sought to be covered by the permit, as well as the number, age, and sex of such species, if known[.]" 50 C.F.R. § 17.22(b)(1)(i)-(ii) (endangered wildlife); 50 C.F.R. § 17.32(b)(1)(iii)(A)-(B) (threatened wildlife).

Upon receiving a complete application package, the Service must publish notice in the Federal Register and provide the public an opportunity to comment on whether the Service should issue the permit. 16 U.S.C. § 1539(a)(2)(B); 50 C.F.R. § 17.22 ("The Director [of the Service] shall publish notice in the Federal Register of each application for [an incidental take permit]. Each notice shall invite the submission from interested parties, within 30 days after the date of the notice, of written data, views, or arguments with respect to the application."); 50 C.F.R. § 17.32(b)(1)(ii); *see, e.g.,* Notice of Receipt of an Application for an Incidental Take Permit, 61 Fed. Reg. 9716 (1996) (summarizing Volusia County's application). Upon expiration of the public comment period, the Service must issue the permit if it finds that:

> (i) the taking will be incidental;
>
> (ii) the applicant will, to the maximum extent practicable, minimize and mitigate the impacts of such taking;
>
> (iii) the applicant will ensure that adequate funding for the plan will be provided;
>
> (iv) the taking will not appreciably reduce the likelihood of the survival and recovery of the species in the wild; . . .
>
> (v) the measures, if any, required under [16 U.S.C. § 1539(a)(2)(A)(iv)] will be met; [and]
>
> [the Service] has received such other assurances as [it] may require that the [habitat conservation plan] will be implemented[.]

16 U.S.C. § 1539(a)(2)(B); 50 C.F.R. § 17.22(b)(2); 50 C.F.R. § 17.32(b)(2).

An incidental take permit "may authorize a single transaction, a series of transactions, or a number of activities over a specific period of time." 50 C.F.R. § 17.22; 50 C.F.R. § 17.32. Additionally,

> [t]he authorizations on the face of a permit which set forth specific times, dates, places, methods of taking, numbers and kinds of wildlife or plants, location of activity, authorize certain circumscribed transactions, or otherwise permit a specifically limited matter, are to be strictly construed and shall not be interpreted to permit similar or related matters outside the scope of strict construction.

50 C.F.R. § 13.42; *see also* 50 C.F.R. § 220.42. Finally, the applicant's failure to comply "with the terms and conditions of the permit" requires the Service to revoke the permit. 16 U.S.C. § 1539(a)(2)(C).

We turn first to the Turtles' contention that Volusia County's incidental take permit does not expressly authorize takings through artificial beachfront lighting. Such express authority, if it exists, can be found only within the four corners of the permit. *See generally* 16 U.S.C. § 1539(a) (issuing official must "prescribe" the permit's "terms and conditions"). In its introductory headline, Volusia County's incidental take permit states that the Service "authorizes incidental take within the Defined Area or County Beaches, associated with the activities described in Condition F below, of [appellant loggerhead sea turtle, appellant green sea turtle, leatherback sea turtle, hawksbill sea turtle (*Eretmochelys imbricata*) and Kemp's ridley sea turtle (*Lepidochelys kempii*)] conditioned upon implementation of the terms and conditions of this Permit." Condition F, in turn, lists eleven "authorized" types of incidental take:

F. The following types of incidental take are authorized herein, subject to the continued validity of this Permit:

1. Harassment, injury, and/or death to sea turtle eggs and/or hatchlings resulting from public and emergency and/or safety *vehicles* driving over unmarked/unprotected sea turtle nests located in designated traffic lane/driving area(s) or ramp [illegible] area(s) on County Beaches.
2. Harassment, injury, and/or death to sea turtle eggs and/or hatchlings resulting from emergency and/or safety *vehicles* driving over unmarked/unprotected sea turtles nests located within the Defined Area.
3. Harassment, injury, and/or death to sea turtle eggs and/or hatchlings resulting from emergency and/or safety *vehicles* driving over marked sea turtle nests located within the Defined Areas.
4. Harassment, injury, and/or death to hatchling sea turtles emerging from unmarked/unprotected nests and subsequently caught in *vehicle* ruts in areas where no rut removal has taken place.
5. Harassment, injury, and/or death to adult, hatchling, stranded, or post-hatchling washback [sic] sea turtles resulting from collisions with emergency and/or safety *vehicles* operating within the Defined Area; such vehicles may also disorient/harass adults and/or hatchling sea turtles with headlights while in motion or at rest for less than one minute, or harass adult sea turtles during nesting activity.
6. Harassment, injury, and/or death to adult female sea turtles attempting to nest in the Transitional and/or Urban Areas of the County Beaches between 8 a.m. and 7 p.m., resulting from collisions with *vehicles* operated by the general public.
7. Harassment, injury, and/or death to hatchling sea turtles emerging from the nest and/or crawling from the Transitional and/or Urban Areas of the County Beaches to the ocean between 8 a.m. and 7 p.m., resulting from collisions with *vehicles* operated by the general public pursuant to terms and conditions of this permit.
8. Harassment, injury, and/or death to post-hatchling sea turtles that have emerged from a nest and entered the ocean by

having been washed back onto Transitional and/or Urban Areas of the County Beaches resulting from collisions with *vehicles* operated by the general public pursuant to terms and conditions of this permit.

9. Harassment, injury, and/or death to nesting female turtles attempting to nest in the Defined Areas, resulting from physiological stress of potentially increasing the number of false crawls during the nesting season, or from sand compaction due to *vehicles* operating within the Defined Area pursuant to the terms and conditions of this permit.

10. Harassment, injury, and/or death of sea turtle and/or hatchlings in unmarked/unprotected nests due to physical crushing by activities associated with (1) marking the established Conservation Zone in the Transitional and Urban Areas of the County Beaches; (2) placement of trash receptacles on County Beaches; (3) placement of portable toilets as outlined in the [habitat conservation plan]; and (4) beach maintenance activities, including ramp maintenance.

11. Harassment, injury, and/or death of sea turtle eggs and/or nests laid outside the normal sea turtle nesting season, May 1 through October 31, when a nest monitoring/marking program is not in place.

(Emphasis added.) Indisputably, these eleven types of incidental take relate only to vehicular access on Volusia County's beaches. None of the eleven authorized activities listed in Condition F concerns artificial beachfront lighting. The only form of lighting mentioned in Condition F is vehicular headlights.

Although the majority of its conditions concern beach driving, the incidental take permit does address artificial beachfront lighting. Condition G of the permit, entitled "Mitigation/ Minimization Measures," lists fifteen categories of "measures [to] be employed by the Permittee to ensure that take is minimized and mitigated." * * * The mitigation measures relative to artificial beachfront lighting occupy less than two out of twenty-five pages of Volusia County's incidental take permit:

13. Artificial Beachfront Lighting.

> i. Beachfront Lighting Management Plan. By November [illegible date] 1997, the Permittee shall have developed a Beach Lighting Management Plan. The U.S. Fish and Wildlife Service must approve the Beach Lighting Management Plan prior to its implementation. * * *
>
> The time frame for developing scope of work for the Beach Lighting Management Plan is one year from adoption of the [habitat conservation plan]. The Beach Lighting Management Plan will be implement-

> ed during the second and third years following adoption. Lighting inventories will be conducted during the first year of implementation. The annual lighting maintenance program will be initiated during the third year after [habitat conservation plan] adoption, and a mitigation plan for uncorrectable lighting problems will be implemented during the fourth and fifth years following adoption.
>
> ii. Lighting Surveys. By April 1, 1997, Permittee shall develop, with further consultation and assistance from the U.S. Fish and Wildlife Service and Florida Department of Environmental Protection, a methodology for implementing and citing light sources that disorient sea turtles. Permittee will conduct lighting surveys and compile lists of infractions for Code Enforcement action or referral to the U.S. Fish and Wildlife Service. Lighting surveys will be conducted monthly, at a minimum, from April 1 through October 31 of each year.
>
> iii. County-owned and Operated Lights. The Permittee will survey all beachfront lights owned or operated by Volusia County to identify those that are not in compliance with State guidelines. The Permittee will ensure that the individual responsible for surveying the lights coordinates with the U.S. Fish and Wildlife Service for concurrence with the results. Any lights deemed to be a problem for sea turtles as a result of the survey will be brought into compliance by the County. The U.S. Fish and Wildlife Service will be notified to conduct a survey to ensure compliance; Volusia County personnel or their contractor will be present for the survey. All of the above measures will take place prior to May 1, 1997.
>
> iv. Light Management Training. By July 1, 1997, the Permittee will establish a training manual and hold at least two Permittee-sponsored workshops on lighting and beach crime to provide information on the effects of lighting in compliance with Volusia County Code protecting sea turtles and crime occurrences.

Condition G does not contain any language expressly authorizing takes of sea turtles through artificial beachfront lighting like that contained within Condition F.

In light of the foregoing, it is readily apparent that the incidental take permit exhaustively lists all authorized activities within Condition F and all mitigation measures within Condition G. Activities relative to driving on the beach are mentioned in both conditions. Activities relative to artificial beachfront lighting, however, are mentioned only in Condition G. Given the permit's structure, the express authority to take sea turtles through artificial beachfront lighting—if the Service had so intended—

would be memorialized in Condition F. This absence is dispositive. Accordingly, Volusia County lacks the Service's express permission to take sea turtles incidentally through artificial beachfront lighting.

Volusia County argues that even if it lacks the Service's express permission, it has the Service's implied permission to take sea turtles incidentally through artificial beachfront lighting because the Service expressly conditioned the permit on Volusia County's implementation of detailed lighting-related mitigatory measures. This argument presents an issue of first impression in this and other circuits, whether the incidental take permit exception (16 U.S.C. § 1539(a)) to the "take" prohibition (16 U.S.C. § 1538(a)(1)(B)) applies to, and thus excepts from liability, an activity performed as a purely mitigatory measure upon which the Service conditions the permit. We hold that it does not.

The ESA's text and the Service's regulations provide every indication that incidental take permission must be express and activity-specific. To be excepted from liability, the ESA mandates that the "take" be "incidental to ... the carrying out of an ... *activity*." 16 U.S.C. § 1539(a)(1)(B) (emphasis added). Moreover, in addressing the requirements of the habitat conservation plan, the ESA semantically separates the "action[]" at issue from the applicant's intentions to "mitigate" the taking. *Compare* 16 U.S.C. § 1539(a)(2)(A)(iii) ("what alternative *actions* to such taking the applicant considered") (emphasis added) *with* 16 U.S.C. § 1539(a)(2)(A)(ii) ("what steps the applicant will take to minimize and *mitigate* such impacts") (emphasis added). *See generally Friends of Endangered Species, Inc. v. Jantzen,* 760 F.2d 976, 984 (9th Cir. 1985) (separating semantically the activity for which the applicants sought an incidental take permit—a development "project"—from the mitigatory measures—"restrictions" on the development). Furthermore, before the Service issues an incidental take permit, the fact-finding official must resolve at least two statutorily distinct questions: (1) whether the *activity* will be free of purposeful takes; and (2) whether the applicant will *mitigate* the authorized takes' effect. *Compare* 16 U.S.C. § 1539(a)(2)(B)(i) ("the *taking* will be incidental") (emphasis added) *with* 16 U.S.C. § 1539(a)(2)(B)(ii) ("the applicant will ... minimize and *mitigate* the impacts of such taking") (emphasis added).

The statutory dividing line between activities sought to be permitted and mitigatory measures is further reinforced in the Service's regulations. The Service requires applicants to describe completely "the *activity* sought to be authorized." 50 C.F.R. §§ 17.22(b)(1)(i), 17.32(b)(1)(iii)(A) (emphasis added); *see also* 50 C.F.R. § 222.22(b)(4) (incidental take permit applications to the National Marine Fisheries Service must include a "detailed description of the proposed *activity*") (emphasis added). The incidental take permit, in turn, "may authorize a single transaction, a series of transactions, or a number of *activities*[.]" 50 C.F.R. §§ 17.22, 17.32 (emphasis added). Finally, the Service emphasizes that the "authorizations on the face of a permit which set forth specific ... *methods of taking* ... are to be strictly construed and shall not be interpreted to permit similar or related matters outside the scope of strict construction." 50

C.F.R. § 13.42 (emphasis added); *see also* 50 C.F.R. § 222.22(d) (incidental take permits that the National Marine Fisheries Service issues must "contain such terms and conditions as the Assistant Administrator deems necessary and appropriate, including ... [t]he authorized *method of taking*") (emphasis added).

Even the Service's informal publication advises applicants to describe specifically "all *actions* ... that ... are likely to result in incidental take" so that the permit holder "can determine the applicability of the incidental take authorization to the *activities* they undertake." United States Fish & Wildlife Serv., Dep't of the Interior; Nat'l Marine Fisheries Serv., Dep't of Commerce, *Habitat Conservation Planning Handbook* (Nov.1996), at 3–12 to 3–13 (emphasis added). Otherwise, the Service warns, "broadly defined types of *activities* ... generally would not be authorized." *Habitat Handbook*, at 3–13 (emphasis added).

* * * The content of Volusia County's application and correspondence with the Service reflects the statutory and regulatory dividing line between authorized activities and mitigatory measures. In its initial application to the Service, Volusia County "complete[ly] describ[ed] ... the activity sought to be authorized" as "vehicular access to Volusia County beaches[.]" (Citing 50 C.F.R. §§ 17.22(b)(1)(i).) A follow-up letter from a Service official acknowledging receipt of the application summarized that Volusia County sought "a permit to cover any incidental take of sea turtles that may occur on Volusia County beaches ... as a result of *vehicular access* to county beaches." (Emphasis added.) Another follow-up letter from the Service pointedly expressed that

> it is important to state for the record that the County of Volusia is not seeking incidental take authority for marine sea turtles resulting from lights owned or operated by the County. The purpose of any such discussion in the habitat conservation plan ... is to provide *mitigation* for impacts to marine sea turtles resulting from *permitted activities.* The [incidental take permit] application you submitted requests incidental take authority for sea turtle species from *beach-driving* and associated activities only.

(Emphasis added.) Finally, in a responsive letter to the Service, an assistant county attorney reiterated that "Volusia County is seeking an Incidental Take Permit for vehicles [*sic*] access to the beaches. However, Volusia County has addressed lighting throughout its permit application as a *mitigating* factor." (Emphasis added.)

Contrary to Volusia County's position, no published case law even purports to suggest that purely mitigatory measures fall within the scope of the incidental take permit exception, 16 U.S.C. § 1539(a). In *Ramsey v. Kantor,*i the Ninth Circuit addressed whether the States of Oregon and Washington that were neither federal agencies nor applicants for an incidental take statement issued under 16 U.S.C. § 1536(b) may lawfully take federally protected fish without first obtaining an incidental take permit under 16 U.S.C. § 1539(a). 96 F.3d 434, 437 (9th Cir. 1996). The court answered the question in the affirmative "provided the actions in question are contemplated by an incidental take statement issued under [16 U.S.C. § 1536(b)] and are conducted in compliance with the requirements of that statement." *Ramsey,* 96 F.3d at 442. Because the incidental take statement "clearly anticipated" that Oregon and Washington would regulate the fishing of unprotected salmon, the court held that those states were not liable for takes of endangered and threatened salmon that "intermingle with and are all but indistinguishable from" unprotected salmon. *Ramsey,* 96 F.3d at 438, 442.

Volusia County argues that the Service "clearly anticipated" takes resulting from artificial beachfront lighting in the incidental take permit, just as the issuing agency in *Ramsey* "clearly anticipated" takes resulting from salmon fishing regulations in the incidental take statement. 96 F.3d at 442. We are not convinced. As a threshold matter, the *Ramsey* court gave no indication that Oregon's and Washington's salmon fishing regulations served as purely mitigatory measures, as does Volusia County's artificial beachfront lighting activities.

In any event, the law governing incidental take statements issued under 16 U.S.C. § 1536(b), the statutory source in *Ramsey,* differs from the law governing incidental take permits issued under 16 U.S.C. § 1539(a), the statutory source in this case. *See generally Ramsey,* 96 F.3d at 439. First, the issuing agency's prerequisite findings are not the same. To permit an incidental taking under 16 U.S.C. § 1536(b), the issuing agency must conclude, in pertinent part, that:

> [1] the agency action will not [likely jeopardize the continued existence of any protected species or result in the destruction or adverse modification of its critical habitat ("likely jeopardize protected species")], or [the agency] offers reasonable and prudent alternatives which the Secretary believes would not [jeopardize protected species]; [and]
>
> [2] the taking of an endangered species or a threatened species incidental to the agency action will not [likely jeopardize protected species][.]

16 U.S.C. § 1536(b)(4) (incorporating by reference 16 U.S.C. § 1536(a)(2)). To permit an incidental taking under 16 U.S.C. § 1539(a), however, the issuing agency must find, in pertinent part, that:

> [1] the taking will be incidental;
>
> [2] the applicant will ... minimize and mitigate the impacts of such taking;
>
> [3] the applicant will ensure that adequate funding for the [habitat conservation] plan will be provided;
>
> [4] the taking will not appreciably reduce the likelihood of the survival and recovery of the species in the wild; and

[5] the [other measures that the issuing agency may require] will be met[.]

16 U.S.C. § 1539(a)(2)(B) (incorporating by reference 16 U.S.C. § 1539(a)(2)(A)(iv)). Both, of course, require a finding that the take sought to be authorized will be "incidental." Both also focus on the ultimate effect of the incidental take on the species. Only 16 U.S.C. § 1539, however, expressly requires a finding of future mitigation. As such, the holding of *Ramsey*—that a nonapplicant's actions can be excepted from take liability if they are contemplated in an incidental take statement—cannot fairly be read to apply to mitigatory measures contemplated in an incidental take permit. *See* 96 F.3d at 442.

A second important difference between an incidental take statement (16 U.S.C. § 1536(b)) and an incidental take permit (16 U.S.C. § 1539(a)) lies in the broad language of 16 U.S.C. § 1536(*o*), which applies only to holders or beneficiaries of the former. Under section 1536(*o*), "*any* taking that is in compliance with the terms and conditions specified in [an incidental take statement issued under 16 U.S.C. § 1536(b)] shall not be considered to be a prohibited taking of the species concerned." 16 U.S.C. § 1536(*o*)(2). No similar provision applies to "any" taking in compliance with an incidental take permit's terms and conditions, including mitigatory measures. The closest analogous provision in section 1539 appears only in the converse: the issuing official "shall revoke [an incidental take permit] if he finds that the permittee is not complying with the terms and conditions of the permit." 16 U.S.C. § 1539(a)(2)(C).

Finally, the prohibitions that underlie the incidental take exceptions are unique. The prohibition that underlies the incidental take statement exception applies only to federal agencies, and imposes upon them a duty to consult with the statement-issuing agency and ensure that their proposed action will not likely "jeopardize the continued existence of any endangered species or threatened species or result in the destruction or adverse modification of [critical] habitat[.]" 16 U.S.C. § 1536(a)(2) (the "jeopardy" clause). The prohibition that underlies the incidental take permit exception applies to federal, state, local and private actors, and creates no similar duty to consult. *See* 16 U.S.C. §§ 1532(13), 1538(a)(1)(B) (the "take" prohibition). Additionally, the "jeopardy" clause applies to protected fish, wildlife and plants, whereas the "take" prohibition applies only to protected fish and wildlife. *See* 16 U.S.C. §§ 1532(16), 1536(a)(2), 1538(a)(1). Consequently, some activities—especially those relating to land use—are more likely to result in "jeopardy" than a "take." *See Sweet Home,* 115 S.Ct. at 2415 ("Section 7 [16 U.S.C. § 1536] imposes a broad, affirmative duty to avoid adverse habitat modifications that § 9 [16 U.S.C. § 1539] does not replicate, and § 7 does not limit its admonition to habitat modification that actually kills or injures wildlife.") (internal quotation marks and citations omitted)[.] These differences further militate against broadening the scope of the incidental take permit exception (16 U.S.C. § 1539(a)) even if some courts have suggested that section

1536(*o*) serves to broaden the scope of the incidental take statement exception (16 U.S.C. § 1536(b)).

The fact remains that no court has been presented with the issue facing us today. To be sure, protecting troubled wildlife is serious business. *See Tennessee Valley Auth. v. Hill,* 437 U.S. 153, 174 (1978) ("[T]he language, history, and structure of the [Endangered Species Act] indicates beyond doubt that Congress intended endangered species to be afforded the highest of priorities."). Consequently, permits that purport to excuse takes of wildlife must be clear on their face. In this case, "the Secretary ... permit[ted]" only takes of sea turtles incidental to driving on the beach. 16 U.S.C. § 1539(a)(1). Accordingly, the district court erred in dismissing the Turtles' claim that artificial beachfront lighting takes sea turtles. * * *

NOTES

1. **Tracking This Case Through Section 9.** What are the listed species at issue in this case? How have those species been "taken" in violation of section 9, according to the plaintiffs? How, allegedly, is Volusia County responsible for those takings? Does this case raise a section 9 causation issue, as in *Strahan v. Coxe*? If so, why? Does the Eleventh Circuit decide that issue? Why or why not?

2. **Tracking This Case Through Section 10.** Note that neither the district court nor the Eleventh Circuit has yet determined whether Volusia County can be held liable for a section 9 taking. Why, then, would the courts go ahead and analyze the scope of Volusia County's ITP? What procedures did Volusia County go through to get an ITP? For what activities did it seek an ITP? What specific mitigation measures does the ITP require? What kind of HCP did Volusia County create?

3. **Explicit Incidental Taking Authorizations.** What kinds of incidental takings does Volusia County's ITP explicitly allow? Does Volusia County's ITP explicitly authorize it to take the relevant species through artificial lighting? Why or why not? How does the Eleventh Circuit interpret the ITP? What interpretive guidelines have the USFWS and NMFS/NOAA Fisheries provided for ITPs?

4. **Implicit Incidental Taking Authorizations.** How does Volusia County argue that its ITP *implicitly* authorizes incidental takings of the relevant species through artificial lighting? Does the Eleventh Circuit agree? Why or why not? What distinctions does the Eleventh Circuit draw in deciding this issue?

5. **Section 7 Incidental Take Statements and Section 10 ITPs Compared.** How does a section 7 incidental take statement compare to a section 10 ITP, according to the Eleventh Circuit? Why do these exemptions' differences justify differences in interpretive approaches? What do those differences do to the persuasive value of the Ninth Circuit's decision in the *Ramsey* case for the Eleventh Circuit's decision here? Why? How should ITPs

be construed compared section 7 incidental take statements, according to the Eleventh Circuit? Why?

6. **Reliance on Supreme Court Precedent.** How does the Eleventh Circuit use *TVA v. Hill*? Is its decision consistent with *TVA v. Hill*? Why or why not? How does the Eleventh Circuit use *Sweet Home*? Is its decision consistent with *Sweet Home*? Why or why not?

* * *

III. THE ENDANGERED SPECIES ACT AND THE CONVENTION ON INTERNATIONAL TRADE IN ENDANGERED SPECIES OF WILD FAUNA AND FLORA (CITES)

A. INTRODUCTION TO THE CONVENTION

As noted, Congress had two general purposes in enacting the Endangered Species Act of 1973: to implement *domestic* protections for endangered and threatened species; and to implement a variety of international treaties related to species protection. The most general of the treaties that Congress implemented through the ESA is the ***Convention on International Trade in Endangered Species of Wild Fauna and Flora* (CITES)**. Indeed, the ESA defines "Convention," as used in the statute, to refer exclusively to CITES, ESA § 3(4), 16 U.S.C. § 1532(4), despite the other conventions that Congress listed in its findings. CITES was first presented for signature in Washington, D.C., on March 3, 1973. The United States Senate advised ratification on August 3, 1973, and President Richard M. Nixon ratified the Convention on September 13, 1973. CITES entered into force on July 1, 1975.

Let's begin by examining CITES itself.

INTERNATIONAL TRADE IN ENDANGERED SPECIES OF WILD FAUNA AND FLORA

27 U.S.T. 1087, T.I.A.S. No. 8249.

The Contracting States,

RECOGNIZING that wild fauna and flora in their many beautiful and varied forms are an irreplaceable part of the natural systems of the earth which must be protected for this and the generations to come;

CONSCIOUS of the ever-growing value of wild fauna and flora from aesthetic, scientific, cultural, recreational and economic points of view;

RECOGNIZING that peoples and States are and should be the best protectors of their own wild fauna and flora;

RECOGNIZING, in addition, that international cooperation is essential for the protection of certain species of wild fauna and flora against over-exploitation through international trade;

CONVINCED of the urgency of taking appropriate measures to this end;

HAVE AGREED as follows:

ARTICLE I

DEFINITIONS

For the purpose of the present Convention, unless the context otherwise requires:

(a) "Species" means any species, subspecies, or geographically separate population thereof;

(b) "Specimen" means:

  (i) any animal or plant, whether alive or dead;

  (ii) in the case of an animal: for species included in Appendices I and II, any readily recognizable part or derivative thereof; and for species included in Appendix III, any readily recognizable part or derivative thereof specified in Appendix III in relation to the species; and

  (iii) in the case of a plant: for species included in Appendix I, any readily recognizable part or derivative thereof; and for species included in Appendices II and III, any readily recognizable part or derivative thereof specified in Appendices II and III in relation to the species;

(c) "Trade" means export, re-export, import and introduction from the sea;

(d) "Re-export" means export of any specimen that has previously been imported;

(e) "Introduction from the sea" means transportation into a State of specimens of any species which were taken in the marine environment not under the jurisdiction of any State;

(f) "Scientific Authority" means a national scientific authority designated in accordance with Article IX;

(g) "Management Authority" means a national management authority designated in accordance with Article IX;

(h) "Party" means a State for which the present Convention has entered into force.

ARTICLE II

FUNDAMENTAL PRINCIPLES

1. Appendix I shall include all species threatened with extinction which are or may be affected by trade. Trade in specimens of these species must be subject to particularly strict regulation in order not to

endanger further their survival and must only be authorized in exceptional circumstances.

2. Appendix II shall include:

   (a) all species which although not necessarily now threatened with extinction may become so unless trade in specimens of such species is subject to strict regulation in order to avoid utilization incompatible with their survival; and

   (b) other species which must be subject to regulation in order that trade in specimens of certain species referred to in sub-paragraph (a) of this paragraph may be brought under effective control.

3. Appendix III shall include all species which any Party identifies as being subject to regulation within its jurisdiction for the purpose of preventing or restricting exploitation, and as needing the cooperation of other parties in the control of trade.

4. The Parties shall not allow trade in specimens of species included in Appendices I, II and III except in accordance with the provisions of the present Convention.

ARTICLE III

REGULATION OF TRADE IN SPECIMENS OF SPECIES INCLUDED IN APPENDIX I

1. All trade in specimens of species included in Appendix I shall be in accordance with the provisions of this Article.

2. The export of any specimen of a species included in Appendix I shall require the prior grant and presentation of an export permit. An export permit shall only be granted when the following conditions have been met:

   (a) a Scientific Authority of the State of export has advised that such export will not be detrimental to the survival of that species;

   (b) a Management Authority of the State of export is satisfied that the specimen was not obtained in contravention of the laws of that State for the protection of fauna and flora;

   (c) a Management Authority of the State of export is satisfied that any living specimen will be so prepared and shipped as to minimize the risk of injury, damage to health or cruel treatment; and

   (d) a Management Authority of the State of export is satisfied that an import permit has been granted for the specimen.

3. The import of any specimen of a species included in Appendix I shall require the prior grant and presentation of an import permit and either an export permit or a re-export certificate. * * *

4. The re-export of any specimen of a species included in Appendix I shall require the prior grant and presentation of a re-export certificate. A re-export certificate shall only be granted when the following conditions have been met:

(a) a Management Authority of the State of re-export is satisfied that the specimen was imported into that State in accordance with the provisions of the present Convention;

(b) a Management Authority of the State of re-export is satisfied that any living specimen will be so prepared and shipped as to minimize the risk of injury, damage to health or cruel treatment; and

(c) a Management Authority of the State of re-export is satisfied that an import permit has been granted for any living specimen.

5. The introduction from the sea of any specimen of a species included in Appendix I shall require the prior grant of a certificate from a Management Authority of the State of introduction. * * *

ARTICLE IV

REGULATION OF TRADE IN SPECIMENS OF SPECIES INCLUDED IN APPENDIX II

1. All trade in specimens of species included in Appendix II shall be in accordance with the provisions of this Article.

2. The export of any specimen of a species included in Appendix II shall require the prior grant and presentation of an export permit. An export permit shall only be granted when the following conditions have been met:

(a) a Scientific Authority of the State of export has advised that such export will not be detrimental to the survival of that species;

(b) a Management Authority of the State of export is satisfied that the specimen was not obtained in contravention of the laws of that State for the protection of fauna and flora; and

(c) a Management Authority of the State of export is satisfied that any living specimen will be so prepared and shipped as to minimize the risk of injury, damage to health or cruel treatment.

3. A Scientific Authority in each Party shall monitor both the export permits granted by that State for specimens of species included in Appendix II and the actual exports of such specimens. Whenever a Scientific Authority determines that the export of specimens of any such species should be limited in order to maintain that species throughout its range at a level consistent with its role in the ecosystems in which it occurs and well above the level at which that species might become eligible for inclusion in Appendix I, the Scientific Authority shall advise the appropriate Management Authority of suitable measures to be taken to limit the grant of export permits for specimens of that species.

4. The import of any specimen of a species included in Appendix II shall require the prior presentation of either an export permit or a re-export certificate.

5. The re-export of any specimen of a species included in Appendix II shall require the prior grant and presentation of a re-export certifi-

cate. A re-export certificate shall only be granted when the following conditions have been met:

(a) a Management Authority of the State of re-export is satisfied that the specimen was imported into that State in accordance with the provisions of the present Convention; and

(b) a Management Authority of the State of re-export is satisfied that any living specimen will be so prepared and shipped as to minimize the risk of injury, damage to health or cruel treatment.

6. The introduction from the sea of any specimen of a species included in Appendix II shall require the prior grant of a certificate from a Management Authority of the State of introduction. * * *

7. Certificates referred to in paragraph 6 of this Article may be granted on the advice of a Scientific Authority, in consultation with other national scientific authorities or, when appropriate, international scientific authorities, in respect of periods not exceeding one year for total numbers of specimens to be introduced in such periods.

ARTICLE V

REGULATION OF TRADE IN SPECIMENS OF SPECIES INCLUDED IN APPENDIX III

1. All trade in specimens of species included in Appendix III shall be in accordance with the provisions of this Article.

2. The export of any specimen of a species included in Appendix III from any State which has included that species in Appendix III shall require the prior grant and presentation of an export permit. An export permit shall only be granted when the following conditions have been met:

(a) a Management Authority of the State of export is satisfied that the specimen was not obtained in contravention of the laws of that State for the protection of fauna and flora; and

(b) a Management Authority of the State of export is satisfied that any living specimen will be so prepared and shipped as to minimize the risk of injury, damage to health or cruel treatment.

3. The import of any specimen of a species included in Appendix III shall require, except in circumstances to which paragraph 4 of this Article applies, the prior presentation of a certificate of origin and, where the import is from a State which has included that species in Appendix III, an export permit.

4. In the case of re-export, a certificate granted by the Management Authority of the State of re-export that the specimen was processed in that State or is being re-exported shall be accepted by the State of import as evidence that the provisions of the present Convention have been complied with in respect of the specimen concerned.

* * * ARTICLE VIII

MEASURES TO BE TAKEN BY THE PARTIES

1. The Parties shall take appropriate measures to enforce the provisions of the present Convention and to prohibit trade in specimens in violation thereof. These shall include measures:

   (a) to penalize trade in, or possession of, such specimens, or both; and

   (b) to provide for the confiscation or return to the State of export of such specimens.

2. In addition to the measures taken under paragraph 1 of this Article, a Party may, when it deems it necessary, provide for any method of internal reimbursement for expenses incurred as a result of the confiscation of a specimen traded in violation of the measures taken in the application of the provisions of the present Convention.

3. As far as possible, the Parties shall ensure that specimens shall pass through any formalities required for trade with a minimum of delay. To facilitate such passage, a Party may designate ports of exit and ports of entry at which specimens must be presented for clearance. The Parties shall ensure further that all living specimens, during any period of transit, holding or shipment, are properly cared for so as to minimize the risk of injury, damage to health or cruel treatment.

* * *6. Each Party shall maintain records of trade in specimens of species included in Appendices I, II and III which shall cover:

   (a) the names and addresses of exporters and importers; and

   (b) the number and type of permits and certificates granted; the States with which such trade occurred; the numbers or quantities and types of specimens, names of species as included in Appendices I, II and III and, where applicable, the size and sex of the specimens in question.

7. Each Party shall prepare periodic reports on its implementation of the present Convention and shall transmit to the Secretariat:

   (a) an annual report containing a summary of the information specified in sub-paragraph (b) of paragraph 6 of this Article; and

   (b) a biennial report on legislative, regulatory and administrative measures taken to enforce the provisions of the present Convention.

8. The information referred to in paragraph 7 of this Article shall be available to the public where this is not inconsistent with the law of the Party concerned.

ARTICLE IX

MANAGEMENT AND SCIENTIFIC AUTHORITIES

1. Each Party shall designate for the purposes of the present Convention:

(a) one or more Management Authorities competent to grant permits or certificates on behalf of that Party; and

(b) one or more Scientific Authorities. * * *

* * * ARTICLE XIV

EFFECT ON DOMESTIC LEGISLATION AND INTERNATIONAL CONVENTIONS

1. The provisions of the present Convention shall in no way affect the right of Parties to adopt:

   (a) stricter domestic measures regarding the conditions for trade, taking possession or transport of specimens of species included in Appendices I, II and III, or the complete prohibition thereof; or

   (b) domestic measures restricting or prohibiting trade, taking possession, or transport of species not included in Appendices I, II or III.

2. The provisions of the present Convention shall in no way affect the provisions of any domestic measures or the obligations of Parties deriving from any treaty, convention, or international agreement relating to other aspects of trade, taking, possession, or transport of specimens which is in force or subsequently may enter into force for any Party including any measure pertaining to the Customs, public health, veterinary or plant quarantine fields.

3. The provisions of the present Convention shall in no way affect the provisions of, or the obligations deriving from, any treaty, convention or international agreement concluded or which may be concluded between States creating a union or regional trade agreement establishing or maintaining a common external customs control and removing customs control between the parties thereto insofar as they relate to trade among the States members of that union or agreement.

* * * ARTICLE XIX

SIGNATURE

The present Convention shall be open for signature at Washington until 30th April 1973 and thereafter at Berne until 31st December 1974.

ARTICLE XX

RATIFICATION, ACCEPTANCE, APPROVAL

The present Convention shall be subject to ratification, acceptance or approval. Instruments of ratification, acceptance or approval shall be deposited with the Government of the Swiss Confederation which shall be the Depositary Government.

ARTICLE XXI

ACCESSION

The present Convention shall be open indefinitely for accession. Instruments of accession shall be deposited with the Depositary Government.

ARTICLE XXII

ENTRY INTO FORCE

1. The present Convention shall enter into force 90 days after the date of deposit of the tenth instrument of ratification, acceptance, approval or accession, with the Depositary Government.
2. For each State which ratifies, accepts or approves the present Convention or accedes thereto after the deposit of the tenth instrument of ratification, acceptance, approval or accession, the present Convention shall enter into force 90 days after the deposit by such State of its instrument of ratification, acceptance, approval or accession.

* * * IN WITNESS WHEREOF the undersigned Plenipotentiaries, being duly authorized to that effect, have signed the present Convention.

DONE at Washington this third day of March, One Thousand Nine Hundred and Seventy-three.

NOTES

1. **Ratification of the Convention by the United States.** Representatives of the United States signed CITES on March 3, 1973. What steps did the United States then take to ratify the Convention? When were those steps taken? How do these steps track the requirements regarding treaties in the U.S. Constitution? What other requirements does CITES itself add to the ratification process?

2. **Bringing CITES into Force.** Treaties generally specify when or how they will ***come into force***—that is, operate as international law binding on the ratifying countries. These provisions often specify that a certain number of countries must ratify the treaty before it comes into force among the parties. Why did CITES come into force only on July 1, 1975, despite numerous signatures in 1973?

3. **The Convention's Regulatory Focus.** How, most generally, does CITES seek to protect endangered and threatened species internationally? Why is such a focus appropriate for an international treaty? Given that focus, is CITES sufficient (even with domestic implementation) to protect threatened and endangered species worldwide? Why or why not?

4. **The Three Appendices to CITES.** The heart of CITES is its three appendices, each of which lists species entitled to protection under the Convention. According to the Convention, what are the differences between Appendix I, Appendix II, and Appendix III species? What requirements apply to species listed in each appendix?

5. **Coordination with Other Law.** According to Article XIV, what is the relationship between CITES and domestic law? What is the relationship between CITES and other treaties? Do these provisions make sense, given the CITES' goals? Why or why not?

* * *

B. IMPLEMENTATION OF CITES THROUGH THE ENDANGERED SPECIES ACT

1. Statutory Provisions Related to CITES

The ESA is the primary statute through which the United States implements CITES. The ESA designates the Secretary of the Interior "as the Management Authority and the Scientific Authority for the purposes of" CITES and commands that "the respective functions of each such Authority shall be carried out through the United States Fish and Wildlife Service." ESA § 8A(a), 16 U.S.C. § 1537a(a). These agencies must "do all things necessary and appropriate to carry out the functions" of the Management Authority and Scientific Authority under the Convention. ESA § 8A(b), (c), 16 U.S.C. § 1537a(b), (c). The Secretary of State, in turn, must explain the United States' responses to proposed amendments to Appendices I and II:

> If the United States votes against including any species in Appendix I or II of the Convention and does not enter a reservation pursuant to paragraph (3) of Article XV of the Convention with respect to that species, the Secretary of State, before the 90th day after the last day on which such a reservation could be entered, shall submit to the Committee on Merchant Marine and Fisheries of the House of Representatives, and to the Committee on the Environment and Public Works of the Senate, a written report setting forth the reasons why such a reservation was not entered.

ESA § 8A(d), 16 U.S.C. § 1537a(d).

Substantively, the ESA makes it "unlawful for any person subject to the jurisdiction of the United States to engage in any trade in any specimens contrary to the provisions of the Convention, or to possess any specimens traded contrary to the provisions of the Convention, including the definitions of terms in article I thereof." ESA § 9(c)(1), 16 U.S.C. § 1538(c)(1). Moreover, importers and exporters of fish, wildlife, plants, and African elephant ivory must generally have the Secretary of the Interior's permission, must keep records as the Secretary requires, are subject to inspections, must file reports as the Secretary requires, and must import and export from designated ports. ESA § 9(d), (e), (f), 16 U.S.C. § 1538(d), (e), (f).

There are several exceptions to the ESA's CITES-related trade provisions. First, a person is not subject to the import/export requirements if he or she is importing "shellfish or fishery products" that: (1) are not listed for protection under the ESA itself; and (2) "are imported for purposes of human or animal consumption or taken in waters under the jurisdiction of the United States or on the high seas for recreational purposes * * *." ESA § 9(d)(1)(A), (e), (f)(1). Second, if a person seeks to import fish or wildlife listed in Appendix II of CITES but *not* listed for protection under the ESA itself and: (1) CITES does not prohibit the taking or export of that fish or wildlife species; (2) the person is not importing the fish or wildlife in the course of a commercial activity; and (3) the person has complied with the Secretary of the Interior's permission, recordkeeping, inspection, reporting, and import/export requirements, then the importation is presumed not to violate CITES. *Id.* § 9(c)(2), 16 U.S.C. § 1538(c)(2). Finally, the ESA provision prohibiting violation of CITES does not apply to articles made in whole or part out of endangered or threatened species that are more than 100 years old, so long as the article has not been repaired or modified with listed species parts since December 28, 1973 (the day that the ESA took effect) and so long as the article enters the United States through a properly designated port. *Id.* § 10(h), 16 U.S.C. § 1539(h).

How much authority does the ESA actually give the federal government to implement CITES and to ensure that people and companies within the United States are not trading in internationally recognized endangered and threatened species? That issue was the subject of the following case.

CASTLEWOOD PRODUCTS, L.L.C. v. NORTON

365 F.3d 1076 (D.C. Cir. 2004).

HARRY T. EDWARDS, CIRCUIT JUDGE:

This case concerns the United States' detention of several shipments of bigleaf mahogany from Brazil. The United States and Brazil are both signatories to the Convention on International Trade in Endangered Species of Wild Fauna and Flora, Mar. 3, 1973, 27 U.S.T. 1087 ("CITES" or "Convention"). The Convention governs trade in endangered species that are listed in its appendices. Article V provides that an export permit for species included in Appendix III can be granted by the exporting country only when, *inter alia,* the designated Management Authority of the exporting country is satisfied that the specimen was not obtained in contravention of its laws. CITES, art. V(2)(a), 27 U.S.T. at 1097. Brazil has included bigleaf mahogany in Appendix III. In the United States, the Endangered Species Act, 16 U.S.C. §§ 1531–44 (2000) ("ESA"), prohibits trade in violation of the Convention and authorizes the Secretary of the Interior and the Secretary of Agriculture to enforce the ESA.

This case arose when the Animal and Plant Health Inspection Service ("APHIS") of the United States Department of Agriculture ("USDA") refused entry at U.S. ports to certain shipments of bigleaf mahogany after Brazil's Management Authority gave information to the United States Department of the Interior's Fish and Wildlife Service ("FWS") suggest-

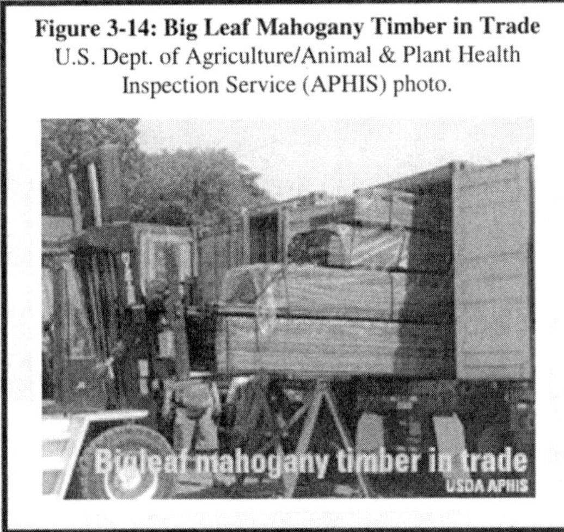

Figure 3-14: Big Leaf Mahogany Timber in Trade
U.S. Dept. of Agriculture/Animal & Plant Health Inspection Service (APHIS) photo.

ing that the specimens in the shipments were not legally obtained. On July 23, 2002, Castlewood Products, L.L.C., Interforest Corp., M. Bohlke Veneer Corp., Marwood, Inc., United Veneer, L.L.C., Veneer Technologies, Inc., and Aljoma Lumber, Inc., the U.S. corporate consignees of the disputed shipments, brought this action in the United States District Court for the District of Columbia to compel delivery of the shipments. The plaintiffs claimed that, because the export permits accompanying the shipments were signed and issued by Brazil's Management Authority, APHIS's detention of the shipments was arbitrary and capricious. The District Court denied the plaintiffs' motion for summary judgment and granted summary judgment to the Government, holding that the decision to detain the shipments was authorized by treaty, statute, and regulation. Interforest, Marwood, Veneer Technologies, and Aljoma Lumber appealed and we now affirm the judgment of the District Court.

I. BACKGROUND

A. Regulatory Background

The Convention governs the import and export of certain species of endangered fauna and flora that are listed in its appendices. This case concerns bigleaf mahogany, which Brazil has included in Appendix III. Article V of CITES provides that the export of any species listed in Appendix III requires "the prior grant and presentation of an export permit." CITES, art. V(2), 27 U.S.T. at 1097. That article provides:

> An export permit shall only be granted when the following conditions have been met:
>
> (a) a Management Authority of the State of export is satisfied that the specimen was not obtained in contravention of the laws of that State for the protection of fauna and flora;

(b) a Management Authority of the State of export is satisfied that any living specimen will be so prepared and shipped as to minimize the risk of injury, damage to health or cruel treatment.

Id.

A Management Authority is designated by each state to "grant permits or certificates on behalf of that Party." *Id.,* art. IX(1)(a), 27 U.S.T. at 1103. The United States has designated the Secretary of the Interior as the CITES Management Authority, and the Secretary's functions in this capacity are carried out through FWS. *See* 16 U.S.C. § 1537a(a). In Brazil, the Instituto Brasileiro do Meio Ambiente e dos Recursos Naturais Renovaveis or the Brazilian Institute of the Environment and Renewable Natural Resources (also known as "IBAMA") is the Management Authority under CITES.

Article VIII of the Convention provides:

(1) The Parties shall take appropriate measures to enforce the provisions of the present Convention and to prohibit trade in specimens in violation thereof. These shall include measures:

(a) to penalize trade in, or possession of, such specimens, or both; and

(b) to provide for the confiscation or return to the State of export of such specimens.

CITES, art. VIII(1)(a), 27 U.S.T. at 1101. Article XIV makes it clear that the Convention does not purport to limit the right of the Parties to adopt "stricter domestic measures regarding the conditions for trade, taking possession or transport of specimens of species included in Appendices I, II, and III, or complete prohibition thereof. . . ." *Id.,* art. XIV(1)(a), 27 U.S.T. at 1108.

Article XI provides for regular meetings of the Parties to the Convention, at which they may, *inter alia,* "make recommendations for improving the effectiveness of the present Convention." *Id.,* art. XI(3)(e), 27 U.S.T. at 1105. These recommendations, adopted through resolutions, are intended to give guidance to the Parties in implementing the Convention. Since ratification, the Parties have adopted two resolutions recommending specific measures to strengthen enforcement of the Convention. One, Resolution 11.3, recommends that,

(c) if an importing country has reason to believe that an Appendix–II or -III species is traded in contravention of the laws of any country involved in the transaction, it:

(i) immediately inform the country whose laws were thought to have been violated and, to the extent possible, provide that country with copies of all documentation relating to the transaction; and

(ii) where possible, apply stricter domestic measures to that transaction as provided for in Article XIV of the Convention.

CITES, Resolution 11.3 (2000). The other, Resolution 12.3, recommends that "the Parties refuse to accept any permit or certificate that is invalid, including authentic documents that do not contain all the required information ... or that contain information that brings into question the validity of the permit or certificate." CITES Resolution 12.3 § XIV(d) (2002) (recalling and incorporating CITES Resolution 10.2 § II(h) (1997)).

Congress implemented the Convention into U.S. law in the Endangered Species Act of 1973, Pub. L. No. 93–205, 87 Stat. 884 (codified as amended at 16 U.S.C. §§ 1531–44 (2000)). The ESA makes it unlawful to "engage in any trade in any specimens contrary to the provisions of the Convention." 16 U.S.C. § 1538(c)(1). It provides that any fish, wildlife or plants possessed or transferred in violation of the ESA or its regulations "shall be subject to forfeiture to the United States." 16 U.S.C. § 1540(e)(4)(A). The Secretary of the Interior is authorized to promulgate regulations as may be appropriate to enforce the ESA. 16 U.S.C. § 1540(f). The statute also provides for the coordination of the administration of the ESA between the Secretary of Agriculture and the Secretary of the Interior. 16 U.S.C. § 1540(h). FWS and APHIS work together to enforce the provisions of CITES.

The Department of the Interior has promulgated regulations to implement the ESA. *See* 50 C.F.R. pt. 23 (2003). One regulation provides: "In order to import into the United States any wildlife or plant listed in appendix III from a foreign country that has listed such animal or plant in appendix III, a valid foreign export permit or re-export certificate issued by such country must be obtained prior to such importation." 50 C.F.R. § 23.12(a)(3)(i). Another regulation states: "Only export permits, re-export certificates, certificates of origin, or other certificates issued and signed by a management authority will be accepted as a valid foreign document from a country that is a party to the Convention." 50 C.F.R. § 23.14(a).

B. *Factual Background*

The facts are largely undisputed. In the fall of 2001, FWS and APHIS learned that the Brazilian government had imposed a moratorium on the logging, transport, and export of bigleaf mahogany timber. In February 2002, APHIS placed holds on shipments of bigleaf mahogany from Brazil. FWS sent a letter to IBAMA, noting that "none of the permits accompanying the shipments were endorsed ... by the export inspection authorities in Brazil," and stating that USDA was detaining the shipments until officials in the United States could gain "verification of the validity of accompanying CITES permits." IBAMA informed FWS that recent shipments of bigleaf mahogany arriving in the United States from Brazil were accompanied by export permits that IBAMA had issued pursuant to preliminary judicial injunctions. IBAMA stated that its issuance of these permits did not reflect its independent judgment that the mahogany had been obtained lawfully.

IBAMA informed FWS that it had appealed these decisions, the merits of which were pending. * * * The letter noted that bigleaf mahogany trade had ceased by law in Brazil, with an exception for certified timber. It also acknowledged that bigleaf mahogany continued to be logged illegally. FWS and IBAMA had a similar exchange about two other shipments of mahogany in March 2002. FWS then received letters from Randolf Zachow, an IBAMA official, confirming the validity of some of the permits in question, and questioning the validity of the ban on the harvesting of mahogany.

On May 2, 2002, the President of IBAMA, Rômulo José Fernandes Barreto Mello, sent a letter to FWS invalidating Zachow's statements. Mello informed FWS that Zachow's letters did not express the point of view of the Brazilian government or IBAMA, and that Zachow had since been dismissed from his post. Mello's letter also stated that IBAMA's law enforcement officials and technicians would determine the entire wood chain of custody for bigleaf mahogany from the forests and the trading companies in 2000 and 2001. * * *

In a letter dated May 22, 2002, Mello clarified IBAMA's position regarding the permits issued pursuant to judicial command. He wrote that IBAMA "must not say that a judicial decision is not legal or not valid." * * * However, Mello also noted that "the controls available nowadays at IBAMA do not allow us to state exactly the legality of each particular shipment." The letter provided survey data indicating that shipments of mahogany up to a certain volume had legal origin, but that "the legal origin of such exceeding volume is not confirmed by IBAMA, as required in Article V, paragraph 2(a) of the Convention."

Subsequently, IBAMA presented tables to the CITES Secretariat showing the total volume of legally harvested timber by exporter. On June 20, 2002, APHIS released five shipments of bigleaf mahogany for which IBAMA had identified the origin and chain of custody. However, APHIS continued to detain other shipments of bigleaf mahogany.

On July 23, 2002, the plaintiffs commenced this action in the United States District Court for the District of Columbia to compel the delivery of the mahogany shipments that were still being detained. * * * The plaintiffs argued that, pursuant to the ESA and its implementing regulations, APHIS is required to validate a shipment for import upon presentment of all documentation required by the implementing regulations, and that a valid foreign export permit is the only document from the exporting country that is required under the Convention.

* * * II. ANALYSIS

A. Standard of Review

We review *de novo* the District Court's grant of summary judgment, which means that we review the agency's decision on our own. Under the applicable provisions of the Administrative Procedure Act, we must determine whether the agency's decision is "arbitrary, capricious, an abuse of discretion, or otherwise not in accordance with law." 5 U.S.C. § 706(2)(A) (2000). And, in the course of our review, "[w]e must give substantial deference to an agency's interpretation of its own regulations. Our task is not to decide which among several competing interpretations best serves the regulatory purpose. Rather, the agency's interpretation must be given controlling weight unless it is plainly erroneous or inconsistent with the regulation." *Thomas Jefferson Univ. v. Shalala,* 512 U.S. 504, 512 (1994) (inner quotations and citations omitted). Thus, "[w]e accord an agency's interpretation of its own regulations a 'high level of deference,' accepting it 'unless it is plainly wrong.' " *Gen. Elec. Co. v. EPA,* 53 F.3d 1324, 1327 (D.C. Cir. 1995) (quoting *Gen. Carbon Co. v. OSHRC,* 860 F.2d 479, 483 (D.C. Cir. 1988)).

B. The Requirement of a "Valid Foreign Export Permit"

Appellants challenge the decision by FWS and APHIS to detain the mahogany shipments as arbitrary and capricious, claiming that it rests on impermissible interpretations of 50 C.F.R. §§ 23.12(a) and 23.14(a). We find no merit in this challenge.

Section 23.12(a)(3)(i) provides:

> In order to import into the United States any wildlife or plant listed in appendix III from a foreign country that has listed such animal or plan in appendix III, a valid foreign export permit or re-export certificate issued by such country must be obtained prior to such importation.

50 C.F.R. § 23.12(a)(3)(i). APHIS detained the mahogany shipments at issue here, because, in its representations to FWS, "IBAMA indicated it had not determined whether the mahogany had been legally acquired, which is a prerequisite to the issuance of a CITES export permit for this species." This application of the regulation reflects the Government's position that a foreign export permit cannot be "valid" under CITES absent an assurance from the exporting country "that the specimen was not obtained in contravention of the laws of that State." *See* CITES, art. V(2)(a), 27 U.S.T. at 1097.

Appellants argue that the Government's interpretation of § 23.12(a)(3)(i) is at odds with the plain text of § 23.14(a), which states:

> Only export permits, re-export certificates, certificates of origin, or other certificates issued and signed by a management authority will be accepted as a valid foreign document from a country that is a party to the Convention.

50 C.F.R. § 23.14(a). * * *

Section 23.12(a)(3)(i) merely requires a *valid* foreign export permit, but it does not specify the conditions that a foreign export permit must meet in order for U.S. officials to regard the permit as valid, *i.e.,* to conclude that the exporting Management Authority was "satisfied that the specimen was not obtained in contravention of the laws of that State." CITES, art. V(2)(a), 27 U.S.T. at 1097. Section 23.14(a) requires that an export permit be issued and signed by the foreign Management Authority in order be accepted, but it does not say that these requirements are the only conditions that an agency may lawfully require before accepting a permit. Therefore, the language of the regulations is ambiguous as to whether U.S. officials may "look behind" a lawfully signed and issued export permit to determine whether the substantive requirements of CITES (*i.e.,* that the Management Authority was satisfied that the specimen was not obtained unlawfully) had actually been met.

* * * In light of these statutory and regulatory provisions, the Government acted reasonably in requiring more than facial satisfaction of § 23.14(a) when determining whether an export permit is "valid" (*i.e.,* issued in compliance with CITES) under § 23.12(a)(3)(i). The regulations were promulgated to implement the ESA, which was itself passed, in part, to implement the Convention. The ESA specifically prohibits trade contrary to the provisions of the Convention, 16 U.S.C. § 1538(c), and provides that any specimens that are imported in violation of the ESA are subject to forfeiture to the United States, 16 U.S.C. § 1540(e)(4)(A). The Convention requires that an export permit for an Appendix III species shall only be granted when "a Management Authority of the State of export is satisfied that the specimen was not obtained in contravention of the laws of that State for the protection of fauna and flora." CITES, art. V(2)(a), 27 U.S.T. at 1097.

Furthermore, Article XI provides for regular meetings of the Parties to the Convention, at which they may, *inter alia,* "make recommendations for improving the effectiveness of the present Convention." *Id.,* art. XI(3)(e), 27 U.S.T. at 1105. These recommendations, adopted through resolutions, are intended to give guidance to the Parties in implementing the Convention. Resolution 11.3 recommends that, "if an importing country has reason to believe that an Appendix ... III species is traded in contravention of the laws of any country involved in the transaction, it ... immediately inform the country whose laws were thought to have been violated." CITES Resolution 11.3 (2000). And Resolution 12.3 recommends that "the Parties refuse to accept any permit or certificate that is invalid, including authentic documents that do not contain all the required information ... or that contain information that brings into question the validity of the permit or certificate." CITES Resolution 12.3 § XIV(d) (2002) (repealing and incorporating CITES Resolution 10.2 § II(h) (1997)).

These provisions, taken together, make it clear that the agencies' interpretation of the applicable regulations is perfectly reasonable. It is also clear here that, to date, there are no "valid" export permits for the disputed shipments. There is no dispute that Brazil's Management Authority questioned whether the goods in the disputed shipments were obtained legally. The United States thus had a reasonable basis for inquiring further and detaining the shipments until a finding of legal acquisition could be made.

* * * We also reject appellants' argument that the decision by a Brazilian federal court in *Bianchini E Serafim LTDA v. IBAMA,* Writ of Mandamus No.2002.001437–0 (10th Fed. Dist. Ct. of Curitiba, June 28, 2002), J.A. 262–65 (trans. Berlitz GlobalNet, J.A. 253–61), compels reversal in this case. The decision in *Bianchini* has no bearing on the shipments at issue in this case.

The Government acknowledges that the United States will release detained shipments when judicial review in a foreign state concludes that the goods were legally obtained, regardless of whether the foreign Management Authority disagrees with the judicial decision. There is no serious dispute over this point. Indeed, the Government followed this precept in this case in response to the *Bianchini* decision.

The Brazilian federal district court's decision in *Bianchini* upheld a mandatory injunction directing IBAMA to issue an export permit for one exporter's shipment of bigleaf mahogany. * * * Following this decision, IBAMA informed FWS that, pursuant to that final judicial decision, "such wood was legally acquired and must be released." Although IBAMA had appealed the *Bianchini* decision, IBAMA declared that "such appeal must not uphold (impede) its accomplishment." APHIS then authorized the release of the shipment at issue in *Bianchini.*

However, *Bianchini* does not detract in any way from the reasonableness of APHIS's decision to detain other shipments for which no court or Management Authority has confirmed legal acquisition. * * *

It is undisputed that *Bianchini* involved a different shipment than those at issue here. In contrast to *Bianchini,* there was no final judicial disposition as to the legal acquisition of the wood in the shipments at issue in this case. For the shipments at issue here, the Brazilian court had issued *ex parte* orders requiring IBAMA to issue the export permits. These preliminary injunctions did not purport to find that the mahogany in the shipments at issue here was legally obtained. Therefore, APHIS reasonably detained the shipments for want of assurance, either from IBAMA or pursuant to judicial decree, that the wood in the disputed shipments was legally obtained. In the absence of a valid export permit for these shipments, the Government had the authority to detain them. * * *

NOTES

1. **Tracking This Case Through CITES.** What two countries are involved in this CITES dispute? Why does CITES apply to them? Which is the exporting country and which is the importing country? What species is involved? How was that species listed under CITES? What protections thus apply to that species?

2. **Standard of Review.** What standard of review does the D.C. Circuit use to review the Secretary of the Interior's actions in this case? Why?

3. **The CITES/ESA Violation.** What provision *of the ESA* did the importers allegedly violate in this case? What violation *of CITES* underlay that alleged ESA violation? Was any other violation of the ESA involved? Why or why not?

4. **The Factual Evidence of CITES Trade Violations.** The plaintiffs in this case had the documentation required under CITES for their shipment. Why did the Secretary of the Interior nevertheless believe that a violation of CITES might be in progress? What exchanges occurred between the two countries? What do these exchanges suggest about the implementation of CITES in the exporting country? Why didn't the *Bianchini* decision in the exporting country resolve any remaining factual disputes?

5. **The Plaintiffs' Arguments and the Secretary's Responses.** How did the plaintiffs argue that the Secretary of the Interior had to release the impounded shipments? Did they rely on domestic law or international law? What provisions, specifically, did they rely upon? How did the Secretary of the Interior respond? Did she rely on international law or domestic law? What provisions, specifically, did she rely upon?

6. **CITES Resolutions.** What are CITES Resolutions? What legal status do they have? What two resolutions were involved in this case? How did they influence the D.C. Circuit's decision? *Should* they have influenced the D.C. Circuit's decision? Why or why not?

7. **Other Views of CITES Permits.** The ability of customs officials to "look behind" a CITES permit at the underlying legality of the harvest/capture and export, as the D.C. Circuit did here, is a highly contested issue in CITES enforcement. The year before this case, for example, a court in the United Kingdom arguably came to the opposite conclusion in another case involving allegedly illegal shipments of mahogany from Brazil, holding that importing countries were not *required* to look behind the permits. *R (on the Application of Greenpeace) v. Secretary of State for the Environment, Food and Rural Affairs*, 2002 EWCA Civ. 1036 (July 25, 2003). Note, however, that the UK case raised the question of whether such investigation was *mandatory*, while the D.C. Circuit in *Castlewood* merely had to decide whether APHIS has the *discretion* to look behind the permit.

8. **Recent Implementation of CITES:** In January 2009, the U.S. government called public meetings to discuss CITES permitting in the United States for the harvest and export of American ginseng, which is listed in CITES Appendix II. *See* 74 Fed. Reg. 725 (Jan. 7, 2009). In addition, a recent proposal to downlist the Wood bison from endangered to threatened under the Endangered Species Act corresponded to a change in the species' CITES status, from Appendix I to Appendix II. 74 Fed. Reg. 5908, 5910 (Feb. 3, 2009).

* * *

2. Coordinating CITES, the ESA, and State Species Protections

CITES and the ESA potentially create two layers of protection for any given species. In addition, as was noted at the beginning of this chapter, in the ESA Congress actively sought to engage states within the United States in the protection of endangered and threatened species. The following case discusses how these various levels of species protection interact.

MAN HING IVORY AND IMPORTS, INC. v. DEUKMEJIAN

702 F.2d 760 (9th Cir. 1983).

FLETCHER, CIRCUIT JUDGE:

This case calls for a determination of the preemptive scope of the Convention on International Trade in Endangered Species of Wild Fauna and Flora, March 3, 1973, 27 U.S.T. 1087, T.I.A.S. No. 8249 (Convention), the Endangered Species Act of 1973, 16 U.S.C. §§ 1531–1543, and federal regulations enacted pursuant to the Endangered Species Act. Appellee Man Hing Ivory and Imports, Inc., is a wholesale importer of African elephant ivory products. In 1977, Man Hing filed suit in district court seeking a declaration that Cal. Penal Code § 653o (West Supp. 1981), which prohibits trade in elephant parts within the State of California, is preempted by the Convention and the Endangered Species Act.

* * * ANALYSIS

The facts in this case are not in dispute. Appellee wishes to conduct wholesale trade in African elephant ivory within the State of California. In 1970, the California legislature enacted Cal. Penal Code § 653o which currently provides that:

> (a) It is unlawful to import into this state for commercial purposes, to possess with intent to sell, or to sell within the state, the dead body, or any part or product thereof, of any alligator, crocodile, polar bear, leopard, ocelot, tiger, cheetah, jaguar, sable antelope, wolf (Canis lupus), zebra, whale, cobra, python, sea turtle, colobus monkey, kangaroo, vicuna, sea otter, free-roaming feral horse, dolphin or porpoise (Delphinidae), Spanish lynx, or elephant.
>
> Any person who violates any provision of this section is guilty of a misdemeanor and shall be subject to a fine of not less than one thousand dollars ($1,000) and not to exceed five thousand ($5,000) or imprisonment in the county jail for not to exceed six months, or both such fine and imprisonment, for each violation.

A 1976 amendment to the statute added elephants to the proscription of section 653o. *See* 1976 Cal. Stat. ch. 692, § 1. Absent any preempting federal law, section 653o would clearly prohibit the activities in which appellee wishes to engage.

A. Convention on International Trade in Endangered Species of Wild Fauna and Flora.

In 1975, President Ford proclaimed the United States' agreement to the Convention on International Trade in Endangered Species of Wild

Fauna and Flora. 27 U.S.T. at 1089. The purpose of this multilateral convention is to protect "certain species of wild fauna and flora against over-exploitation through international trade. . . ." *Id.* at 1090 (Preamble).

To accomplish this goal, the Convention lists animals in three categories. In the first are animals that all contracting countries agree are endangered; in the second are animals whose survival may be endangered; and in the third, animals that one country has identified as subject to protective regulation within its jurisdiction. The African elephant is listed in the second category. Trade in the parts or products of animals listed in this category is permitted so long as the trader obtains a trade permit from the country of the animal's origin. Man Hing argues that because it has the required permit, the California prohibition on trade in elephant products cannot be applied to it consistent with the obligations of the United States under the Convention.

Figure 3-15: African Elephant
Photo care of U.S. Department of State.

The district court rejected this argument because "[t]he Convention, standing alone, is in nowise the law of the United States. It is not self-executing. Legislation must be enacted if any of its provisions are to have the force of United States law." The district court may well be correct. We agree that "courts are empowered to give direct legal effect to treaties only insofar as they are self-executing and therefore operate as the law of the land." *Hopson v. Kreps,* 622 F.2d 1375, 1380 (9th Cir. 1980); *see Head Money Cases,* 112 U.S. 580, 598 (1884); *see also* L. HENKIN, FOREIGN AFFAIRS AND THE CONSTITUTION 156–67 (1972). But we need not decide if the Convention is itself self-executing, since the terms of section 1(a) of Article XIV of the Convention state that the provisions of the Convention shall in no way affect the right of parties to adopt stricter domestic measures regulating or even prohibiting the trade or transport of any part or derivative of certain species, including the African elephant. 27 U.S.T. at 1108. Thus, any rights to import African elephant products purportedly established under the Treaty are conditioned on the absence of prohibitory domestic measures. State laws are deemed domestic measures. *See* Convention, art. XIV, 27 U.S.T. at 1108–09; L. HENKIN, FOREIGN AFFAIRS AND THE CONSTITUTION 244–45 & nn. 63–64 at 479–80 (1972) (and cases cited therein). The Convention, therefore, cannot itself preempt California law.

B. The Endangered Species Act of 1973.

The Endangered Species Act of 1973 implements, *inter alia,* the International Convention on Trade in Endangered Species of Wild Fauna and Flora. *See* 16 U.S.C. §§ 1531(a)(4)(F), 1532(4), 1537a, 1538(c). The Act "represent[s] the most comprehensive legislation for the preservation of endangered species ever enacted by any nation. Its stated purposes [are] 'to provide a means whereby the ecosystems upon which endangered species and threatened species depend may be conserved,' and 'to provide a program for the conservation of such ... species....' " *TVA v. Hill,* 437 U.S. 153, 180 (1978) (quoting 16 U.S.C. § 1531(b) (1976)). Whether, as Man Hing argues, such extensive federal legislation preempts otherwise valid state law is a question of Congressional intent. * * *

Section 6(f) of the Endangered Species Act, while not explicitly prohibiting state regulation, does directly address the scope of federal preemption intended for the Endangered Species Act. The section provides:

> Any State law or regulation which applies with respect to the importation or exportation of, or interstate or foreign commerce in, endangered species or threatened species is void to the extent that it may effectively (1) permit what is prohibited by this chapter or by any regulation which implements this chapter, or (2) prohibit what is authorized pursuant to an exemption or permit provided for in this chapter or in any regulation which implements this chapter. This chapter shall not otherwise be construed to void any State law or regulation which is intended to conserve migratory, resident, or introduced fish or wildlife, or to permit or prohibit sale of such fish or wildlife. Any State law or regulation respecting the taking of an endangered species or threatened species may be more restrictive than the exemptions or permits provided for in this chapter or in any regulation which implements this chapter but not less restrictive than the prohibitions so defined.

16 U.S.C. § 1535(f) (1976). This general language, by its terms, does not forbid state statutes such as California Penal Code § 653o. Rather, it allows full implementation of section 653o so long as the state statute does not prohibit what the federal statute or its implementing regulations permit. The Act itself nowhere authorizes the importation or sale of African elephant products by permit or by exemption. Indeed, it prohibits the sale or import of endangered species unless such import or sale is

specifically authorized or exempted. 16 U.S.C. § 1538(a). Thus, only by reference to the federal regulations adopted to implement the Act may the precise scope of what the Act permits be determined. In fact, the legislative history of the Endangered Species Act unequivocally shows that Congress meant for federal law to preempt state law pursuant to the first sentence of section 6(f) only where the species was listed as endangered on the federal list and where the federal permission or ban related to interstate or foreign trade in, or exportation or importation of, that species:

> The question of preemption of state laws [regarding the taking of listed species] was of great interest during the hearings, due in part to the fact that the language in the Administration bill was susceptible of alternative interpretations. Accordingly, the Committee rewrote the language of the Administration bill to make it clear that the states would and should be free to adopt legislation or regulations that might be more restrictive than that of the Federal government and to enforce the legislation. *The only exception to this would be in cases where there was a specific Federal permission for or a ban on importation, exploitation or interstate commerce; in any such case the State could not override the Federal action.* In every other respect, the State powers to regulate in a more restrictive fashion or to include additional species remain unimpaired.

H.R. REP. NO. 412, 93d Cong., 1st Sess. 7–8 (1973) (emphasis added).

C. *Federal Regulation Under the Endangered Species Act of Trade in African Elephant Products.*

Section 4 of the Endangered Species Act, 16 U.S.C. § 1533 (1976), delegates to the Secretaries of Interior and Commerce the power to adopt specific regulations for implementation of the Act. In the exercise of this delegated authority, the Secretaries are empowered to compile a list of threatened or endangered species. *Id.* § 1533(c)(1). The Secretary of Interior is also authorized to adopt regulations for the protection of listed species, *id.* § 1533(d); the scope of such protective regulations may include prohibition of any of the proscribed activities set forth in section 9 of the Act, 16 U.S.C. § 1538.

Pursuant to these powers, the Secretary of the Interior, in May, 1978, added the African elephant to the list of threatened and endangered species. 43 Fed. Reg. 20,504 (1978). The ordinary effect of this listing would be to prohibit trade in African elephant parts or products. 50 C.F.R. § 1731(a) (1981); *see* 16 U.S.C. §§ 1533(d), 1538(a)(1)(A). By the terms of section 6(f) of the Act, such a result would be consistent with, and not preemptive of, Cal. Penal Code § 653o.

Contemporaneous with the listing of the African elephant, however, the Secretary adopted regulations permitting limited trade in elephant products. 50 C.F.R. § 17.40(e) (1981). These regulations provide:

> (e) African elephant (*Loxodona africana*).

(1) Except as provided in paragraph (e)(2) or (3) of this section, the prohibitions incorporated into § 17.31(a) shall apply to any African elephant, alive or dead, and to any part, product, or offspring thereof.

(2) The prohibition against importation referred to in paragraph (e)(1) of this section shall not apply to any such wildlife which:

(i) Has originated in the wild in a country that is a party to the Convention on International Trade in Endangered Species of Wild Fauna and Flora, March 3, 1973, TIAS No. 8249; and

(ii) Has been exported from such country of origin, and, in any case of reexportation has been reexported, in accordance with Article IV of such Convention: *Provided,* That: Neither compliance with Article VII, Paragraph 2 of such Convention nor compliance with Article VII, Paragraph 3 of such Convention shall constitute compliance with this paragraph (e)(2)(ii); and

(iii) Has remained in customs control and in an unaltered condition in any country not a party to such Convention that it enters while in transit to the United States.

(3) A special purpose permit may be issued in accordance with the provisions of § 17.32 authorizing any activity otherwise prohibited with regard to such wildlife, upon submission of proof that such wildlife was already in the United States on June 11, 1978 or that such wildlife was imported into the United States in accordance with paragraph (e)(2) of this section.

Id. Since no claim is raised here that the Secretary abused his discretion in adopting section 17.40(e) we assume as did the district court, that section 17.40(e) is indeed a "regulation which implements [the Act]" in the sense of section 6(f).

The district court determined that the effect of section 17.40(e) is to preempt operation of California Penal Code § 653o insofar as the state statute prohibits trade in elephant products by an authorized federal permittee. We agree. The pertinent language of section 6(f) states, "[a]ny state law . . . is void to the extent that it may effectively . . . (2) prohibit what is authorized pursuant to an exemption or permit provided for . . . in any regulation which implements this chapter." 16 U.S.C. § 1535(f) (1976). This language, together with the provisions of 50 C.F.R. § 17.40(e), preclude California's enforcement of section 653o where it would prohibit federally authorized trade in African elephant products. The state appellants do not seriously contend otherwise.

Appellants do, however, argue that one of the conditions of the federal permit alters the otherwise preemptive effect of the federal statute and regulation. Condition 11(B), printed on the front of the federal permit states:

> THE VALIDITY OF THIS PERMIT IS ALSO CONDITIONED UPON STRICT OBSERVANCE OF ALL APPLICABLE FOREIGN, STATE, AND OTHER FEDERAL LAW.

To appellant, this language means that the federal permit authorizing trade in elephant parts is void where such trade is prohibited by state law. Essentially, the state argues that this condition, together with the third sentence of section 6(f) of the Endangered Species Act (permitting state laws more restrictive than the federal statute), allows any state to nullify federally permitted trade in endangered species.

We find appellants' position intriguing but conclude that it ultimately cannot withstand scrutiny. Federal regulations provide that no federal permit for trade in endangered species, including an elephant permit issued pursuant to 50 C.F.R. § 17.40(e),

> shall be construed to relieve a person from any other requirements imposed by a statute or regulation of any state or the United States, including any applicable health, quarantine, agricultural, or customs laws or regulations, or other Service enforced statutes or regulations.

50 C.F.R. § 10.3 (1981). This general provision is the source of condition 11(B). The condition is a part of the printed form used for all federal fish and wildlife permits issued for trade in endangered species. Plainly, condition 11(B) is intended to do no more than implement the section 10.3 requirement that any trade under a federal permit meet state or federal health, quarantine, customs, and agricultural laws. To read the condition more broadly, as appellants would have us do, would open the way for states to impose regulation to supersede federal regulation of trade in imported endangered species or their export or interstate commerce, a form of state preemption clearly contrary to the intent of Congress in passing the Endangered Species Act.

Accordingly, we affirm the district court's well-considered judgment that section 6(f) of the Endangered Species Act, together with 50 C.F.R. § 17.40(e), preempts California's statutory prohibition on trade in African elephant products by a trader who has secured all necessary federal permits. * * *

NOTES

1. **Tracking the African Elephant Through CITES.** How is the African elephant listed for protection under CITES? To what protections does that listing entitle it? Specifically, does CITES prohibit trade in the African elephant and its parts, or does it allow such trade?

2. **Tracking the African Elephant Through the ESA.** Has the African elephant been listed for protection under the ESA? If so, to what

statutory protections would it ordinarily be entitled? How has the USFWS altered those statutory protections through its regulations? Why does the USFWS have authority to make such alterations for the African elephant? As a result of these regulations, does the ESA prohibit trade in the African elephant and its parts, or does it allow such trade?

3. **Tracking the African Elephant Through the California Penal Code.** How has California protected the African elephant? Does the California Penal Code prohibit trade in the African elephant and its parts, or does it allow such trade?

4. **Preemption of the California Penal Code.** As was noted at the beginning of this chapter, the Supremacy Clause of the U.S. Constitution provides that both treaties and federal statutes are the supreme law of the law. As a result, both sources of law can preempt state statutes. Does CITES preempt the California Penal Code with respect to the African elephant? Why or why not? What does CITES itself say about its relationship to domestic law, including state statutes?

Does the ESA preempt the California Penal Code with respect to African elephants? Why or why not? What does the ESA itself say about its relationship to state law? When is state law *not* preempted? If the USFWS had not enacted special regulations for the African elephant, would the California Penal Code have been preempted? Why or why not? Why do the regulations make a difference?

5. **Increased Protections for African Elephants.** African elephants are now included in CITES Appendix I, except for the populations of Botswana, Namibia, South Africa, and Zimbabwe, which are included in CITES Appendix II. Would that changed categorization for the elephant change the outcome of this case? Why or why not?

6. **Self-Executing Treaties.** California argued that CITES is not self-executing and hence could not preempt the California statute. What does it mean for a statute to be self-executing? Why would that status make a difference to its ability to preempt state law? What did the district court decide about whether CITES is self-executing? Do you agree? How did the Ninth Circuit resolve this issue?

7. **One-Way Preemption and Federal Environmental Law.** Notice that the ESA most emphatically preempts: (1) state law that actually contradicts federal law; and (2) state law that is less protective than federal law. As the Ninth Circuit notes, states like California remain free to more stringently protect species than the ESA does and to provide protections for species not listed under the federal ESA—so long as such state laws do not actually contradict the federal law, as was the case here. This "one-way" preemption—preemption of any state law that is less protective of the environment but allowance of more protective state laws—is typical of the federal environmental statutes and helps to promote a system of ***cooperative federalism***, which will be discussed in more detail in Chapters 4 and 5.

* * *

IV. OTHER INTERSECTIONS OF SPECIES PROTECTION, INTERNATIONAL LAW, AND INTERNATIONAL TRADE

A. INTRODUCTION TO THE GATT AND THE WTO

CITES is not the only international treaty that can affect international trade in species of concern. In 1947, the international community concluded negotiations on the ***General Agreement on Tariffs and Trade*** **(GATT)**, Oct. 30, 1947, 55 U.N.T.S. 187, T.I.A.S. No. 1700, which came into force on January 1, 1948. The GATT's objectives and methods have been described as follows:

> The objective of GATT is the progressive reduction of trade barriers among members to remove distortions in international markets and to ensure that goods and, more recently, services are not discriminated on the basis of their national origin. To understand the GATT and its progeny, one must recognize its underlying diplomatic objective: that increased trade ties will foster political ties and enhance international security. It was widely believed by the GATT's architects that the spiraling protectionism of the 1930s had directly contributed to the economic instability accompanying the rise of fascism. Just two years after the bloodiest war in human history, protectionist trade barriers represented far more than mere commercial preferences.
>
> The GATT's provisions are almost entirely negative; in order to liberalize trade they prescribe the scope of national regulatory discretion, rather than requiring governments to positively enact regulations. The "Most Favored Nation" (MFN) obligation seeks to prevent nations from discriminating between products from competing importing Member States (e.g., the United States cannot favor products from Uruguay over similar goods from Venezuela). The GATT, through the "National Treatment" obligation, also prevents nations from discriminating against Member States' imports in favor of domestic products (e.g., the United States cannot favor its products over "like" foreign products from Uruguay or Venezuela). It further requires the removal of a variety of restrictions that would limit the quantity of imports permitted.

DAVID HUNTER, JAMES SALZMAN, & DURWOOD ZAELKE, INTERNATIONAL ENVIRONMENTAL LAW AND POLICY 1147 (2d Ed. 2002).

Negotiations regarding and amendments to the GATT continued long after 1947. At the most recent "Uruguay Round" of negotiations, completed in December 1993, the parties laid the basis for what became the ***World Trade Organization*** **(WTO)**, which came into being on January 1, 1995. Parties to the ***Marrakesh Agreement Establishing the World Trade Organization***, April 15, 1994, 33 I.L.M. 1125 (1994) ("the WTO

Agreement"), agreed, through an "all or nothing" package agreement, to abide by:

- The original 1947 GATT, plus certain interim understandings and agreements, collectively referred to as the ***GATT 1994***;
- The Agreement on Agriculture;
- The Agreement on Application of Sanitary and Phytosanitary Measures (the ***SPS Agreement***);
- The Agreement on Textiles and Clothing;
- The Agreement on Technical Barriers to Trade (the ***TBT Agreement***);
- The Agreement on Trade–Related Investment Measures;
- The Agreement on Implementation of Article VI of the GATT 1994;
- The Agreement on Implementation of Article VII of the GATT 1994;
- The Agreement on Preshipment Inspection;
- The Agreement on Rules of Origin;
- The Agreement on Import Licensing Procedures;
- The Agreement on Subsidies and Counterveiling Measures;
- The Agreement on Safeguards;
- The General Agreement on Trade in Services;
- The Agreement on Trade–Related Aspects of Intellectual Property Rights (the ***TRIPS Agreement***);
- The Understanding on Rules and Procedures Governing the Settlement of Disputes;
- The Agreement on Government Procurement; and
- The International Bovine Meat Agreement.

The United States is a party to the Marrakesh Agreement and implements this package through the Uruguay Round Agreements Act, Pub. L. No. 103–465, 108 Stat. 4809 (Dec. 8, 1994).

B. THE GATT'S ENVIRONMENTAL PROVISIONS

The GATT, as noted, is primarily a trade agreement. Nevertheless, both the original 1947 GATT and the GATT 1994 address environmental issues in ***Article XX***:

Article XX

General exceptions

Subject to the requirement that such measures are not applied in a manner which would constitute a means of arbitrary or unjustifiable discrimination between countries where the same conditions prevail,

> or a disguised restriction on international trade, nothing in this Agreement shall be construed to prevent the adoption or enforcement by any contracting party of measures:
>
> * * * (b) necessary to protect human, animal or plant life or health;
>
> * * * (d) necessary to secure compliance with laws or regulations which are not inconsistent with the provisions of this Agreement * * *;
>
> * * * (g) relating to the conservation of exhaustible natural resources if such measures are made effective in conjunction with restrictions on domestic production or consumption * * *.

Moreover, the parties to the GATT 1994 issued the ***Decision on Trade and the Environment***, April 14, 1994, 33 I.L.M. 1267 (1994), because "there should not be, nor need be, any policy contradiction between upholding and safeguarding an open, non-discriminatory and equitable multilateral trading system on the one hand, and acting for the protection of the environment, and the promotion of sustainable development, on the other." 33 I.L.M. at 1267. The Decision directed the "General Council of the WTO to establish a Committee on Trade and Environment open to all members of the WTO," *id.* at 1268, with the Committee empowered to recommend rules "to enhance positive interaction between trade and environmental measures." *Id.*

C. THE ESA AND THE GATT: THE SHRIMP/TURTLE DISPUTE

Within the United States, "[a]ll sea turtles that occur in U.S. waters are listed as either endangered or threatened under the Endangered Species Act of 1973 ("ESA")," including the green (threatened or endangered, depending on location), hawksbill (endangered), Kemp's ridley (endangered), leatherback (endangered), and loggerhead (threatened) sea turtles. 61 Fed. Reg. 18,102, 18,102 (April 24, 1996). Trawling for shrimp can kill or injure sea turtles that get caught in the shrimp nets, particularly because the sea turtles—which are reptiles that need to breathe air at the surface—can drown. As a result, shrimp trawlers in U.S. waters risked violating the ESA's section 9 "take" prohibition every time they went fishing. Moreover, in a 1994 Biological Opinion issued pursuant to section 7 of the ESA, NMFS concluded "that the long-term operation of the shrimp fishery [in the Gulf of Mexico and southwestern Atlantic Ocean], resulting in mortality of Kemp's ridleys at levels observed in 1994, was likely to jeopardize the continued existence of the Kemp's ridley population and could prevent the recovery of the loggerhead population." 61 Fed. Reg. 18,102, 18,103 (April 24, 1996).

Figure 3-16: Loggerhead Turtle Escaping a Fishing Net through a Turtle Excluder Device (TED)
NOAA photo.

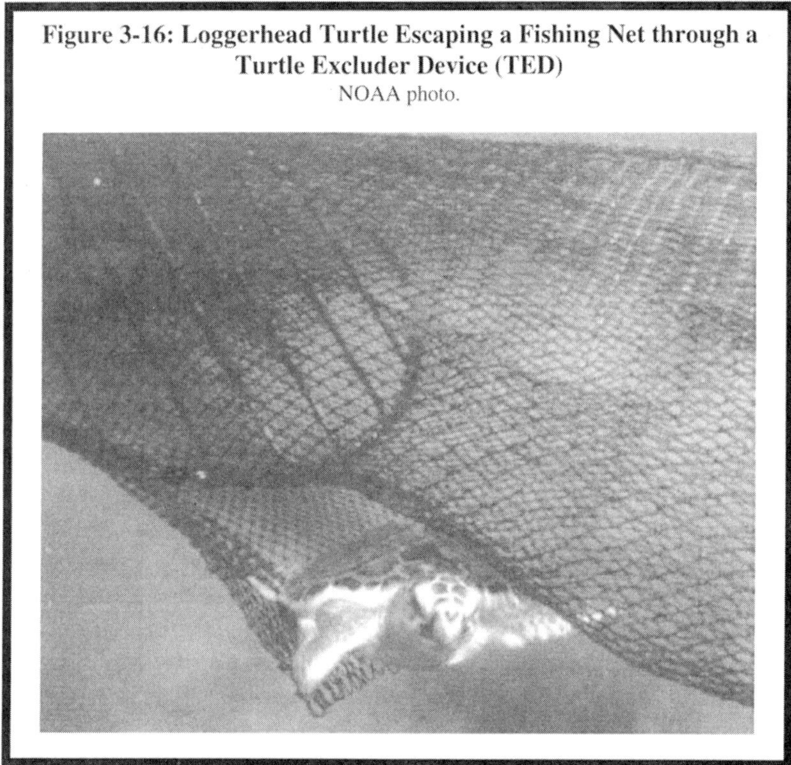

NMFS/NOAA Fisheries and the USFWS have been working to reduce sea turtle mortality from shrimp trawling since 1983. The primary technological means for reducing sea turtle drownings is the ***Turtle Excluder Device* (TED)**, which shrimp fishers attach to their trawling nets. The TEDs exclude the large sea turtles from the nets while allowing the much smaller shrimp to be caught. NMFS and NOAA created a voluntary TED program in 1983, in part to generate studies regarding the value of TEDs in preserving the listed sea turtles. In early 1987, NOAA and NMFS proposed the first mandatory TED rule for U.S. shrimp trawlers. 52 Fed. Reg. 6179 (March 2, 1987). Shrimp trawlers commenting on the rule complained about increased insurance rates and loss of fishing revenue, but NMFS concluded that the costs of installing the TEDs would be small compared to the total costs of shrimping. As a result, it promulgated a final, mandatory TED rule. 52 Fed. Reg. 24,244, 24,244 (June 29, 1987).

Undaunted, the shrimp trawlers appealed to Congress, which addressed the TED requirements in the Endangered Species Act Amendments of 1988, Pub. L. No. 100–478, 102 Stat. 2306 (Oct. 7, 1988). Specifically, the Amendments delayed the effective date of NMFS's 1987 TED regulations until May 1, 1990, for inshore areas and until May 1, 1989, for offshore areas, to allow for an independent review of the TEDs' efficacy. *Id.* § 1008(a). In addition, "[t]he Secretary [of Commerce] shall undertake an educational effort among shrimp fishermen, either directly or by contract with competent persons or entities, to instruct fishermen in the usage of the turtle excluder device or any other device which might be imposed upon such fishermen * * *." *Id.* § 1008(b)(8).

Congress acted again in November 1989, this time involving the Secretary of State in sea turtle protections. Specifically, in section 609 of Public Law No. 101–162, 103 Stat. 988 (November 21, 1989), Congress ordered the Secretary of State, "with respect to those species of sea turtles the conservation of which is the subject of regulations promulgated by the Secretary of Commerce [acting through NOAA and NMFS] on June 29, 1987," to negotiate agreements with other countries to protect sea turtles and to report to Congress within one year on commercial shrimp fishing operations in other countries and the effects of those fisheries on sea turtles. *Id.* § 609(a).

In addition, Congress established that "[t]he importation of shrimp or products from shrimp which have been harvested with commercial fishing technology which may affect adversely such species of sea turtles shall be prohibited not later than May 1, 1991," unless countries exporting shrimp to the United States complied with the section 609 certification procedure. *Id.* § 609(b)(1). This procedure allowed the President to certify shrimp and shrimp products for importation into the United States if:

(A) the government of the harvesting nation has provided documentary evidence of the adoption of a regulatory program governing the incidental taking of such sea turtles in the course of such harvesting that is comparable to the United States; and

(B) the average rate of that incidental taking by vessels of the harvesting nation is comparable to the average rate of incidental taking of sea turtles by United States vessels in the course of such harvesting; or

(C) the particular fishing environment of the harvesting nation does not pose a threat of the incidental taking of such sea turtles in the course of such harvesting.

Id. § 609(b)(2). In December 1990, President George H.W. Bush delegated his certification authority under section 609 to the Secretary of State. 56 Fed. Reg. 357 (Dec. 19, 1990).

Cognizant of the fact that section 609 was likely to create trade issues, including potential violations of the GATT, the Secretary of State issued initial guidelines to implement section 609 that limited section 609's applicability to nations in the wider Caribbean region, reasoning that "[i]n passing section 609, Congress recognized that these conservation measures taken by U.S. shrimp fishermen would be of limited effectiveness unless a similar level of protection is afforded throughout the turtles' migratory range across the Gulf of Mexico, Caribbean, and western Atlantic Ocean." 56 Fed. Reg. 1051 (Jan. 10, 1991). Moreover, the guidelines excluded aquacultured shrimp from the import ban and provided that a harvesting country's regulatory programs would be deemed comparable to the United States' if the country provided for use of TEDs by its shrimp trawlers, phased in over three years.

In February 1993, the Secretary of State revised the Guidelines to require TEDs on all commercial shrimp trawlers by May 1, 1994, keeping the section 609 comparability requirements parallel with NOAA's and NMFS's requirements for U.S. shrimp trawlers. 58 Fed. Reg. 9015 (Feb. 18, 1993). However, the Secretary continued to limit section 609's applicability to the wider Caribbean region.

Almost immediately, the Earth Island Institute challenged the Secretary's application of section 609, arguing that section 609 applied to *all* nations harvesting shrimp, not just those in the Caribbean. Earth Island initially filed suit in the U.S. District Court for the Northern District of California, only to have the district court and the Ninth Circuit determine that exclusive jurisdiction lay in the U.S. Court of International Trade. *See Earth Island Institute v. Christopher*, 6 F.3d 648, 650–52 (9th Cir. 1993) (relying on 28 U.S.C. § 1581(i)(3), (4)). The Ninth Circuit also invalidated section 609(a), concluding that Congress had violated principles of separation of powers by ordering the Secretary of State to engage in foreign affairs. *Id.* at 652–54.

Earth Island refiled its lawsuit in the Court of International Trade, which, relying on both *TVA v. Hill* and *Babbitt v. Sweet Home Chapter of Communities for a Great Oregon*, decided in 1995 that section 609 applies to *all* foreign governments. *Earth Island Institute v. Christopher*, 913 F. Supp. 559, 575–79 (CIT 1995). The court recognized the potential conflict with the GATT, *id.* at 579, but it nevertheless directed the Secretary of State "to prohibit not later than May 1, 1996 the importation of shrimp or products of shrimp wherever harvested in the wild with commercial fishing technology which may affect adversely those species of sea turtles the conservation of which is the subject of regulations promulgated by the Secretary of Commerce on June 29, 1987 * * *." *Id.* at 580. The court later denied the Secretary's request for a one-year enforcement delay. *Earth Island Institute v. Christopher*, 922 F. Supp. 616 (CIT 1996).

As expected, other shrimp harvesting nations protested the United States' full implementation of section 609. In particular, on October 8, 1996, India, Malaysia, Pakistan, and Thailand, relying on the WTO Agreement's Understanding on Rules and Procedures Governing the Settlement of Disputes, requested consultations with the United States regarding the section 609 import ban. Unsatisfied with those negotiations, in January 1997 Malaysia, Thailand, and Pakistan requested the WTO's Dispute Settlement Body to establish a dispute resolution panel to evaluate their claims that the United States was violating the GATT 1994. The WTO Panel issued its findings on May 15, 1998, concluding that the United States, in implementing section 609, had violated Article XI:1 of the GATT 1994 by imposing a prohibition or restriction on the importation of shrimp. Report of the WTO Panel, *United States–Import Prohibition of Certain Shrimp and Shrimp Products*, WT/DS58/R, at ¶ 7.17. More disturbing to the United States—which had virtually admitted this violation—was the Panel's finding that the United States could not justify section 609 under Article XX. The Panel found that "the chapeau [introductory provisions of] Article XX, interpreted within its context and in light of the object and purpose of GATT and of the WTO Agreement, only allows Members to derogate from GATT provisions so long as, in doing so, they do not undermine the WTO multilateral trading system, thus also abusing the exceptions contained in Article XX." *Id.* ¶ 7.44. Pursuant to this interpretation, it concluded that section 609 "constitutes unjustifiable discrimination between countries where the same conditions prevail," *id.* ¶ 7.49, particularly because the United States was taking unilateral action to protect sea turtles without negotiating with other countries. *Id.* ¶ 7.61.

The United States appealed this decision to the WTO's Appellate Body, resulting in the decision below.

UNITED STATES—IMPORT PROHIBITION OF CERTAIN SHRIMP AND SHRIMP PRODUCTS

Report of the Appellate Body
World Trade Organization
WT/DS58/AB/R
(October 12, 1998).

I. INTRODUCTION: STATEMENT OF THE APPEAL

1. This is an appeal by the United States from certain issues of law and legal interpretations in the Panel Report, *United States–Import Prohibition of Certain Shrimp and Shrimp Products*. * * *

2. * * * The United States issued regulations in 1987 pursuant to the Endangered Species Act of 1973 requiring all United States shrimp trawl vessels to use approved Turtle Excluder Devices ("TEDs") or tow-time restrictions in specified areas where there was a significant mortality of sea turtles in shrimp harvesting. These regulations, which became fully effective in 1990, were modified so as to require the use of approved TEDs at all times and in all areas where there is a likelihood that shrimp trawling will interact with sea turtles, with certain limited exceptions.

* * * 5. The 1996 Guidelines provide that all shrimp imported into the United States must be accompanied by a Shrimp Exporter's Declaration form attesting that the shrimp was harvested either in the waters of a nation currently certified under Section 609 or "under conditions that do not adversely affect sea turtles", that is: (a) "Shrimp harvested in an aquaculture facility in which the shrimp spend at least 30 days in ponds prior to being harvested"; (b) "Shrimp harvested by commercial shrimp trawl vessels using TEDs comparable in effectiveness to those required in the United States"; (c) "Shrimp harvested exclusively by means that do not involve the retrieval of fishing nets by mechanical devices or by vessels using gear that, in accordance with the U.S. program ... , would not require TEDs"; and (d) "Species of shrimp, such as the pandalid species, harvested in areas where sea turtles do not occur." On 8 October 1996,

the United States Court of International Trade ruled that the 1996 Guidelines were in violation of Section 609 in allowing the import of shrimp from non-certified countries if accompanied by a Shrimp Exporter's Declaration form attesting that they were caught with commercial fishing technology that did not adversely affect sea turtles. A 25 November 1996 ruling of the United States Court of International Trade clarified that shrimp harvested by manual methods which did not harm sea turtles could still be imported from non-certified countries. On 4 June 1998, the United States Court of Appeals for the Federal Circuit vacated the decisions of the United States Court of International Trade of 8 October and 25 November 1996. In practice, however, exemption from the import ban for TED-caught shrimp from non-certified countries remained unavailable while this dispute was before the Panel and before us.

6. The 1991 Guidelines limited the geographical scope of the import ban imposed by Section 609 to countries in the wider Caribbean/western Atlantic region, and granted these countries a three-year phase-in period. The 1993 Guidelines maintained this geographical limitation. On 29 December 1995, the United States Court of International Trade held that the 1991 and 1993 Guidelines violated Section 609 by limiting its geographical scope to shrimp harvested in the wider Caribbean/western Atlantic region, and directed the Department of State to extend the ban worldwide not later than 1 May 1996. On 10 April 1996, the United States Court of International Trade refused a subsequent request by the Department of State to postpone the 1 May 1996 deadline. On 19 April 1996, the United States issued the 1996 Guidelines, extending Section 609 to shrimp harvested in *all* foreign countries effective 1 May 1996.

* * * IV. ISSUES RAISED IN THIS APPEAL

79. The issues raised in this appeal by the appellant, the United States, are the following:

> * * *(b) whether the Panel erred in finding that the measure at issue constitutes unjustifiable discrimination between countries where the same conditions prevail and thus is not within the scope of measures permitted under Article XX of the GATT 1994.

* * * VI. APPRAISING SECTION 609 UNDER ARTICLE XX OF THE GATT 1994

92. We turn to the second issue raised by the appellant, the United States, which is whether the Panel erred in finding that the measure at issue constitutes unjustifiable discrimination between countries where the same conditions prevail and, thus, is not within the scope of measures permitted under Article XX of the GATT 1994.

A. The Panel's Findings and Interpretative Analysis

* * * 94. Article XX of the GATT 1994 reads, in its relevant parts:

Article XX
General Exceptions

Subject to the requirement that such measures are not applied in a manner which would constitute a means of arbitrary or unjustifiable discrimination between countries where the same conditions prevail, or a disguised restriction on international trade, nothing in this Agreement shall be construed to prevent the adoption or enforcement by any Member of measures:

. . .

(*b*) necessary to protect human, animal or plant life or health;

. . .

(*g*) relating to the conservation of exhaustible natural resources if such measures are made effective in conjunction with restrictions on domestic production or consumption;

95. The Panel did not follow all of the steps of applying the "customary rules of interpretation of public international law" as required by Article 3.2 of the DSU. As we have emphasized numerous times, these rules call for an examination of the ordinary meaning of the words of a treaty, read in their context, and in the light of the object and purpose of the treaty involved. A treaty interpreter must begin with, and focus upon, the text of the particular provision to be interpreted. It is in the words constituting that provision, read in their context, that the object and purpose of the states parties to the treaty must first be sought. Where the meaning imparted by the text itself is equivocal or inconclusive, or where confirmation of the correctness of the reading of the text itself is desired, light from the object and purpose of the treaty as a whole may usefully be sought.

* * * 99. In *United States—Gasoline*, we enunciated the appropriate method for applying Article XX of the GATT 1994:

> In order that the justifying protection of Article XX may be extended to it, the measure at issue must not only come under one or another of the particular exceptions—paragraphs (a) to (j)—listed under Article XX; it must also satisfy the requirements imposed by the opening clauses of Article XX. *The analysis is*, in other words, *two-tiered: first, provisional justification by reason of characterization of the measure under XX(g); second, further appraisal of the same measure under the introductory clauses of Article XX.* (emphasis added) * * *

* * * *B. Article XX(g): Provisional Justification of Section 609*

106. In claiming justification for its measure, the United States primarily invokes Article XX(g). * * *

107. Paragraph (g) of Article XX covers measures:

relating to the conservation of exhaustible natural resources if such measures are made effective in conjunction with restrictions on domestic production or consumption;

"Exhaustible Natural Resources"

108. We begin with the threshold question of whether Section 609 is a measure concerned with the conservation of "exhaustible natural resources" within the meaning of Article XX(g). * * * India, Pakistan and Thailand contended that a "reasonable interpretation" of the term "exhaustible" is that the term refers to "finite resources such as minerals, rather than biological or renewable resources." In their view, such finite resources were exhaustible "because there was a limited supply which could and would be depleted unit for unit as the resources were consumed." * * *

109. We are not convinced by these arguments. Textually, Article XX(g) is *not* limited to the conservation of "mineral" or "non-living" natural resources. The complainants' principal argument is rooted in the notion that "living" natural resources are "renewable" and therefore cannot be "exhaustible" natural resources. We do not believe that "exhaustible" natural resources and "renewable" natural resources are mutually exclusive. One lesson that modern biological sciences teach us is that living species, though in principle, capable of reproduction and, in that sense, "renewable", are in certain circumstances indeed susceptible of depletion, exhaustion and extinction, frequently because of human activities. Living resources are just as "finite" as petroleum, iron ore and other non-living resources.

110. The words of Article XX(g), "exhaustible natural resources", were actually crafted more than 50 years ago. They must be read by a treaty interpreter in the light of contemporary concerns of the community of nations about the protection and conservation of the environment. While Article XX was not modified in the Uruguay Round, the preamble attached to the *WTO Agreement* shows that the signatories to that Agreement were, in 1994, fully aware of the importance and legitimacy of environmental protection as a goal of national and international policy. The preamble of the *WTO Agreement*—which informs not only the GATT 1994, but also the other covered agreements—explicitly acknowledges "the objective of *sustainable development*" * * *.

* * * 112. Given the recent acknowledgement by the international community of the importance of concerted bilateral or multilateral action to protect living natural resources, and recalling the explicit recognition by WTO Members of the objective of sustainable development in the preamble of the *WTO Agreement*, we believe it is too late in the day to suppose that Article XX(g) of the GATT 1994 may be read as referring only to the conservation of exhaustible mineral or other non-living natural resources. Moreover, two adopted GATT 1947 panel reports previously found fish to be an "exhaustible natural resource" within the meaning of Article XX(g). We hold that, in line with the principle of effectiveness in

treaty interpretation, measures to conserve exhaustible natural resources, whether *living* or *non-living*, may fall within Article XX(g).

113. We turn next to the issue of whether the living natural resources sought to be conserved by the measure are "exhaustible" under Article XX(g). That this element is present in respect of the five species of sea turtles here involved appears to be conceded by all the participants and third participants in this case. The exhaustibility of sea turtles would in fact have been very difficult to controvert since all of the seven recognized species of sea turtles are today listed in Appendix 1 of the Convention on International Trade in Endangered Species of Wild Fauna and Flora ("CITES"). The list in Appendix 1 includes "all species *threatened with extinction* which are or may be affected by trade." (emphasis added)

* * *115. For all the foregoing reasons, we find that the sea turtles here involved constitute "exhaustible natural resources" for purposes of Article XX(g) of the GATT 1994.

"Relating to the Conservation of [Exhaustible Natural Resources]"

116. Article XX(g) requires that the measure sought to be justified be one which "relat[es] to" the conservation of exhaustible natural resources. In making this determination, the treaty interpreter essentially looks into the relationship between the measure at stake and the legitimate policy of conserving exhaustible natural resources. It is well to bear in mind that the policy of protecting and conserving the endangered sea turtles here involved is shared by all participants and third participants in this appeal, indeed, by the vast majority of the nations of the world. None of the parties to this dispute question the genuineness of the commitment of the others to that policy.

* * *118. In the present case, we must examine the relationship between the general structure and design of the measure here at stake, Section 609, and the policy goal it purports to serve, that is, the conservation of sea turtles.

119. Section 609(b)(1) imposes an import ban on shrimp that have been harvested with commercial fishing technology which may adversely affect sea turtles. This provision is designed to influence countries to adopt national regulatory programs requiring the use of TEDs by their shrimp fishermen. In this connection, it is important to note that the general structure and design of Section 609 *cum* implementing guidelines is fairly narrowly focused. There are two basic exemptions from the import ban, both of which relate clearly and directly to the policy goal of conserving sea turtles. First, Section 609, as elaborated in the 1996 Guidelines, excludes from the import ban shrimp harvested "under conditions that do not adversely affect sea turtles". Thus, the measure, by its terms, excludes from the import ban: aquaculture shrimp; shrimp species (such as *pandalid* shrimp) harvested in water areas where sea turtles do not normally occur; and shrimp harvested exclusively by artisanal meth-

ods, even from non-certified countries. The harvesting of such shrimp clearly does not affect sea turtles. Second, under Section 609(b)(2), the measure exempts from the import ban shrimp caught in waters subject to the jurisdiction of certified countries.

120. There are two types of certification for countries under Section 609(b)(2). First, under Section 609(b)(2)(C), a country may be certified as having a fishing environment that does not pose a threat of incidental taking of sea turtles in the course of commercial shrimp trawl harvesting. There is no risk, or only a negligible risk, that sea turtles will be harmed by shrimp trawling in such an environment.

121. The second type of certification is provided by Section 609(b)(2)(A) and (B). Under these provisions, as further elaborated in the 1996 Guidelines, a country wishing to export shrimp to the United States is required to adopt a regulatory program that is comparable to that of the United States program and to have a rate of incidental take of sea turtles that is comparable to the average rate of United States' vessels. This is, essentially, a requirement that a country adopt a regulatory program requiring the use of TEDs by commercial shrimp trawling vessels in areas where there is a likelihood of intercepting sea turtles. This requirement is, in our view, directly connected with the policy of conservation of sea turtles. It is undisputed among the participants, and recognized by the experts consulted by the Panel, that the harvesting of shrimp by commercial shrimp trawling vessels with mechanical retrieval devices in waters where shrimp and sea turtles coincide is a significant cause of sea turtle mortality. Moreover, the Panel did "not question ... the fact generally acknowledged by the experts that TEDs, when properly installed and adapted to the local area, would be an effective tool for the preservation of sea turtles."

122. In its general design and structure, therefore, Section 609 is not a simple, blanket prohibition of the importation of shrimp imposed without regard to the consequences (or lack thereof) of the mode of harvesting employed upon the incidental capture and mortality of sea turtles. Focusing on the design of the measure here at stake, it appears to us that Section 609, *cum* implementing guidelines, is not disproportionately wide in its scope and reach in relation to the policy objective of protection and conservation of sea turtle species. The means are, in principle, reasonably related to the ends. The means and ends relationship between Section 609 and the legitimate policy of conserving an exhaustible, and, in fact, endangered species, is observably a close and real one * * *.

123. In our view, therefore, Section 609 is a measure "relating to" the conservation of an exhaustible natural resource within the meaning of Article XX(g) of the GATT 1994.

"If Such Measures are Made Effective in conjunction with Restrictions on Domestic Production or Consumption"

124. In *United States–Gasoline*, we held that the above-captioned clause of Article XX(g),

> ... is appropriately read as a requirement that the measures concerned impose restrictions, not just in respect of imported gasoline but also with respect to domestic gasoline. The clause is a requirement of *even-handedness* in the imposition of restrictions, in the name of conservation, upon the production or consumption of exhaustible natural resources.

In this case, we need to examine whether the restrictions imposed by Section 609 with respect to imported shrimp are also imposed in respect of shrimp caught by United States shrimp trawl vessels.

125. We earlier noted that Section 609, enacted in 1989, addresses the mode of harvesting of imported shrimp only. However, two years earlier, in 1987, the United States issued regulations pursuant to the Endangered Species Act requiring all United States shrimp trawl vessels to use approved TEDs, or to restrict the duration of tow-times, in specified areas where there was significant incidental mortality of sea turtles in shrimp trawls. These regulations became fully effective in 1990 and were later modified. They now require United States shrimp trawlers to use approved TEDs "in areas and at times when there is a likelihood of intercepting sea turtles", with certain limited exceptions. Penalties for violation of the Endangered Species Act, or the regulations issued thereunder, include civil and criminal sanctions. The United States government currently relies on monetary sanctions and civil penalties for enforcement. The government has the ability to seize shrimp catch from trawl vessels fishing in United States waters and has done so in cases of egregious violations. We believe that, in principle, Section 609 is an even-handed measure.

126. Accordingly, we hold that Section 609 is a measure made effective in conjunction with the restrictions on domestic harvesting of shrimp, as required by Article XX(g).

C. The Introductory Clauses of Article XX: Characterizing Section 609 under the Chapeau's Standards

127. As noted earlier, the United States invokes Article XX(b) only if and to the extent that we hold that Section 609 falls outside the scope of Article XX(g). Having found that Section 609 does come within the terms of Article XX(g), it is not, therefore, necessary to analyze the measure in terms of Article XX(b).

128. Although provisionally justified under Article XX(g), Section 609, if it is ultimately to be justified as an exception under Article XX, must also satisfy the requirements of the introductory clauses—the "chapeau"—of Article XX, that is,

> Article XX
> *General Exceptions*
>
> Subject to the requirement that such measures are *not applied in a manner which would constitute a means of arbitrary or unjustifiable*

> *discrimination between countries where the same conditions prevail*, or *a disguised restriction on international trade*, nothing in this Agreement shall be construed to prevent the adoption or enforcement by any Member of measures: (emphasis added)

We turn, hence, to the task of appraising Section 609, and specifically the manner in which it is applied under the chapeau of Article XX; that is, to the second part of the two-tier analysis required under Article XX.

1. General Considerations

* * *131. We commence the second tier of our analysis with an examination of the ordinary meaning of the words of the chapeau. The precise language of the chapeau requires that a measure not be applied in a manner which would constitute a means of "arbitrary or unjustifiable discrimination between countries where the same conditions prevail" or a "disguised restriction on international trade." There are three standards contained in the chapeau: first, arbitrary discrimination between countries where the same conditions prevail; second, unjustifiable discrimination between countries where the same conditions prevail; and third, a disguised restriction on international trade. In order for a measure to be applied in a manner which would constitute "arbitrary or unjustifiable discrimination between countries where the same conditions prevail", three elements must exist. First, the application of the measure must result in *discrimination*. * * * Second, the discrimination must be *arbitrary* or *unjustifiable* in character. We will examine this element of *arbitrariness* or *unjustifiability* in detail below. Third, this discrimination must occur *between countries where the same conditions prevail*. * * * Thus, the standards embodied in the language of the chapeau are not only different from the requirements of Article XX(g); they are also different from the standard used in determining that Section 609 is violative of the substantive rules of Article XI:1 of the GATT 1994.

* * *134. We note once more that [language in the WTO Agreement's Preamble] demonstrates a recognition by WTO negotiators that optimal use of the world's resources should be made in accordance with the objective of sustainable development. As this preambular language reflects the intentions of negotiators of the *WTO Agreement*, we believe it must add colour, texture and shading to our interpretation of the agreements annexed to the *WTO Agreement*, in this case, the GATT 1994. We have already observed that Article XX(g) of the GATT 1994 is appropriately read with the perspective embodied in the above preamble.

135. We also note that since this preambular language was negotiated, certain other developments have occurred which help to elucidate the objectives of WTO Members with respect to the relationship between trade and the environment. The most significant, in our view, was the Decision of Ministers at Marrakesh to establish a permanent Committee on Trade and Environment (the "CTE"). In their Decision on Trade and Environment, Ministers expressed their intentions, in part, as follows:

> . . . *Considering* that there should not be, nor need be, any policy contradiction between upholding and safeguarding an open, non-discriminatory and equitable multilateral trading system on the one hand, and acting for the protection of the environment, and the promotion of sustainable development on the other, . . .

In this Decision, Ministers took "note" of the Rio Declaration on Environment and Development, Agenda 21, and "its follow-up in the GATT, as reflected in the statement of the Council of Representatives to the CONTRACTING PARTIES at their 48th Session in 1992 . . . ." * * *

* * * 138. In our view, the language of the chapeau makes clear that each of the exceptions in paragraphs (a) to (j) of Article XX is a *limited and conditional* exception from the substantive obligations contained in the other provisions of the GATT 1994, that is to say, the ultimate availability of the exception is subject to the compliance by the invoking Member with the requirements of the chapeau. This interpretation of the chapeau is confirmed by its negotiating history. The language initially proposed by the United States in 1946 for the chapeau of what would later become Article XX was unqualified and unconditional. Several proposals were made during the First Session of the Preparatory Committee of the United Nations Conference on Trade and Employment in 1946 suggesting modifications. In November 1946, the United Kingdom proposed that "in order to prevent abuse of the exceptions of Article 32 [which would subsequently become Article XX]", the chapeau of this provision should be qualified. This proposal was generally accepted, subject to later review of its precise wording. Thus, the negotiating history of Article XX confirms that the paragraphs of Article XX set forth *limited and conditional* exceptions from the obligations of the substantive provisions of the GATT. Any measure, to qualify finally for exception, must also satisfy the requirements of the chapeau. This is a fundamental part of the balance of rights and obligations struck by the original framers of the GATT 1947.

139. The chapeau of Article XX is, in fact, but one expression of the principle of good faith. This principle, at once a general principle of law and a general principle of international law, controls the exercise of rights by states. One application of this general principle, the application widely known as the doctrine of *abus de droit*, prohibits the abusive exercise of a state's rights and enjoins that whenever the assertion of a right "impinges on the field covered by [a] treaty obligation, it must be exercised bona fide, that is to say, reasonably." * * *

* * *141. With these general considerations in mind, we address now the issue of whether the *application* of the United States measure, although the measure itself falls within the terms of Article XX(g), nevertheless constitutes "a means of arbitrary or unjustifiable discrimination between countries where the same conditions prevail" or "a disguised restriction on international trade". We address, in other words, whether the application of this measure constitutes an abuse or misuse of the provisional justification made available by Article XX(g). * * *

2. *"Unjustifiable Discrimination"*

142. We scrutinize first whether Section 609 has been applied in a manner constituting "unjustifiable discrimination between countries where the same conditions prevail". Perhaps the most conspicuous flaw in this measure's application relates to its intended and actual coercive effect on the specific policy decisions made by foreign governments, Members of the WTO. Section 609, in its application, is, in effect, an economic embargo which requires *all other exporting Members*, if they wish to exercise their GATT rights, to adopt *essentially the same* policy (together with an approved enforcement program) as that applied to, and enforced on, United States domestic shrimp trawlers. * * * [A]ny flexibility that may have been intended by Congress when it enacted the statutory provision has been effectively eliminated in the implementation of that policy through the 1996 Guidelines promulgated by the Department of State and through the practice of the administrators in making certification determinations.

* * *144. The actual *application* of the measure, through the implementation of the 1996 Guidelines and the regulatory practice of administrators, *requires* other WTO Members to adopt a regulatory program that is not merely *comparable*, but rather *essentially the same*, as that applied to the United States shrimp trawl vessels. Thus, the effect of the application of Section 609 is to establish a rigid and unbending standard by which United States officials determine whether or not countries will be certified, thus granting or refusing other countries the right to export shrimp to the United States. Other specific policies and measures that an exporting country may have adopted for the protection and conservation of sea turtles are not taken into account, in practice, by the administrators making the comparability determination.

* * * 146. Furthermore, when this dispute was before the Panel and before us, the United States did not permit imports of shrimp harvested by commercial shrimp trawl vessels using TEDs comparable in effectiveness to those required in the United States if those shrimp originated in waters of countries not certified under Section 609. In other words, *shrimp caught using methods identical to those employed in the United States* have been excluded from the United States market solely because they have been caught in waters of *countries that have not been certified by the United States*. The resulting situation is difficult to reconcile with the declared policy objective of protecting and conserving sea turtles. This suggests to us that this measure, in its application, is more concerned with effectively influencing WTO Members to adopt essentially the same comprehensive regulatory regime as that applied by the United States to its domestic shrimp trawlers, even though many of those Members may be differently situated. We believe that discrimination results not only when countries in which the same conditions prevail are differently treated, but also when the application of the measure at issue does not allow for any inquiry into the appropriateness of the regulatory program for the conditions prevailing in those exporting countries.

147. Another aspect of the application of Section 609 that bears heavily in any appraisal of justifiable or unjustifiable discrimination is the failure of the United States to engage the appellees, as well as other Members exporting shrimp to the United States, in serious, across-the-board negotiations with the objective of concluding bilateral or multilateral agreements for the protection and conservation of sea turtles, before enforcing the import prohibition against the shrimp exports of those other Members. * * *

* * * 149. Second, the protection and conservation of highly migratory species of sea turtles, that is, the very policy objective of the measure, demands concerted and cooperative efforts on the part of the many countries whose waters are traversed in the course of recurrent sea turtle migrations. The need for, and the appropriateness of, such efforts have been recognized in the WTO itself as well as in a significant number of other international instruments and declarations[, including Agenda 21, the Convention on Biological Diversity, and the Convention on the Conservation of Migratory Species of Wild Animals.] * * *

150. Third, the United States did negotiate and conclude one regional international agreement for the protection and conservation of sea turtles: The Inter–American Convention. * * *

151. * * * The Inter–American Convention demonstrates the conviction of its signatories, including the United States, that consensual and multilateral procedures are available and feasible for the establishment of programs for the conservation of sea turtles. Moreover, the Inter–American Convention emphasizes the continuing validity and significance of Article XI of the GATT 1994, and of the obligations of the *WTO Agreement* generally, in maintaining the balance of rights and obligations under the *WTO Agreement* among the signatories of that Convention.

152. The Inter–American Convention thus provides convincing demonstration that an alternative course of action was reasonably open to the United States for securing the legitimate policy goal of its measure, a course of action other than the unilateral and non-consensual procedures of the import prohibition under Section 609. * * *

153. Clearly, the United States negotiated seriously with some, but not with other Members (including the appellees), that export shrimp to the United States. The effect is plainly discriminatory and, in our view, unjustifiable. * * * The unilateral character of the application of Section 609 heightens the disruptive and discriminatory influence of the import prohibition and underscores its unjustifiability.

154. The application of Section 609, through the implementing guidelines together with administrative practice, also resulted in other differential treatment among various countries desiring certification. Under the 1991 and 1993 Guidelines, to be certifiable, fourteen countries in the wider Caribbean/western Atlantic region had to commit themselves to require the use of TEDs on all commercial shrimp trawling vessels by 1 May 1994. These fourteen countries had a "phase-in" period of three

years during which their respective shrimp trawling sectors could adjust to the requirement of the use of TEDs. With respect to all other countries exporting shrimp to the United States (including the appellees, India, Malaysia, Pakistan and Thailand), on 29 December 1995, the United States Court of International Trade directed the Department of State to apply the import ban on a world-wide basis not later than 1 May 1996. On 19 April 1996, the 1996 Guidelines were issued by the Department of State bringing shrimp harvested in *all* foreign countries within the scope of Section 609, effective 1 May 1996. Thus, all countries that were not among the fourteen in the wider Caribbean/ western Atlantic region had only four months to implement the requirement of compulsory use of TEDs. * * *

* * * 157. When the foregoing differences in the means of application of Section 609 to various shrimp exporting countries are considered in their cumulative effect, we find, and so hold, that those differences in treatment constitute "unjustifiable discrimination" between exporting countries desiring certification in order to gain access to the United States shrimp market within the meaning of the chapeau of Article XX.

3. "Arbitrary Discrimination"

158. We next consider whether Section 609 has been applied in a manner constituting "arbitrary discrimination between countries where the same conditions prevail". We have already observed that Section 609, in its application, imposes a single, rigid and unbending requirement that countries applying for certification under Section 609(b)(2)(A) and (B) adopt a comprehensive regulatory program that is essentially the same as the United States' program, without inquiring into the appropriateness of that program for the conditions prevailing in the exporting countries. Furthermore, there is little or no flexibility in how officials make the determination for certification pursuant to these provisions. In our view, this rigidity and inflexibility also constitute "arbitrary discrimination" within the meaning of the chapeau.

* * *165. We find, accordingly, that the United States measure is applied in a manner which amounts to a means not just of "unjustifiable discrimination", but also of "arbitrary discrimination" between countries where the same conditions prevail, contrary to the requirements of the chapeau of Article XX. The measure, therefore, is not entitled to the justifying protection of Article XX of the GATT 1994. Having made this finding, it is not necessary for us to examine also whether the United States measure is applied in a manner that constitutes a "disguised restriction on international trade" under the chapeau of Article XX.

* * * FINDINGS AND CONCLUSIONS

168. For the reasons set out in this Report, the Appellate Body:

* * *(b) reverses the Panel's finding that the United States measure at issue is not within the scope of measures permitted under the chapeau of Article XX of the GATT 1994, and

(c) concludes that the United States measure, while qualifying for provisional justification under Article XX(g), fails to meet the requirements of the chapeau of Article XX, and, therefore, is not justified under Article XX of the GATT 1994.

169. The Appellate Body *recommends* that the DSB request the United States to bring its measure found in the Panel Report to be inconsistent with Article XI of the GATT 1994, and found in this Report to be not justified under Article XX of the GATT 1994, into conformity with the obligations of the United States under that Agreement.

NOTES

1. **So, Who Won?** Was the Appellate Body's decision a victory for the United States? Why or why not?

2. **The Rest of the Story, Internationally.** On November 6, 1998, the WTO Dispute Resolution Board adopted the Appellate Body Report. On November 25, the United States notified the Board that it intended to comply with the Appellate Body's decision, and the United States, India, Malaysia, Pakistan, and Thailand agreed that 13 months (*i.e.*, by December 1999) was a reasonable time for the United States to implement the Appellate Body's decision.

In March 1999, the Secretary of State proposed revisions to the section 609 Guidelines. At the same time, the Secretary noted that the United States had taken steps to comply with the Appellate Body's decision: (1) the Secretary had clarified the regulations regarding comparability and specified that the Secretary would consider all proffered evidence; (2) the Secretary had changed the exemption procedures to make the certification process more transparent; (3) the Secretary had clarified that shrimp harvested by vessels using TEDs could be imported into the United States, regardless of the nation of origin's certification status; (4) the Secretary had begun negotiations regarding sea turtle protection with the Indian Ocean nations; and (5) the United States had announced that it would provide technical training regarding TEDs to any nation that wanted such training. 64 Fed. Reg. 14,481 (March 25, 1999).

The Secretary of State issued the Revised Guidelines for the Implementation of Section 609 of Public Law 101–162 in July 1999. 64 Fed. Reg. 36,946 (July 8, 1999). Australia, India, Malaysia, Thailand, and the USFWS had all commented on the proposed revisions. Under the revised Guidelines, the Secretary will grant certification under section 609(b)(2)(C) if: (1) there are no turtles in the nation's waters; (2) shrimp trawlers from the nation harvest shrimp exclusively by means that do not pose a threat; or (3) shrimp trawling operations take place exclusively in waters where sea turtles do not occur. The Secretary considers four types of shrimp harvesting "not harmful" to sea turtles: aquaculture; use of TEDs comparable to those used in the United States; retrieval of fishing nets exclusively by nonmechanical means; and individual determinations by the Secretary. As for section 609(b)(2)(A) and (B) (the comparability requirements), "[t]he Department of State is presently aware of no measure or series of measures that can minimize the capture and drowning of sea turtles in [standard otter trawl] nets that is comparable in effectiveness to the required use of TEDs." *Id.* at 36,950.

In January 2000, the United States informed the WTO Dispute Resolution Board that it had implemented the Appellate Body's recommendations. On October 23, 2000, Malaysia requested another dispute resolution panel, arguing that section 609 still violated the GATT 1994 and that the United States must remove all import restrictions on shrimp and shrimp products. The European Communities, Japan, Ecuador, Australia, India, Thailand, Canada, Mexico, Pakistan, and Hong Kong participated in the panel as third parties. On June 15, 2001, the panel issued its Report, holding that the United States was making good faith efforts to negotiate for sea turtle protections and that section 609 "is justified under Article XX of the GATT 1994" as long as the United States continued "serious good faith efforts to reach a multilateral agreement." Report of the WTO Panel, *United States–Import Prohibition of Certain Shrimp and Shrimp Products*, WT/DS58/RW, at ¶ 6.1 (June 15, 2001). Malaysia appealed, but the Appellate Body upheld the panel's decision. Report of the Appellate Body, *United States–Import Prohibition of Certain Shrimp and Shrimp Products*, WT/DS58/23, at ¶ 153 (Oct. 22, 2001). The Dispute Resolution Body adopted the Appellate Body Report on November 26, 2001.

The Secretary of State continues to issue certifications to shrimp-harvesting nations pursuant to section 609. For instance, on April 30, 2004, the Secretary certified that Belize, Colombia, Costa Rica, Ecuador, El Salvador, Guatemala, Guyana, Honduras, Mexico, Nicaragua, Pakistan, Panama, Suriname, and Trinidad and Tobago had comparable programs for purposes of section 609(b)(2). *See* 69 Fed. Reg. 26,916 (May 14, 2004). Fifteen other nations received certifications because their cold-water shrimp fisheries posed no danger to sea turtles: Belgium, Canada, Chile, Denmark, Finland, Germany, Iceland, Ireland, the Netherlands, New Zealand, Norway, Russia, Sweden, the United Kingdom, and Uruguay. *Id.* Finally, eight nations—the Bahamas, China, the Dominican Republic, Fiji, Jamaica, Oman, Peru, and Sri Lanka—and Hong Kong received certifications because their commercial shrimpers use small-scale technology and small boats and therefore did not pose a danger to sea turtles. *Id.*

Certifications remained largely the same through 2007. On May 22, 2007, the Secretary of State certified that 16 countries had adopted programs for protecting sea turtles comparable to those of the United States. New countries compared to the 2004 list included Madagascar, Nigeria, and Venezuela; Trinidad and Tobago had dropped off the list. 72 Fed. Reg. 28,753 (May 22, 2007). Argentina joined the list of nations with certified cold-water fisheries, *id.*, while the list of certifications on the basis of small-scale fisheries remained the same. *Id.*

In May 2009, the United States again caused controversy when it issued its new Section 609 certifications. 74 Fed. Reg. 21,048 (May 6, 2009). The Secretary of State certified that 15 shrimping countries have protections for sea turtles comparable to the United States': Belize, Colombia, Ecuador, El Salvador, Guatemala, Guyana, Honduras, Madagascar, Mexico, Nicaragua, Nigeria, Pakistan, Panama, Suriname, and Venezuela. Twenty-four countries were certified because their cold-water shrimp fisheries posed no danger to sea turtles: Argentina, Belgium, Canada, Chile, Denmark, Finland, Germany, Iceland, Ireland, the Netherlands, New Zealand, Norway, Russia, Sweden, the United Kingdom, and Uruguay. Finally, eight countries and one economic unit (Hong Kong) were certified because their small-technology shrimp fisheries posed no danger to sea turtles: Bahamas, China, the Dominican Republic, Fiji, Hong Kong, Jamaica, Oman, Peru, and Sri Lanka. The controversy arose because the Secretary of State de-certified Costa Rica, on the grounds that Costa Rica was ineffectively enforcing its TED requirements. The de-certification was important news in Costa Rica.

3. **The Rest of the Story, Domestically.** The Earth Island Institute, later the Turtle Island Restoration Network, did not stop litigating issues under section 609. As noted in the 1998 Appellate Body report presented above, in 1996, the Court of International Trade determined that, under section 609, shrimp harvested on trawlers equipped with TEDs could *not* be imported into the United States if the nation of origin was not certified under section 609(b)(2). *Earth Island Institute v. Christopher*, 942 F. Supp. 597, 604–05 (CIT 1996). When the Secretary of State again allowed such importation in the 1998 Revised Guidelines, Earth Island sued again, and the Court of International Trade again held that the Revised Guidelines violated section 609 by allowing importation of TED-caught shrimp from uncertified nations. *Earth Island Institute v. Daley*, 48 F. Supp. 2d 1064, 1079–81 (CIT 1999). However, the Federal Circuit reversed on appeal. *Turtle Island Restoration Network v. Evans*, 284 F.3d 1282, 1291–96 (2002).

Interestingly, in reaching its decision, the Federal Circuit thoroughly explored the legislative history of section 609, concluding that, "to the extent legislative history is available, we find that Congress with remarkable unanimity was focused on protecting the domestic shrimp industry, not the sea turtle, when it enacted section 609. Many comments made on the Senate floor reflected deep skepticism about the effectiveness of TED requirements, and about the wisdom of placing sea turtle conservation above the economic well-being of domestic shrimpers." *Id.* at 1294–95. Does this conclusion have any bearing on the United States' ability to justify section 609 under Article XX of the GATT? Why or why not?

4. **Justifying Environmental Measures Under the GATT.** One of the most significant aspects of the Appellate Body's decision presented above was its reversal of the Panel's approach to analyzing Article XX exemption claims. What did the Panel do wrong in its analysis? How did the Appellate Body analyze the United States' claim of exemption? Why does that approach make a difference?

5. **The Article XX(g) Exemption Claim for Section 609.** According to the Appellate Body, what are the elements of a claim for exemption under Article XX(g)? What elements did the appellees dispute, and how? How did the Appellate Body define or refine each element? Did section 609 meet each of these elements? Why or why not? How was the Endangered Species Act relevant to the Appellate Body's conclusions?

6. **Article XX's Chapeau and Section 609.** How does the chapeau (introductory language) of Article XX relate to the specific exemptions listed

in that Article? According to the Appellate Body, what limitations does the chapeau impose on Article XX exemption claims? Did Section 609 fall within these limitations? Why or why not? What other obligations does the United States have?

7. **Treaty Interpretation Tools.** What tools did the Appellate Body use to interpret Article XX? How do these tools of treaty interpretation compare to the statutory interpretation tools that United States courts use to interpret statutes? What other treaties did the Appellate Body reference, and why were they relevant to Article XX? In particular, what role did CITES play in its interpretation?

Chapter 4

The Clean Air Act, the Risks of Pollution, and the Costs and Benefits of Environmental Regulation

■ ■ ■

I. INTRODUCTION TO THE CLEAN AIR ACT

A. AIR POLLUTION BEFORE THE 1970 AMENDMENTS

Air pollution is a long-recognized consequence of industrialization. By the first half of the 20th century, residents of cities were accustomed to breathing polluted air, and such conditions persist in many large cities around the world, such as Los Angeles, Mexico City and Beijing. What prompted the United States to try to control such pollution?

One answer lies in "killer fog" events in the United States and other parts of the world. For example, in 1930, fog trapped pollution in the city of Liège, Belgium, killing dozens of people. More important for U.S. air pollution regulation was the 1948 killer fog at Donora, Pennsylvania, a steelmaking town with a population of 14,000. The steel mills generated chemical fumes. In particular, the zinc smelters emitted sulfur dioxide, carbon monoxide, and metal dust, which normally blew away. However, when a heavy fog settled over the town in October 1948, those air pollutants could not escape. Between October 26 and 31, "20 people were asphyxiated and over 7,000 were hospitalized or became ill as the result of severe air pollution * * *." Pennsylvania Department of Environmental Protection, *Donora Smog Kills 20*,http://www.dep.state.pa.us/dep/DEPUTATE/polycomm/update/10–30–98/10309839.htm.

The Donora killer fog is considered the United States' worst pollution disaster. Four years later, a similar event in London, England, proved that Donora was not a fluke and that industrial air pollution was a serious threat to human health. In the 1952 London "killer fog," an atmospheric inversion created a "toxic mix of dense fog and sooty black coal smoke," made worse by the residents' increased burning of coal to keep warm as the temperature dropped. The sooty fog lasted four days, and at its worst, visibility within the city was only one foot. The fog was made deadly because of particulates and sulfur dioxide in the soot, which caused inflammations in the already-weakened lungs of long-time London residents. On the second day of the fog, 500 people in London died; 900 people died on the last day. Overall, "[e]stimates sat the smog killed anywhere from 4,000 to 11,000 people." National Public Radio, *The Killer Fog of '52*, http://discover.npr.org/templates/story/story.php?storyid=873954 (Dec. 11, 2002). This 1952 disaster, according to some historians, changed several countries' attitudes toward air pollution. "Before the incident, people in cities tended to accept pollution as a part of life. Afterward, more and more, they fought to limit the poisonous side effects of the industrial age." *Id.*

Federal regulation of air pollution in the United States began shortly after the London Killer Fog. In 1955, Congress enacted the Air Pollution Control Act. Pub. L. No. 84–159, 69 Stat. 322. Like many early federal pollution-related statutes, this Act functioned mainly to provide states with research money and technical assistance—it did not impose any actual requirements on air polluters. "Killer fogs" in New York and other United States locations, however, prompted Congress to improve its efforts, resulting in the 1963 Clean Air Act. Pub. L. No. 88–206, 77 Stat. 392. Like the Air Pollution Control Act, this first version of the Clean Air Act established grant and research programs to help states in their air pollution control efforts. In addition, however, the new statute authorized the Department of Health, Education, and Welfare (HEW; the EPA did not exist until 1970) to abate *interstate* air pollution.

Federal air regulation expanded again in 1967, when Congress passed the Air Quality Act. Pub. L. No. 90–148, 81 Stat. 485. The Air Quality Act amended the 1963 Clean Air Act to require HEW to set *national air quality criteria*. States were then supposed to set *ambient air quality standards* based on these criteria and to submit *implementation plans* to HEW, which were supposed to become the mechanisms for enforcing the state-set ambient air quality standards. A major shortcoming of the 1967 Act, however, was its lack of effective enforcement procedures. As a result, air pollution tended to be "regulated," if at all, only through nuisance cases. What does the following famous nuisance case suggest about the effectiveness of both the 1967 Act and common-law nuisance in achieving air quality goals?

BOOMER v. ATLANTIC CEMENT COMPANY, INC.

26 N.Y.2d 219 (N.Y. App. 1970).

BERGAN, JUDGE.

Defendant operates a large cement plant near Albany. These are actions for injunction and damages by neighboring land owners alleging injury to property from dirt, smoke and vibration emanating from the plant. A nuisance has been found after trial, temporary damages have been allowed; but an injunction has been denied.

The public concern with air pollution arising from many sources in industry and in transportation is currently accorded ever wider recognition accompanied by a growing sense of responsibility in State and Federal Governments to control it. Cement plants are obvious sources of air pollution in the neighborhoods where they operate.

Figure 4-1: The Round Top Portland Cement Factory, 1882
National Park Service photo.

But there is now before the court private litigation in which individual property owners have sought specific relief from a single plant operation. The threshold question raised by the division of view on this appeal is whether the court should resolve the litigation between the parties now before it as equitably as seems possible; or whether, seeking promotion of the general public welfare, it should channel private litigation into broad public objectives.

A court performs its essential function when it decides the rights of parties before it. Its decision of private controversies may sometimes greatly affect public issues. Large questions of law are often resolved by the manner in which private litigation is decided. But this is normally an incident to the court's main function to settle controversy. It is a rare exercise of judicial power to use a decision in private litigation as a purposeful mechanism to achieve direct public objectives greatly beyond the rights and interests before the court.

Effective control of air pollution is a problem presently far from solution even with the full public and financial powers of government. In large measure adequate technical procedures are yet to be developed and some that appear possible may be economically impracticable.

It seems apparent that the amelioration of air pollution will depend on technical research in great depth; on a carefully balanced consideration of the economic impact of close regulation; and of the actual effect on public health. It is likely to require massive public expenditure and to demand more than any local community can accomplish and to depend on regional and interstate controls.

A court should not try to do this on its own as a by-product of private litigation and it seems manifest that the judicial establishment is neither equipped in the limited nature of any judgment it can pronounce nor prepared to lay down and implement an effective policy for the elimination of air pollution. This is an area beyond the circumference of one private lawsuit. It is a direct responsibility for government and should not thus be undertaken as an incident to solving a dispute between property owners and a single cement plant—one of many—in the Hudson River valley.

The cement making operations of defendant have been found by the court of Special Term to have damaged the nearby properties of plaintiffs in these two actions. That court, as it has been noted, accordingly found defendant maintained a nuisance and this has been affirmed at the Appellate Division. The total damage to plaintiffs' properties is, however, relatively small in comparison with the value of defendant's operation and with the consequences of the injunction which plaintiffs seek.

The ground for the denial of injunction, notwithstanding the finding both that there is a nuisance and that plaintiffs have been damaged substantially, is the large disparity in economic consequences of the nuisance and of the injunction. * * *

The rule in New York has been that such a nuisance will be enjoined although marked disparity be shown in economic consequence between the effect of the injunction and the effect of the nuisance.

* * * There are cases where injunction has been denied. [However, if] the damage to plaintiffs in these present cases from defendant's cement plant is "not unsubstantial", an injunction should follow.

* * * Th[e] result at Special Term and at the Appellate Division is a departure from a rule that has become settled; but to follow the rule literally in these cases would be to close down the plant at once. This court is fully agreed to avoid that immediately drastic remedy; the difference in view is how best to avoid it.

One alternative is to grant the injunction but postpone its effect to a specified future date to give opportunity for technical advances to permit defendant to eliminate the nuisance; another is to grant the injunction conditioned on the payment of permanent damages to plaintiffs which would compensate them for the total economic loss to their property present and future caused by defendant's operations. For reasons which will be developed the court chooses the latter alternative.

If the injunction were to be granted unless within a short period—*e.g.*, 18 months—the nuisance be abated by improved methods, there would be no assurance that any significant technical improvement would occur.

The parties could settle this private litigation at any time if defendant paid enough money and the imminent threat of closing the plant would build up the pressure on defendant. If there were no improved techniques found, there would inevitably be applications to the court at Special Term for extensions of time to perform on showing of good faith efforts to find such techniques.

Moreover, techniques to eliminate dust and other annoying by-products of cement making are unlikely to be developed by any research the defendant can undertake within any short period, but will depend on the total resources of the cement industry nationwide and throughout the world. The problem is universal wherever cement is made.

For obvious reasons the rate of the research is beyond control of defendant. If at the end of 18 months the whole industry has not found a technical solution a court would be hard put to close down this one cement plant if due regard be given to equitable principles.

On the other hand, to grant the injunction unless defendant pays plaintiffs such permanent damages as may be fixed by the court seems to do justice between the contending parties. All of the attributions of economic loss to the properties on which plaintiffs' complaints are based will have been redressed.

* * * It seems reasonable to think that the risk of being required to pay permanent damages to injured property owners by cement plant owners would itself be a reasonable effective spur to research for improved techniques to minimize nuisance.

* * * The orders should be reversed, without costs, and the cases remitted to Supreme Court, Albany County to grant an injunction which shall be vacated upon payment by defendant of such amounts of permanent damage to the respective plaintiffs as shall for this purpose be determined by the court.

NOTES

1. **The Rest of the Story.** From the plaintiffs' perspective, the primary problems with Atlantic Cement's operations were dust from the cement manufacturing process and blasting from the associated mining operations. The named plaintiffs, Oscar and June Boomer, owned an auto junkyard and body shop about a mile from the Atlantic Cement plant. Another plaintiff "couple lived in a ranch house about half a mile from the quarry. The blasting caused large cracks in the walls, ceiling, and even the exterior of their house.... Fine dust from the cement operation coated the interior with what the [plaintiffs] described at trial as a 'plastic-like coating.' " Daniel A. Farber,

The Story of Boomer: *Pollution and the Common Law*, *in* RICHARD J. LAZARUS & OLIVER A. HOUCK, ENVIRONMENTAL LAW STORIES 7, 10 (2005).

Nevertheless, Atlantic Cement "had built one of the largest and most modern cement factories in the world at a cost of $45 million, and had installed the most effective devices then available to control the dust and noise created by the operations of its plant. [Atlantic Cement] was also the largest taxpayer and employer in town, with over 300 workers at its plant." Joseph C. Sweeney, *Protection of the Environment in the United States*, 1 FORDHAM ENVTL. L. REP. 1, 9–10 (1989). "Its anti-pollution equipment was said to have cost over $2,000,000." Joel C. Dobris, *Boomer Twenty Years Later: An Introduction, With Some Footnotes About "Theory,"* 54 ALBANY L. REV. 171, 172 (1990). Moreover, "[b]efore the litigation was over, the company had spent an additional $1.6 million installing a spray system, a fiberglass bag collector, and converting from coal to oil." Farber, *supra*, at 9. Do these facts help to explain why the New York courts deviated from prior law and refused to issue an injunction?

The plaintiffs were not uncompensated, however. "The total recovery by the plaintiffs, including interest on the one claim that was not settled prior to judgment, was $710,737.56, nearly four times the amount of permanent damages set forth in the trial court's initial opinion." Jeff F. Lewin, *Boomer and the American Law of Nuisance: Past, Present, and Future*, 54 ALBANY L. REV. 189, 218 (1990). Moreover, "Atlantic belatedly purchased most of the plantiffs' properties to create a buffer zone. Several of the plaintiffs moved away after receiving damages. But at age 80 [in 2005], Mr. Boomer himself still runs a business in the areas." Farber, *supra*, at 23.

Still, having proven that the cement factory was a nuisance, should the plaintiffs have had to accept this remedy, especially considering that the court recognized that air pollution causes health problems? Why or why not? Consider that "[t]he plant remains the second largest cement facility in the United States. The plant's most recent [Toxic Release Inventory report, required by the Emergency Planning and Community Right-to-Know Act, 42 U.S.C. §§ 11001–11050,] lists 142,000 pounds of hydrochloric acid, 29 pounds of lead, 37 pounds of mercury compounds, and small amounts of dioxins in 2002." Farber, *supra*, at 25. Mr. Boomer is still living with these emissions. Should he have to?

2. **Air Pollution and Nuisance.** How does the majority view the air pollution problem in the United States? How effective is the doctrine of nuisance in addressing that problem? Did the plaintiffs prove a public or a private nuisance? Does that distinction really matter?

3. **The Role of Technology in Air Pollution Control.** What role does technology play in this decision? How does the majority of the judges on the New York Court of Appeals view the court's role in forcing particular sources of air pollution to improve their technology?

Ironically, "[t]echnology was already available (of which the court was unaware) that could have controlled the emissions." Bradford C. Wynche, *A Guide to the Common Law of Nuisance in South Carolina*, 45 SOUTH CAROLINA L. REV. 337, 378 n.282 (Winter 1994). Assuming that the parties know about this technology, would either party necessarily bring it to the court's attention? Why or why not? Might knowledge of that technology have affected the court's remedy? Why or why not?

4. **The Resurgence of Nuisance in a Climate Change Era.** Climate change, and the federal government's failure to enact comprehensive climate change legislation, has prompted a resurgence in air emissions-based nuisance suits. In June 2011, for example, the U.S. Supreme Court decided *American Electric Power Co. v. Connecticut*, ___ U.S. ___, 131 S.Ct. 2527 (2011), addressing the claims of eight states, New York City, and three land trusts that the emissions from fossil-fuel electric power plants owned by four private power companies and the Tennessee Valley Authority constituted nuisances because their emissions contributed to climate change. The plaintiffs raised nuisance claims based on both federal and state law, but the Supreme Court addressed only the former. It held that the claims based on the federal law of nuisance were displaced by the EPA's authority to regulate greenhouse gas emissions pursuant to the federal Clean Air Act—authority that the Court had recognized in 2007 in *Massachusetts v. EPA*, presented in Part II.A.3. *AEP v. Connecticut*, ___ U.S. ___, 131 S. Ct. at 2536–38. However, because neither the U.S. Court of Appeals for the Second Circuit nor the parties had addressed the issue of state-law nuisance, the Supreme Court expressly left open the question of whether the plaintiffs could bring their state-law nuisance claims.

Why does climate change inspire plaintiffs to reach for common-law claims such as nuisance? Given the court's response to nuisance and air pollution in *Boomer*, how do you think courts would resolve a nuisance case based on climate change? Does climate change lend itself to this kind of common law nuisance litigation? Why or why not?

* * *

B. AIR POLLUTION AFTER 1970: THE FEDERAL CLEAN AIR ACT AMENDMENTS OF 1970

The Clean Air Act was one of the first environmental pollution control statutes that Congress enacted. Congress substantially changed the structure of the 1967 Clean Air Act in the Clean Air Act Amendments of 1970, which are considered the source of the contemporary federal Clean Air Act.

The 1970 amendments, like the 1967 Act, combined federal and state regulation, a type of regulatory structure known as ***cooperative federalism***. Under the 1970 Act's scheme of cooperative federalism, however, the federal government (working through the Environmental Protection Agency, or EPA) sets basic requirements for ambient air quality with respect to various pollutants. These basic requirements are known as the ***National Ambient Air Quality Standards***, or NAAQS. Acknowledging air pollution's direct relationship to public health, Congress had the EPA set primary NAAQS to protect the public health, including an adequate margin of safety.

The EPA also sets certain emissions standards for particular kinds of sources of air pollution, based on the technology that can control various kinds of air pollutants. Thus, the Clean Air Act is a ***technology-based*** statute. However, the Clean Air Act is also a ***technology-forcing*** statute: Unlike the New York Court of Appeals in *Boomer*, Congress in 1970 demanded that entire industries develop better air pollution control technologies or risk being shut down entirely.

The Clean Air Act gives *each state* the primary responsibility for figuring out how to meet the EPA-set NAAQS in each of the various ***Air Quality Control Regions*** **(AQCRs)**—basically, the natural airsheds—within that state's borders. Each state establishes its air quality program to meet the NAAQS through a ***State Implementation Plan*** **(SIP)**. In some regions, such as the Great Plains states, air quality was already good enough in 1970 to meet the NAAQS that the EPA established. However, in others, such as the areas around Los Angeles and Washington, D.C., states had more difficulty. AQCRs with air quality sufficient to meet the NAAQS are ***attainment regions***. AQCRs with air quality that does not meet the NAAQS are ***nonattainment regions***. The Clean Air Act's requirements for individual stationary sources vary depending on the AQCR's attainment or nonattainment status.

The Clean Air Act has been a work-in-progress for over three decades now. Congress amended the statute in 1977, 1981, 1990, 1998, and 1999 to address additional air quality problems and to fine-tune regulation of previously-addressed problems. As a result of all these amendments and the variety of air quality issues that exist, the current Clean Air Act, 42 U.S.C. §§ 7401–7671q, is a very large statute that rivals the U.S. Internal Revenue Code for length and complexity. What follows is an introduction to the most important provisions of this Act.

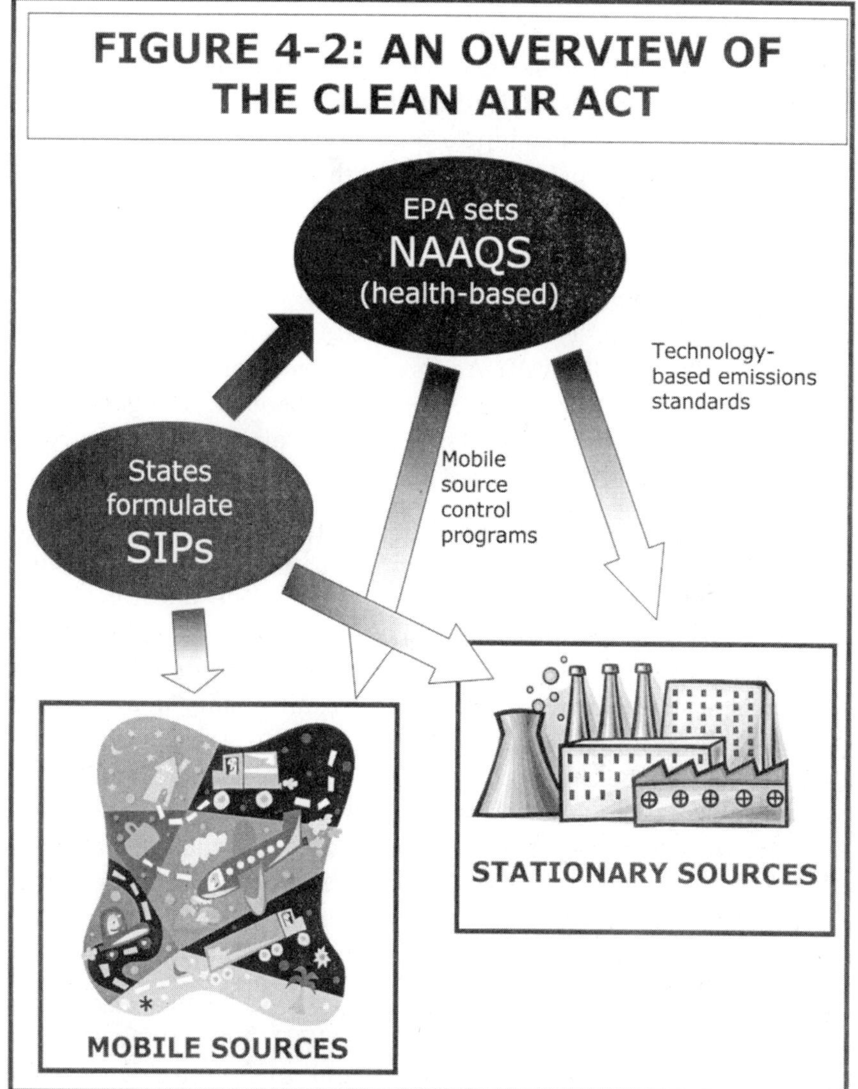

II. CRITERIA POLLUTANTS, NAAQS, SIPS, AND THE CLEAN AIR ACT'S COOPERATIVE FEDERALISM

A. ESTABLISHING CRITERIA POLLUTANTS

In the Clean Air Act Amendments of 1970, Congress gave the EPA 30 days to produce a list of air pollutants whose emission "cause[s] or contribute[s] to air pollution which may reasonably be anticipated to endanger public health or welfare"; whose presence "in the ambient air results from numerous or diverse mobile and stationary sources"; and "for which air quality criteria had not been issued * * *." CAA § 108(a)(1), 42 U.S.C. § 7408(a)(1).

After the EPA listed these ***criteria pollutants***, it had to issue ***air quality criteria*** for them within 12 months. CAA § 108(a)(2), 42 U.S.C. § 7408(a)(2). The air quality criteria had to "accurately reflect the latest scientific knowledge," indicate "the kind and extent of all identifiable effects on public health or welfare which may be expected from the presence of such pollutant in the ambient air," and include information on other variable factors that can alter the effects of the pollutant, other air pollutants that the criteria pollutant might interact with, and "any known or anticipated adverse effects on welfare." *Id.*

1. Criteria Pollutants vs. Mobile Source Controls, Part 1: Establishing Lead as a Criteria Pollutant

The EPA fairly immediately established five criteria pollutants—ozone, particulate matter (PM), carbon monoxide (CO), nitrogen oxides (NOx), and sulfur dioxide (SO_2). However, it then resisted the addition of any more. An additional candidate pollutant, lead, became the subject of litigation.

Lead is a very useful metal in industry, because: (1) it is easy to separate from its ores; (2) it is malleable and thus easy to shape; (3) it does not corrode; and (4) it is relatively abundant in the earth's crust. However, lead is also extremely toxic. Public health officials currently deem a person to be suffering from lead poisoning when he or she has a blood-lead concentration (the amount of lead dissolved in the blood) of 10 micrograms per deciliter of blood or higher. Lead Poisoning Resource Center, http://www.aboutlead.com. Lead poisoning in children can cause speech delay, hyperactivity, attention deficient disorder, learning disabilities, behavioral disorders, neurological damage, renal damage, stunted growth, anemia, hearing loss, and mental retardation. *Id.* In adults, lead poisoning can lead to kidney damage, neurological damage, anemia, hypertension, impotence, sterility, and miscarriages. *Id.*

Public health officials estimate that, in the 1970s, 88% of the children in the United States had blood-lead levels greater than 10 micrograms per liter—*i.e.*, that *most* children in the United States were suffering from lead poisoning from a very early age. *Id.* Childhood lead poisoning had been recognized as a medical phenomenon since at least 1887, and the United States Public Health Service began warning of the dangers of lead in 1922. Jamie Lincoln Kitman, *8,500 Years of Lead ... 79 Years of Leaded Gasoline*, THE NATION (March 20, 2000).

Because the Clean Air Act is a complex statute, the EPA often appears to have several options when it decides to regulate air pollutants. For example, as we'll see in more detail, one important distinction is between stationary and mobile sources. Criteria pollutants are most relevant to stationary source regulation. Thus, if an air pollutant is a problem mostly because of *mobile* sources like cars and trucks, designating that pollutant a criteria pollutant might not seem to be the best regulatory strategy.

For example, at the time that the EPA was dealing with the issue of whether lead should be a criteria pollutant, EPA officials knew that one source of childhood lead poisoning was lead-based paint, such as house paint, now outlawed under ***Lead-Based Paint Poisoning Prevention Act***. 42 U.S.C. § 4822. However, the far more important source of blood lead poisoning, for both children and adults, was emissions from automobiles that used leaded gasoline. As a result, when the EPA initially sought to protect public health from lead emission, it preferred to target leaded gasoline, based on its Clean Air Act mobile source authority to regulate fuel additives.

Figure 4-3: Sources of Lead Emissions, 1970
EPA graphic.

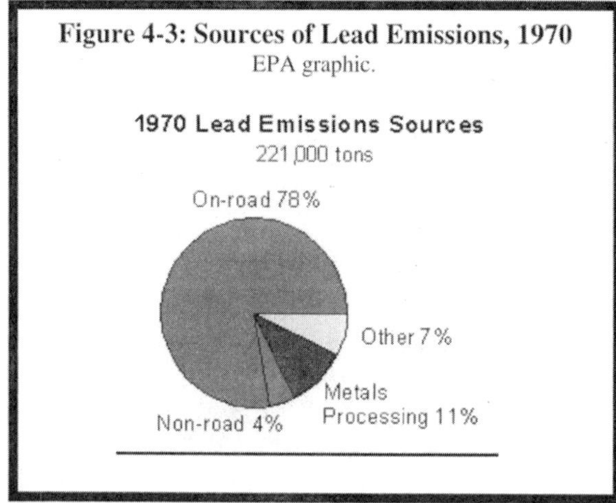

QUESTIONS: Consider Figure 4–3. What does it suggest about the EPA's choice of regulatory mechanism for addressing lead air pollution? Did the EPA make an illogical choice of regulatory mechanism? Why or why not?

The EPA began phasing out leaded gasoline in 1976. It did so pursuant to its authority under Section 211 of the Clean Air Act, which allows the EPA to regulate fuel additives "if in the judgment of the Administrator any emission product of such fuel or fuel additive causes, or contributes, to air pollution which may reasonably be anticipated to endanger the public health or welfare...." CAA § 211(c)(1), 42 U.S.C. § 7545(c)(1).

QUESTIONS: How does the standard in Section 211 for regulating fuel additives compare to Section 108's requirements for establishing criteria pollutants? In particular, can the EPA make an "endangerment" finding under Section 211 without simultaneously making an "endangerment" finding under Section 108? What other elements does Section 108 require before the EPA must list a pollutant as a criteria pollutant?

In *Natural Resources Defense Council v. Train*, 411 F. Supp. 864 (S.D.N.Y. 1976), *aff'd sub nom Natural Resources Defense Council, Inc. v. Train*, 545 F.2d 320 (2d Cir. 1976), U.S. District Judge Stewart concluded that the EPA could not avoid listing lead as a criteria pollutant simply because the EPA preferred to regulate lead by phasing out leaded gasoline pursuant to Section 211 of the Clean Air Act. Judge Stewart emphasized that "the language of § 108 indicates that upon certain enumerated conditions, one factual and one judgmental, the Administrator 'shall' list a pollutant which triggers the remedial provisions of §§ 108–110. The statute does not provide, as defendants would have it, that the Administrator has authority to determine whether the statutory remedies which follow a § 108 listing are appropriate for a given pollutant. . . ." *Id.* at 867. Judge Stewart concluded that, "[i]n the instant case, the Administrator has conceded that, in his judgment, lead 'has an adverse effect on health' and comes from 'numerous or diverse mobile or stationary sources.' The two statutory criteria having been met and this court having determined that a duty thereafter arises, it is ordered that the Administrator place lead on the list of pollutants, in accordance with the mandate of § 108, within 30 days from the date of this decision." *Id.* at 871.

Moreover, the EPA Administrator's preference for dealing with the lead problem through regulation of gasoline could not eliminate his duty to list lead as a criteria pollutant under Section 108:

> The benefits of uniform standards, of federal controls and of averting "another major regulatory task" for the states can all accrue from regulations under § 211 when lead is listed under § 108. If the Administrator sets standards under § 211 which effectively decrease the level of lead in the ambient air by taking lead out of gasoline, then the decrease in pollution brought about by the § 211 regulations will be taken into account by each state when it submits its plan to meet the national standard set under § 110. In fact, § 211(c)(4)(C) provides that the only circumstances under which the Administrator may approve the regulation of motor vehicle fuel or fuel additive in an implementation plan promulgated pursuant to § 108 is where "he finds that the State control or prohibition is necessary to achieve the national primary or secondary ambient air quality standard which the plan implements." Therefore, if the Administrator had made the necessary regulations under § 211, he cannot permit the states to regulate lead emissions through the implementation plans provided for in § 110. In the event that regulation under § 211 causes a decrease in air lead sufficient to meet any national standard set under § 108, then there will be uniform standards, federal regulation and no further regulatory task for the states. Despite regulation under § 211, however, the Administrator must nevertheless list lead as a pollutant since it concededly meets the two criteria of § 108 and must set in motion the collection of scientific data and the issuance of criteria and national standards.

Id. at 869–70. As a result of this litigation, the EPA listed lead as a criteria pollutant on March 31, 1976. *See* 43 Fed. Reg. 46,246, 46,246.

2. The Current Criteria Pollutants

Lead was the last criteria pollutant that the EPA designated under section 108, bringing the total number of criteria pollutants to six. In 1999, the EPA described the criteria pollutants and their effects and human health and welfare as follows:

The Common Air Pollutants (Criteria Air Pollutants)

Ozone (ground-level ozone is the principal component of smog)

- **Source**—chemical reaction of pollutants; VOCs and NOx
- **Health Effects**—breathing problems, reduced lung function, asthma, irritates eyes, stuffy nose, reduced resistance to colds and other infections, may speed up aging of lung tissue
- **Environmental Effects**—ozone can damage plants and trees; smog can cause reduced visibility
- **Property Damage**—Damages rubber, fabrics, etc.

Nitrogen Dioxide (One of the NOx); smog-forming chemical

- **Source**—burning of gasoline, natural gas, coal, oil etc. Cars are an important source of NO2.
- **Health Effects**—lung damage, illnesses of breathing passages and lungs (respiratory system)
- **Environmental Effects**—nitrogen dioxide is an ingredient of acid rain (acid aerosols), which can damage trees and lakes. Acid aerosols can reduce visibility.
- **Property Damage**—acid aerosols can eat away stone used on buildings, statues, monuments, etc.

Carbon Monoxide (CO)

- **Source**—burning of gasoline, natural gas, coal, oil etc.
- **Health Effects**—reduces ability of blood to bring oxygen to body cells and tissues; cells and tissues need oxygen to work. Carbon monoxide may be particularly hazardous to people who have heart or circulatory (blood vessel) problems and people who have damaged lungs or breathing passages

Particulate Matter (PM–10); (dust, smoke, soot)

- **Source**—burning of wood, diesel and other fuels; industrial plants; agriculture (plowing, burning off fields); unpaved roads
- **Health Effects**—nose and throat irritation, lung damage, bronchitis, early death
- **Environmental Effects**—particulates are the main source of haze that reduces visibility

- **Property Damage**—ashes, soots, smokes and dusts can dirty and discolor structures and other property, including clothes and furniture

Sulfur Dioxide

- **Source**—burning of coal and oil, especially high-sulfur coal from the Eastern United States; industrial processes (paper, metals)
- **Health Effects**—breathing problems, may cause permanent damage to lungs
- **Environmental Effects**—SO2 is an ingredient in acid rain (acid aerosols), which can damage trees and lakes. Acid aerosols can also reduce visibility.
- **Property Damage**—acid aerosols can eat away stone used in buildings, statues, monuments, etc.

Lead

- **Source**—leaded gasoline (being phased out), paint (houses, cars), smelters (metal refineries); manufacture of lead storage batteries
- **Health Effects**—brain and other nervous system damage; children are at special risk. Some lead-containing chemicals cause cancer in animals. Lead causes digestive and other health problems.
- **Environmental Effects**—Lead can harm wildlife.

Office of Air Regulation, U.S. E.P.A., *The Common Air Pollutants*, *in* THE PLAIN ENGLISH GUIDE TO THE CLEAN AIR ACT (1999). The EPA currently describes the criteria air pollutants at its urban air quality web site. *See* Office of Air, U.S. EPA, *What Are the Six Common Air Pollutants?*, http://www.epa.gov/air/urbanair.

3. Criteria Pollutants vs. Mobile Source Controls, Part 2: Is Carbon Dioxide the Next Criteria Pollutant?

Climate change, like lead, presents serious questions regarding how best to regulate—even about whether the Clean Air Act is the best statute to use. Most scientists have acknowledged that climate change is real and that human activities are at least partly responsible for it by increasing atmospheric concentrations of greenhouse gases, such as carbon dioxide, a byproduct of combustion of fossil fuels. In addition, the EPA, on its climate change web site, states that:

> The warmest global average temperatures on record have all occurred within the past 15 years, with the warmest two years being 1998 and 2005. Most of the warming in recent decades is likely the result of human activities. * * * If greenhouse gases continue to increase, climate models predict that the average temperature at the Earth's surface could increase from 2.5 to 10.4°F above 1990 levels by the end

> of this century. Scientists are certain that human activities are changing the composition of the atmosphere, and that increasing the concentration of greenhouse gases will change the planet's climate.

U.S. EPA, *Climate Change: Basic Information*, http://www.epa.gov/climatechange/basicinfo.html (as updated May 4, 2007). Some of the projected effects of climate change include unstable weather, increased flooding, increased drought, more frequent outbreaks of tropical diseases such as West Nile virus, rising sea levels, and the potential elimination of several island nations.

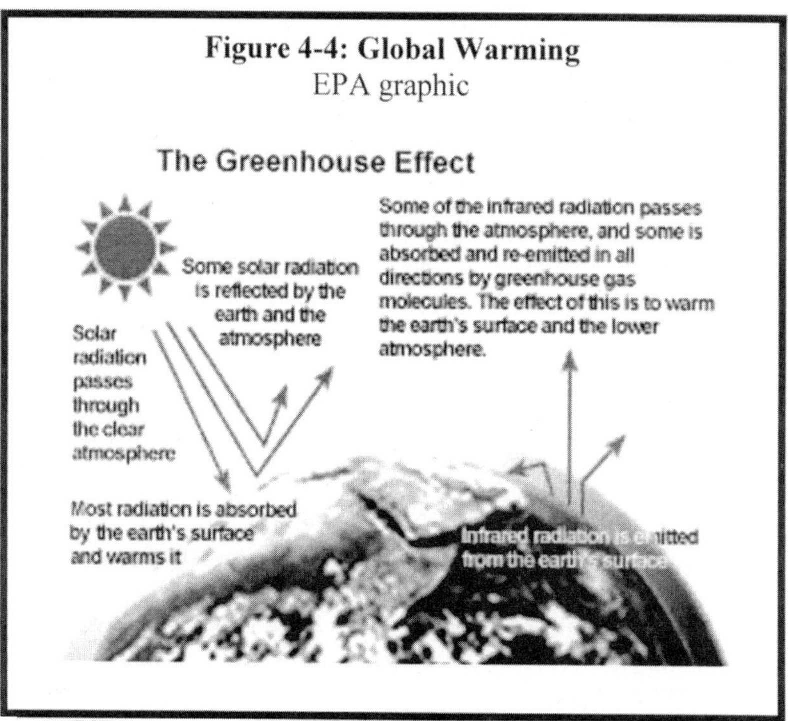

Figure 4-4: Global Warming
EPA graphic

In light of this growing scientific consensus, toward the end of the Clinton Administration, the International Center for Technology Assessment (ICTA) and other parties began to lobby the EPA to regulate carbon dioxide and other greenhouse gases under the Clean Air Act. The Clinton Administration EPA declared that it had authority to regulate carbon dioxide; nevertheless, it did nothing to add carbon dioxide to the list of criteria pollutants. In 1999, the ICTA formally petitioned the EPA to regulate greenhouse gas emissions from new motor vehicles pursuant to Section 202 of the Clean Air Act. Under Section 202, the EPA "shall by regulation prescribe . . . standards applicable to the emission of any air pollutant from any class or classes of new motor vehicles . . . which in his judgment cause, or contribute to, air pollution which may reasonably be anticipated to endanger public health or welfare." CAA § 202(a)(1), 42 U.S.C. § 7521(a)(1).

After three years of the EPA's inaction, the ICTA filed suit in December 2002 to force the EPA to decide its petition. While that lawsuit was pending, two other legal proceedings arose: (1) in February 2003, New York, Connecticut, Maine, Massachusetts, New Jersey, Rhode Island, and Washington sent a notice of intent to sue the EPA for the EPA's failure to set new source performance standards (NSPS) for fossil fuel-fired power plants' emissions of carbon dioxide pursuant to Section 111; and (2) in June 2003, Connecticut, Maine, and Massachusetts independently filed suit to force the EPA to list carbon dioxide as a criteria pollutant. While both of these lawsuits were still pending, in August 2003, the Bush Administration EPA concluded that it lacked authority to regulate carbon dioxide because the Clean Air Act does not address climate change.

Following this declaration of lack of authority, the EPA formally denied the ICTA's petition on September 8, 2003. 68 Fed. Reg. 52,922. In October 2003, eleven states joined the ICTA in appealing this petition denial to the D.C. Circuit. In 2005, the D.C. Circuit upheld a fractured decision upholding the EPA: Judge Randolph determined that the EPA could use its discretion to not regulate carbon dioxide and other greenhouse gases, while Judge Sentelle held that the plaintiffs lacked standing (see Chapter 6). Judge Tatel dissented. *Massachusetts v. EPA*, 415 F.3d 50 (D.C. Cir. 2005). The D.C. Circuit denied a rehearing *en banc* in December 2005, 433 F.3d 66 (D.C. Cir. 2005), but the U.S. Supreme Court granted *certiorari*. 548 U.S. 903, 126 S.Ct. 2960 (June 26, 2006).

On April 2, 2007, the Supreme Court issued the following decision.

MASSACHUSETTS v. ENVIRONMENTAL PROTECTION AGENCY

549 U.S. 497 (2007).

STEVENS, J., delivered the opinion of the Court, in which KENNEDY, SOUTER, GINSBURG, and BREYER, JJ., joined.

A well-documented rise in global temperatures has coincided with a significant increase in the concentration of carbon dioxide in the atmosphere. Respected scientists believe the two trends are related. For when carbon dioxide is released into the atmosphere, it acts like the ceiling of a greenhouse, trapping solar energy and retarding the escape of reflected heat. It is therefore a species—the most important species—of a "greenhouse gas."

Calling global warming "the most pressing environmental challenge of our time," a group of States,[2] local governments,[3] and private organizations,[4] alleged in a petition for certiorari that the Environmental Protec-

2. California, Connecticut, Illinois, Maine, Massachusetts, New Jersey, New Mexico, New York, Oregon, Rhode Island, Vermont, and Washington.

3. District of Columbia, American Samoa, New York City, and Baltimore.

4. Center for Biological Diversity, Center for Food Safety, Conservation Law Foundation, Environmental Advocates, Environmental Defense, Friends of the Earth, Greenpeace, International Center for Technology Assessment, National Environmental Trust, Natural Resources

tion Agency (EPA) has abdicated its responsibility under the Clean Air Act to regulate the emissions of four greenhouse gases, including carbon dioxide. Specifically, petitioners asked us to answer two questions concerning the meaning of § 202(a)(1) of the Act: whether EPA has the statutory authority to regulate greenhouse gas emissions from new motor vehicles; and if so, whether its stated reasons for refusing to do so are consistent with the statute.

* * * I

Section 202(a)(1) of the Clean Air Act ... provides:

> "The [EPA] Administrator shall by regulation prescribe (and from time to time revise) in accordance with the provisions of this section, standards applicable to the emission of any air pollutant from any class or classes of new motor vehicles or new motor vehicle engines, which in his judgment cause, or contribute to, air pollution which may reasonably be anticipated to endanger public health or welfare...."

The Act defines "air pollutant" to include "any air pollution agent or combination of such agents, including any physical, chemical, biological, radioactive ... substance or matter which is emitted into or otherwise enters the ambient air." § 7602(g). "Welfare" is also defined broadly: among other things, it includes "effects on ... weather ... and climate." § 7602(h).

When Congress enacted these provisions, the study of climate change was in its infancy. In 1959, shortly after the U.S. Weather Bureau began monitoring atmospheric carbon dioxide levels, an observatory in Mauna Loa, Hawaii, recorded a mean level of 316 parts per million. * * * By the time Congress drafted § 202(a)(1) in 1970, carbon dioxide levels had reached 325 parts per million.

In the late 1970's, the Federal Government began devoting serious attention to the possibility that carbon dioxide emissions associated with human activity could provoke climate change. In 1978, Congress enacted the National Climate Program Act, 92 Stat. 601, which required the President to establish a program to "assist the Nation and the world to understand and respond to natural and man-induced climate processes and their implications," *id.,* § 3. President Carter, in turn, asked the National Research Council, the working arm of the National Academy of Sciences, to investigate the subject. The Council's response was unequivocal: "If carbon dioxide continues to increase, the study group finds no reason to doubt that climate changes will result and no reason to believe that these changes will be negligible.... A wait-and-see policy may mean waiting until it is too late."

Congress next addressed the issue in 1987, when it enacted the Global Climate Protection Act, Title XI of Pub. L. 100–204, 101 Stat. 1407, note following 15 U.S.C. § 2901. * * *

Defense Council, Sierra Club, Union of Concerned Scientists, and U.S. Public Interest Research Group.

Meanwhile, the scientific understanding of climate change progressed. In 1990, the Intergovernmental Panel on Climate Change (IPCC), a multinational scientific body organized under the auspices of the United Nations, published its first comprehensive report on the topic. Drawing on expert opinions from across the globe, the IPCC concluded that "emissions resulting from human activities are substantially increasing the atmospheric concentrations of ... greenhouse gases [which] will enhance the greenhouse effect, resulting on average in an additional warming of the Earth's surface."

* * * Some five years later—after the IPCC issued a second comprehensive report in 1995 concluding that "[t]he balance of evidence suggests there is a discernible human influence on global climate"—the UNFCCC signatories met in Kyoto, Japan, and adopted a protocol that assigned mandatory targets for industrialized nations to reduce greenhouse gas emissions. Because those targets did not apply to developing and heavily polluting nations such as China and India, the Senate unanimously passed a resolution expressing its sense that the United States should not enter into the Kyoto Protocol. President Clinton did not submit the protocol to the Senate for ratification.

II

On October 20, 1999, a group of 19 private organizations[15] filed a rulemaking petition asking EPA to regulate "greenhouse gas emissions from new motor vehicles under § 202 of the Clean Air Act." * * * Fifteen months after the petition' submission, EPA requested public comment on "all the issues raised in [the] petition," adding a "particular" request for comments on "any scientific, technical, legal, economic or other aspect of these issues that may be relevant to EPA's consideration of this petition." 66 Fed. Reg. 7486, 7487 (2001). EPA received more than 50,000 comments over the next five months. See 68 Fed. Reg. 52924 (2003).

Before the close of the comment period, the White House sought "assistance in identifying the areas in the science of climate change where there are the greatest certainties and uncertainties" from the National Research Council, asking for a response "as soon as possible." The result was a 2001 report titled *Climate Change: An Analysis of Some Key Questions* (NRC Report), which, drawing heavily on the 1995 IPCC report, concluded that "[g]reenhouse gases are accumulating in Earth's atmosphere as a result of human activities, causing surface air temperatures and subsurface ocean temperatures to rise. Temperatures are, in fact, rising." *NRC Report* 1.

---

15. Alliance for Sustainable Communities; Applied Power Technologies, Inc.; Bio Fuels America; The California Solar Energy Industries Assn.; Clements Environmental Corp.; Environmental Advocates; Environmental and Energy Study Institute; Friends of the Earth; Full Circle Energy Project, Inc.; The Green Party of Rhode Island; Greenpeace USA; International Center for Technology Assessment; Network for Environmental and Economic Responsibility of the United Church of Christ; New Jersey Environmental Watch; New Mexico Solar Energy Assn.; Oregon Environmental Council; Public Citizen; Solar Energy Industries Assn.; The SUN DAY Campaign.

On September 8, 2003, EPA entered an order denying the rulemaking petition. 68 Fed. Reg. 52922. The agency gave two reasons for its decision: (1) that contrary to the opinions of its former general counsels, the Clean Air Act does not authorize EPA to issue mandatory regulations to address global climate change, see *id.*, at 52925–52929; and (2) that even if the agency had the authority to set greenhouse gas emission standards, it would be unwise to do so at this time, *id.*, at 52929–52931.

In concluding that it lacked statutory authority over greenhouse gases, EPA observed that Congress "was well aware of the global climate change issue when it last comprehensively amended the [Clean Air Act] in 1990," yet it declined to adopt a proposed amendment establishing binding emissions limitations. *Id.*, at 52926. Congress instead chose to authorize further investigation into climate change. *Ibid.* (citing §§ 103(g) and 602(e) of the Clean Air Act Amendments of 1990, 104 Stat. 2652, 2703, 42 U.S.C. §§ 7403(g)(1) and 7671a(e)). * * *

EPA stated that it was "urged on in this view" by this Court's decision in *FDA v. Brown & Williamson Tobacco Corp.*, 529 U.S. 120 (2000). In that case, relying on "tobacco['s] unique political history," *id.*, at 159, we invalidated the Food and Drug Administration's reliance on its general authority to regulate drugs as a basis for asserting jurisdiction over an "industry constituting a significant portion of the American economy," *ibid.*

EPA reasoned that climate change had its own "political history": Congress designed the original Clean Air Act to address *local* air pollutants rather than a substance that "is fairly consistent in its concentration throughout the *world's* atmosphere," 68 Fed. Reg. 52927 (emphasis added); declined in 1990 to enact proposed amendments to force EPA to set carbon dioxide emission standards for motor vehicles, *ibid.* (citing H.R. 5966, 101st Cong., 2d Sess. (1990)); and addressed global climate change in other legislation, 68 Fed. Reg. 52927. Because of this political history, and because imposing emission limitations on greenhouse gases would have even greater economic and political repercussions than regulating tobacco, EPA was persuaded that it lacked the power to do so. *Id.*, at 52928. In essence, EPA concluded that climate change was so important that unless Congress spoke with exacting specificity, it could not have meant the agency to address it.

Having reached that conclusion, EPA believed it followed that greenhouse gases cannot be "air pollutants" within the meaning of the Act. * * * *Id.*, at 52929.

Even assuming that it had authority over greenhouse gases, EPA explained in detail why it would refuse to exercise that authority. The agency began by recognizing that the concentration of greenhouse gases has dramatically increased as a result of human activities, and acknowledged the attendant increase in global surface air temperatures. *Id.*, at 52930. EPA nevertheless gave controlling importance to the NRC Report's statement that a causal link between the two " 'cannot be unequivocally established.' " *Ibid.* (quoting *NRC Report* 17). Given that residual uncertainty, EPA concluded that regulating greenhouse gas emissions would be unwise. 68 Fed. Reg. 52930.

The agency furthermore characterized any EPA regulation of motor-vehicle emissions as a "piecemeal approach" to climate change, *id.*, at 52931, and stated that such regulation would conflict with the President's "comprehensive approach" to the problem, *id.*, at 52932. That approach involves additional support for technological innovation, the creation of nonregulatory programs to encourage voluntary private-sector reductions in greenhouse gas emissions, and further research on climate change—not actual regulation. *Id.*, at 52932–52933. According to EPA, unilateral EPA regulation of motor-vehicle greenhouse gas emissions might also hamper the President's ability to persuade key developing countries to reduce greenhouse gas emissions. *Id.*, at 52931.

III

Petitioners, now joined by intervenor States and local governments, sought review of EPA's order in the United States Court of Appeals for the District of Columbia Circuit. Although each of the three judges on the panel wrote a separate opinion, two judges agreed "that the EPA Administrator properly exercised his discretion under § 202(a)(1) in denying the petition for rule making." 415 F.3d 50, 58 (2005). The court therefore denied the petition for review.

* * * IV

[The majority found that Massachusetts had standing to bring this lawsuit. The Court's standing analysis is presented in Chapter 6.]

V

The scope of our review of the merits of the statutory issues is narrow. As we have repeated time and again, an agency has broad discretion to choose how best to marshal its limited resources and personnel to carry out its delegated responsibilities. See *Chevron U.S.A. Inc. v. Natural Resources Defense Council, Inc.*, 467 U.S. 837, 842–845 (1984). That discretion is at its height when the agency decides not to bring an enforcement action. * * *

* * * EPA concluded in its denial of the petition for rulemaking that it lacked authority under 42 U.S.C. § 7521(a)(1) to regulate new vehicle emissions because carbon dioxide is not an "air pollutant" as that term is defined in § 7602. In the alternative, it concluded that even if it possessed authority, it would decline to do so because regulation would conflict with other administration priorities. As discussed earlier, the Clean Air Act expressly permits review of such an action. § 7607(b)(1). We therefore "may reverse any such action found to be . . . arbitrary, capricious, an abuse of discretion, or otherwise not in accordance with law." § 7607(d)(9).

VI

On the merits, the first question is whether § 202(a)(1) of the Clean Air Act authorizes EPA to regulate greenhouse gas emissions from new motor vehicles in the event that it forms a "judgment" that such emissions contribute to climate change. We have little trouble concluding that it does. In relevant part, § 202(a)(1) provides that EPA "shall by regulation prescribe ... standards applicable to the emission of any air pollutant from any class or classes of new motor vehicles or new motor vehicle engines, which in [the Administrator's] judgment cause, or contribute to, air pollution which may reasonably be anticipated to endanger public health or welfare." 42 U.S.C. § 7521(a)(1). Because EPA believes that Congress did not intend it to regulate substances that contribute to climate change, the agency maintains that carbon dioxide is not an "air pollutant" within the meaning of the provision.

The statutory text forecloses EPA's reading. The Clean Air Act's sweeping definition of "air pollutant" includes "*any* air pollution agent or combination of such agents, including *any* physical, chemical ... substance or matter which is emitted into or otherwise enters the ambient air...." § 7602(g) (emphasis added). On its face, the definition embraces all airborne compounds of whatever stripe, and underscores that intent through the repeated use of the word "any." Carbon dioxide, methane, nitrous oxide, and hydrofluorocarbons are without a doubt "physical [and] chemical ... substance [s] which [are] emitted into ... the ambient air." The statute is unambiguous.

Rather than relying on statutory text, EPA invokes postenactment congressional actions and deliberations it views as tantamount to a congressional command to refrain from regulating greenhouse gas emissions. Even if such postenactment legislative history could shed light on the meaning of an otherwise-unambiguous statute, EPA never identifies any action remotely suggesting that Congress meant to curtail its power to treat greenhouse gases as air pollutants. * * *

EPA's reliance on *Brown & Williamson Tobacco Corp.*, 529 U.S. 120, is similarly misplaced. In holding that tobacco products are not "drugs" or "devices" subject to Food and Drug Administration (FDA) regulation pursuant to the Food, Drug and Cosmetic Act (FDCA), see 529 U.S., at 133, we found critical at least two considerations that have no counterpart in this case.

First, we thought it unlikely that Congress meant to ban tobacco products, which the FDCA would have required had such products been classified as "drugs" or "devices." *Id.*, at 135–137. Here, in contrast, EPA jurisdiction would lead to no such extreme measures. EPA would only *regulate* emissions, and even then, it would have to delay any action "to permit the development and application of the requisite technology, giving appropriate consideration to the cost of compliance," § 7521(a)(2). However much a ban on tobacco products clashed with the "common sense" intuition that Congress never meant to remove those products from circulation, *Brown & Williamson,* 529 U.S., at 133, there is nothing counterintuitive to the notion that EPA can curtail the emission of substances that are putting the global climate out of kilter.

Second, in *Brown & Williamson* we pointed to an unbroken series of congressional enactments that made sense only if adopted "against the backdrop of the FDA's consistent and repeated statements that it lacked authority under the FDCA to regulate tobacco." *Id.,* at 144. We can point to no such enactments here: EPA has not identified any congressional action that conflicts in any way with the regulation of greenhouse gases from new motor vehicles. * * *

EPA finally argues that it cannot regulate carbon dioxide emissions from motor vehicles because doing so would require it to tighten mileage standards, a job (according to EPA) that Congress has assigned to DOT. See 68 Fed. Reg. 52929. But that DOT sets mileage standards in no way licenses EPA to shirk its environmental responsibilities. * * *

While the Congresses that drafted § 202(a)(1) might not have appreciated the possibility that burning fossil fuels could lead to global warming, they did understand that without regulatory flexibility, changing circumstances and scientific developments would soon render the Clean Air Act obsolete. The broad language of § 202(a)(1) reflects an intentional effort to confer the flexibility necessary to forestall such obsolescence. Because greenhouse gases fit well within the Clean Air Act's capacious definition of "air pollutant," we hold that EPA has the statutory authority to regulate the emission of such gases from new motor vehicles.

VII

The alternative basis for EPA's decision—that even if it does have statutory authority to regulate greenhouse gases, it would be unwise to do so at this time—rests on reasoning divorced from the statutory text. While the statute does condition the exercise of EPA's authority on its formation of a "judgment," 42 U.S.C. § 7521(a)(1), that judgment must relate to whether an air pollutant "cause[s], or contribute[s] to, air pollution which may reasonably be anticipated to endanger public health or welfare," *ibid.* Put another way, the use of the word "judgment" is not a roving license to ignore the statutory text. It is but a direction to exercise discretion within defined statutory limits.

* * * Under the clear terms of the Clean Air Act, EPA can avoid taking further action only if it determines that greenhouse gases do not contribute to climate change or if it provides some reasonable explanation as to why it cannot or will not exercise its discretion to determine whether they do. To the extent that this constrains agency discretion to pursue other priorities of the Administrator or the President, this is the congressional design.

EPA has refused to comply with this clear statutory command. Instead, it has offered a laundry list of reasons not to regulate. * * * Although we have neither the expertise nor the authority to evaluate these policy judgments, it is evident they have nothing to do with whether greenhouse gas emissions contribute to climate change. Still less do they amount to a reasoned justification for declining to form a scientific judgment. In particular, while the President has broad authority in foreign affairs, that authority does not extend to the refusal to execute domestic laws. * * *

Nor can EPA avoid its statutory obligation by noting the uncertainty surrounding various features of climate change and concluding that it would therefore be better not to regulate at this time. See 68 Fed. Reg. 52930–52931. If the scientific uncertainty is so profound that it precludes EPA from making a reasoned judgment as to whether greenhouse gases contribute to global warming, EPA must say so. That EPA would prefer not to regulate greenhouse gases because of some residual uncertainty—which, contrary to Justice SCALIA's apparent belief, is in fact all that it said, see 68 Fed. Reg. 52929 ("We do not believe . . . that it would be either effective or appropriate for EPA *to establish [greenhouse gas] standards for motor vehicles* at this time" (emphasis added))—is irrelevant. The statutory question is whether sufficient information exists to make an endangerment finding.

In short, EPA has offered no reasoned explanation for its refusal to decide whether greenhouse gases cause or contribute to climate change. Its action was therefore "arbitrary, capricious, . . . or otherwise not in accordance with law." 42 U.S.C. § 7607(d)(9)(A). We need not and do not reach the question whether on remand EPA must make an endangerment finding, or whether policy concerns can inform EPA's actions in the event that it makes such a finding. We hold only that EPA must ground its reasons for action or inaction in the statute.

VIII

The judgment of the Court of Appeals is reversed, and the case is remanded for further proceedings consistent with this opinion.

It is so ordered.

JUSTICE SCALIA, with whom THE CHIEF JUSTICE, JUSTICE THOMAS, and JUSTICE ALITO join, dissenting.

* * * I

A

The provision of law at the heart of this case is § 202(a)(1) of the Clean Air Act (CAA), which provides that the Administrator of the Environmental Protection Agency (EPA) "shall by regulation prescribe . . . standards applicable to the emission of any air pollutant from any class or classes of new motor vehicles or new motor vehicle engines, which *in his judgment* cause, or contribute to, air pollution which may reasonably be anticipated to endanger public health or welfare." 42 U.S.C. § 7521(a)(1) (emphasis added). As the Court recognizes, the statute "condition[s] the exercise of EPA's authority on its formation of a 'judgment.' " There is no dispute that the Administrator has made no such judgment in this case.

The question thus arises: Does anything *require* the Administrator to make a "judgment" whenever a petition for rulemaking is filed? Without citation of the statute or any other authority, the Court says yes. * * * Where does the CAA say that the EPA Administrator is required to come to a decision on this question whenever a rulemaking petition is filed? The Court points to no such provision because none exists. * * *

B

Even on the Court's own terms, however, the same conclusion follows. As mentioned above, the Court gives EPA the option of determining that the science is too uncertain to allow it to form a "judgment" as to whether greenhouse gases endanger public welfare. * * * But EPA *has* said precisely that—and at great length, based on information contained in a 2001 report by the National Research Council (NRC) entitled *Climate Change Science: An Analysis of Some Key Questions*:

> "As the NRC noted in its report, concentrations of [greenhouse gases (GHGs)] are increasing in the atmosphere as a result of human activities (pp. 9–12). It also noted that '[a] diverse array of evidence points to a warming of global surface air temperatures' (p. 16). The report goes on to state, however, that '[b]ecause of the large and still uncertain level of natural variability inherent in the climate record and the uncertainties in the time histories of the various forcing agents (and particularly aerosols), a [causal] linkage between the buildup of greenhouse gases in the atmosphere and the observed climate changes during the 20th century cannot be unequivocally established. The fact that the magnitude of the observed warming is large in comparison to natural variability as simulated in climate models is suggestive of such a linkage, but it does not constitute proof of one because the model simulations could be deficient in natural variability on the decadal to century time scale' (p. 17).
>
> "The NRC also observed that 'there is considerable uncertainty in current understanding of how the climate system varies naturally and reacts to emissions of [GHGs] and aerosols' (p. 1). * * *
>
> "The science of climate change is extraordinarily complex and still evolving. Although there have been substantial advances in climate change science, there continue to be important uncertainties in our understanding of the factors that may affect future climate change and how it should be addressed. * * * Substantial scientific uncertainties limit our ability to assess each of these factors and to separate out those changes resulting from natural variability from those that are directly the result of increases in anthropogenic GHGs.
>
> "Reducing the wide range of uncertainty inherent in current model predictions will require major advances in understanding and modeling of the factors that determine atmospheric concentrations of green-

house gases and aerosols, and the processes that determine the sensitivity of the climate system."

68 Fed. Reg. 52930.

I simply cannot conceive of what else the Court would like EPA to say.

II

A

Even before reaching its discussion of the word "judgment," the Court makes another significant error when it concludes that "§ 202(a)(1) of the Clean Air Act *authorizes* EPA to regulate greenhouse gas emissions from new motor vehicles in the event that it forms a 'judgment' that such emissions contribute to climate change." For such authorization, the Court relies on what it calls "the Clean Air Act's capacious definition of 'air pollutant.' "

"Air pollutant" is defined by the Act as "any air pollution agent or combination of such agents, including any physical, chemical, ... substance or matter which is emitted into or otherwise enters the ambient air." 42 U.S.C. § 7602(g). The Court is correct that "[c]arbon dioxide, methane, nitrous oxide, and hydrofluorocarbons," fit within the second half of that definition: They are "physical, chemical, ... substance[s] or matter which [are] emitted into or otherwise ente[r] the ambient air." But the Court mistakenly believes this to be the end of the analysis. In order to be an "air pollutant" under the Act's definition, the "substance or matter [being] emitted into ... the ambient air" must also meet the *first* half of the definition—namely, it must be an "air pollution agent or combination of such agents." The Court simply pretends this half of the definition does not exist.

* * * It is perfectly reasonable to view the definition of "air pollutant" in its entirety: An air pollutant *can* be "any physical, chemical, ... substance or matter which is emitted into or otherwise enters the ambient air," but only if it retains the general characteristic of being an "air pollution agent or combination of such agents." This is precisely the conclusion EPA reached.... Once again, in the face of textual ambiguity, the Court's application of *Chevron* deference to EPA's interpretation of the word "including" is nowhere to be found. Evidently, the Court defers only to those reasonable interpretations that it favors.

B

Using (as we ought to) EPA's interpretation of the definition of "air pollutant," we must next determine whether greenhouse gases are "agent[s]" of "air pollution." If so, the statute would authorize regulation; if not, EPA would lack authority.

Unlike "air pollutants," the term "air pollution" is not itself defined by the CAA; thus, once again we must accept EPA's interpretation of that ambiguous term, provided its interpretation is a "permissible construction of the statute." *Chevron,* 467 U.S., at 843. * * * EPA began with the commonsense observation that the "[p]roblems associated with atmospheric concentrations of CO_2," *id.,* at 52927, bear little resemblance to what would naturally be termed "air pollution" * * *. In other words, regulating the buildup of CO_2 and other greenhouse gases in the upper reaches of the atmosphere, which is alleged to be causing global climate change, is not akin to regulating the concentration of some substance that is *polluting* the *air.*

* * * In the end, EPA concluded that since "CAA authorization to regulate is generally based on a finding that an air pollutant causes or contributes to air pollution," 68 Fed. Reg. 52928, the concentrations of CO_2 and other greenhouse gases allegedly affecting the global climate are beyond the scope of CAA's authorization to regulate. "[T]he term 'air pollution' as used in the regulatory provisions cannot be interpreted to encompass global climate change." *Ibid.* Once again, the Court utterly fails to explain why this interpretation is incorrect, let alone so unreasonable as to be unworthy of *Chevron* deference.

* * *

The Court's alarm over global warming may or may not be justified, but it ought not distort the outcome of this litigation. This is a straightforward administrative-law case, in which Congress has passed a malleable statute giving broad discretion, not to us but to an executive agency. No matter how important the underlying policy issues at stake, this Court has no business substituting its own desired outcome for the reasoned judgment of the responsible agency.

NOTES

1. **What Next for Motor Vehicle Emissions?** Given the Supreme Court's decision in *Massachusetts v. EPA,* will the EPA have to regulate greenhouse gas emissions from new motor vehicles? Why or why not? Review the quotation from the EPA's web site and the Supreme Court's opinion. Has the EPA already made an endangerment finding regarding carbon dioxide and other greenhouse gases? Why or why not? Is there any other way that the EPA can justify its decision not to regulate greenhouse gas emissions? Why or why not?

2. **Regulating Emissions from New Motor Vehicles vs. Establishing New Criteria Pollutants.** How does the standard in Section 202 for regulating new motor vehicle emissions compare to Section 108's requirements for establishing criteria pollutants? In particular, can the EPA make an "endangerment" finding under Section 202 without simultaneously making an "endangerment" finding under Section 108? What other elements does Section 108 require before the EPA must list a pollutant as a criteria pollutant? After the Supreme Court's decision in *Massachusetts v. EPA,* can the EPA avoid listing carbon dioxide and other greenhouse gases as criteria pollutants? Why or why not? If the EPA decides to regulate greenhouse gas

emissions from new motor vehicles, will it be able to avoid listing carbon dioxide and other greenhouse gases as criteria pollutants? Why or why not?

3. **The Aftermath of *Massachusetts v. EPA*.** On May 14, 2007, President George W. Bush issued Executive Order No. 13432, declaring that "it is the policy of the United States to ensure the coordinated and effective exercise of the authorities of the President and the heads of the Department of Transportation, the Department of Energy, and the Environmental Protection Agency to protect the environmental with respect to greenhouse gas emissions from motor vehicles, nonroad vehicles, and nonroad engines, in a manner consistent with sound science, analysis of benefits and costs, public safety, and economic growth." § 1, 72 Fed. Reg. 27,717, 27,717. The order requires that, if a federal agency undertakes "a regulatory action that can reasonably be expected to directly regulate emissions, or to substantially and predictably affect emissions, of greenhouse gases from motor vehicles, nonroad vehicles, nonroad engines, or the use of motor fuels," that agency must regulate jointly with the other affected agencies and coordinate with them. § 3, 72 Fed. Reg. at 27,717–18.

On July 30, 2008, in response to pressure to respond to the *Massachusetts v. EPA* decision, the Bush Administration's EPA issued an Advance Notice of Proposed Rulemaking to gather comments on "Regulating Greenhouse Gas Emissions Under the Clean Air Act." 73 Fed. Reg. 44,354 (July 30, 2008). Within this announcement, the EPA stated that "it has become clear that if EPA were to regulate greenhouse gas emissions from motor vehicles under the Clean Air Act, then regulation of smaller stationary sources that also emit GHGs—such as apartment buildings, large home, schools, and hospitals—could also be triggered. One point is clear: The potential regulation of greenhouse gases under any portion of the Clean Air Act could result in an unprecedented expansion of EPA authority that would have a profound effect on virtually every sector of the economy and touch every household in the land." *Id.* at 44,355.

4. **The Obama Administration's EPA's Endangerment Finding:** On April 24, 2009, the EPA for the new Obama Administration issued, in response to *Massachusetts v. EPA*, a proposed endangerment finding not just for carbon dioxide but also for five other greenhouse gases—methane, nitrous oxide, hydrofluorocarbons, perfluorocarbons, and sulfur hexafluoride. 74 Fed. Reg. 18,886 (April 24, 2009). The EPA declined to include several other known greenhouse gases—including water vapor, chlorofluorocarbons (CFCs), hydochlorofluorocarbons (HCFCs), halons, tropospheric ozone, black carbon, and fluorinated ethers—in the endangerment finding. *Id.* at 18.896–97. The EPA concluded that the total body of scientific evidence compellingly supports a positive endangerment finding for both public health and welfare. *Id.* at 18,888. It concluded that the six greenhouse gases are causing and will continue to cause impacts, including increasing temperatures, changes in precipitation patterns, ice melt, rising sea levels, and stronger and more frequent storm events. *Id.* at 18,898–18,901. Public health impacts from these effects will be generally worsening over time and include heat-related health problems, increases in regional ozone pollution, increases in food- and water-borne pathogens and disease, and changes in allergen patterns. *Id.* at 18,901–02. The EPA virtually admitted that these are indirect impacts from green-

house gas pollution but nevertheless asserted that the Clean Air Act's endangerment criteria extend to indirect health impacts:

> Some have argued that a positive endangerment finding for public health cannot be made because the health effects associated with elevated atmospheric concentrations of greenhouse gases occur via climate change, and not directly through inhalation or other exposure to the greenhouse gases themselves. These commenters argue that because 'climate' is included in the definition of welfare, the Act requires that all effects which may flow from a welfare effect must themselves be considered a welfare effect. The Administrator disagrees with this narrow view of the endangerment criteria. Mortality and morbidity that result from the effects of climate change are clearly public health problems. It would be anomalous to argue that a person who is injured or dies from heat exhaustion or increased exposure to a pathogen has not suffered a health impact.

Id. at 18,902. Public welfare impacts, in turn, including the various impacts from heavy precipitation (flooding, runoff, erosion, and water quality impacts); reductions in water supplies; crop failures; problems in livestock production; forest fires, insect outbreaks, and tree mortality in forests of the interior West, Southwest, and Alaska; coastal storm surges and flooding; damage to water infrastructure; ocean acidification; and rearrangements of and other impacts on ecosystems and biodiversity. *Id.* at 18, 902–03. Finally, the EPA also considered international effects. *Id.* at 18,903.

Comments on the endangerment finding closed on June 23, 2009. On June 25, 2009, the Competitive Enterprise Institute released an internal EPA report from Alan Carlin and John Davidson of the EPA's National Center for Environment and Economics, which questioned the science behind the EPA's endangerment finding. Robin Bravender, "Two EPA Staffers Question Science Behind Climate 'Endangerment' Proposal," *The New York Times* (June 26, 2009). The report itself is available at http://www.eenews.net/public/25/11519/features/documents/2009/06/26/document_gw_01.pdf.

On December 7, 2009, the EPA Administrator, Lisa Jackson, formally signed both an endangerment finding and a "cause or contribute" finding under Section 202. These finding were published in the Federal Register on December 15, 2009, 74 Fed. Reg. 66,496 (Dec. 15, 2009), and took effect on January 14, 2010. As the EPA explains:

> On December 7, 2009, the Administrator signed two distinct findings regarding greenhouse gases under section 202(a) of the Clean Air Act:
>
> **Endangerment Finding:** The Administrator finds that the current and projected concentrations of the six key well-mixed greenhouse gases—carbon dioxide (CO_2), methane (CH_4), nitrous oxide (N_2O), hydrofluorocarbons (HFCs), perfluorocarbons (PFCs), and sulfur hexafluoride (SF_6)—in the atmosphere threaten the public health and welfare of current and future generations.
>
> **Cause or Contribute Finding:** The Administrator finds that the combined emissions of these well-mixed greenhouse gases from new motor

> vehicles and new motor vehicle engines contribute to the greenhouse gas pollution which threatens public health and welfare.
>
> These findings do not themselves impose any requirements on industry or other entities. However, this action was a prerequisite for implementing greenhouse gas emissions standards for vehicles. In collaboration with the National Highway Traffic Safety Administration, EPA finalized emission standards for light-duty vehicles (2012–2016 model years) in May of 2010 and heavy-duty vehicles (2014–2018 model years) in August of 2011.

U.S. EPA, *Proposed Endangerment and Cause or Contribute Findings for Greenhouse Gases under the Clean Air Act*, http://epa.gov/climatechange/endangerment.html (as updated Nov. 9, 2011). Thus, climate change is now affecting regulation of mobile sources under the Clean Air Act.

* * *

B. SETTING NAAQS

Once the EPA has identified a criteria air pollutant pursuant to section 108, 42 U.S.C. § 7408, the Clean Air Act then requires it to publish ***National Ambient Air Quality Standards* (NAAQS)** for that pollutant. Specifically, for each criteria air pollutant, the EPA had to publish a ***national primary ambient air quality standard*** and a ***national secondary ambient air quality standard***. CAA § 109(a)(1), 42 U.S.C. § 7409(a)(1). The EPA sets *primary* NAAQS at levels "requisite to protect the public health," based on the air quality criteria and including "an adequate margin of safety." CAA § 109(b)(1), 42 U.S.C. § 7409(b)(1). *Secondary* NAAQS, in contrast, "protect the public welfare from any known or anticipated adverse effects associated with the presence of such air pollutant in the ambient air." CAA § 109(b)(2), 42 U.S.C. § 7409(b)(2).

On its face, section 109, 42 U.S.C. § 7409, gives the EPA no leeway to consider anything besides public health requirements when it sets the primary NAAQS. Two issues emerge from this health focus. First, what does it mean to write a standard that protects the "public health"? Should the standard protect the most sensitive individuals, such as those with asthma, or only the "average" individuals? Second, can the EPA consider the costs involved when it sets NAAQS?

Consider both of these questions as you read the D.C. Circuit's opinion considering the legitimacy of the EPA's NAAQS for lead, which the EPA published in 1978.

LEAD INDUSTRIES ASSOCIATION, INC. v. ENVIRONMENTAL PROTECTION AGENCY

647 F.2d 1130 (D.C. Cir. 1980), *cert. denied*, 449 U.S. 1042.

J. SKELLY WRIGHT, CHIEF JUDGE:

* * * In the present consolidated cases we are asked to review EPA regulations establishing national ambient air quality standards for lead.

These air quality standards prescribe the maximum concentrations of lead that will be permitted in the air of our country. * * * Petitioners are the Lead Industry Association, Inc. (LIA), a nonprofit trade association whose 78 members include most of the country's producers and commercial consumers of lead, and St. Joe Minerals Corporation (St. Joe).

* * * II. THE STATUTORY SCHEME

The first step toward establishing national ambient air quality standards for a particular pollutant is its addition to a list, compiled by EPA's Administrator, of pollutants that cause or contribute to air pollution "which may reasonably be anticipated to endanger public health or welfare[.]" Section 108(a)(1), 42 U.S.C. § 7408(a)(1). Within twelve months of the listing of a pollutant under Section 108(a) the Administrator must issue "air quality criteria" for the pollutant. * * * This criteria document must "accurately reflect the latest scientific knowledge useful in indicating the kind and extent of all identifiable effects on public health or welfare which may be expected from the presence of such pollutant in the ambient air, in varying quantities." Section 108(a)(2), 42 U.S.C. § 7408(a)(2).

At the same time as he issues air quality criteria for a pollutant, the Administrator must also publish proposed national primary and secondary air quality standards for the pollutant. Section 109(a)(2), 42 U.S.C. § 7409(a) (2). National primary ambient air quality standards are standards "the attainment and maintenance of which in the judgment of the Administrator, based on such criteria and allowing an adequate margin of safety, are requisite to protect the public health." Section 109(b)(1), 42 U.S.C. § 7409(b)(1). Secondary air quality standards "specify a level of air quality the attainment and maintenance of which in the judgment of the Administrator, based on such criteria, is requisite to protect the public welfare from any known or anticipated adverse effects associated with the presence of such air pollutant in the ambient air." Section 109(b)(2), 42 U.S.C. § 7409(b)(2). Effects on "the public welfare" include "effects on soils, water, crops, vegetation, manmade materials, animals, wildlife, weather, visibility, and climate, damage to and deterioration of property, and hazards to transportation, as well as effects on economic values and on personal comfort and well-being." Section 302(h), 42 U.S.C. § 7602(h). The Administrator is required to submit the proposed air quality standards for public comment in a rulemaking proceeding, the procedure for which is prescribed by Section 307(d) of the Act, 42 U.S.C. § 7607(d).

* * * III. THE LEAD STANDARDS RULEMAKING PROCEEDINGS

As required by statute, EPA's first step toward promulgating air quality standards for lead was to prepare a criteria document. The Lead Criteria Document was the culmination of a process of rigorous scientific and public review, and thus is a comprehensive and thoughtful analysis of the most current scientific information on the subject. The Lead Criteria Document went through three major drafts, and three separate reviews, including public meetings by the Subcommittee on Scientific Criteria for Environmental Lead of EPA's Science Advisory Board (SAB Lead Subcommittee). The Agency reviewed over 280 public comments, most of a sophisticated scientific nature, before it issued the final Criteria Document. Members of the public, industry (including the petitioners in these cases), environmental groups, the scientific community, and state and federal government agencies actively participated in the review of the drafts. Notice of the meetings of the SAB Lead Subcommittee was published in the Federal Register, and the drafts of the Criteria Document which were to be reviewed were available before the meetings. A formal record and a transcript of the proceedings were kept, and a review of the transcript shows that scientists with differing views could and did exchange ideas with each other as well as agency staff, and that all were questioned by the members of the Subcommittee.

A. The Lead Criteria Document

EPA released its "Air Quality Criteria For Lead" on December 14, 1977. 42 Fed. Reg. 63076. * * * The Criteria Document concluded that, among the major organ systems, the hematopoietic (blood-forming) and neurological systems are the areas of prime concern. Its discussion of the effects of lead on these two organ systems is central to our review of the lead standards.

The Criteria Document identified a variety of effects of lead exposure on the blood-forming system. We will discuss only the effects that played an important role in the Administrator's analysis. Anemia, which can be caused by lead-induced deformation and destruction of erythrocytes (red blood cells) and decreased hemoglobin synthesis, is often the earliest clinical manifestation of lead intoxication. * * * The Criteria Document concluded * * * that in "children, a threshold level for anemia is about 40 μg Pb/dl, whereas the corresponding value for adults is about 50 μg Pb/dl." (The concentration of lead in the blood is measured in micrograms of lead per deciliter of blood, μg Pb/dl.)

The Criteria Document also examined other more subtle effects on the blood-forming system, associated with lower levels of lead exposure. The most pertinent of these "subclinical" effects for purposes of these cases is lead-related elevation of erythrocyte protoporphyrin (EP elevation). According to the Criteria Document, this phenomenon must, for a number of reasons, be regarded as an indication of an impairment of human health. First, EP elevation indicates an impairment in the functioning of the mitochondria, the subcellular units which play a crucial role in the production of energy in the body, and in cellular respiration. Second, it indicates that lead exposure has begun to affect one of the basic biological functions of the body production of heme within the red blood cells. Heme is critical to transporting oxygen to every cell in the body. Third, EP elevation may indicate that any reserve capacity there may be in the heme synthesis system has been reduced. Finally, the Criteria Document noted that lead's interference with the process of heme synthesis in the blood may suggest that lead interferes with production of heme proteins in other organ systems, particularly the renal and neurological systems. The Criteria Document reported that the threshold for EP elevation in children and women is at blood lead levels of 15–20 μg Pb/dl, and 25–30 μg Pb/dl in adult males. * * *

* * * In addition to examining the health effects of lead exposure, the Criteria Document also discussed other issues critical to the task of setting air quality standards for lead. One of these issues is the relationship between air lead exposure and blood lead levels a relationship commonly referred to as the air lead/blood lead ratio. The Criteria Document acknowledged that derivation of a functional relationship between air lead exposure and blood lead levels is made difficult by the fact that the relationship is not a linear one; rather, the ratio tends to increase as air lead levels are reduced. The Document was nevertheless able to conclude, after a detailed examination of the relevant studies that air lead/blood lead ratios fall within a range of 1:1 to 1:2 (μg Pb/m^3 air):(μg Pb/dl blood) at the levels of lead exposure generally encountered by the population, *i.e.*, blood lead levels increase by between 1 and 2 μg Pb/dl of blood for every 1 μg Pb/m^3 of air. (Air lead content is measured in micrograms of lead per cubic meter of air, μg Pb/m^3.) The Criteria Document reported that the studies indicate that the ratio for children is at the upper end of this range or even slightly above it.

Finally, the Criteria Document also examined the distribution of blood lead levels throughout the population, concluding that there is a significant variability in individual blood lead responses to any particular level of air lead exposure. * * * The Criteria Document looked into the question whether any sub-groups within the population are particularly vulnerable to the effects of lead exposure. It concluded that preschool-age children and pregnant women are particularly sensitive to lead exposure, the latter mainly because of the risk to the unborn child.

** * * D. The Final Air Quality Standards for Lead*

The Administrator promulgated the final air quality standards on October 5, 1978, prescribing national primary and secondary ambient air quality standards for lead of 1.5 μg Pb/m^3, averaged over a calendar quarter. 43 Fed. Reg. 46246. Although the final standards were the same as the proposed standards (with the exception of the change in the averaging period from 30 to 90 days), the Administrator arrived at the final standards through somewhat different analysis. * * * In particular, he seemed to feel that legitimate questions had been raised concerning the health significance of the early stages of EP elevation and about the threshold blood lead level for this condition. 43 Fed. Reg. 46248, 46253. The Administrator's reexamination focused on two key questions: (1) What is the maximum safe individual blood lead level for children? and (2) what proportion of the target population should be kept below this blood lead level? *Id.* at 46249, 46252–46253. Addressing the first issue required a review of the health effects of lead exposure discussed in the Criteria Document. The Administrator concluded that, although EP elevation beginning at blood lead levels of 15–20 μg Pb/dl is potentially adverse to the health of children, only when blood lead concentration reaches a level of 30 μg Pb/dl is this effect significant enough to be considered adverse to health. *Id.* at 46253. Accordingly, he selected 30 μg Pb/dl as the maximum safe individual blood lead level for children. *Id.* The Administrator based this choice on three mutually supporting grounds. First, it is at this blood lead level that the first adverse health effect of lead exposure impairment of heme synthesis begins to occur in children. Second, a maximum safe individual blood lead level of 30 μg Pb/dl would allow an adequate margin of safety in protecting children against more serious effects of lead exposure anemia, symptoms of which begin to appear in children at blood lead levels of 40 μg Pb/dl, and central nervous system deficits which start to occur in children at blood lead levels of 50 μg Pb/dl. Third, the Administrator reasoned that the maximum safe individual blood lead level should be no higher than the blood lead level used by the Center for Disease Control in screening children for lead poisoning 30 μg Pb/dl. *Id.*

Having determined the maximum safe individual blood lead level for the target population, the Administrator next focused on the question of what percentage of children between the ages of 1 and 5 years the standard should attempt to keep below this blood lead level. According to the 1970 census, there are approximately 20 million children under the age of 5 years in the United States, 12 million of them in urban areas and 5 million in inner cities where lead exposure may be especially high. The Administrator concluded that in order to provide an adequate margin of safety, and to protect special high risk sub-groups, the standards should aim at keeping 99.5% of the target population below the maximum safe individual blood lead level of 30 μg Pb/dl. *Id.* at 46253, 46255. The next step in the analysis was to determine what target mean population blood lead level would ensure that 99.5% of the children below the age of 5 years would be kept below the maximum safe individual blood lead level of 30 μg Pb/dl. Using the lognormal statistical technique he had alluded to in the proposed standards, he calculated that a target mean population blood lead level of 15 μg Pb/dl (the same number as in the proposed standards, but arrived at through different analysis), would accomplish this task. *Id.* at 46253, 46254. Thereafter, the Administrator used the same estimate of the contribution from non-air sources, 12 μg Pb/dl, and the same air lead/blood lead ratio, 1:2, that he had used in calculating the proposed standards, to compute the final ambient air quality standards for lead. The result was an ambient air quality standard of 1.5 μg Pb/m 3, the same as the proposed standard. *Id.* at 46254. The Administrator did, however, change the averaging period for the standards from one calendar month to one calendar quarter, *id.* at 46255, because he felt that this change would significantly improve the validity of the data to be used in monitoring the progress toward attainment of the standards without rendering the standards less protective. *Id.*

* * * IV. STANDARD OF REVIEW

The scope of judicial review of the Administrator's decisions and actions is delineated by Section 307(d) of the Act, 42 U.S.C. § 7607(d). We must uphold the Administrator's actions unless we find that they were: (1) "arbitrary, capricious, an abuse of discretion, or otherwise not in accordance with law"; (2) "contrary to constitutional right, power, privilege, or immunity"; (3) "in excess of statutory jurisdiction, authority, or limitations, or short of statutory right[.]" Section 307(d)(9), 42 U.S.C. § 7607(d)(9). In addition, we may set aside any action found to be "without observance of procedure required by law," if (i) the failure to follow the prescribed procedure was arbitrary or capricious, (ii) the procedural objection was raised during the public comment period, or there were good reasons why it was not, and (iii) the procedural errors "were so serious and related to matters of such central relevance to the rule that there is a substantial likelihood that the rule would have been significantly changed if such errors had not been made." *Id.* Section 307(d)(8), 42 U.S.C. § 7607(d)(8).

* * * It is also important to note that although the pertinent sections of the Clean Air Act outline the policy objectives to be sought and the procedural framework to be followed in promulgating ambient air quality standards, Congress left the formulation of the specific standards to EPA's Administrator. This task presents complex questions of science, law, and social policy under the Act. The record is lengthy approximately 10,000 pages and it is highly technical. * * *

* * * Thus mindful of our restricted role, we turn to consider petitioners' claims. Petitioners posit three basic questions for decision. First, did the Administrator exceed his authority under the statute in promulgating the lead standards? Second, were key elements in the Administrator's analysis arbitrary or capricious? Third, do alleged procedural shortcomings in the lead standards rulemaking warrant a remand of the regulations to EPA?

V. STATUTORY AUTHORITY

The petitioners' first claim is that the Administrator exceeded his authority under the statute by promulgating a primary air quality standard for lead which is more stringent than is necessary to protect the public health because it is designed to protect the public against "subclinical" effects which are not harmful to health. * * * In developing this argument St. Joe contends that EPA erred by refusing to consider the issues of economic and technological feasibility in setting the air quality standards for lead. * * *

This argument is totally without merit. St. Joe is unable to point to anything in either the language of the Act or its legislative history that offers any support for its claim that Congress, by specifying that the Administrator is to allow an "adequate margin of safety" in setting primary air quality standards, thereby required the Administrator to consider economic or technological feasibility. To the contrary, the statute and its legislative history make clear that economic considerations play no part in the promulgation of ambient air quality standards under Section 109.

Where Congress intended the Administrator to be concerned about economic and technological feasibility, it expressly so provided. For example, Section 111 of the Act, 42 U.S.C. § 7411, directs the Administrator to consider economic and technological feasibility in establishing standards of performance for new stationary sources of air pollution based on the best available control technology. In contrast, Section 109(b) speaks only of protecting the public health and welfare. Nothing in its language suggests that the Administrator is to consider economic or technological feasibility in setting ambient air quality standards.

The legislative history of the Act also shows the Administrator may not consider economic and technological feasibility in setting air quality standards; the absence of any provision requiring consideration of these factors was no accident; it was the result of a deliberate decision by Congress to subordinate such concerns to the achievement of health goals. Exasperated by the lack of significant progress toward dealing with the problem of air pollution under the Air Quality Act of 1967, 81 Stat. 485, and prior legislation, Congress abandoned the approach of offering suggestions and setting goals in favor of "taking a stick to the States in the form of the Clean Air Amendments of 1970 * * *." *Train v. Natural Resources Defense Council, Inc.*, 421 U.S. at 64; see *Union Electric Co. v. EPA*, 427 U.S. 246, 256–257 (1976). Congress was well aware that, together with Sections 108 and 110, Section 109 imposes requirements of a "technology-forcing" character. *Id.* at 257; *Train v. Natural Resources Defense Council, Inc.*, 421 U.S. at 91; *Ethyl Corp. v. EPA*, 541 F.2d at 14. * * * The "technology-forcing" requirements of the Act "are expressly designed to force regulated sources to develop pollution control devices that might at the time appear to be economically or technologically infeasible." *Union Electric Co. v. EPA*, 427 U.S. at 257.

* * * Section 109(b) does not specify precisely what Congress had in mind when it directed the Administrator to prescribe air quality standards that are "requisite to protect the public health." The legislative history of the Act does, however, provide some guidance. The Senate Report explains that the goal of the air quality standards must be to ensure that the public is protected from "adverse health effects." S. REP. NO. 91–1196, at 10. And the report is particularly careful to note that especially sensitive persons such as asthmatics and emphysematics are included within the group that must be protected. * * *

* * * This court has previously noted that some uncertainty about the health effects of air pollution is inevitable. And we pointed out that

"[a]waiting certainty will often allow for only reactive, not preventive regulat[ory action]." *Ethyl Corp. v. EPA*, 541 F.2d at 25. Congress apparently shares this view; it specifically directed the Administrator to allow an adequate margin of safety to protect against effects which have not yet been uncovered by research and effects whose medical significance is a matter of disagreement. * * * Moreover, it is significant that Congress has recently acknowledged that more often than not the "margins of safety" that are incorporated into air quality standards turn out to be very modest or nonexistent, as new information reveals adverse health effects at pollution levels once thought to be harmless. Congress' directive to the Administrator to allow an "adequate margin of safety" alone plainly refutes any suggestion that the Administrator is only authorized to set primary air quality standards which are designed to protect against health effects that are known to be clearly harmful.

Furthermore, we agree with the Administrator that requiring EPA to wait until it can conclusively demonstrate that a particular effect is adverse to health before it acts is inconsistent with both the Act's precautionary and preventive orientation and the nature of the Administrator's statutory responsibilities. Congress provided that the Administrator is to use his judgment in setting air quality standards precisely to permit him to act in the face of uncertainty. And as we read the statutory provisions and the legislative history, Congress directed the Administrator to err on the side of caution in making the necessary decisions. * * * All that is required by the statutory scheme is evidence in the record which substantiates his conclusions about the health effects on which the standards were based. Accordingly, we reject LIA's claim that the Administrator exceeded his statutory authority and turn to LIA's challenge to the evidentiary basis for the Administrator's decisions.

VI. HEALTH BASIS FOR THE LEAD STANDARDS

LIA does not question a number of the steps in the Administrator's analysis. It does not disagree with his selection of children between the ages of one and five years as the target population, or the decision to set a standard that would keep 99.5 percent of the children below the maximum safe individual blood lead level. In addition, LIA does not challenge the Administrator's suggestion that the standards should be based on an assumption that non-air sources contribute 12 μg Pb/dl to blood lead levels. LIA does, however, challenge other key elements in the Administrator's analysis.

A. Maximum Safe Individual Blood Lead Level

LIA attacks the Administrator's determination that 30 μg Pb/dl should be considered the maximum safe individual blood lead level for children, maintaining that there is no evidence in the record indicating that children suffer any health effects that can be considered adverse at this blood lead level. As previously noted, the Administrator's selection was based on his finding that EP elevation at 30 μg Pb/dl is the first adverse health effect of lead exposure, and his determination that a maximum safe individual blood lead level of 30 μg Pb/dl will allow an adequate margin of safety in protecting children against the more serious effects of lead exposure anemia, symptoms of which appear at blood lead levels of 40 μg Pb/dl and central nervous system deficits which begin to occur at blood lead levels of 50 μg Pb/dl.

* * * Our review of the record persuades us that there is adequate support for each of the Administrator's conclusions about the health effects of lead exposure and, consequently, that LIA's challenges to the evidentiary support for these findings must be rejected. Under the statutory scheme enacted by Congress, the Criteria Document prepared with respect to each pollutant is to provide the scientific basis for promulgation of air quality standards for the pollutant. We have already noted that the Lead Criteria Document was the product of a process that allowed the rigorous scientific and public review that are essential to the preparation of a document "accurately reflect[ing] the latest scientific knowledge useful in indicating the kind and extent of all identifiable effects [of lead exposure] on [the] public health * * *." In our view, the Criteria Document provides ample support for the Administrator's findings.

The Criteria Document concluded that EP elevation, which begins in children at blood levels of 15–20 μg Pb/dl, is one of the more significant effects of low level lead exposure because it indicates that lead has already begun to affect basic biological functions in the body. * * * Relying on the Criteria Document's discussion, as well as other evidence in the record, the Administrator made a judgment that for purposes of setting air quality standards for lead, EP elevation at 30 μg Pb/dl must be considered the first adverse effect on the health of children, and he determined that the maximum safe individual blood lead level should be no higher than 30 μg Pb/dl.

The Administrator's judgment echoes the consensus of a group of clinicians who, in 1975, participated in preparation of a statement issued by the Center For Disease Control and endorsed by the American Academy of Pediatrics. These experts agreed that EP elevation "should be used as an indicator of a significant and worrisome body burden of lead." Moreover, the Center For Disease Control uses EP elevation at 30 μg Pb/dl as the cutoff point for detection of lead poisoning in children in its screening programs, a factor that influenced the Administrator's decision. 43 Fed. Reg. 46253. The Administrator's reliance on this was, in our view, entirely appropriate. * * * Further support for the Administrator's decisions is provided by the testimony of various medical and other scientific experts who participated in the lead standards rulemaking. These experts endorsed the Administrator's (and Criteria Document's) conclusions about the effects of low level lead exposures, and agreed with his assessment of the health significance of these effects. The Administrator's decision is, of course, precisely the sort of issue that Congress specifically left to his judgment, and where there is evidence in the record which supports these judgments, this court is not at liberty to substitute its judgment for the

Administrator's. In this instance the Administrator has acted properly under the terms of the statute. He has explained his factual findings and policy judgments, and there is an adequate basis in the record for these decisions. No more is required of him.

* * * We also reject LIA's claim that the evidence in the record does not support the Administrator's determination that the blood lead threshold for symptoms of anemia in children is 40 μg Pb/dl. According to the Criteria Document, the onset of anemia is marked by a decline in the level of hemoglobin per unit of blood. * * * The Criteria Document's conclusions were reached after a review of various studies that have examined the subject, and we cannot, in light of these findings, say that the Administrator's decision about the threshold blood lead level for the symptoms of anemia in children does not have an adequate basis in the record.

Finally, our examination of the record also reveals ample support for the Administrator's determination that lead-induced central nervous system deficits begin to occur in children at blood lead levels of 50 μg Pb/dl. The central nervous system damage about which the Administrator was concerned was not the severe brain damage that can occur at relatively high levels of lead exposure 80–100 μg Pb/dl. Rather, his focus was on more subtle and largely irreversible neurological and behavioral impairment that has been detected in children at lower blood lead levels, 43 Fed. Reg. 46253. The Criteria Document candidly admitted that "[t]he literature on this subject is somewhat limited and controversial," but it was nevertheless able to conclude that "certain statements [can] be made about the possible hazard of low to moderate lead exposure levels." * * * The Criteria Document reported that the blood lead levels associated with these neurobehavioral deficits are 50–60 μg Pb/dl. These conclusions were endorsed by several of the experts who participated in the lead standards rulemaking proceedings, including one of LIA's experts. Some of these experts even suggested that these effects may occur at blood lead levels lower than the levels indicated by the Criteria Document. Contrary to LIA's suggestion, the evidence in the Criteria Document and the testimony of the experts provides an adequate basis for this court to undertake a review of the Administrator's findings concerning these effects. Accordingly, we reject LIA's challenge to the Administrator's conclusion that central nervous system deficits begin to occur in children at blood lead levels of 50 μg Pb/dl.

Our conclusion that there is ample support for the Administrator's determination that EP elevation at 30 μg Pb/dl is the first adverse health effect that children experience as a result of lead exposure is, of course, sufficient to sustain his selection of 30 μg Pb/dl as the maximum safe individual blood lead level. Given this, we cannot say that his further determination that a maximum safe individual blood lead level of 30 μg Pb/dl would in addition provide protection against the more serious adverse health effects of lead exposure was irrational.

* * * Having determined that we must uphold the Administrator's decisions concerning the health effects that are the basis for the lead standards, we turn to petitioners' other challenges to the Administrator's analysis.

B. Margin of Safety

Both LIA and St. Joe argue that the Administrator erred by including multiple allowances for margins of safety in his calculation of the lead standards. * * * They argue that margin of safety allowances were reflected in the choice of the maximum safe individual blood lead level for children, in the decision to place 99.5 percent of the target population group below that blood lead level, in the selection of an air lead/blood lead ratio at 1:2, and in the Administrator's estimate of the contribution to blood lead levels that should be attributed to non-air sources. The net result of these multiple allowances for margins of safety, petitioners contend, was a standard far more stringent than is necessary to protect the public health. * * *

* * * We agree with the Administrator that nothing in the statutory scheme or the legislative history requires him to adopt the margin of safety approach suggested by St. Joe. Adding the margin of safety at the end of the analysis is one approach, but it is not the only possible method. * * * Where, as here, the Administrator has provided an explanation of why he chose one method rather than another, and this explanation and his choice are not irrational, we must accept his decision. * * *

VII. ALLEGED ARBITRARY AND CAPRICIOUS DECISIONS

Petitioners contend that a number of the findings which constitute the very core of the Administrator's analysis violate one or more of the decisionmaking requirements of the Act. * * *

A. Air Lead/Blood Lead Ratio

LIA contends that the Administrator's choice of an air lead/blood lead ratio of 1:2 as the appropriate ratio for calculating the lead standards was arbitrary and capricious. LIA's claim is largely based on its disagreement with the Administrator's interpretation of the results of three studies that have examined the relationship between air lead exposure and blood lead levels. * * * LIA maintains that the Administrator would have arrived at a ratio of 1:1.3, had he focused solely on the studies involving children.

We do not agree that the Administrator's selection of an air lead/blood lead ratio of 1:2 was arbitrary or capricious. The Criteria Document reported that air lead/blood lead ratios for the whole population, adults as well as children, range between 1:1 and 1:2, with children at the upper end of the range or even slightly above it. And the range of ratios for children reported by the studies that were reviewed in the Criteria Document was 1:1.2 to 1:2.3. The Administrator's choice of a ratio of 1:2 for purposes of calculating the lead standards is consistent with each of these findings. Moreover, the Administrator calculated that each of three particularly relevant and well-documented studies that were reviewed by the Criteria Document suggested an air lead/blood lead ratio close to 1:2. 43 Fed. Reg. 46250, 46254. Finally, the Administrator's choice of a ratio of 1:2 was endorsed by several experts who participated in the rulemaking proceedings. Indeed, the issue of the proper relationship between air lead exposure and blood lead levels was extensively discussed in the comments on the initial drafts of the Criteria Document, with several experts severely criticizing the suggestions in early drafts that the appropriate ratio is 1:1. Given all the evidence in the record which supports the Administrator's choice of a ratio of 1:2, we would be exceeding the scope of our reviewing function if we were to agree with LIA's suggestion that the Administrator's decision was either arbitrary or capricious.

B. Changes in Method

LIA next argues that the Administrator contravened the decisionmaking requirements of Section 307(d), 42 U.S.C. § 7607(d), by failing to explain the reasons for a change in the method he used in calculating the lead standards between the proposed and the final standards. LIA correctly points out that the final standard was based on an adverse health effects threshold of 30 μg Pb/dl, whereas the proposed standards had been based on a threshold of 15 μg Pb/dl. It notes that one reason why both the proposed and the final standards nevertheless arrived at an air quality standard of 1.5 μg Pb/m^3 was that the Administrator employed different statistical procedures in determining the target mean population blood level for the two standards. While intimating that the change in methods was not unrelated to EPA's desire to arrive at a final standard of 1.5 μg Pb/m^3, LIA contends that the Administrator did not explain the reasons for this change in method as required by the Act. * * *

We find LIA's contentions to be without substantial merit. In evaluating the significance of these claims, we cannot help noticing that in spite of the misgivings the Administrator had expressed about the lognormal statistical procedure, both LIA and its experts endorsed the use of this procedure in their comments on the proposed standards, and in fact used it to calculate the alternative standards that they recommended. LIA's newly discovered objection to the use of this procedure thus really seems directed at the result it produced, rather than the mere fact that the Administrator used it. Be that as it may, we are satisfied that the Administrator complied with the requirements of Section 307(d). At the time he issued the proposed standards the Administrator informed the public that use of lognormal statistical procedures was an alternative approach to the method he had employed in calculating the proposed standards, and he candidly explained that he had some reservations about the procedure. 42 Fed. Reg. 63079. A fair reading of the Administrator's discussion of the issue in the final regulations suggests that the comments on the proposed standards, including the comments submitted by LIA and its experts, persuaded him to reexamine his analysis, and to conclude that his earlier misgivings about the lognormal procedure were exaggerated. 43

Fed. Reg. 46252–46253. And we are satisfied that it is possible to discern the reasons why the Administrator decided to adopt this procedure from his discussion. *Id.* Accordingly, we must conclude that his discussion of the alternative methods and the reasons for the change in his approach were more than adequate to comply with the requirements of Section 307(d).

Finally, we have uncovered nothing in the record that indicates that the procedure is unreliable, or that the Administrator's decision to use it was unreasonable. Moreover, so far as we can tell, at no time during the course of the rulemaking proceedings did LIA raise any objections to, or even express any reservations about, the lognormal statistical procedure, this in spite of the misgivings the Administrator expressed in the proposed standards. LIA did not even mention this issue in the petition it filed with EPA for reconsideration and stay of the lead standards. In these circumstances, remanding the regulations to EPA is totally unwarranted. * * *

* * * IX. THE SECONDARY AIR QUALITY STANDARD

The final challenge to the Administrator's actions that we must consider is LIA's objection to his decision to promulgate a national secondary ambient air quality standard for lead of 1.5 μg Pb/m^3, the same level as the primary standard. The Administrator explained that this decision was based on his conclusion that the evidence on the "welfare effects" of lead exposure did not justify promulgation of a secondary standard more stringent than the primary standard. LIA argues that the Administrator had no authority to adopt the secondary standard without making supporting findings showing that the standard is necessary to protect the public welfare. * * * LIA argues that the Administrator should have considered whether the welfare effects of lead exposure would permit him to set a secondary air quality standard higher than the primary standard. Pointing out that the primary standards are supposed to protect public health and that they are based on a 90–day averaging period, LIA argues that it follows that primary standards need be met only in inhabited areas, whereas the secondary standards must also be met in uninhabited areas. Consequently, LIA contends, the Administrator's failure to consider the possibility of setting a higher secondary standard will impose an additional burden on industrial sources located in uninhabited areas which may not be justified by the requirements of protecting the public welfare.

LIA's complaint is based on a misconception about the reach of the primary standard. As EPA notes, the primary standard must be met in all parts of the country, whether inhabited or uninhabited. Thus by setting the secondary standard at the same level as the primary standard, the

Administrator imposed no additional burdens on the industry, and he properly concentrated his attention on whether the welfare effects of lead exposure justified promulgation of a more stringent secondary standard. * * *

* * * XI. CONCLUSION

The national ambient air quality standards for lead were the culmination of a process of rigorous scientific and public review which permitted a thorough ventilation of the complex scientific and technical issues presented by this rulemaking proceeding. Interested parties were allowed a number of opportunities to participate in exploration and resolution of the issues raised by the standard-setting exercise. EPA, and ultimately the public whose health these air quality standards protect, have benefitted from their contribution. To be sure, even the experts did not always agree about the answers to the questions that were raised. Indeed, they did not always agree on what the relevant questions were. These disagreements underscore the novelty and complexity of the issues that had to be resolved, and both the EPA and the participants in the rulemaking proceeding deserve to be commended for the diligence with which they approached the task of coming to grips with these difficult issues.

We have accorded these cases the most careful consideration, combining as we must careful scrutiny of the evidence in the record with deference to the Administrator's judgments. We conclude that in this rulemaking proceeding the Administrator complied with the substantive and procedural requirements of the Act, and that his decisions are both adequately explained and amply supported by evidence in the record. Accordingly, we reject petitioners' claims of error. The regulations under review herein are

Affirmed.

NOTES

1. **The Stakes in Setting NAAQS.** Who does the Lead Industries Association represent? Why would the Association so vigorously challenge the EPA's lead NAAQS? Why would it argue that the EPA should consider costs and technological feasibility when setting NAAQS?

2. **The Current NAAQS.** The EPA has charted out the current NAAQS as follows. "Units of measure for the standards are parts per million (ppm) by volume, milligrams per cubic meter of air (mg/m^3), and micrograms per cubic meter of air ($\mu g/m^3$)."

National Ambient Air Quality Standards

POLLUTANT (YEAR)	PRIMARY/ SECONDARY	AVERAGING TIME	LEVEL	FORM
Carbon monoxide (2011)	Primary	8-hour 1-hour	9 ppm 35 ppm	Not to be exceeded more than once per year.
Lead (2008)	Primary & Secondary	Rolling 3-month average	0.15 µg/m³	Not to be exceeded.
Nitrogen dioxide (2010 & 1996)	Primary	1-hour	100 ppb	98th percentile, averaged over 3 years
	Primary & Secondary	Annual	53 ppb	Annual Mean
Ozone (2008)	Primary & Secondary	8-hour	0.075 ppm	Annual fourth-highest daily maximum 8-hr concentration, averaged over 3 years
PM2.5 (2006)	Primary & Secondary	Annual	15 µg/m³	Annual mean, averaged over 3 years
		24-hour	35µg/m³	98th percentile, averaged over 3 years
PM10 (2006)	Primary & Secondary	24-hour	150 µg/m³	Not to be exceeded more than once per year on average over 3 years
Sulfur Dioxide (2010 & 1973)	Primary	1-hour	75 ppb	99th percentile of 1-hour daily maximum concentrations, averaged over 3 years
	Secondary	3-hour	0.5ppm	Not to be exceeded more than once per year

3. **The Legality of Cost Considerations in NAAQS Determinations.** Why can't the EPA consider costs of implementation in setting primary NAAQS? What provisions of the Clean Air Act helped to convince the D.C. Circuit that costs are *not* relevant to primary NAAQS? What other tools of statutory construction did the court consider?

The issue of costs and NAAQS did not go away after this case. In July 1997, the EPA revised the NAAQS for particulate matter and ozone, and the American Trucking Associations challenged the new standards in court, arguing, in part, that the EPA must complete a cost-benefit analysis before promulgating NAAQS. The D.C. Circuit unanimously rejected this argument, and in 2001 the U.S. Supreme Court affirmed that costs play no role in the EPA's setting of primary NAAQS. *Whitman v. American Trucking Associations*, 531 U.S. 457 (2001).

4. **NAAQS "Requisite to Protect the Public Health."** How does the EPA interpret "requisite to protect the public health" in setting the lead NAAQS? *Whose* health, precisely, does it seek to protect? Why? What risks does the EPA try to eliminate? Why? How exactly did it set the lead NAAQS? How did it incorporate a margin of safety? How did it deal with uncertainty in the science? What did the D.C. Circuit conclude about the relationship among science, uncertainty, risk, and the public health in the setting of NAAQS, and why?

5. **The D.C. Circuit's Standard of Review.** What standard of review does the D.C. Circuit use to review the EPA's lead NAAQS? Notice that this standard comes from the Clean Air Act itself, not the federal Administrative Procedures Act (APA). Why would Congress include a specific standard of review within the Clean Air Act? Does this standard of review differ from that in the APA? Why or why not?

How did the standard of review affect the D.C. Circuit's ability to review the EPA's scientific and policy judgments? In particular, what is the relationship between this standard of review and scientific uncertainty? Did the D.C. Circuit attempt to figure out whether the EPA's lead NAAQS is scientifically "correct"? Why or why not? Could the EPA have chosen a different lead NAAQS? Why or why not?

6. **The Lead NAAQS and Environmental Justice.** As noted in *Lead Industries Association*, the EPA set the primary lead NAAQS with a goal of protecting 99.5% of inner city children from acquiring blood-lead levels greater than 30 micrograms per deciliter. The standard that the EPA chose for the primary NAAQS was 1.5 micrograms per cubic meter of air. Under this standard, the EPA projected that, out of a central urban population of 5 million children, 693,000 children would have blood-lead levels greater than 20 micrograms per deciliter, 126,500 children would have blood-lead levels greater than 25 micrograms per deciliter, and 20,605 would have blood-lead levels greater than 30 micrograms per deciliter. EPA, *National Primary and Secondary Ambient Air Quality Standards for Lead*, 43 Fed. Reg. 46,246 (Oct. 5, 1978).

Given the fact that central urban children, statistically, are more likely to be from low-income families and/or to be racial minorities, does the EPA's lead NAAQS raise environmental justice concerns? Why or why not? Why should *any* children have to have blood-lead levels high enough to be of concern? Did the EPA implicitly include some cost-benefit balancing in choosing to protect only 99.5% of inner city children? Did it discriminate against inner-city children?

7. **The Costs of the Clean Air Act.** Despite the health-based nature of the NAAQS, the EPA has in fact performed a series of cost-benefit analyses of the Clean Air Act's regulatory requirements. In section 312 of the Act, Congress required that the EPA Administrator "conduct a comprehensive analysis of the impact of this chapter on the public health, economy, and environment of the United States." CAA § 312(a), 42 U.S.C. § 7612(a). Moreover, Congress specifically required that the EPA "consider the costs, benefits and other effects associated with compliance with" the NAAQS. *Id.* § 312(a)(1), 42 U.S.C. § 7612(a)(1). "In describing the benefits of [the NAAQS], the Administrator shall consider all of the economic, public health, and environmental benefits of efforts to comply with such standards. In any case where numerical values are assigned to such benefits, a default assumption of zero *shall not* be assigned to such benefits unless supported by specific data." *Id.* § 312(b), 42 U.S.C. § 7612(b). In turn, "[i]n describing the costs of [these standard], the Administrator shall consider the effects of such standard on employment, productivity, cost of living, economic growth, and the overall economy of the United States." *Id.* § 312(c), 42 U.S.C. § 7612(c).

The EPA's first cost-benefit report was due to Congress on November 15, 1991, CAA § 312(d), 42 U.S.C. § 7612(d), and updates were due to Congress every two years thereafter. *Id.* § 312(e), 42 U.S.C. § 7612(e). The EPA's methodology for conducting these cost-benefit analyses was discussed in the Introduction to this casebook.

As Figure 4–5 illustrates, the EPA concluded in its initial cost-benefit report to Congress (belatedly submitted in 1997) that the benefits of the Clean Air Act greatly exceeded the costs associated with the Act. As the Introduction noted, moreover, many of the Act's benefits came from avoided health problems and avoided medical treatment, including avoided air-pollution-related deaths, asthma reduction, and even retained intelligence from the removal of lead.

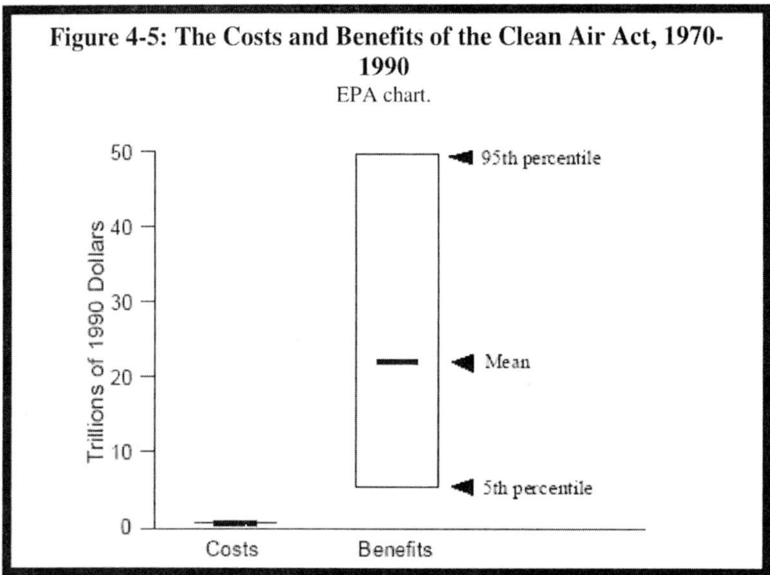

Figure 4-5: The Costs and Benefits of the Clean Air Act, 1970-1990
EPA chart.

In 1999, the EPA calculated the projected continued costs and benefits of the Clean Air Act through 2010. Those calculations are shown in Figure 4–6. This time, the range of benefit calculations (which depend on various assumptions that the EPA makes about value) allow for the possibility that the Clean Air Act will impose more costs than it creates benefits. Nevertheless, the central and high-end estimates of benefits still result in benefit:cost ratios of 4:1 and 8:1 to 10:1, respectively.

Of course, the benefits of the Clean Air Act derive from more than just the health-based primary NAAQS. As will be discussed, the Clean Air Act also reduces pollution from hazardous air pollutants and from various fuels, as is evident in the EPA's elimination of lead from gasoline.

Figure 4-6: Projected Costs and Benefits of the Clean Air Act, 2000 to 2010

EPA chart.

Summary Comparison of Benefits and Costs (Estimates in millions 1990$)

Titles I through V		
	Annual Estimates	
	2000	2010
Monetized Direct Costs:		
Low [a]		
Central	$19,000	$27,000
High [a]		
Monetized Direct Benefits:		
Low[b]	$16,000	$26,000
Central	$71,000	$110,000
High[b]	$160,000	$270,000
Net Benefits:		
Low	($3,000)	($1,000)
Central	$52,000	$83,000
High	$140,000	$240,000
Benefit/Cost Ratio:		
Low[c]	less than 1/1	less than 1/1
Central	4/1	4/1
High[c]	more than 8/1	more than 10/1

[a] The cost estimates for this analysis are based on assumptions about future changes in factors such as consumption patterns, input costs, and technological innovation. We recognize that these assumptions introduce significant uncertainty into the cost results; however the degree of uncertainty or bias associated with many of the key factors cannot be reliably quantified. Thus, we are unable to present specific low and high cost estimates.

[b] Low and high benefits estimates are based on primary results and correspond to 5th and 95th percentile results from statistical uncertainty analysis, incorporating uncertainties in physical effects and valuation steps of benefits analysis. Other significant sources of uncertainty not reflected include the value of unquantified or unmonetized benefits that are not captured in the primary estimates and uncertainties in emissions and air quality modeling.

[c] The low benefit/cost ratio reflects the ratio of the low benefits estimate to the central costs estimate, while the high ratio reflects the ratio of the high benefits estimate to the central costs estimate. Because we were unable to reliably quantify the uncertainty in cost estimates, we present the low estimate as "less than X," and the high estimate as "more than Y", where X and Y are the low and high benefit/cost ratios, respectively.

8. **Actual NAAQS and Health Effects.** Note that in setting the lead NAAQS, the EPA chose to average airborne lead concentrations over 90 days. In 1997, the EPA chose final PM2.5 (fine particulate matter) NAAQS of 15 micrograms per cubic meter *averaged over a year* and 65 micrograms per cubic meter *averaged over a day*. Why would the EPA set both yearly and daily standards for PM2.5? Why would the daily standard be so much higher than the yearly standard? What do the differences between the daily and annual standards imply about the health risks from fine particulate matter? In contrast, under the EPA's 1997 NAAQS for ozone, air quality control regions must not exceed 0.08 parts per million averaged *over eight hours* or 0.12 parts per million averaged *over an hour*. What do these standards imply about the health risks from ozone, as compared to the health risks from PM2.5?

9. **Why *National* Ambient Air Quality Standards?** At the end of *Lead Industries Association*, LIA challenged the secondary lead NAAQS on the grounds that they impose additional burdens on industry in places that are not densely populated. As the D.C. Circuit pointed out, LIA botched its argument by mischaracterizing the role of secondary NAAQS. Nevertheless, LIA raised an interesting point: Why *should* the NAAQS be the same for the

entire country? Does it make sense to require the air above New York City or Los Angeles to be as clean as the air in Wyoming or Montana? As a practical matter, isn't it harder—and hence more expensive—for some areas of the country to comply with the NAAQS than others? Why do you think that Congress went ahead and imposed such a national requirement, knowing that practical and economic disparities would arise?

10. **The New Ozone NAAQS.** On June 20, 2007, the EPA proposed new, more stringent NAAQS for ground-level ozone, which is the primary component of smog. Office of Air & Radiation, U.S. EPA, *Fact Sheet–Proposal to Revise the National Ambient Air Quality Standards for Ozone*, http://www.epa.gov/glo/pdfs/20070620_fs.pdf (last updated June 21, 2007). Under the EPA proposal, the new primary ozone NAAQS would be reset "to a level within the range of 0,070–0.075 ppm (70–75 ppb)," although the agency also sought comments "on alternative levels of the 8–hour primary ozone standard, within a range from 0.060 ppm up to and including retention of the current standard. . . ." *Id.* The EPA is also considering a new secondary ozone NAAQS "designed specifically to protect sensitive plants from damage caused by repeated ozone exposure throughout the growing season. This cumulative standard would add daily ozone concentrations across a three-month period. EPA is proposing to set the level of the cumulative standard within the range of 7 to 21 ppm-hours." *Id.* The EPA plans to issue the new standards on March 12, 2008, then designate attainment and nonattainment areas by June 2010, with state implementation plans (see below) due in 2013 and final attainment to be achieved by 2030. *Id.*

On September 2, 2011, however, President Obama announced that the new ozone regulations would be delayed until 2013. On October 11, 2011, EarthJustice, the American Lung Association, the Natural Resources Defense Council, the Appalachian Mountain Club, and the Environmental Defense Fund sued the EPA about the delay, seeking earlier release of the regulations. Opponents claim that the regulations would cost between $20 billion and $90 billion per year to implement, whereas the plaintiffs in the lawsuit claim that improved health and other benefits would more than make up for the costs of the regulations.

11. **Implementing the New Particulate Matter NAAQS:** The particulate matter NAAQS in the chart are the result of the EPA's 2006 rulemaking. 71 Fed. Reg. 61,143 (2006). These rules reduced the daily standard for PM2.5—particulate matter of 2.5 microns in diameter or less—from 65 micrograms per cubic meter of air to 35 micrograms per cubic meter and set an annual standard for PM2.5 of 15 micrograms per cubic meter. The daily standard for PM10—particulate matter of between 2.5 and 10 microns in diameter—was reduced from 150 micrograms per cubic meter to 70 micrograms per cubic meter. The final deadline for implementing the standards through SIPs was December 18, 2008. The American Farm Bureau Federation and several states challenged the new particulate matter NAAQS. In February 2009, the U.S. Court of Appeals for the D.C. Circuit remanded the yearly NAAQS for PM2.5 to the EPA, concluding that the EPA had failed to adequately explain why that standard was sufficient, given harms to human health from short-term exposures to particulate matter. The EPA had acknowledged that it failed to consider short-term effects in setting the annual

standard for PM2.5. *American Farm Bureau Federation v. EPA*, 559 F.3d 512, 520–22 (D.C. Cir. 2009). In reporting on the D.C. Circuit's decision, the *Los Angeles Times* referred to the 2006 standard as "a Bush-era decision to water down rules controlling the fine soot particles that cause lung cancer, heart disease, and asthma." Margot Roosevelt, Bush-era soot measure overturned, *Los Angeles Times Greenspace*, http://latimesblogs.latimes.com/greenspace/2009/02/soot-pollution.html (February 24, 2009). The EPA maintains a web site about its 2006 Particulate Matter NAAQS: http://www.epa.gov/particles/naaqsrev2006.html.

12. **NAAQS for Greenhouse Gases?** Despite issuing an endangerment finding for mobile source regulation, the EPA has not, as of late 2011, established nationwide NAAQS for greenhouse gases. Nevertheless, the EPA clearly intends to regulate greenhouse gas emissions under the Clean Air Act. Its regulations through the end of 2011 include:

- Mandatory Reporting of Greenhouse Gases, 74 Fed. Reg. 56,260 (Oct. 30, 2009): Required a variety of emitters to submit greenhouse gas emission reports beginning with 2010 emissions data. The first reports were originally due on March 18, 2011, but EPA extended the deadline to September 30, 2011. 76 Fed. Reg. 14,812 (March 18, 2011).
- Prevention of Significant Deterioration and Title V Greenhouse Gas Tailoring Rule ("the Tailoring Rule"), 75 Fed. Reg. 31514 (June 3, 2010): Changes the 100–tons-per-year and 250–tons-per-year emissions thresholds for permitting of stationary sources for greenhouse gas emissions. Specifically, under the rule, as of January 2, 2011, the requirements of the Prevention of Significant Deterioration (PSD) Program (see Part IV.C.1) would apply to projects causing a net increase of greenhouse gas emissions of 75,000 tons per year or more of carbon dioxide equivalents. Then, on July 1, 2011, new and existing stationary sources that emit or have the potential to emit 100,000 tons per year of carbon dioxide equivalents would become subject to permitting requirements.
- PSD and Title V Permitting Guidance for Greenhouse Gases, 75 Fed. Reg. 70,254 (Nov. 17, 2010). This document provides guidance to permitting authorities on how to do the permitting for stationary sources of greenhouse gases. The EPA updated the Guidance in March 2011, and the revised version is available at http://www.epa.gov/nsr/ghgdocs/ghgpermittingguidance.pdf.
- Inventory of U.S. Greenhouse Gas Emissions and Sinks: 1990–2009, 76 Fed. Reg. 10,026 (Feb. 23, 2011).
- Deferral for CO_2 Emissions From Bioenergy and Other Biogenic Sources Under the Prevention of Significant Deterioration (PSD) and Title V Programs, 76 Fed. Reg. 43,490 (July 20, 2011): Defers for three years the application of Clean Air Act permitting to carbon dioxide emissions from bioenergy sources, such as biomass plants.

Nevertheless, the exact scope of Clean Air Act regulation of greenhouse gas emissions remains unclear. As of November 2011, both the Tailoring Rule and the biomass deferral rule were being challenged in federal courts. In June

2011 and again in September 2011, the EPA delayed promulgating greenhouse gas emissions limitations for power plants, announcing on November 17 that the rules would come out in early 2012. However, on November 22, 2011, the EPA announced that it would delay its regulations setting greenhouse gas emission limitations for refineries, which were supposed to be promulgated by mid-December.

* * *

C. SIPS

As part of the Clean Air Act's cooperative federalism, Congress announced that "[e]ach State shall have the primary responsibility for assuring air quality within the entire geographic area comprising such State by submitting an ***implementation plan*** for such State which will specify the manner in which national primary and secondary ambient air quality standards will be achieved and maintained within each air quality control region in such State." CAA § 107(a), 42 U.S.C. § 7407(a) (emphasis added). To carry out this responsibility, States delineated the ***air quality control regions*** (AQCRs) within their boundaries. CAA § 109(b), 42 U.S.C. § 7409(b). For each criteria air pollutant, moreover, the state Governor designated each AQCR as ***attainment***, ***nonattainment***, or ***unclassifiable*** for each criteria air pollutant, depending on whether or not air quality in the AQCR met the NAAQS for that pollutant. CAA § 109(d), 42 U.S.C. § 7409(d). Because such designations are pollutant-specific, an AQCR can simultaneously be in attainment for some criteria pollutants and in nonattainment for others.

Three years after the EPA designated each primary and secondary NAAQS, each state had to submit "a plan which provides for implementation, maintenance, and enforcement of such primary standard in each air quality control region * * *." CAA § 110 (a)(1), 42 U.S.C. § 7410(a)(1). These ***State Implementation Plans* (SIPs)** must ensure that no source of air pollutants contributes to nonattainment or undermines attainment of the NAAQS. More specifically, section 110, 42 U.S.C. § 7410, imposes a total of 13 requirements on SIPs:

Each plan shall—

(A) include enforceable emissions limitations and other control measures, means, or techniques (including economic incentives such as fees, marketable permits, and auctions of emissions rights), as well as schedules and timetables for compliance, as may be necessary or appropriate to meet the requirements of this chapter;

(B) provide for the establishment and operation of appropriate devices, methods, systems, and procedures necessary to—

(i) monitor, compile, and analyze data on ambient air quality, and

(ii) upon request, make such data available to the Administrator;

(C) include a program to provide for the enforcement of the measures described in subparagraph (A), and regulation of the modification and construction of any stationary source within the areas covered by the plan as necessary to assure that national ambient air quality standards are achieved, including a permit program * * *;

(D) contain adequate provisions—

(i) prohibiting, consistent with the provisions of this subchapter, any source or other type of emissions activity within the State from emitting any air pollutant in amounts which will—

(I) contribute significantly to nonattainment in, or interfere with maintenance by, any other State with respect to any such national primary or secondary ambient air quality standard, or

(II) interfere with measures required to be included in the applicable implementation plan for any other State under part C of this subchapter to prevent significant deterioration of air quality or to protect visibility.

(ii) insuring compliance with the applicable requirements of sections 7426 and 7415 of this title (relating to interstate and international pollution abatement);

(E) provide (i) necessary assurances that the State * * * will have adequate personnel, funding, and authority under State * * * law to carry out such implementation plan * * *, (ii) requirements that the State comply with the requirements respecting State boards under section 7428 of this title, and (iii) necessary assurances that, where the State has relied on a local or regional government, agency, or instrumentality for the implementation of any plan provision, the State has responsibility for ensuring adequate implementation of such plan provision;

(F) require, as may be prescribed by the Administrator—

(i) the installation, maintenance, and replacement of equipment, and the implementation of other necessary steps, by owners or operators of stationary sources to monitor emissions from such sources,

(ii) periodic reports on the nature and amounts of emissions and emissions-related data from such sources, and

(iii) correlation of such reports by the State agency with any emissions limitations or standards established pursuant to this chapter, which reports shall be available at reasonable times for public inspection;

(G) provide for authority comparable to that in section 7603 of this title [Emergency Powers] and adequate contingency plans to implement such authority;

(H) provide for revision of such plan—

(i) from time to time as may be necessary to take account of revisions of such national primary or secondary ambient air quality standard or the availability of improved or more expeditious methods of attaining such standard, and

(ii) except as provided in paragraph (3)(C), whenever the Administrator finds on the basis of information available to the Administrator the the plan is substantially inadequate to attain the national ambient air quality standard which it implements or to otherwise comply with any additional requirements established under this chapter;

(I) in the case of a plan or plan revision for an area designated as a nonattainment area, meet the applicable requirements of part D of this subchapter (relating to nonattainment areas);

(J) meet the applicable requirements of section 7421 of this title (relating to consultation), section 7427 of this title (relating to public notification) and part C of this subchapter (relating to prevention of significant deterioration of air quality and visibility protection);

(K) provide for—

(i) the performance of such air quality modeling as the Administrator may prescribe for the purpose of predicting the effect on ambient air quality of any emissions of any air pollutant for which the Administrator has established a national ambient air quality standard, and

(ii) the submission, upon request, of data related to such air quality modeling to the Administrator;

(L) require the owner or operator of each major stationary source to pay to the permitting authority, as a condition of any permit required under this chapter, a fee sufficient to cover—

(i) the reasonable costs of reviewing and acting upon any application for such a permit, and

(ii) if the owner or operator receives a permit for such source, the reasonable costs of implementing and enforcing the terms and conditions of any such permit (not including any court costs or other costs associated with any enforcement action), until such fee requirement is superseded with respect to such sources by the Administrator's approval of a fee program under subchapter V of this chapter; and

(M) provide for consultation and participation by local political subdivisions affected by the plan.

CAA § 110(a)(2), 42 U.S.C. § 7410(a)(2). In addition, the states may—but are not required—to include an indirect source review program to address sources of air pollution not governed by the regular regulatory program. CAA § 110(a)(5)(A)(i), 42 U.S.C § 7410(a)(5)(A)(i).

Before the state can receive the EPA's approval, its SIP submission must meet the EPA's ***minimum completeness criteria***. *See* CAA § 110(k)(1)(A), 42 U.S.C. § 7410(k)(1)(A). The EPA has 60 days in which to assess whether the SIP submission meets these criteria. CAA § 110(k)(1)(B), 42 U.S.C. § 7410(k)(1)(B). If the completeness criteria are met, then the EPA has 12 months in which to approve or disapprove of the SIP. CAA § 110(k)(2), 42 U.S.C. § 7410(k)(2). If the EPA "finds that a State has failed to make a required submission or finds that the plan or plan revision submitted by the State does not satisfy the minimum criteria * * *, or * * * disapproves a State implementation plan in whole or in part," the EPA can write a ***Federal Implementation Plan*** **(FIP)** for the state within two years. CAA § 110(c)(1), 42 U.S.C. § 7410(c)(1). However, the FIP will take effect only if the state does not correct the deficiency to the Administrator's satisfaction. CAA § 110(c)(1)(B), 42 U.S.C. § 7410(c)(1)(B).

A reasonable question at this point is why most states went ahead and wrote their own SIPs, rather than just letting the EPA write FIPs for them. One answer is that in cases of state noncooperation, the EPA has the authority to impose sanctions against the state. CAA § 110(m), 42 U.S.C. § 7410(m). The most controversial of these sanctions are reductions in federal highway funds granted to states. CAA § 179(b)(1), 42 U.S.C. § 7509(b)(1). Another explanation lies in the perception that the EPA dislikes writing FIPs and in the states' fears that any EPA-generated FIP would impose draconian requirements on the state that would be much more expensive than the state would incur in writing its own SIP.

As the 13 SIP requirements indicate, SIP writing is a continual process, and states must amend their SIPs any time that the EPA amends the NAAQS or other requirements in the Act. In addition, the EPA itself has the authority to issue ***SIP calls*** "[w]henever the Administrator finds that the applicable implementation plan for any area is substantially inadequate to attain or maintain the relevant national ambient air quality standard * * * or to otherwise comply with any requirement of this chapter * * *." CAA § 110(k)(5), 42 U.S.C. § 7410(k)(5). SIP calls force states to revise their SIPs, with deadlines no longer than 18 months. *Id.* The SIP revisions, moreover, are subject to all of the requirements—and all of the potential sanctions—that original SIP submissions and state-motivated SIP revisions are subject to. *Id.*

If a state's SIP submission *does* meet the minimum completeness criteria and *does* meet all thirteen requirements, "the Administrator shall approve such a submittal * * *." CAA § 110(k)(3), 42 U.S.C. § 7410(k)(3). As the following case demonstrates, the federal courts have interpreted this provision as giving the EPA little authority to "tweak" state SIPs, regardless of the real-life consequences of those SIPs.

UNION ELECTRIC COMPANY v. ENVIRONMENTAL PROTECTION AGENCY

427 U.S. 246 (1976).

Mr. JUSTICE MARSHALL delivered the opinion of the Court.

After the Administrator of the Environmental Protection Agency (EPA) approves a state implementation plan under the Clean Air Act, the plan may be challenged in a court of appeals within 30 days, or after 30 days have run if newly discovered or available information justifies subsequent review. We must decide whether the operator of a regulated emission source, in a petition for review of an EPA-approved state plan filed after the original 30–day appeal period, can raise the claim that it is economically or technologically infeasible to comply with the plan.

[T]he Clean Air Amendments of 1970 * * * reflect congressional dissatisfaction with the progress of existing air pollution programs and a determination to "tak[e] a stick to the States," in order to guarantee the prompt attainment and maintenance of specified air quality standards. The heart of the Amendments is the requirement that each State formulate, subject to EPA approval, an implementation plan designed to achieve national primary ambient air quality standards[,] those necessary to protect the public health[,] "as expeditiously as practicable but . . . in no case later than three years from the date of approval of such plan." § 110(a)(2)(A) of the Clean Air Act, 42 U.S.C. § 1857c–5(a)(2)(A). The plan must also provide for the attainment of national secondary ambient air quality standards[,] those necessary to protect the public welfare[,] within a "reasonable time." *Ibid.* Each State is given wide discretion in formulating its plan, and the Act provides that the Administrator "shall approve" the proposed plan if it has been adopted after public notice and hearing and if it meets eight specified criteria. § 110(a)(2).

Figure 4-7: Sources of SO_2 Emissions
EPA graph.

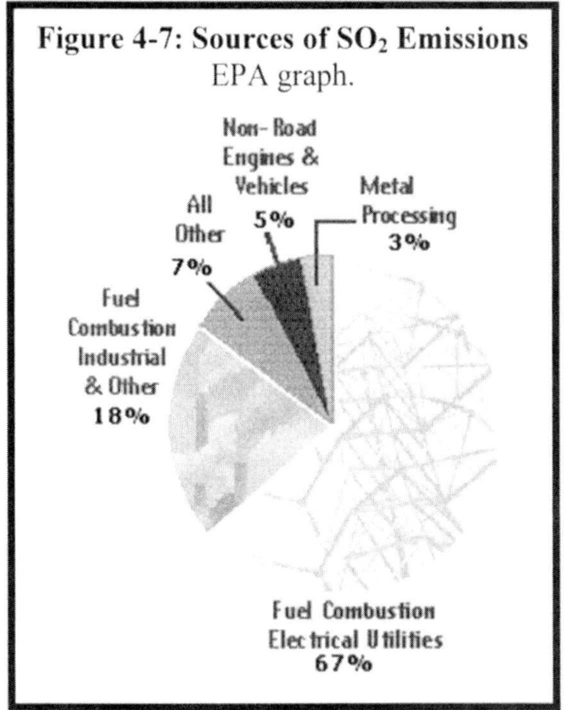

On April 30, 1971, the Administrator promulgated national primary and secondary standards for six air pollutants he found to have an adverse effect on the public health and welfare. Included among them was sulfur dioxide, at issue here. After the promulgation of the national standards, the State of Missouri formulated its implementation plan and submitted it for approval. Since sulfur dioxide levels exceeded national primary standards in only one of the State's five air quality regions the Metropolitan St. Louis Interstate region, the Missouri plan concentrated on a control strategy and regulations to lower emissions in that area. The plan's emission limitations were effective at once, but the State retained authority to grant variances to particular sources that could not immediately comply. The Administrator approved the plan on May 31, 1972.

Petitioner is an electric utility company servicing the St. Louis metropolitan area, large portions of Missouri, and parts of Illinois and Iowa. Its three coal-fired generating plants in the metropolitan St. Louis area are subject to the sulfur dioxide restrictions in the Missouri implementation plan. Petitioner did not seek review of the Administrator's approval of the plan within 30 days, as it was entitled to do under § 307(b)(1) of the Act, 42 U.S.C. § 1857h–5(b)(1), but rather applied to the appropriate state and county agencies for variances from the emission limitations affecting its three plants. Petitioner received one-year variances, which could be extended upon reapplication. The variances on two of petitioner's three plants had expired and petitioner was applying for extensions when, on May 31, 1974, the Administrator notified petitioner that sulfur dioxide emissions from its plants violated the emission limitations contained in the Missouri plan. Shortly thereafter petitioner filed a petition in the Court of Appeals for the Eighth Circuit for review of the Administrator's 1972 approval of the Missouri implementation plan.

* * * II

* * * B

Since a reviewing court regardless of when the petition for review is filed may consider claims of economic and technological infeasibility only if the Administrator may consider such claims in approving or rejecting a state implementation plan, we must address ourselves to the scope of the Administrator's responsibility. * * * After surveying the relevant provisions of the Clean Air Amendments of 1970 and their legislative history, we agree that Congress intended claims of economic and technological infeasibility to be wholly foreign to the Administrator's consideration of a state implementation plan.

As we have previously recognized, the 1970 Amendments to the Clean Air Act were a drastic remedy to what was perceived as a serious and otherwise uncheckable problem of air pollution. The Amendments place the primary responsibility for formulating pollution control strategies on the States, but nonetheless subject the States to strict minimum compliance requirements. These requirements are of a "technology-forcing character," and are expressly designed to force regulated sources to develop pollution control devices that might at the time appear to be economically or technologically infeasible.

This approach is apparent on the face of § 110(a)(2). The provision sets out [] criteria that an implementation plan must satisfy, and provides that if these criteria are met and if the plan was adopted after reasonable notice and hearing, the Administrator "shall approve" the proposed state plan. The mandatory "shall" makes it quite clear that the Administrator is not to be concerned with factors other than those specified, and none of the [] factors appears to permit consideration of technological or economic infeasibility. Nonetheless, if a basis is to be found for allowing the Administrator to consider such claims, it must be among [those] criteria, and so it is here that the argument is focused.

It is suggested that consideration of claims of technological and economic infeasibility is required by the first criterion that the primary air quality standards be met "as expeditiously as practicable but . . . in no case later than three years . . ." and that the secondary air quality standards be met within a "reasonable time." § 110(a)(2)(A). The argument is that what is "practicable" or "reasonable" cannot be determined without assessing whether what is proposed is possible. This argument does not survive analysis.

Section 110(a)(2)(A)'s three-year deadline for achieving primary air quality standards is central to the Amendments' regulatory scheme and, as both the language and the legislative history of the requirement make clear, it leaves no room for claims of technological or economic infeasibility. The 1970 congressional debate on the Amendments centered on whether technology forcing was necessary and desirable in framing and attaining air quality standards sufficient to protect the public health, standards later termed primary standards. The House version of the Amendments was quite moderate in approach, requiring only that health-related standards be met "within a reasonable time." The Senate bill, on the other hand, flatly required that, possible or not, health-related standards be met "within three years."

The Senate's stiff requirement was intended to foreclose the claims of emission sources that it would be economically or technologically infeasible for them to achieve emission limitations sufficient to protect the public health within the specified time. * * *

The Conference Committee and, ultimately, the entire Congress accepted the Senate's three-year mandate for the achievement of primary air quality standards, and the clear import of that decision is that the Administrator must approve a plan that provides for attainment of the primary standards in three years even if attainment does not appear feasible. In rejecting the House's version of reasonableness, however, the conferees strengthened the Senate version. The Conference Committee made clear that the States could not procrastinate until the deadline approached. Rather, the primary standards had to be met in less than three years if possible; they had to be met "as expeditiously as practicable." § 110(a)(2)(A). Whatever room there is for considering claims of infeasibility in the attainment of primary standards must lie in this phrase, which is, of course, relevant only in evaluating those implementation plans that attempt to achieve the primary standard in less than three years.

It is argued that when such a state plan calls for proceeding more rapidly than economics and the available technology appear to allow, the plan must be rejected as not "practicable." Whether this is a correct reading of § 110(a)(2)(A) depends on how that section's "as expeditiously as practicable" phrase is characterized. * * *

Secondary air quality standards, those necessary to protect the public welfare, were subject to far less legislative debate than the primary standards. The House version of the Amendments treated welfare-related standards together with health-related standards, and required both to be met "within a reasonable time." The Senate bill, on the other hand, treated health- and welfare-related standards separately and did not require that welfare-related standards met in any particular time at all, although the Committee Report expressed the desire that they be met "as rapidly as possible." The final Amendments also separated welfare-related standards from health-related standards, labeled them secondary air quality standards, and adopted the House's requirement that they be met within a "reasonable time." §§ 109(b), 110(a)(2)(A). Thus, technology forcing is not expressly required in achieving standards to protect the public welfare.

It does not necessarily follow, however, that the Administrator may consider claims of impossibility in assessing a state plan for achieving secondary standards. As with plans designed to achieve primary standards in less than three years, the scope of the Administrator's power to reject a plan depends on whether the State itself may decide to engage in technology forcing and adopt a plan more stringent than federal law demands. * * * We read the "as may be necessary" requirement of § 110(a)(2)(B) to demand only that the implementation plan submitted by the State meet the "minimum conditions" of the Amendments. Beyond that, if a State makes the legislative determination that it desires a particular air quality by a certain date and that it is willing to force technology to attain it or lose a certain industry if attainment is not possible such a determination is fully consistent with the structure and purpose of the Amendments, and § 110(a)(2)(B) provides no basis for the EPA Administrator to object to the determination on the ground of infeasibility.

In sum, we have concluded that claims of economic or technological infeasibility may not be considered by the Administrator in evaluating a state requirement that primary ambient air quality standards be met in the mandatory three years. And, since we further conclude that the States may submit implementation plans more stringent than federal law requires and that the Administrator must approve such plans if they meet the minimum requirements of § 110(a)(2), it follows that the language of § 110(a)(2)(B) provides no basis for the Administrator ever to reject a state implementation plan on the ground that it is economically or technologically infeasible. Accordingly, a court of appeals reviewing an approved plan under § 307(b)(1) cannot set it aside on those grounds, no matter when they are raised.

III

Our conclusion is bolstered by recognition that the Amendments do allow claims of technological and economic infeasibility to be raised in situations where consideration of such claims will not substantially interfere with the primary congressional purpose of prompt attainment of the national air quality standards. * * *

Perhaps the most important forum for consideration of claims of economic and technological infeasibility is before the state agency formulating the implementation plan. So long as the national standards are met, the State may select whatever mix of control devices it desires, and industries with particular economic or technological problems may seek special treatment in the plan itself. Moreover, if the industry is not exempted from, or accommodated by, the original plan, it may obtain a variance, as petitioner did in this case; and the variance, if granted after notice and a hearing, may be submitted to the EPA as a revision of the plan. § 110(a) (3)(A), 42 U.S.C. § 1857c–5(a)(3)(A) (1970 ed., Supp. IV). Lastly, an industry denied an exemption from the implementation plan, or denied a subsequent variance, may be able to take its claims of economic or technological infeasibility to the state courts. *See, e.g.*, MO. REV. STAT. § 203.130 (1972); CAL. HEALTH & SAFETY CODE § 39506 (West 1973); PA. STAT. ANN., Tit. 71, § 1710.41 (1962).

* * * In short, the Amendments offer ample opportunity for consideration of claims of technological and economic infeasibility. Always, however, care is taken that consideration of such claims will not interfere substantially with the primary goal of prompt attainment of the national standards. Allowing such claims to be raised by appealing the Administrator's approval of an implementation plan, as petitioner suggests, would frustrate congressional intent. It would permit a proposed plan to be struck down as infeasible before it is given a chance to work, even though Congress clearly contemplated that some plans would be infeasible when proposed. And it would permit the Administrator or a federal court to reject a State's legislative choices in regulating air pollution, even though Congress plainly left with the States, so long as the national standards were met, the power to determine which sources would be burdened by regulation and to what extent. Technology forcing is a concept somewhat new to our national experience and it necessarily entails certain risks. But Congress considered those risks in passing the 1970 Amendments and decided that the dangers posed by uncontrolled air pollution made them worth taking. Petitioner's theory would render that considered legislative judgment a nullity, and that is a result we refuse to reach.

Affirmed.

Mr. JUSTICE POWELL, with whom THE CHIEF JUSTICE joins, concurring.

I join the opinion of the Court because the statutory scheme and the legislative history, thoroughly described in the Court's opinion, demonstrate irrefutably that Congress did not intend to permit the Administrator of the Environmental Protection Agency to reject a proposed state implementation plan on the grounds of economic or technological infeasibility. * * * But it is difficult to believe that Congress would adhere to its absolute position if faced with the potentially devastating consequences to the public that this case vividly demonstrates.

Petitioner is an electric utility supplying power demands in the St. Louis metropolitan area, a large part of Missouri, and parts of Illinois and Iowa. It alleges that it cannot continue to operate if forced to comply with the sulfur dioxide restrictions contained in the Missouri implementation plan approved by the Administrator. Specifically, petitioner alleges that since the Administrator's approval of the plan, low-sulfur coal has become too scarce and expensive to obtain; reliable and satisfactory sulfur dioxide removal equipment that would enable it to comply with the plan's requirements simply has not been devised; the installation of the unsatisfactory equipment that is available would cost over $500 million, a sum impossible to obtain by bonds that are contingent on approval by regulatory bodies and public acceptance; and, even if the financing could be obtained, the carrying, operating, and maintenance costs of over $120 million a year would be prohibitive. Petitioner further alleges that recent evidence has disclosed that sulfur dioxide in the ambient air is not the hazard to public health that it was once thought to be, and that compliance with the sulfur regulation in the Missouri plan is not necessary to the attainment of national primary and secondary ambient air standards in the St. Louis area.

At the risk of civil and criminal penalties enforceable by both the State and Federal Governments, as well as possible citizens' suits, 42 U.S.C. §§ 1857c–8, 1857h–2, petitioner is being required either to embark upon the task of installing allegedly unreliable and prohibitively expensive equipment or to shut down. Yet the present Act permits neither the Administrator, in approving the state plan, nor the courts, in reviewing that approval under § 307 of the Act, 42 U.S.C. § 1857h–5, even to consider petitioner's allegations of infeasibility.

Environmental concerns, long neglected, merit high priority, and Congress properly has made protection of the public health its paramount consideration. But the shutdown of an urban area's electrical service could have an even more serious impact on the health of the public than that created by a decline in ambient air quality. The result apparently required by this legislation in its present form could sacrifice the well-being of a large metropolitan area through the imposition of inflexible demands that may be technologically impossible to meet and indeed may no longer even be necessary to the attainment of the goal of clean air.

I believe that Congress, if fully aware of this Draconian possibility, would strike a different balance.

NOTES

1. **SIPs and the Clean Air Act's Cooperative Federalism.** How does the Supreme Court view the Clean Air Act's structure of cooperative federalism? What are the relative roles and powers of the EPA and the states with respect to SIPs? Specifically, to what extent can EPA "interfere with" SIPs? What statutory provisions does the Supreme Court rely on in its analysis? What other tools of statutory construction does it use in reaching its conclusion?

2. ***Union Electric* and Revisions to the SIP Requirements.** As noted, Congress has amended the Clean Air Act several times, and the list of SIP requirements is one of the provisions that it has revised. At the time of the *Union Electric* case, SIPs had to meet only eight requirements—none of which, as the Court points out, required the EPA to examine the SIP submission for technological and economic feasibility. Under the current Act, Congress has specified 13 requirements, as quoted above. Did Congress heed the concurring Justices' plea in *Union Electric* to revise the Clean Air Act?

3. **The Three-Year Compliance Deadline.** One of the more obvious revisions Congress has made to the SIP requirements since the *Union Electric*

decision is the elimination of the three-year mandatory requirement in section 110(2)(A). Why would Congress have eliminated that timing requirement?

4. **The Draconian Clean Air Act: An Improvement Over Nuisance**? As noted after *Lead Industries Association*, in 2001 the Supreme Court confirmed the D.C. Circuit's long-held conclusion that the EPA cannot consider costs when establishing the NAAQS. In *Union Electric*, the Supreme Court determined that the EPA cannot consider either economic or technological infeasibility when deciding whether to approve a state's SIP, and even the concurring Justices agree that Congress intended to force industries to develop new technologies or go out of business. Do these two cases together mean that the EPA and the states could force entire industries to shut down in pursuit of clean air? Is that what Congress intended? Isn't this the same dilemma that the New York courts faced in *Boomer v. Atlantic Cement*? Did Congress simply make the opposite decision?

5. **Cooperative Federalism and Federal Regulatory "Floors."** As the *Union Electric* Court explains, the Clean Air Act embodies a common approach that Congress uses when writing environmental statutes: the federal government establishes minimum requirements for environmental protection but leaves the states free to regulate more stringently than federal law requires. CAA § 116, 42 U.S.C. § 7416. Given the history of air quality regulation in the United States, why do you think that Congress decided to mandate a **"floor"** level of environmental protection rather than capping the **"ceiling"**? Why might states choose to be more protective than federal law requires?

6. **Sulfur Dioxide, Power Plants, and the Clean Air Act.** As Figure 4–7 indicates, electrical power plants like the Union Electric Company are significant sources of sulfur dioxide emissions, especially when those power plants burn high-sulfur coal as fuel. Power plant emissions of sulfur dioxide continue to be a significant problem under the Clean Air Act, particularly because sulfur dioxide is an important component of ***acid rain*** and because many outdated power plants in the Midwest have managed to continue in operation under the emissions standards for existing plants, escaping ***new source review***. These continuing issues will be discussed later in this chapter.

* * *

D. FEDERAL CONSISTENCY REVIEW

As part of the Clean Air Act's cooperative federalism, Congress acted to ensure that the federal government would not unduly interfere with states' efforts to comply with the NAAQS through their SIPs. As a result, section 176 of the Act provides that "[n]o department, agency, or instrumentality of the Federal Government shall engage in, support in any way or provide financial assistance for, license or permit, or approve, any activity which does not conform to an implementation plan after it has been approved or promulgated under section 7410 * * *." CAA § 176(c)(1), 42 U.S.C. § 7506(c)(1). This provision makes assurance of conformity with SIPs "an affirmative responsibility of the head of such department, agency, or instrumentality." *Id.* Moreover, section 176 defines "conformity" to require:

(A) conformity to an implementation plan's purpose of eliminating or reducing the severity and number of violations of the national ambient air quality standards and achieving expeditious attainment of such standards; and

(B) that such activities will not—

(i) cause or contribute to any new violation of any standard in any area;

(ii) increase the frequency or severity of any existing violation of any standard in any area; or

(iii) delay timely attainment of any standard or required interim emission reductions or other milestones in any area.

CAA § 176(c)(1), 42 U.S.C. § 7506(c)(1).

How far does this conformity requirement extend? Can it, for instance, limit the President's implementation of the North America Free Trade Agreement (NAFTA), 32 I.L.M. 289, 605 (Dec. 17, 1992, in force Jan. 1, 1994), an international treaty governing trade relations between the United States, Canada, and Mexico? The Supreme Court considered that issue in the following case.

DEPARTMENT OF TRANSPORTATION v. PUBLIC CITIZEN

541 U.S. 752 (2004).

JUSTICE THOMAS delivered the opinion of the Court.

In this case, we confront the question whether * * * the Clean Air Act (CAA), 42 U.S.C. §§ 7401–7671q, require[s] the Federal Motor Carrier Safety Administration (FMCSA) to evaluate the environmental effects of cross-border operations of Mexican-domiciled motor carriers, where FMCSA's promulgation of certain regulations would allow such cross-border operations to occur. Because FMCSA lacks discretion to prevent these cross-border operations, we conclude that th[is] statute[] impose[s] no such requirement on FMCSA.

* * * I

* * * A

* * * 2

What is known as the CAA became law in 1963. In 1970, Congress substantially amended the CAA into roughly its current form. The 1970 amendments mandated national air quality standards and deadlines for their attainment, while leaving to the States the development of "implementation plan[s]" to comply with the federal standards.

In 1977, Congress again amended the CAA to prohibit the Federal Government and its agencies from "engag[ing] in, support[ing] in any way or provid[ing] financial assistance for, licens[ing] or permit[ting], or approv[ing], any activity which does not conform to [a state] implementation plan." 42 U.S.C. § 7506(c)(1). The definition of "conformity" includes restrictions on, for instance, "increas[ing] the frequency or severity of any existing violation of any standard in any area," or "delay[ing] timely attainment of any standard ... in any area." § 7506(c)(1)(B). These safeguards prevent the Federal Government from interfering with the States' abilities to comply with the CAA's requirements.

3

FMCSA, an agency within the Department of Transportation (DOT), is responsible for motor carrier safety and registration. See 49 U.S.C. § 113(f). FMCSA has a variety of statutory mandates, including "ensur[ing]" safety, § 31136, establishing minimum levels of financial responsibility for motor carriers, § 31139, and prescribing federal standards for safety inspections of commercial motor vehicles, § 31142. Importantly, FMCSA has only limited discretion regarding motor vehicle carrier registration: It must grant registration to all domestic or foreign motor carriers that are "willing and able to comply with" the applicable safety, fitness, and financial-responsibility requirements. § 13902(a)(1). FMCSA has no statutory authority to impose or enforce emissions controls or to establish environmental requirements unrelated to motor carrier safety.

B

We now turn to the factual and procedural background of this case. Before 1982, motor carriers domiciled in Canada and Mexico could obtain certification to operate within the United States from the Interstate Commerce Commission (ICC). In 1982, Congress, concerned about discriminatory treatment of United States motor carriers in Mexico and Canada, enacted a 2-year moratorium on new grants of operating authority. Congress authorized the President to extend the moratorium beyond the 2-year period if Canada or Mexico continued to interfere with United States motor carriers, and also authorized the President to lift or modify the moratorium if he determined that doing so was in the national interest. 49 U.S.C. § 10922*(l)* (1982 ed.). Although the moratorium on Canadian motor carriers was quickly lifted, the moratorium on Mexican motor carriers remained, and was extended by the President.

In December 1992, the leaders of Mexico, Canada, and the United States signed the North American Free Trade Agreement (NAFTA), 32 I.L.M. 605 (1993). As part of NAFTA, the United States agreed to phase out the moratorium and permit Mexican motor carriers to obtain operating authority within the United States' interior by January 2000. On NAFTA's effective date (January 1, 1994), the President began to lift the trade moratorium by allowing the licensing of Mexican carriers to provide some bus services in the United States. The President, however, did not continue to ease the moratorium on the timetable specified by NAFTA, as concerns about the adequacy of Mexico's regulation of motor carrier safety remained.

The Government of Mexico challenged the United States' implementation of NAFTA's motor carrier provisions under NAFTA's dispute-resolution process, and in February 2001, an international arbitration panel determined that the United States' "blanket refusal" of Mexican motor carrier applications breached the United States' obligations under NAFTA. Shortly thereafter, the President made clear his intention to lift the moratorium on Mexican motor carrier certification following the preparation of new regulations governing grants of operating authority to Mexican motor carriers.

In May 2001, FMCSA published for comment proposed rules concerning safety regulation of Mexican motor carriers. One rule (the Application Rule) addressed the establishment of a new application form for Mexican motor carriers that seek authorization to operate within the United States. Another rule (the Safety Monitoring Rule) addressed the establishment of a safety-inspection regime for all Mexican motor carriers that would receive operating authority under the Application Rule.

Figure 4-8: Truck and Other Traffic at the Mexican Border

Federal Highway Administration photo.

In December 2001, Congress enacted the Department of Transportation and Related Agencies Appropriations Act, 2002, 115 Stat. 833. Section 350 of this Act provided that no funds appropriated under the Act could be obligated or expended to review or to process any application by a Mexican motor carrier for authority to operate in the interior of the United States until FMCSA implemented specific application and safety-monitoring requirements for Mexican carriers. Some of these requirements went beyond those proposed by FMCSA in the Application and Safety Monitoring Rules. Congress extended the § 350 conditions to appropriations for Fiscal Years 2003 and 2004.

In January 2002, acting pursuant to NEPA's [National Environmental Policy Act's] mandates, FMCSA issued a programmatic EA [Environmental Assessment] for the proposed Application and Safety Monitoring Rules. * * * Vital to the EA's analysis * * * was the assumption that there would be no change in trade volume between the United States and Mexico due to the issuance of the regulations. * * * Because FMCSA concluded that the entry of the Mexican trucks was not an "effect" of its regulations, it did not consider any environmental impact that might be caused by the increased presence of Mexican trucks within the United States.

* * * On March 19, 2002, FMCSA issued the two interim rules, delaying their effective date until May 3, 2002, to allow public comment on provisions that FMCSA added to satisfy the requirements of § 350. In the regulatory preambles, FMCSA * * * addressed the CAA * * *, determining that it did not need to perform a "conformity review" of the proposed regulations under 42 U.S.C. § 7506(c)(1) because the increase in emissions from these regulations would fall below the Environmental Protection Agency's (EPA's) threshold levels needed to trigger such a review.

In November 2002, the President lifted the moratorium on qualified Mexican motor carriers. Before this action, however, respondents filed petitions for judicial review of the Application and Safety Monitoring Rules, arguing that the rules were promulgated in violation of * * * the CAA. The Court of Appeals agreed with respondents, granted the petitions, and set aside the rules.

* * * The Court of Appeals [for the Ninth Circuit] directed FMCSA to prepare a full CAA conformity determination for the challenged regulations. It concluded that FMCSA's determination that emissions attributable to the challenged rules would be below the threshold levels was not reliable because the agency's CAA determination reflected the "illusory distinction between the effects of the regulations themselves and the effects of the presidential rescission of the moratorium on Mexican truck entry."

We granted certiorari and now reverse.

* * * III

Under the CAA, a federal "department, agency, or instrumentality" may not, generally, "engage in, support in any way or provide financial assistance for, license or permit, or approve, any activity" that violates an applicable State air-quality implementation plan. 42 U.S.C. § 7506(c)(1);

40 CFR § 93.150 (2003). Federal agencies must, in many circumstances, undertake a conformity determination with respect to a proposed action, to ensure that the action is consistent with § 7506(c)(1). See 40 CFR §§ 93.150(b), 93.153(a)-(b). However, an agency is exempt from the general conformity determination under the CAA if its action would not cause new emissions to exceed certain threshold emission rates set forth in § 93.153(b). FMCSA determined that its proposed regulations would not cause emissions to exceed the relevant threshold amounts and therefore concluded that the issuance of its regulations would comply with the CAA. Critical to its calculations was its consideration of only those emissions that would occur from the increased roadside inspections of Mexican trucks; * * * FMCSA's CAA analysis did not consider any emissions attributable to the increased presence of Mexican trucks within the United States.

EPA's rules provide that "a conformity determination is required for each pollutant where the total of direct and indirect emissions in a nonattainment or maintenance area caused by a Federal action would equal or exceed" the threshold levels established by the EPA. 40 CFR § 93.153(b). "Direct emissions" are defined as those covered emissions "that are caused or initiated by the Federal action and occur at the same time and place as the action." § 93.152. The term "indirect emissions" means covered emissions that

> "(1) Are caused by the Federal action, but may occur later in time and/or may be further removed in distance from the action itself but are still reasonably foreseeable; and (2) The Federal agency can practicably control and will maintain control over due to a continuing program responsibility of the Federal agency." *Ibid.*

[T]he EPA's CAA regulations have defined the term "[c]aused by." *Ibid.* In particular, emissions are "[c]aused by" a Federal action if the "emissions ... would not ... occur in the absence of the Federal action." *Ibid.* Thus, the EPA has made clear that for purposes of evaluating causation in the conformity review process, some sort of "but for" causation is sufficient.

Although arguably FMCSA's proposed regulations would be "but for" causes of the entry of Mexican trucks into the United States, the emissions from these trucks are neither "direct" nor "indirect" emissions. First, the emissions from the Mexican trucks are not "direct" because they will not occur at the same time or at the same place as the promulgation of the regulations.

Second, FMCSA cannot practicably control, nor will it maintain control, over these emissions. As discussed above, FMCSA does not have the ability to countermand the President's decision to lift the moratorium, nor could it act categorically to prevent Mexican carriers from being registered or Mexican trucks from entering the United States. Once the regulations are promulgated, FMCSA would have no ability to regulate any aspect of vehicle exhaust from these Mexican trucks. FMCSA could not refuse to register Mexican motor carriers simply on the ground that their trucks would pollute excessively. FMCSA cannot determine whether registered carriers actually will bring trucks into the United States, cannot control the routes the carriers take, and cannot determine what the trucks will emit. Any reduction in emissions that would occur at the hands of FMCSA would be mere happenstance. It cannot be said that FMCSA "practicably control[s]" or "will maintain control" over the vehicle emissions from the Mexican trucks, and it follows that the emissions from the Mexican trucks are not "indirect emissions."

The emissions from the Mexican trucks are neither "direct" nor "indirect" emissions caused by the issuance of FMCSA's proposed regulations. Thus, FMCSA did not violate the CAA or the applicable regulations by failing to consider them when it evaluated whether it needed to perform a full "conformity determination." * * *

NOTES

1. **The Scope of the Clean Air Act's Conformity Review.** Why did the Supreme Court uphold the FMCSA's decision *not* to engage in a Clean Air Act conformity review? How do the EPA's regulations interpret the conformity review requirement? Why is causation an issue in this case?

2. **Public Citizen's Choice of Defendant.** Was this a case of Public Citizen simply choosing the wrong defendant? Note that the Supreme Court emphasizes that the FMCSA will not have continuing authority over the emissions from the Mexican trucks. Does that mean that Public Citizen should have sued the EPA instead? Why or why not? Or, given the suggestions that the President's decision to lift the moratorium is the cause of increased emissions from Mexican trucks, should Public Citizen have sued the President of the United States? Review the statutory language quoted before this case. Does the Clean Air Act's conformity review requirement apply to the President's implementation of international treaties? Why or why not? If it does apply, would Public Citizen have a cause of action against the President? Why or why not?

3. **Environmental Justice and Mexican Trucks.** Does this case raise environmental justice concerns? Why or why not? If so, how would you describe those concerns?

4. **The Rest of the Story: Environmental Protection and International Trade, Revisited.** Environmental organizations were not the only groups to protest President George W. Bush's lifting of the Mexican truck moratorium. Attorneys General from nine states—Arizona, California, Illinois, Massachusetts, New Mexico, Oklahoma, Oregon, Washington, and Wisconsin—filed briefs in support of Public Citizen. In addition, labor and trucking organizations in the United States also fought the entry of Mexican trucks. As early as 1997, Ron Carey, then president of the Teamsters Union, protested the entry of "unsafe" Mexican trucks into the United States, and the Teamsters Union was a plaintiff in *Public Citizen*.

Originally, under NAFTA, United States roads were supposed to be open to Mexican trucks by summer 1996, but the United States blocked their entry in December 1995. By November 2002, the FMCSA had 130 applications from Mexican-domiciled truck and bus companies. Federal Motor Carrier Safety Administration, *Mexican Motor Carrier Main Page*, http://www.fmcsa.dot.gov/español/english/mmc_english.htm. During the moratorium, Mexican trucks made 4.5 million trips to the border each year, "and the value of goods crossing the border tops $160 billion annually." Anne Gearan, AP, *Mexican trucks can roll in U.S., high court rules* (June 8, 2004). Against American claims "that Mexican trucks are typically older and more polluting than American trucks," Mexico claimed that "the moratorium has cost it more than $2 billion." CNN.com, *U.S. roadways opened to Mexican trucks* (June 8, 2004), http://www.cnn.com/2004/LAW/06/07/scotus.mexican.trucks.ap/. Given these facts, does this case raise other issues of environmental discrimination in trade? If so, how? Does this case raise concerns roughly parallel to the Shrimp–Turtle dispute before the World Trade Organization, discussed in Chapter 3?

5. **Consistency for Everything?** There are other ways that federal agencies can avoid a consistency review of their actions. For example, on June 12, 2009, the U.S. Court of Appeals for the Ninth Circuit upheld the Federal Aviation Administration (FAA) in refusing to undergo a consistency review for flight path changes at airports. Interpreting the EPA's regulations, the Ninth Circuit concluded that consistency review was not required when the effects of the federal action on air quality would be *de minimis*. *City of Las Vegas v. FAA*, 570 F.3d 1109, 1117–18 (9th Cir. 2009). *Accord*, *County of Rockland, New York v. FAA*, 335 Fed. Appx. 52, 56 (D.C. Cir. 2009) (holding that the FAA's redesign of flight paths for the New York/New Jersey/Philadelphia metropolitan area was exempt from Clean Air Act conformity under the *de minimis* exemption). The Federal Energy Regulatory Commission (FERC), in turn, did not have to comply with Clean Air Act conformity requirements when it approved a northward-flowing natural gas pipeline that would bring foreign natural gas into California because, although the pipeline would be the "but for" cause of indirect emissions, FERC could not practicably control those emissions. *South Coast Air Quality Management District v. FERC*, 621 F.3d 1085, 1100–01 (9th Cir. 2010).

III. REGULATING CRITERIA POLLUTANT EMISSIONS: MOBILE SOURCES

A. WHAT IS A MOBILE SOURCE?

In the section on criteria pollutants, you have already seen two issues involving air quality and mobile sources: (1) the EPA's phasing out of leaded gasoline; and (2) the petition to have the EPA regulate greenhouse gas emissions from new motor vehicles. More generally, Subchapter II of the Clean Air Act, 42 U.S.C. §§ 7521–7590, establishes the Act's basic requirements to reduce air pollution from ***mobile sources***.

The Act defines mobile sources in contrast to ***stationary sources***. A "***stationary source***," for purposes of the Act, is "any source of an air pollutant except those emissions resulting directly from an internal combustion engine for transportation purposes or from a nonroad engine or nonroad vehicle as defined in section 7550 of this title." CAA § 302(z), 43 U.S.C. § 7602(z). By implication, therefore, ***mobile sources*** are sources of air pollutants that use an internal combustion engine for transportation purposes, that have a nonroad engine, or that are nonroad vehicles.

Subchapter II defines a "***motor vehicle***" to be "any self-propelled vehicle designed for transporting persons or property on a street or highway." CAA § 216(2), 42 U.S.C. § 7550(2). Trucks and automobiles are two obvious and common motor vehicles that the Clean Air Act regulates.

A "***nonroad engine***," in turn, is "an internal combustion engine (including the fuel system) that is not used in a motor vehicle or a vehicle used solely for competition, or that is not subject to standards promulgated under section 7411 or section 7521 of this title." *Id.* § 216(10), 42 U.S.C. § 7550(10). A "***nonroad vehicle***" is "a vehicle that is powered by a nonroad engine and that is not a motor vehicle or a vehicle used solely for competition." *Id.* § 216(11), 42 U.S.C. § 7550(11). The EPA considers the following kinds of engines and vehicles to be nonroad engines and vehicles:

- *Compression-ignition engines*, often operating with diesel fuel, such as those used in tractors, combines, and other farm, construction, and mining equipment.
- *Small spark-ignition engines*, such as those in lawnmowers, leaf blowers, and chainsaws.
- *Large spark-ignition engines*, often fueled by gas or propane, such as those in forklifts and generators.
- *Marine diesel engines*, found primarily in commercial ships.
- *Marine spark-ignition engines*, found in smaller boats and personal watercraft.
- *Recreational vehicles*, such as snowmobiles, dirt bikes, and all-terrain vehicles.
- *Locomotives*.
- *Aviation vehicles and engines*, including both aircraft and ground support.

Office of Transportation & Air Quality, EPA, *Nonroad Engines, Equipment, and Vehicles*, http://www.epa.gov/otaq/nonroad.htm. As a result of this extension to nonroad vehicles and engines, Subpart II governs quite a few different kinds of sources of air pollution.

B. MOTOR VEHICLE EMISSION AND FUEL STANDARDS

1. Motor Vehicle Emission Standards

As you've already seen in connection with *Massachusetts v. EPA*, under section 202 of the Clean Air Act, the Administrator of the EPA must establish, through regulations, "standards applicable to the emission of any air pollutant from any class or classes of new motor vehicles or new motor vehicle engines, which in his judgment cause, or contribute to, air pollution which may reasonably be anticipated to endanger public health or welfare." CAA § 202(a)(1), 42 U.S.C. § 7521(a)(1). Three aspects of this mandate are notable. First, the EPA's standard-setting authority concentrates on "new motor vehicles" and "new motor vehicle engines." Subchapter II defines a "***new motor vehicle***" to be "a motor vehicle the equitable or legal title to which has never been transferred to an ultimate purchaser," while a "***new motor vehicle engine***" is "an engine in a new motor vehicle or a motor vehicle engine the equitable or legal title to which has never been transferred to the ultimate purchaser * * *." CAA § 216(3), 42 U.S.C. § 7550(3). Congress concentrated emission reduction requirements in new sources because such sources can generally install the best emission-control technology for the least cost, especially compared to retrofitting existing sources.

Second, the EPA's emissions controls for motor vehicles have traditionally focused on emissions of hydrocarbons, carbon monoxide (CO), nitrogen oxides (NOx), and particulate matter. CAA § 202(a)(3), 42 U.S.C. § 7521(a)(3). Figures 4–9 through 4–12 indicate why Congress chose to concentrate on these emissions.

Finally, emissions standards for these four pollutants for heavy-duty vehicles and for motor vehicle engines manufactured during or after model year 1983 must

> reflect the greatest degree of emission reduction achievable through the application of technology which the Administrator determines will be available for the model year to which such standards apply, giving appropriate consideration to cost, energy, and safety factors associated with the application of such technology.

CAA § 202(a)(3)(A)(i), 42 U.S.C. § 7521(a)(3)(A)(i). In other words, vehicle emissions standards are both ***technology-based*** and ***technology-forcing*** standards, because the EPA has the authority to *predict* what technologies *will be* available to control emissions in each new model year of cars and trucks. As such, the EPA is not limited to imposing requirements based on existing technology, as the next case will make clear; it can force manufacturers to make technological improvements. Congress did give manufacturers limited predictability, however, by requiring that emissions standards for heavy duty vehicles or engines "apply for a period of no less than three model years beginning no earlier than the model year commencing 4 years after such revised standard is promulgated." CAA § 202(a)(3)(C), 42 U.S.C. § 7521(a)(3)(C).

Subchapter II makes it illegal for importers, manufacturers, and owners to import or manufacture any motor vehicle that does not meet the emissions standards or to tamper with motor vehicles to bypass the emission control equipment, CAA § 203, 42 U.S.C. § 7522; allows the United States to enjoin illegal behavior, CAA § 204, 42 U.S.C. § 7523; and subjects violators to administrative and civil penalties. CAA § 205, 42 U.S.C. § 7524. It also gives the EPA authority to test or require testing of new motor vehicles to ensure compliance with the emissions standards. CAA § 206, 42 U.S.C. § 7525.

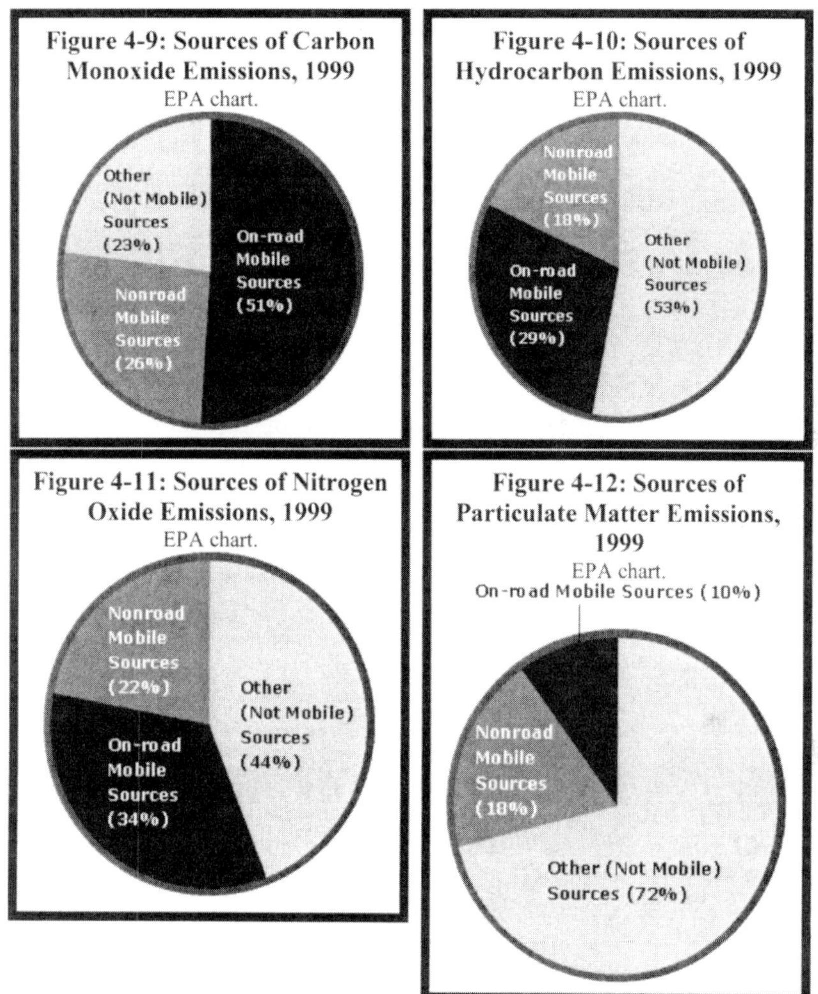

Motor vehicle manufacturers resisted the imposition of these new technology-based emissions standards. One of the earliest and biggest battles between the EPA and auto manufacturers involved the EPA's requirement that motor vehicles use catalytic converters by model year 1975.

INTERNATIONAL HARVESTER COMPANY v. RUCKELSHAUS

478 F.2d 615 (D.C. Cir. 1973).

LEVENTHAL, CIRCUIT JUDGE:

These consolidated petitions of International Harvester and the three major auto companies, Ford, General Motors and Chrysler, seek review of a decision by the Administrator of the Environmental Protection Agency denying petitioners' applications, filed pursuant to Section 202 of the Clean Air Act, for one-year suspensions of the 1975 emission standards prescribed under the statute for light duty vehicles in the absence of suspension.

I. STATEMENT OF THE CASE

The tension of forces presented by the controversy over automobile emission standards may be focused by two central observations:

(1) The automobile is an essential pillar of the American economy. Some 28 per cent of the nonfarm workforce draws its livelihood from the automobile industry and its products.

(2) The automobile has had a devastating impact on the American environment. As of 1970, authoritative voices stated that "[a]utomotive pollution constitutes in excess of 60% of our national air pollution problem" and more than 80 per cent of the air pollutants in concentrated urban areas.

A. Statutory Framework

Congressional concern over the problem of automotive emissions dates back to the 1950's, but it was not until the passage of the Clean Air Act in 1965 that Congress established the principle of Federal standards for automobile emissions. Under the 1965 act and its successor, the Air Quality Act of 1967, the Department of Health, Education and Welfare was authorized to promulgate emission limitations commensurate with existing technological feasibility.

* * * The legislative background must also take into account the fact that in 1969 the Department of Justice brought suit against the four largest automobile manufacturers on grounds that they had conspired to delay the development of emission control devices.

On December 31, 1970, Congress grasped the nettle and amended the Clean Air Act to set a statutory standard for required reductions in levels of hydrocarbons (HC) and carbon monoxide (CO) which must be achieved for 1975 models of light duty vehicles. Section 202(b) of the Act added by the Clean Air Amendments of 1970, provides that, beginning with the 1975 model year, exhaust emission of hydrocarbons and carbon monoxide from "light duty vehicles" must be reduced at least 90 per cent from the permissible emission levels in the 1970 model year. In accordance with the

Congressional directives, the Administrator on June 23, 1971, promulgated regulations limiting HC and CO emissions from 1975 model light duty vehicles to .41 and 3.4 grams per vehicle mile respectively. 36 Fed. Reg. 12,657 (1971). At the same time, as required by section 202(b)(2) of the Act, he prescribed the test procedures by which compliance with these standards is measured.

Congress was aware that these 1975 standards were "drastic medicine," designed to "force the state of the art." There was, naturally, concern whether the manufacturers would be able to achieve this goal. Therefore, Congress provided, in Senator Baker's phrase, a "realistic escape hatch": the manufacturers could petition the Administrator of the EPA for a one-year suspension of the 1975 requirements, and Congress took the precaution of directing the National Academy of Sciences to undertake an ongoing study of the feasibility of compliance with the emission standards. * * * Under section 202(b)(5)(D) of the Act, 42 U.S.C. § 1857f–1(b)(5)(D), the Administrator is authorized to grant a one-year suspension

> only if he determines that (i) such suspension is essential to the public interest or the public health and welfare of the United States, (ii) all good faith efforts have been made to meet the standards established by this subsection, (iii) the applicant has established that effective control technology, processes, operating methods, or other alternatives are not available or have not been available for a sufficient period of time to achieve compliance prior to the effective date of such standards, and (iv) the study and investigation of the National Academy of Sciences conducted pursuant to subsection (c) of this section and other information available to him has not indicated that technology, processes, or other alternatives are available to meet such standards.

The statute provides that an application for suspension may be filed any time after January 1, 1972, and that the Administrator must issue a decision thereon within 60 days. On March 13, 1972, Volvo, Inc., filed an application for suspension and thereby triggered the running of the 60 day period for a decision. 37 Fed. Reg. 5766 (March 21, 1972.) Additional suspension requests were filed by International Harvester on March 31, 1972, and by Ford Motor Company, Chrysler Corporation, and General Motors Corporation on April 5, 1972. * * * The decision to deny suspension to all applicants was issued on May 12, 1972. * * *

B. Initial Decision of the Administrator

The data available from the concerned parties related to 384 test vehicles run by the five applicants and the eight other vehicle manufacturers subpoenaed by the Administrator. * * * At the outset of his Decision, the Administrator determined that the most effective system so far developed was the noble metal oxidizing catalyst. * * * It was this system to which the data base was initially narrowed: only cars using this kind of system were to be considered in making the "available technology" determination.

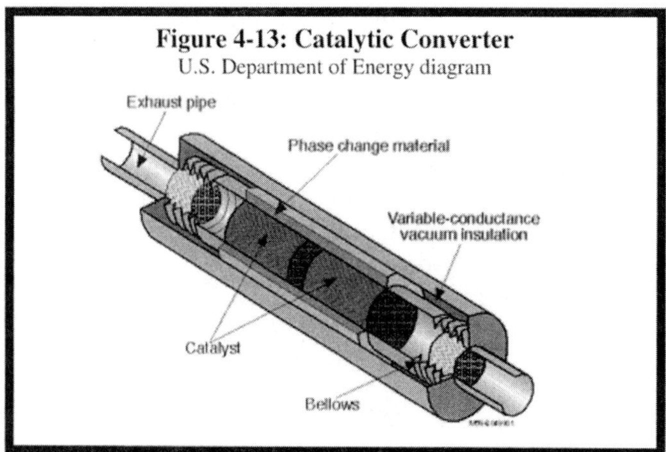

Figure 4-13: Catalytic Converter
U.S. Department of Energy diagram

The problem the Administrator faced in making a determination that technology was available, on the basis of these data, was that actual tests showed only one car with actual emissions which conformed to the standard prescribing a maximum of .41 grams, per mile, of HC and 3.4 grams per mile of CO. No car had actually been driven 50,000 miles, the statutory "useful life" of a vehicle and the time period for which conformity to the emission standards is required. * * *

Instead, certain data of the auto companies were used as a starting point for making a prediction, but remolded into a more useable form for this purpose. * * * [T]he Administrator "adjusted" the data of the auto companies by use of several critical assumptions.

First, he made an adjustment to reflect the assumption that fuel used in 1975 model year cars would either contain an average of .03 grams per gallon or .05 grams per gallon of lead. This usually resulted in an increase of emissions predicted, since many companies had tested their vehicles on lead-free gasoline.

Second, the Administrator found that the attempt of some companies to reduce emissions of nitrogen oxides below the 1975 Federal standard of 3.0 grams per vehicle mile resulted in increased emissions of hydrocarbons and carbon monoxide. This adjustment resulted in a downward adjustment of observed HC and CO data, by a specified factor.

Third, the Administrator took into account the effect the "durability" of the preferred systems would have on the emission control obtainable. This required that observed readings at one point of usage be increased by a deterioration factor (DF) to project emissions at a later moment of use. The critical methodological choice was to make this adjustment from a base of emissions observed at 4000 miles. Thus, even if a car had actually been tested over 4000 miles, predicted emissions at 50,000 miles would be determined by multiplying 4000 mile emissions by the DF factor.

Fourth, the Administrator adjusted for "prototype-to-production slippage." This was an upward adjustment made necessary by the possibility that prototype cars might have features which reduced HC and CO emissions, but were not capable of being used in actual production vehicles.

Finally, in accord with a regulation assumed, as to substance, in the text of the Decision, but proposed after the suspension hearing, a downward adjustment in the data readings was made on the basis of the manufacturers' ability, in conformance with certification procedures, to replace the catalytic converter "once during 50,000 miles of vehicle operation," a change they had not used in their testing.

With the data submitted and the above assumptions, the Administrator concluded that no showing had been made that requisite technology was not available. * * *

C. This Court's December 1972 Remand

After oral argument to this court on December 18, 1972, in a per curiam order issued December 19, 1972, we remanded the record to the Administrator, directing him to supplement his May 12, 1972 decision by setting forth:

> (a) the consideration given by the Administrator to the January 1, 1972 Semiannual Report on Technological Feasibility of the National Academy of Sciences; and (b) the basis for his disagreement, if any, with the findings and conclusion in that study concerning the availability of effective technology to achieve compliance with the 1975 model year standards set forth in the Act.

* * * We were [] troubled by arguments advanced by petitioners that the methodology used by the Administrator in reaching his conclusion, and indeed the conclusion itself, was inconsistent with that of the Academy. It was our view that if and to the extent such differences existed they should be explained by EPA, in order to aid us in determining whether the Administrator's conclusion under (iii) rested on a reasoned basis.

D. Supplement to the Decision of the Administrator

Our remand of the record resulted in a "Supplement to Decision of the Administrator" issued December 30, 1972. The Administrator in his Supplement stated that "In general I consider the factual findings and technical conclusions set forth in the NAS report and in the subsequent Interim Standards Report dated April 26, 1972 . . . to be consistent with my decision of May 12, 1972."

The Report made by the NAS, pursuant to its obligation under 202(b)(5) (D) of the Clean Air Act, had concluded: "The Committee finds that the technology necessary to meet the requirements of the Clean Air

Act Amendments for 1975 model year light-duty motor vehicles is not available at this time."

The Administrator apparently relied, however, on the NAS Report to bolster his conclusion that the applicants had not established that technology was unavailable. The same NAS Report had stated:

> ... the status of development and rate of progress made it possible that the larger manufacturers will be able to produce vehicles that will qualify, provided that provisions are made for catalyst replacement and other maintenance, for averaging emissions of production vehicles, and for the general availability of fuel containing suitably low levels of catalyst poisons.

The Administrator pointed out that two of NAS's provisos—catalytic converter replacement and low lead levels—had been accounted for in his analysis of the auto company data, and provision therefore had been insured through regulation. As to the third, "averaging emissions of production vehicles," the Administrator offered two reasons for declining to make a judgment about this matter: (1) The significance of averaging related to possible assembly-line tests, as distinct from certification test procedure, and such tests had not yet been worked out. (2) If there were an appropriate assembly-line test it would be expected that each car's emissions could be in conformity, without a need for averaging, since the assembly line vehicles "equipped with fresh catalysts can be expected to have substantially lower emissions at zero miles than at 4000 miles."

The Administrator also claimed that he had employed the same methodology as the NAS used in its Interim Standards Report, evidently referring to the use of 4000 mile emissions as a base point, and correction for a deterioration factor and a prototype-production slippage factor. The identity of methodology was also indicated, in his view, by the fact the EPA and NAS both agreed on the component parts of the most effective emission control system.

The Administrator did refer to the "severe driveability problems" underscored by the NAS Report, which in the judgment of NAS "could have significant safety implications," stating that he had not been presented with any evidence of "specific safety hazard" nor knew of any presented to the NAS. He did not address himself to the issue of performance problems falling short of specific safety hazards.

II. REJECTION OF MANUFACTURERS' GENERAL CONTENTIONS

We begin with consideration, and rejection, of the broad objections leveled by petitioners against EPA's over-all approach.

A. *Future Technological Developments*

We cannot accept petitioners' arguments that the Administrator's determination whether technology was "available," within the meaning of section 202(b)(5)(D) of the Act, must be based solely on technology in being as of the time of the application, and that the requirement that this be "available" precludes any consideration by the Administrator of what he determines to be the "probable" or likely sequence of the technology already experienced. Congress recognized that approximately two years' time was required before the start of production for a given model year, for the preparation of tooling and manufacturing processes. But Congress did not decide—and there is no reason for us to do so—that all development had to be completed before the tooling up period began. The manufacturers' engineers have admitted that technological improvements can continue during the two years prior to production. Thus there was a sound basis for the Administrator's conclusion that the manufacturers could "improve, test, and apply" technology during the lead time period.

* * * While we reject the contention as broadly stated, principally by General Motors, we hasten to add that the Administrator's latitude for projection is subject to the restraints of reasonableness, and does not open the door to " 'crystal ball' inquiry." The Administrator's latitude for projection is unquestionably limited by relevant considerations of lead time needed for production. Implicit also is a requirement of reason in the reliability of the EPA projection. In the present case, the Administrator's prediction of available technology was based on known elements of existing catalytic converter systems. This was a permissible approach subject, of course, to the requirement that any technological developments or refinements of existing systems, used as part of the EPA methodology, would have to rest on a reasoned basis.

* * * III. OVERALL PERSPECTIVE OF SUSPENSION ISSUE

This case ultimately involves difficult issues of statutory interpretation, as to the showing required for applicants to sustain their burden that technology is not available. It also taxes our ability to understand and evaluate technical issues upon which that showing, however it is to be defined, must rest. At the same time, however, larger questions are at stake. As Senator Baker put it, "This may be the biggest industrial judgment that has been made in the United States in this century." 116 Cong. Rec. 33,085 (1970). * * *

Two principal considerations compete for our attention. On the one hand, if suspension is not granted, and the prediction of the EPA Administrator that effective technology will be available is proven incorrect, grave economic consequences could ensue. * * * On the other hand, if suspension is granted, and it later be shown that the Administrator's prediction of feasibility was achievable in 1975 there may be irretrievable ecological costs. It is to this second possibility we first turn.

A. Potential Environmental Costs

The most authoritative estimate in the record of the ecological costs of a one year suspension is that of the NAS Report. Taking into account such "factors as the vehicle-age distribution among all automobiles, the decrease in vehicle miles driven per year, per car as vehicle age increases, the predicted nationwide growth in vehicle miles driven each year" and the effect of emission standards on exhaust control, NAS concluded that:

> . . . the effect on total emissions of a one-year suspension with no additional interim standards appears to be small. The effect is not more significant because the emission reduction now required of model year 1974 vehicles, as compared with uncontrolled vehicles (80 percent for HC and 69 percent for CO), is already so substantial.

* * * The question in this context is not whether these are costs the consumer should rightly bear if ecological damage is to be minimized, but rather the general effect on consumer purchasing of 1975 model year cars in anticipation of lower performance. A drop-off in purchase of 1975 cars will result in a prolonged usage of older cars with *less* efficient pollution control devices. If the adverse performance effect deterred purchasing significantly enough, resulting in greater retention of "older" cars in the "mix" of cars in use, it might even come to pass that total actual emissions (of all cars in use) would be greater under the 1975 than the 1974 standards.

* * * The NAS Report states that the effects of emission controls on vehicle driveability are difficult to quantify, but nevertheless makes the following qualitative evaluation:

> Driveability after a cold-engine start, and especially with cold ambient conditions, is likely to be impaired. To reduce HC and CO emissions during engine warmup, the choke is set to release quickly, and the fuel-air mixture is leaned out as early as possible after engine startup. Under these conditions, problems of engine stall, and vehicle stumble and hesitation on rapid acceleration, have been prevalent.

The willingness of the consumer to buy 1975 model year cars may also be affected, to some degree, by the anticipated significant costs of pollution control devices. The problem is further bedeviled by the possibility that consumers albeit rightly assigned the cost burden of pollution devices, may seek to avoid that burden, however modest, and to exercise, at least in some measure, an option to use older cars. Again, this would have the thrust of increasing actual total emissions of cars in use.

We may also note that it is the belief of many experts—both in and out of the automobile industry—that air pollution cannot be effectively checked until the industry finds a substitute for the conventional automotive power plant—the reciprocating internal combustion (*i.e.*, "piston") engine. * * *

The NAS estimated that there would be a small environmental cost to suspension of 1975 standards even if 1974 standards were retained, but further recommended intermediate standards that would dilute even such modest environmental cost. The following table shows the various standards, and one put forward by Ford for 1975:

Maximum emissions (grams per mile)

	HC	CO
1974 standards	3.4	39.0
Ford proposal	1.6	19.0
NAS recommendation for intermediate standards:		
No catalyst change	1.1	8.2
One catalyst change	0.8	6.3
1975 Standards	0.41	3.4

* * * On balance the record indicates the environmental costs of a one-year suspension are likely to be relatively modest. This must be balanced against the potential economic costs—and ecological costs—if the Administrator's prediction on the availability of effective technology is incorrect.

B. Potential Economic Costs

Theoretical possibility of industry shutdown

If in 1974, when model year 1975 cars start to come off the production line, the automobiles of Ford, General Motors and Chrysler cannot meet the 1975 standards and do not qualify for certification, the Administrator of EPA has the theoretical authority, under the Clean Air Act, to shut down the auto industry, as was clearly recognized in Congressional debate. We cannot put blinders on the facts before us so as to omit awareness of the reality that this authority would undoubtedly never be exercised, in light of the fact that approximately 1 out of every 7 jobs in this country is dependent on the production of the automobile. Senator Muskie, the principal sponsor of the bill, stated quite clearly in the debate on the Act that he envisioned the Congress acting if an auto industry shutdown were in sight.

The economic consequence of an approach geared to stringency, relying on relaxation as a safety valve

A more likely forecast, and one which enlightens what influenced the EPA decision to deny the suspension, was articulated by George Allen, Deputy Assistant Administrator for General Enforcement and a member of EPA's Hearing Panel:

> The problem really comes down to this: A decision has to be made next month, early next month. If the decision is to suspend the standards and adopt an interim standard . . . and in 1975 it turns out that technology exists to meet the statutory standard, today's decision turns out to be wrong.
>
> * * * If, on the other hand, a decision is made today that the standards cannot lawfully be suspended, and we go down to 1975 and nobody can meet the standard, today's decision was wrong.

> In [the first] case, there is not much to do about the wrong decision; it was made, many people relied on it; it turns out the standard could have been met, but I doubt if we could change it.
>
> In the second case, if a wrong decision is made, there is probably a remedy, a re-application and a recognition by the agency that it is not technically feasible to meet the standards. You can correct the one; you probably can't correct the other.

Grave problems are presented by the assumption that if technical feasibility proves to be a "wrong decision" it can be remedied by a relaxation.

* * * The record before us suggests that there already exists a technological gap between Ford and General Motors, in Ford's favor. General Motors did not make the decision to concentrate on what EPA found to be the most effective system at the time of its decision—the noble metal monolithic catalyst. Instead it relied principally on testing the base metal catalyst as its first choice system. * * *

* * * If in 1974, when certification of production vehicles begins, any one of the three major companies cannot meet the 1975 standards, it is a likelihood that standards will be set to permit the higher level of emission control achievable by the laggard. This will be the case whether or not the leader has or has not achieved compliance with the 1975 standards. Even if the relaxation is later made industry-wide, the Government's action, in first imposing a standard not generally achievable and then relaxing it, is likely to be detrimental to the leader who has tooled up to meet a higher standard than will ultimately be required.

** * * D. The Issue of Feasibility Sufficient for Basic Auto Demand*

* * * A difficult problem is posed by the companies' contention that the production and major retooling capacity does not exist to shift production from a large number of previous models and engine types to those capable of complying with the 1975 standards and meeting the demand for new cars. The Administrator made no finding as to this problem. We believe the statute requires such a finding, explaining how the Administrator estimates "basic demand" and how his definition conforms to the statutory objective. The emission standards set for 1976 cannot be breached, since they represent an absolute judgment of Congress. But as to the decision on a one year suspension, and the underlying issue of technological feasibility, Congress intended, we think, that the Administrator should take into account such "demand" considerations.

A significant decrease in auto production will have a major economic impact on labor and suppliers to the companies. We have no reason to believe that "effective technology" did not comport within its meaning sufficient technology to meet a basic level of consumer demand.

E. Balancing of Risks

This case inevitably presents, to the court as to the Administrator, the need for a perspective on the suspension that is informed by an analysis which balances the costs of a "wrong decision" on feasibility against the gains of a correct one. These costs include the risks of grave maladjustments for the technological leader from the eleventh-hour grant of a suspension, and the impact on jobs and the economy from a decision which is only partially accurate, allowing companies to produce cars but at a significantly reduced level of output. Against this must be weighed the environmental savings from denial of suspension. The record indicates that these will be relatively modest. There is also the possibility that failure to grant a suspension may be counter-productive to the environment, if there is significant decline in performance characteristics.

Another consideration is present, that the real cost to granting a suspension arises from the symbolic compromise with the goal of a clean environment. We emphasize that our view of a one year suspension, and the intent of Congress as to a one year suspension, is in no sense to be taken as any support for further suspensions. This would plainly be contrary to the intent of Congress to set an absolute standard in 1976. On the contrary, we view the imperative of the Congressional requirement as to the significant improvement that must be wrought no later than 1976, as interrelated with the provision for one-year suspension. The flexibility in the statute provided by the availability of a one year suspension only strengthens the impact of the absolute standard. Considerations of fairness will support comprehensive and firm, even drastic, regulations, provided a "safety valve" is also provided—ordinarily a provision for waiver, exception or adjustment, in this case a provision for suspension. * * * To hold the safety valve too rigidly is to interfere with the relief that was contemplated as an integral part of the firmness of the overall, enduring program.

We approach the question of the burden of proof on the auto companies with the previous considerations before us.

IV. THE REQUIRED SHOWING ON "AVAILABLE TECHNOLOGY"

It is with utmost diffidence that we approach our assignment to review the Administrator's decision on "available technology." * * * Nevertheless we must proceed to the task of judicial review assigned by Congress.

The Act makes suspension dependent on the Administrator's determination that:

> the applicant has established that effective control technology, processes, operating methods, or other alternatives are not available or have not been available for a sufficient period of time to achieve compliance prior to the effective data of such standards....

A. Requirement of Observed Data From Manufacturers

Clearly this requires that the applicants come forward with data which showed that they could not comply with the contemplated standards. The normal rules place such a burden on the party in control of the relevant information. It was the auto companies who were in possession of the data about emission performance of their cars.

The submission of the auto companies unquestionably showed that no car had actually been driven 50,000 miles and achieved conformity of emissions to the 1975 standards. The Administrator's position is that on the basis of the methodology outlined, he can predict that the auto companies can meet the standards, and that the ability to make a prediction saying the companies can comply means that the petitioners have failed to sustain their burden of proof that they cannot comply.

B. *Requisite Reliability of Methodology Relied on by EPA To Predict Feasibility Notwithstanding Lack of Actual Experience*

We agree with the Administrator's proposition in general. Its validity as applied to this case rests on the reliability of his prediction, and the nature of his assumptions. One must distinguish between prediction and prophecy. In a matter of this importance, the predictor must make a showing of reliability of the methodology of prediction, when that is being relied on to overcome this "adverse" actual test data of the auto companies. The statute does not contemplate use of a "crystal ball."

* * * The underlying issue is the reasonableness and reliability of the Administrator's methodology, for it alone offsets the data adduced by petitioners in support of suspension. It is the Administrator who must bear the burden on this matter, because the development and use of the methodology are attributable to his knowledge and expertise. * * * In the context of this proceeding, this requires that EPA bear a burden of adducing a reasoned presentation supporting the reliability of its methodology.

C. *Analysis of EPA Assumptions*

The multiple assumptions used by the Administrator in making his prediction are subject to serious doubts.

The basic formula used to make the prediction that each of the manufacturers could meet the 1975 standards was based on 1975 certification requirements, so that in part it paralleled testing procedures which would be used in 1975 to certify automobiles for sale. The formula is:

50,000 mile emissions = 4000 mile emissions x deterioration factor

Four kinds of assumptions were used in making the 50,000 mile emission prediction: (1) regulatory, (2) engineering or scientific, (3) techniques of application of basic formula to particular companies, and (4) statistical reliability of the final prediction.

1. *Regulatory assumptions*

First, EPA assumed that certain types of maintenance would have to be performed on 1975 model year cars, if its 50,000 miles emission predictions were to be meaningful. * * * This assumption was necessary because much of the data supplied by the companies was obtained from cars that were under rigid controls during testing. The problem with such maintenance assumptions is whether the ordinary driver will actually pay for this kind of maintenance just to reduce the emission levels of his automobile. * * *

Secondly, the predicted emission level assumes that there will be one total replacement of the catalytic converter at some time after 25,000 miles. * * * The critical question is how much will the one replacement reduce emissions otherwise obtainable by use of a single catalyst. * * *

The third regulatory assumption relates to the average lead level which will exist in gasoline available for 1975 model year cars. Lead levels in gasoline contribute to the levels of HC and CO both in terms of normal emission control achievable (the 4000 mile emission) and to the deterioration in emissions over time (deterioration factor). * * *

On December 27, 1972, a regulation was promulgated "designed to assure general availability by July 1, 1974, of suitable gasolines containing no more than .05 grams per gallon of lead. . . ." It was the assumption of the Administrator that the .05 maximum would result in gas containing on the average .03 grams per gallon of lead. The discrepancy between the maximum and average is accounted for by the contamination of lead free gasoline from its point of production to its marketing outlet. Thus EPA will allow a maximum of .05 but anticipates that on the average fuel will be at .03. * * *

2. *Engineering and scientific assumptions*

Engineering or scientific assumptions are made in predicting 4000 mile emissions and deterioration factors, and we shall give separate consideration to each independent variable.

a. The 4000 mile emission factor

The use of 4000 mile emissions as a starting point is based on certification procedures. No challenge has been made to this mileage as a base point, largely because it appears that at this mileage the engine is broken in and emission levels are relatively stabilized. * * *

Lead adjustment factor

This Lead Adjustment Factor was calculated using only Ford cars, but the value of the factor was assumed to be the same in adjusting Chrysler 4000 mile emissions with this factor. The cars had been tested with a dynamometer, a type of test equipment used for laboratory testing of an engine. A measurement of the efficiency of the catalytic converter at the 4000 mile mark was the critical value which had to be obtained from the dynamometer since this would indicate what the proper lead adjustment factor would be.

* * * Petitioners claim that the high temperature readings on the dynamometer reflect a higher RPM, and hence that a testing below 200 hours corresponded to 4000 miles of use. * * *

The cause of higher than expected temperature readings cannot be ascertained from the record, and we are left with the alternative contentions of the parties. It is up to EPA, however, to support its methodology as reliable, and this requires more than reliance on the unknown, either by speculation, or mere shifting back of the burden of proof.

b. Deterioration factor

Methodological problems also existed with the calculation of the deterioration factor, which took account of possible deterioration in emission quality from 4000 miles to 50,000 miles. Different questions arose as to the calculation of this factor for Ford and Chrysler.

In the case of Ford, the Administrator predicted that emissions would *improve* from 4000 to 50,000 miles, and arrived at a deterioration factor of less than 1. * * * The Administrator never explained why there should be no deterioration. Nor does EPA explain how this result can be squared with other data on Ford catalyst efficiencies, which was used in the case of the General Motors prediction, showing 50,000 mile catalyst efficiencies ranging from 21% to 53% for HC and 47% to 72% for CO.

In the case of Chrysler, the deterioration factor was also calculated to be less than 1, but this figure was only arrived at after eliminating some data points from the emission measurement on the tested car #333, due to what EPA claimed were unrepresentative points resulting from non-catalyst malfunctions. Although it may be, as EPA argues here, that including the data points would still produce predicted 50,000 emission levels in conformity with the 1975 standard, the fact remains that these data points were removed. Moreover, it is not apparent why one should ignore malfunctions of a car which contribute to high emissions, even if they are not malfunctions of the converter. Malfunctions of cars occur to some degree, and cars operating in 1975 will undoubtedly be subject to them.

Lead adjustment factor

A lead adjustment factor is applied to the deterioration factor, as well as to 4000 mile emissions. EPA estimated on the basis of the questionable Ford dynamometer data, that lead levels had no observable effect, which was contrary to industry testimony on the subject. The Administrator evidently had doubts as to the dependability of these results as well, and therefore assumed a 10% factor for lead adjustment. No explanation is given of the origins of this 10% figure. * * *

3. EPA methodology for General Motors

In the case of General Motors an entirely different methodology from that used for Ford and Chrysler was employed. * * * The catalyst efficiency data were taken from Engelhard converters used principally on Ford cars and applied against the raw emissions of a General Motors engine. This assumed, with no explanation of the validity of such an assumption, that Engelhard catalysts will function as efficiently in General Motors cars as in those of Ford. A prediction was made on the basis of a hypothetical case. One cannot help be troubled by the adoption of this technique for General Motors. It was apparently recognized as at best a second best approach, in terms of the reliability of the prediction, or the same catalyst efficiency procedure would also have been used for Ford and Chrysler.

4. Statistical reliability of assumptions

In this case the Administrator is necessarily making a prediction. No tests exist on whether this prediction is or is not reliable. It would, therefore, seem incumbent on the Administrator to estimate the possible degree of error in his prediction. The NAS, for example, said that the data of the manufacturers were subject to +-20–30% margin of error, and this is separate from any margin of error that may be due to the various assumptions made by the Administrator. * * *

V. CONCLUSION AND DISPOSITION

* * * In this case technical issues permeate the "available technology" determination which the Administrator made the focal point of his decision. In approaching our judicial task we conclude that the requirement of a "reasoned decision" by the Environmental Protection Agency means, in present context, a reasoned presentation of the reliability of a prediction and methodology that is relied upon to overcome a conclusion, of lack of available technology, supported prima faciely by the only actual and observed data available, the manufacturers' testing.

The number of unexplained assumptions used by the Administrator, the variance in methodology from that of the Report of the National Academy of Sciences, and the absence of an indication of the statistical reliability of the prediction, combine to generate grave doubts as to whether technology is available to meet the 1975 statutory standards. * * * These grave doubts have a legal consequence. This is customarily couched, by legal convention, in terms of "burden of proof." * * * We think the vehicle manufacturers established by a preponderance of the evidence, in the record before us, that technology was not available, within the meaning of the Act, when they adduced the tests on actual vehicles; that the Administrator's reliance on technological methodology to offset the actual tests raised serious doubts and failed to meet the burden of proof which in our view was properly assignable to him, in the light of accepted legal doctrine and the intent of Congress discerned, in part, by taking into account that the risk of an "erroneous" denial of suspension outweighed the risk of an "erroneous" grant of suspension. We do not use the burden of proof in the conventional sense of civil trials, but the Administrator must sustain the burden of adducing a reasoned presentation supporting the reliability of EPA's methodology.

* * * These factors combine to convince us that, under our view of Congressional intent, we cannot affirm the EPA's denial of suspension as stated. That is not necessarily to assume, as at least some petitioners do, that the EPA's process must be brought to nullity.

* * * Following our suggestion in *Environmental Defense Fund, Inc. v. EPA*, 465 F.2d 528 (1972), the Administrator may consider possible use of interim standards short of complete suspension. The statute permits conditioning of suspension on the adoption, by virtue of the information adduced in the suspension proceeding, of interim standards, higher than those set for 1974.

* * * The case is remanded for further proceedings not inconsistent with this opinion.

NOTES

1. **The Rest of the Story.** In 1970, 36% of the nation's total hydrocarbon emissions and 20% of its NOx emissions came from automobiles. Michael Koontz, *Clean Air and Transportation: The Facts May Surprise You*, 62:1 PUBLIC ROADS (July/Aug. 1998). A typical 1960s model year car emitted about 11 grams of hydrocarbons, 4 grams of NOx, and 80 grams of carbon monoxide over *every mile of use*. *Id.* Prior to the 1970 amendments to the Clean Air Act, Congress had required auto makers to reduce hydrocarbon emissions to 3.4 grams per mile and carbon monoxide emissions to 39 grams per mile—the 1974 standards charted in *International Harvester*. In 1970, Congress somewhat unexpectedly required automobile manufacturers to achieve 90% reductions in auto emissions, reducing hydrocarbon emissions to 0.41 grams per mile and carbon monoxide emissions to 3.4 grams per mile for the 1975 model year. These are the standards at issue in this case.

As a result of this case, the EPA delayed the implementation of Congress's emission reduction requirements by one year. It also granted a one-year extension of the 1976 NOx emission reduction requirement.

Under pressure from the auto industry, the original 1975 reduction requirement for hydrocarbon emissions was eventually delayed until 1980, after two waivers from the EPA and two extensions from Congress. Carbon monoxide emission reductions were delayed even longer, until model year 1983. Nevertheless, auto manufacturers met the emissions reductions for hydrocarbons and carbon monoxide by 1980—only 10 years after Congress originally imposed them.

NOx was more difficult. The first catalytic converters actually resulted in emission of *more* NOx as a consequence of reducing hydrocarbon emissions. In other words, there was an unavoidable trade-off that made it technologically impossible to achieve both the hydrocarbon and the NOx emission reductions simultaneously. As a result, after the EPA granted an extension, Congress granted an additional extension, then voted in the 1977 amendments to the Act to impose a less stringent 1 gram per mile standard instead, to take effect in the 1981 model year. That standard was also subject to a series of waivers, finally taking effect in 1984.

In the 1990 amendments to the Clean Air Act, Congress again required significant improvements in auto emissions. For 1994 model year cars, NOx emissions had to be reduced to 0.4 grams per mile, reinstating the 90% reduction requirement. For 1996 model year cars, hydrocarbon emissions had to be reduced to 0.25 grams, or about one-half of one percent of the 1960s models' emissions.

Litigation and lobbying are expensive activities, yet the automobile industry has lobbied against, and then litigated against, every set of emissions reduction requirements that Congress and the EPA have imposed. Why would the automobile industry take the time and expense to so stringently fight emissions reductions? Consider this: In the early 1970s, "GM estimated that catalytic converters and other pollution controls would raise the price of a car by two percent. Ford and Chrysler estimated that it would cost an additional five percent." William Kovarik & Matthew E. Hermes, *Fuels and Society C: 14. Impact of Catalytic Converters on Auto Manufacturing*, http://chemcases.com/converter/converter–22.htm. The overall costs of catalytic converters and other hardware turned out to be $10 billion per year. Benefit estimates, on the other hand, ranged from one economist's estimate of $2 billion per year, based on well-documented acute health effects, to the American Lung Association's estimate of $93 billion per year and the Natural Resources Defense Council's estimate of $120–220 billion per year. *Id.* Did the lobbying and litigating produce benefits for the industry? If so, how? Do you think that Congress or the EPA would ever allow the automobile industry to go out of business? Why or why not? *See, e.g.*, 116 Cong. Rec. 32,905 (1970) (comments of Senator Muskie).

2. **Catalytic Converters and Lead Reductions.** As part II.A discussed, *supra*, early litigation forced the EPA to add lead as a criteria pollutant under the Clean Air Act. The EPA preferred to reduce lead emissions by regulating fuel. Beginning in the 1920s, gasoline producers added tetraethyl lead to gasoline to reduce engine "knock," and by 1936, over 90% of the gasoline sold in the United States was "leaded." Jamie Lincoln Kitman, *8,500 Years of Lead . . . 79 Years of Leaded Gasoline*, THE NATION (March 20, 2000), *available at* http://www.mindfully.org/Pesticide/Lead–History.htm. Even though lead became a criteria pollutant, the EPA continued its regulation of leaded fuel.

Based on its 1972 Clean Air Act regulations, the EPA began phasing out leaded gasoline in 1976. The EPA's phase-out of leaded gasoline and the emissions requirements for new cars are linked, because the active element of catalytic converters—platinum—is contaminated by leaded gas, a fact discovered in 1970. Thus, for automobiles to be able to take advantage of this technological advance, which would so dramatically reduce automobile emissions, unleaded gasoline had to become the norm.

Of course, the change to unleaded gasoline not only allowed catalytic converters to reduce hydrocarbon, NOx, and carbon monoxide emissions but also reduced lead emissions from automobiles. By 1980, lead levels in gasoline had dropped 50% and blood-lead levels in United States residents had dropped 37%. Kitman, *supra.* The EPA calculated in 1983 that even in 1980, before the phase-out was complete, the benefits of the lead phase-out exceeded its costs by $700 million. *Id.* The primary phase-out of leaded gasoline was complete in 1986, and by 1991, blood-lead levels for U.S. residents had dropped by 78%. *Id.* Currently, only 9% of children have blood-lead levels that exceed 10 micrograms per deciliter, the level currently designated as lead poisoning.

Lead Poisoning Resource Center, *What Is Lead Poisoning?*, http://www.aboutlead.com.

3. **The Role of the "Wrong Decision."** What was the D.C. Circuit's concern with the "wrong decision" in this case? Did its analysis of the "wrong decision" amount to a risk assessment of the EPA's decision that catalytic converters were "available" for model year 1975 vehicles? Why or why not? How did the court's cost-benefit balancing affect its decision? How did the court's "wrong decision" analysis affect its legal evaluation of the case?

4. **Predictions vs. Prophecies: The EPA's Authority to Designate Technological Standards.** According to the D.C. Circuit, can the EPA require emission standards for future model years based on technology that does not yet exist? Why or why not? What is the limit of the EPA's authority to designate specific technologies?

5. **Light Duty Vehicles, Light Duty Trucks, and Heavy Duty Vehicles.** The emissions standards at issue in *International Harvester* apply only to ***light duty vehicles***. In a portion of *International Harvester* not reproduced above, International Harvester won its claim that trucks should not be considered "light duty vehicles" subject to the 1975 emissions standards.

The Clean Air Act now imposes separate emissions requirements on ***light-duty trucks*** and on ***heavy duty vehicles***. Light-duty trucks include trucks and sport utility vehicles (SUVs), as well as non-passenger motor vehicles. CAA § 202(g), 42 U.S.C. § 7521(g). The Clean Air Act currently requires that by the 1994 model year, light duty trucks weighing up to 3,750 pounds had to meet the same emission standards for hydrocarbons, carbon monoxide, and NOx as light duty vehicles—that is, 0.25 grams per mile, 3.4 grams per mile, and 0.4 grams per mile, respectively. *Id.* & Table G. Light duty trucks weighing 3,751–5,750 pounds are subject to more relaxed standards of 0.32 grams per mile of hydrocarbons, 4.4 grams per mile of carbon monoxide, and 0.7 grams per mile of NOx. *Id.* & Table G. Light duty trucks weighing more than 5,750 pounds are subject to emissions standards of 0.39 grams per mile of hydrocarbons, 5.0 grams per mile of carbon monoxide, and 1.1 grams per mile of NOx by the model year 1995. CAA § 202(h), 42 U.S.C. § 7521(h) & Table H. Diesel-burning light trucks of all weights are subject to less stringent NOx emissions requirements. *Id.* § 202(g), (h), 42 U.S.C. § 7521(g), (h), & Tables G, H.

A ***heavy duty vehicle*** is "a truck, bus, or other vehicle manufactured primarily for use on the public streets, roads, and highways * * * which has a gross vehicle weight * * * in excess of 6000 pounds. Such term includes any such vehicle which has special features enabling off-street or off-highway operation and use," but the term does not include railway vehicles. CAA § 202(b)(3)(C), 42 U.S.C. § 7521(b)(3)(C). Beginning in model year 1983, emissions of hydrocarbons, carbon monoxide, NOx, *and particulate matter* from heavy duty vehicles shall be subject to "standards which reflect the greatest degree of emission reduction achievable through the application of technology which the Administrator determines will be available for the model year to which such standards apply, giving appropriate consideration to cost, energy, and safety factors associated with the application of such technology." CAA § 202(a)(3)(A)(i), 42 U.S.C. § 7521(a)(3)(A)(i).

The EPA promulgated new emissions standards for heavy duty vehicles in January 2001. 66 Fed. Reg. 5,001 (Jan. 18, 2001). This rule "establish[es] a comprehensive national control program that will regulate the heavy-duty vehicle and its fuel as a single system," and the requirements take effect in model year 2007. *Id.* at 5002. Estimating "that heavy-duty trucks and buses today account for about one-third of nitrogen oxides emissions," *id.*, the EPA requires trucks to use low-sulfur diesel fuel and calls for a 97% reduction in diesel fuel sulfur content. *Id.* The rule also requires manufacturers to equip trucks with high efficiency emissions control devices. The EPA expects that, "[b]y 2030, this program will reduce annual emissions of nitrogen oxides, nonmethane hydrocarbons, and particulate matter by a projected 2.6 million, 115,000 and 109,000 tons, respectively. We project that these reductions and the resulting significant environmental benefits of this program will come out at an average cost increase of about $2000 to $3,200 per vehicle in the near terms and about $1,200 to $1,900 per new vehicle in the long term, depending on the vehicle size." *Id.*

6. **Greenhouse Gas Emissions Standards for Motor Vehicles.** In September 2011, the EPA and the National Highway Traffic Safety Administration (NHTSA) finalized regulations that establish greenhouse gas emission emissions standards and fuel efficiency standards for medium- and heavy-duty engines and vehicles. Greenhouse Gas Emissions Standards and Fuel Efficiency Standard for Medium- and Heavy–Duty Engines and Vehicles, 76 Fed. Reg. 57,106 (Sept. 15, 2011). The EPA, for its part, set emissions standards for carbon dioxide, nitrous oxide, and methane, which will become mandatory with the 2014 model year for covered vehicles.

On November 16, 2011, the two agencies proposed regulations to establish greenhouse gas emissions standards and fuel economy standards for light-duty vehicles and engines, which would cover normal passenger vehicles. 2017 and Later Model Year Light–Duty Vehicle Greenhouse Gas Emissions and Corporate Average Fuel Economy Standards, 76 Fed. Reg. 74,854 (Dec. 1, 2011). Comments were due to the agencies on January 30, 2012. The proposed rules build on an existing program for model years 2010 to 2016 and would apply to vehicles in model years 2017 to 2025. According to the two agencies:

> Combined with the standards already in effect for MYs 2012–2016, as well as the MY 2011 CAFE standards, the proposed standards would result in MY 2025 light-duty vehicles with nearly double the fuel economy, and approximately one-half of the GHG emissions compared to MY 2010 vehicles—representing the most significant federal action ever taken to reduce GHG emissions and improve fuel economy in the U.S. EPA is proposing standards that are projected to require, on an average industry fleet wide basis, 163 grams/mile of carbon dioxide (CO_2) in model year 2025, which is equivalent to 54.5 mpg if this level were achieved solely through improvements in fuel efficiency.
>
> * * * From a societal standpoint, this second phase of the National Program is projected to save approximately 4 billion barrels of oil and 2 billion metric tons of GHG emissions over the lifetimes of those vehicles

> sold in MY 2017–2025. The agencies estimate that fuel savings will far outweigh higher vehicle costs, and that the net benefits to society of the MYs 2017–2025 National Program will be in the range of $311 billion to $421 billion (7 and 3 percent discount rates, respectively) over the lifetimes of those vehicles sold in MY 2017–2025.

Id. at 74,859.

Compared to the greenhouse gas emission reduction proposals for stationary sources, these regulations have been generally accepted. In large part, that lack of controversy resulted because the EPA and NHTSA involved all of the important stakeholders in the rule negotiations. Why would automobile manufacturers be willing to participate in such negotiations with the agencies? Why would public health and environmental organizations?

* * *

2. State Emissions Standards for Motor Vehicles

Section 209 of the Clean Air Act provides that "[n]o State or any political subdivision thereof shall adopt or attempt to enforce any standard relating to the control of emissions from new motor vehicles or new motor vehicle engines subject to this part." CAA § 209(a), 42 U.S.C. § 7543. A similar prohibition applies to state certification and inspection requirements. *Id.* As a result, federal emissions standards for new motor vehicles generally ***preempt*** any state law on the same subject.

Nevertheless, section 209 also allows the EPA Administrator to waive its prohibitions for "any State which has adopted standards * * * for the control of emissions from new motor vehicles or new motor vehicle engines prior to March 30, 1966, if the State determines that the State standards will be, in the aggregate, at least as protective of public health and welfare as applicable Federal standards." CAA § 209(b)(1), 42 U.S.C. § 7543(b)(1). If the waiver is granted, "compliance with such State standards shall be treated as compliance with applicable Federal standards for purposes of this subchapter." *Id.* § 209(b)(3), 42 U.S.C. § 7543(c).

For many years, California was the only state to have its own state emissions standards program under section 209. In 1990, however, Congress added section 177 to the CAA, which allows states that have AQCRs that are nonattainment for ozone or carbon monoxide to "adopt and enforce for any model year standards relating to control of emissions from new motor vehicles or new motor vehicle engines * * * if * * * such standards are identical to the California standards for which a waiver has been granted for such model year * * *." CAA § 177(1), 42 U.S.C. § 7507(1). Northeastern states, in particular, have begun to take advantage of this option. *See generally Association of International Auto Manufacturers, Inc. v. Commissioner, Massachusetts Department of Environmental Protection*, 208 F.3d 1 (1st Cir. 2000) (regarding Massachusetts' use of the California requirements); *American Auto Manufacturers Association v. Cahill*, 152 F.3d 196 (2d Cir. 1998) (regarding New York's use of the California requirements).

How far, otherwise, does section 209's preemption of state law extend? The U.S. Supreme Court recently addressed that issue in the context of a California air quality management district's Fleet Rules in the following case.

ENGINE MANUFACTURERS ASSOCIATION v. SOUTH COAST AIR QUALITY MANAGEMENT DISTRICT

541 U.S. 246 (2004).

JUSTICE SCALIA delivered the opinion of the Court.

Respondent South Coast Air Quality Management District (District) is a political subdivision of California responsible for air pollution control in the Los Angeles metropolitan area and parts of surrounding counties that make up the South Coast Air Basin. It enacted six Fleet Rules that generally prohibit the purchase or lease by various public and private fleet operators of vehicles that do not comply with stringent emission requirements. The question in this case is whether these local Fleet Rules escape pre-emption under § 209(a) of the Clean Air Act (CAA), 42 U.S.C. § 7543(a), because they address the purchase of vehicles, rather than their manufacture or sale.

I

The District is responsible under state law for developing and implementing a "comprehensive basinwide air quality management plan" to reduce emission levels and thereby achieve and maintain "state and federal ambient air quality standards." CAL. HEALTH & SAFETY CODE ANN. § 40402(e) (West 1996). Between June and October 2000, the District adopted six Fleet Rules. The Rules govern operators of fleets of street sweepers (Rule 1186.1), of passenger cars, light-duty trucks, and medium-duty vehicles (Rule 1191), of public transit vehicles and urban buses (Rule 1192), of solid waste collection vehicles (Rule 1193), of airport passenger transportation vehicles, including shuttles and taxicabs picking up airline passengers (Rule 1194), and of heavy-duty on-road vehicles (Rule 1196). All six Rules apply to public operators; three apply to private operators as well (Rules 1186.1, 1193, and 1194).

The Fleet Rules contain detailed prescriptions regarding the types of vehicles that fleet operators must purchase or lease when adding or replacing fleet vehicles. Four of the Rules (1186.1, 1192, 1193, and 1196) require the purchase or lease of "alternative-fuel vehicles," and the other two (1191 and 1194) require the purchase or lease of either "alternative-fueled vehicles" or vehicles that meet certain emission specifications established by the California Air Resources Board (CARB). CARB is a statewide regulatory body that California law designates as "the air pollution control agency for all purposes set forth in federal law." CAL. HEALTH & SAFETY CODE ANN. § 39602 (West 1996). The Rules require operators to keep records of their purchases and leases and provide access to them upon request. *See, e.g.,* Rule 1186.1(g)(1), App. 23. Violations expose fleet operators to fines and other sanctions. *See* CAL. HEALTH & SAFETY CODE ANN. §§ 42400–42410, 40447.5 (West 1996 and Supp. 2004).

In August 2000, petitioner Engine Manufacturers Association sued the District and its officials, also respondents, claiming that the Fleet Rules are pre-empted by § 209 of the CAA, which prohibits the adoption or attempted enforcement of any state or local "standard relating to the control of emissions from new motor vehicles or new motor vehicle engines." 42 U.S.C. § 7543(a). The District Court granted summary judgment to respondents, upholding the Rules in their entirety. It held that the Rules were not "standard[s]" under § 209(a) because they regulate only the purchase of vehicles that are otherwise certified for sale in California. The District Court recognized that the First and Second Circuit Courts of Appeals had previously held that CAA § 209(a) pre-empted state laws mandating that a specified percentage of a manufacturer's in-state sales be of "zero-emission vehicles." See *Association of Int'l Automobile Mfrs., Inc. v. Commissioner, Mass. Dept. of Environmental Protection,* 208 F.3d 1, 6–7 (C.A. 1 2000); *American Automobile Mfrs. Assn. v. Cahill,* 152 F.3d 196, 200 (C.A. 2 1998). It did not express disagreement with these rulings, but distinguished them as involving a restriction on vehicle sales rather than vehicle purchases: "Where a state regulation does not compel manufacturers to meet a new emissions limit, but rather affects the purchase of vehicles, as the Fleet Rules do, that regulation is not a standard." 158 F. Supp. 2d 1107, 1118 (C.D. Cal. 2001).

The Ninth Circuit affirmed on the reasoning of the District Court. We granted certiorari.

II

Section 209(a) of the CAA states:

> "No State or any political subdivision thereof shall adopt or attempt to enforce any standard relating to the control of emissions from new motor vehicles or new motor vehicle engines subject to this part. No State shall require certification, inspection, or any other approval relating to the control of emissions ... as condition precedent to the initial retail sale, titling (if any), or registration of such motor vehicle, motor vehicle engine, or equipment." 42 U.S.C. § 7543(a).

The District Court's determination that this express pre-emption provision did not invalidate the Fleet Rules hinged on its interpretation of the word "standard" to include only regulations that compel manufacturers to meet specified emission limits. This interpretation of "standard" in turn caused the court to draw a distinction between purchase restrictions (not pre-empted) and sale restrictions (pre-empted). Neither the manufacturer-specific interpretation of "standard" nor the resulting distinction between purchase and sale restrictions finds support in the text of § 209(a) or the structure of the CAA.

"Statutory construction must begin with the language employed by Congress and the assumption that the ordinary meaning of that language accurately expresses the legislative purpose." *Park 'N Fly, Inc. v. Dollar Park & Fly, Inc.*, 469 U.S. 189, 194 (1985). Today, as in 1967 when § 209(a) became law, "standard" is defined as that which "is established by authority, custom, or general consent, as a model or example; criterion; test." WEBSTER'S SECOND NEW INTERNATIONAL DICTIONARY 2455 (1945). The criteria referred to in § 209(a) relate to the emission characteristics of a vehicle or engine. To meet them the vehicle or engine must not emit more than a certain amount of a given pollutant, must be equipped with a certain type of pollution-control device, or must have some other design feature related to the control of emissions. This interpretation is consistent with the use of "standard" throughout Title II of the CAA (which governs emissions from moving sources) to denote requirements such as numerical emission levels with which vehicles or engines must comply, *e.g.*, 42 U.S.C. § 7521(a)(1)(B)(ii), or emission-control technology with which they must be equipped, *e.g.*, § 7521(a)(6).

Respondents, like the courts below, engraft onto this meaning of "standard" a limiting component, defining it as only "[a] *production* mandat[e] that require[s] *manufacturers* to ensure that the vehicles they produce have particular emissions characteristics, whether individually or in the aggregate." This confuses standards with the means of enforcing standards. Manufacturers (or purchasers) can be made responsible for ensuring that vehicles *comply* with emission standards, but the standards themselves are separate from those enforcement techniques. While standards target vehicles or engines, standard-enforcement efforts that are proscribed by § 209 can be directed to manufacturers or purchasers.

The distinction between "standards," on the one hand, and methods of standard enforcement, on the other, is borne out in the provisions immediately following § 202. These separate provisions enforce the emission criteria—*i.e.*, the § 202 standards. Section 203 prohibits manufacturers from selling any new motor vehicle that is not covered by a "certificate of conformity." 42 U.S.C. § 7522(a). Section 206 enables manufacturers to obtain such a certificate by demonstrating to the EPA that their vehicles or engines conform to the § 202 standards. § 7525. Sections 204 and 205 subject manufacturers, dealers, and others who violate the CAA to fines imposed in civil or administrative enforcement actions. §§ 7523–7524. By defining "standard" as a "production mandate directed toward manufacturers," respondents lump together § 202 and these other distinct statutory provisions, acknowledging a standard to be such only when it is combined with a mandate that prevents manufacturers from selling noncomplying vehicles.

That a standard is a standard even when not enforced through manufacturer-directed regulation can be seen in Congress's use of the term in another portion of the CAA. As the District Court recognized, CAA § 246 (in conjunction with its accompanying provisions) requires state-adopted and federally approved "restrictions on the purchase of fleet vehicles *to meet clean-air standards*." 158 F. Supp. 2d, at 1118 (emphasis added); see also 42 U.S.C. §§ 7581–7590. (Respondents do not defend the

District's Fleet Rules as authorized by this provision; the Rules do not comply with all of the requirements that it contains.) Clearly, Congress contemplated the enforcement of emission standards through purchase requirements.

Respondents contend that their qualified meaning of "standard" is necessary to prevent § 209(a) from pre-empting "far too much" by "encompass[ing] a broad range of state-level clean-air initiatives" such as voluntary incentive programs. But it is hard to see why limitation to mandates on manufacturers is necessary for this purpose; limitation to mandates on manufacturers and purchasers, or to mandates on *anyone,* would have the same salvific effect. We need not resolve application of § 209(a) to voluntary incentive programs in this case, since all the Fleet Rules are mandates.

In addition to having no basis in the text of the statute, treating sales restrictions and purchase restrictions differently for pre-emption purposes would make no sense. The manufacturer's right to sell federally approved vehicles is meaningless in the absence of a purchaser's right to buy them. It is true that the Fleet Rules at issue here cover only certain purchasers and certain federally certified vehicles, and thus do not eliminate all demand for covered vehicles. But if one State or political subdivision may enact such rules, then so may any other; and the end result would undo Congress's carefully calibrated regulatory scheme.

A command, accompanied by sanctions, that certain purchasers may buy only vehicles with particular emission characteristics is as much an "attempt to enforce" a "standard" as a command, accompanied by sanctions, that a certain percentage of a manufacturer's sales volume must consist of such vehicles. We decline to read into § 209(a) a purchase/sale distinction that is not to be found in the text of § 209(a) or the structure of the CAA.

* * * IV

The courts below held all six of the Fleet Rules to be entirely outside the pre-emptive reach of § 209(a) based on reasoning that does not withstand scrutiny. In light of the principles articulated above, it appears likely that at least certain aspects of the Fleet Rules are pre-empted. * * *

It does not necessarily follow, however, that the Fleet Rules are pre-empted *in toto.* We have not addressed a number of issues that may affect the ultimate disposition of petitioners' suit, including the scope of petitioners' challenge, whether some of the Fleet Rules (or some applications of them) can be characterized as internal state purchase decisions (and, if so, whether a different standard for pre-emption applies), and whether § 209(a) pre-empts the Fleet Rules even as applied beyond the purchase of new vehicles (*e.g.,* to lease arrangements or to the purchase of used vehicles). These questions were neither passed on below nor presented in the petition for certiorari. They are best addressed in the first instance by the lower courts in light of the principles articulated above.

The judgment is vacated, and the case is remanded for further proceedings consistent with this opinion.

It is so ordered.

NOTES

1. **The Rest of the Story.** On June 4, 2004, the South Coast Air Quality Management District sought a waiver from the EPA pursuant to Section 209 for its Fleet Rules. In the interim, however, the U.S. District Court for the Central District of California decided the *Engine Manufacturers Association* remand, concluding that California's Fleet Rules were not preempted by the Clean Air Act. *Engine Manufacturers Association v. South Coast Air Quality Management District*, CV 00–090–065 FMC (C.D. Cal. May, 5, 2005), *available at* http://www.nrdc.org/media/docs/050509.pdf. Given the U.S. Supreme Court's decision above, what was left for the district court judge to decide? How could the district judge have left the Fleet Rules in force?

2. **What Are the Fleet Rules?** How did the South Coast Air Quality Management District try to argue that the Clean Air Act did *not* preempt its Fleet Rules? What was it trying to accomplish with those Fleet Rules? Do the rules change the type of vehicle sold in California? Why or why not?

3. **Interpreting Section 209(a).** What word in section 209(a) of the Clean Air Act is at issue in this case? Why? How did Justice Scalia and the majority interpret that word? What tools of statutory construction did they rely upon?

4. **Federal Preemption and Cooperative Federalism.** The federal government's ability to preempt state law is rooted in the Supremacy Clause of the U.S. Constitution, which states that "[t]his Constitution, and the Laws of the United States which shall be made in Pursuance thereof; and all Treaties made, or which shall be made, under the Authority of the United States, shall be the supreme Law of the Land; and the Judges in every State shall be bound thereby, any Thing in the Constitution or Laws of any State to the Contrary notwithstanding." U.S. CONST., art VI, cl. 2. What is the relationship between section 209(a) and the cooperative federalism that operates throughout the Clean Air Act? Why would Congress want to preempt the states from enacting state-level emissions standards for motor vehicles? Is its concern related to the automobile industry's concerns in *International Harvester*? Why or why not?

5. **California, Low Emission Vehicle Standards, Climate Change, and *Massachusetts v. EPA*.** On July 22, 2002, Governor Gray Davis of California signed into law Assembly Bill 1493, which required the California Air Resources Board (CARB) to establish vehicle emissions rules to reduce greenhouse gases, especially CO_2 emissions. In September 2004, CARB approved its Low Emission Vehicle (LEV) standards, which would require auto manufacturers to cut CO_2 from cars and light duty trucks by 22% by 2009 and by 30% by 2016.

On December 21, 2005, California petitioned the EPA to waive the Clean Air Act's preemption of these standards. However, the EPA refused to act on

California's petition until the U.S. Supreme Court resolved the issue of the agency's authority to regulate greenhouse gas emissions pursuant to the Clean Air Act. The U.S. Supreme Court, as noted above, decided *Massachusetts v. EPA* on April 2, 2007. On April 30, the EPA announced two public hearings on California's petition, which were held in May 2007. EPA, *California State Motor Vehicle Pollution Control Standards; Request for Waiver of Federal Preemption; Opportunity for Public Hearing*, 72 Fed. Reg. 21260 (April 30, 2007). On June 21, 2007, EPA Administrator Stephen Johnson informed California Governor Arnold Schwarzenegger that the EPA would be deciding California's petition by the end of 2007.

In the meantime, several other states began announcing their intentions to adopt the California LEV standards. By December 2007, 12 states—mainly on the coasts—had done so: California, Oregon, Washington, Maine, Maryland, Massachusetts, Connecticut, New York, Rhode Island, Vermont, Pennsylvania, and New Jersey. Four other states—Arizona, Colorado, Florida, and Utah—planned to do so. This widespread state adoption prompted three lawsuits by auto makers against the states—one in California, one in Rhode Island, and one in Vermont—claiming that the California LEV rules were invalid because the Clean Air Act did not apply to greenhouse gases and because the auto makers could not meet the new standards. All three courts stayed the lawsuits while the Supreme Court decided *Massachusetts v. EPA*, but by June 2007 all three were back in force, with the Vermont lawsuit the first to go to trial.

On September 12, 2007, the Vermont District Court held that neither the Clean Air Act nor the Energy Policy and Conservation Act preempted Vermont regulations adopting the California LEV standards, assuming that California received its anticipated waiver. *Green Mountain Chrysler Plymouth Dodge Jeep v. Crombie*, 508 F. Supp. 2d 295 (D. Vt. 2007). The Eastern District of California, three months later, reached the same conclusion regarding California's standards. *Central Valley Chrysler–Jeep, Inc. v. Goldstene*, 529 F. Supp. 2d 1151 (E.D. Cal. 2007).

Less than a week after the California decision, however, the EPA announced that it would deny California's waiver application. The EPA issued its official denial and explanation on February 29, 2008. 73 Fed. Reg. 12,156 (March 6, 2008). The EPA "concluded that Section 209(b) was intended to allow California to promulgate state standards applicable to emissions from new motor vehicles to address pollution problems that are local or regional. [The EPA does] not believe section 209(b)(1)(B) was intended to allow California to promulgate state standards for emissions from new motor vehicles to address global climate change problems; nor, in the alternative, [does the EPA] believe that the effects of climate change in California are compelling and extraordinary compared to the effects in the rest of the country." *Id.* at 12,156–57.

Protests were immediate, and even Congress began to investigate the EPA's denial of California's waiver request. With the change in presidential administration, however, California's request is being reconsidered. On February 12, 2009, the Obama Administration's EPA announced that it would review California's request for a waiver, and on June 30, 2009, the EPA granted that waiver, effective for the current model year of cars. 74 Fed. Reg. 32,744 (July 8, 2009). In June 2011, the EPA confirmed that this waiver applied to California's amendments to its greenhouse gas emissions standards or, in the alternative, granted California a new waiver. 76 Fed. Reg. 34,693 (June 14, 2011).

It is worth noting, however, that the denial in the greenhouse gas context was truly unusual, even for the Bush Administration. For example, six months later, the Bush Administrative granted California's waiver request to allow it to require 2010 model year heavy-duty vehicles and engines to have on-board diagnostic systems. 73 Fed. Reg. 52,042 (September 8, 2008).

In the meantime, in September 2006, California sued six major automobile manufacturers, alleging that those automobile makers' contributions to greenhouse gases in California amounted to a public nuisance. As the California Attorney General's Office explains the reasoning behind and fate of that case:

> The companies produce vehicles that emit over 289 million metric tons of carbon dioxide in the United States each year. Carbon dioxide emissions from their products in this country account for over 20 percent of carbon dioxide emissions in the United States, and over 30 percent of emissions in California. California sought monetary compensation for the large-scale damages that the companies' contributions to global warming are already causing in this state. Invoking what is known as the "political question" doctrine, the trial court dismissed the complaint, agreeing with the defendants that it is for Congress and the President, not the courts, to address the injuries that California is experiencing from global warming. We believe that trial court misapplied the political question doctrine; federal courts not only have the ability to provide a forum for the states' grievances, they have a duty to do so, particularly while Congress and the President fail to act.
>
> California appealed the auto case to the Ninth Circuit Court of Appeals. In the almost three years that the case had been pending, however, progress had been made in regulating vehicle GHG emissions, due in large part to the efforts of California. Accordingly, before the matter went to hearing, California filed a motion to dismiss its appeal. In June, 2009, the Ninth Circuit issued an order granting California's motion to dismiss in light of the actions taken by the federal government to reduce greenhouse gas emissions from motor vehicles. These federal actions include EPA's draft determination that greenhouse gases from motor vehicles threaten public health and welfare and must be regulated under the Clean Air Act and President Obama's directive to the U.S. Department of Transportation to establish improved national fuel economy standards in line with California's greenhouse gas automobile stan-

> dards. While California continues to believe the trial court in the auto case erred, this recent progress hopefully will afford the state some relief against the effects of global warming to which the auto companies' emissions contribute.

Office of the Attorney General, State of California Department of Justice, *Public Nuisance Litigation*, http://ag.ca.gov/globalwarming/litigation.php (2011).

What do you think about California's role in motivating regulation of greenhouse gas emissions from motor vehicles? Does this series of events suggest that states are the true leaders in dealing with climate change, or is the federal government finally catching up? Notably, the California agency responsible for air quality was a major participant in the EPA's and NHTSA's rulemakings for greenhouse gas emissions from motor vehicles, and the California waiver was an important consideration in establishing the federal requirements.

6. **The Breadth of the Clean Air Act's Preemption of Mobile Source Emissions.** It is worth noting that the Section 209 preemption can apply to many mobile sources. For example, in late 2008, the U.S. Court of Appeals for the Ninth Circuit held that the Clean Air Act preempted California's regulations limiting emissions from the auxiliary diesel engines of ocean-going vessels within 24 miles of California's coast. *Pacific Merchant Shipping Ass'n v. Goldstene*, 517 F.3d 1108 (9th Cir. 2008).

* * *

3. Motor Vehicle Fuel Standards

Under section 211 of the Clean Air Act, "[t]he Administrator [of the EPA] may by regulation designate any fuel or fuel additive * * * and, after such date or dates as may be prescribed by him, no manufacturer or possessor of any such fuel or additive may sell, offer for sale, or introduce into commerce such fuel or additive * * *." CAA § 211(a), 42 U.S.C. § 7545.

The Administrator can also register fuels and fuel additives. *Id.* § 211(b), 42 U.S.C. § 7545(b). Registration allows the EPA to require manufacturers to notify it of any fuel additives, their commercial names, their concentrations, their chemical compositions, and their purposes, and to conduct tests on the health effects of such additives. *Id.* Registration allows manufacturers to continue to sell the fuel or fuel additive, *id.* § 211(a), 42 U.S.C. § 7545(a), but the Administrator may also use the information obtained to

> control or prohibit the manufacture, introduction into commerce, offering for sale, or sale of any fuel or fuel additive for use in a motor vehicle, motor vehicle engine, or nonroad engine or nonroad vehicle (A) if in the judgment of the Administrator any emission product of such fuel or fuel additive causes, or contributes, to air pollution which may reasonably be anticipated to endanger the public health or welfare, or (B) if emission products of such fuels or fuel additive will

> impair to a significant degree the performance of any emission control device or system which is in general use, or which the Administrator finds has been developed to a point where in a reasonable time it would be in general use were such regulation to be promulgated.

Id. § 211(c)(1), 42 U.S.C. § 7545(c)(1).

Before promulgating such regulations, however, the Administrator must consider "all relevant medical and scientific evidence available to him, including consideration of other technologically or economically feasible means of achieving" the new motor vehicle emissions standards. *Id.* § 7545(c)(2), 42 U.S.C. § 7545(c)(2). Moreover, the Administrator must conduct "a cost benefit analysis comparing emission control devices or systems which are or will be in general use and require the proposed control or prohibition with emission control devices or systems which are or will be in general use and do not require the proposed control or prohibition" before issuing any such regulation and must hold a public hearing and publish findings regarding the results of that analysis. *Id.* Finally, the Administrator cannot prohibit any fuel or fuel additive "unless he finds, and publishes such finding, that in his judgment such prohibition will not cause the use of any other fuel or fuel additive which will produce emissions which will endanger the public health or welfare to the same or greater degree that the use of the fuel or fuel additive proposed to be prohibited." *Id.*

In general, states are preempted from regulating fuels and fuel additives if the Administrator has found that no control or prohibition is required for that fuel or fuel additive *or* if the Administrator has prescribed a control or prohibition and the state requirement is not identical. CAA § 211(c)(4), 42 U.S.C. § 7545(c)(4). However, states can try to include such regulations in their SIPs, which the Administrator can approve "only if he finds that the State control or prohibition is necessary to achieve the national primary or secondary ambient air quality standard which the plan implements." *Id.*

The most famous fuel additive that the EPA has regulated is, of course, lead, as has already been discussed. The EPA called for a phase-out of leaded gasoline in its 1972 Clean Air Act regulations, and, after those regulations survived challenge in court, the phase-out began in 1976, with the primary phase-out ending in 1986.

However, the elimination of lead did not eliminate fuel additive issues. Beginning in 1979, gasoline manufacturers began to replace lead in gasoline with ***Methyl Tertiary Butyl Ether*** **(MTBE)**, a chemical that, like lead, can reduce engine "knock." MTBE use increased after the 1990 amendments to the Clean Air Act, when Congress required an oxygenated fuels program to reduce emissions of certain kinds of pollutants. CAA § 211(k) (***reformulated gasoline*** requirements to reduce smog-causing emissions), § 211(m) (***oxygenated fuel*** requirements to reduce carbon monoxide emissions), 42 U.S.C. § 7545(k), (m). Increased oxygen content (Congress requires reformulated gasoline to be 2% oxygen by weight) allows gasoline to burn more completely, reducing automobile emissions of carbon monoxide, volatile organic compounds (VOCs), NOx, and certain toxics like benzene.

Since 1995, Congress has required that ***reformulated gasoline*** be available in the cities with the worst levels of ground-level ozone, CAA § 211(k)(1), 42 U.S.C. § 7545(k)(1), and 30% of the gasoline sold in the United States is now reformulated gasoline. About 87% of that reformulated gasoline contains MTBE. Manufacturers generally prefer MTBE for economic reasons and because it blends easily, but other oxygenating additives are available. For example, ethanol is the additive usually used to reduce carbon monoxide emissions under the oxygenated fuels program.

As an additive, MTBE is thus a lower-cost means of reducing automobile pollution emissions in general and smog in particular. Unfortunately, like lead, MTBE is also toxic. Problems arise not so much from exhaust emissions of MTBE but rather from its contamination of soil and groundwater. In 2000, then-EPA Administrator Christine Whitman commissioned a blue-ribbon study of MTBE to address, in part, whether the EPA should regulate MTBE under the Clean Air Act. So far, the EPA has preferred to pursue other means of regulation, including regulation of underground gasoline storage tanks, regulation pursuant to the Toxic Substances Control Act, 15 U.S.C. §§ 2601–2692, and regulation pursuant to the Safe Drinking Water Act. 42 U.S.C. §§ 300f to 300j–26. *See* EPA, *Methyl Tertiary Butyl Ether*, http://www.epa.gov/mtbe/gas.htm. For examples of *state* attempts to regulate MTBE, see *Oxygenated Fuels Ass'n, Inc. v. Davis*, 331 F.3d 665, 673 (9th Cir. 2003) (holding that the Clean Air Act did not preempt California's ban on MTBE); *In re Methyl Tertiary Butyl Ether ("MTBE") Products Liability Litigation*, 175 F. Supp. 2d 593, 611–16 (S.D.N.Y. 2001) (holding that the Clean Air Act did not preempt state-law tort claims regarding MTBE contamination).

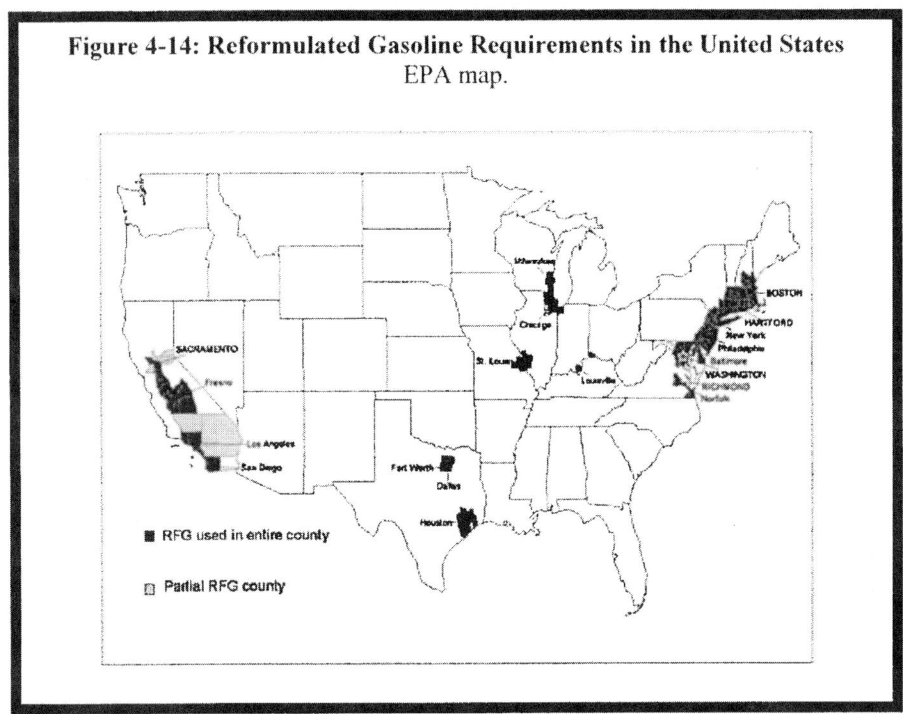

Figure 4-14: Reformulated Gasoline Requirements in the United States
EPA map.

Fuel standards under the Clean Air Act have also become caught up with more general federal energy policies, especially use of renewable fuels. As one example, in April 2009, the EPA granted a waiver request from Growth Energy and 54 ethanol manufacturers pursuant to Section 211(f) to allow the use of gasoline that is 15% ethanol. 74 Fed. Reg. 18,228 (April 21, 2009).

More comprehensively, the Energy Policy Act of 2005 created, in Section 211(*o*) of the Clean Air Act, the Renewable Fuel Standard Program. These amendments imposed an expanded renewable fuel requirement and recognized four categories of renewable fuels: cellulosic biofuel, biomass-based diesel, advanced biofuel, and total renewable fuel. Criteria for renewable fuels now include life cycle greenhouse gas emission performance, and the fuels covered include not only gasoline but also diesel and certain nonroad fuels. Cellulosic biofuels also received the benefits of waiver provisions and EPA credits. Under the Renewable Fuels Standard Program, the EPA sets a yearly standard for renewable fuels, expressed as a percentage of applicable fuels, in November of the previous year. For 2011, the renewable fuels standards were:

Cellulosic biofuel	0.003%
Biomass-based diesel	0.69%
Advanced biofuel	0.78%
Renewable fuel	8.01%

For 2012, the standards proposed in November 2011 are:

Cellulosic biofuel	0.002 to 0.010%
Biomass-based diesel	0.91%
Advanced biofuel	1.21%
Renewable fuel	9.21%

C. NONROAD ENGINES AND VEHICLES

Under section 213, the Administrator of the EPA had to study "emissions from nonroad engines and nonroad vehicles (other than locomotives or engines used in locomotives) to determine if such emissions cause, or significantly contribute to, air pollution which may reasonably be anticipated to endanger public health or welfare." CAA § 213(a)(1), 42 U.S.C. § 7547(a)(1). If the EPA concluded that nonroad emissions had such an effect, or that nonroad emissions contributed to ozone or carbon monoxide nonattainment, then the EPA was supposed to promulgate nonroad emissions regulations within a year. *Id.* § 213(a)(3), 42 U.S.C. § 7547(a)(3).

The EPA issued its new nonroad diesel rule in June 2004. EPA, Control of Emissions of Air Pollution from Nonroad Diesel Engines and Fuel, 69 Fed. Reg. 38,957 (June 29, 2004). This regulation requires a more than 90% reduction in pollutant emissions from nonroad diesel engines by 2030. According to the EPA, nonroad diesel engines account for 60% of the total diesel particulate matter emissions and 30% of the total NOx emissions from all mobile sources. EPA, *Clean Air Nonroad Diesel Final Rule*, http://www.epa.gov/nonroad-diesel/2004fr.htm. The new rule covers the more than 650,000 pieces of new nonroad diesel equipment sold in the United States each year, and the EPA has calculated a benefit:cost ratio of 40:1 for the new requirements. EPA, *Clean Air Nonraod Diesel Rule Summary*, http://www.epa.gov/nonroad-diesel/2004fr/420f04029.htm. Many of the benefits are health-related. For example, the EPA expects that, by 2030, the emissions reductions mandated by the rule will "prevent 12,000 premature deaths, 8,900 hospitalizations, and one million work days lost." EPA, *Clean Air Nonroad Diesel Final Rule*, http://www.epa.gov/nonroad-diesel/2004fr.htm.

The EPA was also supposed to promulgate emissions standards for locomotives and locomotive engines by November 1995. CAA § 213(a)(5), 42 U.S.C. § 7547(a)(5). In June 2004, the EPA issued an Advanced Notice of Proposed Rule Making proposing to issue new standards for locomotive emissions of NOx, particulate matter, hydrocarbons, and toxic air pollutants through the use of high efficiency catalytic aftertreatment and the use of clean (low-sulfur) diesel fuel. EPA, Control of Emissions of Air Pollution from New Locomotive Engines and New Marine Compression–Ignition Engines, 69 Fed. Reg. 39,275 (June 29, 2004).

IV. REGULATING CRITERIA POLLUTANT EMISSIONS: STATIONARY SOURCES

In addition to regulating mobile sources, the Clean Air Act regulates ***stationary sources*** of air pollutants. As noted above, a "***stationary source***" is "any source of an air pollutant except those emissions resulting directly from an internal combustion engine for transportation purposes or from a nonroad engine or nonroad vehicle as defined in section 7550 of this title." CAA § 302(z), 43 U.S.C. § 7602(z). The EPA regulates stationary sources through ***technology-based emissions limitations***. What exact emissions limitations apply to a particular stationary source depends on four factors: (1) the pollutants that the source is discharging; (2) the location of the source—whether it is in an ***attainment area*** or a ***nonattainment area***; (3) the source's status as either an ***existing stationary source*** or a ***new stationary source***; and (4) whether the source qualifies as a ***major stationary source***. Stationary source regulation under the Clean Air Act, therefore, depends on a ***multi-factor trigger***.

A. STATIONARY SOURCES, THE "BUBBLE" CONCEPT, AND DEFERENCE TO THE EPA

Despite the Clean Air Act's global definition of "stationary source," identifying stationary sources is not as obvious as it might appear. For example, the provision of the Clean Air Act that governs new stationary sources, CAA § 111, 42 U.S.C. § 7411, defines "stationary source" to mean "any building, structure, facility, or installation which emits or may emit any air pollutant." However, a "facility" may consist of several "buildings." Is each building regulated individually? Similarly, a single building may have several vents and/or pipes that emit air pollutants to the outside world. Is each of these sources of emissions a separate "stationary source," or is the entire building a single source?

Who gets to decide how to interpret the term "stationary source"? From the time of the U.S. Supreme Court's decision in *Marbury v. Madison*, federal courts have reserved to themselves the final authority to interpret federal law. As you've already seen in prior chapters, however, in the context of administrative agencies, federal courts regularly ***defer*** to an agency's interpretation of a statute that the agency implements, particularly if the statutory program is complex and highly technical. In the following Clean Air Act case involving the EPA's definition of "stationary source," the Supreme Court established one of the most important tests for determining how much deference to give an agency's interpretation of a federal statute—a standard of review now referred to as ***Chevron deference***.

CHEVRON U.S.A., INC. v. NATURAL RESOURCES DEFENSE COUNCIL, INC.

467 U.S. 837 (1984).

JUSTICE STEVENS delivered the opinion of the Court.

In the Clean Air Act Amendments of 1977, Congress enacted certain requirements applicable to States that had not achieved the national air quality standards established by the Environmental Protection Agency (EPA) pursuant to earlier legislation. The amended Clean Air Act required these "nonattainment" States to establish a permit program regulating "new or modified major stationary sources" of air pollution. * * * The EPA regulation promulgated to implement this permit requirement allows a State to adopt a plantwide definition of the term "stationary source." Under this definition, an existing plant that contains several pollution-emitting devices may install or modify one piece of equipment without meeting the permit conditions if the alteration will not increase the total emissions from the plant. The question presented by these cases is whether EPA's decision to allow States to treat all of the pollution-emitting devices within the same industrial grouping as though they were encased within a single "bubble" is based on a reasonable construction of the statutory term "stationary source."

I

The EPA regulations containing the plantwide definition of the term stationary source were promulgated on October 14, 1981. 46 Fed. Reg. 50766. * * * The Court of Appeals [for the D.C. Circuit] set aside the regulations. * * *

II

When a court reviews an agency's construction of the statute which it administers, it is confronted with two questions. First, always, is the question whether Congress has directly spoken to the precise question at issue. If the intent of Congress is clear, that is the end of the matter; for the court, as well as the agency, must give effect to the unambiguously expressed intent of Congress. If, however, the court determines Congress has not directly addressed the precise question at issue, the court does not simply impose its own construction on the statute, as would be necessary in the absence of an administrative interpretation. Rather, if the statute is silent or ambiguous with respect to the specific issue, the question for the court is whether the agency's answer is based on a permissible construction of the statute.

"The power of an administrative agency to administer a congressionally created . . . program necessarily requires the formulation of policy and the making of rules to fill any gap left, implicitly or explicitly, by Congress." *Morton v. Ruiz*, 415 U.S. 199, 231 (1974). If Congress has explicitly left a gap for the agency to fill, there is an express delegation of authority to the agency to elucidate a specific provision of the statute by regulation. Such legislative regulations are given controlling weight unless they are arbitrary, capricious, or manifestly contrary to the statute. Sometimes the legislative delegation to an agency on a particular question is implicit rather than explicit. In such a case, a court may not substitute its own construction of a statutory provision for a reasonable interpretation made by the administrator of an agency.

* * * [I]t is clear that the Court of Appeals misconceived the nature of its role in reviewing the regulations at issue. Once it determined, after its own examination of the legislation, that Congress did not actually have an intent regarding the applicability of the bubble concept to the permit program, the question before it was not whether in its view the concept is "inappropriate" in the general context of a program designed to improve air quality, but whether the Administrator's view that it is appropriate in the context of this particular program is a reasonable one. Based on the examination of the legislation and its history which follows, we agree with the Court of Appeals that Congress did not have a specific intention on the applicability of the bubble concept in these cases, and conclude that the EPA's use of that concept here is a reasonable policy choice for the agency to make.

III

In the 1950's and the 1960's Congress enacted a series of statutes designed to encourage and to assist the States in curtailing air pollution. The Clean Air Amendments of 1970 "sharply increased federal authority and responsibility in the continuing effort to combat air pollution," [*Train v. NRDC*, 421 U.S. 60,] at 64, but continued to assign "primary responsibility for assuring air quality" to the several States. Section 109 of the 1970 Amendments directed the EPA to promulgate National Ambient Air Quality Standards (NAAQS's) and § 110 directed the States to develop plans (SIP's) to implement the standards within specified deadlines. In addition, § 111 provided that major new sources of pollution would be required to conform to technology-based performance standards; the EPA was directed to publish a list of categories of sources of pollution and to establish new source performance standards (NSPS) for each. Section 111(e) prohibited the operation of any new source in violation of a performance standard.

Section 111(a) defined the terms that are to be used in setting and enforcing standards of performance for new stationary sources. It provided:

"For purposes of this section:

. . .

"(3) The term 'stationary source' means any building, structure, facility, or installation which emits or may emit any air pollutant."

In the 1970 Amendments that definition was not only applicable to the NSPS program required by § 111, but also was made applicable to a requirement of § 110 that each state implementation plan contain a procedure for reviewing the location of any proposed new source and preventing its construction if it would preclude the attainment or maintenance of national air quality standards.

* * * *Nonattainment*

The 1970 legislation provided for the attainment of primary NAAQS's by 1975. In many areas of the country, particularly the most industrialized States, the statutory goals were not attained. * * * In light of this situation, the EPA published an Emissions Offset Interpretative Ruling in December 1976, *see* 41 Fed. Reg. 55524, to "fill the gap," as respondents put it, until Congress acted. * * * In general, the Ruling provided that "a major new source may locate in an area with air quality worse than a national standard only if stringent conditions can be met." *Id.*, at 55525. The 1976 Ruling did not, however, explicitly adopt or reject the "bubble concept."

IV

The Clean Air Act Amendments of 1977 are a lengthy, detailed, technical, complex, and comprehensive response to a major social issue. A small portion of the statute [Part D] expressly deals with nonattainment areas. The focal point of this controversy is one phrase in that portion of the Amendments.

Basically, the statute required each State in a nonattainment area to prepare and obtain approval of a new SIP by July 1, 1979. In the interim those States were required to comply with the EPA's interpretative Ruling of December 21, 1976. * * *

Most significantly for our purposes, the statute provided that each plan shall

> "(6) require permits for the construction and operation of new or modified major stationary sources in accordance with section 173...." * * *

* * * The 1977 Amendments contain no specific reference to the "bubble concept." Nor do they contain a specific definition of the term "stationary source," though they did not disturb the definition of "stationary source" contained in § 111(a)(3), applicable by the terms of the Act to the NSPS program. Section 302(j), however, defines the term "major stationary source" as follows:

> "(j) Except as otherwise expressly provided, the terms 'major stationary source' and 'major emitting facility' mean any stationary facility or source of air pollutants which directly emits, or has the potential to emit, one hundred tons per year or more of any air pollutant (including any major emitting facility or source of

fugitive emissions of any such pollutant, as determined by rule by the Administrator).''

V

The legislative history of the portion of the 1977 Amendments dealing with nonattainment areas does not contain any specific comment on the "bubble concept" or the question whether a plantwide definition of a stationary source is permissible under the permit program. It does, however, plainly disclose that in the permit program Congress sought to accommodate the conflict between the economic interest in permitting capital improvements to continue and the environmental interest in improving air quality. * * *

* * * VI

As previously noted, prior to the 1977 Amendments, the EPA had adhered to a plantwide definition of the term "source" under a NSPS program. After adoption of the 1977 Amendments, proposals for a plantwide definition were considered in at least three formal proceedings.

* * * In April, and again in September 1979, the EPA published additional comments in which it indicated that revised SIP's could adopt the plantwide definition of source in nonattainment areas in certain circumstances. On the latter occasion, the EPA made a formal rulemaking proposal that would have permitted the use of the "bubble concept" for new installations within a plant as well as for modifications of existing units. It explained:

> " 'Bubble' Exemption: The use of offsets inside the same source is called the 'bubble.' EPA proposes use of the definition of 'source' * * * to limit the use of the bubble under nonattainment requirements in the following respects:
>
> "i. Part D SIPs that include all requirements needed to assure reasonable further progress and attainment by the deadline under section 172 and that are being carried out need not restrict the use of a plantwide bubble, the same as under the PSD proposal.
>
> "ii. Part D SIPs that do not meet the requirements specified must limit use of the bubble by including a definition of 'installation' as an identifiable piece of process equipment."

Significantly, the EPA expressly noted that the word "source" might be given a plantwide definition for some purposes and a narrower definition for other purposes. * * *

The EPA's summary of its proposed Ruling discloses a flexible rather than rigid definition of the term "source" to implement various policies and programs * * *.

In August 1980, however, the EPA adopted a regulation that, in essence, applied the basic reasoning of the Court of Appeals in these cases.

The EPA took particular note of the two then-recent Court of Appeals decisions, which had created the bright-line rule that the "bubble concept" should be employed in a program designed to maintain air quality but not in one designed to enhance air quality. Relying heavily on those cases, EPA adopted a dual definition of "source" for nonattainment areas that required a permit whenever a change in either the entire plant, or one of its components, would result in a significant increase in emissions even if the increase was completely offset by reductions elsewhere in the plant. The EPA expressed the opinion that this interpretation was "more consistent with congressional intent" than the plantwide definition because it "would bring in more sources or modifications for review," 45 Fed. Reg. 52697 (1980), but its primary legal analysis was predicated on the two Court of Appeals decisions.

In 1981 a new administration took office and initiated a "Government-wide reexamination of regulatory burdens and complexities." 46 Fed. Reg. 16281. In the context of that review, the EPA reevaluated the various arguments that had been advanced in connection with the proper definition of the term "source" and concluded that the term should be given the same definition in both nonattainment areas and PSD areas.

In explaining its conclusion, the EPA first noted that the definitional issue was not squarely addressed in either the statute or its legislative history and therefore that the issue involved an agency "judgment as how to best carry out the Act." *Ibid.* It then set forth several reasons for concluding that the plantwide definition was more appropriate. It pointed out that the dual definition "can act as a disincentive to new investment and modernization by discouraging modifications to existing facilities" and "can actually retard progress in air pollution control by discouraging replacement of older, dirtier processes or pieces of equipment with new, cleaner ones." *Ibid.* Moreover, the new definition "would simplify EPA's rules by using the same definition of 'source' for PSD, nonattainment new source review and the construction moratorium. This reduces confusion and inconsistency." *Ibid.* Finally, the agency explained that additional requirements that remained in place would accomplish the fundamental purposes of achieving attainment with NAAQS's as expeditiously as possible. These conclusions were expressed in a proposed rulemaking in August 1981 that was formally promulgated in October. *See id.*, at 50766.

VII

In this Court respondents expressly reject the basic rationale of the Court of Appeals' decision. That court viewed the statutory definition of the term "source" as sufficiently flexible to cover either a plantwide definition, a narrower definition covering each unit within a plant, or a dual definition that could apply to both the entire "bubble" and its components. It interpreted the policies of the statute, however, to mandate the plantwide definition in programs designed to maintain clean air and to forbid it in programs designed to improve air quality. Respondents place a fundamentally different construction on the statute. They contend that the text of the Act requires the EPA to use a dual definition—if either a component of a plant, or the plant as a whole, emits over 100 tons of pollutant, it is a major stationary source. They thus contend that the EPA rules adopted in 1980, insofar as they apply to the maintenance of the quality of clean air, as well as the 1981 rules which apply to nonattainment areas, violate the statute.

Statutory Language

The definition of the term "stationary source" in § 111(a)(3) refers to "any building, structure, facility, or installation" which emits air pollution. This definition is applicable only to the NSPS program by the express terms of the statute; the text of the statute does not make this definition applicable to the permit program. Petitioners therefore maintain that there is no statutory language even relevant to ascertaining the meaning of stationary source in the permit program aside from § 302(j), which defines the term "major stationary source." We disagree with petitioners on this point.

The definition in § 302(j) tells us what the word "major" means—a source must emit at least 100 tons of pollution to qualify—but it sheds virtually no light on the meaning of the term "stationary source." It does equate a source with a facility—a "major emitting facility" and a "major stationary source" are synonymous under § 302(j). The ordinary meaning of the term "facility" is some collection of integrated elements which has been designed and constructed to achieve some purpose. Moreover, it is certainly no affront to common English usage to take a reference to a major facility or a major source to connote an entire plant as opposed to its constituent parts. Basically, however, the language of § 302(j) simply does not compel any given interpretation of the term "source."

Respondents recognize that, and hence point to § 111(a)(3). Although the definition in that section is not literally applicable to the permit program, it sheds as much light on the meaning of the word "source" as anything in the statute. As respondents point out, use of the words "building, structure, facility, or installation," as the definition of source, could be read to impose the permit conditions on an individual building that is a part of a plant. * * * The language may reasonably be interpreted to impose the requirement on any discrete, but integrated, operation which pollutes. This gives meaning to all of the terms—a single building, not part of a larger operation, would be covered if it emits more than 100 tons of pollution, as would any facility, structure, or installation. Indeed, the language itself implies a "bubble concept" of sorts: each enumerated item would seem to be treated as if it were encased in a bubble. * * *

We are not persuaded that parsing of general terms in the text of the statute will reveal an actual intent of Congress. We know full well that this language is not dispositive; the terms are overlapping and the language is not precisely directed to the question of the applicability of a given term in the context of a larger operation. To the extent any congressional "intent" can be discerned from this language, it would appear that the listing of overlapping, illustrative terms was intended to enlarge, rather than to confine, the scope of the agency's power to regulate particular sources in order to effectuate the policies of the Act.

Legislative History

In addition, respondents argue that the legislative history and policies of the Act foreclose the plantwide definition, and that the EPA's interpretation is not entitled to deference because it represents a sharp break with prior interpretations of the Act.

Based on our examination of the legislative history, we agree with the Court of Appeals that it is unilluminating. * * * We find that the legislative history as a whole is silent on the precise issue before us. It is, however, consistent with the view that the EPA should have broad discretion in implementing the policies of the 1977 Amendments.

More importantly, that history plainly identifies the policy concerns that motivated the enactment; the plantwide definition is fully consistent with one of those concerns—the allowance of reasonable economic growth—and, whether or not we believe it most effectively implements the other, we must recognize that the EPA has advanced a reasonable explanation for its conclusion that the regulations serve the environmental objectives as well. Indeed, its reasoning is supported by the public record developed in the rulemaking process, as well as by certain private studies.

Our review of the EPA's varying interpretations of the word "source"—both before and after the 1977 Amendments—convinces us that the agency primarily responsible for administering this important legislation has consistently interpreted it flexibly—not in a sterile textual vacuum, but in the context of implementing policy decisions in a technical and complex arena. The fact that the agency has from time to time changed its interpretation of the term "source" does not, as respondents argue, lead us to conclude that no deference should be accorded the agency's interpretation of the statute. An initial agency interpretation is not instantly carved in stone. * * *

Significantly, it was not the agency in 1980, but rather the Court of Appeals that read the statute inflexibly to command a plantwide definition for programs designed to maintain clean air and to forbid such a definition for programs designed to improve air quality. The distinction the court drew may well be a sensible one, but our labored review of the problem has surely disclosed that it is not a distinction that Congress ever articulated itself, or one that the EPA found in the statute before the courts began to review the legislative work product. We conclude that it was the Court of Appeals, rather than Congress or any of the decisionmakers who are authorized by Congress to administer this legislation, that was primarily responsible for the 1980 position taken by the agency.

Policy

The arguments over policy that are advanced in the parties' briefs create the impression that respondents are now waging in a judicial forum a specific policy battle which they ultimately lost in the agency and in the 32 jurisdictions opting for the "bubble concept," but one which was never waged in the Congress. Such policy arguments are more properly addressed to legislators or administrators, not to judges.

In these cases, the Administrator's interpretation represents a reasonable accommodation of manifestly competing interests and is entitled to deference: the regulatory scheme is technical and complex, the agency considered the matter in a detailed and reasoned fashion, and the decision involves reconciling conflicting policies. Congress intended to accommodate both interests, but did not do so itself on the level of specificity presented by these cases. * * *

Judges are not experts in the field, and are not part of either political branch of the Government. Courts must, in some cases, reconcile competing political interests, but not on the basis of the judges' personal policy preferences. In contrast, an agency to which Congress has delegated policy-making responsibilities may, within the limits of that delegation, properly rely upon the incumbent administration's views of wise policy to inform its judgments. While agencies are not directly accountable to the people, the Chief Executive is, and it is entirely appropriate for this political branch of the Government to make such policy choices—resolving the competing interests which Congress itself either inadvertently did not resolve, or intentionally left to be resolved by the agency charged with the administration of the statute in light of everyday realities.

When a challenge to an agency construction of a statutory provision, fairly conceptualized, really centers on the wisdom of the agency's policy, rather than whether it is a reasonable choice within a gap left open by Congress, the challenge must fail. * * *

We hold that the EPA's definition of the term "source" is a permissible construction of the statute which seeks to accommodate progress in reducing air pollution with economic growth. "The Regulations which the Administrator has adopted provide what the agency could allowably view as ... [an] effective reconciliation of these twofold ends...." *United States v. Shimer*, 367 U.S., at 383. * * *

NOTES

1. ***Chevron* Deference.** The *Chevron* Court created a test that is known as the "*Chevron* Two–Step." In the first step, the reviewing court examines the statute to determine whether Congress has directly spoken to the issue at hand. If so, both the court and the administrative agency must give effect to Congress's intent. If the statute leaves a gap, however, or if congressional intent is ambiguous, then the court will uphold the agency's interpretation unless that interpretation is unreasonable. As a practical

matter, if a federal court is going to overturn an agency's interpretation under *Chevron*, the agency's interpretation is far more likely to fail at Step 1 than at Step 2. As a result, the determination of Congress' intent within a statute is often critical to the outcome of a *Chevron* analysis.

2. ***Chevron* Deference and Legislative History.** The *Chevron* Court examined the Clean Air Act's language and structure *and* its legislative history to determine Congress's intent with respect to the "bubble" conception of stationary sources. As has been discussed in previous chapters, however, since the *Chevron* decision some Justices of the Supreme Court—notably Justice Scalia—have ignored or even refused to consider legislative history. As a result, the actual application of the *Chevron* test in federal courts can vary considerably.

3. **Interpreting "Stationary Source."** Why did the *Chevron* Court uphold the EPA's interpretation of "stationary source"? What *is* the EPA's interpretation of "stationary source"? How did the plaintiffs try to challenge that interpretation?

4. **Supreme Court Clarifications of *Chevron*'s Applicability.** The Supreme Court has emphasized recently that the *Chevron* test applies only when a federal agency issues an *interpretation* of a statute that it administers through fairly structured proceedings, such as notice-and-comment rulemaking or formal adjudication. *United States v. Mead Corp.*, 533 U.S. 218 (2001). If the agency issues its interpretation through less considered proceedings, such as through a letter of advice or through guidance documents, federal courts will give that interpretation less deference, although the interpretation is still "entitled to respect." *Id.*; *see also Skidmore v. Swift & Co.*, 323 U.S. 134 (1944); *Christensen v. Harris County*, 529 U.S. 576 (2000). To determine how much deference to give to these less formal interpretations, federal courts consider "the thoroughness evident in [the agency's] consideration, the validity of its reasoning, its consistency with earlier and later pronouncements, and all those factors which give it power to persuade, if lacking power to control." *Skidmore*, 323 U.S. at 140.

5. **Deference to the EPA's Interpretations of Its Own Regulations.** As has been discussed in previous chapters, Congress is not the only body that writes environmental laws. The EPA has written volumes of regulations to implement the federal environmental statutes. Like the statutes themselves, not all of these regulations are crystal clear, and the EPA often has to clarify the meaning of its regulations. When the EPA interprets *its own regulations*—as opposed to the statute that Congress wrote—federal courts are ***highly deferential*** to the EPA's interpretation and will only reverse EPA's interpretation of its own regulation if that interpretation is ***plainly wrong***.

6. **Costs and Benefits of Clean Air Act "Bubble."** According to the Supreme Court, in interpreting "stationary source" so as to allow states to employ the "bubble" concept, the EPA was balancing two potentially conflicting congressional goals in the Clean Air Act's regulation of stationary sources: improving environmental quality and allowing for continued economic growth. What are the costs and benefits associated with use of the "bubble"

concept? Why would the Natural Resources Defense Council, an environmental organization, *oppose* the use of the "bubble" concept? What costs did it see to environmental protection? Why would industry embrace the "bubble" concept? What economic benefits does the "bubble" concept allow? Are there potential environmental benefits from this concept as well?

7. **"Bubbles" and Emissions Trading.** Capping an entire facility under a single regulatory "bubble" for emissions purposes is one of the most basic examples of ***emissions trading***. Within a single facility, reductions in emissions of an air pollutant from one source can be balanced against emissions of that same pollutant from another source, allowing overall reductions in emissions at the entire facility without necessarily improving every single source of those emissions. As will be discussed in connection with transboundary air pollution, emissions trading has become important in addressing larger-scale air pollution problems, as well.

8. **Indirect Sources: A Mix of Stationary and Mobile Sources.** A third type of "source" under the Clean Air Act, besides mobile sources and stationary sources, is the ***indirect source***. In 1977, Congress amended section 110 to exclude indirect sources from mandatory coverage in SIPs. 42 U.S.C. § 7410(a)(5)(A). Section 110 defines an "indirect source" to be "a facility, building, structure, installation, real property, road, or highway which attracts, or may attract, mobile sources of pollution. Such term includes parking lots, parking garages, and other facilities subject to any measure for management of parking supply * * *." *Id.* § 110(a)(5)(C), 42 U.S.C. § 7410(a)(5)(C).

Given this definition, is the harbor tunnel section of Interstate 93, which runs under Boston Harbor in Massachusetts, a stationary source or an indirect source? The tunnel system includes six buildings that contain ducts and fans to direct carbon monoxide- and hydrocarbon-containing air from the tunnel through stacks 90 to 225 feet tall into the atmosphere. The Massachusetts Department of Public Works did not intend to install any pollution control equipment on these stacks to reduce pollution emissions, as would be required if the stacks qualified as stationary sources. *See Sierra Club v. Larson*, 2 F.3d 462 (1st Cir. 1993).

* * *

B. REGULATION OF STATIONARY SOURCES EMITTING CRITERIA POLLUTANTS IN NONATTAINMENT AREAS

As the Supreme Court indicated in *Chevron*, an AQCR with air quality insufficient to meet the NAAQS for one or more criteria pollutants is in ***nonattainment*** for those pollutants. "[T]he 1970 Act envisioned attainment by 1975, but in no case later than 1977." Robert A. Wyman, Thomas R. Freeman, & J. Wesley Skow, *Air and Water Pollution Control Law: The Clean Air Act Nonattainment Program*, C432 ALI–ABA 479 (May 25, 1989). Obviously, the country did not meet that goal. The EPA has mapped the nonattainment regions of the United States, shown in Figure 4–13. What does this map tend to suggest about nonattainment?

As a result, in the 1977 amendments to the Clean Air Act, Congress added Part D, CAA §§ 171–193, 42 U.S.C. §§ 7501–7515, to address the nonattainment problem, arguably the most important problem under the Clean Air Act. The amendments required all AQCRs to come into attainment by December 31, 1982, but also allowed for attainment extensions for ozone and carbon monoxide until December 31, 1987.

The country did not meet these revised attainment deadlines, either, prompting Congress to again address nonattainment in the 1990 Amendments to the Clean Air Act. Under the current requirements, in general, states must ensure that a nonattainment AQCR meets primary and secondary NAAQS "as expeditiously as practicable," with a deadline for attaining primary NAAQS within five years of nonattainment designation. CAA § 172(a)(2), 42 U.S.C. § 7502(a)(2). In addition, states must amend their SIPs to regulate ***existing*** and ***new stationary sources'*** emissions. "New" or "existing" is judged by the date of the nonattainment designation. The Clean Air Act's nonattainment provisions require ***existing major stationary sources*** to meet emissions limitations based on ***reasonably available control technology*** **(RACT)**, CAA § 172(c)(1), 42 U.S.C. § 7502(c)(1), and require all ***new and modified major stationary sources*** to get permits. CAA § 172(c)(5), 42 U.S.C. § 7502(c)(5). A stationary source is ***major*** if it "directly emits, or has the potential to emit, one hundred tons per year or more of any pollutant * * *." CAA § 302(j), 42 U.S.C. § 7602(j).

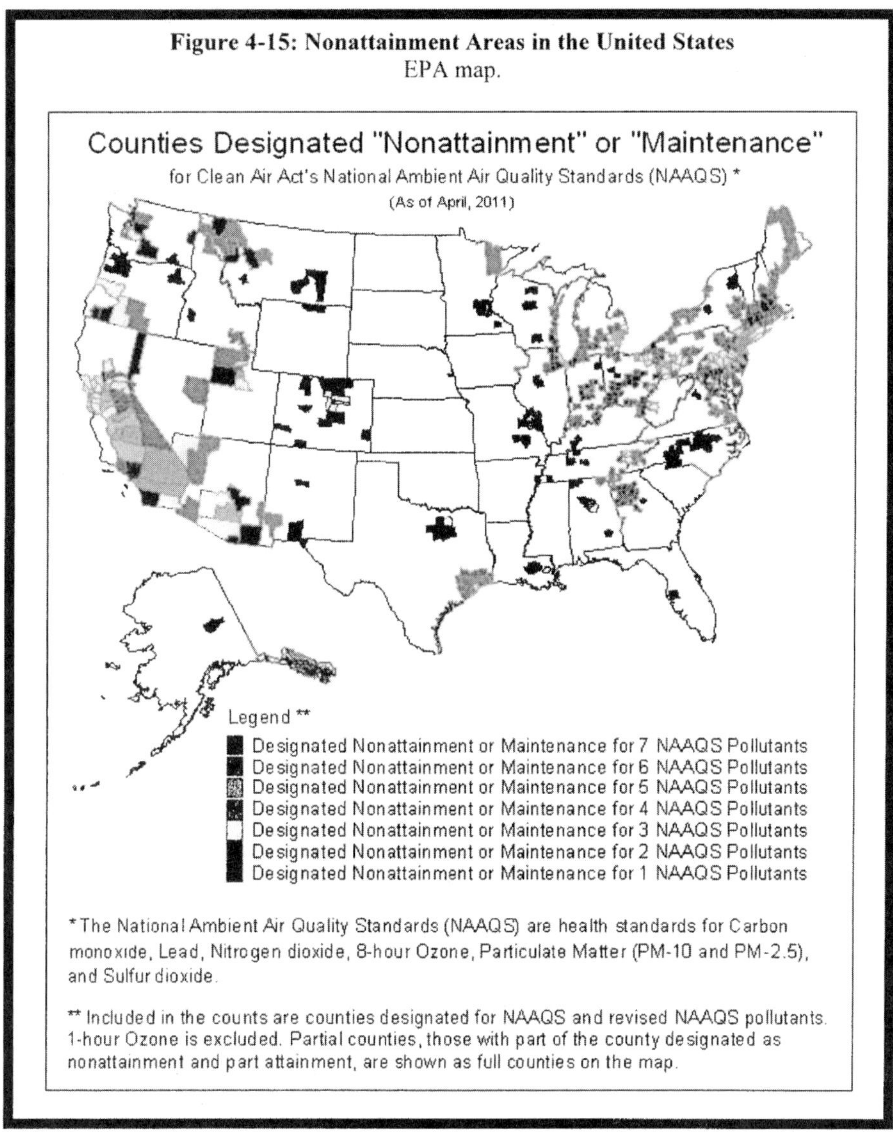

Figure 4-15: Nonattainment Areas in the United States
EPA map.

In order to receive a permit, a new or modified stationary source must comply with emissions limitations based on the ***lowest achievable emission rate*** **(LAER)**, CAA § 173(a)(2), 42 U.S.C. § 7503(a)(2), and can begin operation only if other sources have reduced their emissions sufficiently to ***offset*** the new source's emissions. CAA § 173(a)(1), 42 U.S.C. § 7503(a)(1). LAER is the most stringent *categorical* (industry– rather than individual facility-based) emission limitation for stationary sources in the Clean Air Act. To establish LAER, states or the EPA must choose "the most stringent limitation which is contained in the implementation plan of any State for such class or category of source" or "the most stringent emission limitation achieved in practice by such class or category of source," "whichever is more stringent." CAA § 171(3), 42 U.S.C. § 7501(3). Moreover, "[i]n no event shall the application of this term permit a proposed new or modified stationary source to emit any pollutant in excess of the amount allowable under applicable new source standards of performance." *Id.*

TABLE 4–1: CRITERIA POLLUTANT EMISSIONS STANDARDS IN NONATTAINMENT AREAS		
	NEW MAJOR STATIONARY SOURCES	**EXISTING MAJOR STATIONARY SOURCES**
NONATTAINMENT AREA: PART D:	Major Source = 100 tons/year of pollutants: LAER + OFFSETS + PERMIT (incorporated into Title V permitting)	Major Source = 100 tons/year pollutants: RACT + PERMIT (incorporated into Title V permitting)

The Clean Air Act's nonattainment provisions thus effectively shifted the Act's regulatory focus from the SIPs to the individual stationary sources. Congress continued this shift in focus in later amendments to the Act, culminating in its 1990 creation of the comprehensive Title V permit program for *all* major stationary sources.

Nevertheless, states still implement the individual source requirements through their SIPs. If a state fails to comply with the nonattainment requirements, the EPA can sanction the state by prohibiting federal highway grants for highway projects in the nonattainment region and/or by increasing the emissions offset requirement for new or modified major stationary sources so that "the ratio of emission reductions to increased emissions shall be at least 2 to 1." CAA § 179(b), 42 U.S.C. § 7509(b).

In addition to these general requirements, nonattainment AQCRs are subject to requirements particular to the pollutant for which the region is in nonattainment. As the cases will suggest, ozone nonattainment has been a particularly thorny air pollution issue to resolve. Regions in nonattainment for ozone, for example, are further classified as being in ***marginal, moderate, serious, severe, or extreme nonattainment***, with deadlines for attainment varying from three to 20 years accordingly. CAA § 181(a)(1), 42 U.S.C. § 7511(a)(1). Offset requirements for new and modified major stationary sources also vary depending on the severity of nonattainment, from 1.1 to 1 in marginal areas, CAA § 182(a)(4), 42 U.S.C. § 7511a(a)(4), to 1.2 to 1 in severe areas. CAA § 182(e)(1), 42 U.S.C. § 7511a(e)(1). Special requirements also exist for AQCRs in nonattainment for carbon monoxide, CAA §§ 186–187, 42 U.S.C. §§ 7512–7512a; particulates, CAA §§ 188–190, 42 U.S.C. §§ 7513–7513b; and sulfur oxides, nitrogen dioxide, and lead, CAA §§ 191–192, 42 U.S.C. §§ 7514–7514a.

Ozone nonattainment raised other issues regarding the ability of states to achieve attainment. The EPA determines whether an AQCR is in attainment for ozone by reviewing the last three years' measurements of pollution in that AQCR. The EPA responded to Congress's 1990 amendments, therefore, by calculating AQCRs' ozone nonattainment based on air quality monitoring in the year 1987 through 1989. As fate would have it, ozone concentrations in 1988 were among the highest ever recorded—but not because pollutant emissions had drastically increased. "A very stagnant weather pattern dominated the summer of 1988 in the eastern US. Polluted air was recirculated, leading to repeating severe ozone violations. High temperatures were oppressive and persistent. An extensive drought resulted in dry conditions conducive to ozone formation. Peak ozone levels in 1988 were the highest recorded at Mid–Atlantic ozone monitors in the past ten years * * *." Mid–Atlantic Regional Air Management Association, *Air Quality Improvement: Ozone Levels in 1988 and 1995*, http://www.marama.org/atlas/improvement.html (last revised Nov. 17, 1998) (citing Eric Luebehusen, personal communication, Feb. 14, 1996).

Given the 1988 problems, when the EPA listed the ozone nonattainment areas for 1990, 100 AQCRs around the country qualified. Forty-one areas were "marginal" nonattainment areas; 32 were "moderate" nonattainment areas; 18 were "serious" nonattainment areas; five (Chicago, Illinois; Milwaukee/Racine, Wisconsin; Muskegon, Michigan; Philadelphia, Pennsylvania; and San Diego, California) were "Severe I" nonattainment areas; three (Baltimore, Maryland; Houston, Texas; and New York, New York) were "Severe II" nonattainment areas; and one—Los Angeles, California—was an "extreme" nonattainment area for ozone. Robert A. Wyman, *Clean Air Act Amendments: The Potential Impact of the Nonattainment and Permit Rules*, 15 PLI/Crim 323, 325 (Nov./Dec. 1990). Given the unusual year in 1988, however, many of these areas managed to achieve attainment status relatively quickly: before 1995, thirty-three of the original ozone nonattainment areas had achieved the ozone NAAQS, and in 1995, the EPA redesignated 30 more of the remaining nonattainment areas for ozone as being in attainment. U.S. EPA, *AirTrends 1995 Report*, http://www.epa.gov/air/airtrends/aqtrnd95/brochure/o3co.html (last updated Sept. 21, 2004). Thus, almost two-thirds of the original ozone nonattainment areas achieved attainment within five years—a result that suggests that the EPA's use of the 1988 monitoring data led to unrealistic assessments of the ozone nonattainment problem.

The following case addresses the process through which nonattainment areas can become redesignated as attainment areas.

SOUTHWESTERN PENNSYLVANIA GROWTH ALLIANCE v. BROWNER

121 F.3d 106 (3d Cir. 1997).

ALITO, CIRCUIT JUDGE:

The Southwestern Pennsylvania Growth Alliance ("SWPGA") has petitioned for review of a final rule of the Environmental Protection Agency ("EPA"), 61 Fed. Reg. 19,193 (May 1, 1996). In this rule, the EPA denied the Commonwealth of Pennsylvania's request that the EPA redesignate the Pittsburgh–Beaver Valley nonattainment area (the "Area") to attainment status for ozone, pursuant to the Clean Air Act, 42 U.S.C. § 7407(d)(3). * * * Although we are sympathetic to the view expressed by many within the Area that this rule threatens serious economic harm, we recognize that our role as a reviewing court is strictly limited. We conclude that under the applicable legal standards, we are constrained to deny the petition for review.

I.

A. Congress enacted the Clean Air Act to "protect and enhance the quality of the Nation's air resources so as to promote the public health and welfare and the productive capacity of its population." 42 U.S.C. § 7401(b)(1). To achieve this purpose, the Act authorizes the EPA to identify air pollutants that are sufficiently dangerous to warrant federal regulation. *See* 42 U.S.C. § 7408(a). For each pollutant that the EPA identifies, the Act authorizes the EPA to promulgate a national ambient air quality standard (NAAQS), which is the maximum allowable concentration of the pollutant in the ambient air. *See* 42 U.S.C. § 7409(a).

One pollutant for which the EPA has promulgated a NAAQS is ozone, whose chemical precursors are emitted by industrial and transportation sources. *See* 40 C.F.R. § 50.9(a) (1996). The EPA measures ozone levels at monitoring sites located throughout the country. When a monitoring site measures that a given day's "maximum hourly average ozone concentration" has exceeded the NAAQS, an "exceedance" has occurred. *See* 40 C.F.R. § 50, App. H (1996). If a monitoring site registers more than an average of one exceedance per year, over a three-year period, that site is in noncompliance with the NAAQS. *Id.*

The Clean Air Act's 1990 amendments provide that the EPA designate areas of the country as either "attainment" areas, "nonattainment" areas, or "unclassifiable" areas for particular pollutants, depending on whether an area has complied with the NAAQS for that pollutant. *See* 42 U.S.C. § 7407(d). If one monitoring site within an area is in noncompliance with a NAAQS, then the entire area is designated a nonattainment area for that pollutant. *See* 40 C.F.R. Pt. 50.9(a); 40 C.F.R. Pt. 50, App. H (1996). Nonattainment areas are further classified as "marginal," "moderate," "serious," "severe," or "extreme" nonattainment areas, according to the extent to which the area's monitor readings exceed the NAAQS. *See* 42 U.S.C. § 7511(a). The Clean Air Act assigns to the states the responsibility for assuring air quality within each state. *See* 42 U.S.C. § 7407(a). The Act provides that within three years of the EPA's promulgation of a NAAQS for a pollutant, each state must submit to the EPA a state implementation plan ("SIP") specifying measures that will attain, maintain, and enforce the NAAQS. *See* 42 U.S.C. § 7410(a). All SIPs must meet the substantive requirements enumerated at 42 U.S.C. § 7410(a)(2). Once the EPA finds that a SIP complies with the Act, the EPA will approve the SIP. *See* 42 U.S.C. § 7410(k). When the EPA has designated an area within a state as a nonattainment area for a particular pollutant, that state must modify its SIP to include increasingly strict pollution controls delineated in the Act, depending on the area's nonattainment classification. *See* 42 U.S.C. § 7511(a).

The Act specifies the procedures through which the EPA may redesignate an area from nonattainment to attainment. The process begins when the governor of a state submits a request for redesignation. *See* 42 U.S.C. § 7407(d)(3)(D). Then, "[w]ithin 18 months of receipt of a complete State redesignation submittal, the [EPA] Administrator shall approve or deny such redesignation." *Id.* Under 42 U.S.C. § 7407(d)(3)(E), the EPA Administrator "may not promulgate a redesignation of a nonattainment area . . . to attainment unless" the following five criteria are met:

> (i) the Administrator determines that the area has attained the national ambient air quality standard;
>
> (ii) the Administrator has fully approved the applicable implementation plan for the area under section 7410(k) of this title;
>
> (iii) the Administrator determines that the improvement in air quality is due to permanent and enforceable reductions in emissions resulting from implementation of the applicable implementation plan and applicable Federal air pollutant control regulations and other permanent and enforceable reductions;
>
> (iv) the Administrator has fully approved a maintenance plan for the area as meeting the requirements of section 7505a of this title; and
>
> (v) the State containing such area has met all requirements applicable to the area under section 7410 of this title and part D of this subchapter.

Id. Thus, in order for the EPA to redesignate an area from nonattainment to attainment, the EPA must find that all five of these criteria have been satisfied.

B. In 1990, the EPA classified the Pittsburgh–Beaver Valley Area (the "Area") as a moderate nonattainment area for ozone. *See* 56 Fed. Reg. 56,694, 56,820 (Nov. 6, 1991). The EPA based this designation on ozone exceedances during the three-year period from 1987 to 1989. *See id.* In November 1993, the Pennsylvania Department of Environmental Resources submitted to the EPA a request to redesignate the Area to attainment status for ozone. The redesignation request pointed out that the Area had attained the NAAQS for ozone during the three-year period from 1991–1993, with only two exceedances in 1991, zero exceedances in 1992, and one exceedance in 1993. *See* 61 Fed. Reg. 19,193, 19,195 (May 1, 1996). Pennsylvania's request acknowledged that its SIP had not yet been fully approved by the EPA, but stated that the state expected to receive full EPA approval shortly. The request also included a maintenance plan, under which Pennsylvania demonstrated how it planned to maintain the NAAQS in the area until the year 2004.

In July 1995, the EPA published a final notice of determination that the Area was in attainment of the NAAQS for ozone. *See* 60 Fed. Reg. 37,015 (July 19, 1995). Later in the summer of 1995, however, ozone monitors in the Area recorded 16 exceedances over a seven-day period. Two of these monitors recorded more than three exceedances each. After confirming these data, the EPA revoked its earlier determination that the Area had attained the NAAQS for ozone. *See* 61 Fed. Reg. 28,061 (June 4, 1996).

The EPA also published a notice of proposed rulemaking stating its intention to disapprove Pennsylvania's redesignation request and maintenance plan. *See* 61 Fed. Reg. 4,598 (Feb. 7, 1996). The EPA expressed various reasons for proposing disapproval. One of the EPA's reasons was that the 1995 summer ozone exceedances indicated that the Area had not attained the NAAQS. The EPA also reasoned that these exceedances indicated that the underlying basis for Pennsylvania's maintenance plan was no longer valid. *See id.* After public comment, the EPA promulgated a final rule disapproving Pennsylvania's redesignation request and maintenance plan. *See* 61 Fed. Reg. 19,193 (May 1, 1996).

C. The petitioner in this case is the Southwestern Pennsylvania Growth Alliance, which is an organization of major manufacturers and local governments in the Pittsburgh–Beaver Valley Area.

SWPGA contests the EPA's denial of Pennsylvania's request to redesignate the Area to attainment status. * * * Since the EPA's final rule stated that none of these five criteria had been satisfied, the petitioner, if it is to prevail, must demonstrate that the EPA erred in its determinations as to all five of § 7407(d)(3)(E)'s criteria.

The petitioner thus faces an exacting burden. Under the Administrative Procedure Act, 5 U.S.C. § 706(2)(A), this court must uphold the EPA's action unless it is "arbitrary, capricious, an abuse of discretion, or otherwise not in accordance with law." In applying this standard, our "only task is to determine whether [the EPA] considered the relevant factors and articulated a rational connection between the facts found and the choice made." *Baltimore Gas & Elec. Co. v. Natural Resources Defense Council, Inc.*, 462 U.S. 87, 105 (1983). The EPA's disapproval of Pennsylvania's redesignation request "would be arbitrary and capricious if the agency has relied on factors which Congress has not intended it to consider". *Motor Vehicle Mfrs. Ass'n v. State Farm Auto Ins. Co.*, 463 U.S. 29, 43 (1983).

II.

SWPGA first argues that the EPA erred when it determined that the Area did not attain the NAAQS for ozone. In so arguing, SWPGA contends that the EPA had no basis for concluding that the first of 42 U.S.C. § 7407(d)(3)(E)'s five requirements was not satisfied. We hold, however, that it was proper for the EPA to determine that the Area did not attain the NAAQS for ozone.

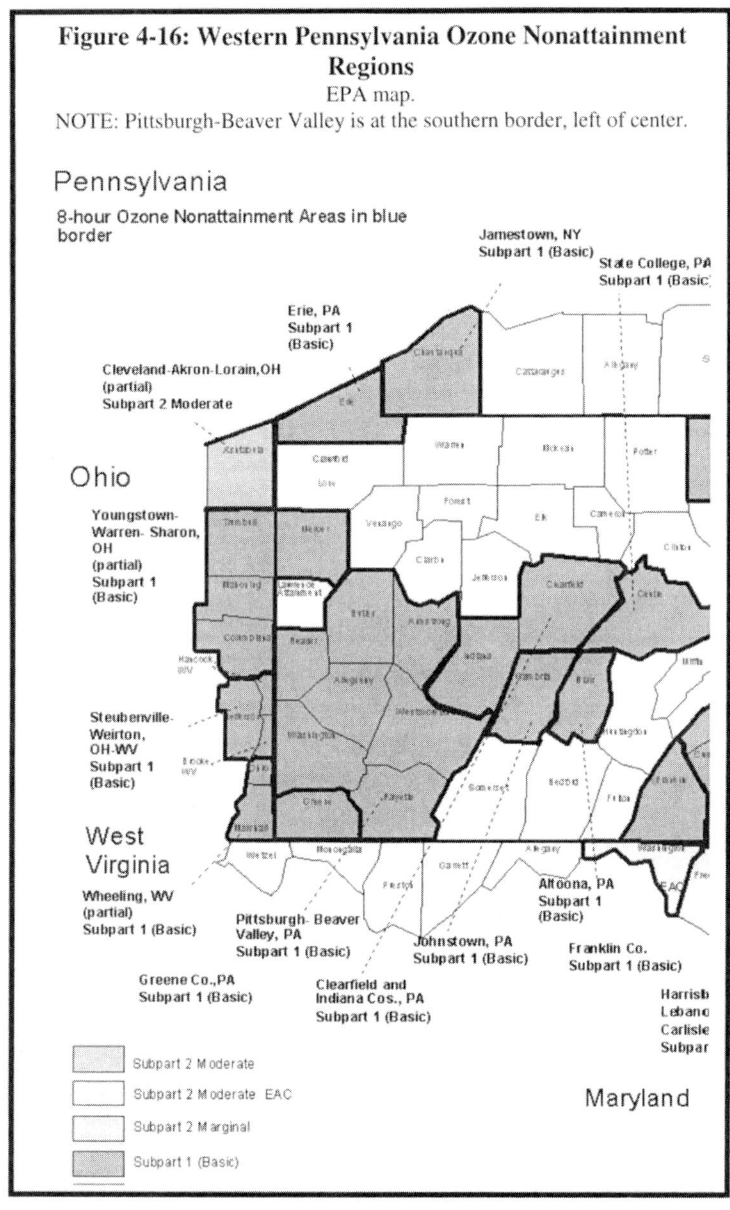

Figure 4-16: Western Pennsylvania Ozone Nonattainment Regions
EPA map.
NOTE: Pittsburgh-Beaver Valley is at the southern border, left of center.

A. The petitioner contends that the EPA acted contrary to the language of the Clean Air Act when it took into consideration the ozone exceedances that were recorded in the summer of 1995. The petitioner points to language in the Act stating that "[w]ithin 18 months of receipt of a complete State redesignation submittal, the Administrator *shall* approve or deny such redesignation." 42 U.S.C. § 7407(d)(3)(D) (emphasis added). The petitioner argues that the use of the word "shall" in this provision imposes upon the EPA a mandatory duty to act on a state's redesignation request within 18 months of submission. According to the petitioner, the EPA violated this mandatory duty when it took into consideration the 1995 ozone exceedance data, because these data did not exist during the 18–month period. The petitioner concludes that without these improperly considered data, there was no valid reason for the EPA to deny redesignation.

We agree with the EPA that the petitioner may not raise this argument on appeal because this argument was not raised during the rulemaking process. * * * Moreover, even if we were to reach the merits of the petitioner's argument, we would hold that 42 U.S.C. § 7407(d)(3)(D) did not preclude the EPA from considering the summer 1995 exceedance data. The language of the provision that enumerates the redesignation criteria tends to support this result. Under 42 U.S.C. § 7407(d)(3)(E)(i), the EPA Administrator "may not" promulgate a redesignation of a nonattainment area unless, among other things, "the Administrator determines that the area has attained the national ambient air quality standard." The use of the term "has attained" instead of "attained" may be interpreted as suggesting that the attainment must continue until the date of the redesignation.

In any event, even if we assume for present purposes that the language of 42 U.S.C. § 7407(d)(3)(E) is ambiguous as to whether the EPA may disregard data arising after the expiration of the 18–month period, we must defer to the EPA's interpretation of this provision under the rule of *Chevron, U.S.A., Inc. v. Natural Resources Defense Council, Inc.,* 467 U.S. 837 (1984). *Chevron* instructs reviewing courts that if Congress has not "directly spoken to the precise question at issue . . . the question for the court is whether the agency's answer is based on a permissible construction of the statute." *Id.* at 842–43. The EPA has published numerous legislative rules that have interpreted 42 U.S.C. § 7407(d)(3)(E) as obliging the EPA to deny a redesignation request if the EPA knows that the area is not in present attainment of the NAAQS. Because the EPA's interpretation is a reasonable construction of the statute, we defer to the EPA's interpretation.

The petitioners contend that § 7407(d)(3)(D) prohibits the EPA from considering any data acquired more than 18 months after the submission of Pennsylvania's redesignation request. They assert—correctly, in our view—that the use of the word "shall" in § 7407(d)(3)(D) imposes upon the EPA a mandatory duty to act on a state's redesignation request within 18 months. The petitioner's argument fails, however, because § 7407(d)(3)(D)'s use of the word "shall" does not conclusively indicate that Congress, as embodied in these formal rules, intended to prohibit the EPA from taking action after the expiration of the statutorily specified time period.

* * * [T]he petitioner has not brought to our attention anything in the Clean Air Act itself (other than the use of the word "shall" in 42 U.S.C. § 7407(d)(3)(D)), or anything in the Act's legislative history that shows that Congress intended for the EPA to lose its power to consider data brought to its attention after the expiration of the 18–month deadline. To the contrary, two important aspects of the Clean Air Act strongly suggest that Congress did not intend for the EPA to lose its power to act after 18 months. The first is the Act's failure to specify a consequence for noncompliance with the 18–month deadline. As the Supreme Court has observed, "if a statute does not specify a consequence for noncompliance with statutory timing provisions, the federal courts will not in the ordinary course impose their own coercive sanction." *United States v. James Daniel Good Real Property,* 510 U.S. 43, 63 (1993).

Second, the Clean Air Act affords a less drastic remedy than that urged by the petitioner. * * * [E]ither the petitioner or the Commonwealth of Pennsylvania could have brought an action to enforce the 18–month deadline in 42 U.S.C. § 7407(d)(3)(D). The petitioner has not called to our attention any provision of the Clean Air Act that would have precluded such an action. Had the petitioner brought such an action, the result would have been far less drastic than that which the petitioner now urges, which is the redesignation of an area that is not in attainment of the NAAQS.

* * * B. The petitioner further attacks the EPA's conclusion that the Area did not attain the NAAQS by arguing that the EPA failed to take into account data demonstrating that much of the offending ozone originated outside the Area. The petitioner contends that ozone readings from border monitors demonstrate that much of the ozone contributing to the exceedances during the summer of 1995 originated in neighboring states and was transported into the Area by wind. * * *

The petitioner contends that the EPA "failed to adequately analyze and consider the role transported ozone and ozone precursors played in the Area's 1995 exceedances." Although the petitioner does not seem to argue that these exceedances were caused solely by transported ozone, the petitioner maintains that such ozone plainly contributed to the 1995 exceedances. The petitioner states that "[t]here is nothing in the record upon which the EPA bases its assumption that exceedances are attributable solely to sources within the border when high ozone levels are being transported into the Area."

In response, the EPA argues that the Clean Air Act and its implementing regulations "require that EPA determine whether or not an area has met the NAAQS and satisfied the first criterion for redesignation without regard to why the NAAQS and the criterion many not have been met." In essence, then, the EPA maintains that the origin of the ozone that caused the 1995 exceedances was legally irrelevant. *See* 61 Fed. Reg. at 19,193, 19,194 (the EPA's final rule denying Pennsylvania's request to redesignate the Area). The EPA goes on, however, to defend its scientific analysis of the role of transported ozone in the Area.

In evaluating the EPA's interpretation of the Clean Air Act, we must apply the familiar *Chevron* analysis to which we previously referred. Under this analysis, if "Congress has directly spoken to the precise question at issue . . . the court . . . must give effect to the unambiguously expressed intent of Congress." *Chevron,* 467 U.S. at 842–43. If, however, the "precise question at issue" is one about which Congress has been either "silent or ambiguous," then a reviewing court must defer to the agency's statutory interpretation if it is "based on a permissible construction of the statute." *Id.* at 843.

Here, the EPA contends that the Clean Air Act itself prohibited allowances for ozone transported from outside the Area. The EPA relies in part on 42 U.S.C. § 7407(d)(1)(A)(ii), which provides that an attainment area is one that "meets" the NAAQS, and 42 U.S.C. § 7407(d)(3)(E)(i), which prohibits the EPA from redesignating an area to attainment unless the EPA determines that the area "has attained" the NAAQS. These provisions are certainly consistent with and lend some support to the EPA's interpretation.

Somewhat stronger support for the EPA's argument is furnished by other provisions of the Act. The first of these is 42 U.S.C. § 7511a(h), which establishes "rural transport areas." These are areas that do not attain the NAAQS for ozone, despite not producing any significant amount of ozone themselves. Congress addressed the problem that ozone transport causes rural transport areas by exempting such areas from certain pollution control requirements, provided that the areas make certain submissions to the EPA. Although such areas can enjoy relaxed control requirements, they must remain in nonattainment status, because they have not attained the NAAQS for ozone.

Congress also addressed the problem of ozone transport in 42 U.S.C. § 7511(a)(4), which describes certain circumstances under which the EPA may adjust a nonattainment area's classification (*e.g.,* from "severe" to "serious"). Under this provision, if a nonattainment area meets criteria making it eligible for adjustment of its classification, there are several factors that the EPA may consider when making the adjustment. One of these factors is "the level of pollution transport between the area and other affected areas, including both intrastate and interstate transport." *Id.* Thus, under this provision, the EPA may consider pollutant transport when adjusting a nonattainment area's classification, but pollution transport does not affect the area's designation as a nonattainment area.

* * * Accordingly, we accept the EPA's position that the origin of the ozone that caused the exceedances at issue is legally irrelevant.

* * * D. We thus conclude that the EPA did not act arbitrarily or capriciously, did not abuse its discretion, and did not act contrary to law when it determined that the Pittsburgh–Beaver Valley area was not attaining the national ambient air quality standard for ozone. Since 42

U.S.C. § 7407(d)(E)(i) prohibits the EPA from redesignating an area that is not in attainment of the NAAQS, the EPA correctly denied Pennsylvania's request for redesignation. We thus do not need to consider the petitioner's arguments that the EPA erred in determining that § 7407(d)(E)'s four other criteria were also not met, since § 7407(d)(E) provides that nonfulfillment of any one of its five criteria will prohibit the EPA from redesignating a nonattainment area to attainment status. * * *

NOTES

1. **Requirements for Attainment Redesignation.** What are the five statutory criteria that the EPA must evaluate when determining whether a nonattainment area can be redesignated as an attainment area? In the Third Circuit's approach to these criteria, who had the burden of proof regarding redesignation? What must that party prove?

2. **The Pittsburgh–Beaver Valley's Nonattainment.** What went wrong with Pennsylvania's request to have the Pittsburgh–Beaver Valley area redesignated as an attainment area? For what pollutant was it in nonattainment? Which redesignation criterion or criteria did the area fail, according to the EPA? Why was the timing of the EPA's decisionmaking important in this case? NOTE: Like 1988, 1995 was an unusually bad year for ozone pollution in the United States. Mid–Atlantic Regional Air Management Association, *Air Quality Improvement: Ozone Levels in 1988 and 1995*, http://www.marama.org/atlas/improvement.html (last revised Nov. 17, 1998).

3. **Applying the *Chevron* Standard of Review.** For what issues in this case did the Third Circuit use the *Chevron* standard of review? Why? What aspects of the Clean Air Act was the EPA interpreting?

4. **Arbitrary and Capricious Review.** For what issues in this case did the Third Circuit use the arbitrary and capricious standard of review? Why? What issues of fact did the EPA determine?

5. **Interstate Air Pollution and Nonattainment.** The EPA and the Third Circuit essentially consider interstate air pollution to be irrelevant to whether the Pittsburgh–Beaver Valley can be redesignated attainment or not. Nevertheless, as the Third Circuit pointed out, the EPA *can* consider interstate sources of air pollution when classifying the *level* of nonattainment. Is it fair that certain regions of the country must endure nonattainment status because of air pollution coming from somewhere else?

As we shall see in later sections of this chapter, Congress was quite aware of the interstate pollution problem and enacted several provisions to address those issues.

6. **The Economics of Nonattainment.** Why would the Southwestern Pennsylvania *Growth* Alliance fight so hard to get the Pittsburgh–Beaver Valley redesignated an attainment area, when the July measurements made it clear that this AQCR continued to violate the NAAQS? As a practical matter, what effect can a nonattainment designation have on economic growth?

7. **The 2004 Administrative Redesignations for Ozone.** In July 1997, the EPA amended the ozone NAAQS, establishing a new standard of

0.08 parts per million, averaged over eight hours. The U.S. Supreme Court upheld this standard in its 2001 decision in *American Trucking Associations*, and the EPA has been implementing the new standard ever since—including re-evaluating ozone nonattainment. On April 30, 2004, the EPA issued its final nonattainment designations, 69 Fed. Reg. 23,858 (April 30, 2004), but designated areas that fell within 5% of the cutoff for each level of nonattainment were eligible to apply for redesignation within 90 days. On September 15, 2004, the EPA reclassified nine nonattainment areas from moderate to marginal based on these redesignation requests. U.S. EPA, *Reclassification Fact Sheet*, http://www.epa.gov/ozonedesignations/documents/bumpDown/factsheet.htm.

* * *

C. REGULATION OF STATIONARY SOURCES' EMISSIONS OF CRITERIA POLLUTANTS IN ATTAINMENT AREAS

1. The PSD Program

In ***attainment areas***, by definition, the air quality meets the NAAQS and hence should be adequate to protect human health and welfare. Nevertheless, the states are not free to set whatever emissions limitations they want for attainment (or unclassifiable) AQCRs. Concerned that unfettered expansion of stationary sources in attainment areas would lead to air quality deterioration, and perhaps even the creation of new nonattainment areas, Congress created the ***Prevention of Significant Deterioration* (PSD) *program*** to impose emissions limitations on certain stationary sources in these areas. CAA Title I, Part C, §§ 160–169B, 42 U.S.C. §§ 7470–7492. Under this program, each SIP "shall contain emissions limitations and such other measures as may be necessary * * * to prevent significant deterioration of air quality in each region (or portion thereof) designated * * * as attainment or unclassifiable." CAA § 161, 42 U.S.C. § 7471. The PSD program is thus an exceptional program in the Clean Air Act because it demands air quality that is *better* than the NAAQS' health-based minimums.

The PSD program begins by classifying all attainment or unclassifiable AQCRs as Class I or Class II areas. Class I areas include all international parks, all national wilderness areas and national memorial parks comprising more than 5000 acres, all national parks comprising more than 6000 acres, and all other areas designated Class I before August 7, 1977. All other attainment and unclassifiable AQCRs start out as Class II areas, but the relevant state may redesignate a Class II area as a Class I area. CAA § 162, 42 U.S.C. § 7472; CAA § 164, 42 U.S.C. § 7474.

The classification of an AQCR as Class I or Class II determines the ***maximum allowable increases*** of sulfur dioxide and particulates within that region. For example, the average concentration of sulfur dioxide in a Class I region can increase only two micrograms per cubic liter per year, while the average concentration of sulfur dioxide in a Class II region can increase up to 20 micrograms per cubic liter per year. CAA § 163(b)(1), (2), 42 U.S.C. § 7473(b)(1), (2). Such allowable increases are designed to allow new sources to locate in the AQCR without destruction of air quality. For other air pollutants of concern—specifically, hydrocarbons, carbon monoxide, photochemical oxidants, and nitrogen oxides—the EPA promulgates regulations to prevent the significant deterioration of air quality. CAA § 166, 42 U.S.C. § 7476.

To further ensure that new sources do not push attainment AQCRs into nonattainment, the PSD program requires each ***major new emitting facility*** to get an individual permit specifying emissions limitations for that facility. CAA § 165(a)(1), 42 U.S.C. § 7475(a)(1). The PSD program defines two categories of "***major emitting facilities***." First, any stationary source "with the potential to emit two hundred and fifty tons per year or more of any air pollutant" qualifies. CAA § 169(1), 42 U.S.C. § 7479(1). Second, a stationary source qualifies as a "major emitting facility" if it can emit 100 tons per year or more of any air pollutant and it falls into one of the following categories:

> fossil-fuel fired steam electric plants of more than two hundred and fifty million British thermal units per hour heat input, coal cleaning plants (thermal dryers), kraft pulp mills, Portland Cement plants, primary zinc smelters, iron and steel mill plants, primary aluminum ore reduction plants, primary copper smelters, municipal incinerators capable of charging more than 50 tons of refuse per day, hydrofluoric, sulfuric, and nitric acid plants, petroleum refineries, lime plants, phosphate rock processing plants, coke oven batteries, sulfur recovery plants, carbon black plants (furnace process), primary lead smelters, fuel conversion plants, sintering plants, secondary metal production facilities, chemical process plants, fossil-fuel boilers of more than two hundred and fifty million British thermal units per hour heat input, petroleum storage and transfer facilities with a capacity exceeding three hundred thousand barrels, taconite ore processing facilities, glass fiber processing plants, charcoal production facilities.

Id. A "major emitting facility" is considered "***new***" under the PSD program if construction of that facility began after August 7, 1997. CAA § 165(a)(1), 42 U.S.C. § 7475(a)(1).

In order to receive an operating permit, the owner or operator of the major new emitting facility in an attainment or unclassifiable AQCR must show that its emissions will not cause the AQCR to exceed the maximum allowable increases, the NAAQS, or any other standard. CAA § 165(a)(2), 42 U.S.C. § 7475(a)(2). In addition, the facility is subject to emissions limitations based on the ***best available control technology*** **(BACT)** for each criteria pollutant that it emits. BACT is a ***technology-based emission standard*** and is defined as "an emission limitation based on the maximum degree of reduction of each pollutant * * * which the permitting authority, on a case-by-case basis, taking into account energy, environmental, and economic impacts and other costs, determines is achievable for such facility through application of production processes and available methods, systems, and techniques * * *." CAA § 169(3), 42 U.S.C. § 7479(3). In other words, in setting BACT, the permitting authority (which can be either the EPA or the state) must take into account not only costs but also the individual circumstances and practical considerations of the individual facility. As a result, BACT is, effectively, more constraining than LAER, the standard for new sources in nonattainment areas, because the EPA sets LAER on an industry-wide (*i.e.*, averaging) basis.

Other new sources of criteria pollutants in attainment areas may also be subject to emissions limitations. The Clean Air Act requires the EPA to set ***new source performance standards*** **(NSPS)** for new stationary sources, CAA § 111, 42 U.S.C. § 7411, which reflect "the greatest degree of emission limitation achievable through application of the best technological system of continuous emission which (taking into consideration the cost of achieving such emission reduction, and any non-air quality health and environmental impact and energy requirements) has been adequately demonstrated * * *." CAA § 111(g)(4)(B), 42 U.S.C. § 7411(g)(4)(B). This technology-based emission standard is more commonly known as the ***Best Available Demonstrated Technology*** **(BADT).**

In the 1990 amendments to the Clean Air Act, Congress generalized the permit requirement to require all ***major sources*** of air pollutants to get permits. CAA Title V, §§ 501–507, 42 U.S.C. §§ 7661–7661f. A "***major source***" for permitting purposes includes any stationary source "which directly emits, or has the potential to emit, one hundred tons per year or more of any air pollutant," whether that source is new or existing. CAA § 501(2), 42 U.S.C. § 7661(2); § 302(j), 42 U.S.C. § 7602(j).

Thus, to summarize emissions limitations for stationary sources so far:

TABLE 4–2: EMISSIONS STANDARDS FOR CRITERIA POLLUTANTS IN NONATTAINMENT AREAS & UNDER THE PSD PROGRAM

	NEW MAJOR STATIONARY SOURCES	EXISTING MAJOR STATIONARY SOURCES
NONATTAINMENT AREA: PART D:	Major Source = 100 tons/year of pollutants: LAER + OFFSETS + PERMIT (incorporated into Title V permitting)	Major Source = 100 tons/year pollutants: RACT + PERMIT (incorporated into Title V permitting)
ATTAINMENT/ UNCLASSIFIABLE AREA: PSD PROGRAM:	Major Emitting Facility = 250 tons/year of pollutants or 100 tons/year and source is in one of the 26 special categories: BACT + PERMIT	NOT APPLICABLE

As the following case demonstrates, one of the most frequently litigated issues in attainment areas is what constitutes BACT.

ALASKA DEPARTMENT OF ENVIRONMENTAL CONSERVATION v. ENVIRONMENTAL PROTECTION AGENCY

540 U.S. 461 (2004).

JUSTICE GINSBURG delivered the opinion of the Court.

This case concerns the authority of the Environmental Protection Agency (EPA or Agency) to enforce the provisions of the Clean Air Act's (CAA or Act) Prevention of Significant Deterioration (PSD) program. Under that program, no major air pollutant emitting facility may be constructed unless the facility is equipped with "the best available control technology" (BACT). As added by § 165, 91 Stat. 735, and amended, 42 U.S.C. § 7475(a)(4). BACT, as defined in the CAA, means, for any major air pollutant emitting facility, "an emission limitation based on the maximum degree of [pollutant] reduction ... which the permitting authority, on a case-by-case basis, taking into account energy, environmental, and economic impacts and other costs, determines is achievable for [the] facility...." § 7479(3).

* * * In the case before us, "the permitting authority" under § 7479(3) is the State of Alaska, acting through Alaska's Department of Environmental Conservation (ADEC). The question presented is what role EPA has with respect to ADEC's BACT determinations. Specifically, may EPA act to block construction of a new major pollutant emitting facility permitted by ADEC when EPA finds ADEC's BACT determination unreasonable in light of the guides § 7479(3) prescribes? We hold that the Act confers that checking authority on EPA.

I

A

* * * The PSD requirements, enacted as part of 1977 amendments to the Act, Title I, § 160 *et seq.*, 91 Stat. 731, "are designed to ensure that the air quality in attainment areas or areas that are already 'clean' will not degrade," [R. BELDEN, CLEAN AIR ACT 43 (2001)]. *See* 42 U.S.C. § 7470(1) (purpose of PSD program is to "protect public health and welfare from any actual or potential adverse effect which in [EPA's] judgment may reasonably be anticipate[d] to occur from air pollution ... notwithstanding attainment and maintenance of all national ambient air quality standards"). * * *

* * * Northwest Alaska, the region this case concerns, is classified as an attainment or unclassifiable area for nitrogen dioxide, 40 CFR § 81.302

(2002), therefore, the PSD program applies to emissions of that pollutant in the region. In 2002, the Agency reported that "[a]ll areas of the country that once violated the NAAQS for [nitrogen dioxide] now meet that standard." EPA, LATEST FINDINGS ON NATIONAL AIR QUALITY 7 (Aug. 2003).

Section 165 of the Act, 42 U.S.C. § 7475, installs a permitting requirement for any "major emitting facility," defined to include any source emitting more than 250 tons of nitrogen oxides per year, § 7479(1). No such facility may be constructed or modified unless a permit prescribing emission limitations has been issued for the facility. § 7475(a)(1); *see* § 7479(2)(C) (defining "construction" to include "modification"). Alaska's SIP imposes an analogous requirement. 18 ALASKA ADMIN. CODE § 50.300(c)(1) (2003). Modifications to major emitting facilities that increase nitrogen oxide emissions in excess of 40 tons per year require a PSD permit. 40 CFR § 51.166(b)(23)(i) (2002); 18 ALASKA ADMIN. CODE § 50.300(h)(3)(B)(ii) (2003).

The Act sets out preconditions for the issuance of PSD permits. *Inter alia,* no PSD permit may issue unless "the proposed facility is subject to the best available control technology for each pollutant subject to [CAA] regulation ... emitted from ... [the] facility." 42 U.S.C. § 7475(a)(4). As described in the Act's definitional provisions, "best available control technology" (BACT) means:

> "[A]n emission limitation based on the maximum degree of reduction of each pollutant subject to regulation under this chapter emitted from or which results from any major emitting facility, which the permitting authority, on a case-by-case basis, taking into account energy, environmental, and economic impacts and other costs, determines is achievable for such facility through application of production processes and available methods, systems, and techniques.... In no event shall application of 'best available control technology' result in emissions of any pollutants which will exceed the emissions allowed by any applicable standard established pursuant to section 7411 or 7412 of this title [emission standards for new and existing stationary sources]." § 7479(3).

40 CFR § 51.166(b)(12) (2002) (repeating statutory definition). Alaska's SIP contains provisions that track the statutory BACT requirement and definition. 18 ALASKA ADMIN. CODE §§ 50.310(d)(3) and 50.990(13) (2003). The State, with slightly variant terminology, defines BACT as "the emission limitation that represents the maximum reduction achievable for each regulated air contaminant, taking into account energy, environmental and economic impacts, and other costs." *Ibid.* Under the federal Act, a limited class of sources must gain advance EPA approval for the BACT prescribed in the permit. 42 U.S.C. § 7475(a)(8).

CAA also provides that a PSD permit may issue only if a source "will not cause, or contribute to, air pollution in excess of any ... maximum allowable increase or maximum allowable concentration for any pollutant" or any NAAQS. § 7475(a)(3). * * *

Among measures EPA may take to ensure compliance with the PSD program, two have special relevance here. The first prescription, § 113(a)(5) of the Act, provides that "[w]henever, on the basis of any available information, [EPA] finds that a State is not acting in compliance with any requirement or prohibition of the chapter relating to the construction of new sources or the modification of existing sources," EPA may "issue an order prohibiting the construction or modification of any major stationary source in any area to which such requirement applies." 42 U.S.C. § 7413(a)(5)(A). The second measure, § 167 of the Act, trains on enforcement of the PSD program; it requires EPA to "take such measures, including issuance of an order, or seeking injunctive relief, as necessary to prevent the construction or modification of a major emitting facility which does not conform to the [PSD] requirements." § 7477. * * *

B

Teck Cominco Alaska, Inc. (Cominco), operates a zinc concentrate mine, the Red Dog Mine, in northwest Alaska approximately 100 miles north of the Arctic Circle and close to the native Alaskan villages of Kivalina and Noatak. The mine is the region's largest private employer. It supplies a quarter of the area's wage base. * * *

In 1988, Cominco obtained authorization to operate the mine, a "major emitting facility" under the Act and Alaska's SIP. The mine's PSD permit authorized five 5,000 kilowatt Wartsila diesel electric generators, MG–1 through MG–5, subject to operating restrictions; two of the five generators were permitted to operate only in standby status. Petitioner Alaska Department of Environmental Conservation (ADEC) issued a second PSD permit in 1994 allowing addition of a sixth full-time generator (MG–6), removing standby status from MG–2, and imposing a new operational cap that allowed all but one generator to run full time.

In 1996, Cominco initiated a project, with funding from the State, to expand zinc production by 40%. Anticipating that the project would increase nitrogen oxide emissions by more than 40 tons per year, Cominco applied to ADEC for a PSD permit to allow, *inter alia,* increased electricity generation by its standby generator, MG–5. On March 3, 1999, ADEC preliminarily proposed as BACT for MG–5 the emission control technology known as selective catalytic reduction (SCR),[1] which reduces nitrogen oxide emissions by 90%. In response, Cominco amended its application to add a seventh generator, MG–17, and to propose as BACT an alternative control technology—Low NOx[2]—that achieves a 30% reduction in nitrogen oxide pollutants.

---

1. SCR requires injections of "ammonia or urea into the exhaust before the exhaust enters a catalyst bed made with vanadium, titanium, or platinum. The reduction reaction occurs when the flue gas passes over the catalyst bed where the NOx and ammonia combine to become nitrogen, oxygen, and water. . . ."

2. In Low NOx, changes are made to a generator to improve fuel atomization and modify the combustion space to enhance the mixing of air and fuel.

On May 4, 1999, ADEC, in conjunction with Cominco's representative, issued a first draft PSD permit and preliminary technical analysis report that concluded Low NOx was BACT for MG–5 and MG–17. To determine BACT, ADEC employed EPA's recommended top-down methodology:

> "In brief, the top-down process provides that all available control technologies be ranked in descending order of control effectiveness. The PSD applicant first examines the most stringent—or 'top'—alternative. That alternative is established as BACT unless the applicant demonstrates, and the permitting authority in its informed judgment agrees, that technical considerations, or energy, environmental, or economic impacts justify a conclusion that the most stringent technology is not 'achievable' in that case. If the most stringent technology is eliminated in this fashion, then the next most stringent alternative is considered, and so on." EPA, NEW SOURCE REVIEW WORKSHOP MANUAL B2 (Draft Oct. 1990) (hereinafter New Source Review Manual).

Applying top-down methodology, ADEC first homed in on SCR as BACT for MG–5, and the new generator, MG–17. "[W]ith an estimated reduction of 90%," ADEC stated, SCR "is the most stringent" technology. Finding SCR "technically and economically feasible," ADEC characterized as "overstated" Cominco's cost estimate of $5,643 per ton of nitrogen oxide removed by SCR. Using Cominco's data, ADEC reached a cost estimate running between $1,586 and $2,279 per ton. Costs in that range, ADEC observed, "are well within what ADEC and EPA conside[r] economically feasible." Responding to Cominco's comments on the preliminary permit, engineering staff in ADEC's Air Permits Program pointed out that, according to information Cominco provided to ADEC, "SCR has been installed on similar diesel-fired engines throughout the world."

Despite its staff's clear view "that SCR (the most effective individual technology) [was] technologically, environmentally, and economically feasible for the Red Dog power plant engines," ADEC endorsed the alternative proffered by Cominco. * * *

On the final day of the public comment period, July 2, 1999, the United States Department of the Interior, National Parks Service (NPS), submitted comments to ADEC. NPS objected to the projected offset of new emissions from MG–5 and MG–17 against emissions from other existing generators that were not subject to BACT. * * *

Following NPS' lead, EPA wrote to ADEC on July 29, 1999, commenting: "Although ADEC states in its analysis that [SCR], the most stringent level of control, is economically and technologically feasible, ADEC did not propose to require SCR.... [O]nce it is determined that an emission unit is subject to BACT, the PSD program does not allow the imposition of a limit that is less stringent than BACT." A permitting authority, EPA agreed with NPS, could not offset new emissions "by imposing new controls on other emission units" that were not subject to BACT. New emissions could be offset only against reduced emissions from sources covered by the same BACT authorization. EPA further agreed with NPS that, based on the existing information, BACT would be required for MG–1, MG–3, MG–4, and MG–5.

After receiving EPA comments, ADEC issued a second draft PSD permit and technical analysis report on September 1, 1999, again finding Low NOx to be BACT for MG–17. Abandoning the emissions-offsetting justification advanced in the May 4 draft permit, ADEC agreed with NPS and EPA that "emission reductions from sources that were not part of the permit action," here MG–1, MG–2, MG–3, MG–4, MG–5, and MG–6, could not be considered in determining BACT for MG–17.

ADEC conceded that, lacking data from Cominco, it had made "no judgment . . . as to the impact of . . . [SCR] on the operation, profitability, and competitiveness of the Red Dog Mine." Contradicting its May 1999 conclusion that SCR was "technically and economically feasible," ADEC found in September 1999 that SCR imposed "a disproportionate cost" on the mine. ADEC concluded, on a "cursory review," that requiring SCR for a rural Alaska utility would lead to a 20% price increase, and that in comparison with other BACT technologies, SCR came at a "significantly higher" cost. No economic basis for a comparison between the mine and a rural utility appeared in ADEC's technical analysis.

EPA protested the revised permit. * * * To justify the September 1, 1999, permit, EPA suggested, ADEC could "include an analysis of whether requiring Cominco to install and operate [SCR] would have any adverse economic impacts upon Cominco specifically." Stating that such an inquiry was unnecessary and expressing "concerns related to confidentiality," Cominco declined to submit financial data. In this regard, Cominco simply asserted, without detail, that the company's "overall debt remains quite high" despite continuing profits. Cominco also invoked the need for "[i]ndustrial development in rural Alaska."

On December 10, 1999, ADEC issued the final permit and technical analysis report. Once again, ADEC approved Low NOx as BACT for MG–17 "[t]o support Cominco's Red Dog Mine Production Rate Increase Project, and its contributions to the region." ADEC did not include the economic analysis EPA had suggested. * * *

The same day, December 10, 1999, EPA issued an order to ADEC, under §§ 113(a)(5) and 167 of the Act, 42 U.S.C. §§ 7413(a)(5) and 7477, prohibiting ADEC from issuing a PSD permit to Cominco "unless ADEC satisfactorily documents why SCR is not BACT for the Wartsila diesel generator [MG–17]." In the letter accompanying the order, the Agency stated that "ADEC's own analysis supports the determination that BACT is [SCR], and that ADEC's decision in the proposed permit therefore is both arbitrary and erroneous."

On February 8, 2000, EPA, again invoking its authority under §§ 113(a)(5) and 167 of the Act, issued a second order, this time prohibiting Cominco from beginning "construction or modification activities at the

Red Dog mine." A third order, issued on March 7, 2000, superseding and vacating the February 8 order, generally prohibited Cominco from acting on ADEC's December 10 PSD permit but allowed limited summer construction. On April 25, 2000, EPA withdrew its December 10 order. Once ADEC issued the permit, EPA explained, that order lacked utility. On July 16, 2003, ADEC granted Cominco a PSD permit to construct MG–17 with SCR as BACT. Under the July 16, 2003, permit, SCR ceases to be BACT "if and when the case currently pending before the Supreme Court of the United States of America is decided in favor of the State of Alaska."

The day EPA issued its first order against Cominco, February 8, 2000, ADEC and Cominco petitioned the Court of Appeals for the Ninth Circuit for review of EPA's orders. * * * EPA had properly exercised its discretion in issuing the three orders, the Ninth Circuit ultimately determined, because (1) Cominco failed to "demonstrat[e] that SCR was economically infeasible," and (2) "ADEC failed to provide a reasoned justification for its elimination of SCR as a control option." We granted certiorari to resolve an important question of federal law, *i.e.,* the scope of EPA's authority under §§ 113(a)(5) and 167, and now affirm the Ninth Circuit's judgment.

* * * III

A

Centrally at issue in this case is the question whether EPA's oversight role, described by Congress in CAA §§ 113(a)(5) and 167, extends to ensuring that a state permitting authority's BACT determination is reasonable in light of the statutory guides. Sections 113(a)(5) and 167 lodge in the Agency encompassing supervisory responsibility over the construction and modification of pollutant emitting facilities in areas covered by the PSD program. 42 U.S.C. §§ 7413(a)(5) and 7477. In notably capacious terms, Congress armed EPA with authority to issue orders stopping construction when "a State is not acting in compliance with any [CAA] requirement or prohibition ... relating to the construction of new sources or the modification of existing sources," § 7413(a)(5), or when "construction or modification of a major emitting facility ... does not conform to the requirements of [the PSD program]," § 7477.

The federal Act enumerates several "[p]reconstruction requirements" for the PSD program. § 7475. Absent these, "[n]o major emitting facility ... may be constructed." *Ibid.* One express preconstruction requirement is inclusion of a BACT determination in a facility's PSD permit. §§ 7475(a)(1) and (4). As earlier set out, the Act defines BACT as "an emission limitation based on the maximum degree of reduction of [a] pollutant ... which the permitting authority, on a case-by-case basis, taking into account energy, environmental, and economic impacts and other costs, determines is achievable for [a] facility." § 7479(3). Under this formulation, the permitting authority, ADEC here, exercises primary or initial responsibility for identifying BACT in line with the Act's definition of that term.

All parties agree that one of the "many requirements in the PSD provisions that the EPA may enforce" is "that a [PSD] permit contain a BACT limitation." It is therefore undisputed that the Agency may issue an order to stop a facility's construction if a PSD permit contains no BACT designation.

EPA reads the Act's definition of BACT, together with CAA's explicit listing of BACT as a "[p]reconstruction requiremen[t]," to mandate not simply *a* BACT designation, but a determination of BACT faithful to the statute's definition. In keeping with the broad oversight role §§ 113(a)(5) and 167 vest in EPA, the Agency maintains, it may review permits to ensure that a State's BACT determination is reasonably moored to the Act's provisions. We hold, as elaborated below, that the Agency has rationally construed the Act's text and that EPA's construction warrants our respect and approbation.

BACT's statutory definition requires selection of an emission control technology that results in the "maximum" reduction of a pollutant "achievable for [a] facility" in view of "energy, environmental, and economic impacts, and other costs." 42 U.S.C. § 7479(3). This instruction, EPA submits, cabins state permitting authorities' discretion by granting only "authority to make *reasonable* BACT determinations," *i.e.,* decisions made with fidelity to the Act's purpose "to insure that economic growth will occur in a manner consistent with the preservation of existing clean air resources," 42 U.S.C. § 7470(3). Noting that state permitting authorities' statutory discretion is constrained by CAA's strong, normative terms "maximum" and "achievable," § 7479(3), EPA reads §§ 113(a)(5) and 167 to empower the federal Agency to check a state agency's unreasonably lax BACT designation.

EPA stresses Congress' reason for enacting the PSD program—to prevent significant deterioration of air quality in clean-air areas within a State and in neighboring States. §§ 7470(3), (4). That aim, EPA urges, is unlikely to be realized absent an EPA surveillance role that extends to BACT determinations. * * *

* * * The CAA construction EPA advances in this litigation is reflected in interpretive guides the Agency has several times published. We "normally accord particular deference to an agency interpretation of 'longstanding' duration," *Barnhart v. Walton,* 535 U.S. 212, 220 (2002) (quoting *North Haven Bd. of Ed. v. Bell,* 456 U.S. 512, 522, n. 12 (1982)), recognizing that "well-reasoned views" of an expert administrator rest on " 'a body of experience and informed judgment to which courts and litigants may properly resort for guidance,' " *Bragdon v. Abbott,* 524 U.S. 624, 642 (1998) (quoting *Skidmore v. Swift & Co.,* 323 U.S. 134, 139–140 (1944)).

We have previously accorded dispositive effect to EPA's interpretation of an ambiguous CAA provision. *See Chevron U.S.A. Inc. v. Natural Resources Defense Council, Inc.,* 467 U.S. 837, 865–866 (1984); *Union Elec.,* 427 U.S., at 256. The Agency's interpretation in this case, presented in internal guidance memoranda, however, does not qualify for the dispositive force described in *Chevron. See Christensen v. Harris County,* 529 U.S. 576, 587 (2000) ("Interpretations such as those in . . . policy statements, agency manuals, and enforcement guidelines, all of which lack the force of law—do not warrant *Chevron*-style deference."); *accord, United States v. Mead Corp.,* 533 U.S. 218, 234 (2001). Cogent "administrative interpretations . . . not [the] products of formal rulemaking . . . nevertheless warrant respect." *Washington State Dept. of Social and Health Servs. v. Guardianship Estate of Keffeler,* 537 U.S. 371, 385 (2003). We accord EPA's reading of the relevant statutory provisions, §§ 7413(a)(5), 7470(3), 7470(4), 7475(a)(4), 7477, and 7479(3), that measure of respect.

B

ADEC assails the Agency's construction of the Act on several grounds. Its arguments do not persuade us to reject as impermissible EPA's longstanding, consistently maintained interpretation.

ADEC argues that the statutory definition of BACT, § 7479(3), unambiguously assigns to "the permitting authority" alone determination of the control technology qualifying as "best available." Because the Act places responsibility for determining BACT with "the permitting authority," ADEC urges, CAA excludes federal Agency surveillance reaching the substance of the BACT decision. EPA's enforcement role, ADEC maintains, is restricted to the requirement "that the permit contain a BACT limitation."

Understandably, Congress entrusted state permitting authorities with initial responsibility to make BACT determinations "case-by-case." § 7479(3). A state agency, no doubt, is best positioned to adjust for local differences in raw materials or plant configurations, differences that might make a technology "unavailable" in a particular area. But the fact that the relevant statutory guides—"maximum" pollution reduction, considerations of energy, environmental, and economic impacts—may not yield a "single, objectively 'correct' BACT determination," surely does not signify that there can be no *unreasonable* determinations. Nor does Congress' sensitivity to site-specific factors necessarily imply a design to preclude in this context meaningful EPA oversight under §§ 113(a)(5) and 167. EPA claims no prerogative to designate the correct BACT; the Agency asserts only the authority to guard against unreasonable designations.

Nor do we find enlightening Congress' inclusion of the word "determines" in the BACT definition. [S]tate permitting authorities' BACT determinations are not "conclusiv[e] and authoritativ[e]." * * *

Under ADEC's interpretation, EPA properly inquires whether a BACT determination appears in a PSD permit, but not whether that BACT determination "was made on reasonable grounds properly supported on the record," 63 Fed. Reg., at 13797. Congress, however, vested EPA with explicit and sweeping authority to enforce CAA "requirements" relating to the construction and modification of sources under the PSD program, including BACT. We fail to see why Congress, having expressly endorsed an expansive surveillance role for EPA in two independent CAA provisions, would then implicitly preclude the Agency from verifying substantive compliance with the BACT provisions and, instead, limit EPA's superintendence to the insubstantial question whether the state permitting authority had uttered the key words "BACT."

We emphasize, however, that EPA's rendition of the Act's less than crystalline text leaves the "permitting authority" considerable leeway. The Agency acknowledges "the need to accord appropriate deference" to States' BACT designations and disclaims any intention to " 'second guess' state decisions," 63 Fed. Reg., at 13797. Only when a state agency's BACT determination is "not based on a reasoned analysis" may EPA step in to ensure that the statutory requirements are honored. EPA adhered to that limited role here, explaining why ADEC's BACT determination was "arbitrary" and contrary to ADEC's own findings. EPA's limited but vital role in enforcing BACT is consistent with a scheme that "places primary responsibilities and authority with the States, backed by the Federal Government." S. REP. NO. 95–127, p. 29.

* * * In sum, EPA interprets the Act to allow substantive federal Agency surveillance of state permitting authorities' BACT determinations subject to federal court review. We credit EPA's longstanding construction of the Act and confirm EPA's authority, pursuant to §§ 113(a)(5) and 167, to rule on the reasonableness of BACT decisions by state permitting authorities.

IV

A

We turn finally, and more particularly, to the reasons why we conclude that EPA properly exercised its statutory authority in this case. * * * Treating the case-specific issue as embraced within the sole question presented, we are satisfied that EPA did not act arbitrarily in finding that ADEC furnished no tenable accounting for its determination that Low NOx was BACT for MG–17.

Because the Act itself does not specify a standard for judicial review in this instance, we apply the familiar default standard of the Administrative Procedure Act, 5 U.S.C. § 706(2)(A), and ask whether the Agency's action was "arbitrary, capricious, an abuse of discretion, or otherwise not in accordance with law." Even when an agency explains its decision with "less than ideal clarity," a reviewing court will not upset the decision on that account "if the agency's path may reasonably be discerned." *Bowman Transp., Inc. v. Arkansas–Best Freight System, Inc.*, 419 U.S. 281, 286 (1974). EPA's three skeletal orders to ADEC and Cominco surely are not composed with ideal clarity. These orders, however, are properly read together with accompanying explanatory correspondence from EPA; so read, the Agency's comments and orders adequately ground the determination that ADEC's acceptance of Low NOx for MG–17 was unreasonable given the facts ADEC found.

In the two draft permits and the final permit, ADEC formally followed the EPA-recommended top-down methodology to determine BACT, as Cominco had done in its application. Employing that methodology in the May 1999 draft permit, ADEC first concluded that SCR was the most stringent emission-control technology that was both "technically and economically feasible." That technology should have been designated BACT absent "technical considerations, or energy, environmental, or economic impacts justif[ying] a conclusion that [SCR was] not 'achievable' in [this] case." ADEC nevertheless selected Low NOx as BACT; ADEC did so in May 1999 based on Cominco's suggestion that fitting all Red Dog Mine generators with Low NOx would reduce aggregate emissions.

In September and December 1999, ADEC again rejected SCR as BACT but no longer relied on Cominco's suggestion that it could reduce aggregate emissions by equipping all generators with Low NOx. ADEC candidly stated that it aimed "[t]o support Cominco's Red Dog Mine Production Rate Increase Project, and its contributions to the region." In these second and third rounds, ADEC rested its selection of Low NOx squarely and solely on SCR's "disproportionate cost."

EPA concluded that ADEC's switch from finding SCR economically feasible in May 1999 to finding SCR economically infeasible in September 1999 had no factual basis in the record. In the September and December 1999 technical analyses, ADEC acknowledged that "no judgment [could then] be made as to the impact of [SCR's] cost on the operation, profitability, and competitiveness of the Red Dog Mine." ADEC nevertheless concluded that SCR would threaten both the Red Dog Mine's "unique and continuing impact on the economic diversity" of northwest Alaska and the mine's "world competitiveness." ADEC also stressed the mine's role as employer in an area with "historical high unemployment and limited permanent year-round job opportunities."

We do not see how ADEC, having acknowledged that no determination "[could] be made as to the impact of [SCR's] cost on the operation . . . and competitiveness of the [mine]," could simultaneously proffer threats to the mine's operation or competitiveness as reasons for declaring SCR economically infeasible. ADEC, indeed, forthrightly explained why it was disarmed from reaching any judgment on whether, or to what extent, implementation of SCR would adversely affect the mine's operation or profitability: Cominco had declined to provide the relevant financial data, disputing the need for such information and citing "confidentiality" concerns[.] No record evidence suggests that the mine, were it to use SCR for its new generator, would be obliged to cut personnel, or raise zinc prices. Absent evidence of that order, ADEC lacked cause for selecting Low NOx as BACT based on the more stringent control's impact on the mine's operation or competitiveness.

Nor has ADEC otherwise justified its choice of Low NOx. To bolster its assertion that SCR was too expensive, ADEC invoked four BACT determinations made in regard to diesel generators used for primary power production; BACT's cost, in those instances, ranged from $0 to $936 per ton of nitrogen oxide removed. ADEC itself, however, had previously found SCR's per-ton cost, then estimated as $2,279, to be "well within what ADEC and EPA considers economically feasible." Tellingly, as to examples of low-cost BACT urged by Cominco, ADEC acknowledged: "The cited examples of engines permitted in Alaska without requiring SCR are not valid examples as they either took place over 18 months ago or were not used for similar purposes." ADEC added that it has indeed "permitted [Alaska] projects requiring SCR." Further, EPA rejected ADEC's comparison between the mine and a rural utility, because "no facts exist to suggest that the 'economic impact' of the incrementally higher cost of SCR on the world's largest producer of zinc concentrates would be anything like its impact on a rural, non-profit utility that must pass costs on to a small base of individual consumers."

ADEC's basis for selecting Low NOx thus reduces to a readiness "[t]o support Cominco's Red Dog Mine Production Rate Increase Project, and its contributions to the region." This justification, however, hardly meets ADEC's own standard of a "source-specific ... economic impac[t] which demonstrate[s] [SCR] to be inappropriate as BACT." In short, as the Ninth Circuit determined, EPA validly issued stop orders because ADEC's BACT designation simply did not qualify as reasonable in light of the statutory guides. * * *

B

We emphasize that today's disposition does not impede ADEC from revisiting the BACT determination in question. In letters and orders throughout the permitting process, EPA repeatedly commented that it was open to ADEC to prepare "an appropriate record" supporting its selection of Low NOx as BACT. At oral argument, counsel for EPA reaffirmed that, "absolutely," ADEC could reconsider the matter and, on an "appropriate record," endeavor to support Low NOx as BACT. We see no reason not to take EPA at its word.

* * *

In sum, we conclude that EPA has supervisory authority over the reasonableness of state permitting authorities' BACT determinations and may issue a stop construction order, under §§ 113(a)(5) and 167, if a BACT selection is not reasonable. We further conclude that, in exercising that authority, the Agency did not act arbitrarily or capriciously in finding that ADEC's BACT decision in this instance lacked evidentiary support. EPA's orders, therefore, were neither arbitrary nor capricious. The judgment of the Court of Appeals is accordingly

Affirmed.

JUSTICE KENNEDY, with whom THE CHIEF JUSTICE, JUSTICE SCALIA, and JUSTICE THOMAS join, dissenting.

The majority, in my respectful view, rests its holding on mistaken premises, for its reasoning conflicts with the express language of the Clean Air Act (CAA or Act), with sound rules of administrative law, and with principles that preserve the integrity of States in our federal system. The State of Alaska had in place procedures that were in full compliance with the governing statute and accompanying regulations promulgated by the Environmental Protection Agency (EPA). As I understand the opinion of the Court and the parties' submissions, there is no disagreement on this point. Alaska followed these procedures to determine the best available control technology (BACT). EPA, however, sought to overturn the State's decision, not by the process of judicial review, but by administrative fiat. The Court errs, in my judgment, by failing to hold that EPA, based on nothing more than its substantive disagreement with the State's discretionary judgment, exceeded its powers in setting aside Alaska's BACT determination. * * *

NOTES

1. **Cooperative Federalism?** What was the relationship between the EPA and the State of Alaska in the setting of BACT and the issuance of PSD permits? What kind of enforcement authority does the EPA possess to ensure that Alaska and Cominco comply with the Clean Air Act's requirements, according to the majority? Why did Alaska and the dissent disagree?

2. **The Economics of BACT Decisions.** Why did Cominco make such an effort to bargain its way out of the SCR technology, do you suppose? Why did the EPA object to such bargaining? Was its objection consistent with the "bubble" concept it espoused in *Chevron*? Why or why not?

3. **The Standard of Review.** What standard did the majority use to review the EPA's interpretation of its own authority? Why?

4. **Determining BACT.** How do states and the EPA determine BACT, according to this case? Why did the Supreme Court majority uphold the EPA in overturning the State of Alaska's determination that Low NOx was BACT for Cominco?

* * *

Chapter 1 raised the issue of environmental justice in connection with permitting for Treatment, Storage, and Disposal (TSD) facilities under RCRA and noted that the EPA has expressed renewed interest in considering environmental justice issues in its permitting decisions. Environmental justice issues can also arise in the context of the Clean Air Act's PSD permitting. Consider, for example: in the case you just read, *Alaska Department of Environmental Conservation v. EPA*, was ADEC making an environmental justice argument in favor of Low NOx? Why or why not? Should the EPA have considered the environmental justice aspects of that case? Why or why not?

The EPA's Environmental Appeals Board (EAB)—the internal administrative review board for the EPA—*has* recently explicitly considered environmental justice in another Alaska-based PSD permitting appeal.

IN RE: SHELL GULF OF MEXICO, INC., SHELL OFFSHORE, INC. (FRONTIER DISCOVERY DRILLING UNIT)

2010 WL 5478647 (E.A.B. E.P.A. Dec. 30, 2010)

Opinion of the Board by Judge Wolgast:

I. *STATEMENT OF THE CASE*

On March 31, 2010, pursuant to Clean Air Act ("CAA" or the "Act") section 328, 42 U.S.C. § 7627, U.S. Environmental Protection Agency ("EPA" or "Agency") Region 10 ("Region") issued an Outer Continental Shelf ("OCS") Prevention of Significant Deterioration ("PSD") Permit to Construct, Permit Number R10OCS/PSD–AK–09–01 ("Chukchi Permit"), to Shell Gulf of Mexico, Inc. ("SGOMI"). On April 9, 2010, the Region issued another OCS PSD Permit to Construct, Permit Number R10OCS/PSD–AK–2010–01 ("Beaufort Permit"), to Shell Offshore, Inc. ("SOI").

The Chukchi and Beaufort Permits ("Permits") authorize SGOMI and SOI (collectively, "Shell") "to construct and operate the Frontier Discoverer drillship and its air emission units and to conduct other air pollutant emitting activities" for the purpose of oil exploration in the Chukchi and Beaufort Seas off the North Slope of Alaska. Both Permits provide for the use of an associated fleet of support ships, such as icebreakers and a supply ship, in addition to the Frontier Discoverer. * * *

Three groups filed petitions requesting that the Environmental Appeals Board ("Board") grant review of both the Chukchi and Beaufort Permits: 1) Center for Biological Diversity ("CBD"); 2) Earthjustice, on behalf of several conservation groups ("EJ Petitioners"), and; 3) Alaska Eskimo Whaling Commission and Inupiat Community of the Arctic Slope ("AEWC"). Both the Region and Shell filed responses to the petitions, arguing that the Board should not grant review.

In this decision, the Board addresses three issues the EJ Petitioners and AEWC raise and concludes that the Permits must be remanded to the Region with respect to two of those issues. Having determined that a remand is necessary, the Board further concludes that the remand will significantly alter the administrative record as it pertains to certain other issues AEWC and CBD raise and that the Region should review those issues as part of its analysis on remand.

II. *ISSUES CONSIDERED ON APPEAL*

* * * 3. Did the Region clearly err when it relied solely on compliance with the national ambient air quality standard ("NAAQS") for nitrogen

dioxide ("NO_2") in effect at the time the Permits were issued to demonstrate that Shell's operations will not have "disproportionately high and adverse human health or environmental effects" on Alaska Natives living in North Slope communities, given that the Administrator published a proposed rule in the Federal Register on July 15, 2009, several months before the Permits were issued, setting forth updated scientific evidence and proposing to supplement the annual NO_2 NAAQS with a 1–hour NO_2 NAAQS, and published a final rule in the Federal Register on February 9, 2010, several weeks before the Permits were issued, concluding that the annual NO_2 NAAQS no longer provided requisite protection of public health and establishing a supplemental 1–hour NO_2 NAAQS?

III. *SUMMARY OF DECISION*

* * * With respect to the environmental justice analysis, the Board concludes that the Region clearly erred when it relied solely on demonstrated compliance with the then-existing annual NO_2 NAAQS as sufficient to find that the Alaska Native population would not experience disproportionately high and adverse human health or environmental effects from the permitted activity. The Region's reliance solely on compliance with the annual NO_2 standard when it issued the Chukchi and Beaufort Permits on March 31 and April 9, 2010, was clearly erroneous given that the Administrator proposed a rule, published in the Federal Register on July 15, 2009, which made available updated scientific evidence supporting the Administrator's proposal to supplement the annual NO_2 NAAQS with a 1–hour NO_2 NAAQS. The Administrator concluded that the annual NO_2 NAAQS alone did not provide requisite protection of public health and established a supplemental 1–hour NO_2 NAAQS in a final rule published in the Federal Register on February 9, 2010, several weeks prior to the Region issuing the Chukchi and Beaufort Permits.

Having found clear error in these aspects of the Region's decisions, the Board remands the Permits to the Region. * * *

IV. *STANDARD OF REVIEW*

When evaluating a permit appeal, the Board determines whether the permit issuer's rationale for its conclusions is adequately explained and supported by the administrative record. In other words, the record must demonstrate that the permit issuer "exercised his or her considered judgment" when making permit determinations. As this Board has previously observed, "[w]ithout an articulation by the permit writer of his analysis, [the Board] cannot properly perform any review whatsoever of that analysis and, therefore, cannot conclude that it meets the requirements of rationality."

V. *FACTUAL AND PROCEDURAL HISTORY*

A. *Factual History of the Permits*

As stated above, the Permits authorize Shell, subject to conditions, "to construct and operate the Frontier Discoverer drillship and its air emissions units and to conduct other air pollutant emitting activities" during exploratory drilling activities undertaken on oil and gas lease blocks in the Chukchi and Beaufort Seas off the North Slope of Alaska. The Chukchi Permit authorizes exploratory drilling activities beyond twenty-five miles of the state of Alaska's seaward boundary, whereas the Beaufort Permit authorizes exploratory drilling activities both within and beyond the twenty-five mile boundary. Both Permits provide for the use of an associated fleet of support ships, such as icebreakers and a supply ship, in addition to the Frontier Discoverer.

B. *Procedural History Before the Board*

On May 10, 2010, the Board issued an order granting Shell's motion to participate in the proceedings and setting a scheduling conference for May 13, 2010. Immediately following the scheduling conference, the Board consolidated the petitions for review and scheduled oral argument for June 18, 2010.

Two weeks later, the President and the Department of the Interior ("DOI") announced the suspension of any plans to drill exploratory wells in the Beaufort and Chukchi Seas until 2011. Specifically, DOI stated that Shell's Applications for Permits to Drill ("APDs") in the Chukchi and Beaufort Seas would not be considered until 2011 pending further information-gathering, evaluation of proposed drilling technology, and evaluation of oil spill response mechanisms in the Arctic. In response to the Administration's announcement, the Region and Petitioners filed motions requesting, respectively, that the Board hold matters in abeyance, or that the Board vacate the Permits and remand them.

The Board postponed the oral argument on the merits of the petitions scheduled for June 18, 2010, and instead held oral argument regarding the Region's and Petitioners' respective motions on that same date. The Board subsequently scheduled oral argument on the merits of the petitions to take place on August 17, 2010, and further requested that the parties focus their arguments on the three issues set forth above in Part II[.] The Board stated that it was particularly interested in hearing argument on the three issues identified "because they are legal in nature, and thus the analyses set forth in the documentation supporting the Permits are unlikely to be affected by any subsequent DOI announcement of new requirements or mandates pertaining to future exploratory drilling on the OCS." At the time, the Board made clear that it had not yet decided whether it would proceed to issue a decision on the merits.

After several revisions to the oral argument schedule, and after the Region withdrew its request for abeyance as to the three issues scheduled for oral argument, the Board held argument on October 7, 2010. The case now stands ready for decision.

VI. *ANALYSIS*

* * *C. *Did the Region Clearly Err By Limiting the Scope of Its Environmental Justice Analysis Based on the Area's Attainment of the NAAQS for NO_2 In Effect On the Date of Permit Issuance?*

The Executive Order entitled "Federal Actions To Address Environmental Justice in Minority Populations and Low–Income Populations" states in relevant part that "each Federal agency shall make achieving environmental justice part of its mission by identifying and addressing, as appropriate, disproportionately high and adverse human health or environmental effects of its programs, policies, and activities on minority populations and low-income populations." Exec. Order 12,898, 59 Fed. Reg. 7629, 7629 (Feb. 11, 1994) ("Executive Order"). Federal agencies are required to implement this order "consistent with, and to the extent permitted by, existing law." The Board has held that environmental justice issues must be considered in connection with the issuance of PSD permits.

In the present case, AEWC and the Region agree that the North Slope communities potentially impacted by Shell's proposed operations include a "significantly high percentage of Alaskan Natives, who are considered a minority under [Executive Order] 12898." AEWC contends that the Region clearly erred when it concluded that compliance with the existing annual NO_2 NAAQS demonstrates compliance with the Executive Order.

* * * At the outset, the Board notes that the Region engaged in significant outreach to residents of communities on the North Slope in these OCS PSD permitting processes. The record demonstrates that several public hearings were held in communities across the North Slope for both the Chukchi and Beaufort Permits. While the Region's actions in this regard are laudable, the instant appeals do not contest the Region's public participation procedures for soliciting input on environmental justice issues. As such, the Board turns its attention to the substance of the Region's environmental justice analysis.

A brief synopsis of the juxtaposed time lines for the issuance of both the 1–hour NO_2 NAAQS rule and the Chukchi and Beaufort Permits aids in providing context to the environmental justice claims in these appeals. On July 15, 2009, the Administrator published in the Federal Register a proposed rule to revise the primary NAAQS for oxides of nitrogen as measured by NO_2 to provide requisite protection to public health. The Region proposed the modified Chukchi draft permit and accompanying statement of basis on January 8, 2010. One month later, on February 9, 2010, the Administrator published the final 1–hour NO_2 NAAQS rule in the Federal Register, setting the new 1–hour NO_2 NAAQS at 100 ppb. Eight days later, on February 17, 2010, the public comment period on the modified Chukchi draft permit ended, and the Region proposed the Beaufort draft permit and accompanying statement of basis. The public comment period for the Beaufort draft permit ended on March 22, 2010. The Region issued the Chukchi and Beaufort Permits on March 31, 2010, and

April 9, 2010, respectively. The Final Rule became effective on April 12, 2010.

* * * The Region's adherence to prior Board precedent stating that compliance with the NAAQS is sufficient to demonstrate compliance with the Executive Order is misplaced. In the context of PSD permit challenges, the Region correctly states that the Board has accepted compliance with the NAAQS as sufficient to demonstrate that emissions from a proposed facility will not have disproportionately high and adverse human health or environmental effects on a minority or low-income population. However, the Region ignores the unusual context of this case, as well as the reasons that underlie the Board's precedent of looking in part to NAAQS compliance to satisfy the Executive Order.

The cases the Region cites as support for its decisions in the Chukchi and Beaufort Permits, in which the Board upheld a permit issuer's environmental justice analysis based on demonstrated compliance with the NAAQS, do not support the Region's position in this case. First and foremost, in each of the cases the Region cites, no party argued that a later-in-time standard had been proposed or finalized prior to the permit issuer's decision, and thus application of the then-effective standard was not an issue raised in any of the petitions. In addition, in each of the cases cited, the permit issuer provided some analysis or record evidence to demonstrate compliance with the Executive Order that the Board could look to in evaluating petitioners' claims regarding environmental justice. Thus, the cases the Region cites to support its argument that compliance with the then-applicable NAAQS also indicates de facto compliance with the Executive Order are all distinguishable from the Petitions at issue here. Further, the Region's arguments belie the basis upon which the Board relies on the Agency's NAAQS decisions.

The Agency sets the NAAQS using technical and scientific expertise, ensuring that the primary NAAQS protects the public health with an adequate margin of safety.

* * * The Board's concerns in this case lie with the Region's stated reliance on its demonstration of compliance with the NAAQS in effect at the time of the Permits' issuance despite the fact that the Administrator had finalized the new 1–hour NO_2 NAAQS prior to the issuance of the Permits, and thus the Administrator had already concluded, prior to the issuance of the Permits, that the annual NO_2 NAAQS alone did not provide requisite protection of the public health. Despite the Administrator's unequivocal determination, made prior to the issuance of either final Permit, that the annual NO_2 NAAQS alone was not requisite to protect the public health with an adequate margin of safety, the Region nonetheless solely relies on compliance with the then-applicable annual NO_2 NAAQS to demonstrate that Alaska Natives living in North Slope communities will not experience disproportionately high and adverse human health or environmental effects.

* * * The Region does not address the 1–hour NO_2 NAAQS Final Rule, which was published in the Federal Register on February 9, 2010, in the Chukchi Response to Comments. The Region's environmental justice analysis states in relevant part:

> EPA has determined that this permitting action will not have disproportionately high and adverse human health or environmental effects on minority or low-income populations because it does not affect the level of protection to human health or the environment. * * * [T]he final permit is designed to meet the requirements of the CAA. The emission limits in the permit are expected to curb air pollution sufficiently so that air quality in the region continues to attain the applicable NAAQS. *The level of the NAAQS is set low enough to protect public health, including sensitive individuals, with an adequate margin of safety. Numerous health studies and comments from experts and the public are used in determining the NAAQS level that will be protective of public health. After the level of a NAAQS is set, compliance with the NAAQS is used to assess health impacts.* A modeled impact less than the NAAQS indicates that public health is protected, at least for the particular pollutant addressed by the NAAQS. Objections to the NAAQS themselves must be addressed during the NAAQS review process, which occurs every few years.

The italicized portions of the Region's analysis are apparently intended to support the Region's decision to rely on attainment of the "applicable NAAQS," in other words the then-current annual NO_2 standard, and to demonstrate that the population of the North Slope will not experience disproportionately high and adverse human health or environmental effects due to exposure to unhealthy levels of NO_2. However, these statements in support of the Region's reliance on the NO_2 NAAQS effective prior to April 12, 2010, are directly contravened by the preamble to the final rule supplementing the annual NO_2 standard with the 1–hour NO_2 standard.

In multiple parts of the preamble, the Administrator makes clear that since the last review of the NO_2 NAAQS in 1996, substantial new evidence and insight into the relationship between NO_2 exposure and health effects has developed. For example, the Final Rule states that "epidemiologic evidence has grown substantially" with the addition of several different types of studies and that, as a result, "[t]his body of evidence focuses the current review on NO_2-related respiratory effects at lower ambient and exposure concentrations than considered in the previous review." With respect to the adequacy of the current standard, presented as part of the rationale for the final decision to revise the primary NO_2 NAAQS, the Administrator concludes that "[g]iven the * * * consideration of the evidence, particularly the epidemiologic studies reporting NO_2-associated health effects in locations that meet the current standard, * * * the scientific evidence calls into question the adequacy of the current standard to protect public health." In summarizing the final decisions with respect to revising the NO_2 primary NAAQS and explaining the Administrator's rationale, the preamble to the Final Rule states:

> In addition to setting a new 1-hour standard, the Administrator retains the current annual standard with a level of 53 ppb. The new 1-hour standard, in combination with the annual standard, will provide protection for susceptible groups against adverse respiratory health effects associated with short-term exposures to NO_2 and effects potentially associated with long-term exposures to NO_2.

Nowhere in the record before the Board does the Region acknowledge or provide a rationale for why it reached a determination about NO_2 health effects that is inconsistent with the Administrator's findings. The scientific evidence informing the development of the supplemental 1-hour NO_2 standard was available to the public at the time the 1-hour NO_2 standard was proposed on July 15, 2009, more than eight months prior to the issuance of either permit. Yet the Region relied on compliance with the outdated science, embodied in the then-current NO_2 NAAQS, at the time the Permits were finalized to support its determination that the Alaska Native population would not experience disproportionately high and adverse human health or environmental effects and conducted no further environmental justice analysis. The Board cannot condone the Region's failure to account for the updated scientific and technical reviews that accompanied the publication of the proposed and final 1-hour NO_2 NAAQS when the Region considered environmental justice issues pursuant to the Executive Order. Given these facts, the Board concludes that the Region clearly erred in relying on compliance with the NO_2 NAAQS effective when the Chukchi and Beaufort Permits were issued to demonstrate that its environmental justice analysis is adequate. The Region's sole reliance on attainment of the NO_2 NAAQS in effect prior to April 12, 2010, to demonstrate that the Permits sufficiently complied with the Executive Order is clearly erroneous in light of the fact that the Administrator had already both proposed, and later finalized, a new, more stringent standard prior to the issuance of the Chukchi and Beaufort Permits in which the Administrator determined that the body of evidence supporting the existing annual NO_2 NAAQS was outdated and that the newer data indicated that the standard was no longer adequate to protect public health.

VII. *ORDER*

In summary, the Board concludes that the Region clearly erred * * * in the limited scope of its analysis of the impact of NO_2 emissions on Alaska Native "environmental justice" communities located in the affected area. The Board concludes that the Region did not include in the administrative record an adequate explanation of its determination of when Frontier Discoverer becomes and ceases to be an OCS source in light of the statutory terms and the criteria set forth in 40 C.F.R. § 55.2 and remands the Chukchi and Beaufort Permits to the Region.

With respect to the environmental justice analysis, the Board concludes that the Region clearly erred when it relied solely on demonstrated compliance with the then-existing annual NO_2 NAAQS as sufficient to find that the Alaska Native population would not experience disproportionately high and adverse human health or environmental effects from the permitted activity. The Region's reliance solely on compliance with the annual NO_2 standard when it issued the Chukchi and Beaufort Permits on March 31 and April 9, 2010, was clearly erroneous given that the Administrator proposed a rule, published in the Federal Register on July 15, 2009, which made available updated scientific evidence supporting the Administrator's proposal to supplement the annual NO_2 NAAQS with a 1–hour NO_2 NAAQS. The Administrator concluded that the annual NO_2 NAAQS alone did not provide requisite protection of public health and established a supplemental 1–hour NO_2 NAAQS in a final rule published in the Federal Register on February 9, 2010, several weeks prior to the Region issuing the Chukchi and Beaufort Permits. Having found clear error in these aspects of the Region's decisions, the Board remands both the Chukchi and Beaufort Permits to the Region.

NOTES

1. **Where Are We? The Administrative Law Aspects of Permit Appeals.** As noted, this review of Shell's offshore drilling permits occurred before the Environmental Appeals Board, or EAB. The EAB is a part of the EPA, and hence this case was the result of an *administrative agency appeal* of the region's—here, EPA Region 10's—initial decisions on the two PSD permits. After completing the administrative appeals process, challengers can also appeal to federal court, as the *Alaska Department of Environmental Conservation v. EPA* case made clear. Indeed, as you may have learned in Administrative Law, an avenue to federal court is deemed necessary to prevent administrative agencies, housed within the Executive Branch, from violating the U.S. Constitution's separation of powers principles.

2. **NAAQS and Environmental Justice.** What is the EPA's standard view regarding the relationship between the Clean Air Act's NAAQS and compliance with the Environmental Justice Executive Order? Why didn't that view work in this case? What was the significance of the EPA's revision of the NO_2 NAAQS as these permits were being issued?

3. **Environmental Law Offshore.** While it is often easy to forget about the oceans in an initial overview of environmental law, it is important to remember that most of the major federal statutes apply at sea as well as on land, at least in some respects. For example, in Chapter 3 we saw that the National Marine Fisheries Service has delegated authority under the Endangered Species Act to list ocean species for protection under the Act, and we examined how sea turtles have been the subject of international protections for species through international trade regulations. The Clean Water Act, as we'll see in Chapter 5, also extends to the ocean. CERCLA can apply to marine releases of hazardous substances, although marine oil spills are largely governed through the Oil Pollution Act of 1990, 33 U.S.C. §§ 2701 to 2762.

As this case suggests, offshore oil drilling operations are subject to the Clean Air Act. Why? Why would drilling operations result in the emission of air pollutants? NOTE: Offshore oil drilling operations also need permits issued through the Outer Continental Shelf Lands Act (OCSLA), 43 U.S.C. §§ 1331 to 1356, and almost always need Clean Water Act permits, as well. Moreover, the involvement of federal agencies in such permitting will also trigger NEPA, as discussed in Chapter 2.

4. **Shell's Alaska Permits and the BP Oil Disaster in the Gulf of Mexico.** Notice that the EAB notes that Shell's permits were effectively put on hold in June 2010. Shell's permits for offshore oil construction got caught in the regulatory aftermath of the BP *Deepwater Horizon* blowout and oil spill that started in April 2010 and lasted through most of the summer of 2010.

* * *

2. Regional Haze

The second part of the PSD program in attainment areas, added through amendments in 1977 and 1990, addresses ***visibility protection***. Most of these provisions focus on Class I areas, with Congress declaring "as a national goal the prevention of any future, and the remedying of any existing, impairment of visibility in mandatory class I federal areas which impairment results from manmade air pollution." CAA § 169A(a)(1), 42 U.S.C. § 7491(a)(1). After studies by the Secretary of the Interior and the EPA to identify Federal Class I areas "where visibility is an important value in the area" and "methods for preventing and remedying such manmade air pollution and resulting visibility impairment," CAA § 169A(a)(2), (3), 42 U.S.C. § 7491(a)(2), (3), the EPA was required to promulgate visibility regulations that would assure "reasonable progress" toward meeting the visibility goal. CAA § 169A(a)(4), 42 U.S.C. § 7491(a)(4). Relevant states then had to revise their SIPs to implement these regulations. CAA § 169A(b), 42 U.S.C. § 7491(b).

As part of their SIP revisions, states had to require existing major stationary sources that were less than 15 years old as of August 7, 1977, to adhere to emissions standards based on the ***best available retrofit technology*** **(BART)**. CAA § 169A(b)(1)(A), 42 U.S.C. § 7491(b)(1)(A). This was the first time that Congress had imposed a technology-based emissions standard on *existing* stationary sources, reducing states' flexibility in regulating those sources. In determining the BART standards, states or the EPA "take into consideration the costs of compliance, the energy and non-air quality environmental impacts of compliance, any existing pollution control technology in use at the source, the remaining useful life of the source, and the degree of improvement in visibility which may reasonably be anticipated to result from the use of such technology * * *." CAA § 169A(g)(2), 42 U.S.C. § 7491(g)(2). A ***"major stationary source"*** for BART purposes includes all of the specifically designated "major emitting facilities" for the PSD program—fossil-fuel fired steam electric plants of more than 250 million British thermal units per hour heat input, and so forth—but only if the particular source has the potential to emit 250 tons or more of any pollutant. CAA § 169A(g)(7), 42 U.S.C. § 7491(g)(7). (Recall that these kinds of sources qualify as new "major emitting facilities" for PSD permit purposes if they have the potential to discharge *100* tons or more of any pollutant.)

Thus, to summarize emissions limitations so far:

TABLE 4–3: EMISSIONS STANDARDS FOR CRITERIA AIR POLLUTANTS		
	NEW MAJOR STATIONARY SOURCES	EXISTING MAJOR STATIONARY SOURCES
NONATTAINMENT AREA: PART D:	Major Source = 100 tons/year of pollutants: LAER + OFFSETS + PERMIT (incorporated into Title V permitting)	Major Source = 100 tons/year pollutants: RACT + PERMIT (incorporated into Title V permitting)
ATTAINMENT/ UNCLASSIFIABLE AREA: PSD PROGRAM:	Major Emitting Facility = 250 tons/year of pollutants or 100 tons/year and source is in one of the 26 special categories: BACT + PERMIT	NOT APPLICABLE
REGIONAL HAZE:	NOT APPLICABLE	Major Source = 250 tons/year pollutants and source is in one of the 26 special categories: BART + PERMIT
TITLE V:	Major Source = 100 tons/year of pollutants: NSPS + PERMIT	Major Source = 100 tons/year of pollutants: PERMIT

The 1990 amendments to the visibility protection provisions established funding for the EPA and the National Park Service to study progress in visibility attainment in Class I areas and require the EPA to assess progress toward the visibility goal every five years. CAA § 169B(a), (b), 42 U.S.C. § 7492(a), (b). In addition, Congress authorized the EPA to establish ***visibility transport regions***, with governing ***visibility transport commissions***, when interstate transportation of air pollutants "contributes significantly" to visibility impairment in a Class I region. CAA § 169B(c), 42 U.S.C. § 7492(c). Finally, Congress ordered the EPA to establish a visibility transport commission for the Grand Canyon National Park. CAA § 169B(f), 42 U.S.C. § 7492(f).

D. NEW SOURCE REVIEW AND MODIFIED STATIONARY SOURCES

As the previous two sections have made clear, a stationary source's status as "new" or "existing" can make a significant difference regarding the stringency of the emissions standards to which it is subject. This status is rarely problematic for brand new sources or long-existing, unchanged sources. However, a stationary source is also considered "new" for purposes of the Clean Air Act if "the construction *or modification* [of that source] commenced after the publication of regulations * * * prescribing" an NSPS under section 111 of the Act. CAA § 111(a)(2), 42 U.S.C. § 7411(a)(2) (emphasis added).

Thus, in both the PSD and new source provisions of the Clean Air Act, ***modified sources*** are subject to the same emissions controls as new sources. Section 111 defines "***modification***" to be "any physical change in, or change in the method of operation of, a stationary source which increases the amount of any air pollutant emitted by such source or which results in the emission of any air pollutant not previously emitted." CAA § 111(a)(4), 42 U.S.C. § 7411(a)(4). The EPA's regulations define "modification" in essentially the same way. 40 C.F.R. § 60.14(a).

The process of determining whether an existing source has undergone sufficient modifications to be considered a modified source is known as ***new source review*** **(NSR).** Congress included the NSR requirement to ensure that as older stationary sources of air pollutants were remodeled, rebuilt, expanded, or upgraded, they would incorporate more stringent air pollution control technology as part of the rebuilding process.

However, not every change in a source's operation counts as a "modification" that triggers the NSR requirements. For example, the EPA has long excluded from NSR ***routine maintenance, repair, and replacement*** (the **RMRR** exception), increases in production rate, and increases in the hours of operation. 40 C.F.R. § 60.14(e) (NSPS program); 40 C.F.R. § 52.21(b)(2)(iii) (PSD program). Drawing the line between RMRR and "modifications" that trigger the NSR requirements has not always been easy, but the courts have generally held that an NSR "modification" requires both a physical change in the facility and in increase in emissions. *See Wisconsin Electric Power Co. v. Reilly*, 893 F.2d 901 (7th Cir. 1990).

Given some of the confusions surrounding NSR and the potential expense for the utility industry, the George W. Bush Administration made regulatory reform of the NSR process a priority. On December 31, 2002, the EPA issued its rules regarding the **RMRR** exclusion. 67 Fed. Reg. 80,290 (Dec. 31, 2002). These rules changed the existing case-by-case, factor-based approach to assessing whether an NSR-triggering "modification" has occurred. Two changes in the new rules were particularly important: (1) the annual maintenance, repair, and replacement allowance; and (2) the ***equipment replacement provision*** **(ERP).**

The annual maintenance, repair, and replacement allowance provisions excluded capital expenditures that were "relatively small" compared to the replacement cost of the facility—less than 20% of that replacement cost—from the new source review requirements. 67 Fed. Reg. at 80, 294. The ERP, in turn,

> specifies that the replacement of components of a process unit with identical components or their functional equivalents will come within the scope of the [RMRR] exclusion, provided the cost of replacing the component falls below 20% of the replacement value of the process unit of which the component is a part, the replacement does not change the unit's basic design parameters, and the unit continues to meet enforceable emission and operational limitations.

68 Fed. Reg. 61,248, 61,251 (Oct. 27, 2003).

By July 2003, the EPA had received petitions to reconsider its RMRR rules from most of the northeastern states (Connecticut, Maine, Maryland, Massachusetts, New Hampshire, New Jersey, New York, Pennsylvania, Rhode Island, and Vermont), California's South Coast Air Quality Management District, the Natural Resources Defense Council, Earthjustice, the Clean Air Task Force, Environmental Defense, Newmont Mining Corp., the National Cattlemen's Beef Association, and the National Mining Association. The EPA addressed most of these petitions in early November 2003, clarifying that sources can "use an actual-to-projected-actual applicability test to determine whether installing a replacement unit results in a significant emissions increase," that replacement units include reconstructed units, and that sources receive no emissions reduction credit for emissions reductions attributable to the shutdown of a replaced emissions unit. 68 Fed. Reg. 63,021, 63,024 (Nov. 7, 2003). Otherwise, however, the EPA left the amended new source rules in place.

The states immediately challenged the rules in the D.C. Circuit. In *New York v. U.S. EPA*, 413 F.3d 3 (D.C. Cir. 2005), the D.C. Circuit upheld parts of the rules and rejected parts of the rules. In particular, the court upheld the EPA's baseline calculation regulations, its demand growth exclusion, and its use of the "bubble concept" for calculating emissions. However, the court disallowed the EPA's exceptions for sources that employ environmentally helpful "clean units" and/or pollution control projects, and it concluded that the EPA had not adequately explained the new recordkeeping and reporting requirements. In June 2007, the EPA finally amended its 2002 NSR regulations to remove the vacated "clean unit" and pollution control project exceptions. EPA, *Prevention of Significant Deterioration (PSD) and Nonattainment New Source Review (NSR): Removal of Vacated Elements*, 72 Fed. Reg. 32526 (June 13, 2007).

The ERP had a slightly different fate. The EPA issued its final ERP rule in October 2003. 68 Fed. Reg. 61,248 (Oct. 27, 2003). The states immediately challenged this rule in the D.C. Circuit, which stayed the rule pending litigation. *New York v. EPA*, No. 03–1380 (D.C. Cir. 2003). Less than a year later, the EPA offered to reconsider the ERP. 69 Fed. Reg. 40,278 (July 1, 2004). Hearings and comments related to this reconsideration continued through the end of 2004, but the EPA denied the request for reconsideration in June 2005. EPA, *Prevention of Significant Deterioration (PSD) and Nonattainment New Source Review (NSR): Equipment Replacement Provision of the Routine Maintenance, Repair, and Replace-*

ment Exclusion: Reconsideration, *70 Fed. Reg. 33,838, 33,838 (June 10, 2005). About nine months later, the D.C. Circuit vacated the ERP provisions of the 2002 rulemaking, concluding that the 20% annual allowance violated the Clean Air Act because there is no* de minimis *exception to the NSR requirements.* New York v. EPA, *443 F.3d 880 (D.C. Cir. 2006).*

Meanwhile, in the midst of all of this new rulemaking and litigation related to the 2002 regulations, litigation was still ongoing regarding the Clinton Administration's NSR enforcement efforts under the old (1980) regulations. This litigation often involved the issue of how to assess whether a "modification" had occurred and whether the EPA had to treat "modification" the same for both the PSD and the NSPS NSR programs. In 2007, the Supreme Court addressed the relationship of the two NSR programs in the following case.

ENVIRONMENTAL DEFENSE v. DUKE ENERGY CORPORATION

549 U.S. 561 (2007).

SOUTER, J., delivered the opinion of the Court, in which ROBERTS, C. J., and STEVENS, SCALIA, KENNEDY, GINSBURG, BREYER, and ALITO, JJ., joined, and in which THOMAS, J., joined as to all but Part III–A.

In the 1970s, Congress added two air pollution control schemes to the Clean Air Act: New Source Performance Standards (NSPS) and Prevention of Significant Deterioration (PSD), each of them covering modified, as well as new, stationary sources of air pollution. The NSPS provisions define the term "modification," 42 U.S.C. § 7411(a)(4), while the PSD provisions use that word "as defined in" NSPS, § 7479(2)(C). The Court of Appeals concluded that the statute requires the Environmental Protection Agency (EPA) to conform its PSD regulations on "modification" to their NSPS counterparts, and that EPA's 1980 PSD regulations can be given this conforming construction. * * *

I

The Clean Air Amendments of 1970, 84 Stat. 1676, broadened federal authority to combat air pollution, see *Chevron U.S.A. Inc. v. Natural Resources Defense Council, Inc.,* 467 U.S. 837, 845–846 (1984), and directed EPA to devise National Ambient Air Quality Standards (NAAQS) limiting various pollutants, which the States were obliged to implement and enforce, 42 U.S.C. §§ 7409, 7410. The amendments dealing with NSPS authorized EPA to require operators of stationary sources of air pollutants to use the best technology for limiting pollution, both in newly constructed sources and those undergoing "modification," 42 U.S.C. § 7411(a)(2). Section 111(a) of the 1970 amendments defined this term within the NSPS scheme as "any physical change in, or change in the method of operation of, a stationary source which increases the amount of any air pollutant emitted by such source or which results in the emission of any air pollutant not previously emitted," 42 U.S.C. § 7411(a)(4).

EPA's 1975 regulations implementing NSPS provided generally that "any physical or operational change to an existing facility which results in an increase in the emission rate to the atmosphere of any pollutant to which a standard applies shall be considered a modification within the meaning of [S]ection 111." 40 CFR § 60.14(a) (1976). Especially significant here is the identification of an NSPS "modification" as a change that "increase[s] . . . the emission rate," which "shall be expressed as kg/hr of any pollutant discharged into the atmosphere." § 60.14(b).

NSPS, however, did too little to "achiev[e] the ambitious goals of the 1970 Amendments," R. BELDEN, CLEAN AIR ACT 7 (2001) (hereinafter BELDEN), and the Clean Air Act Amendments of 1977, 91 Stat. 685, included the PSD provisions, which aimed at giving added protection to air quality in certain parts of the country "notwithstanding attainment and maintenance of" the NAAQS. 42 U.S.C. § 7470(1). The 1977 amendments required a PSD permit before a "major emitting facility" could be "constructed" in an area covered by the scheme. § 7475(a). As originally enacted, PSD applied only to newly constructed sources, but soon a technical amendment added the following subparagraph: "The term 'construction' when used in connection with any source or facility, includes the modification (as defined in [S]ection 111(a)) of any source or facility." 42 U.S.C. § 7479(2)(C). In other words, the "construction" requiring a PSD permit under the statute was made to include (though it was not limited to) a "modification" as defined in the statutory NSPS provisions.

In 1980, EPA issued PSD regulations, which "limited the application of [PSD] review" of modified sources to instances of " 'major' modificatio[n]," BELDEN 46, defined as "any physical change in or change in the method of operation of a major stationary source that would result in a significant net emissions increase of any pollutant subject to regulation under the Act." 40 CFR § 51.166(b)(2)(i) (1987). Further regulations in turn addressed various elements of this definition, three of which are to the point here. First, the regulations specified that an operational change consisting merely of "[a]n increase in the hours of operation or in the production rate" would not generally constitute a "physical change or change in the method of operation." § 51.166(b)(2)(iii)(*f*). For purposes of a PSD permit, that is, such an operational change would not amount to a "modification" as the Act defines it. Second, the PSD regulations defined a "net emissions increase" as "[a]ny increase in actual emissions from a particular physical change or change in the method of operation," net of other contemporaneous "increases and decreases in actual emissions at the source." § 51.166(b)(3). "Actual emissions" were defined to "equal the average rate, in tons per year, at which the unit actually emitted the pollutant during a two-year period which precedes the particular date and which is representative of normal source operation." § 51.166(b)(21)(ii). "[A]ctual emissions" were to be "calculated using the unit's actual operating hours [and] production rates." *Ibid.* Third, the term "significant" was defined as "a rate of emissions that would equal or exceed" one or another enumerated threshold, each expressed in "tons per year." § 51.166(b)(23)(i).

It would be bold to try to synthesize these statutory and regulatory provisions in a concise paragraph, but three points are relatively clear about the regime that covers this case:

(a) The Act defines modification of a stationary source of a pollutant as a physical change to it, or a change in the method of its operation, that increases the amount of a pollutant discharged or emits a new one.

(b) EPA's NSPS regulations require a source to use the best available pollution-limiting technology only when a modification would increase the rate of discharge of pollutants measured in kilograms per hour.

(c) EPA's 1980 PSD regulations require a permit for a modification (with the same statutory definition) only when it is a major one and only when it would increase the actual annual emission of a pollutant above the actual average for the two prior years.

The Court of Appeals held that Congress's provision defining a PSD modification by reference to an NSPS modification caught not only the statutory NSPS definition, but also whatever regulatory gloss EPA puts on that definition at any given time (for the purposes of the best technology requirement). When, therefore, EPA's PSD regulations specify the "change" that amounts to a "major modification" requiring a PSD permit, they must measure an increase in "the amount of any air pollutant emitted," 42 U.S.C. § 7411(a)(4), in terms of the hourly rate of discharge, just the way NSPS regulations do. Petitioners and the United States say, on the contrary, that when EPA addresses the object of the PSD scheme it is free to put a different regulatory interpretation on the common statutory core of "modification," by measuring increased emission not in terms of hourly rate but by the actual, annual discharge of a pollutant that will follow the modification, regardless of rate per hour. This disagreement is the nub of the case.

II

Respondent Duke Energy Corporation runs 30 coal-fired electric generating units at eight plants in North and South Carolina. The units were placed in service between 1940 and 1975, and each includes a boiler containing thousands of steel tubes arranged in sets. Between 1988 and 2000, Duke replaced or redesigned 29 tube assemblies in order to extend the life of the units and allow them to run longer each day.

The United States filed this action in 2000, claiming, among other things, that Duke violated the PSD provisions by doing this work without permits. Environmental Defense, North Carolina Sierra Club, and North Carolina Public Interest Research Group Citizen Lobby/ Education Fund intervened as plaintiffs and filed a complaint charging similar violations.

Duke moved for summary judgment, one of its positions being that none of the projects was a "major modification" requiring a PSD permit because none increased hourly rates of emissions. The District Court agreed with Duke's reading of the 1980 PSD regulations. * * *

* * * The Court of Appeals for the Fourth Circuit affirmed, "albeit for somewhat different reasons." "[T]he language and various interpretations of the PSD regulations ... are largely irrelevant to the proper analysis of this case," reasoned the Court of Appeals, "because Congress' decision to create identical statutory definitions of the term 'modification'" in the NSPS and PSD provisions of the Clean Air Act "has affirmatively mandated that this term be interpreted identically" in the regulations promulgated under those provisions. * * *

* * * We granted the petition for certiorari brought by intervenor-plaintiffs, and now vacate.

III

* * * A

In applying the 1980 PSD regulations to Duke's conduct, the Court of Appeals thought that, by defining the term "modification" identically in its NSPS and PSD provisions, the Act required EPA to conform its PSD interpretation of that definition to any such interpretation it reasonably adhered to under NSPS. But principles of statutory construction are not so rigid. Although we presume that the same term has the same meaning when it occurs here and there in a single statute, the Court of Appeals mischaracterized that presumption as "effectively irrebuttable." We also understand that "[m]ost words have different shades of meaning and consequently may be variously construed, not only when they occur in different statutes, but when used more than once in the same statute or even in the same section." *Atlantic Cleaners & Dyers, Inc. v. United States,* 286 U.S. 427, 433 (1932). Thus, the "natural presumption that identical words used in different parts of the same act are intended to have the same meaning ... is not rigid and readily yields whenever there is such variation in the connection in which the words are used as reasonably to warrant the conclusion that they were employed in different parts of the act with different intent." *Ibid.* A given term in the same statute may take on distinct characters from association with distinct statutory objects calling for different implementation strategies.

The point is the same even when the terms share a common statutory definition, if it is general enough * * *. * * * Context counts.

It is true that the Clean Air Act did not merely repeat the term "modification" or the same definition of that word in its NSPS and PSD sections; the PSD language referred back to the section defining "modification" for NSPS purposes. 42 U.S.C. § 7479(2)(C). However, nothing in the text or the legislative history of the technical amendments that added the cross-reference to NSPS suggests that Congress had details of regulatory implementation in mind when it imposed PSD requirements on modified sources; the cross-reference alone is certainly no unambiguous congressional code for eliminating the customary agency discretion to resolve questions about a statutory definition by looking to the surroundings of the defined term, where it occurs. Absent any iron rule to ignore the reasons for regulating PSD and NSPS "modifications" differently, EPA's construction need do no more than fall within the limits of what is reasonable, as set by the Act's common definition.

B

The Court of Appeals's reasoning that the PSD regulations must conform to their NSPS counterparts led the court to read those PSD regulations in a way that seems to us too far a stretch for the language used. The 1980 PSD regulations on "modification" simply cannot be taken to track the agency's regulatory definition under the NSPS.

* * * We think [the Court of Appeals'] understanding of the 1980 PSD regulations makes the mistake of overlooking the difference between the two separate components of the regulatory definition of "major modification": "[1] any physical change in or change in the method of operation of a major stationary source that [2] would result in a significant net emissions increase of any pollutant subject to regulation under the Act." § 51.166(b)(2)(i). The exclusion of "increase in ... hours ... or ... production rate," § 51.166(b)(2)(iii)(*f*), speaks to the first of these components ("physical change ... or change in ... method," § 51.166(b)(2)(i)), but not to the second ("significant net emissions increase," *ibid.*). As the preamble to the 1980 PSD regulations explains, forcing companies to obtain a PSD permit before they could simply adjust operating hours "would severely and unduly hamper the ability of any company to take advantage of favorable market conditions." In other words, a mere increase in the hours of operation, standing alone, is not a "physical change or change in the method of operation." 40 CFR § 51.166(b)(2)(iii).

* * * In sum, the text of the 1980 PSD regulations on "modification" doomed the Court of Appeals's attempt to equate those regulations with their NSPS counterpart. * * *

IV

Finally, Duke assumes for argument that the Act and the 1980 regulations may authorize EPA to construe a PSD "modification" as it has done, but it charges that the agency has taken inconsistent positions and is now "retroactively targeting twenty years of accepted practice." This claim, too, has not been tackled by the District Court or the Court of Appeals; to the extent it is not procedurally foreclosed, Duke may press it on remand.

* * *

The judgment of the Court of Appeals is vacated, and the case is remanded for further proceedings consistent with this opinion.

It is so ordered.

JUSTICE THOMAS, concurring in part.

I join all but Part III–A of the Court's opinion. I write separately to note my disagreement with the dicta in that portion of the opinion, which states that the statutory cross-reference does not mandate a singular regulatory construction.

The Prevention of Significant Deterioration (PSD) statute explicitly links the definition of the term "modification" to that term's definition in the New Source Performance Standard (NSPS) statute:

> "The term 'construction' when used in connection with any source or facility, includes the modification (as defined in section 7411(a) of this title) of any source or facility."

42 U.S.C. § 7479(2)(C).

Section 7411(a) contains the NSPS definition of "modification," which the parties agree is the relevant statutory definition of the term for both PSD and NSPS. Because of the cross-reference, the definitions of "modification" in PSD and NSPS are one and the same. The term "modification" therefore has the same meaning despite contextual variations in the two admittedly different statutory schemes. Congress' explicit linkage of PSD's definition of "modification" to NSPS' prevents the Environmental Protection Agency (EPA) from adopting differing regulatory definitions of "modification" for PSD and NSPS.

* * * Even if the cross-reference were merely the equivalent of repeating the words of the definition, we must still apply our usual presumption that the same words repeated in different parts of the same statute have the same meaning. That presumption has not been overcome here. While the broadly stated regulatory goals of PSD and NSPS differ, these contextual differences do not compel different definitions of "modification." * * * EPA demonstrated as much when it recently proposed regulations that would unify the regulatory definitions of "modification." See 70 Fed. Reg. 61083, n. 3 (2005) (terming the proposal "an appropriate exercise of our discretion" and stating that the unified definition better serves PSD's goals).

The majority opinion does little to overcome the presumption that the same words, when repeated, carry the same meaning. Instead, it explains that this Court's cases do not compel identical language to be interpreted identically in all situations. Granting that point, the majority still has the burden of stating why our general presumption does not control the outcome here. It has not done so.

NOTES

1. **So, Who Won?** Who won this case, Environmental Defense or Duke Energy? What are the consequences for the government's enforcement action against Duke Energy? What was the EPA's position in this case? Do we yet

know whether Duke Energy has triggered the new source review provisions? Why or why not? What will be the effect of the EPA's new regulations, mentioned in Justice Thomas' concurrence?

2. **Interpreting "Modification."** Whose statutory construction argument do you find most convincing, the majority's or Justice Thomas'? Why? Should it matter that the PSD provisions actually cross-reference the NSPS provisions' definition of "modification," instead of merely repeating the word "modification"? Why or why not? Should it matter that Congress defined "major source" in several places in the statute for different purposes, but did not bother to re-define "modification"? Why or why not? Why, despite his disagreement with the majority, is Justice Thomas's opinion a concurring opinion instead of a dissenting opinion?

3. ***Chevron* Deference?** Note that the majority cites to *Chevron*. Is this decision based on *Chevron* deference? Why or why not? Should *Chevron* deference be relevant in this situation? Why or why not?

4. **What Triggers New Source Review?** According to the majority and the EPA, when are existing sources subject to new source review? Let's say that a power plant increases its hours of operation to keep up with increasing demand for electricity. As a result, its total annual emissions of pollutants increase. Is the power plant subject to new source review under the NSPS provisions? Why or why not? Is it subject to new source review under the PSD provisions? Why or why not?

5. **Predicting the Supreme Court.** The U.S. Supreme Court issued its opinion in *Duke Energy* the same day that it issued its opinion in *Massachusetts v. EPA*, presented in Part II of this chapter in the discussion of criteria pollutants. *Massachusetts v. EPA* split the Court, if you recall. Why is *Duke Energy* a nearly unanimous decision?

6. **New Source Review Enforcement under the Clinton and George W. Bush Administrations.** Toward the end of the Clinton Administration, the EPA and the U.S. Department of Justice began a concerted effort to force aging power plants—some of the nation's biggest new source review violators—to comply with the new source review requirements. *Duke Energy* emerged from those enforcement efforts.

However, when President George W. Bush took office in January 2001, these enforcement priorities changed. As a result, as of October 2004, the EPA had finalized new source review settlements with only seven companies, representing 74 power-generating units. "CITGO, DOJ Settle NSR Violations; First Consent Decree in a Year," 19:38 *Octane Week*, 2004 WLNR 19590927, at *1 (Oct. 11, 2004).

The 2002 NSR Reform regulations were part of the change in enforcement priorities. In all of its NSR rulemaking Federal Register notices, the EPA noted that the sources most affected by the NSR Reform rules include electric plants, petroleum refiners, industrial chemical manufacturers, natural gas producers and transporters, pulp and paper mills, auto manufacturers, and pharmaceutical companies—most of which have strong political lobbies. Many of the affected electric plants had been the targets of the Clinton Administration's increased enforcement efforts. At the end of September

2004, EPA Inspector General Nikki Tinsley issued a report concluding that the new NSR rules "have seriously hampered" the EPA's enforcement efforts against the power plants. "Bush NSR reforms harmed enforcement efforts," *Greenwire*, Oct. 1, 2004, at 1.

Nevertheless, the NSR settlements give concrete evidence of why the economics of new source review and upgrading pollution controls encourage power companies to continue to resist the imposition of new source review requirements. In October 2004, for example, the EPA settled with CITGO, which agreed to pay $3.6 million in civil penalties and $320 million to upgrade the air pollution controls at its facilities. *Id.* A year earlier, the EPA's settlement with ChevronTexaco required the company to spend $275 million for pollution control upgrades. "CITGO to spend $320 million on pollution upgrades," *Greenwire*, Oct. 1, 2004, at 1.

In 2007, just before the Supreme Court issued its opinion in *Duke Energy*, the EPA resumed filing NSR cases against electric utilities. Specifically, on March 12, 2007, it filed its first contested NSR case against Kentucky Utilities Co. with respect to alleged modifications made in 1997 at its E.W. Brown power plant in Mercer County, Kentucky. The agency then announced on March 28, 2007—five days before the Supreme Court decided *Duke Energy*—that it expected to file several more NSR challenges against electric utilities during the rest of 2007. Steven D. Cook, "EPA Preparing New Source Review Cases Against Utilities Lacking Modern Controls," 60 *Daily Environment* (BNA, Inc.), at A–1 (March 29, 2007).

7. **Calculating Emissions in New Source Review.** As the *Duke Energy* decision suggests, there are several ways to calculate whether physical changes in a stationary source will increase emissions and hence trigger the NSR requirements. How did the calculations differ in that case between the PSD and NSPS programs?

The EPA is still struggling with how to best calculate emissions increases. In 2005, for example, it proposed new emissions tests for Electric Generating Units. EPA, *Prevention of Significant Deterioration, Nonattainment New Source Review, and New Source Performance Standards: Emissions Test for Electric Generating Units*, 70 Fed. Reg. 61,081 (Oct. 20, 2005). In this proposed rule, the EPA intended to make the emissions test for the PSD and nonattainment programs the same as that for the NSPS program—that is, a comparison of the maximum hourly emissions achievable by the source over the last five years to the maximum hourly emissions achievable after the changes to the facility. *Id.* at 61,081. However, the EPA has recognized that several other tests are possible: (1) a comparison of maximum hourly emissions actually achieved (as opposed to achievable); (2) an output-based hourly emissions test; and (3) achievable or achieved emissions tests based on annual, rather than hourly, emissions. The difficulty in choosing among these tests is suggested by the fact that in May 2007, the EPA supplemented its October 2005 proposed rulemaking with a broader range of choices while simultaneously deciding that the output-based test should be used only as a means of calculating achievable or achieved emissions. EPA, *Supplemental Notice*, 72 Fed. Re. 26,202, 26,202 (May 8, 2007).

8. **Counting Emissions for New Source Review in the PSD Program.** NSR regulations have been potentially ambiguous because they refer to changes in a source's emissions—arguably, *any* change in the emissions of *any* air pollutant, regardless of whether that air pollutant is otherwise regulated under the Clean Air Act. Toward the end of the Bush Administration, the EPA interpreted its own regulations in a December 18, 2008 memorandum, then gave notice in the Federal Register that "[a]s of the date of the memorandum, EPA interprets this definition of 'regulated NSR pollutant' to exclude pollutants for which EPA regulations only require monitoring or reporting but include all pollutants subject to a provision in the Act or regulation adopted by EPA pursuant to the Act that requires actual control of emissions of that pollutant." 73 Fed. Reg. 80,300, 80,301 (Dec. 31, 2008). Nevertheless, with the EPA's recent regulation of emissions of carbon dioxide and other greenhouse gases, many sources will qualify for Clean Air Act regulation than has been true in the past—one reason that the EPA promulgated its Tailoring Rule, discussed earlier in this chapter in connection with *Massachusetts v. EPA*.

9. **New Source Review Regulations and the Change in Presidential Administration.** As *Environmental Defense v. Duke Energy Corp.* makes clear, new source review has been controversial—and subject to administration-by-administration changes—for some time. The transition from the Bush Administration to the Obama Administration was no different. The EPA keeps track of the status of the various new source review regulations at U.S. EPA, *New Source Review: Regulations and Standards*, http://www.epa.gov/nsr/actions.html. As the Bush Administration was leaving office, it published two new NSR regulations for the PSD program—the "aggregation" rule and the "flexible air permitting" rule—in addition to several earlier regulations, as Note 7 indicates. PSD & NSR: Aggregation and Project Netting, 74 Fed. Reg. 2376 (Jan. 15, 2009). In response to petitions for reconsideration, the Obama EPA stayed the effective date of these new regulations until May 18, 2009, in order to review them. On May 14, 2009, it extended that deadline to May 18, 2010. In late September 2009, the Obama Administration EPA finalized the flexible air permitting rule in essentially the same form as the Bush Administration EPA proposed it. Flexible Air Permitting Rule, 74 Fed. Reg. 51,418 (Oct. 6, 2009). The EPA proposed to revoke the aggregation rule in April 2010, 75 Fed. Reg. 19,567 (April 15, 2010), but as of early December 2011 had not yet repealed it.

In addition, on April 24, 2009, the Obama Administration's EPA granted several petitions to review three other aspects of the Bush Administration's NSR rules. These petitions cover the regulations governing fugitive emissions; the regulations governing the "reasonable possibility standard"; and the regulations governing the PM2.5 NSR Permitting Rule, which allowed "grandfathering" of certain facilities. The EPA formally repealed the PM2.5 rule in May 2011. 76 Fed. Reg. 28,646 (May 18, 2011). However, the current EPA has retained the 2007 regulation requiring recordkeeping if there is a "reasonable possibility" that the project will result in a net emissions increase.

The 2008 fugitive emissions rule required fugitive or escaping emissions to be included in determining whether a physical or operational change results in a major modification only for sources in certain industries. At the end of March 2010, the EPA stayed the fugitive emissions rule for 18 months, until the end of October 3, 2011. 75 Fed. Reg. 16,012 (March 31, 2010). In March 2011, the EPA issued an interim Fugitive Emissions Rule "to revert the treatment of fugitive emissions in applicability determinations to the approach that applied prior to the Fugitive Emissions Rule on an interim basis, while EPA completes the reconsideration." 76 Fed. Reg. 17,548, 17,551 (March 30, 2011). The EPA expected to finalize its reconsideration of the 2008 rule in October 2012. *Id.*

* * *

V. REGULATION OF HAZARDOUS AIR POLLUTANTS (HAPs)

A. HAZARDOUS AIR POLLUTANTS

1. Introduction

Criteria air pollutants are the common air pollutants emitted into the air from a variety of sources, which cumulatively have adverse health effects. In 1970, however, Congress was also concerned about ***hazardous air pollutants*** **(HAPs)**. These pollutants, also known as toxic air pollutants, generally create more acute and/or more severe health problems than the criteria air pollutants, although they are generally less pervasive in the air. Specifically, HAPs are air pollutants "which are known to be, or may reasonably be anticipated to be, carcinogenic, mutagenic, teratogenic, neurotoxic, which cause reproductive dysfunction, or which are acutely or chronically toxic" or which cause "adverse environmental effects whether through ambient concentrations, bioaccumulation, deposition, or otherwise * * *." CAA § 112(b)(2), 42 U.S.C. § 7412(b)(2).

As the EPA has graphically demonstrated (*see* Figure 4–16), HAPs derive from a variety of sources and reach humans and the environment through a variety of pathways. In addition, as Figure 4–17 shows, toxic pollutants emitted into the air can pollute a variety of media.

2. Establishing the HAP List

Congress dramatically altered the regulation of HAPs in the 1990 amendments to the Clean Air Act. Initially, in 1970, Congress established that the Administrator of the EPA would establish the list of HAPs on a health-based standard, much as the Administrator still establishes the list of criteria air pollutants. Specifically, the 1970 Act provided that "[t]he Administrator shall, within 90 days after December 31, 1970, publish (and shall from time to time thereafter revise) a list which includes each hazardous air pollutant for which he intends to establish an emission standard under this section." CAA § 112(b)(1)(A), 42 U.S.C. § 7412(b)(1)(A) (1982). Moreover:

> Within 180 days after the inclusion of any air pollutant in such list, the Administrator shall publish proposed regulations establishing emission standards for such pollutant together with a notice of a public hearing within thirty days. Not later than 180 days after such publication, the Administrator shall prescribe an emission standard for such pollutant, unless he finds, on the basis of information presented at such hearings, that such pollutant clearly is not a hazardous air pollutant. The Administrator shall establish any such standard at the level which in his judgment provides an ample margin of safety to protect the public health from such hazardous air pollutant.

CAA § 112(b)(1)(B), 42 U.S.C. § 7412(b)(1)(B) (1982).

Figure 4-17: Sources of Hazardous Air Pollutants
EPA diagram.

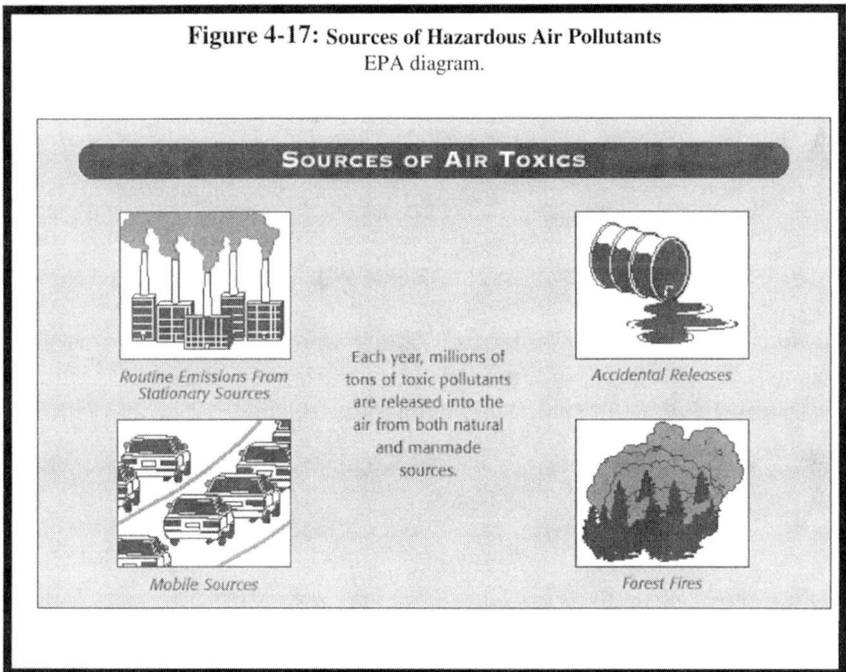

Nevertheless, the EPA's establishment of the list of HAPs was slow. As the Second Circuit recounted in 1989:

> From 1970 to the enactment of the Clean Air Act Amendments of 1977, the EPA listed only five pollutants: asbestos (1971), beryllium (1971), mercury (1971), vinyl chloride (1975), and benzene (1977). *See* 40 C.F.R. § 61.01 (1988). The House report on the 1977 amendments criticized the EPA for its preoccupation with criteria pollutants (regulated pursuant to Act §§ 108–110) and the paucity of its activity in regulating hazardous air pollutants pursuant to section 112. *See* H.R. REP. NO. 294, 95th Cong., 1st Sess. 36 (1977), U.S. Code Cong. & Admin. News 1977, p. 1077.

> The 1977 amendments included an "agency-forcing" provision which required the Administrator to decide whether to list arsenic, cadmium, and polycyclic organic matter within one year, and radioactive pollutants within two years, pursuant to Act §§ 108, 111 and/or 112. *See* Act § 122(a), 42 U.S.C. § 7422(a) (1982). From 1977 to 1983, nonetheless, the Administrator added only radionuclides (1979) and inorganic arsenic (1980) to the List. In November, 1983, then Administrator Ruckelshaus conceded at a Congressional hearing that "delays in implementing Section 112 have been substantial and, to a large extent, avoidable." * * * The Administrator told the subcommittee: "we believe we can complete, by the end of 1985, decisions for approximately 20 to 25 substances on the list of 37" that the EPA had identified as possible candidates for the List.

Natural Resources Defense Council, Inc. v. Thomas, 885 F.2d 1067, 1071 (2d Cir. 1989).

The reason for the EPA's delay in listing HAPs was simple: given the HAPs' toxic nature, the only adequate health-based emissions standard known was a zero emissions standard—*i.e.*, a complete prohibition on all HAP emissions. However, a complete ban on HAP emissions would have been practically unworkable for United States industry—worse than shutting down the automobile industry. As a result, in the 1990 amendments to section 112, Congress determined that, rather than leave the listing of HAPs to the EPA, Congress itself would establish a list of HAPs that the EPA had to regulate. CAA § 112(b)(1), 42 U.S.C. § 7412(b)(1). These amendments reflected two emerging themes in federal environmental law: increasing congressional micromanagement; and disgust with general agency foot-dragging under President Ronald Reagan's administration.

Congress's initial statutory list of HAPs contained 189 pollutants. You can view the original list at U.S. EPA, *The Clean Air Act Amendments of 1990 List of Hazardous Air Pollutants,* http://www.epa.gov/ttn/atw/orig189.html. However, Congress did not intend this initial list to remain static. It required the EPA to "periodically review the list * * * and,

Figure 4-18: The Fate of Air Toxics
EPA diagram.

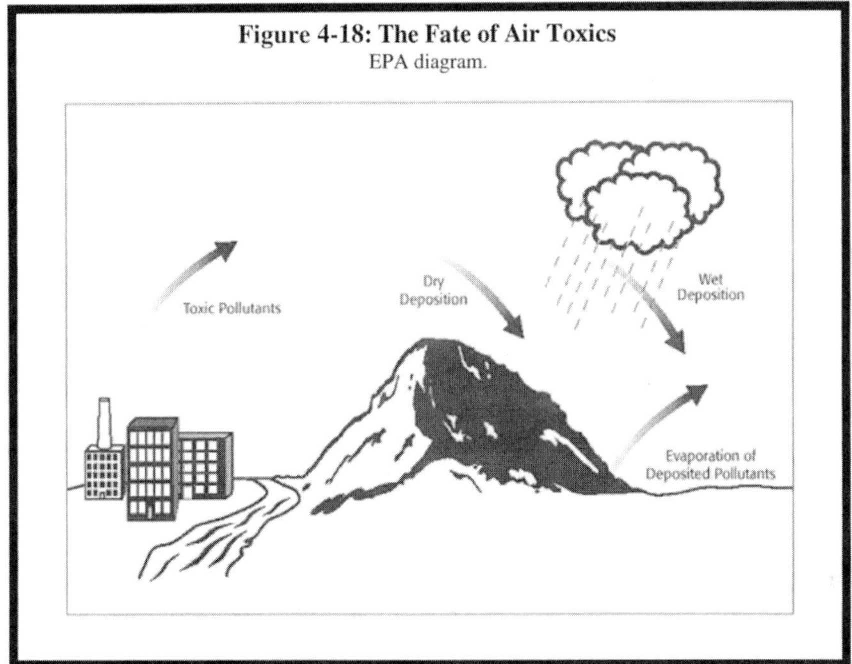

where appropriate, revise such list by rule * * *." CAA § 112(b)(2), 42 U.S.C. § 7412(b)(2). In addition, it also allowed "any person" to petition the EPA to modify the list, either by adding pollutants to or subtracting pollutants from the list.

The following case addresses the statutory and regulatory requirements for delisting a HAP.

AMERICAN FOREST AND PAPER ASSOCIATION, INC. v. ENVIRONMENTAL PROTECTION AGENCY

294 F.3d 113 (D.C. Cir. 2002).

KAREN LECRAFT HENDERSON, CIRCUIT JUDGE:

The American Forest and Paper Association, Inc. (Association), a national trade association of the forest, paper and wood products industry, seeks review of a notice published by the Environmental Protection Agency (EPA) denying the Association's petition to delete the substance methanol from the list of "hazardous air pollutants" (HAPs) pursuant to section 112(b) of the Clean Air Act (CAA), 42 U.S.C. § 7412(b). * * * For the reasons set out below, we conclude EPA's explanation of its reasons for denying the delisting petition satisfies the statutory standard and we therefore deny the Association's petition for review.

I.

Section 112 requires EPA to set emission standards for "hazardous air pollutants." *See* 42 U.S.C. § 7412. In 1990 the Congress amended section 112 to establish a statutory list of HAPs, including methanol. *See* 42 U.S.C. § 7412(b)(1). * * * Section 7412(b)(3) provides that "any person may petition the Administrator to modify the list of hazardous air pollutants under this subsection by adding or deleting a substance." *Id.* § 7412(b)(3)(A). EPA is required (1) to "add a substance to the list upon a showing by the petitioner or on the Administrator's own determination that the substance is an air pollutant and that emissions, ambient concentrations, bioaccumulation or deposition of the substance are known to cause or may reasonably be anticipated to cause adverse effects to human health or adverse environmental effects," *id.* § 7412(b)(3)(B); and (2) to "delete a substance from the list upon a showing by the petitioner or on the Administrator's own determination that there is adequate data on the health and environmental effects of the substance to determine that emissions, ambient concentrations, bioaccumulation or deposition of the substance may not reasonably be anticipated to cause any adverse effects to the human health or adverse environmental effects," *id.* § 7412(b)(3)(C).

The Association petitioned EPA to delist methanol in March 1996, relying on information it claimed shows exposure to methanol does not result in adverse effects to human health. "[T]o assess the potential for adverse human health effects due to inhalation exposure" to a particular substance EPA generally uses an "inhalation reference concentration" (RfC), which "represents the estimated maximum exposure to a pollutant, as extrapolated from animal studies, that a human can tolerate continuously for 70 years without experiencing any adverse health effect," *Chem. Mfrs. Ass'n v. EPA*, 28 F.3d 1259, 1265 (D.C. Cir. 1994). Because EPA had not yet established an inhalation RfC for methanol, the Association proposed a "safe exposure level" (SEL) for the substance, asserting that "exposures at or below the SEL can be expected to produce no adverse human health effects from lifetime inhalation exposures." 66 Fed. Reg. at 21,931. The Association derived its SEL from the "Rogers Study," which examined the effect on mice of methanol exposure for seven hours per day. The Association converted the No–Observable–Adverse–Effect–Level (NOAEL) derived from the Rogers Study to a human equivalent and adjusted it for interspecies extrapolation and for individual variation. The Association offered the resulting level of 83 milligrams per cubic meter (mg/m^3) as the SEL for methanol. The Association further asserted that the highest predicted 24–hour average concentration of methanol from known sources is 3.65 mg/m^3. Because this maximum exposure level was below its proposed SEL, the Association claimed that methanol exposure does not cause adverse effects and therefore should be delisted pursuant to section 112(b)(3)(C). The Association supplemented its petition periodically until EPA published a "notice of receipt of a complete petition" on July 19, 1999. Subsequently the Association submitted additional materials addressing the "Burbacher Study," published in October 1999, which examined the effects of methanol inhalation on primates and which the Association contended supports delisting methanol.

Following a comment period, EPA issued its notice of denial on May 2, 2001. While generally approving the studies and the methodology the Association had used, EPA disagreed with the Association's analysis in three crucial respects.

First, EPA took issue with the Association's SEL, contending it should have incorporated a "duration adjustment," to account for the difference between the Rogers Study's 7–hour daily exposure and potential human daily exposure of 24 hours; and, in addition, it should have been derived using the "benchmark dose" (BMD) methodology rather than using the NOAEL methodology as the Association did. EPA determined that recalculating the SEL using a duration adjustment and the BMD methodology "would yield an SEL on the order of 4–6 mg/m^3." 66 Fed. Reg. at 21,932. Because these values "are at the approximate midpoint of the values (0.3–30 mg/m^3) that might be derived from the data of the Burbacher Primate Study," EPA concluded that "a range of 0.3 to 30 mg/m^3 represents the most appropriate criterion for determining whether methanol emissions may reasonably be anticipated to cause adverse human health effects" and that "24–hour exposures below 0.3 mg/m^3 are not likely to result in adverse human health effects." 66 Fed. Reg. at 21,935–36. EPA cautioned that it was "unable to make a more precise determination at this time regarding the exposure levels at which adverse effects are likely to occur." 66 Fed. Reg. at 21,936.

Second, EPA challenged the Association's maximum 24–hour exposure level as too low. Based on the data initially submitted by the Association, EPA suggested that the "maximum 24–hour exposures to methanol emissions could be in the range of 2 to 7 mg/m^3, but that such exposures may not reasonably be expected to exceed 7 mg/m^3." 66 Fed. Reg. at 21,939.

Third, EPA determined that, contrary to the Association's contention, the Burbacher Study in fact supports retaining methanol on the list because it revealed several possible adverse health effects, namely, a decrease in gestation time, an increase in the number of required caesarian-section births, and, in prenatally exposed offspring, instances of a "severe wasting syndrome," concentration-related delay in sensorimotor development and lower performance on an infant intelligence test. 66 Fed. Reg. at 21,932–33. EPA concluded that, "based on the weight of evidence, ... there are reproductive and developmental health consequences following exposure to methanol in primates (Burbacher *et al.*) and that these effects should be considered relevant to potential risks in humans." 66 Fed. Reg. at 21,935.

Because EPA's maximum exposure level exceeded the floor of its SEL range and because the Burbacher Study, as EPA construed it, indicated potential adverse effects from methanol, EPA determined it "c[ould] not conclude that there are adequate data to determine that emissions of methanol may not reasonably be anticipated to cause any adverse effects to human health." 66 Fed. Reg. at 21,920.

The Association petitioned for review of the notice of denial on July 2, 2001.

II.

The Association raises a series of challenges to the EPA's notice of denial. We find none of them persuasive.

First, the Association asserts EPA misinterpreted the statutory standard for delisting a substance to permit it to rely on mere speculation about adverse effects. * * * EPA construed the statutory language to impose a "burden . . . on a petitioner to demonstrate that the available data support an affirmative determination that emissions of a substance may not be reasonably anticipated to result in adverse effects on human health or the environment" so that "EPA will not remove a substance from the list of HAP based merely on the inability to conclude that emissions of the substance will cause adverse effects on human health or the environment." 66 Fed. Reg. at 21,930. We review EPA's construction of the statutory language under the familiar *Chevron* analysis[.] * * * EPA's interpretation easily passes muster under *Chevron*. The statutory language unambiguously places on a delisting petitioner the burden to make a "showing" that "there is adequate data" about a substance to determine exposure to it "*may* not reasonably be anticipated to cause" adverse effects. This is precisely what EPA has construed it to require. * * *

* * * The Association argues that EPA's decision fails a "reality check" in two respects. First, the Association points out that methanol levels far higher than the maximum predicted for industrial source exposure have been reported in unexposed, healthy humans and primates, particularly in the expelled breath of study subjects who had recently consumed substantial amounts of fruit. In the notice of denial, EPA set forth specific reasons why the methanol levels in study subjects' mouths after fruit consumption may not correspond to—and may in fact considerably exceed—the actual methanol levels in the subjects' blood. EPA also noted that the high levels of methanol measured represented "an extreme case" and that consumption of fruit sufficient to produce them "most likely involves acute GI effects sufficient to discourage the attempt." Second, the Association contends that pharmacokinetic models show that an SEL of 0.3 mg/m^3 causes only a minuscule and inconsequential increase in an exposed subject's blood methanol level. EPA has reasonably rejected the Association's pharmacokinetic models as "not targeted to humans likely to be the most sensitive to methanol," notably pregnant women, developing fetuses and persons with enzyme and vitamin deficiencies. In

addition, EPA noted the possible short window of exposure for adverse developmental effects to occur in developing fetuses and its consequent concern that, despite natural fluctuations in background methanol blood levels, there is a risk of negative effects from even short term peaks.

Next, the Association challenges EPA's decision to calculate the SEL using the BMD methodology (specifically, the BMDL–5 lower confidence level) rather than the NOAEL. In the Association's view, the BMD introduces an "unexplained, unacknowledged level of conservativism," and is, in any event, an untested, experimental approach. "We may reject an agency's choice of a scientific model 'only when the model bears no rational relationship to the characteristics of the data to which it is applied.' " *National Wildlife Fed'n v. EPA*, 286 F.3d 554, 562 (D.C. Cir. 2002) (quoting *Appalachian Power Co. v. EPA*, 135 F.3d 791, 802 (D.C. Cir. 1998)). That is not the case here. EPA has long advocated the BMD as superior to the NOAEL because "[u]nlike the NOAEL, the BMD takes into account dose-response information." The BMD's advantages over NOAEL have also been acknowledged by private researchers, including those in the Rogers Study who calculated a BMD for methanol. Thus, EPA's choice of the BMD methodology was not arbitrary.

* * * The Association also challenges EPA's determination that the "maximum 24–hour exposures could be in the range of 2 to 7 mg/m^3." We need not resolve this issue, however, because the lower exposure level the Association proposed—3.65 mg/m^3—also exceeds EPA's threshold SEL of 0.3 mg/m^3 (which we uphold) and therefore does not support delisting.

Next, the Association, relying on a report by the Health Effect Institute (HEI), which sponsored the Burbacher Study, asserts EPA arbitrarily attributed to methanol exposure the adverse effects observed in the Burbacher Study. We believe EPA's findings were reasonable. * * * [T]he HEI Report confirms EPA's position that the study data indicate methanol *may* reasonably be anticipated to cause adverse health effects but are insufficient at this time to determine conclusively that it does or does not.

Finally, the Association claims EPA violated the express directive in section 112(b)(3)(A) that EPA "may not deny a petition solely on the basis of inadequate resources or time for review." 42 U.S.C. § 7412(b)(3)(A). We disagree. EPA reviewed the Association's petition thoroughly and at great length, repeatedly requesting additional submissions before it deemed the Association's petition complete. In the end, based on its analyses, EPA concluded, consistently with the statute, that the Association had not produced sufficient data to satisfy its statutory burden. * * *

NOTES

1. **Listing vs. Delisting HAPs.** What standard does the Clean Air Act establish for eliminating particular pollutants from the HAP list? How does that standard compare to the standard for *listing* hazardous air pollutants?

2. **The EPA's Construction of the HAP Delisting Standard.** How has the EPA construed the statutory delisting standard? What standard of review did the D.C. Circuit use to review the EPA's construction? Why? Does the EPA's construction further Congress's purposes in section 112? Why or why not? What is the effect of EPA's interpretation of the burden of proof for delisting petitions on actual removal of chemicals from the HAP list, do you think?

What *factual* determinations did the EPA have to make in reviewing the petition to delist methanol? Why did the EPA disagree with the petitioners' scientific findings? What standard of review did the D.C. Circuit use to review those disagreements?

3. **Methanol as a HAP.** Why is methanol considered a hazardous air pollutant? What adverse effects does it have on human health? Who is particularly at risk from methanol exposure? Why? What uncertainties still remain regarding the effects of methanol? How did the EPA treat those uncertainties in the face of the petition to delist methanol?

4. **The Economics of HAP Emission Standards.** Why would the American Forest and Paper Association petition the EPA to delist methanol as a HAP? Consider the amount of information that the Association needed to provide to the EPA to complete its petition. Is the petitioning process cost-free? Why or why not? Now consider the litigation. Is litigation cost-free? Why or why not? Why would the Association be willing to fight so hard to delist methanol? Does it help your analysis to know that papermaking companies generate methanol during the pulping process at a rate of 12 to 20 pounds per ton of production, and that the paper bleaching process can increase that total to 25 pounds, making methanol the largest component of those companies' wastes?

* * *

B. REGULATION OF MOBILE SOURCES OF HAPS

Section 112 of the Clean Air Act, by its own terms, applies only to stationary sources. *See* CAA § 112(a)(1), 42 U.S.C. § 7412(a)(1) (defining "major source" to refer only to stationary sources). However, the EPA has worked to eliminate mobile source emissions of some HAPs—notably, lead and benzene—through its regulation of fuel requirements, discussed in Part III.B.3.

C. REGULATION OF STATIONARY SOURCES OF HAPS

1. Major Stationary Sources and MACT

Congress took a slightly different approach to regulating HAP emissions from stationary sources than it used in regulating their emissions of criteria air pollutants. Emission standards for the seven criteria air pollutants, as we have seen, depend on three factors: (1) whether the stationary source is a new or modified, as opposed to existing, source; (2) whether the source is located in an attainment or nonattainment area; and (3) whether the source is a major source. Emissions standards for HAPs, in contrast, depend primarily only on one factor: whether the stationary source is considered a ***major source*** of HAPs. Under the statutory definitions in section 112, a stationary source of HAPs is a "major source" for purposes of section 112 if it "emits or has the potential to emit considering controls, in the aggregate, 10 tons per year or more of any hazardous air pollutant or 25 tons per year or more of any combination of hazardous air pollutants." CAA § 112(a)(1), 42 U.S.C. § 7412(a)(1).

Congress required the EPA to set ***National Emission Standards for Hazardous Air Pollutants*** **(NESHAPs)** based initially on the ***Maximum Achievable Control Technology*** **(MACT)** for both new and existing major stationary sources that emit HAPs. CAA § 112(d)(2), 42 U.S.C. § 7412(d)(2). The Clean Air Act defines MACT as "the maximum degree of reduction of emissions of the hazardous air pollutants * * * (including a prohibition on emissions, where achievable) that the Administrator, taking into consideration the cost of achieving such emission reduction, and any non-air quality health and environmental impacts and energy requirements, determines achievable for new or existing sources in the category or subcategory to which such emission standard applies * * *." *Id.*

Nevertheless, while both new and existing major stationary sources of HAPs are subject to the MACT standard, the process of setting MACT is different for the two categories. Relying on the Clean Air Act itself, CAA § 112(d)(3), 42 U.S.C. § 7412(d)(3), the EPA has summarized these statutory differences as follows.

> EPA's MACT standards are based on the emissions levels already achieved by the best-performing similar facilities. This straightforward, performance-based approach yields standards that are both reasonable and effective in reducing toxic emissions. This approach also provides a level economic playing field by ensuring that facilities with good controls are not disadvantaged relative to competitors with poorer controls.
>
> When developing a MACT standard for a particular source category, EPA looks at the level of emissions currently being achieved by the best-performing similar sources through clean processes, control devices, work practices, or other methods. These emissions levels set a baseline (often referred to as the "MACT floor") for the new standard. At a minimum, a MACT standard must achieve, throughout the industry, a level of emissions control that is at least equivalent to the MACT floor. EPA can establish a more stringent standard when this makes economic, environmental, and public health sense.
>
> The MACT floor is established differently for existing sources and new sources:

- For **existing sources**, the MACT floor must equal the average emissions limitations currently achieved by the best-performing 12 percent of sources in that source category, if there are 30 or more existing sources. If there are fewer than 30 existing sources, then the MACT floor must equal the average emissions limitation achieved by the best-performing five sources in the category.
- For **new sources**, the MACT floor must equal the level of emissions control currently achieved by the best-controlled similar source.

Wherever feasible, EPA writes the final MACT standard as an emissions limit (i.e., as a percent reduction in emissions or a concentration limit that regulated sources must achieve). Emissions limits provide flexibility for industry to determine the most effective way to comply with the standard.

Office of Air Quality, Planning, and Standards, U.S. EPA, *Taking Toxics Out of the Air*, http://www.epa.gov/oar/oaqps/takingtoxics/p1.html#1 (last updated March 7, 2007).

New and existing major sources also differ in *when* they must comply with the MACT emissions standards. New sources must comply with any applicable MACT standards as they are being constructed and getting a permit under Title V. CAA § 112(i)(1), 42 U.S.C. § 7412(i)(1). Modified existing sources, similarly, must comply with MACT during the reconstruction process. *Id.* In contrast, the EPA establishes compliance dates for existing sources, but all existing sources must comply with the relevant MACT standards within three years of the EPA establishing those standards, subject to a possible one-year extension and several statutory exemptions. CAA § 112(i)(3), 42 U.S.C. § 7412(i)(3). For example, any source that has already installed BART or LAER technology does not have to comply with the MACT standard for five years. CAA § 112(i)(6), 42 U.S.C. § 7412(i)(6).

The EPA sets the actual MACT standards on the basis of industrial categories. As a result, all industrial sources of the same basic type emitting the same basic pollutants are subject to the same MACT standards, but the MACT standards for the same HAPs emitted by sources in a different industry may be different.

Congress put the EPA on a schedule for establishing these industrial categories and promulgating the NESHAPs for them. CAA § 112(c)(1), (e)(1), 42 U.S.C. § 7412(c)(1), (e)(1). Under this schedule, the EPA should have finished establishing MACT standards for all categories by November 15, 2000. CAA § 112(e)(1)(E), 42 U.S.C. § 7412(e)(1)(E). While the EPA has indeed approached NESHAP promulgation in stages labeled—as Congress envisioned—the "2–Year," "4–Year," "7–Year," and "10–Year" MACT rules, the EPA did not finish the first stage of NESHAP promulgation until 2004. Between 1993 and 2004, it published 96 MACT standards for 156 source categories ("industry sectors").

In addition, Congress required the EPA to investigate, by 1996, the possibility that even more stringent controls would be necessary to protect the public health and to revise MACT standards by 2004 if necessary "in order to provide an ample margin of safety to protect public health * * * or to prevent, taking into consideration costs, energy, safety, and other relevant factors, an adverse environmental effect." CAA § 112(f)(1), (2), 42 U.S.C. § 7412(f)(1), (2). Thus, while the NESHAPs begin as ***technology-based emissions limitations***, they are supposed to end as ***health-based emissions limitations***.

The EPA issued its report on the residual health risks from HAPs in 1999. OFFICE OF AIR QUALITY PLANNING AND STANDARDS, U.S. E.P.A., RESIDUAL RISK REPORT TO CONGRESS (EPA–453/R–99–001) (March 1999), *available at* http://www.wpa.gov/ttn/oarpg/t3/reports/risk_rep.pdf. It then began implementing the health-based NESHAPs in phases. Phase 1, which lasted from 2005 to 2007, consisted of the first 8 "residual risk" NESHAP standards that the EPA promulgated, for: coke ovens; dry cleaning; industrial cooling towers; hazardous organic NESHAP; gasoline distribution; ethylene oxide sterilizers; magnetic tape; and halogenated solvents. Technology Transfer Network Air Toxics Website, U.S. E.P.A., *Risk and Technology Review*, http://www.epa.gov/ttn/atw/rrisk/rtrpg.html (last updated Dec. 12, 2007); *see also, e.g.*, EPA, *National Air Emissions Standards for Hazardous Air Pollutants: Halogenated Solvent Cleaning*, 72 Fed. Reg. 25,138 (May 3, 2007); EPA, *National Emission Standards for Coke Oven Batteries*, 70 Fed. Reg. 19,992 (April 15, 2005).

In March 2007, the EPA launched Phase II of its "residual risk" NESHAP work with an Advanced Notice of Proposed Rulemaking that explained the data that the EPA intends to use in analyzing, simultaneously, the residual health risks from toxics emitted from sources in 22 industry categories. EPA, *Risk and Technology Review, Phase II*, 72 Fed. Reg. 14,734 (March 29, 2007). At the end of the original 60–day comment period, the EPA extended comments for another 30 days, until June 29, 2007. 72 Fed. Reg. 29,287 (May 25, 2007).

2. Minor Stationary Sources of HAPs and the Urban Air Toxics Strategy

Unlike for criteria air pollutants, under section 112's ***urban air toxics strategy***, Congress did regulate some ***minor stationary sources*** that emit HAPs. Congress found "that emissions of hazardous air pollutants from ***area sources*** may individually, or in the aggregate, present significant risks to public health in urban areas." CAA § 112(k)(1), 42 U.S.C. § 7412(k)(1) (emphasis added). "Area sources" are non-major, non-mobile sources that emit HAPs in urban areas. CAA § 112(a)(2), 42 U.S.C. § 7412(a)(2). They include such minor but cumulatively dangerous sources such as dry cleaners and gas stations.

Figure 4-19: Urban Sources of HAPs
EPA graphic.

The purpose of the urban air toxic strategy is "to achieve a substantial reduction in emissions of hazardous air pollutants from area sources and an equivalent reduction in the public health risks associated with such sources including a reduction of not less than 75 per centum in the incidence of cancer attributable to emissions from such sources." CAA § 112(k)(1), 42 U.S.C. § 7412(k)(1). To achieve this goal, the EPA had to identify at least 30 HAPs that "present the greatest threat to public health in the largest number of urban areas" and identify the categories of sources emitting those HAPs that "account[] for 90 per centum or more of the aggregate emissions of each of the 30 identified hazardous air pollutants * * *." CAA § 112(k)(3)(B), 42 U.S.C. § 7412(k)(3)(B). These identified sources are then subject to, in the Administrator's discretion, technology-based emissions standards based either on MACT or the ***Generally Available Control Technologies or management practices* (GACT)**. CAA § 112(d)(5), 42 U.S.C. § 7412(d)(5).

3. The Clean Air Act Emissions Standards Chart for Stationary Sources

With the addition of section 112, the chart of Clean Air Act emissions regulation can now be updated as shown in Table 4–4.

TABLE 4–4: CLEAN AIR ACT EMISSIONS STANDARDS FOR STATIONARY SOURCES			
	NEW MAJOR STATIONARY SOURCES	EXISTING MAJOR STATIONARY SOURCES	MINOR STATIONARY SOURCES
NONATTAINMENT AREA:			
PART D:	Major Source = 100 tons/year of pollutants: LAER + OFFSETS + PERMIT (incorporated into Title V permitting)	Major Source = 100 tons/year pollutants: RACT + PERMIT (incorporated into Title V permitting)	NOT APPLICABLE

TABLE 4–4: CLEAN AIR ACT EMISSIONS STANDARDS FOR STATIONARY SOURCES

	NEW MAJOR STATIONARY SOURCES	EXISTING MAJOR STATIONARY SOURCES	MINOR STATIONARY SOURCES
SECTION 112:	Major Source = 10 tons/year 1 HAP or 25 tons/year >1 HAP: MACT + PERMIT	Major Source = 10 tons/year 1 HAP or 25 tons/year >1 HAP: MACT + PERMIT	Urban Area Source: MACT or GACT
ATTAINMENT/ UNCLASSIFIABLE AREA:			
PSD PROGRAM:	Major Emitting Facility = 250 tons/ year of pollutants or 100 tons/year and source is in one of the 26 special categories: BACT + PERMIT	NOT APPLICABLE	NOT APPLICABLE
REGIONAL HAZE:	NOT APPLICABLE	Major Source = 250 tons/year pollutants and source is in one of the 26 special categories: BART + PERMIT	NOT APPLICABLE
TITLE V:	Major Source = 100 tons/year of pollutants: NSPS + PERMIT	Major Source = 100 tons/year of pollutants: PERMIT	NOT APPLICABLE
SECTION 112:	Major Source = 10 tons/year 1 HAP or 25 tons/year >1 HAP: MACT + PERMIT	Major Source = 10 tons/year 1 HAP or 25 tons/year >1 HAP: MACT + PERMIT	Urban Area Source: MACT or GACT

VI. TRANSBOUNDARY AIR POLLUTION

A. INTRODUCTION

One of the quintessential properties of air pollution is that it moves with the winds, irrespective of state and international boundaries. As a result, regulation of air pollution often must address the transboundary effects of the pollution. We have already seen, for example, how transboundary air pollution, especially ozone, can interfere with an AQCR's ability to meet the NAAQS. The Clean Air Act and the EPA have addressed a variety of transboundary air pollution problems.

B. THE CLEAN AIR ACT'S INTERSTATE AIR POLLUTION PROVISIONS

1. Addressing Interstate Air Pollution through SIPs

In order to receive EPA approval, each SIP must ensure that sources of air pollutants within that state will not:

> (I) contribute significantly to nonattainment in, or interfere with maintenance by, any other State with respect to any national primary or secondary ambient air quality standard, or
>
> (II) interfere with measures required to be included in the applicable implementation plan for any other State under part C of this subchapter to prevent significant deterioration of air quality or to protect visibility.

CAA § 110(a)(2)(D)(i), 42 U.S.C. § 7410(a)(2)(D)(i). SIPs must also ensure compliance with section 126, the Clean Air Act's interstate pollution provision. CAA § 110(a)(2)(D)(ii), 42 U.S.C. § 7410(a)(2)(D)(ii).

More expansively, section 126 requires each new or modified proposed major source to provide written notice to all nearby states if that new or modified source is subject to the PSD program or "may significantly contribute to levels of air pollution in excess of the national ambient air quality standards in any air quality control region outside the State in which such source intends to locate (or make such modification)." CAA § 126(a)(1), 42 U.S.C. § 7426(a)(1). In addition, each SIP must identify existing major stationary sources with similar effects, and the state must notify nearby states of such sources. CAA § 126(a)(2), 42 U.S.C. § 7426(a)(2). Affected states can also petition EPA for a determination that a major source in another state is or will be interfering with their air quality. CAA § 126(b), 42 U.S.C. § 7427(b).

Once the EPA makes such a finding of interference, it is illegal for any new or modified major stationary source to be constructed or to operate in violation of the section 110 interstate SIP requirements, or "for any major existing source to operate more than three months after such finding has been made with respect to it." CAA § 126(c), 42 U.S.C. § 7426(c). However, existing sources can continue to operate beyond three months if they meet the EPA's emissions limitations and compliance schedules. *Id.*

Nevertheless, a problem in coordinating section 110 and section 126 arises because the cross-references in section 126 to section 110 all reference section 110(a)(2)(D)*(ii)*—the provision that requires SIPs to ensure compliance with section 126. Thus, read literally, section 126 requires compliance with section 110(a)(2)(D)(ii), which requires compliance with section 126. Sounds a bit circular, doesn't it? The following case deals with this apparent circularity and the relationship Congress intended between sections 110 and 126.

NORTH CAROLINA v. ENVIRONMENTAL PROTECTION AGENCY

531 F.3d 896 (D.C. Cir. 2008).

PER CURIAM:

These consolidated petitions for review challenge various aspects of the Clean Air Interstate Rule. Because we find more than several fatal flaws in the rule and the Environmental Protection Agency ("EPA") adopted the rule as one, integral action, we vacate the rule in its entirety and remand to EPA to promulgate a rule that is consistent with this opinion.

I. Background

A. Title I of the Clean Air Act

* * * One provision of Title I requires SIPs to

> contain adequate provisions—(i) prohibiting, consistent with the provisions of this subchapter, any source or other type of emissions activity within the State from emitting any air pollutant in amounts which will—(I) contribute significantly to nonattainment in, or interfere with maintenance by, any other State with respect to any [NAAQS]....

42 U.S.C. § 7410(a)(2)(D)(i)(I) (statutory provision to which we refer throughout this opinion as "section 110(a)(2)(D)(i)(I)"). In 1998, EPA relied on this provision to promulgate the NO_x SIP Call, which imposed a duty on certain upwind sources to reduce their NO_x emissions by a specified amount so that they no longer " 'contribute significantly to nonattainment in, or interfere with maintenance by,' a downwind State." The NO_x SIP Call created an optional cap-and-trade program for nitrogen oxides ("NO_x"). Like the NO_x SIP Call, the Clean Air Interstate Rule—Rule To Reduce Interstate Transport of Fine Particulate Matter and Ozone (Clean Air Interstate Rule); Revisions to Acid Rain Program; Revisions to the NO_x SIP Call, 70 Fed. Reg. 25,162 (May 12, 2005) ("CAIR")—which is the rule at issue in these consolidated petitions for review, also derives its statutory authority from section 110(a)(2)(D)(i)(I).

B. Title IV of the Clean Air Act

Title IV of the CAA, 42 U.S.C. §§ 7651–7651*o*, aims to reduce acid rain deposition nationwide and in doing so creates a cap-and-trade program for sulfur dioxide ("SO_2") emitted by fossil fuel-fired combustion devices. Congress capped SO_2 emissions for affected units, or electric generating units ("EGUs"), at 8.9 million tons nationwide, *id.* § 7651b(a)(1), and distributed "allowances" among those units. One "allowance" is an authorization for an EGU to emit one ton of SO_2 in a year. * * *

Title IV exempts EGUs that are "simple combustion turbines, or units which serve a generator with a nameplate capacity of 25 Mwe [megawatt electrical] or less," those that are not fossil fuel-fired, those that do not sell electricity, and those that cogenerate steam and electricity unless they sell a certain amount of electricity. It also provides that certain exempt units—"qualifying small power production facilities" and "qualifying cogeneration facilities," * * * and certain "new independent power production facilities," * * *—may elect to become a part of Title IV.

C. Clean Air Interstate Rule

Pursuant to its Title I authority to ensure that states have plans in place that implement the requirements in section 110(a)(2)(D)(i)(I), EPA promulgated CAIR. CAIR's purpose is to reduce or eliminate the impact of upwind sources on out-of-state downwind nonattainment of NAAQS for fine particulate matter ("$PM_{2.5}$"), a pollutant associated with respiratory and cardiovascular problems, and eight-hour ozone, a pollutant commonly known as smog. For the most part, EPA defines sources at the state level. EPA determined that 28 states and the District of Columbia ("upwind states") contribute significantly to out-of-state downwind nonattainment of one or both NAAQS. Because SO_2 "is a precursor to $PM_{2.5}$ formation, and NO_x is a precursor to both ozone and $PM_{2.5}$ formation," CAIR requires upwind states "to revise their [SIPs] to include control measures to reduce emissions" of SO_2 and NO_x. CAIR requires upwind states to reduce their emissions in two phases. NO_x reductions are to start in 2009, SO_2 reductions are to start in 2010, and the second reduction phase for each air pollutant is to start in 2015. To implement CAIR's emission reductions, the rule also creates optional interstate trading programs for each air pollutant, to which, in the absence of approved SIPs, all upwind sources are now subject. In addition, CAIR revises Title IV's Acid Rain Program regulations governing the SO_2 cap-and-trade program and replaces the NO_x SIP Call with the CAIR ozone-season NO_x trading program.

* * *CAIR uses a different air quality threshold for each of the two pollutants it regulates. A state meets the air quality threshold for $PM_{2.5}$ (and is therefore subject to CAIR) if it contributes 0.2 micrograms per cubic meter ("g/m^3") or more of $PM_{2.5}$ to out-of-state downwind areas that are in nonattainment. CAIR uses a more complicated process to define the air quality threshold for ozone NAAQS. CAIR first eliminates a state from inclusion in the CAIR ozone program if it has the following characteristics (1) it contributes less than 2 parts per billion ("ppb") to a nonattainment area's ozone concentration as measured using either a "zero-out method" or a "source apportionment method," or (2) its relative contribution to the nonattainment area's excess ozone concentration (the number of particles exceeding 85 ppb) is less than one percent. States that survive the screening criteria are then assessed to determine if they contribute significantly to ozone nonattainment in another state using three metrics:

(1) magnitude of contribution, (2) frequency of contribution, and (3) relative amount of contribution to the area's ozone concentration that exceeds attainment levels.

States that "contribute significantly" to nonattainment for ozone NAAQS are subject to CAIR's ozone-season limits for NO_x and those that "contribute significantly" to nonattainment for $PM_{2.5}$ NAAQS are subject to CAIR's annual limits for NO_x and SO_2. The ozone-season NO_x limits are a percentage reduction in the annual limits for NO_x calculated for $PM_{2.5}$ contributors. In order to eliminate a state's significant contribution to $PM_{2.5}$ NAAQS, CAIR sets an annual cap on NO_x and SO_2 emissions in the region. Each state participating in CAIR's allowance-trading programs receives a budget of allowances, calculated according to a different formula for SO_2 and NO_x. If a state develops a SIP that opts out of the trading programs to which all its upwind sources are now subject in the absence of an approved SIP, the state must limit its emissions to a cap specified by CAIR.

* * * II. Analysis

* * * A. North Carolina Issues

Petitioner North Carolina challenges CAIR's programs for pollution-trading, EPA's interpretation of the "interfere with maintenance" provision in section 110(a)(2)(D)(i)(I), the 2015 compliance deadline for Phase Two of CAIR, the NO_x Compliance Supplement Pool, EPA's interpretation of the word "will" that precedes "contribute significantly" in section 110(a)(2)(D)(i)(I), and EPA's use of a 0.2 g/m^3 air quality threshold for including upwind states in CAIR's $PM_{2.5}$ program. We grant North Carolina's petition as to the trading programs, the "interfere with maintenance" language, and the 2015 compliance deadline, deny its petition as to its interpretation of "will" and the air quality threshold, and take no action on the NO_x Compliance Supplement Pool issue.

1. Pollution–Trading Programs

North Carolina challenges the lawfulness of CAIR's trading programs for SO_2 and NO_x. * * * EPA designed CAIR to eliminate the significant contribution of upwind states, as a whole, to downwind nonattainment. EPA did not purport to measure each state's significant contribution to specific downwind nonattainment areas and eliminate them in an isolated, state-by-state manner. Reasoning that capping emissions in each state would not achieve reductions in the most cost-effective manner, EPA decided to take a regionwide approach to CAIR and include voluntary emissions trading programs. * * * In CAIR's trading system, states are given initial emissions budgets, but sources can choose to sell or purchase emissions credits from sources in other states. As a result, states may emit more or less pollution than their caps would otherwise permit.

Because EPA evaluated whether its proposed emissions reductions were "highly cost effective," at the regionwide level assuming a trading program, it never measured the "significant contribution" from sources within an individual state to downwind nonattainment areas. Using EPA's method, such a regional reduction, although equivalent to the sum of reductions required by all upwind states to meet their budgets, would never equal the aggregate of each state's "significant contribution" for two reasons. State budgets alone, without trading, would not be "highly cost effective." And although EPA has measured the "air quality factor" to include states in CAIR, it has not measured the unlawful amount of pollution for each upwind-downwind linkage. * * * Thus EPA's apportionment decisions have nothing to do with each state's "significant contribution" because under EPA's method of analysis, state budgets do not matter for significant contribution purposes.

But according to Congress, individual state contributions to downwind nonattainment areas do matter. Section 110(a)(2)(D)(i)(I) prohibits sources "*within the State*" from "contribut[ing] significantly to nonattainment *in* ... *any other State* ..." (emphasis added). Yet under CAIR, sources in Alabama, which contribute to nonattainment of $PM_{2.5}$ NAAQS in Davidson County, North Carolina, would not need to reduce their emissions at all. Theoretically, sources in Alabama could purchase enough NO_x and SO_2 allowances to cover all their current emissions, resulting in no change in Alabama's contribution to Davidson County, North Carolina's nonattainment. CAIR only assures that the entire region's significant contribution will be eliminated. It is possible that CAIR would achieve section 110(a)(2)(D)(i)(I)'s goals. EPA's modeling shows that sources contributing to North Carolina's nonattainment areas will at least reduce their emissions even after opting into CAIR's trading programs. But EPA is not exercising its section 110(a)(2)(D)(i)(I) duty unless it is promulgating a rule that achieves something measurable toward the goal of prohibiting sources "within the State" from contributing to nonattainment or interfering with maintenance "in any other State."

* * *Because CAIR is designed as a complete remedy to section 110(a)(2)(D)(i)(I) problems, as EPA claims, CAIR must do more than achieve something measurable; it must actually require elimination of emissions from sources that contribute significantly and interfere with maintenance in downwind nonattainment areas. To do so, it must measure each state's "significant contribution" to downwind nonattainment even if that measurement does not directly correlate with each state's individualized air quality impact on downwind nonattainment relative to other upwind states. Otherwise, the rule is not effectuating the statutory mandate of prohibiting emissions moving from one state to another, leaving EPA with no statutory authority for its action. Whether EPA could promulgate a section 110(a)(2)(D)(i)(I) remedy that would bar alternate relief, such as would be available under section 126, 42 U.S.C. § 7426, is a question that is not before the court.

2. "Interfere With Maintenance"

Section 110(a)(2)(D)(i)(I) requires EPA to ensure that SIPs "contain adequate provisions" prohibiting sources within a state from emitting air pollutants in amounts which will "contribute significantly to nonattainment in, *or* interfere with maintenance by, any other State with respect to any [NAAQS]." North Carolina argues that EPA unlawfully ignored the "interfere with maintenance" language in section 110(a)(2)(D)(i)(I), divesting it of independent effect in CAIR. It contends that instead of limiting the beneficiaries of CAIR to downwind areas that were monitored to be in nonattainment when EPA promulgated CAIR *and* were modeled to be in nonattainment in 2009 and 2010, when CAIR goes into effect, EPA should have also included in CAIR upwind states, such as Georgia, that send pollution into downwind areas that are projected to barely meet attainment levels of NAAQS in 2010. North Carolina only contests EPA's interpretation of the "interfere with maintenance" prong as applied to EPA's determination of which states are beneficiaries of CAIR for the ozone NAAQS.

North Carolina explains that even though all of its counties are projected to attain NAAQS for ozone by 2010, several of its counties are at risk of returning to nonattainment due to interference from upwind sources. * * * EPA has stated that "historical data indicates that attaining counties with air quality levels within 3 ppb of the standard are at risk of returning to nonattainment." * * * And in the case of Fulton County, Georgia, EPA determined that the "interfere with maintenance" provision justified imposing controls on upwind states in 2015 even though it is projected to attain the NAAQS by a margin of 7 or 8 ppb because its ozone levels have varied by at least that margin several times in the recent past. North Carolina argues that EPA must utilize this "historic variability" standard to determine which downwind areas suffer interference with their maintenance in 2010, not just 2015. If it did so, EPA would see that Mecklenburg County, North Carolina, has varied by at least 3 ppb (the relevant margin between attainment and nonattainment for that county in 2010) six times in the recent past and consequently would include in CAIR any state, such as Georgia, that is contributing an unlawful amount of pollution to this downwind area.

* * * Under EPA's reading of the statute, a state can never "interfere with maintenance" unless EPA determines that at one point it "contribute[d] significantly to nonattainment." EPA stated clearly on two occasions "that it would apply the interfere with maintenance provision in section 110(a)(2)(D) in conjunction with the significant contribution to nonattainment provision and so did not use the maintenance prong to separately identify upwind States subject to CAIR." EPA reasoned that this interpretation "avoid[s] giving greater weight to the potentially lesser environmental effect" and strikes "a reasonable balance between controls in upwind states and in-state controls." EPA stated that an interpretation that permitted states that are able to attain NAAQS on their own to benefit from CAIR "could even create a perverse incentive for downwind states to increase local emissions."

All the policy reasons in the world cannot justify reading a substantive provision out of a statute. Areas that find themselves barely meeting attainment in 2010 due in part to upwind sources interfering with that attainment have no recourse under EPA's interpretation of the interference prong of section 110(a)(2)(D)(i)(I).2010 is not insignificant because that is the deadline for downwind areas to attain ozone NAAQS. An outcome that fails to give independent effect to the "interfere with maintenance" prong violates the plain language of section 110(a)(2)(D)(i)(I). The provision at issue is written in the disjunctive: SIPs must "contain adequate provisions prohibiting ... any source or other type of emissions activity within the State from emitting any air pollutant in amounts which will contribute significantly to nonattainment in, *or* interfere with maintenance by, any other State...." 42 U.S.C. § 7410(a)(2)(D)(i)(I) (emphasis added). "Canons of construction ordinarily suggest that terms connected by a disjunctive be given separate meanings, unless the context dictates otherwise...." There is no context in section 110(a)(2)(D)(i)(I) directing an alternate result; therefore EPA must give effect to both provisions in the statute.

* * * Because EPA describes CAIR as a complete remedy to a section 110(a)(2)(D)(i)(I) violation and does not give independent significance to the "interfere with maintenance" language to identify upwind states that interfere with downwind maintenance, it unlawfully nullifies that aspect of the statute and provides no protection for downwind areas that, despite EPA's predictions, still find themselves struggling to meet NAAQS due to upwind interference in 2010. For this reason, we grant North Carolina's petition on this issue. Although North Carolina challenged CAIR on the "interfere with maintenance" issue only with regard to ozone, the rule includes the same flaw with regard to $PM_{2.5}$. The court does not address North Carolina's separate contention that EPA failed to comply with notice-and-comment requirements regarding its proposed test for an "interfere with maintenance" violation, or the propriety of the test itself.

3. 2015 Compliance Deadline

North Carolina argues that the 2015 deadline for upwind states to eliminate their "significant contribution" to downwind nonattainment ignores the plain language of section 110(a)(2)(D)(i), contradicts EPA's goal of "balanc[ing] the burden for achieving attainment between regional-scale and local-scale control programs," violates the Supreme Court's holding that EPA may not consider economic and technological infeasibility when approving a SIP, and departs from the contrary approach it took in the NO_x SIP Call without explanation.

North Carolina challenges the 2015 Phase Two deadline for upwind states to come into compliance with CAIR as incompatible with section 110(a)(2)(D)(i)(I)'s mandate that SIPs contain adequate provisions prohibiting significant contributions to nonattainment "consistent with the provisions of [Title I]." 42 U.S.C. § 7410(a)(2)(D)(i)(I). Title I dictates the deadlines for states to attain particular NAAQS. $PM_{2.5}$ attainment must be achieved "as expeditiously as practicable, but no later than 5 years from the date such area was designated nonattainment ... except that the

Administrator may extend the attainment date ... for a period no greater than 10 years from the date of designation as nonattainment...." 42 U.S.C. § 7502(a)(2)(A). North Carolina, along with the rest of the CAIR states, must meet $PM_{2.5}$ NAAQS by 2010. Ozone nonattainment areas must attain permissible levels of ozone "as expeditiously as practicable," but no later than the assigned date in the table the statute provides. 42 U.S.C. § 7511. North Carolina's statutory deadline is June 2010, but it could be even sooner if EPA upon repromulgating its regulations sets an earlier deadline. North Carolina argues that despite the statutory mandate that section 110(a)(2)(D)(i), 42 U.S.C. § 7410(a)(2)(D)(i), be consistent with the rest of Title I, which requires compliance with $PM_{2.5}$ and ozone NAAQS by 2010, CAIR gives states that "contribute significantly" to nonattainment until 2015 to comply based solely on reasons of feasibility.

EPA contends that the phrase "consistent with the provisions of [Title I]" does not require incorporating Title I's NAAQS attainment deadlines into CAIR. It argues that section 110(a)(2)(D)(i)(I) does not mandate any particular time frame and that the language about consistency only requires EPA to make a rule consistent with *procedural* provisions in Title I, not substantive ones. * * * If there were any ambiguity as to Congress's intent in excluding the limiting language EPA proposes, an examination of the relevant language in the context of the whole CAA dispels any doubts as to its meaning. In the CAA, Congress differentiates between requiring consistency with provisions in a title and requiring consistency "with the *procedures* established" under a title. Section 110(a)(2) (D)(i), 42 U.S.C. § 7410(a)(2)(D)(i), is not limited to procedural provisions in Title I; thus it requires EPA to consider all provisions in Title I—both procedural and substantive—and to formulate a rule that is consistent with them.

Despite section 110(a)(2)(D)(i)'s requirement that prohibitions on upwind contributions to downwind nonattainment be "consistent with the provisions of [Title I]," EPA did not make any effort to harmonize CAIR's Phase Two deadline for upwind contributors to eliminate their significant contribution with the attainment deadlines for downwind areas. As a result, downwind nonattainment areas must attain NAAQS for ozone and $PM_{2.5}$ without the elimination of upwind states' significant contribution to downwind nonattainment, forcing downwind areas to make greater reductions than section 110(a)(2)(D)(i)(I) requires. Because EPA ignored its statutory mandate to promulgate CAIR consistent with the provisions in Title I mandating compliance deadlines for downwind states in 2010, we grant North Carolina's petition challenging the 2015 Phase Two deadline. We need not address petitioner's other arguments against this provision.

* * * B. SO_2 and NO_x Budgets

SO_2 Petitioners and petitioner Entergy challenge CAIR's budgets for the SO_2 and NO_x trading programs. EPA set states' SO_2 budgets for 2010 to 50% (35% in 2015) of the allowances the states' EGUs receive under Title IV. SO_2 Petitioners argue EPA never explained how these budgets related to section 110(a)(2)(D)(i)(I)'s mandate of prohibiting significant contributions to downwind nonattainment. Therefore, they claim, the budgets and the regionwide cap, are "arbitrary, capricious, ... or otherwise not in accordance with law," 42 U.S.C. § 7607(d)(9)(A). As for NO_x, EPA reduced states' budgets to the extent their EGUs burned oil or gas. Entergy claims EPA made this adjustment purely in the interests of fairness-an improper reason under section 110(a)(2)(D)(i)(I). We grant the petitions, agreeing EPA chose the budgets for both pollutants in an improper manner. In short, the fact that SO_2 and NO_x are precursors to ozone and $PM_{2.5}$ pollution does not give EPA plenary authority to reduce emissions of these substances. Section 110(a)(2)(D)(i)(I) obligates states to prohibit emissions that contribute significantly to nonattainment or interfere with maintenance downwind, and EPA must exercise its authority under this provision to make measurable progress towards those goals.

1. SO_2 Budgets

We first address EPA's choice of SO_2 budgets. EPA claims to have based state budgets for SO_2 and NO_x on the amount of emissions sources can eliminate by applying controls EPA deems "highly cost-effective controls" * * *. We observe initially that state SO_2 budgets are unrelated to the criterion (the "air quality factor") by which EPA included states in CAIR's SO_2 program. Significant contributors, for purposes of inclusion only, are those states EPA projects will contribute at least 0.2 g/m^3 of $PM_{2.5}$ to a nonattainment area in another state. While we would have expected EPA to require states to eliminate contributions above this threshold, EPA claims to have used the measure of significance we mentioned above: emissions that sources within a state can eliminate by applying "highly cost-effective controls." * * *

* * * EPA's choice of SO_2 budgets does not track the requirements of section 110(a)(2)(D)(i)(I). That much is evident from EPA's decision to base the budgets on allowances states' EGUs receive under Title IV. Those allowances are not, as EPA asserts, a "logical starting point" for setting CAIR's SO_2 emissions caps. Congress designed the Title IV allowance scheme using EGU data from 1985 to 1987 to address the national acid rain problem. Nowhere does EPA explain how reducing Title IV allowances will adequately prohibit states from contributing significantly to downwind nonattainment of the $PM_{2.5}$ NAAQS. And while "Congress chose a policy of not revisiting and revising these allocations and, apparently, believed that its allocation methodology would be appropriate for future time periods," it is unclear how the quantitative number of allowances created by 1990 legislation to address one substance, acid rain, could be relevant to 2015 levels of an air pollutant, $PM_{2.5}$.

* * * Because EPA did not explain how the objectives in section 110(a)(2)(D)(i)(I) relate to its choice of SO_2 emissions caps based on Title IV allowances, we conclude that choice was "arbitrary, capricious, ... or not otherwise in accordance with law," 42 U.S.C. § 7607(d)(9)(A).

2. NO_x Budgets

Next, we address EPA's use of "fuel factors" to allocate the regional NO_x cap among the CAIR states. EPA determined the cap by multiplying NO_x emissions rates (0.15 mmBtu in 2010 and 0.125 mmBtu in 2015) by the heat input of states in the CAIR region. Then, EPA distributed to each state, as its budget of NO_x emissions allowances, its proportionate share of the regional cap. But in determining these shares, EPA adjusted each state's heat input for the mix of fuels its power plants used: while a coal-fired EGU contributed its full heat input to the state total, an oil-fired EGU counted for only 60% of its heat input and a gas-fired EGU only 40%. Entergy argues this fuel adjustment was irrational because EPA made it purely for the sake of sharing the burden of emissions reductions fairly. We agree EPA's notion of fairness has nothing to do with states' section 110(a)(2)(D)(i)(I) obligations to prohibit significant contributions to downwind nonattainment.

* * * Not all methods of developing state emission budgets are equally valid, because an agency may not "trespass beyond the bounds of its statutory authority by taking other factors into account" than those to which Congress limited it, nor "substitute new goals in place of the statutory objectives without explaining how [doing so comports with] the statute." Section 110(a)(2)(D)(i)(I) addresses emissions "within the State" that contribute significantly to downwind pollution. Naturally we defer to EPA's interpretation of the Clean Air Act so far as it is reasonable, *Chevron,* 467 U.S. 837, and we have recognized that significance may include cost. However, EPA's interpretation cannot extend so far as to make one state's significant contribution depend on another state's cost of eliminating emissions.

Yet that is exactly what EPA has done. For example, Louisiana's EGUs use more gas and oil than most states' EGUs. Consequently, instead of the budget of 42,319 tons per year that would be Louisiana's proportional share of the regionwide cap without fuel adjustment, the State only received 29,593 tons per year. The rest of those credits went to states with more coal-fired EGUs than average, which necessarily received "larger NO_x emissions budgets" than their unadjusted proportional shares. EPA favored coal-fired EGUs in this way because they face a "greater burden . . . to control emissions" than gas-and oil-fired EGUs. In essence, a state having mostly coal-fired EGUs gets more credits because Louisiana can control emissions more cheaply.

* * * Each state must eliminate its own significant contribution to downwind pollution. While CAIR should achieve something measurable towards that goal, it may not require some states to exceed the mark. Because the fuel-adjustment factors shifted the burden of emission reductions solely in pursuit of equity among upwind states-an improper reason-the resulting state budgets were arbitrary and capricious.

* * *D. Border State Issues

Under Title I of the CAA, there is a presumption of state-level regulation generally, and the text of section 110, 42 U.S.C. § 7410, establishes the state as the appropriate primary administrative unit to address interstate transport of emissions. To take action regarding a state pursuant to section 110(a)(2)(D)(i)(I) EPA need only have evidence that emissions "within the State" contribute significantly to another state's nonattainment or interfere with its maintenance of a national ambient air quality standard ("NAAQS"), unless there is evidence that exculpates part of the upwind state from that determination. Thus, in developing a rule, EPA may select states as the unit of measurement. The burden is on the party challenging inclusion of part of a state to present "finer-grained computations" showing that it is "innocent of material contributions" to the state's overall downwind pollution. In response to such data, EPA must ensure that the contested area makes a "measurable contribution," such that it is "part of the problem" of the state's aggregate downwind impact.

Various utilities and one municipality, but not the States themselves, challenge inclusion in CAIR of the upwind States of Texas, Florida, and Minnesota. The court denies all except Minnesota Power's petition.

* * *3. Minnesota

In the proposed rule, EPA included the State of Minnesota after determining that its downwind contribution of $PM_{2.5}$ was 0.39 g/m^3, well above the air quality threshold of 0.2 g/m^3 needed for inclusion in CAIR. In the preamble to the final rule, however, EPA indicated that it had recalculated Minnesota's contribution to be 0.21 g/m^3, and included the State in CAIR. Upon reconsideration, EPA again recalculated and determined that the State's contribution was actually 0.20 g/m^3, the exact threshold for inclusion.

Minnesota Power challenges the inclusion of the State for $PM_{2.5}$ as resting on two types of unaddressed flawed data resulting in an overstatement of emissions: (1) projecting units' emissions as of 2010 to be at a significantly higher rate than as of 2001, with some above the permitted level, and (2) misallocating energy production or heat input projections between units. In view of these claimed errors, Minnesota Power contends that EPA has failed to provide a "complete analytic defense" of its model's treatment of Minnesota. The court grants the petition because EPA's failure to address the claimed errors was unjustifiable. * * *

* * * III. Remedy

The petitioners disagree about the proper remedy, with positions ranging from Minnesota Power's demand that we vacate CAIR with respect to Minnesota to North Carolina's request that we vacate only the Compliance Supplement Pool but remand most of CAIR for EPA to make changes to the compliance date, the set of included states, and the trading program. Unfortunately, we cannot pick and choose portions of CAIR to preserve. * * * EPA has been quite consistent that CAIR was one, integral action. It developed both the SO_2 and NO_x programs assuming all states would participate in the trading programs as implemented in CAIR's Model Rule, and it modeled the crucial cost-effectiveness of the caps "assum[ing] interstate emissions trading." The model also took into account "the use of the existing title IV bank of SO_2 allowances." Moreover, EPA justified the SO_2 and NO_x portions of CAIR as complementary measures to mitigate $PM_{2.5}$ pollution. In sum, CAIR is a single, regional program, as EPA has always maintained, and all its components must stand or fall together.

Indeed, they must fall. * * * We must vacate CAIR because very little will "survive[ ] remand in anything approaching recognizable form."

* * * *So ordered.*

NOTES

1. **The United States' Prevailing Winds.** In the United States, the prevailing winds blow west to east (the Jet Stream) and, on the east coast, south to north. As a result, this case is typical of interstate air pollution cases in deriving from the complaints of the northeastern states about interstate air pollution arriving from southern and Midwestern states. Because the Rocky Mountains form a fairly effective barrier to air pollution, western states escape many regional interstate air pollution issues.

2. **The Multiplicity of Interstate Programs**. As the U.S. Court of Appeals for the D.C. Circuit notes, Congress had already addressed some of the interstate effects of SO_2 and NOx in the Clean Air Act's acid rain program. Why did the EPA go ahead and provide additional requirements for these two pollutants in CAIR? What other interstate air pollution problems do these pollutants contribute to?

3. **Nonattainment Compliance and CAIR Compliance.** Why did North Carolina complain about the deadlines that the EPA had set in CAIR? How did those deadlines compare to states' deadlines for coming into attainment? Does the mismatch make sense? Why not?

4. **Regional Measures?** Geographically, how did the EPA attempt to address the interstate air pollution issues raised in CAIR? Why was that approach impermissible, according to the D.C. Circuit? What is the proper geographical focus under Section 110?

* * *

2. Ozone–Specific Provisions

As the previous case makes clear, ozone is a particularly significant interstate pollution problem. As part of the ozone nonattainment provisions added to the Clean Air Act in 1990, Congress required the EPA to study nitrogen oxides (NOx) and volatile organic compounds (VOCs), which are ozone precursors. CAA § 185B, 42 U.S.C. § 7511f. The EPA has since provided the following information about ozone.

How Can Ozone Be Both Good and Bad?

Ozone occurs in two layers of the atmosphere. The layer surrounding the earth's surface is the troposphere. Here, ground-level or "bad" ozone is an air pollutant that damages human health, vegetation, and many common materials. It is a key ingredient of urban smog. The troposphere extends to a level about 10 miles up, where it meets the second layer, the stratosphere. The stratospheric or "good" ozone layer extends upward from about 10 to 30 miles and protects life on earth from the sun's harmful ultraviolet rays (UV-b).

What Causes "Bad" Ozone?

Motor vehicle exhaust and industrial emissions, gasoline vapors, and chemical solvents are some of the major sources of NOX and VOC, also known as ozone precursors. Strong sunlight and hot weather cause ground-level ozone to form in harmful concentrations in the air. Many urban areas tend to have high levels of "bad" ozone, but other areas are also subject to high ozone levels as winds carry NOX emissions hundreds of miles away from their original sources.

Ozone concentrations can vary from year to year. Changing weather patterns (especially the number of hot, sunny days), periods of air stagnation, and other factors that contribute to ozone formation make long-term predictions difficult.

* * *

How Does "Bad" Ozone Affect Human Health and the Environment?

Repeated exposure to ozone pollution may cause permanent damage to the lungs. Even when ozone is present in low levels, inhaling it triggers a variety of health problems including chest pains, coughing, nausea, throat irritation, and congestion. It also can worsen bronchitis, heart disease, emphysema, and asthma, and reduce lung capacity.

Healthy people also experience difficulty in breathing when exposed to ozone pollution. Because ozone pollution usually forms in hot weather, anyone who spends time outdoors in the summer may be affected, particularly children, the elderly, outdoor workers and people exercising. Millions of Americans live in areas where the national ozone health standards are exceeded.

Ground-level ozone damages plant life and is responsible for 500 million dollars in reduced crop production in the United States each year. It interferes with the ability of plants to produce and store food, making them more susceptible to disease, insects, other pollutants, and harsh weather. "Bad" ozone damages the foliage of trees and other plants, ruining the landscape of cities, national parks and forests, and recreation areas.

What is Being Done About Bad Ozone?

The Clean Air Act Amendments of 1990 require EPA, states, and cities to implement programs to further reduce emissions of ozone precursors from sources such as cars, fuels, industrial facilities, power plants, and consumer/commercial products. Power plants will be reducing emissions, cleaner cars and fuels are being developed, many gas stations are using special nozzles at the pumps to recapture gasoline vapors, and vehicle inspection programs are being improved to reduce emissions.

Office of Air Quality, Planning, and Standards, U.S. E.P.A., *Ozone: Good Up High, Bad Nearby* (Oct. 1997), *available at* http://www.epa.gov/oar/oaqps/gooduphigh (last updated Oct. 16, 2006).

In 1990, Congress added special provisions to the Clean Air Act to address interstate ozone pollution. Congress statutorily designated Connecticut, Delaware, Maine, Maryland, Massachusetts, New Hampshire, New Jersey, New York, Pennsylvania, Rhode Island, Vermont, and the District of Columbia as an ozone transport region, CAA § 184(a), 42 U.S.C. § 7511c(a)—that is, as a region where the interstate transportation of ozone pollutants "contributes significantly to a violation of a national ambient air quality standard * * *." CAA § 176A(a), 42 U.S.C. § 7506a(a). States within the ozone transport region had to amend their SIPs to comply with the enhanced vehicle inspection and maintenance requirements that apply to ozone serious nonattainment areas, *see* CAA §§ 184(b)(1)(A), 182(c)(2)(A), 42 U.S.C. §§ 7511c(b)(1)(A), 7511a(c)(3), and to subject all sources of VOCs to RACT requirements. CAA

§ 184(b)(1)(B), 42 U.S.C. § 7511c(b)(1)(B). The EPA was also free to recommend additional control requirements for these states. CAA § 184(c)(1), 42 U.S.C. § 7511c(c)(1).

Nevertheless, ozone transportation remains a regionally divisive issue in the United States. What happens when upwind states struggling with ozone nonattainment requirements confront demands from downwind states that their efforts are insufficient? Or what if the emissions controls necessary to protect downwind states would increase ozone emissions within the nonattainment state? The following case addresses the perpetual tension between midwestern and eastern states over the issue of ozone attainment.

NEW YORK v. ENVIRONMENTAL PROTECTION AGENCY

133 F.3d 987 (7th Cir. 1998).

POSNER, CHIEF JUDGE.

Before us is a petition to review a final rule issued by the Environmental Protection Agency granting the four states that abut Lake Michigan (Illinois, Indiana, Michigan, and Wisconsin) an exemption from limitations that the Clean Air Act, 42 U.S.C. §§ 7401 *et seq.*, requires states to impose on the emission of nitrogen oxides. Approval of Section 182(f) Exemption, 61 Fed. Reg. 2428 (1996), codified in 40 C.F.R. §§ 52.726(k), 52.778(i), 52.1174(*l*), 52.2585(i). The petition for review was filed by New York (joined by Pennsylvania and Vermont), which being downwind from the Lake Michigan states wants the level of nitrogen oxide emissions originating in those states to be as low as possible.

When carbon compounds known as "volatile organic compounds" (VOCs) mix with nitrogen oxides (NOX) in the presence of sunlight, the result is ozone, a major factor in urban smog. (Carbon monoxide also contributes to the formation of ozone, but it is not a VOC and is not at issue in this case.) Yet once ozone is formed, a further addition of nitrogen oxides may react with the ozone in a way that will cause the ozone level to fall in the immediate area; at the same time, the additional nitrogen oxides, drifting downwind, may raise the ozone level elsewhere. And, conversely, reducing the quantity of nitrogen oxides in the air may raise rather than lower the ozone level in the area in which the mixing of the nitrogen oxides and the ozone takes place, while at the same time reducing the ozone level downwind. (A further complication, but not one at issue in this litigation, is that reducing the ozone level in the atmosphere may increase the incidence of skin cancer.) Thus, predicting the total effect on ozone (and therefore on smog) of a reduction in nitrogen oxide emissions, and the geographical incidence of that effect, is a tricky business; and the uncertainties of prediction have generated the interstate conflict that gives rise to the petition for review. New York is convinced that reducing the amount of nitrogen oxide emissions from sources in the Lake Michigan states will reduce the ozone level in New York. The Lake

Michigan states believe that such a reduction might raise the ozone level in midwestern cities. And of course they are also concerned because the benefits of a reduction (if any) in the ozone level in the Midwest are unlikely to be as great as the costs of the pollution-control requirements that the EPA has waived in the rule under attack, for most of the benefits from reducing the emission of nitrogen oxides in the emitting states will be received by the downwind states.

* * * In 1990, the Clean Air Act was amended to deal specifically with ozone. Section 185B of the amended Act, 42 U.S.C. § 7511f, directs the EPA (in conjunction with other bodies) to conduct a study of, among other things, the role of nitrogen oxides in the formation of ozone, and to report the results of the study to Congress; the report was submitted in 1993. Section 182(f)(1), 42 U.S.C. § 7511a(f)(1), imposes on the states a duty to control emissions of nitrogen oxides, but goes on (in section 182(f)(1)(A)) to lift the duty if "the [EPA] determines (when the [EPA] approves a [state implementation] plan or plan revision) that additional reductions of oxides of nitrogen would not contribute to attainment of the national ambient air quality standard for ozone in the area," "area" being defined in a way that, so far as the present case is concerned, includes the Lake Michigan states and excludes the downwind states. 42 U.S.C. § 7511a(f)(1)(A). And section 182(f)(3) provides that "at any time after the final report under section [185B] is submitted to Congress, a person may petition the [EPA] for a determination under [section 182(f)(1)]." It was after the submission of the section 185B report that the Lake Michigan states petitioned under section 182(f)(3) for the exemption that the EPA granted and that New York and two other eastern states challenge.

Their principal argument is that the EPA can grant an exemption from the normal restrictions on the emission of nitrogen oxides—as opposed to making a mere "determination" under section 182(f)(3) that reducing the level of those emissions (by insisting on compliance with the restrictions) would not aggravate the ozone problem in the petitioning states—only in conjunction with the approval of a state implementation plan or a revision of such a plan. The effect of this interpretation would be to require the EPA to defer action on the Lake Michigan states' request for an exemption until it approves, in the recently begun section 110(a)(2)(D) proceeding, appropriate revisions in the states' implementation plans. Section 182(f) confines the EPA's consideration to the ozone problem in the states of emission and thus excludes consideration of downwind effects, but those effects will be at the center of the EPA's consideration of the revision of the Lake Michigan states' implementation plans. The effect of the rule challenged in this case is thus to allow the Lake Michigan states to continue to emit nitrogen oxides without regard to downwind effects until the completion and implementation of the section 110(a)(2)(D) proceeding, which will be years from now.

The EPA's interpretation of section 182(f) is at least as plausible as New York's, and that makes this an easy case under the *Chevron* doctrine. Immediate compliance with the requirements for limiting the emission of nitrogen oxides would require power plants and other stationary-source emitters of these oxides to install expensive pollution-control equipment at a time when the effect of nitrogen oxides on pollution is uncertain. That is why Congress authorized the EPA in section 182(f)(3), upon petition by affected persons, including states, 42 U.S.C. § 7602(e), to waive the standards for NOX if satisfied that compliance with those standards would not improve the ozone situation in the area, without regard to any downwind effects. Of course later on, when the EPA considered downwind effects pursuant to the mandate of section 110(a)(2)(D), it would have in effect to rescind the permission granted under section 182(f)(3) if it found the downwind effects significant. But meanwhile states would not have to require expensive measures of compliance that might prove wasted should those effects ultimately be found not to be serious after all.

On New York's interpretation, section 182(f)(3) is empty. For having obtained the EPA's favorable determination under that subsection, the states would still have to submit an implementation plan revised in accordance with the determination and then ask the EPA for the exemption. Since they could have submitted the revised plan and asked for the exemption without bothering to first seek a favorable determination under section 182(f)(3), proceeding under that section would be a waste of everybody's time—a superfluous gesture not plausibly imputed to congressional design. Of course, the direct route, by channeling the states' request for relief through the plan or plan-revision route, would bring section 110(a)(2)(D) into play and require consideration of downwind effects. That is why New York wants to confine the Lake Michigan states to that route. But it would defeat the apparent purpose of section 182(f)(3), which is to allow the postponement of full compliance with the control requirements for nitrogen oxides until the downwind effects are determined, provided that the effects of postponement in the emitting area are not adverse. So New York's interpretation really does read this section out of the statute, even though the section appears to be the key to a sensible response to the manifold uncertainties involved in the control of ozone. On New York's view, even if the Lake Michigan states could show that reducing their nitrogen oxide emissions would significantly worsen air quality in the Midwest, and even if the downwind effects of such a reduction were totally unknown, the EPA could not relax its NOX requirements until the completion, years from now, of the section 110(a)(2)(D) proceeding. That doesn't make a lot of sense.

New York has another string to its bow, however. It argues that the EPA was mistaken to think that further reductions in nitrogen oxide emissions by stationary sources in the Lake Michigan states would do nothing for the ozone problem in those states. If that is right, the EPA should not have granted the states' section 182(f)(3) petition, quite apart from any downwind effects. * * *

To determine the effects of the exemption in the emitting area, the EPA compares the effects on the ozone level of substantial reductions in the emission of VOCs (carbon compounds that, the reader will recall, react with nitrogen oxides in the presence of sunlight to form ozone) with the effects of substantial reductions in the level of nitrogen oxides and, more to the point, of VOCs plus nitrogen oxides. If the effects on the ozone level of just reducing the emission of VOCs to the level required by the Clean Air Act are as great as the effects of the alternatives that involve reducing the emission of nitrogen oxides, the exemption will be granted. The thinking behind this approach is that if reducing the level of nitrogen oxides has no *incremental* effect on the ozone level, that is, no effect given required reductions in the cofactor in ozone pollution, forcing a reduction in the level of nitrogen oxides would not contribute to attaining the ozone standard. This is a sensible reading of the statute, and, under *Chevron,* miles away from anything we could properly reverse.

* * * The petition for review is DENIED.

NOTES

1. **Interpreting Section 182(f).** How did the eastern states and the EPA differ in their views of § 182(f)? Why did the choice matter to the downwind states? What standard did the Seventh Circuit use to review the EPA's view of § 182(f)? Why? Using that standard of review, why did the Seventh Circuit uphold the EPA's view of § 182(f)? What were the consequences for the northeastern states?

2. **The Economics of VOC and NOx Reduction.** How did economics play into the EPA's and the Seventh Circuit's view of section 182(f)? Are economics a proper consideration at this stage? Why shouldn't the Lake Michigan state sources have to install pollution control equipment as soon as possible?

3. **Progress in Reducing Ozone.** As Figure 4–20 shows, although the ozone problem persists, recent studies by the EPA indicate that the overall progress in reducing ozone pollution has been positive.

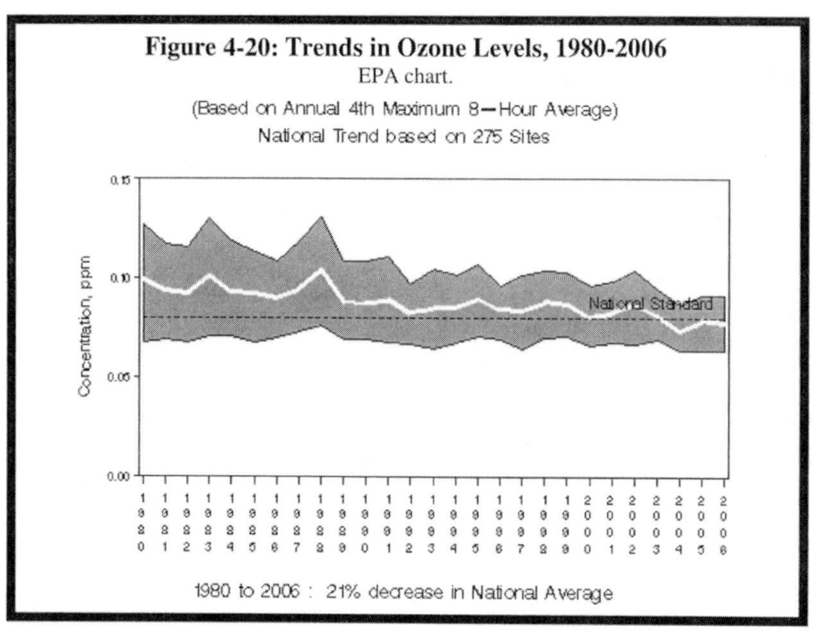

Figure 4-20: Trends in Ozone Levels, 1980-2006
EPA chart.

* * *

3. Nitrogen Oxides, Sulfur Dioxide, and Acid Rain

STATE OF GEORGIA v. TENNESSEE COPPER COMPANY

206 U.S. 230 (1907).

Mr. JUSTICE HOLMES delivered the opinion of the court:

This is a bill in equity filed in this court by the state of Georgia, in pursuance of a resolution of the legislature and by direction of the governor of the state, to enjoin the defendant copper companies from discharging noxious gas from their works in Tennessee over the plaintiff's territory. It alleges that, in consequence of such discharge, a wholesale destruction of forests, orchards, and crops is going on, and other injuries are done and threatened in five counties of the state. It alleges also a vain application to the state of Tennessee for relief. * * *

The case has been argued largely as if it were one between two private parties; but it is not. The very elements that would be relied upon in a suit between fellow citizens as a ground for equitable relief are wanting here. The state owns very little of the territory alleged to be affected, and the damage to it capable of estimate in money, possibly, at least, is small. This is a suit by a state for an injury to it in its capacity of quasi-sovereign. In that capacity the state has an interest independent of and behind the titles of its citizens, in all the earth and air within its domain. It has the last word as to whether its mountains shall be stripped of their forests and its inhabitants shall breathe pure air. It might have to pay individuals before it could utter that word, but with it remains the final power. The alleged damage to the state as a private owner is merely a makeweight, and we may lay on one side the dispute as to whether the destruction of forests has led to the gullying of its roads.

* * * It is a fair and reasonable demand on the part of a sovereign that the air over its territory should not be polluted on a great scale by sulphurous acid gas, that the forests on its mountains, be they better or worse, and whatever domestic destruction they have suffered, should not be further destroyed or threatened by the act of persons beyond its control, that the crops and orchards on its hills should not be endangered from the same source. If any such demand is to be enforced this must be notwithstanding the hesitation that we might feel if the suit were between private parties, and the doubt whether, for the injuries which they might be suffering to their property, they should not be left to an action at law.

The proof requires but a few words. It is not denied that the defendants generate in their works near the Georgia line large quantities of sulphur dioxid which becomes sulphurous acid by its mixture with the air. It hardly is denied, and cannot be denied with success, that this gas often is carried by the wind great distances and over great tracts of Georgia land. On the evidence the pollution of the air and the magnitude of that pollution are not open to dispute. Without any attempt to go into details immaterial to the suit, it is proper to add that we are satisfied, by a preponderance of evidence, that the sulphurous fumes cause and threaten damage on so considerable a scale to the forests and vegetable life, if not to health, within the plaintiff state, as to make out a case * * *. Whether Georgia, by insisting upon this claim, is doing more harm than good to her own citizens, is for her to determine. The possible disaster to those outside the state must be accepted as a consequence of her standing upon her extreme rights.

* * * If the state of Georgia adheres to its determination, there is no alternative to issuing an injunction, after allowing a reasonable time to the defendants to complete the structures that they now are building, and the efforts that they are making to stop the fumes. The plaintiff may submit a form of decree on the coming in of this court in October next.

Injunction to issue.

NOTES

1. **Acid Rain and Interstate Nuisance.** The *Tennessee Copper* litigation was an early example of interstate air pollution resulting in ***acid rain***. "***Acid rain***" refers to atmospheric conditions that create acidic precipitation—not just rain but also fog and snow. Acid rain became a more generally noticeable problem in the 1960s and 1970s in the eastern United States and Canada, acidifying rivers, lakes, and streams, which in turn killed fish, damaged forests, depleted soil, and eroded buildings. In the 1970s,

researchers discovered that power plants and other major stationary sources in the Midwest that burn high-sulfur coal and emit sulfur dioxide and nitrogen oxides are the primary causes of acid rain in the Northeast.

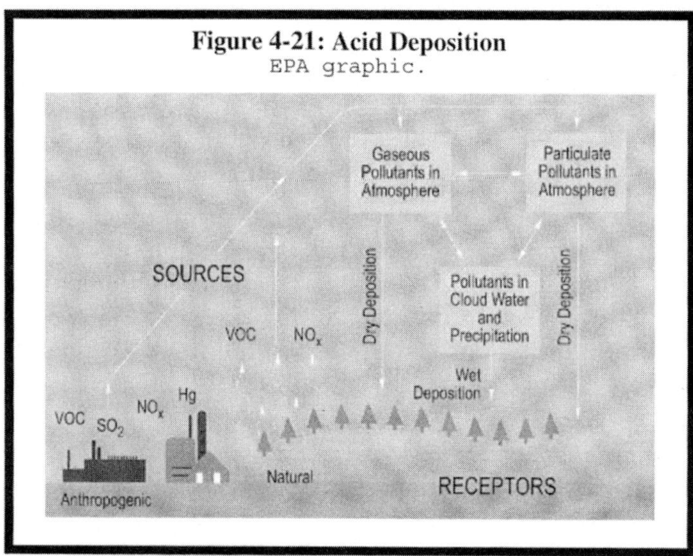

Figure 4-21: Acid Deposition
EPA graphic.

The EPA describes the acid rain issue as follows:

> "Acid rain" is a broad term referring to a mixture of wet and dry deposition (deposited material) from the atmosphere containing higher than normal amounts of nitric and sulfuric acids. The precursors, or chemical forerunners, of acid rain formation result from both natural sources, such as volcanoes and decaying vegetation, and man-made sources, primarily emissions of sulfur dioxide (SO_2) and nitrogen oxides (NO_x) resulting from fossil fuel combustion. In the United States, roughly 2/3 of all SO_2 and 1/4 of all NO_x come from electric power generation that relies on burning fossil fuels, like coal. Acid rain occurs when these gases react in the atmosphere with water, oxygen, and other chemicals to form various acidic compounds. The result is a mild solution of sulfuric acid and nitric acid. When sulfur dioxide and nitrogen oxides are released from power plants and other sources, prevailing winds blow these compounds across state and national borders, sometimes over hundreds of miles.

U.S. E.P.A., *Acid Rain: What Is Acid Rain?*, http://www.epa.gov/acidrain/what/index.html (as updated June 8, 2007).

How did the Supreme Court attempt to deal with interstate acid rain problems in *Tennessee Copper*? Should states get special consideration when bringing interstate pollution cases?

2. **Interstate Pollution Cases and the Supreme Court's Original Jurisdiction**. The U.S. Constitution gives the U.S. Supreme Court ***original jurisdiction*** to hear cases in which a state is a party. U.S. CONST., art. III, § 2. As a result, before Congress enacted the federal environmental statutes, states often applied directly to the Supreme Court for resolution of interstate

pollution issues. The Court developed a limited body of federal common law to address these issues, and it has since held that the federal environmental statutes preempt this federal common law of nuisance. In *Missouri v. Illinois*, an interstate water pollution case cited in *Tennessee Copper*, the Court imposed a rather high burden of proof on complaining states seeking an injunction against polluting states, and the Court generally resisted imposing specific pollution controls on offending states.

Tennessee Copper is an exception to the Court's general reluctance to control interstate pollution from the bench. Not only did the Court find that Georgia was entitled to an injunction, it later imposed specific emissions requirements on the offending companies. For example, in 1916 the Court determined that the Ducktown Sulphur, Copper & Iron Co., a co-defendant in the principal case, could emit no more than 25 tons per day of sulfur gases from April 10 to October 1, and no more than 50 tons per day the rest of the year. *Georgia v. Tennessee Copper Co.*, 240 U.S. 650, 650 (1916).

Why might the Supreme Court have been inclined to find for Georgia in the *Tennessee Copper* litigation and to impose such specific injunctions? Did it matter, do you think, that Georgia was suing two copper companies instead of—as had been the case in *Missouri v. Illinois*—another state? Why or why not?

* * *

As was discussed in Note 1 after *Tennessee Copper*, acid rain has continued to be an important interstate air pollution problem. After attempts to use the Clean Air Act's general interstate air pollution provisions—sections 110 and 126, the SIP-related process—failed to adequately address the acid rain problem, Congress in 1990 added specific acid rain reduction provisions to the Act. CAA §§ 401–416, 42 U.S.C. §§ 7651–7651o. Congress's motivations for enacting the program came from increasing scientific certainties about the dangers of acid rain:

> [Scientists] have concluded that acid rain and its precursors are responsible for between 50,000 and 70,000 premature deaths per year. In addition, acid deposition is responsible for massive damage to buildings and other man-made structures, poisoning lakes and streams to the extent that they can no longer support fish and other life, altering the chemical composition of soils and upsetting the natural balance which enables their productive use, and reducing visibility throughout the United States.

S. REP. NO. 101–228, 1990 U.S.C.C.A.N. 3385, 3389–90 (Dec. 20, 1989).

Congress's goal in 1990 was to reduce sulfur dioxide emissions to 10 million tons below 1980 emission levels and to reduce nitrogen oxide emissions to 2 million tons below 1980 emission levels. CAA § 401(b), 42 U.S.C. § 7651(b). Congress sought to achieve this goal through an innovative ***"cap-and-trade"*** program. Under this program, EPA sets annual sulfur dioxide allowances for the relevant sources. CAA § 403, 42 U.S.C. § 7651b. Stationary sources may emit sulfur dioxide only to the amount of the allowance. However, if a source emits less sulfur dioxide than its allowance, it can trade or sell the "excess" allowance to other sources that cannot meet their allowances, in accordance with EPA regulations. Sources emitting more sulfur dioxide than allowed for that year are subject to penalties of $2000 per ton of excess pollutant emitted. CAA § 411(a), 42 U.S.C. § 7651j(a). In addition, the source may have to offset its emissions the following year by the amount of its excess discharge. CAA § 411(b), 42 U.S.C. § 7651j(b).

Issuance of acid rain emissions allowances occurred in two stages. Phase I primarily affected large electricity generators, took effect in 1995, and remained in effect until January 1, 2000. Congress set the general Phase I allowances. CAA § 404, 42 U.S.C. § 7651c. The EPA then "allocated allowances at an emission rate of 2.5 pounds of SO_2/mmBtu (million British thermal units) of heat input, multiplied by the unit's baseline mmBtu (the average fossil fuel consumed from 1985 through 1987). * * * Alternative or additional allowance allocations were made for various units, including affected units in Illinois, Indiana, and Ohio, which were allocated a pro rata share of 200,000 additional allowances each year from 1995 to 1999." U.S. E.P.A., *Clean Air Markets: Acid Rain Program SO_2 Allowances Fact Sheet* http://www.epa.gov/airmarkets/trading/factsheet.html (as updated Feb. 1, 2007).

Figure 4-22: State-by-State Reductions in SO2 Emissions, 1990-2010
EPA graphic.

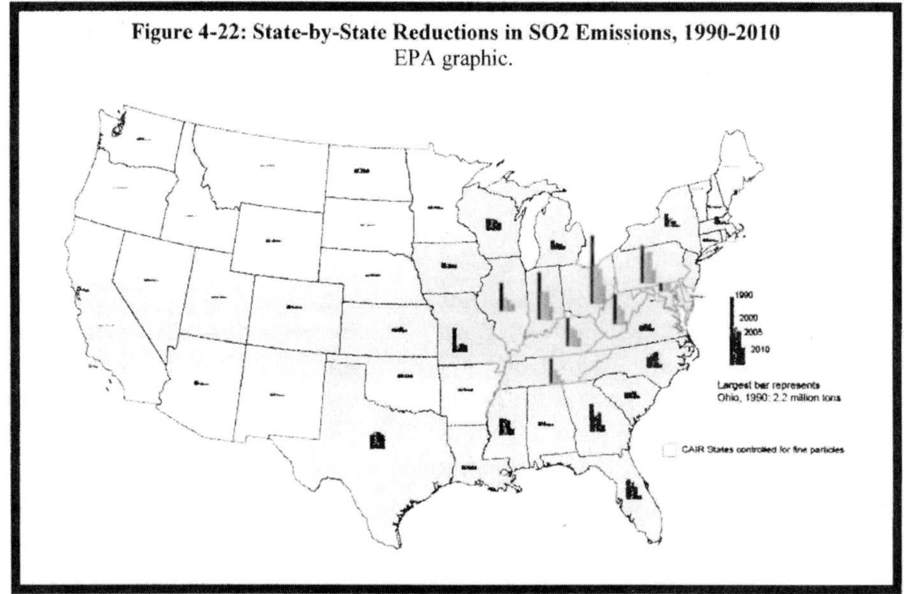

On January 1, 2000, the Phase II allowances took effect, requiring further sulfur dioxide reductions on a category-by-category basis, with allowances keyed to the sources' 1985 emissions rates. CAA § 405, 42 U.S.C. § 7651d. Phase II applies to almost all reasonably sized generating facilities. In Phase II, "[a]llowance allocation calculations were made for various types of units, such as coal- and gas-fired units with low and high emissions rates or low fuel consumption. EPA allocated allowances to each unit at an emission rate of 1.2 pounds of SO_2/mmBtu of heat input, multiplied by the unit's baseline. During Phase II, the Act places a cap at 8.95 million on the number of allowances issued to units each year. This effectively caps emissions at 8.95 million tons annually and ensures that the mandated emissions reductions are maintained over time." U.S. E.P.A., *Clean Air Markets: Acid Rain Program SO_2 Allowances Fact Sheet* http://www.epa.gov/airmarkets/trading/factsheet.html (as updated Feb. 1, 2007).

As sources become ***affected sources*** subject to the sulfur dioxide emission reduction requirements, they also become subject to the ***nitrogen oxides emission reduction program***. CAA § 407, 42 U.S.C. § 7651f. This is *not* a cap-and-trade program. Instead, EPA establishes nitrogen oxides emission limitations based "on the degree of reduction achievable through retrofit application of the best system of continuous emission reduction, taking into account available technology, costs and energy and environmental impacts," or BART. CAA § 407(b)(2), 42 U.S.C. § 7651f(b)(2).

Sources subject to the acid rain program are also subject to the Title V permit program. CAA § 408, 42 U.S.C. § 7651g. Finally, sources that emit sulfur dioxide that are not *required* to participate in the acid rain reduction program may nevertheless opt into that program. CAA § 410, 42 U.S.C. § 7651i.

In November 1999, EPA issued a progress report on the acid rain program, generally concluding that the sulfur dioxide portion of the program was quite successful. First, the costs of the program were far less than first predicted. In 1990, EPA estimated that sulfur dioxide emission reductions would cost $4.6 billion per year by 2010, the year in which Congress's acid rain goal is supposed to be met. By 1994, the Government Accountability Office had reevaluated the cost to be $2 billion per year by 2010, and in 1998 projected costs were less than $1 billion per year by 2010. At the same time, emissions reductions occurred faster than predicted. In 1995, the first year of sulfur dioxide emissions allowances, sulfur dioxide emissions dropped by 3 million tons. By 1999, the utilities with the highest rates of sulfur dioxide emissions had decreased their emissions to 5 million tons below their 1980 levels. As a result of these early decreases, by 1999 sulfate deposition levels in the Northeast and Mid-Atlantic regions had dropped by about 25 percent. OFFICE OF AIR QUALITY, PLANNING, AND STANDARDS, U.S. E.P.A., PROGRESS REPORT ON THE EPA ACID RAIN PROGRAM 5–6 (Nov. 1999), *available at* http://www.epa.gov/airmarkets/progress/docs/1999report.pdf.

Reduction in nitrogen oxides has been less successful, in part because other sources of nitrogen oxides have kept total emission levels about even since 1995. Nevertheless, the average emission rates of NOx by utilities in the Phase I program dropped about 42 percent between 1996 and 1999, resulting in a 35 percent decrease in actual NOx emissions from electric utilities. *Id.*

4. Other Interstate Trading Programs

a. *Clean Air Interstate Rule (CAIR)*

In May 2005, the EPA promulgated the ***Clean Air Interstate Rule* (CAIR)** to address interstate pollution from fine particulates and ozone in the eastern United States. EPA, *Rule to Reduce Interstate Transport of Fine Particulate Matter and Ozone (Clean Air Interstate Rule)*, 70 Fed. Reg. 72,268 (May 12, 2005). CAIR establishes regional caps on SO_2 and NO_x emissions to reduce ozone and particulate matter nonattainment in eastern states (sulfur dioxide is a precursor to both) and will operate concurrently with the acid rain program. In its rulemaking, the EPA found that 28 states and the District of Columbia contribute significantly to ozone and $PM_{2.5}$ nonattainment in the eastern states and imposed a SIP call. Moreover, the rule caps annual SO_2 emissions in the region at 3.7 million tons in 2010 and 2.6 million tons in 2015, while it caps NO_x emissions at 1.5 million tons in 2009 and 1.3 million tons in 2015.

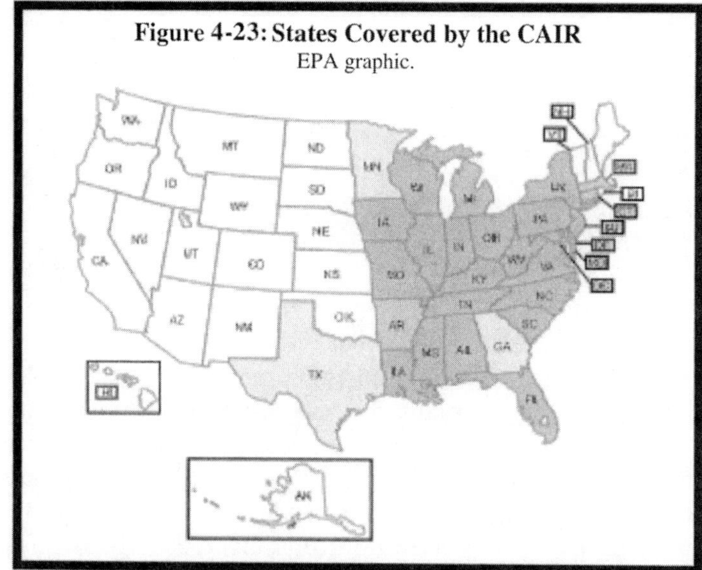

Figure 4-23: States Covered by the CAIR
EPA graphic.

b. *Clean Air Visibility Rule (CAVR)*

The EPA promulgated the ***Clean Air Visibility Rule* (CAVR)** in July 2005. EPA, *Regional Haze Regulations and Guidelines for Best Available Retrofit Technology (BART) Determinations*, 70 Fed. Reg. 39,104 (July 6, 2005). CAVR requires non-CAIR sources located in the West and parts of New England to reduce SO_2 and NO_x emissions that impair visibility in the national parks. In addition, the EPA allowed power plants and other stationary sources to establish regional cap-and-trade programs to achieve the required reductions.

c. *Clean Air Mercury Rule (CAMR)*

In May 2005, the EPA promulgated the Clean Air Mercury Rule (CAMR) to establish a cap-and-trade program for mercury emissions, to begin in 2010. EPA, *Standards of Performance for New and Existing Stationary Sources: Electric Utility Steam Generating Units*, 70 Fed. Reg. 28,606 (May 18, 2005). The rule imposed new mercury emissions requirements on both new and existing coal-fired power plants; it also required all states to come up with methods to reduce mercury emissions. In 2005, these utilities emitted approximately 48 tons per year of mercury. Under the new trading program, total emissions will be capped at 38 tons per year in 2010 and 15 tons per year in 2018.

Figure 4-24: Mercury Deposition in the United States
EPA graphic.

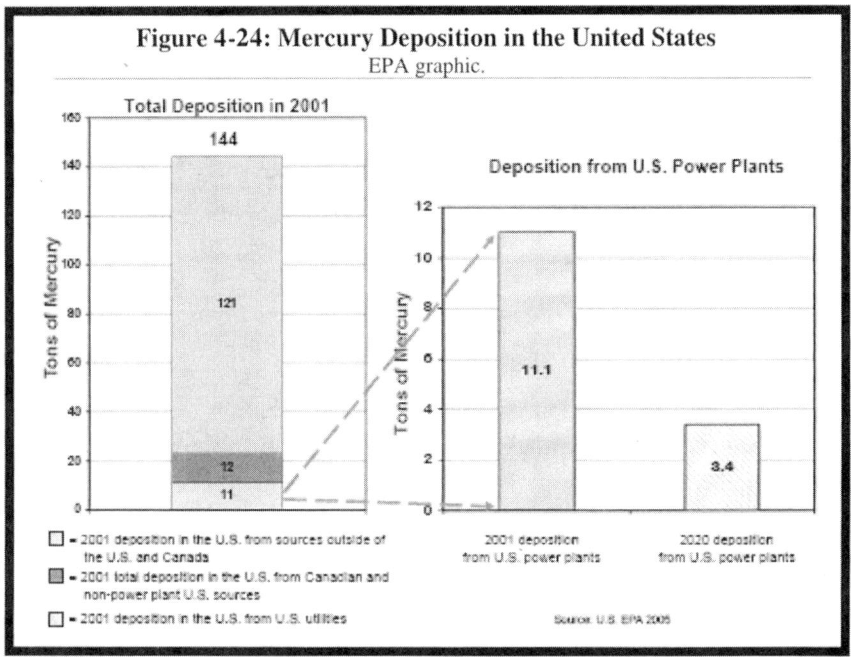

C. INTERNATIONAL AIR POLLUTION: SECTION 115 OF THE CLEAN AIR ACT

Congress addressed problems of international air pollution through section 115 of the Clean Air Act. 42 U.S.C. § 7415. Section 115 provides that:

> Whenever the Administrator, upon receipt of reports, surveys or studies from any duly constituted international agency has reason to believe that any air pollutant or pollutants emitted in the United States cause or contribute to air pollution which may reasonably be anticipated to endanger public health or welfare in a foreign country or whenever the Secretary of State requests him to do so with respect to such pollution which the Secretary of State alleges is of such a

> nature, the Administrator shall give formal notification thereof to the Governor of the State in which such emissions originate.

CAA § 115(a), 42 U.S.C. § 7415(a). This notification from the EPA to the state is deemed a requirement that the state revise its SIP, and "[a]ny foreign country so affected by such emission of pollutant or pollutants shall be invited to appear at any public hearing association with any revision of the appropriate portion of the applicable state implementation plan." *Id.* § 115(b), 42 U.S.C. § 7415(b). However, section 115 applies "only to a foreign country which the Administrator determines has given the United States essentially the same rights with respect to the prevention or control of air pollution occurring in that country as is given that country by this section." *Id.* § 115(c), 42 U.S.C. § 7415(c).

Perhaps unsurprisingly, the only litigated use of section 115 involved acid rain and Canada. On January 13, 1981—days before Ronald Reagan succeeded Jimmy Carter as President of the United States—then-EPA Administrator Douglas M. Costle sent a letter to President Carter's Secretary of State, Edmund S. Muskie, finding that sources in the United States were contributing to acid rain in Canada, endangering Canadian health and welfare. *Thomas v. State of New York*, 802 F.2d 1443, 1445 (D.C. Cir. 1986). In addition, Administrator Costle found that newly enacted Canadian legislation afforded the United States the same rights that Canada had under section 115, meeting the reciprocity requirement. *Id.* When Administrator Costle's successor at the EPA did nothing to implement this finding, states, environmental groups, and property owners sued the EPA, claiming that the EPA had mandatory duties to identify the states responsible and to issue notices requiring SIP revisions in those states. *Id.* at 1444–45. The District Court for the District of Columbia found for the plaintiffs and issued an injunction, *id.* at 1446, but the D.C. Circuit reversed, concluding that Administrator Costle's findings were substantive "rules" under the federal Administrative Procedure Act (APA) and hence could only be effective if the EPA issued them through notice-and-comment rulemaking procedures, which it had not. *Id.* at 1446–47.

Undaunted, Canada then petitioned the EPA to issue the required rules. The following decision resulted.

HER MAJESTY THE QUEEN IN RIGHT OF ONTARIO v. UNITED STATES ENVIRONMENTAL PROTECTION AGENCY

912 F.2d 1525 (D.C. Cir. 1990).

BUCKLEY, CIRCUIT JUDGE:

The question before us is whether the Environmental Protection Agency has any present obligation to take action under section 115 of the Clean Air Act, which establishes a procedure for the prevention of air pollutants in the United States from causing harm in the form of acid deposition to the public health and welfare in Canada. The Province of Ontario and a number of States and environmental groups have petitioned the EPA for a rulemaking that would essentially set in motion section 115's international pollution abatement procedures. We conclude, first, that section 115 does not require the EPA to initiate those procedures until it is able to identify the specific sources in the United States of pollutants that cause harm in Canada; and second, we are satisfied that the EPA is not as yet able to do so.

I. BACKGROUND

Section 115(a) of the Clean Air Act provides in relevant part as follows:

> Whenever the Administrator, upon receipt of reports, surveys or studies from any duly constituted international agency has reason to believe that any air pollutant or pollutants emitted in the United States cause or contribute to air pollution which may reasonably be anticipated to endanger public health or welfare in a foreign country . . . , the Administrator shall give formal notification thereof to the Governor of the State in which such emissions originate.

42 U.S.C. § 7415(a) (1982). The Administrator's finding that pollution emitted in the United States contributes to such air pollution is referred to as an "endangerment finding."

* * * The remedy provided by section 115 is applicable "only to a foreign country which the Administrator determines has given the United States essentially the same rights with respect to the prevention or control of air pollution occurring in that country as is given that country by this section." *Id.* § 7415(c). This determination is known as a "reciprocity finding."

The dispute in this case is whether the EPA has a present obligation, under section 115, to promulgate endangerment and reciprocity findings as proposed rules with respect to U.S. emissions that allegedly result in harmful levels of acid deposition in Canada. Acid deposition is believed to result primarily from the transportation of sulphur and nitrogen oxide emissions into the atmosphere where they are converted, by chemical processes, into acids that, in combination with water vapors, precipitate in the form of "acid rain," often many hundreds of miles from their source.

* * * The EPA's view of section 115 is that the endangerment finding under section 115(a) is inextricably linked to the requirement that it notify the States whose SIP's must be revised under section 115(b); in other words, the EPA believes that it need not make an endangerment finding until it is able to identify the sources of the pollutants. Otherwise, it will not be able to give the required notification. It then argues that because it currently lacks sufficient information to be able to trace pollutants affecting the Canadian health and welfare to specific sources in the United States, it is not obliged to make endangerment findings at this

time. In sum, under the EPA's interpretation, section 115 requires a "unitary proceeding."

Conversely, in petitioners' view the section 115 remedial process may be implemented in stages. * * * They conclude that the EPA has already effectively made endangerment and reciprocity determinations, and therefore it is obliged to publish them as proposed rules; and having made those determinations, the agency may not simply refuse to take *any* corrective action while it continues to study the problem. Petitioners do not base their argument on a belief that the EPA can in fact trace pollutants to their specific sources at the present time.

* * * II. DISCUSSION

Petitioners argue that the EPA has denied their rulemaking petitions, and that its denial was arbitrary, capricious, and not in accordance with law because once the EPA is able to make endangerment and reciprocity findings, it *must* publish them for notice and comment and thereby initiate the remedial process established by section 115. The EPA * * * defends its interpretation of section 115 as reasonable. * * *

* * * In reviewing an agency's interpretation of a statute it administers, we first determine, using traditional tools of statutory construction, "whether Congress has directly spoken to the precise question at issue." *Chevron U.S.A. Inc. v. NRDC, Inc.,* 467 U.S. 837, 842–43 & n. 9 (1984). If the intent of Congress is clear and unambiguous, "that intention is the law and must be given effect." *Id.* at 843 n. 9. If, on the other hand, the statute is silent or ambiguous with respect to a specific issue, then we "must defer to the agency's interpretation ... so long as it is reasonable and consistent with the statutory purpose." *Ohio v. United States Dep't of the Interior,* 880 F.2d 432, 441 (D.C. Cir. 1989); *see also Chevron,* 467 U.S. at 843.

We are unable to draw any "unmistakable conclusion" as to whether Congress intended proceedings under section 115 to be unitary or divisible. The statutory language can be read either way, and the legislative history is meager and unilluminating. And although, as we explain below, the structure of the statute tends to support the EPA's view, we believe it falls short of expressing a clear and unambiguous congressional intent. Under the second step of the *Chevron* analysis, however, we comfortably conclude that the EPA's view of section 115 is permissible, as it is both entirely reasonable and consistent with the statutory plan.

Section 115(a) provides that "[w]henever" the Administrator, based on certain reports or studies, has "reason to believe" that an air pollutant emitted in the United States causes or contributes to air pollution that may reasonably be anticipated to endanger health or welfare in a foreign country, he "*shall* give formal notification thereof to the Governor of the State in which such emissions originate." 42 U.S.C. § 7415(a) (emphasis added). The words "whenever" the Administrator "has reason to believe" imply a degree of discretion underlying the endangerment finding. Once that finding is made, however, the remedial action that follows is both specific and mandatory—the Administrator "shall" notify the Governor of the specific State emitting the pollution and require it to revise its SIP.

The statute thus creates a specific linkage between the endangerment finding and the remedial procedures: Once the endangerment finding is made, the SIP revision process *must* follow. As a result, if there is insufficient information to enable the Administrator to implement those remedies, the promulgation of an endangerment finding alone would largely be pointless. For this reason, the EPA's view that the Administrator must have sufficient evidence correlating the endangerment to sources of pollution within a particular State before he can exercise his discretion to make endangerment findings is both reasonable and consistent with the statute.

Our view of the EPA's interpretation is further supported by section 115(b), which mandates a revision of the polluting State's SIP. Under subsection (b), the Administrator's notice to the Governor represents a finding that the State's SIP must be revised "with respect to so much of the ... plan *as is inadequate to prevent or eliminate the endangerment referred to in subsection (a) of this section.*" 42 U.S.C. § 7415(b) (emphasis added). This provision reinforces the linkage between the endangerment finding and the remedy that Congress has prescribed. If the EPA does not have a sufficient base of knowledge to trace endangering pollutants to sources within specific States, then a simple endangerment finding would leave subsection (b) without effect. The unitary approach adopted by the EPA avoids that result.

* * * Our reluctance to intrude into the EPA's decisionmaking process at this time is consistent with the great deference we generally accord to an agency's "predictions within [its] area of special expertise, at the frontiers of science." *New York v. EPA,* 852 F.2d 574, 580 (D.C. Cir. 1988), *cert. denied,* ___ U.S. ___, 109 S.Ct. 1338 (1989). In addition, the agency's position as to the *application* of section 115 does not have any direct and immediate effect on the rights of petitioners, because the section 115 abatement process—as permissibly construed by the EPA—may yet be undertaken. Thus, * * * we conclude that the EPA has not taken final action on petitioners' request for rulemaking—except, of course, to the extent they have requested a two-step proceeding.

* * * We are, of course, fully aware that more than nine years have elapsed since Administrator Costle advised Secretary of State Muskie and Senator Mitchell of his conclusion that pollutants from sources in the United States were endangering the public welfare in Canada. But we are also aware of the unusual complexity of the factors facing the agency in determining the effects of acid rain and in tracing the pollutants from the point of deposition back to their sources. In fact, it was for the purpose, among others, of developing a better understanding of the acid rain phenomenon that Congress enacted the Acid Precipitation Act of 1980, 42 U.S.C. §§ 8901–8912 (1982).

This statute initiated a ten-year program, commonly known as the National Acid Precipitation Assessment Program ("NAPAP"), that is designed to identify the causes and sources of acid rain, to evaluate its environmental, social, and economic effects, and to assess potential methods of control. *See* 42 U.S.C. § 8903. We note that the final NAPAP report is due in December 1990. At oral argument the EPA pointed to this study as evidence of specific research being conducted that could enable the agency to take action under section 115; the EPA also asserted that the report should provide it with a sufficient basis to make a reasoned decision on the petitioners' rulemaking petitions.

It is in part on the basis of this information that we conclude that the EPA's delay in acting on the petitions has been neither arbitrary, nor capricious, nor contrary to law. * * *

NOTES

1. **Scientific Uncertainty and International Air Pollution Problems.** What role did scientific uncertainty play in this case? Why did the D.C. Circuit determine that the EPA was justified in delaying action to address the harm to Canada, despite Administrator Costle's findings almost a decade earlier?

2. **Canada and the 1990 Amendments to the Clean Air Act.** Notice the timing of Canada's lawsuit—just prior to and during Congress's 1990 amendments to the Clean Air Act that added the acid rain trading program. Nevertheless, while Congress acknowledged that acid rain was affecting eastern Canada as well as the eastern United States, *see* S. REP. NO. 101–228, 1990 U.S.C.C.A.N. 3385, 3653 (noting that southeastern Canada was affected), 3655 (noting that 10,000 lakes in Ontario were affected by acid rain), 3657 (noting that acid rain was harming Canadian sugar maples) (Dec. 20, 1989), the United States' obligations to Canada played little role in the 1990 amendments.

Nevertheless, on March 13, 1991, the United States and Canada entered the Agreement Between the Government of the United States of America and the Government of Canada on Air Quality. The initial focus of this Agreement was acid rain, and Annex 1 to the Agreement is the Acid Rain Annex. (The two countries have since expanded the Agreement to address transboundary ozone and transboundary particular matter pollution.) Under this Agreement, the easternmost provinces of Canada agreed to reduce their sulfur dioxide emissions to 2.3 million tonnes (a tonne is equivalent to 1.1 American tons) by 1994 and to maintain that level through December 1999. Canada would then maintain a permanent national cap of 3.2 million tonnes of sulfur dioxide per year from 2000 on. The United States, in turn, agreed to a 10 million ton reduction in sulfur dioxide emissions by 2000 (with credits for reductions already achieved under the acid rain program) and to a permanent national cap on sulfur dioxide emissions from electric utilities of 8.95 million tons per year by 2010. U.S. E.P.A., *Progress Under the Air Quality Agreement*, http://www.epa.gov/airmarkets/progsregs/usca/cooperation.html (last updated Oct. 2,

2003). The Agreement itself is available at http://www.epa.gov/airmarkets/progsregs/usca/agreement.html.

3. **Transboundary Air Pollution and Mexico.** Transboundary air pollution is also an issue along the United States–Mexico border. In 1983, the United States and Mexico entered into the Agreement on Cooperation for the Protection and Improvement of the Environment in the Border Area, also known as the La Paz Agreement. More recently, the EPA and its counterpart in Mexico have built upon the La Paz Agreement to create the U.S.–Mexico Border 2012 Framework, a program designed to achieve a variety of environmental goals along the border by 2012. Goal #2 of this Framework is to "Reduce Air Pollution." In November 2002, the parties outlined the Border Air Quality Strategy, which has as its objective to, "[b]y 2012 or sooner, reduce air emissions as much as possible toward attainment of respective national ambient air quality standards, and reduce exposure in the border region * * *." U.S. E.P.A., *U.S. Mexico Border 2012 Framework*, http://www.epa.gov/usmexicoborder.

4. **Section 115 and Climate Change.** The United States has, rather famously, refused to ratify the Kyoto Protocol, which requires nations to reduce their emissions of carbon dioxide, a greenhouse pollutant, in an attempt to slow climate change. Climate change is a *global* air pollution issue, arguably the biggest transboundary air pollution currently facing the world. Some of the projected effects of climate change include increasingly severe weather in many parts of the globe and elevated sea levels, which may eliminate several island nations entirely and threaten many other coastal nations, such as the Netherlands.

Can other nations use section 115 of the Clean Air Act to force the United States to address its emissions of carbon dioxide and other greenhouse gases? Why or why not? Does it matter that the United States has not listed carbon dioxide as a criteria pollutant? Why or why not? Does the decision in *Massachusetts v. EPA* affect your analysis? Why or why not?

* * *

CHAPTER 5

THE CLEAN WATER ACT AND FEDERALISM

■ ■ ■

I. INTRODUCTION TO THE CLEAN WATER ACT

Like the Clean Air Act, the federal ***Clean Water Act***, 33 U.S.C. §§ 1251–1387, has a relatively long history. Early versions of the Act were known as the ***Federal Water Pollution Control Act*** (**FWPCA**); the name "Clean Water Act" derives from the Clean Water Act Amendments of 1977. Congress first enacted the FWPCA in 1948 in response to growing concerns about water quality, but early versions of the statute gave most regulatory authority over water quality to the states and limited the federal role to interstate enforcement and financial encouragement to states to set ***water quality standards*** and to build sewage treatment plants.

However, state regulation proved ineffective, and several events in the late 1960s and early 1970s inspired the federal government to act. In 1969, for example, a substantial oil spill occurred off the coast of Santa Barbara, California, causing several environmental problems and raising public awareness of the problem of water pollution. By the early 1970s, Lake Erie was dying and many major rivers, such as the Potomac River, were clearly suffering because of water pollution. Indeed, the nation's water pollution problems became acutely obvious when several rivers, most famously the Cuyahoga River in Ohio, caught fire and burned.

Congress enacted the current version of the Clean Water Act in 1972, Pub. L. No. 92–500, 86 Stat. 816 (Oct. 18, 1972), imposing federally set ***technology-based effluent limitations*** and ***permit requirements*** onto the existing system of state water quality standards. The goal of the current Clean Water Act "is to restore and maintain the chemical, physical, and biological integrity of the Nation's waters." CWA § 101(a), 33 U.S.C. § 1251(a). The EPA has graphically summarized the "nation's waters," as is shown in Figure 5–1.

The Clean Water Act has two major components. First, the Act provides funding to municipalities and states to encourage them to build sewage treatment plants, often referred to as ***Publicly Owned Treat-***

ment Works* (POTWs)**. Second, the Act prohibits all discharges of pollutants except as in conformance with the Act, CWA § 301(a), 33 U.S.C.§ 1311(a), and establishes two main permit programs—the ***Section 402 National Pollutant Discharge Elimination System* (NPDES)** permit program, CWA § 402, 33 U.S.C. § 1342, and the ***Section 404 "dredge and fill" permit program, CWA § 404, 33 U.S.C. § 1344, to regulate individual dischargers. The EPA and the U.S. Army Corps of Engineers are in charge of administering these permit programs, but states can apply for authority to implement them if the states comply with certain requirements. As a practical matter, most states now implement the NPDES permit program, but the Army Corps still issues most section 404 permits, subject to the EPA's oversight.

Figure 5-1: The Waters of the United States
EPA graphic.

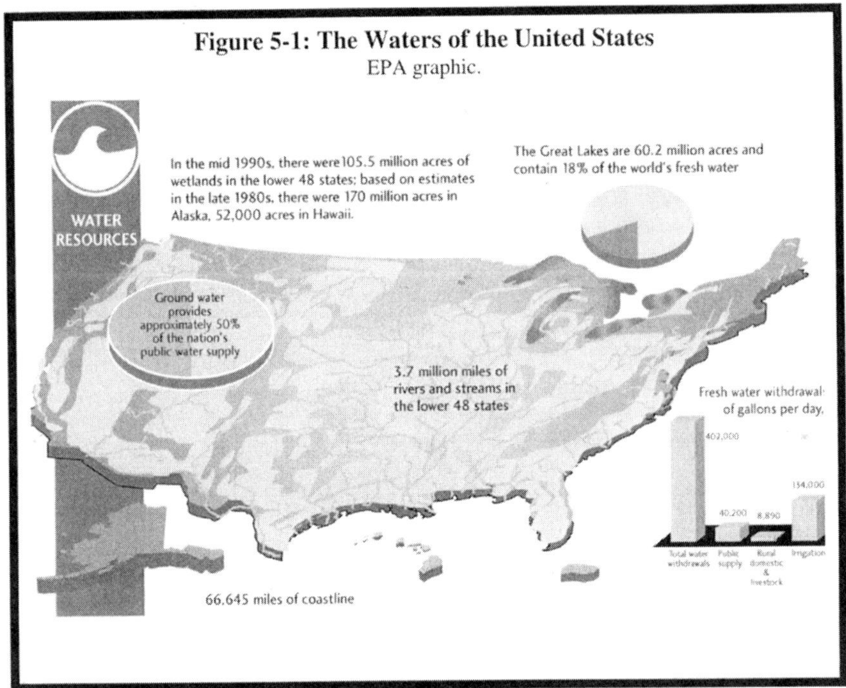

Thus, even though the 1972 Act decidedly increased the role of the federal government in the regulation of the nation's water quality, the structure of the Clean Water Act (even more than the Clean Air Act) is a structure of ***cooperative federalism***, where the state and federal governments each have distinct and important roles to play. Indeed, Congress explicitly recognized the authority of states in maintaining water quality:

> It is the policy of Congress to recognize, preserve, and protect the primary responsibilities and rights of States to prevent, reduce, and eliminate pollution, to plan the development and use (including restoration, preservation, and enhancement) of land and water resources, and to consult with the Administrator in the exercise of his authority

> under this chapter. It is the policy of Congress that the States manage the construction grant program [for POTWs] under this chapter and implement the permit programs under sections 1342 and 1344 of this title.

CWA § 101(b), 33 U.S.C. § 1251(b).

The Clean Water Act has enjoyed considerable success in cleaning up the most obvious water quality problems. In 1972, "[o]nly a third of the nation's waters were safe for fishing and swimming. Wetlands losses were estimated at about 460,000 acres annually. Agricultural runoff resulted in the erosion of 2.25 billion tons of soil and the deposit of large amounts of phosphorus and nitrogen into many waters. Sewage treatment plants served only 85 million people." U.S. EPA, CLEAN WATER ACT: A BRIEF HISTORY 2 (2001). In contrast, by the late 1990s, "[t]wo-thirds of the nation's waters are safe for fishing and swimming. The rate of annual wetlands losses is estimated at about 70,000 to 90,000 acres according to recent studies. The amount of soil lost due to agricultural runoff has been cut by one billion tons annually, and phosphorus and nitrogen levels in water sources are down. Modern wastewater treatment facilities serve 173 million people." *Id.*

II. TRIGGERING FEDERAL JURISDICTION UNDER THE CLEAN WATER ACT

A. THE CLEAN WATER ACT'S BASIC PROHIBITION

Both the statutory language and the U.S. Constitution, especially the Interstate Commerce Clause, limit federal jurisdiction under the Clean Water Act. The main ***statutory*** trigger for federal jurisdiction is found in section 301(a), which provides that:

> Except as in compliance with this section and sections 1312, 1316, 1317, 1328, 1342, and 1344 of this title, ***the discharge of any pollutant by any person shall be unlawful***.

CWA § 301(a), 33 U.S.C. § 1311(a) (emphasis added).

While this statutory trigger seems simple, the Clean Water Act's definitions add several layers of complexity to it. For example, a ***"person"*** for purposes of section 301(a) is "an individual, corporation, partnership, association, State, municipality, commission, or political subdivision of a State, or any interstate body." CWA § 502(5), 33 U.S.C. § 1362(5). The statutory definition thus expands the regulatory scope of section 301(a) beyond individuals to business entities and to state and local governments.

More complex is the statutory definition of ***"discharge of a pollutant."*** According to the Clean Water Act's definition section,

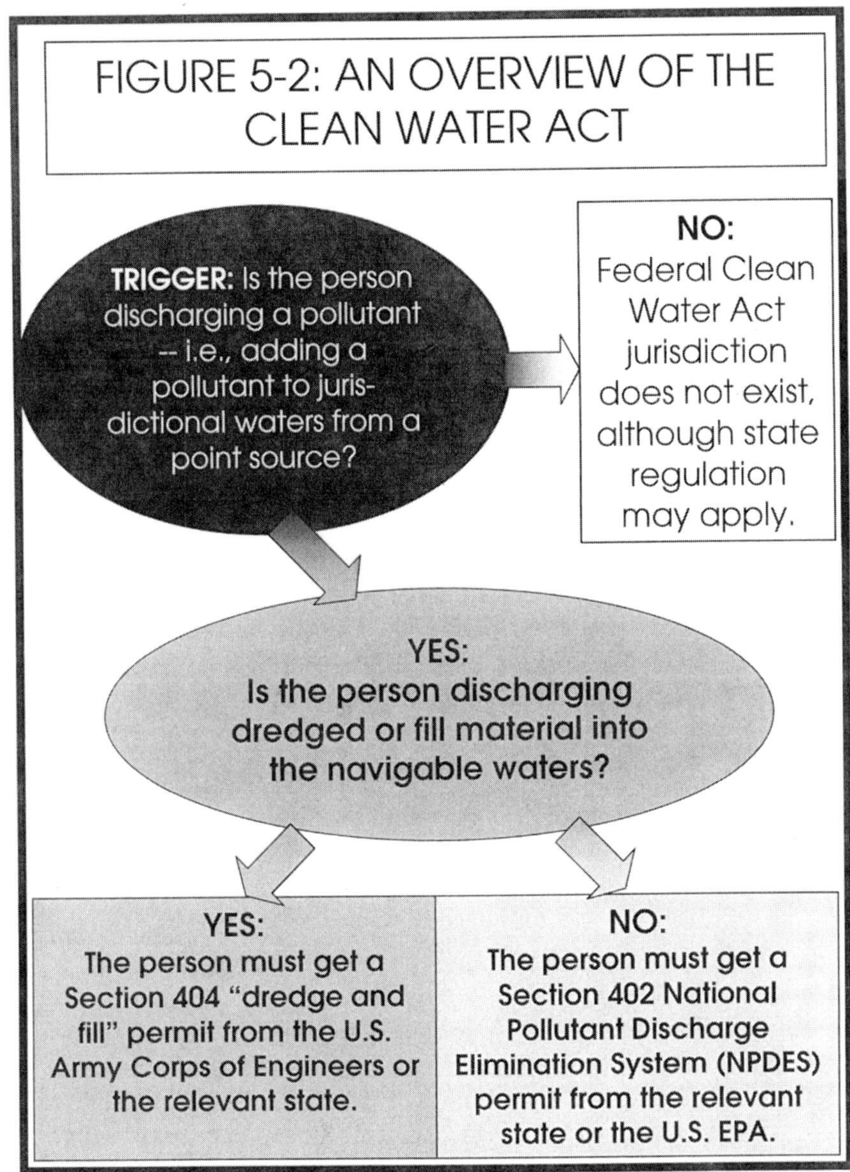
FIGURE 5-2: AN OVERVIEW OF THE CLEAN WATER ACT
TRIGGER: Is the person discharging a pollutant -- i.e., adding a pollutant to juris-dictional waters from a point source?
NO: Federal Clean Water Act jurisdiction does not exist, although state regulation may apply.
YES: Is the person discharging dredged or fill material into the navigable waters?
YES: The person must get a Section 404 "dredge and fill" permit from the U.S. Army Corps of Engineers or the relevant state.
NO: The person must get a Section 402 National Pollutant Discharge Elimination System (NPDES) permit from the relevant state or the U.S. EPA.

> [t]he term "discharge of a pollutant" and the term "discharge of pollutants" each means (A) any addition of any pollutant to navigable waters from any point source, [and] (B) any addition of any pollutant to the waters of the contiguous zone or the ocean from any point source other than a vessel or other floating craft.

CWA § 502(14), 33 U.S.C. § 1362(14). Given this statutory definition of "discharge of a pollutant," the elements of federal Clean Water Act jurisdiction are: (1) an "addition" (2) of a "pollutant" (3) to jurisdictional waters ("navigable waters," "contiguous zone," or the "ocean") (4) from a "point source." Let's examine each of these elements in more detail.

B. "ADDITION"

1. Additions in General

The Clean Water Act itself does not further define "addition," nor has the EPA defined that term in regulations. As a result, explication of that element has come almost entirely through case law. Most of the time, deciding whether an "addition" of a pollutant has occurred is relatively easy. "Addition" generally implies that the polluter discharges something into the water from the "outside world"—*i.e.*, adds material to a waterway that was not present in that waterway before. But what if the alleged polluter is merely shifting water around? Can the transfer of water constitute an "addition" of pollutants? Consider the following case.

DUBOIS v. UNITED STATES DEPARTMENT OF AGRICULTURE

102 F.3d 1273 (1st Cir. 1996).

BOWNES, SENIOR CIRCUIT JUDGE.

The defendant-intervenor Loon Mountain Recreation Corporation ("Loon Corp.") operates a ski resort in the White Mountain National Forest in Lincoln, New Hampshire. In order to expand its skiing facilities, Loon Corp. sought and received a permit to do so from the United States Forest Service. Appellant Roland Dubois sued the Forest Service alleging violations of the * * * Clean Water Act ("CWA"), 33 U.S.C. § 1251, *et seq.* * * *. * * * The district court granted the Forest Service's motion for summary judgment and denied the other motions. * * *

I. STATEMENT OF THE CASE

A. Facts

The White Mountain National Forest ("WMNF") is a public resource managed by the United States Forest Service for a wide range of competing public uses and purposes, including "outdoor recreation, range, timber, watershed, ... wildlife and fish purposes," 16 U.S.C. § 528 (1994), and skiing, 16 U.S.C. § 497(b) (1994). Pursuant to the National Forest Management Act of 1976, the Forest Service makes long-term plans to coordinate these competing uses, 16 U.S.C. § 1604(e)(1) (1994), and issues "special use" permits authorizing private recreational services on national forest land, 36 C.F.R. §§ 251.50–.65 (1995). The Forest Service's exercise of its permitting authority is legally constrained by environmental considerations emanating, *inter alia,* from [] the CWA * * *.

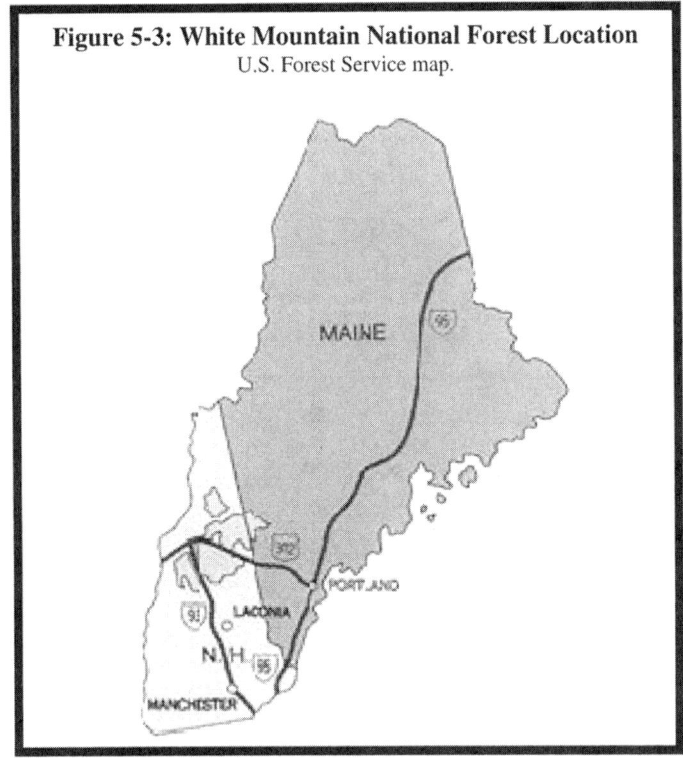

Figure 5-3: White Mountain National Forest Location
U.S. Forest Service map.

Loon Pond is located in the WMNF at an elevation of 2,400 feet. It has a surface area of 19 acres, with shallow areas around the perimeter and a central bowl 65 feet deep. It is unusual for its relatively pristine nature. There is virtually no human activity within the land it drains except skiing at the privately owned Loon Mountain Ski Area. New Hampshire Department of Environmental Services ("NHDES") regulations classify Loon Pond as a Class A waterbody, protected by demanding water quality standards under a variety of criteria, *see* N.H. CODE ADMIN. R. ENV. WS. 432.03, and as an Outstanding Resource Water ("ORW"), protected against any measurable long-term degradation by the State's anti-degradation rules, *see id.* 437.06; 40 C.F.R. § 131.12(a)(3) (1995). It ranks in the upper 95th percentile of all lakes and ponds in northern New England for low levels of phosphorus, which results in limited plant growth and therefore high water clarity and higher total biological production. The pond supports a rich variety of life in its ecosystem. Loon Pond also constitutes a major source of drinking water for the town of Lincoln 1,600 feet below it. A dam across the outlet of the Pond regulates the flow of water from the Pond to Lincoln's municipal reservoir.

Loon Corp., defendant-intervenor herein, owns the Loon Mountain Ski Area, which has operated since the 1960s not far from Loon Pond. Prior to the permit revision that gave rise to this litigation, Loon Corp. held a special use permit to operate on 785 acres of WMNF land. That permit allowed Loon Corp. to draw water ("drawdown") for snowmaking from Loon Pond, as well as from the East Branch of the Pemigewasset River ("East Branch") and from nearby Boyle Brook. In order to use water from Loon Pond, Loon Corp. also needed authorization from the Town of Lincoln and the State of New Hampshire. Beginning in 1974, Loon Corp. was authorized to pump snowmaking water from Loon Pond down to 18 inches below full level. A 1988 amendment to this agreement permitted drawdown below the 18–inch level on a case-by-case basis. Combined uses by Lincoln and Loon Corp. during the period governed by these agreements typically caused four- to six-foot fluctuations in the level of Loon Pond.

In addition to being used as a source of water for snowmaking, Loon Pond has been the repository for disposal of water after it is pumped through the snowmaking system. This includes water that originally came from Loon Pond, as well as water that originated in the East Branch or in Boyle Brook. Approximately 250,000 gallons of East Branch water have been transferred into Loon Pond each year in this manner. Obviously the water discharged into Loon Pond contains at least the same pollutants that were present in the intake water. Evidence in the record indicates that intake water taken from the East Branch contains bacteria, other aquatic organisms such as *Giardia lambia*, phosphorus, turbidity and heat. Evidence was also introduced in court * * * that oil and grease were present in the discharge water, although their source was disputed.

In 1986, Loon Corp. applied to the Forest Service for an amendment to its special use permit to allow expansion of its facilities within the WMNF. * * *

Many individuals and groups, including both plaintiffs, filed comments pointing out various environmental problems with each alternative that involved expanding the ski area. One lengthy comment from the U.S. Environmental Protection Agency ("EPA") expressed its concern that the use of Loon Pond for snowmaking purposes would "use Loon Pond like a cistern" instead of treating it "with care" because it is "acknowledged to be one of the rare high altitude ponds of its size in the White Mountains." Other commenters suggested that Loon Corp. be required to build artificial water storage ponds, in order to eliminate the problem of depleting Loon Pond when withdrawing water for snowmaking as well as the problem of adding pollutants to Loon Pond when discharging water into the Pond after use.

* * * The Forest Service [nevertheless endorsed a plan whereby] Loon Corp. would more than double the amount of water used for snowmaking, from 67 million gallons per year to 138 million gallons. Seventeen million gallons of the increase would be drawn from the East Branch, and 54 million gallons from Loon Pond. In addition, Loon Corp. was authorized to draw the Pond down for snowmaking by fifteen feet, compared to the current eighteen inches. The Forest Service assumed that the Town of Lincoln would need up to an additional five feet of Pond

water, making a total of twenty feet that the Pond was expected to be drawn down each year. This would constitute approximately 63% of the Pond's water. * * *

Dubois and RESTORE appealed the [decision] to the Regional Forester and, thereafter, to the Chief of the Forest Service. These appeals were denied. On March 16, 1994, the Forest Service issued a special use permit to Loon Corp., implementing the decision * * *.

B. Proceedings Below

Plaintiff Dubois filed a complaint in the United States District Court for the District of Columbia, challenging the Forest Service's approval of the Loon Mountain expansion project. He * * * argued that the Forest Service violated the CWA, 33 U.S.C. § 1311, by failing to obtain a National Pollutant Discharge Elimination System ("NPDES") permit before approving Loon Corp.'s expansion plans, which entailed removing water from the East Branch, using it to pressurize and prevent freezing in its snowmaking equipment, and then discharging the used water into Loon Pond. According to Dubois, an NPDES permit was required in order for Loon Corp. to discharge pollutants into Loon Pond, including the discharge from Loon Corp.'s snowmaking equipment.

Plaintiff RESTORE, a membership organization, intervened on behalf of its members to challenge the project. RESTORE [] reiterated Dubois' claim that an NPDES permit was required. * * *

The parties cross-moved for summary judgment. * * * The district court denied Loon Corp.'s motion to dismiss, granted summary judgment for the Forest Service, and denied the plaintiffs' cross-motions for summary judgment.

* * * VII. THE CLEAN WATER ACT ISSUES

The Clean Water Act (CWA) was "bold and sweeping legislative initiative," *United States v. Commonwealth of P.R.*, 721 F.2d 832, 834 (1st Cir. 1983), enacted to "restore and maintain the chemical, physical, and biological integrity of the Nation's waters." 33 U.S.C. § 1251(a) (1994). "This objective incorporated a broad, systemic view of the goal of maintaining and improving water quality: as the House Report on the legislation put it, 'the word "integrity" ... refers to a condition in which the natural structure and function of ecosystems [are] maintained.' " *United States v. Riverside Bayview Homes, Inc.*, 474 U.S. 121, 132 (1985) (quoting H.R. REP. NO. 92–911, at 76 (1972), U.S. Code Cong. & Admin. News 1972, at 3744).

The most important component of the Act is the requirement that an NPDES permit be obtained; *see* 33 U.S.C. § 1342 (1994). In addition, the CWA requires states to adopt water quality standards which protect against degradation of the physical, chemical, or biological attributes of the state's waters. 33 U.S.C. §§ 1251(a), 1313(d)(4)(B) (1994); 40 C.F.R. § 131.12 (1995). * * *

* * * *B. NPDES Permit*

Section 301(a) of the Clean Water Act prohibits the "discharge of any pollutant" into navigable waters from any "point source" without an NPDES permit. 33 U.S.C. § 1311(a) (1994). Plaintiffs argue that the Forest Service violated Section 301(a) by failing to obtain an NPDES permit before approving Loon's plan to remove water from the East Branch, use it to pressurize and prevent freezing in its snowmaking equipment, and then discharge the used water into Loon Pond. Section 301(a) prohibits the "discharge of any pollutant by any person" except as authorized pursuant to a permit issued under the Act. *Id.; see* 33 U.S.C. §§ 1342, 1344 (1994). The term "discharge of a pollutant" is defined as "any addition of any pollutant to navigable waters from any point source." 33 U.S.C. § 1362(12)(A) (1994). The definition of a "pollutant" includes "dredged spoil, solid waste, . . . sewage, garbage, . . . biological materials, . . . heat, . . . sand, . . . and agricultural waste." 33 U.S.C. § 1362(6) (1994). "Navigable waters" is defined as "the waters of the United States." 33 U.S.C. § 1362(7) (1994). The district court found and the parties agree that Loon Pond is a water of the United States, that the East Branch water discharged from Loon Corp.'s snowmaking pipes into Loon Pond is a pollutant within the meaning of the CWA, and that the pipe discharging the water into Loon Pond is a point source. The question, then, is whether there is an "addition" of pollutants to Loon Pond when water containing pollutants is discharged from Loon Corp.'s snowmaking equipment into Loon Pond.

The district court answered this question in the negative. The court reasoned that the intake water from the East Branch of the Pemigewasset River and the water in Loon Pond are all part of "a singular entity, '*the* waters of the United States,' " and therefore that "the bodies of water are not to be considered individually in this context." Because it interpreted the East Branch and Loon Pond to be part of the same "singular entity," the court concluded that the transfer of water from the East Branch into Loon Pond would not constitute an "addition" into the Pond, at least if the pipes added no new pollutants.

There is no basis in law or fact for the district court's "singular entity" theory. The error in the court's reasoning is highlighted by an analogy the court drew: it hypothesized a pond in which "we place a pipe . . . and we pump the pond water from the bottom to the surface. No one would reasonably contend that internal pumping causes an 'addition' of pollutants to the pond. Instead, we would consider the pumping to be a redistribution of pollutants from one part of the pond to another." Such a situation is not at all analogous to the instant case. There is no barrier separating the water at the top of a pond from the water at the bottom of the same pond; chemicals, organisms, and even heat are able to pass from the top to the bottom or *vice versa,* at rates determined only by the laws of science.

In contrast, the transfer of water or its contents from the East Branch to Loon Pond would not occur naturally. This is more analogous to the example the district court gave from the opposite end of the spectrum: where water is added "from an external source" to the pond and an NPDES permit is required. As in this converse example, the East Branch and Loon Pond are not the same body of water; the East Branch is indeed a source "external" to Loon Pond. We can take judicial notice that the Pemigewasset River was for years one of the most polluted rivers in New England, the repository for raw sewage from factories and towns. It emitted an overwhelming odor and was known to peel the paint off buildings located on its banks. Yet, under the district court's theory, even if such conditions still prevailed, a proposal to withdraw water from the Pemigewasset to discharge it into Loon Pond would be analogous to moving water from the top to the bottom of a single pond; it would not constitute an "addition" of pollutants "from an external source" because both the East Branch and Loon Pond are part of the "singular" waters of the United States. The district court apparently would reach the same conclusion regardless of how polluted the Pemigewasset was or how pristine Loon Pond was. We do not believe Congress intended such an irrational result.

The district court's analysis also ignores the fact that water would pass through Loon Corp.'s privately owned pipes on its way from the East Branch to Loon Pond. Thus, nature would not regulate—and neither the Forest Service nor the court could know in advance—whether any pollutants would be added to the water as it passes through the pipes. * * * The district court's analysis would apply equally if the water passed through a paper mill on its way to Loon Pond, instead of through snowmaking pipes. And the analysis is equally unpersuasive in either circumstance. Either way, the water leaves the domain of nature and is subject to private control rather than purely natural processes. As such, it has lost its status as waters of the United States.

Other courts have held that an NPDES permit is required before pollutants may be moved from one body of water of the United States to another. * * *

Even the Forest Service does not support the district court's conclusion that mere transfers of water from one water body to another, without more, never result in an addition of pollutants to waters of the United States. * * * It argues that Loon Corp. "moves water between hydrologically connected water bodies containing water of like quality" which, therefore, does not "introduce pollutants 'from the outside world' into the receiving waters." Accordingly, the Forest Service argues no permit is required. We disagree with the Forest Service's qualification.

First, there is nothing in the statute evincing a Congressional intent to distinguish between "unrelated" water bodies and related or "hydrologically connected" water bodies. The CWA simply addresses "any addition of any pollutant to navigable waters from any point source." 33 U.S.C.

§ 1362(12)(A). Nor is the purpose of the CWA served by means of such a distinction. If anything, the purpose would be better served by a distinction between *de minimis* transfers of water and transfers which add some not insignificant amount of pollutants to the transferee water body. But no such distinction appears in the statute, and to imply one would thrust some agencies with no expertise on environmental issues into the role of deciding whether the CWA's environmental protections should even be considered.

More compellingly, the Forest Service's "hydrological connectedness" proposal ignores a fundamental fact about water: the direction of flow. It is true that Loon Pond and the East Branch of the Pemigewasset River are "hydrologically connected" in the sense that water from the Pond flows *down* and eventually empties into the River. But water from the East Branch certainly does not flow *uphill* into Loon Pond, carrying with it the pollutants that have undisputedly accumulated in the East Branch water from some of the other sources of water entering the East Branch from upstream. Under such circumstances, defendants cannot credibly argue that these water bodies are so related that the transfer of water *from* the East Branch *to* Loon Pond is not an "addition" of water from one of the "waters of the United States" to another. We therefore reject the Forest Service's "hydrological connectedness" proposal.

Likewise, we reject its assertion, unsupported by the record, that in some general sense the two bodies of water are "of like quality." First, this is the kind of substantive question to which the EPA would apply its technical expertise in deciding whether to issue an NPDES permit and what conditions to attach to such a permit in order to protect water quality. It is not the kind of threshold question that the Forest Service or this court should address in deciding whether to subject the Loon Corp. expansion proposal to the NPDES permitting process.

Second, the Forest Service does not contest plaintiffs' assertion that there are at least some pollutants in the East Branch that do not exist naturally in Loon Pond. [T]he East Branch has been designated by the New Hampshire legislature as a Class B Waterway, a lower quality designation than the Class A quality rating of Loon Pond. The difference in classifications—the East Branch as a Class B waterway, Loon Pond as Class A—evinces a higher quality level for the Pond than for the River, and belies the Forest Service's assertion that the two bodies of water are "of like quality."

Even if the East Branch were rated in the same general class as Loon Pond (Class A), that would not mean the two bodies of water were identical in quality, such that an NPDES permit would be unnecessary. The East Branch contains different organisms than Loon Pond, *inter alia, Giardia lambia*. Loon Pond is also colder overall than the East Branch, and its lower depths are significantly colder. The two bodies of water also have different chemistries, especially the low level of phosphorus in Loon Pond, which affects its biological composition. Nor has the Forest Service argued that *all* such pollutants would be eliminated before any East Branch water would be pumped up to refill Loon Pond after depletion by Loon Corp.'s snowmaking. The Service cannot say, therefore, that the discharge of East Branch water into Loon Pond would not result in "any pollutants" being added to the Pond. 33 U.S.C. § 1362(12)(A).

Aside from the difficulty of defining a general concept such as "of like quality," it would defeat the purpose of the CWA's permit process to interpret the statutory language "discharge of *any* pollutant," 33 U.S.C. § 1311(a), to be implicitly qualified by the phrase "except when the transferee body of water is of like quality." * * * We cannot allow such a watering down of Congress' clear statutory protections.

We hold that the Pemigewasset River and Loon Pond are two distinct "waters of the United States," and that the proposed transfer of water from one to the other constitutes an "addition." Where, as is undisputed here, the discharge is through a point source and the intake water contains pollutants, an NPDES permit is required. The Forest Service's determination to the contrary was arbitrary and capricious and not in accordance with law. *See* 5 U.S.C. § 706(2)(A). * * *

NOTES

1. **Natural Flow and Clean Water Act "Additions."** *Dubois* is typical of "addition" cases. The Second Circuit has applied a similar "natural flow" test to determine whether an addition of pollutants has occurred. *See, e.g., Catskill Mountains Chapter of Trout Unlimited, Inc. v. City of New York*, 273 F.3d 481, 491–93 (2d Cir. 2001); *Dague v. City of Burlington*, 935 F.2d 1343, 1354–55 (2d Cir. 1991).

2. **Another Perspective? The "But–For" Test for Additions of Pollutants.** In *Miccosukee Tribe of Indians of Florida v. South Florida Water Management District*, 280 F.3d 1364 (11th Cir. 2002), the Eleventh Circuit adopted a slightly different test to determine whether an "addition" of "pollutants" has occurred. In that case, a pump that was part of a levee system in the Florida Everglades pumped water against the system's natural flow from one canal, the C–11 Canal, into another canal. The water in the C–11 Canal had a higher concentration of phosphorus than the receiving water. In the Eleventh Circuit's analysis, "for an addition of pollutants to be from a point source, the relevant inquiry is whether—but for the point source—the pollutants would have been added to the receiving body of water. We, therefore, conclude that an addition from a point source occurs if a point source is the cause-in-fact of the release of pollutants into navigable waters." *Id.* at 1368. This "but-for" causation test is met, moreover, "[w]hen a point source changes the natural flow of a body of water which contains pollutants and causes that water to flow into another distinct body of navigable water into which it would not have otherwise flowed * * *. And, because the pollutants would not have entered the second body of water *but for* the change in flow caused by the point source, an addition of pollutants from a point source occurs." *Id.* at 1368–69. Because, in the case before it, "without the operation of the S–9 pump station, the polluted waters from the C–11 Canal

would not normally flow east into the'' receiving canal, ''the S–9 pump station, therefore, is the cause-in-fact of the addition of pollutants to the WCA–3A. We, therefore, conclude that the release of water caused by the S–9 pump station's operation constitutes an addition of pollutants from a point source.'' *Id.* at 1369.

On appeal, the U.S. Supreme Court vacated the Eleventh Circuit's decision. *South Florida Water Management District v. Miccosukee Tribe of Indians*, 541 U.S. 95, 112 (2004). The Court refused to resolve the ''unitary waters'' issue, leaving it open for the government to argue on remand—although the Court did express doubts about the validity of that theory. *Id.* at 1543–45. The Court also decided that factual issues remained regarding whether the two canals were separate waterbodies, precluding summary judgment. *Id.* at 1545–47. However, the Court did not discuss the ''but for'' test for additions.

Is the Eleventh Circuit's ''but-for'' analysis significantly different from the First Circuit's ''natural flow analysis''? Why or why not? Can you think of any circumstances where an ''addition'' might exist under one test but not under the other? Which is the more broadly applicable test?

The newest complication for Clean Water Act ''additions'' as the result of moving water around is the EPA's Water Transfers Rule, 73 Fed. Reg. 33,697 (June 13, 2008), which took effect on August 12, 2008. This rule exempts from federal regulation any ''activity that conveys waters of the United States to another water of the United States without subjecting the water to intervening industrial, municipal, or commercial use,'' although states remain free to regulate such transfers. *Id.* The Second Circuit has indicated that it thinks this Rule violates the Act, *see Catskill Mountains Chapter of Trout Unlimited, Inc. v. City of New York*, 451 F.3d 77, 82 (2d Cir. 2006), but the Eleventh Circuit upheld the Rule and the Supreme Court declined to review the decision. *Friends of the Everglades v. South Florida Water Management Dist.*, 570 F.3d 1210, 1218–28 (11th Cir. 2009), *cert. denied*, ___ U.S. ___, 131 S.Ct. 643 (2010). Would this Rule have changed the outcome in *Dubois*? Why or why not?

3. **''Additions'' from Dams, Part 1: Dam–Induced Changes to Water Quality.** There is no statutory reason why courts should analyze additions of pollutants from dams differently than additions of pollutants from any other source. Nevertheless, early in the history of the Clean Water Act, the EPA determined that mere passage of water through a dam could *not* constitute an addition of pollutants for Clean Water Act purposes unless the dam itself added pollutants like grease. When the National Wildlife Federation challenged that interpretation in court, the D.C. Circuit, deferring to the EPA's interpretation of ''addition,'' issued a highly influential opinion that the mere movement of water through a dam did *not* constitute an addition of pollutants. *National Wildlife Federation v. Gorsuch*, 693 F.2d 156, 174–77 (D.C. Cir. 1982).

In *Gorsuch*, the D.C. Circuit acknowledged that ''[d]ams cause a variety of interrelated water quality problems, both in reservoirs and in river water downstream from a dam.'' *Id.* at 161. The five specific dam-related water quality problems that the plaintiffs and the D.C. Circuit identified were:

reductions in dissolved oxygen in the downstream water, interfering with fish survival and the water's ability to break down pollutants; increased heavy metal leaching into low-oxygen and anaerobic areas; changes in the temperature of water; sediment trapping and consequential increased scouring of downstream shorelines; and supersaturation of air in the water after the water plunges over the dam, which can kill fish. *Id.* at 161–64. Nevertheless, the D.C. Circuit excluded dams from Clean Water Act regulation because, despite inducing these changes in water quality, dams did not "add" pollutants to the water that passed through them. *Id.* at 174–83.

In 1988, the National Wildlife Federation again tried to argue that dams triggered Clean Water Act jurisdiction, this time in the Sixth Circuit. *National Wildlife Federation v. Consumers Power Co.*, 862 F.2d 580 (6th Cir. 1988). The facts in the Sixth Circuit case were arguably more compelling than those in *Gorsuch*, involving the entrainment—trapping and chopping up—of fish at a hydroelectric dam on Lake Michigan. *Id.* at 581–82. Nevertheless, the Sixth Circuit followed *Gorsuch* and held that the dam did not "add" pollutants to Lake Michigan. Following the EPA's argument, the Sixth Circuit noted that, unlike seafood processors, who *are* regulated under the Clean Water Act because they remove fish from the oceans, process them, and then throw dead fish and fish parts back into the ocean, the hydroelectric dam in question never removed the fish from the waters. *Id.* at 585. Thus, even though "the manipulation of water by the Ludington facility's turbine changes the form of the pollutant from live fish to a mixture of live and dead fish in the process of generating electricity," the dam did not "add" anything to the waters of Lake Michigan. *Id.* "There can be no doubt that the Ludington facility does not create the fish which become entrained in the process of generating electricity." *Id.*

Are the D.C. Circuit's and Sixth Circuit's decisions in *Gorsuch* and *Consumers Power Co.* consistent with either the First Circuit's "natural flow" test from *Dubois* or the Eleventh Circuit's "but-for" causation test from *Miccosukee*? Why or why not?

4. **"Additions" from Dams, Part 2: Section 208 and the Federalism Implications of Permitting Dams**. Through section 208 of the Clean Water Act, 33 U.S.C. § 1288, Congress tried to encourage states to enact areawide waste treatment management plans. After the EPA issued guidelines for such plans, state governors had 60 days to "identify each area within the State which, as a result of urban-industrial concentrations or other factors, has substantial water quality control problems." CWA § 208(a)(2), 33 U.S.C. § 1288(a)(2). Such designation was supposed to lead to a "continuing areawide waste treatment management planning process," CWA § 208(b)(1)(A), 33 U.S.C. § 1288(b)(1)(A), including: identification of necessary ***publicly owned treatment works*** (**POTWs**, or sewage treatment plants); establishment of construction schedules; establishment of a regulatory program; and identification and control of various kinds of water pollution, including nonpoint sources, mining-related sources, construction-related sources, and salt water intrusions. CWA § 208(b)(2), 33 U.S.C. § 1288(b)(2). Complying states were entitled to federal grants and federal technical assistant to help implement their plans. CWA § 1288(f), (g), (h), 33 U.S.C. § 1288(f), (g), (h).

In *Gorsuch*, *supra* Note 3, the D.C. Circuit perceived negative implications for the federalism balance that section 208 sought to achieve between states and the federal government if the federal government were allowed to regulate dams directly, pursuant to section 301 and the Clean Water Act's permit programs:

> The legislative history of the 1977 amendments further bolsters the view that the division of pollution control efforts between discharge permits under § 402 and areawide waste management plans under § 208 was not just a device for separating out pollution sources amenable to NPDES technological controls. Rather, Congress viewed state pollution control programs under § 208 as in part an "experiment" in the effectiveness of state regulation * * *.
>
> * * * The Senate Report also expresses a positive intent to leave certain pollution problems to the states, at least for the time being:
>
>> Section 208 ... may not be adequate. It may be that the States will be reluctant to develop [adequate] control measures ... and it may be that some time in the future a Federal presence can be justified and afforded. But for the moment, it is both necessary and appropriate to make a distinction as to the kinds of activities that are to be regulated by the Federal Government and the kinds of activities which are to be subject to some measure of local control.

Gorsuch, 693 F.2d at 176. The D.C. Circuit concluded in *Gorsuch* that "we cannot say, on the record before us, that federal intervention is needed because the states have abdicated their § 208 responsibility over a truly pressing national problem. The record does not show how vigorous state enforcement has been, but at least some efforts have been made to remedy dam-caused pollution." *Id.* at 183.

Though ambitious, the section 208 program is largely considered a failure. To deal with section 208's ineffectiveness in dealing with nonpoint source pollution in particular, Congress added section 319, 33 U.S.C. § 1329, to the Act in 1987. Did the 1987 amendments thus suggest that the *Gorsuch* court was wrong? Why or why not?

5. **"Additions" from Dams, Part 3: Does the EPA's Interpretation Deserve the Deference It Has Received?** In 2001, the Second Circuit considered the issue of deference to the EPA's view of dams and reached a very different conclusion from the D.C. and Sixth Circuits. Noting that the EPA's interpretation that dams do not "add" pollutants for purposes of section 301(a) had never gone through notice-and-comment rulemaking or formal adjudication, the Second Circuit relied on *United States v. Mead Corp.*, 533 U.S. 218 (2001), and *Christensen v. Harris County,* 529 U.S. 576 (2000), to hold that that interpretation not only was not entitled to *Chevron* deference but also was not entitled to much deference whatsoever. *Catskill Mountains Chapter of Trout Unlimited, Inc. v. City of New York*, 273 F.3d 481, 489–91 (2d Cir. 2001). Instead, the Second Circuit reviewed the dam cases in light of its *Dubois*-like "natural flow" analysis:

> The EPA's position, upheld by the *Gorsuch* and *Consumers Power* courts, is that for there to be an "addition," a "point source must introduce the

pollutant into navigable water from the outside world." *Gorsuch,* 693 F.2d at 165. We agree with this view provided that "outside world" is construed as any place outside the particular water body to which pollutants are introduced. Given that understanding of "addition," the transfer of water containing pollutants from one body of water to another, distinct body of water is plainly an addition and thus a "discharge" that demands an NPDES permit.

Both *Gorsuch* and *Consumers Power* essentially involved the recirculation of water, without anything added "from the outside world." Such recirculation, they concluded, could not be an "addition." In *Gorsuch,* water was released from a reservoir through a dam to the stream below. Plaintiffs complained that such a release amounted to a regulated discharge under the Act, requiring a permit. The reservoir above the dam and the stream below, at least arguably, were sufficiently the "same" water that the release might not be considered an "addition"; nothing was introduced to the water that was not, in some sense, already there. * * *

In *Consumers Power,* the defendant had withdrawn water from Lake Michigan, along with some surprised fish, for hydroelectric power generation. The water and fish were then returned to the Lake after passing through hydroelectric generators, which puréed some of the fish. The court found that returning the fish to the Lake, albeit in a different form, was not an "addition" because the fish had already been there. * * * Indeed, the court concluded that "[t]he water which passes through the [defendant's hydropower works] never loses its status as water of the United States." * * * The navigable water was recirculated, but nothing was added. The Sixth Circuit therefore also concluded that the releases from the defendant's hydropower works were not "introduced from the outside world." * * *

The *Gorsuch* and *Consumers Power* decisions comport with the plain meaning of "addition," assuming that the water from which the discharges came is the same as that to which they go. If one takes a ladle of soup from a pot, lifts it above the pot, and pours it back into the pot, one has not "added" soup or anything else to the pot (beyond, perhaps, a *de minimis* quantity of airborne dust that fell into the ladle). In requiring a permit for such a "discharge," the EPA might as easily require a permit for Niagara Falls.

The present case, however, strains past the breaking point the assumption of "sameness" made by the *Gorsuch* and *Consumers Power* courts. Here, water is artificially diverted from its natural course and travels several miles from the Reservoir through Shandaken Tunnel to Esopus Creek, a body of water utterly unrelated in any relevant sense to the Schoharie Reservoir and its watershed. No one can reasonably argue that the water in the Reservoir and the Esopus are in any sense the "same," such that "addition" of one to the other is a logical impossibility. When the water and the suspended sediment therein passes from the Tunnel into the Creek, an "addition" of a "pollutant" from a "point source" has been made to a "navigable water," and the terms of the statute are satisfied.

Id. at 491–92. Did the Second Circuit create a split among the circuits regarding the status of dams under the Clean Water Act? Why or why not?

* * *

2. Additions of Dredged Material: The Redeposit Issue

In the *Catskill Mountains* case, as quoted in Note 5 above, the Second Circuit casually noted that "ladling" of pollutants—lifting pollutants out of a waterbody only to pour them back into the same waterbody—would not qualify as an "addition" of pollutants. However, the Clean Water Act clearly requires that dischargers of *dredged material* get a permit. *See* CWA § 404(a), 33 U.S.C. § 1344(a) (requiring permits for discharges of dredged material). Discharges of dredged material underscore the problem of what constitutes an "addition" because "dredged material" is, by definition, material that has been taken out of the navigable waters. 33 C.F.R. § 323.2(c). *Discharges* of dredged material, therefore, always involve some kind of *redeposit* of the dredged material into the navigable waters, and hence the line between unregulated "ladling" and regulated "redeposits" is not always clear, as in the following case.

UNITED STATES v. DEATON

209 F.3d 331 (4th Cir. 2000).

MICHAEL, CIRCUIT JUDGE:

The United States sued James and Rebecca Deaton, alleging that they violated §§ 301 and 404 of the Clean Water Act, 33 U.S.C. §§ 1311, 1344, by sidecasting dredged material as they dug a drainage ditch through a wetland. The district court ultimately awarded summary judgment to the Deatons, and the government appeals. We reverse, holding that sidecasting in a jurisdictional wetland is the discharge of a pollutant under the Clean Water Act. * * *

I.

On November 22, 1988, James Deaton signed a contract to buy a twelve-acre parcel of land in Wicomico County, Maryland, subject to the condition that it was suitable for developing a small residential subdivision. Deaton immediately applied to the Wicomico County Health Department for a sewage disposal permit for a five-lot "single family subdivision." The Health Department denied the permit on April 26, 1989, because the groundwater elevations were unacceptably high at the disposal sites proposed by Deaton and his consultant. The department commented that "[t]he majority of the parcel ... is very poorly drained and would severely restrict the function of the on-site sewage disposal systems." There was a "very limited area" that might warrant evaluation, the department said, if it proved to be within the property boundary. In late April 1989, after the permit was denied, Deaton contacted the U.S. Department of Agriculture, Soil Conservation Service (SCS), to discuss the wetness problem on the twelve-acre parcel. Deaton was referred to Glen

Richardson, who agreed to examine the site. According to Deaton, Richardson suggested that the problem could be corrected by digging a ditch through the middle of the property. Deaton and his wife (Rebecca) decided to go ahead with the purchase of the land, and title was transferred to them in June 1989.

Before any ditching work began, the property was also inspected by Michael Sigrist, District Conservationist at the SCS in Wicomico County. Deaton and Sigrist walked over the property together, and Deaton told Sigrist that he wanted to dig a large ditch to drain the area. Sigrist saw hydric soils (which are typical of wetland areas), areas of standing water, "a large, low wet area" in the center of the parcel, and nontidal wetlands. Water was flowing from the property into a culvert that connects to (or is part of) Perdue Creek. (The waters of Perdue Creek end up in the Wicomico River, a tributary of the Chesapeake Bay.) Sigrist advised Deaton that a large portion of his property contained nontidal wetlands and that he would need a permit from the U.S. Army Corps of Engineers (the Corps) before undertaking any ditching work. Deaton ignored Sigrist's advice and hired a contractor to dig a drainage ditch across the property. Using a back hoe, a front-end track loader, and a bulldozer, the contractor dug a 1,240 foot ditch that intersected the areas that Sigrist had identified as wetlands. As he dug, the contractor piled the excavated dirt on either side of the ditch, a practice known as sidecasting.

Figure 5-4: An Example of Wetland Drainage
U.S. Geological Survey photo.

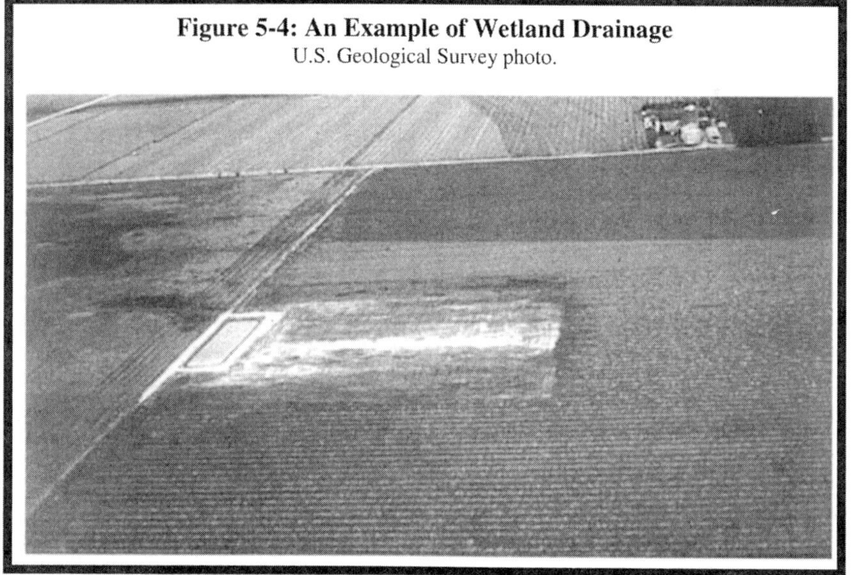

In July 1990 the Corps learned of possible Clean Water Act violations on the Deaton property. A Corps ecologist, Alex Dolgos, inspected the site and concluded that it contained wetlands, that those wetlands were "waters of the United States" under the Clean Water Act, and that the ditching and fill work that had taken place required a permit. On August

7 and 8, 1990, the Corps issued stop-work orders to Deaton and his contractor, warning them that their placement of fill material in a nontidal wetland violated § 404 of the Clean Water Act, 33 U.S.C. § 1344, and that no further work should be done without a permit. Deaton filed a joint state and federal application in December 1990, seeking permits to ditch and fill wetlands in order to construct an eighteen-lot subdivision. That application was returned as incomplete on February 15, 1991, and was never resubmitted. Over the next three years Deaton engaged several consultants to inspect the property, negotiate with the Corps, and prepare a remediation plan. No remediation ever took place, however, and on July 21, 1995, the government filed a civil complaint alleging that the Deatons had violated the Clean Water Act by discharging fill material (the dirt excavated from the ditch) into a regulated wetland.

The government moved for partial summary judgment, seeking rulings that jurisdictional wetlands (waters of the United States) existed on the property, that the Deatons had violated the Clean Water Act by filling those wetlands, and that the Deatons were therefore liable for the restoration of the property and subject to civil penalties. The Deatons cross-moved for summary judgment, asserting that the portions of the property affected by the fill material were not wetlands under the Corps' regulations, that the property was not a wetland adjacent to waters of the United States (and thus was not subject to the Clean Water Act), *see* 33 C.F.R. § 328.3, and that sidecasting dirt excavated from a ditch in a wetland did not require a permit under the Act. On September 22, 1997, the district court granted partial summary judgment to the government, holding that any wetlands on the property were subject to the Clean Water Act and that sidecasting excavated material into those wetlands was the discharge of a pollutant under the Act. The Deatons' motion for summary judgment was denied. * * *

On December 23, 1997, this court decided *United States v. Wilson,* 133 F.3d 251 (4th Cir. 1997). One issue in that case was whether side-casting in a wetland without a permit violated the Clean Water Act. The panel split three ways, with one judge concluding that sidecasting did not constitute the discharge of a pollutant under the Act, one judge concluding that it did, and one judge concurring in the judgment without reaching the sidecasting question. After *Wilson* was decided, the district court reconsidered its award of partial summary judgment to the government. In a subsequent order (entered June 23, 1998) the district court noted that although it agreed with the judge in *Wilson* who said that unauthorized sidecasting in a wetland is against the law, it predicted that this court would adopt the reasoning of the judge who concluded that sidecasting is not the discharge of a pollutant. On that analysis the district court vacated its prior determination that sidecasting is the discharge of a pollutant under the Act; it then granted summary judgment for the Deatons.

The government now appeals the judgment awarded to the Deatons * * *. For the reasons discussed below, we hold that sidecasting is the discharge of a pollutant that violates the Act. * * *

II.

The Clean Water Act prohibits the discharge, without a permit, of any pollutant into "navigable waters." *See* 33 U.S.C. §§ 1311(a), 1362(6), (7), (12). The Act defines "navigable waters" as "the waters of the United States, including the territorial seas." *Id.* § 1362(7). Consistent with the intent of Congress, the Corps has construed "waters of the United States" to include the territorial seas, interstate waters, waters used or susceptible to use in interstate commerce, tributaries of any of these waters, and wetlands adjacent to all of these waters. *See* 33 C.F.R. § 328.3(a); *United States v. Riverside Bayview Homes, Inc.*, 474 U.S. 121, 132–35 (1985). The Corps argues and we assume for purposes of this appeal that the Deatons' property contains wetlands that are subject to the Clean Water Act. The narrow issue before us today is whether sidecasting (that is, the deposit of dredged or excavated material from a wetland back into that same wetland) constitutes the discharge of a pollutant under the Clean Water Act. We hold that it does.

The Clean Water Act defines "discharge of a pollutant" to mean "any addition of any pollutant to navigable waters from any point source." 33 U.S.C. § 1362(12)(A). The definition of pollutant, in turn, specifically includes "dredged spoil" that has been "discharged into water." *Id.* § 1362(6). The piles of dirt dredged up by the Deatons' contractor were, without question, "pollutants" within the meaning of the Act. This conclusion, instead of resolving the dispute, merely brings us to its center because the parties disagree fundamentally about what it means to "discharge . . . a pollutant" into the waters of the United States.

The Deatons seize on the word "addition" in the phrase "addition of any pollutant" in the statutory definition of discharge. [33] U.S.C. § 1362(12). They argue that the "ordinary and natural meaning of 'addition' means something *added, i.e.*, the addition of something not previously present." Thus, according to the Deatons, no pollutant is discharged unless there is an "introduction of new material into the area, or an increase in the amount of a type of material which is already present." Because sidecasting results in no net increase in the amount of material present in the wetland, the Deatons argue, it does not involve the "addition" (or discharge) of a pollutant. We are not convinced by this argument.

Contrary to what the Deatons suggest, the statute does not prohibit the addition of material; it prohibits "the addition of any pollutant." The idea that there could be an addition of a pollutant without an addition of material seems to us entirely unremarkable, at least when an activity transforms some material from a nonpollutant into a pollutant, as occurred here. In the course of digging a ditch across the Deaton property, the contractor removed earth and vegetable matter from the wetland.

Once it was removed, that material became "dredged spoil," a statutory pollutant and a *type* of material that up until then was not present on the Deaton property. It is of no consequence that what is now dredged spoil was previously present on the same property in the less threatening form of dirt and vegetation in an undisturbed state. What is important is that once that material was excavated from the wetland, its redeposit in that same wetland *added* a pollutant where none had been before. *See* 33 U.S.C. § 1362(6), (12). Thus, even under the definition of "addition" (that is, "something added") offered by the Deatons, sidecasting adds a pollutant that was not present before.

Although we conclude that the Clean Water Act's definition of discharge and its use of the term "addition" are unambiguous, the underlying rationale for defining dredged spoil as a pollutant provides further support for our conclusion. In deciding to classify dredged spoil as a pollutant, Congress determined that plain dirt, once excavated from waters of the United States, could not be redeposited into those waters without causing harm to the environment. Indeed, several seemingly benign substances like rock, sand, cellar dirt, and biological materials are specifically designated as pollutants under the Clean Water Act. *See* 33 U.S.C. § 1362(6). Congress had good reason to be concerned about the reintroduction of these materials into the waters of the United States, including the wetlands that are a part of those waters.

Wetlands perform a vital role in maintaining water quality by trapping sediment and toxic and nontoxic pollutants before they reach streams, rivers, or other open bodies of water. *See* OFFICE OF TECHNOLOGY ASSESSMENT, U.S. CONGRESS, WETLANDS: THEIR USE AND REGULATION 48–50 (1984). Given sufficient time, many (but not all) of these pollutants will decompose, degrade, or be absorbed by wetland vegetation. *See id.* at 48–49. When a wetland is dredged, however, and the dredged spoil is redeposited in the water or wetland, pollutants that had been trapped may be suddenly released. *See id.* at 49; *Wilson*, 133 F.3d at 273–74. At the same time, the increased drainage brought about by the dredging may render the surrounding wetland unable to reabsorb and filter those pollutants and sediment (the very purpose of dredging is to destroy wetland characteristics). *See* 40 C.F.R. § 230.41(b). Even in a pristine wetland or body of water, the discharge of dredged spoil, rock, sand, and biological materials threatens to increase the amount of suspended sediment, harming aquatic life. *See* OFFICE OF TECHNOLOGY ASSESSMENT, *supra*, at 48; *see also Wilson*, 133 F.3d at 274.

These effects are no less harmful when the dredged spoil is redeposited in the same wetland from which it was excavated. The effects on hydrology and the environment are the same. Surely Congress would not have used the word "addition" (in "addition of any pollutant") to prohibit the discharge of dredged spoil in a wetland, while intending to prohibit such pollution only when the dredged material comes from outside the wetland. * * *

For these reasons, we hold that the Clean Water Act's definition of discharge as "any addition of any pollutant to navigable waters" encompasses sidecasting in a wetland. We therefore reverse the district court's June 23, 1998, judgment to the contrary. * * *

NOTES

1. **"Addition" of What, Exactly?** What distinction did the Fourth Circuit draw between the addition of *material* and the addition of *pollutants*? Why was that distinction important to the outcome of the case? Why did the court adopt that distinction, as a matter of statutory interpretation?

The theory that the Fourth Circuit adopted might be termed the "legal transformation" theory of additions. The court accepted that material dredged or otherwise removed from the beds of various waters—material that is not and cannot be a pollutant *in situ*—is transformed into a pollutant upon its removal. As a result, an addition of a pollutant occurs when the discharger redeposits the removed material—even if the discharger returns the removed material to essentially the same place from which it was removed. As noted, the Clean Water Act requires some version of a "legal transformation" theory, because section 404(a) clearly requires permits for the discharge of dredged material—that is, for the discharge of material removed from the bottoms of waterbodies. *See* 33 U.S.C. § 1344(a). Why would Congress have expressly subjected discharges of dredged material to federal jurisdiction?

2. **Additions of Dredged Material and Deep Ripping of Wetlands.** The Ninth Circuit relied on *Deaton* and the legal transformation theory to hold that "deep ripping" of wetlands—the mechanized destruction of the bottom clay layer under wetlands, allowing the water to drain away—constituted an "addition" of pollutants to the wetland in violation of the Clean Water Act. *Borden Ranch Partnership v. U.S. Army Corps of Engineers*, 261 F.3d 810, 814–15 (9th Cir. 2001). According to the Ninth Circuit:

> The[] cases recognize that activities that destroy the ecology of a wetland are not immune from the Clean Water merely because they do not involve the introduction of material brought in from somewhere else. In this case, the Corps alleges that Tsakopoulos has essentially poked a hole in the bottom of protected wetlands. That is, by ripping up the bottom layer of soil, the water that was trapped can now drain out. While it is true, that in so doing, no new material has been "added," a "pollutant" has certainly been "added." Prior to the deep ripping, the protective layer of soil was intact, holding the wetland in place. Afterwards, that soil was wrenched up, moved around, and redeposited somewhere else. We can see no meaningful distinction between this activity and the activities at issue in * * * *Deaton*. We therefore conclude that deep ripping, when undertaken in the context at issue here, can constitute a discharge of a pollutant under the Clean Water Act.

Id. The Supreme Court granted *certiorari* to review the Ninth Circuit's decision in *Borden Ranch*, and on December 16, 2002, to the surprise of many, eight equally divided Justices upheld the Ninth Circuit's decision. However, the two-sentence opinion gives little guidance regarding "additions" of pollutants into wetlands, stating only that "[t]he judgment is affirmed by an equally divided Court" and that "Justice KENNEDY took no part in the consideration or decision of this case." *Borden Ranch Partnership v. United States Army Corps of Engineers*, 537 U.S. 99, 100 (2002).

3. **Incidental Fallback as a Clean Water Act "Addition."** The D.C. Circuit took a narrow view of "addition" in *National Mining Association v. U.S. Army Corps of Engineers*, 145 F.3d 1399 (D.C. Cir. 1998). The issue in *National Mining Association* was whether the U.S. Army Corps of Engineers and the EPA had the authority to regulate incidental fallback of material in connection with dredging and construction activities. "Incidental fallback" refers to the small amounts of dredged material that fall off of machinery *as* the dredged material is being lifted out of the waterbody. *Id.* at 1403. According to the D.C. Circuit, incidental fallback is *not* an addition of a pollutant. "Because incidental fallback represents a net withdrawal, not an addition, of material, it cannot be a discharge. * * * The agencies' primary counterargument—that fallback constitutes an 'addition of any pollutant' because material becomes a pollutant only upon being dredged—is ingenious but unconvincing. Regardless of any legal metamorphosis that may occur at the moment of dredging, we fail to see how there can be an addition of *dredged material* when there is no addition of *material.* * * * Congress could not have contemplated that the attempted removal of 100 tons of that substance could constitute an addition simply because only 99 tons of it were actually taken away." *National Mining Association*, 145 F.3d at 1403–04.

* * *

C. "POLLUTANT"

Unlike "addition," the Clean Water Act *does* define "pollutant."

> The term "pollutant" means dredged spoil, solid waste, incinerator residue, sewage, garbage, sewage sludge, munitions, chemical wastes, biological materials, radioactive materials, heat, wrecked or discarded equipment, rock, sand, cellar dirt and *industrial, municipal, and agricultural waste discharged into water.*

CWA § 502(6), 33 U.S.C. § 1362(6) (emphasis added). This definition is very broad, especially given that it includes all "industrial, municipal, and agricultural waste."

Nevertheless, the definition of "pollutant" also includes two exceptions—materials that are *not* considered pollutants under the Act, so that the discharge of these materials does *not* trigger Clean Water Act jurisdiction.

> ["Pollutant"] does not mean (A) "sewage from vessels or a discharge incidental to the normal operation of a vessel of the Armed Forces" within the meaning of section 1323 of this title; or (B) water, gas, or other material which is injected into a well to facilitate production of oil or gas, or water derived in association with oil or gas production and disposed of in a well, if the well used either to facilitate produc-

> tion or for disposal purposes is approved by authority of the State in which the well is located, and if such State determines that such injection or disposal will not result in the degradation of ground or surface water resources.

Id. Notice that these two exceptions are of two different types. Congress exempted sewage discharges from vessels and discharges incidental to the operation of military vessels from section 301(a) and the Act's two permit programs because the EPA and the Coast Guard regulate these discharges pursuant to section 313 of the Act. 33 U.S.C. § 1323. Thus, the exemption prevents double regulation. The oil and gas exemption, in contrast, functions more as a complete exemption, entirely eliminating certain oil and gas processes from Clean Water Act jurisdiction.

In addition, although the definition of "pollutant" is broad, not every material qualifies, even if Congress did not specifically exempt it. Consider the following case.

ASSOCIATION TO PROTECT HAMMERSLEY, ELD, AND TOTTEN INLETS v. TAYLOR RESOURCES, INC.

299 F.3d 1007 (9th Cir. 2002).

GOULD, CIRCUIT JUDGE.

This case poses the interesting question whether the mussel shells, mussel feces and other biological materials emitted from mussels grown on harvesting rafts, and thereby entering the beautiful waters of Puget Sound, constitute the discharge of pollutants from a point source without a permit in violation of the Clean Water Act ("the Act"), 33 U.S.C. §§ 1251–1376. * * *

The Association to Protect Hammersley, Eld, and Totten Inlets ("APHETI"), a non-profit organization composed of about 3,000 persons who reside along the southern shores of Puget Sound, sued Taylor Resources, Inc. ("Taylor"), a mussel-harvesting company, under the citizen suit provisions of the Act. APHETI sought: (1) a judgment declaring that Taylor discharged pollutants from its mussel-harvesting facilities without a National Pollutant Discharge Elimination System ("NPDES") permit; (2) an order enjoining Taylor from discharging pollutants from its facilities until it obtained such a permit; and (3) an order imposing civil penalties for Taylor's alleged violations of the Act. The district court granted summary judgment in favor of Taylor, holding that Taylor's mussel-harvesting rafts did not violate the Clean Water Act. APHETI appeals. We reach the Clean Water Act claim and review de novo the district court's grant of summary judgment. We affirm.

I

The Clean Water Act, 33 U.S.C. §§ 1251–1376, aims to restore and maintain the "chemical, physical and biological integrity of [the] Nation's waters." 33 U.S.C. § 1251(a). To achieve these desirable goals, the Act "establishes a comprehensive statutory system for controlling water pollution. To that end, it establishes the ... NPDES permit system for regulating discharges of pollutants into waters of the United States." *Nat'l Wildlife Fed'n v. Consumers Power Co.*, 862 F.2d 580, 582 (6th Cir. 1988).

A cornerstone of the Clean Water Act is that the "discharge of any pollutant" from a "point source" into navigable waters of the United States is unlawful unless the discharge is made according to the terms of an NPDES permit obtained from either the United States Environmental Protection Agency ("EPA") or from an authorized state agency. 33 U.S.C. §§ 1311(a), 1342; *see also Comm. To Save Mokelumne River v. E. Bay Mun. Util. Dist.*, 13 F.3d 305, 308 (9th Cir. 1993). In Washington State, the Department of Ecology ("Ecology") is authorized by the EPA to administer the Clean Water Act's NPDES program. *See* 33 U.S.C. § 1342(c)(1) (suspending the availability of federal NPDES permits once a state-permitting program has been submitted and approved by the EPA). With these salient legal principles in mind, we consider the dispute between APHETI and Taylor.

II

Since the early 1990s, Taylor has run two mussel-harvesting facilities in Puget Sound's Totten Inlet, producing more than 20,000 pounds of mussels each year. With these facilities, Taylor harvests gallo mussels, a species of mussels present in Puget Sound for about twenty-five years.

Taylor attaches what are termed "mussel brood stock" or mussel "seeds"—that is, what we might consider to be "infant" mussels if personified—to suspension ropes that hang from floating rafts. Leading from Taylor's rafts, the suspension ropes are immersed and then anchored to the sea floor, surrounded by mesh netting designed to protect the mussels from predators. Taylor does not add fish food or chemicals to the water; the mussels are nurtured exclusively by the nutrients found naturally in the waters of Puget Sound, with nothing added. It is nature and the vibrant waters of Puget Sound that transform the mussel "seeds" into edible mussels worthy of admiration and human appetite.

But here's the rub, the environmental issue, as APHETI sees it: The tiny mussels have their commensurate physical and chemical processes. And as a byproduct of their metabolism, the mussels harvested at Taylor's facilities produce and release, as particulate matter, feces and pseudofeces, and they generate dissolved materials in the form of ammonium and inorganic phosphate (collectively, "mussel byproduct"). Also, gallo mussel shells have appeared on the beaches of Totten Inlet since the mid–1990s. There is no doubt that mussel byproduct and mussel shells are released from Taylor's facilities and, in this sense, they are adding something, however small, to the Sound's abundant waters. But it must also be recognized that the mussels act as filters and are considered by many to enhance water quality by filtering excess nutrients or other matter in the water that can be destructive to marine environments.[1]

Figure 5-5: Four-Month Old Mussels in Puget Sound (with Kelp Crabs)
National Oceanic and Atmospheric Administration photo.

Taylor's mussel-harvesting rafts, although not welcomed by all who reside along Puget Sound's southern shores, are not a rogue operation. Since Taylor began its operations, it has applied for and received all required permits for compliance with both the Washington State Environmental Policy Act and the National Environmental Policy Act. To comply with the Clean Water Act, Taylor sought to acquire an NPDES permit. Ecology, however, told Taylor that it would neither accept nor process Taylor's application for an NPDES permit. In Ecology's view, an NPDES permit was not required for Taylor's mussel-harvesting facilities.

On August 18, 1997, the Director of Ecology responded in a letter to an APHETI member who had inquired whether an NPDES permit was required for mussel harvesting rafts. The Director of Ecology wrote that

1. Several Puget Sound area Native American Tribes submitted letters as *amicus curiae* in strong and unequivocal support of Taylor and argued, among other things, that their own historical shellfish-harvesting methods, which are similar in design to Taylor's methods, serve to enhance water quality. For example, the Squaxin Island Tribe wrote that it relies on a high standard of water quality for its aquacultural activities and that "shellfish populations are a regulating species, helping to consume and control excess nutrients added to the water from other sources." Similarly, the Port Gamble S'Klallam Tribe wrote that "because of their formidable water filtration capabilities, mussel rafts have actually been proposed as a means to improve water quality in embayments where poor circulation and point source discharges threaten water quality." Although we cannot make factual findings in our appellate review, we need not close our eyes to the positions of these independent Tribes, which have a deep historic familiarity with Puget Sound waters, with harvesting shellfish, and with concern for the environment.

mussel-harvesting facilities do not violate the Clean Water Act because "shellfish farmers do not need to add fish food (nutrients) to the water to promote shellfish growth." Not persuaded, APHETI, on August 18, 1999, filed a complaint under the citizen suit provision of the Clean Water Act, 33 U.S.C. § 1365, alleging that Taylor had violated the Act by "discharging pollutants," such as mussel feces, mussel shells, and ammonia from its rafts into the Puget Sound without an NPDES permit. *See* 33 U.S.C. §§ 1311, 1342. APHETI claimed that particles and chemicals emitted from the mussels were "pollutants," that Taylor's harvesting rafts were "point sources," and that Taylor therefore needed an NPDES permit to operate. APHETI sought civil penalties and an order enjoining Taylor from discharging pollutants from its facilities until Taylor obtained an NPDES permit.

The district court granted summary judgment to Taylor, holding that Taylor's facilities did not "discharge a pollutant" and that the mussels and mussel rafts were not "point sources." In this appeal, we must assess whether the district court's conclusions on these novel interpretive issues under the Clean Water Act were correct.

* * * IV

We recur to the fundamental law described at the outset of our opinion: The "discharge of any pollutant" from a "point source" into navigable waters is unlawful under the Clean Water Act unless made per the terms of an NPDES permit obtained from Ecology as the authorized state agency. Because no permit was obtained before commencing the raft operations in the navigable waters of Puget Sound, we now address whether the materials naturally released by gallo mussels are "pollutant[s]" under the Clean Water Act.

The Act states:

> The term "pollutant" means dredged spoil, solid waste, incinerator residue, sewage, garbage, sewage sludge, munitions, chemical wastes, *biological materials,* radioactive materials, heat, wrecked or discarded equipment, rock, sand, cellar dirt and industrial, municipal, and agricultural waste discharged into water.

33 U.S.C. § 1362(6) (emphasis added). APHETI argues that the chemicals, fluids, shells and other materials released by Taylor's mussels meet the statutory definition of "pollutant" because these materials are "biological materials" and thus "pollutants" under the Act. A novel question is presented, but we conclude that APHETI's contention must be rejected to preserve the integrity of the Clean Water Act.

"It is well settled that the starting point for interpreting a statute is the language of the statute itself." *Gwaltney of Smithfield, Ltd. v. Chesapeake Bay Found., Inc.*, 484 U.S. 49, 56 (1987) (internal quotation marks and citations omitted). We begin with the language of the Clean Water Act and consider its illustrative pollutants. *See* 33 U.S.C. § 1362(6). The Act lists diverse examples of a "pollutant," and in this context the meaning of "biological materials" is not readily apparent.

The doctrine of *ejusdem generis* suggests that the definition of "biological materials" is not as broad as APHETI argues. Under that doctrine, "[w]hen a statute contains a list of specific items and a general item, we usually deem the general item to be of the same category or class as the more specifically enumerated items." *Sutton v. Providence St. Joseph Med. Ctr.*, 192 F.3d 826, 834 (9th Cir. 1999). Here, the more specific items in the illustrative list of pollutants, such as "radioactive materials," "wrecked or discarded equipment," "garbage," "sewage sludge," "solid waste," and "incinerator residue" support an understanding of the more general statutory term, "biological materials," as waste material of a human or industrial process.

Viewed in this context, mussel shells, mussel feces and other natural byproduct of live mussels do not appear to be the type of materials the drafters of the Act would classify as "pollutants." But it must also be acknowledged that the phrase "biological materials" could literally embrace the emissions at issue. For this reason, the statute is ambiguous on whether "biological materials" means *all* biological matter regardless of quantum and nature and regardless of whether generated by living creatures, or whether the term is limited to biological materials that are a waste product of some human process. In light of this ambiguity, we consider the congressional intent in passing the Clean Water Act.

In 1972, Congress passed the Clean Water Act amendments, 33 U.S.C. §§ 1251–1387, to respond to environmental degradation of the nation's waters. In the text of the Act, Congress plainly and explicitly listed the "protection and *propagation* of ... shellfish" as one of the goals of reduced pollution and cleaner water. 33 U.S.C. § 1251(a)(2) (emphasis added); *see also* 33 U.S.C. §§ 1312(a), 1314(a)(2). It would be anomalous to conclude that the living shellfish sought to be *protected* under the Act are, at the same time, "pollutants," the discharge of which may be *proscribed* by the Act. Such a holding would contravene clear congressional intent, give unintended effect to the ambiguous language of the Act and undermine the integrity of its prohibitions.

This conclusion is strengthened by further analysis. When faced with an ambiguous statutory term, we may apply other tools of reason in assessing what Congress proscribed. Interpreting the ambiguous term, "biological materials," in its context, we consider that the addition of this material to the waters, so far as the record shows, does not add any identifiable harm, let alone appreciable or significant damage, to the Puget Sound environment. Moreover, there may be countervailing environmental benefits for encouraging shellfish farming in Puget Sound. We are persuaded that Congress did not intend that living shellfish and the natural chemicals and particulate biological matter emitted from them, or the occasional shells that separate from them, be considered pollutants.

By holding that mussel shells and mussel byproduct are not pollutants, we do not suggest that materials found naturally in the water can never be "biological materials" considered pollutants under the Act. A facility that processes fish on land or sea and that discards skin, scales, bones and entrails into the waters might be discharging pollutants under the Act. Similarly, if shellfish are processed and shells discarded in the water, this might be the discharge of pollutants, even though the biological materials had been in the water before processing. Such materials, although naturally occurring, are altered by a human or industrial process and, as waste material in significant amounts, might affect the biological composition of the water. * * * In our case, however, the shells and natural byproduct of living mussels released from Taylor's facilities are the result of the natural biological processes of the mussels, not the waste product of a transforming human process.[9] Accordingly, we do not view Taylor's mussel shells and mussel byproduct as pollutants under the Clean Water Act.

That "biological materials" means the waste product of a human or industrial process is in accord with the views of other courts that have examined what constitutes "biological materials" under the Act. These cases support that the "biological materials" that are "pollutants" under the Act are materials that are transformed by human activity. We reject a broader interpretation in this case. Moreover, our conclusion that the statutory term "biological materials" means the waste product of a human process is further reinforced by the Act's use of the term "pollution," which is defined as the "*man-made* or *man-induced* alteration of the chemical, physical, biological, and radiological integrity of water." 33 U.S.C. § 1362(19) (emphasis added).

We conclude that Taylor's mussel shells and the byproduct from these living mussels are not "biological materials" under the Act because these materials come from the natural growth and development of the mussels and not from a transformative human process. We hold that the mussel shells, mussel feces and other mussel byproduct released from Taylor's live mussels thus do not fall within the statutory definition and meaning of "pollutant." * * *

NOTES

1. **Interpreting "Pollutant" for Purposes of the Clean Water Act.** Why did the Ninth Circuit conclude that the mussel shells and mussel feces are not "pollutants" under the Clean Water Act? What tools of statutory interpretation did it use? Did the Ninth Circuit interpret "pollutant" and

9. As a caveat, the record does not indicate that the biological materials released by Taylor's facilities were released in concentrations significantly greater than would otherwise be found in the waters of the Puget Sound. Accordingly, we need not decide whether the addition of biological materials to the water in concentrations significantly higher than natural concentrations could support a conclusion that such biological materials are "pollutant[s]" under the Act by virtue of their high concentrations. In this case, feces and chemicals exuded from live mussels have not been shown in the record significantly to alter the character of Puget Sound waters, and the record suggests instead that the mussel-harvesting operations generally purify the waters.

"biological materials" as broadly as it could have? Why or why not? How did its interpretation serve the broader purposes of the Clean Water Act, arguably? Is a different view of the Act's purposes possible? Could mussel shells and mussel feces *ever* qualify as "pollutants"? When?

2. **Waste Disposal, RCRA, and the Clean Water Act.** Why would fish processing wastes qualify as "pollutants" when the mussel byproducts at issue in this case did not? Did the Ninth Circuit transform the Clean Water Act into a waste disposal statute, like RCRA? How does the Ninth Circuit's decision in this case relate to RCRA's definition of "solid waste"? Recall that under RCRA a person does not need to get a RCRA permit if the person already has a Clean Water Act NPDES permit for the disposal of the "solid wastes" at issue. RCRA § 1004(27), 42 U.S.C. § 6903(27). Does this case help explain why Congress saw no need for both statutory regimes to regulate the same discharge? To what extent do RCRA and the Clean Water Act serve parallel purposes, according to the Ninth Circuit's view of the Clean Water Act?

3. **An Implied *De Minimis* Exception?** Read footnotes 2 and 9 carefully. To what extent did the Ninth Circuit rely on lack of harm to reach its conclusion that the mussel byproducts in this case were not "pollutants"? What else do mussels do to water quality besides add mussel byproducts? Should such considerations be relevant in assessing whether Clean Water Act jurisdiction exists? Why or why not?

4. **Native American and Environmental Justice Issues.** Re-read footnote 2. Why would the Native American Tribes in the Puget Sound area submit *amici* briefs in this litigation? How did the Ninth Circuit treat the Tribes' arguments? Is its consideration of the Tribes' arguments a form of environmental justice? Why or why not?

5. **Discharger Culpability and Clean Water Act Liability**. Compare Taylor's conduct in this case with the Deatons' conduct in *United States v. Deaton*. If the Ninth Circuit had found that mussel byproducts *were* pollutants, would Taylor have been as culpable in violating the Clean Water Act as the Deatons were? Why or why not? Should such culpability matter? Why or why not?

The short answer is that relative culpability is irrelevant to a discharger's administrative or civil liability for violating the Clean Water Act because such violations are strict liability offenses. *United States v. Allegheny Ludlum Corp.*, 366 F.3d 164, 174–75 (3rd Cir. 2004); *United States v. Winchester Municipal Utilities*, 944 F.2d 301, 304 (6th Cir. 1991); *United States v. West of England Ship Owner's Mutual Protection & Indemnity Ass'n*, 872 F.2d 1192, 1198 (5th Cir. 1989); *Stoddard v. Western Carolina Regional Sewer Authority*, 784 F.2d 1200, 1208 (4th Cir. 1986); *Matter of Oswego Barge Corp.*, 664 F.2d 327, 343 (2d Cir. 1981); *United States v. Earth Sciences, Inc.*, 599 F.2d 368, 374 (10th Cir. 1979); *United States v. Marathon Pipeline Co.*, 589 F.2d 1305, 1309 (7th Cir. 1978). However, a violator's culpability *does* become relevant when the agency assesses administrative penalties, CWA § 309(g)(3), 33 U.S.C. § 1319(g)(3), or the court assesses civil penalties. *Id.* § 309(d), 33 U.S.C. § 1319(d).

Taylor's situation also raises a potential equitable issue regarding Clean Water Act liability. Taylor actually applied to the Washington Department of Ecology, the authorized NPDES permitting agency, and Ecology refused to issue the permit, claiming that it was unnecessary. APHETI then sued *Taylor* pursuant to the Clean Water Act's citizen suit provision, CWA § 505, 33 U.S.C. § 1365, seeking to impose liability on Taylor. Should Taylor have a defense to the citizen suit based on the Department of Ecology's refusal to issue the permit? Why or why not? *Compare Hughey v. JMS Development Corp.*, 78 F.3d 1523, 1530 (11th Cir. 1996), *with Mississippi River Revival, Inc. v. City of Minneapolis, Minn.*, 319 F.3d 1013, 1015–18 (8th Cir. 2003); *Sierra Club, Lone Star Chapter v. Cedar Point Oil Co., Inc.*, 73 F.3d 546, 552–59 (5th Cir. 1996); *U.S. Public Interest Research Group v. Atlantic Salmon of Maine*, 215 F.Supp.2d 239, 257–58 (D. Me. 2002).

* * *

D. JURISDICTIONAL WATERS

1. "Navigable Waters"

In order for a discharge to trigger the Clean Water Act's prohibition, the regulated entity must add pollutants to a jurisdictional water. Under subsection (A) of the definition of "discharge of a pollutant," a person must add a pollutant to the ***navigable waters***. CWA § 502(14)(A), 33 U.S.C. § 1362(14)(A). "Navigable waters" is a term with a long history in federal law, important to common law concepts like the public trust doctrine and the navigation servitude as well as to pre-Clean Water Act statutes like the Rivers and Harbors Act of 1899. Traditionally, "navigable waters" referred to waters with some direct connection to navigation. Depending on the exact legal context, such waters can include:

- Waters that are currently "navigable in fact"—that is, ships and boats can actually sail on the waterbody. *See United States v. Appalachian Elec. Power Co.*, 311 U.S. 377, 407–09 (1940).
- Waters that had been navigable in fact at some point in the past, such as when a state became part of the United States. *See Oregon ex rel. State Land Board v. Corvallis Sand & Gravel Co.*, 429 U.S. 363, 370–71 (1977).
- Waters that can be made navigable in fact through feats of engineering, such as by deepening channels or by building a system of locks. *See* 33 C.F.R. § 321.1(a).
- Waters subject to the ebb and flow of the tide. *See Phillips Petroleum Co. v. Mississippi*, 484 U.S. 469, 478–81 (1988).

By the time Congress enacted the Federal Water Pollution Control Act Amendments in 1972, its constitutional authority to regulate these traditional "navigable waters" was undisputed. Thus, the Clean Water Act's applicability to waters that are navigable in the traditional sense, especially to waters that are currently "navigable in fact," is similarly undisputed.

In the 1972 amendments, however, Congress purposefully expanded federal jurisdiction beyond the traditional "navigable waters" for purposes of the Clean Water Act. The Clean Water Act defines "***navigable waters***" to be "the waters of the United States, including the territorial seas." CWA § 502(7), 33 U.S.C. § 1362(7). The Act does not further define "waters of the United States," but the ***territorial seas*** are the first three miles of ocean extending from the coast. CWA § 502(8), 33 U.S.C. § 1362(8). States generally control these waters through the federal Submerged Lands Act. 43 U.S.C. §§ 1301–1315.

Congress's expanded statutory definition of "navigable waters" and the Act's legislative history indicated that Congress intended to expand federal jurisdiction over water pollution. *See* CONF. REP. NO. 92–1236 (Sept. 28, 1972), *reprinted in* 1972 U.S.C.C.A.N. 3776, 3821 (noting that "[t]he conferees fully intend the term 'navigable waters' be given the broadest possible constitutional interpretation"). After 1972, therefore, most federal courts concluded or assumed that federal Clean Water Act jurisdiction over "navigable waters" extended to the limits of the Commerce Clause. *Leslie Salt Co. v. United States*, 896 F.2d 354, 360 (9th Cir. 1990); *United States v. Rivera Torres*, 826 F.2d 151, 155 (1st Cir. 1987); *Utah v. Marsh*, 740 F.2d 799, 804 (10th Cir. 1984); *Avoyelles Sportsmen's League v. Marsh*, 715 F.2d 897, 916 n.33 (5th Cir. 1983); *United States v. Lambert*, 695 F.2d 536, 538 (11th Cir. 1983); *Minnesota v. Hoffman*, 543 F.2d 1198, 1200 n.1 (8th Cir. 1976); *United States v. Ashland Oil & Transportation Co.*, 504 F.2d 1317, 1325 (6th Cir. 1974).

In addition, by 1977 the EPA and the Army Corps of Engineers had expansively defined "waters of the United States" in their Clean Water Act regulations. Under these virtually identical sets of regulations, "waters of the United States" include:

(a) All waters which are currently used, were used in the past, or may be susceptible to use in interstate or foreign commerce, including all waters which are subject to the ebb and flow of the tide;

(b) All interstate waters, including interstate "wetlands;"

(c) ***All other waters such as intrastate*** lakes, rivers, streams (including intermittent streams), mudflats, sandflats, "***wetlands***," sloughs, prairie potholes, wet meadows, playa lakes, or natural lakes ***the use, degradation, or destruction of which would affect or could affect interstate or foreign commerce*** including any such waters:

(1) Which are or could be used by interstate or foreign travelers for recreation or other purposes;

(2) From which fish or shellfish are or could be taken and sold in interstate or foreign commerce; or

(3) Which are or could be used for industrial purposes by industries in interstate commerce;

(d) All impoundments of waters otherwise defined as waters of the United States under this definition;

(e) Tributaries of waters identified in paragraphs (a) through (d) of this definition;

(f) The territorial sea; and

(g) "Wetlands" adjacent to waters (other than waters that are themselves wetlands) identified in paragraphs (a) through (f) of this definition.

40 C.F.R. § 122.2 (emphasis added); *see also* 40 C.F.R. § 230.3(s) (both EPA); 33 C.F.R. § 328.3(a) (Army Corps).

Of all of these regulatory categories of "waters of the United States," it is the third—intrastate waters that could affect interstate commerce—that has been the most controversial, particularly with respect to intrastate wetlands. "Wetlands" are soggy areas, often commonly referred to as "swamps" or "sloughs." Wetlands are critical habitat areas for birds and other wildlife, and they play critical roles in flood control and water purification.

Figure 5-6: Acres of Wetlands Losses in the United States
EPA graph.

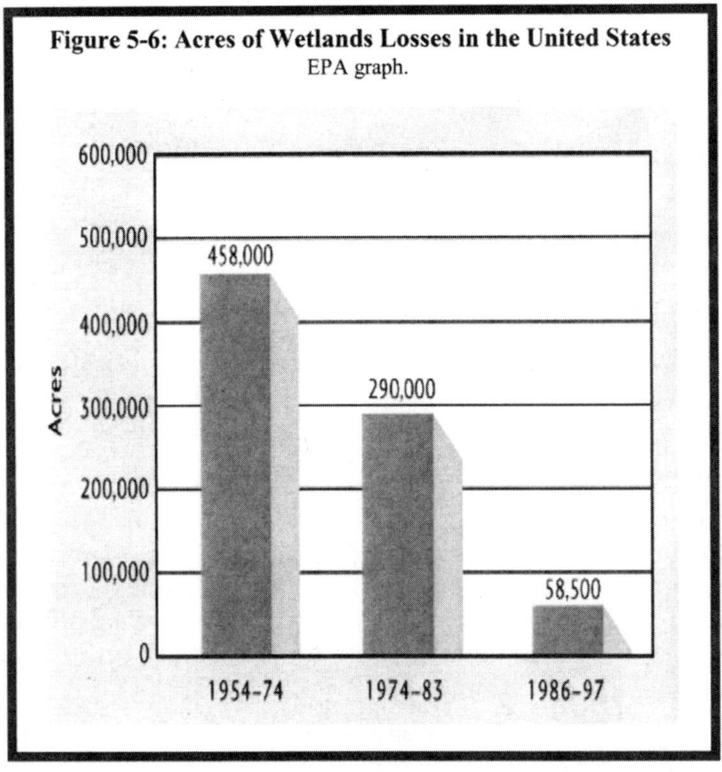

People wishing to develop property containing wetlands often need to fill those wetlands in order to build. The resulting losses of wetlands are obvious, as Figure 5–6 demonstrates. Federal assertions of jurisdiction over such filling, usually by the Army Corps of Engineers pursuant to its permitting authority under section 404, have spawned much litigation over the status of wetlands as "navigable waters."

In a trilogy of cases covering more than two decades, the U.S. Supreme Court has discussed the Clean Water Act's applicability to wetlands. In the first of these cases, ***United States v. Riverside Bayview Homes, Inc.***, 474 U.S. 121 (1985), the Court *unanimously* held that the U.S. Army Corps can assert Clean Water Act jurisdiction over wetlands adjacent to larger bodies of water. The defendant, Riverside Bayview Homes, Inc., owned 80 acres of low-lying, marshy land near the shores of Lake St. Clair in Macomb County, Michigan. In 1976, it began to fill these wetlands to build a housing development.

Giving *Chevron* deference to the Army Corps' regulatory interpretation of "waters of the United States," the U.S. Supreme Court concluded that applying the Clean Water Act to "***adjacent wetlands***" made sense. According to the *Riverside Bayview* Court:

> Congress chose to define the waters covered by the Act broadly. Although the Act prohibits discharges into "navigable waters," *see* CWA §§ 301(a), 404(a), 502(12), 33 U.S.C. §§ 1311(a), 1344(a), 1362(12), the Act's definition of "navigable waters" as "the waters of the United States" makes it clear that the term "navigable" as used in the Act is of limited import. In adopting this definition of "navigable waters," Congress evidently intended to repudiate limits that had been placed on federal regulation by earlier water pollution control statutes and to exercise its powers under the Commerce Clause to regulate at least some waters that would not be deemed "navigable" under the classical understanding of that term. *See* S. CONF. REP. NO. 92–1236, p. 144 (1972); 118 Cong. Rec. 33756–33757 (1972) (statement of Rep. Dingell).
>
> Of course, it is one thing to recognize that Congress intended to allow regulation of waters that might not satisfy traditional tests of navigability; it is another to assert that Congress intended to abandon traditional notions of "waters" and include in that term "wetlands" as well. Nonetheless, the evident breadth of congressional concern for protection of water quality and aquatic ecosystems suggests that it is reasonable for the Corps to interpret the term "waters" to encompass wetlands adjacent to waters as more conventionally defined. Following the lead of the Environmental Protection Agency, *see* 38 Fed. Reg. 10834 (1973), the Corps has determined that wetlands adjacent to navigable waters do as a general matter play a key role in protecting and enhancing water quality * * *.
>
> * * * We cannot say that the Corps' conclusion that adjacent wetlands are inseparably bound up with the "waters" of the United States—based as it is on the Corps' and EPA's technical expertise—is unreasonable. In view of the breadth of federal regulatory authority contemplated by the Act itself and the inherent difficulties of defining

> precise bounds to regulable waters, the Corps' ecological judgment about the relationship between waters and their adjacent wetlands provides an adequate basis for a legal judgment that adjacent wetlands may be defined as waters under the Act.
>
> This holds true even for wetlands that are not the result of flooding or permeation by water having its source in adjacent bodies of open water. The Corps has concluded that wetlands may affect the water quality of adjacent lakes, rivers, and streams even when the waters of those bodies do not actually inundate the wetlands. For example, wetlands that are not flooded by adjacent waters may still tend to drain into those waters. In such circumstances, the Corps has concluded that wetlands may serve to filter and purify water draining into adjacent bodies of water, *see* 33 CFR § 320.4(b)(2)(vii) (1985), and to slow the flow of surface runoff into lakes, rivers, and streams and thus prevent flooding and erosion, *see* §§ 320.4(b)(2)(iv) and (v). In addition, adjacent wetlands may "serve significant natural biological functions, including food chain production, general habitat, and nesting, spawning, rearing and resting sites for aquatic . . . species." § 320.4(b)(2)(i). In short, the Corps has concluded that wetlands adjacent to lakes, rivers, streams, and other bodies of water may function as integral parts of the aquatic environment even when the moisture creating the wetlands does not find its source in the adjacent bodies of water. Again, we cannot say that the Corps' judgment on these matters is unreasonable, and we therefore conclude that a definition of "waters of the United States" encompassing all wetlands adjacent to other bodies of water over which the Corps has jurisdiction is a permissible interpretation of the Act. Because respondent's property is part of a wetland that actually abuts on a navigable waterway, respondent was required to have a permit in this case.

Riverside Bayview Homes, 474 U.S. at 130–31.

Nevertheless, in a footnote, the *Riverside Bayview* Court specified that "[w]e are not called upon to address the question of the authority of the Corps to regulate discharges of fill material into wetlands that are not adjacent to bodies of open water, *see* 33 CFR §§ 323.2(a)(2) and (3) (1985), and we do not express any opinion on that question." *Id.* at 131–32 n.8. This footnote, therefore, set up the next problem for Clean Water Act jurisdiction over wetlands: the problem of non-adjacent, or so-called ***"isolated" wetlands***.

In 1986, in the wake of *Riverside Bayview*'s broad interpretation of "navigable waters," the Army Corps of Engineers revised its regulations. In the preamble to those revisions—but not in the regulations themselves—the Corps noted that it would assert federal Clean Water Act jurisdiction over any intrastate waters:

> (i) Which are or would be used as habitat by birds protected by Migratory Bird Treaties; or

(ii) Which are or would be used as habitat by other migratory birds which cross state lines; or

(iii) Which are or would be used as habitat for endangered species; or

(iv) Used to irrigate crops sold in interstate commerce.

Final Rule for Regulatory Programs of the Corps of Engineers, 51 Fed. Reg. 41,206, 41,217 (Nov. 13, 1986). These non-regulatory assertions of jurisdiction have become known, collectively, as the "Migratory Bird Rule." The Migratory Bird Rule emphasized the Army Corps' (and the EPA's) belief that federal jurisdiction under the Clean Water Act extends to the limits of the Commerce Clause.

In 2001, the Supreme Court disagreed in the second case of the "navigable waters" trilogy, ***Solid Waste Agency of Northern Cook County v. U.S. Army Corps of Engineers***, 531 U.S. 159 (2001) (better known as *SWANCC*). *SWANCC* involved an abandoned sand and gravel mining site that 23 cities and villages in suburban Chicago wanted to convert to a sanitary landfill. Several of the abandoned gavel pits had filled with water, and, while the Army Corps did not consider them "wetlands" for purposes of the Clean Water Act, over 121 species of birds used the new ponds, including migratory birds. The Army Corps asserted Clean Water Act jurisdiction over the site on the basis of the Migratory Bird Rule and denied SWANCC a Section 404 permit to fill the ponds. When SWANCC appealed, a split Supreme Court held, 5–4, that the Army Corps and EPA could not use the Migratory Bird Rule to assert Clean Water Act jurisdiction over intrastate, isolated waters. *Id.* at 174.

However, the case had further implications for Clean Water Act "navigable waters." For example, consider how the *SWANCC* majority characterized *Riverside Bayview Homes*. The dissent, following *Riverside Bayview*, would have accorded the Army Corps and EPA deference and extended Clean Water Act jurisdiction to the limits of the Commerce Clause. *SWANCC*, 531 U.S. at 175–77, 192–93 (J. Stevens, dissenting). In contrast, the majority limited the holding and import of *Riverside Bayview Homes*.

> This is not the first time we have been called upon to evaluate the meaning of § 404(a). In *United States v. Riverside Bayview Homes, Inc.,* 474 U.S. 121 (1985), we held that the Corps had § 404(a) jurisdiction over wetlands that actually abutted on a navigable waterway. In so doing, we noted that the term "navigable" is of "limited import" and that Congress evidenced its intent to "regulate at least some waters that would not be deemed 'navigable' under the classical understanding of that term." *Id.*, at 133. But our holding was based in large measure upon Congress' unequivocal acquiescence to, and approval of, the Corps' regulations interpreting the CWA to cover wetlands adjacent to navigable waters. *See id.*, at 135–139. We found that Congress' concern for the protection of water quality and aquatic ecosystems indicated its intent to regulate wetlands "inseparably bound up with the 'waters' of the United States." *Id.*, at 134.

> It was the significant nexus between the wetlands and "navigable waters" that informed our reading of the CWA in *Riverside Bayview Homes.* Indeed, we did not "express any opinion" on the "question of the authority of the Corps to regulate discharges of fill material into wetlands that are not adjacent to bodies of open water. . . ." *Id.*, at 131–132, n.8. In order to rule for respondents here, we would have to hold that the jurisdiction of the Corps extends to ponds that are *not* adjacent to open water. But we conclude that the text of the statute will not allow this.

SWANCC, 532 U.S. at 167–68. Thus, the majority concluded that the Clean Water Act did not extend to waters on the basis that migratory birds used those waters ***as a matter of statutory interpretation***—the Clean Water Act's definition of "navigable waters" was simply not that broad. Moreover, it emphasized the "***significant nexus***" between adjacent wetlands and larger waters—a nexus that isolated ponds and isolated wetlands do not have. Finally, it re-invigorated the importance of Congress's choice of "navigable waters" as the jurisdictional term:

> We thus decline respondents' invitation to take what they see as the next ineluctable step after *Riverside Bayview Homes:* holding that isolated ponds, some only seasonal, wholly located within two Illinois counties, fall under § 404(a)'s definition of "navigable waters" because they serve as habitat for migratory birds. As counsel for respondents conceded at oral argument, such a ruling would assume that "the use of the word navigable in the statute . . . does not have any independent significance." We cannot agree that Congress' separate definitional use of the phrase "waters of the United States" constitutes a basis for reading the term "navigable waters" out of the statute. We said in *Riverside Bayview Homes* that the word "navigable" in the statute was of "limited import" and went on to hold that § 404(a) extended to nonnavigable wetlands adjacent to open waters. But it is one thing to give a word limited effect and quite another to give it no effect whatever. The term "navigable" has at least the import of showing us what Congress had in mind as its authority for enacting the CWA: its traditional jurisdiction over waters that were or had been navigable in fact or which could reasonably be so made. *See, e.g., United States v. Appalachian Elec. Power Co.*, 311 U.S. 377, 407–408 (1940).

SWANCC, 531 U.S. at 171–72.

The *SWANCC* majority also refused to defer to the Army Corps' (and by implication, the EPA's) regulatory definition of "waters of the United States" because that definition caused constitutional federalism problems:

> We find § 404(a) to be clear, but even were we to agree with respondents, we would not extend *Chevron* deference here.
>
> Where an administrative interpretation of a statute invokes the outer limits of Congress' power, we expect a clear indication that Congress intended that result. This requirement stems from our

> prudential desire not to needlessly reach constitutional issues and our assumption that Congress does not casually authorize administrative agencies to interpret a statute to push the limit of congressional authority. This concern is heightened where the administrative interpretation alters the federal-state framework by permitting federal encroachment upon a traditional state power. * * *
>
> * * * [There] are significant constitutional questions raised by respondents' application of their regulations, and yet we find nothing approaching a clear statement from Congress that it intended § 404(a) to reach an abandoned sand and gravel pit such as we have here. Permitting respondents to claim federal jurisdiction over ponds and mudflats falling within the "Migratory Bird Rule" would result in a significant impingement of the States' traditional and primary power over land and water use. Rather than expressing a desire to readjust the federal-state balance in this manner, Congress chose to "recognize, preserve, and protect the primary responsibilities and rights of States ... to plan the development and use ... of land and water resources...." 33 U.S.C. § 1251(b). We thus read the statute as written to avoid the significant constitutional and federalism questions raised by respondents' interpretation, and therefore reject the request for administrative deference.

SWANCC, 531 U.S. at 172–73.

While the *SWANCC* majority clearly invalidated the use of the Migratory Bird Rule to assert federal jurisdiction over isolated gravel pits pursuant to section 404, the exact scope of the decision beyond the majority's precise holding was unclear. As a result, in the wake of *SWANCC*, federal courts split regarding the scope of Clean Water Act jurisdiction over intrastate, non-navigable waterways. Moreover, because the same definition of "navigable waters" applies in section 301(a), section 402, and section 404, the vast majority of federal courts assumed that *SWANCC* affected *all* federal jurisdiction under the Clean Water Act—not just the Army Corps' jurisdiction under section 404.

The majority of federal courts assumed or declared that *SWANCC* eliminated all federal Clean Water Act jurisdiction over isolated, non-navigable, intrastate waterways. At the same time, however, the majority of federal courts—and Administrative Law Judges (ALJs) within the EPA—determined that federal Clean Water Act jurisdiction remains over any waterway that has a surface water connection to waters that are navigable in fact, no matter how intermittent, convoluted, or human-made the connection might be. *See United States v. Krilich*, 303 F.3d 784, 791 (7th Cir. 2002) (noting that the *SWANCC* decision did not eliminate Clean Water Act jurisdiction over waters not immediately adjacent to traditional navigable waters); *United States v. Interstate General Co.*, 2002 WL 1421411, at *1 (4th Cir. 2002) (upholding Clean Water Act jurisdiction over wetlands adjacent to headwaters of small streams that flow into larger creeks and eventually into the Potomac River and Chesapeake Bay);

Headwaters, Inc. v. Talent Irrigation District, 243 F.3d 526, 533–34 (9th Cir. 2001) (upholding Clean Water Act jurisdiction over irrigation canals when such canals were occasionally open to other navigable waters). In other words, these courts equated *Riverside Bayview*'s emphasis on a "hydrological connection" with the *SWANCC* Court's demand for a "significant nexus."

Several minority rules also emerged. A few federal courts read *SWANCC* very narrowly, determining that *SWANCC* eliminated only the Migratory Bird Rule, and that all other parts of the EPA and Army Corps regulations defining "waters of the United States" remain valid. Under this interpretation, the EPA and the Army Corps retained authority to regulate isolated waters if those waters affect interstate commerce. *See, e.g.*, *Brace v. United States*, 51 Fed. Cl. 649, 653 (Fed. Cl. 2002) (implying that the Army Corps still had authority to regulate isolated ponds and wetlands connected to interstate commerce); *Colvin v. United States*, 181 F. Supp. 2d 1050, 1055 (C.D. Cal. 2001) (noting that *SWANCC* invalidated the Migratory Bird Rule but did not invalidate the Army Corps' other interpretation of "navigable waters"); *United States v. Krilich*, 152 F. Supp. 2d 983, 988 (N.D. Ill. 2001) (noting that "*SWANCC* does indicate * * * that wetlands likely need to have a substantial connection to interstate commerce or a connection to navigable waters (in the traditional sense) in order to be waters of the United States").

In contrast, a very few federal courts read *SWANCC* very broadly, holding that the Supreme Court effectively invalidated *all* of the EPA's and Army Corps' regulatory definitions of "waters of the United States." These courts limited Clean Water Act jurisdiction to those waters that are "navigable" in the traditional sense and to other waters that are *immediately adjacent* to waters that are navigable in the traditional sense. For example, in 2003, the New Jersey District Court concluded:

> In light of *Solid Waste*, it is the view of this court that the "hydrological connection" test is no longer the valid mode of analysis. In this context, the language of Chief Justice Rehnquist's opinion is instructive: it is the "significant nexus between the wetlands and 'navigable waters'" that must inform our reading of the CWA * * *. [A] "significant nexus" must constitute more than a mere "hydrological connection."

FD & P Enterprises, Inc. v. U.S. Army Corps of Engineers, 239 F.Supp.2d 509, 517 (D.N.J. 2003); *see also United States v. Bay-Houston Towing Co., Inc.*, 197 F. Supp. 2d 788, 790–92 (E.D. Mich. 2002) (holding that Clean Water Act jurisdiction did not exist over a very large wetland even though its drainage water reached the Black River and Lake Huron); *United States v. Newdunn Associates*, 195 F. Supp. 2d 751, 764 (E.D. Va. 2002) (calling into question the entirety of the Army Corps of Engineers' 1986 regulations defining "waters of the United States" and denying Clean Water Act jurisdiction over wetlands connected via several intermediary conveyances to traditionally navigable waters); *United States v. Rapanos*,

190 F. Supp. 2d 1011, 1014–16 (E.D. Mich. 2002) (holding that Clean Water Act jurisdiction did not exist over wetlands that were twenty miles from a traditional navigable water, even though a surface water connection existed).

In 2006, the Supreme Court again took up the scope of "navigable waters" in the context of wetlands in two consolidated cases, *Rapanos v. United States* and *Carabell v. U.S. Army Corps of Engineers*. Both cases raised the issue of the "significant nexus" from *Solid Waste Agency*; in addition, the Supreme Court granted *certiorari* on the issue of the Commerce Clause limitation on federal jurisdiction under the Clean Water Act.

In issuing their decision in *Rapanos*, the Justices published five opinions—three of which were fairly lengthy—and no clear decision. However, a majority made up of the Justice Scalia plurality (Justices Scalia, Alito, Roberts, and Thomas) and Justice Kennedy's concurrence agreed that the cases had to be remanded for reconsideration of the "proper" analysis for ***wetlands adjacent to* tributaries *of actual navigable waters***. See if you can discern what that "proper" analysis should be—and any other majority views—as you read the following excerpts.

NOTE: Because the Justices issued only plurality opinions, and because those opinions (1) are each individually lengthy and complex; and (2) present views of federal Clean Water Act jurisdiction that are in some ways radically different from each other, the *Rapanos* "opinion" is in effect three separate opinions. As a result, this casebook includes all three of those major opinions.

RAPANOS v. UNITED STATES

547 U.S. 715 (2006).

JUSTICE SCALIA announced the judgment of the Court, and delivered and opinion, in which THE CHIEF JUSTICE, JUSTICE THOMAS, and JUSTICE ALITO join.

In April 1989, petitioner John A. Rapanos backfilled wetlands on a parcel of land in Michigan that he owned and sought to develop. This parcel included 54 acres of land with sometimes-saturated soil conditions. The nearest body of navigable water was 11 to 20 miles away. Regulators had informed Mr. Rapanos that his saturated fields were "waters of the United States," 33 U.S.C. § 1362(7), that could not be filled without a permit. Twelve years of criminal and civil litigation ensued.

The burden of federal regulation on those who would deposit fill material in locations denominated "waters of the United States" is not trivial. In deciding whether to grant or deny a permit, the U.S. Army Corps of Engineers (Corps) exercises the discretion of an enlightened despot, relying on such factors as "economics," "aesthetics," "recreation," and "in general, the needs and welfare of the people," 33 CFR § 320.4(a) (2004). The average applicant for an individual permit spends 788 days and $271,596 in completing the process, and the average applicant for a nationwide permit spends 313 days and $28,915—not counting costs of mitigation or design changes. Sunding & Zilberman, *The Economics of Environmental Regulation by Licensing: An Assessment of Recent Changes to the Wetland Permitting Process*, 42 NATURAL RESOURCES J. 59, 74–76 (2002). "[O]ver $1.7 billion is spent each year by the private and public sectors obtaining wetlands permits." *Id.,* at 81. These costs cannot be avoided, because the Clean Water Act "impose[s] criminal liability," as well as steep civil fines, "on a broad range of ordinary industrial and commercial activities." *Hanousek v. United States,* 528 U.S. 1102, 1103 (2000) (THOMAS, J., dissenting from denial of certiorari). In this litigation, for example, for backfilling his own wet fields, Mr. Rapanos faced 63 months in prison and hundreds of thousands of dollars in criminal and civil fines.

The enforcement proceedings against Mr. Rapanos are a small part of the immense expansion of federal regulation of land use that has occurred under the Clean Water Act—without any change in the governing statute—during the past five Presidential administrations. In the last three decades, the Corps and the Environmental Protection Agency (EPA) have interpreted their jurisdiction over "the waters of the United States" to cover 270-to-300 million acres of swampy lands in the United States—including half of Alaska and an area the size of California in the lower 48 States. And that was just the beginning. The Corps has also asserted jurisdiction over virtually any parcel of land containing a channel or conduit—whether man-made or natural, broad or narrow, permanent or ephemeral—through which rainwater or drainage may occasionally or intermittently flow. On this view, the federally regulated "waters of the United States" include storm drains, roadside ditches, ripples of sand in the desert that may contain water once a year, and lands that are covered by floodwaters once every 100 years. Because they include the land containing storm sewers and desert washes, the statutory "waters of the United States" engulf entire cities and immense arid wastelands. In fact, the entire land area of the United States lies in some drainage basin, and an endless network of visible channels furrows the entire surface, containing water ephemerally wherever the rain falls. Any plot of land containing such a channel may potentially be regulated as a "water of the United States."

I

Congress passed the Clean Water Act (CWA or Act) in 1972. The Act's stated objective is "to restore and maintain the chemical, physical, and biological integrity of the Nation's waters." 86 Stat. 816, 33 U.S.C. § 1251(a). The Act also states that "[i]t is the policy of Congress to recognize, preserve, and protect the primary responsibilities and rights of States to prevent, reduce, and eliminate pollution, to plan the development and use (including restoration, preservation, and enhancement) of land and water resources, and to consult with the Administrator in the exercise of his authority under this chapter." § 1251(b).

One of the statute's principal provisions is 33 U.S.C. § 1311(a), which provides that "the discharge of any pollutant by any person shall be unlawful." "The discharge of a pollutant" is defined broadly to include "any addition of any pollutant to navigable waters from any point source," § 1362(12), and "pollutant" is defined broadly to include not only traditional contaminants but also solids such as "dredged spoil, ... rock, sand, [and] cellar dirt," § 1362(6). And, most relevant here, the CWA defines "navigable waters" as "the waters of the United States, including the territorial seas." § 1362(7).

The Act also provides certain exceptions to its prohibition of "the discharge of any pollutant by any person." § 1311(a). Section 1342(a) authorizes the Administrator of the EPA to "issue a permit for the discharge of any pollutant, ... notwithstanding section 1311(a) of this title." Section 1344 authorizes the Secretary of the Army, acting through the Corps, to "issue permits ... for the discharge of dredged or fill material into the navigable waters at specified disposal sites." § 1344(a), (d). It is the discharge of "dredged or fill material"—which, unlike traditional water pollutants, are solids that do not readily wash downstream—that we consider today.

For a century prior to the CWA, we had interpreted the phrase "navigable waters of the United States" in the Act's predecessor statutes to refer to interstate waters that are "navigable in fact" or readily susceptible of being rendered so. After passage of the CWA, the Corps initially adopted this traditional judicial definition for the Act's term "navigable waters." After a District Court enjoined these regulations as too narrow, the Corps adopted a far broader definition. The Corps' new regulations deliberately sought to extend the definition of "the waters of the United States" to the outer limits of Congress's commerce power.

The Corps' current regulations interpret "the waters of the United States" to include, in addition to traditional interstate navigable waters, 33 CFR § 328.3(a)(1) (2004), "[a]ll interstate waters including interstate wetlands," § 328.3(a)(2); "[a]ll other waters such as intrastate lakes, rivers, streams (including intermittent streams), mudflats, sandflats, wetlands, sloughs, prairie potholes, wet meadows, playa lakes, or natural ponds, the use, degradation or destruction of which could affect interstate or foreign commerce," § 328.3(a)(3); "[t]ributaries of [such] waters," § 328.3(a)(5); and "[w]etlands adjacent to [such] waters [and tributaries] (other than waters that are themselves wetlands)," § 328.3(a)(7). The regulation defines "adjacent" wetlands as those "bordering, contiguous [to], or neighboring" waters of the United States. § 328.3(c). It specifically provides that "[w]etlands separated from other waters of the United States by man-made dikes or barriers, natural river berms, beach dunes and the like are 'adjacent wetlands.' " *Ibid.*

We first addressed the proper interpretation of 33 U.S.C. § 1362(7)'s phrase "the waters of the United States" in *United States v. Riverside Bayview Homes, Inc.*, 474 U.S. 121 (1985). That case concerned a wetland that "was adjacent to a body of navigable water," because "the area characterized by saturated soil conditions and wetland vegetation extended beyond the boundary of respondent's property to ... a navigable waterway." *Id.*, at 131; see also 33 CFR § 328.3(b) (2004). Noting that "the transition from water to solid ground is not necessarily or even typically an abrupt one," and that "the Corps must necessarily choose some point at which water ends and land begins," 474 U.S., at 132, we upheld the Corps' interpretation of "the waters of the United States" to include wetlands that "actually abut[ted] on" traditional navigable waters. *Id.*, at 135.

Following our decision in *Riverside Bayview*, the Corps adopted increasingly broad interpretations of its own regulations under the Act. For example, in 1986, to "clarify" the reach of its jurisdiction, the Corps announced the so-called "Migratory Bird Rule," which purported to extend its jurisdiction to any intrastate waters "[w]hich are or would be used as habitat" by migratory birds. 51 Fed. Reg. 41217; see also *SWANCC, supra*, at 163–164. In addition, the Corps interpreted its own regulations to include "ephemeral streams" and "drainage ditches" as "tributaries" that are part of the "waters of the United States," see 33 CFR § 328.3(a)(5), provided that they have a perceptible "ordinary high water mark" as defined in § 328.3(e). 65 Fed. Reg. 12823 (2000). This interpretation extended "the waters of the United States" to virtually any land feature over which rainwater or drainage passes and leaves a visible mark—even if only "the presence of litter and debris." 33 CFR § 328.3(e). Prior to our decision in *SWANCC*, lower courts upheld the application of this expansive definition of "tributaries" to such entities as storm sewers that contained flow to covered waters during heavy rainfall and dry arroyos connected to remote waters through the flow of groundwater over "centuries[.]"

In *SWANCC*, we considered the application of the Corps' "Migratory Bird Rule" to "an abandoned sand and gravel pit in northern Illinois." 531 U.S., at 162. Observing that "[i]t was the *significant nexus* between the wetlands and 'navigable waters' that informed our reading of the CWA in *Riverside Bayview*," *id.*, at 167 (emphasis added), we held that *Riverside Bayview* did not establish "that the jurisdiction of the Corps extends to ponds that are not adjacent to open water." 531 U.S., at 168 (emphasis deleted). On the contrary, we held that "nonnavigable, isolated, intrastate waters," *id.*, at 171—which, unlike the wetlands at issue in *Riverside Bayview*, did not "actually abu[t] on a navigable waterway," 531 U.S., at 167—were not included as "waters of the United States."

Following our decision in *SWANCC*, the Corps did not significantly revise its theory of federal jurisdiction under § 1344(a). The Corps provided notice of a proposed rulemaking in light of *SWANCC*, 68 Fed. Reg. 1991 (2003), but ultimately did not amend its published regulations.

Because *SWANCC* did not directly address tributaries, the Corps notified its field staff that they "should continue to assert jurisdiction over traditional navigable waters ... and, generally speaking, their tributary systems (and adjacent wetlands)." 68 Fed. Reg. 1998. In addition, because *SWANCC* did not overrule *Riverside Bayview,* the Corps continues to assert jurisdiction over waters " 'neighboring' " traditional navigable waters and their tributaries. 68 Fed. Reg. 1997 (quoting 33 CFR § 328.3(c) (2003)).

Even after *SWANCC*, the lower courts have continued to uphold the Corps' sweeping assertions of jurisdiction over ephemeral channels and drains as "tributaries." For example, courts have held that jurisdictional "tributaries" include the "intermittent flow of surface water through approximately 2.4 miles of natural streams and manmade ditches (paralleling and crossing under I–64)," *Treacy v. Newdunn Assoc.,* 344 F.3d 407, 410 (C.A.4 2003); a "roadside ditch" whose water took "a winding, thirty-two-mile path to the Chesapeake Bay," *United States v. Deaton,* 332 F.3d 698, 702 (C.A.4 2003); irrigation ditches and drains that intermittently connect to covered waters, *Community Assn. for Restoration of Environment v. Henry Bosma Dairy,* 305 F.3d 943, 954–955 (C.A.9 2002); *Headwaters, Inc. v. Talent Irrigation Dist.,* 243 F.3d 526, 534 (C.A.9 2001); and (most implausibly of all) the "washes and arroyos" of an "arid development site," located in the middle of the desert, through which "water courses ... during periods of heavy rain," *Save Our Sonoran, Inc. v. Flowers,* 408 F.3d 1113, 1118 (C.A.9 2005).

These judicial constructions of "tributaries" are not outliers. Rather, they reflect the breadth of the Corps' determinations in the field. * * * They have also applied that definition to such manmade, intermittently flowing features as "drain tiles, storm drains systems, and culverts." *Id.,* at 24 (footnote omitted).

In addition to "tributaries," the Corps and the lower courts have also continued to define "adjacent" wetlands broadly after *SWANCC.* For example, some of the Corps' district offices have concluded that wetlands are "adjacent" to covered waters if they are hydrologically connected "through directional sheet flow during storm events," GAO Report 18, or if they lie within the "100–year floodplain" of a body of water—that is, they are connected to the navigable water by flooding, on average, once every 100 years, *id.,* at 17, and n. 16. Others have concluded that presence within 200 feet of a tributary automatically renders a wetland "adjacent" and jurisdictional. *Id.,* at 19. And the Corps has successfully defended such theories of "adjacency" in the courts, even after *SWANCC's* excision of "isolated" waters and wetlands from the Act's coverage. One court has held since *SWANCC* that wetlands separated from flood control channels by 70–foot-wide berms, atop which ran maintenance roads, had a "significant nexus" to covered waters because, *inter alia,* they lay "within the 100 year floodplain of tidal waters." *Baccarat Fremont Developers, LLC v. Army Corps of Engineers,* 425 F.3d 1150, 1152, 1157 (C.A.9 2005). In one of the cases before us today, the Sixth Circuit held, in agreement with "[t]he majority of courts," that "while a hydrological connection between the non-navigable and navigable waters is required, there is no 'direct abutment' requirement" under *SWANCC* for " 'adjacency.' " 376 F.3d 629, 639 (2004) *(Rapanos II)*. And even the most insubstantial hydrologic connection may be held to constitute a "significant nexus." One court distinguished *SWANCC* on the ground that "a molecule of water residing in one of these pits or ponds [in *SWANCC*] could not mix with molecules from other bodies of water"—whereas, in the case before it, "water molecules currently present in the wetlands will inevitably flow towards and mix with water from connecting bodies," and "[a] drop of rainwater landing in the Site is certain to intermingle with water from the [nearby river]." *United States v. Rueth Development Co.*, 189 F. Supp. 2d 874, 877–878 (N.D. Ind. 2002).

II

In these consolidated cases, we consider whether four Michigan wetlands, which lie near ditches or man-made drains that eventually empty into traditional navigable waters, constitute "waters of the United States" within the meaning of the Act. [T]he Rapanos and their affiliated businesses[] deposited fill material without a permit into wetlands on three sites near Midland, Michigan: the "Salzburg site," the "Hines Road site," and the "Pine River site." The wetlands at the Salzburg site are connected to a man-made drain, which drains into Hoppler Creek, which flows into the Kawkawlin River, which empties into Saginaw Bay and Lake Huron. The wetlands at the Hines Road site are connected to something called the "Rose Drain," which has a surface connection to the Tittabawassee River. And the wetlands at the Pine River site have a surface connection to the Pine River, which flows into Lake Huron. It is not clear whether the connections between these wetlands and the nearby drains and ditches are continuous or intermittent, or whether the nearby drains and ditches contain continuous or merely occasional flows of water.

The United States brought civil enforcement proceedings against the Rapanos petitioners. The District Court found that the three described wetlands were "within federal jurisdiction" because they were "adjacent to other waters of the United States," and held petitioners liable for violations of the CWA at those sites. On appeal, the United States Court of Appeals for the Sixth Circuit affirmed, holding that there was federal jurisdiction over the wetlands at all three sites because "there were hydrological connections between all three sites and corresponding adjacent tributaries of navigable waters."

[T]he Carabells[] were denied a permit to deposit fill material in a wetland located on a triangular parcel of land about one mile from Lake St. Clair. A man-made drainage ditch runs along one side of the wetland, separated from it by a 4–foot-wide man-made berm. The berm is largely or entirely impermeable to water and blocks drainage from the wetland, though it may permit occasional overflow to the ditch. The ditch empties into another ditch or a drain, which connects to Auvase Creek, which empties into Lake St. Clair.

After exhausting administrative appeals, the Carabell petitioners filed suit in the District Court, challenging the exercise of federal regulatory jurisdiction over their site. The District Court ruled that there was federal jurisdiction because the wetland "is adjacent to neighboring tributaries of navigable waters and has a significant nexus to 'waters of the United States.' " Again the Sixth Circuit affirmed, holding that the Carabell wetland was "adjacent" to navigable waters.

We granted certiorari and consolidated the cases to decide whether these wetlands constitute "waters of the United States" under the Act, and if so, whether the Act is constitutional.

III

The Rapanos petitioners contend that the terms "navigable waters" and "waters of the United States" in the Act must be limited to the traditional definition of *The Daniel Ball,* which required that the "waters" be navigable in fact, or susceptible of being rendered so. See 10 Wall., at 563. But this definition cannot be applied wholesale to the CWA. The Act uses the phrase "navigable waters" as a *defined* term, and the definition is simply "the waters of the United States." 33 U.S.C. § 1362(7). Moreover, the Act provides, in certain circumstances, for the substitution of state for federal jurisdiction over "navigable waters ... *other than* those waters which are presently used, or are susceptible to use in their natural condition or by reasonable improvement as a means to transport interstate or foreign commerce ... including wetlands adjacent thereto." § 1344(g)(1) (emphasis added). This provision shows that the Act's term "navigable waters" includes something more than traditional navigable waters. We have twice stated that the meaning of "navigable waters" in the Act is broader than the traditional understanding of that term, *SWANCC,* 531 U.S., at 167; *Riverside Bayview,* 474 U.S., at 133. We have also emphasized, however, that the qualifier "navigable" is not devoid of significance, *SWANCC, supra,* at 172.

We need not decide the precise extent to which the qualifiers "navigable" and "of the United States" restrict the coverage of the Act. Whatever the scope of these qualifiers, the CWA authorizes federal jurisdiction only over "waters." 33 U.S.C. § 1362(7). The only natural definition of the term "waters," our prior and subsequent judicial constructions of it, clear evidence from other provisions of the statute, and this Court's canons of construction all confirm that "the waters of the United States" in § 1362(7) cannot bear the expansive meaning that the Corps would give it.

The Corps' expansive approach might be arguable if the CWA defined "navigable waters" as "water of the United States." But "the waters of the United States" is something else. The use of the definite article ("the") and the plural number ("waters") show plainly that § 1362(7) does not refer to water in general. In this form, "the waters" refers more narrowly to water "[a]s found in streams and bodies forming geographical features such as oceans, rivers, [and] lakes," or "the flowing or moving masses, as of waves or floods, making up such streams or bodies." WEBSTER'S NEW INTERNATIONAL DICTIONARY 2882 (2d ed. 1954) (hereinafter WEBSTER'S SECOND). On this definition, "the waters of the United States" include only relatively permanent, standing or flowing bodies of water. The definition refers to water as found in "streams," "oceans," "rivers," "lakes," and "bodies" of water "forming geographical features." *Ibid.* All of these terms connote continuously present, fixed bodies of water, as opposed to ordinarily dry channels through which water occasionally or intermittently flows. Even the least substantial of the definition's terms, namely "streams," connotes a continuous flow of water in a permanent channel—especially when used in company with other terms such as "rivers," "lakes," and "oceans." None of these terms encompasses transitory puddles or ephemeral flows of water.

* * * In addition, the Act's use of the traditional phrase "navigable waters" (the defined term) further confirms that it confers jurisdiction only over relatively *permanent* bodies of water. The Act adopted that traditional term from its predecessor statutes. See *SWANCC,* 531 U.S., at 180 (STEVENS, J., dissenting). On the traditional understanding, "navigable waters" included only discrete *bodies* of water. * * * Plainly, because such "waters" had to be navigable in fact or susceptible of being rendered so, the term did not include ephemeral flows. As we noted in *SWANCC*, the traditional term "navigable waters"—even though defined as "the waters of the United States"—carries *some* of its original substance: "[I]t is one thing to give a word limited effect and quite another to give it no effect whatever." 531 U.S., at 172. That limited effect includes, at bare minimum, the ordinary presence of water.

* * * Most significant of all, the CWA itself categorizes the channels and conduits that typically carry intermittent flows of water separately from "navigable waters," by including them in the definition of " 'point source.' " The Act defines " 'point source' " as "any discernible, confined and discrete conveyance, including but not limited to any pipe, ditch, channel, tunnel, conduit, well, discrete fissure, container, rolling stock, concentrated animal feeding operation, or vessel or other floating craft, from which pollutants are or may be discharged." 33 U.S.C. § 1362(14). It also defines " 'discharge of a pollutant' " as "any addition of any pollutant *to* navigable waters *from* any point source." § 1362(12)(A) (emphases added). The definitions thus conceive of "point sources" and "navigable waters" as separate and distinct categories. The definition of "discharge" would make little sense if the two categories were significantly overlapping. The separate classification of "ditch[es], channel[s], and conduit[s]"—which are terms ordinarily used to describe the watercourses through which *intermittent* waters typically flow—shows that these are, by and large, *not* "waters of the United States."

Moreover, only the foregoing definition of "waters" is consistent with the CWA's stated "policy of Congress to recognize, preserve, and protect the primary responsibilities and rights of the States to prevent, reduce, and eliminate pollution, [and] to plan the development and use (including restoration, preservation, and enhancement) of land and water resources.... " § 1251(b). * * *

Even if the phrase "the waters of the United States" were ambiguous as applied to intermittent flows, our own canons of construction would establish that the Corps' interpretation of the statute is impermissible. As we noted in *SWANCC*, the Government's expansive interpretation would "result in a significant impingement of the States' traditional and primary power over land and water use." 531 U.S., at 174. Regulation of land use, as through the issuance of the development permits sought by petitioners in both of these cases, is a quintessential state and local power. The extensive federal jurisdiction urged by the Government would authorize the Corps to function as a *de facto* regulator of immense stretches of intrastate land—an authority the agency has shown its willingness to exercise with the scope of discretion that would befit a local zoning board. See 33 CFR § 320.4(a)(1) (2004). We ordinarily expect a "clear and manifest" statement from Congress to authorize an unprecedented intrusion into traditional state authority. The phrase "the waters of the United States" hardly qualifies.

Likewise, just as we noted in *SWANCC*, the Corps' interpretation stretches the outer limits of Congress's commerce power and raises difficult questions about the ultimate scope of that power. See 531 U.S., at 173 (In developing the current regulations, the Corps consciously sought to extend its authority to the farthest reaches of the commerce power. See 42 Fed. Reg. 37127 (1977).) Even if the term "the waters of the United States" were ambiguous as applied to channels that sometimes host ephemeral flows of water (which it is not), we would expect a clearer statement from Congress to authorize an agency theory of jurisdiction that presses the envelope of constitutional validity.

In sum, on its only plausible interpretation, the phrase "the waters of the United States" includes only those relatively permanent, standing or continuously flowing bodies of water "forming geographic features" that are described in ordinary parlance as "streams[,] ... oceans, rivers, [and] lakes." See WEBSTER'S SECOND 2882. The phrase does not include channels through which water flows intermittently or ephemerally, or channels that periodically provide drainage for rainfall. The Corps' expansive interpretation of the "the waters of the United States" is thus not "based on a permissible construction of the statute." *Chevron U.S.A. Inc. v. Natural Resources Defense Council, Inc.*, 467 U.S. 837, 843 (1984).

IV

In *Carabell*, the Sixth Circuit held that the nearby ditch constituted a "tributary" and thus a "water of the United States" under 33 CFR § 328.3(a)(5) (2004). Likewise in *Rapanos*, the Sixth Circuit held that the nearby ditches were "tributaries" under § 328(a)(5). But *Rapanos II* also stated that, even if the ditches were not "waters of the United States," the wetlands were "adjacent" to *remote* traditional navigable waters in virtue of the wetlands' "hydrological connection" to them. This statement reflects the practice of the Corps' district offices, which may "assert jurisdiction over a wetland without regulating the ditch connecting it to a water of the United States." GAO Report 23. We therefore address in this Part whether a wetland may be considered "adjacent to" remote "waters of the United States," because of a mere hydrologic connection to them.

In *Riverside Bayview,* we noted the textual difficulty in including "wetlands" as a subset of "waters": "On a purely linguistic level, it may appear unreasonable to classify 'lands,' wet or otherwise, as 'waters.' " 474 U.S., at 132. We acknowledged, however, that there was an inherent ambiguity in drawing the boundaries of any "waters":

> "[T]he Corps must necessarily choose some point at which water ends and land begins. Our common experience tells us that this is often no easy task: the transition from water to solid ground is not necessarily or even typically an abrupt one. Rather, between open waters and dry land may lie shallows, marshes, mudflats, swamps, bogs—in short, a huge array of areas that are not wholly aquatic but nevertheless fall far short of being dry land. Where on this continuum to find the limit of 'waters' is far from obvious."

Ibid.

Because of this inherent ambiguity, we deferred to the agency's inclusion of wetlands "actually abut[ting]" traditional navigable waters: "Faced with such a problem of defining the bounds of its regulatory authority," we held, the agency could reasonably conclude that a wetland that "adjoin[ed]" waters of the United States is itself a part of those waters. *Id.,* at 132. The difficulty of delineating the boundary between water and land was central to our reasoning in the case: "In view of the breadth of federal regulatory authority contemplated by the Act itself and *the inherent difficulties of defining precise bounds to regulable waters,* the Corps' ecological judgment about the relationship between waters and their adjacent wetlands provides an adequate basis for a legal judgment that adjacent wetlands may be defined as waters under the Act." *Id.,* at 134 (emphasis added).

When we characterized the holding of *Riverside Bayview* in *SWANCC,* we referred to the close connection between waters and the wetlands that they gradually blend into: "It was the *significant nexus* between the wetlands and 'navigable waters' that informed our reading of the CWA in *Riverside Bayview Homes.*" 531 U.S., at 167 (emphasis added). In particular, *SWANCC* rejected the notion that the ecological considerations upon which the Corps relied in *Riverside Bayview*—and upon which the dissent repeatedly relies today—provided an *independent* basis for including entities like "wetlands" (or "ephemeral streams") within the phrase "the waters of the United States." * * *

Therefore, *only* those wetlands with a continuous surface connection to bodies that are "waters of the United States" in their own right, so that there is no clear demarcation between "waters" and wetlands, are "adjacent to" such waters and covered by the Act. Wetlands with only an intermittent, physically remote hydrologic connection to "waters of the United States" do not implicate the boundary-drawing problem of *Riverside Bayview,* and thus lack the necessary connection to covered waters that we described as a "significant nexus" in *SWANCC*. 531 U.S., at 167. Thus, establishing that wetlands such as those at the Rapanos and Carabell sites are covered by the Act requires two findings: First, that the adjacent channel contains a "wate[r] of the United States," (*i.e.,* a relatively permanent body of water connected to traditional interstate navigable waters); and second, that the wetland has a continuous surface connection with that water, making it difficult to determine where the "water" ends and the "wetland" begins.

V

Respondents and their *amici* urge that such restrictions on the scope of "navigable waters" will frustrate enforcement against traditional water polluters under 33 U.S.C. §§ 1311 and 1342. Because the same definition of "navigable waters" applies to the entire statute, respondents contend that water polluters will be able to evade the permitting requirement of § 1342(a) simply by discharging their pollutants into noncovered intermittent watercourses that lie upstream of covered waters.

That is not so. Though we do not decide this issue, there is no reason to suppose that our construction today significantly affects the enforcement of § 1342, inasmuch as lower courts applying § 1342 have not characterized intermittent channels as "waters of the United States." The Act does not forbid the "addition of any pollutant *directly* to navigable waters from any point source," but rather the "addition of any pollutant *to* navigable waters." § 1362(12)(A) (emphasis added); § 1311(a). Thus, from the time of the CWA's enactment, lower courts have held that the discharge into intermittent channels of any pollutant *that naturally washes downstream* likely violates § 1311(a), even if the pollutants discharged from a point source do not emit "directly into" covered waters, but pass "through conveyances" in between. *United States v. Velsicol Chemical Corp.,* 438 F. Supp. 945, 946–947 (W.D. Tenn. 1976) (a municipal sewer system separated the "point source" and covered navigable waters).

* * * In contrast to the pollutants normally covered by the permitting requirement of § 1342(a), "dredged or fill material," which is typically deposited for the sole purpose of staying put, does not normally wash downstream, and thus does not normally constitute an "addition . . . to navigable waters" when deposited in upstream isolated wetlands. §§ 1344(a), 1362(12). The Act recognizes this distinction by providing a separate permitting program for such discharges in § 1344(a). It does not

appear, therefore, that the interpretation we adopt today significantly reduces the scope of § 1342 of the Act. * * *

* * * VIII

Because the Sixth Circuit applied the wrong standard to determine if these wetlands are covered "waters of the United States," and because of the paucity of the record in both of these cases, the lower courts should determine, in the first instance, whether the ditches or drains near each wetland are "waters" in the ordinary sense of containing a relatively permanent flow; and (if they are) whether the wetlands in question are "adjacent" to these "waters" in the sense of possessing a continuous surface connection that creates the boundary-drawing problem we addressed in *Riverside Bayview*.

* * *

We vacate the judgments of the Sixth Circuit * * * and remand both cases for further proceedings.

It is so ordered.

CHIEF JUSTICE ROBERTS, concurring.

Five years ago, this Court rejected the position of the Army Corps of Engineers on the scope of its authority to regulate wetlands under the Clean Water Act, 86 Stat. 816, as amended, 33 U.S.C. § 1251 *et seq. Solid Waste Agency of Northern Cook Cty. v. Army Corps of Engineers,* 531 U.S. 159 (2001) *(SWANCC).* The Corps had taken the view that its authority was essentially limitless; this Court explained that such a boundless view was inconsistent with the limiting terms Congress had used in the Act. *Id.,* at 167–174.

In response to the *SWANCC* decision, the Corps and the Environmental Protection Agency (EPA) initiated a rulemaking to consider "issues associated with the scope of waters that are subject to the Clean Water Act (CWA), in light of the U.S. Supreme Court decision in *[SWANCC].*" 68 Fed. Reg.1991 (2003). * * *

Agencies delegated rulemaking authority under a statute such as the Clean Water Act are afforded generous leeway by the courts in interpreting the statute they are entrusted to administer. See *Chevron U.S.A. Inc. v. Natural Resources Defense Council, Inc.,* 467 U.S. 837, 842–845 (1984). Given the broad, somewhat ambiguous, but nonetheless clearly limiting terms Congress employed in the Clean Water Act, the Corps and the EPA would have enjoyed plenty of room to operate in developing *some* notion of an outer bound to the reach of their authority.

The proposed rulemaking went nowhere. Rather than refining its view of its authority in light of our decision in *SWANCC*, and providing guidance meriting deference under our generous standards, the Corps chose to adhere to its essentially boundless view of the scope of its power. The upshot today is another defeat for the agency. * * *

JUSTICE KENNEDY, concurring in the judgment.

These consolidated cases require the Court to decide whether the term "navigable waters" in the Clean Water Act extends to wetlands that do not contain and are not adjacent to waters that are navigable in fact. In *Solid Waste Agency of Northern Cook Cty. v. Army Corps of Engineers,* 531 U.S. 159 (2001) *(SWANCC),* the Court held, under the circumstances presented there, that to constitute " 'navigable waters' " under the Act, a water or wetland must possess a "significant nexus" to waters that are or were navigable in fact or that could reasonably be so made. *Id.,* at 167, 172. In the instant cases neither the plurality opinion nor the dissent by Justice STEVENS chooses to apply this test; and though the Court of Appeals recognized the test's applicability, it did not consider all the factors necessary to determine whether the lands in question had, or did not have, the requisite nexus. In my view the cases ought to be remanded to the Court of Appeals for proper consideration of the nexus requirement.

I

Although both the plurality opinion and the dissent by Justice STEVENS (hereinafter the dissent) discuss the background of these cases in some detail, a further discussion of the relevant statutes, regulations, and facts may clarify the analysis suggested here.

A

The "objective" of the Clean Water Act (Act), is "to restore and maintain the chemical, physical, and biological integrity of the Nation's waters." 33 U.S.C. § 1251(a). * * *

The statutory term to be interpreted and applied in the two instant cases is the term "navigable waters." The outcome turns on whether that phrase reasonably describes certain Michigan wetlands the Corps seeks to regulate. Under the Act "[t]he term 'navigable waters' means the waters of the United States, including the territorial seas." § 1362(7). In a regulation the Corps has construed the term "waters of the United States" to include not only waters susceptible to use in interstate commerce—the traditional understanding of the term "navigable waters of the United States[]"—but also tributaries of those waters and, of particular relevance here, wetlands adjacent to those waters or their tributaries. 33 CFR §§ 328.3(a)(1), (5), (7) (2005). * * *

Contrary to the plurality's description, wetlands are not simply moist patches of earth. They are defined as "those areas that are inundated or saturated by surface or ground water at a frequency and duration sufficient to support, and that under normal circumstances do support, a prevalence of vegetation typically adapted for life in saturated soil conditions. Wetlands generally include swamps, marshes, bogs, and similar areas." § 328.3(b). The Corps' *Wetlands Delineation Manual,* including over 100 pages of technical guidance for Corps officers, interprets this definition of wetlands to require: (1) prevalence of plant species typically adapted to saturated soil conditions, determined in accordance with the United States Fish and Wildlife Service's National List of Plant Species that Occur in Wetlands; (2) hydric soil, meaning soil that is saturated, flooded, or ponded for sufficient time during the growing season to become anaerobic, or lacking in oxygen, in the upper part; and (3) wetland hydrology, a term generally requiring continuous inundation or saturation to the surface during at least five percent of the growing season in most years. See WETLANDS RESEARCH PROGRAM TECHNICAL REPORT Y–87–1 (on-line edition), pp. 12–34 (Jan.1987), http://www.saj.usace. army.mil/permit/documents /87manual.pdf. Under the Corps' regulations, wetlands are adjacent to tributaries, and thus covered by the Act, even if they are "separated from other waters of the United States by man-made dikes or barriers, natural river berms, beach dunes and the like." § 328.3(c).

* * * II

Twice before the Court has construed the term "navigable waters" in the Clean Water Act. In *United States v. Riverside Bayview Homes, Inc.,* 474 U.S. 121 (1985), the Court upheld the Corps' jurisdiction over wetlands adjacent to navigable-in-fact waterways. *Id.,* at 139. The property in *Riverside Bayview,* like the wetlands in the *Carabell* case now before the Court, was located roughly one mile from Lake St. Clair, though in that case, unlike *Carabell,* the lands at issue formed part of a wetland that directly abutted a navigable-in-fact creek, 474 U.S., at 131. In regulatory provisions that remain in effect, the Corps had concluded that wetlands perform important functions such as filtering and purifying water draining into adjacent water bodies, 33 CFR § 320.4(b)(2)(vii), slowing the flow of runoff into lakes, rivers, and streams so as to prevent flooding and erosion, §§ 320.4(b)(2)(iv), (v), and providing critical habitat for aquatic animal species, § 320.4(b)(2)(i). 474 U.S., at 134–135. Recognizing that "[a]n agency's construction of a statute it is charged with enforcing is entitled to deference if it is reasonable and not in conflict with the expressed intent of Congress," *id.,* at 131 (citing *Chemical Mfrs. Assn. v. Natural Resources Defense Council, Inc.,* 470 U.S. 116, 125 (1985), and *Chevron U.S.A. Inc. v. Natural Resources Defense Council, Inc.,* 467 U.S. 837, 842–845 (1984)), the Court held that "the Corps' ecological judgment about the relationship between waters and their adjacent wetlands provides an adequate basis for a legal judgment that adjacent wetlands may be defined as waters under the Act," 474 U.S., at 134. The Court reserved, however, the question of the Corps' authority to regulate wetlands other than those adjacent to open waters. See *id.,* at 131–132, n.8.

In *SWANCC,* the Court considered the validity of the Corps' jurisdiction over ponds and mudflats that were isolated in the sense of being unconnected to other waters covered by the Act. 531 U.S., at 171. The property at issue was an abandoned sand and gravel pit mining operation where "remnant excavation trenches" had "evolv[ed] into a scattering of permanent and seasonal ponds." *Id.,* at 163. Asserting jurisdiction pursuant to a regulation called the "Migratory Bird Rule," the Corps argued that these isolated ponds were "waters of the United States" (and thus "navigable waters" under the Act) because they were used as habitat by migratory birds. *Id.,* at 164–165. The Court rejected this theory. "It was the significant nexus between wetlands and 'navigable waters,'" the Court held, "that informed our reading of the [Act] in *Riverside Bayview Homes.*" *Id.,* at 167. Because such a nexus was lacking with respect to isolated ponds, the Court held that the plain text of the statute did not permit the Corps' action. *Id.,* at 172.

Riverside Bayview and *SWANCC* establish the framework for the inquiry in the cases now before the Court: Do the Corps' regulations, as applied to the wetlands in *Carabell* and the three wetlands parcels in *Rapanos,* constitute a reasonable interpretation of "navigable waters" as in *Riverside Bayview* or an invalid construction as in *SWANCC?* Taken together these cases establish that in some instances, as exemplified by *Riverside Bayview,* the connection between a nonnavigable water or wetland and a navigable water may be so close, or potentially so close, that the Corps may deem the water or wetland a "navigable water" under the Act. In other instances, as exemplified by *SWANCC,* there may be little or no connection. Absent a significant nexus, jurisdiction under the Act is lacking. Because neither the plurality nor the dissent addresses the nexus requirement, this separate opinion, in my respectful view, is necessary.

A

The plurality's opinion begins from a correct premise. As the plurality points out, and as *Riverside Bayview* holds, in enacting the Clean Water Act Congress intended to regulate at least some waters that are not navigable in the traditional sense. *Riverside Bayview,* 474 U.S., at 133; see also *SWANCC, supra,* at 167. This conclusion is supported by "the evident breadth of congressional concern for protection of water quality and aquatic ecosystems." *Riverside Bayview, supra,* at 133; see also *Milwaukee v. Illinois,* 451 U.S. 304, 318 (1981) (describing the Act as "an all-encompassing program of water pollution regulation"). It is further compelled by statutory text, for the text is explicit in extending the coverage of the Act to some nonnavigable waters. In a provision allowing States to assume some regulatory functions of the Corps (an option Michigan has exercised), the Act limits States to issuing permits for:

> "the discharge of dredged or fill material into the navigable waters (other than those waters which are presently used, or are susceptible to use in their natural condition or by reasonable improvement as a means to transport interstate or foreign commerce shoreward to their ordinary high water mark, including all waters which are subject to the ebb and flow of the tide shoreward to their ordinary high water mark, or mean higher high water mark on the west coast, including wetlands adjacent thereto) within its jurisdiction."

33 U.S.C. § 1344(g)(1).

Were there no Clean Water Act "navigable waters" apart from waters "presently used" or "susceptible to use" in interstate commerce, the "other than" clause, which begins the long parenthetical statement, would overtake the delegation of authority the provision makes at the outset. Congress, it follows, must have intended a broader meaning for navigable waters. The mention of wetlands in the "other than" clause, moreover, makes plain that at least some wetlands fall within the scope of the term "navigable waters." See *Riverside Bayview, supra,* at 138–139, and n.11.

From this reasonable beginning the plurality proceeds to impose two limitations on the Act; but these limitations, it is here submitted, are without support in the language and purposes of the Act or in our cases interpreting it. * * *

* * * In sum the plurality's opinion is inconsistent with the Act's text, structure, and purpose. * * *

* * * B

While the plurality reads nonexistent requirements into the Act, the dissent reads a central requirement out—namely, the requirement that the word "navigable" in "navigable waters" be given some importance. Although the Court has held that the statute's language invokes Congress' traditional authority over waters navigable in fact or susceptible of being made so, *SWANCC,* 531 U.S., at 172 (citing *Appalachian Power,* 311 U.S., at 407–408), the dissent would permit federal regulation whenever wetlands lie alongside a ditch or drain, however remote and insubstantial, that eventually may flow into traditional navigable waters. The deference owed to the Corps' interpretation of the statute does not extend so far.

Congress' choice of words creates difficulties, for the Act contemplates regulation of certain "navigable waters" that are not in fact navigable. Nevertheless, the word "navigable" in the Act must be given some effect. See *SWANCC, supra,* at 172. Thus, in *SWANCC* the Court rejected the Corps' assertion of jurisdiction over isolated ponds and mudflats bearing no evident connection to navigable-in-fact waters. And in *Riverside Bayview,* while the Court indicated that "the term 'navigable' as used in the Act is of limited import," 474 U.S., at 133, it relied, in upholding jurisdiction, on the Corps' judgment that "wetlands adjacent to lakes, rivers, streams, and other bodies of water may function as integral parts of the aquatic environment even when the moisture creating the wetlands does not find its source in the adjacent bodies of water," *id.,* at 135. The implication, of course, was that wetlands' status as "integral parts of the aquatic environment"—that is, their significant nexus with navigable waters—was what established the Corps' jurisdiction over them as waters of the United States.

Consistent with *SWANCC* and *Riverside Bayview* and with the need to give the term "navigable" some meaning, the Corps' jurisdiction over wetlands depends upon the existence of a significant nexus between the wetlands in question and navigable waters in the traditional sense. The required nexus must be assessed in terms of the statute's goals and purposes. Congress enacted the law to "restore and maintain the chemical, physical, and biological integrity of the Nation's waters," 33 U.S.C. § 1251(a), and it pursued that objective by restricting dumping and filling in "navigable waters," §§ 1311(a), 1362(12). With respect to wetlands, the rationale for Clean Water Act regulation is, as the Corps has recognized, that wetlands can perform critical functions related to the integrity of other waters—functions such as pollutant trapping, flood control, and runoff storage. 33 CFR § 320.4(b)(2). Accordingly, wetlands possess the requisite nexus, and thus come within the statutory phrase "navigable waters," if the wetlands, either alone or in combination with similarly situated lands in the region, significantly affect the chemical, physical, and biological integrity of other covered waters more readily understood as "navigable." When, in contrast, wetlands' effects on water quality are speculative or insubstantial, they fall outside the zone fairly encompassed by the statutory term "navigable waters."

* * * As applied to wetlands adjacent to navigable-in-fact waters, the Corps' conclusive standard for jurisdiction rests upon a reasonable inference of ecologic interconnection, and the assertion of jurisdiction for those wetlands is sustainable under the Act by showing adjacency alone. That is the holding of *Riverside Bayview*. Furthermore, although the *Riverside Bayview* Court reserved the question of the Corps' authority over "wetlands that are not adjacent to bodies of open water," 474 U.S., at 131–132, n. 8, and in any event addressed no factual situation other than wetlands adjacent to navigable-in-fact waters, it may well be the case that *Riverside Bayview*'s reasoning—supporting jurisdiction without any inquiry beyond adjacency—could apply equally to wetlands adjacent to certain major tributaries. Through regulations or adjudication, the Corps may choose to identify categories of tributaries that, due to their volume of flow (either annually or on average), their proximity to navigable waters, or other relevant considerations, are significant enough that wetlands adjacent to them are likely, in the majority of cases, to perform important functions for an aquatic system incorporating navigable waters.

The Corps' existing standard for tributaries, however, provides no such assurance. As noted earlier, the Corps deems a water a tributary if it feeds into a traditional navigable water (or a tributary thereof) and possesses an ordinary high-water mark, defined as a "line on the shore established by the fluctuations of water and indicated by [certain] physical characteristics," § 328.3(e). This standard presumably provides a rough measure of the volume and regularity of flow. Assuming it is subject to reasonably consistent application, it may well provide a reasonable measure of whether specific minor tributaries bear a sufficient nexus with other regulated waters to constitute "navigable waters" under the Act. Yet the breadth of this standard—which seems to leave wide room for regulation of drains, ditches, and streams remote from any navigable-in-fact water and carrying only minor water-volumes towards it—precludes its adoption as the determinative measure of whether adjacent wetlands are likely to play an important role in the integrity of an aquatic system comprising navigable waters as traditionally understood. Indeed, in many cases wetlands adjacent to tributaries covered by this standard might appear little more related to navigable-in-fact waters than were the isolated ponds held to fall beyond the Act's scope in *SWANCC*.

When the Corps seeks to regulate wetlands adjacent to navigable-in-fact waters, it may rely on adjacency to establish its jurisdiction. Absent more specific regulations, however, the Corps must establish a significant nexus on a case-by-case basis when it seeks to regulate wetlands based on adjacency to nonnavigable tributaries. Given the potential overbreadth of the Corps' regulations, this showing is necessary to avoid unreasonable applications of the statute. Where an adequate nexus is established for a particular wetland, it may be permissible, as a matter of administrative convenience or necessity, to presume covered status for other comparable wetlands in the region. That issue, however, is neither raised by these facts nor addressed by any agency regulation that accommodates the nexus requirement outlined here.

This interpretation of the Act does not raise federalism or Commerce Clause concerns sufficient to support a presumption against its adoption. To be sure, the significant nexus requirement may not align perfectly with the traditional extent of federal authority. Yet in most cases regulation of wetlands that are adjacent to tributaries and possess a significant nexus with navigable waters will raise no serious constitutional or federalism difficulty. As explained earlier, moreover, and as exemplified by *SWANCC*, the significant-nexus test itself prevents problematic applications of the statute. See 531 U.S., at 174. The possibility of legitimate Commerce Clause and federalism concerns in some circumstances does not require the adoption of an interpretation that departs in all cases from the Act's text and structure.

III

In both the consolidated cases before the Court the record contains evidence suggesting the possible existence of a significant nexus according to the principles outlined above. Thus the end result in these cases and many others to be considered by the Corps may be the same as that suggested by the dissent, namely, that the Corps' assertion of jurisdiction is valid. Given, however, that neither the agency nor the reviewing courts properly considered the issue, a remand is appropriate, in my view, for application of the controlling legal standard. * * *

* * * In these consolidated cases I would vacate the judgments of the Court of Appeals and remand for consideration whether the specific wetlands at issue possess a significant nexus with navigable waters.

JUSTICE STEVENS, with whom JUSTICE SOUTER, JUSTICE GINSBURG, and JUSTICE BREYER join, dissenting.

In 1972, Congress decided to "restore and maintain the chemical, physical, and biological integrity of the Nation's waters" by passing what we now call the Clean Water Act, 33 U.S.C. § 1251 *et seq*. The costs of achieving the Herculean goal of ending water pollution by 1985, see § 1251(a), persuaded President Nixon to veto its enactment, but both Houses of Congress voted to override that veto by overwhelming margins. To achieve its goal, Congress prohibited "the discharge of any pollutant"—defined to include "any addition of any pollutant to navigable waters from any point source"—without a permit issued by the Army Corps of Engineers (Army Corps or Corps) or the Environmental Protection Agency (EPA). §§ 1311(a), 1362(12)(A). Congress further defined "navigable waters" to mean "the waters of the United States." § 1362(7).

The narrow question presented in [*Rapanos*] is whether wetlands adjacent to tributaries of traditionally navigable waters are "waters of the United States" subject to the jurisdiction of the Army Corps; the question in [*Carabell*] is whether a manmade berm separating a wetland from the adjacent tributary makes a difference. The broader question is whether regulations that have protected the quality of our waters for decades, that were implicitly approved by Congress, and that have been repeatedly enforced in case after case, must now be revised in light of the creative criticisms voiced by the plurality and Justice KENNEDY today. Rejecting more than 30 years of practice by the Army Corps, the plurality disregards the nature of the congressional delegation to the agency and the technical and complex character of the issues at stake. Justice KENNEDY similarly fails to defer sufficiently to the Corps, though his approach is far more faithful to our precedents and to principles of statutory interpretation than is the plurality's.

In my view, the proper analysis is straightforward. The Army Corps has determined that wetlands adjacent to tributaries of traditionally navigable waters preserve the quality of our Nation's waters by, among other things, providing habitat for aquatic animals, keeping excessive sediment and toxic pollutants out of adjacent waters, and reducing downstream flooding by absorbing water at times of high flow. The Corps' resulting decision to treat these wetlands as encompassed within the term "waters of the United States" is a quintessential example of the Executive's reasonable interpretation of a statutory provision. See *Chevron U.S.A. Inc. v. Natural Resources Defense Council, Inc.*, 467 U.S. 837, 842–845 (1984).

Our unanimous decision in *United States v. Riverside Bayview Homes, Inc.*, 474 U.S. 121 (1985), was faithful to our duty to respect the work product of the Legislative and Executive Branches of our Government. Today's judicial amendment of the Clean Water Act is not.

* * * II

Our unanimous opinion in *Riverside Bayview* squarely controls these cases. There, we evaluated the validity of the very same regulations at issue today. These regulations interpret "waters of the United States" to cover all traditionally navigable waters; tributaries of these waters; and wetlands adjacent to traditionally navigable waters or their tributaries. 33

CFR §§ 328.3(a)(1), (5), and (7) (2005); §§ 323.2(a)(1), (5), and (7) (1985). Although the particular wetland at issue in *Riverside Bayview* abutted a navigable creek, we framed the question presented as whether the Clean Water Act "authorizes the Corps to require landowners to obtain permits from the Corps before discharging fill material into wetlands adjacent to navigable bodies of water *and their tributaries*." 474 U.S., at 123 (emphasis added).

We held that, pursuant to our decision in *Chevron,*

> "our review is limited to the question whether it is reasonable, in light of the language, policies, and legislative history of the Act for the Corps to exercise jurisdiction over wetlands adjacent to but not regularly flooded by rivers, streams, and other hydrographic features more conventionally identifiable as 'waters.' "

474 U.S., at 131.

Applying this standard, we held that the Corps' decision to interpret "waters of the United States" as encompassing such wetlands was permissible. We recognized the practical difficulties in drawing clean lines between land and water, *id.,* at 132, and deferred to the Corps' judgment that treating adjacent wetlands as "waters" would advance the "congressional concern for protection of water quality and aquatic ecosystems," *id.,* at 133.

Contrary to the plurality's revisionist reading today, *Riverside Bayview* nowhere implied that our approval of "adjacent" wetlands was contingent upon an understanding that "adjacent" means having a "continuous surface connection" between the wetland and its neighboring creek. Instead, we acknowledged that the Corps defined "adjacent" as including wetlands " 'that form the border of or are in reasonable proximity to other waters' " and found that the Corps reasonably concluded that adjacent wetlands are part of the waters of the United States. 474 U.S., at 134 (quoting 42 Fed. Reg. 37128 (1977)). Indeed, we explicitly acknowledged that the Corps' jurisdictional determination was reasonable even though

> "not every adjacent wetland is of great importance to the environment of adjoining bodies of water.... If it is reasonable for the Corps to conclude that in the majority of cases, adjacent wetlands have significant effects on water quality and the ecosystem, its definition can stand. That the definition may include some wetlands that are not significantly intertwined with the ecosystem of adjacent waterways is of little moment, for where it appears that a wetland covered by the Corps' definition is in fact lacking in importance to the aquatic environment ... the Corps may always allow development of the wetland for other uses simply by issuing a permit."

474 U.S., at 135 n.9.

In closing, we emphasized that the scope of the Corps' asserted jurisdiction over wetlands had been specifically brought to Congress' attention in 1977, that Congress had rejected an amendment that would have narrowed that jurisdiction, and that even proponents of the amendment would not have removed wetlands altogether from the definition of "waters of the United States." *Id.,* at 135–139.

Disregarding the importance of *Riverside Bayview,* the plurality relies heavily on the Court's subsequent opinion in *Solid Waste Agency of Northern Cook Cty. v. Army Corps of Engineers,* 531 U.S. 159 (2001) *(SWANCC).* In stark contrast to *Riverside Bayview,* however, *SWANCC* had nothing to say about wetlands, let alone about wetlands adjacent to traditionally navigable waters or their tributaries. Instead, *SWANCC* dealt with a question specifically reserved by *Riverside Bayview,* namely, the Corps' jurisdiction over isolated waters—" 'waters that are *not* part of a tributary system to interstate waters or to navigable waters of the United States, the degradation or destruction of which could affect interstate commerce.' " 531 U.S., at 168–169 (quoting 33 CFR § 323.2(a)(5) (1978); emphasis added); see also 531 U.S., at 163 (citing 33 CFR § 328.2(a)(3) (1999), which is the later regulatory equivalent to § 323.2(a)(5) (1978)). At issue in *SWANCC* was "an abandoned sand and gravel pit ... which provide[d] habitat for migratory birds" and contained a few pools of "nonnavigable, isolated, intrastate waters." 531 U.S., at 162, 166. The Corps had asserted jurisdiction over the gravel pit under its 1986 Migratory Bird Rule, which treated isolated waters as within its jurisdiction if migratory birds depended upon these waters. The Court rejected this jurisdictional basis since these isolated pools, unlike the wetlands at issue in *Riverside Bayview,* had no "significant nexus" to traditionally navigable waters. 531 U.S., at 167. In the process, the Court distinguished *Riverside Bayview*'s reliance on Congress' decision to leave the Corps' regulations alone when it amended the Act in 1977, since " '[i]n both Chambers, debate on the proposals to narrow the definition of navigable waters centered largely on the issue of wetlands preservation' " rather than on the Corps' jurisdiction over truly isolated waters. 531 U.S., at 170 (quoting 474 U.S., at 136).

Unlike *SWANCC* and like *Riverside Bayview,* the cases before us today concern wetlands that are adjacent to "navigable bodies of water [or] their tributaries," 474 U.S., at 123. Specifically, these wetlands abut tributaries of traditionally navigable waters. As we recognized in *Riverside Bayview,* the Corps has concluded that such wetlands play important roles in maintaining the quality of their adjacent waters, see *id.,* at 134–135, and consequently in the waters downstream. Among other things, wetlands can offer "nesting, spawning, rearing and resting sites for aquatic or land species"; "serve as valuable storage areas for storm and flood waters"; and provide "significant water purification functions." 33 CFR § 320.4(b)(2) (2005); 474 U.S., at 134–135. These values are hardly "*independent*" ecological considerations as the plurality would have it—instead, they are integral to the "chemical, physical, and biological integrity of the Nation's waters," 33 U.S.C. § 1251(a). Given that wetlands serve these important water quality roles and given the ambiguity inherent in the phrase "waters of the United States," the Corps has reasonably interpreted its jurisdiction to cover non-isolated wetlands. See 474 U.S., at 131–135.

This conclusion is further confirmed by Congress' deliberate acquiescence in the Corps' regulations in 1977. *Id.,* at 136. Both Chambers conducted extensive debates about the Corps' regulatory jurisdiction over wetlands, rejected efforts to limit this jurisdiction, and appropriated funds for a " 'National Wetlands Inventory' " to help the States " 'in the development and operation of programs under this Act.' " *Id.,* at 135–139 (quoting 33 U.S.C. § 1288(i)(2)). We found these facts significant in *Riverside Bayview,* see 474 U.S., at 135–139, as we acknowledged in *SWANCC.* See 531 U.S., at 170–171 (noting that "*[b]eyond Congress' desire to regulate wetlands adjacent to 'navigable waters,'* respondents point us to no persuasive evidence" of congressional acquiescence (emphasis added)).

The Corps' exercise of jurisdiction is reasonable even though not every wetland adjacent to a traditionally navigable water or its tributary will perform all (or perhaps any) of the water quality functions generally associated with wetlands. *Riverside Bayview* made clear that jurisdiction does not depend on a wetland-by-wetland inquiry. 474 U.S., at 135 n.9. Instead, it is enough that wetlands adjacent to tributaries generally have a significant nexus to the watershed's water quality. If a particular wetland is "not significantly intertwined with the ecosystem of adjacent waterways," then the Corps may allow its development "simply by issuing a permit." *Ibid.* Accordingly, for purposes of the Corps' jurisdiction it is of no significance that the wetlands in [*Rapanos*] serve flood control and sediment sink functions, but may not do much to trap other pollutants, or that the wetland in [*Carabell*] keeps excess water from Lake St. Clair but may not trap sediment.

Seemingly alarmed by the costs involved, the plurality shies away from *Riverside Bayview*'s recognition that jurisdiction is not a case-by-case affair. I do not agree with the plurality's assumption that the costs of preserving wetlands are unduly high. It is true that the cost of § 404 permits are high for those who must obtain them—but these costs amount to only a small fraction of 1% of the $760 billion spent each year on private and public construction and development activity. More significant than the plurality's exaggerated concern about costs, however, is the fact that its omission of any discussion of the benefits that the regulations at issue have produced sheds a revelatory light on the quality (and indeed the impartiality) of its cost-benefit analysis. The importance of wetlands for water quality is hard to overstate. Unsurprisingly, the Corps' approach has the overwhelming endorsement of numerous *amici curiae,* including 33 States and the county in which the property in [*Carabell*] is located.

In final analysis, however, concerns about the appropriateness of the Corps' 30–year implementation of the Clean Water Act should be addressed to Congress or the Corps rather than to the Judiciary. Whether the benefits of particular conservation measures outweigh their costs is a classic question of public policy that should not be answered by appointed judges. The fact that large investments are required to finance large developments merely means that those who are most adversely affected by the Corps' permitting decisions are persons who have the ability to communicate effectively with their representatives. Unless and until they succeed in convincing Congress (or the Corps) that clean water is less important today than it was in the 1970's, we continue to owe deference to regulations satisfying the "evident breadth of congressional concern for protection of water quality and aquatic ecosystems" that all of the Justices on the Court in 1985 recognized in *Riverside Bayview,* 474 U.S., at 133.

* * * IV

While I generally agree with Parts I and II–A of Justice KENNEDY's opinion, I do not share his view that we should replace regulatory standards that have been in place for over 30 years with a judicially crafted rule distilled from the term "significant nexus" as used in *SWANCC.* To the extent that our passing use of this term has become a statutory requirement, it is categorically satisfied as to wetlands adjacent to navigable waters or their tributaries. *Riverside Bayview* and *SWANCC* together make this clear. *SWANCC*'s only use of the term comes in the sentence: "It was the significant nexus between the wetlands and 'navigable waters' that informed our reading of the [Clean Water Act] in *Riverside Bayview.*" 531 U.S., at 167. Because *Riverside Bayview* was written to encompass "wetlands adjacent to navigable waters and their tributaries," 474 U.S., at 123, and reserved only the question of isolated waters, see *id.,* at 131–132, n. 8; its determination of the Corps' jurisdiction applies to the wetlands at issue in these cases.

Even setting aside the apparent applicability of *Riverside Bayview,* I think it clear that wetlands adjacent to tributaries of navigable waters generally have a "significant nexus" with the traditionally navigable waters downstream. Unlike the "nonnavigable, isolated, intrastate waters" in *SWANCC,* 531 U.S., at 171, these wetlands can obviously have a cumulative effect on downstream water flow by releasing waters at times of low flow or by keeping waters back at times of high flow. This logical connection alone gives the wetlands the "limited" connection to traditionally navigable waters that is all the statute requires, see *id.,* at 172; 474 U.S., at 133—and disproves Justice KENNEDY's claim that my approach gives no meaning to the word " 'navigable[.]' " Similarly, these wetlands can preserve downstream water quality by trapping sediment, filtering toxic pollutants, protecting fish-spawning grounds, and so forth. While there may exist categories of wetlands adjacent to tributaries of traditionally navigable waters that, taken cumulatively, have no plausibly discernable relationship to any aspect of downstream water quality, I am skeptical. And even given Justice KENNEDY's "significant nexus" test, in the absence of compelling evidence that many such categories do exist I see no reason to conclude that the Corps' longstanding regulations are overbroad.

Justice KENNEDY's "significant nexus" test will probably not do much to diminish the number of wetlands covered by the Act in the long run. Justice KENNEDY himself recognizes that the records in both cases contain evidence that "should permit the establishment of a significant nexus," and it seems likely that evidence would support similar findings as to most (if not all) wetlands adjacent to tributaries of navigable waters. But Justice KENNEDY's approach will have the effect of creating additional work for all concerned parties. Developers wishing to fill wetlands adjacent to ephemeral or intermittent tributaries of traditionally navigable waters will have no certain way of knowing whether they need to get § 404 permits or not. And the Corps will have to make case-by-case (or category-by-category) jurisdictional determinations, which will inevitably increase the time and resources spent processing permit applications. These problems are precisely the ones that *Riverside Bayview*'s deferential approach avoided. See 474 U.S., at 135 n.9 (noting that it "is of little moment" if the Corps' jurisdiction encompasses some wetlands "not significantly intertwined" with other waters of the United States). Unlike Justice KENNEDY, I see no reason to change *Riverside Bayview*'s approach—and every reason to continue to defer to the Executive's sensible, bright-line rule.

V

As I explained in *SWANCC*, Congress passed the Clean Water Act in response to wide-spread recognition-based on events like the 1969 burning of the Cuyahoga River in Cleveland—that our waters had become appallingly polluted. 531 U.S., at 174–175 (dissenting opinion). The Act has largely succeeded in restoring the quality of our Nation's waters. Where the Cuyahoga River was once coated with industrial waste, "[t]oday, that location is lined with restaurants and pleasure boat slips." EPA, *A Benefits Assessment of the Water Pollution Control Programs Since 1972*, p. 1–2 (Jan. 2000), http://www.epa.gov/ost/economics/assessment.pdf. By curtailing the Corps' jurisdiction of more than 30 years, the plurality needlessly jeopardizes the quality of our waters. In doing so, the plurality disregards the deference it owes the Executive, the congressional acquiescence in the Executive's position that we recognized in *Riverside Bayview*, and its own obligation to interpret laws rather than to make them. While Justice KENNEDY's approach has far fewer faults, nonetheless it also fails to give proper deference to the agencies entrusted by Congress to implement the Clean Water Act.

I would affirm the judgments in both cases, and respectfully dissent from the decision of five Members of this Court to vacate and remand. I close, however, by noting an unusual feature of the Court's judgments in these cases. It has been our practice in a case coming to us from a lower federal court to enter a judgment commanding that court to conduct any further proceedings pursuant to a specific mandate. That prior practice has, on occasion, made it necessary for Justices to join a judgment that did not conform to their own views. In these cases, however, while both the plurality and Justice KENNEDY agree that there must be a remand for further proceedings, their respective opinions define different tests to be applied on remand. Given that all four Justices who have joined this opinion would uphold the Corps' jurisdiction in both of these cases—and in all other cases in which either the plurality's or Justice KENNEDY's test is satisfied—on remand each of the judgments should be reinstated if *either* of those tests is met.

JUSTICE BREYER, dissenting.

In my view, the authority of the Army Corps of Engineers under the Clean Water Act extends to the limits of congressional power to regulate interstate commerce. I therefore have no difficulty finding that the wetlands at issue in these cases are within the Corps' jurisdiction, and I join Justice STEVENS' dissenting opinion.

My view of the statute rests in part upon the nature of the problem. The statute seeks to "restore and maintain the chemical, physical, and biological integrity of the Nation's waters." 33 U.S.C. § 1251(a). Those waters are so various and so intricately interconnected that Congress might well have decided the only way to achieve this goal is to write a statute that defines "waters" broadly and to leave the enforcing agency with the task of restricting the scope of that definition, either wholesale through regulation or retail through development permissions. That is why I believe that Congress, in using the term "waters of the United States," § 1362(7), intended fully to exercise its relevant Commerce Clause powers.

I mention this because the Court, contrary to my view, has written a "nexus" requirement into the statute. *SWANCC, supra,* at 167. But it has left the administrative powers of the Army Corps of Engineers untouched. That agency may write regulations defining the term—something that it has not yet done. And the courts must give those regulations appropriate deference.

If one thing is clear, it is that Congress intended the Army Corps of Engineers to make the complex technical judgments that lie at the heart of the present cases (subject to deferential judicial review). In the absence of updated regulations, courts will have to make ad hoc determinations that run the risk of transforming scientific questions into matters of law. That is not the system Congress intended. Hence I believe that today's opinions, taken together, call for the Army Corps of Engineers to write new regulations, and speedily so.

NOTES

1. **What Exactly Is the *Rapanos* Court Deciding?** How does the Scalia plurality define and frame the issues in *Rapanos*? How does Justice Kennedy define those issues? How does the Stevens dissent define and frame the issues? Does the definition of the issues in each opinion affect the focus and outcome of that opinion? Why or why not?

2. **What Is a "Water of the United States"?** How does each of the three major opinions ultimately define "waters of the United States"? Are any two of the three opinions reconcilable regarding their definitions? Why or why not? What wrinkle does Justice Breyer add? Is his argument viable after *Solid Waste Agency*? Why or why not?

3. **What Is an "Adjacent Wetland"?** How does each of the three major opinions ultimately define "adjacent wetland"? Do you think the United States can win on remand under Justice Scalia's definition? Why or why not? How about under Justice Kennedy's definition? Under Justice Stevens'? Are any two of the three opinions reconcilable regarding their definitions?

4. **Use and Abuse of Precedent, Part 1: Groundwater Inundation in *Riverside Bayview*.** The wetlands at issue in *Riverside Bayview* were wetlands because they were inundated by *groundwater*; indeed, the Supreme Court first had to establish that surface inundation was not necessary to meet the Army Corps' definition of "wetland" before it could reach the larger issue of whether wetlands could be "waters of the United States." Does that detail regarding the facts of *Riverside Bayview* undermine any of the three major opinions in *Rapanos*? Why or why not?

Groundwater has been an issue for Clean Water Act jurisdiction since before the *Riverside Bayview* decision, and the federal courts are currently split on whether Clean Water Act jurisdiction extends to discharges into underground waters. *Compare Friends of Santa Fe County v. LAC Minerals, Inc.,* 892 F. Supp. 1333, 1357–58 (D.N.M. 1995) (holding that the Clean Water Act applies to discharges into ground water that is hydrologically connected to surface water); *Washington Wilderness Coalition v. Hecla Mining Co.,* 870 F. Supp. 983, 989–90 (E.D. Wash. 1994) (holding that, although "Congress did not intend to include *isolated* groundwater as part of the 'navigable waters' " that the Clean Water Act regulates, the Clean Water Act does apply to discharges of pollutants that reach surface waters through ground water); *Sierra Club v. Colorado Refining Co.,* 838 F. Supp. 1428, 1434 (D. Colo. 1993) (holding that discharges into "navigable waters" include discharges into hydrologically connected ground water); *McClellan Ecological Seepage Situation v. Weinberger,* 707 F. Supp. 1182, 1193–96 (E.D. Cal. 1988), *vacated on other grounds,* 47 F.3d 325 (9th Cir.), *cert. denied,* 516 U.S. 807 (1995) (noting that although "Congress did not intend to require NPDES permits for discharges of pollutants to isolated groundwater," plaintiff could state a claim if it could "establish that the groundwater is naturally connected to surface waters that constitute 'navigable waters' under the Clean Water Act"); *with Town of Norfolk v. United States Army Corps of Engineers,* 968 F.2d 1438, 1451 (1st Cir. 1992) (holding that the Army Corps' regulatory definition of "waters of the United States" limited Clean Water Act coverage to surface waters); *Kelley v. United States,* 618 F. Supp. 1103, 1106–07 (W.D. Mich. 1985) (holding that Congress's intent was to leave regulation of contaminated groundwater to the states); *United States v. GAF Corp.,* 389 F. Supp. 1379, 1383–84 (S.D. Tex. 1975) (holding that Clean Water Act jurisdiction did not extend to discharges to groundwater); *Village of Oconomowoc Lake v. Dayton Hudson Corp.,* 24 F.3d 962 (7th Cir.), *cert. denied* 513 U.S. 930 (1994) (holding that a possible hydrological connection between ground water and surface waters could not justify Clean Water Act regulation); *Exxon Corp. v. Train,* 554 F.2d 1310, 1312 n. 1, 1318–19 (5th Cir. 1977) (noting that EPA "disclaims 'jurisdiction and authority to regulate subsurface disposal directly.' ").

At the statutory level, it is worth noting that when Congress wanted certain provisions of the Clean Water Act to apply to groundwater, it stated so explicitly. Thus, for example, in section 102(a) of the Act, Congress provided that "[t]he Administrator shall * * * prepare or develop comprehensive programs for preventing, reducing, or eliminating the pollution of the navigable waters and *ground waters* and improving the sanitary condition of surface and *underground waters.*" 33 U.S.C. § 1252(a) (emphasis added). Similarly, under section 104(a)(5), the Administrator shall "establish, equip, and maintain a water quality surveillance system for the purpose of monitoring the quality of the navigable waters and *ground waters* and the contiguous zone and the oceans * * *." 33 U.S.C. § 1254(a)(5) (emphasis added). In contrast, section 1342, which establishes the NPDES permitting system, makes no explicit reference to ground water or underground waters; neither does the definition of "discharge of a pollutant," quoted above. Are these statutory references relevant in determining whether the Clean Water Act prohibits discharges of pollutants to ground water? Why or why not?

5. **Use and Abuse of Precedent, Part 2: What Exactly Did *Riverside Bayview* Decide?** How does each of the three major opinions in *Rapanos* use the Supreme Court's decision in *Riverside Bayview*? How does each characterize the holding(s) of *Riverside Bayview*? On what points do the three opinions disagree? How does each Justice's choice of what to emphasize from *Riverside Bayview* affect his reasoning in *Rapanos*?

6. **Use and Abuse of Precedent, Part 3: What Exactly Did *SWANCC* Decide?** How does each of the three major opinions in *Rapanos* use the Supreme Court's decision in *SWANCC*? How does each of those three opinions characterize the holding in *SWANCC*? Which decision—*Riverside Bayview* or *SWANCC*—is more controlling in *Rapanos*, according to each decision? Why? How does each Justices's choice of what to emphasize from *SWANCC* affect his reasoning in *Rapanos*?

7. **Constitutional Considerations and the *Rapanos* Decision.** As noted, when the Supreme Court granted *certiorari* in *Rapanos*, it accepted two questions: the statutory questions regarding whether the wetlands at issue could be considered "waters of the United States"; but also the constitutional question of the Commerce Clause limitations on Clean Water Act jurisdiction. Did any opinion reach the constitutional issue? Was the Commerce Clause at all relevant to the opinions? If so, how?

In addition, of course, there was a lingering federalism concern from the decision in *SWANCC*. What role did federalism considerations play in the *Rapanos* opinions? Did the Justices see the federalism concerns at stake in regulation of these wetlands the same way? Why or why not? How should lower courts now think about federalism concerned under the Clean Water Act, in light of *Rapanos* and *SWANCC*?

8. ***Chevron* Deference and the Agencies' Regulations.** What role did *Chevron* deference play in each of the three major opinions? Is each

opinion's use of *Chevron* consistent with the Court's view of *Chevron* deference in *SWANCC*? Why or why not? Is each opinion's use of *Chevron* deference consistent with *Chevron* itself? Why or why not?

Chief Justice Roberts suggests that the Army Corps and the EPA would have been afforded more deference—and had a better chance of succeeding in *Rapanos*—if they had revised their Clean Water Act regulations after *SWANCC*. He also suggests—as does Justice Stevens—that the agencies are now foreclosed from amending their regulations to re-define "waters of the United States" and/or "adjacent wetlands"? Do you agree? Why or why not?

9. **Wetlands Delineation.** Determining whether wetlands exist is one factual issue relevant to certain Clean Water Act cases. Another is how far wetlands extend—*i.e.*, where does an admitted wetland transform into unregulated upland ("dry" ground)? The Army Corps resolves both of these issues through a ***wetlands delineation***, a potentially complex physical evaluation of the site at issue. Specifically, to implement its regulatory definition of "wetlands," the Corps relies on its 1987 *Wetlands Delineation Manual*. The Corps identifies wetlands through three categories of general diagnostic environmental characteristics: vegetation, soil classification, and hydrology. WATERWAYS EXPERIMENT STATION, U.S. DEPARTMENT OF THE ARMY, ARMY CORPS OF ENGINEERS WETLANDS DELINEATION MANUAL 13–14 (Jan. 1987), *available at* http://www.wetlands.com/ regs/tlpage02e.htm (last updated 1999). Regarding vegetation, the Corps looks for hydrophytic, or water-loving, plants that grow where soils are inundated or frequently saturated with water. *Id.* at 14. One indication of a wetland, for example, is that more than 50 percent of the plants in a given area are hydrophytic plants. *Id.* at 18. As for soils, the Corps looks for hydric soils—that is, "a soil that is saturated, flooded, or ponded long enough during the growing season to develop anaerobic [oxygen-deprived] conditions that favor the growth and regeneration of hydrophytic vegetation * * *." *Id.* at 19. Finally, the Corps looks at the hydrology of the area to determine whether it is an area that is "periodically inundated or [has] soils saturated to the surface at some time during the growing season." *Id.* at 24.

10. **State Regulation of Isolated Wetlands After *SWANCC* and *Rapanos*.** *SWANCC* and *Rapanos* are both federal law decision limiting federal jurisdiction over certain kinds of waters under a federal statute, the Clean Water Act. Nothing in either case prevents—and, indeed, the majority's and plurality's, respectively, emphasis on state powers and rights would apparently actively encourage—state regulation of any waters excluded from Clean Water Act coverage.

After the *SWANCC* decision, the Association of State Wetlands Managers (ASWM) conducted a survey of state laws to determine whether state regulation would fill the gaps that *SWANCC* left in wetlands regulation. According to this survey, fifteen states offered "considerable protection for isolated freshwater wetlands": Connecticut, Florida, Maine, Maryland, Massachusetts, Michigan, Minnesota, New Hampshire, New Jersey, New York, Oregon, Pennsylvania, Rhode Island, Vermont, and Virginia. Jon Kusler, *The* SWANCC *Decision and State Regulation of Wetlands*, ALI-ABA CLE: WETLANDS LAW AND REGULATION (May 29–31, 2002), SG096 ALI–ABA 79; Association of State Wetlands Managers, *State Wetland Programs: State Wetland Protection Statutes*, at http://www.aswm.org/swp/states.htm (last updated June 29, 2002). Eleven states provided little or no protection for isolated freshwater wetlands: Alaska, Georgia, Kansas, Louisiana, Mississippi, Nebraska, North Carolina, North Dakota, South Carolina, South Dakota, and Texas. *Id.*

The *SWANCC* decision also prompted states to change their water quality protection laws to ensure that isolated waters, especially isolated wetlands, are regulated. Wisconsin has successfully expanded its water quality legislation to cover isolated, nonnavigable wetlands. *See* Charlie Luthin, Wisconsin Wetlands Association, *Crisis and Victory for Wisconsin Wetlands*, WISCONSIN WETLANDS (Summer 2001). The Indiana Department of Environmental Management administratively extended Indiana's state NPDES permit program to isolated, nonnavigable, intrastate waters, but that extension has been subject to administrative law challenges and proper rulemaking is still pending. Office of Water Quality, Indiana Department of Environmental Management, *NPDES Permit for Discharges of Dredged and Fill Material to Isolated Waters No Longer Subject to Federal Jurisdiction*, http://www.in.gov/idem/water/planbr/401/wnpdes.html (updated March 28, 2002).

11. **Federalism in Other Clean Water Act Contexts: State Regulation of Discharges to Underground Waters.** In *Umatilla Waterquality Protective Association, Inc. v. Smith Frozen Foods, Inc.*, 962 F. Supp. 1312 (D. Or. 1997), the United States District Court for the District of Oregon spent much time considering the relationship between Oregon's water quality regulatory scheme and the Clean Water Act in determining whether the Clean Water Act applied to discharges to underground waters. The State of Oregon, like most states, administers the Clean Water Act NPDES permit program for discharges of pollutants into the "navigable waters" within its boundaries, and Oregon law defines "navigable waters" to parallel the Clean Water Act definition. However, the Oregon Department of Environmental Quality (DEQ) also administers a state permit program, the Water Pollution Control Facility (WPCF) permit program, for other discharges into the "waters of the state." "Waters of the state" include:

> lakes, bays, ponds, impounding reservoirs, springs, wells, rivers, streams, creeks, estuaries, marshes, inlets, canals, the Pacific Ocean within the territorial limits of the State of Oregon and all other bodies of surface or *underground waters,* natural or artificial, inland or coastal, fresh or salt, public or private (except those private waters which do not combine or effect a junction with natural surface or underground waters), which are wholly or partially within or bordering the state or within its jurisdiction.

OR. REV. STAT. 468B.005(8) (emphasis added). This definition, unlike Clean Water Act "waters of the United States," clearly includes underground waters. By the time the Oregon District Court was deciding the *Umatilla* case, the State of Oregon had, for over 25 years, required dischargers to surface waters to get Clean Water Act NPDES permits but required dischargers to underground waters to get state WPCF permits.

The *Umatilla* court found Oregon's surface water/underground water distinction relevant to the issue of whether the Clean Water Act applied to discharges to underground waters "because EPA retains oversight jurisdiction of the state's NPDES program. Thus, EPA has a statutory duty to inform the state when that 'state is not administering [an approved NPDES program] in accordance with requirements of this section,' 33 U.S.C. § 1342(c)(3), and can withdraw such program approval if the state does not correct its administration problems. *Id.* * * * Nevertheless, to the court's knowledge, EPA has never objected to Oregon's dual permitting system nor required that a person discharging to groundwater pursuant to a WPCF permit obtain an NPDES permit instead." *Umatilla Waterquality Protective Ass'n*, 962 F. Supp. at 1316. As a result, because "EPA has apparently not seen fit to require Oregon to modify its NPDES permit program, and DEQ's interpretation of the CWA is reasonable in light of Congress's language, the Act's legislative history, and EPA's regulatory actions," the court concluded that, "while Oregon's interpretation of the CWA is by no means controlling here, that interpretation in combination with EPA's initial approval and continued unwillingness to order a modification lends weight to my conclusion that the CWA's NPDES program does not apply to any discharges to groundwater." *Id.* at 1320.

Do you agree? Is the EPA's failure to exercise its oversight authority over a state NPDES program sufficient reason to uphold a *state's* interpretation of federal law? Why or why not? Consider this: The EPA has exercised its oversight authority over delegated state programs only rarely, and never to "correct" a state's view of whether discharges to ground water should be included in the Clean Water Act's NPDES permitting program. Couldn't the Oregon District Court's logic therefore support another state in concluding that discharges to ground water *are* part of the NPDES permit program? Should the Clean Water Act apply differently in different states? Why or why not? Should states have the freedom to regulate their water quality more stringently than the federal Act requires? Why or why not?

What about the dischargers who had been operating in Oregon pursuant to state WPCF permits? What could have happened to them if the Oregon District Court had decided that discharges to ground water required NPDES permits instead? Is that consideration relevant? Why or why not?

What does the *Umatilla* case indicate about uncertainty in the law governing Clean Water Act jurisdiction? Did the *SWANCC* or *Rapanos* decision make Clean Water Act jurisdiction more or less certain? Why? Is such uncertainty good for the goal of restoring water quality? Why or why not?

* * *

Was the *Rapanos* decision helpful, in any sense of the word? If you were a federal judge in the lower courts on remand—or facing a similar jurisdictional issue in a different case—would you know how to rule on evidentiary submissions? How to instruct the jury? How to decide the case? Why or why not? Which of the three major opinions would you try to follow? Why? What is the "law" in this area of Clean Water Act jurisdiction? Are you sure?

The next case provides one example of how the lower courts have dealt with the *Rapanos* decision.

UNITED STATES v. ROBISON

505 F.3d 1208 (11th Cir. 2007).

HULL, CIRCUIT JUDGE:

Defendants McWane, Inc. ("McWane"), James Delk ("Delk"), and Michael Devine ("Devine") appeal their convictions for their roles in a Clean Water Act ("CWA") conspiracy (Count 1), as well as their convictions for substantive violations of the CWA (Counts 2, 3, 5, 7–19, 21, and 22). After the defendants' convictions, the United States Supreme Court addressed how to define "navigable waters" under the CWA in *Rapanos v. United States,* 547 U.S. 715 (2006). The definition of "navigable waters" in the jury charge in this case was erroneous under *Rapanos,* and the government has not shown that the error was harmless. Accordingly, we must vacate defendants' CWA convictions and remand the case for a new trial. * * *

I. BACKGROUND

A. *Defendants*

Defendant McWane is a large manufacturer of cast iron pipe, flanges, valves, and fire hydrants. McWane has numerous manufacturing plants. This case concerns McWane's plant in Birmingham, Alabama (hereinafter "the plant" or "McWane's plant").

Defendants Delk and Devine, along with Charles "Barry" Robison and Donald Harbin, worked in management positions at McWane's plant at all relevant times.

Robison was McWane's Vice President of Environmental Affairs. Defendant Delk was the General Manager of the plant. Defendant Devine was the Plant Manager, and he reported to defendant Delk. Harbin was the Maintenance Manager, and he reported to defendant Devine.

B. *Avondale Creek*

The CWA violations at issue involve McWane's discharge of pollutants into Avondale Creek, which is adjacent to McWane's plant.

Avondale Creek flows into another creek called Village Creek. In turn, Village Creek flows approximately twenty-eight miles into and through Bayview Lake, which was created by damming Village Creek. On the other side of Bayview Lake, Village Creek becomes Locust Fork, and Locust Fork flows approximately twenty miles out of Bayview Lake before it flows into the Black Warrior River.

At trial, the government presented testimony, *inter alia,* from an EPA investigator (Fritz Wagoner) that Avondale Creek is a perennial stream with a "continuous uninterrupted flow" into Village Creek. Wagoner testified that there is "a continuous uninterrupted flow" not only from Avondale Creek into Village Creek, but also from Village Creek through

Bayview Lake and into Locust Fork, and ultimately into the Black Warrior River.

On cross-examination, Wagoner admitted that he did not conduct a "tracer test" to check the flow of Avondale Creek into the Black Warrior River. Wagoner explained that a "tracer test" is a procedure whereby a "concentrated dye" is put into a body of water and tracked to determine "where that water body flows." Wagoner conducted no tests to measure the volume of water discharged from Avondale Creek or between the bodies of water that connect Avondale Creek and the Black Warrior River. He conceded that the water level in Avondale Creek was so low that he was able to walk through Avondale Creek all the way down to its intersection with Village Creek. Furthermore, Wagoner testified that Village Creek is dammed (creating Bayview Lake) and that the dam runs "all the way across Village Creek." Wagoner's only site visit was in April 2005. This was more than four years after the violations at issue in this case.

The government presented no evidence, through Wagoner or otherwise, of the chemical, physical, or biological effect that Avondale Creek's waters had or might have had on the Black Warrior River. Indeed, the district court observed that there was no evidence of any actual harm or injury to the Black Warrior River.

C. Defendants' conduct

McWane's plant manufactures eighteen-foot and twenty-foot lengths of pipe. McWane utilizes a great deal of water in its pipe manufacturing processes. The water that runs out of the pipe manufacturing machines is generally referred to as "process wastewater." * * * The process wastewater contained various contaminants, including hydraulic oil, excess iron, and trash.

* * * McWane obtained an NPDES permit from [the Alabama Department of Environmental Management (ADEM)] that authorized McWane to discharge some process wastewater. Specifically, McWane's NPDES permit allowed it to discharge some treated process wastewater into Avondale Creek, but only from one discharge point at the plant ("DSN001"), and only if other discharge limits and bookkeeping requirements were met. McWane's NPDES permit also allowed it to discharge "storm water runoff from industrial activity" from other discharge points at the plant ("DSN002" through "DSN020"). McWane, however, was not permitted to discharge process wastewater from any point at the plant other than DSN001.

At trial, the government established that McWane discharged process wastewater into Avondale Creek from discharge points other than DSN001, in violation of the express provisions of its NPDES permit. * * * One McWane employee described the extent of the process wastewater discharges as "[e]nough to drown a small village." Indeed, multiple witnesses testified that process wastewater from McWane's plant was regularly discharged into Avondale Creek. * * *

McWane's NPDES permit listed defendant Delk as one of two people with the authority and responsibility to prevent and abate violations of ADEM's regulations. Trial testimony established that defendant Delk was "everybody's boss" at the plant, and that on multiple occasions, defendant Delk ordered McWane employees to pump process wastewater from the basements, despite knowing that the wastewater had nowhere to go but Avondale Creek. Further testimony established that defendant Delk watched as wastewater spilled or was pumped into the center courtyard of the plant, and that Delk once instructed Harbin to falsify a water sample for inspectors.

Likewise, defendant Devine also ordered McWane employees to violate the NPDES permit. * * *

** * * D. Indictment*

In May 2004, a twenty-five count indictment was issued against McWane, Delk, Devine, Robison, and Donald Bills (the plant engineer). * * *

E. Trial

A jury trial was held in May and June 2005. * * * On June 10, 2005, the jury returned guilty verdicts on all remaining counts except Counts 4, 6, and 20. All three appellants here, McWane, Delk, and Devine, were convicted of conspiracy to violate the CWA (Count 1), as well as multiple substantive violations of the CWA. * * *

F. Sentences

On December 5, 2005, the district court sentenced the defendants. The district court sentenced: (1) Delk to 36 months' probation (including 6 months of nighttime home detention), and a fine of $90,000; (2) Devine to 24 months' probation (including 3 months of nighttime home detention), and a fine of $35,000; and (3) McWane to 60 months' probation and a fine of $5 million.

II. DISCUSSION

The parties' disagreement as to what constitutes a "navigable water" under the CWA is at the heart of this appeal.

A. Jury instruction on "navigable waters"

The CWA generally prohibits the discharge of pollutants into "navigable waters." *See* 33 U.S.C. §§ 1311(a), 1362(12). Under the CWA, "navigable waters" are defined as "the waters of the United States, including the territorial seas." *Id.* § 1362(7). The parties agree that the definition of "navigable waters" is a key element of the CWA criminal offenses in this case.

Based on the Supreme Court's *Rapanos* decision, defendants contend that Avondale Creek is not a "navigable water" within the meaning of the CWA, and that the district court erroneously instructed the jury as to the definition of the term "navigable waters." The government responds that Avondale Creek's connection with the Black Warrior River and/or Village Creek renders Avondale Creek a "navigable water" within the meaning of the CWA.

The problem in this case arises because the district court charged the jury that "navigable waters" include "any stream which may eventually flow into a navigable stream or river," and that such stream may be man-made and flow "only intermittently," as follows:

> [A] "water of the United States" includes any stream which may eventually flow into a navigable stream or river. The Government does not have to prove that the stream into which the discharge is made is itself navigable in fact. What it must prove is that the stream into which the discharge is made may eventually flow directly or indirectly into a navigable stream or river. *The stream into which the discharge is made may be a natural or manmade [stream] and may flow continuously or only intermittently, as long as it may eventually flow directly or indirectly into a navigable stream or river whose use affects interstate commerce.*
>
> A navigable stream or river is defined as one that is used or is susceptible of being used in its ordinary condition, as a highway for interstate commerce, over which trade and travel are or may be conducted in the customary modes of trade and travel on water.

(Emphasis added.)

The district court's jury charge was based, *inter alia,* on this Court's decision in *United States v. Eidson,* 108 F.3d 1336 (11th Cir. 1997). In *Eidson,* we observed: (1) that Congress chose to define broadly the waters covered by the CWA; (2) that it was "well established that Congress intended to regulate the discharge of pollutants into all waters that may eventually lead to waters affecting interstate commerce"; and (3) that courts repeatedly had recognized that tributaries to waters affecting interstate commerce—even when man-made or intermittently flowing—were subject to the CWA. *Eidson,* 108 F.3d at 1341–42.

However, the defendants' trial occurred before *Rapanos,* and the Supreme Court indicated in *Rapanos* that *Eidson*'s "expansive definition" of " 'tributaries' " is no longer good law. *Rapanos,* 126 S.Ct. at 2217 (plurality opinion) (citing, *inter alia, Eidson,* 108 F.3d at 1340–42). Even the government here tacitly concedes that the jury charge given by the district court in this case was erroneous to some extent in light of *Rapanos.* Nevertheless, the government contends that any error in the jury charge was harmless and does not require reversal.

Accordingly, we consider *Rapanos* in detail in order to determine exactly how and to what extent the district court's "navigable waters" instruction was erroneous. We then consider whether the incorrect jury instruction was harmless error.

B. Rapanos and the proper definition of "navigable waters"

In *Rapanos,* which involved two consolidated cases, the Supreme Court addressed how the statutory term "navigable waters" should be construed under the CWA. * * * The entire Supreme Court agreed that the term "navigable waters" encompasses something more than traditionally "navigable-in-fact" waters. However, five Justices concluded that remand was necessary for consideration of whether the wetlands at issue were "navigable waters" covered by the CWA, and whether the EPA and the Army Corps of Engineers had impermissibly extended their regulatory authority under the CWA.

Despite agreeing that the remand was necessary for further consideration of whether the wetlands at issue were covered by the CWA, the five-Justice majority fractured with regard to the proper definition of the term "navigable waters." Justice Scalia wrote for a four-Justice plurality, while Justice Kennedy provided the fifth vote for reversal. Justice Stevens dissented, joined by the remaining three Justices.

1. Justice Scalia's plurality opinion

* * * According to the plurality, "navigable waters" include only "relatively permanent, standing or continuously flowing bodies of water 'forming geographic features' that are described in ordinary parlance as 'streams[,] ... oceans, rivers, [and] lakes.'" The plurality emphasized that bodies of water such as streams, oceans, rivers, and lakes (i.e., "navigable waters") are "continuously present, fixed bodies of water, as opposed to ordinarily dry channels through which water occasionally or intermittently flows."

Moreover, while the plurality was of the view that "relatively continuous flow is a *necessary* condition for qualification as a 'water,'" relatively continuous flow, in and of itself, is "not an *adequate* condition" under the plurality's test.

* * * Noting that under prior precedent wetlands "adjacent to" navigable bodies of water were considered "waters of the United States," the plurality stated that "*only* those wetlands with a *continuous surface connection* to bodies that are 'waters of the United States' in their own right, so that there is no clear demarcation between 'waters' and wetlands, are 'adjacent to' such waters and covered by the Act." "Wetlands with only an intermittent, physically remote hydrologic connection to 'waters of the United States' ... lack the necessary connection to covered waters...." To summarize, the plurality's test for "establishing that wetlands ... are covered by the Act requires two findings: First, that the adjacent channel [to the wetland] contains 'a water of the United States,' (i.e., a relatively permanent body of water connected to traditional interstate navigable waters); and second, that the wetland has a continuous

surface connection with that water, making it difficult to determine where the 'water' ends and the 'wetland' begins."

* * * 2. Justice Kennedy's concurrence

Justice Kennedy supplied the fifth vote for reversal and agreed with the plurality that the Sixth Circuit had failed to apply the proper test as to what constitutes a "navigable water." However, Justice Kennedy disagreed with the plurality over the substance of the proper test.

According to Justice Kennedy, the Supreme Court actually established the test for determining whether a "water or wetland" constitutes a "navigable water" under the CWA five years prior to *Rapanos,* in *Solid Waste Agency of Northern Cook County v. United States Army Corps of Engineers,* 531 U.S. 159 (2001) ("*SWANCC*"). Citing *SWANCC*, Justice Kennedy wrote in his *Rapanos* concurrence that the applicable test for determining whether or not a "water or wetland" is "navigable" is the so-called "significant nexus" test. In Justice Kennedy's view, a "water or wetland" can only be "navigable" under the CWA if it possesses a " 'significant nexus' to waters that are or were navigable in fact or that could reasonably be so made."

Because *Rapanos* was a wetlands case, Justice Kennedy's concurrence then focused on when a wetland meets the "significant nexus" test. A wetland meets the "significant nexus" test if, "either alone or in combination with similarly situated lands in the region, [it] significantly affect[s] the chemical, physical, and biological integrity of other covered waters more readily understood as 'navigable.' " "When, in contrast, wetlands' effects on water quality are speculative or insubstantial, they fall outside the zone fairly encompassed by the statutory term 'navigable waters.' "

Justice Kennedy also emphasized that a "mere hydrologic connection" between a wetland and a navigable-in-fact body of water would not necessarily be sufficiently substantial to meet his "significant nexus" test. According to Justice Kennedy, a "mere hydrologic connection . . . may be too insubstantial for the hydrologic linkage to establish the required nexus with navigable waters as traditionally understood." Under Justice Kennedy's test, the "required nexus must be assessed in terms of the statute's goals and purposes," which are to " 'restore and maintain the chemical, physical, and biological integrity of the Nation's waters.' "

3. Justice Stevens's dissent

Justice Stevens, writing for himself and three other Justices, would have upheld the Army Corps of Engineers' and EPA's broad interpretation of CWA jurisdiction and concluded that the wetlands at issue in *Rapanos* were "navigable waters," i.e., "waters of the United States."

* * * Justice Stevens's dissent then stated that the four Justices joining his opinion would uphold CWA jurisdiction in all cases in which either the plurality's or Justice Kennedy's test is met, as follows:

> Given that all four Justices who have joined this opinion would uphold the Corps' jurisdiction in both of these cases—and in all other

cases in which either the plurality's *or* Justice Kennedy's test is satisfied—on remand each of the judgments should be reinstated if *either* of those tests is met.

C. *The governing rule of Rapanos*

Given the various opinions, the parties dispute what constitutes the governing definition of "navigable waters" under *Rapanos.* The defendants argue that only Justice Kennedy's concurrence (i.e., the "significant nexus" test) applies. The government responds that if Avondale Creek can be shown to satisfy *either* the plurality's test or Justice Kennedy's test, that is sufficient to sustain CWA jurisdiction in this case.

The circuits likewise are split on the question of which *Rapanos* opinion provides the holding. Both the Seventh and the Ninth Circuits concluded that Justice Kennedy's concurrence controls and adopted the "significant nexus" test. *See N. Cal. River Watch v. City of Healdsburg,* 496 F.3d 993, 999–1000 (9th Cir. 2007) ("*River Watch II*"); *United States v. Gerke Excavating, Inc.,* 464 F.3d 723, 724–25 (7th Cir. 2006), *cert. denied,* 128 S.Ct. 45 (Oct. 1, 2007). The First Circuit, on the other hand, concluded that because the dissenting *Rapanos* Justices would find jurisdiction under either Justice Scalia's plurality test or Justice Kennedy's "significant nexus" test, " 'the United States may elect to prove jurisdiction under either test.' " *United States v. Johnson,* 467 F.3d 56, 64 (1st Cir. 2006) (citation omitted), *cert. denied,* 128 S.Ct. 375 (Oct. 9, 2007). Because the Ninth Circuit in *River Watch II* expressly adopted the Seventh Circuit's reasoning in *Gerke,* we review *Gerke* in detail, and then *Johnson.*

In *Gerke,* the Seventh Circuit, faced with a Supreme Court remand "in light of *Rapanos,*" addressed which *Rapanos* opinion governed the further stages of the case before it. *Gerke,* 464 F.3d at 724–25. Citing *Marks v. United States,* 430 U.S. 188 (1977), the Seventh Circuit first noted that when a majority of the Supreme Court agrees only on the result of a case, lower courts "are to follow the narrowest ground to which a majority of the Justices would have assented if forced to choose." *Gerke,* 464 F.3d at 724. The *Gerke* court explained that it found Justice Kennedy's test to be "narrower (so far as reining in federal authority is concerned) ... in most cases, though not in all...." *Id.* at 724–25.

* * * The *Gerke* court surmised that in some wetlands cases Justice Kennedy would vote against finding CWA jurisdiction due to the lack of a "significant nexus," even when the plurality and the dissenting Justices would vote for CWA jurisdiction due to a "surface-water connection" between "wetlands (however remote)" and "a continuously flowing stream (however small)." *Id.* at 725 (quotation marks and citation omitted). However, the *Gerke* court dismissed such instances as "rare" and concluded that, "as a practical matter," Justice Kennedy's concurrence provides "the least common denominator." *Id.*

In contrast, the First Circuit in *Johnson* determined that it would uphold CWA jurisdiction in those cases in which *either* Justice Scalia's test *or* Justice Kennedy's test was satisfied. *Johnson,* 467 F.3d at 64–65. Since—per Justice Stevens's dissent—the four dissenting Justices in *Rapanos* would vote to uphold CWA jurisdiction whenever either of the two tests were met, the First Circuit reasoned that the "simple and pragmatic" way to determine the governing standard was to find CWA jurisdiction in either situation. *Id.* at 64.

The First Circuit acknowledged *Marks*'s language that the holding of a fractured decision "is the position of the Justices 'who *concurred in the judgments* on the narrowest grounds. . . .' " *Id.* at 65 (quoting *Marks,* 430 U.S. at 193). The First Circuit nevertheless cited various post-*Marks* cases in which, in the First Circuit's view, the Supreme Court itself had examined not only plurality and concurring opinions, but also dissenting opinions, in order to determine the holding of an earlier, fragmented Supreme Court decision. *See id.* at 65–66. The First Circuit concluded that its approach was therefore "particularly sound given that the Supreme Court itself has moved away from [rigid application of] the *Marks* formula." *Id.* at 65.

Marks expressly directs lower courts, including this Court, that "[w]hen a fragmented [Supreme] Court decides a case and no single rationale explaining the result enjoys the assent of five Justices, the holding . . . may be viewed as that position taken by those Members *who concurred in the judgments* on the narrowest grounds." Marks, 430 U.S. at 193 (emphasis added) (quotation marks and citation omitted). The "narrowest grounds" is understood as the "less far-reaching" common ground. *Johnson v. Bd. of Regents,* 263 F.3d 1234, 1247 (11th Cir. 2001). We simply cannot avoid the command of *Marks.*

* * * Thus, pursuant to *Marks,* we are left to determine which of the positions taken by the *Rapanos* Justices *concurring in the judgment* is the "narrowest," i.e., the least "far-reaching." *See Marks*, 430 U.S. at 193. The issue becomes whether the definition of "navigable waters" in the plurality or concurring opinions in *Rapanos* was less far-reaching (i.e., less restrictive of CWA jurisdiction). *See Gerke,* 464 F.3d at 724–25.

Notably, Justice Kennedy's test, at least in wetlands cases such as *Rapanos,* will classify a water as "navigable" more frequently than Justice Scalia's test. *See Gerke,* 464 F.3d at 724–25; *Rapanos,* 126 S.Ct. at 2265 n. 14 (Stevens, J., dissenting); *see also Johnson,* 467 F.3d at 64. This is because Justice Kennedy's concurrence rejected two "limitations" imposed by the plurality's test on the definition of "navigable waters." Specifically, Justice Kennedy's concurrence rejected the plurality's requirement that "navigable waters" must be "relatively permanent, standing or flowing bodies of water," and also rejected the plurality's requirement of a "continuous surface connection." As discussed later, in factual circumstances different from *Rapanos,* Justice Scalia's test may be less restrictive of CWA jurisdiction; however, in determining the governing holding in *Rapanos,* we cannot disconnect the facts in the case from the various opinions and determine which opinion is narrower in the abstract. Thus, pursuant to *Marks,* we adopt Justice Kennedy's "significant nexus" test as the governing definition of "navigable waters" under *Rapanos.*

D. The jury instruction was erroneous and not harmless error

We next consider whether the district court's jury charge comported with Justice Kennedy's "significant nexus" test.

Again, under Justice Kennedy's concurrence, a water can be considered "navigable" under the CWA only if it possesses a "significant nexus" to waters that "are or were navigable in fact or that could reasonably be so made." Moreover, a "mere hydrologic connection" will not necessarily be enough to satisfy the "significant nexus" test. The district court here did not mention the phrase "significant nexus" in its "navigable waters" instruction to the jury or advise the jury to consider the chemical, physical, or biological effect of Avondale Creek on the Black Warrior River. Rather, the district court instructed the jury that a continuous or intermittent flow into a navigable-in-fact body of water would be sufficient to bring Avondale Creek within the reach of the CWA. As such, the instruction did not satisfy Justice Kennedy's "significant nexus" test and was erroneous.

Moreover, the government bears the burden of establishing that the jury charge error was harmless. In order to carry its burden, the government must establish that the error did not "affect [defendants'] substantial rights." Fed. R. Crim. P. 52(a). * * *

Here, the government failed to satisfy its burden. Although Wagoner (the EPA investigator) testified that in his opinion there is a continuous uninterrupted flow between Avondale Creek and the Black Warrior River, he did not testify as to any "significant nexus" between Avondale Creek and the Black Warrior River. The government did not present any evidence, through Wagoner or otherwise, about the possible chemical, physical, or biological effect that Avondale Creek may have on the Black Warrior River, and there was also no evidence presented of any actual harm suffered by the Black Warrior River. Thus, the government failed to establish that the jury instruction error did not affect the jury's verdict or had but very slight effect, and the district court's "navigable waters" instruction was not harmless error.

* * * This case arguably is one in which Justice Scalia's test may actually be more likely to result in CWA jurisdiction than Justice Kennedy's test, despite the fact that Justice Kennedy's test, as applied in *Rapanos,* would treat more waters as within the scope of the CWA. To be sure, the district court's jury instruction was still erroneous even under Justice Scalia's plurality opinion, because the instruction allowed the jury to find that defendants' discharges were into a "navigable water" even if the jury also concluded that Avondale Creek flowed "only intermittently." But under *Justice Scalia's* test, that error may well have been harmless,

because Wagoner, the EPA investigator, clearly and unambiguously testified that there is a continuous, uninterrupted flow between Avondale Creek and the Black Warrior River. Under Justice Scalia's test, the district court's jury instruction error arguably "did not affect the verdict, 'or had but very slight effect.'" Thus, the decision as to which *Rapanos* test applies may be outcome-determinative in this case, and so it is not surprising that the government advocates a practical, *Johnson*-style approach whereby all votes—from plurality, concurring, and dissenting Justices—are counted.

Nevertheless, as we have already discussed, *Marks* requires us to adopt the narrowest view of the Justices who concurred in the judgment in *Rapanos*. Thus, Justice Kennedy's test is the test against which we have measured the district court's jury instruction for harmless error. Justice Kennedy's test is also the test that the district court must apply on remand, for the reasons explained.

* * * III. CONCLUSION

For the foregoing reasons, defendants' convictions are reversed. * * * The case is remanded for a new trial as to all defendants on the CWA conspiracy count (Count 1) and for a new trial as to all defendants charged in the remaining substantive CWA counts (Counts 2, 3, 5, 7–19, 21, and 22).

NOTES

1. **Choosing Among the *Rapanos* Opinions.** As the Eleventh Circuit notes, the federal Courts of Appeal (and the district courts where there is no controlling circuit court decision) are currently split regarding the controlling test for a "navigable water" under the Clean Water Act. What approach did the First Circuit take in *Johnson*? Why? Which *Rapanos* opinion essentially controls under *Johnson*? Why?

What approach did the Eleventh Circuit take here, in *Robison*, and the Seventh Circuit take in *Gerke*? Why? Which *Rapanos* opinion controls under *Gerke* and *Robison*? Does that result make sense?

2. **The *Marks* Test for Resolving Plurality Opinions.** What is the *Marks* test for finding a controlling rule of law from a plurality or split Supreme Court decision? How did the Eleventh Circuit apply that test here? Do you agree with the Eleventh Circuit's analysis? Why or why not? What do you make of the fact that, under the facts of the *Robison* case, jurisdiction was *more* likely to exist under the Scalia plurality's view of "waters of the United States" than under Justice Kennedy's "significant nexus" test? Doesn't that fact suggest that the *Marks* test doesn't apply well to the *Rapanos* decision? (By the way, in *Johnson*, the First Circuit emphasized that the Supreme Court has been backing away from the *Marks* test.)

3. **The *Rapanos* Guidance.** On June 5, 2007, the EPA the Army Corps issued guidance regarding their application of the *Rapanos* decision. U.S. EPA & U.S. Army Corps of Engineers, *Clean Water Act Jurisdiction Following the*

U.S. Supreme Court's Decision in Rapanos v. United States & Carabell v. United States (June 2007). This Guidance and other information regarding the definition of "waters of the United States" is available from the EPA at: Office of Water, U.S. EPA, *Clean Water Act Definition of "Waters of the United States,"* http://www.epa.gov/wetlands/guidance/CWAwaters.html (as updated Jan. 17, 2008). The two agencies asked for public comment on the guidance, presumably as a prelude to rulemaking, and on November 27, 2007, the agencies extended the deadline for such comments to January 21, 2008.

According to the guidance, the two agencies will assert Clean Water Act jurisdiction over: (1) traditional navigable waters; (2) wetlands adjacent to traditional navigable waters; (3) "[n]on-navigable tributaries of traditional navigable waters that are relatively permanent where the tributaries typically flow year-round or have continuous flow at least seasonally (e.g. typically three months)"; and (4) wetlands that directly abut such tributaries. *Clean Water Act Jurisdiction* at 1.

The agencies will use a case-by-case analysis to determine whether three other types of waters "have a significant nexus with a traditionally navigable water": (1) "[n]on-navigable tributaries that are not relatively permanent"; (2) "[w]etlands adjacent to non-navigable tributaries that are not relatively permanent"; and (3) "[w]etlands adjacent to but that do not directly abut a relatively permanent non-navigable tributary." *Id.* "In considering how to apply the significant nexus standard, the agencies have focused on the integral relationship between the ecological characteristics of tributaries and those of their adjacent wetlands, which determines in part their contribution to restoring and maintaining the chemical, physical, and biological integrity of the Nation's navigable waters." *Id.* at 8. "Principal considerations when evaluating significant nexus include the volume, duration, and frequency of the flow of water of the tributary to a traditional navigable water," but "[i]f the tributary has adjacent wetlands, the significant nexus evaluation needs to recognize the ecological relationship between tributaries and their adjacent wetlands, and their closely linked role in protecting the chemical, physical, and biological integrity of downstream traditional waters." *Id.* at 9. "In addition, the agencies will consider other relevant factors, including the functions performed by the tributary together with the functions performed by any adjacent wetlands," including pollution sequestration and flood control. *Id.* at 10.

Finally, the EPA and the Army Corps concluded that they would generally *not* assert Clean Water Act jurisdiction over "[s]wales or erosional features (e.g. gullies, small washes) characterized by low volume, infrequent, or short duration flow" or over "[d]itches (including roadside ditches) excavated wholly in and draining only uplands and that do not carry a relatively permanent flow of water." *Id.* at 1.

How are the EPA and the Army Corps of Engineers interpreting the *Rapanos* opinion? Which Justice's or Justices' opinion(s) did the agencies find controlling? Why do you say that?

Revised *Rapanos* Guidance appeared on December 2, 2008, although with very few changes from the initial Guidance. *See* http://www.usace.army.mil/CECW/Documents/cecwo/reg/cwa_guide/cwa_juris_2dec08.pdf. However, in

April 2011, the EPA and the Army Corps of Engineers proposed new guidance on how to apply *Rapanos*. They received about 230,000 public comments, many of which urged the agencies to engage in actual rulemaking. As a result, as of December 2011, the EPA anticipates proposing a new regulation to define "waters of the United States" in early 2012. For more information, *see* http://water.epa.gov/lawsregs/guidance/wetlands/CWAwaters.cfm.

4. **The Rest of the *Rapanos* Story.** The federal government's litigation with John Rapanos began in 1994. A jury criminally convicted Rapanos of Clean Water Act violations in 1995, and Rapanos was sentenced to three years' probation and paid a $185,000 criminal fine. The civil litigation that led to the Supreme Court's fractured decision presented in this chapter finally settled on December 29, 2008. As part of that settlement, Rapanos and the other defendants agreed, as compensation for the 54 acres of wetlands that they destroyed: (1) to pay a $150,000 penalty; (2) to construct 100 acres of new wetlands at a cost of $750,000; (3) to preserve 134 acres of wetlands in Midland County; and (4) to create a mitigation endowment of $25,000. The federal court approved the consent decree on March 18, 2009. The consent decree is available from the EPA at http://www.epa.gov/compliance/resources/decrees/civil/cwa/rapanos-cd.pdf. At the time of the settlement, John Rapanos was 73 years old, and his fight over "waters of the United States" had lasted about 15 years.

* * *

2. The "Contiguous Zone" and the "Ocean"

Under subsection (B) of the definition of "discharge of a pollutant," a "discharge of a pollutant" occurs if there is "any addition of any pollutant to the waters of the ***contiguous zone*** or the ***ocean*** from any point source other than a vessel or other floating craft." CWA § 502(12)(B), 33 U.S.C. § 1362(12)(B) (emphasis added). According to the Act's definitions, "[t]he term 'contiguous zone' means the entire zone established or to be established by the United States under article 24 of the Convention of the Territorial Sea and the Contiguous Zone." CWA § 502(9), 33 U.S.C. § 1362(9). This definition references one of the four international agreements that make up the 1958 United Nations Convention on the Law of the Sea (UNCLOS I), which allowed signatory countries to establish a three-mile-wide territorial sea and a contiguous zone that could reach up to twelve nautical miles out to sea. In the ***territorial sea***, a nation exercises complete sovereignty, the same as it does for its land territory, and the Clean Water Act includes the territorial sea as part of the "navigable waters." CWA § 502(7), 33 U.S.C. § 1362(7). In contrast, a nation can use its ***contiguous zone*** primarily for enforcement purposes—to pursue and catch violators for breaches of domestic law.

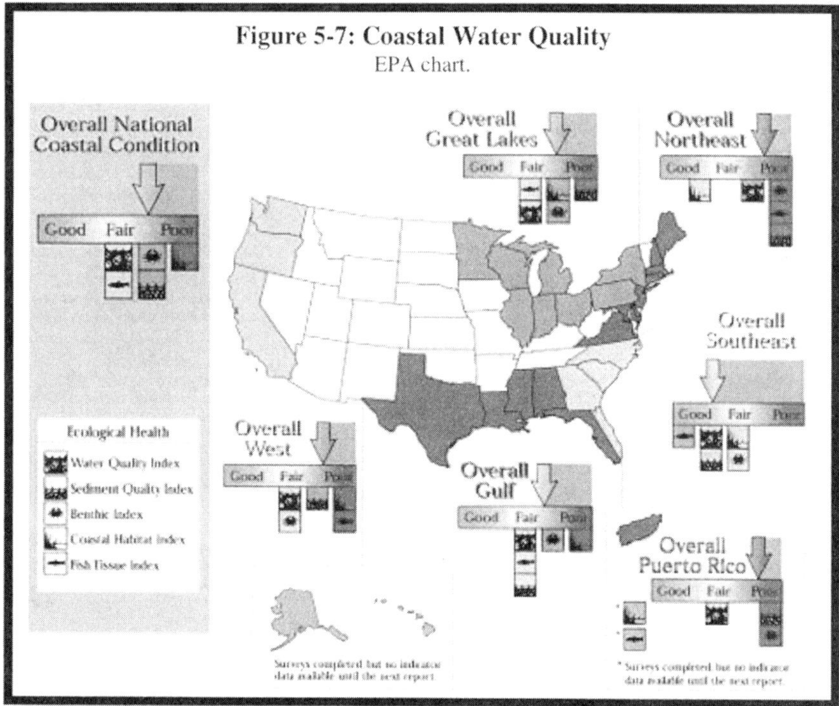

Figure 5-7: Coastal Water Quality
EPA chart.

UNCLOS III, which came into force in 1994, largely superseded UNCLOS I in terms of international ocean jurisdiction. UNCLOS III expanded the territorial sea to twelve nautical miles and the contiguous zone to 24 nautical miles. The United States is not a signatory to UNCLOS III, but in 1999 President Clinton proclaimed a 24–mile contiguous zone for the United States. Nevertheless, the statutory definition of "contiguous zone" in the Clean Water Act appears to preserve the 12–mile limitation from UNCLOS I, just as the Clean Water Act's definition of "territorial sea" preserves the three-mile "norm" from UNCLOS I.

Any ambiguities regarding the "contiguous zone," however, are largely irrelevant, because the Clean Water Act also prohibits discharges of pollutants into the "ocean." The Act defines "***ocean***" as "any portion of the high seas beyond the contiguous zone." CWA § 502(10), 33 U.S.C. § 1362(10). Read literally, this definition would appear to extend Clean Water Act jurisdiction across all of the oceans—at least until other nations' contiguous zones. As a practical matter, however, presidential proclamation and customary international law limits the scope of the Clean Water Act's "oceans" to a band of waters extending 200 nautical miles out to sea. International law more commonly refers to this portion of the ocean as a nation's ***Exclusive Economic Zone*** **(EEZ)**, and under UNCLOS III and United States presidential proclamation, nations can regulate in the EEZ to protect the environment.

Other issues do arise with respect to regulating discharges into the contiguous zone and the ocean. First, federal regulation of activities at sea is far more complex than regulation of activities in other waters. For example, the Marine Protection, Research, and Sanctuaries Act, also known as the Ocean Dumping Act, 33 U.S.C. §§ 1401–1445, regulates discharges into the ocean directly from vessels.

Second, even under the Clean Water Act, discharges into the territorial sea, the contiguous zone and the ocean are subject to different regulatory requirements than discharges into the other jurisdictional waters. For example, under section 403, 33 U.S.C. § 1343, all discharges into the territorial sea, the contiguous zone, or the ocean must comply with the EPA's ***ocean discharge criteria***. The ocean discharge criteria are guidelines to regulate the degradation of the ocean waters to prevent harm to marine life or to other human uses of the ocean.

As Figure 5–7 demonstrates, protection of the United States's ocean waters is an increasingly important component of the Clean Water Act's mission. In 2005, the EPA assessed the overall condition of the United States' coastal waters to be somewhere between "fair" and "poor," with the waters along the West and Northeast coasts and the waters surrounding Puerto Rico to be in the worst shape.

E. POINT SOURCE

Figure 5-8: Sources of Water Pollution
EPA graphic.

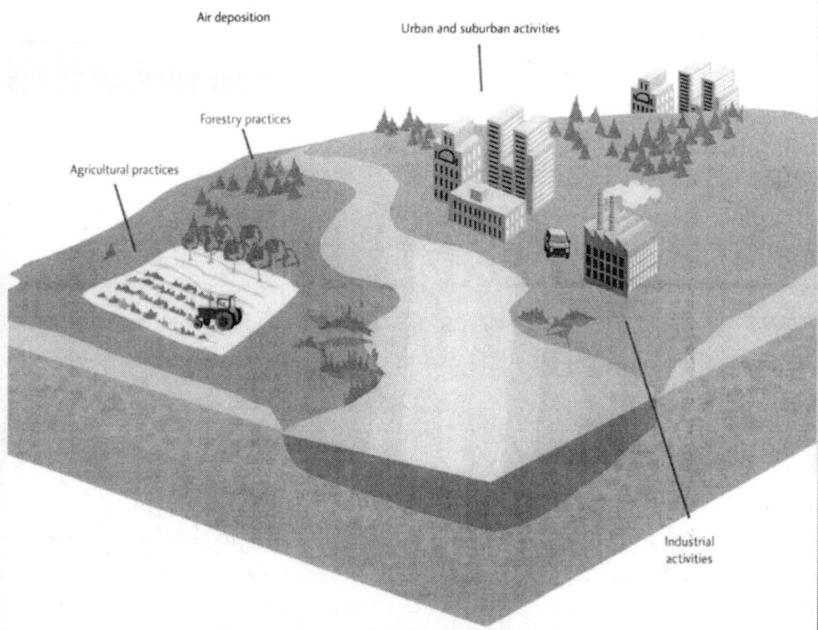

As Figure 5–8 illustrates, a host of activities can cause water pollution. Jurisdiction under the Clean Water Act, however, extends only to discharges of pollutants from ***point sources***. Indeed, one of the Act's major jurisdictional distinctions is between point sources and ***nonpoint sources***, with the former subject to Clean Water Act jurisdiction and the latter being left to the states to regulate, if states so choose.

The Clean Water Act defines a "point source" to be:

> any discernible, confined and discrete conveyance, including but not limited to any pipe, ditch, channel, tunnel, conduit, well, discrete fissure, container, rolling stock, concentrated animal feeding operation, or vessel or other floating craft, from which pollutants are or may be discharged.

CWA § 502(14), 33 U.S.C. § 1362(14). The definition also specifies two exceptions, however. The term "point source" "does *not* include agricultural stormwater discharges and return flows from irrigated agriculture." *Id.* (emphasis added).

Thus, like many of the terms comprising the definition of a "discharge of a pollutant," the Clean Water Act broadly defines "point source." In general, most every human-controlled conveyance of pollutants to water comes within its purview. Nevertheless, the following case illustrates some of the limits of "point source."

UNITED STATES v. PLAZA HEALTH LABORATORIES, INC.

3 F.3d 643 (2d Cir. 1993).

GEORGE C. PRATT, CIRCUIT JUDGE:

Defendant Geronimo Villegas appeals from a judgment entered in the United States District Court for the Eastern District of New York * * * convicting him of two counts of knowingly discharging pollutants into the Hudson River in violation of the Clean Water Act ("CWA"). *See* 33 U.S.C. §§ 1311 and 1319(c)(2). * * *

FACTS AND BACKGROUND

Villegas was co-owner and vice president of Plaza Health Laboratories, Inc., a blood-testing laboratory in Brooklyn, New York. On at least two occasions between April and September 1988, Villegas loaded containers of numerous vials of human blood generated from his business into his personal car, and drove to his residence at the Admirals Walk Condominium in Edgewater, New Jersey. Once at his condominium complex, Villegas removed the containers from his car and carried them to the edge of the Hudson River. On one occasion he carried two containers of the vials to the bulkhead that separates his condominium complex from the river, and placed them at low tide within a crevice in the bulkhead that was below the high-water line.

On May 26, 1988, a group of eighth graders on a field trip at the Alice Austin House in Staten Island, New York, discovered numerous glass vials containing human blood along the shore. Some of the vials had washed up on the shore; many were still in the water. Some were cracked, although most remained sealed with stoppers in solid-plastic containers or ziplock bags. Fortunately, no one was injured. That afternoon, New York City workers recovered approximately 70 vials from the area.

On September 25, 1988, a maintenance worker employed by the Admirals Walk Condominium discovered a plastic container holding blood vials wedged between rocks in the bulkhead. New Jersey authorities retrieved numerous blood vials from the bulkhead later that day.

Ten of the retrieved vials contained blood infected with the hepatitis-B virus. All of the vials recovered were eventually traced to Plaza Health Laboratories.

Based upon the May 1988 discovery of vials, Plaza Health Laboratories and Villegas were indicted on May 16, 1989, on two counts each of violating §§ 1319(c)(2) and (3) of the Clean Water Act. 33 U.S.C. §§ 1251 *et seq.* * * * Counts II and IV of the superseding indictment charged Villegas with knowingly discharging pollutants from a "point source" without a permit. *See* 33 U.S.C. §§ 1311(a), 1319(c)(2). Counts I and III alleged that Villegas had discharged pollutants, knowing that he placed others in "imminent danger of death or serious bodily injury." *See* 33 U.S.C. § 1319(c)(3). On January 31, 1991, following a trial before Judge Korman, the jury found Villegas guilty on all four counts.

* * * Villegas contends that one element of the CWA crime, knowingly discharging pollutants from a "point source," was not established in his case. He argues that the definition of "point source," 33 U.S.C. § 1362(14), does not include discharges that result from the individual acts of human beings. Raising primarily questions of legislative intent and statutory construction, Villegas argues that at best, the term "point source" is ambiguous as applied to him, and that the rule of lenity should result in reversal of his convictions. * * *

DISCUSSION

Because "discharge from a point source" is an essential element of a "knowing" violation as well as a "knowing endangerment" violation, *see* 33 U.S.C. §§ 1319(c)(2)-(3), we need not address the government's contentions regarding the CWA's definition of "imminent danger" if we should conclude that Villegas's discharges were not "from a point source." We therefore consider the "point source" issue first.

A. *Navigating the Clean Water Act.*

The basic prohibition on discharge of pollutants is in 33 U.S.C. § 1311(a), which states:

> Except as in compliance with this section and sections 1312, 1316, 1317, 1328, *1342,* and 1344 of this title, the *discharge* of any *pollutant* by any person shall be unlawful.

Id. (emphasis added)

The largest exception to this seemingly absolute rule is found in 33 U.S.C. § 1342, which establishes the CWA's national pollutant discharge elimination system, or NPDES * * *.

* * * Reading § 1311(a), the basic prohibition, and § 1342(a)(1), the permit section, together, we can identify the basic rule, our rhumb line to clean waters, that, absent a permit, "the discharge of any pollutant by any person" is unlawful. 33 U.S.C. § 1311(a).

We must then adjust our rhumb line by reference to two key definitions—"pollutant" and "discharge." "Pollutant" is defined, in part, as "biological materials ... *discharged* into water." 33 U.S.C. § 1362(6) (emphasis added). "Discharge," in turn, is "any addition of any pollutant to navigable waters *from any point source*...." (emphasis added). 33 U.S.C. § 1362(12).

As applied to the facts of this case, then, the defendant "added" a "pollutant" (human blood in glass vials) to "navigable waters" (the Hudson River), and he did so without a permit. The issue, therefore, is whether his conduct constituted a "discharge," and that in turn depends on whether the addition of the blood to the Hudson River waters was "from any point source."

For this final course adjustment in our navigation, we look again to the statute.

> (14) The term "point source" means any discernible, confined and discrete conveyance, including but not limited to any pipe, ditch, channel, tunnel, conduit, well, discrete fissure, container, rolling stock, concentrated animal feeding operation, or vessel or other floating craft, from which pollutants are or may be discharged. This term does not include agricultural stormwater discharges and return flows from irrigated agriculture.

33 U.S.C. § 1362(14). * * * As the parties have presented the issue to us in their briefs and at oral argument, the question is "whether a human being can be a point source." * * *

* * * To determine the scope of the CWA's "point source" definition, we first consider the language and structure of the act itself. If the language is not plain, an excursion into legislative history and context may prove fruitful. Judicial interpretations of the term can be instructive as well, as may be interpretive statements by the agency in charge of implementing the statute. If we conclude after this analysis that the statute is ambiguous as applied to Villegas, then the rule of lenity may apply.

1. Language and Structure of Act.

Human beings are not among the enumerated items that may be a "point source". Although by its terms the definition of "point source" is nonexclusive, the words used to define the term and the examples given ("pipe, ditch, channel, tunnel, conduit, well, discrete fissure," *etc.*) evoke images of physical structures and instrumentalities that systematically act as a means of conveying pollutants from an industrial source to navigable waterways.

In addition, if every discharge involving humans were to be considered a "discharge from a point source," the statute's lengthy definition of "point source" would have been unnecessary. It is elemental that Congress does not add unnecessary words to statutes. Had Congress intended to punish any human being who polluted navigational waters, it could readily have said: "any person who places pollutants in navigable waters without a permit is guilty of a crime."

The Clean Water Act generally targets industrial and municipal sources of pollutants, as is evident from a perusal of its many sections. Consistent with this focus, the term "point source" is used throughout the statute, but invariably in sentences referencing industrial or municipal discharges. *See, e.g.,* 33 U.S.C. § 1311 (referring to "owner or operator" of point source); § 1311(e) (requiring that effluent limitations established under the Act "be applied to all point sources of discharge"); § 1311(g)(2) (allows an "owner or operator of a point source" to apply to EPA for modification of its limitations requirements); § 1342(f) (referring to classes, categories, types, and sizes of point sources); § 1314(b)(4)(B) (denoting "best conventional pollutant control technology measures and practices" applicable to any point source within particular category or class); § 1316 ("any point source ... which is constructed as to meet all applicable standards of performance"); § 1318(a) (administrator shall require owner or operator of any point source to install, use and maintain monitoring equipment or methods); and § 1318(c) (states may develop procedures for inspection, monitoring, and entry with respect to point sources located in state).

This emphasis was sensible, as "[i]ndustrial and municipal point sources were the worst and most obvious offenders of surface water quality. They were also the easiest to address because their loadings emerge from a discrete point such as the end of a pipe." David Letson, *Point/Nonpoint Source Pollution Reduction Trading: An Interpretive Survey*, 32 NAT. RESOURCES J. 219, 221 (1992).

* * * *2. Legislative History and Context.*

The broad remedial purpose of the CWA is to "restore and maintain the chemical, physical, and biological integrity of the Nation's waters." 33 U.S.C. § 1251(a). The narrow questions posed by this case, however, may not be resolved merely by simple reference to this admirable goal. * * * We agree [] that "even if we accept the purposes section at face value, it is only suggestive, not dispositive of [the issue before us]. Caution is always advisable in relying on a general declaration of purpose to alter the apparent meaning of a specific provision." [*National Wildlife Fed'n v. Gorsuch*, 693 F.2d 156, 178 (D.C. Cir. 1982)].

The legislative history of the CWA, while providing little insight into the meaning of "point source," confirms the act's focus on industrial polluters. Congress required NPDES permits of those who discharge from a "point source." The term "point source," introduced to the act in 1972, was intended to function as a means of identifying industrial polluters—generally a difficult task because pollutants quickly disperse throughout the subject waters. The senate report for the 1972 amendments explains:

> In order to further clarify the scope of the regulatory procedures in the Act the Committee had added a definition of point source to distinguish between control requirements where there are *specific confined conveyances, such as pipes,* and control requirements which are imposed to control runoff. The control of pollutants from runoff is applied pursuant to section 209 and the authority resides in the State or other local agency.

S. REP. NO. 92–414, *reprinted in* 1972 U.S.C.C.A.N. 3668, 3744.

* * * We find no suggestion either in the act itself or in the history of its passage that Congress intended the CWA to impose criminal liability on an individual for the myriad, random acts of human waste disposal, for example, a passerby who flings a candy wrapper into the Hudson River, or a urinating swimmer. Discussions during the passage of the 1972 amendments indicate that Congress had bigger fish to fry.

* * * *3. Caselaw.*

Our search for the meaning of "point source" brings us next to judicial constructions of the term. The "point source" element was clearly established in the few CWA criminal decisions under § 1319(c) that are reported.

[With one exception,] the cases that have interpreted "point source" have done so in civil-penalty or licensing settings, where greater flexibility of interpretation to further remedial legislative purposes is permitted, and the rule of lenity does not protect a defendant against statutory ambiguities.

* * * *4. Regulatory Structure.*

Finally, not even the EPA's regulations support the government's broad assertion that a human being may be a "point source." The EPA stresses that the discharge be "through pipes, sewers, or other conveyances:"

> *Discharge of a pollutant* means:
>
> (a) Any addition of any "pollutant" or combination of pollutants to "waters of the United States" from any "point source."

> . . . This definition includes additions of pollutants into waters of the United States from: surface runoff which is collected or channelled by man; *discharges through pipes, sewers, or other conveyances* owned by a State, municipality, or other person which do not lead to a treatment works; and discharges through pipes, sewers, or other conveyances, leading into privately owned treatment works. This term does not include an addition of pollutants by any "indirect discharger."

40 C.F.R. § 122.2 (1992) (emphasis supplied).

In sum, although Congress had the ability to so provide, § 1362(14) of the CWA does not expressly recognize a human being as a "point source"; nor does the act make structural sense when one incorporates a human being into that definition. The legislative history of the act adds no light to the muddy depths of this issue, and cases urging a broad interpretation of the definition in the civil-penalty context do not persuade us to do so here, where Congress has imposed heavy criminal sanctions. Adopting the government's suggested flexibility for the definition would effectively read the "point source" element of the crime out of the statute, and not even the EPA has extended the term "point source" as far as is urged here.

We accordingly conclude that the term "point source" as applied to a human being is at best ambiguous.

B. *Rule of Lenity.*

In criminal prosecutions the rule of lenity requires that ambiguities in the statute be resolved in the defendant's favor. In other words, we cannot add to the statute what congress did not provide. "[B]efore a man can be punished as a criminal under the Federal law his case must be 'plainly and unmistakably' within the provisions of some statute." *United States v. Gradwell*, 243 U.S. 476, 485 (1917).

Since the government's reading of the statute in this case founders on our inability to discern the "obvious intention of the legislature", *Huddleston* [*v. United States*], 415 U.S. [814,] 831 [(1974)], to include a human being as a "point source," we conclude that the criminal provisions of the CWA did not clearly proscribe Villegas's conduct and did not accord him fair warning of the sanctions the law placed on that conduct. Under the rule of lenity, therefore, the prosecutions against him must be dismissed. * * *

OAKES, CIRCUIT JUDGE, dissenting:

I agree that this is not the typical Clean Water Act prosecution—though, as criminal prosecutions under the Act are infrequent, or at least result in few published judicial opinions, what is "typical" is as yet ill-defined. * * * However, because I do not agree that a person can never be a point source, and because I believe that Mr. Villegas' actions, as the jury found them, fell well within the bounds of activity proscribed by the Clean

Water Act's bar on discharge of pollutants into navigable waters, I am required to dissent.

Point source.

I begin with the proposition that the Clean Water Act bars "the discharge of any pollutant by any person," except as authorized elsewhere in the Act. 33 U.S.C. § 1311(a) (1988). The only limiting factors are definitional: the Act bars "discharges" from "point sources" of "pollutants" to "navigable waters." It does not bar nonpoint source pollution, pollution of dry land or nonnavigable waters, or the movement of existing pollution within the navigable waters.

The key in this case is the definition of a point source. The term is introduced as part of the definition of "discharge of a pollutant": "any addition of any pollutant to navigable waters from any point source." 33 U.S.C. § 1362(12)(A) (1988). The term "point source," in turn, is defined as

> *any discernible, confined and discrete conveyance, including but not limited to* any pipe, ditch, channel, tunnel, conduit, well, discrete fissure, container, rolling stock, concentrated animal feeding operation, or vessel or other floating craft, from which pollutants are or may be discharged. This term does not include agricultural stormwater discharges and return flows from irrigated agriculture.

33 U.S.C. § 1362(14) (1988) (emphasis added).

The language of this definition indicates that it encompasses a wide range of means of placing pollutants into navigable waters. The question before us is what, in addition to the listed examples, is a "discernible, confined and discrete conveyance."

I begin with the obvious, in hopes that it will illuminate the less obvious: the classic point source is something like a pipe. This is, at least in part, because pipes and similar conduits are needed to carry large quantities of waste water, which represents a large proportion of the point source pollution problem. Thus, devices designed to convey large quantities of waste water from a factory or municipal sewage treatment facility are readily classified as point sources. Because not all pollutants are liquids, however, the statute and the cases make clear that means of conveying solid wastes to be dumped in navigable waters are also point sources. *See, e.g.,* 33 U.S.C. § 1362(14) ("rolling stock," or railroad cars, listed as an example of a point source).

What I take from this look at classic point sources is that, at the least, an organized means of channeling and conveying industrial waste in quantity to navigable waters is a "discernible, confined and discrete conveyance." The case law is in accord: courts have deemed a broad range of means of depositing pollutants in the country's navigable waters to be point sources. Nor have courts been inclined to exclude mining or agricultural point sources, despite the fact that portions of the Clean Water Act protect these industries to some extent. Further, the legislative history indicates that the Act was meant to control periodic, as well as continuous, discharges. S. REP. NO. 92–414, 92d Cong. 1st Sess. (1971), *reprinted at* 1972 U.S.C.C.A.N. 3668, 3705.

In short, the term "point source" has been broadly construed to apply to a wide range of polluting techniques, so long as the pollutants involved are not just humanmade, but reach the navigable waters by human effort or by leaking from a clear point at which waste water was collected by human effort. * * * In explaining why a broad definition was needed, [courts have] noted that the statute sets as its goal the "attainment of the no discharge objective," and that this objective could not be achieved if the term "point source" were read narrowly.

This broad reading of the term "point source" is essential to fulfill the mandate of the Clean Water Act * * *. * * * Nonetheless, the term "point source" sets significant definitional limits on the reach of the Clean Water Act. Fifty percent or more of all water pollution is thought to come from nonpoint sources. So, to further refine the definition of "point source," I consider what it is that the Act does not cover: nonpoint source discharges.

Nonpoint source pollution is, generally, runoff: salt from roads, agricultural chemicals from farmlands, oil from parking lots, and other substances washed by rain, in diffuse patterns, over the land and into navigable waters. The sources are many, difficult to identify and difficult to control. Indeed, an effort to greatly reduce nonpoint source pollution could require radical changes in land use patterns which Congress evidently was unwilling to mandate without further study. The structure of the statute—which regulates point source pollution closely, while leaving nonpoint source regulation to the states under the Section 208 program—indicates that the term "point source" was included in the definition of discharge so as to ensure that nonpoint source pollution would *not* be covered. Instead, Congress chose to regulate first that which could easily be regulated: direct discharges by identifiable parties, or point sources.

This rationale for regulating point and nonpoint sources differently—that point sources may readily be controlled and are easily attributable to a particular source, while nonpoint sources are more difficult to control without radical change, and less easily attributable, once they reach water, to any particular responsible party—helps define what fits within each category. * * *

While Villegas' activities were not prototypical point source discharges—in part because he was disposing of waste that could have been disposed of on land, and so did not need a permit or a pipe—they much more closely resembled a point source discharge than a nonpoint source discharge. First, Villegas and his lab were perfectly capable of avoiding discharging their waste into water: they were [] a "controllable" source.

Furthermore, the discharge was directly into water, and came from an identifiable point, Villegas. Villegas did not dispose of the materials on land, where they could be washed into water as nonpoint source pollution.

Rather, he carried them, from his firm's laboratory, in his car, to his apartment complex, where he placed them in a bulkhead below the high tide line. I do not think it is necessary to determine whether it was Mr. Villegas himself who was the point source, or whether it was his car, the vials, or the bulkhead: in a sense, the entire stream of Mr. Villegas' activity functioned as a "discrete conveyance" or point source. The point is that the source of the pollution was clear, and would have been easy to control. Indeed, Villegas was well aware that there were methods of controlling the discharge (and that the materials were too dangerous for casual disposal): his laboratory had hired a professional medical waste handler. He simply chose not to use an appropriate waste disposal mechanism.

* * * I am of course given pause, however, by the nature of the criminal sanctions attached to point source discharges under § 1319. Given the broad statutory definitions of pollutant and point source, it would appear that a knowing violation would include intentionally throwing a candy wrapper into the ocean—and that this is an activity which could subject the thrower to a $25,000 fine and three years in jail. It seems improbable to me that this could have been Congress' intent. Consequently, I would with the majority read the statute as ambiguous as it pertains to individual litterers, as opposed to disposers of industrial and municipal waste. The latter were the principal targets of the authors of the CWA, and, as professional creators of waste, charged with knowledge that disposal of waste into navigable waters is a crime.

Furthermore, no factual dispute essential to finding Villegas' activities to have been a point source discharge remains. The jury concluded that Villegas did in fact place pollutants—the materials he brought from the laboratory—into navigable waters; the only question for us is whether this activity is point source pollution. Thus, I do not believe that the difficulty the prosecutors had here in defining Villegas' offense resulted in their failing to prove that Villegas violated the law. * * *

NOTES

1. **The Criminal Context of *Plaza Health Laboratories* and Interpretation of "Point Source."** Did the fact that Mr. Villegas was being *criminally* prosecuted under the Clean Water Act affect the Second Circuit's interpretation of "point source"? If so, how? What principles of statutory construction did the court rely upon? What other tools of statutory construction did the Second Circuit use in deciding whether or not a human being can be a "point source" under the Clean Water Act?

2. **The True Basis of the Second Circuit's Decision.** Was this a rule of lenity case or a "point source" case? Why? Why does the distinction

matter? Would the Second Circuit have decided this case differently if the federal government had sought only civil penalties against Mr. Villegas? Why or why not? What values does the rule of lenity protect? As the Second Circuit correctly noted, criminal prosecutions under the Clean Water Act are comparatively rare. Why did the federal government pursue a criminal prosecution in this case, do you suppose?

3. **"Knowing" Violations of the Clean Water Act.** As has been discussed, administrative and civil violations of the Clean Water Act are strict liability offenses. However, as the Second Circuit noted in *Plaza Health Laboratories*, criminal violations of the Clean Water Act require that the defendant have acted "knowingly" or "negligently"—*i.e.*, there is a *mens rea* requirement. CWA § 309(c), 33 U.S.C. § 1319(c). However, the Clean Water Act does not define "knowing," and significant debate has occurred regarding what exactly the criminal defendant must know: Must the defendant have known that he or she was breaking the law, or only that the defendant was engaged in the acts that constituted a violation? Most federal Courts of Appeals have adopted the latter approach. *United States v. Technic Services, Inc.*, 314 F.3d 1031, 1042 (9th Cir. 2002); *United States v. Sinskey*, 119 F.3d 712, 715–17 (8th Cir. 1997); *United States v. Hopkins*, 53 F.3d 533, 537–41 (2d Cir. 1995); *United States v. Weitzenhoff*, 35 F.3d 1275, 1285–86 (9th Cir. 1993); *United States v. Baytank (Houston), Inc.*, 934 F.2d 599, 618–19 (5th Cir. 1991).

Given what you know of the *Plaza Health Laboratory* facts, do you have any doubts that Mr. Villegas knew he was acting illegally when he disposed of the hepatitis B-contaminated vials of blood? Why or why not? Assuming that he knew that he was acting illegally, why should he receive the benefit of the rule of lenity?

4. **The Dissent's View of "Point Sources."** Why did Judge Oakes dissent? What approach did Judge Oakes take in construing the term "point source"? How did this approach differ from the majority's approach? Which view of "point source" do you find more persuasive? Why?

5. **The Wrong "Point Source" Argument? A Problem.** Judge Oakes suggested in dissent that the majority focused too narrowly on the issue of whether *Mr. Villegas* could qualify as a point source. Could you argue that the *vials* that contained the blood were the relevant point sources? How? Could you argue that *Mr. Villegas's car*, which he used to transport the vials from the lab to the Hudson River, was the point source? How? Do either of these possibilities fit the definition of "point source" better than Mr. Villegas himself? Why or why not?

6. **Nonpoint Source Pollution**. As Judge Oakes noted in dissent, if water pollution does not come from a point source it is ***nonpoint source pollution*** **(NPS).** The Clean Water Act imposes no federal requirements on nonpoint source pollution, although it does encourage states to enact NPS management plans. *See* CWA §§ 208, 319, 33 U.S.C. §§ 1288, 1329. In 1998, as part of the Clean Water Action Plan, the EPA concluded that nonpoint

source pollution, particularly agricultural nonpoint source pollution, is the most significant remaining cause of water quality impairment in the United States. We shall look more closely at various attempts to bring nonpoint source pollution within the Clean Water Act's federal regulatory regime later in this chapter. For now, look again at Figure 5–8, *supra*. Which sources of water pollution depicted are nonpoint sources of pollution?

7. **The EPA's "Point Source" Regulations and Clean Water Act Regulation of Other Federal Agencies.** As part of its authority to implement the Clean Water Act, the EPA can promulgate regulations that clarify statutory terms. As was true for the Clean Air Act, such regulatory interpretations of statutory terms by the agency charged with implementing the statute are accorded *Chevron* deference—the EPA's interpretation will be upheld if: (1) Congress has not clearly spoken to the specific issue involved; and (2) the EPA's interpretation is reasonable. The EPA has promulgated a number of regulations that clarify—or attempt to clarify—how the term "point source" applies to a variety of particular activities. Recently, for example, the U.S. Forest Service tried to argue that its aerial spraying of pesticides was exempt from Clean Water Act regulation on the basis of an EPA regulation, 40 C.F.R. § 122.27, which declares that silvicultural (forestry-related) nonpoint source activities like pest control are not subject to Clean Water Act regulation. The Ninth Circuit disagreed, concluding that the EPA had not intended to exclude silvicultural activities that qualified as point source discharges and that even if it had, the EPA lacked authority to create point source exemptions under the Act. *League of Wilderness Defenders/Blue Mountains Biodiversity Project v. Forsgren*, 309 F.3d 1181, 1185–88 (9th Cir. 2002).

8. **Vessels, "Other Floating Craft," and Point Source Discharges into the Ocean.** Recall that under subsection (B) of the definition of "discharge of a pollutant," discharges into the contiguous zone or the ocean—that is, discharges more than three miles out to sea—trigger Clean Water Act jurisdiction only if they come from a "point source other than a vessel or other floating craft." CWA § 502(12)(B), 33 U.S.C. § 1362(12)(B). In addition, the normal Clean Water Act permitting requirements do not apply to discharges of sewage from vessels, wherever in the ocean those discharges occur. *See* CWA §§ 502(6), 312, 33 U.S.C. §§ 1362(6), 1322. As a result, the definitions of "vessel" and "other floating craft" can be crucial to Clean Water Act jurisdiction in the oceans.

In *United States v. West Indies Transport, Inc.*, 127 F.3d 299 (3rd Cir. 1997), the Third Circuit addressed the issue of whether five fixed barges floating in Krum Bay, St. Thomas, could qualify as non-vessel "point sources" for purposes of the Clean Water Act. The bay was part of the territorial sea, but West Indies Transport used the barges for housing, resulting in discharges of sewage into the Bay, raising the issue of whether the barges were "vessels." The Third Circuit quickly concluded that West Indies Transport was liable for violating the Clean Water Act because the barges were "floating craft," not "vessels":

> 33 U.S.C. § 1322(a)(1) defines "new vessel" and "existing vessel" to include "every description of watercraft or other artificial contrivance used, or capable of being used, as a means of transportation on water." This definition contrasts vessels with "other floating craft," a term which the Clean Water Act does not define, but which suggests by its terms and

> in the context of the statute an artificial water-borne contrivance that, in contrast to a vessel, is not used or capable of being used for transportation purposes. *See* 33 U.S.C. § 1362(12). At all relevant times, the barge in question was moored permanently to shore. It was used to house foreign workers, not as a means of transport. Nor could the barge have been used for transport. According to testimony at trial, defendants' barge was half submerged in the water of Krum Bay, with part of the hull resting on the bottom and with water visible below decks. The barge could not be moved from its mooring. There was sufficient evidence therefore for the trier of fact to conclude that the barge was not a vessel within the meaning of the Clean Water Act.

Id. at 309.

* * *

III. NPDES PERMITS

As many of the cases presented so far have noted, the practical import of section 301(a), 33 U.S.C. § 1311(a), is that a person cannot discharge pollutants without a permit. The most common type of permit under the Clean Water Act is the ***National Pollutant Discharge Elimination System*** **(NPDES)** permit. The Administrator of the EPA received the initial authority to issue NPDES permits, CWA § 402(a), 33 U.S.C. § 1342(a), but states may apply to the EPA for authority to issue such permits to the dischargers within their borders. CWA § 402(b), 33 U.S.C. § 1342(b). States seeking to obtain NPDES permitting authority must meet nine statutory requirements, but "[t]he Administrator shall approve each such submitted program unless he determines that adequate authority does not exist" to meet those nine requirements. *Id.*

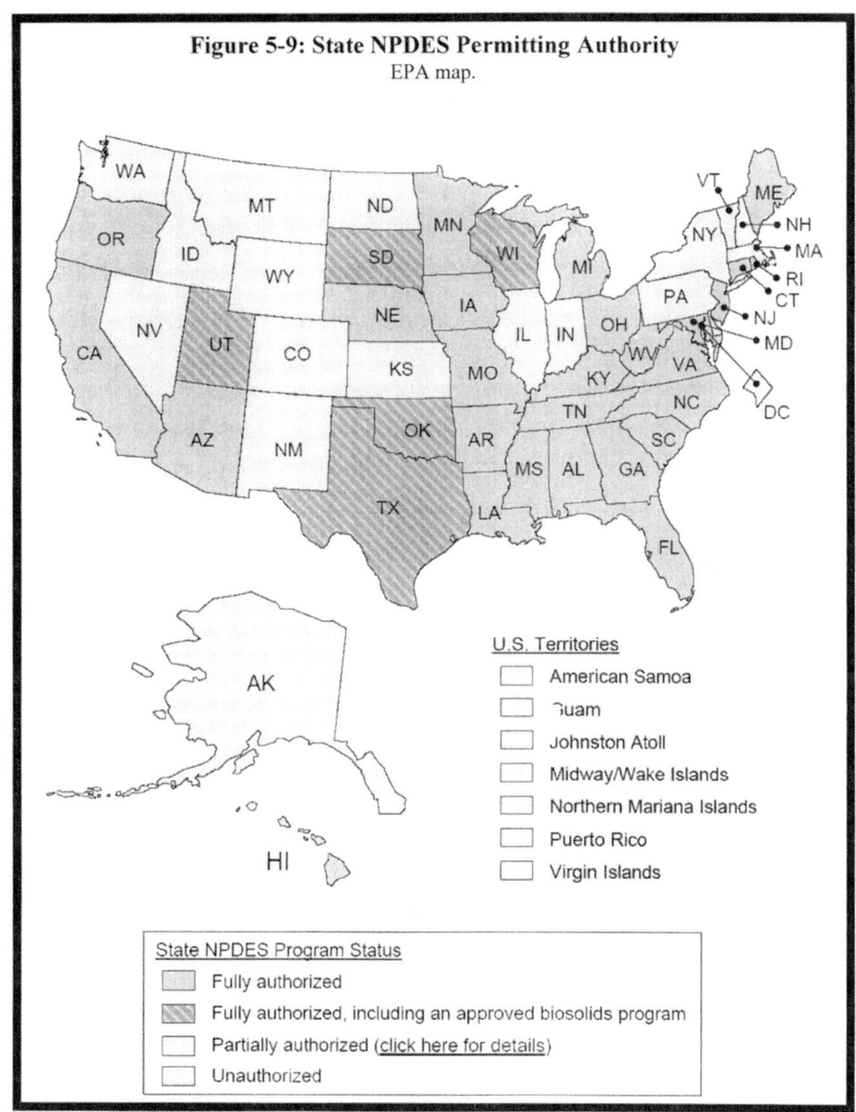

Thus, the Clean Water Act expresses a clear preference that states take over the NPDES permit program, a preference that Congress made explicit in the policies section of the Act. CWA § 101(b), 33 U.S.C. § 1251(b). Moreover, because the Clean Water Act requires the EPA to consider partial state permit program applications, CWA § 402(n), 33 U.S.C. § 1342(n), the EPA has divided state NPDES permitting authority into several components: (1) *base NPDES permitting authority*, through which the state issues individual NPDES permits to non-federal dischargers; (2) *federal facility permitting authority*, through which the state can issue NPDES permits or federal dischargers; (3) *general NPDES permitting authority*, through which the state can create general permits for relatively innocuous dischargers; (4) *municipal sewage sludge regulatory*

authority, more formally referred to as the *biosolids program*; and (5) *pretreatment requirement authority*, which allows the state to set pretreatment requirements for *indirect dischargers—i.e.*, dischargers who send pollutants directly into POTWs/sewage treatment plants.

States have rather enthusiastically sought NPDES permitting authority, as Figure 5–9 demonstrates. Nevertheless, the standards and requirements in an NPDES permit remain the same, regardless of what governmental authority issues the permit. According to section 402 of the Clean Water Act, NPDES permits must ensure that the "discharge will meet * * * all applicable requirements under sections 1311, 1312, 1316, 1317, 1318, and 1343 of this title." CWA § 402(a)(1), 33 U.S.C. § 1342(a)(1). Let's examine each of these requirements in order.

A. SECTION 1311: TECHNOLOGY–BASED EFFLUENT LIMITATIONS

1. Effluent Limitations in General

The core of any NPDES permit are the ***technology-based effluent limitations*** that the EPA establishes pursuant to section 301, 33 U.S.C. § 1311. States can establish effluent limitations as well, but the EPA received the primary authority from Congress to establish them and has issued most of the effluent limitations in use. In general, an ***effluent limitation*** is "any restriction established by a State or the Administrator on quantities, rates, and concentrations of chemical, physical, biological, and other constituents which are discharged from point sources into navigable waters, the waters of the contiguous zone, or the ocean, including schedules of compliance." CWA § 502(11), 33 U.S.C. § 1342(11). As such, effluent limitations tend to be *numeric* limitations on the quantities or concentrations of pollutants that point sources discharge. Many effluent limitations impose ***end-of-the-pipe*** standards on point sources—that is, standards regarding the pollutant content of the point source's effluent as it leaves the point source.

Like emissions standards under the Clean Air Act, Clean Water Act effluent limitations are ***technology-based*** standards. The EPA sets these standards on a pollutant-by-pollutant and industry-by-industry basis, based on the amount of pollutant reduction achievable through pollution control technology.

As in the Clean Air Act, moreover, Congress established several levels of technology-based controls, depending on the type of pollutant. Originally (1973–1976), existing ordinary point sources were subject to two kinds of effluent limitations: (1) for non-toxic pollutants, initial effluent limitations were based on the ***Best Practicable Control Technology Currently Available*** **(BPT)** and had to be achieved by July 1, 1977; and (2) for toxic pollutants, effluent limitations were based on ***Best Available Technology Economically Achievable*** **(BAT)** and had to be achieved immediately. Discharges of non-toxic pollutants would become subject to

BAT-based limitations by July 1, 1983. "EPA defined BPT as the average of the best existing performance by well operating plants within each industrial category or sub-category. BPT standards had to be justified in terms of the industry-wide cost of implementing the technology in relation to the pollutant reduction benefits." Office of Wastewater Management, EPA, *Water Permitting 101*, at 3, *available at* http://www.epa.gov/npdes/pubs/101pape.htm (last viewed April 24, 2002). In contrast, "EPA defined BAT as the performance associated with the best control and treatment measures that have been, or are capable of being, achieved. For BAT, EPA must still consider the cost of attainability; however, it is not required to balance the cost of implementation against the pollutant reduction benefit." *Id.*

Figure 5-10: Secondary Treatment-Based Effluent Limitations

EPA chart.

Secondary Treatment Standards

Parameter	30-Day Average	7-Day Average
5-Day BOD	30 mg/l	45 mg/l
TSS	30 mg/l	45 mg/l
pH	6 - 9 s.u. (instantaneous)	–
Removal	85% BOD_5 and TSS	–

Publicly-owned treatment works **(POTWs)**—sewage treatment plants—were subject to effluent limitations based on ***secondary treatment***. Unlike ***primary treatment***, which generally consists of simple settling out of the solids contained in sewage, or ***tertiary treatment***, which requires full-blown chemical treatment of sewage to bring water quality back to "clean" levels, secondary treatment is biological treatment of sewage, which eliminates the worst qualities of sewage-contaminated water. The EPA's effluent limitations for POTWs, based on secondary treatment, are shown in Figure 5–10.

In the 1977 amendments to the Clean Water Act, Congress added a new category of pollutants—the ***conventional pollutants***—and a new technology-based effluent limitation. The five conventional pollutants are: ***five-day biochemical oxygen demand*** **(BOD_5)**, a measure of how quickly oxygen is used up in water; ***total suspended solids*** **(TSS)**; **pH**, a measure of how acidic or basic water is (pure water is neutral, with a pH of 7; acids have pH values less than 7, while bases have pH values greater than 7); ***fecal coliform***, an indicator of sewage pollution; and ***oil and grease***. Effluent limitations for these conventional pollutants are based on the ***Best Conventional Pollutant Control Technology*** **(BCT)**, and existing point sources had to meet the BCT-based effluent limitations by July 1, 1984. The 1977 amendments also extended the deadline for existing point sources to comply with BAT for ***non-conventional*** and ***toxic*** pollutants to July 1, 1984.

In 1987, Congress again extended the compliance deadline for existing point sources for both BCT- and BAT-based effluent limitations to March 31, 1989. It also subjected stormwater discharges to NPDES permitting, including to BCT- and BAT-based effluent limitations.

2. Variances from the EPA–Set Effluent Limitations

The EPA's decisions regarding industry-wide effluent limitations often enrage an entire industry. However, those industry-wide effluent limitations can also cause difficulties for individual dischargers. To address these individual difficulties, Congress included a number of ***variance*** provisions that would allow a discharger to temporarily escape the Clean Water Act's timetables for coming into compliance with the applicable effluent limitations.

Section 301 provides for a number of statutory variances. For example, under the economic hardship variance, the EPA can modify the effluent limitation schedule for any point source upon a showing that the point source is using "the maximum use of technology within the economic capability of the owner or operator" and that the technology being used "will result in reasonable further progress toward the elimination of the discharge of pollutants." CWA § 301(c), 33 U.S.C. § 1311(c). Statutory variances also exist for: (1) effluent limitations for ammonia, chlorine, color, iron, and total phenols, CWA § 301(g), 33 U.S.C. § 1311(g); (2) POTWs, CWA § 301(h), 33 U.S.C. § 1311(h); (3) municipalities, CWA § 301(i), (j), 33 U.S.C. § 1311(i), (j); and (4) point sources discharging BOD or pH into the deep waters, CWA § 301(m), 33 U.S.C. § 1311(m).

The EPA also created variance procedures. The most important EPA variance was the ***fundamentally different factors* (FDF) *variance***, through which a point source that differed in some significant way from the other point sources in its industrial category could apply to the EPA for a variance from the standard effluent limitations for that category. Congress eventually codified this regulatory variance at CWA § 301(n), 33 U.S.C. § 1311(n). In order to receive an FDF variance, "the owner or operator of [the] facility [must] demonstrate[] to the satisfaction of the Administrator that—"

> (A) the facility is fundamentally different with respect to the factors (other than cost) specified in section 1314(b) or 1314(g) of this title and considered by the Administrator in establishing such national effluent limitation guidelines or categorical pretreatment standards;
>
> (B) the application—
>
>> (i) is based solely on information and supporting data submitted to the Administrator during the rulemaking for establishment of the applicable national effluent guidelines or categor-

ical pretreatment standard specifically raising the factors that are fundamentally different for such facility; or

(ii) is based on information and supporting data referred to in clause (i) and information and supporting data the applicant did not have a reasonable opportunity to submit during such rulemaking;

(C) the alternative requirement is no less stringent than justified by the fundamental difference; and

(D) the alternative requirement will not result in a non-water quality environmental impact which is markedly more adverse than the impact considered by the Administrator in establishing such national effluent limitation guidelines or categorical pretreatment standard.

CWA § 301(n)(1), 33 U.S.C. § 1311(n)(1). Dischargers seeking an FDF variance must apply to the Administrator within 180 days of the EPA promulgating or revising the effluent limitation at issue, *id.* § 301(n)(2), 33 U.S.C. § 1311(n)(2), and the EPA then has 180 days to decide on the variance application. *Id.* § 301(n)(3), 33 U.S.C. § 1311(n)(3).

As the FDF variance provision emphasizes, the factors that the EPA uses to set the effluent limitations, other than cost, are critical in determining whether the applicant is "fundamentally different" enough from the EPA's assumptions to warrant a different effluent limitation. Under section 304, in setting BPT the EPA shall take into consideration, besides cost, "the age of equipment and facilities involved, the process employed, the engineering aspects of the application of various types of control techniques, process changes, non-water quality environmental impact (including energy requirements), and such other factors as the Administrator deems appropriate * * *." CWA § 304(b)(1)(B), 33 U.S.C. § 1314(b)(1)(B). Almost identical factors apply to the EPA's determination of BAT, *id.* § 304(b)(2)(B), 33 U.S.C. § 1314(b)(2)(B), and BCT. *Id.* § 304(b)(4)(B), 33 U.S.C. § 1314(b)(4)(B).

B. SECTION 1312: WATER–QUALITY–RELATED EFFLUENT LIMITATIONS

1. Section 1313: Water Quality Standards

While the industry-wide, EPA-set effluent limitations established pursuant to section 301, 33 U.S.C. § 1311, govern most discharge requirements in a typical NPDES permit, Congress also realized that such nationwide standards might not be sufficient to achieve the desired levels of water quality for particular waterbodies. As a result, ***water quality standards*** serve as a backstop to federal effluent limitations, ensuring that all waters achieve the Clean Water Act's goals. As one facet of the Clean Water Act's cooperative federalism, moreover, *states* retained the primary authority to set water quality standards for the waters within their borders even after the 1972 amendments. CWA § 303(a), 33 U.S.C. § 1313(a).

States set water quality standards on a waterbody-by-waterbody basis. The standards dictate the overall water quality that the state desires the waterbody to achieve, based on the proposed or actual uses of the waterbody. Specifically, water quality standards consist of the ***designated uses*** of the waterbody and ***water quality criteria*** that ensure that the waterbody is fit for those uses. CWA § 303(c)(2)(A), 33 U.S.C. § 1313(c)(2)(A). Congress advised states that:

> Such standards shall be such as to protect the public health or welfare, enhance the quality of water and serve the purposes of this chapter. Such standards shall be established taking into consideration their use and value for public water supplies, propagation of fish and wildlife, recreational purposes, and also for taking into consideration their use and value for navigation.

Id. Congress also suggested in the Clean Water Act that all waters should be "fishable and swimmable." *See* CWA § 101(a)(2), 33 U.S.C. § 1251(a)(2). Finally, both the EPA and Congress require states to include an ***antidegradation policy*** in their water quality standards, 40 C.F.R. §§ 131.6(d), 131.12, preventing states from allowing their waters to degrade below the water quality levels that existed when the Clean Water Act took effect.

Nevertheless, states have considerable discretion in setting water quality standards for the waterbodies within their borders, as the next case discusses.

NATURAL RESOURCES DEFENSE COUNCIL, INC. v. UNITED STATES ENVIRONMENTAL PROTECTION AGENCY

16 F.3d 1395 (4th Cir. 1993).

BRITT, DISTRICT JUDGE:

This appeal arises out of consolidated suits brought by the Natural Resources Defense Council ("NRDC") and Environmental Defense Fund ("EDF") to challenge the approval by the United States Environmental Protection Agency ("EPA") of state water quality standards implemented by Maryland and Virginia. Specifically, NRDC and EDF contest the approval of these state standards as they relate to dioxin.[2]

The district court below issued two published opinions regarding this action * * *.

* * * In *NRDC II,* the district court granted EPA's motions to dismiss and for partial summary judgment. The court held that EPA

2. The term "dioxin" generally encompasses a broad range of closely-related toxic organic chemical compounds. The specific dioxin compound at issue on this appeal is 2,3,7,8–Tetrachloro-dibenzo-p-dioxin ("2,3,7,8–TCDD"). It is highly probable that dioxin is a potent carcinogen. Dioxin is primarily a by-product of the chlorine bleaching of pulp associated with paper manufacturing.

sufficiently reviewed the Maryland and Virginia dioxin standards in accordance with the CWA and that EPA did not abuse its discretion in determining that Maryland and Virginia relied on scientifically defensible assumptions in setting dioxin standards. * * *

NRDC and EDF appeal the district court's decisions and make the following assignments of error: (1) that the district court applied an incorrect legal standard in deciding whether EPA properly approved the state water quality standards; (2) that the district court erred in affirming EPA's approval of the state dioxin standards; and (3) that the district court erred in dismissing both the original and amended Count One of the Maryland complaint. Finding no error, we affirm.

I. Facts

* * * For ease of reference, this court summarizes the facts as follows: On 11 September 1989, the Maryland Department of the Environment ("MDE") sought to revise Maryland's water quality standards to allow its waters to contain dioxin in the amount of 1.2 parts per quadrillion ("ppq"), an amount indisputably less protective than EPA's own guidance criterion of .0013 ppq. However, MDE chose this 1.2 ppq criterion because it had been based on the Food and Drug Administration's ("FDA") less conservative cancer potency factor and because MDE felt that EPA's cancer potency factor overestimated the carcinogenic potential of dioxin. After public hearings were held on the matter, Maryland adopted the 1.2 ppq standard and submitted it to EPA for review and approval.

Similar events took place in Virginia. * * *

EPA approved the Maryland standard on 12 September 1990, and approved the Virginia standard on 25 February 1991. * * * EPA concluded that Maryland's and Virginia's use of the 1.2 ppq standard for dioxin was scientifically defensible, protective of human health, and in full compliance with the CWA.

Plaintiffs then initiated this suit in the district court to challenge EPA's 1984 dioxin criteria document and EPA's approval of the Maryland and Virginia water quality standards. * * *

II. Statutory Scheme

The main purpose of the CWA is to "restore and maintain the chemical, physical, and biological integrity of the Nation's waters" by reducing, and eventually eliminating, the discharge of pollutants into these waters. 33 U.S.C. § 1251(a) (Supp. 1993). While the states and EPA share duties in achieving this goal, primary responsibility for establishing appropriate water quality standards is left to the states. *See id.* § 1251(b) (1982). EPA sits in a reviewing capacity of the state-implemented standards, with approval and rejection powers only. 33 U.S.C. § 1313(c) (1982 & Supp. 1993). Water quality standards are a critical component of the

CWA regulatory scheme because such standards serve as a guideline for setting applicable limitations in individual discharge permits.

In an effort to meet the CWA's primary goal, section 402 of the Act (33 U.S.C. § 1342) establishes the National Pollutant Discharge Elimination System ("NPDES") permit program. Under this program, permits are issued by either the EPA or by states that have been allocated NPDES permitting authority. *Id.* § 1342 (1982 & Supp. 1993). However, a state's exercise of NPDES permitting authority is subject to EPA approval. *Id.* §§ 1342(c), (d) (1982 & Supp. 1993). All NPDES permits must take into account technology-based effluent limitations that reflect the pollution reduction achievable based on specific equipment or process changes, without reference to the effect on the receiving water, and, where necessary, more stringent limitations representing the level of control necessary to ensure that the receiving waters attain and maintain state water quality standards. *Id.* §§ 1311(b) (1982), 1313(c) (1982 & Supp. 1993).

Additionally, the CWA requires each state to adopt water quality standards for all waters of that state and to review them at least every three years. *Id.* §§ 1313(a), (b), (c)(1) (1982 & Supp. 1993). To adopt these standards, states must first classify the uses for which the water is to be protected, such as fishing and swimming, and then each state must determine the level of water quality necessary to protect those uses. Thus, the following three factors are considered when adopting or evaluating a water quality standard: (1) one or more designated uses of the state waters involved; (2) certain water quality criteria, expressed as numeric pollutant concentration levels or narrative statements representing a quality of water that supports a particular designated use; and (3) an antidegradation policy to protect existing uses and high quality waters. *Id.* § 1313(c)(2)(A) (Supp. 1993); 40 C.F.R. § 131.

States are directed to adopt numerical water quality criteria for specific toxic pollutants, such as dioxin, for which EPA has published numerical criteria guidance under 33 U.S.C. § 1314(a), if that pollutant can reasonably be expected to interfere with the designated uses of the states' waters. *Id.* § 1313(c)(2)(B) (Supp. 1993). As mentioned previously, states must submit their new or revised water quality standards to EPA for review. *Id.* § 1313(c)(2)(A) (Supp. 1993). On review, each submission must contain at least six elements: (1) use designations consistent with the CWA; (2) a description of methods used and analyses conducted to support revisions of water quality standards; (3) water quality criteria sufficient to protect the designated uses; (4) an antidegradation policy; (5) certification of compliance with state law; and (6) general information to assist EPA in determining the adequacy of the scientific basis for standards that do not include the "fishable/swimmable" uses as set forth in 33 U.S.C. § 1251(a)(2). 40 C.F.R. § 131.6.

EPA regulations also provide that states should develop numerical criteria based on EPA's criteria guidance under § 304(a) of the CWA, EPA's criteria guidance modified to reflect site-specific conditions, or other scientifically defensible methods. 40 C.F.R. § 131.11(b)(1). Alternatively, states should establish narrative criteria or criteria based on biomonitoring methods if numerical criteria cannot be ascertained, or to supplement numerical criteria. *Id.* § 131.11(b)(2).

III. DISCUSSION

* * * *B. The District Court's Statutory Review of EPA's Approval of the State Water Quality Standards*

NRDC argues that the district court applied an incorrect legal standard in reviewing EPA's approval of the state dioxin standards. To support this argument, NRDC contends that EPA's approval of the state dioxin standards is governed principally by § 303(c) of the CWA, 33 U.S.C. § 1313(c). * * * Specifically, NRDC suggests that under sections 101(a) and 303(c), EPA has an independent duty to objectively ensure that state water quality standards meet the requirements of the CWA, and that nothing in the CWA allows EPA to defer to states on this issue. * * * In sum, NRDC maintains that EPA, as well as the district court, had a duty under the CWA to assert a more dominant role in the review process. The court is unpersuaded.

At the outset it is important to note, as the district court correctly found, that *states* have the primary role, under § 303 of the CWA (33 U.S.C. § 1313), in establishing water quality standards. EPA's sole function, in this respect, is to review those standards for approval. 33 U.S.C. § 1313(c) (1982 & Supp. 1993). * * * EPA [] asserts that its duty under the CWA is not to determine whether the states used EPA's recommended criterion but instead to review state water quality standards and determine whether the states' decision is *scientifically defensible and protective of designated uses. See* 40 C.F.R. §§ 131.5(a), 131.6(c), 131.11(a) & (b). While the CWA admittedly is less than crystal clear on this precise issue, the court realizes that it must give due weight to EPA's interpretation and administration of this highly complex statute, particularly when its determination appears to be reasonable and is supported by substantial evidence in the administrative record.

In each Technical Support Document ("TSD") issued by the EPA, the agency conducted an analysis regarding every assumption used by Maryland and Virginia in deriving their respective water quality standards. EPA independently found that each factor and assumption was scientifically defensible. In reviewing the criteria as a whole, EPA also found that they protected the uses that they were designed to protect.

In light of this extensive agency review, the court reiterates that it does not sit as a scientific body and is not called on to meticulously inspect each and every bit of technical evidence. Rather, the court's function is to determine whether proper legal standards were applied. The court agrees with EPA that its duty, under the CWA and the accompanying regulations, is to ensure that the underlying criteria, which are used as the basis of a particular state's water quality standard, are scientifically defensible and are protective of designated uses. * * *

We hold that the district court applied the correct legal standard under the CWA in reviewing EPA's approval of the state water quality standards at issue.

C. The District Court's Affirmance of EPA's Approval of the Maryland and Virginia Dioxin Standards

Appellants argue that the district court's affirmance of EPA's approval of the Maryland and Virginia water standards should be reversed primarily for two reasons. First, they assert that EPA's approval was arbitrary and capricious because it was not based on all relevant factors, ignored key aspects of the record before it, and failed to show a rational connection between the facts found and the choices made. Second, they maintain that EPA's action was contrary to law because it did not ensure, as required by § 303(c) of the CWA (33 U.S.C. § 1313(c)), that state standards were consistent with the CWA; that is, that the standard protected all designated water uses.

Specifically, NRDC attacks EPA's assessment of the Maryland and Virginia standards regarding the first four factors used in the numeric dioxin criteria determination, namely: (1) cancer potency, (2) risk level, (3) fish consumption, and (4) bioconcentration factor ("BCF"). Of these four, NRDC emphasizes its challenge with respect to the latter two factors, fish consumption and BCF. NRDC contends that these two factors, when considered together, are important because they determine the ultimate "exposure" of an individual to dioxin, while the remaining factors only involve choices about risk or toxicity.

1. Fish Consumption

EPA estimates, on a national average, that an individual eats 6.5 grams of fish per day. Maryland and Virginia used this estimate, *inter alia,* in calculating the 1.2 ppq water quality standard. Appellants argue that by affirming EPA's approval of the states' use of this estimate, the district court failed to require EPA to protect subpopulations with higher than average fish consumption, particularly recreational and subsistence fishers. * * * They emphasize that Maryland and Virginia are coastal states and, as such, are entitled—according to EPA recommendations—to higher than average values for fish consumption.

EPA points out that the 6.5 grams per day value is not intended to represent *total* fish consumption but, rather, that *subset* of fish containing the *maximum* residues of dioxin permissible under state law. In setting this value, EPA was establishing a national standard and was well aware that subpopulations might very well consume more than 6.5 *total* grams of fish per day. No evidence was presented that the subpopulations referred to are consuming more than 6.5 grams per day of *maximum residue fish.*

Appellants argue that the risk is especially high for the Mattaponi and Pamunkey Native American peoples who live near a major paper mill in Virginia and who, it is argued, consume higher-than-average amounts of fish. EPA counters that the fish consumption of these subpopulations is speculative at best, that it is based on anecdotal evidence, and that there is no evidence that the fish that actually are consumed are maximum residue fish. In fact, EPA argues that the Native Americans fish in the streams primarily for shad and herring, both of which are anadromous fish that spend a large part of their lives in the oceans and migrate to the rivers only at certain stages during their lives.

The District Court concluded that the EPA, in exercising its judgment, "relied on scientifically defensible means to reach reasoned judgments regarding fish consumption levels." We agree.

2. Bioconcentration Factor (BCF)

Based on EPA laboratory studies, dioxin is more soluble in fat tissues than it is in water. As a result, it tends to accumulate in fish fat tissues at concentrations higher than those present in the water. By averaging the fat content of fish likely to be eaten by an exposed population, a generic BCF can be calculated that reflects dioxin's presence in fish as some multiple of its concentration in ambient water. In its 1984 dioxin criteria document, EPA calculates a dioxin BCF of 5000 for fish of average (3%) lipid content. Maryland and Virginia used this BCF figure, *inter alia,* to derive their numeric water quality criteria.

Appellants challenge EPA's use and approval of a 5000 BCF. They essentially contend that the 5000 BCF figure is outdated because the latest scientific research suggests that a higher BCF should be used. Citing the administrative record, appellants emphasize that: (1) EPA admits that scientific literature and research has changed significantly since preparation of the 1984 dioxin criteria document; (2) EPA further admits that BCF factors now range from 26,000 to 150,000, depending on test species; (3) Virginia conducted a state-specific study which revealed a BCF calculation of 22,000; and (4) Maryland refused to conduct such a study. Appellants contend that, taking all of these factors into account, EPA ignored all the current scientific data and simply "defaulted" to its old BCF assumption. Appellants argue that EPA acted arbitrarily and improperly in not requiring a higher BCF, especially when Virginia and Maryland chose less stringent factors for cancer potency and risk. We disagree.

Once again, we are confronted with an area dominated by complex scientific inquiry and judgment. Although EPA is aware that some recent BCF studies suggested a higher BCF than 5000, EPA maintains that such results are inconclusive and that no compelling scientific evidence indicates that a 5000 BCF is no longer within the range of scientific defensibility. We simply are not in a position to second-guess this technical decision by administrative experts. A review of the record does indicate that several more recent BCF studies have been conducted and that some have suggested a higher BCF; however, the court concludes that the best course of action is to leave this debate to the world of science to ultimately be resolved by those with specialized training in this field. Upon a careful review of the administrative record, we find no clear evidence showing that the 5000 BCF figure is not supported by sound scientific rationale. Accordingly, we hold that EPA did not act arbitrarily in approving the BCF figure used by Maryland and Virginia, and that EPA has made a rational connection between the facts found in the administrative record and its choice to approve the BCF figure. EPA's approval of the 5000 BCF will not be disturbed.

3. Protection of All Stream Uses

Appellants next contend that the district court ratified EPA's approval of the state dioxin standards without ensuring protection of all stream uses. Appellants suggest that when EPA adopted the 1.2 ppq standard, it was required to demonstrate that other stream uses were protected. They maintain that EPA ignored record evidence revealing that the 1.2 ppq standard could cause serious, direct, toxic effects to aquatic life and other wildlife that consume fish tainted with dioxin. Appellants thus argue that EPA did not follow the CWA, its regulations, or its own guidelines by asserting that the water quality criteria were intended to address only one of the minimum statutory uses, human health protection. Essentially, appellants claim that states must adopt a single criterion for dioxin that protects against all identifiable effects on human health, aquatic life, and wildlife. We disagree.

Section 303(c)(2)(A) of the CWA (33 U.S.C. § 1313(c)(2)(A) (Supp. 1993)) requires that new or revised water quality standards "consist of designated uses of the navigable waters involved and the water quality criteria for such waters based upon such uses." * * *

Reference to the regulations also is instructive: "A water quality standard ... defines the water quality goals of a water body, or portion thereof, by designating the use or uses to be made of the water and by setting criteria necessary to protect the uses." 40 C.F.R. §§ 130.3, 131.2. The regulations define "criteria" as "elements of State water quality standards, expressed as constituent concentrations, levels, or narrative statements, representing a quality of water that supports a particular use. When criteria are met, water quality will generally protect the designated use." *Id.* § 131.3(b). Section 131.11(a) further provides that "[s]tates must adopt those water quality criteria that protect the designated use. Such criteria must be based on sound scientific rationale and must contain sufficient parameters or constituents to protect the designated use. For waters with multiple use designations, the criteria shall support the most sensitive use." *Id.* § 131.11(a).

As previously indicated, states should develop either numerical criteria based upon CWA guidance (or other scientific methods), or narrative criteria, if numerical criteria cannot be established. Narrative criteria might also be developed to supplement numerical criteria. *Id.* § 131.11(b).

Clearly, the form of a particular state's water criteria may be either numeric *or narrative,* depending upon the designated use, as the district court correctly recognized.

In view of the above, we find that use of the term "criteria" in CWA § 303(c)(2)(A) and the regulations means that states may adopt multiple criteria for the same pollutant. Thus, where multiple uses are designated for a body of water, there may be multiple criteria applicable to it, as long as the criteria support the most sensitive use of that particular body of water. States have exclusive responsibility to designate water uses. *See* 40 C.F.R. § 131.10. * * *

EPA avers that its review of the Maryland and Virginia standards was limited exclusively to protection of human health against any potential adverse effects (both cancerous and non-cancerous) caused by dioxin. The TSDs reflect this position. * * *

* * * Thus, EPA duly acknowledged that dioxin may have adverse effects on aquatic life. However, EPA also noted that application of existing, separate narrative criteria protecting such aquatic life and wildlife could require more stringent controls in some cases than would be required through use of the human health criteria alone.

EPA conducted an extensive review of the adequacy of the states' criteria to protect human health, aquatic life and wildlife. Appellants have failed to cite any convincing authority showing that states have an obligation under the CWA or its accompanying regulations to adopt a *single* numeric criterion for dioxin that protects against all identifiable effects to human health, aquatic life, and wildlife. * * *

NOTES

1. **Suing the EPA About State Water Quality Standards.** Note that this was a lawsuit filed against *the EPA* regarding standards that Maryland and Virginia—two *states*—adopted. Why would the NRDC choose to sue the EPA rather than Maryland and Virginia? Could the NRDC have pursued lawsuits against the states? If so, where?

2. **The EPA's Role in Approving Water Quality Standards.** How did the Fourth Circuit define the respective roles of the EPA and the states in setting water quality standards? How much authority does the EPA have over water quality standards under this view?

Note the recommended and adopted water quality standards for dioxin involved in this case. The EPA recommends a water quality standard of 0.0013 parts per *quadrillion* (*i.e.*, per 1,000,000,000,000,000 parts water), while Maryland and Virginia adopted a standard of 1.2 parts per quadrillion (ppq). These numbers should give you some sense of how potent a carcinogen (cancer-causing substance) dioxin is—and it is actually worse because the fat-soluble dioxin bioaccumulates, as the case discussed. Nevertheless, although the concentrations involved are small by absolute standards, the water quality standards that Maryland and Virginia adopted allow almost 1000 times more dioxin into the state waterbodies than the EPA recommended. Why did the Fourth Circuit accept the EPA's approval of the dioxin water quality standards? What standard does the EPA apply when reviewing state water quality standards? Why did Maryland and Virginia's dioxin standards meet that test?

3. **Dioxin and Environmental Justice.** Note that the NRDC challenged the dioxin standards in part because, it argued, subsistence fishers, who are often poor, and Native Americans would consume more dioxin-contaminated fish than citizens on average and hence that the water quality standards would not protect these populations. Should the EPA have considered environmental justice issues before it approved the states' dioxin standards? Why or why not?

4. **Scientific Uncertainty, Public Health, and Water Quality Standards.** What role did scientific uncertainty play in Maryland's and Virginia's decisions to adopt the 1.2 ppq dioxin standards? What role did such uncertainty play in the EPA's approval of those standards? What role did it play in the Fourth Circuit's review of the EPA's approval? Should Maryland and Virginia be able to rely on scientific uncertainty to be *less* protective of public health than the EPA recommends? Why or why not? Are water quality standards health-based standards like National Ambient Air Quality Standards (NAAQS) under the Clean Air Act? Why or why not?

5. **Multiple Water Quality Standards for Dioxin?** What do you think of the Fourth Circuit's conclusion that states can set different water quality standards for the same pollutant when a waterbody has multiple designated uses? As a *legal* matter, how does that conclusion square with the EPA's regulatory requirement that water quality criteria "support the most sensitive use"? 40 C.F.R. § 131.11(a). As a *practical* matter, does it make sense for Maryland and Virginia to set multiple dioxin standards for the same waterbody? Why or why not?

6. **Water Quality Standards and Nonpoint Source Pollution.** How far does state discretion in setting water quality standards extend? Can a state, for example, exempt nonpoint sources of pollution from antidegradation review? The Tenth Circuit said yes, further delineating the division of regulatory authority between the EPA and the states under the Clean Water Act:

> It is the position of American Wildlands in this case that Montana's [] antidegradation policy, which does not consider nonpoint source pollution, is not consistent with the Act and must be disapproved by the EPA. The EPA maintains that the Act does not grant it authority to regulate nonpoint sources of pollution, and therefore, it is powerless to disapprove state antidegradation review policies on the basis of how those policies deal with nonpoint source pollution.
>
> The district court, ruling in favor of the EPA, held that "nothing in the CWA demands that a state adopt a regulatory system for nonpoint sources." We agree. In the Act, Congress has chosen not to give the EPA the authority to regulate nonpoint source pollution.
>
> Because the Act nowhere gives the EPA the authority to regulate nonpoint source discharges, the EPA's determination—that Montana's water

> quality standards exempting nonpoint source discharges from antidegradation review are consistent with the Act—is a permissible construction of the Act.

American Wildlands v. Browner, 260 F.3d 1192, 1197 (10th Cir. 2001).

* * *

2. Water Quality Related Effluent Limitations

Water quality standards can affect NPDES permit requirements in two ways. First, under section 301, point source dischargers must comply not only with the relevant EPA-set effluent limitations but also with "any more stringent limitation, including those necessary to meet water quality standards * * * established pursuant to any State law or regulations * * * or any other Federal law or regulation, or required to implement any applicable water quality standard established pursuant to this chapter." CWA §§ 301(b)(1)(C), 33 U.S.C. §§ 1311(b)(1)(C).

Second, states must prepare a list of all waterbodies that currently do not meet their water quality standards, known as ***water-quality-limited waterbodies***. Each state must then establish a priority ranking of the water-quality-limited waterbodies within its jurisdiction and establish a ***total maximum daily load* (TMDL)** for each pollutant contributing to the non-compliance of the waterbody. A TMDL is the total amount of a given pollutant that can be added to a waterbody every day without the water body exceeding the relevant water quality standard. The amount of pollutant established in the TMDL is then divided among the natural background sources of pollution, the nonpoint sources of pollution (known as the ***load allocation* (LA)**), and the point sources of pollution (known as the ***waste load allocation* (WLA)**). As a result, the terms of the point sources' NPDES permits often have to be adjusted to comply with the TMDL.

TMDLs are governed by section 303(d), 33 U.S.C. § 1313(d), and will be discussed in more detail *infra*. Water-quality-related effluent limitations, in contrast, are governed by section 302, 33 U.S.C. § 1312. Under this section,

> Whenever * * * discharges of pollutants from a point source or group of point sources, with the application of effluent limitations required under section 1311(b)(2) of this title, would interfere with the attainment or maintenance of that water quality in a specific portion of the navigable waters which shall assure protection of public health, public water supplies, agricultural and industrial uses, and the protection and propagation of shellfish, fish and wildlife, and allow recreational activities in and on the water, effluent limitations * * * for such point source or sources shall be established which can reasonably be expected to contribute to the attainment or maintenance of such water quality.

CWA § 302(a), 33 U.S.C. § 1312(a). Thus, the EPA has clear authority to modify effluent limitations for particular point sources on particular water bodies to ensure that water quality goals—including and especially the water quality standards—for those particular water bodies are met.

3. Translating Water Quality Standards into Permit Limitations

Translating water quality standards into specific NPDES permit limitations is not always an easy task, especially considering that states and Tribes can establish ***narrative water quality standards and criteria***. The EPA has described the translation process as follows:

1. The process begins when a state or Indian tribe establishes water quality standards for a water body within its jurisdiction, as required by the Clean Water Act. Water quality standards include designated uses for a water body (*e.g.*, public water supply, propagation of fish and wildlife, recreation); water quality criteria necessary to support the designated uses; and a policy for preventing degradation of the quality of water bodies. Water quality criteria include numeric criteria for specific parameters (*e.g.*, copper, chlorine, temperature, pH); toxicity criteria to protect against the aggregate effects of toxic pollutants; and narrative criteria that describe the desired condition of the water body (*e.g.*, free from visible oil sheen).
2. States and tribes assess water bodies to determine whether they are attaining the established standards.
3. After identifying potential water quality problems, the state or tribe sets priorities for which water bodies to target first for further evaluation.
4. The state or tribe may then evaluate the appropriateness of the established water quality standards for specific waters and reaffirm or refine the standards as appropriate.
5. Next, the state or tribe defines what controls on point and nonpoint sources are necessary either through an analysis of the entire water body or by assessing the impact of individual sources of pollution (*e.g.*, a single industrial process wastewater discharge). When assessing point source discharges to determine whether controls based on water quality standards are necessary, an NPDES permitting authority should conduct an analysis to determine whether the discharge causes, has the "reasonable potential" to cause, or contributes to an excursion of any water quality criteria in the receiving water. Where effluent limits based on water quality standards are necessary, the permitting authority allocates responsibility for controls through wasteload allocations and then effluent limits in NPDES permits consistent with those wasteload allocations.

6. Controls on individual sources are established through nonpoint source programs or NPDES permits.
7. Point source effluent monitoring allows the NPDES authority to assess compliance with the required controls and take enforcement actions where necessary.
8. Finally, the state or tribe uses the information gathered from monitoring sources of pollution and the quality of the water body itself to measure progress in attaining water quality standards.

Office of Water, U.S. EPA, *Overview of the Water Quality Standards to Permit Process*, http://cfpub.epa.gov/npdes/wqbasedpermitting/wqoverview.cfm (last updated June 25, 2002). However, the practical difficulty of translating water quality standards into meaningful NPDES permit requirements remains, as can be seen in the following case.

AMERICAN PAPER INSTITUTE, INC. v. UNITED STATES ENVIRONMENTAL PROTECTION AGENCY

996 F.2d 346 (D.C. Cir. 1993).

WALD, CIRCUIT JUDGE:

In these consolidated petitions for review, the American Paper Institute, Inc., the USX Corporation, Westvaco Corporation, the City of Akron, Ohio and a host of utilities contest several new Environmental Protection Agency ("EPA") regulations interpreting the Clean Water Act ("CWA" or the "Act") and its amendments. The petitioners primarily take issue with an EPA rule requiring writers of pollution discharge permits to use one of three methods to interpret state water quality standards containing so-called "narrative criteria" (*e.g.,* "no toxics in toxic amounts") so as to create precise chemical-specific effluent limitations in those permits. For the reasons discussed below, we find the regulation in question * * * to constitute reasonable, authorized attempts at necessary gap-filling in the CWA statutory scheme. Accordingly, we deny the petitions for review.

I.

In enacting the CWA, Congress sought to "restore and maintain the chemical, physical, and biological integrity of the Nation's waters." 33 U.S.C. § 1251(a). Toward that end, Congress constructed a system in which discharges of pollutants into the waters of the United States from "point source[s]"—"discernable [*sic*], confined and discrete conveyance[s]," 33 U.S.C. § 1362(14), such as factory pipes—are normally permissible only if made pursuant to the terms of a National Pollution Discharge Elimination System ("NPDES") permit. *See* 33 U.S.C. §§ 1311(a), 1342. Under the Act, those licenses must be obtained from the EPA or, in the approximately 40 states the EPA has authorized to administer their own NPDES program, from a designated state agency. *See* 33 U.S.C. § 1342(a)-(d); *see also* 57 Fed. Reg. 43,733, 43,734–35

(1992). In either case, section 301 of the Act mandates that every permit contain (1) effluent limitations that reflect the pollution reduction achievable by using technologically practicable controls, *see* 33 U.S.C. § 1311(b)(1)(A), and (2) any more stringent pollutant release limitations necessary for the waterway receiving the pollutant to meet "water quality standards." 33 U.S.C. § 1311(b)(1)(C).

Of primary importance in this case is section 301's second requirement—*i.e.,* that permits contain discharge limitations sufficient to assure that the receiving waterway satisfies water quality standards. Under the CWA, the water quality standards referred to in section 301 are primarily the states' handiwork. * * *

In accord with Congress' intent to cast the states in the featured role in the promulgation of water quality standards, the EPA may step in and promulgate water quality standards itself only in limited circumstances. It may act only where (1) it determines that a state's proposed new or revised standard does not measure up to CWA requirements *and* the state refuses to accept EPA-proposed revisions to the standard or (2) a state does not act to promulgate or update a standard but, in the EPA's view, a new or revised standard is necessary to meet CWA muster. *See* 33 U.S.C. § 1313(c)(3)-(4).

The water quality standards that emerge from this state/federal *pas de deux* have two primary components: designated "uses" for a body of water (*e.g.,* public water supply, recreation, agriculture) and a set of "criteria" specifying the maximum concentration of pollutants that may be present in the water without impairing its suitability for designated uses. *See* 33 U.S.C. § 1313(c)(2)(A). Criteria, in turn, come in two varieties: specific numeric limitations on the concentration of a specific pollutant in the water (*e.g.,* no more than .05 milligrams of chromium per liter) or more general narrative statements applicable to a wide set of pollutants (*e.g.,* no toxic pollutants in toxic amounts). In deciding what criteria suit particular designated uses, the states are not left entirely to their own devices. As required by the CWA, *see* 33 U.S.C. § 1314(a)(1), the EPA has promulgated a set of *recommended* numeric criteria for certain listed pollutants that the states can, and quite often do, refer to in selecting appropriate criteria. *See* 57 Fed. Red. 60,848, 50,874 (1992).

Of course, the water quality standards by themselves have no effect on pollution; the rubber hits the road when the state-created standards are used as the basis for specific effluent limitations in NPDES permits. As noted above, once a water quality standard has been promulgated, section 301 of the CWA requires all NPDES permits for point sources to incorporate discharge limitations necessary to satisfy that standard. On its face, section 301 imposes this strict requirement as to all standards—*i.e.,* permits must incorporate limitations necessary to meet standards that rely on narrative criteria to protect a designated use as well as standards that contain specific numeric criteria for particular chemicals. The distinctive nature of each kind of criteria, however, inevitably leads to significant distinctions in how the two types of criteria are applied to derive effluent limitations in individual permits. When the standard includes numeric criteria, the process is fairly straightforward: the permit merely adopts a limitation on a point source's effluent discharge necessary to keep the concentration of a pollutant in a waterway at or below the numeric benchmark. Narrative criteria, however, present more difficult problems: How is a state or federal NPDES permit writer to divine what limitations on effluent discharges are necessary to assure that the waterway contains, for example, "no toxics in toxic amounts"? Faced with this conundrum, some permit writers threw up their hands and, contrary to the Act, simply ignored water quality standards including narrative criteria altogether when deciding upon permit limitations. Additionally, when standards containing narrative criteria were enforced—often through the device of whole effluent discharge limitations based on biological monitoring techniques, *see* 57 Fed. Reg. 51,400, 51,402 (1983)—the lack of standardized procedures made it impossible to even approximate consistency in the translation of criteria into permit limitations. *Cf.* 57 Fed. Reg. 60,848, 60,851 (1992). Thus, in the EPA's view, the lack of a required procedure for developing water-quality-based permit limits from narrative criteria hamstrung attempts to fulfill the statutory requirement that NPDES permits contain limitations necessary to meet all water quality standards. *See* 54 Fed. Reg. 23,868, 23,877 (1989).

II.

A. *Interpreting Narrative Criteria to Create Chemical–Specific Limitations*

To address these difficulties, the EPA promulgated the regulation under attack here, 40 C.F.R. § 122.44(d)(1)(vi). That rule requires NPDES permit writers to use one of three mechanisms to translate relevant narrative criteria into *chemical-specific* effluent limitations. Specifically, the regulation provides that a permit writer must establish effluent limits from narrative criteria by using (1) a calculated numeric water quality criterion derived from such tools as a proposed state numeric criterion or an "explicit state policy or regulation interpreting its narrative water quality criterion"; (2) the EPA recommended numeric water quality criteria, but only on a "case-by-case basis" and "supplemented where necessary by other relevant information"; and/or (3) assuming certain conditions are met, limitations on the discharge of an "indicator parameter," *i.e.,* a different pollutant also found in the point source's effluent.

We employ familiar principles in reviewing the disputed regulation. Unless we find that the EPA's rule contravenes the unambiguously conveyed intent of Congress as to this precise issue, we will reject the petitioners' challenge so long as the regulation appears designed to implement the statutory scheme by reasonable means. *See generally Chevron USA Inc. v. Natural Resources Defense Council, Inc.,* 467 U.S. 837, 843–44 (1984).

In arguing that the EPA's rule flunks the first prong of this test, the petitioners highlight the alleged tension between the regulation's delegation of authority to a permit writer to interpret narrative criteria in each particular case and the CWA system, outlined above, in which generally applicable water quality standards are adopted by the states only after public input and the weighing of the competing policy considerations set out in the Act. In function if not in form, petitioners argue, the EPA regulation requires states to cede their standard-setting authority to an unaccountable bureaucrat * * *.

We are unpersuaded. As we understand it, the regulation does not supplant—either formally or functionally—the CWA's basic statutory framework for the creation of water quality standards; rather, it provides alternative mechanisms through which *previously adopted* water quality standards containing narrative criteria may be applied to create effective limitations on effluent emissions. As long as narrative criteria are permissible—and the petitioners do not contend that they are not—and must be enforced through limitations in particular permits, a permit writer will inevitably have some discretion in applying the criteria to a particular case. * * * The EPA's new regulation merely requires that permit writers engage in this task to create chemical-specific limitations on discharges of pollutants and gives those writers three tools with which to do this work in a fairly regularized fashion. *See* 54 Fed. Reg. 23,868, 23,877 (1989); *see also id.* at 23,875. The regulation thus seems to provide an eminently reasonable means of effectuating the intent of the previously adopted narrative criteria as well as Congress' own intent, made explicit in section 301 of the CWA, that *all* state water quality standards be enforced through meaningful limitations in individual NPDES permits.

Petitioners' related argument that the regulation clashes with Congress' intent to give the states the leading role in creating water quality standards also fails, despite petitioners' highlighting of two additional factors they say expose improper federal usurpation of state prerogatives. First, they note that one of the three alternative interpretive mechanisms allowed under the regulation relies on the recommended federal numeric criteria to determine what a state narrative criterion means. But that option is of course only one of three choices enumerated in the regulation. *See id.* at 23,876–77. Moreover, the option in question does not require state or federal permit writers to apply the federal guidelines "whole hog"; the federal standard is to be employed on a "case-by-case basis," and may be "supplemented where necessary by other relevant information." 40 C.F.R. § 122.44(d)(1)(vi)(B). Thus, this alternative requires a permit writer to tailor the federal standard to any relevant site-specific circumstances in order to effectuate the intent of a particular state narrative criterion. In sum, we are not persuaded that the regulation's inclusion—as one of three choices—of an interpretive mechanism that uses the recommended federal criteria only as a starting point impermissibly alters the statutorily created balance of state and federal power.

Petitioners' second argument based on federalism concerns stresses the fact that in the handful of states where the federal government still runs the NPDES permit program, a *federal* permit writer is now charged with interpreting the state standard. Of course, federal writers had been performing this function long before the promulgation of the regulation at issue here. Moreover, the CWA provides states with ample legal recourse if the federal employee strays from the state's understanding of its yardstick. Specifically, under section 401 of the Act, a state may refuse to certify a permit—and thus stop its issuance—if the permit limitations do not "comply" with the state's interpretation of its water quality standards. *See* 33 U.S.C. § 1341(a)(1). The state's ability to deny certification ultimately assures that, under the new regulatory regime as well as under the old, it has sufficient firepower to insist that its standards are accurately interpreted by federal employees. * * *

NOTES

1. **The D.C Circuit's Standard of Review.** What standard did the D.C. Circuit use to review the EPA's permit-writing regulation? Why?

2. **The Federalism Implications of Translating Water Quality Standards into NPDES Permit Requirements.** Why did the American Paper Institute object to the EPA's regulation? What principles of federalism did it rely upon? What did the D.C. Circuit decide about the federalism implications of the EPA's regulation? Why? In general, how did the D.C. Circuit view the relationship between the EPA and the states in implementing the Clean Water Act? Was this view consistent with other cases that you have read? Why or why not?

* * *

C. SECTION 1316: NATIONAL STANDARDS OF PERFORMANCE FOR NEW SOURCES

As noted above, the EPA sets effluent limitations for *existing* sources pursuant to section 301. *New* point sources, in contrast, are subject to the ***new source performance standards*** **(NSPS)** that the EPA establishes pursuant to section 306, 33 U.S.C. § 1316. A "new source," for purposes of section 306, is "any source, the construction of which is commenced after the publication of proposed regulations prescribing a standard of performance under this section which will be applicable to such source, if such standard is thereafter promulgated in accordance with this section." CWA § 306(a)(2), 33 U.S.C § 1316(a)(2). In other words, the EPA's pace in setting NSPS determines whether a source is "new" or not. However, once the EPA promulgates NSPS for a particular category of dischargers, "it shall be unlawful for any owner or operator of any new source to operate such source in violation of any standard of performance applicable to such source." CWA § 306(e), 33 U.S.C. § 1316(e).

NSPS, like effluent limitations, are technology-based standards. Specifically, an NSPS is "a standard for the control of the discharge of pollutants which reflects the greatest degree of effluent reduction which the Administrator determines to be achievable through application of the ***best available demonstrated control technology*** **[BADT]**, processes, operating methods, or other alternatives, including, where practicable, a standard permitting no discharge of pollutants." CWA § 306(a)(1), 33 U.S.C. § 1316(a)(1) (emphasis added).

D. SECTION 1317: TOXIC AND PRETREATMENT EFFLUENT STANDARDS

1. Toxic Pollutants: Effluent Limitations and Effluent Standards

In section 307(a) of the Clean Water Act, 33 U.S.C. § 1317(a), Congress addressed toxic pollutants. It established an initial list of toxic pollutants for the EPA to regulate, then authorized the EPA to add and remove pollutants from the list as needed. In revising the list, the Administrator of the EPA "shall take into account toxicity of the pollutant, its persistence, degradability, the usual or potential presence of the affected organisms in any waters, the importance of affected organisms, and the nature and extent of the effect of the toxic pollutant on such organisms." CWA § 307(a)(1), 33 U.S.C. § 1317(a)(1).

Congress then reiterated section 301's basic technology-based standard for toxic effluent limitations: **BAT**. CWA § 307(a)(2), 33 U.S.C. § 1317(a)(2). In addition, however:

> The Administrator, in his discretion, may publish in the Federal Register a proposed effluent standard (which may include a prohibition) establishing requirements for a toxic pollutant which, if an effluent limitation is applicable to a class or category of point sources, shall be applicable to such category or class only if such standard imposes more stringent requirements. Such published effluent standard (or prohibition) shall take into account the toxicity of the pollutant, its persistence, degradability, the usual or potential presence of the affected organisms in any waters, the importance of the affected organisms and the nature and extent of the effect of the toxic pollutant on such organisms, and the extent to which effective control is being or may be achieved under other regulatory authority.

Id. Thus, the EPA-set ***toxic effluent standards*** are even more stringent than the BAT-based ***toxic effluent limitations*** and can include a complete prohibition on the discharge of a particular toxic pollutant. In addition, the EPA must set toxic effluent standards to "provide[] an ample margin of safety." CWA § 307(a)(4), 33 U.S.C. § 1317(a)(4).

In the context of toxic pollutant effluent limitations and standards, it is worth noting that Congress itself was willing to prohibit the discharge of certain pollutants. For example, section 301 makes it illegal for any point source "to discharge any radiological, chemical, or biological warfare agent, and high-level radioactive waste, or any medical waste into the navigable waters." CWA § 301(f), 33 U.S.C. § 1311(f). Thus, the effluent limitations for these particular pollutants are effectively set, by statute, at zero.

2. Pretreatment Standards

In section 307(b) of the Clean Water Act, 33 U.S.C. § 1317(b), Congress established the ***pretreatment standards***. Pretreatment standards apply to ***indirect dischargers***—that is, to point sources that discharge into a POTW rather than into navigable waters or the ocean. Because these point sources do not discharge into jurisdictional waters, they do not have to get an individual NPDES permit. Nevertheless, their activities can disrupt the effectiveness of POTWs, especially if the indirect dischargers were allowed to overload the POTW with toxic pollutants, which most POTWs are not equipped to treat.

To prevent water quality problems arising from overloaded POTWs, Congress directed the EPA to promulgate pretreatment standards for existing sources "for the introduction of pollutants into treatment works * * * which are publicly owned for those pollutants which are determined not to be susceptible to treatment by such treatment works or which would interfere with the operation of such treatment works." CWA § 307(b)(1), 33 U.S.C. § 1317(b)(1). Rather complexly, for toxic pollutants Congress noted that:

> If, in the case of any toxic pollutant under [§ 1317(a)] introduced by a source into a publicly owned treatment works, the treatment by such works removes all or any part of such toxic pollutant and the discharge from such works does not violate that effluent limitation or standard which would be applicable to such toxic pollutant if it were discharged by such source other than through a publicly owned treatment works, and does not prevent sludge use or disposal by such works in accordance with section 1345 of this title, then the pretreatment requirements for the sources actually discharging such toxic pollutant into such publicly owned treatment works may be revised by the owner or operator of such works to reflect the removal of such toxic pollutant by such works.

Id. In other words, if the POTW can in fact handle the toxic pollutants sent to it, so that neither its own effluent discharge nor its sewage sludge violates the Clean Water Act's toxics standards, then the *POTW* can adjust the pretreatment standards. In addition, state and local governments remain free to impose any pretreatment requirements they desire, so long as those requirements do not conflict with the EPA's pretreatment standards. CWA § 307(b)(4), 33 U.S.C. § 1317(b)(4).

The EPA is supposed to set pretreatment standards for new indirect dischargers in various industry categories at the same time that it sets the NSPS for those categories. The pretreatment standards "shall prevent the discharge of any pollutant into such treatment works, which pollutant may interfere with, pass through, or otherwise be incompatible with such works." CWA § 307(c), 33 U.S.C. § 1317(c). Once the EPA sets pretreatment standards, moreover, noncompliance with those standards is unlawful. CWA § 307(d), 33 U.S.C. § 1317(d).

With this review of section 307, the discussion of the actual NPDES discharge standards is complete. These requirements can be charted out as shown in Figure 5–11.

Figure 5-11: The NPDES Permit Requirements

	CONVENTIONAL POLLUTANTS	TOXIC POLLUTANTS	NON-CONVENTIONAL POLLUTANTS
POTWs	Secondary Treatment	Secondary Treatment, + Pretreatment Requirements	Secondary Treatment
EXISTING POINT SOURCES	BPT by 1977; BCT by 1984	BAT, unless a toxic effluent standard applies	BPT by 1977; BAT by 1989
NEW POINT SOURCES	NSPS (BADT)	BAT, unless a toxic effluent standard applies	NSPS (BADT)
INDIRECT DISCHARGERS	Pretreatment Standards	Pretreatment Standards	Pretreatment Standards

E. SECTION 1318: MONITORING, REPORTING, AND INSPECTION REQUIREMENTS

Enforcement of the Clean Water Act often depends on section 308, 33 U.S.C. § 1318. Under section 308, every Clean Water Act permit must require

> the owner or operator of any point source to (i) establish and maintain such records, (ii) make such reports, (iii) install, use, and maintain such monitoring equipment or methods (including, where appropriate, biological monitoring methods), (iv) sample such effluents (in accordance with such methods, at such locations, at such intervals, and in such manner as the Administrator shall prescribe), and (v) provide such other information as [the enforcing agency] may reasonably require * * *.

CWA § 308(a)(4)(A), 33 U.S.C. § 1318(a)(4)(A). In addition, the enforcing agency or its authorized contractor has a right to enter any point source, to inspect the point source's records and monitoring equipment, and to sample the effluents. CWA § 308(a)(4)(B), 33 U.S.C. § 1318(a)(4)(B).

In general, the EPA and the state permitting agencies require point sources to monitor their discharges and report on a daily basis. These reports are called ***Daily Monitoring Reports*** **(DMRs)**, and, by statute, they are public records. CWA § 308(b), 33 U.S.C. § 1318(b). As a result, it is very easy for both the state and federal enforcement agencies *and* for private citizens to determine whether a particular point source is violating the Clean Water Act—particularly because the Act criminally punishes "[a]ny person who knowingly makes any false material statement, representation, or certification in any application, record, report, plan, or other document filed or required to be maintained * * * or who knowingly falsifies, tampers with, or renders inaccurate any monitoring device or method required to be maintained * * *." CWA § 309(c)(4), 33 U.S.C. § 1319(c)(4). Conviction for false reporting can "be punished by a fine of not more than $10,000 or by imprisonment for not more than 2 years, or by both." *Id.*

F. SECTION 1343: OCEAN DISCHARGE CRITERIA

The final section that contributes to the terms of an NPDES permit is section 403, 33 U.S.C. § 1343. Under section 403, no NPDES permit "for a discharge into *the territorial sea, the waters of the contiguous zone, or the oceans* shall be issued" except in compliance with EPA-issued guidelines for such discharges, known as the ***ocean discharge criteria***. CWA § 403(a), 33 U.S.C. § 1343(a) (emphasis added). According to the statute, the ocean discharge criteria are "guidelines for determining the degradation of the waters of the territorial seas, the contiguous zone, and the oceans" and must include:

(A) the effect of the disposal of pollutants on human health or welfare, including but not limited to plankton, fish, shellfish, wildlife, shorelines, and beaches;

(B) the effect of disposal of pollutants on marine life including the transfer, concentration, and dispersal of pollutants or their byproducts through biological, physical, and chemical processes; changes in marine ecosystem diversity, productivity, and stability; and species and community population changes;

(C) the effects of disposal of pollutants on esthetic, recreation, and economic values;

(D) the persistence and permanence of the effects of disposal of pollutants;

(E) the effect of the disposal at varying rates, of particular volumes and concentrations of pollutants;

(F) other possible locations and methods of disposal or recycling of pollutants including land-based alternatives; and

(G) the effect on alternative uses of the oceans, such as mineral exploitation and scientific study.

CWA § 403(c), 33 U.S.C. § 1343(c).

The EPA promulgated the current ocean discharge criteria in 1980. 45 Fed. Reg. 65,942 (Oct. 3, 1980). It indicated in 2000 that it would be issuing new ocean discharge criteria, 65 Fed. Reg. 42,936 (July 12, 2000), but those new regulations were stalled when the Bush Administration took office in January 2001 and have not reappeared.

G. WATER INTAKE REGULATION

Other NPDES permit requirements do exist. One of the NPDES permit program's more unusual requirements regulates water *intake* at certain kinds of large facilities, rather than discharges of pollutants. Many facilities such as power plants need to take in large quantities of water from nearby waterbodies for cooling purposes, and both the pumping itself and the amount of water taken in can affect the waterbody's integrity.

Congress sought to address these issues through Section 316 of the Act, 33 U.S.C. § 1326. Section 316(a) allows more stringent controls of thermal discharges from point sources if necessary "to assure the protection and propagation of a balanced, indigenous population of shellfish, fish, and wildlife in and on the body of water into which the discharge is to be made. . . ." Section 316(b) also can impose requirements on NPDES permits, but it is a very unusual provision because it deals with water *intake*—not discharges of pollutants. Under this provision, "[a]ny standard established pursuant to section 1311 of this title [standard technology-based effluent limitations for existing sources] or section 1316 of this title [new source performance standards] and applicable to a point source shall require that the location, design, construction, and capacity of cooling water intake structures reflect ***the best technology available for minimizing adverse environmental impact***." 33 U.S.C. § 1326(b) (emphasis added).

In April 2009, the U.S. Supreme Court addressed the EPA's application of Section 316(b) to existing sources, mostly power plants. While doing so, the Court provided a helpful comparison of the Clean Water Act's various technology-based standards—and extensively discussed the role of economics and cost-benefit analysis in establishing those standards.

ENTERGY CORPORATION v. RIVERKEEPER, INC.

556 U.S. 208 (2009).

SCALIA, J., delivered the opinion of the Court, in which ROBERTS, C.J., and KENNEDY, THOMAS, and ALITO, JJ., joined. BREYER, J., filed an opinion concurring in part and dissenting in part. STEVENS, J., filed a dissenting opinion, in which SOUTER and GINSBURG, JJ., joined.

These cases concern a set of regulations adopted by the Environmental Protection Agency (EPA or agency) under § 316(b) of the Clean Water Act, 33 U.S.C. § 1326(b). 69 Fed. Reg. 41576 (2004). Respondents—

environmental groups and various States[1]—challenged those regulations, and the Second Circuit set them aside. The issue for our decision is whether, as the Second Circuit held, the EPA is not permitted to use cost-benefit analysis in determining the content of regulations promulgated under § 1326(b).

I

Petitioners operate—or represent those who operate—large power-plants. In the course of generating power, those plants also generate large amounts of heat. To cool their facilities, petitioners employ "cooling water intake structures" that extract water from nearby water sources. These structures pose various threats to the environment, chief among them the squashing against intake screens (elegantly called "impingement") or suction into the cooling system ("entrainment") of aquatic organisms that live in the affected water sources. Accordingly, the facilities are subject to regulation under the Clean Water Act, 33 U.S.C. § 1251 *et seq.,* which mandates:

> "Any standard established pursuant to section 1311 of this title or section 1316 of this title and applicable to a point source shall require that the location, design, construction, and capacity of cooling water intake structures reflect the best technology available for minimizing adverse environmental impact." § 1326(b).

Sections 1311 and 1316, in turn, employ a variety of "best technology" standards to regulate the discharge of effluents into the Nation's waters.

The § 1326(b) regulations at issue here were promulgated by the EPA after nearly three decades in which the determination of the "best technology available for minimizing [cooling water intake structures'] adverse environmental impact" was made by permit-issuing authorities on a case-by-case basis, without benefit of a governing regulation. The EPA's initial attempt at such a regulation came to nought when the Fourth Circuit determined that the agency had failed to adhere to the procedural requirements of the Administrative Procedure Act. The EPA withdrew the regulation, 44 Fed. Reg. 32956 (1979), and instead published "draft guidance" for use in implementing § 1326(b)'s requirements via site-specific permit decisions under § 1342.

In 1995, the EPA entered into a consent decree which, as subsequently amended, set a multiphase timetable for the EPA to promulgate regulations under § 1326(b). In the first phase the EPA adopted regulations governing certain new, large cooling water intake structures. 66 Fed. Reg. 65256 (2001) (Phase I rules); see 40 CFR §§ 125.80(a), 125.81(a) (2008). Those rules require new facilities with water-intake flow greater than 10 million gallons per day to, among other things, restrict their inflow "to a level commensurate with that which can be attained by a

1. The EPA and its Administrator appeared as respondents in support of petitioners. References to "respondents" throughout the opinion refer only to those parties challenging the EPA rules at issue in these cases.

closed-cycle recirculating cooling water system."[2] § 125.84(b)(1). New facilities with water-intake flow between 2 million and 10 million gallons per day may alternatively comply by, among other things, reducing the volume and velocity of water removal to certain levels. § 125.84(c). And all facilities may alternatively comply by demonstrating, among other things, "that the technologies employed will reduce the level of adverse environmental impact ... to a comparable level" to what would be achieved by using a closed-cycle cooling system. § 125.84(d). These regulations were upheld in large part by the Second Circuit in *Riverkeeper, Inc. v. EPA,* 358 F.3d 174 (2004).

The EPA then adopted the so-called "Phase II" rules at issue here.[3] 69 Fed. Reg. 41576. They apply to existing facilities that are point sources, whose primary activity is the generation and transmission (or sale for transmission) of electricity, and whose water-intake flow is more than 50 million gallons of water per day, at least 25 percent of which is used for cooling purposes. Over 500 facilities, accounting for approximately 53 percent of the Nation's electric-power generating capacity, fall within Phase II's ambit. Those facilities remove on average more than 214 billion gallons of water per day, causing impingement and entrainment of over 3.4 billion aquatic organisms per year. 69 Fed. Reg. 41586.

To address those environmental impacts, the EPA set "national performance standards," requiring Phase II facilities (with some exceptions) to reduce "impingement mortality for all life stages of fish and shellfish by 80 to 95 percent from the calculation baseline"; a subset of facilities must also reduce entrainment of such aquatic organisms by "60 to 90 percent from the calculation baseline." 40 CFR § 125.94(b)(1), (2); see § 125.93 (defining "calculation baseline"). Those targets are based on the environmental improvements achievable through deployment of a mix of remedial technologies, 69 Fed. Reg. 41599, which the EPA determined were "commercially available and economically practicable," *id.,* at 41602.

In its Phase II rules, however, the EPA expressly declined to mandate adoption of closed-cycle cooling systems or equivalent reductions in impingement and entrainment, as it had done for new facilities subject to the Phase I rules. It refused to take that step in part because of the "generally high costs" of converting existing facilities to closed-cycle operation, and because "other technologies approach the performance of this option." Thus, while closed-cycle cooling systems could reduce impingement and entrainment mortality by up to 98 percent, the cost of rendering all Phase II facilities closed-cycle-compliant would be approximately $3.5 billion per year, nine times the estimated cost of compliance with the Phase II performance standards. Moreover, Phase II facilities compelled to convert

2. Closed-cycle cooling systems recirculate the water used to cool the facility, and consequently extract less water from the adjacent waterway, proportionately reducing impingement and entrainment.

3. The EPA has also adopted Phase III rules for facilities not subject to the Phase I and Phase II regulations. 71 Fed. Reg. 35006 (2006). A challenge to those regulations is currently before the Fifth Circuit, where proceedings have been stayed pending disposition of these cases.

to closed-cycle cooling systems "would produce 2.4 percent to 4.0 percent less electricity even while burning the same amount of coal," possibly requiring the construction of "20 additional 400–MW plants ... to replace the generating capacity lost." The EPA thus concluded that "[a]lthough not identical, the ranges of impingement and entrainment reduction are similar under both options.... [Benefits of compliance with the Phase II rules] can approach those of closed-cycle recirculating at less cost with fewer implementation problems."

The regulations permit the issuance of site-specific variances from the national performance standards if a facility can demonstrate either that the costs of compliance are "significantly greater than" the costs considered by the agency in setting the standards, 40 CFR § 125.94(a)(5)(i), or that the costs of compliance "would be significantly greater than the benefits of complying with the applicable performance standards," § 125.94(a)(5)(ii). Where a variance is warranted, the permit-issuing authority must impose remedial measures that yield results "as close as practicable to the applicable performance standards." § 125.94(a)(5)(i), (ii).

Respondents challenged the EPA's Phase II regulations, and the Second Circuit granted their petition for review and remanded the regulations to the EPA. The Second Circuit identified two ways in which the EPA could permissibly consider costs under 33 U.S.C. § 1326(b): (1) in determining whether the costs of remediation "can be 'reasonably borne' by the industry," and (2) in determining which remedial technologies are the most cost-effective, that is, the technologies that reach a specified level of benefit at the lowest cost. It concluded, however, that cost-benefit analysis, which "compares the costs and benefits of various ends, and chooses the end with the best net benefits," is impermissible under § 1326(b).

* * * We then granted certiorari limited to the following question: "Whether [§ 1326(b)] ... authorizes the [EPA] to compare costs with benefits in determining 'the best technology available for minimizing adverse environmental impact' at cooling water intake structures."

II

In setting the Phase II national performance standards and providing for site-specific cost-benefit variances, the EPA relied on its view that § 1326(b)'s "best technology available" standard permits consideration of the technology's costs and of the relationship between those costs and the environmental benefits produced. That view governs if it is a reasonable interpretation of the statute—not necessarily the only possible interpretation, nor even the interpretation deemed *most* reasonable by the courts.

As we have described, § 1326(b) instructs the EPA to set standards for cooling water intake structures that reflect "the best technology available for minimizing adverse environmental impact." The Second Circuit took that language to mean the technology that achieves the greatest reduction in adverse environmental impacts at a cost that can reasonably be borne by the industry. * * * But "best technology" may also describe the technology that *most efficiently* produces some good. In common parlance one could certainly use the phrase "best technology" to refer to that which produces a good at the lowest per-unit cost, even if it produces a lesser quantity of that good than other available technologies.

Respondents contend that this latter reading is precluded by the statute's use of the phrase "for minimizing adverse environmental impact." Minimizing, they argue, means reducing to the smallest amount possible, and the "best technology available for minimizing adverse environmental impacts," must be the economically feasible technology that achieves the greatest possible reduction in environmental harm. But "minimize" is a term that admits of degree and is not necessarily used to refer exclusively to the "greatest possible reduction." For example, elsewhere in the Clean Water Act, Congress declared that the procedures implementing the Act "shall encourage the drastic minimization of paperwork and interagency decision procedures." 33 U.S.C. § 1251(f). If respondents' definition of the term "minimize" is correct, the statute's use of the modifier "drastic" is superfluous.

Other provisions in the Clean Water Act also suggest the agency's interpretation. When Congress wished to mandate the greatest feasible reduction in water pollution, it did so in plain language: The provision governing the discharge of toxic pollutants into the Nation's waters requires the EPA to set "effluent limitations [which] shall require the *elimination* of discharges of all pollutants if the Administrator finds ... that such elimination is technologically and economically achievable," § 1311(b)(2)(A) (emphasis added). See also § 1316(a)(1) (mandating "where practicable, a standard [for new point sources] permitting *no discharge* of pollutants" (emphasis added)). Section 1326(b)'s use of the less ambitious goal of "minimizing adverse environmental impact" suggests, we think, that the agency retains some discretion to determine the extent of reduction that is warranted under the circumstances. That determination could plausibly involve a consideration of the benefits derived from reductions and the costs of achieving them. It seems to us, therefore, that the phrase "best technology available," even with the added specification "for minimizing adverse environmental impact," does not unambiguously preclude cost-benefit analysis.

Respondents' alternative (and, alas, also more complex) argument rests upon the structure of the Clean Water Act. The Act provided that during its initial implementation period existing "point sources"—discrete conveyances from which pollutants are or may be discharged, 33 U.S.C. § 1362(14)—were subject to "effluent limitations ... which shall require the application of the *best practicable control technology* currently available." § 1311(b)(1)(A) (emphasis added). (We shall call this the "BPT" test.) Following that transition period, the Act initially mandated adoption, by July 1, 1983 (later extended to March 31, 1989), of stricter effluent limitations requiring "application of the *best available technology economically achievable* for such category or class, which will result in reasonable further progress toward the national goal of eliminating the discharge of all pollutants." § 1311(b)(2)(A) (emphasis added). (We shall call this the "BATEA" test.) Subsequent amendment limited application of this standard to toxic and nonconventional pollutants, and for the remainder established a (presumably laxer) test of "best conventional-pollutant control technology." § 1311(b)(2)(E). (We shall call this "BCT.") Finally, § 1316 subjected certain categories of new point sources to "the greatest degree of effluent reduction which the Administrator determines to be achievable through application of the *best available demonstrated control technology*." § 1316(a)(1) (emphasis added); § 1316(b)(1)(B). (We shall call this the "BADT" test.) The provision at issue here, applicable not to effluents but to cooling water intake structures, requires, as we have described, "the *best technology available for minimizing adverse environmental impact*," § 1326(b) (emphasis added). (We shall call this the "BTA" test.)

The first four of these tests are elucidated by statutory factor lists that guide their implementation. To take the standards in (presumed) order of increasing stringency: In applying the BPT test the EPA is instructed to consider, among other factors, "the total cost of application of technology in relation to the effluent reduction benefits to be achieved." § 1314(b)(1)(B). In applying the BCT test it is instructed to consider "the *reasonableness of the relationship* between the costs of attaining a reduction in effluents and the effluent reduction benefits derived." § 1314(b)(4)(B) (emphasis added). And in applying the BATEA and BADT tests the EPA is instructed to consider the "cost of achieving such effluent reduction." §§ 1314(b)(2)(B), 1316(b)(1)(B). There is no such elucidating language applicable to the BTA test at issue here. * * *

The Second Circuit, in rejecting the EPA's use of cost-benefit analysis, relied in part on the propositions that (1) cost-benefit analysis is precluded under the BATEA and BADT tests; and (2) that, insofar as the permissibility of cost-benefit analysis is concerned, the BTA test (the one at issue here) is to be treated the same as those two. It is not obvious to us that the first of these propositions is correct, but we need not pursue that point, since we assuredly do not agree with the second. It is certainly reasonable for the agency to conclude that the BTA test need not be interpreted to permit only what those other two tests permit. Its text is not identical to theirs. It has the relatively modest goal of "minimizing adverse environmental impact" as compared with the BATEA's goal of "eliminating the discharge of all pollutants." And it is unencumbered by specified statutory factors of the sort provided for those other two tests, which omission can reasonably be interpreted to suggest that the EPA is accorded greater discretion in determining its precise content.

* * * This extended consideration of the text of § 1326(b), and comparison of that with the text and statutory factors applicable to four parallel provisions of the Clean Water Act, lead us to the conclusion that it was well within the bounds of reasonable interpretation for the EPA to

conclude that cost-benefit analysis is not categorically forbidden. Other arguments may be available to preclude such a rigorous form of cost-benefit analysis as that which was prescribed under the statute's former BPT standard, which required weighing "the total cost of application of technology" against "the . . . benefits to be achieved." But that question is not before us.

In the Phase II requirements challenged here the EPA sought only to avoid extreme disparities between costs and benefits. The agency limited variances from the Phase II "national performance standards" to circumstances where the costs are "significantly greater than the benefits" of compliance. 40 CFR § 125.94(a)(5)(ii). In defining the "national performance standards" themselves the EPA assumed the application of technologies whose benefits "approach those estimated" for closed-cycle cooling systems at a fraction of the cost: $389 million per year, 69 Fed. Reg. 41666, as compared with (1) at least $3.5 billion per year to operate compliant closed-cycle cooling systems, and (2) significant reduction in the energy output of the altered facilities. And finally, EPA's assessment of the relatively meager financial benefits of the Phase II regulations that it adopted—reduced impingement and entrainment of 1.4 billion aquatic organisms, with annualized use-benefits of $83 million and non-use benefits of indeterminate value—when compared to annual costs of $389 million, demonstrates quite clearly that the agency did not select the Phase II regulatory requirements because their benefits equaled their costs.

While not conclusive, it surely tends to show that the EPA's current practice is a reasonable and hence legitimate exercise of its discretion to weigh benefits against costs that the agency has been proceeding in essentially this fashion for over 30 years. As early as 1977, the agency determined that, while § 1326(b) does not *require* cost-benefit analysis, it is also not reasonable to "interpret Section [1326(b)] as requiring use of technology whose cost is wholly disproportionate to the environmental benefit to be gained." While the EPA's prior "wholly disproportionate" standard may be somewhat different from its current "significantly greater than" standard, there is nothing in the statute that would indicate that the former is a permissible interpretation while the latter is not.

Indeed, in its review of the EPA's Phase I regulations, the Second Circuit seemed to recognize that § 1326(b) permits some form of cost-benefit analysis. In considering a challenge to the EPA's rejection of dry cooling systems[7] as the "best technology available" for Phase I facilities the Second Circuit noted that "while it certainly sounds substantial that dry cooling is 95 percent more effective than closed-cycle cooling, it is undeniably relevant that that difference represents a relatively small improvement over closed-cycle cooling at a very significant cost." And in the decision below rejecting the use of cost-benefit analysis in the Phase II

7. Dry cooling systems use air drafts to remove heat, and accordingly remove little or no water from surrounding water sources.

regulations, the Second Circuit nonetheless interpreted "best technology available" as mandating only those technologies that can "be reasonably borne by the industry." But whether it is "reasonable" to bear a particular cost may well depend on the resulting benefits; if the only relevant factor was the feasibility of the costs, their reasonableness would be irrelevant.

In the last analysis, even respondents ultimately recognize that some form of cost-benefit analysis is permissible. They acknowledge that the statute's language is "plainly not so constricted as to require EPA to require industry petitioners to spend billions to save one more fish or plankton." This concedes the principle—the permissibility of at least some cost-benefit analysis—and we see no statutory basis for limiting its use to situations where the benefits are *de minimis* rather than significantly disproportionate.

* * *

We conclude that the EPA permissibly relied on cost-benefit analysis in setting the national performance standards and in providing for cost-benefit variances from those standards as part of the Phase II regulations. The Court of Appeals' reliance in part on the agency's use of cost-benefit analysis in invalidating the site-specific cost-benefit variance provision, was therefore in error, as was its remand of the national performance standards for clarification of whether cost-benefit analysis was impermissibly used. * * * The judgment of the Court of Appeals is reversed, and the cases are remanded for further proceedings consistent with this opinion.

It is so ordered.

APPENDIX TO OPINION OF THE COURT

Statutory Standard	Statutorily Mandated Factors	Entities Subject to Regulation
BPT: "[E]ffluent limitations . . . which shall require the application of the *best practicable control technology currently available*." 33 U.S.C. § 1311(b)(1)(A) (emphasis added).	"Factors relating to the assessment of best practicable control technology currently available . . . shall include consideration of the total cost of application of technology in relation to the effluent reduction benefits to be achieved." 33 U.S.C. § 1314(b)(1)(B) .	Existing point sources during the Clean Water Act's initial implementation phase.
BCT: "[E]ffluent limitations . . . which shall require application of the *best conventional pollutant control technology*." 33 U.S.C.	"Factors relating to the assessment of best conventional pollutant control technology . . . shall include consideration of the reasonable-	Existing point sources that discharge "conventional pollutants" as defined by the EPA under 33 U.S.C. § 1314(a)(4).

Statutory Standard	Statutorily Mandated Factors	Entities Subject to Regulation
§ 1311(b)(2)(E)(emphasis added).	ness of the relationship between the costs of attaining a reduction in effluents and the effluent reduction benefits derived." 33 U.S.C. § 1314(b)(4)(B).	
BATEA: "[E]ffluent limitations ... which ... shall require application of the *best available technology economically achievable* ... which will result in reasonable further progress toward the national goal of eliminating the discharge of all pollutants." 33 U.S.C. § 1311(b)(2)(A)(emphasis added).	"Factors relating to the assessment of best available technology shall take into account ... the cost of achieving such affluent reduction." 33 U.S.C. § 1314(b)(2)(B).	Existing point sources that discharge toxic pollutants and non-conventional pollutants.
BADT: "[A] standard for the control of the discharge of pollutants which reflects the greatest degree of effluent reduction with the Administrator determines to be achievable through application of the *best available demonstrated control technology*." 33 U.S.C. § 1316(a)(1)(emphasis added)	"[T]he Administrator shall take into consideration the cost of achieving such effluent reduction, and any non-water quality environmental impact and energy requirements." 33 U.S.C. § 1316(b)(1)(B).	New point sources within the categories of sources identified by the EPA under 33 U.S.C. § 1316(b)(1)(A).
BTA: "Any standard ... applicable to a point source shall require that the location, design, construction, and capacity of cooling water intake structures reflect the best technology available for minimizing adverse environmental impact." 33 U.S.C. § 1326(b).	N/A	Point sources that operate cooling water intake structures.

Justice BREYER, concurring in part and dissenting in part.

I agree with the Court that the relevant statutory language authorizes the Environmental Protection Agency (EPA) to compare costs and benefits. Nonetheless the drafting history and legislative history of related provisions make clear that those who sponsored the legislation intended the law's text to be read as restricting, though not forbidding, the use of cost-benefit comparisons. And I would apply that text accordingly. * * *

* * * Consequently, like the majority, I would remand these cases to the Court of Appeals. But unlike the majority I would permit that court to remand the cases to the EPA so that the EPA can either apply its traditional "wholly disproportionate" standard or provide an adequately reasoned explanation for the change.

JUSTICE STEVENS, with whom JUSTICE SOUTER and JUSTICE GINSBURG join, dissenting.

Section 316(b) of the Clean Water Act (CWA), 33 U.S.C. § 1326(b), which governs industrial powerplant water intake structures, provides that the Environmental Protection Agency (EPA or Agency) "shall require" that such structures "reflect the best technology available for minimizing adverse environmental impact." The EPA has interpreted that mandate to authorize the use of cost-benefit analysis in promulgating regulations under § 316(b). For instance, under the Agency's interpretation, technology that would otherwise qualify as the best available need not be used if its costs are "significantly greater than the benefits" of compliance. 40 CFR § 125.94(a)(5)(ii) (2008).

Like the Court of Appeals, I am convinced that the EPA has misinterpreted the plain text of § 316(b). Unless costs are so high that the best technology is not "available," Congress has decided that they are outweighed by the benefits of minimizing adverse environmental impact. Section 316(b) neither expressly nor implicitly authorizes the EPA to use cost-benefit analysis when setting regulatory standards; fairly read, it prohibits such use.

I

As typically performed by the EPA, cost-benefit analysis requires the Agency to first monetize the costs and benefits of a regulation, balance the results, and then choose the regulation with the greatest net benefits. The process is particularly controversial in the environmental context in which a regulation's financial costs are often more obvious and easier to quantify than its environmental benefits. And cost-benefit analysis often, if not always, yields a result that does not maximize environmental protection.

For instance, although the EPA estimated that water intake structures kill 3.4 billion fish and shellfish each year, the Agency struggled to calculate the value of the aquatic life that would be protected under its § 316(b) regulations. To compensate, the EPA took a shortcut: Instead of monetizing all aquatic life, the Agency counted only those species that are commercially or recreationally harvested, a tiny slice (1.8 percent to be precise) of all impacted fish and shellfish. This narrow focus in turn skewed the Agency's calculation of benefits. When the EPA attempted to value all aquatic life, the benefits measured $735 million. But when the EPA decided to give zero value to the 98.2 percent of fish not commercially or recreationally harvested, the benefits calculation dropped dramatically—to $83 million. Agency acknowledged that its failure to monetize the other 98.2 percent of affected species " 'could result in serious misallocation of resources,' " because its "comparison of complete costs and incomplete benefits does not provide an accurate picture of net benefits to society."

Because benefits can be more accurately monetized in some industries than in others, Congress typically decides whether it is appropriate for an agency to use cost-benefit analysis in crafting regulations. * * * Accordingly, we should not treat a provision's silence as an implicit source of cost-benefit authority, particularly when such authority is elsewhere expressly granted and it has the potential to fundamentally alter an agency's approach to regulation. * * *

* * * II

In 1972, Congress amended the CWA to strike a careful balance between the country's energy demands and its desire to protect the environment. The Act required industry to adopt increasingly advanced technology capable of mitigating its detrimental environmental impact. Not all point sources were subject to strict rules at once. Existing plants were granted time to retrofit with the best technology while new plants were required to incorporate such technology as a matter of design. Although Congress realized that technology standards would necessarily put some firms out of business, the statute's steady march was toward stricter rules and potentially higher costs.

Section § 316(b) was an integral part of the statutory scheme. The provision instructs that "[a]ny standard established pursuant to section 1311 of this title or section 1316 of this title and applicable to a point source shall require that the location, design, construction, and capacity of cooling water intake structures reflect the *best technology available for minimizing adverse environmental impact*." 33 U.S.C. § 1326(b) (2006 ed.) (emphasis added). The "best technology available," or "BTA," standard delivers a clear command: To minimize the adverse environmental impact of water intake structures, the EPA must require industry to adopt the best technology available.

* * * The appropriate analysis requires full consideration of the CWA's structure and legislative history to determine whether Congress contemplated cost-benefit analysis and, if so, under what circumstances it directed the EPA to utilize it. This approach reveals that Congress granted the EPA authority to use cost-benefit analysis in some contexts but not others, and that Congress intend to control, not delegate, when cost-benefit analysis should be used.

Powerful evidence of Congress' decision not to authorize cost-benefit analysis in the BTA standard lies in the series of standards adopted to regulate the outflow, or effluent, from industrial powerplants. Passed at the same time as the BTA standard at issue here, the effluent limitation standards imposed increasingly strict technology requirements on industry. In each effluent limitation provision, Congress distinguished its willingness to allow the EPA to consider costs from its willingness to allow the Agency to conduct a cost-benefit analysis. And to the extent Congress permitted cost-benefit analysis, its use was intended to be temporary and exceptional.

* * * It is in this light that the BTA standard regulating water intake structures must be viewed. The use of cost-benefit analysis was a critical component of the CWA's structure and a key concern in the legislative process. We should therefore conclude that Congress intended to forbid cost-benefit analysis in one provision of the Act in which it was silent on the matter when it expressly authorized its use in another. This is particularly true given Congress' decision that cost-benefit analysis would play a temporary and exceptional role in the CWA to help existing plants transition to the Act's ambitious environmental standards. Allowing cost-benefit analysis in the BTA standard, a permanent mandate applicable to all powerplants, serves no such purpose and instead fundamentally weakens the provision's mandate.

Accordingly, I would hold that the EPA is without authority to perform cost-benefit analysis in setting BTA standards. To the extent the EPA relied on cost-benefit analysis in establishing its BTA regulations, that action was contrary to law, for Congress directly foreclosed such reliance in the statute itself. * * *

III

Because the Court unsettles the scheme Congress established, I respectfully dissent.

NOTES

1. **Cost-Benefit Analysis and Clean Water Act Permitting.** Both the majority and the dissent closely examine the history and structure of the Clean Water Act to decide whether Section 316 allows the EPA to engage in a cost-benefit analysis when establishing the technology-based requirements for water intake structures. Why is a cost-benefit analysis important, according to the majority? What does a cost-benefit analysis leave out, according to the dissent?

The majority provides a good overview of the Clean Water Act's technology-based requirements and their language regarding costs. How do these standards compare, according to both the majority and the dissent? What has been the general trend of the Clean Water Act's evolution, according to the dissent?

As a more basic question, what do both sets of Justices mean by "cost-benefit analysis"? Or, to put the question another way, how could the EPA consider costs in implementing Section 316 without actually performing a cost-benefit analysis?

2. **Section 316's Silence.** Part of the interpretive problem for Section 316, as both the majority and the dissent note, is that Congress did not say

much of anything about cost-benefit analysis in Section 316. What should congressional silence indicate about a statutory provision? One the one hand, the Court could adopt a presumption that anything not explicitly prohibited is allowed. On the other, it could decide instead that anything not explicitly allowed is prohibited. Would *either* presumption work for all statutes? Why or why not? Does the Court, by default, have to be at least somewhat attentive to statutory context? Why or why not? Aren't some interpretations necessarily implicit?

3. **Update on Section 316 Regulations.** As the Supreme Court mentioned, the EPA had also promulgated "Phase III" regulations pursuant to Section 316. 71 Fed. Reg. 35,006 (June 16, 2006). These regulations applied to existing and new offshore and coastal oil and gas extraction facilities and were being challenged in the U.S. Court of Appeals for the Fifth Circuit at the time of the Supreme Court's decision. In August 2010, the Fifth Circuit agreed to the EPA's voluntary request of a remand for the regulations governing existing facilities and upheld the regulations for new facilities. *ConocoPhillips Co. v. U.S. EPA*, 612 F.3d 822, 832, 838–42 (5th Cir. 2010). Under a November 2010 settlement with Riverkeeper, the EPA agreed to propose regulations for existing facilities by March 14, 2011, and to finalize those regulations by July 27, 2012. Under a negotiated extension of that settlement, the proposed regulations appeared in the Federal Register on April 20, 2011, 76 Fed. Reg. 22,174 (April 20, 2011), and the comment period closed on August 18, 2011. *See* 76 Fed. Reg. 43,230 (July 20, 2011). The EPA is also conducting a "willingness to pay" preference study for evaluating the benefits of various cooling water intake regulatory options.

4. **The Water–Energy Nexus.** Section 316 and the intake regulations for power plants and offshore and coastal oil and gas facilities are just one example of the ***water-energy nexus***, a term describing the intense and tangled interrelationship between water and energy. Almost all forms of power production—coal-fired power plants, nuclear power plants, and even solar energy facilities—require huge amounts of water for their operations. In addition, significant quantities of energy are needed to treat water, move it from one location to another, and heat or cool it for use. Unfortunately, in the United States, water policies and energy policies have generally developed independently, although—especially in light of climate change's impacts on water resources—various governmental bodies, including the U.S. Department of Energy, are increasingly thinking about ways to harmonize energy policy with regulation of water quality and water quantity (the latter of which is generally the subject of courses in Water Law).

* * *

H. STATE VARIATIONS IN SPDES PROGRAMS

The cases in this section have all discussed the federal requirements for NPDES permits. Nevertheless, as the Supreme Court emphasized in *SWANCC* and *Rapanos*, the Clean Water Act leaves much room for states to regulate water quality more stringently and/or more extensively than the Act requires. Oregon's explicit regulation of discharges to ground water under the state WPCF permit program and states' expansion of state regulation to isolated wetlands in the wake of the *SWANCC* decision are two examples of state regulation that arguably extends beyond the Act's reach. In addition, section 510 of the Clean Water Act explicitly encourages more stringent state water quality regulation:

> Except as expressly provided in this chapter, nothing in this chapter shall (1) preclude or deny the right of any State or political subdivision thereof or interstate agency to adopt or enforce (A) any standard or limitation respecting the discharges of pollutants, or (B) any requirement respecting control or abatement of pollution; except that if an effluent limitation, or other limitation, effluent standard, prohibition, pretreatment standard, or standard of performance is in effect under this chapter, each State or political subdivision or interstate agency may not adopt any effluent limitation, or other limitation, effluent standard, prohibition, pretreatment standard, or standard of performance which is less stringent than the effluent limitation, or other limitation, effluent standard, prohibition, pretreatment standard, or standard of performance under this chapter; or (2) be construed as impairing or in any manner affecting any right or jurisdiction of the States with respect to the waters (including boundary waters) of such States.

CWA § 510, 33 U.S.C. § 1370. Thus, states can pursue their own regulatory goals, so long as their requirements are at least as stringent as any required federal minimum standards, and so long as they do not interfere with the jurisdictional authority of other states.

Thus, if a state incorporates these state-law expansions of basic Clean Water Act regulation, the ***State Pollutant Discharges Elimination Systems* (SPDES)** permit program may effectively be more comprehensive than the NPDES permit program. Nevertheless, expanded state regulation of water quality can have its own complexities, as the following case demonstrates.

MAPLE LEAF FARMS, INC. v. WISCONSIN DEPARTMENT OF NATURAL RESOURCES

633 N.W.2d 720 (Wis. App. 2001).

¶ 1 Brown, P.J.

Maple Leaf Farms, Inc. (Maple Leaf) appeals from a trial court order upholding the administrative determination by the Wisconsin Department of Natural Resources (DNR) under the Wisconsin Pollution Discharge Elimination System (WPDES). Specifically, Maple Leaf contends that the DNR has no authority to prescribe conditions under which it landspreads off-site manure generated from its duck-growing facilities. We affirm the decision of the circuit court, which upheld the DNR's authority to regulate Maple Leaf's landspreading of manure.

FACTS

¶ 2 Maple Leaf is the largest duck producer and processor in Wisconsin. It operates two duck-growing facilities in Racine County. The Downy Duck facility, located in the Town of Dover, houses 100,000 ducks and generates 34,000 tons of manure annually. The Main Farm, located in the Town of Yorkville, houses 250,200 ducks and generates 57,000 tons of manure annually. The operation of each of these facilities results in an actual or potential "discharge of pollutants" into the waters of the state within the meaning of WIS. STAT. § 283.01(5) (1999–2000). Because of their size, both Downy Duck and Main Farm are "point sources" subject to the WPDES program, specifically as concentrated animal feeding operations (CAFO) within the meaning of § 283.01(12)(a). Both facilities are also large animal feeding operations within the meaning of WIS. ADMIN. CODE § NR 243.04(13).

¶ 3 The manure produced by Maple Leaf's duck operations is valuable as a nutrient supplement for agricultural crops. Some of the manure is applied on fields located on company property, but Maple Leaf also contracts with a number of farmers for land application of the waste. The off-site landspreading is undertaken by Maple Leaf. * * * The farmers pay Maple Leaf according to the quantity of manure that Maple Leaf applies to their fields.

¶ 4 On June 25, 1997, the DNR issued WPDES wastewater permits to Downy Duck and Main Farm. These permits require Maple Leaf to maintain runoff control structures and to implement procedures for the storage and disposal of animal wastes, including an animal waste management plan. *See* WIS. ADMIN. CODE §§ NR 243.13, 243.14. * * * On this appeal, Maple Leaf raises a single issue: the DNR's authority to regulate the land application of manure on off-site croplands.

STANDARD OF REVIEW

¶ 5 This court reviews the agency's decision rather than the decision of the circuit court. An agency's decision must be upheld when it is based on an accurate interpretation of the law and supported by substantial evidence in the record. WIS. STAT. § 227.57(5), (6). Courts apply one of three levels of deference to an agency's interpretation of a statute: great weight, due weight or de novo. The de novo standard applies if construction of the statute involves interpreting the scope of an agency's power. The parties agree that this appeal addresses the scope of the DNR's authority under the WPDES permit program. Therefore, we engage in a de novo analysis of the applicable law.

DISCUSSION

¶ 6 This case arises in the context of striking changes in the livestock production industries. "The character of livestock production in many parts of the world . . . is changing rapidly and dramatically. Economies of scale, specialization, and regional concentration in all major livestock production sectors have fueled a trend toward fewer, larger operations that confine thousands of animals on limited acreage." Larry C. Frarey and Staci J. Pratt, *Environmental Regulation of Livestock Production Operations*, 9 NAT. RESOURCES & ENV'T 8 (1995). Land disposal is the prevailing manure management strategy for most of these facilities. *Id.* at 11. Animal waste disposal is thus a prime concern in our state and across the nation. *See generally* J.B. Ruhl, *Farms, Their Environmental Harms, and Environmental Law*, 27 ECOLOGY L.Q. 263, 285–87 (2000).

Figure 5-12: An Example of a Hog CAFO
U.S. Geological Survey photo.

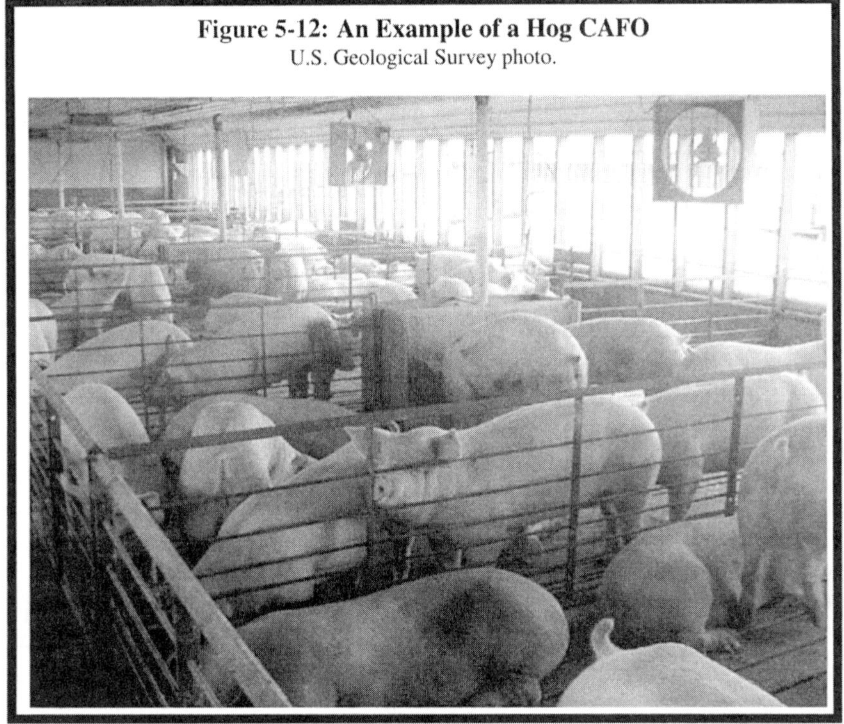

¶ 7 According to expert testimony elicited at the administrative hearing, landspreading manure improperly results in the release of pollutants to surface water or groundwater. If applied near streams, or on fields with drainage tile systems, runoff of pollutants into surface waters is likely. Soluble and fixed phosphorus can be carried away by surface water runoff and discharged into nearby surface waters. Runoff of phosphorus adds to the eutrophication of surface water, a condition where the dissolved nutrients stimulate excessive plant growth which can cause oxygen loss and subsequent harm to the fishery. When nitrogen leaches into groundwater, high levels of nitrate-nitrogen can make groundwater an unsafe source of drinking water.

¶ 8 To determine whether the DNR may regulate off-site manure applications, we first must determine if the exercise of such authority has been granted by the legislature. * * *

¶ 9 We preface our analysis with a brief review of the federal and state water pollution control programs. The federal Clean Water Act (CWA) prohibits the discharge of any pollutant by any person to navigable waters from any point source. 33 U.S.C. §§ 1311(a), 1362(12) (2000). "Pollutant" includes "solid waste" and "agricultural waste." *Id.* at § 1362(6). A "point source" includes "any discernible, confined and discrete conveyance" such as a ditch, channel or conduit, as well as any "concentrated animal feeding operation" (CAFO). *Id.* at § 1362(14). * * *

¶ 10 The CWA authorizes states to implement their own permit programs as long as the state programs impose standards at least as stringent as those of the federal program. The WPDES program differs from the CWA in two important respects. First, it defines waters of the state, which are subject to regulatory protection, to include groundwater, WIS. STAT. § 283.01(20), whereas waters of the United States, as defined in 40 C.F.R. § 122.2 (2001), do not include groundwater. Second, the Wisconsin legislature has authorized the DNR to establish more stringent effluent limitations if necessary to meet water quality standards. WIS. STAT. § 283.13(5).

¶ 11 According to Maple Leaf, a key provision of the enabling statute is the uniformity provision contained in WIS. STAT. § 283.11(2):

> [A]ll rules promulgated by the [DNR] under this chapter as they relate to point source discharges, effluent limitations, municipal monitoring requirements, standards of performance for new sources, toxic effluent standards or prohibitions and pretreatment standards shall comply with and not exceed the requirements of the [CWA] and regulations adopted under that act.

Maple Leaf asserts that because the federal program does not regulate off-site manure spreading, the uniformity provision effectively eliminates the DNR's authority to impose permit conditions on this activity.

¶ 12 The DNR asserts that its authority to regulate this activity originates in a broad delegation of power enunciated in WIS. STAT. § 283.001, and its authority to condition permits on compliance with groundwater protection standards under WIS. STAT. § 283.31. * * *

¶ 13 * * * WISCONSIN STAT. ch. 283 does not expressly authorize the DNR to regulate off-site manure applications; therefore, we must determine whether such regulatory power is fairly implied from the language of the statute. * * *

¶ 14 WISCONSIN STAT. § 283.001(1) sets forth the policy and purpose of Wisconsin's WPDES program. It recognizes that

> [u]nabated pollution of the waters of this state continues to ... endanger public health; to threaten fish and aquatic life, scenic and ecological values; and to limit the domestic, municipal, recreational, industrial, agricultural and other uses of water. It is the policy of this state to restore and maintain the chemical, physical, and biological integrity of its waters to protect public health, safeguard fish and

aquatic life and scenic and ecological values, and to enhance the domestic, municipal, recreational, industrial, agricultural, and other uses of water.

¶ 15 The legislature granted the DNR "all authority necessary to establish, administer and maintain a state pollutant discharge elimination system to effectuate the policy set forth under sub. (1) and consistent with all the requirements of the federal water pollution control act." WIS. STAT. § 283.001(2). This broad grant of power authorizes the DNR to implement a permit program that protects groundwater as well as surface water. As we noted previously, in this respect, the state regulatory program is broader and more stringent than the federal program. This far-reaching power complements the DNR's broad regulatory power to protect waters of the state in other legislative enactments as well. Reading § 283.001(1) and (2) together, we find that the enabling statute clearly and unambiguously empowers the DNR to regulate where groundwater may be affected by the discharge of pollutants. We perceive no implication that the legislature intended to limit the DNR's authority to protect waters of the state to discharges of pollutants occurring on sites owned by the discharger.

¶ 16 Maple Leaf asserts that the uniformity provision constricts the authority of the DNR to regulate off-site by providing that state rules "as they relate to point source discharges [and] effluent limitations ... shall comply with and not exceed the requirements of the federal water pollution control act ... and regulations adopted under that act." WIS. STAT. § 283.11(2). This provision appears in subchapter III entitled "Standards; Effluent Limitations." We agree with the position of the DNR that this provision applies only where the federal program regulates the activity in question, for example, where the EPA has imposed specific discharge limits for defined categories of industrial discharges and the DNR has superimposed more stringent limits. It would not apply where the federal government has chosen not to regulate at all.

* * * ¶ 21 Having concluded that the uniformity provision is not relevant to our statutory analysis, we must now consider whether the DNR's authority in WIS. STAT. § 283.001(2) can be harmonized with WIS. STAT. § 283.31 for conferring authority to regulate off-site applications of manure. Section 283.31 is found in subchapter IV entitled "Permits" and contains the following relevant language:

283.31 Water pollutant discharge elimination system; permits, terms and conditions.

(1) The discharge of any pollutant into any waters of the state ... by any person is unlawful unless such discharge ... is done under a permit issued by the department under this section ...

... (3) The department may issue a permit under this section for the discharge of any pollutant ... upon condition that such discharges will meet all the following, whenever applicable:

(a) Effluent limitations.

(b) Standards of performance for new sources.

(c) Effluent standards, effluent prohibitions and pretreatment standards.

(d) Any more stringent limitations, including those:

1. Necessary to meet federal or state water quality standards, or schedules of compliance established by the department . . .

. . . (f) Groundwater protection standards established under ch. 160.

(4) The department shall prescribe conditions for permits issued under this section to assure compliance with the requirements of sub. (3). . . .

¶ 22 Looking at WIS. STAT. § 283.31(1), the first sentence explicitly states that if a person discharges any pollutant into waters of the state, such discharge will be unlawful unless it is done in compliance with a permit. WISCONSIN STAT. § 283.01(5) defines "discharge of pollutants" as the addition of any pollutant to the waters of this state from any point source. Section 283.01(12) states that a "point source" means either of the following:

(a) A discernible, confined and discrete conveyance, including but not limited to any pipe, ditch, channel, tunnel, conduit, well, discrete fissure, container, rolling stock, *concentrated animal feeding operation* . . . from which pollutants may be discharged . . . into the waters of the state. . . .

(b) A discernable, confined and discrete conveyance of storm water for which a permit is required under § 283.33(1). (Emphasis added.)

¶ 23 Maple Leaf does not challenge that it is a concentrated animal feeding operation and therefore a point source subject to the permit requirements of WIS. STAT. § 283.31. Moreover, Maple Leaf does not challenge the DNR's authority under this statute to regulate its spreading of manure on land that it owns. We understand Maple Leaf to argue that this statute cannot be used to authorize the DNR to issue a permit regulating manure applications to off-site croplands. The plain language of the statute does not distinguish between discharges that occur off-site or on-site. The statute's focus is on whether there is a discharge from a point source to waters of the state. We focus our inquiry therefore on whether landspreading of manure off-site is a discharge to waters of the state by Maple Leaf. If we conclude that it is not, then the DNR has no authority under the statute to regulate this activity by permit.

¶ 24 There is no Wisconsin case which has analyzed landspreading practices under the WPDES permit program. In *Concerned Area Residents for the Environment v. Southview Farm,* 34 F.3d 114 (2nd Cir. 1994), the

Second Circuit held that the entire farm of a large dairy, not just the barns and pens, was a point source requiring an NPDES permit. Moreover, the Second Circuit ruled that the dairy's method of applying animal manure to its farmlands was a point source because the manure spreaders themselves were point sources. *Id.* at 119. Refusing to apply the CWA's exemption for agricultural storm water discharge, the court determined that any other result would allow farmers to get away with spreading animal waste on fields without regard for absorption capacity or runoff potential. *See id.* at 120–21.

¶ 25 Similarly, in *Community Ass'n for Restoration of the Environment v. Henry Bosma Dairy,* 65 F. Supp. 2d 1129 (E.D. Wash. 1999), the district court held that wastes removed from NPDES-regulated manure holding ponds and spread on land as fertilizer remain subject to the continuing jurisdiction of the NPDES permit. *See id.* at 1155. As a result of *Bosma,* noncompliance with a permit's waste management practices that results in discharges of runoff from manure laden fields is illegal.

¶ 26 We find these cases helpful to our determination of whether WIS. STAT. § 283.31 authorizes the DNR to issue permits that encompass manure applications to off-site croplands. We agree with the courts in *Bosma* and *Southview Farm* that a CAFO includes not only the ground where the animals are confined, but also the equipment that distributes and/or applies the animal waste produced at the confinement area to fields outside the confinement area. Any overapplication of manure by Maple Leaf through its landspreading activities would then be a discharge, either because of runoff to surface waters or percolation of pollutants to groundwater. Because the off-site croplands are used by Maple Leaf to dispose of waste produced at its on-site facility, the permit conditions imposed on Maple Leaf to enforce groundwater protection standards are as applicable to Maple Leaf's off-site landspreading operations as they are on-site. Therefore, because a CAFO's overapplication of manure to fields can be a discharge to groundwater under the statute, we determine that the DNR has authority to issue permits regulating Maple Leaf's off-site landspreading operations.

¶ 27 Under our analysis of WIS. STAT. §§ 283.001 and 283.31, we conclude that the legislature has conferred authority on the DNR to regulate discharges, in the form of overapplication of manure, by CAFOs regardless of whether the discharge occurs on land owned by the CAFO. We now must determine if WIS. ADMIN. CODE ch. NR 243, governing animal waste management practices, implements this authority.

¶ 28 We begin by examining the purpose of the animal waste management regulation. "The purpose of this chapter is to establish design standards and accepted animal waste management practices for the large animal feeding operations category of point sources." WIS. ADMIN. CODE § NR 243.01(1). Subsection (2) provides that "[o]nly those animal feeding operations which improperly manage their wastes and as a result cause ground or surface water pollution, or those subject to the requirements for large animal feeding operations will be regulated under this code." WISCONSIN ADMIN. CODE § NR 243.02 further states that this chapter applies to discharges of pollutants resulting from large animal feeding operations within the subcategories specified in § NR 243.11, Table 2. There is no question that Maple Leaf qualifies as a large animal feeding operation category of point source under these provisions and is therefore subject to the permitting requirements contained in the chapter. Like the enabling statute, these provisions are not concerned with where the discharge occurs with respect to its off-site or on-site location.

¶ 29 Subchapter II of the regulation requires an owner or operator of a large animal feeding operation to apply for a permit with the DNR. As part of the permit process, the applicant is required to submit an animal waste management plan for approval. In approving the management plan, the DNR is required to consider the following factors:

1. Potential impacts on waters of the state due to overapplication of the animal wastes.
2. Soil limitations such as permeability, infiltration rate, drainage class and flooding hazard.
3. Volume and water content of the waste material.
4. Available storage capacity and method of application.
5. Nutrient requirements of the crop or crops to be grown on the fields utilizing the animal wastes.

WIS. ADMIN. CODE § NR 243.14(2)(a). The DNR views these measures as creating a pollution prevention program with respect to large animal feeding operations. We agree with the DNR that the effect of these measures is to require permit holders to implement sound environmental practices as a means to enforce compliance with surface and groundwater standards. *See* WIS. STAT. § 283.31(3)(f) (conditioning issuance of permits on compliance with groundwater protection standards established by DNR). * * *

* * * ¶ 34 Maple Leaf's core issue concerns the requirement that it submit nutrient management plans for off-site applications. Nutrient management plans require Maple Leaf to report the quantity of manure to be spread, the nutrient needs of the crop and the corresponding nutrient content of the manure to be spread. This information insures manure application only at agronomic rates (*i.e.*, no greater than the capacity of crops to utilize the nitrogen or phosphorus present in the manure applied). Maple Leaf and the *amici curiae* object to such burdensome conditions that call for extensive study, observations and reports required for lands other than the land they own. In particular, Maple Leaf points out that it has no control over the landowner's tillage practices, crop rotation, or application of other sources of fertilizer. Nevertheless, as a CAFO under the WPDES program, Maple Leaf would be held liable for discharges that occur from overapplication of manure.

¶ 35 These issues raise serious policy concerns regarding the wisdom of the DNR's decision to hold Maple Leaf ultimately responsible for the manure it generates and applies off-site. We cannot rule, however, on the wisdom of an agency's decision. We simply must determine whether the DNR is empowered by the legislature to exercise its authority in this manner and we have concluded that it is. There is nothing in WIS. ADMIN. CODE ch. NR 243 which distinguishes between on-site and off-site landspreading activities. In either case, the purpose of the code is to prevent the discharge of pollutants to waters of the state. Furthermore, the WPDES statutory prohibition on discharges of pollutants from CAFOs would be of little value if the owners of the CAFOs could avoid responsibility merely by placing those pollutants onto the ground of third parties without regard to rates and quantities so that the pollutants would predictably leach into groundwater or runoff to surface waters. Our interpretation of the statute and regulation is consistent with the overall legislative goal to "restore and maintain the . . . integrity of [our state's] waters." WIS. STAT. § 283.001(1). The order affirming the agency's determination is affirmed.

NOTES

1. **Wisconsin Jurisdiction over Water Quality.** How did the Wisconsin Department of Natural Resource's (WDNR's) jurisdiction over water quality issues differ from federal jurisdiction under the Clean Water Act? What elements of jurisdiction were the same? Why were Maple Leaf Farms' landspreading activities *not* subject to federal jurisdiction under the Clean Water Act, according to the Wisconsin Court of Appeals?

2. **Wisconsin's Uniformity Rule.** What is Wisconsin's "uniformity rule"? What does this state law effectively do to WDNR's potential authority under section 510 of the Clean Water Act? Why would a state legislature enact such a "uniformity" requirement? Why did the uniformity requirement *not* apply to the WDNR's regulation of Maple Leaf Farms?

3. **Wisconsin's Standards for Review of Administrative Agency Actions.** What standard of review did the Wisconsin Court of Appeals use to review the WDNR's decision to subject Maple Leaf Farms to regulation? Why? What administrative standards of review does Wisconsin law recognize? How do the Wisconsin standards compare to the federal standards of review found in the federal Administrative Procedure Act? Do Wisconsin's standards strike you as being easier or more difficult to apply than the federal standards of review? Why?

4. **Statutory Permitting Authority vs. Regulatory Permitting Authority.** Why did the WDNR need both statutory and regulatory authority in order to require Maple Leaf Farms to get a permit? How does this hierarchy of authority compare to the hierarchy governing federal agency authority under the Clean Water Act? Compare this case, for example, to *Riverside Bayview Homes* and the U.S. Army Corps' authority to regulate adjacent wetlands.

5. **Concentrated Animal Feeding Operations (CAFOs).** The Clean Water Act's definition of "point source" explicitly includes "***concentrated***

animal feeding operations," better known as CAFOs, CWA § 501(14), 33 U.S.C. § 1362(14), and the duck farms at issue in this case were CAFOs. As a practical matter, CAFOs are the large "factory farms" that have become increasingly prevalent in agriculture, where farmers keep large numbers of animals in very small areas. As this case indicates, CAFOs generate huge amounts of animal wastes, which are then often used as fertilizers but which can (and often do) result in water pollution, especially when combined with excess rainfall.

To qualify as a CAFO under the federal regulations, a farm must first qualify as an ***animal feeding operation* (AFO)**. According to the EPA's regulations, a farm is an AFO if it keeps and raises animals in confined situations. Specifically, the farm is an AFO if: (1) animals are confined or stabled for a total of 45 days or more a year; and (2) crops are not grown in the same facility. 40 C.F.R. § 122.23(b)(1). Approximately 257,000 AFOs exist in the United States. OFFICE OF WATER, U.S. EPA, NPDES PERMIT WRITERS' GUIDANCE MANUAL AND EXAMPLE NPDES PERMIT FOR CONCENTRATED ANIMAL FEEDING OPERATIONS 1–1 (Dec. 31, 2003), *available at* http://www.epa.gov/npdes/pubs/cafo_permit_guidance_chapters.pdf.

If a farm qualifies as an AFO, then there are three ways that it can qualify as a CAFO. First, an AFO is a large CAFO if the AFO confines 1,000 or more ***animal units***. 40 C.F.R. § 122.23(b)(2), (4). The number of animals in an "animal unit" varies by the species involved, based on the amount of wastes it can generate. For example, 1 beef cow equals 1 animal unit, but it takes only 0.7 dairy cows to qualify as 1 animal unit and only 0.5 horses. *Id.* § 122.23(b)(4). Conversely, a farm must have 5 ducks, 10 sheep, 55 turkeys or 100 chickens before it has 1 animal unit. *Id.*

Second, an AFO qualifies as a medium CAFO if it confines 300 to 1000 animal units *and* it either discharges pollutants through a human-made structure or discharges pollutants into waters that run through the facility or come into contact with the confined animals. *Id.* § 122.23(b)(6).

Finally, the authority that issues the Clean Water Act permit (the EPA or the state) may designate any AFO as a small CAFO if that AFO is a significant source of water pollution. *Id.* § 122.23(c).

6. **Ongoing Controversies Regarding the EPA's CAFO Regulations.** On February 12, 2003, the EPA issued a highly controversial rule to govern CAFOs under the Clean Water Act. The rule addressed several of the issues raised in the *Maple Leaf Farms* decision, providing for example that the EPA could regulation runoff from the land application of manure from CAFOs. In addition, the EPA's regulation required all CAFOs to apply for an NPDES permit so that the permitting agency could decide whether a discharge would actually occur, and it addressed Nutrient Management Plans like those Wisconsin required. Finally, the rule created effluent limitations for CAFOs, including BCT-based effluent limitations for fecal coliform and NSPS.

In February 2005, the Second Circuit addressed challenges to the CAFO regulations, upholding some parts of the regulations and overturning others. Significantly for this case, the court upheld the EPA's authority to address runoff and other water quality issues from land application of manure. However, the court invalidated the Nutrient Management Plan requirements because the EPA did not require that those plans be made part of the resulting NPDES permit. In addition, the court invalidated the "duty to apply" provisions on the ground that no Clean Water Act jurisdiction existed unless a discharge occurred. Finally, the court remanded the technology-based effluent limitations for a variety of reasons. *Waterkeeper Alliance, Inc. v. U.S. EPA*, 399 F.3d 486 (2d Cir. 2005).

In response to the Second Circuit's decision, the EPa proposed new CAFO regulations on June 30, 2006. 71 Fed. Reg. 37,744 (2006). The proposed regulation would require only dischargers to apply for a permit; requires that Nutrient Management Plans be incorporated into NPDES permits; allows certain CAFOs to request best management, zero discharge effluent limitations; and re-established the technology-based effluent limitations. The EPA finalized the CAFO regulations in November 2008 and made them effective as of December 22, 2008. Revised National Pollutant Discharge Elimination System Permit Regulation and Effluent Limitations Guideline for Concentrated Animal Feeding operations in Response to the *Waterkeeper* Decision; Final Rule, 73 Fed. Reg. 70,418 (Nov. 20, 2008). In addition to the features described for the proposed rule, unpermitted CAFOs can certify that their facilities have no discharge. The consolidated CAFO regulations are found in 40 C.F.R. Part 122.

Nevertheless, the EPA's regulation of CAFOs is limited by its lack of knowledge regarding how specific CAFO facilities operate. To remedy this problem, in October 2011 the EPA proposed its CAFO Reporting Rule, 76 Fed. Reg. 65,431 (October 21, 2011), through which the EPA will require CAFOs to submit facility-specific information.

7. **State Water Quality Regulation and RCRA.** In this case, Maple Leaf Farms sold duck manure as a means of disposing of its excess manure. As has been noted, RCRA exempts discharges of pollutants regulated pursuant to Clean Water Act NPDES permits from the definition of "solid waste," and hence from RCRA regulation. Is Maple Leaf Farms exempt from RCRA here? Why or why not? If not, would the duck manure otherwise be considered RCRA "solid waste"? Why or why not?

* * *

I. TRIBAL REGULATORY JURISDICTION UNDER THE CLEAN WATER ACT

In 1987, Congress added a new section to the Clean Water Act, section 518, that recognized the authority of Native American Tribes to exercise Clean Water Act jurisdiction. 33 U.S.C. § 1377. Under section 518(e), the Administrator of the EPA can treat a Tribe as a state for purposes of Clean Water Act permitting,

but only if—

(1) the Indian tribe has a governing body carrying out substantial governmental duties and powers;

(2) the functions to be exercised by the Indian tribe pertain to the management and protection of water resources which are held by

an Indian tribe, held by the United States in trust for Indians, held by a member of an Indian tribe is such property interest is subject to a trust restriction on alienation, or otherwise within the borders of an Indian reservation; and

(3) the Indian tribe is reasonably expected to be capable, in the Administrator's judgment, of carrying out the functions to be exercised in a manner consistent with the terms and purposes of this chapter and of all applicable regulations.

CWA § 518(e), 33 U.S.C. § 1377(e).

The potential applicability of section 518 is limited, however. Congress defined "Indian tribe" for purposes of this section to be "any Indian tribe, band, group, or community *recognized by the Secretary of the Interior* and *exercising governmental authority over a Federal Indian reservation*." CWA § 518(h), 33 U.S.C. § 1377(h) (emphasis added). As a practical matter, therefore, Treatment-as-a-State (TAS) status under section 518 is limited to those Tribes that the federal government already formally recognizes and that have managed to retain tribal authority over land. As Figure 5–14 shows, there are 562 federally recognized Tribes in the United States. As of January 2008, forty-one Tribes across the country have obtained TAS status and have EPA-approved water quality standards. Office of Water, U.S. EPA, *Indian Tribe Approvals,* http://www.epa.gov/waterscience/tribes/approvtable.htm (as updated July 12, 2007).

Figure 5-13: Federally Recognized Tribes in the United States
U.S. Department of Energy map.

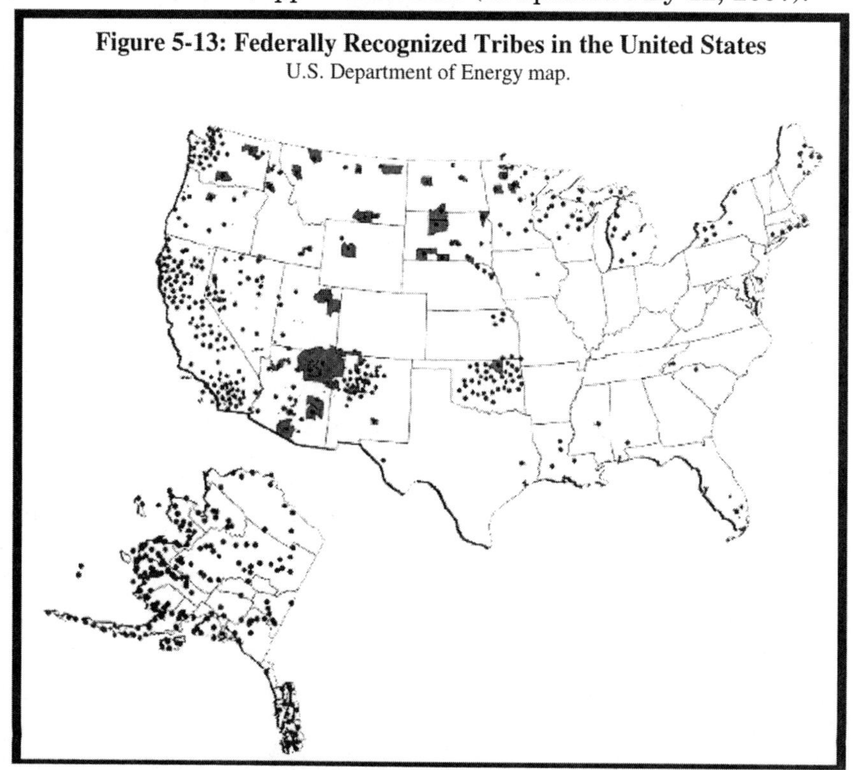

The already-complex scheme of federalism in the Clean Water Act becomes even more complex when Native American Tribes assume a role of regulator. First, when the EPA grants Tribes TAS status under the Clean Water Act, the number of regulatory jurisdictions within the state increases. Second, the law governing tribal regulatory authority in general is federal law—and particularly complex federal law, at that. A complete discussion of Indian law is beyond the scope of an introductory Environmental Law course. Nevertheless, the following case gives the flavor of some of the jurisdictional and federalism issues that tribal TAS status can raise.

WISCONSIN v. ENVIRONMENTAL PROTECTION AGENCY

266 F.3d 741 (7th Cir. 2001).

DIANE P. WOOD, CIRCUIT JUDGE.

* * * In this case, we confront one of the more complex kinds of overlapping sovereignty that exists in the United States today: that between the States and Indian tribes. The Supreme Court addressed one aspect of that relationship in its 2000 Term in *Nevada v. Hicks*, 533 U.S. 353 (2001), which held that tribal authorities lacked legislative jurisdiction to regulate the activities of state officials on reservation land when those officials were investigating off-reservation violations of state law. *Id.* at 2318. A different aspect of the same relationship is before us here: namely, whether the Environmental Protection Agency (EPA), acting through authority delegated to it by statute, was empowered to treat a particular tribe as a "state" for purposes of certain water quality rules. Like the district court, we conclude that the EPA acted properly in doing so, and we thus affirm the district court's judgment rejecting the challenge Wisconsin has brought to the EPA's action.

I

A. The Clean Water Act

The Clean Water Act (the Act) prohibits the discharge of pollutants into navigable waters unless the discharge is sanctioned by a permit or statute. *See* 33 U.S.C. § 1311(a). Permits are issued by the EPA or by state agencies subject to EPA review. *Id.* at § 1342. The Act also gives states the authority to establish water quality standards for waters within their boundaries (*id.* at § 1313), to certify compliance with those standards (*id.* at § 1341), and to issue and enforce discharge permits (*id.* at §§ 1342, 1319), all under the watchful eye of the EPA. Like other states, Wisconsin has enacted its own federally approved comprehensive water pollution regulatory system.

In 1987, Congress amended the Act to authorize the EPA to treat Indian tribes as states under § 518 of the Act. Once a tribe has treatment-as-state (TAS) status, the statute permits it to establish water quality standards for bodies of water within its reservation and to require permits for any action that may create a discharge into those waters. 33 U.S.C. § 1377(e). In 1991, after full notice-and-comment rule-making, the EPA issued a final rule implementing this provision and setting forth the requirements Indian tribes would have to meet in order to be granted TAS status:

(1) the tribe must be federally recognized;

(2) the tribe must have a governing body carrying out substantial governmental duties and powers;

(3) the functions to be exercised by the tribe must pertain to the management and protection of water resources which are held by the tribe, held by the United States in trust for the tribe, or otherwise within the borders of the reservation; and

(4) the tribe must be capable of carrying out the functions of the Act.

40 C.F.R. § 131.8(a); *see also* 33 U.S.C. §§ 1377(e)(1)-(3).

Relying heavily on the Supreme Court's decision in *Montana v. United States*, 450 U.S. 544 (1981), the EPA concluded that this was neither a plenary delegation of inherent authority to tribes to regulate all reservation waters, nor was it a standard that precluded tribal regulation of any non-member or any off-reservation activity. *See* 56 Fed. Reg. at 64877. Instead, the agency chose a case-by-case approach under which a tribe attempting to satisfy element (3) of the regulation would have to show that it possesses inherent authority over the waters in light of evolving case law. *See* 56 Fed. Reg. at 64878. There was no question that tribes could regulate the activities of tribal members, undertaken on the reservation, in order to protect the quality of reservation waters. In addition, the EPA concluded that "a tribe may regulate the activities of non-Indians on fee lands within its reservations when those activities threaten or have a direct effect on the political integrity, the economic security, or the health or welfare of the tribe." *Id.*

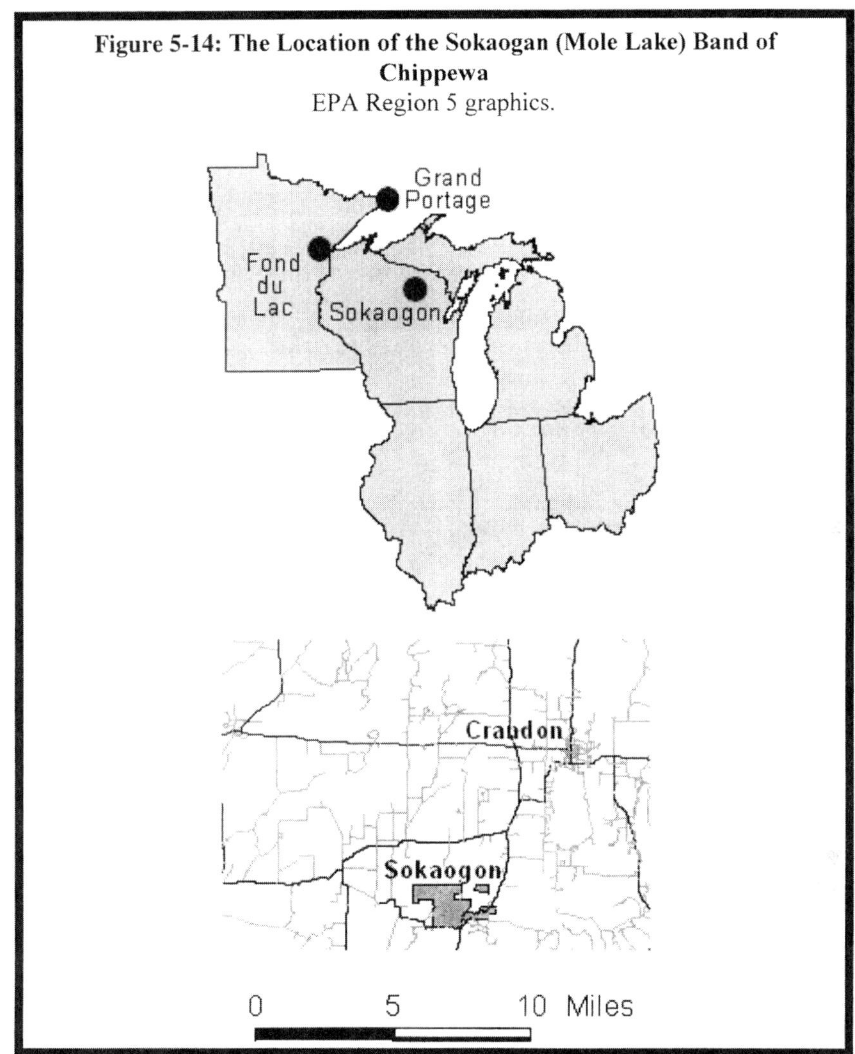

Figure 5-14: The Location of the Sokaogan (Mole Lake) Band of Chippewa
EPA Region 5 graphics.

The EPA acknowledged that this will usually be an easy showing, based on "generalized findings" that water quality is related to human health and welfare. *See id.* Although the EPA stated that it would make a case-specific determination with regard to the scope of each tribe's authority, once a tribe has shown that impairment of the waters on the reservation would have a serious and substantial effect on the health and welfare of the tribe, the EPA presumes that there has been an adequate showing of inherent authority. *Id.* at 64879.

B. The Mole Lake Band and Its Application for TAS Status

The waters at issue in this case are lakes and streams adjacent to or surrounded by the reservation of the Sokaogon Chippewa Community, also known as the Mole Lake Band of Lake Superior Chippewa Indians (the Band), located in northeastern Wisconsin. The Mole Lake reservation is unusual in two respects. First, the Band is heavily reliant on the availability of the water resources within the reservation for food, fresh water, medicines, and raw materials. In particular, Rice Lake, the largest body of water on the reservation, is a prime source of wild rice, which serves as a significant dietary and economic resource for the Band. Second, all of the 1,850 acres within the reservation are held in trust by the United States for the tribe. None of the land within the reservation is controlled or owned in fee by non-members of the tribe.

In August 1994, the Band applied for TAS status under the Act. Wisconsin opposed the application, arguing that it was sovereign over all of the navigable waters in the state, including those on the reservation, and that its sovereignty precluded any tribal regulation. Nevertheless, after elaborate administrative proceedings, on September 29, 1995, the EPA approved the Band's application, finding that the tribe had satisfied all of the requirements of 40 C.F.R. § 131.8, including the necessary demonstration of its inherent authority over all water resources on the reservation. In keeping with its earlier positions, the EPA noted that the inherent authority question did not turn on who had title to the land underneath the waters.

This grant of TAS status alarmed the State of Wisconsin, which saw it as both an affront to the state's sovereignty and, more pragmatically, as an action with the potential to throw a wrench into the state's planned construction of a huge zinc-copper sulfide mine on the Wolf River, upstream from Rice Lake. Concerned about its loss of authority over certain territory within its outer boundaries and worried that the tribal water standards might limit the activities of the mine by prohibiting some or all of the discharge from the mine, Wisconsin filed this action in district court on January 25, 1996, reiterating its challenge to the EPA's grant of TAS status to the Band. (The United States and the EPA waived immunity under 5 U.S.C. § 702.) The state's case raises a fundamental challenge to the TAS grant; the relief it seeks is outright revocation of the grant, rather than mere accommodation for any particular project. * * *

In April 1999, the district court upheld the TAS grant, finding that the EPA's determination that a tribe could regulate all water within the reservation, regardless of ownership, was a reasonable interpretation of the relevant statutes and regulations. Wisconsin now appeals.

II

* * * Wisconsin is challenging the EPA's findings only with respect to the third requirement for TAS status—the demonstration of the tribe's inherent authority to regulate water quality within the borders of the reservation. Wisconsin gives three reasons why the EPA's determination that the tribe had established such authority was unreasonable.

1. Not "Within the Borders"

For the first time on appeal, Wisconsin contends that Rice Lake is not "within the borders" of the reservation because the legal description of the reservation runs only to the Lake's highwater mark. This argument is waived, however, because Wisconsin did not present it to the EPA. Furthermore, even if we could overlook this waiver and considered the argument on its merits, we would reject it. [] Rice Lake is almost completely surrounded by reservation land (and the small percentage that is not abuts off-reservation trust lands). If the EPA had been given a chance to consider this point, it would have been completely reasonable for it to interpret the phrase "within the borders" to include such a body of water.

2. No Authority Because No Title

Second, Wisconsin argues that the tribe does not have authority over the water resources on the reservation because the state has ownership of the underlying lake beds. We will assume for the purposes of this appeal that, pursuant to the Equal Footing Doctrine, the state does indeed have title to the lake beds within the reservation.

This court has indeed held that, in some situations, state ownership of lake beds may restrict a tribe's authority to regulate the waters running over those beds. In *Wisconsin v. Baker*, 698 F.2d 1323, 1335 (7th Cir. 1983), we found that, because the state of Wisconsin held title to the underlying lake beds in a reservation, the Chippewa Band was precluded from restricting hunting and fishing in the reservation waters.

But contrary to Wisconsin's assertions, *Baker* does not dispose of this case. Most importantly, *Baker* did not involve a particular statute under which Congress specified that tribes would be entitled to be treated as states under particular circumstances, and both Congress and the responsible agency outlined the regulatory authority tribes were to exercise. The legal structure governing *Baker* involved only the treaty that created the reservation, and that treaty did not contain any language regarding the tribe's powers to regulate reservation waters. The Clean Water Act, by contrast, explicitly gives authority over waters within the borders of the reservation to the tribe and does not even discuss ownership rights. Secondly, * * * the *Baker* court left open the possibility that state ownership of lake beds may not preclude tribal authority over the waters if tribal regulation was necessary to protect the "political integrity, the economic security, or the health or welfare" of the Band, as both parties concede is the case here. Thirdly, *Baker* was about hunting and fishing rights, which have traditionally been the subject of state regulation, while the ultimate authority for the water quality standards lies with the federal EPA, not the state of Wisconsin (which itself has acted only pursuant to federal delegation).

Baker therefore has little or no application to the case before us. We find pertinent instead a number of legal principles all of which support the EPA's determination that a state's title to a lake bed does not in itself exempt the waters from all outside regulation. First, "the power of Congress to regulate commerce among the states involves the control of the navigable waters of the United States." *Coyle v. Smith*, 221 U.S. 559,

573 (1911). Unlike the situation in *SWANCC of Northern Cook County v. U.S. Army Corps of Engineers*, 531 U.S. 159 (2001), here no one disputes that the waters at issue are "navigable waters" for purposes of either the Clean Water Act or the Commerce Clause.

The breadth of federal authority over Indian affairs is equally well-established: "The Constitution vests the Federal Government with exclusive authority over relations with Indian tribes." *Montana v. Blackfeet Tribe*, 471 U.S. 759, 764 (1985); U.S. CONST., Art. I, § 8, cl.3. In fact, in the absence of tribal TAS status, the EPA and not the state of Wisconsin might well be the proper authority to administer Clean Water Act programs for the reservation, because state laws may usually be applied to Indians on their reservations only if Congress so expressly provides. *See California v. Cabazon Band of Mission Indians*, 480 U.S. 202, 207 (1987).

Because the state does not contend that its ownership of the beds would preclude the federal government from regulating the waters within the reservation, it cannot now complain about the federal government allowing tribes to do so. It was reasonable for the EPA to determine that ownership of the waterbeds did not preclude federally approved regulation of the quality of the water, and we uphold that determination.

3. No Inherent Authority over Off–Reservation Activities

Finally, Wisconsin argues that the Band did not make the required showing of authority over those activities potentially affected by its imposition of water quality standards. Because the EPA has determined that, unlike the Clean Air Act, the Clean Water Act is not an express delegation of power to tribes, *see* 56 Fed. Reg. at 64880, the EPA requires tribes to show that they already possessed inherent authority over the activities undoubtedly affected by the water regulations. EPA regulations allow a tribe to establish this authority by showing that impairment of the reservation's waters would affect "the political integrity, the economic security, or the health or welfare of the tribe." 56 Fed. Reg. at 64877.

This regulatory language tracks the Supreme Court's decision in *Montana v. United States, supra*, in which the Court recognized the general rule that "the inherent sovereign powers of an Indian tribe do not extend to the activities of nonmembers of the tribe," 450 U.S. at 565, but went on to hold that "[a] tribe may also retain inherent power to exercise civil authority over the conduct of non-Indians on fee lands within its reservation when that conduct threatens or has some direct effect on the political integrity, the economic security, or the health or welfare of the tribe." *Id.* at 566. The regulations also track the more recent Supreme Court language in *Strate v. A–1 Contractors*, 520 U.S. 438 (1997), by noting that authority is usually proper because "water quality management serves the purpose of protecting public health and safety, which is a core governmental function, whose exercise is critical to self-government." 56 Fed. Reg. at 64879. * * *

Once a tribe is given TAS status, it has the power to require upstream off-reservation dischargers, conducting activities that may be economically valuable to the state (*e.g.*, zinc and copper mining), to make sure that their activities do not result in contamination of the downstream on-reservation waters (assuming for the sake of argument that the reservation standards are more stringent than those the state is imposing on the upstream entity). Such compliance may impose higher compliance costs on the upstream company, or in the extreme case it might have the effect of prohibiting the discharge or the activities altogether. This is a classic extraterritorial effect, which Wisconsin argues is impermissible and takes this case beyond the scope of *Montana*, which concerned only tribal authority over non-member activities on reservation fee lands.

But this is not the only situation where upstream and downstream users may have different standards and some accommodation is necessary. Wisconsin's argument could be made equally if the downstream regulator were Illinois, yet in that case the need for the two states to coordinate their standards, or for the upstream company to comply with the more stringent rules, would be clear. In fact, Congress anticipated this very problem in the statute, and it had the following to say about it:

> The Administrator shall, in promulgating such regulations [for TAS status], consult affected States sharing common water bodies and provide a mechanism for the resolution of any unreasonable consequences that may arise as a result of differing water quality standards that may be set by States and Indian tribes located on common bodies of water. Such mechanism shall provide for explicit consideration of relevant factors including, but not limited to, the effects of differing water quality permit requirements on upstream and downstream dischargers, economic impacts, and present and historical uses and quality of the waters subject to such standards. Such mechanism should provide for the avoidance of such unreasonable consequences in a manner consistent with the objective of this chapter.

33 U.S.C. § 1377(e).

The EPA has developed the mechanism called for by the statute, which allows it to mediate conflicting interests when a tribe's standards differ from those of a state. *See also* 33 U.S.C. § 1341(a). In addition, once a tribe is given TAS status, the Act gives it the same right as that given to states to object to permits issued for upstream off-reservation activities. *See* 56 Fed. Reg. at 64887. * * * This mechanism, rather than a futile effort to avoid extraterritorial effects, is the way both Congress and the agency sought to accommodate the inevitable differences that would arise.

We say "inevitable" because activities located outside the regulating entity (here the reservation), and the resulting discharges to which those activities can lead, can and often will have "serious and substantial" effects on the health and welfare of the downstream state or reservation. There is no case that expressly rejects an application of *Montana* to off-reservation activities that have significant effects within the reservation, and it would be exceedingly hard to say that the EPA's interpretation is contrary to law in the face of the express recognition of this issue and the choice of a solution in the statute itself. It was reasonable for the EPA to determine that, since the Supreme Court has held that a tribe has inherent authority over activities having a serious effect on the health of the tribe, this authority is not defeated even if it exerts some regulatory force on off-reservation activities.

* * * Because the Band has demonstrated that its water resources are essential to its survival, it was reasonable for the EPA, in line with the purposes of the Clean Water Act and the principles of *Montana*, to allow the tribe to regulate water quality on the reservation, even though that power entails some authority over off-reservation activities. Since a state has the power to require upstream states to comply with its water quality standards, to interpret the statutes to deny that power to tribes because of some kind of formal view of authority or sovereignty would treat tribes as second-class citizens. Nothing in § 1377(e) indicates that Congress authorized any such hierarchy. Particularly in light of the deference we owe to the EPA's decisions here, we see nothing that would justify our setting aside the agency's action. * * *

NOTES

1. **State Ownership of the Bed and Banks.** One of Wisconsin's arguments in this case was that the Mole Lake Band could have no authority over Rice Lake because the state owns the beds and banks of that lake. Wisconsin relied on the federal ***Equal Footing*** and ***public trust doctrines***. The original 13 colonies received title to the beds and banks of the navigable (in the traditional sense) waters when they defeated England in the Revolutionary War. Through the ***Equal Footing Doctrine***, the U.S. Supreme Court extended ownership of the beds and banks of waters navigable-in-fact at the time of statehood to states that joined the United States *after* the Revolutionary War. *Bonelli Cattle Co. v. Arizona*, 414 U.S. 313, 317–18 (1973). The beds and banks of waters that were not navigable-in-fact could be privately owned.

Why did the Seventh Circuit discount Wisconsin's "title" argument? Does its decision make more sense when you consider that (1) under the Equal Footing and public trust doctrines, states own only the beds and banks, not the water itself; and (2) state ownership is still subject to both a ***public trust***—the right of the people to use the waters—and the federal ***navigation servitude***—essentially, the right of the federal government to keep the waterway open to actual navigation? *See, e.g., Phillips Petroleum Co. v. Mississippi*, 484 U.S. 469, 473–76 (1988) (applying the federal public trust doctrine); *United States v. Certain Parcels of Land Situated in City of Valdez*, 666 F.2d 1236, 1238 (9th Cir. 1982) (applying the federal navigation servitude).

2. **The Relationship Between States and Tribes under the Clean Water Act.** Wisconsin had two reasons for challenging the EPA's grant of TAS status to the Mole Lake Band. What were they? Which reason probably supplied the stronger motivation for litigation, do you suppose? Why?

3. **Interstate Relations and Extra–Territorial Effect under the Clean Water Act.** One of Wisconsin's concerns in this case was that the Mole Lake Band would establish more stringent water quality standards than Wisconsin and that these standards would affect discharges upstream of the reservation. As the Seventh Circuit noted, the Clean Water Act expressly allows for such extra-territorial effects, even though states (and Tribes) generally cannot regulate outside of their own jurisdictions. Section 401 of the Act, discussed more fully *infra*, requires the EPA to give downstream states (and Tribes) notice of any federally permitted discharge upstream that might interfere with the downstream state or Tribe's water quality standards, and the downstream state or Tribe can object to the discharge and request that the upstream state or tribe impose more stringent limitations on the discharge. CWA § 401(a)(2), 33 U.S.C. § 1341(a)(2).

4. **Federalism and the Presence of Tribes.** How does the presence of Tribes within a state affect the balance of Clean Water Act regulatory authority between the state and the EPA, even before the Tribes receive TAS status? What is the relationship between the Tribes and the federal government? Do states ordinarily have authority to regulate activities on tribal lands?

5. **Tribal Authority Under the Clean Air Act.** As the Seventh Circuit noted, the Clean Air Act, unlike the Clean Water Act, directly grants Tribes authority to engage in air quality regulation; tribal authority does *not* depend on the Tribe's inherent authority. Under the Clean Air Act, the EPA Administrator "is authorized to treat Indian tribes as States" and "may provide under such Indian tribe grant and contract assistance to carry out functions provided" in the Act. CAA § 301(d)(1), 42 U.S.C. § 7601(d)(1). To be eligible for such authority, a Tribe must "ha[ve] a governing body carrying out substantial governmental duties and powers," propose to exercise its Clean Air Act authority to manage and protect "air resources within the exterior boundaries of the reservation or other areas within the tribe's jurisdiction," and be "reasonably expected to be capable, in the judgment of the Administrator, of carrying out the functions to be exercised in a manner consistent with the terms and purposes of [the Clean Air Act] and all applicable regulations." CAA § 301(d)(2), 42 U.S.C. § 7601(d)(2).

What is different about the language of the Clean Air Act and the Clean Water Act with respect to the EPA's authority to treat Tribes as states? Why has the EPA treated the Clean Air Act provisions as supplying Tribes with a specific congressional grant of regulatory authority, while the Clean Water Act rests on Tribes' inherent authority? What difference does that distinction make to tribal regulatory authority, according to the Seventh Circuit? *See Arizona Public Service Co. v. EPA*, 211 F.3d 1280, 1287 (D.C. Cir. 2000).

* * *

J. ENFORCING THE NPDES PERMIT PROGRAM

Since 1972, the number of dischargers covered by NPDES permits has grown significantly, as Figure 5–15 demonstrates. The number of NPDES permittees makes enforcement a critical component of the NPDES program, and the Act authorizes both the EPA and delegated states to enforce its provisions. Under section 309, states and the EPA can pursue administrative, civil, and criminal remedies against a point source that: (1) discharges without a permit; (2) discharges in violation of its NPDES permit; (3) fails to comply with the pretreatment standards, if the point source is an indirect discharger; (4) files inaccurate DMRs; or (5) violates a prior state or EPA enforcement order. 33 U.S.C. § 1319. Section 402, moreover, specifies that the federal government retains full enforcement authority even after a state has assumed NPDES permitting authority for point sources within that state. CWA § 402(i), 33 U.S.C. § 1342(i).

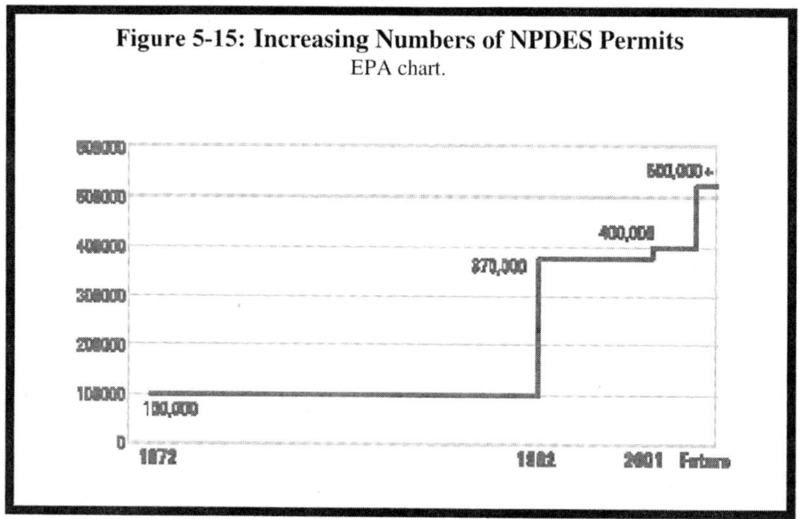

Figure 5-15: Increasing Numbers of NPDES Permits
EPA chart.

In addition, under section 505, citizens may file a citizen enforcement action "against any person * * * who is alleged to be in violation of (A) an effluent standard or limitation under this chapter or (B) an order issued by the Administrator or State with respect to such a standard or limitation * * *." CWA § 505(a)(1), 33 U.S.C. § 1365(a)(1). This section defines "effluent standard or limitation" to include:

> (1) effective July 1, 1973, an unlawful act under subsection (a) of section 1311 of this title [*i.e.*, the discharge of pollutants without a permit]; (2) an effluent limitation or other limitation under section 1311 or 1312 of this title; (3) standard of performance under section 1316 of this title; (4) prohibition, effluent standard or pretreatment standards under section 1317 of this title; (5) certification under section 1341 of this title; (6) permit or condition thereof issued under section 1342 of this title, which is in effect under this chapter (including a requirement applicable by reason of section 1323 of this title); or (7) a regulation under section 1345(d) of this title.

CWA § 505(f), 33 U.S.C. § 1365(f). We will discuss "certifications under section 1341" (item 4) later. The reference to section 1323 in item 6 ensures that federal facilities are also subject to citizen suits. Finally, regulations under section 1345(d) (item 7) govern the disposal of sewage sludge from POTWs.

Government and citizen enforcement authority against permitted point sources, however, is a bit more limited. Once a point source has an NPDES permit, compliance with the permit shields the point source from most kinds of Clean Water Act enforcement:

> Compliance with a permit issued pursuant to this section shall be deemed compliance, for purposes of sections 1319 and 1365 of this title, with sections 1311, 1312, 1316, 1317, and 1343 of this title, except any standard imposed under section 1317 of this title for a toxic pollutant injurious to human health.

CWA § 402(k), 33 U.S.C. § 1342(k). As a result of this protection, section 402(k) is often referred to as the ***"permit shield"*** provision.

IV. SECTION 404 "DREDGE AND FILL" PERMITS

A. INTRODUCTION AND OVERVIEW

The section 402 NPDES permit program is the Clean Water Act's most extensive permit program. However, certain kinds of "discharges of pollutants" are regulated instead under the ***section 404 "dredge and fill" permit program***. Under section 404, "[t]he Secretary may issue permits * * * for the discharge of dredged or fill material into the navigable waters at specified disposal sites." CWA § 404(a), 33 U.S.C. § 1344(a). The section 404 permit program differs in several significant respects from the NPDES permit program.

1. Federal Agency Administration of the Act

First, Congress gave the primary regulatory authority for the section 404 permit program to the Secretary of the Army, acting through the ***U.S. Army Corps of Engineers***. CWA § 404(d), 33 U.S.C. § 1344(d). Nevertheless, the EPA retains oversight authority over the section 404 permit program. Moreover, the EPA issued the ***section 404(b)(1) Guidelines***, CWA § 404(b)(1), 33 U.S.C. § 1344(b)(1), and the EPA can veto any particular permit or discharge. *See* CWA § 404(c), 33 U.S.C. § 1344(c).

Nevertheless, the Clean Water Act's structure of "cooperative federalism" continues into the section 404 permit program. As in the NPDES permit program, states (and Tribes) can obtain section 404 permitting authority. CWA § 404(g), (h), 33 U.S.C. § 1344(g), (h). Moreover, section 404(t) provides that:

> Nothing in this section shall preclude or deny the right of any State or interstate agency to control the discharge of dredged or fill material in any portion of the navigable waters within the jurisdiction of such State, including any activity of any Federal agency, and each such agency shall comply with such State or interstate requirements both

> substantive and procedural to control the discharge of dredged or fill material to the same extent that any person is subject to such requirements. This section shall not be construed as affecting or impairing the authority of the Secretary to maintain navigation.

CWA § 404(t), 33 U.S.C. § 1344(t). Nevertheless, only two states—Michigan and New Jersey—have received section 404 permitting authority. U.S. EPA, *State or Tribal Assumption of the Section 404 Permit Program*, http://www.epa.gov/owow/wetlands/facts/fact23.html (last updated Sept. 26, 2003). Lack of state acquisition of section 404 permitting authority thus stands in sharp contrast to the widespread state acquisition of section 402 NPDES permitting authority. According to the EPA, states give several reasons for their reluctance to acquire section 404 permitting authority: (1) lack of funding; (2) section 404's limitation on state permitting to non-navigable waters, *see* CWA § 404(g)(1), 33 U.S.C. § 1344(g)(1); (3) concerns regarding federal requirements and oversight; (4) availability of alternative mechanisms for regulating; and (5) the controversial nature of section 404 permitting. *Id.*

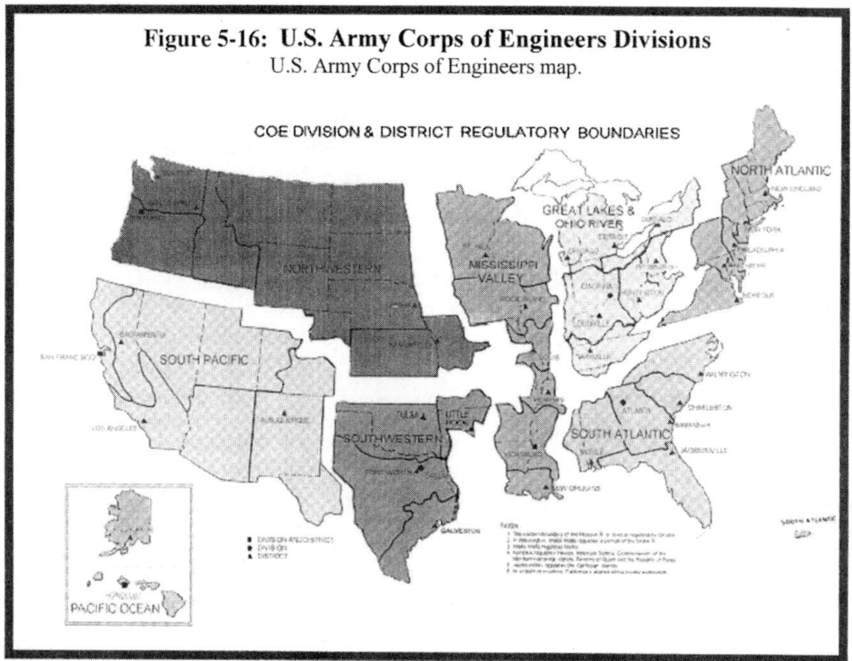

Figure 5-16: U.S. Army Corps of Engineers Divisions
U.S. Army Corps of Engineers map.

Because of states' reluctance to acquire section 404 permitting authority, section 404 permitting has remained an area where the federal government—embodied mainly in the Army Corps of Engineers—dominates water quality regulation.

2. Navigable Waters

Second, unlike the NPDES permit program, the section 404 permit program is limited to discharges into the ***navigable waters***. CWA

§ 404(a), 33 U.S.C. § 1344(a). As was discussed in connection with federal regulatory jurisdiction pursuant to section 301(a), the navigable waters are the inland freshwaters and the territorial sea—the first three miles of the ocean. The section 404 permit program does not apply in the deeper waters of the ocean.

3. Discharges of Dredged or Fill Material

Third, the section 404 permit program applies to discharges of only two kinds of pollutants—specifically, to "discharge[s] of ***dredged or fill material*** * * *." CWA § 404(a), 33 U.S.C. § 1344(a). The Clean Water Act itself does not further define "dredged materials" or "fill materials." Nevertheless, section 404 exempts a number of activities from the permit requirement. No permit is required for "the discharge of dredged or fill material—"

> (A) from normal farming, silviculture [forestry], and ranching activities such as plowing, seeding, cultivating, minor drainage, harvesting for the production of food, fiber, and forest products, or upland soil and water conservation practices;
>
> (B) for the purpose of maintenance, including emergency reconstruction of recently damaged parts, of currently serviceable structures such as dikes, dams, levees, groins, riprap, breakwaters, causeways, and bridge abutments or approaches, and transportation structures;
>
> (C) for the purpose of construction or maintenance of farm or stock ponds or irrigation ditches, or the maintenance of drainage ditches;
>
> (D) for the purpose of construction of temporary sedimentation basins on a construction site which does not include the placement of fill material into the navigable waters;
>
> (E) for the purpose of construction or maintenance of farm roads or forest roads, or temporary roads for moving mining equipment, where such roads are constructed and maintained, in accordance with best management practices, to assure that flow and circulation patterns and chemical and biological characteristics of the navigable waters are not impaired, that the reach of the navigable waters is not reduced, and that any adverse effect on the aquatic environment will be otherwise minimized; [or]
>
> (F) resulting from any activity with respect to which a State has an approved [areawide waste treatment management] plan under section 1288(b)(4) of [the Clean Water Act] which meets [the consultation and best management practices requirements in section 1288(b)(4)(B) and (C)] * * *.

CWA § 404(f)(1), 33 U.S.C. § 1344(f)(1). Nevertheless, these statutory exemptions are not as broad as they appear, because section 404(f)(2), the "***recapture provision***," provides that:

> Any discharge of dredged or fill material into the navigable waters incidental to any activity having as its purpose bringing an area of the navigable waters into a use to which it was not previously subject, where the flow or circulation of navigable waters may be impaired or the reach of such waters be reduced, shall be required to have a permit under this section.

CWA § 404(f)(2), 33 U.S.C. § 1344(f)(2).

The Army Corps' regulations provide further clarification of "dredged material" and "fill material." The Corps has defined ***"discharge of dredged material"*** to be "the addition of dredged material into, including redeposit of dredged material other than incidental fallback within, the waters of the United States." 33 C.F.R. § 323.2(d)(1). ***"Dredged material,"*** in turn, is "material that is excavated or dredged from waters of the United States." *Id.* § 323.2(c). Thus, as was discussed in connection with "addition," dredged material must originate from navigable waters and then be replaced back into the navigable waters.

According to the Army Corps, discharges of dredged material normally *include*:

(1) "The addition of dredged material to a specified disposal site located in waters of the United States;"

(2) "The runoff or overflow from a contained land or water disposal area;"

(3) "Any addition, including redeposit other than incidental fallback, of dredged material, including excavated material, into waters of the United States which is incidental to any activity, including mechanized landclearing, ditching, channelization, or other excavation."

33 C.F.R. § 323.2(d)(1). The Corps and the EPA "regard the use of mechanized earth-moving equipment to conduct landclearing, ditching, channelization, in-stream mining or other earth-moving activity in waters of the United States as resulting in a discharge of dredged material unless project-specific evidence shows that the activity results in only incidental fallback." 33 C.F.R. § 323.2(d)(2). As a result, any construction activity in or near waters of the United States is likely to include a discharge of dredged material that requires a section 404 permit, unless only incidental fallback results. As was discussed in connection with "additions," "***incidental fallback*** is the redeposit of small volumes of dredged material that is incidental to excavation activity in waters of the United States when such material falls back to substantially the same place as the initial removal." 33 C.F.R. § 323.2(d)(2)(ii) (emphasis added).

According to the Army Corps, the "***discharge of fill material***" is "the addition of fill material into waters of the United States." 33 C.F.R. § 323.2(f). The Corps also notes in its regulations that "discharges of fill material" generally *include* the following activities:

(1) "Placement of fill that is necessary for the construction of any structure or infrastructure in a water of the United States;"

(2) "[T]he building of any structure or infrastructure or impoundment requiring rock, sand, dirt, or other material for its construction;"

(3) "[S]ite-development fills for recreational, industrial, commercial, residential, or other uses;"

(4) "[C]auseways or road fills;"

(5) "[D]ams and dikes;"

(6) "[A]rtificial islands;"

(7) "[P]roperty protection and/or reclamation devices such as riprap, groins, seawalls, breakwaters, and revetments;"

(8) "[B]each nourishment;"

(9) "[L]evees;"

(10) "[F]ill for structures such as sewage treatment facilities, intake and outfall pipes associated with power plants and subaqueous utility lines; placement of fill material for construction or maintenance of any liner, berm, or other infrastructure associated with solid waste landfills; placement of overburden, slurry, or tailings of similar mining-related materials; and"

(11) "[A]rtificial reefs."

33 C.F.R. § 323.2(f). However, "discharge of fill material" does *not* include "plowing, cultivating, seeding, and harvesting for the production of food, fiber, and forest products." *Id.*

"***Fill material***," in turn, is "material placed in waters of the United States where the material has the effect of:"

(i) Replacing any portion of a water of the United States with dry land; or

(ii) Changing the bottom elevation of any portion of a water of the United States.

33 C.F.R. § 323.2(e) (as amended, 67 Fed. Reg. 31,129 (May 9, 2002)).

4. Choosing Between Section 402 and Section 404 Permitting

Most of the time, it is fairly obvious which of the Clean Water Act's two permitting programs applies to a discharge of pollutants—but not always. In 2009, the U.S. Supreme Court decided the following case raising that issue. Do you think that the Court properly distinguished the two permit programs? Why or why not?

COEUR ALASKA, INC. v. SOUTHEAST ALASKA CONSERVATION COUNCIL

557 U.S. 261 (2009).

KENNEDY, J., delivered the opinion of the Court, in which ROBERTS, C.J., and THOMAS, BREYER, and ALITO, JJ., joined, and in which SCALIA, J., joined in part. BREYER, J., filed a concurring opinion. SCALIA, J., filed an opinion concurring in part and concurring in the judgment. GINSBURG, J., filed a dissenting opinion, in in which STEVENS and SOUTER, JJ., joined.

These cases require us to address two questions under the Clean Water Act (CWA or Act). The first is whether the Act gives authority to the United States Army Corps of Engineers, or instead to the Environmental Protection Agency (EPA), to issue a permit for the discharge of mining waste, called slurry. The Corps of Engineers has issued a permit to petitioner Coeur Alaska, Inc. (Coeur Alaska), for a discharge of slurry into a lake in Southeast Alaska. The second question is whether, when the Corps issued that permit, the agency acted in accordance with law. We conclude that the Corps was the appropriate agency to issue the permit and that the permit is lawful.

* * * I

A

Petitioner Coeur Alaska plans to reopen the Kensington Gold Mine, located some 45 miles north of Juneau, Alaska. The mine has been closed since 1928, but Coeur Alaska seeks to make it profitable once more by using a technique known as "froth flotation." Coeur Alaska will churn the mine's crushed rock in tanks of frothing water. Chemicals in the water will cause gold-bearing minerals to float to the surface, where they will be skimmed off.

At issue is Coeur Alaska's plan to dispose of the mixture of crushed rock and water left behind in the tanks. This mixture is called slurry. Some 30 percent of the slurry's volume is crushed rock, resembling wet sand, which is called tailings. The rest is water.

The standard way to dispose of slurry is to pump it into a tailings pond. The slurry separates in the pond. Solid tailings sink to the bottom, and water on the surface returns to the mine to be used again.

Rather than build a tailings pond, Coeur Alaska proposes to use Lower Slate Lake, located some three miles from the mine in the Tongass National Forest. This lake is small—800 feet at its widest crossing, 2,000 feet at its longest, and 23 acres in area. Though small, the lake is 51 feet deep at its maximum. The parties agree the lake is a navigable water of the United States and so is subject to the CWA. They also agree there can be no discharge into the lake except as the CWA and any lawful permit allow.

Over the life of the mine, Coeur Alaska intends to put 4.5 million tons of tailings in the lake. This will raise the lakebed 50 feet—to what is now the lake's surface—and will increase the lake's area from 23 to about 60 acres. To contain this wider, shallower body of water, Coeur Alaska will dam the lake's downstream shore. The transformed lake will be isolated from other surface water. Creeks and stormwater runoff will detour around it. Ultimately, lakewater will be cleaned by purification systems and will flow from the lake to a stream and thence onward.

B

Numerous state and federal agencies reviewed and approved Coeur Alaska's plans. At issue here are actions by two of those agencies: the Corps of Engineers and the EPA.

1

The CWA classifies crushed rock as a "pollutant." 33 U.S.C. § 1362(6). On the one hand, the Act forbids Coeur Alaska's discharge of crushed rock "[e]xcept as in compliance" with the Act. CWA § 301(a), 33 U.S.C. § 1311(a). Section 404(a) of the CWA, on the other hand, empowers the Corps to authorize the discharge of "dredged or fill material." 33 U.S.C. § 1344(a). The Corps and the EPA have together defined "fill material" to mean any "material [that] has the effect of . . . [c]hanging the bottom elevation" of water. 40 CFR § 232.2. The agencies have further defined the "discharge of fill material" to include "placement of . . . slurry, or tailings or similar mining-related materials." *Ibid.*

In these cases the Corps and the EPA agree that the slurry meets their regulatory definition of "fill material." On that premise the Corps evaluated the mine's plan for a § 404 permit. After considering the environmental factors required by § 404(b), the Corps issued Coeur Alaska a permit to pump the slurry into Lower Slate Lake.

In granting the permit the Corps followed the steps set forth by § 404. Section 404(b) requires the Corps to consider the environmental consequences of every discharge it allows. 33 U.S.C. § 1344(b). The Corps must apply guidelines written by the EPA pursuant to § 404(b). Applying those guidelines here, the Corps determined that Coeur Alaska's plan to use Lower Slate Lake as a tailings pond was the "least environmentally damaging practicable" way to dispose of the tailings. To conduct that analysis, the Corps compared the plan to the proposed alternatives.

The Corps determined that the environmental damage caused by placing slurry in the lake will be temporary. And during that temporary disruption, Coeur Alaska will divert waters around the lake through pipelines built for this purpose. Coeur Alaska will also treat water flowing from the lake into downstream waters, pursuant to strict EPA criteria. Though the slurry will at first destroy the lake's small population of common fish, that population may later be replaced. After mining operations are completed, Coeur Alaska will help "recla[im]" the lake by "[c]apping" the tailings with about 4 inches of "native material." The Corps concluded that

> "[t]he reclamation of the lake will result in more emergent wetlands/vegetated shallows with moderate values for fish habitat, nutrient recycling, carbon/detrital export and sediment/toxicant retention, and high values for wildlife habitat."

If the tailings did not go into the lake, they would be placed on nearby wetlands. The resulting pile would rise twice as high as the Pentagon and cover three times as many acres. If it were chosen, that alternative would destroy dozens of acres of wetlands—a permanent loss. On the premise that when the mining ends the lake will be at least as environmentally hospitable, if not more so, than now, the Corps concluded that placing the tailings in the lake will cause less damage to the environment than storing them above ground: The reclaimed lake will be "more valuable to the aquatic ecosystem than a permanently filled wetland . . . that has lost all aquatic functions and values."

2

The EPA had the statutory authority to veto the Corps permit, and prohibit the discharge, if it found the plan to have "an unacceptable adverse effect on municipal water supplies, shellfish beds and fishery areas . . . , wildlife, or recreational areas." CWA § 404(c), 33 U.S.C. § 1344(c). After considering the Corps findings, the EPA did not veto the Corps permit, even though, in its view, placing the tailings in the lake was not the "environmentally preferable" means of disposing of them. By declining to exercise its veto, the EPA in effect deferred to the judgment of the Corps on this point.

The EPA's involvement extended beyond the agency's veto consideration. The EPA also issued a permit of its own—not for the discharge from the mine into the lake but for the discharge from the lake into a downstream creek. Section 402 grants the EPA authority to "issue a permit for the discharge of any pollutant," "[e]xcept as provided in [CWA § 404]." 33 U.S.C. § 1342(a). The EPA's § 402 permit authorizes Coeur Alaska to discharge water from Lower Slate Lake into the downstream creek, subject to strict water-quality limits that Coeur Alaska must regularly monitor.

The EPA's authority to regulate this discharge comes from a regulation, termed a "new source performance standard," that it has promulgated under authority granted to it by § 306(b) of the CWA. Section 306(b) gives the EPA authority to regulate the amount of pollutants that certain categories of new sources may discharge into the navigable waters of the United States. 33 U.S.C. § 1316(b). Pursuant to this authority, the EPA in 1982 promulgated a new source performance standard restricting discharges from new froth-flotation gold mines like Coeur Alaska's. The standard is stringent: It allows "no discharge of process wastewater" from these mines. 40 CFR § 440.104(b)(1).

Applying that standard to the discharge of water from Lower Slate Lake into the downstream creek, the EPA's § 402 permit sets strict limits on the amount of pollutants the water may contain. The permit requires Coeur Alaska to treat the water using "reverse osmosis" to remove aluminum, suspended solids, and other pollutants. Coeur Alaska must monitor the water flowing from the lake to be sure that the pollutants are kept to low, specified minimums.

C

SEACC brought suit against the Corps of Engineers and various of its officials in the United States District Court for the District of Alaska. The Corps permit was not in accordance with law, SEACC argued, for two reasons. First, in SEACC's view, the permit was issued by the wrong agency—Coeur Alaska ought to have sought a § 402 permit from the EPA, just as the company did for the discharge of water from the lake into the downstream creek. Second, SEACC contended that regardless of which agency issued the permit, the discharge itself is unlawful because it will violate the EPA new source performance standard for froth-flotation gold mines. (This is the same performance standard described above, which the EPA has already applied to the discharge of water from the lake into the downstream creek.) SEACC argued that this performance standard also applies to the discharge of slurry into the lake. It contended further that the performance standard is a binding implementation of § 306. Section 306(e) of the CWA makes it "unlawful" for Coeur Alaska to "operate" the mine "in violation of" the EPA's performance standard. 33 U.S.C. § 1316(e).

Coeur Alaska and the State of Alaska intervened as defendants. Both sides moved for summary judgment. The District Court granted summary judgment in favor of the defendants.

The Court of Appeals for the Ninth Circuit reversed and ordered the District Court to vacate the Corps of Engineers' permit. The court acknowledged that Coeur Alaska's slurry "facially meets the Corps' current regulatory definition of 'fill material,'" because it would have the effect of raising the lake's bottom elevation. But the court also noted that the EPA's new source performance standard "prohibits discharges from froth-flotation mills." The Court of Appeals concluded that "[b]oth of the regulations appear to apply in this case, yet they are at odds." To resolve the conflict, the court turned to what it viewed as "the plain language of the Clean Water Act." The court held that the EPA's new source performance standard "applies to discharges from the froth-flotation mill at Coeur Alaska's Kensington Gold Mine into Lower Slate Lake."

* * * The decision of the Court of Appeals in effect reallocated the division of responsibility that the Corps and the EPA had been following. The Court granted certiorari. We now hold that the decision of the Court of Appeals was incorrect.

II

The question of which agency has authority to consider whether to permit the slurry discharge is our beginning inquiry. We consider first the authority of the EPA and second the authority of the Corps. Our conclusion is that under the CWA the Corps had authority to determine whether Coeur Alaska was entitled to the permit governing this discharge.

A

Section 402 gives the EPA authority to issue "permit[s] for the discharge of any pollutant," with one important exception: The EPA may not issue permits for fill material that fall under the Corps' § 404 permitting authority. Section 402(a) states:

> "*Except as provided in* . . . *[CWA § 404, 33 U.S.C. § 1344],* the Administrator may . . . issue a permit for the discharge of any pollutant, . . . notwithstanding [CWA § 301(a), 33 U.S.C. § 1311(a)], upon condition that such discharge will meet either (A) all applicable requirements under [CWA § 301, 33 U.S.C. § 1311(a); CWA § 302, 33 U.S.C. § 1312; CWA § 306, 33 U.S.C. § 1316; CWA § 307, 33 U.S.C. § 1317; CWA § 308, 33 U.S.C. § 1318; CWA § 403, 33 U.S.C. § 1343], or (B) prior to the taking of necessary implementing actions relating to all such requirements, such conditions as the Administrator determines are necessary to carry out the provisions of this chapter." 33 U.S.C. § 1342(a)(1) (emphasis added).

Section 402 thus forbids the EPA from exercising permitting authority that is "provided [to the Corps] in" § 404.

This is not to say the EPA has no role with respect to the environmental consequences of fill. The EPA's function is different, in regulating fill, from its function in regulating other pollutants, but the agency does exercise some authority. Section 404 assigns the EPA two tasks in regard to fill material. First, the EPA must write guidelines for the Corps to follow in determining whether to permit a discharge of fill material. CWA § 404(b); 33 U.S.C. § 1344(b). Second, the Act gives the EPA authority to "prohibit" any decision by the Corps to issue a permit for a particular disposal site. CWA § 404(c); 33 U.S.C. § 1344(c). We, and the parties, refer to this as the EPA's power to veto a permit.

The Act is best understood to provide that if the Corps has authority to issue a permit for a discharge under § 404, then the EPA lacks authority to do so under § 402.

Even if there were ambiguity on this point, the EPA's own regulations would resolve it. Those regulations provide that "[d]ischarges of dredged or fill material into waters of the United States which are regulated under section 404 of CWA" "do not require [§ 402] permits" from the EPA. 40 CFR § 122.3.

* * * The question whether the EPA is the proper agency to regulate the slurry discharge thus depends on whether the Corps of Engineers has

authority to do so. If the Corps has authority to issue a permit, then the EPA may not do so. We turn to the Corps' authority under § 404.

B

Section 404(a) gives the Corps power to "issue permits ... for the discharge of dredged or fill material." 33 U.S.C. § 1344(a). As all parties concede, the slurry meets the definition of fill material agreed upon by the agencies in a joint regulation promulgated in 2002. That regulation defines "fill material" to mean any "material [that] has the effect of ... [c]hanging the bottom elevation" of water—a definition that includes "slurry, or tailings or similar mining-related materials." 40 CFR § 232.2.

SEACC concedes that the slurry to be discharged meets the regulation's definition of fill material. Its concession on this point is appropriate because slurry falls well within the central understanding of the term "fill," as shown by the examples given by the regulation. * * *

Rather than challenge the agencies' decision to define the slurry as fill, SEACC instead contends that § 404 contains an implicit exception. According to SEACC, § 404 does not authorize the Corps to permit a discharge of fill material if that material is subject to an EPA new source performance standard.

But § 404's text does not limit its grant of power in this way. Instead, § 404 refers to all "fill material" without qualification. Nor do the EPA regulations support SEACC's reading of § 404. The EPA has enacted guidelines, pursuant to § 404(b), to guide the Corps permitting decision. 40 CFR pt. 230. Those guidelines do not strip the Corps of power to issue permits for fill in cases where the fill is also subject to an EPA new source performance standard.

SEACC's reading of § 404 would create numerous difficulties for the regulated industry. As the regulatory regime stands now, a discharger must ask a simple question—is the substance to be discharged fill material or not? The fill regulation, 40 CFR § 232.2, offers a clear answer to that question; and under the agencies' view, that answer decides the matter—if the discharge is fill, the discharger must seek a § 404 permit from the Corps; if not, only then must the discharger consider whether any EPA performance standard applies, so that the discharger requires a § 402 permit from the EPA.

Under SEACC's interpretation, however, the discharger would face a more difficult problem. The discharger would have to ask—is the fill material also subject to one of the many hundreds of EPA performance standards, so that the permit must come from the EPA, not the Corps? The statute gives no indication that Congress intended to burden industry with that confusing division of permit authority.

The regulatory scheme discloses a defined, and workable, line for determining whether the Corps or the EPA has the permit authority. Under this framework, the Corps of Engineers, and not the EPA, has authority to permit Coeur Alaska's discharge of the slurry.

III

A second question remains: In issuing the permit did the Corps act in violation of a statutory mandate so that the issuance was "not in accordance with law"? 5 U.S.C. § 706(2)(A). SEACC contends that the slurry discharge will violate the EPA's new source performance standard and that the Corps permit is made "unlawful" by CWA § 306(e). Petitioners and the agencies argue that the permit is lawful because the EPA performance standard, and § 306(e), do not apply to fill material regulated by the Corps. In order to determine whether the Corps permit is lawful we must answer the question: Do EPA performance standards, and § 306(e), apply to discharges of fill material?

* * * A

As for the statutory argument, SEACC claims the CWA § 404 permit is unlawful because § 306(e) forbids the slurry discharge. Petitioners and the federal agencies, in contrast, contend that § 306(e) does not apply to the slurry discharge.

1

To address SEACC's statutory argument, it is necessary to review the EPA's responsibilities under the CWA. As noted, § 306 empowers the EPA to regulate the froth-flotation gold mining industry. See 33 U.S.C. § 1316(b). Pursuant to this authority, EPA promulgated the new source performance standard relied upon by SEACC. The standard is stringent. If it were to apply here, it would allow "no discharge of process wastewater" from the mine. 40 CFR § 440.104(b)(1).

The term "process wastewater" includes solid waste. So the regulation forbids not only pollutants that dissolve in water but also solid pollutants suspended in water—what the agency terms "total suspended solids," or TSS. See § 440.104(a) (limiting the amount of TSS from other kinds of mines).

Were there any doubt about whether the EPA's new source performance standard forbade solids as well as soluble pollutants, the agency's action in these cases would resolve it. Here, the EPA's § 402 permit authorizes Coeur Alaska to discharge water from Lower Slate Lake into a downstream creek, provided the water meets the quality requirements set by the performance standard. This demonstrates that the performance standard regulates solid waste. The EPA's permit not only restricts the amount of total suspended solids, but also forbids the mine from allowing any "floating solids" to flow from the lake. No party disputes the EPA's authority to regulate these discharges of solid mining waste; and no party questions the validity of the EPA's new source performance standard when it is applicable.

When the performance standard applies to a point source, § 306(e) makes it "unlawful" for that point source to violate it: "[I]t shall be unlawful for any owner or operator of any new source to operate such source in violation of any standard of performance applicable to such source." CWA § 306(e), 33 U.S.C. § 1316(e).

SEACC argues that this provision, § 306(e), forbids the mine from discharging slurry into Lower Slate Lake. SEACC contends the new source performance standard is, in the words of § 306(e), "applicable to" the mine. Both the text of the performance standard and the EPA's application of it to the discharge of mining waste from Lower Slate Lake demonstrate that the performance standard is "applicable to" Coeur Alaska's mine in some circumstances. And so, SEACC reasons, it follows that because the new source performance standard forbids even minute discharges of solid waste, it also forbids the slurry discharge, 30% of which is solid waste.

2

For their part, the State of Alaska and the federal agencies claim that the Act is unambiguous in the opposite direction. They rely on § 404 of the Act. As explained above, that section authorizes the Corps of Engineers to determine whether to issue a permit allowing the discharge of the slurry. Petitioners and the agencies argue that § 404 grants the Corps authority to do so without regard to the EPA's new source performance standard or the § 306(e) prohibition discussed above.

Petitioners and the agencies make two statutory arguments based on § 404's silence in regard to § 306. First, they note that nothing in § 404 requires the Corps to consider the EPA's new source performance standard or the § 306(e) prohibition. That silence advances the argument that § 404's grant of authority to "issue permits" contradicts § 306(e)'s declaration that discharges in violation of new source performance standards are "unlawful."

Second, petitioners and the agencies point to § 404(p), which protects § 404 permitees from enforcement actions by the EPA or private citizens:

> "Compliance with a permit issued pursuant to this section . . . shall be deemed compliance, for purposes of sections 1319 [CWA § 309] and 1365 [CWA § 505] of this title, with sections 1311 [CWA § 301], 1317 [CWA § 307], and 1343 [CWA § 403] of this title." 33 U.S.C. § 1344(p).

Here again, their argument is that silence is significant. Section 404(p) protects the permitee from lawsuits alleging violations of CWA § 301 (which bars the discharge of "any pollutant" "except as in compliance" with the Act), § 307 (which bars the discharge of "toxic pollutants"); and § 403 (which bars discharges into the sea). But § 404(p) does not in express terms protect the permitee from a lawsuit alleging a violation of § 306(e) or of the EPA's new source performance standards. Section 404(p)'s silence regarding § 306 is made even more significant because a parallel provision in § 402 does protect a § 402 permitee from an enforcement action alleging a violation of § 306. CWA § 402(k), 33 U.S.C. § 1342(k).

In our view, Congress' omission of § 306 from § 404, and its inclusion of § 306 in § 402(k), is evidence that Congress did not intend § 306(e) to apply to Corps § 404 permits or to discharges of fill material. If § 306 did apply, then the Corps would be required to evaluate each permit application for compliance with § 306, and issue a permit only if it found the discharge would comply with § 306. But even if that finding were made, it is not clear that the § 404 permitee would be protected from a suit seeking a judicial determination that the discharge violates § 306.

3

The CWA is ambiguous on the question whether § 306 applies to discharges of fill material regulated under § 404. On the one hand, § 306 provides that a discharge that violates an EPA new source performance standard is "unlawful"—without any exception for fill material. On the other hand, § 404 grants the Corps blanket authority to permit the discharge of fill material—without any mention of § 306. This tension indicates that Congress has not "directly spoken" to the "precise question" of whether § 306 applies to discharges of fill material.

B

Before turning to how the agencies have resolved that question, we consider the formal regulations that bear on §§ 306 and 404. The regulations, like the statutes, do not address the question whether § 306, and the EPA new source performance standards promulgated under it, apply to § 404 permits and the discharges they authorize. There is no regulation, for example, interpreting § 306(e)'s text—"standard of performance applicable to such source"—to mean that a performance standard ceases to be "applicable" the moment the discharge qualifies as fill material, which would resolve the cases in petitioners' favor. Nor is there a regulation providing that the Corps, in deciding whether to grant a permit under § 404, must deny that permit if the discharge would violate § 306(e), which would decide the cases for SEACC.

* * * C

The regulations do not give a definitive answer to the question whether § 306 applies to discharges regulated by the Corps under § 404, but we do find that agency interpretation and agency application of the regulations are instructive and to the point. The question is addressed and resolved in a reasonable and coherent way by the practice and policy of the two agencies, all as recited in a memorandum written in May 2004 by Diane Regas, then the Director of the EPA's Office of Wetlands, Oceans and Watersheds, to Randy Smith, the Director of the EPA's regional Office of Water with responsibility over the mine. The Memorandum, though not subject to sufficiently formal procedures to merit *Chevron* deference is entitled to a measure of deference because it interprets the agencies' own regulatory scheme.

The Regas Memorandum explains:

"As a result [of the fact that the discharge is regulated under § 404], the regulatory regime applicable to discharges under section 402, including effluent limitations guidelines and standards, such as those applicable to gold ore mining ... do not apply to the placement of tailings into the proposed impoundment [of Lower Slate Lake]. See 40 CFR § 122.3(b)."

The regulation that the Memorandum cites—40 CFR § 122.3—is one we considered above and found ambiguous. That regulation provides: "[d]ischarges of dredged or fill material into waters of the United States which are regulated under section 404 of CWA" "do not require [§ 402] permits." The Regas Memorandum takes an instructive interpretive step when it explains that because the discharge "do[es] not require" an EPA permit, the EPA's performance standard "do[es] not apply" to the discharge. The Memorandum presents a reasonable interpretation of the regulatory regime. We defer to the interpretation because it is not "plainly erroneous or inconsistent with the regulation[s]." * * *

* * * The Court requested the parties to submit supplemental briefs addressing whether the CWA contemplated that both agencies would issue a permit for a discharge. A two-permit regime would allow the EPA to apply its performance standard, while the Corps could apply its § 404(b) criteria. The parties agree, however, that a two-permit regime is contrary to the statute and the regulations. We conclude that this is correct. A two-permit regime would cause confusion, delay, expense, and uncertainty in the permitting process. In agreement with all of the parties, we conclude that, when a permit is required to discharge fill material, either a § 402 or a § 404 permit is necessary. Here, we now hold, § 404 applies, not § 402.

The Regas Memorandum's interpretation of the agencies' regulations is consistent with the regulatory scheme as a whole. The Memorandum preserves a role for the EPA's performance standards; it guards against the possibility of evasion of those standards; it employs the Corps' expertise in evaluating the effects of fill material on the aquatic environment; it does not allow toxic pollutants to be discharged; and we have been offered no better way to harmonize the regulations. We defer to the EPA's conclusion that its performance standard does not apply to the initial discharge of slurry into the lake but applies only to the later discharge of water from the lake into the downstream creek.

* * * The agencies' published statements indicate adherence to the EPA's previous application and interpretation of its performance standards. SEACC cannot show that the agencies have changed their interpretation or application of their regulations.

SEACC cites no instance in which the EPA has applied one of its performance standards to a discharge of fill material. By contrast, Coeur Alaska cites two instances in which the Corps issued a § 404 permit authorizing a mine to discharge solid waste (tailings) as fill material. SEACC objects that those two § 404 permits authorized discharges that used the tailings to construct useful structures—a dam in one case, a tailings pond in another. Here, by contrast, SEACC contends that the primary purpose of the discharge is to use a navigable water to dispose of waste. But that objection misses the point. The two § 404 permits cited by Coeur Alaska illustrate that the agencies did not have a prior practice of applying EPA performance standards to discharges of mining wastes that qualify as fill material.

SEACC has not demonstrated that the agencies have changed their policy, and it cannot show that the Regas Memorandum is contrary to the agencies' published statements.

* * *

We accord deference to the agencies' reasonable decision to continue their prior practice.

The judgment of the Court of Appeals is reversed, and these cases are remanded for further proceedings consistent with this opinion.

It is so ordered.

JUSTICE BREYER, concurring.

As I understand the Court's opinion, it recognizes a legal zone within which the regulating agencies might reasonably classify material either as "dredged or fill material" subject to § 404 of the Clean Water Act, 33 U.S.C. § 1344(a), or as a "pollutant," subject to §§ 402 and 306, 33 U.S.C. §§ 1342(a), 1316(a). Within this zone, the law authorizes the environmental agencies to classify material as the one or the other, so long as they act within the bounds of relevant regulations, and provided that the classification, considered in terms of the purposes of the statutes and relevant regulations, is reasonable.

This approach reflects the difficulty of applying §§ 402 and 306 literally to *every* new-source-related discharge of a "pollutant." * * *

To literally apply these performance standards so as to forbid the use of any of these substances as "fill," even when, say, they constitute no more than trace elements in dirt, crushed rock, or sand that is clearly being used as "fill" to build a levee or to replace dirt removed from a lake bottom may prove unnecessarily strict, to the point that such application would undermine the objective of § 404, which foresees the use of "dredged or fill material" in certain circumstances and with approval of the relevant agencies. § 1344. At minimum, the EPA might reasonably read the statute and the applicable regulations as allowing the use of such material, say crushed rock, as "fill" in some of these situations.

At the same time, I recognize the danger that Justice GINSBURG warns against, namely, that "[w]hole categories of regulated industries" might "gain immunity from a variety of pollution-control standards," if, say, a § 404–permit applicant simply adds "sufficient solid matter" to a pollutant "to raise the bottom of a water body," thereby turning a "pollutant" governed by § 306 into "fill" governed by § 404.

Yet there are safeguards against that occurring. For one thing, as the Court recognizes, it is not the case that *any* material that has the " 'effect of . . . [c]hanging the bottom elevation' " of the body of water is automatically subject to § 404, not § 402. The EPA has never suggested that it would interpret the regulations so as to turn § 404 into a loophole, permitting evasion of a "performance standard" simply because a polluter discharges enough pollutant to raise the bottom elevation of the body of water. For another thing, even where a matter is determined reasonably to be "fill" and consequently falls within § 404, the EPA can retain an important role in the permitting process. That is because the EPA may veto any § 404 plan that it finds has an "unacceptable adverse effect on municipal water supplies, shellfish beds and fishery areas . . . , wildlife, or recreational areas." § 1344(c). Finally, EPA's decision not to apply § 306, but to allow permitting to proceed under § 404, must be a reasonable decision; and court review will help assure that is so. 5 U.S.C. § 706.

In these cases, it seems to me that the EPA's interpretation of the statute as permitting the EPA/Corps of Engineers "fill" definition to apply to the cases at hand is reasonable, hence lawful. Lower Slate Lake, located roughly three miles from the Kensington Gold Mine, is 51 feet deep, 800 feet wide, and 2,000 feet long; downstream from the lake is Slate Creek. Faced with a difficult choice between creating a huge pile of slurry on nearby wetlands or using part of the lake as a storage facility for mine tailings, the EPA arrived at a compromise. On the one hand, it would treat mine tailings placed directly into the lake as "fill" under the § 404 permitting program. The tailings, the EPA recognized, would have the "immediate effect of filling the areas of water into which they are discharged." But it would also treat any spillover of the tailings, or chemicals from the tailings, into any nearby waterway, most particularly Slate Creek (running out of Slate Lake) as requiring a § 402 permit. The EPA's § 306 "performance standard" would apply and that standard insists upon *no discharge of process wastewater at all.* The EPA reached this result because it recognized that, even though pollutants discharged into the creek might come "in the form of suspended and settleable solids," such solids would "have, at most, an incidental filling effect." The EPA thereby sought to apply the distinction it had previously recognized between discharges that have the immediate effect of raising the bottom elevation of water, and those that only have the "associated effect, over time, of raising the bottom elevation of a water due to settling of waterborne pollutants."

I cannot say whether the EPA's compromise represents the best overall environmental result; but I do believe it amounts to the kind of detailed decision that the statutes delegate authority to the EPA, not the courts, to make (subject to the bounds of reasonableness). I believe the Court's views are consistent with those I here express. And with that understanding, I join its opinion.

[JUSTICE SCALIA's concurring opinion on deference is omitted.]

JUSTICE GINSBURG, with whom JUSTICE STEVENS and JUSTICE SOUTER join, dissenting.

Petitioner Coeur Alaska, Inc., proposes to discharge 210,000 gallons per day of mining waste into Lower Slate Lake, a 23–acre subalpine lake in Tongass National Forest. The "tailings slurry" would contain concentrations of aluminum, copper, lead, and mercury. Over the life of the mine, roughly 4.5 million tons of solid tailings would enter the lake, raising the bottom elevation by 50 feet. It is undisputed that the discharge would kill all of the lake's fish and nearly all of its other aquatic life.

Coeur Alaska's proposal is prohibited by the Environmental Protection Agency (EPA) performance standard forbidding any discharge of process wastewater from new "froth-flotation" mills into waters of the United States. See 40 CFR § 440.104(b)(1) (2008). Section 306 of the Clean Water Act directs EPA to promulgate such performance standards, 33 U.S.C. § 1316(a), and declares it unlawful for any discharger to violate them, § 1316(e). Ordinarily, that would be the end of the inquiry.

Coeur Alaska contends, however, that its discharge is not subject to EPA's regulatory regime, but is governed, instead, by the mutually exclusive permitting authority of the Army Corps of Engineers. The Corps has authority, under § 404 of the Act, § 1344(a), to issue permits for discharges of "dredged or fill material." By regulation, a discharge that has the effect of raising a water body's bottom elevation qualifies as "fill material." See 33 CFR § 323.2(e) (2008). Discharges properly within the Corps' permitting authority, it is undisputed, are not subject to EPA performance standards.

The litigation before the Court thus presents a single question: Is a pollutant discharge prohibited under § 306 of the Act eligible for a § 404 permit as a discharge of fill material? In agreement with the Court of Appeals, I would answer no. The statute's text, structure, and purpose all mandate adherence to EPA pollution-control requirements. A discharge covered by a performance standard must be authorized, if at all, by EPA.

I

A

Congress enacted the Clean Water Act in 1972 "to restore and maintain the chemical, physical, and biological integrity" of the waters of the United States. 33 U.S.C. § 1251(a). "The use of any river, lake, stream or ocean as a waste treatment system," the Act's drafters stated, "is unacceptable." Congress announced in the Act itself an ambitious objective: to eliminate, by 1985, the discharge of all pollutants into the Nation's navigable waters. 33 U.S.C. § 1251(a).

In service of its goals, Congress issued a core command: "[T]he discharge of any pollutant by any person shall be unlawful," except in compliance with the Act's terms. § 1311(a). The Act's substantive requirements—housed primarily in Subchapter III, "Standards and Enforcement"—establish "a comprehensive regulatory program supervised by an expert administrative agency[.]"

* * * Of key importance, new sources must meet stringent "standards of performance" adopted by EPA under § 306. That section makes it "unlawful for *any* ... new source to operate ... in violation of" an applicable performance standard. 33 U.S.C. § 1316(e) (emphasis added). * * * Moreover, new sources, unlike existing sources, are not eligible for EPA-granted variances from applicable limitations.

In 1982, EPA promulgated new source performance standards for facilities engaged in mining, including those using a froth-flotation milling process. Existing mills, the Agency found, were already achieving zero discharge; it was therefore practicable, EPA concluded, for new mills to do as well. Accordingly, under 40 CFR § 440.104(b)(1), new mines using the froth-flotation method, as Coeur Alaska proposes to do, may not discharge wastewater directly into waters of the United States.

B

The nationwide pollution-control requirements just described are implemented through the National Pollution Discharge Elimination System (NPDES), a permitting scheme set forth in § 402 and administered by EPA and the States. The NPDES is the linchpin of the Act, for it transforms generally applicable effluent limitations into the individual obligations of each discharger. The discharge of a pollutant is generally prohibited unless the source has obtained a NPDES permit.

The Act also establishes a separate permitting scheme, administered by the Corps, for discharges of "dredged or fill material." 33 U.S.C. § 1344(a). Section 404 hews to the Corps' established expertise in matters of navigability and construction. The § 404 program does not implement the uniform, technology-based pollution-control standards set out, *inter alia,* in § 306. Instead, § 404 permits are subject to regulatory guidelines based generally on the impact of a discharge on the receiving environment.

As the above-described statutory background indicates, Coeur Alaska's claim to a § 404 permit carries weighty implications. If eligible for that permit, Coeur Alaska can evade the exacting performance standard prescribed by EPA for froth-flotation mills. It may, instead, use Lower Slate Lake "as the settling pond and disposal site for the tailings."

II

Is a pollutant discharge prohibited under § 306(e) eligible to receive a § 404 permit as a discharge of fill material? All agree on preliminary matters. Only one agency, the Corps or EPA, can issue a permit for the discharge. Only EPA, through the NPDES program, issues permits that implement § 306. Further, § 306(e) and EPA's froth-flotation performance standard, unless inapplicable here, bar Coeur Alaska's proposed discharge.

No part of the statutory scheme, in my view, calls into question the governance of EPA's performance standard. The text of § 306(e) states a clear proscription: "[I]t shall be unlawful for any owner or operator of any new source to operate such source in violation of any standard of performance applicable to such source." 33 U.S.C. § 1316(e). Under the standard of performance relevant here, "there shall be no discharge of process wastewater to navigable waters from mills that use the froth-flotation process" for mining gold. 40 CFR § 440.104(b)(1). The Act imposes these requirements without qualification.

Section 404, stating that the Corps "may issue permits" for the discharge of "dredged or fill material," does not create an exception to § 306(e)'s plain command. 33 U.S.C. § 1344(a). Section 404 neither mentions § 306 nor states a contrary requirement. The Act can be home to both provisions, with no words added or omitted, so long as the category of "dredged or fill material" eligible for a § 404 permit is read in harmony with § 306. Doing so yields a simple rule: Discharges governed by EPA performance standards are subject to EPA's administration and receive permits under the NPDES, not § 404.

* * * The Court's reading, in contrast, strains credulity. A discharge of a pollutant, otherwise prohibited by firm statutory command, becomes lawful if it contains sufficient solid matter to raise the bottom of a water body, transformed into a waste disposal facility. Whole categories of regulated industries can thereby gain immunity from a variety of pollution-control standards. The loophole would swallow not only standards governing mining activities, see 40 CFR pt. 440 (effluent limitations and new source performance standards for ore mining and dressing); *id.,* pt. 434 (coal mining); *id.,* pt. 436 (mineral mining), but also standards for dozens of other categories of regulated point sources, see, *e.g., id.,* pt. 411 (cement manufacturing); *id.,* pt. 425 (leather tanning and finishing); *id.,* pt. 432 (meat and poultry products processing). Providing an escape hatch for polluters whose discharges contain solid matter, it bears noting, is particularly perverse; the Act specifically focuses on solids as harmful pollutants.

* * * In sum, it is neither necessary nor proper to read the statute as allowing mines to bypass EPA's zero-discharge standard by classifying slurry as "fill material." The use of waters of the United States as "settling ponds" for harmful mining waste, the Court of Appeals correctly held, is antithetical to the text, structure, and purpose of the Clean Water Act.

* * *

For the reasons stated, I would affirm the judgment of the Ninth Circuit.

NOTES

1. **Identifying the Interpretive Problem.** Why did Coeur Alaska's proposed mine create an interpretation difficulty for Clean Water Act permitting? What two standards were in conflict? Why did the Supreme Court decide both that: (1) Coeur Alaska's mine was subject to Section 404; and (2) Coeur Alaska's mine was *not* subject to the otherwise applicable Section 306 new source performance standard? How does Section 404 permitting differ from Section 402 permitting?

2. **Identifying Differences in Interpretive Approach.** The majority and dissenting Justices differ not only in the conclusions they reach but also in how they approach the interpretive problem that this case posed. Where do the majority Justices start? How do they view the relationship between Section 404 and Section 402 permitting? What question do they ask first in deciding which permit program—and which permit terms—apply to the Coeur Alaska mine? Conversely, where do the dissenting Justices start? What aspect of the Clean Water Act do they most prominently try to effect? How does that approach affect their views of how the Section 402 and Section 404 permitting programs should work together?

3. **Justice Breyer's Concurrence.** Why does Justice Breyer—who often sides with environmental protection—concur in this case? What compromise(s) does he see occurring? What does Coeur Alaska's filling of the lake *prevent*? Think back to the many wetlands cases you read in connection with establishing Clean Water Act jurisdiction—is this a "better" solution?

Note that one criticism that has been leveled at this case is that most of the parties—and most of the Justices—seem to assume that the mining should go forward in some form. As Section B.1 will explore in more detail, however, the EPA's Section 404(b)(1) Guidelines are designed to *limit* the number of Section 404 permits that the Army Corps issues that have detrimental environmental impacts.

4. **The EPA's Role in Section 404 Permitting.** Another important feature of this case is that the EPA concurred in the conclusion that Section 404 permitting applied. What could the EPA have done if it had disagreed? Who would—or should—the Court have deferred to then—the EPA or the Army Corps? This issue is not completely resolved, but the fact that the EPA writes the Section 404(b)(1) Guidelines and can veto Army Corps permits suggests that the EPA should be accorded more deference than the Army Corps. We will return to this issue in the *Bersani* case, *infra*.

5. **The Rest of the Story.** Coeur Alaska began production at its Kensington Gold Mine on June 24, 2010, and expects to produce about 125,000 ounces of gold per year for at least 10 years. Construction of the mine employed 500 people, and 200 employees operate the mine. Videos and pictures of the mine are available at the company's web site, http://www.kensingtongold.com/images.html#Videos. In addition, Coeur Alaska supplies a video of the Juneau, Alaska, celebration of the Supreme Court's decision at http://vimeo.com/5529874. The Alaska Department of Natural Resources maintains a comprehensive web site for the Kensington Gold Mine, through

which copies of all water quality permits, monitoring reports, and inspection reports are available; *see* http://dnr.alaska.gov/mlw/mining/largemine/kensington/.

In December 2010, Coeur Alaska paid the EPA $170,000 in fines for unpermitted discharges of sediment and acidic stormwater into a nearby creek and pond during the five years of the mine's construction (2005–2010). Coeur Alaska apparently knew about the acid mine drainage problem since March 2007 but neglected to inform the EPA. State of Alaska inspectors spotted the tell-tale orange drainage water in April 2008. In addition, as expected, the mining operation has transformed Lower Slate Lake. EarthJustice provides a slide show of "before and after" pictures, with explanations, at http://earthjustice.org/slideshows/images-from-the-kensington-mine-case#/sites/default/files/slideshows/09–2010/slate_01.jpg.

* * *

B. THE TERMS OF SECTION 404 "DREDGE AND FILL" PERMITS

Unlike section 402, section 404 does not include a list of statutory provisions governing the terms of the section 404 permit. *Compare* CWA § 404(a), 33 U.S.C. § 1344(a), *with* CWA § 402(a), 33 U.S.C. § 1342(a). Instead, two sets of standards govern section 404 permit requirements: the EPA's ***Section 404(b)(1) Guidelines*** and the Corps' ***public interest review***.

Discharges of dredged or fill material subject to the section 404 program can significantly alter, or even completely obliterate, the navigable waters and their associated habitats and ecosystem functions. The Section 404(b)(1) Guidelines and the public interest review work to ensure that such discharges will not, in fact, destroy navigable waters when such destruction is not absolutely required. If all else fails, moreover, the EPA can veto or restrict a section 404 permit if the discharge of dredged or fill materials "will have an unacceptable adverse effect on municipal water supplies, shellfish beds and fishery areas (including spawning and breeding areas), wildlife, or recreational areas." CWA § 404(c), 33 U.S.C. § 1344(c).

1. The EPA's Section 404(b)(1) Guidelines

a. The EPA's Basic Approach

Historically, the EPA's concern in its oversight role under section 404 has been to limit the impact of dredging and filling on waters of the United States. This bias emerges, for example, from the fundamental principle of the EPA's Section 404(b)(1) Guidelines:

> dredged or fill material should not be discharged into the aquatic ecosystem, unless it can be demonstrated that such a discharge will not have an unacceptable adverse impact either individually or in

> combination with known and/or probable impacts of other activities affecting the ecosystems of concern.

40 C.F.R. § 230.1(c). In accordance with this fundamental principle, the Guidelines specify that "[n]o discharge of dredged or fill material shall be permitted if it:"

> (1) Causes or contributes, after consideration of disposal site dilution and dispersion, to violations of any applicable State water quality standard;
>
> (2) Violates any applicable toxic effluent standard or limitation under section 307 of the Act;
>
> (3) Jeopardizes the continued existence of species listed as endangered or threatened under the Endangered Species Act of 1973, as amended * * *; or
>
> (4) Violates any requirement imposed by the Secretary of Commerce to protect any [National Marine Sanctuary].

40 C.F.R. § 230.10(b). Similarly, the Guidelines also specify that "no discharge of dredged or fill material shall be permitted which will cause or contribute to significant degradation of the waters of the United States." 40 C.F.R. § 230.10(c). According to the EPA, the following examples would constitute "significant degradation":

> (1) Significantly adverse effects of the discharge of pollutants on human health or welfare, including but not limited to effects on municipal water supplies, plankton, fish, shellfish, wildlife, and special aquatic sites;
>
> (2) Significantly adverse effects of the discharge of pollutants on life stages of aquatic life and other wildlife dependent on aquatic ecosystems, including the transfer, concentration, and spread of pollutants or their byproducts outside of the disposal site through biological, physical, and chemical processes;
>
> (3) Significantly adverse effects of the discharge of pollutants aquatic ecosystem diversity, productivity, and stability. Such effects may include, but are not limited to, loss of fish and wildlife habitat or loss of the capacity of a wetland to assimilate nutrients, purify water, or reduce wave energy; or
>
> (4) Significantly adverse effects of discharge of pollutants on recreational, aesthetic, and economic values.

40 C.F.R. § 230.10(c). Otherwise, "no discharge of dredged or fill material shall be permitted unless appropriate and practicable steps have been taken which will minimize potential adverse impacts of the discharge on the aquatic ecosystem." 40 C.F.R. § 230.10(d). These "appropriate and practicable steps" become conditions of the section 404 permit.

b. Special Aquatic Sites and Practicable Alternatives

One of the EPA's tools for minimizing the adverse effects of the section 404 permit program is its ***practicable alternatives*** analysis.

Under the Section 404(b)(1) Guidelines, "no discharge of dredged or fill material shall be permitted if there is a ***practicable alternative*** to the proposed discharge which would have less adverse impact on the aquatic ecosystem, so long as the alternative does not have other significant adverse environmental consequences." 40 C.F.R. § 230.10(a) (emphasis added). According to the EPA, "*[a]n alternative is practicable if it is available and capable of being done after taking into consideration cost, existing technology, and logistics in light of overall project purposes.*" 40 C.F.R. § 230.10(a)(2) (emphasis added). Practicable alternatives include:

> (i) Activities which do not involve a discharge of dredged or fill material into waters of the United States or ocean waters;
>
> (ii) Discharge of dredged or fill material at other locations in waters of the United States or ocean waters.

40 C.F.R. § 230.10(a)(1). Thus, for example, acquisition of additional land can be a practicable alternative. 40 C.F.R. § 230.10(a)(2). Moreover, while the permit applicant usually includes information about practicable alternatives in the section 404 permit application, the EPA and the Army Corps are not bound by the applicant's determination.

In addition, the EPA will presume that a practicable alternative exists if the permit applicant proposes to discharge into a ***special aquatic site*** and the activity is not ***water dependent***. 40 C.F.R. § 230.10(a)(3). This presumption then requires permit applicants to prove that no upland sites were available for development. *Carabell v. U.S. Army Corps of Engineers*, 257 F. Supp. 2d 917, 933 (E.D. Mich. 2003) (holding that the applicant's lack of explanation of why an upland site was unavailable was insufficient to overcome the presumption, and upholding the Army Corps' denial of the section 404 permit). *But see generally James City County, Va. v. U.S. E.P.A.*, 758 F. Supp. 348 (E.D. Va. 1990) (holding that the EPA could *not* presume that alternatives existed when the project was a water-dependent reservoir construction project).

Special aquatic sites include: (1) sanctuaries and refuges designated under state and federal laws to conserve fish and wildlife, 40 C.F.R. § 230.40(a); (2) wetlands, 40 C.F.R. § 230.41(a); (3) mud flats, 40 C.F.R. § 230.42(a); (4) vegetated shallows, 40 C.F.R. § 230.43(a); (5) coral reefs, 40 C.F.R. § 230.44(a); and (6) riffle and pool complexes. 40 C.F.R. § 230.45(a).

A proposed activity is ***water dependent*** if it requires access to or proximity to or siting within the water to accomplish its basic purpose. Of course, sorting "basic" purposes from "incidental" purposes often leads to litigation, especially when developers want to build waterfront housing. *See generally, e.g., National Wildlife Federation v. Whistler*, 27 F.3d 1341 (8th Cir. 1994) (upholding the Army Corps' determination that boat access to a river, rather than housing development, was the primary purpose of a waterfront development project).

c. *When Is an Alternative "Available"?*

As noted, under the EPA's Section 404(b)(1) Guidelines, practicable alternatives exist to discharging dredged or fill material into the navigable waters when those alternatives are "available and capable of being done * * *." When, exactly, does a developer have to look for available alternatives? The next case discusses that issue.

BERSANI v. UNITED STATES ENVIRONMENTAL PROTECTION AGENCY

850 F.2d 36 (2d Cir. 1988).

TIMBERS, CIRCUIT JUDGE:

Appellants John A. Bersani, the Pyramid Companies, Newport Galleria Group and Robert J. Congel ("Pyramid", collectively) appeal from a judgment entered October 23, 1987 in the Northern District of New York * * * granting summary judgment in favor of appellees, the United States Environmental Protection Agency ("EPA") [and] the United States Army Corps of Engineers (the "Corps") * * * (the "Federal Appellees" collectively), and denying Pyramid's motion for summary judgment.

This case arises out of Pyramid's attempt to build a shopping mall on certain wetlands in Massachusetts known as Sweedens Swamp. Acting under the Clean Water Act, 33 U.S.C. § 1251 *et seq.* (1982), EPA vetoed the approval by the Corps of a permit to build the mall because EPA found that an alternative site had been available to Pyramid at the time it entered the market to search for a site for the mall. The alternative site was purchased later by another developer and arguably became unavailable by the time Pyramid applied for a permit to build the mall.

On appeal, the thrust of Pyramid's argument is a challenge to what it calls EPA's "market entry" theory, *i.e.*, the interpretation by EPA of the relevant regulation, which led EPA to consider the availability of alternative sites at the time Pyramid entered the market for a site, instead of at the time it applied for a permit. * * *

We hold (1) that the market entry theory is consistent with both the regulatory language and past practice; (2) that EPA's interpretation, while not necessarily entitled to deference, is reasonable; and (3) that EPA's application of the regulation is supported by the administrative record. We agree with the district court's conclusion that EPA's findings were not arbitrary and capricious. * * *

* * * I.

We shall summarize only those facts and prior proceedings believed necessary to an understanding of the issues raised on appeal.

A. Statutory and Regulatory Framework

One of the sections of the Clean Water Act (the "Act") relevant to the instant case is § 301(a), 33 U.S.C. § 1311(a) (1982), which prohibits the discharge of any pollutant, including dredged or fill materials, into the nation's navigable waters, except in compliance with the Act's provisions, including § 404. It is undisputed that Sweedens Swamp is a "navigable water," as defined in 33 U.S.C. § 1362 (1982), and that Pyramid's shopping center proposal will involve the discharge of dredged or fill materials.

Section 404 of the Act, 33 U.S.C. § 1344 (1982 & Supp. III 1985), focusing on dredged or fill materials, provides that the United States Army and EPA will share responsibility for implementation of its provisions. EPA and the Corps also share responsibility for enforcing the Act. 33 U.S.C. §§ 1311 (1982), 1319 (1982), 1344(n) and (s) (1982). Section 404(a) authorizes the Secretary of the Army, acting through the Corps, to issue permits for the discharge of dredged or fill materials at particular sites. 33 U.S.C. § 1344(a) (1982). Section 404(b) provides that, subject to § 404(c), the Corps must base its decisions regarding permits on guidelines (the "404(b)(1) guidelines") developed by EPA in conjunction with the Secretary of the Army. 33 U.S.C. § 1344(b) (Supp. III 1985).

The 404(b)(1) guidelines, published at 40 C.F.R. Part 230 (1987), are regulations containing the requirements for issuing a permit for discharge of dredged or fill materials. 40 C.F.R. § 230.10(a) covers "non-water dependent activities" (*i.e.*, activities that could be performed on non-wetland sites, such as building a mall) and provides essentially that the Corps must determine whether an alternative site is available that would cause less harm to the wetlands. Specifically, it provides that "no discharge of dredged or fill material shall be permitted if there is a practicable alternative" to the proposal that would have a "less adverse impact" on the "aquatic ecosystem." It also provides that a practicable alternative may include "an area not presently owned by the applicant which could reasonably be obtained, utilized, expanded or managed in order to fulfill the basic purpose of the proposed activity." 40 C.F.R. 230.10(a)(2). It further provides that, "unless clearly demonstrated otherwise", practicable alternatives are (1) "presumed to be available" and (2) "presumed to have less adverse impact on the aquatic ecosystem." 40 C.F.R. 230.10(a)(3). Thus, an applicant such as Pyramid must rebut both of these presumptions in order to obtain a permit. Sections 230.10(c) and (d) require that the Corps not permit any discharge that would contribute to significant degradation of the nation's wetlands and that any adverse impacts must be mitigated through practicable measures.

In addition to following the 404(b)(1) guidelines, the Corps may conduct a "public interest review." 33 C.F.R. § 320.4 (1987). This public interest review is not mandatory under § 404, unlike consideration of the 404(b) guidelines. In a public interest review, the Corps' decision must reflect the "national concern" for protection and use of resources but must also consider the "needs and welfare of the people." *Id.*

Under § 404(c) of the Act, 33 U.S.C. § 1344(c), EPA has veto power over any decision of the Corps to issue a permit. It is this provision that is at the heart of the instant case.

* * * In short, both EPA and the Corps are responsible for administering the program for granting permits for discharges of pollutants into wetlands under § 404. The Corps has the authority to issue permits following the 404(b)(1) guidelines developed by it and EPA; EPA has the authority under § 404(c) to veto any permit granted by the Corps. The Corps processes about 11,000 permit applications each year. EPA has vetoed five decisions by the Corps to grant permits.

B. Factual Background of the Sweedens Swamp Project

Sweedens Swamp is a 49.5 acre wetland which is part of an 80 acre site near Interstate 95 in South Attleboro, Massachusetts. Although some illegal dumping and motorbike intrusions have occurred, these activities have been found to have had little impact on the site which remains a "high-quality red maple swamp" providing wildlife habitat and protecting the area from flooding and pollution.

The effort to build a mall on Sweedens Swamp was initiated by Pyramid's predecessor, the Edward J. DeBartolo Corporation ("DeBartolo"). DeBartolo purchased the Swamp some time before April 1982. At the time of this purchase an alternative site was available in North Attleboro (the "North Attleboro site"). * * * Pyramid took over the project in 1983. * * *

One of the key issues in dispute in the instant case is just when did Pyramid begin searching for a suitable site for its mall. EPA asserts that Pyramid began to search in the Spring of 1983. Pyramid asserts that it began to search several months later, in September 1983. The difference is crucial because on July 1, 1983—a date between the starting dates claimed by EPA and Pyramid—a competitor of Pyramid, the New England Development Co. ("NED"), purchased options to buy the North Attleboro site. This site was located upland and could have served as a "practicable alternative" to Sweedens Swamp, *if* it had been "available" at the relevant time. Thus, if the relevant time to determine whether an alternative is "available" is the time the applicant is searching for a site (an issue that is hotly disputed), and if Pyramid began to search at a time *before* NED acquired options on the North Attleboro site, there definitely would have been a "practicable alternative" to Sweedens Swamp, and Pyramid's application should have been denied. On the other hand, if Pyramid did not begin its search until *after* NED acquired options on the North Attleboro site, then the site arguably was not "available" and the permit should have been granted. * * *

In December 1983, Pyramid purchased Sweedens Swamp from DeBartolo. In August 1984, Pyramid applied under § 404(a) to the New England regional division of the Corps (the "NE Corps") for a permit. It sought to fill or alter 32 of the 49.6 acres of the Swamp; to excavate nine acres of uplands to create artificial wetlands; and to alter 13.3 acres of existing wetlands to improve its environmental quality. Later Pyramid proposed to mitigate the adverse impact on the wetlands by creating 36 acres of replacement wetlands in an off-site gravel pit.

During the review of Pyramid's application by EPA, by the Fish and Wildlife Service ("FWS") and by the Corps, Pyramid submitted information on "practicable alternatives," especially the North Attleboro site. In rejecting that site as an alternative, Pyramid asserted that building a mall there was not *feasible,* not that the site was *unavailable.* * * *

In November 1984, EPA and FWS submitted official comments to the NE Corps recommending denial of the application because Pyramid's proposal was inconsistent with the 404(b)(1) guidelines. Pyramid had failed (1) to overcome the presumption of the availability of alternatives and (2) to mitigate adequately the adverse impact on wildlife. EPA threatened a § 404(c) review. Pyramid then proposed to create additional artificial wetlands at a nearby upland site, a proposal it eventually abandoned.

In January 1985, the NE Corps hired a consultant to investigate the feasibility of Sweedens Swamp and the North Attleboro site. The consultant reported that either site was feasible but that from a commercial standpoint only one mall could survive in the area. On February 19, 1985, the NE Corps advised Pyramid that denial of its permit was imminent. On May 2, 1985, the NE Corps sent its recommendation to deny the permit to the national headquarters of the Corps. Although the NE Corps ordinarily makes the final decision on whether to grant a permit, *see* 33 C.F.R. § 325.8 (1982), in the instant case, because of widespread publicity, General John F. Wall, the Director of Civil Works at the national headquarters of the Corps, decided to review the NE Corps' decision. Wall reached a different conclusion. He decided to grant the permit after finding that Pyramid's offsite mitigation proposal would reduce the adverse impacts sufficiently to allow the "practicable alternative" test to be deemed satisfied. * * * Although he did not explicitly address the issue, Wall apparently assumed that the relevant time to determine whether there was a practicable alternative was the time of the application, not the time the applicant entered the market. * * *

On May 31, 1985, Wall ordered the NE Corps to send Pyramid, EPA and FWS a notice of its intent to grant the permit. The NE Corps complied on June 28, 1985.

On July 23, 1985, EPA's RA [Regional Administrator] initiated a § 404(c) review of the Corps' decision. Following the procedure set forth in 40 C.F.R. Part 231 [], EPA published notice of its intent to prohibit the project in the *Federal Register;* held a public hearing on September 26, 1985; and permitted a period for public comment which closed on October 4, 1985. A second hearing was held on November 18, 1985.

On March 4, 1986, the RA recommended that EPA veto the permit because of adverse impacts on wildlife and available "practicable alternatives". * * *

On May 13, 1986, EPA issued its final determination, which prohibited Pyramid from using Sweedens Swamp. It found (1) that the filling of the Swamp would adversely affect wildlife; (2) that the North Attleboro site could have been available to Pyramid at the time Pyramid investigated the area to search for a site; (3) that considering Pyramid's failure or unwillingness to provide further materials about its investigation of alternative sites, it was uncontested that, at best, Pyramid never checked the availability of the North Attleboro site as an alternative; (4) that the North Attleboro site was feasible and would have a less adverse impact on the wetland environment; and (5) that the mitigation proposal did not make the project preferable to other alternatives because of scientific uncertainty of success. In the second of these findings, EPA used what Pyramid calls the "market entry" approach.

On July 1, 1986, Pyramid commenced the instant action in the district court to vacate EPA's final determination as arbitrary and capricious. * * *

On October 6, 1987, the court granted EPA's motion for summary judgment. The court stated that, with regard to the market entry theory, EPA's interpretation of its regulations was entitled to deference. This appeal followed.

For the reasons which follow, we affirm.

II.

One of Pyramid's principal contentions is that the market entry approach is inconsistent with both the language of the 404(b)(1) guidelines and the past practice of the Corps and EPA.

A.

With regard to the language of the regulations, Pyramid reasons that the 404(b)(1) guidelines are framed in the present tense, while the market entry approach focuses on the *past* by considering whether a practicable alternative *was* available at the time the applicant entered the market to search for a site. To support its argument that the 404(b)(1) guidelines are framed in the present tense, Pyramid quotes the following language:

> "An alternative is practicable if it *is* available.... If it is otherwise a practicable alternative, an area not *presently* owned by the applicant which *could* reasonably *be* obtained, utilized, expanded or managed in order to fulfill the basic purpose of the proposed activity *may be* considered."

40 C.F.R. § 230.10(a)(2) (emphasis added). It then argues that EPA says "is" means "was." * * *

While this argument has a certain surface appeal, we are persuaded that it is contrary to a common sense reading of the regulations; that it entails an overly literal and narrow interpretation of the language; and that it creates requirements not intended by Congress.

First, while it is true that the language is in the present tense, it does not follow that the "most natural" reading of the regulations would create a time-of-application rule. As EPA points out, "the regulations do not indicate *when* it is to be determined whether an alternative 'is' available," (emphasis in original), *i.e.*, the "present" of the regulations might be the time the application is submitted; the time it is reviewed; or any number of other times. Based upon a reading of the language in the context of the controlling statute and the regulations as a whole, moreover, we conclude that when the agencies drafted the language in question they simply were not thinking of the specific issues raised by the instant case, in which an applicant had available alternatives at the time it was selecting its site but these alternatives had evaporated by the time it applied for a permit. We therefore agree with the district court that the regulations are essentially silent on the issue of timing and that it would be appropriate to consider the objectives of the Act and the intent underlying the promulgation of the regulations.

Second, as EPA has pointed out, the preamble to the 404(b)(1) guidelines states that the purpose of the "practicable alternatives" analysis is "to recognize the special value of wetlands and to avoid their unnecessary destruction, particularly where practicable alternatives *were* available in non-aquatic areas to achieve the basic purpose of the proposal." 45 Fed. Reg. 85,338 (1980) (emphasis added). In other words, the purpose is to create an incentive for developers to avoid choosing wetlands when they could choose an alternative upland site. Pyramid's reading of the regulations would thwart this purpose because it would remove the incentive for a developer to search for an alternative site at the time such an incentive is needed, *i.e.*, at the time it is making the decision to select a particular site. * * *

* * * In short, we conclude that a common-sense reading of the statute can lead only to the use of the market entry approach used by EPA.

B.

With regard to the past practice of the Corps and EPA, Pyramid asserts that neither has ever applied a market entry approach. * * * Our examination of these prior decisions has satisfied us, however, that the issue raised in the instant case simply has not been addressed before. * * *

We believe that the issue essentially is one of first impression. We view EPA's action in the instant case as an application of the regulatory language to the specific needs of this case which arose here for the first time. We therefore hold that EPA has not acted contrary to prior practice under the regulations.

III.

We turn next to the issue of whether EPA's interpretation of the 404(b)(1) guidelines is entitled to the deference usually accorded an agency with regard to its interpretation of regulations it is charged with administering and participated in formulating. * * *

Pyramid contends that such deference was unwarranted because two agencies—EPA and the Corps—developed and administered the regulations, and the Corps reached a different conclusion from that of EPA on the market entry issue. * * *

In response, EPA asserts that the Corps did not take a developed opposing policy position on the issue of what time is relevant in the "practicable alternatives" analysis. The reason for this is that the Corps, acting through General Wall, based its decision primarily on its finding that Pyramid's mitigation proposal was workable. EPA also asserts, on the issue of its expertise, that its "selective and most infrequent invocation" of its veto power underscores EPA's "seriousness" about using the veto. Finally EPA asserts that the Act's legislative history indicates that Congress intended EPA to have the "final word" on any disputes with the Corps.

While none of EPA's assertions is entirely persuasive, there also are difficulties with Pyramid's position. It is undeniable, for example, that Wall in fact did find that the North Attleboro site was "unavailable" and thus it appears that the Corps tacitly was applying a time-of-application test. On the other hand, it is possible that Wall believed that Pyramid did not enter the market until after NED had purchased the North Attleboro site. Accordingly, Wall may have found the alternative site "unavailable" under the market entry approach. Pyramid's and EPA's other arguments similarly cut both ways or are inconclusive.

Even if we are not thoroughly persuaded that EPA's interpretation was entitled to deference, however, we nevertheless conclude that the district court's decision in its favor must be upheld. As Pyramid itself points out (to the detriment of its argument), the issue of deference is separate from the issue of the standards of review of the district court and of our Court.

* * * Applying these standards, we are convinced that EPA's market entry interpretation was reasonable, and therefore was neither "arbitrary and capricious" nor "not in accordance with law." We therefore hold that the district court correctly found that EPA's interpretation of the regulations was reasonable. * * *

NOTES

1. **The EPA's Use of Its Veto Authority Under Section 404(c).** Why did the EPA choose to veto the section 404 permit at issue in this case? How often has the EPA used its veto authority, according to the Second Circuit?

The EPA itself emphasized in September 2003 that it "has completed only 11 'veto' actions out of an estimated 150,000 permit applications received since the regulations went into effect in October 1979." U.S. EPA, *EPA's Clean Water Act Section 404(c): Veto Authority*, http://www.epa.gov/owow/wetlands/facts/fact14.html (last updated Sept. 26, 2003). What does this statistic suggest about the effectiveness of section 404(c) as a regulatory oversight mechanism? What does it suggest about the permits that the EPA chooses to "veto"?

It should be noted, however, that the EPA and the Army Corps have entered into a series of agreements regarding the implementation of the section 404 permitting program designed to reduce the friction between them. For example, the agencies outlined their respective roles in enforcing section 404 permits in their 1989 *Memorandum Between the Department of the Army and the Environmental Protection Agency: Federal Enforcement for the Section 404 Program of the Clean Water Act*, available at http://www.epa.gov/owow/wetlands/regs/enfmoa.html (last updated Jan. 17, 2003). In another memorandum specifically governing the agencies' dispute resolution procedures, moreover, the agencies agreed that elevated review of individual section 404 permits would be "limited to those cases that involve aquatic resources of national importance." U.S. EPA & U.S. Army Corps of Engineers, *Clean Water Act Section 404(q): Memorandum of Agreement* (Aug. 11, 1992), *available at* http://www.epa.gov/owow/wetlands/regs/dispmoa.html (last updated Jan. 17, 2003).

2. **Market Entry vs. Time of Permitting Theories of Availability.** What is the "time of permitting" theory of available alternatives? Why did Pyramid (and perhaps the Army Corps) prefer this approach to determining availability? What interests does the "time of permitting" approach serve? What is the "market entry" theory of available alternatives? Why did the EPA prefer this approach? What goals does the market theory approach serve? Why did the Second Circuit uphold this approach?

3. **Who Gets the Deference Under Section 404?** One of the difficulties regarding implementation of the section 404 permit program is the question of *which* federal agency—the EPA or the Army Corps—is entitled to deference regarding its interpretations of the Act when the two agencies disagree in their interpretations. How did the EPA argue in this case that *it* was entitled to deference? Did the Second Circuit agree? Why or why not? What kind of deference did the Second Circuit give to the EPA's interpretation? How could you argue that the *Army Corps* should be the agency entitled to deference?

In general, the Army Corps *is* entitled to deference when it implements the section 404 permit program. However, no court has yet conclusively determined which agency is entitled to prevail when the EPA and the Army Corps disagree.

* * *

2. The Army Corps' Public Interest Review

As noted in *Bersani*, applications for section 404 permits are potentially subject to the Army Corps' ***public interest review*** as well as to review under the section 404(b)(1) Guidelines. The Corps' "review" consists of application of a series of policies that the Army Corps uses to assess "the probable impacts, including the cumulative impacts, of the proposed activity and its intended use on the public interest." 33 C.F.R.

§ 320.4(a)(1). The Corps looks broadly at all relevant factors in the proposed project to balance the benefits of the project against its costs and detriments. *Id.* The Corps will deny the permit, moreover, if the project does not comply with the EPA's Section 404(b)(1) Guidelines. *Id.*

The specific considerations under the public interest review include:

- ***Wetlands review***. The Army Corps will deny a section 404 permit if the project will alter important wetlands or contribute to the cumulative destruction of wetlands, unless the relevant District Engineer concludes "that the benefits of the proposed alteration outweigh the damage to the wetlands resource." 33 C.F.R. § 320.4(b)(4).
- ***Fish and wildlife review***. The Army Corps consults with state and federal fish and wildlife conservation agencies to prevent "direct and indirect loss" or damage to fish and wildlife resources from the proposed project. 33 C.F.R. § 320.4(c).
- ***Water quality review***. The Army Corps evaluates section 404 permit applications to see whether the project will comply with relevant effluent limitations and water quality standards. 33 C.F.R. § 320.4(d). This review considers both point source discharges and nonpoint source pollution. *Id.*
- ***Review for historic, cultural, scenic, and recreational values***. The Army Corps considers the impact of the proposed project on "wild and scenic rivers, historic properties and National Landmarks, National Rivers, National Wilderness Areas, National Seashores, National Recreation Areas, National Lakeshores, National Parks, National Monuments, estuarine and marine sanctuaries, archeological resources, including Indian religious or cultural sites, and such other areas as may be established under federal or state law for similar and related purposes." 33 C.F.R. § 320.4(e).
- ***Baseline review***. The Army Corps scrutinizes projects in the territorial sea that will alter the coastline or the baselines for measuring state and federal jurisdiction. 33 C.F.R. § 320.4(f). Moreover, permittees and the Corps must coordinate such projects with the United States Attorney General and the Department of the Interior. *Id.*
- ***Private property review***. The Army Corps considers the proposed project's effect on private property interests such as riparian rights. 33 C.F.R. § 320.4(g).
- ***Coastal zone management coordination***. When a proposed project will take place in the coastal zone of a state with an approved coastal zone management plan under the federal Coastal Zone Management Act, the state must certify that the project complies with the requirements of its plan before the Army Corps will issue the permit. 33 C.F.R. § 320.4(h).

- ***National Marine Sanctuary coordination***. When a proposed project will take place in a National Marine Sanctuary, the Secretary of Commerce must certify that the project will comply with the requirements for that Sanctuary. 33 C.F.R. § 320.4(i).
- ***Other requirements review***. The Army Corps considers the proposed project's compliance with other federal, state, and local requirements. 33 C.F.R. § 320.4(j)(1).
- ***Dams or other impoundments review***. The Corps can require non-federal permit applicants to prove that the dam or other structure is safe. 33 C.F.R. § 320.4(k).
- ***Floodplain management review***. When a proposed project is located in a floodplain, the Army Corps seeks to avoid "long and short term significant adverse impacts associated with the occupancy and modification of floodplains, as well as the direct and indirect support of floodplain development whenever there is a practicable alternative." 33 C.F.R. § 320.4(*l*)(2). If the Army Corps decides that the project can proceed, it will nevertheless ensure "that the impacts of potential flooding on human health, safety, and welfare are minimized, the risks of flood losses are minimized, and, whenever practicable the natural and beneficial values served by floodplains are restored and preserved." *Id.*
- ***Water supply and conservation review***. The state's allocations of water rights control when the proposed project will affect water supplies. 33 C.F.R. § 320.4(m).
- ***Energy conservation and development review***. If a proposed project is related to energy production, the Army Corps will prioritize issuance of the section 404 permit. 33 C.F.R. § 320.4(n).
- ***Navigation review***. The Army Corps will deny a section 404 permit application for a project that will substantially impair navigation and anchorage. 33 C.F.R. § 320.4(*o*).
- ***Environmental benefit review***. The Army Corps balances any environmental benefits from the proposed project against the environmental harms that it will cause. 33 C.F.R. § 320.4(p).
- ***Economic review***. The Army Corps considers potential economic benefits from the proposed project, such as jobs in the local community, tax revenues, and property values. 33 C.F.R. § 320.4(q).
- ***Mitigation review***. The Army Corps usually requires the permit applicant to agree to mitigation measures before it will issue the section 404 permit. 33 C.F.R. § 320.4(r).

As the Army Corps' regulations make clear, moreover, these various facets of the public interest review process are directly relevant to the eventual terms of a section 404 permit.

> District engineers will add special conditions to Department of the Army permits when such conditions are necessary to satisfy legal

> requirements or to otherwise satisfy the public interest requirement. Permit conditions will be directly related to the impact of the proposal, appropriate to the scope and degree of those impacts, and reasonably enforceable.

33 C.F.R. § 325.4(a).

C. GENERAL PERMITS

The federal agencies and authorized states may issue general permits under both the NPDES and section 404 permit programs, but general permits have been a more significant (and controversial) part of the latter program. Section 404 provides that:

> In carrying out his functions relating to the discharge of dredged or fill material under this section, the Secretary [of the Army, acting through the Army Corps of Engineers] may * * * issue general permits on a State, regional, or nationwide basis for any category of activities involving discharges of dredged or fill material *if the Secretary determines that the activities in such category are similar in nature, will cause only minimal adverse environmental effect when performed separately, and will have only minimal cumulative adverse effect on the environment.*

CWA § 404(e)(1), 33 U.S.C. § 1344(e)(1) (emphasis added). The Army Corps must follow the Section 404(b)(1) Guidelines when establishing such general permits. *Id.*

On March 12, 2006, the Army Corps re-issued its ***nationwide permits* (NWPs)**, as it does every five years. The 2007 regulations create 49 NWPs, subject to 28 conditions. In general, these permits apply to minor discharges, to environmentally helpful activities, and to necessary safety and maintenance activities. *See generally* U.S. Army Corps of Engineers, *2007 Nation Wide Permits, Conditions, Further Information, and Definitions (with Corrections)*, http://www.usace.army.mil/cw/cecwo/reg/nwp/nwp2007_gen_conditions_def.pdf. For example, wetlands restoration activities are covered by NWP 17.

For years, the most controversial general permit was NWP 26, which originally allowed developers to fill up to five acres of wetlands without getting an individual section 404 permit. By 1996, the Army Corps had reduced the maximum filled acreage to three acres, and by 2002 NWP 26 had ceased to exist. However, NWP 39 allows residential, commercial, and institutional developers to operate under a general permit if the project will fill half an acre or less of nontidal wetlands.

The advantage of general permits for dischargers is the ease of acquiring one. If a discharger's proposed project meets the Army Corps' criteria for a general permit, the discharger can "acquire" such a permit simply by notifying the Army Corps of its project and of the discharger's intent to be covered by the general permit. Unlike individual section 404 permits, the Army Corps does not individually review the discharger's project pursuant to the Section 404(b)(1) Guidelines or the public interest review.

D. EFFECT OF A SECTION 404 PERMIT

Like NPDES permits, section 404 permits shield the permittee from enforcement actions under the Clean Water Act. Section 404's permit shield provision states that:

> Compliance with a permit issued pursuant to this section, including any activity carried out pursuant to a general permit issued under this section, shall be deemed compliance, for purposes of sections 1319 and 1365 of this title, with sections 1311, 1317, and 1343 of this title.

CWA § 404(p), 33 U.S.C. § 1344(p). Note that, unlike NPDES permits, section 404 permits completely shield the permittee from liability for discharges of toxic pollutants.

E. SECTION 404 PERMITS AND REGULATORY TAKINGS

Under the Fifth Amendment of the U.S. Constitution, the federal government cannot take private property for public use without paying just compensation. U.S. CONST., Amend. V. Originally, this so-called "takings" prohibition applied only to the government's ***physical takings*** of property—such as, for example, condemnation of private property to build a public highway or building. However, in *Penn Central Transportation Co. v. New York City*, 438 U.S. 104 (1978), the U.S. Supreme Court recognized the possibility of a ***regulatory taking***—that is, the possibility that government regulation would so cripple a landowner's ability to use the property that the government should have to pay the landowner compensation. *Id.* at 123. Because landowners often seek a section 404 permit before developing their properties, denials of section 404 permits have given rise to several Fifth Amendment regulatory takings claims.

While the full scope of Fifth Amendment "takings" jurisprudence is beyond the scope of this textbook, the following case gives some of the flavor of section 404 takings litigation.

JENTGEN v. UNITED STATES

657 F.2d 1210 (Ct. Cl. 1981).

KUNZIG, JUDGE:

In this case, plaintiff contends that he has suffered an uncompensated taking as the consequence of federal regulation affecting his development of a planned residential community near the Everglades. The statutes in question, § 10 of the Rivers and Harbors Appropriation Act of 1899, 33 U.S.C. § 403, and § 404 of the Federal Water Pollution Control Act Amendments of 1972, 33 U.S.C. § 1344 and implementing regulations thereunder, prohibit, *inter alia*, obstructions, dredging and filling in navigable waters without the authorization of the Army Corps of Engineers. The latter, stressing environmental factors, has thus far refused to grant plaintiff the permits for which he has applied. We hold that while plaintiff may indeed have sustained some economic loss, the loss is not such as to constitute a taking under the circumstances herein.

I

Plaintiff, Jentgen, in 1971 purchased for $150,000 a 101.8 acre tract located within the city limits of Everglades City, Florida, in an area neighboring the Everglades National Park. Jentgen planned to develop there a water-oriented residential community. The property, completely undeveloped, lay astride the mean high water mark and contained large areas of dense mangrove vegetation, including wetlands. The project would necessitate considerable earth-moving, dredging and filling, and the erection of a dock and marina.

As of 1971, the purchase date, these proposed activities were subject to § 10 of the Rivers and Harbors Appropriation Act of 1899, 33 U.S.C. § 403 (1976) (Rivers and Harbors Act), which requires a permit from the Army Corps of Engineers to the extent that "any obstruction" is created in the "navigable waters of the United States." The Corps defines "navigable waters of the United States" to encompass tidal waters shoreward to the mean high water mark and/or waters suitable for use in commercial navigation. *See* 33 C.F.R. § 322.2(a) (1980).

In 1972, Congress enacted § 404 of the Federal Water Pollution Control Act Amendments, 33 U.S.C. § 1344 (1976) (FWPCA), which prohibits the "discharge of dredged or fill material ... into navigable waters" without a permit from the Army Corps of Engineers. The most significant feature of the new statute for the case at bar was the extension of Corps jurisdiction from "navigable waters of the United States" to "navigable waters." It is now well settled that Congress, in adopting the latter term, "asserted federal jurisdiction over the nation's waters to the maximum extent permissible under the Commerce Clause." *Natural Resources Defense Council v. Callaway*, 392 F. Supp. 685, 686 (D.D.C. 1975). Notably, both the Corps and the courts have interpreted "navigable waters" to include "adjacent wetlands." *See* 33 C.F.R. § 323.2 (1980); *United States v. Holland*, 373 F. Supp. 665, 673–674 (M.D. Fla. 1974).

The implication for Jentgen was that, as of 1972, a greater proportion of his property fell within the regulatory jurisdiction of the Corps than had previously been the case and the areas subject to the need for a permit had been widened.

Until 1968, the Corps' sole criterion in granting permits within its jurisdiction was the likely adverse impact upon commercial navigation. However, on December 18, 1968, in response to a growing national concern for environmental values and related federal legislation, the Corps stiffened its requirements, adding the following relevant considerations:

fish and wildlife; conservation; pollution; aesthetics; ecology; and the general public interest.

On April 4, 1974, the Corps published further revised regulations so as to:

1) incorporate new permit programs under section 404 of the FWPCA;
2) incorporate the requirements of new federal legislation by adding to the factors to be weighed in the so-called "public interest review," including: economics; historic values; flood damage prevention; land-use classification; recreation; water supply and water quality;
3) inaugurate a full-fledged wetlands policy to protect wetlands subject to the Corps' jurisdiction from unnecessary destruction.

See 42 Fed. Reg. 37122–37164 (1977); 33 C.F.R. §§ 320.1–329.16 (1980). These stiffening requirements are the main source of the difficulties which have brought Jentgen before this court.

In 1973, plaintiff applied for a permit under § 10 of the Rivers and Harbors Act and in 1975 applied for the requisite permit under § 404 of the FWPCA. The applications related to approximately 80 acres of the Jentgen tract; the remaining 20 acres are uplands and can be developed without dredging and filling and, consequently, without the need for Corps authorization. Of the 80 acres covered by the applications, 60 were proposed for development and 20 were to be preserved in the natural state. On July 5, 1977, Jentgen was informed that his applications had been denied as "not in the public interest." The Corps especially stressed the "direct adverse physical impact" upon the mangrove wetlands located on Jentgen's property. Of crucial importance, however, Jentgen was offered modified permits which would have allowed for development of over 20 of the 80 acres covered by the applications, but the permits were declined. At no time has Jentgen sought judicial review of the permit denials. Instead, Jentgen filed suit in this court on August 9, 1977, seeking "just compensation" under the Fifth Amendment for the alleged taking of his property as the consequence of the Government's refusal to allow him to go forward with his original plans. He seeks approximately $6,000,000. Under the specific facts of this case, and the tests enunciated by the courts, we hold that there has been no taking in this case.

II

It is well established as a matter of law that government regulation can effect a Fifth Amendment taking. *See, e.g., Penn Central Transp. Co. v. New York City*, 438 U.S. 104, 123 (1978) (no taking found on the specific facts of that case); *Benenson v. United States*, 212 Ct. Cl. 375, 388, 390, 548 F.2d 939, 947, 948 (1977) (taking found). The rationale, as stated by Justice Brennan, is that "[p]olice power regulations such as zoning ordinances and other land-use restrictions can destroy the use and enjoyment of property in order to promote the public good just as effectively as formal condemnation or physical invasion of property." *San Diego Gas & Electric Co. v. San Diego*, 450 U.S. 621, ___, 101 S.Ct. 1287, 1304 (1981) (Brennan, J., dissenting). While, "Government hardly could go on if to some extent values incident to property could not be diminished without paying for every such change in the general law," *Pennsylvania Coal Co. v. Mahon*, 260 U.S. 393, 413 (1922), the principle generally applied is that "if regulation goes too far it will be recognized as a taking," *id.* at 415; *see San Diego Gas, supra*, 450 U.S. at ___, 101 S. Ct. at 1302.

"The determination that governmental action constitutes a taking is, in essence, a determination that the public at large, rather than a single owner, must bear the burden of an exercise of state power in the public interest." *Agins v. City of Tiburon*, 447 U.S. 255, 260 (1980). It is frequently stated that the question whether a particular restriction effects a taking depends largely upon the particular circumstances of the case. *See, e.g., Penn Central Transp. Co., supra*, 438 U.S. at 124. Generally speaking, the Just Compensation Clause preserves governmental power to regulate subject to the dictates of "justice and fairness." *Andrus v. Allard*, 444 U.S. 51, 61, 65 (1979).

While "[t]he economic impact of the regulation on the claimant and, particularly, the extent to which the regulation has interfered with distinct investment-backed expectations are, of course, relevant considerations," *Penn Central Transp. Co., supra*, the decisions of the Supreme Court "uniformly reject the proposition that diminution in property value, standing alone, can establish a 'taking.'" *Id.* at 131, citing, *Euclid v. Ambler Realty Co.*, 272 U.S. 365 (1926) (75% diminution in value caused by zoning law); *Hadachek v. Sebastian*, 239 U.S. 394 (1915) (87.5% diminution in value). Similarly, the Court has branded as fallacious the "contention that a 'taking' must be found to have occurred whenever the land-use restriction may be characterized as imposing a 'servitude' on the claimant's parcel." *Penn Central Transp. Co., supra*, 438 U.S. at 130 n.27. Instead, "the 'taking' issue in these contexts is resolved by focusing on the uses the regulations permit." *Id.* at 131. In one of its most recent pronouncements, the Court crystallized its thinking as follows: "The application of a general zoning law to particular property effects a taking if the ordinance does not substantially advance legitimate state interests ... or denies a(n) owner economically viable use of his land...." *Agins, supra*, 447 U.S. at 260, *accord, Hodel v. Virginia Surface Mining and Reclamation Ass'n*, 452 U.S. 264, ___, 101 S. Ct. 2352, 2370 (1981); *Penn Central Transp. Co., supra*, 438 U.S. at 138; *Benenson v. United States*, 212 Ct. Cl. 375, 388–389, 548 F.2d 939, 947–948 (1977).

In applying the foregoing considerations, it is important to bear in mind the Supreme Court's admonition:

> "Taking" jurisprudence does not divide a single parcel into discrete segments and attempt to determine whether rights in a particular segment have been entirely abrogated. In deciding whether a particular governmental action has effected a taking, this Court focuses

rather both on the character of the action and on the nature and extent of the interference with rights in the parcel as a whole. . . .

Penn Central Transp. Co., *supra*, 438 U.S. at 130–131 (emphasis supplied).

III

Plaintiff initially contends that, as the consequence of *post hoc* government regulation during the early 1970's, he has been deprived of the economically viable use of his property and has therefore suffered a taking. The facts, however, thoroughly refute this contention. They show that the Corps did offer plaintiff the necessary permits to develop over 20 acres of the 80 acres covered by his applications, but that plaintiff refused. Overall, the tract contains approximately 20 additional acres of developable uplands which can be developed without first obtaining Corps permits. The record shows that the market value of the property, post-denial, is still between $80,000 and $150,000: the latter figure being the amount plaintiff paid for the property in 1971. These factors are flatly inconsistent with the proposition that plaintiff's property has been rendered valueless as the consequence of government regulation. In our view, the facts of this case are exceedingly weak * * *.

Plaintiff alternatively contends that he has suffered a taking solely by virtue of the fact that he has been deprived of the highest and best economic use for his property if not the entire use. This argument is merely another way of saying that there has been some diminution in the value of the property, rather than the complete destruction of all economically viable uses. The Supreme Court, however, has clearly held that mere diminution in value, standing alone, cannot establish a taking. *See Penn Central Transp. Co.*, *supra*, 438 U.S. at 131. Despite the changed phraseology, plaintiff's alternative argument fails as a matter of law.

By and large, we do not believe that "justice and fairness" require us to find a taking in this case. Reduced to its essentials, this case merely presents an instance of some diminution in value, or frustration of reasonable investment-backed expectations, stemming from changes in applicable statutes and regulations an insufficient basis, under *Penn Central*, to establish a taking. We note that in a number of recent cases the Supreme Court has refused to find takings under circumstances arguably far more compelling than those presented by the case at bar. *See, e.g.*, *Agins*, *supra*; *Penn Central Transp. Co.*, *supra*.

We feel that these considerations are dispositive of plaintiff's claim and hold that there has been no taking. * * *

NOTES

1. **The Basic Law of Regulatory Takings.** When does a regulatory taking occur, according to the U.S. Court of Claims? Why had no taking occurred here? Would it have made a difference if Mr. Jentgen had purchased the land for $3 million, in the expectation that he would make $6 million off the development? Why or why not?

2. **Wetlands Development and the "Denominator" Problem.** As the Court of Claims noted in *Jentgen*, the federal courts generally will not hold the government liable for a constitutional "taking" on the basis that *part* of the property is undevelopable. Thus, section 404 permit denials have not constituted "takings" even when those denials prevented the landowner from developing 12.3 out of 14.5 acres or destroyed 98.5 percent of the property's value. *Walcek v. United States*, 303 F.3d 1349, 1355–56 (Fed. Cir. 2002); *Cooley v. United States*, 324 F.3d 1297, 1304–05 (Fed. Cir. 2003).

As a result, property owners claiming that a constitutional "taking" has occurred often try to argue for the smallest parcel of property possible, making it easier to argue that the permit denial resulted in an absolute destruction of the property's value. Although the federal courts have varied somewhat in how they analyze this issue, most look for the "single economic unit" that the property owner was looking to develop at the time the property owner submitted the section 404 permit application. *See, e.g., Forest Properties, Inc. v. United States*, 177 F.3d 1360, 1365 (Fed. Cir. 1999). Given this rule, had a "taking" occurred when the property owner sought a permit to fill 9.4 acres of lake bottom to develop in conjunction with 53 upland acres, and the Army Corps denied the permit? *See Forest Properties, Inc. v. United States*, 39 Fed. Cl. 56, 6, 72–74 (Fed. Cl. 1997). What if the property owner originally purchased 250 acres but, by the time the owner applied for the section 404 permit: (1) he had sold all but 6.4 developed acres and 51 undeveloped acres; (2) state regulation prohibited development on all but 12.5 acres of the remaining undeveloped land; and (3) the Army Corps denied the section 404 permit application, preventing development of that 12.5 acres? *See Loveladies Harbor, Inc. v. United States*, 28 F.3d 1171, 1179–82 (Fed. Cir. 1994).

3. **The United State Court of Claims/Court of Federal Claims.** The United States Court of Claims, which decided the *Jentgen* case, was the predecessor to the current U.S. Court of Federal Claims. The jurisdiction of the U.S. Court of Federal Claims can be complex. *See* 28 U.S.C. §§ 1491–1509; *see also generally, e.g., Brown v. United States*, 389 F.3d 1296 (D.C. Cir. 2004); *Clark v. United States*, 2004 WL 2404076 (Fed. Cir. 2004); *Todd v. United States*, 386 F.3d 1091, 1093–94 (Fed. Cir. 2004). Nevertheless, most generally, the Court of Federal Claims has jurisdiction to hear claims against the United States based on the Constitution, federal statutes, or contract, or "for liquidated or unliquidated damages in cases not sounding in tort." 28 U.S.C. § 1491(a)(1). As a result, this court has jurisdiction to hear Fifth Amendment takings claims against the federal government. The Court of Federal Claims has its own rules of procedure, *see* 28 U.S.C., References and Annotations, and parties appeal its decisions exclusively to the U.S. Court of Appeals for the Federal Circuit. 28 U.S.C. § 1295(a)(3).

4. **Property Development and Environmental Regulation, Revisited.** Like the Endangered Species Act, section 404 of the Clean Water Act is occasionally attacked for "unreasonably" interfering with development. Indeed, as noted, states have cited takings liability as one reason for not assuming section 404 permitting authority. It is important to remember, however, that no Fifth Amendment takings liability exists until the Army Corps and the EPA *deny* the section 404 permit; if they grant it, the developer

can proceed with the project. Army Corps statistics indicate that it denies less than one percent of the section 404 permit applications that it receives (although five percent are eventually withdrawn). U.S. Army Corps of Engineers, *All Permit Decisions FY 2002*, http://www.usace.army.mil/inet/functions/cw/cecwo/reg/2002webcharts.pdf. In FY2002, this amounted to 128 permit denials. *Id.* In comparison, the Army Corps granted over 4,000 individual section 404 permits, close to 36,000 nationwide permits, and over 38,000 regional general permits. *Id.*

5. **State Liability for Regulatory Takings.** The Fifth Amendment prohibition on government takings of private property without just compensation applies to the states by way of the Fourteenth Amendment. *Palazzolo v. Rhode Island*, 533 U.S. 606, 617 (2001); *Chicago, B. & Q.R. Co. v. Chicago*, 166 U.S. 226, 233–34 (1897). In addition, many state constitutions also prohibit government takings. State water quality regulation, like Army Corps permitting, can thus also provoke regulatory "takings" claims, especially when states regulate nonpoint sources through land-use-related ***best management practices*** **(BMPs)**.

For example, in the 1980s, the California Water Resources Control Board sought to protect the water quality of Lake Tahoe by instituting a permit system to control nonpoint source runoff of sediments into the lake. *Tahoe-Sierra Preservation Council v. State Water Resources Control Board*, 210 Cal.App.3d 1421, 1425–26 (1989). Specifically, the Water Board's regulatory program "prohibit[ed] discharge of waste attributable to new development in environmental zones or new development which is not in accordance with the classification system." *Id.* at 1429. Landowners sued to challenge the system, claiming that the classification system would prohibit them from constructing residences on their Lake Tahoe properties, *id.*, which in turn constituted a regulatory taking. *Id.* at 1426. The California Court of Appeals held that the taking claim was not ripe for adjudication because the regulatory plan had not yet been applied to the plaintiffs' properties, nor had the plaintiffs had an opportunity to use the administrative review processes available to challenge the classification of their lots. *Id.* at 1443–44.

Tahoe-Sierra Preservation Council is not the only case in which attempts to protect Lake Tahoe have resulted in "takings" claims. Lake Tahoe straddles the California–Nevada border, and the interstate Tahoe Regional Planning Agency (TRPA) has enacted land use planning requirements to try to control development around the lake. While engaged in studies to support a comprehensive plan for Lake Tahoe development, the TRPA imposed two moratoria on further development, effectively preventing development of Lake Tahoe properties for 32 months, from August 1981 until April 1984. Property owners sued in federal court, claiming that the moratoria constituted a "taking" of their property in violation of the U.S. Constitution. In May 2002, a divided U.S. Supreme Court disagreed, determining that temporary moratoria on development for legitimate environmental and planning purposes do not automatically amount to a regulatory "taking" of private property. *Tahoe-Sierra Preservation Council, Inc. v. Tahoe Regional Planning Agency*, 535 U.S. 302, 342–43 (2002).

* * *

V. OTHER PROVISIONS FOR PROTECTING WATER QUALITY

A. NONPOINT SOURCE POLLUTION REGULATION

Nonpoint source water pollution is any pollution of water that does not come from a point source—that is, from a "discernible, confined, and discrete conveyance." The most typical nonpoint source pollution is ***runoff***, as when rain or snow melt flows over streets, parking lots, crop fields, or disturbed soil and picks up dirt, trash, oil, grease, nutrients, fertilizers, pesticides, and sediments along its way to a river or lake. Impervious surfaces such as streets, parking lots, and sidewalks dramatically increase natural levels of runoff.

Runoff is not the only kind of nonpoint source pollution, however. Another nonpoint source of water pollution is ***atmospheric deposition*** of pollutants—the transportation of pollutants to waterways via the air, as in acid rain. The most significant pollutants that reach waterways via atmospheric deposition are nitrogen compounds, mercury, other metals, and pesticides. Office of Water, U.S. EPA, *Air Deposition of Pollutants*, http://www.epa.gov/ owow/oceans/airdep/air2.html.

Nonpoint source pollution is the leading remaining cause of water pollution in the United States. U.S. EPA, *Executive Summary*, at ES–3, *in* WATER QUALITY REPORT (2000), *available at* http://www.epa.gov/305b/2000 report/execsum.pdf. According to the EPA, "at least 50% of water quality problems in the U.S. result from NPS pollution." Office of Water, U.S. EPA, *Pointer No. 4: The Nonpoint Source Management Program* (EPA 841–F–96–0040), http://www.epa.gov/owow/nps/facts/point4.htm (last updated Aug. 28, 2002). The importance of nonpoint source pollution was clear in 1994, as is summarized in Figure 5–17. Nor had that picture changed much by 2003, when the EPA reported the following major remaining causes of water pollution to Congress, as is shown in Figure 5–18.

Figure 5-17: The Five Leading Sources of Water Quality Impairment, 1994
EPA chart.

Rank	Rivers	Lakes	Estuaries
1	Agriculture	Agriculture	Urban Runoff/ Storm Sewers
2	Municipal Sewage Treatment Plants	Municipal Sewage Treatment Plants	Municipal Sewage Treatment Plants
3	Hydrologic/Habitat Modification	Urban Runoff/ Storm Sewers	Agriculture
4	Urban Runoff/ Storm Sewers	Unspecified Nonpoint Sources	Industrial Point Sources
5	Resource Extraction	Hydrologic/Habitat Modification	Petroleum Activities

Figure 5-18: The Five Leading Sources of Water Quality Impairment, 2003
EPA chart.

Rank	Rivers	Lakes	Estuaries
1	Agriculture	Agriculture	Industrial Discharges
2	Municipal Point Sources	Unspecified Nonpoint Sources	Urban Runoff/ Storm Sewers
3	Hydrologic Modification	Atmospheric Deposition	Municipal Point Sources
4	Habitat Modification	Urban Runoff/ Storm Sewers	Upstream Sources
5	Urban Runoff/ Storm Sewers	Municipal Point Sources	Agriculture

Congress was aware of nonpoint source pollution problem as it debated the 1972 Clean Water Act. Congressional hearings made it clear that "[a]gricultural runoff, animal wastes, soil erosion, fertilizers, pesticides and other farm chemicals that are a part of runoff, construction runoff and siltation from mines and acid mine drainage are major contributors to the Nation's water pollution problem." S. REP. NO. 92–414 (1971), *reprinted in* 1972 U.S.C.C.A.N. 3668, 3705. Congress even concluded that "[i]t has become clearly established that the waters of the Nation cannot be restored and their quality maintained unless the very complex and difficult problem of nonpoint sources is addressed." *Id.* Nevertheless, Congress left this "very complex and difficult problem" to the states' experimentation, because "many nonpoint sources of pollution are beyond present technology to control." *Id.* Thus, regulation of nonpoint source pollution is part of the Clean Water Act's scheme of federalism.

In encouraging states to experiment with nonpoint source pollution regulation, Congress originally relied solely on ***section 208*** of the Clean Water Act, 33 U.S.C. § 1288, which encourages states to enact ***area-wide waste management plans***. These plans were to address, *inter alia*, various forms of nonpoint source pollution. CWA § 208(b)(2)(F), (G), (H), 33 U.S.C. § 1288(b)(2)(F), (G), (H). In return, states would receive federal financial and technological assistance. CWA § 208(f), (g), (h), (j), 33 U.S.C. § 1288(f), (g), (h), (j).

By 1987, however, it was clear to Congress that section 208 was not effectively addressing nonpoint source pollution. As a result, Congress added a new ***section 319*** to the Act. 33 U.S.C. § 1329. Section 319 established "a national policy that programs for the control of nonpoint sources of pollution be developed and implemented in an expeditious manner so as to enable the goals of the Act to be met through the control of both point and nonpoint sources of pollution." WATER QUALITY ACT OF 1987, SECTION-BY-SECTION ANALYSIS PREPARED BY THE HON. JAMES J. HOWARD, CHAIRMAN OF THE HOUSE COMMITTEE ON PUBLIC WORKS AND TRANSPORTATION, 133 Cong. Rec. H131 (1987), *reprinted in* 1987 U.S.C.C.A.N. 7, 30. Section 319 encourages states to adopt ***nonpoint source management plans*** in exchange for federal funding. In order to receive federal nonpoint source grants, however, the state had to submit to the EPA a nonpoint source management plan that meets section 319's requirements, and the EPA had to approve that plan. CWA § 319(a), (b), 33 U.S.C. § 1329(a), (b). States also had to set milestones for themselves in having nonpoint sources meet ***Best Management Practices* (BMPs)** to control their water pollution, and they have to meet those milestones in order to continue to receive federal funds. CWA § 319(h)(8), 33 U.S.C. § 1329(h)(8). According to the EPA,

> By 1991, all 50 states and the territories had received EPA approval [of their section 319 nonpoint source management plans]; by 1995, 7 tribes also had received approval. Since 1990, recipients of 319 grants have directed approximately 40 percent of awarded funds toward controlling NPS pollution from agricultural lands.

Office of Water, U.S. EPA, *Pointer No. 4: The Nonpoint Source Management Program* (EPA 841–F–96–0040, http://www.epa.gov/owow/nps/facts/point4.htm (last updated Aug. 28, 2002)).

Thus, state and tribal nonpoint source management programs have now existed for over two decades. As Figures 5–17 and 5–18 suggest, however, their success has been limited in effectively addressing the nonpoint source pollution problem. As a result, enterprising citizens have increasingly attempted to use other water-quality-related provisions in the Clean Water Act to establish a *federal* dimension to nonpoint source regulation.

B. TMDLS

1. TMDLs in General

As was noted in connection with the discussion of water-quality-related effluent limitations in NPDES permits, under section 303(d) of the Clean Water Act, 33 U.S.C. § 1313(d), states must prepare a list of all waterbodies that currently do not meet their water quality standards, known as ***water-quality-limited waterbodies***. According to the EPA's estimates, over 40% of waters in the United States do not meet their water quality standards. *See* Figure 5–19.

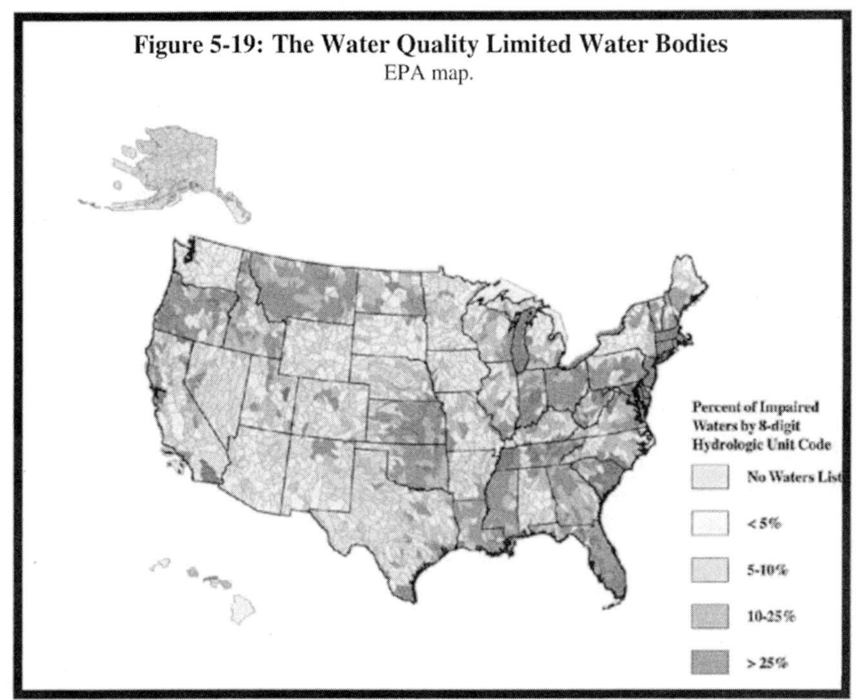

Figure 5-19: The Water Quality Limited Water Bodies
EPA map.

Once a state has determined which waters within its borders are not meeting the relevant water quality standards, the state must rank those water-quality-limited waterbodies in order of priority and establish a ***total maximum daily load*** **(TMDL)** for each pollutant contributing to the non-compliance of the waterbody. A TMDL is the total amount of a given pollutant that can be added to a waterbody every day without the water body exceeding the relevant water quality standard. The amount of pollutant established in the TMDL is then divided among the natural background sources of pollution, the nonpoint sources of pollution (known as the ***load allocation*** **(LA)**), and the point sources of pollution (known as the ***waste load allocation*** **(WLA)**). Section 303(d) most directly requires that the state or the EPA adjust point sources' permits in order to achieve the TMDL, CWA § 303(d)(4), (e)(3), 33 U.S.C. § 1313(d)(4), (e)(3), but the TMDL process can also encourage states to more thoroughly regulate nonpoint sources, as well.

2. Setting TMDLs

In the Clean Water Act's scheme of cooperative federalism, states have the primary authority to set TMDLs, just as states have the primary authority to set water quality standards. As with water quality standards, however, the EPA must set TMDLs for the state if the state refuses to do so. CWA § 303(d)(2), 33 U.S.C. § 1313(d)(2). Neither states nor the EPA showed much inclination to start—let alone finish—the TMDL process. As a result, most of the existing TMDLs are the result of citizen-suit litigation against both states and the EPA. *See generally, e.g., San Francisco BayKeeper v. Whitman*, 297 F.3d 877 (9th Cir. 2002) (California); *Hayes v. Whitman*, 264 F.3d 1017 (10th Cir. 2001) (Oklahoma); *Alaska Center for Environment v. Browner*, 20 F.3d 981 (9th Cir. 1994) (Alaska); *Scott v. City of Hammond, Indiana*, 741 F.2d 992, 996–98 (7th Cir. 1984) (Illinois); *Natural Resources Defense Council, Inc. v. Fox*, 129 F. Supp. 2d 666 (S.D.N.Y. 2001) (New York); *Friends of the Wild Swan, Inc. v. U.S. EPA*, 130 F. Supp. 2d 1207 (D. Mont. 2000) (Montana); *Kingman Park Civic Ass'n v. U.S. EPA*, 84 F.Supp.2d 1 (D.D.C. 1999) (District of Columbia); *American Canoe Ass'n, Inc. v. U.S. EPA*, 30 F.Supp.2d 908 (E.D. Va. 1998) (Virginia); *Idaho Sportsmen's Coalition v. Browner*, 951 F.Supp. 962 (W.D. Wash. 1996) (Idaho); *Sierra Club v. Hankinson*, 939 F.Supp. 865 (N.D. Ga. 1996) (Georgia).

Even under court order, TMDL writing has been a slow process. One reason is that TMDLs are not always easy to calculate, as the following case demonstrates.

NATURAL RESOURCES DEFENSE COUNCIL, INC. v. MUSZYNSKI

268 F.3d 91 (2d Cir. 2001).

POOLER, CIRCUIT JUDGE:

Plaintiffs–Appellants Natural Resources Defense Council, Inc., Environmental Defense Fund, Inc., and Alan G. Hevesi (collectively "NRDC") appeal from a May 30, 2000, judgment of the United States District Court for the Southern District of New York (Peter K. Leisure, *Judge*), entered upon a May 2, 2000, Opinion and Order. NRDC challenges only the district court's dismissal of its claim brought under the APA seeking judicial review of the Environmental Protection Agency's ("EPA") decision to approve total maximum daily loads ("TMDLs") for phosphorous for eight New York reservoirs. The TMDLs were submitted to EPA by the

State of New York pursuant to the CWA, 33 U.S.C. § 1313. We affirm the district court's holding that the CWA does not require TMDLs to be expressed in terms of daily loads, but remand to the district court for remand to EPA for further explanation of why annual loads are appropriate in the case of New York's phosphorus TMDLs.

BACKGROUND

* * * In general, the Clean Water Act protects waterbodies by limiting discharges of pollutants into them through technology based controls. *See* 33 U.S.C. § 1311(b)(2)(A). * * * The Act also requires states to adopt water quality standards for their waterbodies based upon the uses of the waterbodies. *See* 33 U.S.C. § 1313(a)-(c). Where effluent limitations are not "stringent enough to implement any water quality standard applicable" to a waterbody, the CWA requires that the "State shall establish a priority ranking for such waters." 33 U.S.C. § 1313(d)(1)(A). For such waterbodies, the state is required to establish a "total maximum daily load, for those pollutants which the [EPA] Administrator identifies." *Id.* at § 1313(d)(1)(C). Each total maximum daily load ("TMDL") "shall be established at a level necessary to implement the applicable water quality standards with seasonal variations and a margin of safety which takes into account any lack of knowledge concerning the relationship between effluent limitations and water quality." *Id.* In effect, a TMDL posts a limit on the total amount of a pollutant a waterbody may receive over a period of time. *See* 40 C.F.R. § 130.2(i). The TMDL encompasses discharges into the water from specific sites (like factories located along a river) known as point sources, as well as from nonpoint sources, which can consist of, for example, runoff due to the agricultural use of land adjoining a river, as well as, finally, the natural occurrence of the pollutant in the waterbody (*i.e.*, "natural background"). *See id.*; 33 U.S.C. § 1362(14) (defining "point source"); *Trustees for Alaska v. EPA*, 749 F.2d 549, 558 (9th Cir, 1984) (defining "nonpoint source"). The TMDLs the state establishes to limit the loading (or release) of pollutants into a waterbody must in turn be approved by the EPA. *See* 33 U.S.C. § 1313(2).

In recent years, the nineteen upstate water reservoirs which supply New York City its drinking water have suffered increasing phosphorus pollution, due both to discharges of sewage into them and runoff from nonpoint sources. The increasing quantity of phosphorus in these reservoirs has the propensity to make the reservoirs eutrophic: a state which, as one expert explained in the administrative record before us, arises from "the accumulation of phosphorus in ... reservoirs [which] has caused excessive growth or nuisance 'blooms' of algae and aquatic macrophytes which are harmful to a waterbody." Eutrophication "can have adverse effects on drinking water quality, ranging from aesthetic changes to potential public health risks such as the increased production of organic material which, after disinfection, leads to by-products."

In 1994, NRDC filed an environmental citizen suit in the United States District Court for the Southern District of New York, claiming, in pertinent part, that the State of New York had a nondiscretionary duty under the CWA to promulgate TMDLs for the nineteen reservoirs providing New York City drinking water, and that its failure to do so amounted to a constructive submission of no TMDLs, leaving EPA with the nondiscretionary duty to promulgate the TMDLs itself. The district court refused NRDC summary judgment on this claim, holding there was a genuine issue of fact concerning whether New York had submitted TMDLs for the reservoirs.

In January 1995, New York placed the nineteen reservoirs on a list submitted to EPA naming waterbodies for which technology-based pollution controls were "not stringent enough to attain or maintain compliance with applicable state water quality standards," which, for the reservoirs, is "water supply." The waterbodies on the list were given priority in the development of TMDLs for pollutants impairing water quality. In 1996, New York published a report explaining the methodology for calculating the phosphorus TMDLs for the reservoirs. The report explained that developing TMDLs "for a large watershed can be data intensive and a phased approach is often used to protect the water body while additional information is collected," and noted that initial phosphorus TMDLs (the "Phase I TMDLs") would be "based on the best available data and utilize[] simplified models." The Phase I TMDLs were to be supplemented in 1998 by a second set of TMDLS ("Phase II TMDLs") taking into account "improved data." The Phase I TMDLs were established, and after a public comment period during which NRDC offered criticisms, the TMDLs were submitted to EPA for eighteen of the nineteen reservoirs on January 31, 1997. On April 2, 1997, EPA approved the submission for eight of the reservoirs. It also declined to approve the submitted TMDLs for the remaining ten reservoirs because it concluded that pollution levels in those reservoirs did not exceed the level that required resort to TMDLs under the CWA.

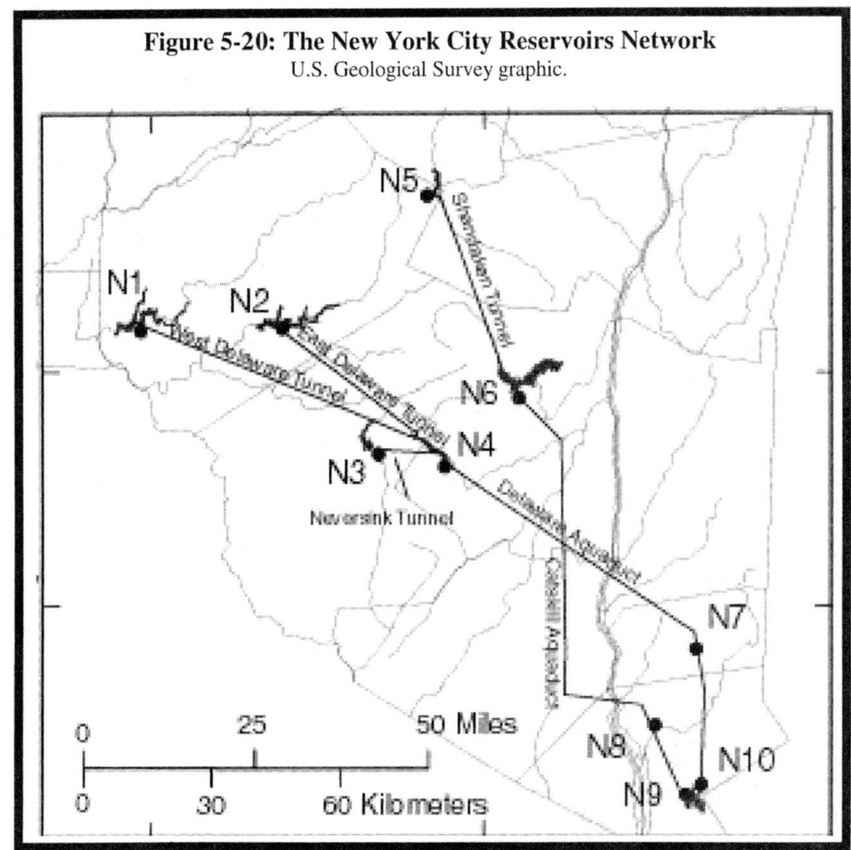

Figure 5-20: The New York City Reservoirs Network
U.S. Geological Survey graphic.

In response, NRDC amended its complaint, claiming that the TMDLs submitted by New York were facially inadequate under the CWA and therefore EPA violated a nondiscretionary duty under the CWA in approving TMDLs for the eight reservoirs, as well as violating the Administrative Procedure Act, 5 U.S.C. § 706 ("APA"). * * *

On May 2, 2000, the district court issued a final ruling, finding, in pertinent part, that EPA's approval of the eight TMDLs was rationally supported by the administrative record and did not constitute a violation of the APA. * * *

* * *On appeal, NRDC renews its arguments that the EPA violated the APA by approving TMDLs that were deficient because they 1) are expressed in terms of annual, not daily, loads; 2) fail to implement the applicable water standard—in this case, a standard appropriate for the water supply use of the reservoirs; and 3) fail to incorporate an adequate margin of safety.

DISCUSSION

This court reviews a district court's review of an agency action de novo. Under the Administrative Procedure Act, a court may "hold unlawful and set aside agency action, findings, and conclusions found to be ... arbitrary, capricious, an abuse of discretion, or otherwise not in accordance with law." 5 U.S.C. § 706. Review under this provision is "narrow," limited to examining the administrative record to determine "whether the [agency] decision was based on a consideration of the relevant factors and whether there has been a clear error of judgment." *City of New York v. Shalala*, 34 F.3d 1161, 1167 (2d Cir. 1994). Thus, while the "court may not substitute its judgment for that of the agency," an agency decision may be set aside where the agency "has relied on factors which Congress has not intended it to consider, entirely failed to consider an important aspect of the problem, offered an explanation for its decision that runs counter to the evidence before the agency, or is so implausible that it could not be ascribed to a difference in view or the product of agency expertise." *Id.* (internal quotations omitted).

I. TOTAL MAXIMUM DAILY LOADS.

The CWA requires states to identify waters that cannot meet their water quality standards even after implementation of the effluent limitations required by 33 U.S.C. §§ 1311(b)(1)(A), (B). *See* 33 U.S.C. § 1313(d)(1)(A). For such waters, "[e]ach State shall establish ... the total maximum daily load, for those pollutants." *Id.* at § 1313(d)(1)(C). "Such load shall be established at a level necessary to implement the applicable water quality standards with seasonal variations and a margin of safety which takes into account any lack of knowledge concerning the relationship between effluent limitations and water quality." *Id.* Further, each state must estimate

> the total maximum daily thermal load required to assure protection and propagation of a balanced, indigenous population of shellfish, fish and wildlife. Such estimates shall take into account the normal water temperatures, flow rates, seasonal variations, existing sources of heat input, and the dissipative capacity of the identified waters or parts thereof. Such estimates shall include a calculation of the maximum heat input that can be made into each such part and shall include a margin of safety which takes into account any lack of knowledge concerning the development of thermal water quality criteria for such protection and propagation in the identified waters or parts thereof.

Id. at § 1313(d)(1)(D). EPA's implementing regulations note that TMDLs "can be expressed in terms of either mass per time, toxicity, or other appropriate measure." 40 C.F.R. § 130.2(i).

NRDC claims the TDMLs approved by EPA are in violation of the CWA because they are presented in terms of annual maximum loads of phosphorus, not daily loads. NRDC argues that an annual expression of TMDLs violates the clear language of the statute, so the matter boils down to one of simple statutory interpretation. EPA, in turn, argues that the statute is silent with regard to how TMDLs should be expressed and that its own regulations make clear that any general expression in terms of units of mass over a period of time is acceptable. * * *

Statutory analysis begins with the plain meaning of a statute. The plain meaning can be extrapolated by giving words their ordinary sense. If the plain meaning of a statute is susceptible to two or more reasonable meanings, *i.e.*, if it is ambiguous, then a court may resort to the canons of statutory construction. Although the canons of statutory interpretation provide a court with numerous avenues for supplementing and narrowing the possible meaning of ambiguous text, most helpful to our interpretation of the CWA in this case are two rules. First, when determining which reasonable meaning should prevail, the text should be placed in the context of the entire statutory structure. Second, "absurd results are to be avoided and internal inconsistencies in the statute must be dealt with." *United States v. Turkette*, 452 U.S. 576, 580 (1981). Finally, if the canons of statutory interpretation and resort to other interpretive aids (like legislative history) do not resolve the issue, we will give deference to the view of the agency tasked with administering the statute, particularly insofar as those views are expressed in rules and regulations that implement the statute. "[C]onsiderable weight should be accorded to an executive department's construction of a statutory scheme it is entrusted to administer." *United States v. Mead Corp.*, 533 U.S. 218, 227–28 (2001) (internal quotations omitted).

If the language of the statute is as plain as NRDC urges, NRDC's reading of the statute easily prevails. The CWA calls for establishment of a "total maximum *daily* load," not an hourly, weekly, monthly, or annual load. We believe, however, that the term "total maximum daily load" is susceptible to a broader range of meanings. Indeed, NRDC's overly narrow reading of the statute loses sight of the overall structure and purpose of the CWA. The CWA contemplates the establishment of TMDLs for an open-ended range of pollutants that are susceptible to effective regulation by such means. *See* 33 U.S.C. § 1313(d)(1)(c) (noting that states must establish TMDLs for all "pollutants which the Administrator identifies ... as suitable for such calculation"). In the case of each pollutant, effective regulation requires agencies to determine how the pollutant enters, interacts with, and, at a certain level or under certain conditions, adversely impacts an affected waterbody. In the case of highly toxic pollutants that may work harmful effects upon a waterbody almost immediately when present at small levels, close regulation at a daily level may be most appropriate. In the case of other pollutants, like phosphorus, the amounts waterbodies can tolerate vary depending upon the waterbody and the season of the year, while the harmful consequences of excessive amounts may not occur immediately. In short, the CWA's effective enforcement requires agency analysis and application of information concerning a broad range of pollutants. We are not prepared to say Congress intended that such far-ranging agency expertise be narrowly confined in application to regulation of pollutant loads on a strictly daily basis. Such a reading strikes us as absurd, especially given that for some pollutants, effective regulation may best occur by some other periodic measure than a diurnal one. Accordingly, we agree with EPA that a "total maximum daily load" may be expressed by another measure of mass per time, where such an alternative measure best serves the purpose of effective regulation of pollutant levels in waterbodies.

* * * [Here,] EPA argues that a daily measure of phosphorus would be inappropriate given that phosphorus concentrations vary seasonally and annually. The record supports this view, indicating that phosphorus concentrations in waterbodies are affected "by the seasonal interplay of temperatures, density, and wind," resulting in the frequent occurrence of "very large short-term yearly variations which characterize the gradually increasing concentration." While the record makes clear why EPA or a State might opt not to measure loads on a daily basis, it remains unclear why an annual measurement of loads would therefore be more appropriate since phosphorus concentrations vary within a waterbody on a seasonal basis.

* * * The record shows that the "flow" or the amount of phosphorus contributed to a waterbody by each source will "vary widely in response to season, storm events, and other random factors." Given this and the fact that phosphorus contributed to a waterbody during one season can impact algal growth during other seasons (when, due to seasonal factors, biological activity increases), seasonal regulation of phosphorus flows may be more appropriate. Of course, we do not suggest how best to regulate phosphorus. Instead, we remand for EPA to justify how the annual period of measurement takes seasonal variations into account.

II. IMPLEMENTATION OF APPLICABLE WATER STANDARDS.

The CWA requires that each TMDL "be established at a level necessary to implement the applicable water quality standards." 33 U.S.C. § 1313(d)(1)(C). The New York State Department of Environmental Conservation ("NYSDEC") has determined that the use, and hence applicable water quality standard, for the reservoirs is "water supply." New York's water quality standard for phosphorus requires the presence of "[n]one in amounts that will result in growths of algae, weeds and slimes that will impair the waters for their best usages." N.Y. COMP. CODES R. & REGS., tit. 6, § 703.2. In 1993, the NYSDEC determined that a numerical guidance value of twenty micrograms of phosphorus per liter of water ("µg/L") would meet the standard imposed by the regulation with regard to waterbodies used for recreational purposes. New York relied on the same figure when determining the TMDLs for the reservoirs, while recognizing that a "guidance value" developed for the "protection of aesthetics for primary and secondary contact recreation ... may not be stringent enough to protect the drinking water supply." New York declared it "will continue to investigate if the [guidance value developed to protect water for aesthetic purposes] is sufficient to maintain water quality in the reservoirs, with the future option to revise this critical concentration." NRDC argues that the TMDLs for these reservoirs are not those necessary, under the CWA, to "implement the applicable water quality standards" because a less stringent standard, designed to protect water for recreational uses, has been applied to waterbodies designated for water supply use, the highest use.

According to the NYSDEC, the value of 0.020 μg/l "total phosphorus" is based upon [waterbody] user surveys conducted in New York as well as Vermont and Minnesota in which citizens "are asked to best describe the physical condition of the lake with respect to algal levels and the recreational suitability of the lake at the time of sampling." During the comment period for New York's proposed TMDLs, New York met NRDC's objection to the use of an aesthetic criteria in determining appropriate phosphorus levels by stating: "We acknowledge that the current guidance value ... is based on aesthetic conditions affecting recreational uses.... Since it is the only presently available phosphorus criteria, it was used for the Phase I TMDL analysis. This is appropriate, especially in New York, where the best use designation of a waterbody for drinking water expressly incorporates all other best uses set forth in our regulations." * * * New York conceded "that a different phosphorus guidance value or standard may be necessary to reduce eutrophication and/or to protect surface waterbodies that are a source of water supply. NYC is in the process of collecting additional data for the development of a phosphorous standard specifically designed for the protection of waters as a water supply source."

While at first blush New York's use of an aesthetic water quality standard to protect drinking water seems a cause for concern, in the end, EPA's primary concern in determining whether to approve the TMDL is whether or not the TMDL will "implement the applicable water quality standard[]." 33 U.S.C. § 1313(d)(1)(C). As the district court concluded, "If 20 μg/L is an appropriate phosphorus guidance value for drinking water as well as for recreational use, then EPA acted reasonably in approving TMDLs that incorporated the 20 μg/L value." In approving New York's TMDLs, EPA noted that the guidance was based on an aesthetic criteria, but stated that nevertheless "the phosphorus guidance value is meant to control excessive and nuisance growths of algae and other aquatic plants. This guidance value is used by the NYSDEC to reduce nuisance algal blooms to acceptable levels and therefore, it indirectly address [*sic*] the effects of eutrophication and cultural eutrophication." Most importantly, EPA concluded that "NYSDEC's guidance value is below EPA's recommended level of 25 μg/L, and should, therefore, be sufficiently protective to control nuisance aquatic growth and to protect against other indirect effects of eutrophication and accelerated cultural eutrophication."

* * * As all the parties recognize, additional research oriented to the specific conditions of New York's reservoirs would be optimal. In the meantime, EPA's hands are not tied just because it must act based on scientific knowledge that is incomplete or disputed. "In the face of conflicting evidence at the frontiers of science, courts' deference to expert determinations should be at its greatest." *Cellular Phone*, 205 F.3d at 90. Therefore, EPA's determination that New York can formulate its TMDL

for phosphorus using an aesthetic criterion is not arbitrary and capricious at this point in time.

III. MARGIN OF SAFETY

The CWA requires that a TMDL incorporate "a margin of safety which takes into account any lack of knowledge concerning the relationship between effluent limitations and water quality." 33 U.S.C. § 1313(d)(1)(C). The TMDLs for the pertinent reservoirs incorporate a margin of safety ("MOS") amounting to ten percent of the critical load. Thus, the critical load for a given reservoir—that is, the estimated maximal amount of phosphorus that the reservoir can receive without becoming eutrophic—is typically reduced by ten percent in order to arrive at the appropriate TMDL. * * * In approving the TMDLs, EPA noted that in lieu of any

> "standard" or guideline for choosing a specific margin of safety, best professional judgment and the available information are used in setting a margin of safety. (In many cases, a separate margin of safety is not used, but is inherent in the conservative assumptions used in the model). The close calibration between the predicted and observed phosphorus concentrations indicates the model and assumptions are justified and that a higher margin of safety is not warranted.

NRDC argues the margin of safety fails to meet "the clearly delineated Congressional specifications" because there are not adequate findings in the record that the margin of safety used addresses "any lack of knowledge concerning the relationship between effluent limitations and water quality," as the CWA requires.

This is not a case where the agency has "relied on factors which Congress has not intended it to consider." *Shalala*, 34 F.3d at 1167. EPA's approval of the MOS was guided in part by the close calibration between predicted and observed phosphorus concentrations in the New York reservoirs. New York relied on the Reckhow Land Use Model to calculate the amount of phosphorus entering the reservoirs. * * * Reliance on the Reckhow Model was justified because it had "been previously applied to several of the New York City reservoirs with good results." * * *

EPA could reasonably conclude that given the close calibration of the Reckhow Model, a larger margin of safety was not warranted. The margin of safety accounts for uncertainty regarding the effects of phosphorus on water quality by ensuring that the TMDL maintains phosphorus levels below the critical load the reservoir can tolerate. The Reckhow model aids in this task since its accuracy ensures a limited range of fluctuation between projected phosphorus levels and actual levels.

NRDC takes issue with the adoption of a ten percent margin of safety, arguing that no scientific or mathematical basis prescribed this percentage as opposed to any other. As EPA explained, because "there is no 'standard' or guideline for choosing a specific margin of safety, best professional judgment and the available information are used in setting [it]." While the MOS may thus be set with an uncomfortable degree of discretion, requiring that EPA show a rigorous scientific methodology dictates one course of action as opposed to another and would effectively prevent the agency from acting in situations where action is required in the face of a clear public health or environmental danger but the magnitude of that danger cannot be effectively quantified. * * * Finally, it is worth noting that approval of the Phase I MOS was based, in part, on the limited information available. The EPA approval contemplates revision of the MOS as more information becomes available: "As additional reservoir data and loading data become available, Phase I model assumptions are being reexamined under Phase II." * * *

NOTES

1. **Tracking This Case Through Section 303.** What water quality standard had New York set for the reservoirs at issue in this case? In particular, what was the designated use of the reservoirs? What were the water quality criteria, especially as relates to phosphorus? Why weren't the effluent limitations sufficient to ensure that the reservoirs met the water quality standards? (HINT: What sources were adding phosphorus to the reservoirs?) How did New York set the TMDLs for the reservoirs? Why did the state pick the phosphorus TMDL that it picked? Given the sources that are polluting the reservoirs, how do you think that New York will actually implement the TMDL?

2. **The States' Authority Over Water Quality, Revisited.** How does a state's authority to set TMDLs compare to its authority to set water quality standards? How much authority does the EPA have to review TMDLs, compared to its authority to review state water quality standards? What standard of review did the court use to review the EPA's approval of New York's TMDLs? Why?

3. **"Daily" Maximum Loads?** How did the Second Circuit construe the "daily" element of TMDLs? What tools of statutory construction did it rely on? Is its construction consistent with the "plain meaning" of section 303? Why or why not? How much deference did the Second Circuit accord to the EPA's understanding of "total daily maximum load"? Why?

Not all courts have agreed with the Second Circuit's reading of the TMDL requirement. The D.C. Circuit, for example, held in 2006 that the Clean Water Act's use of the word "daily" prohibited the EPA from establishing or approving seasonal or annual TMDLs. *Friends of the Earth, Inc. v. EPA*, 446 F.3d 140, 144–45 (D.C. Cir. 2006).

4. **The Role of Science and Scientific Uncertainty in Setting TMDLs.** Why did New York rely on a reference concentration related to *aesthetics* in setting the TMDLs for the reservoirs? How did the Second Circuit treat the need for additional research as it reviewed the EPA's approval of TMDLs based on that reference concentration? Does the Second Circuit's approach make sense, given the overall goals of the Clean Water Act? Why or why not?

Why would Congress require states and the EPA to set TMDLs to include a margin of safety? How does a margin of safety advance the Clean Water Act's overall goals? How did New York incorporate a margin of safety in this case? Why did the EPA approve New York's approach? Why did the Second Circuit uphold the EPA's approval? To what extent did the validity of the TMDL at issue depend upon the scientific validity of the Reckhow Model? What would have happened if the validity of the model was more questionable, do you think?

* * *

3. TMDLs and Nonpoint Source Pollution

TMDLs, by their very nature, must take account of nonpoint source pollution, and hence the TMDL process provides states with one possible motivation for more effectively addressing nonpoint source pollution. In *Muszynski*, for example, New York's reservoirs suffered from eutrophication as a result of both point source discharges of sewage and nonpoint source runoff. New York could therefore address the phosphorus problem by: (1) forcing the point sources to more stringently treat their effluent; (2) forcing the nonpoint sources to more effectively control their runoff; or (3) both. Under what circumstances might option (1) be most attractive to New York? Under what circumstances might option (2) be more attractive? Might it matter whether the point sources were POTWs? Why or why not?

Sometimes, as a practical matter, the state's regulatory choices are limited. Consider the following hypothetical. Suppose that State A's water quality standards for the Blue River and the Green River require that these rivers' water have a phosphorus concentration of 20 micrograms per liter or less. However, both rivers currently have a phosphorus concentration of 50 micrograms per liter—clearly violating their water quality standards. As a result, both rivers are water quality limited waterbodies under section 303(d), and State A must set a TMDL for phosphorus for each one. State A determines that, given the two rivers' volumes and their rates of flow, 100 grams of phosphorus can be added to each river each day without the water quality standards being violated.

BLUE RIVER: Suppose that when State A examines the sources contributing phosphorus to the Blue River, it discovers that:

WASTE LOAD ALLOCATION: 5 industrial point sources (each with an NPDES permit) each contribute 25 grams of phosphorus per day	125 grams/day
LOAD ALLOCATION: Runoff from 1 family farm contributes, on average, 5 grams of phosphorus per day	5 grams/day
BACKGROUND: Natural and uncontrollable sources contribute 15 grams of phosphorus per day	15 grams/day
TOTAL LOAD:	**145 grams/day**

How should State A adjust the phosphorus contributions to the Blue River in order to meet the TMDL? It cannot adjust the natural background levels (15 grams per day), and State A is unlikely in this situation to require the family farm to change its contribution (5 grams per day). Together, these two sources contribute 20 grams per day, leaving 80 grams per day for State A to divide among the five point sources. As a result, State A will probably amend these point sources' NPDES permits to allow each point source to discharge only 16 grams of phosphorus per day (80 grams per day divided by five sources)—requiring each of those point sources to find a way to reduce the phosphorus in its discharged effluent by 9 grams per day (which might not be easy, if the NPDES permit terms for phosphorus were already based on BAT or NSPS). If State A fails to set the TMDL or to adjust the NPDES permits, moreover, the EPA can (and must) do so. Also, given the need for a margin of safety and the fact that the runoff from the farm will vary with rainfall, State A will probably make even more stringent adjustments to the NPDES permits.

GREEN RIVER: In contrast, when State A examines the sources contributing phosphorus to the Green River, State A discovers that:

WASTE LOAD ALLOCATION: 1 industrial point source (with an NPDES permit) contributes 5 grams of phosphorus per day	5 grams/day
LOAD ALLOCATION: Runoff from 5 large farming operations contributes, on average, 150 grams of phosphorus per day	150 grams/day
BACKGROUND: Natural and uncontrollable sources contribute 15 grams of phosphorus per day	15 grams/day
TOTAL LOAD:	**170 grams/day**

What will State A do now? It cannot meet the water quality standard for the Green River just by adjusting the one NPDES permit—even if the point source discharges *no* phosphorus, the Green River will still violate the water quality standard. Because most of the Green River's phosphorus pollution comes from agricultural runoff, promulgation of TMDLs in this case should prompt State A to enact or amend its nonpoint source regulations and BMP requirements for the farms.

But the Green River situation also creates a potential legal problem, so far as cooperative federalism is concerned. Suppose that State A refuses to set the TMDL or to regulate the agricultural nonpoint source pollution. Nonpoint source pollution, remember, is almost exclusively the province of the states—the EPA has no direct or clear authority under the Clean Water Act to regulate such sources. Can the EPA set and enforce TMDLs when *only* nonpoint sources pollute a given waterbody? The following case addressed the relationship of federally set TMDLs to nonpoint source pollution regulation.

PRONSOLINO v. NASTRI

291 F.3d 1123 (9th Cir. 2002).

BERZON, CIRCUIT JUDGE.

The United States Environmental Protection Agency ("EPA") required California to identify the Garcia River as a water body with insufficient pollution controls and, as required for waters so identified, to set so-called "total maximum daily loads" ("TMDLs")—the significance of which we explain later—for pollution entering the river. Appellants challenge the EPA's authority under the Clean Water Act ("CWA" or the "Act") § 303(d), 33 U.S.C. § 1313(d), to apply the pertinent identification and TMDL requirements to the Garcia River. The district court rejected this challenge, and we do as well.

CWA § 303(d) requires the states to identify and compile a list of waters for which certain "effluent limitations" "are not stringent enough" to implement the applicable water quality standards for such waters. § 303(d)(1)(A). Effluent limitations pertain only to point sources of pollution; point sources of pollution are those from a discrete conveyance, such as a pipe or tunnel. Nonpoint sources of pollution are nondiscrete sources; sediment run-off from timber harvesting, for example, derives from a nonpoint source. The Garcia River is polluted only by nonpoint sources. Therefore, neither the effluent limitations referenced in § 303(d) nor any other effluent limitations apply to the pollutants entering the Garcia River.

The precise statutory question before us is whether the phrase "are not stringent enough" triggers the identification requirement both for waters as to which effluent limitations apply but do not suffice to attain water quality standards and for waters as to which effluent limitations do not apply at all to the pollution sources impairing the water. We answer this question in the affirmative, a conclusion which triggers the application of the statutory TMDL requirement to waters such as the Garcia River.

I. STATUTORY BACKGROUND

Resolution of the statutory interpretation question before us, discrete though it is, "requires a familiarity with the history, the structure, and, alas, the jargon of the federal water pollution laws." *Natural Res. Def. Council v. EPA*, 915 F.2d 1314, 1316 (9th Cir. 1990). We therefore begin with a brief overview of the Act.

A. *The Major Goals and Concepts of the CWA*

Congress enacted the CWA in 1972, amending earlier federal water pollution laws that had proven ineffective. *EPA v. California*, 426 U.S. 200, 202 (1976). Prior to 1972, federal water pollution laws relied on "water quality standards specifying the acceptable levels of pollution in a State's interstate navigable waters as the primary mechanism . . . for the control of water pollution." *Id.* The pre–1972 laws did not, however, provide concrete direction concerning how those standards were to be met in the foreseeable future.

In enacting sweeping revisions to the nation's water pollution laws in 1972, Congress began from the premise that the focus "on the tolerable effects rather than the preventable causes of pollution" constituted a major shortcoming in the pre 1972 laws. *Oregon Natural Desert Ass'n v. Dombeck*, 172 F.3d 1092, 1096 (9th Cir. 1998) (quoting *EPA v. State Water Resources Control Board*, 426 U.S. 200, 202–03 (1976)). The 1972 Act therefore sought to target primarily "the preventable causes of pollution," by emphasizing the use of technological controls. *Id.*

At the same time, Congress decidedly did *not* in 1972 give up on the broader goal of attaining acceptable water quality. CWA § 101(a), 33 U.S.C. § 1251(a). Rather, the new statute recognized that even with the application of the mandated technological controls on point source discharges, water bodies still might not meet state-set water quality standards. The 1972 statute therefore put in place mechanisms other than direct federal regulation of point sources, designed to "restore and maintain the chemical, physical, and biological integrity of the Nation's waters." § 101(a).

In so doing, the CWA uses distinctly different methods to control pollution released from point sources and that traceable to nonpoint sources. The Act directly mandates technological controls to limit the pollution point sources may discharge into a body of water. On the other hand, the Act "provides no direct mechanism to control nonpoint source pollution but rather uses the 'threat and promise' of federal grants to the states to accomplish this task," [*Dombeck*, 172 F.3d] at 1097 (citations omitted), thereby "recogniz[ing], preserv[ing], and protect[ing] the primary responsibilities and rights of States to prevent, reduce, and eliminate pollution, [and] to plan the development and use . . . of land and water resources. . . ." § 101(b).

B. The Structure of CWA § 303, 33 U.S.C. § 1313

1. Water Quality Standards

Section 303 is central to the Act's carrot-and-stick approach to attaining acceptable water quality without direct federal regulation of nonpoint sources of pollution. * * *

2. *Section 303(d): "Identification of Areas with Insufficient Controls; Maximum Daily Load"*

Section 303(d)(1)(A) requires each state to identify as "areas with insufficient controls" "those waters within its boundaries for which the effluent limitations required by section [301(b)(1)(A)] and section [301(b)(1)(B)] of this title are not stringent enough to implement any water quality standard applicable to such waters." *Id.* * * *

For waters identified pursuant to § 303(d)(1)(A) (the "§ 303(d)(1) list"), the states must establish the "total maximum daily load" ("TMDL") for pollutants identified by the EPA as suitable for TMDL calculation. § 303(d)(1)(C). "A TMDL defines the specified maximum amount of a pollutant which can be discharged or 'loaded' into the waters at issue from all combined sources." *Dioxin/Organochlorine Center v. Clarke*, 57 F.3d 1517, 1520 (9th Cir. 1995). The TMDL "shall be established at a level necessary to implement the applicable water quality standards...." § 303(d)(1)(C).

Section 303(d)(2), in turn, requires each state to submit its § 303(d)(1) list and TMDLs to the EPA for its approval or disapproval. If the EPA approves the list and TMDLs, the state must incorporate the list and TMDLs into its "continuing planning process," the requirements for which are set forth in § 303(e). § 303(d)(2). If the EPA disapproves either the § 303(d)(1) list or any TMDLs, the EPA must itself put together the missing document or documents. *Id.* The state then incorporates any EPA-set list or TMDL into the state's continuing planning process. *Id.*

* * * The EPA in regulations has made more concrete the statutory requirements. Those regulations, in summary, define "water quality limited segment[s]"—those waters that must be included on the § 303(d)(1) list—as "[a]ny segment where it is known that water quality does not meet applicable water quality standards, and/or is not expected to meet applicable water quality standards, even after the application of the technology-based effluent limitations required by sections 301(b) and 306[, 33 U.S.C. § 1316]." 40 C.F.R. § 130.2(j) (2000). The regulations then divide TMDLs into two types: "load allocations," for nonpoint source pollution, and "wasteload allocations," for point source pollution. § 130.2(g)-(i). Under the regulations, states must identify those waters on the § 303(d)(1) lists as "still requiring TMDLs" if any required effluent limitation or other pollution control requirement (including those for nonpoint source pollution) will not bring the water into compliance with water quality standards. § 130.7(b) (2000).

3. *Continuing Planning Process*

The final pertinent section of § 303, § 303(e), requiring each state to have a "continuing planning process," gives some operational force to the prior information-gathering provisions. The EPA may approve a state's continuing planning process only if it "will result in plans for all navigable waters within such State" that include, *inter alia*, effluent limitations, TMDLs, areawide waste management plans for nonpoint sources of pollution, and plans for "adequate implementation, including schedules of compliance, for revised or new water quality standards." § 303(e)(3).

The upshot of this intricate scheme is that the CWA leaves to the states the responsibility of developing plans to achieve water quality standards if the statutorily-mandated point source controls will not alone suffice, while providing federal funding to aid in the implementation of the state plans. TMDLs are primarily informational tools that allow the states to proceed from the identification of waters requiring additional planning to the required plans. As such, TMDLs serve as a link in an implementation chain that includes federally-regulated point source controls, state or local plans for point and nonpoint source pollution reduction, and assessment of the impact of such measures on water quality, all to the end of attaining water quality goals for the nation's waters.

II. FACTUAL AND PROCEDURAL BACKGROUND

A. *The Garcia River TMDL*

In 1992, California submitted to the EPA a list of waters pursuant to § 303(d)(1)(A). Pursuant to § 303(d)(2), the EPA disapproved California's 1992 list because it omitted seventeen water segments that did not meet the water quality standards set by California for those segments. Sixteen of the seventeen water segments, including the Garcia River, were impaired only by nonpoint sources of pollution. After California rejected an opportunity to amend its § 303(d)(1) list to include the seventeen substandard segments, the EPA, again acting pursuant to § 303(d)(2), established a new § 303(d)(1) list for California, including those segments on it. California retained the seventeen segments on its 1994, 1996, and 1998 § 303(d)(1) lists.

California did not, however, establish TMDLs for the segments added by the EPA. Environmental and fishermen's groups sued the EPA in 1995 to require the EPA to establish TMDLs for the seventeen segments, and in a March 1997 consent decree the EPA agreed to do so. * * *

The Garcia River TMDL for sediment is 552 tons per square mile per year, a sixty percent reduction from historical loadings. The TMDL allocates portions of the total yearly load among the following categories of nonpoint source pollution: a) "mass wasting" associated with roads; b) "mass wasting" associated with timber harvesting; c) erosion related to road surfaces; and d) erosion related to road and skid trail crossings.

B. *The Appellants*

In 1960, appellants Betty and Guido Pronsolino purchased approximately 800 acres of heavily logged timber land in the Garcia River watershed. In 1998, after re-growth of the forest, the Pronsolinos applied for a harvesting permit from the California Department of Forestry ("Forestry").

In order to comply with the Garcia River TMDL, Forestry and/or the state's Regional Water Quality Control Board required, among other things, that the Pronsolinos' harvesting permit provide for mitigation of 90% of controllable road-related sediment run-off and contain prohibitions on removing certain trees and on harvesting from mid-October until May 1. The Pronsolinos' forester estimates that the large tree restriction will cost the Pronsolinos $750,000.

* * * III. ANALYSIS

A. *Deference to the EPA*

As this is a summary judgment case, our review of the district court's decision is, of course, de novo. * * * Harder to answer is the question of the degree of deference we owe the EPA's regulations and decisions interpreting and applying CWA § 303.

The EPA argues that we owe deference to the interpretation of § 303 embodied in its regulations, pursuant to *Chevron U.S.A., Inc. v. Natural Res. Def. Council,* 467 U.S. 837 (1984). An agency's statutory interpretation is entitled to *Chevron* deference if "Congress delegated authority to the agency generally to make rules carrying the force of law, and . . . the agency interpretation claiming deference was promulgated in the exercise of that authority." *United States v. Mead,* 533 U.S. 218, 226–27 (2001). If *Chevron* deference applies, we must defer to the agency's interpretation as long as it is reasonably consistent with the statute. *Id.* at 229.

The Pronsolinos urge an approach at the opposite end of the deference spectrum, asserting that the EPA's interpretation should receive no deference at all because, they maintain, the EPA has inconsistently interpreted § 303(d) and has not included its current interpretation in a regulation that has the force of law. In between *Chevron* deference and no deference, however, lies another possibility. The Supreme Court in *Mead* recently clarified that agency interpretations that do not qualify for *Chevron* deference may nonetheless merit deference pursuant to *Skidmore v. Swift & Co.*, 323 U.S. 134 (1944). 533 U.S. at 237. Under *Skidmore*, we defer to the agency's position according to its persuasiveness. *Mead*, 533 U.S. at 221. Factors relevant to determining persuasiveness include the agency's expertise, care, consistency, and formality, as well as the logic of the agency's position. *Id.* at 228 (citing *Skidmore*, 323 U.S. at 139–40). Thus, we must consider whether the EPA's interpretation is due *Chevron* deference, as the EPA argues; no deference, as the Pronsolinos argue; or, alternatively, *Skidmore* deference (and, if so, to what extent).

The EPA has the statutory authority to enact a rule carrying the force of law as to the issue at hand. The CWA delegates to the EPA the general rule-making authority necessary for the agency to carry out its functions under the Act. CWA § 501(a), 33 U.S.C. § 1361(a). One of those functions is to approve or disapprove the § 303(d)(1) list and any required TMDLs. § 303(d)(2). So the EPA has the delegated authority to enact regulations carrying the force of law regarding the identification of § 303(d)(1) waters and TMDLs.

The Pronsolinos do not contest the EPA's general rule-making authority but maintain that it has not been exercised, because no currently-operative EPA regulation *expressly* precludes the Pronsolinos' position that §§ 303(d)(1)(A) and (C) do not apply to rivers impaired only by nonpoint source pollution. The pertinent regulations do, however, reflect the EPA's interpretation—that is, that the statute requires the identification on § 303(d)(1) lists of waters impaired only by nonpoint sources of pollution—and the EPA so reads its regulations.

* * * In short, the EPA's regulations concerning § 303(d)(1) lists and TMDLs apply whether a water body receives pollution from point sources only, nonpoint sources only, or a combination of the two. The EPA has issued directives concerning the states' CWA § 303(d) requirements in conformity with this understanding of its regulations.

In light of the current regulations and the agency's understanding of those regulations, as well as the delegated authority of the EPA to interpret the CWA, the EPA's interpretation is entitled to *Chevron* deference.

* * * B. *Plain Meaning and Structural Issues*

1. *The Competing Interpretations*

Section 303(d)(1)(A) requires listing and calculation of TMDLs for "those waters within [the state's] boundaries for which the effluent limitations required by section [301(b)(1)(A)] and section [301(b)(1)(B)] of this title *are not stringent enough to implement any water quality standard* applicable to such waters." § 303(d) (emphasis added). The precise statutory question before us is whether, as the Pronsolinos maintain, the term "not stringent enough to implement ... water quality standard[s]" as used in § 303(d)(1)(A) must be interpreted to mean *both* that application of effluent limitations will not achieve water quality standards *and* that the waters at issue are subject to effluent limitations. As only waters with point source pollution are subject to effluent limitations, such an interpretation would exclude from the § 303(d)(1) listing and TMDL requirements waters impaired only by nonpoint sources of pollution.

The EPA, as noted, interprets "not stringent enough to implement ... water quality standard[s]" to mean "not adequate" or "not sufficient ... to implement any water quality standard," and does not read the statute as implicitly containing a limitation to waters initially covered by effluent limitations. According to the EPA, if the use of effluent limitations will not implement applicable water quality standards, the water falls within § 303(d)(1)(A) regardless of whether it is point or nonpoint sources, or a combination of the two, that continue to pollute the water.

2. *The Language and Structure of § 303(d)*

Whether or not the appellants' suggested interpretation is entirely implausible, it is at least considerably weaker than the EPA's competing construction. The Pronsolinos' version necessarily relies upon: (1) understanding "stringent enough" to mean "strict enough" rather than "thorough going enough" or "adequate" or "sufficient"; and (2) reading the phrase "not stringent enough" in isolation, rather than with reference to the stated goal of implementing "any water quality standard applicable to such waters." Where the answer to the question "not stringent enough for what?" is "to implement any [applicable] water quality standard," the meaning of "stringent" should be determined by looking forward to the broad goal to be attained, not backwards at the inadequate effluent limitations. * * * Based on the language of the contested phrase alone, then, the more sensible conclusion is that the § 303(d)(1) list must contain any waters for which the particular effluent limitations will not be adequate to attain the statute's water quality goals.

Placing the phrase in its statutory context supports this conclusion. Section 303(d) begins with the requirement that each state "identify those waters within its boundaries. . . ." § 303(d)(1)(A). So the statute's starting point for the listing project is a compilation of each and every navigable water within the state. Then, only those waters that will attain water quality standards after application of the new point source technology are excluded from the § 303(d)(1) list, leaving all those waters for which that technology will not "implement any water quality standard applicable to such waters." § 303(d)(1)(A). The alternate construction, in contrast, would begin with a subset of all the state's waterways, those that have point sources subject to effluent limitations, and would result in a list containing only a subset of that subset—those waters as to which the applicable effluent limitations are not adequate to attain water quality standards.

* * * Nothing in § 303(d)(1)(A) distinguishes the treatment of point sources and nonpoint sources as such; the only reference is to the "effluent limitations required by" § 301(b)(1). So if the effluent limitations required by § 301(b)(1) are "as a matter of law" "not stringent enough" to achieve the applicable water quality standards for waters impaired by point sources not subject to those requirements, then they are also "not stringent enough" to achieve applicable water quality standards for other waters not subject to those requirements, in this instance because they are impacted only by nonpoint sources. * * *

3. *The Statutory Scheme as a Whole*

The Pronsolinos' objection to this view of § 303(d) * * * is, in essence, that the CWA as a whole distinguishes between the regulatory schemes applicable to point and non-point sources, so we must assume such a distinction in applying §§ 303(d)(1)(A) and (C). We would hesitate in any case to read into a discrete statutory provision something that is not there because it is contained elsewhere in the statute. But here, the premise is wrong: There is no such general division throughout the CWA.

Point sources are treated differently from nonpoint sources for many purposes under the statute, but not all. In particular, there is no such distinction with regard to the basic purpose for which the § 303(d) list and TMDLs are compiled, the eventual attainment of state-defined water quality standards. Water quality standards reflect a state's designated *uses* for a water body and do not depend in any way upon the source of pollution. *See* § 303(a)–(c).

Nor is there any other basis for inferring from the structure of the Act an implicit limitation in §§ 303(d)(1)(A) and (C). The statutory subsection requiring water quality segment identification and TMDLs, § 303(d), appears in the section entitled "Water Quality Standards and Implementation Plans," not in the immediately preceding section, CWA § 302, 33 U.S.C. § 1312, entitled "Water Quality Related Effluent Limitations." So the section heading does not suggest any limitation to waters subject to effluent limitations.

Additionally, § 303(d) follows the subsections setting forth the requirements for water quality standards, § 303(a)-(c)—which, as noted above, apply without regard to the source of pollution—and precedes the "continuing planning process" subsection, § 303(e), which applies broadly as well. Thus, § 303(d) is structurally part of a set of provisions governing an interrelated goal-setting, information-gathering, and planning process that, unlike many other aspects of the CWA, applies without regard to the source of pollution.

* * * The various reporting requirements that apply to nonpoint source pollution are no more impermissibly redundant than are the planning requirements. Congress specifically provided that in preparing the § 319 report, states may rely on information from § 303(e), which incorporates the TMDLs. § 319(a)(2). Moreover, states must produce a § 319 report only once, but must update the § 303(d)(1) list periodically. § 319; § 303(d)(2). Also, the § 319 report requires the identification of a plan to reduce nonpoint source pollution, without regard to the attainment of water quality standards, while the plans generated using the § 303(d)(1) lists and TMDLs are guided by the goal of achieving those standards. § 319; § 303(d), (e).

Essentially, § 319 encourages the states to institute an approach to the elimination of nonpoint source pollution similar to the federally-mandated effluent controls contained in the CWA, while § 303 encompasses a water quality based approach applicable to all sources of water pollution. As various sections of the Act encourage different, and complementary, state schemes for cleaning up nonpoint source pollution in the nation's waterways, there is no basis for reading any of those sections—including § 303(d)—out of the statute.

There is one final aspect of the Act's structure that bears consideration because it supports the EPA's interpretation of § 303(d): The list required by § 303(d)(1)(A) requires that waters be listed if they are impaired by a combination of point sources and nonpoint sources; the language admits of no other reading. Section 303(d)(1)(C), in turn, directs that TMDLs "shall be established at a level necessary *to implement* the applicable water quality standards...." *Id.* (emphasis added). So, at least in blended waters, TMDLs must be calculated with regard to nonpoint sources of pollution; otherwise, it would be impossible "to implement the applicable water quality standards," which do not differentiate sources of pollution. * * *

Nothing in the statutory structure—or purpose—suggests that Congress meant to distinguish, as to § 303(d)(1) lists and TMDLs, between waters with one insignificant point source and substantial nonpoint source pollution and waters with only nonpoint source pollution. Such a distinction would, for no apparent reason, require the states or the EPA to monitor waters to determine whether a point source had been added or removed, and to adjust the § 303(d)(1) list and establish TMDLs accordingly. There is no statutory basis for concluding that Congress intended such an irrational regime.

Looking at the statute as a whole, we conclude that the EPA's interpretation of § 303(d) is not only entirely reasonable but considerably more convincing than the one offered by the plaintiffs in this case.

C. Federalism Concerns

The Pronsolinos finally contend that, by establishing TMDLs for waters impaired only by nonpoint source pollution, the EPA has upset the balance of federal-state control established in the CWA by intruding into the states' traditional control over land use. *See SWANCC of Northern Cook County v. United States Army Corps of Eng'rs,* 531 U.S. 159, 172–73 (2001). That is not the case.

The Garcia River TMDL identifies the maximum load of pollutants that can enter the Garcia River from certain broad categories of nonpoint sources if the river is to attain water quality standards. It does not specify the load of pollutants that may be received from particular parcels of land or describe what measures the state should take to implement the TMDL. Instead, the TMDL expressly recognizes that "implementation and monitoring" "are state responsibilities" and notes that, for this reason, the EPA did not include implementation or monitoring plans within the TMDL.

Moreover, § 303(e) requires—separately from the § 303(d)(1) listing and TMDL requirements—that each state include in its continuing planning process "adequate implementation, including schedules of compliance, for revised or new water quality standards" "for all navigable waters within such State." § 303(e)(3). The Garcia River TMDL thus serves as an informational tool for the creation of the state's implementation plan, independently—and explicitly—required by Congress.

California chose both *if* and *how* it would implement the Garcia River TMDL. States must implement TMDLs only to the extent that they seek to avoid losing federal grant money; there is no pertinent statutory provision otherwise requiring implementation of § 303 plans or providing for their enforcement. *See* CWA § 309, 33 U.S.C. § 1319; CWA § 505, 33 U.S.C. § 1365.

Finally, it is worth noting that the arguments that the Pronsolinos raise here would apply equally to nonpoint source pollution controls for blended waters. Yet, as discussed above, Congress definitely required that the states or the EPA establish TMDLs for all pollutants in waters on § 303(d)(1) lists, including blended waters.

We conclude that the Pronsolinos' federalism basis for reading § 303 against its own words and structure is unfounded. * * *

NOTES

1. **Deference to the EPA's Interpretation.** What kind of deference did the Ninth Circuit give the EPA's interpretation of section 303(d)? Why?

2. **The Scope of Section 303(d).** Why did the Ninth Circuit determine that the section 303(d) TMDL requirement applied to *all* impaired waterbodies, even if the only sources of pollutants were nonpoint sources? What tools of statutory construction did it rely upon? Does the Ninth Circuit's interpretation of section 303(d) make sense in terms of the Clean Water Act's larger goals and purposes? Why or why not? Consider the fact that, according to the EPA, "In California, only 1 percent of impaired waterways fail to meet water quality standards solely because of pollution that comes from pipes, municipal waste treatment works, or other point sources. EPA shows that 54 percent of California's impaired waterways are polluted by nonpoint sources exclusively, while another 45 percent are impaired by a combination of point and nonpoint sources." EPA Region 9, *Federal Appeals Court Upholds Landmark Clean Water Act Decision*, *available through* U.S. EPA, *TMDL Lawsuit Information*, http://www.epa.gov/owow/tmdl/lawsuit.html (last updated Oct. 8, 2004). Do these figures suggest why the EPA considered *Pronsolino* a "landmark" case?

3. **Federalism and TMDLs in the Nonpoint Source Context.** How did the plaintiffs attempt to use the federalism concerns that the Supreme Court raised in *SWANCC* to attack the EPA's position in *Pronsolino*? Why did the Ninth Circuit decide that such federalism concerns were misplaced? Do you agree? Why or why not?

4. **The Pronsolinos' Choice of Defendant.** Why, as a practical matter, did the Pronsolinos challenge the Garcia River sediment TMDL? Why was it *the EPA* that set the TMDL?

Which agency was actually *implementing* the TMDL with respect to the Pronsolinos? Why? Was it the implementation or the setting of the TMDL that actually caused the Pronsolinos problems? Why? Was the EPA challenge the only lawsuit related to the Garcia River TMDL that the Pronsolinos could have brought? Why or why not? Would it help to know that, to comply with the TMDL, the "Pronsolinos had to sharply limit their road-building and were prohibited from harvesting during the rainy season. They also had to leave nearly a million dollars' worth of conifers standing." Phil Zahodiakin, *Supreme Court asked to review TMDL rules*, 31:20 PESTICIDE & TOXIC CHEMICAL NEWS 30 (March 10, 2003).

5. **The Rest of the Story.** In February 2003, the Pronsolinos, along with the American Farm Bureau Federation and the California Farm Bureau Federation, petitioned the Supreme Court to review the Ninth Circuit's decision. The Supreme Court denied the petition. *Pronsolino v. Nastri*, 539 U.S. 926, 926 (2003). Later in 2003, however, the nonprofit Conservation Fund, acting in conjunction with the Nature Conservancy, began negotiations to purchase a 23,780–acre tract of forest along the Garcia River, representing about 40 percent of the Garcia River watershed. Voice of America, *Conservation Fund to Harvest Newly Acquired Timber Tract in California*, 2004 WL 76343629, at *1 (May 9, 2004). The sale was completed in May 2004 for $18 million, and the Conservation Fund plans to engage in timber harvesting on the land in an environmentally protective manner—an experiment in eco-friendly timber practices. *Id.*

* * *

C. SECTION 401 CERTIFICATIONS

1. Introduction to Section 401 Certifications

Like the Endangered Species Act, the Clean Water Act attempts to ensure that federal activities will comply with the Act's larger goals. To this end, section 401 of the Act provides:

> Any applicant for a Federal license or permit to conduct any activity * * * which may result in any discharge into the navigable waters, shall provide the licensing or permitting agency a certification from the State in which the discharge originates or will originate * * * that any such discharge will comply with the applicable provisions of sections 1311, 1312, 1313, 1316, and 1317 of this title. * * * No license or permit shall be granted until the certification required by this section has been obtained or has been waived * * *. No license or permit shall be granted if certification has been denied by the State * * *.

CWA § 401(a), 33 U.S.C. § 1341(a). Moreover, in its certification, the state

> shall set forth any effluent limitations and other limitations, and monitoring requirements necessary to assure that any applicant for a Federal license or permit will comply with any applicable effluent limitations and other limitations, under section 1311 or 1312 of this title, standards of performance under section 1316 of this title, or prohibition, effluent standard, or pretreatment standard under section 1317 of this title, and with any other appropriate requirement of

State law set forth in such certification, and shall become a condition on any Federal license or permit subject to the provisions of this section.

CWA § 401(d), 33 U.S.C. § 1341(d). Section 401, therefore, gives states the authority to veto or condition *any* federal license or permit that might affect water quality in that state. Section 401 is thus a significant provision with respect to federalism concerns, in that it gives states authority over the federal government with regard to water quality protection. Nevertheless, when states began to actively use their section 401 authority to influence federal permitting decisions, their actions were challenged, as in the following case.

PUD NO. 1 OF JEFFERSON COUNTY v. WASHINGTON DEPARTMENT OF ECOLOGY

511 U.S. 700 (1994).

JUSTICE O'CONNOR delivered the opinion of the Court.

Petitioners, a city and a local utility district, want to build a hydroelectric project on the Dosewallips River in Washington State. We must decide whether respondent state environmental agency (hereinafter respondent) properly conditioned a permit for the project on the maintenance of specific minimum stream flows to protect salmon and steelhead runs.

I

This case involves the complex statutory and regulatory scheme that governs our Nation's waters, a scheme that implicates both federal and state administrative responsibilities. The Federal Water Pollution Control Act, commonly known as the Clean Water Act, 86 Stat. 816, as amended, 33 U.S.C. § 1251 *et seq.,* is a comprehensive water quality statute designed to "restore and maintain the chemical, physical, and biological integrity of the Nation's waters." § 1251(a). The Act also seeks to attain "water quality which provides for the protection and propagation of fish, shellfish, and wildlife." § 1251(a)(2).

To achieve these ambitious goals, the Clean Water Act establishes distinct roles for the Federal and State Governments. Under the Act, the Administrator of the Environmental Protection Agency (EPA) is required, among other things, to establish and enforce technology-based limitations on individual discharges into the country's navigable waters from point sources. *See* §§ 1311, 1314. Section 303 of the Act also requires each State, subject to federal approval, to institute comprehensive water quality standards establishing water quality goals for all intrastate waters. §§ 1311(b)(1)(C), 1313. These state water quality standards provide "a supplementary basis ... so that numerous point sources, despite individual compliance with effluent limitations, may be further regulated to prevent water quality from falling below acceptable levels." *EPA v.*

California ex rel. State Water Resources Control Bd., 426 U.S. 200, 205, n.12 (1976).

A state water quality standard "shall consist of the designated uses of the navigable waters involved and the water quality criteria for such waters based upon such uses." 33 U.S.C. § 1313(c)(2)(A). In setting standards, the State must comply with the following broad requirements:

> "Such standards shall be such as to protect the public health or welfare, enhance the quality of water and serve the purposes of this chapter. Such standards shall be established taking into consideration their use and value for public water supplies, propagation of fish and wildlife, recreational [and other purposes.]" *Ibid.*

See also § 1251(a)(2).

A 1987 amendment to the Clean Water Act makes clear that § 303 also contains an "antidegradation policy"—that is, a policy requiring that state standards be sufficient to maintain existing beneficial uses of navigable waters, preventing their further degradation. Specifically, the Act permits the revision of certain effluent limitations or water quality standards "only if such revision is subject to and consistent with the antidegradation policy established under this section." § 1313(d)(4)(B). Accordingly, EPA's regulations implementing the Act require that state water quality standards include "a statewide antidegradation policy" to ensure that "[e]xisting instream water uses and the level of water quality necessary to protect the existing uses shall be maintained and protected." 40 CFR § 131.12 (1993). At a minimum, state water quality standards must satisfy these conditions. The Act also allows States to impose more stringent water quality controls. *See* 33 U.S.C. §§ 1311(b)(1)(C), 1370. *See also* 40 CFR § 131.4(a) (1995).

The State of Washington has adopted comprehensive water quality standards intended to regulate all of the State's navigable waters. *See* WASHINGTON ADMINISTRATIVE CODE (WAC) 173–201–010 to 173–201–120 (1986). The State created an inventory of all the State's waters, and divided the waters into five classes. 173–201–045. Each individual fresh surface water of the State is placed into one of these classes. 173–201–080 The Dosewallips River is classified AA, extraordinary. 173–201–080(32). The water quality standard for Class AA waters is set forth at 173–201–045(1). The standard identifies the designated uses of Class AA waters as well as the criteria applicable to such waters.[1]

---

1. WAC 173–201–045(1) (1986) provides in pertinent part:

"(1) Class AA (extraordinary).

"(a) General characteristic. Water quality of this class shall markedly and uniformly exceed the requirements for all or substantially all uses.

"(b) Characteristic uses. Characteristic uses shall include, but not be limited to, the following:

"(i) Water supply (domestic, industrial, agricultural).

"(ii) Stock watering.

"(iii) Fish and shellfish:
Salmonid migration, rearing, spawning, and harvesting.
Other fish migration, rearing, spawning, and harvesting.

. . . .

"(iv) Wildlife habitat.

In addition to these specific standards applicable to Class AA waters, the State has adopted a statewide antidegradation policy. That policy provides:

"(a) Existing beneficial uses shall be maintained and protected and no further degradation which would interfere with or become injurious to existing beneficial uses will be allowed.

"(b) No degradation will be allowed of waters lying in national parks, national recreation areas, national wildlife refuges, national scenic rivers, and other areas of national ecological importance.

. . . "(f) In no case, will any degradation of water quality be allowed if this degradation interferes with or becomes injurious to existing water uses and causes long-term and irreparable harm to the environment." 173–201–035(8).

As required by the Act, EPA reviewed and approved the State's water quality standards. *See* 33 U.S.C. § 1313(c)(3); 42 Fed. Reg. 56792 (1977). Upon approval by EPA, the state standard became "the water quality standard for the applicable waters of that State." 33 U.S.C. § 1313(c)(3).

States are responsible for enforcing water quality standards on intrastate waters. § 1319(a). In addition to these primary enforcement responsibilities, § 401 of the Act requires States to provide a water quality certification before a federal license or permit can be issued for activities that may result in any discharge into intrastate navigable waters. 33 U.S.C. § 1341. Specifically, § 401 requires an applicant for a federal license or permit to conduct any activity "which may result in any discharge into the navigable waters" to obtain from the State a certifica-

"(v) Recreation (primary contact recreation, sport fishing, boating, and aesthetic enjoyment).

"(vi) Commerce and navigation.

"(c) Water quality criteria

"(i) Fecal coliform organisms.

"(A) Freshwater–fecal coliform organisms shall not exceed a geometric mean value of 50 organisms/100 mL, with not more than 10 percent of samples exceeding 100 organisms/100 mL.

"(B) Marine water–fecal coliform organisms shall not exceed a geometric mean value of 14 organisms/100 mL, with not more than 10 percent of samples exceeding 43 organisms/100 mL.

"(ii) Dissolved oxygen [shall exceed specific amounts].

. . .

"(iii) Total dissolved gas shall not exceed 110 percent of saturation at any point of sample collection.

"(vi) Temperature shall not exceed [certain levels].

. . .

"(v) pH shall be within [a specified range].

"(vi) Turbidity shall not exceed [specific levels].

"(vii) Toxic, radioactive, or deleterious material concentrations shall be less than those which may affect public health, the natural aquatic environment, or the desirability of the water for any use.

"(viii) Aesthetic values shall not be impaired by the presence of materials or their effects, excluding those of natural origin, which offend the senses of sight, smell, touch, or taste."

tion "that any such discharge will comply with the applicable provisions of sections [1311, 1312, 1313, 1316, and 1317 of this title]." 33 U.S.C. § 1341(a). Section 401(d) further provides that "[a]ny certification ... shall set forth any effluent limitations and other limitations, and monitoring requirements necessary to assure that any applicant ... will comply with any applicable effluent limitations and other limitations, under section [1311 or 1312 of this title] ... and with any other appropriate requirement of State law set forth in such certification." 33 U.S.C. § 1341(d). The limitations included in the certification become a condition on any federal license. *Ibid.*

II

Petitioners propose to build the Elkhorn Hydroelectric Project on the Dosewallips River. * * * The project would divert water from a 1.2-mile reach of the river (the bypass reach), run the water through turbines to generate electricity and then return the water to the river below the bypass reach. Under the Federal Power Act (FPA), 41 Stat. 1063, as amended, 16 U.S.C. § 791a *et seq.*, the Federal Energy Regulatory Commission (FERC) has authority to license new hydroelectric facilities. As a result, petitioners must get a FERC license to build or operate the Elkhorn Project. Because a federal license is required, and because the project may result in discharges into the Dosewallips River, petitioners are also required to obtain state certification of the project pursuant to § 401 of the Clean Water Act, 33 U.S.C. § 1341.

The water flow in the bypass reach, which is currently undiminished by appropriation, ranges seasonally between 149 and 738 cubic feet per second (cfs). The Dosewallips supports two species of salmon, coho and chinook, as well as steelhead trout. As originally proposed, the project was to include a diversion dam which would completely block the river and channel approximately 75% of the river's water into a tunnel alongside the streambed. About 25% of the water would remain in the bypass reach, but would be returned to the original riverbed through sluice gates or a fish ladder. Depending on the season, this would leave a residual minimum flow of between 65 and 155 cfs in the river. Respondent undertook a study to determine the minimum stream flows necessary to protect the salmon and steelhead fishery in the bypass reach. On June 11, 1986, respondent issued a § 401 water quality certification imposing a variety of conditions on the project, including a minimum stream flow requirement of between 100 and 200 cfs depending on the season.

Figure 5-21: The Dosewallips River
National Park Service photo.

A state administrative appeals board determined that the minimum flow requirement was intended to enhance, not merely maintain, the fishery, and that the certification condition therefore exceeded respondent's authority under state law. On appeal, the State Superior Court concluded that respondent could require compliance with the minimum flow conditions. Superior Court also found that respondent had imposed the minimum flow requirement to protect and preserve the fishery, not to improve it, and that this requirement was authorized by state law.

The Washington Supreme Court held that the antidegradation provisions of the State's water quality standards require the imposition of minimum stream flows. The court also found that § 401(d), which allows States to impose conditions based upon several enumerated sections of the Clean Water Act and "any other appropriate requirement of State law," 33 U.S.C. § 1341(d), authorized the stream flow condition. Relying on this language and the broad purposes of the Clean Water Act, the court concluded that § 401(d) confers on States power to "consider all state action related to water quality in imposing conditions on section 401 certificates." We granted certiorari to resolve a conflict among the state courts of last resort. We now affirm.

III

The principal dispute in this case concerns whether the minimum stream flow requirement that the State imposed on the Elkhorn Project is a permissible condition of a § 401 certification under the Clean Water Act. To resolve this dispute we must first determine the scope of the State's authority under § 401. We must then determine whether the limitation at issue here, the requirement that petitioners maintain minimum stream flows, falls within the scope of that authority.

A

There is no dispute that petitioners were required to obtain a certification from the State pursuant to § 401. Petitioners concede that, at a minimum, the project will result in two possible discharges—the release of dredged and fill material during the construction of the project, and the discharge of water at the end of the tailrace after the water has been used to generate electricity. Petitioners contend, however, that the minimum stream flow requirement imposed by the State was unrelated to these specific discharges, and that as a consequence, the State lacked the authority under § 401 to condition its certification on maintenance of stream flows sufficient to protect the Dosewallips fishery.

If § 401 consisted solely of subsection (a), which refers to a state certification that a "discharge" will comply with certain provisions of the Act, petitioners' assessment of the scope of the State's certification authority would have considerable force. Section 401, however, also contains subsection (d), which expands the State's authority to impose conditions on the certification of a project. Section 401(d) provides that any certification shall set forth "any effluent limitations and other limitations ... necessary to assure that *any applicant*" will comply with various provisions of the Act and appropriate state law requirements. 33 U.S.C. § 1341(d) (emphasis added). The language of this subsection contradicts petitioners' claim that the State may only impose water quality limitations specifically tied to a "discharge." The text refers to the compliance of the applicant, not the discharge. Section 401(d) thus allows the State to impose "other limitations" on the project in general to assure compliance with various provisions of the Clean Water Act and with "any other appropriate requirement of State law." * * *

Our view of the statute is consistent with EPA's regulations implementing § 401. The regulations expressly interpret § 401 as requiring the State to find that "there is a reasonable assurance that the *activity* will be conducted in a manner which will not violate applicable water quality standards." 40 CFR § 121.2(a)(3) (1993) (emphasis added). EPA's conclusion that *activities*—not merely discharges—must comply with state water quality standards is a reasonable interpretation of § 401, and is entitled to deference.

Although § 401(d) authorizes the State to place restrictions on the activity as a whole, that authority is not unbounded. The State can only ensure that the project complies with "any applicable effluent limitations and other limitations, under [33 U.S.C. §§ 1311, 1312]" or certain other provisions of the Act, "and with any other appropriate requirement of State law." 33 U.S.C. § 1341(d). The State asserts that the minimum stream flow requirement was imposed to ensure compliance with the state water quality standards adopted pursuant to § 303 of the Clean Water Act, 33 U.S.C. § 1313.

We agree with the State that ensuring compliance with § 303 is a proper function of the § 401 certification. Although § 303 is not one of the statutory provisions listed in § 401(d), the statute allows States to impose limitations to ensure compliance with § 301 of the Act, 33 U.S.C. § 1311. Section 301 in turn incorporates § 303 by reference. *See* 33 U.S.C. § 1311(b)(1)(C). As a consequence, state water quality standards adopted pursuant to § 303 are among the "other limitations" with which a State may ensure compliance through the § 401 certification process. This interpretation is consistent with EPA's view of the statute. *See* 40 CFR § 121.2(a)(3) (1992). Moreover, limitations to assure compliance with state water quality standards are also permitted by § 401(d)'s reference to "any other appropriate requirement of State law." We do not speculate on what additional state laws, if any, might be incorporated by this language. But at a minimum, limitations imposed pursuant to state water quality standards adopted pursuant to § 303 are "appropriate" requirements of state law. * * *

B

Having concluded that, pursuant to § 401, States may condition certification upon any limitations necessary to ensure compliance with state water quality standards or any other "appropriate requirement of State law," we consider whether the minimum flow condition is such a limitation. Under § 303, state water quality standards must "consist of the designated uses of the navigable waters involved and the water quality criteria for such waters based upon such uses." 33 U.S.C. § 1313(c)(2)(A). In imposing the minimum stream flow requirement, the State determined that construction and operation of the project as planned would be inconsistent with one of the designated uses of Class AA water, namely "[s]almonid [and other fish] migration, rearing, spawning, and harvesting." The designated use of the river as a fish habitat directly reflects the Clean Water Act's goal of maintaining the "chemical, physical, and biological integrity of the Nation's waters." 33 U.S.C. § 1251(a). Indeed, the Act defines pollution as "the man-made or man induced alteration of the chemical, physical, biological, and radiological integrity of water." § 1362(19). Moreover, the Act expressly requires that, in adopting water quality standards, the State must take into consideration the use of waters for "propagation of fish and wildlife." § 1313(c)(2)(A).

Petitioners assert, however, that § 303 requires the State to protect designated uses solely through implementation of specific "criteria." * * *

We disagree with petitioners' interpretation of the language of § 303(c)(2)(A). Under the statute, a water quality standard must "consist of the designated uses of the navigable waters involved *and* the water quality criteria for such waters based upon such uses." 33 U.S.C. § 1313(c)(2)(A) (emphasis added). The text makes it plain that water quality standards contain two components. We think the language of

§ 303 is most naturally read to require that a project be consistent with *both* components, namely, the designated use *and* the water quality criteria. Accordingly, under the literal terms of the statute, a project that does not comply with a designated use of the water does not comply with the applicable water quality standards.

Consequently, pursuant to § 401(d) the State may require that a permit applicant comply with both the designated uses and the water quality criteria of the state standards. In granting certification pursuant to § 401(d), the State "shall set forth any ... limitations ... necessary to assure that [the applicant] will comply with any ... limitations under [§ 303] ... and with any other appropriate requirement of State law." A certification requirement that an applicant operate the project consistently with state water quality standards—*i.e.,* consistently with the designated uses of the water body and the water quality criteria—is both a "limitation" to assure "compl[iance] with ... limitations" imposed under § 303, and an "appropriate" requirement of state law.

* * * Washington's Class AA water quality standards are typical in that they contain several open-ended criteria which, like the use designation of the river as a fishery, must be translated into specific limitations for individual projects. For example, the standards state that "[t]oxic, radioactive, or deleterious material concentrations shall be less than those which may affect public health, the natural aquatic environment, or the desirability of the water for any use." WAC 173–201–045(1) (1986). Similarly, the state standards specify that "[a]esthetic values shall not be impaired by the presence of materials or their effects, excluding those of natural origin, which offend the senses of sight, smell, touch, or taste." 173–201–045(1)(c)(viii). We think petitioners' attempt to distinguish between uses and criteria loses much of its force in light of the fact that the Act permits enforcement of broad, narrative criteria based on, for example, "aesthetics."

Petitioners further argue that enforcement of water quality standards through use designations renders the water quality criteria component of the standards irrelevant. We see no anomaly, however, in the State's reliance on both use designations and criteria to protect water quality. The specific numerical limitations embodied in the criteria are a convenient enforcement mechanism for identifying minimum water conditions which will generally achieve the requisite water quality. And, in most circumstances, satisfying the criteria will, as EPA recognizes, be sufficient to maintain the designated use. *See* 40 CFR § 131.3(b) (1993). Water quality standards, however, apply to an entire class of water, a class which contains numerous individual water bodies. For example, in the State of Washington, the Class AA water quality standard applies to 81 specified fresh surface waters, as well as to all "surface waters lying within the mountainous regions of the state assigned to national parks, national forests, and/or wilderness areas," all "lakes and their feeder streams within the state," and all "unclassified surface waters that are tributaries to Class AA waters." WAC 173–201–070 (1986). While enforcement of criteria will in general protect the uses of these diverse waters, a complementary requirement that activities also comport with designated uses enables the States to ensure that each activity—even if not foreseen by the criteria—will be consistent with the specific uses and attributes of a particular body of water.

* * * The State also justified its minimum stream flow as necessary to implement the "antidegradation policy" of § 303, 33 U.S.C. § 1313(d)(4)(B). When the Clean Water Act was enacted in 1972, the water quality standards of all 50 States had antidegradation provisions. These provisions were required by federal law. By providing in 1972 that existing state water quality standards would remain in force until revised, the Clean Water Act ensured that the States would continue their antidegradation programs. *See* 33 U.S.C. § 1313(a). EPA has consistently required that revised state standards incorporate an antidegradation policy. And, in 1987, Congress explicitly recognized the existence of an "antidegradation policy established under [§ 303]." § 1313(d)(4)(B).

EPA has promulgated regulations implementing § 303's antidegradation policy, a phrase that is not defined elsewhere in the Act. These regulations require States to "develop and adopt a statewide antidegradation policy and identify the methods for implementing such policy." 40 CFR § 131.12 (1993). These "implementation methods shall, at a minimum, be consistent with the ... [e]xisting instream water uses and the level of water quality necessary to protect the existing uses shall be maintained and protected." *Ibid.* EPA has explained that under its antidegradation regulation, "no activity is allowable ... which could partially or completely eliminate any existing use." EPA, QUESTIONS AND ANSWERS ON ANTIDEGRADATION 3 (Aug. 1985). Thus, States must implement their antidegradation policy in a manner "consistent" with existing uses of the stream. The State of Washington's antidegradation policy in turn provides that "[e]xisting beneficial uses shall be maintained and protected and no further degradation which would interfere with or become injurious to existing beneficial uses will be allowed." WAC 173–201–035(8)(a) (1986). The State concluded that the reduced stream flows would have just the effect prohibited by this policy. The Solicitor General, representing EPA, asserts, and we agree, that the State's minimum stream flow condition is a proper application of the state and federal antidegradation regulations, as it ensures that an "existing instream water us[e]" will be "maintained and protected." 40 CFR § 131.12(a)(1) (1993).

Petitioners also assert more generally that the Clean Water Act is only concerned with water "quality," and does not allow the regulation of water "quantity." This is an artificial distinction. In many cases, water quantity is closely related to water quality; a sufficient lowering of the water quantity in a body of water could destroy all of its designated uses, be it for drinking water, recreation, navigation or, as here, as a fishery. In any event, there is recognition in the Clean Water Act itself that reduced stream flow, *i.e.*, diminishment of water quantity, can constitute water pollution. * * *

NOTES

1. **Tracking This Case Through Section 401.** What was the federal license or permit that triggered section 401 in this case? What water quality effect could that license or permit have? What "discharges" resulted from the project? Why did those discharges "originate" in the State of Washington?

2. **Washington's Conditions in Its Section 401 Certification.** Why could the State of Washington impose a minimum stream flow condition on this permit? How did it justify the imposition of that requirement? Why are water quality standards relevant to section 401 certifications, according to the Supreme Court? How was the minimum stream flow requirement related to Washington's water quality standards? Why was Washington's antidegradation policy relevant to the section 401 certification and the minimum stream flow requirement?

3. **The Supreme Court's Decision in *S.D. Warren*.** In 2006, the U.S. Supreme Court decided *S.D. Warren Co. v. Maine Board of Environmental Protection*, 547 U.S. 370 (2006), which affirmed and re-enforced the holding of *PUD No. 1 of Jefferson County* and states' authority to control water quality impacts from federally permitted project. The case involved a hydroelectric dam in the Presumpscot River in Maine. When S.D. Warren sought a renewal of its license from the Federal Energy Regulatory Commission (FERC) in 1999, the State of Maine imposed conditions on its Section 401 certification—specifically, it "required Warren to maintain a minimum stream flow in the bypassed portions of the river and to allow passage for various migratory fish and eels." *S.D. Warren*, 547 U.S. at 376. Focusing on Section 401's use of the word "discharge," the Court (notably, the same Court that decided *Rapanos* a few weeks later) *unanimously* upheld both the application of Section 401 to the FERC relicensing and the propriety of Maine's conditions. The Court read the term "discharge" broadly, but it also commented at length about the Clean Water Act's federalism:

> Warren's arguments against reading the word "discharge" in its common sense fail on their own terms. They also miss the forest for the trees.
>
> Congress passed the Clean Water Act to "restore and maintain the chemical, physical, and biological integrity of the Nation's waters," 33 U.S.C. § 1251(a); see also *PUD No. 1,* 511 U.S., at 714, the "national goal" being to achieve "water quality which provides for the protection and propagation of fish, shellfish, and wildlife and provides for recreation in and on the water," 33 U.S.C. § 1251(a)(2). To do this, the Act does not stop at controlling the "addition of pollutants," but deals with "pollution" generally, see § 1251(b), which Congress defined to mean "the man-made or man-induced alteration of the chemical, physical, biological, and radiological integrity of water," § 1362(19).
>
> The alteration of water quality as thus defined is a risk inherent in limiting river flow and releasing water through turbines. Warren itself admits that its dams "can cause changes in the movement, flow, and circulation of a river ... caus[ing] a river to absorb less oxygen and to be less passable by boaters and fish." And several *amici* alert us to the

chemical modification caused by the dams, with "immediate impact on aquatic organisms, which of course rely on dissolved oxygen in water to breathe." Then there are the findings of the Maine Department of Environmental Protection that led to this appeal:

> "The record in this case demonstrates that Warren's dams have caused long stretches of the natural river bed to be essentially dry and thus unavailable as habitat for indigenous populations of fish and other aquatic organisms; that the dams have blocked the passage of eels and sea-run fish to their natural spawning and nursery waters; that the dams have eliminated the opportunity for fishing in long stretches of river, and that the dams have prevented recreational access to and use of the river."

Changes in the river like these fall within a State's legitimate legislative business, and the Clean Water Act provides for a system that respects the States' concerns.

State certifications under § 401 are essential in the scheme to preserve state authority to address the broad range of pollution, as Senator Muskie explained on the floor when what is now § 401 was first proposed:

> "No polluter will be able to hide behind a Federal license or permit as an excuse for a violation of water quality standard[s]. No polluter will be able to make major investments in facilities under a Federal license or permit without providing assurance that the facility will comply with water quality standards. No State water pollution control agency will be confronted with a fait accompli by an industry that has built a plant without consideration of water quality requirements." 116 Cong. Rec. 8984 (1970).

These are the very reasons that Congress provided the States with power to enforce "any other appropriate requirement of State law," 33 U.S.C. § 1341(d), by imposing conditions on federal licenses for activities that may result in a discharge, *ibid.*

Reading § 401 to give "discharge" its common and ordinary meaning preserves the state authority apparently intended.

Id. at 384–87.

* * *

2. Section 401 and Nonpoint Sources

Section 401(a) is triggered by "any discharge into the navigable waters"—not, explicitly, by a "discharge of a pollutant." The Clean Water Act provides that "the term 'discharge' when used without qualification includes a discharge of a pollutant, and a discharge of pollutants." CWA § 502(16), 33 U.S.C. § 1362(16). Does that mean that "discharge" in section 401(a) includes more than just point source discharges—*i.e.*, that section 401(a) could apply when the federal government licenses or permits *nonpoint* sources of water pollution? The Ninth Circuit took up this issue in the following case.

OREGON NATURAL DESERT ASSOCIATION v. DOMBECK

172 F.3d 1092 (9th Cir. 1998).

SCHROEDER, CIRCUIT JUDGE:

The United States Forest Service appeals the district court's ruling that pollution from cattle grazing is subject to the certification requirement of § 401 of the Clean Water Act, 33 U.S.C. § 1341. This appeal requires us to consider whether the term "discharge" in § 1341 includes releases from nonpoint sources as well as releases from point sources. We conclude from the language and structure of the Act that the certification requirement of § 1341 was meant to apply only to point source releases. Accordingly, we reverse.

Figure 5-22: The Malheur National Forest
U.S. Forest Service photo.

The background of this case can be briefly described. In 1993 the Forest Service issued a permit allowing Robert and Diana Burril to graze 50 head of cattle in Oregon's Malheur National Forest. The cattle graze several months a year in and around Camp Creek and the Middle Fork of the John Day River, polluting these waterways with their waste, increased sedimentation, and increased temperature. In 1994 Oregon Natural Desert Association (ONDA) filed an action under the citizen suit provision of the Clean Water Act, 33 U.S.C. § 1365, as well as the Administrative Procedures [*sic*] Act, 5 U.S.C. § 702. ONDA alleged that the Forest Service had violated 33 U.S.C. § 1341 by issuing the grazing permit without first obtaining the State of Oregon's certification that the grazing would not violate the state's water quality standards. The Burrils, Grant County, and the Eastern Oregon Public Lands Coalition intervened as defendants and the Confederated Tribes of the Warm Springs Reservation intervened as plaintiffs. The district court granted the plaintiffs' summary judgment motion, concluding that the Forest Service must obtain certification for activities that will potentially cause nonpoint source pollution.

* * * *The Merits*

The crux of this case is whether the Burrils' Forest Service grazing permit requires certification from the State of Oregon. The resolution of this question hinges on the interpretation of the term "discharge" as used in § 1341. That section provides:

> Any applicant for a Federal license or permit to conduct any activity ... which may result in any discharge into the navigable waters, shall provide the licensing or permitting agency a certification from the State in which the discharge originates ... that any such discharge will comply with the applicable provisions of sections 1311, 1312, 1313, 1316, and 1317 of this title.... No license or permit shall be granted until the certification required by this section has been obtained or has been waived....

The Clean Water Act defines point sources as "discernible, confined and discrete conveyances" such as a pipe, ditch, or machine. 33 U.S.C. § 1362. Other pollution sources, such as runoff from agriculture or in this case, animal grazing, are nonpoint sources.

The appellees argued before us and the district court that "discharge" in § 1341 refers to pollution from both point sources and nonpoint sources. In accepting this argument below, the district court relied exclusively on § 502 of the Act, which provides:

> (12) The term "discharge of a pollutant" [means] any addition of any pollutant to navigable waters from any point source....
>
> (16) The term "discharge" when used without qualification includes a discharge of a pollutant....

33 U.S.C. § 1362. The district court reasoned that because the unqualified term "discharge" is defined as including, but not limited to, point source releases, it must include releases from nonpoint sources as well. The court therefore concluded that the term "discharge" encompassed nonpoint source pollution like runoff from grazing. It rejected the government's position that the unqualified term "discharge" is limited to point sources but includes both polluting and nonpolluting releases.

We review this question of law de novo. We examine "the language of the governing statute, guided not by a single sentence or member of a sentence, but look[ing] to the provisions of the whole law, and to its object and policy." *John Hancock Mut. Life Ins. Co. v. Harris Trust and Sav. Bank*, 510 U.S. 86, 94–95 (1993) (quoting *Pilot Life Ins. Co. v. Dedeaux*, 481 U.S. 41, 51 (1987)). The Clean Water Act, when examined as a whole, cannot support the conclusion that § 1341 applies to nonpoint sources.

* * * The [1972] Clean Water Act [] overhauled the regulation of water quality. Direct federal regulation now focuses on reducing the level of effluent that flows from point sources. This is accomplished through the issuance of permits under the National Pollutant Discharge Elimination System (NPDES). *See* 33 U.S.C. § 1342. The Act prohibits the release of pollutants from point sources except in compliance with an NPDES permit. 33 U.S.C. § 1311.

Nonpoint source pollution is not regulated directly by the Act, but rather through federal grants for state wastewater treatment plans. Section 208 of the Act requires each such plan to contain procedures for the identification and control of nonpoint source pollution. 33 U.S.C. § 1288(b)(2). If the EPA approves a state's plan, it may make grants to the state to defray the costs of administering the plan, *see* 33 U.S.C. § 1288(f), or to construct facilities, see 33 U.S.C. § 1288(g). Thus, the Act provides no direct mechanism to control nonpoint source pollution but rather uses the "threat and promise" of federal grants to the states to accomplish this task. Section 1329, added to the Act in 1987, requires states to adopt nonpoint source management programs and similarly provides for grants to encourage a reduction in nonpoint source pollution.

* * * [T]he scope of the term "discharge" in § 1341 [cannot reach nonpoint sources]. Prior to 1972, the provision required the state to certify that a licensed activity would "not violate applicable water quality standards." Pub. L. 91–224, § 21(b)(1), 84 Stat. 91 (1970). Now, the statute requires certification that any discharge from the licensed activity "will comply with the applicable provisions of sections 1311, 1312, 1313, 1316, and 1317" of Title 33. 33 U.S.C. § 1341(a)(1). The statute was thus amended "to assure consistency with the bill's changed emphasis from water quality standards to effluent limitations based on the elimination of any discharge of pollutants." S. REP. NO. 414, at 69 (1971), *reprinted in* 1972 U.S.C.C.A.N. at 3764, 3735. The term "discharge" in § 1341 is limited to discharges from point sources.

All of the sections cross-referenced in § 1341 relate to the regulation of point sources. Appellees contend section 1313, requiring states to establish water quality standards, relates to nonpoint source pollution because it addresses water quality standards and implementation plans. The section does not itself regulate nonpoint source pollution. Water quality standards are established in part to regulate point source pollution. They provide "a supplementary basis ... so that numerous point sources, despite individual compliance with effluent limitations, may be further regulated to prevent water quality from falling below acceptable levels." *EPA v. California ex rel. State Water Resources Control Bd.*, 426 U.S. 200, 205 n.12 (1976). In *Oregon Natural Resources Council*, 834 F.2d at 850, we held that the reference to water quality standards in § 1311(b)(1)(C) did not sweep nonpoint sources into the scope of § 1311. For similar reasons, § 1313 does not sweep nonpoint sources into the scope of § 1341.

Appellees' reliance on the Supreme Court's decision in *PUD No. 1 v. Washington Dep't of Ecology,* 511 U.S. 700 (1994), is similarly misplaced. In that case, the State of Washington issued a § 1341 certification for a dam, conditioned on minimum stream flows in order to protect fisheries. The Court held that such a condition was permissible under § 1341 even though it did not relate to an effluent discharge from the dam. Thus, a state is free to impose such water-quality limitations "once the threshold condition, the existence of a discharge, is satisfied." *Id.* at 712. The Supreme Court in *PUD No. 1* did not broaden the meaning of the term "discharge" under § 1341. All parties conceded that the construction of the dam would result in discharges from both the release of dredge and fill material and the release of water through the dam's tailrace. *See id.* at 711. Both of these releases, however, would involve point sources; the tailrace is a conveyance and the dredge and fill operation presumably would involve a conveyance or rolling stock. *See* 33 U.S.C. 1362(14).

The terminology employed throughout the Clean Water Act cuts against ONDA's argument that the term "discharge" includes nonpoint source pollution like runoff from grazing. Neither the phrase "nonpoint source discharge" nor the phrase "discharge from a nonpoint source" appears in the Act. Rather, the word "discharge" is used consistently to refer to the release of effluent from a point source. By contrast, the term "runoff" describes pollution flowing from nonpoint sources. The term runoff is used throughout 33 U.S.C. § 1288, describing urban wastewater plans, and 33 U.S.C. § 1314(f), providing guidelines for identification of nonpoint sources of pollution. Section 1341 contains no reference to runoff.

Had Congress intended to require certification for runoff as well as discharges, it could easily have written § 1341 to mirror the language of § 1323, which directs federal agencies "engaged in any activity which may result in the discharge or runoff of pollutants" to comply with applicable water quality standards. 33 U.S.C. § 1323(a). Section 1323 plainly applies to nonpoint sources of pollution on federal land. ONDA does not seek relief under this provision, however, because absent the issuance of an NPDES permit under § 1342, a citizen suit under the Clean Water Act may not be based on a violation of 33 U.S.C. § 1323. *See* 33 U.S.C. § 1365(f).

We have recognized the distinction between the terms "discharge" and "runoff":

> Nonpoint source pollution is not specifically defined in the Act, but is pollution that does not result from the "discharge" or "addition" of pollutants from a point source. Examples of nonpoint source pollution include runoff from irrigated agriculture and silvicultural activities.

Oregon Natural Resources Council, 834 F.2d at 849 n.9. We have further noted that "Congress had classified nonpoint source pollution as runoff caused primarily by rainfall around activities that employ or create pollutants. Such runoff could not be traced to any identifiable point of discharge." *Trustees for Alaska v. EPA*, 749 F.2d 549, 558 (9th Cir. 1984).

Appellees contend that we must adopt the district court's interpretation of "discharge" because that term is defined more broadly than "discharge of pollutants ... from any point source." They argue that "discharge" may only be the broader term if it includes releases from nonpoint sources. This is incorrect. "Discharge" is the broader term because it includes all releases from point sources, whether polluting or nonpolluting. * * * This is the logical interpretation of § 1362(16) that comports with the structure and lexicon of the Clean Water Act.

Intervenor/Appellee Confederated Tribes suggests that the grazing of cattle is "sufficiently similar" to point source pollution to require its inclusion in the definition of the term "discharge." The cattle in question wade in the John Day River and thus introduce their waste directly into the stream. The Tribes argue that we should not distinguish between the manmade conveyances that define a point source and cattle, whose range is normally controlled by manmade structures such as fences. The Clean Water Act, however, does not include animals in its definition of point sources. *See* 33 U.S.C. § 1362(14). It would be strange indeed to classify as a point source something as inherently mobile as a cow. We agree with the Second Circuit that the term "point source" does not include a human being, or any other animal. *See United States v. Plaza Health Labs., Inc.*, 3 F.3d 643, 649 (2d Cir. 1993).

The Tribes also suggest that these cattle may constitute a "concentrated animal feeding operation" under § 1362(14). This position is not tenable. Even assuming that open range grazing could be classified as a concentrated animal feeding operation, a question we do not reach, the controlling regulations make the determination as to whether feeding operations of this size must be certified a discretionary decision of the state NPDES program Director. *See* 40 C.F.R. § 122.23(c). Neither the Director nor the record of any state administrative proceeding is before us. * * *

NOTES

1. **Tracking This Case Through Section 401.** What was the federal license or permit at issue in this case that allegedly triggered section 401? How could the permitted activity affect water quality? Why did this activity generate nonpoint source pollution?

2. **The Meaning of a Section 401 "Discharge."** How had the district court construed section 401(a) with respect to its applicability to federally licensed nonpoint sources? Why? How did the Ninth Circuit construe section 401(a) with respect to nonpoint sources? Why? What tools of statutory construction did it rely upon? Did it have an EPA interpretation to work with? Why or why not?

3. **The Tribes' Back–Up Argument: Cattle Grazing as Point Source Pollution.** Notice that, at the end of its discussion, the Ninth Circuit

addressed the Tribes' arguments that cattle grazing should be considered a point source of pollution. What two specific arguments did the Tribes raise? How did the Ninth Circuit address those arguments? Do you agree that *Plaza Health Laboratories*, presented *supra* in this chapter's initial discussion of the point source/nonpoint source distinction, supports the conclusion that grazing cattle are not themselves point sources? Why or why not? Do you agree with the Ninth Circuit that open range cattle grazing would not constitute a concentrated animal feeding operation (CAFO)? Why or why not?

4. **Other Attempts to Address Nonpoint Source Pollution Directly through Federal Law.** Beyond the cases presented in this chapter, most attempts to reach nonpoint sources through the Clean Water Act have sought to enforce the Clean Water Act's requirements against federal agencies and federal facilities. Under section 313 of the Act, such facilities "shall be subject to, and comply with, all Federal, State, interstate, and local requirements, administrative authority, and process and sanctions respecting the control and abatement of water pollution in the same manner, and to the same extent as any nongovernmental entity * * *." 33 U.S.C. § 1323(a). Such attempts have met with only limited success. *See Newton County Wildlife Ass'n v. Rogers*, 141 F.3d 803, 810 (8th Cir. 1998) (holding that the statewide antidegradation policy was so broad that it added nothing to the Forest Service's responsibilities regarding its nonpoint source federal facilities); *Idaho Sporting Congress v. Thomas*, 137 F.3d 1146, 1152–53 (9th Cir. 1998) (holding that the plaintiffs could use the APA to challenge the Forest Service's nonpoint sources' compliance with Idaho's water quality standards, including its antidegradation policy, but concluding that the Idaho antidegradation policy was limited); *Marble Mountain Audubon Society v. Rice*, 914 F.2d 179, 182–83 (9th Cir. 1990) (holding that citizens could use the APA and NEPA to challenge Forest Service nonpoint source pollution); *Oregon Natural Resources Council v. U.S. Forest Service*, 834 F.2d 842, 849–53 (9th Cir. 1987) (holding that citizens could not use the Clean Water Act's citizen suit provision to challenge federal facility nonpoint sources, but concluding that they could use the APA).

Outside of the federal facilities context, the Fourth Circuit decided an intriguing case, holding that the EPA could condition Clean Water Act grants to state and local governments for sewage treatment on those governments adopting standards and programs to minimize nonpoint source pollution. *Shanty Town Assocs. Ltd. Partnership v. EPA*, 843 F.2d 782, 791 (4th Cir. 1988). This decision dovetails nicely with the Supreme Court's Tenth Amendment federalism jurisprudence, which prohibits the federal government from "simply 'commandee[ring] the legislative processes of the States by directly compelling them to enact and enforce a federal regulatory program,'" but allows the federal government to "attach conditions on the receipt of federal funds * * *." *New York v. United States*, 505 U.S. 144, 161–69 (1992) (quoting *South Dakota v. Dole*, 483 U.S. 203, 206 (1987)).

* * *

VI. TRANSBOUNDARY WATER POLLUTION

A. INTERSTATE NUISANCE SUITS REGARDING WATER QUALITY

Many waterbodies subject to the Clean Water Act either cross state lines or form the border between two states, or both. Thus, the interstate aspects of water pollution have always been a significant issue in water quality protection—particularly for the downstream states. As was true of air pollution, the Supreme Court heard many early interstate water pollution cases pursuant to its original jurisdiction to decide disputes between the states. U.S. CONST., art. III, §§ 2, 3. As was also true of transboundary air pollution, the Supreme Court decided these cases pursuant to a federal common law of nuisance.

The first set of interstate water pollution cases involved Missouri's claim against Illinois that sewage released into the Illinois River from the City of Chicago was causing increased outbreaks of typhus in St. Louis. In *Missouri v. Illinois I*, 180 U.S. 208 (1901)—arguably the first significant interstate pollution case of any kind—the Supreme Court determined that it had jurisdiction to hear Missouri's complaint, over Illinois' demurrer, and that Missouri's cause of action would be nuisance. *Id.* at 219–23, 239–43. However, in *Missouri v. Illinois II*, 200 U.S. 496 (1906), Missouri failed to prove to the Court's satisfaction that Illinois's discharges were causing a nuisance in St. Louis:

> There is no pretense that there is a nuisance of the simple kind that was known to older common law. There is nothing which can be detected by the unassisted senses,—no visible increase in filth, no new smell. On the contrary, it is proved that the great volume of pure water from Lake Michigan, which is mixed with the sewage at the start, has improved the Illinois river in these respects to a noticeable extent. Formerly it was sluggish and ill smelling. Now it is a comparatively clear stream to which edible fish have returned. Its water is drunk by fishermen, it is said without evil results.

Id. at 522.

Interstate water pollution cases continued to receive little substantive resolution in the Supreme Court. *See New York v. New Jersey*, 256 U.S. 296, 302–10 (1921) (denying New York's interstate water pollution claims); *West Virginia ex rel. Dyer v. Sims*, 341 U.S. 22, 26–29 (1951) (denying West Virginia's interstate water pollution claims). Moreover, the *federal* common law of interstate nuisance in water pollution cases did not survive the enactment of the Clean Water Act in 1972. *City of Milwaukee v. Illinois and Michigan*, 451 U.S. 304, 313–17 (1981). *State* common law nuisance claims remain viable between states, but only when based on the law of the state that is the source of the water pollution. *International Paper Co. v. Ouellette*, 479 U.S. 481, 490–99 (1987).

B. INTERSTATE COMPACTS

In its reluctance to decide interstate water pollution cases, the U.S. Supreme Court expressly encouraged the states to use another mechanism for addressing transboundary water pollution issues: the ***interstate compact***. *West Virginia*, *supra*, 341 U.S. at 27–29. Interstate compacts are a constitutional form of interstate agreement, and they become fully enforceable as federal law after Congress approves the compact. U.S. CONST., art. I, § 10, cl.3.

Numerous interstate compacts for water regulation exist. For example, Lake Tahoe straddles the California and Nevada borders. The Tahoe Regional Planning Authority, an interstate planning authority for Lake Tahoe created in 1968 through the Tahoe Regional Planning Compact, an interstate compact between California and Nevada, implements water quality planning and regulation in the lake. Congress approved this compact in 1980. Pub. L. 96–551, 94 Stat. 3233 (Dec. 19, 1980).

C. SECTIONS 401 AND 402 OF THE CLEAN WATER ACT

The Clean Water Act also addresses interstate water quality, through both the section 401 certification process and the Clean Water Act permitting requirements. As we have already seen, section 401(a)(1) requires states to certify any activity that requires a federal license or permit that may result in a discharge into the navigable waters. CWA § 401(a)(1), 33 U.S.C. § 1341(a)(1). Section 401 also provides protections to downstream states, through the EPA. The federal licensing or permitting agency must inform the EPA when applications trigger the section 401(a) certification requirement. CWA § 401(a)(2), 33 U.S.C. § 401(a)(2). Then:

> Whenever such a discharge may affect, as determined by the Administrator, the quality of the waters of any other State, the Administrator within thirty days of the date of notice of application for such Federal license or permit shall so notify such other State, the licensing or permitting agency, and the applicant. If, within sixty days of such notification, such other State determines that such discharge will affect the quality of its waters so as to violate any water quality requirement in such State, and within such sixty-day period notifies the Administrator and the licensing or permitting agency in writing of its objection to the issuance of such license or permit and requests a public hearing on such objection, the licensing or permitting agency shall hold such a hearing. The Administrator shall at such hearing submit his evaluation and recommendations with respect to any such objection to the licensing or permitting agency. Such agency, based upon the recommendations of such State, the Administrator, and upon any additional evidence, if any, presented to the agency at the

> hearing, shall condition such license or permit in such manner as may be necessary to insure compliance with applicable water quality requirements. If the imposition of conditions cannot insure such compliance such agency shall not issue such license or permit.

CWA § 401(a)(2), 33 U.S.C. § 1341(a)(2). Thus, like the state in which the discharge occurs, a downstream affected state can effectively veto a federal license or permit (although not as directly) when the permitted activity will adversely affect its water quality. Consider how effective the downstream state's "veto" actually is as you read the following case.

ARKANSAS v. OKLAHOMA

503 U.S. 91 (1992).

JUSTICE STEVENS delivered the opinion of the Court.

Pursuant to the Clean Water Act, 86 Stat. 816, as amended, 33 U.S.C. § 1251 *et seq.*, the Environmental Protection Agency (EPA or agency) issued a discharge permit to a new point source in Arkansas, about 39 miles upstream from the Oklahoma state line. The question presented in this litigation is whether the EPA's finding that discharges from the new source would not cause a detectable violation of Oklahoma's water quality standards satisfied the EPA's duty to protect the interests of the downstream State. Disagreeing with the Court of Appeals, we hold that the Agency's action was authorized by the statute.

I

In 1985, the city of Fayetteville, Arkansas, applied to the EPA, seeking a permit for the city's new sewage treatment plant under the National Pollution Discharge Elimination System (NPDES). After the appropriate procedures, the EPA, pursuant to § 402(a)(1) of the Act, 33 U.S.C. § 1342(a)(1), issued a permit authorizing the plant to discharge up to half of its effluent (to a limit of 6.1 million gallons per day) into an unnamed stream in northwestern Arkansas. That flow passes through a series of three creeks for about 17 miles, and then enters the Illinois River at a point 22 miles upstream from the Arkansas–Oklahoma border.

The permit imposed specific limitations on the quantity, content, and character of the discharge and also included a number of special conditions, including a provision that if a study then underway indicated that more stringent limitations were necessary to ensure compliance with Oklahoma's water quality standards, the permit would be modified to incorporate those limits.

Respondents challenged this permit before the EPA, alleging, *inter alia,* that the discharge violated the Oklahoma water quality standards. Those standards provide that "no degradation [of water quality] shall be allowed" in the upper Illinois River, including the portion of the river immediately downstream from the state line.

Following a hearing, the Administrative Law Judge (ALJ) concluded that the Oklahoma standards would not be implicated unless the contested discharge had "something more than a mere *de minimis* impact" on the State's waters. He found that the discharge would not have an "undue impact" on Oklahoma's waters and, accordingly, affirmed the issuance of the permit.

On a petition for review, the EPA's Chief Judicial Officer first ruled that § 301(b)(1)(C) of the Clean Water Act "requires an NPDES permit to impose any effluent limitations necessary to comply with applicable state water quality standards." He then held that the Act and EPA regulations offered greater protection for the downstream State than the ALJ's "undue impact" standard suggested. He explained the proper standard as follows:

> "[A] mere theoretical impairment of Oklahoma's water quality standards—*i.e.,* an infinitesimal impairment predicted through modeling but not expected to be actually detectable or measurable—should not by itself block the issuance of the permit. In this case, the permit should be upheld if the record shows by a preponderance of the evidence that the authorized discharges would not cause an actual *detectable* violation of Oklahoma's water quality standards."

On remand, the ALJ made detailed findings of fact and concluded that the city had satisfied the standard set forth by the Chief Judicial Officer. Specifically, the ALJ found that there would be no detectable violation of any of the components of Oklahoma's water quality standards. The Chief Judicial Officer sustained the issuance of the permit.

Both the petitioners * * * (collectively Arkansas) and the respondents in this litigation sought judicial review. Arkansas argued that the Clean Water Act did not require an Arkansas point source to comply with Oklahoma's water quality standards. Oklahoma challenged the EPA's determination that the Fayetteville discharge would not produce a detectable violation of the Oklahoma standards.

The Court of Appeals did not accept either of these arguments. The court agreed with the EPA that the statute required compliance with Oklahoma's water quality standards, and did not disagree with the Agency's determination that the discharges from the Fayetteville plant would not produce a detectable violation of those standards. Nevertheless, relying on a theory that neither party had advanced, the Court of Appeals reversed the Agency's issuance of the Fayetteville permit. The court first ruled that the statute requires that "where a proposed source would discharge effluents that would contribute to conditions currently constituting a violation of applicable water quality standards, such [a] proposed source may not be permitted." Then the court found that the Illinois River in Oklahoma was "already degraded," that the Fayetteville effluent would reach the Illinois River in Oklahoma, and that that effluent could "be expected to contribute to the ongoing deterioration of the scenic

[Illinois R]iver" in Oklahoma even though it would not detectably affect the river's water quality.

The importance and the novelty of the Court of Appeals' decision persuaded us to grant certiorari. We now reverse.

II

Interstate waters have been a font of controversy since the founding of the Nation. This Court has frequently resolved disputes between States that are separated by a common river, that border the same body of water, or that are fed by the same river basin.

Among these cases are controversies between a State that introduces pollutants to a waterway and a downstream State that objects. *See, e.g., Missouri v. Illinois*, 200 U.S. 496 (1906). In such cases, this Court has applied principles of common law tempered by a respect for the sovereignty of the States. *Compare id.*, at 521, *with Georgia v. Tennessee Copper Co.*, 206 U.S. 230, 237 (1907). In forging what "may not improperly be called interstate common law," *Illinois v. Milwaukee*, 406 U.S. 91, 105–106 (1972) (*Milwaukee I*), however, we remained aware "that new federal laws and new federal regulations may in time pre-empt the field of federal common law of nuisance." *Id.* at 107.

In *Milwaukee v. Illinois,* 451 U.S. 304 (1981) (*Milwaukee II*), we held that the Federal Water Pollution Control Act Amendments of 1972 did just that. In addressing Illinois' claim that Milwaukee's discharges into Lake Michigan constituted a nuisance, we held that the comprehensive regulatory regime created by the 1972 amendments pre-empted Illinois' federal common law remedy. * * *

In *Milwaukee II,* the Court did not address whether the 1972 amendments had supplanted *state* common law remedies as well as the federal common law remedy. *See id.*, at 310, n.4. * * * This Court subsequently endorsed that [remedy] in *International Paper Co. v. Ouellette,* 479 U.S. 481 (1987), in which Vermont property owners claimed that the pollution discharged into Lake Champlain by a paper company located in New York constituted a nuisance under Vermont law. The Court held the Clean Water Act taken "as a whole, its purposes and its history" pre-empted an action based on the law of the affected State and that the only state law applicable to an interstate discharge is "the law of the State in which the point source is located." *Id.*, at 493, 487. * * *

Unlike the foregoing cases, this litigation involves not a state-issued permit, but a federally issued permit. To explain the significance of this distinction, we comment further on the statutory scheme before addressing the specific issues raised by the parties.

III

The Clean Water Act anticipates a partnership between the States and the Federal Government, animated by a shared objective: "to restore and maintain the chemical, physical, and biological integrity of the Nation's waters." 33 U.S.C. § 1251(a). Toward this end, the Act provides for two sets of water quality measures. "Effluent limitations" are promulgated by the EPA and restrict the quantities, rates, and concentrations of specified substances which are discharged from point sources. *See* §§ 1311, 1314. "[W]ater quality standards" are, in general, promulgated by the States and establish the desired condition of a waterway. *See* § 1313. These standards supplement effluent limitations "so that numerous point sources, despite individual compliance with effluent limitations, may be further regulated to prevent water quality from falling below acceptable levels." *EPA v. California ex rel. State Water Resources Control Bd.*, 426 U.S. 200, 205 n.12 (1976).

The EPA provides States with substantial guidance in the drafting of water quality standards. *See generally* 40 CFR pt. 131 (1991) (setting forth model water quality standards). Moreover, § 303 of the Act requires, *inter alia,* that state authorities periodically review water quality standards and secure the EPA's approval of any revisions in the standards. If the EPA recommends changes to the standards and the State fails to comply with that recommendation, the Act authorizes the EPA to promulgate water quality standards for the State. 33 U.S.C. § 1313(c).

The primary means for enforcing these limitations and standards is the NPDES, enacted in 1972 as a critical part of Congress' "complete rewriting" of federal water pollution law. *Milwaukee II*, 451 U.S., at 317. Section 301(a) of the Act, 33 U.S.C. § 1311(a), generally prohibits the discharge of any effluent into a navigable body of water unless the point source has obtained an NPDES permit. Section 402 establishes the NPDES permitting regime, and describes two types of permitting systems: state permit programs that must satisfy federal requirements and be approved by the EPA, and a federal program administered by the EPA.

Section 402(b) authorizes each State to establish "its own permit program for discharges into navigable waters within its jurisdiction." 33 U.S.C. § 1342(b). Among the requirements the state program must satisfy are the procedural protections for downstream States discussed in *Ouellette* and *Milwaukee II. See* §§ 1342(b)(3), (5). Although these provisions do not authorize the downstream State to veto the issuance of a permit for a new point source in another State, the Administrator retains authority to block the issuance of any state-issued permit that is outside the guidelines and requirements of the Act. § 1342(d)(2).

In the absence of an approved state program, the EPA may issue an NPDES permit under § 402(a) of the Act. (In these cases, for example, because Arkansas had not been authorized to issue NPDES permits when the Fayetteville plant was completed, the permit was issued by the EPA itself.) The EPA's permit program is subject to the "same terms, conditions, and requirements" as a state permit program. 33 U.S.C. § 1342(a)(3). Notwithstanding this general symmetry, the EPA has construed the Act as requiring that EPA-issued NPDES permits also comply with § 401(a). That section, which predates § 402 and the NPDES, applies to a broad category of federal licenses, and sets forth requirements for "[a]ny applicant for a Federal license or permit to conduct any activity including, but not limited to, the construction or operation of facilities, which may result in any discharge into the navigable waters." 33 U.S.C. § 1341(a). Section 401(a)(2) appears to prohibit the issuance of any federal license or permit over the objection of an affected State unless compliance with the affected State's water quality requirements can be ensured.

IV

The parties have argued three analytically distinct questions concerning the interpretation of the Clean Water Act. First, does the Act require the EPA, in crafting and issuing a permit to a point source in one State, to apply the water quality standards of downstream States? Second, even if the Act does not *require* as much, does the Agency have the statutory authority to mandate such compliance? Third, does the Act provide, as the Court of Appeals held, that once a body of water fails to meet water quality standards no discharge that yields effluent that reach the degraded waters will be permitted?

In these cases, it is neither necessary nor prudent for us to resolve the first of these questions. In issuing the Fayetteville permit, the EPA assumed it was obligated by both the Act and its own regulations to ensure that the Fayetteville discharge would not violate Oklahoma's standards. As we discuss below, this assumption was permissible and reasonable and therefore there is no need for us to address whether the Act requires as much. * * *

Our decision not to determine at this time the scope of the Agency's statutory *obligations* does not affect our resolution of the second question, which concerns the Agency's statutory *authority*. Even if the Clean Water Act itself does not require the Fayetteville discharge to comply with Oklahoma's water quality standards, the statute clearly does not limit the EPA's authority to mandate such compliance.

Since 1973, EPA regulations have provided that an NPDES permit shall not be issued "[w]hen the imposition of conditions cannot ensure compliance with the applicable water quality requirements of all affected States." 40 CFR § 122.4(d) (1991); *see also* 38 Fed. Reg. 13533 (1973); 40 CFR § 122.44(d) (1991). Those regulations—relied upon by the EPA in the issuance of the Fayetteville permit—constitute a reasonable exercise of the Agency's statutory authority.

Congress has vested in the Administrator broad discretion to establish conditions for NPDES permits. Section 402(a)(2) provides that for EPA-issued permits "[t]he Administrator shall prescribe conditions ... to assure compliance with the requirements of [§ 402(a)(1)] and *such other requirements as he deems appropriate.*" 33 U.S.C. § 1342(a)(2) (emphasis added). Similarly, Congress preserved for the Administrator broad authority to oversee state permit programs * * *.

The regulations relied on by the EPA were a perfectly reasonable exercise of the Agency's statutory discretion. The application of state water quality standards in the interstate context is wholly consistent with the Act's broad purpose "to restore and maintain the chemical, physical, and biological integrity of the Nation's waters." 33 U.S.C. § 1251(a). Moreover, as noted above, § 301(b)(1)(C) expressly identifies the achievement of state water quality standards as one of the Act's central objectives. The Agency's regulations conditioning NPDES permits are a well-tailored means of achieving this goal.

* * * Arkansas [] argues that regulations requiring compliance with downstream standards are at odds with the legislative history of the Act and with the statutory scheme established by the Act. Although we agree with Arkansas that the Act's legislative history indicates that Congress intended to grant the Administrator discretion in his oversight of the issuance of NPDES permits, we find nothing in that history to indicate that Congress intended to preclude the EPA from establishing a general requirement that such permits be conditioned to ensure compliance with downstream water quality standards.

Similarly, we agree with Arkansas that in the Clean Water Act Congress struck a careful balance among competing policies and interests, but do not find the EPA regulations concerning the application of downstream water quality standards at all incompatible with that balance. Congress, in crafting the Act, protected certain sovereign interests of the States; for example, § 510 allows States to adopt more demanding pollution-control standards than those established under the Act. Arkansas emphasizes that § 510 preserves such state authority only as it is applied to the waters of the regulating State. Even assuming Arkansas' construction of § 510 is correct, * * * that section only concerns *state* authority and does not constrain the *EPA's* authority to promulgate reasonable regulations requiring point sources in one State to comply with water quality standards in downstream States.

For these reasons, we find the EPA's requirement that the Fayetteville discharge comply with Oklahoma's water quality standards to be a reasonable exercise of the Agency's substantial statutory discretion. *Cf. Chevron U.S.A. Inc. v. Natural Resources Defense Council, Inc.,* 467 U.S. 837, 842–845 (1984).

V

The Court of Appeals construed the Clean Water Act to prohibit any discharge of effluent that would reach waters already in violation of existing water quality standards. We find nothing in the Act to support this reading.

The interpretation of the statute adopted by the court had not been advanced by any party during the Agency or court proceedings. * * * Although the Act contains several provisions directing compliance with state water quality standards, *see, e.g.,* § 1311(b)(1)(C), the parties have pointed to nothing that mandates a complete ban on discharges into a waterway that is in violation of those standards. The statute does, however, contain provisions designed to remedy existing water quality violations and to allocate the burden of reducing undesirable discharges between existing sources and new sources. *See, e.g.,* § 1313(d). Thus, rather than establishing the categorical ban announced by the Court of Appeals—which might frustrate the construction of new plants that would improve existing conditions—the Clean Water Act vests in the EPA and the States broad authority to develop long-range, area-wide programs to alleviate and eliminate existing pollution. *See, e.g.,* § 1288(b)(2).

To the extent that the Court of Appeals relied on its interpretation of the Act to reverse the EPA's permitting decision, that reliance was misplaced.

VI

The Court of Appeals also concluded that the EPA's issuance of the Fayetteville permit was arbitrary and capricious because the Agency misinterpreted Oklahoma's water quality standards. The primary difference between the court's and the Agency's interpretation of the standards derives from the court's construction of the Act. Contrary to the EPA's interpretation of the Oklahoma standards, the Court of Appeals read those standards as containing the same categorical ban on new discharges that the court had found in the Clean Water Act itself. Although we do not believe the text of the Oklahoma standards supports the court's reading (indeed, we note that Oklahoma itself had not advanced that interpretation in its briefs in the Court of Appeals), we reject it for a more fundamental reason—namely, that the Court of Appeals exceeded the legitimate scope of judicial review of an agency adjudication. * * *

As discussed above, an EPA regulation requires an NPDES permit to comply "with the applicable water quality requirements of all affected States." 40 CFR § 122.4(d) (1991). This regulation effectively incorporates into federal law those state-law standards the Agency reasonably determines to be "applicable." In such a situation, then, state water quality standards—promulgated by the States with substantial guidance from the EPA and approved by the Agency—are part of the federal law of water pollution control.

* * * Because we recognize that, at least insofar as they affect the issuance of a permit in another State, the Oklahoma standards have a federal character, the EPA's reasonable, consistently held interpretation of those standards is entitled to substantial deference. In these cases, the Chief Judicial Officer ruled that the Oklahoma standards—which require that there be "no degradation" of the upper Illinois River—would only be violated if the discharge effected an "actually detectable or measurable" change in water quality.

This interpretation of the Oklahoma standards is certainly reasonable and consistent with the purposes and principles of the Clean Water Act.

* * * Moreover, this interpretation of the Oklahoma standards makes eminent sense in the interstate context: If every discharge that had some theoretical impact on a downstream State were interpreted as "degrading" the downstream waters, downstream States might wield an effective veto over upstream discharges.

The EPA's application of those standards in these cases was also sound. On remand, the ALJ scrutinized the record and made explicit factual findings regarding four primary measures of water quality under the Oklahoma standards: eutrophication, esthetics, dissolved oxygen, and metals. In each case, the ALJ found that the Fayetteville discharge would not lead to a detectable change in water quality. He therefore concluded that the Fayetteville discharge would not violate the Oklahoma water quality standards. Because we agree with the Agency's Chief Judicial Officer that these findings are supported by substantial evidence, we conclude that the Court of Appeals should have affirmed both the EPA's construction of the regulations and the issuance of the Fayetteville permit. * * *

NOTES

1. **Tracking This Case Through Section 401.** What was the federal license or permit in this case that triggered application of section 401? Did section 401 *have* to apply to this permit? Why or why not? What possible effects on water quality could the permitted activity have? Which state was the upstream state? Which state was the downstream state? Why did the downstream state object to the issuance of the permit? How did the EPA respond?

2. **Federalism Issues in the Interstate Water Pollution Context.** How did the Supreme Court characterize the federalism aspects of interstate water pollution? Why should interstate water quality issues be primarily a federal—as opposed to a state—concern? Notice that this case placed the EPA and the federal courts in the position of interpreting *state* water quality standards. Did these federal interpretations of state law breach the Clean Water Act's federalism balance, according to the Supreme Court? Why or why not? As between the EPA and the federal courts, who was entitled to deference regarding their interpretation of the state water quality standards? Why? Was this a *Chevron* case? Why or why not?

3. **Federal Permits vs. State Permits in Interstate Water Pollution Controversies.** As the *Arkansas v. Oklahoma* Court noted repeatedly, the fact that the EPA issued this NPDES permit was important to Oklahoma's rights as the downstream state. Because the permit was *federally* issued, it triggered (at least in the EPA's interpretation) section 401. As a result, Arkansas had a right to certify the permit pursuant to section 401(a)(1), and Oklahoma had a right to challenge the permit pursuant to section 401(a)(2).

In contrast, when a delegated state issues an NPDES permit, the permit is *not* a federal permit and section 401 does not apply. However, in order to receive NPDES permitting authority, states must: (1) ensure that the EPA receives notice of the permit application; and (2) ensure "that any State * * * whose waters may be affected by the issuance of a permit may submit written recommendations to the permitting State (and the Administrator) with respect to any permit application and, if any part of such written recommendations are not accepted by the permitting State, that the permitting State will notify such affected State (and the Administrator) in writing of its failure to so accept such recommendations together with its reasons for so doing * * *." CWA § 402(b)(4), (5), 33 U.S.C. § 1342(b)(4), (5). In addition, the EPA retains authority to object in writing to any state-issued NPDES permit within 90 days, and the EPA can take over the NPDES permitting if the permitting state does not adequately address the EPA's objections. CWA § 402(d)(2), (4), 33 U.S.C. § 1342(d)(2), (4). Therefore, if a downstream state will be affected by an upstream state's state-issued NPDES permit, section 402 ensures that the downstream state will be notified of the permit, have an opportunity to submit recommendations, and be allowed to complain to the EPA, which can then take over the permitting process.

The EPA has exercised this veto authority only rarely. One example was discussed in *Champion International Corp. v. United States Environmental Protection Agency*, 850 F.2d 182 (4th Cir. 1988), which involved the EPA's takeover of the NPDES permitting for a North Carolina pulp and paper mill located 26 miles upstream from the North Carolina–Tennessee border. Despite this distance, the mill clearly created murky water conditions that persisted past the Tennessee border, contributing to violations of the Tennessee water quality standards. In January 1983, after having received the draft renewed NPDES permit for the mill, Tennessee asked North Carolina to adjust the effluent limitations in that draft permit to address Tennessee's water quality concerns. By July 1983, in the face of North Carolina's reluctance to address Tennessee's concerns, Tennessee also asked the EPA to participate in the mill's permitting process. Nevertheless, in May 1985 North Carolina issued a final NPDES permit that was identical to the draft permit. The EPA formally objected to the permit in August 1985, and, after North Carolina refused to change the permit, the EPA assumed permitting authority in November 1985. The Fourth Circuit upheld the EPA's authority to do so, and thus Tennessee managed to have its interstate water quality concerns addressed. *Id.* at 186–87.

Given the differences between section 401(a)(2) and section 402(b), if you were representing a downstream state, would you prefer to be dealing with a state-issued NPDES permit or an EPA-issued NPDES permit? Why?

4. **Violating a Downstream State's Water Quality Standards.** When would the Arkansas sewage treatment plant actually violate Oklahoma's water quality standards, according to the Supreme Court? How did the EPA and the Court of Appeals differ in their views of this problem? What factual issues had to be resolved under each interpretation? Given the plant's location, would a violation of Oklahoma's water quality standards be likely under the EPA's view? Why or why not? Would a violation be likely under the Court of Appeals' view? Why or why not? What policy issues did the EPA's approach raise? What policy issues did the Court of Appeals' approach raise? Which did you think is the better approach to preventing degradation of downstream water quality? Why?

5. **Interstate Water Pollution and Section 404 "Dredge and Fill" Permits.** As was noted in the section discussing section 404 permits, very few states have sought section 404 permitting authority. As a result, the U.S. Army Corps of Engineers still issues most section 404 permits, which are then federal permits subject to section 401. *PUD No. 1 of Jefferson County v. Washington Dept. of Ecology*, 511 U.S. 700, 722–23 (1994). General permits issued pursuant to section 404 are also subject to section 401 certifications. *United States v. Marathon Development Corp.*, 867 F.2d 96, 100–01 (1st Cir. 1989).

When states do take over the section 404 permit program, however, they must, as in the NPDES permitting program, inform both the EPA and the affected States of potential interstate water quality problems. CWA § 404(h)(1)(D), (E), 33 U.S.C. § 1344(h)(1)(D), (E). Thus, downstream states are again ensured notification of the permit, an opportunity to submit recommendations, and the ability to complain to the EPA.

* * *

D. INTERNATIONAL WATER POLLUTION

Section 310 of the Clean Water Act addressed international pollution abatement. 33 U.S.C. § 1320. Under this provision:

> Whenever the Administrator, upon receipts of reports, surveys, or studies from any duly constituted international agency, has reason to believe that pollution is occurring which endangers the health or welfare of persons in a foreign country, and the Secretary of State requests him to abate such pollution, he shall give formal notification thereof to the State water pollution control agency of the State or States in which such discharge or discharges originate and to the appropriate interstate agency, if any.

CWA § 310(a), 33 U.S.C. § 1320(a). A hearing follows before a specialized hearing board. *Id.* § 310(a), (c), 33 U.S.C. § 1320(a), (c). After the hearing, the board can require the discharger to file a report "furnishing such information as may reasonably be required as to the character, kind, and quantity of such discharges and the use of facilities or other means to prevent or reduce such discharges by the person filing the report." *Id.* § 310(d), 33 U.S.C. § 1320(d). The board then makes recommendations to the Administrator of the EPA, who can take enforcement actions against the discharger on the basis of those recommendations. *Id.* § 310(c), (f), 33 U.S.C. § 1320(c), (f).

Based on interpretations that you have read throughout this chapter, can the EPA use section 310 to address international water pollution resulting from nonpoint source pollution? Why or why not? How does section 310 affect the normal federalism balance between the EPA and the states?

VII. FUTURE DIRECTIONS FOR THE CLEAN WATER ACT

A. HOW EFFECTIVE HAS THE CLEAN WATER ACT BEEN?

In 1998, for the 25th anniversary of the Clean Water Act, the Clinton Administration issued the *Clean Water Action Plan*. CAROL M. BROWNER & DAN GLICKMAN, THE CLEAN WATER ACTION PLAN (1998), *available at* http://www.cleanwater.gov/action/toc.html (last revised Feb. 2, 2002). The Plan acknowledged both that the nation had made significant progress in improving water quality since 1972 and that serious water quality issues remained. As for progress, the Plan noted that in 1972, only 30 to 40 percent of assessed waters in the United States met their water quality standards, whereas in 1998, 60 to 70 percent of them did. *Id.* at http://www.cleanwater.gov/action/c1a.html. Wetland losses had been reduced almost 75 percent from the 1972 figures of 460,000 acres lost per year. *Id.* Erosion of cropland had been reduced by a third since 1982. *Id.* POTWs treated sewage for only 85 million people in 1972, compared to 173 million people in 1998. *Id.* Finally, the EPA by 1998 had established effluent limitations for over 50 categories of industry, resulting in NPDES permits that eliminated *billions* of pounds of pollutants from industrial wastewaters each year. *Id.*

Nevertheless, the Plan also recognized that half of the nation's 2,000 watersheds remained in need of restoration. *Id.* Of the surveyed waters, moreover, 36 percent of rivers and streams, 39 percent of lakes, 38 percent of estuaries, and 97 percent of the Great Lakes shore miles were still impaired. *Id.* In absolute numbers, "[i]n 1996, states and tribes identified about 15,000 waterbodies not meeting water quality goals." *Id.* Only 16 percent of the watersheds in the continental United States had good water quality in 1998, while 36 percent had moderate water quality problems, 21 percent had serious water quality problems, and 27 percent could not be assessed for lack of information about their water quality. *Id.* The Plan also stressed the problem of nonpoint source pollution, concluding that "[p]olluted [r]unoff is the [m]ost [i]mportant [s]ource of [w]ater [p]ollution." *Id.*

In June 2001, the EPA issued its strategic plan for the Clean Water Act. It noted that 400,000 facilities had NPDES permits, and it expects that number to increase to over 500,000 facilities in the near future. U.S. EPA, PROTECTING THE NATION'S WATERS THROUGH EFFECTIVE NPDES PERMITS: A STRATEGIC PLAN FY 2001 AND BEYOND 1 (June 2001). Moreover, the EPA applauded the states' role in permitting, noting that "[a] state's authorization to implement this program allows state managers to set priorities and tailor the program to meet the challenges facing the waters in that state and to satisfy the desires of its citizens. * * * As 'co-regulators,' the authorized states play a unique role by helping to shape and develop the national program." *Id.* at 2. According to the EPA, "State administered programs promote day-to-day decision making at a level more attuned to the situation in individual watersheds." *Id.* at 14.

Nevertheless, in its 2003 *Draft Strategic Plan*, the EPA concluded that further progress was necessary in meeting the Clean Water Act's *interim* goals that all waters be fishable and swimmable. Office of the Chief Financial Office, U.S. EPA, *Goal 2: Clean and Safe Water*, *in* DRAFT: 2003 STRATEGIC PLAN (March 5, 2003), *available at* http://epa.gov/ocfo/plan/2003goal2.pdf. According to this Plan, in 2000 states reported that approximately 90,000 stream miles and 2.6 million lake acres were not suitable for swimming. *Id.* In 2002, states and Tribes reported that 485,205 river miles and 11,277,276 lake acres had fish that were so contaminated by chemical pollution that they posed a potential human health risk. *Id.* The EPA's June 2003 *Draft Report on the Environment* reports similar problems.

B. FUTURE DIRECTIONS IN WATER QUALITY PROTECTION: WATERSHED MANAGEMENT

In the future, the EPA expects that it and the states will address more and more water quality issues on a ***watershed*** basis. According to the EPA, "[a] watershed is the area of land where all of the water that is under it or drains off of it goes into the same place." Office of Water, U.S. EPA, *What Is a Watershed?*, http://www.epa.gov/owow/watershed/whatis.html (last modified December 2002). The EPA's ***Watershed Initiative*** began as a series of recommendations in the 1998 *Clean Water Action Plan*. At the heart of the new watershed focus are the waterbody-specific TMDLs. "EPA and the states are scheduled to develop as many as 40,000 TMDLs over the next 15 years." U.S. EPA, PROTECTING THE NATION'S WATERS THROUGH EFFECTIVE NPDES PERMITS: A STRATEGIC PLAN FY 2001 AND BEYOND 8 (June 2001). The EPA also intends to implement pilot projects to issue NPDES permits on a watershed basis. *Id.* at 10. Since May 2003, the EPA has been awarding grants to implement watershed projects, and in 2005, it issued its draft handbook for developing watershed plans. U.S. EPA, DRAFT HANDBOOK FOR DEVELOPING WATERSHED PLANS TO RESTORE AND PROTECT OUR WATERS, EPA 841–B–05–005 (Oct. 2005), *available at* http://www.epa.gov/owow/nps/watershed_handbook/. In May 2006, the EPA summarized the complete list of its *Watershed Tools* in a brochure, available at http://www.epa.gov/owow/watershed/watershedtools606.pdf.

C. FUTURE DIRECTIONS IN WATER QUALITY MANAGEMENT: POLLUTION TRADING

Unlike the Clean Air Act, the Clean Water Act contains no provisions that explicitly authorize trading of water pollutants. Nevertheless, in

January 2003, the EPA issued its Final Water Quality Trading Policy. In this policy, the EPA stressed that, in the 1972 Clean Water Act, "Congress recognized and preserved the primary responsibilities and rights of the States to prevent, reduce and eliminate pollution." OFFICE OF WATER, U.S. EPA, WATER QUALITY TRADING POLICY 1 (Jan. 13, 2003), *available at* http://www.epa.gov/owow/watershed/trading/tradingpolicy.html. The EPA presented water quality trading as a cost-effective means of addressing many of the Nation's remaining water quality problems:

> Water quality trading is an approach that offers greater efficiency in achieving water quality goals on a watershed basis. It allows one source to meet its regulatory obligations by using pollutant reductions created by another source that has lower pollution control costs. Trading capitalizes on economies of scale and the control cost differentials among and between sources.
>
> The United States Environmental Protection Agency (EPA) believes that market-based approaches such as water quality trading provide greater flexibility and have potential to achieve water quality and environmental benefits greater than would otherwise be achieved under more traditional regulatory approaches. Market-based programs can achieve water quality goals at a substantial economic savings. EPA estimates that in 1997 annual private point source control costs were about $14 billion and public point source costs were about $34 billion. The National Cost to Implement Total Maximum Daily Loads (TMDLs) Draft Report estimates that flexible approaches to improving water quality could save $900 million dollars annually compared to the least flexible approach (EPA, August 2001). Nitrogen trading among publicly owned treatment works in Connecticut that discharge into Long Island Sound is expected to achieve the required reductions under a TMDL while saving over $200 million dollars in control costs. Market-based approaches can also create economic incentives for innovation, emerging technology, voluntary pollution reductions and greater efficiency in improving the quality of the nation's waters.

Id. at 1–2.

Any proposed water quality trade "must be consistent with the CWA." *Id.* at 4. In addition, "[a]ll water quality trading should occur within a watershed or a defined area for which a TMDL has been approved. Establishing defined trading areas that coincide with a watershed or TMDL boundary results in trades that affect the same water body or stream segment and helps ensure that water quality standards are maintained or achieved throughout the trading area and contiguous waters." *Id.* The EPA most strongly supports trading that involves nutrients (total nitrogen and total phosphorus) and sediments, but it does not support trading in toxic water pollutants, especially persistent bioaccumulative toxics, like dioxin. *Id.* In addition, the "EPA does not support trading to comply with existing technology-based effluent limitations except as expressly authorized by federal regulations." *Id.* at 6. Finally, "[s]ources and activities that are required to obtain a federal permit pursuant to Sections 402 or 404 of the CWA must do so to participate in a trade or trading program." *Id*; *see also* U.S. EPA, WATER QUALITY TRADING ASSESSMENT HANDBOOK: CAN WATER QUALITY TRADING ADVANCE YOUR WATERSHED'S GOALS?, EPA 841–B–04–001 (Nov. 2004).

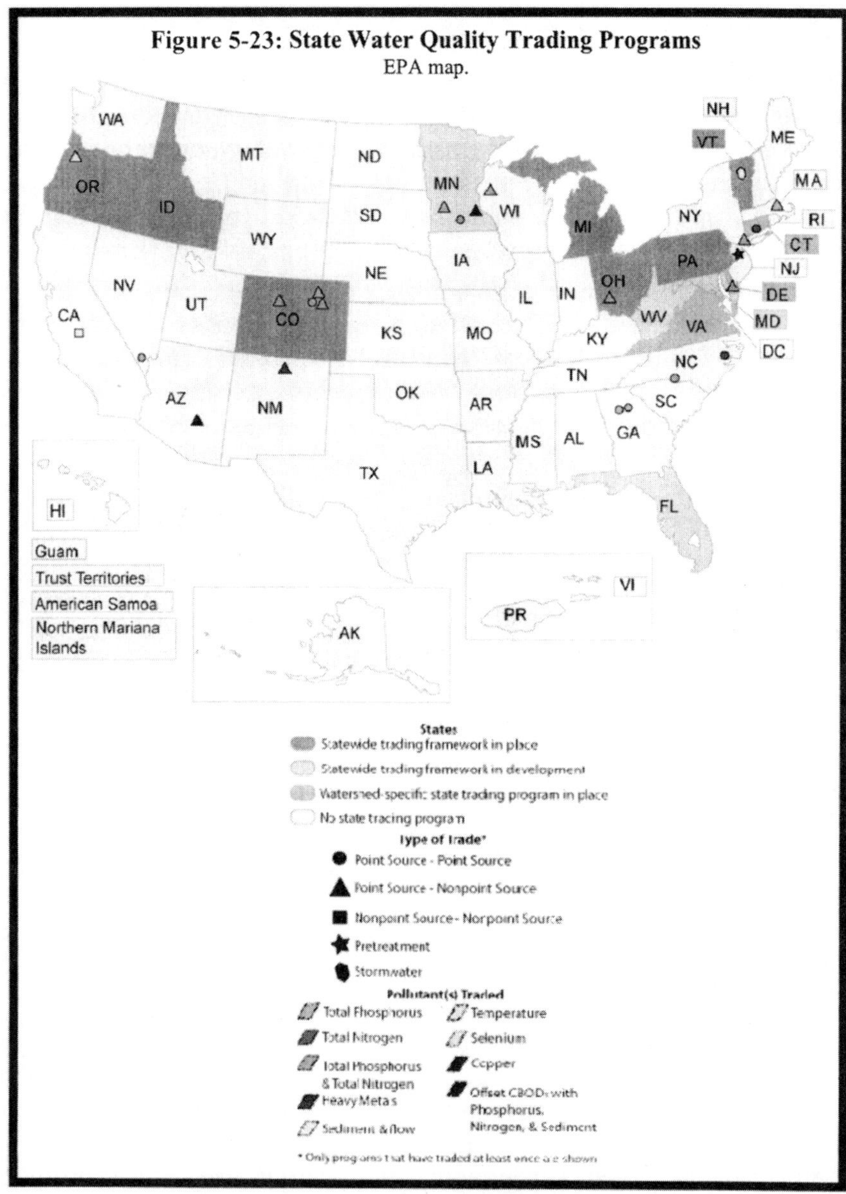

Figure 5-23: State Water Quality Trading Programs
EPA map.

In August 2007, the EPA issued a trading toolkit for NPDES permit writers to facilitate trading. U.S. EPA, Water Quality Trading Toolkit for

Permit Writers, EPA–833–R–07–004 (Aug. 2007), *available at* http://www.epa.gov/owow/watershed/trading/WQTToolkit.html. As of January 2008, as shown in Figure 5–24, seven states—Oregon, Idaho, Colorado, Michigan, Ohio, Pennsylvania, and Vermont—had statewide water quality trading frameworks in place, for a variety of pollutants, while three other states—Virginia, Delaware, and Connecticut—had watershed-specific trading programs in place. Moreover, five other states were in the process of developing trading programs.

CHAPTER 6

ENVIRONMENTAL CITIZEN SUITS AND THE U.S. CONSTITUTION

■ ■ ■

I. INTRODUCTION TO CITIZEN ENVIRONMENTAL LITIGATION

Almost all federal environmental statutes have ***citizen suit provisions***. (NEPA is a notable exception.) These provisions generally allow citizens to sue persons who are violating the Act and/or the federal agency charged with implementing the Act for failure to implement the Act. Under the Clean Water Act, for example:

any citizen may commence a civil action on his own behalf—

(1) against any person (including (i) the United States, and (ii) any other governmental instrumentality or agency to the extent permitted by the eleventh amendment to the Constitution) who is alleged to be in violation of (A) an effluent standard or limitation under this chapter or (B) an order issued by the Administrator or a State with respect to such a standard or limitation, or

(2) against the Administrator where there is alleged a failure of the Administrator to perform any act or duty under this chapter which is not discretionary with the Administrator.

The district courts shall have jurisdiction, without regard to the amount in controversy or the citizenship of the parties, to enforce such an effluent standard or limitation, or such an order, or to order the Administrator to perform any such act or duty, as the case may be, and to apply any appropriate civil penalties under section 1319(d) of this title.

CWA § 505(a), 33 U.S.C. § 1365(a). A "citizen" entitled to bring such actions is "a person or persons having an interest which is or may be adversely affected." *Id.* § 505(g), 33 U.S.C. § 1365(g). Civil penalties assessed in a citizen suit are payable to U.S. Treasury; however, to encourage citizen suits, Congress made litigation costs, "including reasonable attorney and expert witness fees" available to plaintiffs "whenever the court determines such award is appropriate." *Id.* § 505(d), 33 U.S.C. § 1365(d).

Citizens suing federal agencies—but not private parties—have another potential cause of action as well. Under the judicial review provisions of the federal ***Administrative Procedure Act* (APA)**, 5 U.S.C. §§ 701–706, "[a] person suffering a legal wrong because of agency action, or adversely affected or aggrieved by agency action within the meaning of a relevant statute, is entitled to judicial review thereof." 5 U.S.C. § 702. However, the person suing must be "seeking relief other than money damages," *id.*, and can only sue to challenge "[a]gency action made reviewable by statute and final agency action for which there is no adequate remedy in a court * * *." *Id.* § 704. Thus, APA suits can seek only declaratory and injunctive relief.

Both kinds of citizen actions are procedurally and constitutionally complex lawsuits to bring, especially environmental citizen suits, as the rest of this chapter will explore.

II. NOTICE

A. THE BASIC NOTICE REQUIREMENT

The first unusual procedural requirement in environmental citizen suits is the pre-complaint notice that the citizen plaintiff must send. Under the Clean Water Act's citizen suit provision, for example,

> No action may be commenced—
>
> (1) under subsection (a)(1) of this section—
>
> (A) prior to sixty days after the plaintiff has given notice of the alleged violation (i) to the Administrator, (ii) to the State in which the alleged violation occurs, and (iii) to any alleged violator of any standard, limitation, or order, or
>
> (2) under subsection (a)(2) of this section prior to sixty days after the plaintiff has given notice of such actions to the Administrator,
>
> except that such action may be brought immediately after such notification in the case of an action under this section respecting a violation of sections 1316 [new source performance standards] and 1317(a) [toxic effluent standards] of this title. Notice under this subsection shall be given in such manner as the Administrator shall prescribe by regulation.

CWA § 505(b), 33 U.S.C. § 1365(b). The APA, in contrast, contains no notice requirement.

What are the consequences for the lawsuit if the citizen does not strictly comply with these notice requirements? Over time, the federal Courts of Appeals split over whether the notice requirement was merely a procedural requirement, and hence could be waived or corrected later, or a jurisdictional requirement, upon which the federal court's ability to hear the case depended. The following Supreme Court decision resolved that conflict.

HALLSTROM v. TILLAMOOK COUNTY

493 U.S. 20 (1989).

JUSTICE O'CONNOR delivered the opinion of the Court.

The citizen suit provision of the Resource Conservation and Recovery Act of 1976 (RCRA), 90 Stat. 2825, as amended, 42 U.S.C. § 6972 (1982 ed. and Supp. V) permits individuals to commence an action in district court to enforce waste disposal regulations promulgated under the Act. At least 60 days before commencing suit, plaintiffs must notify the alleged violator, the State, and the Environmental Protection Agency (EPA) of their intent to sue. 42 U.S.C. § 6972(b)(1). This 60–day notice provision was modeled upon § 304 of the Clean Air Amendments of 1970, 84 Stat. 1706, as amended, 42 U.S.C. § 7604 (1982 ed.). Since 1970, a number of other federal statutes have incorporated notice provisions patterned after § 304.[1] In this case, we must decide whether compliance with the 60–day notice provision is a mandatory precondition to suit or can be disregarded by the district court at its discretion.

I

Petitioners own a commercial dairy farm located next to respondent's sanitary landfill. In April 1981, believing that the landfill operation violated standards established under RCRA, petitioners sent respondent written notice of their intention to file suit. A year later, petitioners commenced this action. On March 1, 1983, respondent moved for summary judgment on the ground that petitioners had failed to notify Oregon's Department of Environmental Quality (DEQ) and the EPA of their intent to sue, as required by § 6972(b)(1). Respondent claimed that this failure to comply with the notice requirement deprived the District Court of jurisdiction. On March 2, 1983, petitioners notified the agencies of the suit.

---

1. *See, e.g.,* § 505(b) of the Federal Water Pollution Control Act (Clean Water Act), 33 U.S.C. § 1365(b) (1982 ed.); § 310(d)(1) of the Comprehensive Environmental Response, Compensation, and Liability Act of 1980, 42 U.S.C. § 9659(d)(1) (1982 ed., Supp. V); § 105(g)(2) of the Marine Protection, Research, and Sanctuaries Act of 1972, 33 U.S.C. § 1415(g)(2) (1982 ed.); § 12(b) of the Noise Control Act of 1972, 42 U.S.C. § 4911(b) (1982 ed.); § 16(b) of the Deepwater Port Act of 1974, 33 U.S.C. § 1515(b) (1982 ed.); § 1449(b) of the Safe Drinking Water Act, 42 U.S.C. § 300j–8(b) (1982 ed.); § 520(b) of the Surface Mining Control and Reclamation Act of 1977, 30 U.S.C. § 1270(b) (1982 ed.); § 20(b) of the Toxic Substances Control Act, 15 U.S.C. § 2619(b); § 11(g)(2) of the Endangered Species Act of 1973, 16 U.S.C. § 1540(g)(2); § 23(a)(2) of the Outer Continental Shelf Lands Act Amendments of 1978, 43 U.S.C. § 1349(a)(2) (1982 ed.); § 11(b)(1) of the Act to Prevent Pollution from Ships, 33 U.S.C. § 1910(b)(1) (1982 ed.); § 117(b) of the Deep Seabed Hard Mineral Resources Act, 30 U.S.C. § 1427(b) (1982 ed.); § 326(d) of the Emergency Planning and Community Right–To–Know Act of 1986, 42 U.S.C. § 11046(d) (1982 ed., Supp. V); § 335(b) of the Energy Policy and Conservation Act, 42 U.S.C. § 6305(b) (1982 ed.); § 19(b) of the Natural Gas Pipeline Safety Act Amendments of 1976, 49 U.S.C.App. § 1686(b) (1982 ed.); and § 114(b) of the Ocean Thermal Energy Conversion Act of 1980, 42 U.S.C. § 9124(b) (1982 ed.).

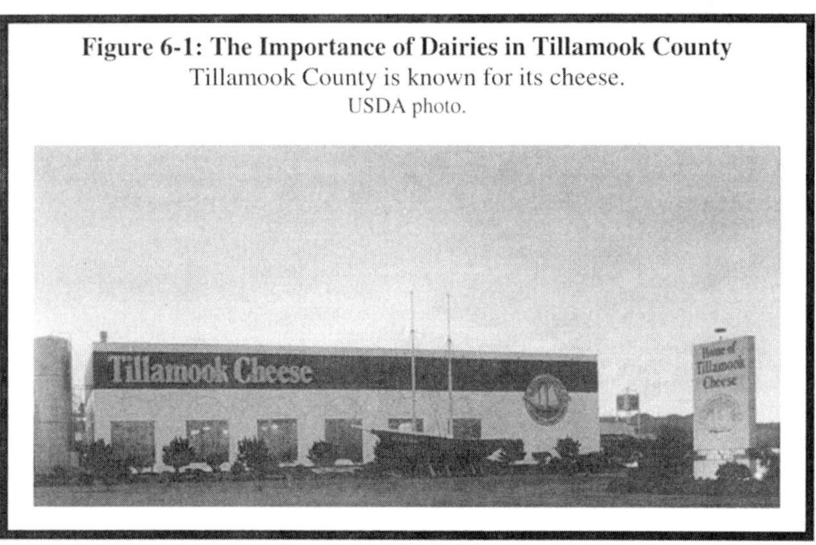

Figure 6-1: The Importance of Dairies in Tillamook County
Tillamook County is known for its cheese.
USDA photo.

The District Court denied respondent's motion. It reasoned that petitioners had cured any defect in notice by formally notifying the state and federal agencies on March 2, 1983. The agencies would then have 60 days to take appropriate steps to cure any violation at respondent's landfill. The court noted that the purpose of the notice requirement was to give administrative agencies an opportunity to enforce environmental regulations. In this case, neither the state nor the federal agency expressed any interest in taking action against respondent. Therefore, the court concluded that dismissing the action at this stage would waste judicial resources.

After the action proceeded to trial, the District Court held that respondent had violated RCRA. The court ordered respondent to remedy the violation but refused to grant petitioners' motion for injunctive relief. * * *

The Court of Appeals for the Ninth Circuit concluded that petitioners' failure to comply with the 60–day notice requirement deprived the District Court of subject matter jurisdiction. Relying on the plain language of § 6972(b)(1), the Court of Appeals determined that permitting the plaintiff to proceed without giving notice would constitute " 'judicial amendment' " of a clear statutory command. The Court of Appeals also determined that strict construction of the notice requirement would best further the goal of giving environmental agencies, rather than courts, the primary responsibility for enforcing RCRA. Therefore, the Court of Appeals remanded the action to the District Court with instructions to dismiss. We granted certiorari to resolve the conflict among the Courts of Appeals regarding the correct interpretation of the notice provision.

II

As we have repeatedly noted, "the starting point for interpreting a statute is the language of the statute itself." *Consumer Product Safety Comm'n v. GTE Sylvania, Inc.*, 447 U.S. 102, 108 (1980). Section 6972(a)(1) permits any person to commence a civil action against an alleged violator of regulations established under RCRA "[except] as provided in subsection (b)." Subsection (b)(1) states:

"(b) Actions prohibited.

"No action may be commenced under paragraph (a)(1) of this section—

"(1) prior to sixty days after the plaintiff has given notice of the violation (A) to the Administrator [of the EPA]; (B) to the State in which the alleged violation occurs; and (C) to any alleged violator of such permit, standard, regulation, condition, requirement, or order...." 42 U.S.C. § 6972(b)(1) (1982 ed.).

The language of this provision could not be clearer. A citizen may not commence an action under RCRA until 60 days after the citizen has notified the EPA, the State in which the alleged violation occurred, and the alleged violator. Actions commenced prior to 60 days after notice are "prohibited." Because this language is expressly incorporated by reference into § 6972(a), it acts as a specific limitation on a citizen's right to bring suit. Under a literal reading of the statute, compliance with the 60–day notice provision is a mandatory, not optional, condition precedent for suit.

Petitioners do not contend that the language of this provision is ambiguous; rather, they assert that it should be given a flexible or pragmatic construction. Thus, petitioners argue that if a suit commenced without proper notice is stayed until 60 days after notice had been given, the District Court should deem the notice requirement to be satisfied. According to petitioners, a 60–day stay would serve the same function as delaying commencement of the suit: it would give the Government an opportunity to take action against the alleged violator and it would give the violator the opportunity to bring itself into compliance.

Whether or not a stay is in fact the functional equivalent of a precommencement delay, such an interpretation of § 6972(b) flatly contradicts the language of the statute. Under Rule 3 of the Federal Rules of Civil Procedure, "[a] civil action is commenced by filing a complaint with the court." Reading § 6972(b)(1) in light of this Rule, a plaintiff may not file suit before fulfilling the 60–day notice requirement. Staying judicial action once the suit has been filed does not honor this prohibition. Congress could have excepted parties from complying with the notice or delay requirement; indeed, it carved out such an exception in its 1984 amendments to RCRA. *See, e.g.*, 42 U.S.C. § 6972(b)(1)(A) (1982 ed., Supp. V) (abrogating the 60–day delay requirement when there is a danger that hazardous waste will be discharged). RCRA, however, contains no exception applicable to petitioners' situation; we are not at liberty to create an exception where Congress has declined to do so.

* * * Petitioners next contend that a literal interpretation of the notice provision would defeat Congress' intent in enacting RCRA; to support this argument, they cite passages from the legislative history of the first citizen suit statute, § 304 of the Clean Air Amendments of 1970, indicating that citizen suits should be encouraged. *See* S. REP. NO. 91–1196, pp. 36–37 (1970), 1 Senate Committee on Public Works, 93d Cong., 2d Sess., A LEGISLATIVE HISTORY OF THE CLEAR AIR ACT AMENDMENTS OF 1970, pp. 436–437 (Comm. Print 1974). This reliance on legislative history is misplaced. We have held that "[a]bsent a clearly expressed legislative intention to the contrary," the words of the statute are conclusive. *Consumer Product Safety Comm'n v. GTE Sylvania, Inc.*, 447 U.S. at 108. Nothing in the legislative history of the citizen suit provision militates against honoring the plain language of the notice requirement. Nor is this one of the " 'rare cases [in which] the literal application of a statute will produce a result demonstrably at odds with the intentions of its drafters.' " *United States v. Ron Pair Enterprises, Inc.*, 489 U.S. 235, 242 (1989), quoting *Griffin v. Oceanic Contractors, Inc.*, 458 U.S. 564, 571 (1982). Rather, the legislative history indicates an intent to strike a balance between encouraging citizen enforcement of environmental regulations and avoiding burdening the federal courts with excessive numbers of citizen suits. *See, e.g.*, 116 Cong. Rec. 32927 (comments of Sen. Muskie). Requiring citizens to comply with the notice and delay requirements serves this congressional goal in two ways. First, notice allows Government agencies to take responsibility for enforcing environmental regulations, thus obviating the need for citizen suits. *See Gwaltney of Smithfield, Inc. v. Chesapeake Bay Foundation, Inc.*, 484 U.S. 49, 60 (1987) ("The bar on citizen suits when governmental enforcement action is under way suggests that the citizen suit is meant to supplement rather than to supplant governmental action"). In many cases, an agency may be able to compel compliance through administrative action, thus eliminating the need for any access to the courts. *See* 116 Cong. Rec. 33104 (1970) (comments of Sen. Hart). Second, notice gives the alleged violator "an opportunity to bring itself into complete compliance with the Act and thus likewise render unnecessary a citizen suit." *Gwaltney, supra,* at 60. This policy would be frustrated if citizens could immediately bring suit without involving federal or state enforcement agencies. Giving full effect to the words of the statute preserves the compromise struck by Congress.

Petitioners next assert that giving effect to the literal meaning of the notice provisions would compel "absurd or futile results." *United States v. American Trucking Assns., Inc.*, 310 U.S. 534, 543 (1940). In essence, petitioners make two arguments. First, petitioners, with *amici,* contend that strictly enforcing the 60–day delay provision would give violators an opportunity to cause further damage or actually accomplish the objective that the citizen was attempting to stop. Similarly, they assert that courts would be precluded from giving essential temporary injunctive relief until

60 days had elapsed. Although we do not underestimate the potential damage to the environment that could ensue during the 60–day waiting period, this problem arises as a result of the balance struck by Congress in developing the citizen suit provisions. Congress has addressed the dangers of delay in certain circumstances and made exceptions to the required notice periods accordingly. *See, e.g.,* the Clean Water Act, as added, 86 Stat. 888, 33 U.S.C. §§ 1365(b) and 1317(a) (1982 ed.) (citizen suits may be brought immediately in cases involving violations of toxic pollutant effluent limitations); the Clean Air Amendments of 1970, 84 Stat. 1706, 42 U.S.C. § 7604(b) (1982 ed.) (citizen suits may be brought immediately in cases involving stationary-source emissions standards and other specified compliance orders). Moreover, it is likely that compliance with the notice requirement will trigger appropriate federal or state enforcement actions to prevent serious damage.

Second, petitioners argue that a strict construction of the notice provision would cause procedural anomalies. For example, petitioners contend that if a citizen notified Government agencies of a violation, and the agencies explicitly declined to act, it would be pointless to require the citizen to wait 60 days to commence suit. While such a result may be frustrating to the plaintiff, it is not irrational: as the Court of Appeals for the First Circuit noted, "[p]ermitting immediate suit ignores the possibility that a violator or agency may change its mind as the threat of suit becomes more imminent." *Garcia v. Cecos, Int'l, Inc.*, 761 F.2d, at 82.

In sum, we conclude that none of petitioners' arguments requires us to disregard the plain language of § 6972(b). "[I]n the long run, experience teaches that strict adherence to the procedural requirements specified by the legislature is the best guarantee of evenhanded administration of the law." *Mohasco Corp. v. Silver*, 447 U.S. 807, 826 (1980). Therefore, we hold that the notice and 60–day delay requirements are mandatory conditions precedent to commencing suit under the RCRA citizen suit provision; a district court may not disregard these requirements at its discretion. * * *

As a general rule, if an action is barred by the terms of a statute, it must be dismissed. * * * Petitioners remain free to give notice and file their suit in compliance with the statute to enforce pertinent environmental standards. * * *

NOTES

1. **Notice and Federal Court Jurisdiction.** Is the citizen suit notice requirement jurisdictional or procedural, according to the Supreme Court? Why? What tools of statutory construction did the Supreme Court use to arrive at its conclusion? For instance, as the *Hallstrom* Court itself notes, Congress itself has created exceptions to the waiting period, generally for lawsuits involving imminent threats. *See, e.g., Francisco Sanchez v. Esso Standard Oil Co.*, 572 F.3d 1, 9 (1st Cir. 2009) (invoking RCRA's notice exception).

2. **The Breadth of *Hallstrom*.** *Hallstrom* involved a RCRA citizen suit. Is the decision limited to RCRA, as a practical matter? Why or why not? How broad a reach does *Hallstrom* arguably have, according to footnote 1?

3. **The Strictness of *Hallstrom*.** If a citizen suit plaintiff does not comply with the statutory requirements for citizen suit notice—giving notice to the entities that the statute requires and waiting the appropriate time that the statute dictates—*Hallstrom* requires that the citizen suit be dismissed. The stringency of this ruling became apparent in *Hawksbill Sea Turtle v. Federal Emergency Management Agency*, 126 F.3d 461 (3rd Cir. 1997). In that Endangered Species Act citizen suit, the plaintiffs (which included the Hawksbill Sea Turtle, the Green Sea Turtle, and the Virgin Islands Tree Boa) alleged that the Federal Emergency Management Agency (FEMA) had violated section 7 of the ESA in building a temporary housing project on St. Thomas island. *Id.* at 463. The plaintiffs gave notice 60 days before filing suit to the Secretary of the Interior (which houses USFWS) and to FEMA. *Id.* at 470. However, USFWS and NMFS share jurisdiction over sea turtles: USFWS has jurisdiction over sea turtles while they are on land, while NMFS has jurisdiction over the turtles when they are in the water. Turtles pass from one agency's jurisdiction to the other when they cross the mean high tide line. *Id.* at 470–71.

Unfortunately for the plaintiffs, NMFS is an agency within the Department of Commerce, not the Department of the Interior. Because the plaintiffs did not give notice to the Secretary of Commerce, and because their complaint included allegations of harm to the sea turtles while the turtles were in the water, *Hallstrom* compelled the Third Circuit to (reluctantly) dismiss the lawsuit—even though the regulations regarding sea turtles were not particularly clear or easy to find. *Id.* at 471–73. The Third Circuit did take the rather unusual step, however, of sending its opinion directly to Congress, opining in a footnote "that Congress and the agencies involved should put their heads together and fashion a simpler and clearer notice scheme." *Id.* at 473 n.7.

* * *

B. THE CONTENTS AND SCOPE OF CITIZEN SUIT NOTICE LETTERS

Hallstrom involved the *statutory* requirements for *timing* of notice found in each environmental citizen suit provision. However, agencies such as the EPA have also enacted *regulatory* requirements governing the *contents* of citizen suit notice. Does *Hallstrom* affect these content-related, regulatory notice requirements? Also, what is the scope of a single notice letter? The Third Circuit addressed these issues in the following highly influential opinion.

PUBLIC INTEREST RESEARCH GROUP OF NEW JERSEY, INC. v. HERCULES, INC.

50 F.3d 1239 (3rd Cir. 1995).

ROTH, CIRCUIT JUDGE:

Plaintiffs, Public Interest Research Group of New Jersey, Inc., (NJPIRG) and Friends of the Earth, Inc., (FOE) brought a citizen suit pursuant to the Federal Water Pollution Control Act (Clean Water Act or Act), 86 Stat. 816, 33 U.S.C. § 1251 *et seq.*, against defendant Hercules, Inc. Pursuant to the Act, plaintiffs notified Hercules, the United States Environmental Protection Agency (EPA), and the New Jersey Department of Environmental Protection and Energy (NJDEPE) that they intended to sue Hercules for alleged violations of its federal and state permits, limiting effluent discharge from its Gibbstown, New Jersey, facility.

Plaintiffs' notice letter claimed that Hercules committed sixty-eight discharge violations from April 1985 through February 1989. A discharge violation involves the release of a pollutant into receiving waters, which release exceeds the quantity, discharge rate, or concentration of the pollutant allowed by the permit. In accord with the citizen suit provision of the Act, plaintiffs waited 60 days and then filed a complaint in federal district court, alleging that Hercules had violated its permit. Plaintiffs attached to the complaint a list of eighty-seven discharge violations. This list omitted several of the originally cited violations and included more than thirty new ones. A majority of the new violations pre-dated the 60-day notice letter; the remainder post-dated it.

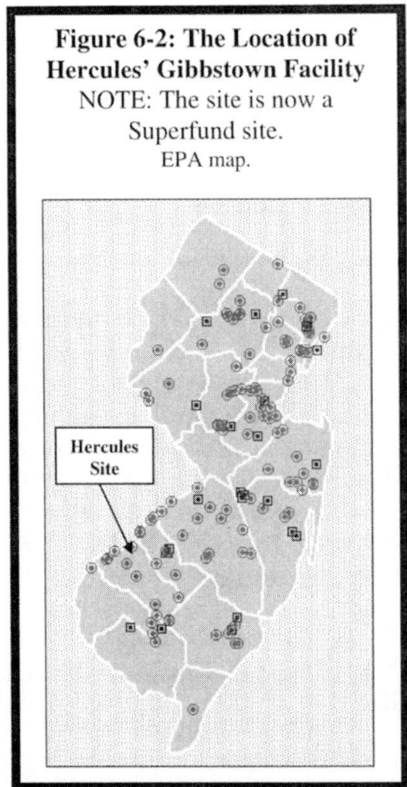

Figure 6-2: The Location of Hercules' Gibbstown Facility
NOTE: The site is now a Superfund site.
EPA map.

Between the time plaintiffs filed their complaint and moved for summary judgment, they supplemented the list of alleged permit violations, committed by Hercules, to include a total of 114 discharge violations, 328 monitoring violations, 58 reporting violations, and 228 recordkeeping violations. At no time prior to plaintiffs' motion for summary judgment did plaintiffs supply Hercules, EPA, or the State of New Jersey (State) with a new notice letter pursuant to the Act. Hercules filed a cross-motion for summary judgment, seeking to dismiss all violations not listed in plaintiffs' notice letter. The violations Hercules sought to dismiss included a majority of the discharge violations and all of the monitoring, reporting and recordkeeping violations.

The district court granted summary judgment for Hercules as to all pre-complaint discharge violations not listed in the notice letter and as to all monitoring, reporting and recordkeeping violations. The court granted summary judgment for plaintiffs as to forty-three discharge violations listed in the notice letter and included in the complaint and as to seventeen post-complaint discharge violations of the same type as those included in the notice letter.

Both parties sought interlocutory review of the district court's decision to grant summary judgment on certain claims and to dismiss others; review was granted. For the reasons stated below, we will affirm the decision of the district court in part, we will reverse it in part, and we will remand this case for further proceedings consistent with this opinion.

I.

The Clean Water Act makes it unlawful to discharge any pollutant into the nation's waters except those discharges made in compliance with the Act. 33 U.S.C. § 1311. In 1975, the federal government issued a National Pollutant Discharge Elimination System (NPDES) permit to Hercules. 33 U.S.C. § 1342. This permit authorized Hercules to discharge certain pollutants from its Gibbstown facility into the Delaware River (outfall 001) and into Clonmell Creek (outfall 002) in strict compliance with conditions specified in the permit. In addition to establishing limits on effluent discharges, the permit required Hercules to monitor its effluent and to submit reports of the results. 33 U.S.C. § 1342(a)(2). The Act requires that such reports, known as Discharge Monitoring Reports (DMRs), be made available to the public. 33 U.S.C. § 1318(b); 40 C.F.R. § 122.41(j), (*l*).

The Clean Water Act allows each state to establish and administer its own permit program, provided that the program meets the requirements established under the Act and is approved by the EPA. 33 U.S.C. § 1342(b). In 1982, the EPA authorized New Jersey to administer a state permit program. After assuming this responsibility, NJDEPE issued a modified Pollutant Discharge Elimination System permit to Hercules for the Gibbstown facility (NJPDES Permit No. NJ 0005134). This permit established monitoring and reporting requirements similar to those of

Hercules' NPDES permit. 40 C.F.R. § 123.25. Under both federal and state law, Hercules was required to make its DMRs available to the public.

The NJPDES permit established the same two outfalls: outfall 001 into the Delaware River and outfall 002 into Clonmell Creek. The permit established discharge limits and monitoring requirements for designated parameters at each outfall, with each parameter defined as a particular attribute of a discharge. Parameters under the Hercules permit included specific pollutants (such as fecal coliform) and discharge characteristics or water quality indicators (such as the color or pH value of the sample or the biochemical oxygen content). The permit established strict limits on these parameters, both as to the overall amount of the pollutant and as to the concentration of the pollutant or water quality.

The Clean Water Act provides that federal or state authorities may take enforcement action against a permit holder who fails to comply with specified permit conditions. 33 U.S.C. §§ 1319 and 1342(b)(7). In addition, the Act provides that private citizens may commence civil actions in certain situations against a permit holder who fails to comply with the Act. 33 U.S.C. § 1365. If the citizen prevails, the court may order injunctive relief and/or impose civil penalties which are payable to the United States.

Following a review of Hercules' DMRs on file with the federal government, NJPIRG notified Hercules, EPA, and the State of its intent to file suit under the citizen suit provision of the Act for Hercules' alleged violation of its permits. Plaintiffs' March 21, 1989, notice letter listed sixty-eight discharges which plaintiffs claimed had occurred from April 1985 through February 1989 in violation of Hercules' permits.

Plaintiffs' notice letter alleged that Hercules violated its permit for the parameters of biological oxygen demand, total residual chlorine, chemical oxygen demand, total suspended solids, phenol, fecal coliform, and bioassay at outfall 001 and the parameters of pH, phenol, chemical oxygen demand, and total suspended solids at outfall 002. The notice letter listed permit violations only in the discharge of a particular pollutant; it did not list any violations for the monitoring required to track that pollutant or for the reporting or recordkeeping which documented the monitoring. It is the discharge violations, however, which are most easily ascertainable from the information available to the public, *i.e.,* the DMRs which Hercules must file.

Plaintiffs filed a citizen suit in federal district court on May 24, 1989, shortly after the 60–day notice period had expired. The complaint alleged eighty-seven discharge violations which had occurred from April 1985 through March 1989. Among these were more than thirty new violations which had not been included in the notice letter; a majority of the new violations pre-dated the notice letter, the remainder post-dated it.

Between the time of the 60–day notice letter on March 21, 1989, and the plaintiffs' final submission for purposes of summary judgment on September 14, 1992, plaintiffs made numerous modifications of their list of alleged violations through "informal" amendments to their complaint. * * * Plaintiffs' final submission to the district court alleged that Hercules had committed 114 discharge violations, 328 monitoring violations, 58 reporting violations, and 228 recordkeeping violations. Plaintiffs did not send a new 60–day letter, giving notice of these additional violations, nor did plaintiffs formally amend their complaint to include them.

* * * *A. District Court Opinion*

Plaintiffs moved for partial summary judgment as to liability and for permanent injunctive relief, enjoining Hercules from future violations of the Clean Water Act. Hercules filed a cross-motion for summary judgment, asserting that plaintiffs had failed to comply with the 60–day notice provision of the Act.

The district court examined the plaintiffs' 60–day notice letter and compared it to the final list of alleged violations submitted by plaintiffs. Finding that the notice letter did not notify Hercules, the EPA, or the State of plaintiffs' intent to sue for monitoring, reporting and recordkeeping violations, the district court granted summary judgment for Hercules on all of these violations.

The district court then placed the discharge violations into three categories: (1) discharge violations included in both the notice letter and the final list; (2) pre-complaint discharge violations not included in the notice letter but included in the final list; and (3) post-complaint discharge violations included in the final list. Finding that plaintiffs had complied with the Act's notice requirement for the violations in category one, the district court denied Hercules' summary judgment motion regarding them. As for the violations in category two, the court granted Hercules' summary judgment motion, holding that plaintiffs had failed to comply with the Act's notice requirement. With regard to category three, the court found no statutory requirement that defendants first be notified by plaintiffs of their intent to sue. It, therefore, granted summary judgment for plaintiffs on these violations.

In support of its decision to distinguish between category two violations and category three violations, the district court, citing *Gwaltney of Smithfield, Ltd. v. Chesapeake Bay Foundation, Inc.*, 484 U.S. 49 (1987), wrote that: "[S]ubsequently occurring violations not noticed in a citizen's 60–day notice letter were specifically contemplated—indeed required—by the Supreme Court as a prerequisite to a district court's jurisdiction over a citizen suit under the Clean Water Act." The court held that such post-complaint violations, being "the 'type of activity' (*e.g.,* discharging pollutants in excess of permit limitations) as have been alleged in the notice letter[,]" survived defendant's summary judgment motion. After reviewing the evidence on violations in categories one and three, a total of 70 violations, the court granted summary judgment (with respect to liability only) in favor of plaintiffs on 60 of these.

In sum, the district court held that, under the Act's notice requirement, the plaintiffs could sue only for those discharge violations that were included in their notice letter or that occurred after the complaint was filed and were a continuation of the same type of violation as contained in the notice letter. The only issue remaining for trial would then be a determination of the size of the penalty for the established discharge violations.

* * * III.

The Clean Water Act authorizes a citizen (defined as a person or persons having an interest which is or may be adversely affected) to bring suit in federal court against any person who is alleged to be in violation of "an effluent standard or limitation" as defined in the Act or "an order issued by the [EPA] Administrator or a State with respect to such a standard or limitation." 33 U.S.C. § 1365(a)(1). In order to commence a suit, a citizen must comply with § 1365(b), which states in part:

> No action may be commenced—
>
> (1) under subsection (a)(1) of this section—
>
> (A) prior to sixty days after the plaintiff has given notice of the alleged violation (i) to the Administrator, (ii) to the State in which the alleged violation occurs, and (iii) to any alleged violator of the standard, limitation, or order.

33 U.S.C. § 1365(b).

In crafting the citizen suit provision, Congress sought to "strike a balance between encouraging citizen enforcement of environmental regulations and avoiding burdening the federal courts with excessive numbers of citizen suits." *Hallstrom v. Tillamook County,* 493 U.S. 20, 29 (1989) (analyzing the legislative history of the citizen suit provision of the Clean Air Amendments of 1970, which served as the precursor to analogous citizen suit provisions in the Clean Water Act and the Resource Conservation and Recovery Act of 1976). * * *

With that [supplemental] purpose in mind for citizen suits, Congress then delegated to the EPA the task of determining the form of the notice letter. Subsection 1365(b) provides that "[n]otice under this subsection shall be given in such manner as the [EPA] Administrator shall prescribe by regulation." The legislative history indicates that Congress sought here to strike a balance between providing notice recipients with sufficient information to identify the basis of the citizen's claim and not placing an undue burden on the citizen.

* * * Pursuant to the statutory directions, EPA drafted a regulation, 40 C.F.R. § 135.3(a), which prescribed the contents of a notice letter:

> *Violation of standard, limitation or order.* Notice regarding an alleged violation of an effluent standard or limitation or of an order with respect thereto, shall include sufficient information to permit the recipient to identify the specific standard, limitation, or order alleged

to have been violated, the activity alleged to constitute a violation, the person or persons responsible for the alleged violation, the location of the alleged violation, the date or dates of such violation, and the full name, address, and telephone number of the person giving notice.

In the present dispute, Hercules does not contend that plaintiffs failed to send a 60-day notice letter. Rather, Hercules asserts that plaintiffs' 60-day notice letter lacked the specificity, required by the Act and its regulation, to put the recipients of the letter on notice of the violations upon which plaintiffs intended to sue. * * *

* * * While there is no doubt that such detailed information is helpful to the recipient of a notice letter in identifying the basis for the citizen suit, such specificity is not mandated by the regulation. The regulation does not require that the citizen identify every detail of a violation. Rather, it states that "[n]otice regarding an alleged violation . . . shall include sufficient information *to permit the recipient to identify*" the components of an alleged violation. 40 C.F.R. § 135.3(a) (emphasis added). We read the regulation to require just what it says: that the citizen provide enough information to enable the *recipient, i.e.,* Hercules, EPA and/or the State, to identify the specific effluent discharge limitation which has been violated, including the parameter violated, the date of the violation, the outfall at which it occurred, and the person or persons involved.

* * * Hercules contends, however, that notice of each individual violation is necessary in order for the recipients of the notice to evaluate the extent of the citizen's claim. Hercules suggests, for example, that whereas the EPA or the State might not pursue an enforcement action against an alleged violator with a small number of individual violations, the government would be more likely to act if each individual violation were included in the notice. Similarly, the larger the number of cited violations, the greater incentive for the permit holder to try to comply.

Hercules' argument ignores the fact that both the federal and state government enforcement agencies have access to the DMRs. Both the Clean Water Act and the New Jersey permit program require that a permittee file DMRs with the EPA and the NJDEPE. The DMRs filed by Hercules list the discharge violations. Once a notice letter from a citizen has been received, the EPA and the State can, with relative ease, check for other discharge violations of the same type. Moreover, as the author of the DMRs, Hercules is surely on notice of the contents of the reports and of the frequency of similar violations.

The district court and Hercules also place great reliance on *Hallstrom* for their interpretation of the statute and regulation. The Supreme Court held in *Hallstrom* that "the notice and 60-day delay requirements are mandatory conditions precedent to commencing suit under the RCRA [Resource Conservation and Recovery Act of 1976] citizen suit provision; a district court may not disregard these requirements at its discretion." 493 U.S. at 31. Hercules and the district court would have us read *Hallstrom* broadly, extending the Supreme Court's interpretation of the notice and 60–day delay requirements to a ruling on the contents of a notice.

We decline to apply *Hallstrom* so broadly. The Supreme Court's focus in *Hallstrom* was on the timing of the notice, not on its contents. [W]hile the literal reading of the statute clearly compels the Court's interpretation of the 60–day delay requirement, there is no express requirement in the statute pertaining to the content of a notice letter. In fact, as we have noted, Congress delegated to the EPA the authority to determine the necessary contents of a notice letter.

* * * This conclusion does not mean, however, that *Hallstrom* is not helpful in our analysis of the notice requirement. In deciding whether the plaintiffs here complied with the content requirements established under the regulation, we must consider whether their notice letter served the purpose that Congress intended: To provide the recipient with effective, as well as timely, notice. *Hallstrom*'s analysis of Congress' intent in crafting the citizen suit provision makes clear that not only is the 60–day notice before filing suit "a mandatory, not optional, condition precedent for suit," 493 U.S. at 26, but also that the content of the notice must be adequate for the recipients of the notice to identify the basis for the citizen's complaint.

The ultimate goal of a citizen suit is to bring the alleged violator into compliance with the nation's environmental laws. This can be achieved through citizen enforcement efforts, government enforcement efforts, or self-enforcement efforts. * * *

Moreover, we note the Supreme Court's statement in *Gwaltney* that "[t]he bar on citizen suits when governmental enforcement action is under way suggests that the citizen suit is meant to supplement rather than to supplant governmental action." 484 U.S. at 60. In deciding whether to initiate an enforcement action, the EPA and the state must be provided with enough information to enable them intelligently to decide whether to do so. At the same time, the alleged violator must be provided with enough information to be able to bring itself into compliance. We will judge the sufficiency of the plaintiffs' 60–day notice letter in terms of whether it accomplishes these purposes.

IV.

Applying these legal precepts to the present dispute, we will analyze the violations in following order: (A) pre-complaint discharge violations, (B) post-complaint discharge violations, and (C) monitoring, reporting and recordkeeping violations.

A. Pre–Complaint Discharge Violations

The district court held that pre-complaint discharge violations not included in plaintiffs' notice letter cannot be included in the suit unless listed in a subsequent notice. * * * We do not agree.

[W]e hold that a notice letter which includes a list of discharge violations, by parameter, provides sufficient information for the recipients of the notice to identify violations of the same type (same parameter, same outfall) occurring during and after the period covered by the notice letter.

The facts of this dispute support this holding. Less than two months after receiving the plaintiffs' 60–day notice letter, the State filed a Notice of Civil Penalty Assessment against Hercules for discharge violations of the permit. Although many of the sixty individual violations included in the State's initial list were exactly the same violation as included in the plaintiff's 60–day notice letter, there were several that were not on the plaintiffs' list. Some of these additional violations occurred in months during which plaintiffs did not identify any discharge violation. We infer from this comparison that the State examined Hercules' DMRs on file to achieve a more comprehensive list of discharge violations. Almost two years later, in March 1991, Hercules and the State executed an ACO [Administrative Consent Order] under which Hercules agreed to pay the State $600,000 as a penalty for 115 discharge violations of its permit. The fact that the State's list of Hercules' discharge violations grew from 60 to 115 in the final ACO demonstrates that once the State received the citizen letter noting that Hercules was violating its permit, the State committed resources to monitoring Hercules' compliance and, in particular, to monitoring Hercules' compliance with the noticed parameters.

We hold, therefore, that the district court erred in granting Hercules' summary judgment motion as to the forty-four pre-complaint discharge violations not included in plaintiffs' notice letter. We will remand this case to the district court to reinstate those alleged violations which are of the same type (same parameter, same outfall) as the alleged violations included in the plaintiffs' 60–day notice letter.

B. Post–Complaint Discharge Violations

Finding that the post-complaint discharge violations included in the plaintiffs' list were a continuation of the type of activity alleged in the notice letter and finding no legal requirement that Hercules first be notified by plaintiffs of their intention to sue upon these violations, the district court held that these violations survived defendant's summary judgment motion.

For the most part, we agree with the district court. We hold that as long as a post-complaint discharge violation is of the same type as a violation included in the notice letter (same parameter, same outfall), no new 60–day notice letter is necessary to include these violations in the suit. In so holding, we do not in effect distinguish between pre-complaint violations and post-complaint violations.

Hercules disagrees, arguing that recipients of the notice letter may be more likely to act (*i.e.,* the government may initiate enforcement action; the permit holder may attempt to remedy the violation) if a citizen is required to file a new notice for post-complaint violations. While it is true that the recipients may be more likely to take action as the number of violations increases, we do not find that this justifies a requirement that a new notice must be given for post-complaint violations before commencing a suit which will include these violations.

Rather, we find that the recipients of the notice are already on notice of violations of the same type, whether past or continuing. As recipients of the permittee's DMRs, the federal and state enforcement agencies have the ability to review the permittee's compliance. The federal and state enforcement agencies are on notice of continuing or intermittent violations of the same type because they are reported to them in the DMRs. Likewise, the permit holder is on notice of continuing or intermittent violations, given the fact that the permit holder is responsible for filing the DMRs.

* * * We have found implicit support for this conclusion regarding post-complaint violations in the Supreme Court's decision in *Gwaltney*. There, the Court held that federal courts do not have jurisdiction over a citizen suit for "wholly past violations." 484 U.S. at 64. Rather, jurisdiction exists "when the citizen-plaintiffs make a good-faith allegation of continuous or intermittent violation." *Id.* In reaching this decision, the Supreme Court noted that "the harm sought to be addressed by the citizen suit lies in the present or the future, not in the past." *Id.* at 59.

Gwaltney requires that for jurisdiction to attach, a citizen must make a good-faith allegation of a continuous or intermittent violation by the defendant at the time the complaint is filed. Because a citizen must delay filing suit for at least 60 days after notice has been sent, it is foreseeable that a complaint will include allegations of more recent violations in an effort to establish "continuous or intermittent violations."

We recognize that the 60–day notice provision in the Act and the holding in *Gwaltney* represent "two separate jurisdictional requirements for bringing a citizen suit." United States' Br. as *Amicus Curae* at 17. Nevertheless, the basis for the Supreme Court's decision in *Gwaltney* is helpful to our analysis. Continuing or intermittent violations of the same type are necessary to create jurisdiction of the citizen suit. They are perforce related to the noticed violations. For this reason, they should be easily identifiable by the notice recipient and, therefore, do not need to be noticed in a new 60–day letter.

C. *Monitoring, Reporting and Recordkeeping Violations*

Finding that the plaintiffs' 60–day notice letter did not notify Hercules, EPA, or the State of plaintiffs' intent to sue for alleged monitoring, reporting or recordkeeping violations, the district court granted Hercules' motion for summary judgment as to all of these alleged violations. We will reverse this holding. [W]e conclude that, when a parameter violation has been noticed, subsequently discovered, directly related violations of discharge limitations or of monitoring, reporting, and recordkeeping requirements for that same parameter at that outfall for that same period may be included in the citizen suit. Monitoring, reporting and recordkeeping requirements are conditions of a permit. When plaintiffs noticed the discharge violations, an investigation by Hercules, EPA, or the State of those excess discharges should uncover related violations of monitoring, reporting or recordkeeping involved in tracking those pollutant parameters.

Support for our conclusion can be found in the legislative history of the citizen suit provision which makes clear that notice serves the important functions of allowing government agencies to take responsibility for enforcing environmental regulations and giving the alleged violator an opportunity to bring itself into complete compliance. The concept of "complete compliance" should consist of the cessation of the offending discharge, with on-going discharges being monitored and recorded in accordance with the permit provisions. All these functions interact to ensure the permit holder's compliance with the permit conditions. The proper performance of each function is required under the permit provisions and a violation of any one may subject the permit holder to a penalty.

The burden on the citizen, however, is to provide sufficient information of a violation, such as an excessive discharge, so that the permit holder and the agency can identify it. If investigation of that discharge by the agency or the permit holder uncovers directly related monitoring, reporting, or recordkeeping violations, "complete compliance" should incorporate the correction of all such interconnected violations. If the agency or the permit holder fails to achieve "complete compliance," the citizen should be able in the citizen suit to seek "complete compliance," eliminating all directly related violations, without the burden of further notice. Correction of an excessive discharge without correction of faulty monitoring of that parameter is not complete compliance. Correction of faulty monitoring without correction of incomplete reporting of that parameter is not complete compliance. * * *

NOTES

1. **Timing of Notice vs. Contents of Notice.** What standard did the Third Circuit use to assess the sufficiency of the citizen suit notice contents? How did this standard differ from the *Hallstrom* standard for timing of notice? What argument did Hercules make about the relevance of *Hallstrom*? What kind of notice requirements did Hercules want? How did the Third Circuit treat *Hallstrom* in its decision?

2. **The Scope of a Notice Letter.** What categories of Clean Water Act violations were at issue in *Hercules*? Which violations did the notice letter *expressly* notice? Why did the Third Circuit hold that the notice letter also covered the other categories of violations? Do you agree with its decision? Why or why not?

3. **The Functional Approach to Notice Letters.** The Third Circuit's approach to citizen suit notice in *Hercules* might be termed a *functional*

approach: the notice letter is adequate if it contains sufficient information to fulfill the statutory purposes of pre-suit notice—namely, allowing the violator to come into compliance and giving the federal and state agencies a change to take over enforcement. The Seventh Circuit has carried this functional approach into other factual contexts. In *Atlantic States Legal Foundation, Inc. v. Stroh Die Casting Co.*, 116 F.3d 814 (7th Cir. 1997), the defendant in a Clean Water Act citizen suit switched outfalls after the citizens gave notice of their suit, then claimed that the notice was invalid because the citizens had not specified the correct outfall. Rejecting the defendant's *Hallstrom*-based arguments and specifically adopting the Third Circuit's approach, the Seventh Circuit concluded that the notice letter had been sufficiently specific to allow Stroh to identify the problem:

> Here, there is no question that Atlantic's April 1989 notice sufficiently informed Stroh about Atlantic's claim that its handling of the die casting wastewater did not comply with the statute. Stroh promptly secured a permit that covered exactly these discharges, under the outfall numbered 3 in the first MMSD permit. It began construction of a treatment facility, which it completed in June of 1990 (at least a month *after* the amended complaint was filed). It then re-routed the very same die casting wastewater to its newly numbered outfall 4. Moreover, it admitted in its May 29, 1990 letter to the MMSD that it was not in compliance and attempted to explain why it missed its deadline for its wastewater treatment system. These are not the actions of a company that has not received enough information for purposes of the statutory notice provisions of the Act.

Id. at 820.

4. **The Formalistic Approach to Citizen Suit Notice.** While the Third Circuit's view of citizen suit notice contents has been widely followed, it is by no means universal, and several federal courts impose strict, *Hallstrom*-like requirements on citizen suit plaintiffs. In these *formalistic* approaches to citizen suit notice, courts often require citizens to explicitly identify all types of violations at issue and, occasionally, all individual violations at issue. Such courts, for example, will reject notice letter language stating that the defendant violated a specific pollutant parameter "on hundreds of occasions" between Date 1 and Date 2. In effect, these courts impose stricter requirements on citizens giving notice 60 days before suit is filed than they impose on plaintiffs filing a complaint, given the federal courts' "notice pleading" standard. *See generally* Robin Kundis Craig, *Notice Letters and Notice Pleading: The Federal Rules of Civil Procedure and the Sufficiency of Environmental Citizen Suit Notice*, 78:1 OREGON LAW REVIEW 105–202 (Spring 1999).

* * *

III. STANDING AND ARTICLE III

The first potential constitutional complexity for citizen suits is ***standing***. Article III of the U.S. Constitution gives federal courts the power to hear only "Cases" or "Controversies." Thus, as a constitutional matter, federal courts are courts of ***limited jurisdiction***. Standing helps the courts to comply with this limitation by requiring the plaintiff have a real and personal stake in the outcome of the litigation. Because standing is a matter of constitutional jurisdiction, moreover, failure to meet the standing requirement results in dismissal of the plaintiff's suit.

In many kinds of litigation, standing is not an issue. For example, in contracts and torts disputes, the plaintiff generally claims to have been directly injured by the defendant and there is a real controversy between them as to their respective fault and liability. Similarly, under federal environmental statutes, ***enforcement actions*** in federal court by the implementing agency do not raise standing issues because the federal government is redressing the injury to the public.

However, the ***citizen suit*** provisions in federal environmental statutes and section 702 of the federal APA could potentially allow "random" third parties—"any person" or "any citizen"—to sue federal agencies and regulated entities for violations of federal environmental laws. For example, a person in Maine might want to sue the EPA about water quality problems in California or sue NMFS about endangered seals in Alaska. Neither the citizen suit provisions nor the APA require the plaintiff to have suffered a traditional kind of injury from the defendant's action; at most, as in the Clean Water Act and section 702 of the APA, they require only that the plaintiff be "adversely affected or aggrieved" by the defendant's action. Thus, both kinds of environmental citizen actions can—and frequently do—raise standing concerns.

A. THE ELEMENTS OF CONSTITUTIONAL STANDING IN ENVIRONMENTAL LAWSUITS

1. The Basic Constitutional Standing Test

The Supreme Court began to issue environmental standing decisions as soon as such suits became possible. Moreover, the Court's environmental standing decisions are almost always split decisions. Justice Scalia, in particular, has argued continuously against the idea of environmental standing. Nevertheless, a majority of Justices have so far been willing to allow environmental standing in certain circumstances. Indeed, as the following case demonstrates, several Justices have been willing to be quite liberal regarding the issue of environmental standing.

SIERRA CLUB v. MORTON

405 U.S. 727 (1972).

Mr. JUSTICE STEWART delivered the opinion of the Court.

I

The Mineral King Valley is an area of great natural beauty nestled in the Sierra Nevada Mountains in Tulare County, California, adjacent to

Sequoia National Park. It has been part of the Sequoia National Forest since 1926, and is designated as a national game refuge by special Act of Congress. Though once the site of extensive mining activity, Mineral King in now used almost exclusively for recreational purposes. Its relative inaccessibility and lack of development have limited the number of visitors each year, and at the same time have preserved the valley's quality as a quasi-wilderness area largely uncluttered by the products of civilization.

The United States Forest Service, which is entrusted with the maintenance and administration of national forests, began in the late 1940's to give consideration to Mineral King as a potential site for recreational development. Prodded by a rapidly increasing demand for skiing facilities, the Forest Service published a prospectus in 1965, inviting bids from private developers for the construction and operation of a ski resort that would also serve as a summer recreation area. The proposal of Walt Disney Enterprises, Inc., was chosen from those of six bidders, and Disney received a three-year permit to conduct surveys and explorations in the valley in connection with its preparation of a complete master plan for the resort.

The final Disney plan, approved by the Forest Service in January 1969, outlines a $35 million complex of motels, restaurants, swimming pools, parking lots, and other structures designed to accommodate 14,000 visitors daily. This complex is to be constructed on 80 acres of the valley floor under a 30–year use permit from the Forest Service. Other facilities, including ski lifts, ski trails, a cog-assisted railway, and utility installations, are to be constructed on the mountain slopes and in other parts of the valley under a revocable special-use permit. To provide access to the resort, the State of California proposes to construct a highway 20 miles in length. A section of this road would traverse Sequoia National Park, as would a proposed high voltage power line needed to provide electricity for the resort. Both the highway and the power line require the approval of the Department of the Interior, which is entrusted with the preservation and maintenance of the national parks.

Representatives of the Sierra Club, who favor maintaining Mineral King largely in its present state, followed the progress of recreational planning for the valley with close attention and increasing dismay. They unsuccessfully sought a public hearing on the proposed development in 1965, and in subsequent correspondence with officials of the Forest Service and the Department of the Interior, they expressed the Club's objections to Disney's plan as a whole and to particular features included in it. In June 1969 the Club filed the present suit in the United States District Court for the Northern District of California, seeking a declaratory judgment that various aspects of the proposed development contravene federal laws and regulations governing the preservation of national parks, forests, and game refuges, and also seeking preliminary and permanent injunctions restraining the federal officials involved from granting their approval or issuing permits in connection with the Mineral King project. The petitioner Sierra Club sued as a membership corporation with "a special interest in the conservation and the sound maintenance of the national parks, game refuges and forests of the country," and invoked the judicial-review provisions of the Administrative Procedure Act, 5 U.S.C. § 701 *et seq.*

Figure 6-3: The Proposed Ski Resort in the Mineral King Valley
National Park Service map.

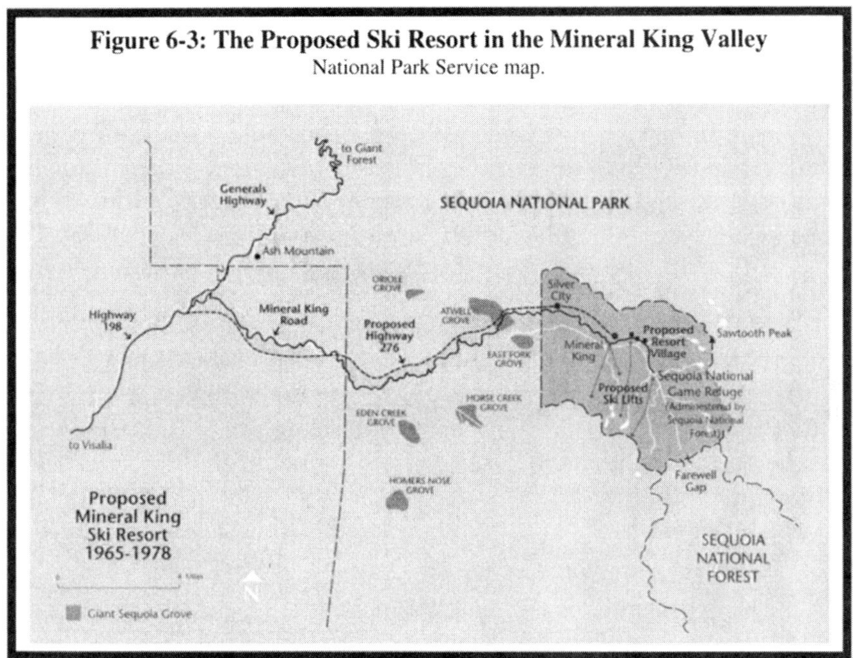

After two days of hearings, the District Court granted the requested preliminary injunction. It rejected the respondents' challenge to the Sierra Club's standing to sue, and determined that the hearing had raised questions "concerning possible excess of statutory authority, sufficiently substantial and serious to justify a preliminary injunction." The respondents appealed, and the Court of Appeals for the Ninth Circuit reversed. With respect to the petitioner's standing, the court noted that there was "no allegation in the complaint that members of the Sierra Club would be affected by the actions of (the respondents) other than the fact that the actions are personally displeasing or distasteful to them," and concluded:

> "We do not believe such club concern without a showing of more direct interest can constitute standing in the legal sense sufficient to challenge the exercise of responsibilities on behalf of all the citizens by two cabinet level officials of the government acting under Congressional and Constitutional authority."

Alternatively, the Court of Appeals held that the Sierra Club had not made an adequate showing of irreparable injury and likelihood of success on the merits to justify issuance of a preliminary injunction. The court thus vacated the injunction. The Sierra Club filed a petition for a writ of certiorari which we granted to review the questions of federal law presented.

II

The first question presented is whether the Sierra Club has alleged facts that entitle it to obtain judicial review of the challenged action. Whether a party has a sufficient stake in an otherwise justiciable controversy to obtain judicial resolution of that controversy is what has traditionally been referred to as the question of standing to sue. Where the party does not rely on any specific statute authorizing invocation of the judicial process, the question of standing depends upon whether the party has alleged such a "personal stake in the outcome of the controversy," *Baker v. Carr*, 369 U.S. 186, 204, as to ensure that "the dispute sought to be adjudicated will be presented in an adversary context and in a form historically viewed as capable of judicial resolution." *Flast v. Cohen*, 392 U.S. 83, 101. Where, however, Congress has authorized public officials to perform certain functions according to law, and has provided by statute for judicial review of those actions under certain circumstances, the inquiry as to standing must begin with a determination of whether the statute in question authorizes review at the behest of the plaintiff.

The Sierra Club relies upon § 10 of the Administrative Procedure Act (APA), 5 U.S.C. § 702, which provides:

> "A person suffering legal wrong because of agency action, or adversely affected or aggrieved by agency action within the meaning of a relevant statute, is entitled to judicial review thereof."

Early decisions under this statute interpreted the language as adopting the various formulations of "legal interest" and "legal wrong" then prevailing as constitutional requirements of standing. But in *Association of Data Processing Service Organizations, Inc. v. Camp*, 397 U.S. 150, and *Barlow v.Collins*, 397 U.S. 159, decided on the same day, we held more broadly that persons had standing to obtain judicial review of federal agency action under § 10 of the APA where they had alleged that the challenged action had caused them "injury in fact," and where the alleged injury was to an interest "arguably within the zone of interests to be protected or regulated" by the statutes that the agencies were claimed to have violated.

* * * [P]alpable economic injuries have long been recognized as sufficient to lay the basis for standing, with or without a specific statutory provision for judicial review. [However, there is still a] question, which has arisen with increasing frequency in federal courts in recent years, as to what must be alleged by persons who claim injury of a noneconomic nature to interests that are widely shared. That question is presented in this case.

III

The injury alleged by the Sierra Club will be incurred entirely by reason of the change in the uses to which Mineral King will be put, and the attendant change in the aesthetics and ecology of the area. Thus, in referring to the road to be built through Sequoia National Park, the complaint alleged that the development "would destroy or otherwise adversely affect the scenery, natural and historic objects and wildlife of the park and would impair the enjoyment of the park for future generations." We do not question that this type of harm may amount to an "injury in fact" sufficient to lay the basis for standing under § 10 of the APA. Aesthetic and environmental well-being, like economic well-being, are important ingredients of the quality of life in our society, and the fact that particular environmental interests are shared by the many rather than the few does not make them less deserving of legal protection through the judicial process. But the "injury in fact" test requires more than an injury to a cognizable interest. It requires that the party seeking review be himself among the injured.

The impact of the proposed changes in the environment of Mineral King will not fall indiscriminately upon every citizen. The alleged injury will be felt directly only by those who use Mineral King and Sequoia National Park, and for whom the aesthetic and recreational values of the area will be lessened by the highway and ski resort. The Sierra Club failed to allege that it or its members would be affected in any of their activities or pastimes by the Disney development. Nowhere in the pleadings or affidavits did the Club state that its members use Mineral King for any purpose, much less that they use it in any way that would be significantly affected by the proposed actions of the respondents.[8]

The Club apparently regarded an allegations of individualized injury as superfluous, on the theory that this was a "public" action involving questions as to the use of natural resources, and that the Club's longstanding concern with and expertise in such matters were sufficient to give it standing as a "representative of the public." This theory reflects a misunderstanding of our cases involving so-called "public actions" in the area of administrative law.

---

8. The only reference in the pleadings to the Sierra Club's interest in the dispute is contained in paragraph 3 of the complaint, which reads in its entirety as follows:

> "Plaintiff Sierra Club is a non-profit corporation organized and operating under the laws of the State of California, with its principal place of business in San Francisco, California since 1892. Membership of the club is approximately 78,000 nationally, with approximately 27,000 members residing in the San Francisco Bay Area. For many years the Sierra Club by its activities and conduct has exhibited a special interest in the conservation and the sound maintenance of the national parks, game refuges and forests of the country, regularly serving as a responsible representative of persons similar interested. One of the principal purposes of the Sierra Club is to protect and conserve the national resources of the Sierra Nevada Mountains. Its interests would be vitally affected by the acts hereinafter described and would be aggrieved by those acts of the defendants as hereinafter more fully appears."

In an *amici curiae* brief filed in this Court by the Wilderness Society and others, it is asserted that the Sierra Club has conducted regular camping trips into the Mineral King area, and that various members of the Club have used and continue to use the area for recreational purposes. These allegations were not contained in the pleadings, nor were they brought to the attention of the Court of Appeals. Moreover, the Sierra Club in its reply brief specifically declines to rely on its individualized interest, as a basis for standing. * * * Our decision does not, of course, bar the Sierra Club from seeking in the District Court to amend its complaint by a motion under Rule 15, Federal Rules of Civil Procedure.

* * * [Under traditional views of standing,] the fact of economic injury is what gives a person standing to seek judicial review under the statute, but once review is properly invoked, that person may argue the public interest in support of his claim that the agency has failed to comply with its statutory mandate. It was in the latter sense that the "standing" * * * existed only as a "representative of the public interest." It is in a similar sense that we have used the phrase "private attorney general" to describe the function performed by persons upon whom Congress has conferred the right to seek judicial review of agency action. *See Data Processing*, *supra*, 397 U.S., at 154.

The trend of cases arising under the APA and other statutes authorizing judicial review of federal agency action has been toward recognizing that injuries other than economic harm are sufficient to bring a person within the meaning of the statutory language, and toward discarding the notion that an injury that is widely shared is *ipso facto* not an injury sufficient to provide the basis for judicial review. We noted this development with approval in *Data Processing*, 397 U.S. at 154, in saying that the interest alleged to have been injured "may reflect 'aesthetic, conservational, and recreational' as well as economic values." But broadening the categories of injury that may be alleged in support of standing is a different matter from abandoning the requirement that the party seeking review must himself have suffered an injury.

* * * [A] mere "interest in a problem," no matter how longstanding the interest and no matter how qualified the organization is in evaluating the problem, is not sufficient by itself to render the organization "adversely affected" or "aggrieved" within the meaning of the APA. The Sierra Club is a large and long-established organization, with a historic commitment to the cause of protecting our Nation's natural heritage from man's depredations. But if a "special interest" in this subject were enough to entitle the Sierra Club to commence this litigation, there would appear to be no objective basis upon which to disallow a suit by any other *bona fide* "special interest" organization however small or short-lived. And if any group with a bona fide "special interest" could initiate such litigation, it is difficult to perceive why any individual citizen with the same *bona fide* special interest would not also be entitled to do so.

The requirement that a party seeking review must allege facts showing that he is himself adversely affected does not insulate executive action from judicial review, nor does it prevent any public interests from being protected through the judicial process. It does serve as at least a rough attempt to put the decision as to whether review will be sought in the hands of those who have a direct stake in the outcome. That goal would be undermined were we to construe the APA to authorize judicial review at the behest of organizations or individuals who seek to do no more than vindicate their own value preferences through the judicial process. The principle that the Sierra Club would have us establish in this case would do just that.

As we conclude that the Court of Appeals was correct in its holding that the Sierra Club lacked standing to maintain this action, we do not reach any other questions presented in the petition, and we intimate no view on the merits of the complaint. The judgment is

Affirmed.

Mr. JUSTICE POWELL and Mr. JUSTICE REHNQUIST took no part in the consideration or decision of this case.

Mr. JUSTICE DOUGLAS, dissenting.

I share the views of my Brother BLACKMUN and would reverse the judgment below.

The critical question of "standing" would be simplified and also put neatly in focus if we fashioned a federal rule that allowed environmental issues to be litigated before federal agencies or federal courts in the name of the inanimate object about to be despoiled, defaced, or invaded by roads and bulldozers and where injury is the subject of public outrage. Contemporary public concern for protecting nature's ecological equilibrium should lead to the conferral of standing upon environmental objects to sue for their own preservation. *See* Stone, *Should Trees Have Standing?—Toward Legal Rights for Natural Objects*, 45 S. CAL. L. REV. 450 (1972). This suit would therefore be more properly labeled as *Mineral King v. Morton*.

Figure 6-4: The Floor of the Mineral King Valley
U.S. Geological Survey photo.

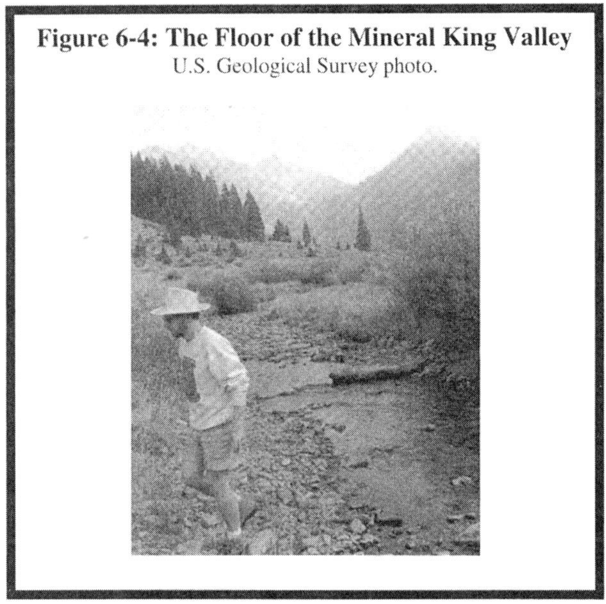

Inanimate objects are sometimes parties in litigation. A ship has a legal personality, a fiction found useful for maritime purposes. The corporation sole—a creature of ecclesiastical law—is an acceptable adversary and large fortunes ride on its cases. The ordinary corporation is a "person" for purposes of the adjudicatory processes, whether it represents proprietary, spiritual, aesthetic, or charitable causes.

So it should be as respects valleys, alpine meadows, rivers, lakes, estuaries, beaches, ridges, proves of trees, swampland, or even air that feels the destructive pressures of modern technology and modern life. The river, for example, is the living symbol of all the life it sustains or nourishes—fish, aquatic insects, water ouzels, otter, fisher, deer, elk, bear, and all other animals, including man, who are dependent on it or who enjoy it for its sight, its sound, or its life. The river as plaintiff speaks for the ecological unit of life that is part of it. Those people who have a meaningful relation to that body of water—whether it be a fisherman, a canoeist, a zoologist, or a logger—must be able to speak for the values which the river represents and which are threatened with destruction. * * *

* * * Those who hike the Appalachian Trail into Sunfish Pond, New Jersey, and camp or sleep there, or run the Allagash in Maine, or climb the Guadalupes in West Texas, or who canoe and portage the Quetico Superior in Minnesota, certainly should have standing to defend those natural wonders before courts or agencies, though they live 3,000 miles away. Those who merely are caught up in environmental news or propaganda and flock to defend these waters or areas may be treated differently. That is why these environmental issues should be tendered by the inanimate object itself. Then there will be assurances that all of the forms of life which it represents will stand before the court—the pileated woodpecker as well as the coyote and bear, the lemmings as well as the trout in the streams. Those inarticulate members of the ecological group cannot speak. But those people who have so frequented the place as to know its values and wonders will be able to speak for the entire ecological community. * * *

Mr. JUSTICE BRENNAN, dissenting.

I agree that the Sierra Club has standing for the reasons stated by my Brother BLACKMUN in Alternative No. 2 of his dissent. I therefore would reach the merits. Since the Court does not do so, however, I simply note agreement with my Brother BLACKMUN that the merits are substantial.

Mr. JUSTICE BLACKMUN, dissenting.

The Court's opinion is a practical one espousing and adhering to traditional notions of standing as somewhat modernized by *Association of Data Processing Service Organizations, Inc. v. Camp*, 397 U.S. 150 (1970); *Barlow v. Collins*, 397 U.S. 159 (1970); and *Flast v. Cohen*, 392 U.S. 83 (1968). If this were an ordinary case, I would join the opinion and the Court's judgment and be quite content.

But this is not ordinary, run-of-the-mill litigation. The case poses—if only we choose to acknowledge and reach them—significant aspects of a wide, growing, and disturbing problem, that is, the Nation's and the world's deteriorating environment with its resulting ecological disturbances. Must our law be so rigid and our procedural concepts so inflexible that we render ourselves helpless when the existing methods and the traditional concepts do not quite fit and do not prove to be entirely adequate for new issues?

* * * Rather than pursue the course the Court has chosen to take by its affirmance of the judgment of the Court of Appeals, I would adopt one of two alternatives:

1. I would reverse that judgment and, instead, approve the judgment of the District Court which recognized standing in the Sierra Club and granted preliminary relief. I would be willing to do this on condition that the Sierra Club forthwith amend its complaint to meet the specifications the Court prescribes for standing. If Sierra Club fails or refuses to take that step, so be it; the case will then collapse. But if it does amend, the merits will be before the trial court once again. As the Court so clearly reveals, the issues on the merits are substantial and deserve resolution. They assay new ground. They are crucial to the future of Mineral King. They raise important ramifications for the quality of the country's public land management. * * *
2. Alternatively, I would permit an imaginative expansion of our traditional concepts of standing in order to enable an organization such as the Sierra Club, possessed, as it is, of pertinent, *bona fide*, and well-recognized attributes and purposes in the area of environment, to litigate environmental issues. * * *

NOTES

1. **The Rest of the Story.** The Sierra Club *did* refile its challenge to the Mineral King development project shortly after the Supreme Court's decision, adding a claim under the National Environmental Policy Act (NEPA), which had not existed at the time the Sierra Club filed its original lawsuit. Tom Turner, Faultline, *Mineral King*, http://www.faultline.org/place/2002/02/mineralking4.html (Feb. 25, 2002). The new NEPA claim proved fatal to the ski resort proposal. The district court judge ordered the Forest Service to complete an EIS. The Forest Service issued the draft EIS in January 1975 and the final EIS in February 1976. *Id.* By this time, "Disney had grown tired of the notoriety the case had generated and pulled out of the project." Earthjustice, *About Us: Our History*, http://www.earthjustice.org/about_us/our_history/index.html (2008). In November 1978, Congress added the Mineral King Valley to the Sequoia National Park through the National Parks and Recreation Act of 1978, Pub. L. 95–625, § 314, 92 Stat. 3467 (Nov. 10, 1978), ending all potential commercial development in the Valley. For a full history of the Valley, including a picture of Justice Douglas's visit, *see* Turner, *supra*.

2. **Theories of Standing.** On what basis did the Sierra Club argue that it had standing in this case? How did the majority conceive of standing? How did Justice Douglas conceive of standing? How did Justice Blackmun conceive of standing? What policy considerations informed each view of environmental standing?

Why did the Sierra Club lose its argument? As the footnotes indicate, the Sierra Club could have easily submitted facts and affidavits that would have guaranteed its standing in this case—and, indeed, several *amici* tried to make such arguments for it. Why would the Sierra Club decline to submit such evidence when it could do so? What was it trying to accomplish?

3. **Species as Plaintiffs.** Recall the Northern Spotted Owl litigation from Chapter 3, related to decisions to list species under the Endangered Species Act. In the Western District of Washington case, the spotted owl itself was the plaintiff. Would the majority accept that such a plaintiff had standing? What or why not? Would the dissenting Justices? Why or why not? This issue recently resurfaced when the Ninth Circuit dismissed an Endangered Species Act case because the named plaintiffs—the cetacean community, a group of whales—lacked standing under both the Endangered Species Act and the APA. *Cetacean Community v. Bush*, 386 F.3d 1169 (9th Cir. 2004).

4. **Organizations as Plaintiffs.** In addition to the injury requirement, the federal courts impose special standing requirements on organizations, like the Sierra Club or Natural Resources Defense Council, that want to pursue environmental litigation. Under the doctrine of ***associational standing*** or ***organization standing***, the organization must show that: (1) at least one member has individual standing; (2) the lawsuit relates to the purposes of the organization; and (3) neither the litigation itself nor the relief provided require the participation of individual plaintiffs, which generally means that the organization is pursuing injunctive and/or declaratory relief, not damages. *See, e.g.*, *Friends of the Earth, Inc. v. Laidlaw Environmental Services (TOC), Inc.*, 528 U.S. 167, 180–81 (2000).

5. ***Sierra Club v. Morton*** **as a Victory?** Despite the fact that the Sierra Club lost its argument in this case, *Sierra Club v. Morton* is generally regarded as a successful standing case for environmental plaintiffs. Can you think of reasons why that might be true?

6. ***Lujan v. National Wildlife Federation.*** *Sierra Club v. Morton* was the main Supreme Court environmental standing case for almost two decades. However, in the 1990s, after the addition of Justice Scalia to the Court, the Supreme Court began to revisit the environmental standing issue. Its first major post-*Morton* decision, *Lujan v. National Wildlife Federation*, 497 U.S. 871 (1990), was an APA challenge to the Bureau of Land Management's decision to open approximately 4500 acres of public lands to mining. The Supreme Court, in an opinion by Justice Scalia, decided that the National Wildlife Federation did not submit sufficient evidence in response to the Government's summary judgment motion to demonstrate that it had standing. Affidavits from National Wildlife Federation members alleged that they used the general area (two million acres) where the mining would occur but failed to specify that they would actually observe the challenged mining. According to the majority, these affidavits did not contain specific enough allegations of injury to survive summary judgment. *Id.* at 885–89. Justices Blackmun, Brennan, Marshall, and Stevens dissented, arguing that the affidavits' allegations that the members' recreational activities had been impaired

created a material issue of fact sufficient to survive summary judgment. *Id.* at 900–04 (J. Blackmun, dissenting).

* * *

In 1992, the Supreme Court again revisited the issue of environmental standing, this time in the context of the Endangered Species Act.

LUJAN v. DEFENDERS OF WILDLIFE

504 U.S. 555 (1992).

JUSTICE SCALIA delivered the opinion of the Court with respect to Parts I, II, III–A, and IV, and an opinion with respect to Part III–B, in which THE CHIEF JUSTICE, JUSTICE WHITE, and JUSTICE THOMAS join.

This case involves a challenge to a rule promulgated by the Secretary of the Interior interpreting § 7 of the Endangered Species Act of 1973 (ESA), 87 Stat. 884, 892, as amended, 16 U.S.C. § 1536, in such fashion as to render it applicable only to actions within the United States or on the high seas. The preliminary issue, and the only one we reach, is whether respondents here, plaintiffs below, have standing to seek judicial review of the rule.

I

The ESA seeks to protect species of animals against threats to their continuing existence caused by man. *See generally TVA v. Hill,* 437 U.S. 153 (1978). The ESA instructs the Secretary of the Interior to promulgate by regulation a list of those species which are either endangered or threatened under enumerated criteria, and to define the critical habitat of these species. 16 U.S.C. §§ 1533, 1536. * * *

In 1978, the Fish and Wildlife Service (FWS) and the National Marine Fisheries Service (NMFS), on behalf of the Secretary of the Interior and the Secretary of Commerce respectively, promulgated a joint regulation stating that the obligations imposed by § 7(a)(2) [of the Act, requiring federal agencies to ensure that their actions do not jeopardize listed species] extend to actions taken in foreign nations. 43 Fed. Reg. 874 (1978). The next year, however, the Interior Department began to reexamine its position. A revised joint regulation, reinterpreting § 7(a)(2) to require consultation only for actions taken in the United States or on the high seas, was proposed in 1983, 48 Fed. Reg. 29990, and promulgated in 1986, 51 Fed. Reg. 19926; 50 CFR 402.01.

Shortly thereafter, respondents, organizations dedicated to wildlife conservation and other environmental causes, filed this action against the Secretary of the Interior, seeking a declaratory judgment that the new regulation is in error as to the geographic scope of § 7(a)(2) and an injunction requiring the Secretary to promulgate a new regulation restoring the initial interpretation. The District Court granted the Secretary's motion to dismiss for lack of standing. The Court of Appeals for the Eighth Circuit reversed by a divided vote. On remand, the Secretary moved for summary judgment on the standing issue, and respondents moved for summary judgment on the merits. The District Court denied the Secretary's motion, on the ground that the Eighth Circuit had already determined the standing question in this case; it granted respondents' merits motion, and ordered the Secretary to publish a revised regulation. The Eighth Circuit affirmed. We granted certiorari.

II

While the Constitution of the United States divides all power conferred upon the Federal Government into "legislative Powers," Art. I, § 1, "[t]he executive Power," Art. II, § 1, and "[t]he judicial Power," Art. III, § 1, it does not attempt to define those terms. To be sure, it limits the jurisdiction of federal courts to "Cases" and "Controversies," but an executive inquiry can bear the name "case" (the Hoffa case) and a legislative dispute can bear the name "controversy" (the Smoot–Hawley controversy). Obviously, then, the Constitution's central mechanism of separation of powers depends largely upon common understanding of what activities are appropriate to legislatures, to executives, and to courts. * * * One of those landmarks, setting apart the "Cases" and "Controversies" that are of the justiciable sort referred to in Article III—"serv[ing] to identify those disputes which are appropriately resolved through the judicial process," *Whitmore v. Arkansas*, 495 U.S. 149, 155 (1990)—is the doctrine of standing. Though some of its elements express merely prudential considerations that are part of judicial self-government, the core component of standing is an essential and unchanging part of the case-or-controversy requirement of Article III.

Over the years, our cases have established that the irreducible constitutional minimum of standing contains three elements. First, the plaintiff must have suffered an "injury in fact"—an invasion of a legally protected interest which is (a) concrete and particularized, *see* [*Allen v. Wright*, 468 U.S. 737,] 756 [(1984)]; *Warth v. Seldin*, 422 U.S. 490, 508 (1975); *Sierra Club v. Morton*, 405 U.S. 727, 740–41, n. 16 (1972); and (b) "actual or imminent, not 'conjectural' or 'hypothetical,' " *Whitmore*, *supra*, 495 U.S. at 155 (quoting *Los Angeles v. Lyons*, 461 U.S. 95, 102 (1983)). Second, there must be a causal connection between the injury and the conduct complained of—the injury has to be "fairly ... trace[able] to the challenged action of the defendant, and not ... th[e] result [of] the independent action of some third party not before the court." *Simon v. Eastern Ky. Welfare Rights Organization*, 426 U.S. 26, 41–42 (1976). Third, it must be "likely," as opposed to merely "speculative," that the injury will be "redressed by a favorable decision." *Id.* at 38, 43.

The party invoking federal jurisdiction bears the burden of establishing these elements. Since they are not mere pleading requirements but rather an indispensable part of the plaintiff's case, each element must be supported in the same way as any other matter on which the plaintiff bears the burden of proof, *i.e.*, with the manner and degree of evidence required at the successive stages of the litigation. At the pleading stage, general factual allegations of injury resulting from the defendant's conduct may suffice, for on a motion to dismiss we "presum[e] that general allegations embrace those specific facts that are necessary to support the claim." *National Wildlife Federation*, *supra*, 497 U.S. at 889. In response to a summary judgment motion, however, the plaintiff can no longer rest on such "mere allegations," but must "set forth" by affidavit or other evidence "specific facts," FED. RULE CIV. PROC. 56(e), which for purposes of the summary judgment motion will be taken to be true. And at the final stage, those facts (if controverted) must be "supported adequately by the evidence adduced at trial." *Gladstone*, *supra*, 441 U.S., at 115, n.31. * * *

III

We think the Court of Appeals failed to apply the foregoing principles in denying the Secretary's motion for summary judgment. Respondents had not made the requisite demonstration of (at least) injury and redressability.

A

Respondents' claim to injury is that the lack of consultation with respect to certain funded activities abroad "increas[es] the rate of extinction of endangered and threatened species." Of course, the desire to use or observe an animal species, even for purely esthetic purposes, is undeniably a cognizable interest for purpose of standing. *See*, *e.g.*, *Sierra Club v. Morton*, 405 U.S. at 734. "But the 'injury in fact' test requires more than an injury to a cognizable interest. It requires that the party seeking review be himself among the injured." *Id.*, at 734–735. To survive the Secretary's summary judgment motion, respondents had to submit affidavits or other evidence showing, through specific facts, not only that listed species were in fact being threatened by funded activities abroad, but also that one or more of respondents' members would thereby be "directly" affected apart from their " 'special interest' in th[e] subject." *Id.*, at 735, 739.

With respect to this aspect of the case, the Court of Appeals focused on the affidavits of two Defenders' members—Joyce Kelly and Amy Skilbred. Ms. Kelly stated that she traveled to Egypt in 1986 and "observed the traditional habitat of the endangered Nile crocodile there and intend[s] to do so again, and hope[s] to observe the crocodile directly," and that she "will suffer harm in fact as the result of [the] American . . . role . . . in overseeing the rehabilitation of the Aswan High Dam on the Nile . . . and [in] develop[ing] . . . Egypt's . . . Master Water Plan." Skilbred averred that she traveled to Sri Lanka in 1981 and "observed th[e] habitat" of "endangered species such as the Asian elephant and the leopard" at what is now the site of the Mahaweli project funded by the Agency for International Development (AID), although she "was unable to see any of the endangered species"; "this development project," she continued, "will seriously reduce endangered, threatened, and endemic species habitat including areas that I visited . . . [, which] may severely shorten the future of these species"; that threat, she concluded, harmed her because she "intend[s] to return to Sri Lanka in the future and hope[s] to be more fortunate in spotting at least the endangered elephant and leopard." When Ms. Skilbred was asked at a subsequent deposition if and when she had any plans to return to Sri Lanka, she reiterated that "I intend to go back to Sri Lanka," but confessed that she had no current plans: "I don't know [when]. There is a civil war going on right now. I don't know. Not next year, I will say. In the future."

Figure 6-5: Asian Elephant
U.S. Fish & Wildlife Service photo.

We shall assume for the sake of argument that these affidavits contain facts showing that certain agency-funded projects threaten listed species—though that is questionable. They plainly contain no facts, however, showing how damage to the species will produce "imminent" injury to Mses. Kelly and Skilbred. That the women "had visited" the areas of the projects before the projects commenced proves nothing. As we have said in a related context, " 'Past exposure to illegal conduct does not in itself show a present case or controversy regarding injunctive relief . . . if unaccompanied by any continuing, present adverse effects.' " *Lyons*, 461 U.S., at 102 (quoting *O'Shea v. Littleton*, 414 U.S. 488, 495–496 (1974)). And the affiants' profession of an "inten[t]" to return to the places they had visited before—where they will presumably, this time, be deprived of the opportunity to observe animals of the endangered species—is simply not enough. Such "some day" intentions—without any description of concrete plans, or indeed even any specification of *when* the some day will be—do not support a finding of the "actual or imminent" injury that our cases require.

Besides relying upon the Kelly and Skilbred affidavits, respondents propose a series of novel standing theories. The first, inelegantly styled "ecosystem nexus," proposes that any person who uses *any part* of a "contiguous ecosystem" adversely affected by a funded activity has standing even if the activity is located a great distance away. This approach, as the Court of Appeals correctly observed, is inconsistent with our opinion in *National Wildlife Federation,* which held that a plaintiff claiming injury from environmental damage must use the area affected by the challenged activity and not an area roughly "in the vicinity" of it. 497 U.S. at 887–889; *see also Sierra Club*, 405 U.S., at 735. It makes no difference that the general-purpose section of the ESA states that the Act was intended in part "to provide a means whereby the ecosystems upon which endangered species and threatened species depend may be conserved," 16 U.S.C. § 1531(b). To say that the Act protects ecosystems is not to say that the Act creates (if it were possible) rights of action in persons who have not been injured in fact, that is, persons who use portions of an ecosystem not perceptibly affected by the unlawful action in question.

Respondents' other theories are called, alas, the "animal nexus" approach, whereby anyone who has an interest in studying or seeing the endangered animals anywhere on the globe has standing; and the "vocational nexus" approach, under which anyone with a professional interest in such animals can sue. Under these theories, anyone who goes to see Asian elephants in the Bronx Zoo, and anyone who is a keeper of Asian elephants in the Bronx Zoo, has standing to sue because the Director of the Agency for International Development (AID) did not consult with the Secretary regarding the AID-funded project in Sri Lanka. This is beyond all reason. Standing is not "an ingenious academic exercise in the conceivable," *United States v. Students Challenging Regulatory Agency Procedures (SCRAP)*, 412 U.S. 669, 688 (1973), but as we have said requires, at the summary judgment stage, a factual showing of perceptible harm. It is clear that the person who observes or works with a particular animal threatened by a federal decision is facing perceptible harm, since the very subject of his interest will no longer exist. It is even plausible—though it goes to the outermost limit of plausibility—to think that a person who observes or works with animals of a particular species in the very area of the world where that species is threatened by a federal decision is facing such harm, since some animals that might have been the subject of his interest will no longer exist. It goes beyond the limit, however, and into pure speculation and fantasy, to say that anyone who observes or works with an endangered species, anywhere in the world, is appreciably harmed by a single project affecting some portion of that species with which he has no more specific connection.

B

Besides failing to show injury, respondents failed to demonstrate redressability. Instead of attacking the separate decisions to fund particular projects allegedly causing them harm, respondents chose to challenge a more generalized level of Government action (rules regarding consultation), the invalidation of which would affect all overseas projects. This programmatic approach has obvious practical advantages, but also obvious difficulties insofar as proof of causation or redressability is concerned. As we have said in another context, "suits challenging, not specifically identifiable Government violations of law, but the particular programs agencies establish to carry out their legal obligations . . . [are], even when premised on allegations of several instances of violations of law, . . . rarely if ever appropriate for federal-court adjudication." *Allen*, 468 U.S., at 759–760.

The most obvious problem in the present case is redressability. Since the agencies funding the projects were not parties to the case, the District Court could accord relief only against the Secretary: He could be ordered to revise his regulation to require consultation for foreign projects. But this would not remedy respondents' alleged injury unless the funding agencies were bound by the Secretary's regulation, which is very much an open question. * * *

Respondents assert that this legal uncertainty did not affect redressability (and hence standing) because the District Court itself could resolve the issue of the Secretary's authority as a necessary part of its standing inquiry. Assuming that it is appropriate to resolve an issue of law such as this in connection with a threshold standing inquiry, resolution by the District Court would not have remedied respondents' alleged injury anyway, because it would not have been binding upon the agencies. They were not parties to the suit, and there is no reason they should be obliged to honor an incidental legal determination the suit produced. The Court of Appeals tried to finesse this problem by simply proclaiming that "[w]e are satisfied that an injunction requiring the Secretary to publish [respondents' desired] regulatio[n] . . . would result in consultation." *Defenders of Wildlife*, 851 F.2d, at 1042, 1043–1044. We do not know what would justify that confidence, particularly when the Justice Department (presumably after consultation with the agencies) has taken the position that the regulation is not binding. The short of the matter is that redress of the only injury in fact respondents complain of requires action (termination of funding until consultation) by the individual funding agencies; and any relief the District Court could have provided in this suit against the Secretary was not likely to produce that action.

A further impediment to redressability is the fact that the agencies generally supply only a fraction of the funding for a foreign project. AID, for example, has provided less than 10% of the funding for the Mahaweli project. Respondents have produced nothing to indicate that the projects they have named will either be suspended, or do less harm to listed species, if that fraction is eliminated. [I]t is entirely conjectural whether the nonagency activity that affects respondents will be altered or affected by the agency activity they seek to achieve. There is no standing. * * *

NOTES

1. **The Elements of Constitutional Standing for Individuals and Defenders of Wildlife's Standing.** What are the three elements of constitutional standing, according to the majority of Supreme Court Justices? Which of those elements did Defenders of Wildlife fail? Why?

2. **Civil Procedure and Proof of Standing.** The majority in *Defenders of Wildlife* explicitly connected proof of standing to the various stages of litigation—motions to dismiss, motions for summary judgment, trial. At what stage of litigation did the standing challenge come in this case? How did that stage affect Defenders of Wildlife's burden of proof regarding standing? What did the majority demand in terms of proof of standing? Why weren't the submitted affidavits good enough, according to the majority? Given what you know about civil procedure, do you agree? Why or why not?

* * *

The U.S. Supreme Court's most recent discussion of environmental standing was its 2009 decision in *Summers v. Earth Island Institute.* As you read that decision, think about the different approaches of the majority and the dissent. Was standing the right ground on which to decide this case? Or, for students who have taken administrative law, did this case really involve a ripeness issue? As a matter of litigation strategy after this case, should an environmental citizen suit plaintiff EVER settle the one live controversy if there are larger issues at stake?

SUMMERS v. EARTH ISLAND INSTITUTE

555 U.S. 488 (2009).

SCALIA, J., delivered the opinion of the Court, in which ROBERTS, C.J., and KENNEDY, THOMAS, and ALITO, JJ., joined. KENNEDY, J., filed a concurring opinion. BREYER, J., filed a dissenting opinion, in which STEVENS, SOUTER, and GINSBURG, JJ., joined.

Respondents are a group of organizations dedicated to protecting the environment. (We will refer to them collectively as "Earth Island.") They seek to prevent the United States Forest Service from enforcing regulations that exempt small fire-rehabilitation and timber-salvage projects from the notice, comment, and appeal process used by the Forest Service for more significant land management decisions. We must determine whether respondents have standing to challenge the regulations in the absence of a live dispute over a concrete application of those regulations.

I

In 1992, Congress enacted the Forest Service Decisionmaking and Appeals Reform Act (Appeals Reform Act or Act), Pub. L. 102–381, Tit. III, § 322, 106 Stat. 1419, note following 16 U.S.C. § 1612. Among other things, this required the Forest Service to establish a notice, comment, and appeal process for "proposed actions of the Forest Service concerning projects and activities implementing land and resource management plans developed under the Forest and Rangeland Renewable Resources Planning Act of 1974." *Ibid.*

The Forest Service's regulations implementing the Act provided that certain of its procedures would not be applied to projects that the Service considered categorically excluded from the requirement to file an environmental impact statement (EIS) or environmental assessment (EA). 36 CFR §§ 215.4(a) (notice and comment), 215.12(f) (appeal) (2008). Later amendments to the Forest Service's manual of implementing procedures, adopted by rule after notice and comment, provided that fire-rehabilitation activities on areas of less than 4,200 acres, and salvage-timber sales of 250 acres or less, did not cause a significant environmental impact and thus would be categorically exempt from the requirement to file an EIS or EA. This had the effect of excluding these projects from the notice, comment, and appeal process.

In the summer of 2002, fire burned a significant area of the Sequoia National Forest. In September 2003, the Service issued a decision memo approving the Burnt Ridge Project, a salvage sale of timber on 238 acres damaged by that fire. Pursuant to its categorical exclusion of salvage sales of less than 250 acres, the Forest Service did not provide notice in a form consistent with the Appeals Reform Act, did not provide a period of public comment, and did not make an appeal process available.

In December 2003, respondents filed a complaint in the Eastern District of California, challenging the failure of the Forest Service to apply to the Burnt Ridge Project § 215.4(a) of its regulations implementing the Appeals Reform Act (requiring prior notice and comment), and § 215.12(f) of the regulations (setting forth an appeal procedure). * * *

The District Court granted a preliminary injunction against the Burnt Ridge salvage-timber sale. Soon thereafter, the parties settled their dispute over the Burnt Ridge Project and the District Court concluded that "the Burnt Ridge timber sale is not at issue in this case." The Government argued that, with the Burnt Ridge dispute settled, and with no other project before the court in which respondents were threatened with injury in fact, respondents lacked standing to challenge the regulations; and that absent a concrete dispute over a particular project a challenge to the regulations would not be ripe. The District Court proceeded, however, to adjudicate the merits of Earth Island's challenges. It invalidated five of the regulations * * * and entered a nationwide injunction against their application.

The Ninth Circuit * * * affirmed * * * the District Court's determination that §§ 215.4(a) and 215.12(f), which were applicable to the Burnt Ridge Project, were contrary to law, and upheld the nationwide injunction against their application.

The Government sought review of the question whether Earth Island could challenge the regulations at issue in the Burnt Ridge Project, and if so whether a nationwide injunction was appropriate relief. We granted certiorari.

II

In limiting the judicial power to "Cases" and "Controversies," Article III of the Constitution restricts it to the traditional role of Anglo-American courts, which is to redress or prevent actual or imminently threatened injury to persons caused by private or official violation of law. Except when necessary in the execution of that function, courts have no charter to review and revise legislative and executive action. * * *

The doctrine of standing is one of several doctrines that reflect this fundamental limitation. It requires federal courts to satisfy themselves that "the plaintiff has 'alleged such a personal stake in the outcome of the controversy' as to warrant *his* invocation of federal-court jurisdiction." He bears the burden of showing that he has standing for each type of relief sought. To seek injunctive relief, a plaintiff must show that he is under threat of suffering "injury in fact" that is concrete and particularized; the threat must be actual and imminent, not conjectural or hypothetical; it must be fairly traceable to the challenged action of the defendant; and it must be likely that a favorable judicial decision will prevent or redress the injury. *Friends of Earth, Inc. v. Laidlaw Environmental Services (TOC), Inc.,* 528 U.S. 167, 180–181 (2000). This requirement assures that "there is a real need to exercise the power of judicial review in order to protect the interests of the complaining party," *Schlesinger v. Reservists Comm. to Stop the War,* 418 U.S. 208, 221 (1974). Where that need does not exist, allowing courts to oversee legislative or executive action "would significantly alter the allocation of power . . . away from a democratic form of government[.]"

The regulations under challenge here neither require nor forbid any action on the part of respondents. The standards and procedures that they prescribe for Forest Service appeals govern only the conduct of Forest Service officials engaged in project planning. "[W]hen the plaintiff is not himself the object of the government action or inaction he challenges, standing is not precluded, but it is ordinarily 'substantially more difficult' to establish." Here, respondents can demonstrate standing only if application of the regulations by the Government will affect *them* in the manner described above.

It is common ground that the respondent organizations can assert the standing of their members. To establish the concrete and particularized injury that standing requires, respondents point to their members' recreational interests in the National Forests. While generalized harm to the forest or the environment will not alone support standing, if that harm in fact affects the recreational or even the mere esthetic interests of the plaintiff, that will suffice. *Sierra Club v. Morton,* 405 U.S. 727, 734–736 (1972).

Affidavits submitted to the District Court alleged that organization member Ara Marderosian had repeatedly visited the Burnt Ridge site, that he had imminent plans to do so again, and that his interests in viewing the flora and fauna of the area would be harmed if the Burnt Ridge Project went forward without incorporation of the ideas he would have suggested if the Forest Service had provided him an opportunity to comment. The Government concedes this was sufficient to establish Article III standing with respect to Burnt Ridge. Marderosian's threatened injury with regard to that project was originally one of the bases for the present suit. After the District Court had issued a preliminary injunction, however, the parties settled their differences on that score. Marderosian's injury in fact with regard to that project has been remedied, and it is, as the District Court pronounced, "not at issue in this case." We know of no precedent for the proposition that when a plaintiff has sued to challenge the lawfulness of certain action or threatened action but has settled that suit, he retains standing to challenge the basis for that action (here, the regulation in the abstract), apart from any concrete application that threatens imminent harm to his interests. Such a holding would fly in the face of Article III's injury-in-fact requirement.

Respondents have identified no other application of the invalidated regulations that threatens imminent and concrete harm to the interests of their members. The only other affidavit relied on was that of Jim Bensman. He asserted, first, that he had suffered injury in the past from development on Forest Service land. That does not suffice for several reasons: because it was not tied to application of the challenged regulations, because it does not identify any particular site, and because it relates to past injury rather than imminent future injury that is sought to be enjoined.

Bensman's affidavit further asserts that he has visited many National Forests and plans to visit several unnamed National Forests in the future. Respondents describe this as a mere failure to "provide the name of each timber sale that affected [Bensman's] interests[.]" It is much more (or much less) than that. It is a failure to allege that *any* particular timber sale or other project claimed to be unlawfully subject to the regulations will impede a specific and concrete plan of Bensman's to enjoy the National Forests. The National Forests occupy more than 190 million acres, an area larger than Texas. There may be a chance, but is hardly a likelihood, that Bensman's wanderings will bring him to a parcel about to be affected by a project unlawfully subject to the regulations. Indeed, without further specification it is impossible to tell *which* projects are (in respondents' view) unlawfully subject to the regulations. * * * Here we are asked to assume not only that Bensman will stumble across a project tract unlawfully subject to the regulations, but also that the tract is about to be developed by the Forest Service in a way that harms his recreational interests, and that he would have commented on the project but for the regulation. Accepting an intention to visit the National Forests as adequate to confer standing to challenge any Government action affecting any portion of those forests would be tantamount to eliminating the requirement of concrete, particularized injury in fact.

The Bensman affidavit does refer specifically to a series of projects in the Allegheny National Forest that are subject to the challenged regulations. It does not assert, however, any firm intention to visit their locations, saying only that Bensman " 'want[s] to' " go there. This vague desire to return is insufficient to satisfy the requirement of imminent injury: "Such 'some day' intentions—without any description of concrete plans, or indeed any specification of *when* the some day will be—do not support a finding of the 'actual or imminent' injury that our cases require." *Defenders of Wildlife,* 504 U.S., at 564.

Respondents argue that they have standing to bring their challenge because they have suffered procedural injury, namely that they have been denied the ability to file comments on some Forest Service actions and will continue to be so denied. But deprivation of a procedural right without some concrete interest that is affected by the deprivation—a procedural right *in vacuo*—is insufficient to create Article III standing. Only a "person who has been accorded a procedural right to protect *his concrete interests* can assert that right without meeting all the normal standards for redressability and immediacy." *Id.,* at 572 n.7 (emphasis added). Respondents alleged such injury in their challenge to the Burnt Ridge Project, claiming that but for the allegedly unlawful abridged procedures they would have been able to oppose the project that threatened to impinge on their concrete plans to observe nature in that specific area. But Burnt Ridge is now off the table.

It makes no difference that the procedural right has been accorded by Congress. That can loosen the strictures of the redressability prong of our standing inquiry—so that standing existed with regard to the Burnt Ridge Project, for example, despite the possibility that Earth Island's allegedly guaranteed right to comment would not be successful in persuading the Forest Service to avoid impairment of Earth Island's concrete interests. Unlike redressability, however, the requirement of injury in fact is a hard floor of Article III jurisdiction that cannot be removed by statute. * * *

III

The dissent proposes a hitherto unheard-of test for organizational standing: whether, accepting the organization's self-description of the activities of its members, there is a statistical probability that some of those members are threatened with concrete injury. Since, for example, the Sierra Club asserts in its pleadings that it has more than " '700,000 members nationwide, including thousands of members in California' " who " 'use and enjoy the Sequoia National Forest,' " it is probable (according to the dissent) that some (unidentified) members have planned to visit some (unidentified) small parcels affected by the Forest Service's procedures and will suffer (unidentified) concrete harm as a result. This novel approach to the law of organizational standing would make a mockery of our prior cases, which have required plaintiff-organizations to make specific allegations establishing that at least one identified member had suffered or would suffer harm. * * *

* * * A major problem with the dissent's approach is that it accepts the organizations' self-descriptions of their membership, on the simple ground that "no one denies" them. But it is well established that the court has an independent obligation to assure that standing exists, regardless of whether it is challenged by any of the parties. Without individual affidavits, how is the court to assure itself that the Sierra Club, for

example, has " 'thousands of members' " who " 'use and enjoy the Sequoia National Forest' "? And, because to establish standing plaintiffs must show that they "use the area affected by the challenged activity and not an area roughly in the vicinity of" a project site, *Defenders of Wildlife,* 504 U.S., at 566 (internal quotation marks omitted), how is the court to assure itself that some of these members plan to make use of the specific sites upon which projects may take place? Or that these same individuals will find their recreation burdened by the Forest Service's use of the challenged procedures? While it is certainly possible—perhaps even likely—that one individual will meet all of these criteria, that speculation does not suffice. "Standing," we have said, "is not 'an ingenious academic exercise in the conceivable' ... [but] requires ... a factual showing of perceptible harm." *Ibid.* In part because of the difficulty of verifying the facts upon which such probabilistic standing depends, the Court has required plaintiffs claiming an organizational standing to identify members who have suffered the requisite harm—surely not a difficult task here, when so many thousands are alleged to have been harmed.

The dissent would have us replace the requirement of " 'imminent' " harm, which it acknowledges our cases establish, with the requirement of " 'a *realistic* threat' that reoccurrence of the challenged activity would cause [the plaintiff] harm 'in the reasonably near future[.]' " That language is taken, of course, from an opinion that did *not* find standing, so the seeming expansiveness of the test made not a bit of difference. The problem for the dissent is that the timely affidavits no more meet that requirement than they meet the usual formulation. They fail to establish that the affiants' members will *ever* visit one of the small parcels at issue. * * *

* * *

Since we have resolved this case on the ground of standing, we need not reach the Government's contention that plaintiffs have not demonstrated that the regulations are ripe for review under the Administrative Procedure Act. We likewise do not reach the question whether, if respondents prevailed, a nationwide injunction would be appropriate. And we do not disturb the dismissal of respondents' challenge to the remaining regulations, which has not been appealed.

The judgment of the Court of Appeals is reversed in part and affirmed in part.

It is so ordered.

JUSTICE BREYER, with whom JUSTICE STEVENS, JUSTICE SOUTER, and JUSTICE GINSBURG join, dissenting.

The Court holds that the Sierra Club and its members (along with other environmental organizations) do not suffer any " 'concrete injury' " when the Forest Service sells timber for logging on "many thousands" of small (250-acre or less) woodland parcels without following legally required procedures—procedures which, if followed, could lead the Service to cancel or to modify the sales. Nothing in the record or the law justifies this counterintuitive conclusion.

I

A

The plaintiffs, respondents in this case, are five environmental organizations. The Earth Island Institute, a California organization, has over 15,000 members in the United States, over 3,000 of whom "use and enjoy the National Forests of California for recreational, educational, aesthetic, spiritual and other purposes." The Sequoia ForestKeeper, a small organization, has "100 plus" members who "use the forests of the Southern Sierra Nevada for activities such as hiking, bird and animal watching, aesthetic enjoyment, quiet contemplation, fishing and scientific study." Heartwood, Inc., located in Illinois and Indiana, is a coalition of environmental organizations with "members" who "continually use the National Forests for the purposes of ecological health, recreation, aesthetic enjoyment, and other purposes." The Center for Biological Diversity, located in Arizona, California, New Mexico, and Washington, has over 5,000 members who "use Forest Service lands," and who are "dedicated to the preservation, protection, and restoration of biological diversity, native species and ecosystems in the Western United States and elsewhere." The Sierra Club has more than "700,000 members nationwide, including thousands of members in California" who "use and enjoy the Sequoia National Forest," for "outdoor recreation and scientific study of various kinds, including nature study, bird-watching, photography, fishing, canoeing, hunting, backpacking, camping, solitude, and a variety of other activities."

These five organizations point to a federal law that says the Forest Service "shall establish a notice and comment process," along with a procedure for filing administrative "appeals," for "proposed actions ... concerning projects and activities implementing land and resource management plans.... " § 322, 106 Stat. 1419, note following 16 U.S.C. § 1612. They add that the Service has exempted from "notice, comment, and appeal" processes its decisions that allow, among other things, salvage-timber sales on burned forest lands of less than 250 acres in size. And they claim that the Service's refusal to provide notice, comment, and appeal procedures violates the statute.

B

The majority says that the plaintiffs lack *constitutional* standing to raise this claim. It holds that the dispute between the five environmental groups and the Forest Service consists simply of an abstract challenge; it does not amount to the concrete "Cas[e]" or "Controvers[y]" that the Constitution grants federal courts the power to resolve. I cannot agree that this is so.

To understand the *constitutional* issue that the majority decides, it may prove helpful to imagine that Congress enacted a *statutory* provision that expressly permitted environmental groups like the respondents here to bring cases just like the present one, provided (1) that the group has members who have used salvage-timber parcels in the past and are likely to do so in the future, and (2) that the group's members have opposed Forest Service timber sales in the past (using notice, comment, and appeal procedures to do so) and will likely use those procedures to oppose salvage-timber sales in the future. The majority cannot, and does not, claim that such a statute would be unconstitutional. See *Massachusetts v. EPA,* 549 U.S. 497, 516–518 (2007); *Sierra Club v. Morton,* 405 U.S. 727, 734–738 (1972). How then can it find the present case constitutionally unauthorized?

* * * II

How can the majority credibly claim that salvage-timber sales, and similar projects, are unlikely to harm the asserted interests of the members of these environmental groups? The majority apparently does so in part by arguing that the Forest Service actions are not "imminent"—a requirement more appropriately considered in the context of ripeness or the necessity of injunctive relief. I concede that the Court has sometimes used the word "imminent" in the context of constitutional standing. But it has done so primarily to emphasize that the harm in question—the harm that was not "imminent"—was merely "conjectural" or "hypothetical" or otherwise speculative. *Lujan v. Defenders of Wildlife,* 504 U.S. 555, 560 (1992). Where the Court has directly focused upon the matter, *i.e.,* where, as here, a plaintiff has *already* been subject to the injury it wishes to challenge, the Court has asked whether there is a *realistic likelihood* that the challenged future conduct will, in fact, recur and harm the plaintiff. * * * Precedent nowhere suggests that the "realistic threat" standard contains identification requirements more stringent than the word "realistic" implies.

* * * [A] threat of future harm may be realistic even where the plaintiff cannot specify precise times, dates, and GPS coordinates. Thus, we recently held that Massachusetts has *standing* to complain of a procedural failing, namely, EPA's failure properly to determine whether to restrict carbon dioxide emissions, even though that failing would create Massachusetts-based harm which (though likely to occur) might not occur for several decades.

The Forest Service admits that it intends to conduct thousands of further salvage-timber sales and other projects exempted under the challenged regulations "in the reasonably near future." How then can the Court deny that the plaintiffs have shown a "realistic" threat that the Forest Service will continue to authorize (without the procedures claimed necessary) salvage-timber sales, and other Forest Service projects, that adversely affect the recreational, aesthetic, and environmental interests of the plaintiffs' members?

Consider: Respondents allege, and the Government has conceded, that the Forest Service took wrongful actions (such as selling salvage timber) "thousands" of times in the two years prior to suit. The Complaint alleges, and no one denies, that the organizations, the Sierra Club for example, have hundreds of thousands of members who use forests regularly across the Nation for recreational, scientific, aesthetic, and environmental purposes. The Complaint further alleges, and no one denies, that these organizations (and their members), believing that actions such as salvage-timber sales harm those interests, regularly oppose salvage-timber sales (and similar actions) in proceedings before the agency. And the Complaint alleges, and no one denies, that the organizations intend to continue to express their opposition to such actions in those proceedings in the future. * * *

* * *

I recognize that the Government raises other claims and bases upon which to deny standing or to hold that the case is not ripe for adjudication. I believe that these arguments are without merit. But because the majority does not discuss them here, I shall not do so either.

With respect, I dissent.

NOTES

1. **Standing Under What Test, Precisely?** The *Summers* majority mainly applies the analysis from *Lujan v. Defenders of Wildlife*, while the dissent relies more heavily on other cases, such as *Sierra Club v. Morton* and *Massachusetts v. EPA*, which you will read in the next section on state standing. What does that fact suggest about the Supreme Court's standing cases? Has standing really become a lawyer's game? Consider at the end of this chapter whether you can fully reconcile all of the Supreme Court's decisions regarding environmental standing.

With respect to *Summers*, should the plaintiffs have settled the part of the case involving the Burnt Ridge Project? Why or why not? What did that settlement do to the plaintiffs' standing for the rest of the case? Does *Summers* therefore create perverse incentives against settlement when plaintiffs are trying to challenge programmatic agency decisions that they believe are illegal? Why or why not?

2. **Agency Illegality and Citizen Suits.** Like *Sierra Club v. Morton*, *Summers* raised the possibility that a federal agency could act completely illegally and no one would have standing to check that illegality. Is that possibility ever likely to become a reality? Consider that in *Sierra Club v. Morton*, the Sierra Club could have easily found members to establish standing, even under the later *Lujan* test. What about here? Who would have standing to challenge the Forest Service's rulemaking, and when?

3. **Probabilistic Standing and the Problem of *Risk* of Harm.** Notice that the majority in *Summers* characterizes the dissent as allowing

statistical probabilities of harm qualify as sufficient injury-in-fact to qualify for standing, and it dismisses that argument. Why? Why does the majority consider probabilistic standing arguments to be problematic? Why does the dissent support them—or does it?

Lujan itself noted that the plaintiff's injury-in-fact does not have to be actual—it can be imminent. But there is a deeper issue here than just imminence. Like aesthetic and recreational injuries in *Sierra Club v. Morton*, risk of harm raises the more basic question of what counts as a injury-in-fact. Suppose, for example, that a RCRA TSD facility mishandles hazardous waste in a way that exposes people in the surrounding neighborhood to a carcinogen. As a result, those people are now 10,000 times more likely to develop a particular kind of liver cancer than the general population. Have the neighbors suffered an injury-in-fact simply because of the significantly increased risk of liver cancer? Tort law, under the subheading of toxic torts litigation, has wrestled with this problem in the *liability* context, which arguably poses more difficult public policy issues. In contrast, increased risk and probabilistic harm in the standing context merely gives the potential plaintiff a basic right to be in federal court, and lower federal courts have been increasingly tolerant of such arguments.

Consider this issue again when you read *Massachusetts v. EPA* in the next section and *Friends of the Earth v. Laidlaw Environmental Services* in Part V.

* * *

2. Standing for States

Most environmental citizen suit provisions allow states to use those provisions to sue alleged violators and the federal government. For example, the Clean Water Act's citizen suit provision states that "any *citizen* may commence a civil action. . . ." CWA § 505(a), 33 U.S.C. § 1365(a) (emphasis added). That provision then goes on to define "citizen" to mean "a *person* or persons having an interest which is or may be adversely affected." CWA § 505(g), 33 U.S.C. § 1365(g) (emphasis added). The Act explicitly defines "person" to include a "State." CWA § 502(5), 33 U.S.C. § 1362(5). Therefore, states may bring their own citizen suits.

However, as you've seen in many contexts in your study of environmental law, states have special status in federal environmental law, and principles of constitutional federalism and statutory cooperative federalism can be very important to courts' decisions regarding the proper implementation of the statutes. Do federalism concerns extend to standing? Should states have special status in federal courts when they sue to protect their environmental and natural resource interests? Consider the U.S. Supreme Court's treatment of state standing in *Massachusetts v. EPA*, the merits of which were covered in Chapter 4.

MASSACHUSETTS v. ENVIRONMENTAL PROTECTION AGENCY

549 U.S. 497 (2007).

STEVENS, J., delivered the opinion of the Court, in which KENNEDY, SOUTER, GINSBURG, and BREYER, JJ., joined.

* * * Calling global warming "the most pressing environmental challenge of our time," a group of States,[2] local governments,[3] and private organizations,[4] alleged in a petition for certiorari that the Environmental Protection Agency (EPA) has abdicated its responsibility under the Clean Air Act to regulate the emissions of four greenhouse gases, including carbon dioxide. * * * In response, EPA, supported by 10 intervening States[5] and six trade associations,[6] correctly argued that we may not address those two questions unless at least one petitioner has standing to invoke our jurisdiction under Article III of the Constitution. * * *

* * * II

On October 20, 1999, a group of 19 private organizations[15] filed a rulemaking petition asking EPA to regulate "greenhouse gas emissions from new motor vehicles under § 202 of the Clean Air Act." * * * The petition further alleged that climate change will have serious adverse effects on human health and the environment. * * * On September 8, 2003, EPA entered an order denying the rulemaking petition. 68 Fed. Reg. 52922. * * *

III

Petitioners, now joined by intervenor States and local governments, sought review of EPA's order in the United States Court of Appeals for the District of Columbia Circuit. Although each of the three judges on the panel wrote a separate opinion, two judges agreed "that the EPA Adminis-

2. California, Connecticut, Illinois, Maine, Massachusetts, New Jersey, New Mexico, New York, Oregon, Rhode Island, Vermont, and Washington.

3. District of Columbia, American Samoa, New York City, and Baltimore.

4. Center for Biological Diversity, Center for Food Safety, Conservation Law Foundation, Environmental Advocates, Environmental Defense, Friends of the Earth, Greenpeace, International Center for Technology Assessment, National Environmental Trust, Natural Resources Defense Council, Sierra Club, Union of Concerned Scientists, and U.S. Public Interest Research Group.

5. Alaska, Idaho, Kansas, Michigan, Nebraska, North Dakota, Ohio, South Dakota, Texas, and Utah.

6. Alliance of Automobile Manufacturers, National Automobile Dealers Association, Engine Manufacturers Association, Truck Manufacturers Association, CO2 Litigation Group, and Utility Air Regulatory Group.

15. Alliance for Sustainable Communities; Applied Power Technologies, Inc.; Bio Fuels America; The California Solar Energy Industries Assn.; Clements Environmental Corp.; Environmental Advocates; Environmental and Energy Study Institute; Friends of the Earth; Full Circle Energy Project, Inc.; The Green Party of Rhode Island; Greenpeace USA; International Center for Technology Assessment; Network for Environmental and Economic Responsibility of the United Church of Christ; New Jersey Environmental Watch; New Mexico Solar Energy Assn.; Oregon Environmental Council; Public Citizen; Solar Energy Industries Assn.; The SUN DAY Campaign.

trator properly exercised his discretion under § 202(a)(1) in denying the petition for rule making." 415 F.3d 50, 58 (2005). The court therefore denied the petition for review. * * *

IV

Article III of the Constitution limits federal-court jurisdiction to "Cases" and "Controversies." Those two words confine "the business of federal courts to questions presented in an adversary context and in a form historically viewed as capable of resolution through the judicial process." *Flast v. Cohen,* 392 U.S. 83, 95 (1968). It is therefore familiar learning that no justiciable "controversy" exists when parties seek adjudication of a political question, *Luther v. Borden,* 7 How. 1 (1849), when they ask for an advisory opinion, *Hayburn's Case,* 2 Dall. 409 (1792), see also *Clinton v. Jones,* 520 U.S. 681, 700, n. 33 (1997), or when the question sought to be adjudicated has been mooted by subsequent developments, *California v. San Pablo & Tulare R. Co.,* 149 U.S. 308 (1893). This case suffers from none of these defects.

The parties' dispute turns on the proper construction of a congressional statute, a question eminently suitable to resolution in federal court. Congress has moreover authorized this type of challenge to EPA action. See 42 U.S.C. § 7607(b)(1). That authorization is of critical importance to the standing inquiry: "Congress has the power to define injuries and articulate chains of causation that will give rise to a case or controversy where none existed before." *Lujan,* 504 U.S., at 580 (KENNEDY, J., concurring in part and concurring in judgment). "In exercising this power, however, Congress must at the very least identify the injury it seeks to vindicate and relate the injury to the class of persons entitled to bring suit." *Ibid.* We will not, therefore, "entertain citizen suits to vindicate the public's nonconcrete interest in the proper administration of the laws." *Id.,* at 581.

EPA maintains that because greenhouse gas emissions inflict widespread harm, the doctrine of standing presents an insuperable jurisdictional obstacle. We do not agree. At bottom, "the gist of the question of standing" is whether petitioners have "such a personal stake in the outcome of the controversy as to assure that concrete adverseness which sharpens the presentation of issues upon which the court so largely depends for illumination." *Baker v. Carr,* 369 U.S. 186, 204 (1962). As Justice KENNEDY explained in his *Lujan* concurrence:

> "While it does not matter how many persons have been injured by the challenged action, the party bringing suit must show that the action injures him in a concrete and personal way. This requirement is not just an empty formality. It preserves the vitality of the adversarial process by assuring both that the parties before the court have an actual, as opposed to professed, stake in the outcome, and that the legal questions presented ... will be resolved, not in the rarified atmosphere of a debating society, but in a concrete factual context

> conducive to a realistic appreciation of the consequences of judicial action."

504 U.S., at 581 (internal quotation marks omitted).

To ensure the proper adversarial presentation, *Lujan* holds that a litigant must demonstrate that it has suffered a concrete and particularized injury that is either actual or imminent, that the injury is fairly traceable to the defendant, and that it is likely that a favorable decision will redress that injury. See *id.,* at 560–561. However, a litigant to whom Congress has "accorded a procedural right to protect his concrete interests," *id.,* at 572 n.7—here, the right to challenge agency action unlawfully withheld, § 7607(b)(1)—"can assert that right without meeting all the normal standards for redressability and immediacy," *ibid.* When a litigant is vested with a procedural right, that litigant has standing if there is some possibility that the requested relief will prompt the injury-causing party to reconsider the decision that allegedly harmed the litigant. *Ibid.*

Only one of the petitioners needs to have standing to permit us to consider the petition for review. We stress here, as did Judge Tatel below, the special position and interest of Massachusetts. It is of considerable relevance that the party seeking review here is a sovereign State and not, as it was in *Lujan,* a private individual.

Well before the creation of the modern administrative state, we recognized that States are not normal litigants for the purposes of invoking federal jurisdiction. As Justice Holmes explained in *Georgia v. Tennessee Copper Co.,* 206 U.S. 230, 237 (1907), a case in which Georgia sought to protect its citizens from air pollution originating outside its borders:

> "The case has been argued largely as if it were one between two private parties; but it is not. The very elements that would be relied upon in a suit between fellow-citizens as a ground for equitable relief are wanting here. The State owns very little of the territory alleged to be affected, and the damage to it capable of estimate in money, possibly, at least, is small. This is a suit by a State for an injury to it in its capacity of *quasi*-sovereign. In that capacity the State has an interest independent of and behind the titles of its citizens, in all the earth and air within its domain. It has the last word as to whether its mountains shall be stripped of their forests and its inhabitants shall breathe pure air."

Just as Georgia's "independent interest . . . in all the earth and air within its domain" supported federal jurisdiction a century ago, so too does Massachusetts' well-founded desire to preserve its sovereign territory today. Cf. *Alden v. Maine,* 527 U.S. 706, 715 (1999) (observing that in the federal system, the States "are not relegated to the role of mere provinces or political corporations, but retain the dignity, though not the full authority, of sovereignty"). That Massachusetts does in fact own a great deal of the "territory alleged to be affected" only reinforces the conclusion that its stake in the outcome of this case is sufficiently concrete to warrant the exercise of federal judicial power.

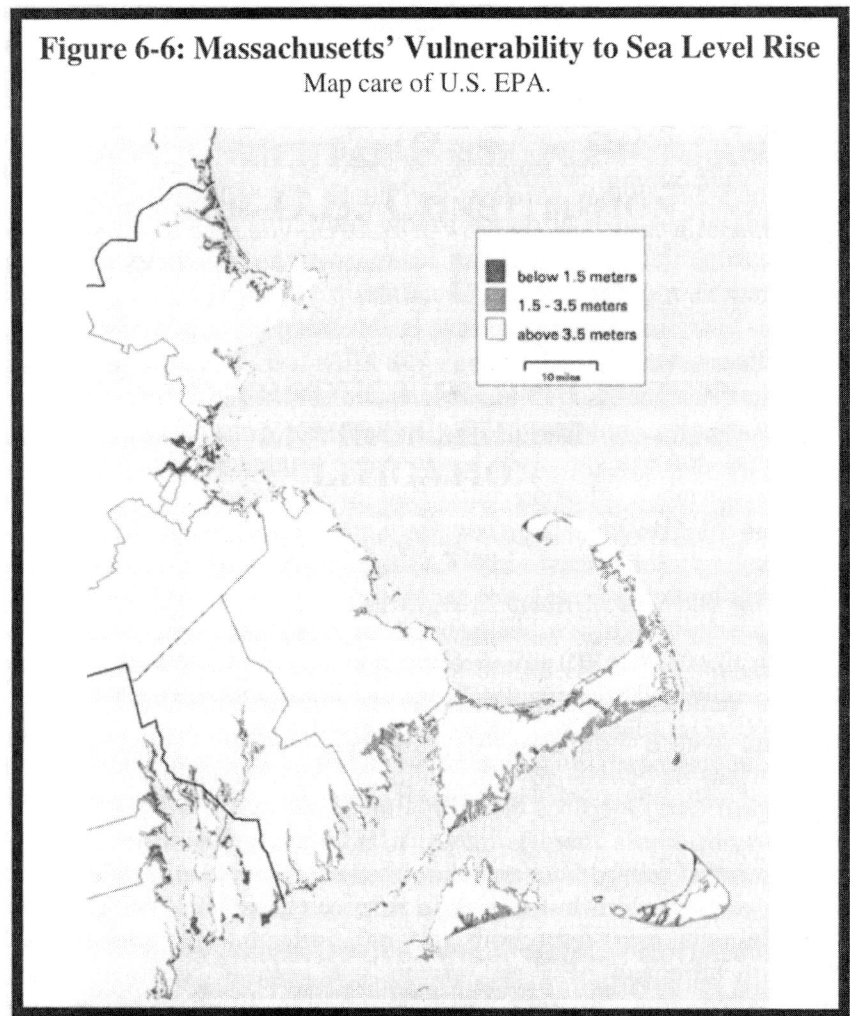

Figure 6-6: Massachusetts' Vulnerability to Sea Level Rise
Map care of U.S. EPA.

When a State enters the Union, it surrenders certain sovereign prerogatives. Massachusetts cannot invade Rhode Island to force reductions in greenhouse gas emissions, it cannot negotiate an emissions treaty with China or India, and in some circumstances the exercise of its police powers to reduce in-state motor-vehicle emissions might well be pre-empted. See *Alfred L. Snapp & Son, Inc. v. Puerto Rico ex rel. Barez,* 458 U.S. 592, 607 (1982) ("One helpful indication in determining whether an alleged injury to the health and welfare of its citizens suffices to give the State standing to sue *parens patriae* is whether the injury is one that the State, if it could, would likely attempt to address through its sovereign lawmaking powers").

These sovereign prerogatives are now lodged in the Federal Government, and Congress has ordered EPA to protect Massachusetts (among others) by prescribing standards applicable to the "emission of any air pollutant from any class or classes of new motor vehicle engines, which in [the Administrator's] judgment cause, or contribute to, air pollution which may reasonably be anticipated to endanger public health or welfare." 42 U.S.C. § 7521(a)(1). Congress has moreover recognized a concomitant procedural right to challenge the rejection of its rulemaking petition as arbitrary and capricious. § 7607(b)(1). Given that procedural right and Massachusetts' stake in protecting its quasi-sovereign interests, the Commonwealth is entitled to special solicitude in our standing analysis.

With that in mind, it is clear that petitioners' submissions as they pertain to Massachusetts have satisfied the most demanding standards of the adversarial process. EPA's steadfast refusal to regulate greenhouse gas emissions presents a risk of harm to Massachusetts that is both "actual" and "imminent." *Lujan,* 504 U.S., at 560 (internal quotation marks omitted). There is, moreover, a "substantial likelihood that the judicial relief requested" will prompt EPA to take steps to reduce that risk. *Duke Power Co. v. Carolina Environmental Study Group, Inc.,* 438 U.S. 59, 79 (1978).

The Injury

The harms associated with climate change are serious and well recognized. Indeed, the NRC Report itself—which EPA regards as an "objective and independent assessment of the relevant science," 68 Fed. Reg. 52930—identifies a number of environmental changes that have already inflicted significant harms, including "the global retreat of mountain glaciers, reduction in snow-cover extent, the earlier spring melting of rivers and lakes, [and] the accelerated rate of rise of sea levels during the 20th century relative to the past few thousand years...." *NRC Report* 16.

Petitioners allege that this only hints at the environmental damage yet to come. According to the climate scientist Michael MacCracken, "qualified scientific experts involved in climate change research" have reached a "strong consensus" that global warming threatens (among other things) a precipitate rise in sea levels by the end of the century, "severe and irreversible changes to natural ecosystems," a "significant reduction in water storage in winter snowpack in mountainous regions with direct and important economic consequences," and an increase in the spread of disease. He also observes that rising ocean temperatures may contribute to the ferocity of hurricanes.

That these climate-change risks are "widely shared" does not minimize Massachusetts' interest in the outcome of this litigation. According to petitioners' unchallenged affidavits, global sea levels rose somewhere between 10 and 20 centimeters over the 20th century as a result of global warming. These rising seas have already begun to swallow Massachusetts' coastal land. Because the Commonwealth "owns a substantial portion of the state's coastal property," it has alleged a particularized injury in its capacity as a landowner. The severity of that injury will only increase over the course of the next century: If sea levels continue to rise as predicted, one Massachusetts official believes that a significant fraction of coastal property will be "either permanently lost through inundation or temporarily lost through periodic storm surge and flooding events." Remediation costs alone, petitioners allege, could run well into the hundreds of millions of dollars.

Causation

EPA does not dispute the existence of a causal connection between man-made greenhouse gas emissions and global warming. At a minimum, therefore, EPA's refusal to regulate such emissions "contributes" to Massachusetts' injuries.

* * * Agencies, like legislatures, do not generally resolve massive problems in one fell regulatory swoop. They instead whittle away at them over time, refining their preferred approach as circumstances change and as they develop a more-nuanced understanding of how best to proceed. That a first step might be tentative does not by itself support the notion that federal courts lack jurisdiction to determine whether that step conforms to law.

And reducing domestic automobile emissions is hardly a tentative step. Even leaving aside the other greenhouse gases, the United States transportation sector emits an enormous quantity of carbon dioxide into the atmosphere—according to the MacCracken affidavit, more than 1.7 billion metric tons in 1999 alone. That accounts for more than 6% of worldwide carbon dioxide emissions. To put this in perspective: Considering just emissions from the transportation sector, which represent less than one-third of this country's total carbon dioxide emissions, the United States would still rank as the third-largest emitter of carbon dioxide in the world, outpaced only by the European Union and China. Judged by any standard, U.S. motor-vehicle emissions make a meaningful contribution to greenhouse gas concentrations and hence, according to petitioners, to global warming.

The Remedy

While it may be true that regulating motor-vehicle emissions will not by itself *reverse* global warming, it by no means follows that we lack jurisdiction to decide whether EPA has a duty to take steps to *slow* or *reduce* it. Because of the enormity of the potential consequences associated with man-made climate change, the fact that the effectiveness of a remedy might be delayed during the (relatively short) time it takes for a new motor-vehicle fleet to replace an older one is essentially irrelevant. Nor is it dispositive that developing countries such as China and India are poised to increase greenhouse gas emissions substantially over the next century: A reduction in domestic emissions would slow the pace of global emissions increases, no matter what happens elsewhere.

We moreover attach considerable significance to EPA's "agree[ment] with the President that 'we must address the issue of global climate change,' " 68 Fed. Reg. 52929 (quoting remarks announcing Clear Skies and Global Climate Initiatives, 2002 Public Papers of George W. Bush, Vol. 1, Feb. 14, p. 227 (2004)), and to EPA's ardent support for various voluntary emission-reduction programs, 68 Fed. Reg. 52932. As Judge Tatel observed in dissent below, "EPA would presumably not bother with such efforts if it thought emissions reductions would have no discernable impact on future global warming." 415 F.3d, at 66.

In sum—at least according to petitioners' uncontested affidavits—the rise in sea levels associated with global warming has already harmed and will continue to harm Massachusetts. The risk of catastrophic harm, though remote, is nevertheless real. That risk would be reduced to some extent if petitioners received the relief they seek. We therefore hold that petitioners have standing to challenge the EPA's denial of their rulemaking petition. * * *

Chief JUSTICE ROBERTS, with whom JUSTICE SCALIA, JUSTICE THOMAS, and JUSTICE ALITO join, dissenting.

* * * I

Article III, § 2, of the Constitution limits the federal judicial power to the adjudication of "Cases" and "Controversies." "If a dispute is not a proper case or controversy, the courts have no business deciding it, or expounding the law in the course of doing so." *DaimlerChrysler Corp. v. Cuno,* 547 U.S. 332, ___, 126 S.Ct. 1854, 1860–1861 (2006). "Standing to sue is part of the common understanding of what it takes to make a justiciable case," *Steel Co. v. Citizens for Better Environment,* 523 U.S. 83, 102 (1998), and has been described as "an essential and unchanging part of the case-or-controversy requirement of Article III," *Defenders of Wildlife, supra,* at 560.

Our modern framework for addressing standing is familiar: "A plaintiff must allege personal injury fairly traceable to the defendant's allegedly unlawful conduct and likely to be redressed by the requested relief." *DaimlerChrysler, supra,* at ___, 126 S.Ct., at 1861 (quoting *Allen v. Wright,* 468 U.S. 737, 751 (1984) (internal quotation marks omitted)). Applying that standard here, petitioners bear the burden of alleging an injury that is fairly traceable to the Environmental Protection Agency's failure to promulgate new motor vehicle greenhouse gas emission standards, and that is likely to be redressed by the prospective issuance of such standards.

Before determining whether petitioners can meet this familiar test, however, the Court changes the rules. It asserts that "States are not normal litigants for the purposes of invoking federal jurisdiction," and that given "Massachusetts' stake in protecting its quasi-sovereign interests, the Commonwealth is entitled to *special solicitude* in our standing analysis."

Relaxing Article III standing requirements because asserted injuries are pressed by a State, however, has no basis in our jurisprudence, and support for any such "special solicitude" is conspicuously absent from the Court's opinion. The general judicial review provision cited by the Court, 42 U.S.C. § 7607(b)(1), affords States no special rights or status. * * * Nor does the case law cited by the Court provide any support for the notion that Article III somehow implicitly treats public and private litigants differently. The Court has to go back a full century in an attempt to justify its novel standing rule, but even there it comes up short. The Court's analysis hinges on *Georgia v. Tennessee Copper Co.,* 206 U.S. 230 (1907)—a case that did indeed draw a distinction between a State and private litigants, but solely with respect to available remedies. The case had nothing to do with Article III standing. * * *

* * * II

It is not at all clear how the Court's "special solicitude" for Massachusetts plays out in the standing analysis, except as an implicit concession that petitioners cannot establish standing on traditional terms. But the status of Massachusetts as a State cannot compensate for petitioners' failure to demonstrate injury in fact, causation, and redressability.

When the Court actually applies the three-part test, it focuses, as did the dissent below, on the State's asserted loss of coastal land as the injury in fact. If petitioners rely on loss of land as the Article III injury, however, they must ground the rest of the standing analysis in that specific injury. That alleged injury must be "concrete and particularized," *Defenders of Wildlife,* 504 U.S., at 560, and "distinct and palpable," *Allen,* 468 U.S., at 741 (internal quotation marks omitted). Central to this concept of "particularized" injury is the requirement that a plaintiff be affected in a "personal and individual way," *Defenders of Wildlife,* 504 U.S., at 560, n. 1, and seek relief that "directly and tangibly benefits him" in a manner distinct from its impact on "the public at large," *id.,* at 573–574. Without "particularized injury, there can be no confidence of 'a real need to exercise the power of judicial review' or that relief can be framed 'no broader than required by the precise facts to which the court's ruling would be applied.'" *Warth v. Seldin,* 422 U.S. 490, 508 (1975) (quoting *Schlesinger v. Reservists Comm. to Stop the War,* 418 U.S. 208, 221–222 (1974)).

The very concept of global warming seems inconsistent with this particularization requirement. Global warming is a phenomenon "harmful to humanity at large," 415 F.3d, at 60 (Sentelle, J., dissenting in part and concurring in judgment), and the redress petitioners seek is focused no more on them than on the public generally—it is literally to change the atmosphere around the world.

If petitioners' particularized injury is loss of coastal land, it is also that injury that must be "actual or imminent, not conjectural or hypothetical," *Defenders of Wildlife, supra,* at 560 (internal quotation marks omitted), "real and immediate," *Los Angeles v. Lyons,* 461 U.S. 95, 102

(1983) (internal quotation marks omitted), and "certainly impending," *Whitmore v. Arkansas,* 495 U.S. 149, 158 (1990) (internal quotation marks omitted).

As to "actual" injury, the Court observes that "global sea levels rose somewhere between 10 and 20 centimeters over the 20th century as a result of global warming" and that "[t]hese rising seas have already begun to swallow Massachusetts' coastal land." But none of petitioners' declarations supports that connection. One declaration states that "a rise in sea level due to climate change is occurring on the coast of Massachusetts, in the metropolitan Boston area," but there is no elaboration. And the declarant goes on to identify a "significan[t]" *non*-global-warming cause of Boston's rising sea level: land subsidence. Thus, aside from a single conclusory statement, there is nothing in petitioners' 43 standing declarations and accompanying exhibits to support an inference of actual loss of Massachusetts coastal land from 20th century global sea level increases. It is pure conjecture.

The Court's attempts to identify "imminent" or "certainly impending" loss of Massachusetts coastal land fares no better. One of petitioners' declarants predicts global warming will cause sea level to rise by 20 to 70 centimeters *by the year 2100.* Another uses a computer modeling program to map the Commonwealth's coastal land and its current elevation, and calculates that the high-end estimate of sea level rise would result in the loss of significant state-owned coastal land. But the computer modeling program has a conceded average error of about 30 centimeters and a maximum observed error of 70 centimeters. * * * [A]ccepting a century-long time horizon and a series of compounded estimates renders requirements of imminence and immediacy utterly toothless. See *Defenders of Wildlife, supra,* at 565 n.2 (while the concept of " 'imminence' " in standing doctrine is "somewhat elastic," it can be "stretched beyond the breaking point"). "Allegations of possible future injury do not satisfy the requirements of Art. III. A threatened injury must be *certainly impending* to constitute injury in fact." *Whitmore, supra,* at 158 (internal quotation marks omitted; emphasis added).

III

Petitioners' reliance on Massachusetts's loss of coastal land as their injury in fact for standing purposes creates insurmountable problems for them with respect to causation and redressability. * * * Petitioners view the relationship between their injuries and EPA's failure to promulgate new motor vehicle greenhouse gas emission standards as simple and direct: Domestic motor vehicles emit carbon dioxide and other greenhouse gases. Worldwide emissions of greenhouse gases contribute to global warming and therefore also to petitioners' alleged injuries. Without the new vehicle standards, greenhouse gas emissions—and therefore global warming and its attendant harms—have been higher than they otherwise would have been; once EPA changes course, the trend will be reversed.

The Court ignores the complexities of global warming, and does so by now disregarding the "particularized" injury it relied on in step one, and using the dire nature of global warming itself as a bootstrap for finding causation and redressability. First, it is important to recognize the extent of the emissions at issue here. Because local greenhouse gas emissions disperse throughout the atmosphere and remain there for anywhere from 50 to 200 years, it is global emissions data that are relevant. According to one of petitioners' declarations, domestic motor vehicles contribute about 6 percent of global carbon dioxide emissions and 4 percent of global greenhouse gas emissions. The amount of global emissions at issue here is smaller still; § 202(a)(1) of the Clean Air Act covers only *new* motor vehicles and *new* motor vehicle engines, so petitioners' desired emission standards might reduce only a fraction of 4 percent of global emissions.

This gets us only to the relevant greenhouse gas emissions; linking them to global warming and ultimately to petitioners' alleged injuries next requires consideration of further complexities. * * * Petitioners are never able to trace their alleged injuries back through this complex web to the fractional amount of global emissions that might have been limited with EPA standards. In light of the bit-part domestic new motor vehicle greenhouse gas emissions have played in what petitioners describe as a 150–year global phenomenon, and the myriad additional factors bearing on petitioners' alleged injury—the loss of Massachusetts coastal land—the connection is far too speculative to establish causation.

IV

Redressability is even more problematic. To the tenuous link between petitioners' alleged injury and the indeterminate fractional domestic emissions at issue here, add the fact that petitioners cannot meaningfully predict what will come of the 80 percent of global greenhouse gas emissions that originate outside the United States. * * * No matter, the Court reasons, because *any* decrease in domestic emissions will "slow the pace of global emissions increases, no matter what happens elsewhere." Every little bit helps, so Massachusetts can sue over any little bit.

The Court's sleight-of-hand is in failing to link up the different elements of the three-part standing test. What must be *likely* to be redressed is the particular injury in fact. The injury the Court looks to is the asserted loss of land. The Court contends that regulating domestic motor vehicle emissions will reduce carbon dioxide in the atmosphere, *and therefore* redress Massachusetts's injury. But even if regulation *does* reduce emissions—to some indeterminate degree, given events elsewhere in the world—the Court never explains why that makes it *likely* that the injury in fact—the loss of land—will be redressed. Schoolchildren know that a kingdom might be lost "all for the want of a horseshoe nail," but "likely" redressability is a different matter. The realities make it pure conjecture to suppose that EPA regulation of new automobile emissions will *likely* prevent the loss of Massachusetts coastal land.

V

Petitioners' difficulty in demonstrating causation and redressability is not surprising given the evident mismatch between the source of their alleged injury—catastrophic global warming—and the narrow subject matter of the Clean Air Act provision at issue in this suit. * * *

When dealing with legal doctrine phrased in terms of what is "fairly" traceable or "likely" to be redressed, it is perhaps not surprising that the matter is subject to some debate. But in considering how loosely or rigorously to define those adverbs, it is vital to keep in mind the purpose of the inquiry. The limitation of the judicial power to cases and controversies "is crucial in maintaining the tripartite allocation of power set forth in the Constitution." *DaimlerChrysler,* 126 S.Ct., at 1860–1861 (internal quotation marks omitted). In my view, the Court today—addressing Article III's "core component of standing," *Defenders of Wildlife, supra,* at 560—fails to take this limitation seriously.

* * * Perhaps the Court recognizes as much. How else to explain its need to devise a new doctrine of state standing to support its result? The good news is that the Court's "special solicitude" for Massachusetts limits the future applicability of the diluted standing requirements applied in this case. The bad news is that the Court's self-professed relaxation of those Article III requirements has caused us to transgress "the proper—and properly limited—role of the courts in a democratic society." *Allen,* 468 U.S., at 750 (internal quotation marks omitted).

I respectfully dissent.

NOTES

1. ***Massachusetts v. EPA* and *Lujan v. Defenders of Wildlife*.** Is the majority's discussion of state standing in *Massachusetts v. EPA* consistent with the decision in *Lujan v. Defenders of Wildlife*? Why or why not? If you think the two cases present different standing analyses, did *Massachusetts v. EPA* change the standing rules for *all* environmental plaintiffs, or just for states? What language in the case leads you to your conclusion?

2. **Climate Change and Standing.** In general, why does global climate change create problems for plaintiffs seeking to bring their lawsuits in federal courts? Under the majority's decision in this case, who can sue about climate change problems? Does the majority essentially recognize increased risk as an injury that can support standing? Why or why not? Under the dissent's approach, could anyone ever sue about any climate change problem? Why or why not? If potential plaintiffs would still exist under the dissent's approach, who would they be?

3. **Massachusetts' Injury-in-Fact.** What injury does Massachusetts claim from the EPA's failure to regulate greenhouse gases, especially carbon dioxide? What are the potential standing problems with this injury-in-fact? How does the majority deal with those potential problems? Is the majority's approach consistent with *Lujan v. Defenders of Wildlife*? Why or why not?

What do the dissenters argue about Massachusetts' injury-in-fact? Is their position consistent with *Lujan*? Why or why not?

4. **Causation and Redressability.** How do the majority and the dissent differ in their views of the causation and redressability elements of standing? In your opinion, which approach is more consistent with *Lujan v. Defenders of Wildlife*? Why?

5. **Standing and Federalism.** Is federalism relevant to the standing analysis, according to the majority? If so, how? What are the implications for state standing in other environmental and natural resources cases? How does the dissent view the federalism issue? Is this view somewhat surprising, given the Justices who dissented? Why or why not?

6. **Standing and Citizen Suit Provisions.** The majority argues that the very existence of the Clean Air Act's citizen suit provision is relevant to the existence of standing for Massachusetts. Why? How does the majority tie this argument to *Lujan v. Defenders of Wildlife*? As a constitutional matter, what role can Congress play in the creation of standing?

7. ***Massachusetts v. EPA* Redux?** On June 20, 2011, the U.S. Supreme Court decided *American Electric Power Co., Inc. v. Connecticut*, ___ U.S. ___, 131 S.Ct. 2527 (2011), another climate change case involving state plaintiffs. Specifically, in this case, eight states, the City of New York, and three private land trusts sued four private power companies and the Tennessee Valley Authority regarding the defendants' emissions of carbon dioxide and other greenhouse gases, arguing that those emissions constituted public nuisances under both federal and state common law. The merits of this decision depended on the merits of *Massachusetts v. EPA* and are discussed in Chapter IV.

The standing issue produced an equally divided Supreme Court, because Justice Sotomayor did not participate in the decision. As a result, the Court's standing analysis was very brief:

> The petitioners contend that the federal courts lack authority to adjudicate this case. Four members of the Court would hold that at least some plaintiffs have Article III standing under *Massachusetts,* which permitted a State to challenge EPA's refusal to regulate greenhouse gas emissions, 549 U.S., at 520–526; and, further, that no other threshold obstacle bars review. Four members of the Court, adhering to a dissenting opinion in *Massachusetts,* 549 U.S., at 535, or regarding that decision as distinguishable, would hold that none of the plaintiffs have Article III standing. We therefore affirm, by an equally divided Court, the Second Circuit's exercise of jurisdiction and proceed to the merits.

Id. at 2535. Thus, *AEP v. Connecticut* did little to elucidate the contours and limits of state standing—although the reference to Justices who would have distinguished *Massachusetts v. EPA* rather than adhere to the dissent suggests that interesting issues remain for the Court to clarify.

* * *

B. THE ZONE OF INTERESTS TEST

While not an element of constitutional standing, the ***zone of interests test*** can also determine whether a citizen plaintiff has standing an environmental suit. The zone of interests test is a ***prudential*** requirement for standing in many environmental citizen suits. That is, federal courts impose the test as a matter of prudence in determining whether the case is one that the court should hear—*not* as a constitutional requirement.

Federal courts presume that the zone of interests test applies. However, because it is not a constitutional requirement, Congress can write statutes to eliminate the zone of interests test from the standing analyses. As a result, the issue of whether the test applies can be very particular to a plaintiff's cause of action. For example, the zone of interest test *always* applies to APA lawsuits, but the citizen suit provisions of many environmental statutes have arguably eliminated that test. Therefore, whether a plaintiff has to meet the zone of interests test—and hence an environmental plaintiff's standing—can depend initially on exactly what the plaintiff's cause of action is, as the following Supreme Court case demonstrates.

BENNETT v. SPEAR

520 U.S. 154 (1997).

JUSTICE SCALIA delivered the opinion of the Court.

This is a challenge to a biological opinion issued by the Fish and Wildlife Service in accordance with the Endangered Species Act of 1973 (ESA), 16 U.S.C. § 1531 *et seq.*, concerning the operation of the Klamath Irrigation Project by the Bureau of Reclamation, and the project's impact on two varieties of endangered fish. The question for decision is whether the petitioners, who have competing economic and other interests in Klamath Project water, have standing to seek judicial review of the biological opinion under the citizen-suit provision of the ESA, § 1540(g)(1), and the Administrative Procedure Act (APA), 5 U.S.C. § 701 *et seq.*

I

The ESA requires the Secretary of the Interior to promulgate regulations listing those species of animals that are "threatened" or "endangered" under specified criteria, and to designate their "critical habitat." 16 U.S.C. § 1533. The ESA further requires each federal agency to "insure that any action authorized, funded, or carried out by such agency . . . is not likely to jeopardize the continued existence of any endangered species or threatened species or result in the destruction or adverse modification of habitat of such species which is determined by the Secretary . . . to be critical." § 1536(a)(2). If an agency determines that action it proposes to take may adversely affect a listed species, it must engage in formal consultation with the Fish and Wildlife Service, as delegate of the Secretary, *ibid.*; 50 CFR § 402.14 (1995), after which the Service must provide the agency with a written statement (the Biological Opinion) explaining how the proposed action will affect the species or its habitat, 16 U.S.C. § 1536(b)(3)(A). If the Service concludes that the proposed action will "jeopardize the continued existence of any [listed] species or threatened species or result in the destruction or adverse modification of [critical habitat]," § 1536(a)(2), the Biological Opinion must outline any "reasonable and prudent alternatives" that the Service believes will avoid that consequence, § 1536(b)(3)(A). Additionally, if the Biological Opinion concludes that the agency action will not result in jeopardy or adverse habitat modification, or if it offers reasonable and prudent alternatives to avoid that consequence, the Service must provide the agency with a written statement (known as the Incidental Take Statement) specifying the "impact of such incidental taking on the species," any "reasonable and prudent measures that the [Service] considers necessary or appropriate to minimize such impact," and setting forth "the terms and conditions ... that must be complied with by the Federal agency ... to implement [those measures]." § 1536(b)(4).

Figure 6-7: Lost River (top) & Shortnose Suckers
U.S. Fish & Wildlife Service photos.

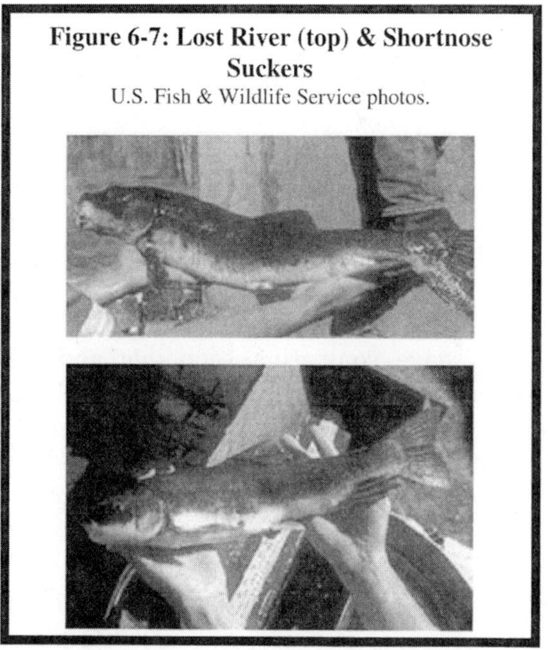

The Klamath Project, one of the oldest federal reclamation schemes, is a series of lakes, rivers, dams, and irrigation canals in northern California and southern Oregon. * * * In 1992, the Bureau notified the Service that operation of the project might affect the Lost River Sucker *(Deltistes luxatus)* and Shortnose Sucker *(Chasmistes brevirostris),* species of fish that were listed as endangered in 1988, *see* 53 Fed. Reg. 27130–

27133 (1988). After formal consultation with the Bureau in accordance with 50 CFR § 402.14 (1995), the Service issued a Biological Opinion which concluded that the " 'long-term operation of the Klamath Project was likely to jeopardize the continued existence of the Lost River and shortnose suckers.' " The Biological Opinion identified "reasonable and prudent alternatives" the Service believed would avoid jeopardy, which included the maintenance of minimum water levels on Clear Lake and Gerber reservoirs. The Bureau later notified the Service that it intended to operate the project in compliance with the Biological Opinion.

Petitioners, two Oregon irrigation districts that receive Klamath Project water and the operators of two ranches within those districts, filed the present action against the director and regional director of the Service and the Secretary of the Interior. Neither the Bureau nor any of its officials is named as defendant. The complaint asserts that the Bureau "has been following essentially the same procedures for storing and releasing water from Clear Lake and Gerber reservoirs throughout the twentieth century[]"; that "[t]here is no scientifically or commercially available evidence indicating that the populations of endangered suckers in Clear Lake and Gerber reservoirs have declined, are declining, or will decline as a result" of the Bureau's operation of the Klamath Project; that "[t]here is no commercially or scientifically available evidence indicating that the restrictions on lake levels imposed in the Biological Opinion will have any beneficial effect on the ... populations of suckers in Clear Lake and Gerber reservoirs[]"; and that the Bureau nonetheless "will abide by the restrictions imposed by the Biological Opinion[.]"

Petitioners' complaint included three claims for relief that are relevant here. The first and second claims allege that the Service's jeopardy determination with respect to Clear Lake and Gerber reservoirs, and the ensuing imposition of minimum water levels, violated § 7 of the ESA, 16 U.S.C. § 1536. The third claim is that the imposition of minimum water elevations constituted an implicit determination of critical habitat for the suckers, which violated § 4 of the ESA, 16 U.S.C. § 1533(b)(2), because it failed to take into consideration the designation's economic impact. Each of the claims also states that the relevant action violated the APA's prohibition of agency action that is "arbitrary, capricious, an abuse of discretion, or otherwise not in accordance with law." 5 U.S.C. § 706(2)(A).

The complaint asserts that petitioners' use of the reservoirs and related waterways for "recreational, aesthetic and commercial purposes, as well as for their primary sources of irrigation water," will be "irreparably damaged" by the actions complained of, and that the restrictions on water delivery "recommended" by the Biological Opinion "adversely affect plaintiffs by substantially reducing the quantity of available irrigation water[.]" In essence, petitioners claim a competing interest in the water the Biological Opinion declares necessary for the preservation of the suckers.

The District Court dismissed the complaint for lack of jurisdiction. It concluded that petitioners did not have standing because their "recreational, aesthetic, and commercial interests . . . do not fall within the zone of interests sought to be protected by ESA[.]" The Court of Appeals for the Ninth Circuit affirmed. It held that the "zone of interests" test limits the class of persons who may obtain judicial review not only under the APA, but also under the citizen-suit provision of the ESA, 16 U.S.C. § 1540(g), and that "only plaintiffs who allege an interest in the *preservation* of endangered species fall within the zone of interests protected by the ESA[.]" We granted certiorari. * * *

II

We first turn to the question the Court of Appeals found dispositive: whether petitioners lack standing by virtue of the zone-of-interests test. Although petitioners contend that their claims lie both under the ESA and the APA, we look first at the ESA because it may permit petitioners to recover their litigation costs, *see* 16 U.S.C. § 1540(g)(4), and because the APA by its terms independently authorizes review only when "there is no other adequate remedy in a court," 5 U.S.C. § 704.

The question of standing "involves both constitutional limitations on federal-court jurisdiction and prudential limitations on its exercise." *Warth v. Seldin*, 422 U.S. 490, 490 (1975) (citing *Barrows v. Jackson*, 346 U.S. 249 (1953)). To satisfy the "case" or "controversy" requirement of Article III, which is the "irreducible constitutional minimum" of standing, a plaintiff must, generally speaking, demonstrate that he has suffered "injury in fact," that the injury is "fairly traceable" to the actions of the defendant, and that the injury will likely be redressed by a favorable decision. *Lujan v. Defenders of Wildlife,* 504 U.S. 555, 560–561 (1992); *Valley Forge Christian College v. Americans United for Separation of Church and State, Inc.*, 454 U.S. 464, 471–472 (1982). In addition to the immutable requirements of Article III, "the federal judiciary has also adhered to a set of prudential principles that bear on the question of standing." *Id.*, at 474–475. * * * Numbered among these prudential requirements is the doctrine of particular concern in this case: that a plaintiff's grievance must arguably fall within the zone of interests protected or regulated by the statutory provision or constitutional guarantee invoked in the suit.

The "zone of interests" formulation was first employed in *Association of Data Processing Service Organizations, Inc. v. Camp,* 397 U.S. 150 (1970). * * * [W]e stated the applicable prudential standing requirement to be "whether the interest sought to be protected by the complainant is arguably within the zone of interests to be protected or regulated by the statute or constitutional guarantee in question." *Data Processing, supra*, at 153. We have made clear, however, that the breadth of the zone of interests varies according to the provisions of law at issue, so that what comes within the zone of interests of a statute for purposes of obtaining judicial review of administrative action under the " 'generous review provisions' " of the APA may not do so for other purposes.

Congress legislates against the background of our prudential standing doctrine, which applies unless it is expressly negated. The first question in the present case is whether the ESA's citizen-suit provision [] negates the zone-of-interests test (or, perhaps more accurately, expands the zone of interests). We think it does. The first operative portion of the provision says that "any person may commence a civil suit"—an authorization of remarkable breadth when compared with the language Congress ordinarily uses. Even in some other environmental statutes, Congress has used more restrictive formulations, such as "[any person] having an interest which is or may be adversely affected," 33 U.S.C. § 1365(g) (Clean Water Act); *see also* 30 U.S.C. § 1270(a) (Surface Mining Control and Reclamation Act) (same); "[a]ny person suffering legal wrong," 15 U.S.C. § 797(b)(5) (Energy Supply and Environmental Coordination Act); or "any person having a valid legal interest which is or may be adversely affected ... whenever such action constitutes a case or controversy," 42 U.S.C. § 9124(a) (Ocean Thermal Energy Conversion Act). * * *

Our readiness to take the term "any person" at face value is greatly augmented by two interrelated considerations: that the overall subject matter of this legislation is the environment (a matter in which it is common to think all persons have an interest) and that the obvious purpose of the particular provision in question is to encourage enforcement by so-called "private attorneys general"—evidenced by its elimination of the usual amount-in-controversy and diversity-of-citizenship requirements, its provision for recovery of the costs of litigation (including even expert witness fees), and its reservation to the Government of a right of first refusal to pursue the action initially and a right to intervene later. * * *

It is true that the plaintiffs here are seeking to prevent application of environmental restrictions rather than to implement them. But the "any person" formulation applies to all the causes of action authorized by § 1540(g)—not only to actions against private violators of environmental restrictions, and not only to actions against the Secretary asserting underenforcement under § 1533, but also to actions against the Secretary asserting overenforcement under § 1533. As we shall discuss below, the citizen-suit provision does favor environmentalists in that it covers all private violations of the ESA but not all failures of the Secretary to meet his administrative responsibilities; but there is no textual basis for saying that its expansion of standing requirements applies to environmentalists alone. The Court of Appeals therefore erred in concluding that petitioners lacked standing under the zone-of-interests test to bring their claims under the ESA's citizen-suit provision.

III

The Government advances several alternative grounds upon which it contends we may affirm the dismissal of petitioners' suit. * * *

A

The Government's first contention is that petitioners' complaint fails to satisfy the standing requirements imposed by the "case" or "controversy" provision of Article III. This "irreducible constitutional minimum" of standing requires: (1) that the plaintiff have suffered an "injury in fact"—an invasion of a judicially cognizable interest which is (a) concrete and particularized and (b) actual or imminent, not conjectural or hypothetical; (2) that there be a causal connection between the injury and the conduct complained of—the injury must be fairly traceable to the challenged action of the defendant, and not the result of the independent action of some third party not before the court; and (3) that it be likely, as opposed to merely speculative, that the injury will be redressed by a favorable decision. *Defenders of Wildlife,* 504 U.S., at 560–561.

Petitioners allege, among other things, that they currently receive irrigation water from Clear Lake, that the Bureau "will abide by the restrictions imposed by the Biological Opinion," and that "[t]he restrictions on lake levels imposed in the Biological Opinion adversely affect [petitioners] by substantially reducing the quantity of available irrigation water[.]" The Government contends, first, that these allegations fail to satisfy the "injury in fact" element of Article III standing because they demonstrate only a diminution in the *aggregate* amount of available water, and do not necessarily establish (absent information concerning the Bureau's water allocation practices) that *petitioners* will receive less water. This contention overlooks, however, the proposition that each element of Article III standing "must be supported in the same way as any other matter on which the plaintiff bears the burden of proof, *i.e.,* with the manner and degree of evidence required at the successive stages of the litigation." *Defenders of Wildlife, supra,* at 561 (quoting *Lujan v. National Wildlife Federation*, 497 U.S. 871, 889 (1990)). * * * Given petitioners' allegation that the amount of available water will be reduced and that they will be adversely affected thereby, it is easy to presume specific facts under which petitioners will be injured—for example, the Bureau's distribution of the reduction pro rata among its customers. The complaint alleges the requisite injury in fact.

The Government also contests compliance with the second and third Article III standing requirements, contending that any injury suffered by petitioners is neither "fairly traceable" to the Service's Biological Opinion, nor "redressable" by a favorable judicial ruling, because the "action agency" (the Bureau) retains ultimate responsibility for determining whether and how a proposed action shall go forward. "If petitioners have suffered injury," the Government contends, "the proximate cause of their harm is an (as yet unidentified) decision by the Bureau regarding the volume of water allocated to petitioners, not the biological opinion itself." This wrongly equates injury "fairly traceable" to the defendant with injury as to which the defendant's actions are the very last step in the chain of causation. * * * By the Government's own account, while the Service's Biological Opinion theoretically serves an "advisory function,"

51 Fed. Reg. 19928 (1986), in reality it has a powerful coercive effect on the action agency[.] * * *

[Moreover,] the action agency must not only articulate its reasons for disagreement (which ordinarily requires species and habitat investigations that are not within the action agency's expertise), but that it runs a substantial risk if its (inexpert) reasons turn out to be wrong. * * * The action agency is technically free to disregard the Biological Opinion and proceed with its proposed action, but it does so at its own peril (and that of its employees), for "any person" who knowingly "takes" an endangered or threatened species is subject to substantial civil and criminal penalties, including imprisonment. *See* §§ 1540(a) and (b) (authorizing civil fines of up to $25,000 per violation and criminal penalties of up to $50,000 and imprisonment for one year); *see also Babbitt v. Sweet Home Chapter, Communities for Great Ore.*, 515 U.S. 687, 708 (1995) (upholding interpretation of the term "take" to include significant habitat degradation).

The Service itself is, to put it mildly, keenly aware of the virtually determinative effect of its biological opinions. The Incidental Take Statement at issue in the present case begins by instructing the reader that any taking of a listed species is prohibited unless "such taking is in compliance with this incidental take statement," and warning that "[t]he measures described below are nondiscretionary, and must be taken by [the Bureau]." Given all of this, and given petitioners' allegation that the Bureau had, until issuance of the Biological Opinion, operated the Klamath Project in the same manner throughout the 20th century, it is not difficult to conclude that petitioners have met their burden—which is relatively modest at this stage of the litigation—of alleging that their injury is "fairly traceable" to the Service's Biological Opinion and that it will "likely" be redressed—*i.e.*, the Bureau will not impose such water level restrictions—if the Biological Opinion is set aside.

B

Next, the Government contends that the ESA's citizen-suit provision does not authorize judicial review of petitioners' claims. The relevant portions of that provision provide that

> "any person may commence a civil suit on his own behalf—
>
> "(A) to enjoin any person, including the United States and any other governmental instrumentality or agency ... who is alleged to be in violation of any provision of this chapter or regulation issued under the authority thereof; or
>
> ... "(C) against the Secretary [of Commerce or the Interior] where there is alleged a failure of the Secretary to perform any act or duty under section 1533 of this title which is not discretionary with the Secretary." 16 U.S.C. § 1540(g)(1).

The Government argues that judicial review is not available under subsection (A) because the Secretary is not "in violation" of the ESA, and under subsection (C) because the Secretary has not failed to perform any nondiscretionary duty under § 1533.

1

Turning first to subsection (C): that it covers only violations of § 1533 is clear and unambiguous. Petitioners' first and second claims, which assert that the Secretary has violated § 1536, are obviously not reviewable under this provision. However, as described above, the third claim alleges that the Biological Opinion implicitly determines critical habitat without complying with the mandate of § 1533(b)(2) that the Secretary "tak[e] into consideration the economic impact, and any other relevant impact, of specifying any particular area as critical habitat." This claim does come within subsection (C).

* * * 2

Having concluded that petitioners' § 1536 claims are not reviewable under subsection (C), we are left with the question whether they are reviewable under subsection (A), which authorizes injunctive actions against any person "who is alleged to be in violation" of the ESA or its implementing regulations. The Government contends that the Secretary's conduct in implementing or enforcing the ESA is not a "violation" of the ESA within the meaning of this provision. In its view, § 1540(g)(1)(A) is a means by which private parties may enforce the substantive provisions of the ESA against regulated parties—both private entities and Government agencies—but is not an alternative avenue for judicial review of the Secretary's implementation of the statute. We agree.

The opposite contention is simply incompatible with the existence of § 1540(g)(1)(C), which expressly authorizes suit against the Secretary, but only to compel him to perform a nondiscretionary duty under § 1533. That provision would be superfluous—and, worse still, its careful limitation to § 1533 would be nullified—if § 1540(g)(1)(A) permitted suit against the Secretary for *any* "violation" of the ESA. It is the " 'cardinal principle of statutory construction' . . . [that] [i]t is our duty 'to give effect, if possible, to every clause and word of a statute' . . . rather than to emasculate an entire section." *United States v. Menasche*, 348 U.S. 528, 538 (1955) (quoting *NLRB v. Jones & Laughlin Steel Corp.*, 301 U.S. 1, 30 (1937), and *Montclair v. Ramsdell*, 107 U.S. 147, 152 (1883)). Application of that principle here clearly requires us to conclude that the term "violation" does not include the Secretary's failure to perform his duties as administrator of the ESA. * * *

* * * IV

The foregoing analysis establishes that the principal statute invoked by petitioners, the ESA, does authorize review of their § 1533 claim, but does not support their claims based upon the Secretary's alleged failure to comply with § 1536. To complete our task, we must therefore inquire whether these § 1536 claims may nonetheless be brought under the

Administrative Procedure Act, which authorizes a court to "set aside agency action, findings, and conclusions found to be . . . arbitrary, capricious, an abuse of discretion, or otherwise not in accordance with law," 5 U.S.C. § 706.

A

No one contends (and it would not be maintainable) that the causes of action against the Secretary set forth in the ESA's citizen-suit provision are exclusive, supplanting those provided by the APA. The APA, by its terms, provides a right to judicial review of all "final agency action for which there is no other adequate remedy in a court," § 704, and applies universally "except to the extent that—(1) statutes preclude judicial review; or (2) agency action is committed to agency discretion by law," § 701(a). Nothing in the ESA's citizen-suit provision expressly precludes review under the APA, nor do we detect anything in the statutory scheme suggesting a purpose to do so. And any contention that the relevant provision of 16 U.S.C. § 1536(a)(2) is discretionary would fly in the face of its text, which uses the imperative "shall."

In determining whether the petitioners have standing under the zone-of-interests test to bring their APA claims, we look not to the terms of the ESA's citizen-suit provision, but to the substantive provisions of the ESA, the alleged violations of which serve as the gravamen of the complaint. The classic formulation of the zone-of-interests test is set forth in *Data Processing*, 397 U.S., at 153: "whether the interest sought to be protected by the complainant is arguably within the zone of interests to be protected or regulated by the statute or constitutional guarantee in question." The Court of Appeals concluded that this test was not met here, since petitioners are neither directly regulated by the ESA nor seek to vindicate its overarching purpose of species preservation. That conclusion was error.

* * * In the claims that we have found not to be covered by the ESA's citizen-suit provision, petitioners allege a violation of § 7 of the ESA, 16 U.S.C. § 1536, which requires, *inter alia,* that each agency "use the best scientific and commercial data available," § 1536(a)(2). Petitioners contend that the available scientific and commercial data show that the continued operation of the Klamath Project will not have a detrimental impact on the endangered suckers, that the imposition of minimum lake levels is not necessary to protect the fish, and that by issuing a Biological Opinion which makes unsubstantiated findings to the contrary the defendants have acted arbitrarily and in violation of § 1536(a)(2). The obvious purpose of the requirement that each agency "use the best scientific and commercial data available" is to ensure that the ESA not be implemented haphazardly, on the basis of speculation or surmise. While this no doubt serves to advance the ESA's overall goal of species preservation, we think it readily apparent that another objective (if not indeed the primary one) is to avoid needless economic dislocation produced by agency officials zealously but unintelligently pursuing their environmental objectives. That economic consequences are an explicit concern of the ESA is evi-

denced by § 1536(h), which provides exemption from § 1536(a)(2)'s no-jeopardy mandate where there are no reasonable and prudent alternatives to the agency action and the benefits of the agency action clearly outweigh the benefits of any alternatives. We believe the "best scientific and commercial data" provision is similarly intended, at least in part, to prevent uneconomic (because erroneous) jeopardy determinations. Petitioners' claim that they are victims of such a mistake is plainly within the zone of interests that the provision protects. * * *

NOTES

1. **Sorting Through the Plaintiffs' Standing: The Plaintiffs' Constitutional Standing.** Did the plaintiffs have *constitutional* standing in this case? Why or why not? Which elements of constitutional standing did the government challenge? How? What did the majority decide about those elements? Why? Was the majority's view of redressability here consistent with its view of redressability in *Defenders of Wildlife*? In particular, did the majority here and plurality in *Defenders of Wildlife* view the USFWS's section 7 authority over other agencies the same way? Why or why not?

2. **Sorting Through the Plaintiffs' Standing: The Plaintiffs' Three Claims and the Applicability of the Zone of Interests Test.** What were the plaintiffs' claims in *Bennett v. Spear*? Which of those claims fell under the Endangered Species Act's citizen suit provision? Why? Which did the plaintiffs have to bring under the APA? Why?

How did the cause of action for each of the plaintiffs' claims affect the application of the zone of interests test? Does that test apply to claims brought pursuant to the Endangered Species Act's citizen suit provision? Why or why not? Does that test apply to claims brought pursuant to the APA? Why or why not? What did the Supreme Court suggest about the applicability of the zone of interests test to *other* environmental citizen suit provisions, such as the Clean Water Act's citizen suit provision?

3. **Sorting Through the Plaintiffs' Standing: Application of the Zone of Interests Test.** How did the majority define the zone of interests test? What provision of the Endangered Species Act was the gravamen of the plaintiffs' complaint? Why? According to the Supreme Court, were the plaintiffs within the zone of interests of that provision? Why or why not? Do you agree?

* * *

IV. THE *GWALTNEY* ISSUE

A second *statutory* limitation on federal courts' jurisdiction over environmental citizen suits arises because most citizen suit provisions allow members of the public to sue regulated entities who are "alleged to be in violation" of the environmental statute. What does that phrase mean for federal court jurisdiction? In particular, can environmental plaintiffs sue a violator for *past* violations of the statute?

GWALTNEY OF SMITHFIELD, LTD. v. CHESAPEAKE BAY FOUNDATION, INC.

484 U.S. 49 (1987).

JUSTICE MARSHALL delivered the opinion of the Court.

In this case, we must decide whether § 505(a) of the Clean Water Act, also known as the Federal Water Pollution Control Act, 33 U.S.C. § 1365(a), confers federal jurisdiction over citizen suits for wholly past violations.

I

The Clean Water Act (Act), 33 U.S.C. § 1251 *et seq.* (1982 ed. and Supp. III), was enacted in 1972 "to restore and maintain the chemical, physical, and biological integrity of the Nation's waters." § 1251(a). In order to achieve these goals, § 301(a) of the Act makes unlawful the discharge of any pollutant into navigable waters except as authorized by specified sections of the Act. 33 U.S.C. § 1311(a).

One of these specified sections is § 402, which establishes the National Pollutant Discharge Elimination System (NPDES). 33 U.S.C. § 1342. Pursuant to § 402(a), the Administrator of the Environmental Protection Agency (EPA) may issue permits authorizing the discharge of pollutants in accordance with specified conditions. § 1342(a). Pursuant to § 402(b), each State may establish and administer its own permit program if the program conforms to federal guidelines and is approved by the Administrator. § 1342(b). The Act calls for the Administrator to suspend the issuance of federal permits as to waters subject to an approved state program. § 1342(c)(1).

The holder of a federal NPDES permit is subject to enforcement action by the Administrator for failure to comply with the conditions of the permit. * * * In the absence of federal or state enforcement, private citizens may commence civil actions against any person "alleged to be in violation of" the conditions of either a federal or state NPDES permit. § 1365(a)(1). If the citizen prevails in such an action, the court may order injunctive relief and/or impose civil penalties payable to the United States Treasury. § 1365(a).

The Commonwealth of Virginia established a federally approved state NPDES program administered by the Virginia State Water Control Board (Board). VA. CODE. § 62.1–44.2 *et seq.* (1950). In 1974, the Board issued a NPDES permit to ITT–Gwaltney authorizing the discharge of seven pollutants from the company's meat-packing plant on the Pagan River in Smithfield, Virginia. The permit, which was reissued in 1979 and modified in 1980, established effluent limitations, monitoring requirements, and other conditions of discharge. In 1981, petitioner Gwaltney of Smithfield acquired the assets of ITT–Gwaltney and assumed obligations under the permit.

Between 1981 and 1984, petitioner repeatedly violated the conditions of the permit by exceeding effluent limitations on five of the seven pollutants covered. These violations are chronicled in the Discharge Monitoring Reports that the permit required petitioner to maintain. The most substantial of the violations concerned the pollutants fecal coliform, chlorine, and total Kjeldahl nitrogen (TKN). Between October 27, 1981, and August 30, 1984, petitioner violated its TKN limitation 87 times, its chlorine limitation 34 times, and its fecal coliform limitation 31 times. Petitioner installed new equipment to improve its chlorination system in March 1982, and its last reported chlorine violation occurred in October 1982. The new chlorination system also helped to control the discharge of fecal coliform, and the last recorded fecal coliform violation occurred in February 1984. Petitioner installed an upgraded wastewater treatment system in October 1983, and its last reported TKN violation occurred on May 15, 1984.

Respondents Chesapeake Bay Foundation and Natural Resources Defense Council, two nonprofit corporations dedicated to the protection of natural resources, sent notice in February 1984 to Gwaltney, the Administrator of EPA, and the Virginia State Water Control Board, indicating respondents' intention to commence a citizen suit under the Act based on petitioner's violations of its permit conditions. Respondents proceeded to file this suit in June 1984, alleging that petitioner "has violated . . . [and] will continue to violate its NPDES permit." Respondents requested that the District Court provide declaratory and injunctive relief, impose civil penalties, and award attorney's fees and costs. The District Court granted partial summary judgment for respondents in August 1984, declaring Gwaltney "to have violated and to be in violation" of the Act. The District Court then held a trial to determine the appropriate remedy.

Before the District Court reached a decision, Gwaltney moved in May 1985 for dismissal of the action for want of subject-matter jurisdiction under the Act. Gwaltney argued that the language of § 505(a), which permits private citizens to bring suit against any person "alleged to be in violation" of the Act, requires that a defendant be violating the Act at the time of suit. * * * Gwaltney contended that because its last recorded violation occurred several weeks before respondents filed their complaint, the District Court lacked subject-matter jurisdiction over respondents' action.

The District Court rejected Gwaltney's argument, concluding that § 505 authorizes citizens to bring enforcement actions on the basis of wholly past violations. * * *

The Court of Appeals affirmed, * * * holding that § 505 "can be read to comprehend unlawful conduct that occurred only prior to the filing of a lawsuit as well as unlawful conduct that continues into the present." * * *

* * * We now vacate the Fourth Circuit's opinion and remand the case.

II

A

It is well settled that "the starting point for interpreting a statute is the language of the statute itself." *Consumer Product Safety Comm'n v. GTE Sylvania, Inc.*, 447 U.S. 102, 108 (1980). * * * The most natural reading of "to be in violation" is a requirement that citizen-plaintiffs allege a state of either continuous or intermittent violation—that is, a reasonable likelihood that a past polluter will continue to pollute in the future. Congress could have phrased its requirement in language that looked to the past ("to have violated"), but it did not choose this readily available option.

Respondents urge that the choice of the phrase "to be in violation," rather than phrasing more clearly directed to the past, is a "careless accident," the result of a "debatable lapse of syntactical precision." But the prospective orientation of that phrase could not have escaped Congress' attention. Congress used identical language in the citizen suit provisions of several other environmental statutes that authorize only prospective relief. *See, e.g.*, Clean Air Act, 42 U.S.C. § 7604; Resource Conservation and Recovery Act of 1976, 42 U.S.C. § 6972 (1982 ed. and Supp. III); Toxic Substances Control Act, 15 U.S.C. § 2619 (1982 ed. and Supp. IV). Moreover, Congress has demonstrated in yet other statutory provisions that it knows how to avoid this prospective implication by using language that explicitly targets wholly past violations.

Respondents seek to counter this reasoning by observing that Congress also used the phrase "is in violation" in § 309(a) of the Act, which authorizes the Administrator of EPA to issue compliance orders. 33 U.S.C. § 1319(a). That language is incorporated by reference in § 309(b), which authorizes the Administrator to bring civil enforcement actions. § 1319(b). Because it is little questioned that the Administrator may bring enforcement actions to recover civil penalties for wholly past violations, respondents contend, the parallel language of § 309(a) and § 505(a) must mean that citizens, too, may maintain such actions.

Although this argument has some initial plausibility, it cannot withstand close scrutiny and comparison of the two statutory provisions. The Administrator's ability to seek civil penalties is not discussed in either § 309(a) or § 309(b); civil penalties are not mentioned until § 309(d), which does not contain the "is in violation" language. 33 U.S.C. § 1319(d). * * *

In contrast, § 505 of the Act does not authorize civil penalties separately from injunctive relief; rather, the two forms of relief are referred to in the same subsection, even in the same sentence. 33 U.S.C. § 1365(a). The citizen suit provision suggests a connection between injunctive relief and civil penalties that is noticeably absent from the provision authorizing agency enforcement. A comparison of § 309 and § 505 thus supports rather than refutes our conclusion that citizens, unlike the Administrator, may seek civil penalties only in a suit brought to enjoin or otherwise abate an ongoing violation.

B

Our reading of the "to be in violation" language of § 505(a) is bolstered by the language and structure of the rest of the citizen suit provisions in § 505 of the Act. These provisions together make plain that the interest of the citizen-plaintiff is primarily forward-looking.

One of the most striking indicia of the prospective orientation of the citizen suit is the pervasive use of the present tense throughout § 505. A citizen suit may be brought only for violation of a permit limitation "which is in effect" under the Act. 33 U.S.C. § 1365(f). Citizen-plaintiffs must give notice to the alleged violator, the Administrator of EPA, and the State in which the alleged violation "occurs." § 1365(b)(1)(A). A Governor of a State may sue as a citizen when the Administrator fails to enforce an effluent limitation "the violation of which is occurring in another State and is causing an adverse effect on the public health or welfare in his State." § 1365(h). The most telling use of the present tense is in the definition of "citizen" as "a person . . . having an interest which is or may be adversely affected" by the defendant's violations of the Act. § 1365(g). This definition makes plain what the undeviating use of the present tense strongly suggests: the harm sought to be addressed by the citizen suit lies in the present or the future, not in the past.

Any other conclusion would render incomprehensible § 505's notice provision, which requires citizens to give 60 days' notice of their intent to sue to the alleged violator as well as to the Administrator and the State. § 1365(b)(1)(A). If the Administrator or the State commences enforcement action within that 60–day period, the citizen suit is barred, presumably because governmental action has rendered it unnecessary. § 1365(b)(1)(B). It follows logically that the purpose of notice to the alleged violator is to give it an opportunity to bring itself into complete compliance with the Act and thus likewise render unnecessary a citizen suit. If we assume, as respondents urge, that citizen suits may target wholly past violations, the requirement of notice to the alleged violator becomes gratuitous. Indeed, respondents, in propounding their interpretation of the Act, can think of no reason for Congress to require such notice other than that "it seemed right" to inform an alleged violator that it was about to be sued.

Adopting respondents' interpretation of § 505's jurisdictional grant would create a second and even more disturbing anomaly. The bar on citizen suits when governmental enforcement action is under way suggests that the citizen suit is meant to supplement rather than to supplant governmental action. The legislative history of the Act reinforces this view of the role of the citizen suit. The Senate Report noted that "[t]he Committee intends the great volume of enforcement actions [to] be brought by the State," and that citizen suits are proper only "if the Federal, State, and local agencies fail to exercise their enforcement responsibility." S. REP. NO. 92–414, p. 64 (1971), *reprinted in* 2 A LEGISLATIVE HISTORY OF THE WATER POLLUTION CONTROL ACT AMENDMENTS OF 1972, p. 1482 (1973) (hereinafter Leg. Hist.). Permitting citizen suits for wholly past violations of the Act could undermine the supplementary role envisioned for the citizen suit. * * * We cannot agree that Congress intended such a result.

C

The legislative history of the Act provides additional support for our reading of § 505. Members of Congress frequently characterized the citizen suit provisions as "abatement" provisions or as injunctive measures. Moreover, both the Senate and House Reports explicitly connected § 505 to the citizen suit provisions authorized by the Clean Air Act, which are wholly injunctive in nature. Congress' acknowledgment of this connection suggests that the identity of the "alleged to be in violation" language of the citizen suit provisions of the two Acts is not accidental; rather, the two provisions share the common central purpose of permitting citizens to abate pollution when the government cannot or will not command compliance. This understanding of the "alleged to be in violation" language as a statutory term of art rather than a mere stylistic infelicity is reinforced by the consistent adherence in the Senate and House Reports to the precise statutory formulation. * * *

* * * III

Our conclusion that § 505 does not permit citizen suits for wholly past violations does not necessarily dispose of this lawsuit, as both lower courts recognized. The District Court found persuasive the fact that "[respondents'] allegation in the complaint, that Gwaltney was continuing to violate its NPDES permit when plaintiffs filed suit[,] appears to have been made fully in good faith." On this basis, the District Court explicitly held, albeit in a footnote, that "even if Gwaltney were correct that a district court has no jurisdiction over citizen suits based entirely on unlawful conduct that occurred entirely in the past, the Court would still have jurisdiction here." The Court of Appeals acknowledged, also in a footnote, that "[a] very sound argument can be made that [respondents'] allegations of continuing violations were made in good faith," but expressly declined to rule on this alternative holding. Because we agree that § 505 confers jurisdiction over citizen suits when the citizen-plaintiffs make a good-faith allegation of continuous or intermittent violation, we remand the case to the Court of Appeals for further consideration.

Petitioner argues that citizen-plaintiffs must prove their allegations of ongoing noncompliance before jurisdiction attaches under § 505. We cannot agree. The statute does not require that a defendant "be in violation" of the Act at the commencement of suit; rather, the statute requires that a defendant be "*alleged* to be in violation." Petitioner's construction of the Act reads the word "alleged" out of § 505. As petitioner itself is quick to note in other contexts, there is no reason to believe that Congress' drafting of § 505 was sloppy or haphazard. We agree with the Solicitor General that "Congress's use of the phrase 'alleged to be in violation' reflects a conscious sensitivity to the practical difficulties of detecting and proving chronic episodic violations of environmental standards." Brief for the United States as *Amicus Curiae* 18. Our acknowledgment that Congress intended a good-faith allegation to suffice for jurisdictional purposes, however, does not give litigants license to flood the courts with suits premised on baseless allegations. Rule 11 of the Federal Rules of Civil Procedure, which requires pleadings to be based on a good-faith belief, formed after reasonable inquiry, that they are "well grounded in fact," adequately protects defendants from frivolous allegations. * * *

Petitioner also worries that our construction of § 505 would permit citizen-plaintiffs, if their allegations of ongoing noncompliance become false at some later point in the litigation because the defendant begins to comply with the Act, to continue nonetheless to press their suit to conclusion. According to petitioner, such a result would contravene both the prospective purpose of the citizen suit provisions and the "case or controversy" requirement of Article III. Longstanding principles of mootness, however, prevent the maintenance of suit when " 'there is no reasonable expectation that the wrong will be repeated.' " *United States v. W.T. Grant Co.*, 345 U.S. 629, 633 (1953) (quoting *United States v. Aluminum Co. of America*, 148 F.2d 416, 448 (CA2 1945)). In seeking to have a case dismissed as moot, however, the defendant's burden "is a heavy one." 345 U.S., at 633. The defendant must demonstrate that it is "*absolutely clear* that the allegedly wrongful behavior could not reasonably be expected to recur." *United States v. Phosphate Export Assn., Inc.*, 393 U.S. 199, 203 (1968) (emphasis added). Mootness doctrine thus protects defendants from the maintenance of suit under the Clean Water Act based solely on violations wholly unconnected to any present or future wrongdoing, while it also protects plaintiffs from defendants who seek to evade sanction by predictable "protestations of repentance and reform." *United States v. Oregon State Medical Society*, 343 U.S. 326, 333 (1952). * * *

NOTES

1. **Citizen Suits for Wholly Past Violations.** Given the Clean Water Act's "alleged to be in violation" language, what kind of violations are beyond the reach of that Act's citizen suit provision, according to the Supreme Court? What kinds of violations are included? What exactly does a citizen suit plaintiff have to allege regarding a defendant's violations in order for the federal court to have jurisdiction? What tools of statutory construction did the Supreme Court use to reach this decision?

2. **The Role of Citizen Enforcement in General.** What is the general role of citizen suits in environmental enforcement, according to the Supreme Court in *Gwaltney*? Why did the Court reach that conclusion? What provisions of the Clean Water Act, besides the citizen suit provision, did it rely

on? How does this view of citizen suits comport with the federalism aspects of the Clean Water Act? How does it comport with the Act's larger goals?

3. **The Clean Air Act and *Gwaltney*.** *Gwaltney* involved the Clean Water Act, which clearly authorizes citizen suits against polluters only if those polluters are "alleged to be in violation" of the Act. In contrast, the Clean Air Act's citizen suit provision allows suits "against any person * * * who is alleged to have violated (if there is evidence that the violation has been repeated) or to be in violation of (A) an emission standard or limitation under this chapter or (B) an order issued by the Administrator or State with respect to such a standard or limitation." CAA § 304(a)(1), 42 U.S.C. § 7604(a)(1). Does the *Gwaltney* analysis apply to Clean Air Act citizen suits? Why or why not?

* * *

After remands all the way back to the district court, the Fourth Circuit eventually addressed the factual issues regarding Gwaltney's ongoing violations in the following case.

CHESAPEAKE BAY FOUNDATION, INC. v. GWALTNEY OF SMITHFIELD, LTD.

890 F.2d 690 (4th Cir. 1989).

SPROUSE, CIRCUIT JUDGE:

This case, a frequent visitor in this court, continues to present serious issues concerning the interpretation of § 505 of the Clean Water Act (the Act). Gwaltney of Smithfield, Ltd. (Gwaltney), appeals the finding of the district court that plaintiffs-appellees Chesapeake Bay Foundation, Inc. (CBF), and Natural Resources Defense Council, Inc. (NRDC), proved ongoing violations by Gwaltney at the time suit was brought. Gwaltney also raises standing and mootness objections to this action. We affirm in part and reverse in part.

I

FACTS AND PROCEDURAL HISTORY

The original action was brought by CBF under the citizen suit provisions of 33 U.S.C. § 1365 (§ 505 of the Act). CBF based its claims on violations by Gwaltney of its National Pollutant Discharge Elimination System (NPDES) permit, and requested both injunctive relief and civil penalties under 33 U.S.C. §§ 1365(a) and 1319(d) (§§ 505(a) and 309(d) of the Act). The district court found that CBF had standing to bring the suit, that the court had subject matter jurisdiction, and that Gwaltney was liable for its violations. Using the Environmental Protection Agency Civil Penalty Policy as a guideline, the court imposed upon Gwaltney a civil penalty of $1,285,322, with interest, of which $289,822 was for violations of Gwaltney's total Kjeldahl nitrogen (TKN) limit, and $995,500 was for violations of the chlorine limit.

* * * The United States Supreme Court granted certiorari on the issue of jurisdiction in order to resolve a split among the circuits and subsequently held that § 1365(a) does not permit citizen suits for wholly past violations. It remanded the case to us to consider whether CBF's complaint had made a good-faith allegation of ongoing violations, holding that such allegation would be sufficient to establish subject matter jurisdiction. The district court, in its initial consideration, had suggested as an alternative holding that CBF had made sufficient good faith allegations of continuing violations to establish jurisdiction. On remand from the Supreme Court, we held that this finding was not clearly erroneous, and remanded the case to the district court "for further findings as to whether, on the merits, plaintiffs proved at trial an ongoing violation."

After remand to the district court, Gwaltney again challenged the subject matter jurisdiction of the court, moving to dismiss the case as moot and, alternatively, to dismiss because the plaintiffs did not have standing. Gwaltney also asserted that even if the court did have jurisdiction to hear the case, it did not have jurisdiction as to Gwaltney's chlorine violations, because no reasonable person could in good faith allege that the chlorine violations were ongoing at the time of trial. Finally, Gwaltney asserted that CBF had failed to meet its burden of proving that there were ongoing violations, even of TKN, at the time of trial.

The district court interpreted our mandate to foreclose any consideration of mootness, standing, or severability of the chlorine and TKN violations, instructing it *only* to determine whether CBF had proved ongoing violations. Finding that CBF had done so, the court reinstated its original judgment of $1,285,322 in civil penalties.

Gwaltney now appeals to this court, claiming there was insufficient evidence to support the district court's finding of ongoing violations. Gwaltney claims that even if there was sufficient evidence the district court erred in reinstating penalties for chlorine as well as TKN violations. Gwaltney also appeals on the standing and mootness issues. Normally, because they are jurisdictional, we would consider the standing and mootness questions first. In this case, however, the jurisdictional issues are intertwined with the finding of ongoing violations; therefore, we address the substantive dispute first.

II

WHETHER THERE WAS AN ONGOING VIOLATION

Gwaltney asserts that the district court erred in finding that there was an ongoing violation at the time suit was brought. As we now know, essentially the last violation occurred on May 15, 1984. Gwaltney claims that at the remand hearing the district court should have considered the evidence of its compliance since that time. Gwaltney also asserts that there was not sufficient evidence adduced at the time of trial to permit a finding of ongoing violation.

In its opinion in this case, the Supreme Court stated that, at trial, the citizen-plaintiff must prove its allegations of ongoing violation in order to prevail. The Court defined a § 1365 ongoing violation to be "a reasonable likelihood that a past polluter will continue to pollute in the future." In our remand to the district court, we instructed that the citizen-plaintiffs could prove an ongoing violation

> either (1) by proving violations that continue on or after the date the complaint is filed, or (2) by adducing evidence from which a reasonable trier of fact could find a continuing likelihood of a recurrence in intermittent or sporadic violations. Intermittent or sporadic violations do not cease to be ongoing until the date when there is no real likelihood of repetition....

* * * There is no doubt that Gwaltney was a past polluter. Its discharge monitoring reports revealed violations in almost every month from the time Gwaltney purchased the plant in 1981 until one month before suit was filed. The question is whether, at the time suit was brought, there was a reasonable likelihood that this past polluter would continue to pollute in the future.

Gwaltney points to its record of near-perfect compliance after May 15, 1984 as conclusive evidence that there was no ongoing violation at the time of trial. However, the proper point from which to assess the likelihood of continuing violations is not the present, with its advantage of hindsight, but the time of the original suit. That is, did CBF carry its burden at trial of proving ongoing violations, either by proving actual violations after the date of filing suit, or by proving a reasonable likelihood that intermittent or sporadic violations would recur at Gwaltney?

The testimony at trial showed the following. Gwaltney purchased the meat processing plant in October of 1981. In June of 1982, it hired a consulting engineer to design modifications so the wastewater treatment facility would adequately treat the plant waste. After various delays, a final plan was approved, and the modifications were completed in October of 1983. Nevertheless, violations of Gwaltney's TKN permit limitation occurred during the winter of 1983–84.

CBF sent notice of intention to sue in February 1984. The last violation of Gwaltney's permit occurred on May 15, 1984. CBF filed suit on June 15, 1984. Trial was held on December 19, 1984. CBF put on as its only witness Dr. Bruce A. Bell. Gwaltney put on, *inter alia,* the testimony of Mr. J. Willis Sneed. Both Dr. Bell and Mr. Sneed testified that a major factor leading to TKN violations is low water temperatures. Dr. Bell's testimony included the following:

> Q. Do you have an opinion based upon your review of the records in this case and your visit to the Gwaltney facility, with regard to whether the Gwaltney facility will meet T.K.N. limits this winter?

A. Assuming we have a normally cold winter, I think it is unlikely that they will.

Q. What is the basis for those doubts?

A. Primarily the question of waste water temperature. They are still using surface aerators, which tend to act to cool the system. And the larger of the two anaerobic lagoons being used has not at this time, or as of a week ago, formed a grease cover over most of the lagoon. And that grease cover is needed to act as an insulating blanket during the cold temperatures.

Mr. Sneed testified that the primary cause of the TKN violations the previous winter had been the lack of an adequate grease cover on the anaerobic lagoon. At another point he testified as follows:

Q. Mr. Sneed, is adequate grease cover important to proper winter T.K.N. treatment of the plant?

A. On the anaerobic lagoon, yes.

Q. You were with us last week when we toured the facility, were you not?

A. Yes.

Q. Isn't it in fact true at that point in time, in December, the lower anaerobic lagoon did not have adequate grease cover?

A. Yes. Earlier in the summer time that lagoon was covered with grease. And that was what we expected would happen. Quite frankly we were very surprised that that grease cover has deteriorated to this point, and we have since taken steps to accelerate the formation of that grease cover.

Q. Given the importance, as you mentioned before, of maintaining adequate grease cover, isn't there some doubt in your mind as to whether the Gwaltney facility would be in compliance with T.K.N. limits this winter?

A. Yes, we have.

Q. Isn't there some doubt? That is all I am asking.

A. Yes, Sir. I think there is some doubt every year that you would expect the plant to go out of compliance at some time.

Thus, at the time of trial, there had been no violations at Gwaltney during the previous summer months, but there had been TKN violations during the previous winter due to an inadequate grease cover. The trial was held on the threshold of another winter, the parties' witnesses agreed that TKN violations were more likely to occur in the winter, there was testimony from both parties' witnesses that the grease cover on the anaerobic lagoon was at the time inadequate to protect against normal winter temperatures, and both witnesses expressed doubt whether Gwaltney could stay in compliance with its TKN limitation through the winter.

There was other evidence adduced at the trial that would indicate recurring violations of the TKN limitation were likely. Dr. Bell expressed concerns about the configuration of the anaerobic lagoon, the use of surface aerators, and the unknown effect of storm water on the system. Dr. Bell and a Gwaltney witness, Mr. Terry L. Rettig, testified that there were problems with the laboratory procedures used at Gwaltney, which would have an adverse effect on Gwaltney's ability to properly assess the operational needs of its treatment facility. There also was evidence that proper wastewater treatment did not receive a high priority at Gwaltney.

Given all of the above, we think that "a reasonable trier of fact could find a continuing likelihood of a recurrence in intermittent or sporadic violations." We therefore affirm the district court in so finding.

III

STANDING

The Supreme Court set forth the elements of Article III standing in *Allen v. Wright*, 468 U.S. 737, 751 (1984): "A plaintiff must allege personal injury fairly traceable to the defendant's allegedly unlawful conduct and likely to be redressed by the requested relief." Gwaltney urges that CBF cannot demonstrate that its injury is "likely to be redressed by the requested relief." It argues that, since its permit violations had ceased at the time suit was filed, the only remedy available to CBF was an assessment of civil penalties against Gwaltney. Since civil penalties are paid into the United States Treasury, Gwaltney urges that such payments could not redress any injury to CBF. However, we already have held that such payments are causally related to a citizen-plaintiff's injury and are therefore likely to redress that injury. * * *

* * * IV

MOOTNESS

Although this jurisdictional issue was not raised in the original trial or on appeal from that judgment and therefore was not specifically included in our order of remand, mootness may be raised at any stage of the proceedings. Moreover, since the record in this respect is fully developed, nothing would be gained by another remand for an initial decision by the district court on this issue. We therefore consider Gwaltney's mootness contention and conclude that the case is not moot.

The Supreme Court's mootness doctrine is well summarized in *Cedar Coal Co. v. United Mine Workers*, 560 F.2d 1153 (4th Cir. 1977), *cert. denied*, 434 U.S. 1047 (1978):

> [C]ourts are not empowered to decide moot questions or abstract propositions, but the exercise of judicial power depends upon the existence of a case or controversy. The suit must be definite and concrete, touching the legal relations of parties having adverse legal interests and be a real and substantial controversy admitting of specific relief through a decree of conclusive character as distin-

guished from an opinion of what the law would be upon a hypothetical statement of facts.

Id. at 1162 (paraphrasing *North Carolina v. Rice*), 404 U.S. 244 (1971).

The question here is whether litigation over penalties imposed for past violations which are linked with ongoing violations presents a live case or controversy, even though primary subject matter jurisdiction is based on alleged continuing violations. In our view, the penalty factor keeps the controversy alive between plaintiffs and defendants in a citizen suit, even though the defendant has come into compliance and even though the ultimate judicial remedy is the imposition of civil penalties assessed for past acts of pollution. This conclusion follows from the structure of both § 1319—authorizing actions by the government against polluters—and § 1365—permitting citizen suits.

It is well established that the simple cessation of illegal activity upon the filing of a complaint does not moot a case. Under the Clean Water Act, civil penalties attach as of the date a permit violation occurs. Liability is fixed by the happening of an event (discharge of effluent with an excessive burden of pollution) that occurred in the past. Thus, the initiation of § 1319 actions by the government can be based on wholly past violations, so that a suit seeking penalties is intrinsically incapable of being rendered moot by the polluter's corrective actions. * * *

A similar rationale governs our consideration of putative mootness arguably brought on by corrective action after a § 1365 citizen suit has been initiated. When the Supreme Court concluded in its *Gwaltney* decision that § 1365 permits citizens' actions against polluters while there are ongoing violations, the Court effectively approved the assessment of penalties based on past violations (the only possible basis for assessing a penalty). Assuming, then, proof of an ongoing violation, a citizen action, like a government action, cannot become moot once there is assessment of civil penalties, so long as the penalties are for past violations that were part of or which contiguously preceded the ongoing violations.

* * * Here, however, we need not speculate—the district court has found as a matter of fact that Gwaltney's violations were ongoing as that term is explained in the Supreme Court's *Gwaltney* decision. As we have explained, that finding is not clearly erroneous, and it shapes the dimensions of this case on appeal. The district court's judgment was based on its conclusion that Gwaltney was guilty of an ongoing violation at the time suit was filed, and the penalty levied against it was based, as it necessarily must be, on past violations. It is both the ongoing nature of the violation and CBF's interest as a private attorney general seeking a remedy for that violation that presents a live controversy in the Article III context.

V

BIFURCATION OF THE TKN AND CHLORINE VIOLATIONS

Our remand instructed the district court to determine whether there had been an ongoing violation at Gwaltney at the time of trial. At the remand hearing, Gwaltney urged that the court should make separate determinations for the TKN and chlorine violations. The court, interpreting our remand quite strictly, deemed it was permitted only to determine whether there was an ongoing violation; finding that there was, the court then reinstated the original judgment, which was based on both TKN and chlorine violations. We reverse.

It is "absolutely clear" that there were no ongoing chlorine violations at the time this suit was brought. Gwaltney had installed new chlorination equipment in March of 1982, had made further modifications over the summer, and had experienced no violations of its chlorine limitations since October of 1982. Clearly Gwaltney had abated its chlorine problems by the time CBF filed suit in June of 1984. Had Gwaltney violated no other permit parameters, the court would have had no subject matter jurisdiction over this suit.

However, Gwaltney did violate other parameters, including the TKN violations which were ongoing at the time suit was filed, and CBF seeks to use that fact to justify imposition of penalties for the chlorine violations. CBF contends that the jurisdictional requirement of § 1365 refers to finding an ongoing violation of the *permit;* having done so, the court may then impose penalties for any past violation of any permit *parameter.* We do not think the statutory language can support that position. Section 1365(a) permits citizen suits against persons alleged to be in violation of "an effluent standard or limitation." Penalties under § 1319(d) may be assessed for violations of "any permit condition or limitation." The entire structure of the Clean Water Act and regulations involves identifying specific pollutants and setting a permit limit for each pollutant of concern. It thus makes sense within this scheme to view each parameter separately for purposes both of determining ongoing violation and of assessing penalties.

CBF's theory also runs against the reasoning of the Supreme Court in finding that there must be an ongoing violation to create subject-matter jurisdiction. If Congress wished to permit citizen suits only when a discharger fails to abate a problem and the government fails to take enforcement action, then it would make little sense to permit penalties for wholly past violations of one parameter simply because there are ongoing violations of another parameter. The chlorine and TKN problems were due to distinct equipment and operational failures, and were corrected by distinct engineering solutions. While it was questionable at the time of suit whether Gwaltney had corrected its TKN violations, it was clear the company had abated its chlorine violations.

We therefore hold that the district court had no jurisdiction to impose penalties for Gwaltney's wholly past chlorine violations. We vacate the judgment for $1,285,322 and remand for the court to enter judgment against Gwaltney in the amount of $289,822—the amount attributable to TKN violations—with interest. * * *

NOTES

1. **Assessing "Ongoing" Violations.** What standard did the Fourth Circuit use to determine whether plaintiffs have met the burden of showing "ongoing" violations? As of *when* must the violations be ongoing?

Notice that the Fourth Circuit assessed ongoing violations on a pollutant-by-pollutant (sometimes referred to as a parameter-by-parameter) basis. Had the plaintiffs in *Gwaltney* shown ongoing TKN violations? Why or why not? Had the plaintiffs shown ongoing chlorine violations? Why or why not? What affect did these determinations have on the amount of civil penalties that the court could assess against Gwaltney?

2. ***Gwaltney* and Standing.** What standing argument did Gwaltney make on remand? How is that argument connected to the Supreme Court's decision that citizens cannot bring citizen suits for wholly past violations?

3. **Mootness and Civil Penalties.** What is mootness? How did Gwaltney try to argue that this citizen suit had become moot? Why did the Fourth Circuit determine that the lawsuit was *not* moot? What role did civil penalty liability play in its decision? What role did the ongoing TKN violations play in its decision?

4. **The Prevalence of the *Gwaltney* Approach.** The Fourth Circuit's approach to ongoing violations and the *Gwaltney* issue has been widely adopted by other circuits. *See, e.g., I.V. Services of America, Inc. v. Inn Development & Management, Inc.*, 182 F.3d 51, 54 (1st Cir. 1999); *Reich v. Occupational Safety & Health Review Com'n*, 102 F.3d 1200, 1202 (11th Cir. 1997); *Natural Resources Defense Council, Inc. v. Texaco Refining & Marketing, Inc.*, 2 F.3d 493, 497 (3rd Cir. 1993); *Atlantic States Legal Foundation, Inc. v. Pan American Tanning Corp.*, 993 F.2d 1017, 1020 (2d Cir. 1993); *Carr v. Alta Verde Industries, Inc.*, 931 F.2d 1055, 1062 (5th Cir. 1991).

5. **Civil Penalty Assessments in Clean Water Act Citizen Suits.** As noted above, the Clean Water Act's citizen suit provision allows the district judge "to apply any appropriate civil penalties under section 1319(d)." CWA § 505(a), 33 U.S.C. § 1365(a). In an important Seventh Amendment decision, the Supreme Court decided that Clean Water Act defendants have a right to a jury trial regarding their *liability*, but that the *judge* could determine the amount of the civil penalty assessed. *Tull v. United States*, 481 U.S. 412, 420–27 (1987).

Section 309(d) of the Clean Water Act allows civil penalties "not to exceed $25,000 per day for each violation." CWA § 309(d), 33 U.S.C. § 1319(d). Moreover:

> In determining the amount of a civil penalty the court shall consider the seriousness of the violation or violations, the economic benefit (if any) resulting from the violation, any history of any such violations, any good-faith efforts to comply with the applicable requirements, the economic impact of the penalty on the violator, and other such matters as justice may require.

Id. In applying these factors, most federal judges start by calculating the maximum penalty allowable—*i.e.*, they multiply $25,000 (or now, by amendment, $27,500) by the total number of days of violation for each parameter violated, then add those totals together. The judge will then reduce this total possible penalty in light of the statutory factors. *See, e.g.*, *United States v. Smithfield Foods, Inc.*, 191 F.3d 516, 528–29 (4th Cir. 1999) (outlining this approach); *but see also United States v. Allegheny Ludlum Corp.*, 366 F.3d 164, 178 n.6 (3rd Cir. 2004) (discussing both the "top-down" approach and the "bottom-up" approach and deeming both valid). The EPA has advocated that the resulting penalty should be at least as much as the economic benefit that the discharger received through the discharger's noncompliance—for example, the savings in not installing new pollution control equipment. *See, e.g.*, U.S. EPA, CIVIL PENALTY POLICY FOR SECTION 311(B)(3) AND SECTION 311(J) OF THE CLEAN WATER ACT 15–16 (Aug. 1998), *available at* http://epa.gov/compliance/resources/policies/civil/cwa/311pen.pdf; *Allegheny Ludlum*, 366 F.3d at 177–78.

* * *

V. STANDING, PART 2: *GWALTNEY* AND THE STANDING ANALYSIS

As Gwaltney's arguments in the remand to the Fourth Circuit indicate, *Gwaltney* and the issue of ongoing violations have implications for standing as well as for statutory citizen suit jurisdiction. The Supreme Court first addressed these implications in *Steel Company v. Citizens for a Better Environment*, 523 U.S. 83 (1998). *Steel Company* involved a citizen suit under the Emergency Planning and Community Right-to-Know Act (EPCRA), 42 U.S.C. § 11046(a)(1). EPCRA requires companies to file hazardous chemical inventory forms every year, listing the pollutants that the company releases into the environment. Steel Company had failed to file these forms since 1988, the first year of EPCRA's deadlines. Upon receiving Citizens for a Better Environment's (CBE's) citizen suit notice, however, Steel Company quickly filed all of its overdue reports. Thus, by the time CBE filed its citizen suit, there was no question that Steel Company's violations were anything other than wholly past violations. Nevertheless, the language of EPCRA's citizen suit provision, unlike the Clean Water Act's, appeared to allow citizen suits for wholly past violations, and the Sixth and Seventh Circuits had split on that issue.

Instead of deciding the EPCRA issue, however, the Supreme Court, in another fractured decision, dismissed the case on standing grounds. According to the opinion issued by Justice Scalia, CBE could show no redressability for its claims:

> The complaint asks for (1) a declaratory judgment that petitioner violated EPCRA; (2) authorization to inspect periodically petitioner's facility and records (with costs borne by petitioner); (3) an order requiring petitioner to provide respondent copies of all compliance reports submitted to the EPA; (4) an order requiring petitioner to pay

civil penalties of $25,000 per day for each violation of §§ 11022 and 11023; (5) an award of all respondent's "costs, in connection with the investigation and prosecution of this matter, including reasonable attorney and expert witness fees, as authorized by Section 326(f) of [EPCRA]"; and (6) any such further relief as the court deems appropriate. None of the specific items of relief sought, and none that we can envision as "appropriate" under the general request, would serve to reimburse respondent for losses caused by the late reporting, or to eliminate any effects of that late reporting upon respondent.

The first item, the request for a declaratory judgment that petitioner violated EPCRA, can be disposed of summarily. There being no controversy over whether petitioner failed to file reports, or over whether such a failure constitutes a violation, the declaratory judgment is not only worthless to respondent, it is seemingly worthless to all the world.

Item (4), the civil penalties authorized by the statute, § 11045(c), might be viewed as a sort of compensation or redress to respondent if they were payable to respondent. But they are not. These penalties—the only damages authorized by EPCRA—are payable to the United States Treasury. In requesting them, therefore, respondent seeks not remediation of its own injury—reimbursement for the costs it incurred as a result of the late filing—but vindication of the rule of law—the "undifferentiated public interest" in faithful execution of EPCRA. This does not suffice. * * * By the mere bringing of his suit, *every* plaintiff demonstrates his belief that a favorable judgment will make him happier. But although a suitor may derive great comfort and joy from the fact that the United States Treasury is not cheated, that a wrongdoer gets his just deserts, or that the Nation's laws are faithfully enforced, that psychic satisfaction is not an acceptable Article III remedy because it does not redress a cognizable Article III injury. Relief that does not remedy the injury suffered cannot bootstrap a plaintiff into federal court; that is the very essence of the redressability requirement.

Item (5), the "investigation and prosecution" costs [], would assuredly benefit respondent as opposed to the citizenry at large. Obviously, however, a plaintiff cannot achieve standing to litigate a substantive issue by bringing suit for the cost of bringing suit. The litigation must give the plaintiff some other benefit besides reimbursement of costs that are a byproduct of the litigation itself. * * *

The remaining relief respondent seeks (item (2), giving respondent authority to inspect petitioner's facility and records, and item (3), compelling petitioner to provide respondent copies of EPA compliance reports) is injunctive in nature. It cannot conceivably remedy any past wrong but is aimed at deterring petitioner from violating EPCRA in the future. The latter objective can of course be "remedial" for Article III purposes, when threatened injury is one of the gravamens of the

> complaint. If respondent had alleged a continuing violation or the imminence of a future violation, the injunctive relief requested would remedy that alleged harm. But there is no such allegation here—and on the facts of the case, there seems no basis for it. Nothing supports the requested injunctive relief except respondent's generalized interest in deterrence, which is insufficient for purposes of Article III.

Id. at 105–09.

Steel Company caused a waive of consternation among citizen suit plaintiffs and their attorneys, because it seemed to indicate that claims for civil penalties could *never* redress a citizen suit plaintiff's injuries—only an injunction could. This interpretation spelled doom for any citizen suit—like *Gwaltney* itself—where the need for an injunction became moot during litigation as a result of the defendant correcting its violations. Two years after deciding *Steel Company*, however, the Supreme Court issued the following decision.

FRIENDS OF THE EARTH, INC. v. LAIDLAW ENVIRONMENTAL SERVICES (TOC), INC.

528 U.S. 167 (2000).

JUSTICE GINSBURG delivered the opinion of the Court.

This case presents an important question concerning the operation of the citizen-suit provisions of the Clean Water Act. Congress authorized the federal district courts to entertain Clean Water Act suits initiated by "a person or persons having an interest which is or may be adversely affected." 33 U.S.C. §§ 1365(a), (g). To impel future compliance with the Act, a district court may prescribe injunctive relief in such a suit; additionally or alternatively, the court may impose civil penalties payable to the United States Treasury. § 1365(a). In the Clean Water Act citizen suit now before us, the District Court determined that injunctive relief was inappropriate because the defendant, after the institution of the litigation, achieved substantial compliance with the terms of its discharge permit. The court did, however, assess a civil penalty of $405,800. The "total deterrent effect" of the penalty would be adequate to forestall future violations, the court reasoned, taking into account that the defendant "will be required to reimburse plaintiffs for a significant amount of legal fees and has, itself, incurred significant legal expenses."

The Court of Appeals vacated the District Court's order. The case became moot, the appellate court declared, once the defendant fully complied with the terms of its permit and the plaintiff failed to appeal the denial of equitable relief. "[C]ivil penalties payable to the government," the Court of Appeals stated, "would not redress any injury Plaintiffs have suffered." Nor were attorneys' fees in order, the Court of Appeals noted, because absent relief on the merits, plaintiffs could not qualify as prevailing parties.

We reverse the judgment of the Court of Appeals. The appellate court erred in concluding that a citizen suitor's claim for civil penalties must be dismissed as moot when the defendant, albeit after commencement of the litigation, has come into compliance. In directing dismissal of the suit on grounds of mootness, the Court of Appeals incorrectly conflated our case law on initial standing to bring suit, *see, e.g., Steel Co. v. Citizens for a Better Environment,* 523 U.S. 83 (1998), with our case law on post-commencement mootness, *see, e.g., City of Mesquite v. Aladdin's Castle, Inc.*, 455 U.S. 283 (1982). A defendant's voluntary cessation of allegedly unlawful conduct ordinarily does not suffice to moot a case. The Court of Appeals also misperceived the remedial potential of civil penalties. Such penalties may serve, as an alternative to an injunction, to deter future violations and thereby redress the injuries that prompted a citizen suitor to commence litigation.

I

A

In 1972, Congress enacted the Clean Water Act (Act), also known as the Federal Water Pollution Control Act, 86 Stat. 816, as amended, 33 U.S.C. § 1251 *et seq.* Section 402 of the Act, 33 U.S.C. § 1342, provides for the issuance, by the Administrator of the Environmental Protection Agency (EPA) or by authorized States, of National Pollutant Discharge Elimination System (NPDES) permits. NPDES permits impose limitations on the discharge of pollutants, and establish related monitoring and reporting requirements, in order to improve the cleanliness and safety of the Nation's waters. Noncompliance with a permit constitutes a violation of the Act. § 1342(h).

Under § 505(a) of the Act, a suit to enforce any limitation in an NPDES permit may be brought by any "citizen," defined as "a person or persons having an interest which is or may be adversely affected." 33 U.S.C. §§ 1365(a), (g). * * *

The Act authorizes district courts in citizen-suit proceedings to enter injunctions and to assess civil penalties, which are payable to the United States Treasury. § 1365(a). In determining the amount of any civil penalty, the district court must take into account "the seriousness of the violation or violations, the economic benefit (if any) resulting from the violation, any history of such violations, any good-faith efforts to comply with the applicable requirements, the economic impact of the penalty on the violator, and such other matters as justice may require." § 1319(d). In addition, the court "may award costs of litigation (including reasonable attorney and expert witness fees) to any prevailing or substantially prevailing party, whenever the court determines such award is appropriate." § 1365(d).

B

In 1986, defendant-respondent Laidlaw Environmental Services (TOC), Inc., bought a hazardous waste incinerator facility in Roebuck,

South Carolina, that included a wastewater treatment plant. (The company has since changed its name to Safety–Kleen (Roebuck), Inc., but for simplicity we will refer to it as "Laidlaw" throughout.) Shortly after Laidlaw acquired the facility, the South Carolina Department of Health and Environmental Control (DHEC), acting under 33 U.S.C. § 1342(a)(1), granted Laidlaw an NPDES permit authorizing the company to discharge treated water into the North Tyger River. The permit, which became effective on January 1, 1987, placed limits on Laidlaw's discharge of several pollutants into the river, including—of particular relevance to this case—mercury, an extremely toxic pollutant. The permit also regulated the flow, temperature, toxicity, and pH of the effluent from the facility, and imposed monitoring and reporting obligations.

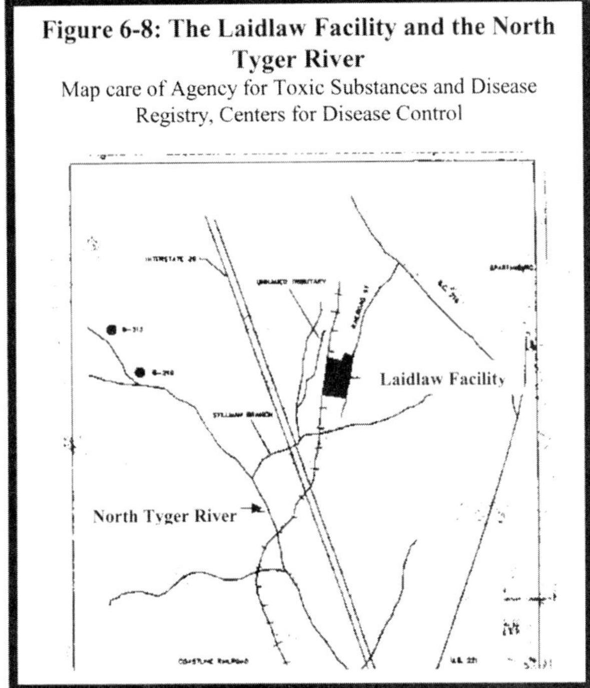

Figure 6-8: The Laidlaw Facility and the North Tyger River
Map care of Agency for Toxic Substances and Disease Registry, Centers for Disease Control

Once it received its permit, Laidlaw began to discharge various pollutants into the waterway; repeatedly, Laidlaw's discharges exceeded the limits set by the permit. In particular, despite experimenting with several technological fixes, Laidlaw consistently failed to meet the permit's stringent 1.3 ppb (parts per billion) daily average limit on mercury discharges. The District Court later found that Laidlaw had violated the mercury limits on 489 occasions between 1987 and 1995.

On April 10, 1992, plaintiff-petitioners Friends of the Earth (FOE) and Citizens Local Environmental Action Network, Inc. (CLEAN) (referred to collectively in this opinion, together with later joined plaintiff-petitioner Sierra Club, as "FOE") took the preliminary step necessary to the institution of litigation. They sent a letter to Laidlaw notifying the company of their intention to file a citizen suit against it under § 505(a) of the Act after the expiration of the requisite 60–day notice period, *i.e.,* on or after June 10, 1992. * * *

On June 12, 1992, FOE filed this citizen suit against Laidlaw under § 505(a) of the Act, alleging noncompliance with the NPDES permit and seeking declaratory and injunctive relief and an award of civil penalties. Laidlaw moved for summary judgment on the ground that FOE had failed to present evidence demonstrating injury in fact, and therefore lacked Article III standing to bring the lawsuit. In opposition to this motion, FOE submitted affidavits and deposition testimony from members of the plaintiff organizations. The record before the District Court also included affidavits from the organizations' members submitted by FOE in support of an earlier motion for preliminary injunctive relief. After examining this evidence, the District Court denied Laidlaw's summary judgment motion, finding—albeit "by the very slimmest of margins"—that FOE had standing to bring the suit.

* * * The record indicates that after FOE initiated the suit, but before the District Court rendered judgment, Laidlaw violated the mercury discharge limitation in its permit 13 times. The District Court also found that Laidlaw had committed 13 monitoring and 10 reporting violations during this period. The last recorded mercury discharge violation occurred in January 1995, long after the complaint was filed but about two years before judgment was rendered.

On January 22, 1997, the District Court issued its judgment. It found that Laidlaw had gained a total economic benefit of $1,092,581 as a result of its extended period of noncompliance with the mercury discharge limit in its permit. The court concluded, however, that a civil penalty of $405,800 was adequate in light of the guiding factors listed in 33 U.S.C. § 1319(d). In particular, the District Court stated that the lesser penalty was appropriate taking into account the judgment's "total deterrent effect." In reaching this determination, the court "considered that Laidlaw will be required to reimburse plaintiffs for a significant amount of legal fees." The court declined to grant FOE's request for injunctive relief, stating that an injunction was inappropriate because "Laidlaw has been in substantial compliance with all parameters in its NPDES permit since at least August 1992."

FOE appealed the District Court's civil penalty judgment, arguing that the penalty was inadequate, but did not appeal the denial of declaratory or injunctive relief. Laidlaw cross-appealed, arguing, among other things, that FOE lacked standing to bring the suit and that DHEC's action qualified as a diligent prosecution precluding FOE's litigation. The United States continued to participate as *amicus curiae* in support of FOE.

On July 16, 1998, the Court of Appeals for the Fourth Circuit issued its judgment. The Court of Appeals assumed without deciding that FOE initially had standing to bring the action, but went on to hold that the case had become moot. The appellate court stated, first, that the elements of Article III standing—injury, causation, and redressability—must persist at every stage of review, or else the action becomes moot. * * * Citing our decision in *Steel Co.,* the Court of Appeals reasoned that the case had become moot because "the only remedy currently available to [FOE]—civil penalties payable to the government—would not redress any injury [FOE has] suffered." The court therefore vacated the District Court's order and remanded with instructions to dismiss the action.

According to Laidlaw, after the Court of Appeals issued its decision but before this Court granted certiorari, the entire incinerator facility in Roebuck was permanently closed, dismantled, and put up for sale, and all discharges from the facility permanently ceased.

We granted certiorari to resolve the inconsistency between the Fourth Circuit's decision in this case and the decisions of several other Courts of Appeals, which have held that a defendant's compliance with its permit after the commencement of litigation does not moot claims for civil penalties under the Act.

II

A

The Constitution's case-or-controversy limitation on federal judicial authority, Art. III, § 2, underpins both our standing and our mootness jurisprudence, but the two inquiries differ in respects critical to the proper resolution of this case, so we address them separately. Because the Court of Appeals was persuaded that the case had become moot and so held, it simply assumed without deciding that FOE had initial standing. But because we hold that the Court of Appeals erred in declaring the case moot, we have an obligation to assure ourselves that FOE had Article III standing at the outset of the litigation. We therefore address the question of standing before turning to mootness.

In *Lujan v. Defenders of Wildlife,* 504 U.S. 555, 560–561 (1992), we held that, to satisfy Article III's standing requirements, a plaintiff must show (1) it has suffered an "injury in fact" that is (a) concrete and particularized and (b) actual or imminent, not conjectural or hypothetical; (2) the injury is fairly traceable to the challenged action of the defendant; and (3) it is likely, as opposed to merely speculative, that the injury will be redressed by a favorable decision. An association has standing to bring suit on behalf of its members when its members would otherwise have standing to sue in their own right, the interests at stake are germane to the organization's purpose, and neither the claim asserted nor the relief requested requires the participation of individual members in the lawsuit.

Laidlaw contends first that FOE lacked standing from the outset even to seek injunctive relief, because the plaintiff organizations failed to show that any of their members had sustained or faced the threat of any "injury in fact" from Laidlaw's activities. In support of this contention Laidlaw points to the District Court's finding, made in the course of setting the penalty amount, that there had been "no demonstrated proof of harm to the environment" from Laidlaw's mercury discharge violations.

The relevant showing for purposes of Article III standing, however, is not injury to the environment but injury to the plaintiff. To insist upon the former rather than the latter as part of the standing inquiry [] is to raise the standing hurdle higher than the necessary showing for success on the merits in an action alleging noncompliance with an NPDES permit. Focusing properly on injury to the plaintiff, the District Court found that FOE had demonstrated sufficient injury to establish standing. For example, FOE member Kenneth Lee Curtis averred in affidavits that he lived a half-mile from Laidlaw's facility; that he occasionally drove over the North Tyger River, and that it looked and smelled polluted; and that he would like to fish, camp, swim, and picnic in and near the river between 3 and 15 miles downstream from the facility, as he did when he was a teenager, but would not do so because he was concerned that the water was polluted by Laidlaw's discharges. Curtis reaffirmed these statements in extensive deposition testimony. For example, he testified that he would like to fish in the river at a specific spot he used as a boy, but that he would not do so now because of his concerns about Laidlaw's discharges.

Other members presented evidence to similar effect. CLEAN member Angela Patterson attested that she lived two miles from the facility; that before Laidlaw operated the facility, she picnicked, walked, birdwatched, and waded in and along the North Tyger River because of the natural beauty of the area; that she no longer engaged in these activities in or near the river because she was concerned about harmful effects from discharged pollutants; and that she and her husband would like to purchase a home near the river but did not intend to do so, in part because of Laidlaw's discharges. CLEAN member Judy Pruitt averred that she lived one-quarter mile from Laidlaw's facility and would like to fish, hike, and picnic along the North Tyger River, but has refrained from those activities because of the discharges. FOE member Linda Moore attested that she lived 20 miles from Roebuck, and would use the North Tyger River south of Roebuck and the land surrounding it for recreational purposes were she not concerned that the water contained harmful pollutants. In her deposition, Moore testified at length that she would hike, picnic, camp, swim, boat, and drive near or in the river were it not for her concerns about illegal discharges. CLEAN member Gail Lee attested that her home, which is near Laidlaw's facility, had a lower value than similar homes located further from the facility, and that she believed the pollutant discharges accounted for some of the discrepancy. Sierra Club member Norman Sharp averred that he had canoed approximately 40 miles downstream of the Laidlaw facility and would like to canoe in the North Tyger River closer to Laidlaw's discharge point, but did not do so because he was concerned that the water contained harmful pollutants.

These sworn statements, as the District Court determined, adequately documented injury in fact. We have held that environmental plaintiffs adequately allege injury in fact when they aver that they use the affected area and are persons "for whom the aesthetic and recreational values of the area will be lessened" by the challenged activity.

Our decision in *Lujan v. National Wildlife Federation,* 497 U.S. 871 (1990), is not to the contrary. In that case an environmental organization assailed the Bureau of Land Management's "land withdrawal review program," a program covering millions of acres, alleging that the program illegally opened up public lands to mining activities. * * * We held that the plaintiff could not survive the summary judgment motion merely by offering "averments which state only that one of [the organization's] members uses unspecified portions of an immense tract of territory, on some portions of which mining activity has occurred or probably will occur by virtue of the governmental action." 497 U.S., at 889.

In contrast, the affidavits and testimony presented by FOE in this case assert that Laidlaw's discharges, and the affiant members' reasonable concerns about the effects of those discharges, directly affected those affiants' recreational, aesthetic, and economic interests. These submissions present dispositively more than the mere "general averments" and "conclusory allegations" found inadequate in *National Wildlife Federation*. *Id.* at 888. Nor can the affiants' conditional statements—that they would use the nearby North Tyger River for recreation if Laidlaw were not discharging pollutants into it—be equated with the speculative " 'some day' intentions" to visit endangered species halfway around the world that we held insufficient to show injury in fact in *Defenders of Wildlife*. 504 U.S., at 564.

* * * Laidlaw argues next that even if FOE had standing to seek injunctive relief, it lacked standing to seek civil penalties. Here the asserted defect is not injury but redressability. Civil penalties offer no redress to private plaintiffs, Laidlaw argues, because they are paid to the government, and therefore a citizen plaintiff can never have standing to seek them.

Laidlaw is right to insist that a plaintiff must demonstrate standing separately for each form of relief sought. But it is wrong to maintain that citizen plaintiffs facing ongoing violations never have standing to seek civil penalties.

We have recognized on numerous occasions that "all civil penalties have some deterrent effect." *Hudson v. United States*, 522 U.S. 93, 102 (1997). More specifically, Congress has found that civil penalties in Clean Water Act cases do more than promote immediate compliance by limiting the defendant's economic incentive to delay its attainment of permit limits; they also deter future violations. This congressional determination warrants judicial attention and respect. "The legislative history of the Act reveals that Congress wanted the district court to consider the need for retribution and deterrence, in addition to restitution, when it imposed civil penalties. . . . [The district court may] seek to deter future violations by basing the penalty on its economic impact." *Tull v. United States*, 481 U.S. 412, 422–423 (1987).

It can scarcely be doubted that, for a plaintiff who is injured or faces the threat of future injury due to illegal conduct ongoing at the time of suit, a sanction that effectively abates that conduct and prevents its recurrence provides a form of redress. Civil penalties can fit that description. To the extent that they encourage defendants to discontinue current violations and deter them from committing future ones, they afford redress to citizen plaintiffs who are injured or threatened with injury as a consequence of ongoing unlawful conduct.

* * * We recognize that there may be a point at which the deterrent effect of a claim for civil penalties becomes so insubstantial or so remote that it cannot support citizen standing. The fact that this vanishing point is not easy to ascertain does not detract from the deterrent power of such penalties in the ordinary case. Justice Frankfurter's observations for the Court, made in a different context nearly 60 years ago, hold true here as well:

> "How to effectuate policy—the adaptation of means to legitimately sought ends—is one of the most intractable of legislative problems. Whether proscribed conduct is to be deterred by *qui tam* action or triple damages or injunction, or by criminal prosecution, or merely by defense to actions in contract, or by some, or all, of these remedies in combination, is a matter within the legislature's range of choice. Judgment on the deterrent effect of the various weapons in the armory of the law can lay little claim to scientific basis." *Tigner v. Texas*, 310 U.S. 141, 148 (1940).

In this case we need not explore the outer limits of the principle that civil penalties provide sufficient deterrence to support redressability. Here, the civil penalties sought by FOE carried with them a deterrent effect that made it likely, as opposed to merely speculative, that the penalties would redress FOE's injuries by abating current violations and preventing future ones—as the District Court reasonably found when it assessed a penalty of $405,800.

Laidlaw contends that the reasoning of our decision in *Steel Co.* directs the conclusion that citizen plaintiffs have no standing to seek civil penalties under the Act. We disagree. *Steel Co.* established that citizen suitors lack standing to seek civil penalties for violations that have abated by the time of suit. 523 U.S., at 106–107 We specifically noted in that case that there was no allegation in the complaint of any continuing or imminent violation, and that no basis for such an allegation appeared to exist. *Id.*, at 108; *see also Gwaltney,* 484 U.S., at 59 ("the harm sought to be addressed by the citizen suit lies in the present or the future, not in the past"). In short, *Steel Co.* held that private plaintiffs, unlike the Federal Government, may not sue to assess penalties for wholly past violations, but our decision in that case did not reach the issue of standing to seek penalties for violations that are ongoing at the time of the complaint and that could continue into the future if undeterred.

B

Satisfied that FOE had standing under Article III to bring this action, we turn to the question of mootness.

The only conceivable basis for a finding of mootness in this case is Laidlaw's voluntary conduct—either its achievement by August 1992 of substantial compliance with its NPDES permit or its more recent shutdown of the Roebuck facility. It is well settled that "a defendant's voluntary cessation of a challenged practice does not deprive a federal court of its power to determine the legality of the practice." *City of Mesquite*, 455 U.S., at 289. "[I]f it did, the courts would be compelled to leave '[t]he defendant . . . free to return to his old ways.'" *Id.*, at 289 n. 10 (citing *United States v. W.T. Grant Co.*, 345 U.S. 629, 632 (1953)). In accordance with this principle, the standard we have announced for determining whether a case has been mooted by the defendant's voluntary conduct is stringent: "A case might become moot if subsequent events made it absolutely clear that the allegedly wrongful behavior could not reasonably be expected to recur." *United States v. Concentrated Phosphate Export Assn.*, 393 U.S. 199, 203 (1968). The "heavy burden of persua[ding]" the court that the challenged conduct cannot reasonably be expected to start up again lies with the party asserting mootness. *Ibid.*

The Court of Appeals justified its mootness disposition by reference to *Steel Co.*, which held that citizen plaintiffs lack standing to seek civil penalties for wholly past violations. In relying on *Steel Co.*, the Court of Appeals confused mootness with standing. The confusion is understandable, given this Court's repeated statements that the doctrine of mootness can be described as "the doctrine of standing set in a time frame: The requisite personal interest that must exist at the commencement of the litigation (standing) must continue throughout its existence (mootness)." *Arizonans for Official English*, 520 U.S., at 68, n. 22 (internal quotation marks omitted).

Careful reflection on the long-recognized exceptions to mootness, however, reveals that the description of mootness as "standing set in a time frame" is not comprehensive. As just noted, a defendant claiming that its voluntary compliance moots a case bears the formidable burden of showing that it is absolutely clear the allegedly wrongful behavior could not reasonably be expected to recur. By contrast, in a lawsuit brought to force compliance, it is the plaintiff's burden to establish standing by demonstrating that, if unchecked by the litigation, the defendant's allegedly wrongful behavior will likely occur or continue, and that the "threatened injury [is] certainly impending." *Whitmore v. Arkansas*, 495 U.S. 149, 158 (1990) (citations and internal quotation marks omitted). * * * The plain lesson of these cases is that there are circumstances in which the prospect that a defendant will engage in (or resume) harmful conduct may be too speculative to support standing, but not too speculative to overcome mootness.

Furthermore, if mootness were simply "standing set in a time frame," the exception to mootness that arises when the defendant's allegedly unlawful activity is "capable of repetition, yet evading review" could not exist. * * * Standing admits of no similar exception; if a plaintiff lacks standing at the time the action commences, the fact that the dispute is capable of repetition yet evading review will not entitle the complainant to a federal judicial forum.

* * * Standing doctrine functions to ensure, among other things, that the scarce resources of the federal courts are devoted to those disputes in which the parties have a concrete stake. In contrast, by the time mootness is an issue, the case has been brought and litigated, often (as here) for years. To abandon the case at an advanced stage may prove more wasteful than frugal. This argument from sunk costs does not license courts to retain jurisdiction over cases in which one or both of the parties plainly lacks a continuing interest, as when the parties have settled or a plaintiff pursuing a nonsurviving claim has died. But the argument surely highlights an important difference between the two doctrines.

* * * Laidlaw also asserts, in a supplemental suggestion of mootness, that the closure of its Roebuck facility, which took place after the Court of Appeals issued its decision, mooted the case. The facility closure, like Laidlaw's earlier achievement of substantial compliance with its permit requirements, might moot the case, but—we once more reiterate—only if one or the other of these events made it absolutely clear that Laidlaw's permit violations could not reasonably be expected to recur. The effect of both Laidlaw's compliance and the facility closure on the prospect of future violations is a disputed factual matter. FOE points out, for example—and Laidlaw does not appear to contest—that Laidlaw retains its NPDES permit. These issues have not been aired in the lower courts; they remain open for consideration on remand. * * *

NOTES

1. **The Dissent.** As might be expected, Justice Scalia (joined by Justice Thomas) issued a lengthy dissent to the majority's decision in *Laidlaw*. He argued that *Steel Company* should have been extended exactly as Laidlaw proposed. *Laidlaw*, 528 U.S. at 205–09 (J. Scalia, dissenting).

2. **Reconciling *Laidlaw* and *Steel Company*.** Is the Supreme Court's decision in *Laidlaw reconcilable* with its decision in *Steel Company*? Why or why not? Is the Supreme Court's decision in *Laidlaw consistent* with its decision in *Steel Co.*? Why or why not?

3. **Injury for Standing Purposes.** What qualifies as an injury for standing purposes, according to the *Laidlaw* Court? What proof of that injury was sufficient? Was the majority's approach to injury in *Laidlaw* consistent with *Sierra Club v. Morton*? *National Wildlife Federation*? *Defenders of Wildlife*? Why or why not?

4. **Mootness.** How did the majority handle the issue of mootness in this case? What *is* mootness? How does it differ from standing, according to the *Laidlaw* Court? Why wasn't the suit against Laidlaw moot, even though Laidlaw's violations had ended and Laidlaw had closed its facility? Is this view of mootness consistent with the Fourth Circuit's discussion of mootness in the remand of *Gwaltney*? Why or why not?

5. **The Next Constitutional Challenge: Citizen Suits and Article II.** In their concurrences with and dissents from *Laidlaw,* Justices Kennedy, Scalia, and Thomas came close to inviting challenges to citizen suits on the grounds that citizen suits interfere with the President's Article II authority to enforce federal law. *Laidlaw*, 528 U.S. at 197 (J. Kennedy, concurring), 209–10 (J. Scalia, dissenting). Four Justices on the current Court have expressed an interest in such issues, enough to grant certiorari. Article II challenges have been raised in lower federal courts, where they have met with universal failure. Nevertheless, such separation of powers challenges are likely to pose the next major constitutional challenge to environmental citizen suits. *See generally* Robin Kundis Craig, *Will Separation of Powers Challenges "Take Care" of Environmental Citizen Suits? Article II, Injury-in-Fact, Private "Enforcers," and Lessons from* Qui Tam *Litigation*, 72:1 UNIVERSITY OF COLORADO LAW REVIEW 93–174 (Winter 2001).

* * *

VI. CITIZEN SUITS AND GOVERNMENT ENFORCEMENT

Every environmental statute includes provisions allowing the government—often both the federal and state governments—to enforce the requirements of the statute. Section 309 of the Clean Water Act, for example, allows the federal government and delegated states to: (1) issue administrative compliance orders and assess administrative penalties, CWA § 309(a), (g), 33 U.S.C. § 1319(a), (g); commence civil actions in federal court for injunctions and civil penalties, CWA § 309(b), (d), 33 U.S.C. § 1319(b), (d); and (3) prosecute violators criminally for negligent violations, knowing violations, knowing endangerment of other persons, or false statements. CWA § 309(c), 33 U.S.C. § 1319(c). Administrative penalties can run to $10,000 per day of violation, to a maximum of $125,000, CWA § 309(g)(2), 33 U.S.C. § 1319(g)(2); civil penalties in court can be up to $25,000 per day of violation, CWA § 309(d), 33 U.S.C. § 1319(d); and criminal penalties can range up to fines of $250,000 for individuals and $100,000 for corporations, plus possible jail sentences of up to 15 years. CWA § 309(c)(3), 33 U.S.C. § 1319(c)(3).

Citizen suits are civil court actions that generally incorporate the governments' civil court remedies. *See, e.g.*, CWA § 505(a), 33 U.S.C. § 1365(a). As the Supreme Court noted in *Gwaltney*, however, citizen suits are *supplemental* to government enforcement. Under the Clean Water Act, for instance, no citizen suit may be commenced "if the Administrator [of EPA] or State has commenced and is diligently prosecuting a civil or criminal action in a court of the United States, or a State to require compliance with the standard, limitation, or order * * *." CWA § 505(b)(1)(B), 33 U.S.C. § 1365(b)(1)(B). Thus, if a state or federal agency pursues ***court*** enforcement against a violator, and is diligently prosecuting that court action, the citizen suit is completely precluded.

Government preclusion is more complex when a federal or state agency pursues *administrative* remedies against the violator. Under the Clean Water Act, members of the public may bring citizen suits "[e]xcept as provided in * * * section 1319(g)(6) of this title." CWA § 505(a), 33 U.S.C. § 1365(a). Section 1319(g) is the Clean Water Act's administrative enforcement provision. It provides:

> (A) Limitations on actions under other sections
>
> Action taken by the Administrator [of the EPA] or the [U.S. Army Corps of Engineers], as the case may be, under this subsection shall not affect or limit the Administrator's or [Army Corps'] authority to enforce any provision of this chapter; except that any violation—
>
> (i) with respect to which the Administrator or the [Army Corps] has commenced and is diligently prosecuting an action under this subsection,
>
> (ii) with respect to which a State has commenced and is diligently prosecuting an action under State law comparable to this subsection, or
>
> (iii) for which the Administrator, the [Army Corps], or the State has issued a final order not subject to further judicial review and the violator has paid a penalty assessed under this subsection, or such comparable State law, as the case may be, shall not be the subject of a civil penalty action under subsection (d) of this section * * * ***or section 1365*** of this title.
>
> (B) Applicability of limitation with respect to citizen suits. The limitations contained in subparagraph (A) on civil penalty actions under section 1365 of this title shall not apply with respect to any violation for which—
>
> (i) a civil action under section 1365(a)(1) of this title has been filed prior to commencement of an action under this subsection, or
>
> (ii) notice of an alleged violation of section 1365(a)(1) of this title has been given in accordance with section 1365(b)(1)(A) of this title prior to commencement of an action under this subsection and an action under section 1365(a)(1) of this title with respect to such alleged violation is filed before the 120th day after the date on which notice is given.

CWA § 309(g)(6), 33 U.S.C. § 1319(g)(6) (emphasis added). Thus, if a state or federal agency chooses to pursue administrative enforcement action instead of litigation in a court, a citizen suit can still proceed if the citizen-plaintiff acts before the government agency does, either by: (1) filing the citizen suit complaint before the government begins its administrative enforcement; or (2) sending a notice letter before the government begins its administrative enforcement action and then filing the complaint for the citizen suit within 120 days of sending the notice letter. Furthermore, government administrative enforcement does not preempt a citizen suit if the government is not diligently prosecuting that enforcement action or, in the case of state administrative enforcement actions, the state law is not "comparable" to the federal law.

Comparability and ***diligent prosecution*** issues have created a split among the federal Courts of Appeals. Federal courts generally use a factor-based test to determine whether the government is diligently prosecuting its enforcement action, either administratively or in court. Factors that courts consider include the timeliness of the government's enforcement, the effectiveness of the enforcement action in bringing about compliance, the length of time allowed for compliance, the amount of penalties assessed, if any, and the availability of citizen participation. *See, e.g.*, *Jones v. City of Lakeland, Tennessee*, 224 F.3d 518, 522–23 (6th Cir. 2000) (*en banc*); *Arkansas Wildlife Federation v. ICI Americas, Inc.*, 29 F.3d 376, 380 (8th Cir. 1994). The Courts of Appeal differ, however, regarding whether to evaluate the government's diligence under a "totality of the circumstances" test, *see id.*, or whether the government's failure to address one factor must result in a finding of no diligence, which in turn allows the citizen suit to proceed. *See, e.g.*, *Citizens for a Better Environment–California v. Union Oil Co. of California*, 83 F.3d 1111, 1115 (9th Cir. 1996) (holding that the government must assess a penalty against the defendant before its enforcement action will preclude a citizen suit); *Proffitt v. Rohm & Haas*, 850 F.2d 1007, 1011–13 (3rd Cir. 1988) (holding that lack of citizen participation in a permit proceeding meant that the government's enforcement action would not preclude a citizen suit).

The same kinds of issues arise when the federal courts assess whether state law is sufficiently ***comparable*** to federal law to allow state enforcement actions to preclude citizen suits. Again, the courts assess comparability by looking at several factors:

> [T]he comparability requirement may be satisfied so long as state law contains comparable penalty provisions which the state is authorized to enforce, has the same overall enforcement goals as the federal [Act], provides interested citizens a meaningful opportunity to participate at significant stages of the decisionmaking process, and adequately safeguards their legitimate substantive interests.

Arkansas Wildlife Federation, 29 F.3d at 381; *see also Lockett v. EPA*, 319 F.3d 678, 684 (5th Cir. 2003) (adopting the Eighth Circuit's factors); *McAbee v. City of Fort Payne*, 318 F.3d 1248, 1254–56 (11th Cir. 2003) (using similar factors). Again, however, the Courts of Appeals split on whether these factors create a "totality of the circumstances" test, *see Lockett*, 319 F.3d at 684; *Arkansas Wildlife Federation*, 29 F.3d at 381; *North & South Rivers Watershed Ass'n v. Town of Scituate*, 949 F.2d 552, 555–56 (1st Cir. 1991); or whether failure of one factor vitiates the state's claim of comparable law, allowing the citizen suit to proceed. *See, e.g., McAbee*, 318 F.3d at 1254–57; *City of Lakeland*, 224 F.3d at 523; *Citizens for a Better Environment*, 83 F.3d at 1115. As a result, conclusions regarding whether state enforcement actions can preclude citizen suits have varied considerably.

VII. CITIZEN SUITS AGAINST STATES: THE ELEVENTH AMENDMENT HURDLE

A. STATES' ELEVENTH AMENDMENT SOVEREIGN IMMUNITY AND ENVIRONMENTAL CITIZEN SUITS

Most environmental citizen suit provisions allow citizen-plaintiffs to sue states for violations of the federal environmental statutes, so long as such lawsuits are consistent with the Eleventh Amendment. The Eleventh Amendment states that:

> The Judicial power of the United States shall not be construed to extend to any suit in law or equity, commenced or prosecuted against one of the United States by Citizens of another State, or by Citizens or Subjects of any Foreign State.

U.S. CONST., amend XI. On its face, the Eleventh Amendment only bars suits brought in federal court against a state by citizens of another state or of a foreign country. However, the Supreme Court has long interpreted the Eleventh Amendment as also barring suits in federal court by citizens against their own state. *See, e.g., Puerto Rico Aqueduct & Sewer Authority v. Metcalf & Eddy, Inc.*, 506 U.S. 139, 144–46 (1993). The Eleventh Amendment does not bar suits by the *federal government* against states in federal court (allowing, in the environmental law context, federal enforcement against states), nor does it address the issue of states' vulnerability to suit in their own courts.

The Eleventh Amendment preserves states' sovereign immunity. However, because under the U.S. Constitution's Supremacy Clause federal law can displace state law, it is sometimes possible for Congress to ***abrogate*** states' Eleventh Amendment sovereign immunity. Congress has most clearly exercised this power in protecting civil liberties pursuant to the Thirteenth, Fourteenth, and Fifteenth Amendments, which were added to the Constitution after the Civil War.

For a time, it also seemed that Congress had eliminated states' Eleventh Amendment defenses to environmental citizen suits. Most relevantly, in *Pennsylvania v. Union Gas Co.*, 491 U.S. 1 (1989), the Supreme

Court held that Congress could constitutionally authorize, pursuant to its Commerce Clause authority, citizen suits for monetary penalties against states in CERCLA's citizen suit provision. *Id.* at 7–12.

Nevertheless, the abrogation of states' Eleventh Amendment immunity by environmental citizen suits was short-lived. In 1996, in *Seminole Tribe of Florida v. Florida*, 517 U.S. 44 (1996), the Supreme Court overruled *Union Gas* in the context of the Indian Gaming Regulatory Act, holding explicitly that Congress did not have the authority under the Indian Commerce Clause to abrogate states' Eleventh Amendment immunity. *Id.* at 63. The Court also made it clear that its logic would extend to the Interstate Commerce Clause, which is the constitutional basis of the federal environmental statutes. *Id.* at 62. As a result, after *Seminole Tribe*, grants of authority to sue states in the environmental statutes' citizen suit provisions are constitutionally very limited in scope, making citizen suits against the states themselves nearly impossible.

B. THE "ARM OF THE STATE" DOCTRINE

Post-*Seminole Tribe*, citizens retain two viable arguments against Eleventh Amendment sovereign immunity. First, the Eleventh Amendment protects only *states* and *state agencies*—not municipalities, counties, or other kinds of governmental entities. Thus, when citizens brought suit against the New York State Thruway Authority for violations of the Clean Water Act, the Second Circuit had to evaluate whether the Thruway Authority enjoyed Eleventh Amendment immunity under the "arm of the state" doctrine. *Mancuso v. New York State Thruway Authority*, 86 F.3d 289, 290 (2d Cir. 1996). The Second Circuit relied on both its own and Supreme Court precedent to outline the test for whether a governmental entity qualifies for Eleventh Amendment immunity under this doctrine:

> The jurisprudence over how to apply the arm-of-the-state doctrine is, at best, confused. In *Feeney v. Port Authority Trans–Hudson Corporation,* 873 F.2d 628, 630–31 (2d Cir. 1989), we considered six factors derived from the Supreme Court's decision in *Lake Country Estates, Inc. v. Tahoe Regional Planning Agency*, 440 U.S. 391 (1979), in deciding whether the Port Authority of New York and New Jersey (the "Port Authority"), a bistate entity created by an interstate compact between those two states, was covered by the Eleventh Amendment: (1) how the entity is referred to in the documents that created it; (2) how the governing members of the entity are appointed; (3) how the entity is funded; (4) whether the entity's function is traditionally one of local or state government; (5) whether the state has a veto power over the entity's actions; and (6) whether the entity's obligations are binding upon the state.
>
> The Supreme Court [] addressed the immunity of bistate entities under the arm-of-the-state doctrine in *Hess v. Port Authority Trans–Hudson Corporation,* ___ U.S. ___, 115 S.Ct. 394 (1994). Justice Ginsburg, writing for the Court, began by distinguishing bistate from

other state-created entities because "the integrity of the compacting States [is not] compromised when the Compact Clause entity is sued in federal court." *Id.* at 401. The Court then discussed the factors that it has examined in *Lake Country*, but found that those factors did not "all point the same way." *Id.* at 402. Under these circumstances, the Court indicated that the Eleventh Amendment's twin rationales—protecting the state's fisc and dignity—"remain our prime guide." *Id.* at 404. The Court rejected the Port Authority's and the dissent's argument that the Eleventh Amendment inquiry should be determined only by looking at the degree of control that New York and New Jersey wielded over the Port Authority. *Id.*, *see also id.* at 411 (O'Connor, J., dissenting). Instead, the Court found that the Eleventh Amendment's central concern was protecting state treasuries and that, under the facts of *Hess*, the proper inquiry was "[i]f the expenditures of the enterprise exceed receipts, is the State in fact obligated to bear and pay the resulting indebtedness of the enterprise?" *Id.* at 406.

> Although *Hess* involved a bistate entity, we nevertheless believe that it is the proper starting place for our Eleventh Amendment inquiry in this case. Thus, following the Supreme Court's lead, we first look to the six *Lake Country* factors identified in *Feeney*. Only if those factors point in different directions do we then turn to the next questions: (a) will allowing the entity to be sued in federal court threaten the integrity of the state? and (b) does it expose the state treasury to risk? We remain mindful of the Supreme Court's emphasis that "the vulnerability of the State's purse [is] the most salient factor." *Hess*, 115 S. Ct. at 404. If all the elements are evenly balanced, this concern will control.

Id. at 293. The six factors split with respect to the Thruway authority. *Id.* at 294–96. As as result, the Second Circuit turned its analysis to the purposes of the Eleventh Amendment:

> We believe that the state sovereignty concern weighs neither in favor nor against Eleventh Amendment immunity. New York law itself provides the same kind of immunity to the Thruway Authority that it accords to the state, subjecting it only to certain tort and breach of contract claims, all of which must be brought in the Court of Claims. Allowing the Thruway Authority to be sued in federal court arguably would interfere with this carefully limited scheme for liability that New York has created. The Thruway Authority, however, is not a traditional state agency, but a public entity that is generally self-funded and, except for the appointment of its members to nine-year terms, it is not under significant state control. Although the Thruway Authority may be identified closely with the state, New York State has given the Thruway Authority an existence quite independent from the state and exercises the most minimal control over the Thruway Authority. We are unable to conclude that subjecting the Thruway Authority to suit in federal court would be an affront to the

> dignity of New York. Because the concern for state liability weighs against a finding of immunity and because the concerns of state sovereignty and dignity are not fully implicated, we hold that the Thruway Authority is not entitled to Eleventh Amendment immunity.

Id. at 296.

C. THE *EX PARTE YOUNG* DOCTRINE

The second exception to the states' Eleventh Amendment immunity that remained viable after *Seminole Tribe* is the *Ex parte Young* doctrine. 209 U.S. 123 (1908). Under this doctrine, the Eleventh Amendment will not bar a lawsuit alleging violations of federal law against a state official in his or her private capacity, on the grounds that such officials are not truly acting in their official capacities if they are violating federal law. *Id.* at 155–60. There are several limitations on the *Ex parte Young* doctrine. For example, the state cannot be liable, directly or indirectly, for damages assessed against the state official. *Papasan v. Allain*, 478 U.S. 265, 278 (1986). The following case discusses the *Ex Parte Young* doctrine in the context of post-*Seminole Tribe* environmental citizen suits.

NATURAL RESOURCES DEFENSE COUNCIL v. CALIFORNIA DEPARTMENT OF TRANSPORTATION

96 F.3d 420 (9th Cir. 1996).

CYNTHIA HOLCOMB HALL, CIRCUIT JUDGE:

This dispute is a citizen enforcement action brought pursuant to the citizens' suit provision of the Clean Water Act, 33 U.S.C. § 1365. Plaintiffs–Appellees filed suit against Defendants–Appellants, the California Department of Transportation ("Caltrans") and its director, James Van Loben Sels, claiming that Caltrans was not in compliance with a Clean Water Act permit that required it to control polluted stormwater runoff from roadways and maintenance yards in Southern California.

The defendants submitted a motion to dismiss for lack of subject matter jurisdiction claiming that the case was barred by the Eleventh Amendment. The district court dismissed all claims against Caltrans because, as an arm of the state, Caltrans is immune from suit under the Eleventh Amendment. In addition, the court dismissed plaintiffs' claims against Van Loben Sels for civil penalties and declaratory relief, because they too were barred by the Eleventh Amendment. However, the court proceeded to trial on plaintiffs' claims for prospective injunctive relief against Van Loben Sels individually.

After a ten-day trial, the district court found that Van Loben Sels had violated the Clean Water Act. Subsequently, the court entered a permanent injunction against Van Loben Sels, requiring a number of specific actions in order to comply with the Clean Water Act permit in the future.

The sole issue raised on appeal is whether the district court correctly held that, as a California state official, Van Loben Sels is subject to suit in federal court for violations of the Clean Water Act. We affirm.

I

The Eleventh Amendment of the United States Constitution prohibits federal courts from hearing suits brought by private citizens against state governments, without the state's consent. State immunity extends to state agencies and to state officers, who act on behalf of the state and can therefore assert the state's sovereign immunity. In general, federal court jurisdiction will not be found against a state official when the state is the real party in interest.

The Supreme Court recognized an important exception to this general rule in *Ex parte Young,* 209 U.S. 123 (1908), which held that the Eleventh Amendment does not bar suit against a state official acting in violation of federal law. *Id.* at 159–60. The doctrine of *Ex parte Young* is premised on the notion that a state can not authorize a state officer to violate the Constitution and laws of the United States. Thus, an action by a state officer that violates federal law is not considered an action of the state and, therefore, is not shielded from suit by the state's sovereign immunity. Therefore, a plaintiff may bring suit in federal court against a state officer accused of violating federal law.

Still, there are some limitations upon *Ex parte Young* suits against state officers. In particular, when a plaintiff brings suit against a state official alleging a violation of federal law, the federal court may award prospective injunctive relief that governs the official's future conduct, but may not award retroactive relief that requires the payment of funds from the state treasury. Therefore, an injunction against the state officer is permitted, even if it might require substantial outlay of funds from the state treasury, provided that it does not award retroactive relief for past conduct.

Although, as appellant points out, many of the cases applying the *Ex parte Young* doctrine address federal constitutional violations, we have held that the doctrine applies to violations of federal statutory law as well. The Supreme Court has recognized that the *Ex parte Young* doctrine is necessary "to permit federal courts to vindicate federal rights and hold state officials responsible to 'the supreme authority of the United States.'" *Pennhurst*, 465 U.S. at 105 (quoting *Ex parte Young*, 209 U.S. at 160). This purpose would be undermined if state officials were not required to act consistently with federal statutes, as well as the federal constitution. Consequently, the *Ex parte Young* exception to Eleventh Amendment immunity applies to violations of federal statutory rights. Indeed, several courts have permitted suits against state officials for injunctive relief pursuant to the Clean Water Act.

In the current case, the district court scrupulously followed the dictates of the Supreme Court's Eleventh Amendment cases. The court dismissed all claims against Caltrans because it is a California state agency which is entitled to immunity from suit. * * * It dismissed all claims against Van Loben Sels for civil penalties and declaratory relief pertaining to past violations of the Clean Water Act. * * * The remaining claims pertained solely to prospective injunctive relief against Van Loben Sels, which is authorized by *Ex parte Young* and *Edelman.* We find no error in the district court's rulings on these points.

II

Next, we must address the Supreme Court's recent Eleventh Amendment decision in *Seminole Tribe of Florida v. Florida,* 517 U.S. 44 (1996). The primary effect of *Seminole Tribe* was to overturn the Court's prior decision in *Pennsylvania v. Union Gas Co.,* 491 U.S. 1 (1989), which held that Congress may abrogate a state's Eleventh Amendment immunity when it legislates pursuant to its powers under the Commerce Clause. Thus, the Court held in *Seminole Tribe* that the Indian Commerce Clause, which for these purposes is indistinguishable from the Interstate Commerce Clause, does not authorize Congress to abrogate a state's immunity to suit without its consent. *Seminole Tribe,* 116 S. Ct. at 1131–32. Nevertheless, this aspect of *Seminole Tribe* does not apply to the current dispute because the district court already dismissed all claims against the State of California, which was represented by its agency, Caltrans.

Yet, the Supreme Court also held in *Seminole Tribe* that the petitioner's claim, which was barred by the Eleventh Amendment, could not be brought as an *Ex parte Young* suit against the state governor either. The Court held that "where Congress has prescribed a detailed remedial scheme for the enforcement against a state of a statutorily created right, a court should hesitate before casting aside those limitations and permitting an action against a state officer based upon *Ex parte Young.*" *Id.* at 1132. Congress may choose to limit the availability of an *Ex parte Young* suit against state officers for violations of federal statutory law, and the Court found that Congress intended to do so when it enacted the statute at issue in *Seminole Tribe. Id.* at 1133 & n. 17.

* * * The statute at issue in the current dispute, the Clean Water Act, is distinguishable from the IGRA, as the Supreme Court noted in *Seminole Tribe. See* 116 S. Ct. at 1133 n. 17. The Court stated that it "[did] not hold that Congress *cannot* authorize federal jurisdiction under *Ex parte Young* over a cause of action with a limited remedial scheme. We find only that Congress did not intend that result in the [IGRA]." *Id.* The Court then contrasted the IGRA to those statutes "where lower courts have found that Congress implicitly authorized suit under *Ex parte Young,*" such as the Clean Water Act. *Id.*

When Congress enacted the Clean Water Act citizen suit provision, it specified that it was legislating to the extent permitted by the Eleventh Amendment. Congress intended to encourage and assist the public to participate in enforcing the standards promulgated to reduce water pollution. *See* 33 U.S.C. § 1251(e). To further that goal, Congress enacted the citizen suit provision so that "a citizen enforcement action might be brought against an individual or a government agency." S. REP. NO. 414, 92d Cong., 2d Sess. (1972), *reprinted in* 1972 U.S.C.C.A.N. 3668, 3749. It would seem reasonable, then, that Congress implicitly intended to authorize citizens to bring *Ex parte Young* suits against state officials with the responsibility to comply with clean water standards and permits. Therefore, we find that the district court did not err when it refused to dismiss the plaintiffs' suit against Van Loben Sels, director of Caltrans. * * *

NOTES

1. ***Seminole Tribe* and the *Ex Parte Young* Doctrine.** How did the Supreme Court limit application of the *Ex Parte Young* doctrine in *Seminole Tribe*? Why didn't the *Ex Parte Young* doctrine apply to the Indian Gaming Regulatory Act in *Seminole Tribe*? Why is the Clean Water Act different, according to the Ninth Circuit? Re-read the Clean Water Act's citizen suit provision, quoted at the beginning of this chapter. Do you agree with the Ninth Circuit? Why or why not?

2. **The *Ex Parte Young* Doctrine and Constitutional Federalism.** How does the *Ex Parte Young* doctrine help to maintain the proper relationship between the federal government and the states, according to the Ninth Circuit? How does the *Ex Parte Young* doctrine relate to the Supremacy Clause?

In 1997, the U.S. Supreme Court emphasized that federal courts applying the *Ex Parte Young* doctrine must ensure that they do not intrude on valid state sovereignty interests. *Idaho v. Coeur d'Alene Tribe of Idaho*, 521 U.S. 261, 281 (1997). According to the Court, the *Ex Parte Young* doctrine is most viable "where there is no state forum available to vindicate federal interests, thereby placing upon Article III courts the special obligation to ensure the supremacy of federal statutory and constitutional law," *id.* at 270, and "when the case calls for interpretation of federal law." *Id.* Does *Couer d'Alene* undermine the Ninth Circuit's decision in *NRDC v. California Department of Transportation*? Why or why not? *See Swartz v. Beach*, 229 F. Supp. 2d 1239, 1255–56 (D. Wyo. 2002) (relying on *ANR Pipeline Co. v. Lafaver*, 150 F.3d 1178, 1190 (10th Cir. 1998)).

3. **The Eleventh Amendment and Environmental Interstate Compacts.** An important exception to states' Eleventh Amendment sovereign immunity arises when states have agreed to an interstate compact and the U.S. Congress has approved that compact. Article I, § 10, cl. 3 of the U.S. Constitution allows interstate compacts with Congress's approval, and states have entered into interstate compacts to address by agreement a number of environmental issues, such as interstate water quality problems and allocation of interstate water bodies.

In the Low Level Radioactive Waste Policy Act, 42 U.S.C. §§ 2021b to 2021j, Congress explicitly encouraged states to enter into interstate compacts to set up regional disposal facilities to handle low-level radioactive waste, such as some medical and industrial waste. *Id.* § 2021d. In 1986, Congress consented to seven interstate compacts negotiated under the Act.

In 2010, the U.S. Supreme Court decided a case involving a dispute among states that had entered one of these compacts. *Alabama v. North Carolina*, ___ U.S. ___, 130 S. Ct. 2295 (2010). The compact involved was, in the Supreme Court's words,

> the Southeast Interstate Low–Level Radioactive Waste Management Compact (Compact), entered into by Alabama, Florida, Georgia, Mississippi, North Carolina, South Carolina, Tennessee, and Virginia. That Compact established an "instrument and framework for a cooperative effort" to develop new facilities for the long-term disposal of low-level radioactive waste generated within the region. The Compact was to be administered by a Southeast Interstate Low–Level Radioactive Waste Management Commission (Commission), composed of two voting members from each party State.

Id. at 2302–03. South Carolina later withdrew from the compact. When North Carolina refused to build a regional disposal facility in accordance with the compact, Alabama, Florida, Tennessee, and Virginia, plus the Commission, sued North Carolina directly in the Supreme Court.

North Carolina claimed that the Commission's claims were barred by the Eleventh Amendment. As the Supreme Court noted, "We have held that an entity created through a valid exercise of the Interstate Compact Clause is not entitled to immunity from suit under the Eleventh Amendment, but we have not decided whether such an entity's suit *against* a State is barred by sovereign immunity." *Id.* at 2314 n.5. The Court determined that, to the extent that the Commission's claims were identical to the plaintiff states', North Carolina's Eleventh Amendment immunity would not bar its claims; however, to the extent that the Commission had different claims, the Eleventh Amendment would require additional analysis later in the litigation. *Id.* at 2314–16.

* * *

VIII. SUITS AGAINST THE FEDERAL GOVERNMENT: FEDERAL FACILITIES AND FEDERAL SOVEREIGN IMMUNITY

Like states, the federal government enjoys sovereign immunity from suit. Unlike states, however, the federal government's sovereign immunity is not explicitly addressed in the Constitution—instead, it is preserved through what might be termed "constitutional common law." The notion of sovereign immunity derives from English common law, which held that the Crown could not be sued without its permission. Accordingly, in order to sue the federal government, plaintiffs must fit within a statutory ***waiver of sovereign immunity***. The federal courts strictly construe such waivers in favor of the federal government.

Federal sovereign immunity becomes an issue in environmental citizen suits when citizens try to sue the United States, federal agencies, or federal facilities for violations of the statute at issue. Most environmental citizen suit provisions provide explicitly for suits against the federal government. The Clean Water Act's citizen suit provision, for example, allows "any citizen to commence a civil action on his own behalf * * * against any person (including (i) the United States * * *." CWA § 505(a)(1), 33 U.S.C. § 1365(a)(1)). Arguably, the inclusion of the "United States" constitutes a waiver of the federal government's sovereign immunity.

In addition, most environmental statutes specifically subject federal facilities to their requirements. Under the Clean Water Act, for example,

> Each department, agency, or instrumentality of the executive, legislative, and judicial branches of the Federal Government (1) having jurisdiction over any property or facility, or (2) engaged in any activity resulting, or which may result, in the discharge or runoff of pollutants, and each officer, agent, or employee thereof in the performance of his official duties, shall be subject to, and comply with, all Federal, State, interstate, and local requirements, administrative authority, and processes and sanctions respecting the control and abatement of water pollution in the same manner, and to the same extent as any nongovernmental entity including the payment of reasonable service charges. The preceding sentence shall apply (A) to any requirement whether substantive or procedural (including any recordkeeping or reporting requirement, any requirement respecting permits and any other requirement, whatsoever), (B) to the exercise of any Federal, State, or local administrative authority, and (C) to any process and sanction, whether enforced in Federal, State. or local courts or in any other manner. This subsection shall apply notwithstanding any immunity of such agencies, officers, agents, or employees under any law or rule of law. * * * No officer, agent, or employee of the United States shall be personally liable for any civil penalty arising from the performance of his official duties, for which he is not otherwise liable, and the United States shall be liable only for those civil penalties arising under Federal law or imposed by a State or local court to enforce an order or the process of such court. * * *

CWA § 313(a), 33 U.S.C. § 1323(a).

The federal facilities provisions in environmental statutes are, decidedly, waivers of federal sovereign immunity. Nevertheless, the federal government has a long history of resisting the breadth of that waiver. For example, in 1977, Congress amended the Clean Water Act's federal facilities provision by adding the second sentence ("substantive or procedural") in order to "correct" the Supreme Court's determination in *Environmental Protection Agency v. California* ex rel. *State Water Resources Control Board*, 426 U.S. 200, 219–27 (1976), that federal facilities did not have to get state-issued NPDES permits in delegated states. Pub. L. No. 95–217, §§ 60, 61(a), 91 Stat. 1597, 1598 (Dec. 27, 1977).

Such arguments against the federal facilities provisions' waiver of federal sovereign immunity continued after the 1977 amendments. For example, under the current language of the Clean Water Act's federal facilities provision, are federal facilities subject to civil penalties? Are you sure? Despite the 1977 amendments to the Clean Water Act, federal Courts of Appeal split regarding this issue, which the following Supreme Court case resolved.

UNITED STATES DEPARTMENT OF ENERGY v. OHIO

503 U.S. 607 (1992).

JUSTICE SOUTER delivered the opinion of the Court.

The question in these cases is whether Congress has waived the National Government's sovereign immunity from liability for civil fines imposed by a State for past violations of the Clean Water Act (CWA), 86 Stat. 816, as amended, 33 U.S.C. § 1251 *et seq.*, or the Resource Conservation and Recovery Act of 1976 (RCRA), 90 Stat. 2795, 2796, as amended, 42 U.S.C. § 6901 *et seq.* We hold it has not done so in either instance.

I

The CWA prohibits the discharge of pollutants into navigable waters without a permit. Section 402, codified at 33 U.S.C. § 1342, gives primary authority to issue such permits to the United States Environmental Protection Agency (EPA), but allows EPA to authorize a State to supplant the federal permit program with one of its own, if the state scheme would include, among other features, sufficiently stringent regulatory standards and adequate provisions for penalties to enforce them. *See generally* 33 U.S.C. § 1342(b) (requirements and procedures for EPA approval of state water-pollution permit plans); *see also* 40 CFR §§ 123.1–123.64 (1991) (detailed requirements for state plans). RCRA regulates the disposal of hazardous waste in much the same way, with a permit program run by EPA but subject to displacement by an adequate state counterpart. *See generally* 42 U.S.C. § 6926 (requirements and procedures for EPA approval of state hazardous-waste disposal permit plans); *see also* 40 CFR §§ 271.1–271.138 (1991) (detailed requirements for state plans).

This litigation began in 1986 when respondent State of Ohio sued petitioner Department of Energy (DOE) in Federal District Court for

Figure 6-9: The Fernald Plant, Before Closure and Conversion to Wetlands
U.S. Department of Energy photo.

violations of state and federal pollution laws, including the CWA and RCRA, in operating its uranium-processing plant in Fernald, Ohio. Ohio sought, among other forms of relief, both state and federal civil penalties for past violations of the CWA and RCRA and of state laws enacted to supplant those federal statutes. Before the District Court ruled on DOE's motion for dismissal, the parties proposed a consent decree to settle all but one substantive claim, and Ohio withdrew all outstanding claims for relief except its request for civil penalties for DOE's alleged past violations. * * * The parties thus left for determination under the motion to dismiss only the issue we consider today: whether Congress has waived the National Government's sovereign immunity from liability for civil fines imposed for past failure to comply with the CWA, RCRA, or state law supplanting the federal regulation.

DOE admits that the CWA and RCRA obligate a federal polluter, like any other, to obtain permits from EPA or the state permitting agency. DOE also concedes that the CWA and RCRA render federal agencies liable for fines imposed to induce them to comply with injunctions or other judicial orders designed to modify behavior prospectively, which we will speak of hereafter as "coercive fines." The parties disagree only on whether the CWA and RCRA, in either their "federal-facilities" or "citizen-suit" sections, waive federal sovereign immunity from liability for fines, which we will refer to as "punitive," imposed to punish past violations of those statutes or state laws supplanting them.

The United States District Court for the Southern District of Ohio held that both statutes waived federal sovereign immunity from punitive fines, by both their federal-facilities and citizen-suit sections. A divided panel of the United States Court of Appeals for the Sixth Circuit affirmed in part, holding that Congress had waived immunity from punitive fines in the CWA's federal-facilities section and RCRA's citizen-suit section, but not in RCRA's federal-facilities section. * * *

* * * II

We start with a common rule, with which we presume congressional familiarity, that any waiver of the National Government's sovereign immunity must be unequivocal. "Waivers of immunity must be 'construed strictly in favor of the sovereign,' ... and not 'enlarge[d] ... beyond what the language requires.' *Eastern Transportation Co. v. United States*, 272 U.S. 675, 686 (1927)." *Ruckelshaus v. Sierra Club*, 463 U.S. 680, 685–686 (1983). By these lights we examine first the two statutes' citizen-suit sections, which can be treated together because their relevant provisions are similar, then the CWA's federal-facilities section, and, finally, the corresponding section of RCRA.

A

So far as it concerns us, the CWA's citizen-suit section reads that

"any citizen may commence a civil action on his own behalf—

"(1) against any person (including ... the United States ...) who is alleged to be in violation of (A) an effluent standard or limitation under this chapter or (B) an order issued by the Administrator or a State with respect to such a standard or limitation....

... "The district courts shall have jurisdiction ... to enforce such an effluent standard or limitation, or such an order ... as the case may be, and to apply any appropriate civil penalties under [33 U.S.C. § 1319(d)]." 33 U.S.C. § 1365(a).

The relevant part of the corresponding section of RCRA is similar:

"[A]ny person may commence a civil action on his own behalf—

"(1)(A) against any person (including ... the United States) ... who is alleged to be in violation of any permit, standard, regulation, condition, requirement, prohibition, or order which has become effective pursuant to this chapter ...

"(B) against any person, including the United States ... who has contributed or who is contributing to the past or present handling, storage, treatment, transportation, or disposal of any solid or hazardous waste which may present an imminent and substantial endangerment to health or the environment....

"... The district court shall have jurisdiction ... to enforce the permit, standard, regulation, condition, requirement, prohibition, or order, referred to in paragraph (1)(A), to restrain any person who has contributed or who is contributing to the past or present handling, storage, treatment, transportation, or disposal of any solid or hazardous waste referred to in paragraph (1)(B), to order such person to take such other action as may be necessary, or both, ... and to apply any appropriate civil penalties under [42 U.S.C. §§ 6928(a) and (g)]." 42 U.S.C. § 6972(a).

A State is a "citizen" under the CWA and a "person" under RCRA, and is thus entitled to sue under these provisions.

Ohio and its *amici* argue that by specifying the United States as an entity subject to suit and incorporating the civil-penalties sections of the CWA and RCRA into their respective citizen-suit sections, "Congress could not avoid noticing that its literal language subject[ed] federal entities to penalties." It is undisputed that each civil-penalties provision authorizes fines of the punitive sort.

The effect of incorporating each statute's civil-penalties section into its respective citizen-suit section is not, however, as clear as Ohio claims. The incorporations must be read as encompassing all the terms of the penalty provisions, including their limitations, ... and significant limitations for present purposes result from restricting the applicability of the civil-penalties sections to "person[s]." While both the CWA and RCRA define "person" to cover States, subdivisions of States, municipalities, and interstate bodies (and RCRA even extends the term to cover governmental corporations), neither statute defines "person" to include the United States. Its omission has to be seen as a pointed one when so many other governmental entities are specified, ... a fact that renders the civil-penalties sections inapplicable to the United States.

Against this reasoning, Ohio argues that the incorporated penalty provisions' exclusion of the United States is overridden by the National Government's express inclusion as a "person" by each of the citizen-suit sections. There is, of course, a plausibility to the argument. Whether that plausibility suffices for the clarity required to waive sovereign immunity is, nonetheless, an issue we need not decide, for the force of Ohio's argument wanes when we look beyond the citizen-suit sections to the full texts of the respective statutes.

What we find elsewhere in each statute are various provisions specially defining "person" and doing so expressly for purposes of the entire section in which the term occurs. * * * Within each statute, then, there is a contrast between drafting that merely redefines "person" when it occurs within a particular clause or sentence and drafting that expressly alters the definition for any and all purposes of the entire section in which the special definition occurs. Such differences in treatment within a given statutory text are reasonably understood to reflect differences in meaning intended, ... and the inference can only be that a special definition not described as being for purposes of the "section" or "subchapter" in which it occurs was intended to have the more limited application to its own clause or sentence alone. Thus, in the instances before us here, the inclusion of the United States as a "person" must go to the clauses subjecting the United States to suit, but no further.

This textual analysis passes the test of giving effect to all the language of the citizen-suit sections. Those sections' incorporations of their respective statutes' civil-penalties sections will have the effect of authorizing punitive fines when a polluter other than the United States is brought to court by a citizen, while the sections' explicit authorizations for suits against the United States will likewise be effective, since those sections concededly authorize coercive sanctions against the National Government.

A clear and unequivocal waiver of anything more cannot be found; a broader waiver may not be inferred. Ohio's reading is therefore to be rejected.

B

The relevant portion of the CWA's federal-facilities section provides that

> "[e]ach department, agency, or instrumentality of the ... Federal Government ... shall be subject to, and comply with, all Federal, State, interstate, and local requirements, administrative authority, and process and sanctions respecting the control and abatement of water pollution in the same manner ... as any nongovernmental entity.... The preceding sentence shall apply (A) to any requirement whether substantive or procedural (including any recordkeeping or reporting requirement, any requirement respecting permits and any other requirement, whatsoever), (B) to the exercise of any Federal, State or local administrative authority, and (C) to any process and sanction, whether enforced in Federal, State, or local courts or in any other manner.... [T]he United States shall be liable only for those civil penalties arising under Federal law or imposed by a State or local court to enforce an order or the process of such court." 33 U.S.C. § 1323(a).

Ohio rests its argument for waiver as to punitive fines on two propositions: first, that the statute's use of the word "sanction" must be understood to encompass such fines * * *; and, second, with respect to the fines authorized under a state permit program approved by EPA, that they "aris[e] under Federal law" despite their genesis in state statutes, and are thus within the scope of the "civil penalties" covered by the congressional waiver * * *.

1

Ohio's first proposition is mistaken. As a general matter, the meaning of "sanction" is spacious enough to cover not only what we have called punitive fines, but coercive ones as well, and use of the term carries no necessary implication that a reference to punitive fines is intended. * * *

* * * The word "sanction" appears twice in § 1323(a), each time within the phrase "process and sanction[s]." The first sentence subjects Government agencies to "process and sanctions," while the second explains that the Government's corresponding liability extends to "any process and sanction, whether enforced in Federal, State, or local courts or in any other manner."

Three features of this context are significant. The first is the separate statutory recognition of three manifestations of governmental power to which the United States is subjected: substantive and procedural requirements; administrative authority; and "process and sanctions," whether "enforced" in courts or otherwise. Substantive requirements are thus distinguished from judicial process, even though each might require the same conduct, as when a statute requires and a court orders a polluter to refrain from discharging without a permit. The second noteworthy feature is the conjunction of "sanction[s]" not with the substantive "requirements," but with "process," in each of the two instances in which "sanction" appears. "Process" normally refers to the procedure and mechanics of adjudication and the enforcement of decrees or orders that the adjudicatory process finally provides. The third feature to note is the statute's reference to "process and sanctions" as "enforced" in courts or otherwise. Whereas we commonly understand that "requirements" may be enforced either by backward-looking penalties for past violations or by the "process" of forward-looking orders enjoining future violations, such forward-looking orders themselves are characteristically given teeth by equity's traditional coercive sanctions for contempt: fines and bodily commitment imposed pending compliance or agreement to comply. The very fact, then, that the text speaks of sanctions in the context of enforcing "process" as distinct from substantive "requirements" is a good reason to infer that Congress was using "sanction" in its coercive sense, to the exclusion of punitive fines.

2

The last relevant passage of § 1323(a), which provides that "the United States shall be liable only for those civil penalties arising under Federal law or imposed by a State or local court to enforce an order or the process of such court," is not to the contrary. * * *

* * * Ohio urges us to find a source of authority good against the United States by reading "arising under Federal law" to include penalties prescribed by state statutes approved by EPA and supplanting the CWA. Ohio argues for treating a state statute as providing penalties "arising under Federal law" by stressing the complementary relationship between the relevant state and federal statutes and the role of such state statutes in accomplishing the purpose of the CWA. This purpose, as Ohio states it, is "to encourage compliance with comprehensive, federally approved water pollution programs while shielding federal agencies from unauthorized penalties." Ohio asserts that "federal facility compliance ... cannot be ... accomplished without the [punitive] penalty deterrent."

The case for such pessimism is not, however, self-evident. To be sure, an agency of the Government may break the law where it might have complied voluntarily if it had faced the prospect of punitive fines for past violations. But to say that its "compliance cannot be ... accomplished" without such fines is to assume that without sanctions for past conduct a federal polluter can never be brought into future compliance, that an agency of the National Government would defy an injunction backed by coercive fines and even a threat of personal commitment. The position seems also to ignore the fact that once such fines start running they can be every dollar as onerous as their punitive counterparts; it could be a very expensive mistake to plan on ignoring the law indefinitely on the assumption that contumacy would be cheap.

Nor does the complementary relationship between state and federal law support Ohio's claim that state-law fines thereby "arise under Federal law." Plain language aside, the far more compelling interpretative case rests on the best known statutory use of the phrase "arising under federal law," appearing in the grant of federal-question jurisdiction to the courts of the United States. *See* 28 U.S.C. § 1331. There, we have read the phrase "arising under" federal law to exclude cases in which the plaintiff relies on state law, even when the State's exercise of power in the particular circumstances is expressly permitted by federal law. Congress' use of the same language in § 1323(a) indicates a likely adoption of our prior interpretation of that language. The probability is enough to answer Ohio's argument that "arising under Federal law" in § 1323(a) is broad enough to cover provisions of state statutes approved by a federal agency but nevertheless applicable *ex proprio vigore.*

Since Ohio's argument for treating state-penalty provisions as arising under federal law thus fails, our reading of the last-quoted sentence from § 1323(a) leaves us with an unanswered question and an unresolved tension between closely related statutory provisions. The question is still what Congress could have meant in using a seemingly expansive phrase like "civil penalties arising under Federal law." Perhaps it used it just in case some later amendment might waive the Government's immunity from punitive sanctions. Perhaps a drafter mistakenly thought that liability for such sanctions had somehow been waived already. Perhaps someone was careless. The question has no satisfactory answer.

We do, however, have a response satisfactory for sovereign immunity purposes to the tension between a proviso suggesting an apparently expansive but uncertain waiver and its antecedent text that evinces a narrower waiver with greater clarity. For under our rules that tension is resolved by the requirement that any statement of waiver be unequivocal: as against the clear waiver for coercive fines the indication of a waiver as to those that are punitive is less certain. The rule of narrow construction therefore takes the waiver no further than the coercive variety.

C

We consider, finally, the federal-facilities section of RCRA, which provides, in relevant part, that the National Government "shall be subject to, and comply with, all Federal, State, interstate, and local requirements, both substantive and procedural (including any requirement for permits or reporting or any provisions for injunctive relief and such sanctions as may be imposed by a court to enforce such relief) ... in the same manner, and to the same extent, as any person is subject to such requirements.... Neither the United States, nor any agent, employee, or officer thereof, shall be immune or exempt from any process or sanction of any State or Federal Court with respect to the enforcement of any such injunctive relief." 42 U.S.C. § 6961.

Ohio and its *amici* stress the statutory subjection of federal facilities to "all ... requirements," which they would have us read as an explicit and unambiguous waiver of federal sovereign immunity from punitive fines. We, however, agree with the Tenth Circuit that "all ... requirements" "can reasonably be interpreted as including substantive standards and the means for implementing those standards, but excluding punitive measures." *Mitzelfelt v. Department of Air Force*, 903 F.2d 1293, 1295 (1990).

We have already observed that substantive requirements can be enforced either punitively or coercively, and the Tenth Circuit's understanding that Congress intended the latter finds strong support in the textual indications of the kinds of requirements meant to bind the Government. Significantly, all of them refer either to mechanisms requiring review for substantive compliance (permit and reporting requirements) or to mechanisms for enforcing substantive compliance in the future (injunctive relief and sanctions to enforce it). In stark contrast, the statute makes no mention of any mechanism for penalizing past violations, and this absence of any example of punitive fines is powerful evidence that Congress had no intent to subject the United States to an enforcement mechanism that could deplete the federal fisc regardless of a responsible officer's willingness and capacity to comply in the future.

The drafters' silence on the subject of punitive sanctions becomes virtually audible after one reads the provision's final sentence, waiving immunity "from any process or sanction of any State or Federal Court with respect to the enforcement of any such injunctive relief." The fact that the drafters' only specific reference to an enforcement mechanism described "sanction" as a coercive means of injunctive enforcement bars any inference that a waiver of immunity from "requirements" somehow unquestionably extends to punitive fines that are never so much as mentioned. * * *

* * * JUSTICE WHITE, with whom JUSTICE BLACKMUN and JUSTICE STEVENS join, concurring in part and dissenting in part.

These cases concern a uranium-processing plant which, the Government concedes, has "contaminated the soil, air and surface waters" of Fernald, Ohio, with radioactive materials, "exceeded certain of the effluent limitations set forth" in its water pollution permit, and "failed to construct portions of the water pollution control facilities in accordance" with the permit.

The situation at the Fernald plant is not an aberration. The Department of Energy (DOE) estimates that taxpayers may pay $40 to $70 billion during the next 20 years to clean up or contain the contamination at its facilities. Federal facilities fail to comply with the Clean Water Act (CWA), 33 U.S.C. § 1251 *et seq.*, twice as frequently as private industry. And the compliance rate of the Departments of Defense and Energy with the Resource Conservation and Recovery Act of 1976 (RCRA), 42 U.S.C. § 6901 *et seq.*, is 10 to 15 percent lower than that of private industry.

In an effort to compel Government agencies to adhere to the environmental laws under which private industry must operate, Congress waived sovereign immunity for civil penalties in the federal facilities and citizen suit provisions of the CWA, 33 U.S.C. §§ 1323, 1365(a), and in the citizen suit provision of the RCRA, 42 U.S.C. § 6972(a). Today, the majority thwarts this effort by adopting "an unduly restrictive interpretation" of both statutes and writing the waivers out of existence. In so doing, the majority ignores the "unequivocally expressed" intention of Congress and deprives the States of a powerful weapon in combating federal agencies that persist in despoiling the environment. * * *

NOTES

1. **Civil Penalties and the Citizen Suit Provisions.** Both RCRA's and the Clean Water Act's citizen suit provisions expressly allow citizen suits against the United States and allow the federal judges to impose civil penalties in citizen suits. Why was the waiver of sovereign immunity nevertheless not completely clear? How did Ohio try to argue that the Clean Water Act's and RCRA's citizen suit provisions expressly waived the federal government's sovereign immunity from civil penalty liability? Why did the majority of the Supreme Court disagree?

2. **Civil Penalties and the Clean Water Act's Federal Facilities Provision.** The Clean Water Act's federal facilities provision states fairly clearly that federal facilities are liable for civil penalties "arising under Federal law" and for all "sanctions." Why was this language still problematic? How did Ohio try to argue that the Clean Water Act's federal facilities provision nevertheless waived the federal government's sovereign immunity from civil penalty liability? Why did the majority of the Supreme Court disagree? What does it mean for federal facilities to be liable for civil penalties arising under federal law?

3. **Civil Penalties and RCRA's Federal Facilities Provision.** How did RCRA's federal facilities provision differ from the Clean Water Act's? Did those differences help or hurt Ohio in its sovereign immunity arguments? Why? Why did the majority decide that RCRA's federal facilities provision did not waive the federal government's sovereign immunity from civil penalty liability? Did the dissenters disagree?

4. **The Rest of the Story.** Shortly after this case, in 1992, Congress amended RCRA's federal facilities provision to clarify that "[t]he Federal, State, interstate, and local substantive and procedural requirements referred to in this subsection include, but are not limited to, all administrative orders and all civil and administrative penalties and fines, regardless of whether such penalties or fines are punitive or coercive in nature or are imposed for isolated, intermittent or continuing violations." RCRA § 6001(a), 42 U.S.C. § 6961(a). Congress has not similarly amended the Clean Water Act. Does the amendment to RCRA "overrule" the Supreme Court's decision in *Department of Energy*? Why or why not?

5. **Federal Facilities and Environmental Enforcement.** According to the EPA, "as of April 1, 2003, there were 7,853 federal facilities that engaged in some type of activity affected by requirements under" federal environmental statutes. U.S. EPA, THE STATE OF FEDERAL FACILITIES: AN OVERVIEW OF COMPLIANCE AT FEDERAL FACILITIES FY2001–2002, at 3 (2004) (EPA 300–R–04–001), *available at* http://www.epa.gov/compliance/resources/reports/accomplishments/federal/soff0102.pdf. Congress has known that federal facilities are significant sources of pollution for decades. For example, during hearings on the 1970 amendments to the Federal Water Pollution Control Act, the precursor to the Clean Water Act, testimony "disclosed many incidents of flagrant violations of air and water pollution requirements by Federal facilities and activities," leading Congress to conclude that "[f]ederal facilities generate considerable water pollution." S. REP. NO. 92–414, *reprinted in* 1972 U.S.C.C.A.N. 3668, 3733, 3746 (Oct. 28, 1971).

Enforcement against federal facilities has long been problematic, however. As the *Department of Energy* case demonstrates, sovereign immunity issues undermine citizen enforcement against federal facilities. In addition, the U.S. Department of Justice, which enforces the various federal environmental laws in court, adheres to a "unitary Executive" theory, under which it can take enforcement actions against other federal agencies only when Congress clearly indicates its intent that such intra-Executive enforcement should occur. *See, e.g.*, U.S. DOJ, AUTHORITY OF DEPARTMENT OF HOUSING AND URBAN DEVELOPMENT TO INITIATE ENFORCEMENT ACTIONS UNDER THE FAIR HOUSING ACT AGAINST OTHER EXECUTIVE BRANCH AGENCIES (1994), *available at* http://www.usdoj.gov/olc/fha.htm. Following this theory, the EPA currently claims authority to assess civil penalties against federal facilities only pursuant to the Clean Air Act, RCRA (after the 1992 amendments), and the Safe Drinking Water Act. Civil Enforcement Division, U.S. EPA, *Federal Facilities and Civil Enforcement*, http://www.epa.gov/compliance/civil/federal/index.html (last updated March 19, 2004).

Nevertheless, other trends in federal facility compliance indicate that the availability of civil penalties does affect federal facility compliance with environmental laws. In a ten-year review of federal facility compliance from FY 1993 to FY 2002—*i.e.*, the ten years following the *Department of Energy* decision and Congress's amendment of RCRA—the EPA reported that:

> From FY 1993 to FY 2002, the federal facility RCRA compliance rate increased steadily from 55 percent to 94 percent. In contrast, the compliance rate for [Clean Water Act]/NPDES decreased from 94 percent to 52

> percent in FY 2001. Although the [Clean Water Act]/NPDES compliance rate in FY 2002 increased from the prior year, it remained nearly 30% below FY 1993 levels. The compliance rate for the [Clean Air Act] fluctuated at a level slightly below 90% for most of the period before increasing to approximately 93% in FY 2002. Similarly, the compliance rate for the [Safe Drinking Water Act] remained above 90% for the entire period, although it declined slightly from 99% in FY 1993 to 96% in FY 2002.

U.S. EPA, THE STATE OF FEDERAL FACILITIES, *supra*, at 1. What does this trend data suggest about the importance of civil penalty availability to federal facility compliance?

* * *

IX. THE IMPORTANCE OF CITIZEN SUIT ENFORCEMENT

Citizen suits have played a significant role in the enforcement of the federal environmental laws. Citizens filed more civil environmental lawsuits in 1997 than the federal government did—indeed, they filed almost as many civil lawsuits as the Department of Justice filed both civilly and criminally. Government enforcement actions still outnumber citizen suits, because state and federal agencies can engage in administrative enforcement. However, both federal and state environmental enforcement efforts have been in decline since 2001, while citizen suits are on the rise, underscoring the continuing role of citizen enforcement in ensuring that statutory provisions effect real environmental improvement.

INDEX

References are to Pages

References are to Pages

References are to Pages

References are to Pages

†